MODERN AUDITING

ASSURANCE SERVICES AND THE INTEGRITY OF FINANCIAL REPORTING

EIGHTH EDITION

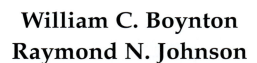

William C. Boynton
Raymond N. Johnson

WILEY

John Wiley & Sons, Inc.

Acquisitions Editor	Mark Bonadeo
Editorial Assistant	Alison Stanley
Marketing Manager	Steve Herdegen
Production Editor	Sandra Dumas
Senior Designer	Dawn Stanley
Media Editor	Allison Morris
Production Management Services	Hermitage Publishing Services

This book was set in 10/12 Palatino by Hermitage Publishing Services and printed and bound by Von Hoffmann Corporation. The cover was printed by Lehigh Press Inc.

The paper in this book was manufactured by a mill whose forest management programs include sustained yield harvesting of its timberlands. Sustained yield harvesting principles ensure that the number of trees cut each year does not exceed the amount of new growth.

This book is printed on acid-free paper. ∞

Boynton, William C., Johnson, Raymond N.
Modern Auditing: Assurance Services, and the Integrity of Financial Reporting

ISBN-13 978-0-471-23011-3
ISBN-10 0-471-23011-1

Printed in the United States of America

10 9 8 7 6 5 4 3 2 1

ABOUT THE AUTHORS

William C. Boynton, Ph.D., CPA received his doctorate in accounting from Michigan State University. He is professor emeritus of accounting at California Polytechnic State University at San Luis Obispo where he formerly served as dean and head of the Accounting Department. He has served on the audit staffs of two international public accounting firms. He has also served as a regional chairperson of the Auditing Section of the American Accounting Association, and on a variety of committees for the American Accounting Association and the Federation of Schools of Accountancy. He is the author or coauthor of several articles and committee reports on accounting and auditing, and has served as codirector of the American Institute of Certified Public Accountants National Banking School. A member of the California Society of Certified Public Accountants, he has served on its Globalization Task Force and its Committees on Accounting Education, the 150-Hour Requirement, and Accounting Principles and Auditing Standards. He is a recipient of the California Society of Certified Public Accountants Faculty Excellence Award.

Raymond N. Johnson, Ph.D., CPA received his doctorate in accounting from the University of Oregon. He is a professor of accounting at Portland State University where he formerly served as head of the Accounting Department, Assistant to the Vice President for Finance and Administration and Assistant to the Provost. He has served on the audit staffs of two international public accounting firms and one local firm. He also served as a consultant to the Auditing Standards Board and was a member of the AICPA Control Risk Audit Guide Task Force. Dr. Johnson currently is a member of the Oregon Board of Accountancy and he is a Past-President of the Oregon Society of CPAs, a former member of AICPA Council (the AICPA's governing body). He led successful legislative and regulatory initiatives in Oregon to expand the pathways to earn the CPA designation. In addition, he has been an American Council on Education Fellow and an Arthur Young McClelland Moores Post-Doctoral Fellow. Dr. Johnson is the recipient of a Leadership Award from the Oregon Entrepreneurs Forum and the Earl Wantland Outstanding Business Professor at Portland State University.

PREFACE

Modern Auditing is designed primarily for the first course in auditing either at the undergraduate or graduate level. Materials in selected chapters and appendices may also serve as the core for a second or advanced course in auditing. Throughout the book, every effort has been made to integrate auditing theory and concepts with auditing methodology and practice. In addition, emphasis is given to the professional responsibilities of independent auditors in upholding the integrity of the financial reporting process.

Our goals in preparing this edition were to (1) open each chapter with real world vignettes that are relevant to chapter material, (2) increase the focus on auditor decision-making, (3) integrate new auditing standards and the Public Companies Accounting Oversight Board (PCAOB) into the book, (4) integrate tools for using generalized audit software in teaching the course, and (5) improve on-line materials that are available for students.

[HIGHLIGHTS OF CHANGES FROM THE PREVIOUS EDITION]

In seeking the goals just enumerated, changes made in this edition include the following:

- Chapter Opening Vignettes use real world examples to relate issues discussed in the chapter discussion.
- Chapter features titled, "Focus on Audit Decisions" highlights key decisions discussed in chapter and chapter summaries reinforce important audit decisions included in the chapter. They will (1) identify the audit decisions discussed in the chapter and provide page references to detailed discussions that (2) identify the factors that influence the auditor's decision, and (3) discuss the audit decision in more detail.
- Discussion of the role of the Public Company Accounting Oversight Board (PCAOB), PCAOB Auditing Standards, and a chapter feature highlight PCAOB standards that differ from Generally Accepted Auditing Standards for private companies.
- Expanded material related to the integrated audit case, "Mt. Hood Furniture" provides a variety of databases that allow students to utilize generalized audit software (IDEA) to accomplish various audit tasks. Multiple databases allow the case to be re-used with different data from term to term.

- Professional simulations for each chapter that provide a more comprehensive problem that addresses the type of professional simulation problems that student will encounter on the CPA exam. This is supported with additional on-line simulations.
- On-line materials available for students include multiple choice questions similar to those encountered on the CPA exam.
- Flowchart style chapter preview at commencement of each chapter.

CONTINUING FEATURES

The following popular features of earlier editions are continued in this edition:

- Clear, accessible writing style has been well-received by students.
- Quality of illustrations.
- Integration of material from authoritative auditing and professional literature throughout the text.
- Abundant illustrations of key concepts, flowcharts, and audit reports.
- Real-world vignettes illustrating contemporary applications of text materials interspersed throughout the text.
- Lists of key terms with page references, now located with the "Learning Checks" at the end of each major section of each chapter.
- An audit case that asks student to make "real world" audit decisions is incorporated in various chapters throughout the text. This provides a consistent and integrated platform for simulating audit conditions.

ORGANIZATION

The organization of the text continues to provide maximum flexibility in choosing the amount and order of material to be covered. For example, the entire audit process is covered outside the cycle chapters. The chapters dealing with ethics, legal liability, and auditors' reports can be covered early or late in the course. The chapter on statistical sampling can be covered before the cycle chapters or be interspersed with the cycle chapters. Various appendices are included to supplement chapter discussion for faculty who wish to pursue topics in more depth.

The Eighth Edition is organized into five parts as follows:

Part	Subject	Chapters
1	The Auditing Environment	1–4
2	Audit Planning	5–10
3	Audit Testing Methodology	11–13
4	Auditing the Transaction Cycles	14–18
5	Completing the Audit/Other Services and Reports	19–23

As shown in the foregoing tabulation, **Part 1, The Auditing Environment,** includes four chapters. Chapter 1, "Auditing and the Public Accounting Profession – Integrity in Financial Reporting ," explains the need for auditing, differentiates the types of services performed by auditors, the roles of the key private and public sector organizations that are associated with or influence the profession, and describes the elements of the multilevel regulatory framework that have as their objective enhancing the quality of services provided by the profession. Chapter 2, entitled "Auditors' Responsibilities and Reports," describes the role and limitations of financial statement audits, introduces generally accepted auditing standards, and explains the concept of reasonable assurance and the auditor's responsibilities regarding the detection of errors and fraud, illegal client acts, and circumstances involving substantial doubt about the client's status as a going concern. Chapter 2 also explains important communications in the auditor's report on financial statements and the auditor's report on internal controls over financial reporting. Appendix 2A provides a number of examples of nonstandard audit reports and explains (1) what they mean, and (2) the criteria for using these reports. Chapter 3, "Professional Ethics," begins with a discussion of ethics and morality from the perspective of both general and professional ethics, and provides in-depth discussions of the profession's *Code of Professional Conduct* and its enforcement. Chapter 4, "Auditors' Legal Liability," includes a thorough discussion of the legal environment and the auditors's exposure to liability under the common law and statutory law, including the Sarbanes-Oxley Act of 2002.

Part 2, Auditing Planning, is comprised of six chapters. Chapter 5, "Overview of the Financial Statement Audit," provides an overview of the six step audit process depicted on the inside front cover. Chapter 6, "Audit Evidence" lays the foundation for audit planning with a discussion of assertions and audit objectives, the sufficiency and competency of evidence, a discussion of audit procedures used by auditors, four important audit decisions made about audit evidence, and audit programs and working papers. Chapter 7, "Accepting the Engagement and Planning the Audit," begins with a discussion of the factors that an auditor should evaluate before accepting or continuing an audit engagement. The chapter then identifies the steps that should be performed in planning the audit, and concludes with a discussion of how understanding the entity and its environment is used in audit planning. Chapter 8, "Materiality Decisions and Analytical Procedures" explains the audit decisions associated with these important audit planning steps. Chapter 9, "Audit Risk, Including the Risk of Fraud" explains the auditor's responsibilities under SAS 99 for planning an audit to obtain reasonable assurance that the financial statements are free of material fraud. In addition, it explores the factors that influence inherent risk decisions and explains preliminary audit strategies often used by auditors. Part 2 concludes with Chapter 10, "Understanding Internal Control." Attention is focused on the definition, fundamental concepts, components, and limitations of the COSO framework for internal control. Particular attention focuses on how the scope of the system of internal control is expanding for public companies. Several appendices to the chapter provide background material about information technology and computer general controls for students that have not completed an accounting information systems class.

Part 3, Audit Testing Methodology, includes three chapters. Chapter 11, "Audit Procedures in Response to Assessed Risks: Tests of Controls," explains the auditor's methodology for meeting the second standard of field work under alternative audit strategies. Attention is given to the nature, timing, and extent of tests of controls in a technology rich environment and to documenting the assessed levels of control risk for assertions pertaining to transaction classes. Consideration is then given to combining control risk assessments for transaction class assertions to arrive at control risk assessments for account balance assertions. Chapter 12, "Audit Procedures in Response to Assessed Risks: Substantive Tests," explains the application of the audit risk model to determine the acceptable level of detection risk for account balance assertions. Consideration is then given to the effects of detection risk on the nature, timing, and extent of substantive tests as well as audit staffing. The chapter includes the development of a general framework that can be used in designing substantive tests for assertions in each of the transaction cycles. The use of statistical and nonstatistical sampling in auditing is explained in Chapter 13. This chapter develops a standard framework for applying audit sampling techniques. The body of the chapter focuses on audit judgments made in implementing an audit sample. It illustrates these judgments with a discussion of nonstatistical approaches for tests of controls and probability proportionate to size sampling for substantive tests. Modules are included in appendices for the application of statistical tests of controls, mean per unit sampling for substantive tests, and nonstatistical sampling for substantive tests.

Part 4, Auditing the Transaction Cycles, has five chapters. Chapters 14 and 15 deal with the revenue and expenditure cycles, respectively. Each chapter starts with an overview of the transaction classes, accounts, and activities associated with the cycle. The audit planning and testing methodologies developed in Parts 2 and 3 are then applied in (1) developing specific audit objectives for the cycle; (2) using an understanding of the business and industry to develop audit strategy and appropriate audit tests; (3) considering materiality, risk, and audit strategy; (4) obtaining an understanding of the internal control structure and assessing control risk; and (5) developing audit programs to meet the acceptable levels of detection risk for assertions pertaining to selected accounts. A similar pattern is followed in both Chapter 16, which covers the production and personnel services cycles that focus on inventory and payroll assertions, respectively, and Chapter 17 continues the discussion in the context of the investing and financing cycles. Since these five cycles affect cash, the audit of cash balances and investment in securities are covered separately in Chapter 18.

The Eighth Edition concludes with Part 5, Completing the Audit, Reporting, and Other Services. Chapter 19 covers four topics: completing the field work, evaluating audit findings, communicating with the client, and fulfilling postaudit responsibilities. Chapter 20, "Attest and Assurance Services and Related Reports," emphasizes the standards and reports associated with other auditing and attest engagements, accounting services, and assurance services offered by CPAs. Chapter 21 is entitled "Internal, Operational, and Governmental Auditing." In addition to describing the standards applicable to each type of auditing, extensive consideration is given under governmental auditing to compliance auditing and the requirements of the Single Audit Act.

END-OF-CHAPTER MATERIALS

As in previous editions, there is an abundance of end-of-chapter materials, including numerous author-prepared questions, questions from professional examinations, and case studies drawn primarily from practice. In addition to the 20 review questions now interspersed throughout each chapter in the "Learning Checks," a typical chapter includes:

- A summary of important auditor knowledge and audit decisions discussed in the chapters with page references.
- Multiple choice questions drawn from the Uniform CPA Examination have been moved out of the text and online in a similar format to that encountered on computer based CPA exams.
- 10 to 15 comprehensive questions that include essay questions from professional examinations.
- 1 to 3 case studies that generally integrate several key concepts covered in the chapter.
- 1 professional simulation problem that requires research to resolve the types of issues discussed in the chapter.

Comprehensive questions from professional examinations are designated as follows: AICPA (Uniform CPA Examination), ICMA (Certified Management Accountant Examination), IIA (Certified Internal Auditor Examination). In total, there are over 900 questions and cases that have been carefully edited to related chapter content.

COMPREHENSIVE CASE

The eighth edition of *Modern Auditing* continues a comprehensive case, which allows students to make actual audit decisions in the context of a growing business in the office furniture industry. This integrated case has 12 assignments over the course of 8 chapters. The case begins in Chapter 7, covering client acceptance and understanding the entity and its environment. Chapter 8 includes two problems on making planning materiality decisions and performing analytical procedures in audit planning. Continuing in Chapter 9, the case assignments cover inherent and fraud risk assessments. The Chapter 11 assignment reflects the topic of Assessing Control Risk. The case continues in Chapter 13 with Statistical Sampling. The Chapter 14 assignments cover Evaluating Internal Controls, Conformation Responses, and the Allowance for Doubtful Accounts. The assignments in Chapter 13 and 14 allow for using generalized audit software. The book is supported by multiple databases such that the same assignment can be used in different terms resulting in different outcomes. The case wraps up in Chapters 19 and 20 by having students concentrate on completing the audit and preparing an audit report. The case assignments within each chapter have students completing a number of exercises, including making audit planning decisions, evaluating evidence and auditing issues, developing working papers related to the case, and preparing an auditor's report.

[SUPPLEMENTARY MATERIALS]

The supplements to this edition of *Modern Auditing* consist of (1) an instructor's resource guide and solutions manual, (2) a test bank, (3) Microtest test-generating software, (4) a student study guide, (5) PowerPoint slides, and (6) databases for use with the comprehensive case embedded in the text. The instructor's resource guide and solutions manual, and test bank will be available for instructors through the book's Web site.

The Instructor's Resource Guide and Solutions Manual contains outlines of the text chapters; suggestions for lectures, classroom activities, and assignments; and references to videos and other supplementary aids the instructor may wish to use. As in previous editions, detailed solutions to the end-of-chapter questions and case studies are provided.

The Test Bank is available electronically through the Web site and in electronic format (Microtest) to facilitate test preparation on a personal computer. The test items are all original and include a large selection of multiple-choice questions, correct/incorrect statements, matching questions, and short essay and analysis questions. Suggested solutions are included.

The comprehensive case includes two cases that allow for the use of generalized audit software. The case in Chapter 13 focuses on audit sampling. The case in Chapter 14 focuses on analyzing the allowance for doubtful accounts. Multiple databases are available for faculty through the Web site, so that solutions can be rotated from term to term. A student version of the Idea software can be obtained free of charge from Idea.

The Student Study Guide to accompany the Eighth Edition includes for each text chapter an expanded outline, 30 chapter highlights, 25 true/false statements, 15 completion questions, and 20 multiple-choice questions. Solutions are included at the end of each chapter.

[ACKNOWLEDGEMENTS]

We take this opportunity to express our sincere appreciation to individuals who have made significant contributions to the Eighth Edition of *Modern Auditing*.

First, we extend thanks to the many adopters of previous editions for their comments and suggestions: Raymond S. Chen, California State University, Northridge; Freddie Choo, San Francisco State University; Robert R. David, Canisius College; John McEldowney, University of North Florida; Marina Nathan, Houston Community College; Patricia Parker, Columbus State Community College; Nile J. Webb, University of Maryland; and T. Sterling Wetzel, Oklahoma State University.

Our sincere thanks are due to the following professors for comprehensive and constructive critiques of this manuscript for the Eighth Edition: Elizabeth Almer, Portland State University; Roselyn Morris, Texas State University–San Marcos; Frank Nekrasz, University of Illinois, Urbana-Champaign; Mark Taylor, Creighton University; Mary Curtis, University of North Texas; and Jane Mutchler, Georgia State University.

We also gratefully acknowledge the permission given by the American Institute of Certified Public Accountants, the Institute of Management Accountants, and

The Institute of Internal Auditors to use materials from their publications, including their professional examinations.

Dr. Johnson also extends his deepest gratitude to his wife and partner in life, Marilyn, who supported this project in a thousand ways and made the vision a reality.

Last, but not least, we express our appreciation to our editor Mark Bonadeo; Sandra Dumas, Production Editor; Dawn Stanley, Designer; and Steve Herdegen, Marketing Manager—as well as all of John Wiley & Sons.

William C. Boynton
Raymond N. Johnson

BRIEF CONTENTS

CONTENTS

PART 2 / AUDIT PLANNING   181

PART

THE AUDITING ENVIRONMENT

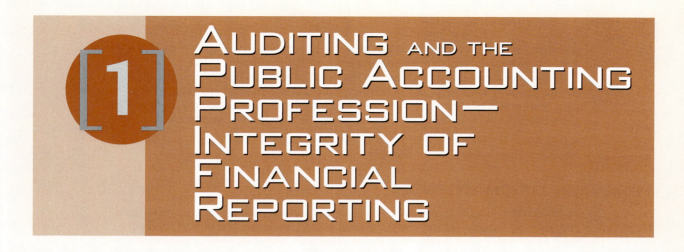

[1] AUDITING AND THE PUBLIC ACCOUNTING PROFESSION— INTEGRITY OF FINANCIAL REPORTING

INTERNAL AUDITORS UNCOVER FINANCIAL FRAUD AT WORLDCOM

In June 2002, WorldCom announced that during the previous two years $3.8 billion in costs had been capitalized rather than expensed. This announcement shook a sagging investor's confidence that was already weakened by the restatement of financial statements by companies like Enron, Waste Management, and Sunbeam and by allegations of dishonesty at the top of other U.S. companies. The size of WorldCom's financial fraud was so significant that this event propelled Congress to pass the Sarbanes-Oxley Act of 2002 to further regulate the financial reporting process.

With hindsight we now see WorldCom as a company that, during price wars that reduced profits in its long-distance markets, relied on aggressive accounting practices to bolster earnings. How do we now know this? The public learned about WorldCom's financial fraud through the hard work of several "auditing heroes" led by Cynthia Cooper (age 38), WorldCom's vice president for Internal Auditing. What did Cynthia Cooper and her staff of internal auditors do to uncover the financial fraud? The internal audit team:

- Followed up on an e-mail with a local newspaper article about a former employee in WorldCom's Texas office who had been fired after he raised questions about a minor accounting matter involving capital expenditures.
- Recognized that $2 billion in capital expenditures had not been authorized as part of the capital budget process.
- Did not settle for glib answers from the director of financial planning who described the $2 billion in capital expenditures as "prepaid capacity" but could not explain the nature of "prepaid capacity."
- Uncovered over $500 million in capitalized computer costs that were not supported by vendor's invoices.
- Demonstrated their independence by continuing to investigate the capitalization of line costs (fees paid to lease portions of other companies' telephone networks) even when instructed by Scott Sullivan, the CFO, to delay this particular audit until the 3rd quarter.

The issue came to a head when Cynthia Cooper and her audit team brought evidence of the improper capitalization of expense to the chairman of WorldCom's audit committee. The audit committee instructed the internal auditors to work with WorldCom's new external auditor, KPMG. Within a week the internal and external auditors compiled evidence of the financial fraud for the audit committee and the external auditors concluded that the accounting treatment was not in accordance with generally accepted accounting principles. Scott Sullivan, the CFO, was given the opportunity to make his case to the audit committee, but the committee members were not persuaded.

The next day the audit committee and the board of directors made public the $3.8 billion restatement of earnings due to the fact that costs had been capitalized that should have been expensed. The audit committee and board of directors also fired the then CFO, Scott Sullivan, who was subsequently indicted by the U.S. Justice Department.

Source: Susan Pulliam and Deborah Solomon, "How Three Unlikely Sleuths Exposed Fraud at WorldCom," *Wall Street Journal,* October 30, 2002, p.1.

[PREVIEW OF CHAPTER 1]

As fraudulent financial reporting and restatements of earnings have become more prevalent, auditing (external audits, internal audits, and governmental audits) has become more important. Financial statement audits provide an important level of assurance about the integrity of financial statement information used by decision makers. Chapter 1 provides an introduction to contemporary auditing and assurance services, describes the organizations associated with the public accounting profession, and ends with a discussion of the regulatory framework that ensures high-quality audit and assurance services. The following diagram provides an overview of the chapter organization and content.

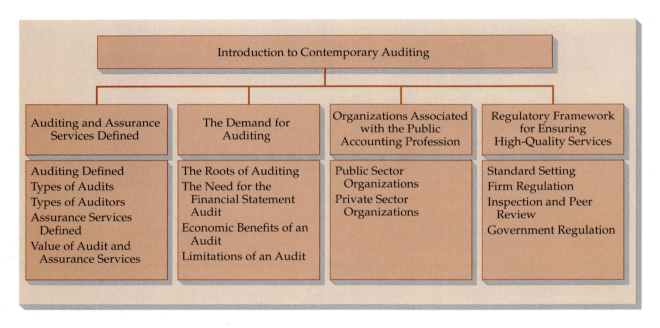

Chapter 1 addresses the following aspects of the auditor's knowledge.

focus on auditor knowledge

After studying this chapter you should understand the following aspects of an auditor's knowledge base:

1. Know the common attributes of activities defined as auditing.
2. Know the differences between the different types of audits and auditors.
3. Know the common attributes of assurance services.

4. Know the variety of services and levels of assurance in the universe of assurance services.
5. Know the value of the audit and other assurance services.
6. Know a historical perspective of the demand for auditing.
7. Know the factors that influence the need for financial statement audits.
8. Know the economic benefits and inherent limitations associated with a financial statement audit.
9. Know the public sector and private sector organizations associated with auditing and assurance services.
10. Know the four components of the auditing profession's multilevel regulatory framework.
11. Know the elements of a system of quality control for a CPA firm's attest practice.

[AUDITING AND ASSURANCE SERVICES DEFINED]

Auditing plays a vital role in business, government, and our economy. Evidence of the importance of auditing is provided by the following:

- Investors and financial analysts value the work of auditors who audit the financial statements of over 15,000 public companies annually, including all companies whose securities are traded on the New York Stock Exchange and NASDAQ. Many investors and financial analysts rely on financial statement audits to provide assurance about the credibility of critical information that they use when making investment decisions.

- Bankers, bonding agencies, and other creditors rely on financial statement audits to ensure that they are using reliable information when extending credit to public and private companies.

- The Sarbanes-Oxley Act of 2002 requires auditors to provide assurance about the quality of internal control over financial reporting in addition to assurance about fair presentation in financial statements.

- The federal government values the work of auditors who audit state and local governments receiving $500,000 or more per year in financial assistance from the federal government under the Single Audit Act.

- The board of directors and audit committees of many public companies value the work of internal auditors who evaluate information systems and report to the board about potential improvements in company operations.

- The federal government values the work of auditors working for the Internal Revenue Service who recommended an additional $4.3 billion in taxes based on corporate audits conducted in 2003.[1]

As a vocation, auditing offers the opportunity for challenging and rewarding careers in public accounting, industry, and government. Many auditors develop a client base with a concentration in one or more key industries. As a result of serving many clients in similar industries, few individuals understand the key competitiveness factors for a business better than the auditor.

---

[1] Reported by the Transactional Records Access Clearing House at Syracuse University, http://trac.syr.edu/tracirs/trends/current/taxpen_corp.html

Individuals choosing an auditing career in a public accounting firm have the opportunity to progress from a starting position of staff assistant to senior auditor, to manager, and then to partner. Becoming a partner ordinarily takes from 10 to 12 years. As auditors progress in their careers, they can expect to be faced with more challenging accounting and auditing issues. In the process of earning a partnership, CPAs develop a reputation for expertise in accounting, auditing, and giving unbiased professional views regarding financial reporting, internal control, business risk, and performance measurement. Auditing career paths in industry and government vary considerably. Some state and local government chief auditor positions are elective offices. Regardless of their career path, most auditors are recognized for their expertise in evaluating organizational performance.

AUDITING DEFINED

Auditor Knowledge 1

■ **Know the common attributes of activities defined as auditing.**

The term *auditing* is used to describe a broad range of activities in our society. The following broad definition of auditing identifies a number of common attributes of most modern auditing activities as depicted in Figure 1-1. The Report of the Committee on Basic Auditing Concepts of the American Accounting Association (*Accounting Review,* vol. 47) defines **auditing** as

> a systematic process of objectively obtaining and evaluating evidence regarding assertions about economic actions and events to ascertain the degree of correspondence between those assertions and established criteria and communicating the results to interested users.

Several attributes of auditing contained in this definition merit special comment:

■ A *systematic process* connotes a logical, structured, and organized series of steps or procedures.
■ *Objectively obtaining and evaluating evidence* means examining the bases for the assertions and judiciously evaluating the results without bias or prejudice either for or against the individual (or entity) making the assertions.

Figure 1-1 ■ Overview of the Audit Process

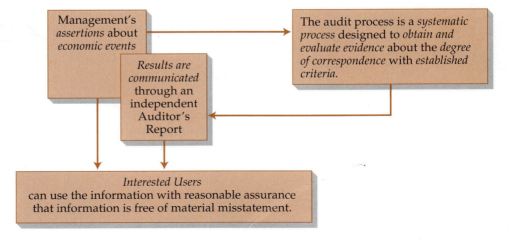

- *Assertions about economic actions and events* are the representations made by the entity or individual. They comprise the subject matter of auditing. Assertions include information contained in financial statements, internal operating reports, and tax returns.
- *Degree of correspondence* refers to the closeness with which the assertions can be identified with established criteria. The expression of correspondence may be quantified, such as the amount of a shortage in a petty cash fund, or it may be qualitative, such as the fairness of financial statements.
- *Established criteria* are the standards against which the assertions or representations are judged. Criteria may be specific rules prescribed by a legislative body, budgets and other measures of performance set by management, or generally accepted accounting principles (GAAP) established by the Financial Accounting Standards Board (FASB) and other authoritative bodies.
- *Communicating the results* is achieved through a written report that indicates the degree of correspondence between the assertions and established criteria. The communication of results either enhances or weakens the credibility of the representations made by another party. The goal of the audit process is to add credibility to management's representations so that interested users can use the information with reasonable assurance that it is free of material misstatement.
- *Interested users* are individuals who use (rely on) the auditor's findings. In a business environment, they include stockholders, management, creditors, governmental agencies, and the public.

These attributes provide a sound description of the auditor's work. Many of these attributes are common to all types of audits. Figure 1-2 compares some of the significant differences between various types of audits: financial statement audits, compliance audits, audit reports on internal control, and operational audits.

Figure 1-2 ■ Comparative Summary of Types of Audits

Type of Audit	Financial Statement Audit	Compliance Audit	Audit Report on Internal Control	Operational Audit
Assertion about economic actions and events	Presentation of financial position, results of operations, and cash flows	Claims or data pertaining to adherence to policies, laws, regulations, etc.	Adequacy of system of internal control over financial reporting	Operational or performance data
Established criteria	Generally accepted accounting principles	Management's policy or laws and regulations	COSO criteria for evaluating internal controls	Objectives set by management
Communication of results	Opinion of independent CPA	Summary of findings or assurance regarding degree of compliance	Opinion of independent CPA	Summary of findings regarding efficiency and effectiveness observed
Interested users	Investors, creditors and others	Management, board of directors, and others	Investors, creditors and others	Management and board of directors

Auditor Knowledge 2

■ Know the differences between the different types of audits and auditors.

TYPES OF AUDITS

Three types of audits normally demonstrate the key characteristics included in the definition of auditing: financial statement audits, compliance audits, and operational audits. The audit report on internal control over financial reporting is a variation of a compliance audit. The nature of each type of audit is briefly described in the following pages.

Financial Statement Audit

A **financial statement audit** involves obtaining and evaluating evidence about an entity's presentation of its financial position, results of operations, and cash flows for the purpose of expressing an opinion on whether they are presented fairly in conformity with established criteria—usually generally accepted accounting principles (GAAP). In most states only CPAs can perform financial statement audits, and the company whose statements are being audited usually hires the external audit firm. The results of financial statement audits are distributed to a wide spectrum of users such as stockholders, creditors, regulatory agencies, and the general public through the auditor's report on financial statements. In addition, the external auditor also prepares a report to the audit committee of the board of directors about the company's accounting policies, internal controls, and other audit findings.

Financial statement audits for major corporations are indispensable to the functioning of our national securities markets. Many lenders and creditors also rely on financial statement audits to obtain assurance about the reliability of information used to support lending decisions. High-quality financial audits significantly reduce the risk that investors and creditors will use poor-quality information when making a variety of investment decisions. In addition, the audit logic developed for financial statement audits is the cornerstone on which auditors have developed compliance audits, operational audits, and a wide array of attest and assurance services. As a result, this text gives extensive consideration to the logic underlying the audit of financial statements.

Compliance Audit

A **compliance audit** involves obtaining and evaluating evidence to determine whether certain financial or operating activities of an entity conform to specified conditions, rules, or regulations. The established criteria in this type of audit may come from a variety of sources. The Sarbanes-Oxley Act of 2002 requires companies to have a dual-purpose audit that audits both the financial statements and management's assertion as to whether it has complied with criteria regarding an adequate system of internal control over financial reporting. Compliance audits may also be based on criteria established by creditors. For instance, a bond covenant may require the maintenance of a specified current ratio. Possibly the widest application of compliance audits relates to criteria based on government regulations. Corporations, for example, must comply with extensive income tax and other government regulations that are subject to audit. Defense contractors must comply with the terms and conditions of government contracts.

audit engagements on compliance with internal controls

A number of studies, beginning with the Trueblood Commission in the 1980s, have come to the conclusion that a sound system of internal control helps prevent fraud. Section 404 of the Sarbanes-Oxley Act of 2002 established a requirement that the management of a public company establish and maintain adequate internal controls over financial reporting and report annually on (1) management's responsibility for internal controls over financial reporting and (2) the effectiveness of such controls.

Each annual report filed with the SEC should include an internal control report:

■ Stating that management is responsible for establishing and maintaining adequate internal controls and procedures over financial reporting.

■ Containing management's assessment, as of the end of the most recent fiscal year, of the effectiveness of the company's internal controls and procedures over financial reporting.

In addition, the independent auditor must audit (provide reasonable assurance about) management's assertions regarding the system of internal control over financial reporting. Under Sarbanes-Oxley, an independent auditor will audit both the financial statement audits and management's assertions regarding compliance with criteria about the adequacy of internal control over financial reporting.

PCAOB
Public Companies
Accounting Oversight Board

Some reports of independent auditors come in the form of an audit report on the adequacy of internal control for general-purpose users. Other reports on compliance audits may be directed to the authority that established the criteria and may include either (1) a summary of findings or (2) an expression of assurance as to the degree of compliance with those criteria.

Operational Audit

An **operational audit** involves obtaining and evaluating evidence about the efficiency and effectiveness of an entity's operating activities in relation to specified objectives. This type of audit is sometimes referred to as a performance audit or a management audit. In a business enterprise, the scope of the audit may encompass all the activities of (1) a department, branch, or division, or (2) a function that may cross business unit lines such as marketing or data processing. In the federal government, an operational audit might extend to all the activities of (1) an agency, such as the Federal Emergency Management Agency (FEMA) or (2) a particular program, such as the distribution of food stamps. The criteria or objectives against which efficiency and effectiveness are measured may be specified, for example, by management or enabling legislation. In other cases, the operational auditor may assist in specifying the criteria to be used. Reports on such audits typically include not only an assessment of efficiency and effectiveness, but also recommendations for improvement. When performed by CPA firms, such audits are likely to involve individuals from the consulting department, or individuals with extensive industry expertise, such as the audit staff.

TYPES OF AUDITORS

Individuals who are engaged to audit economic actions and events for individuals and legal entities are generally classified into three groups: (1) independent auditors, (2) internal auditors, and (3) government auditors.

Independent Auditors

Independent auditors are usually CPAs who are either individual practitioners or members of public accounting firms who render professional auditing services to clients. In general, licensing involves passing the uniform CPA examination and obtaining practical experience in auditing. By virtue of their education, training, and experience, independent auditors are qualified to perform each type of audit described previously. The clients of independent auditors may include profit-making business enterprises, not-for-profit organizations, and governmental agencies.

Like members of the medical and legal professions, independent auditors work on a fee basis. There are similarities between the role of an independent auditor in a public accounting firm and an attorney who is a member of a law firm. However, there is also a major difference: The auditor is expected to be independent of the client in making an audit and in reporting the results, whereas the attorney is expected to be an advocate for the client in rendering legal services. Users rely on the auditor's independence and derive value from the fact that the auditor is unbiased with respect to the client under audit. More attention will be given to independence in later chapters.

Internal Auditors

Internal auditors are employees of the organizations they audit. This type of auditor is involved in an independent evaluation of evidence, called internal auditing, within an organization as a service to the organization. The objective of internal auditing is to assist the management of the organization in the effective discharge of its responsibilities.

The scope of the internal audit function extends to all phases of an organization's activities. Internal auditors are primarily involved with compliance and operational audits. However, as is explained later, the work of internal auditors may supplement the work of independent auditors in financial statement audits.

Many internal auditors hold the certified internal auditor (CIA) credential and some are also CPAs. The international association of internal auditors is the Institute of Internal Auditors (IIA), which prescribes certification criteria and administers the certified internal auditor examination. In addition, the IIA has established practice standards for internal auditing and a code of ethics.

Government Auditors

Government auditors are employed by various local, state, and federal governmental agencies. At the federal level, the three primary agencies are the General Accounting Office (GAO), the Internal Revenue Service (IRS), and the Defense Contract Audit Agency (DCAA).

In performing the audit function for Congress, GAO auditors engage in a wide range of audit activities, including financial statement audits, compliance audits, and operational audits. The results of these audits are reported to the U.S. Congress and the public. GAO auditors are also involved in fact-finding and evaluating alternatives for Congress.

IRS auditors (or agents) audit the returns of taxpayers for compliance with applicable tax laws. Their findings are generally restricted to the agency and the taxpayer. The Defense Contract Audit Agency, as its name suggests, conducts audits of defense contractors and their operations, and reports to the Department of Defense. The national organization for government accountants is the Association of Government Accountants (AGA). Today most government auditors hold CPA and/or CIA certificates.

ASSURANCE SERVICES DEFINED

Auditor Knowledge 3

■ Know the common attributes of assurance services.

Assurance services is a broader term that includes audits and a variety of other assurances about various representations of management. The AICPA Special Committee on Assurance Services[2] developed the following definition.

> **Assurance services** are independent professional services that improve the quality of information, or its context, for decision makers.

There are several important differences between the AAA definition of auditing and the AICPA definition of assurance service that relate to the qualities of the auditor, not just the audit process.

■ The concept of *independence* is a key aspect of assurance services. Users rely on the CPA's independence and derive value from the fact that the CPA is unbiased and objective.

■ The concept of *professional services* encompasses the application of professional judgment that is a unique attribute that the CPA brings to the engagement. CPAs bring their professional skepticism and objectivity to an engagement. Although advances in information technology can speed the accumulation or analysis of data, technology cannot replace the practitioner's professional judgment.

■ The purpose of assurance services is to improve the *quality of information or its context.* Quality, as discussed by the Special Committee on Assurance Services, encompasses the concepts of decision usefulness. Assurance services improve the quality of information by improving its reliability or relevance. The Special Committee defines reliability and relevance as follows:[3]

- Reliability includes representational faithfulness, neutrality, and consistency among periods.
- Relevance includes understandability, comparability with other entities, usability, and completeness.

■ The *decision maker* is featured prominently in the services definition. Assurance services are intended to provide a benefit to the decision maker. Decision makers may be clients or outside third parties.

---

[2] Additional information on assurance services can be found by visiting the Assurance Services web site, which can be accessed through the AICPA homepage at http://www.aicpa.org.

[3] The definitions of reliability and relevance used by the Special Committee on Assurance Services differ somewhat from the description in Statement of Financial Accounting Concepts No. 2.

what it means to be a professional

John Carey's book, *The Rise of the Accounting Profession: From Technician to Professional,* identified seven criteria that distinguish professions from other pursuits. Each of these is discussed here in the context of the requirements to be recognized as a Certified Public Accountant (CPA).

1. *A Body of Specialized Knowledge.* CPAs are recognized as experts in the areas of accounting, auditing, and taxation. This reputation is enhanced by the CPA's expertise in business and organizational success.
2. *A Formal Educational Process.* In most states students must complete 150 semester hours of education including a minimum study in accounting, business, and other subjects in order to qualify to sit for the CPA exam.
3. *Standards Governing Admission.* In order to become a CPA, candidates usually must complete education requirements including the study of accounting, pass the CPA exam, and complete an experience requirement (usually one year of experience).
4. *A Code of Ethics.* The American Institute of CPAs has adopted a code of professional ethics that governs the behavior of CPAs. This code of ethics has been important in establishing a reputation for the CPA profession as one where its members are recognized as acting with integrity and objectivity. In addition, many states have written similar codes into their state accountancy laws.
5. *A Recognized Status Indicated by a License or Special Designation.* Today 54 jurisdictions license CPAs, most of which give CPAs exclusive rights in the practice of accounting and auditing. In addition, CPAs do not have to register as enrolled agents when practicing taxation.
6. *A Public Interest in the Work that the Practitioner's Perform.* CPAs who practice as auditors perform an important role in providing assurance about the reliability of the financial information included in audited financial statements.
7. *A Recognition by Professionals of a Social Obligation.* The auditing profession has recognized the importance of their obligation to the public through self-regulation in the form of peer reviews to ensure high standards in the quality of work. The investing public depends on auditors to provide reasonable assurance that audited financial statements are free of material misstatement.

Auditor Knowledge 4

■ Know the variety of services and levels of assurance in the universe of assurance services.

The audit is only one type of an assurance service. The audit focuses primarily on the information contained in financial statements. Assurance services deal with a wide array of information used by decision makers, not just financial statement users.

Example Assurance Services

Figure 1-3 depicts the universe of assurance services. The following discussion provides examples of assurance and attest services provided by CPAs, along with an explanation of the levels of assurance that are often associated with the various services.

Audit Engagements

The purpose of an **audit engagement** is to provide *reasonable assurance*, not a guarantee, that the financial information is free of material misstatement. This type of

Figure 1-3 ■ Universe of Assurance Services

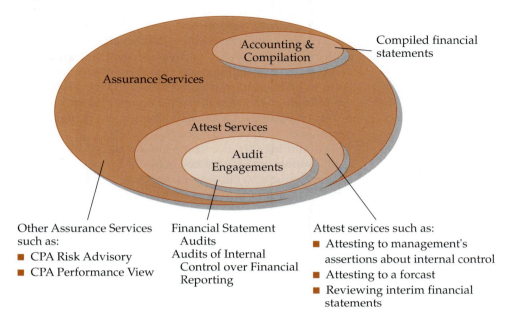

Other Assurance Services such as:
■ CPA Risk Advisory
■ CPA Performance View

Financial Statement Audits
Audits of Internal Control over Financial Reporting

Attest services such as:
■ Attesting to management's assertions about internal control
■ Attesting to a forcast
■ Reviewing interim financial statements

audit involves obtaining and evaluating evidence about an entity's historical financial statements. Although the financial statements of public companies are prepared in accordance with GAAP, financial statements of private companies can be audited in accordance with a federal income tax basis of accounting or a cash basis of accounting. Auditors can also audit only an element of the financial statements such as royalties payable. In addition, auditors of public companies audit the effectiveness of internal controls over financial reporting.

Attest Services

An **attest service** is one in which the CPA firm issues a written communication that expresses a conclusion about the reliability of a written assertion that is the responsibility of another party. In recent years, growing recognition of the skills and experience of CPAs has resulted in a demand from clients, regulating agencies, and others for a variety of attest services.

The term **examination** is used to describe other services that culminate in the positive expression of an opinion as to whether or not another party's assertions conform to stated criteria. Examples include examinations of (1) prospective (rather than historical) financial statements and (2) an entity's compliance with specified laws or regulations. In an examination, as in an audit, the CPA also issues a "positive" expression of opinion on whether management's assertions are presented fairly in conformity with established criteria. Again the goal is to provide *reasonable assurance* that management's assertion is free of material misstatement.

Reviews of financial information also fall under the category of attest services because CPAs provide *negative assurance* about financial information. A **review engagement** consists primarily of inquiries of an entity's management and comparative analyses of financial information. The scope of this service is significantly less than that of an audit or examination. The purpose is to give *negative assurance* as opposed to the positive expression of opinion given in an audit. Thus, instead of stating that financial statements are "presented fairly in conformity with GAAP," a review report states that the reviewer is "not aware of any material modifications that should be made to the statements in order for them to be in conformity with GAAP." This service is sometimes performed on the interim statements of public companies and the annual statements of non-public companies. CPAs may also review management's representation about compliance with debt covenants.

The auditor can also complete an agreed-upon procedures engagement. An **agreed-upon procedures engagement** is one in which the auditor performs specific procedures to attest to management's assertion (for example, the amount of royalties payable) for an outside third party (the entity receiving the royalties). The specific procedures to be performed are agreed upon by the party making the assertion, the party using the assertion, and the CPA. The level of assurance depends on the nature and extensiveness of the attest procedures agreed upon by all parties.

Accounting and Compilation Services

A CPA firm may be engaged by a client to perform a variety of **accounting services,** including doing manual or automated bookkeeping, journalizing, and posting adjusting entries. The CPA may also be engaged to perform a **compilation service** through which the CPA, who is an expert regarding GAAP, drafts and compiles financial statements for the client. When the CPA "compiles" a set of financial statements, the CPA provides *no assurance* about whether the financial statements present fairly in accordance with GAAP, for the CPA has not obtained evidence supporting the financial statements. Nevertheless, this is an important assurance service that improves the relevance of information for decision makers in nonpublic entities. Accounting services are a major activity for some sole practitioners and local CPA firms.

Other Assurance Services

Assurance services are generally focused on improving the relevance or reliability of information used by decision makers. Examples of other types of assurance services include:

- *CPA Risk Advisory* services—services in which the CPA can improve the quality of risk information for internal decision makers through independent assessments of the likelihood that an event or action will adversely affect an organization's ability to achieve its business objectives and execute its strategies successfully.
- *CPA Performance View*—a service that focuses on providing assurance regarding an organization's use of both financial and nonfinancial measures to evaluate the effectiveness and efficiency of its activities.

These services build upon the trust and reputation for integrity and objectivity earned by CPAs, but extend traditional services into totally new areas, as discussed in detail in Chapter 20.

Levels of Assurance

CPAs can provide several levels of assurance when performing assurance services. The common levels of assurance discussed above are as follows:

- **Reasonable assurance.** This is a very high level of assurance but not a guarantee. In audit and examination engagements the CPA needs to obtain sufficient, competent evidence to support a positive opinion that the assertion is presented fairly in all material respects.

- **Negative assurance or review-level assurance.** This is substantially less than an audit or examination. In a review engagement the CPA makes inquiries and performs analytical procedures so that the reviewer can state that he or she is "not aware of any material modifications that should be made to management's assertion."

- **Agreed-upon procedures.** In some cases the entity making an assertion and the entity using an assertion will agree on specific procedures to be performed by the CPA. The level of assurance that is obtained depends on the nature and extensiveness of the agreed-upon procedures performed by the CPA.

- **Compilation without assurance.** In some cases the CPA may compile information to provide decision makers with relevant information. In this case the CPA provides *no assurance* about the underlying reliability of the information.

VALUE OF AUDIT AND ASSURANCE SERVICES

Auditor Knowledge 5

- Know the value of the audit and other assurance services.

Figure 1-4 describes the accountant's value chain. Accountants provide a wide array of services that assist decision makers. Understanding this value chain may help in understanding the value of audit and assurance services. The steps in the accountant's value chain can be described as follows:

- **Capturing business events in the form of data.** This is the job of the accounting information and communication system. In addition, many internal controls function at this level to ensure that accounting data are accurate. In the initial step, for example, data may be input regarding inventory transactions.

- **Communicating the total picture with integrity and objectivity.** This is the process of developing financial statements and other information that might be reported to management, the board of directors, or outside creditors and investors. This second step might be exemplified by developing financial statements that report inventory and other transactions.

- **Transforming complex information into knowledge.** This is the process of provide a context for information and making it usable. An example of the third step might be determining that a company turns inventory four times a year. This information is not very useful, however, without the context of the company, its industry, and its competitors. A retail grocer or a brewer would expect to turn its inventory much more frequently than four times a year. However, this would be an unrealistically high inventory turn for a winery. Jewelry stores and pharmaceutical companies also have slower inventory turns. Significant value is added by establishing a knowledgeable setting for how information will be used.

- **Anticipating and creating opportunities.** If a company is turning its inventory four times a year, and that is slow for the industry, then the next question becomes one of determining how to increase inventory turns. This step might

Figure 1-4 ■ The Accountant's Value Chain

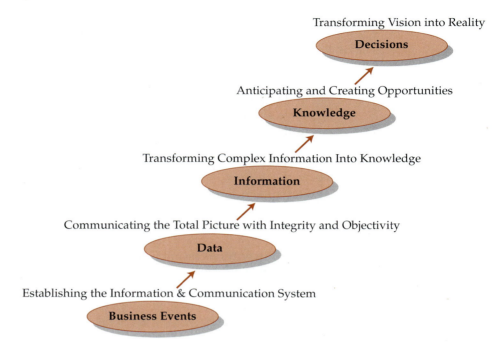

involve identifying slow-moving inventory and determining a strategy for selling off that inventory.

■ **Decision making.** Ultimately, management decide on a course of action to improve inventory management. Management must make the sales and streamline the inventory management process to improve inventory turns.

The role of the financial statement audit is to provide reasonable assurance that the information sets known as financial statements prepared in accordance with GAAP are presented fairly in all material respects. Financial statements that contain material misstatements often lead to poor decisions. For example, many investors in WorldCom made investment decisions based on information that did not accurately reflect the underlying profitability of the company. When the information was corrected, share price declined and investors lost billions of dollars. Imagine the value to investors of having information that was materially correct in the first place. This value is not limited to outside investors. Many directors rely on audited information to fulfill their role in evaluating the performance of management and guiding the company. Management needs reliable information for day-to-day decision making. Without information that is fairly presented, the decisions made by these members of management are significantly handicapped.

Reliable information is the foundation for many decisions. The purpose of an audit is to provide assurance that information used in decision making is reliable. Without audits, outsiders who use information provided by management may not have an adequate foundation on which to make important decisions. The value of every step above *information* on the value chain is dependent upon the credibility of that information.

In addition, internal auditors provide a variety of services in this value chain. For example, they might test internal controls and perform other procedures to provide assurance about the underlying accuracy of information used by management. In addition, they might perform operational audits that use the information coming from the accounting system combined with knowledge of the business and industry to recommend operational improvements. The operational audit assists management in identifying opportunities for improving profitability or for reducing liquidity or solvency risks.

Other assurance services are also aimed at providing valuable information to decision makers. Even though the compilation service provides no assurance about the credibility of underlying information, it usually provides information for decision makers that they would not otherwise have. The review service adds some credibility to underlying information (negative assurance vs. reasonable assurance), but this level of credibility benefits decision makers at a reasonable cost. A service such as *CPA Performance View* is designed to provide decision makers with additional, relevant information that they otherwise might not have. A service such as *CPA Risk Advisory* assists the decision makers in understanding the risks associated with various business opportunities. Each of these services provides value to the decision maker by providing more relevant or more reliable information.

LEARNING CHECK

1-1 Explain the seven attributes that describe the nature of the auditor's work.

1-2 Distinguish among the three principal types of audits and describe the nature of the auditor's report for each.

1-3 Distinguish among the three principal types of auditors and indicate the types of audits each may perform.

1-4 a. Provide two examples of examination engagements and explain the level of assurance provided by the CPA.
b. Provide an example of a review engagement and explain the level of assurance provided by the CPA.

1-5 What assurance is provided by CPAs who perform accounting and compilation services for a client? Explain the benefits received by a client who requests accounting and compilation services.

1-6 Identify two other assurance services provided by CPAs and explain how they improve the relevance or reliability of information used by decision makers.

1-7 a. Explain the value of the audit in the context of the accountant's value chain.
b. Explain the value of the compilation service and the review service in the context of the accountant's value chain.
c. Explain the value of the *CPA Risk Advisory* service in the context of the accountant's value chain.

[KEY TERMS

Accounting services, p. 14
Agreed-upon procedures, p. 15
Agreed-upon procedures
  engagement, p. 14
Assurance services, p. 11
Attest service, p. 13
Audit engagement, p. 12
Auditing, p. 6
Compilation service, p. 14
Compilation without assurance, p. 15
Compliance audit, p. 8

Examination, p. 13
Financial statement audit, p. 8
Government auditors, p. 10
Independent auditors, p. 10
Internal auditors, p. 10
Negative assurance or review-level
  assurance, p. 15
Operational audit, p. 9
Reasonable assurance, p. 15
Review engagement, p. 13

[THE DEMAND FOR AUDITING]

THE ROOTS OF AUDITING

Auditor Knowledge 6

■ **Know a historical
perspective of the
demand for auditing.**

The beginning of the company audit can be linked to British legislation during the industrial revolution in the mid-1800s. Advances in transportation and industrial technology resulted in new economies of scale, larger companies, the advent of professional managers, and the growth of diverse absentee ownership of companies. The development of professional managers who were separate from investors and creditors created a demand for someone to add credibility to management's financial representations. Initially, company audits had to be performed by one or more stockholders, who were not company officers and who were designated by the other stockholders as their representatives. The auditing profession quickly emerged to meet marketplace needs, and legislation was soon revised to permit persons other than stockholders to perform the audits, giving rise to the formation of auditing firms. Some of these early British firms, such as Deloitte & Co., Peat, Marwick, & Mitchell, and Price Waterhouse & Co., can be traced to firms that today practice on an international scale.

The British influence migrated to the United States in the late 1800s as English and Scottish investors sent their own auditors to check on management's statements about the condition of American companies in which they had heavily invested. The focus of these early audits was on finding errors in the balance sheet accounts and stemming the growth of fraud associated with the increasing phenomenon of professional managers and absentee owners. During the early 1900s, the demand for audits expanded greatly owing to rapid growth in the public ownership of corporate securities.

Following the stock market crash of 1929, significant deficiencies were recognized in financial reporting, and the profession was challenged to provide stronger leadership in the further development of accounting and auditing. By then, the income statement had gained status, and attention had to be paid to measures of operating performance and concepts of income as well as financial condition. In order to enhance the credibility of information prepared for investors, the New York Stock Exchange, in 1932, adopted a requirement that all listed corporations obtain an audit certificate from an independent CPA. Passage of the Securities Act of 1933 and the Securities Exchange Act of 1934 further added to the demand for audit services for publicly owned companies.

In response to these demands and growth in the size and complexity of businesses, by the 1940s three important changes in audit practice had evolved: (1) a shift from detailed verification of accounts to sampling or testing as the basis for rendering an opinion on the fairness of financial statements, (2) development of the practice of linking the testing to be done to the auditor's evaluation of a company's internal controls, and (3) deemphasis of the detection of fraud as an audit objective. The auditor's responsibility to find fraud is the subject of controversy to this day and is explained further both in the next chapter and in Chapter 9.

In the 1980s the auditing profession came under scrutiny by Congress following discovery of financial frauds at several public companies such as Equity Funding and National Student Marketing. At this time the public accounting profession took another step in ensuring high-quality audit services. Various states adopted requirements that CPAs engage in annual, continuing professional education in order to maintain their licenses. The public accounting profession also took a voluntary step by instituting a program of peer review. Under this program, a CPA firm would submit its accounting and auditing practice to a review by independent peers every three years.

During the 1980s the accounting profession slowly addressed the issue of its responsibility for finding financial fraud. The National Commission of Fraudulent Financial Reporting made recommendations for improvements in internal controls, and the Auditing Standards Board issued a series of 10 new auditing standards in 1988 to narrow a perceived "expectations gap" in order to bring auditor responsibilities more in line with investor's expectations. The profession also developed new attestation standards as CPAs were asked to render their independent professional judgment about assertions other than financial statement assertions. CPAs were routinely hired to provide review-level assurance to lenders about a company's compliance with debt covenants or to apply agreed-upon procedures to royalty agreements. As information technology advanced and companies subcontracted accounting work to outside organizations, CPAs were asked to attest to the internal controls of the outside service provider.

From 1990 to 2000 CPA firms became professional service firms, hiring a wide variety of business professionals that sold consulting services to their clients. By 2000 consulting revenues exceeded auditing revenues at all the national CPA firms, and in some cases consulting fees to an audit client exceeded the size of the audit fee. The SEC and the investing public began to question how CPAs could be independent on audit issues when the firms were so dependent on consulting revenues. The quality of audits was further questioned when a series of restatements of earnings from public companies such as Sunbeam, Waste Management, Xerox, Adelphia, Enron, and WorldCom brought about a crisis of confidence in the work of auditors. Even though these events were relatively rare out of the approximately 15,000 annual public company audits, the consequences for shareholders amounted to losses in the billions of dollars.

Over the years the demand for auditing has been influenced by professional managers who misled investors by materially misstating the financial performance in their company's financial statements. Investors expect auditors to intervene and find financial statement misstatements. During the 20th century auditors were self-regulated, and the profession set its own standards. The Auditing

Standards Board struggled to find a balance of setting standards to expect auditors to find most financial statement misstatements, but to not set the standard so high that auditors appeared to be self-serving. Corporate management protested standards that would cause significant increases in audit fees.

By 2002 the collapse of Enron and WorldCom led Congress to pass the Sarbanes-Oxley Act of 2002. This Act created the Public Companies Accounting Oversight Board (PCAOB) and gave it responsibility for setting auditing, ethics, independence, and quality control standards for audits of public companies. Congress believed that self-regulation of auditors had not worked and that the SEC was better positioned to protect the investor's interest. The Sarbanes-Oxley Act of 2002 also extended the auditor's work beyond the financial statement audit. A number of important commissions have recognized the importance of good internal controls in preventing financial statement misstatements. Section 404 of the Sarbanes-Oxley Act of 2002 also requires auditors to audit management's assertion about the adequacy of internal controls over financial reporting.

NEED FOR FINANCIAL STATEMENT AUDITS

Auditor Knowledge 7

■ Know the factors that influence the need for financial statement audits.

The FASB, in *Statement of Financial Accounting Concepts No. 2,* states that relevance and reliability are two primary qualities that make accounting information useful for decision makers. Users of financial statements look to the independent auditor's report for assurance about the reliability of information and its conformance to generally accepted accounting principles (a measure of relevance of financial information).

The need for independent audits of financial statements can further be attributed to four conditions as follows:

■ **Conflict of Interest.** Many users of financial statements are concerned about an actual or potential conflict of interest between themselves and the management of the reporting entity. The apprehension extends to a fear that the financial statements prepared by management may be significantly biased in management's favor. A 1998 *Business Week* survey found that 67 percent of CFOs had been asked to misrepresent results and that 12 percent did so.[4] In the same year *CFO Magazine* did a survey that found that 45 percent of CFOs had been asked to misrepresent financial results and that 38 percent of the group did so.[5] Users seek assurance from outside independent auditors that financial statements are free of management bias to combat these pressures.

■ **Consequence.** Published financial statements represent an important and, in some cases, the only source of information used in making significant lending, investment, and other decisions. Thus, users want the financial statement to contain as much relevant and reliable information as possible. This need is recognized by the extensive disclosure requirements imposed by the SEC on the companies under its jurisdiction. It is also recognized by the relevance of GAAP disclosures to many lenders. Financial statement users look to the independent

---

[4] S. Shuster, "The Seventh Annual Business Week Forum of Chief Finanicial Officers," *Business Week,* July 13, 1998.
[5] S. Barr, "Misreporting Results," *CFO: The Magazine for Senior Financial Executives,* December 1998, pp. 36–38.

auditor for assurance that the financial statements have been prepared in conformity with GAAP, including all the appropriate disclosures.

- **Complexity.** Both the subject matter of accounting and the process of preparing financial statements have become increasingly complex. Accounting for the impairment of fixed assets or goodwill, and accounting for leases, pensions, and income taxes are examples of this complexity. As the level of complexity increases, so does the risk of misinterpretations and of intentional or unintentional misstatements. Finding it impossible to evaluate the quality of the financial statements themselves, users rely on the independent auditors to assess the quality of the information contained in the statements.
- **Remoteness.** Distance, time, and cost make it impractical for users of financial statements to seek direct access to the underlying accounting records to perform their own verifications of the financial statement assertions. Rather than accept the quality of the financial data on faith, once again users rely on the independent auditor's report to meet their needs.

These four conditions collectively contribute to **information risk,** which is the risk that the financial statements may be incorrect, incomplete, or biased. Thus, it can be said that financial statement audits enhance the credibility of financial statement by reducing information risk. This information risk was exhibited in cases such as material misstatement of earnings at WorldCom.

<table>
<tr><td>

Auditor Knowledge 8

■ Know the economic benefits and inherent limitations associated with a financial statement audit.

</td></tr>
</table>

ECONOMIC BENEFITS OF AN AUDIT

The annual audit fee for Microsoft, a Fortune 500 company, was disclosed as $15.9 million for the year ended June 30, 2004. Clearly, economic benefits must accrue from audits to justify such costs. Among the economic benefits of financial statement audits are the following:

- **Access to Capital Markets.** As noted previously, public companies must satisfy statutory audit requirements under the federal securities acts in order to register securities and have them traded on securities markets. In addition, stock markets may impose their own requirements for listing securities. Without audits, companies would be denied access to these capital markets and many private companies would be denied access to loans.
- **Lower Cost of Capital.** Small companies often have financial statement audits to obtain bank loans on more favorable borrowing terms. Because of the reduced information risk associated with audited financial statements, creditors may offer loans with lower interest rates.
- **Deterrent to Inefficiency and Fraud.** Research has demonstrated that when employees know that an independent audit is to be made, they take care to make fewer errors in performing accounting functions and are less likely to misappropriate company assets. Thus, the data in company records will be more reliable, and losses from embezzlements and the like will be reduced. In addition, the fact that financial statement assertions are to be verified reduces the likelihood that management will engage in fraudulent financial reporting.
- **Control and Operational Improvements.** Based on observations made during a financial statement audit, the independent auditor often makes suggestions to improve internal control, to evaluate management's assessments of business

risks, to recommend improved performance measures, and to make recommendations to achieve greater operational efficiencies within the client's organization. These benefits are especially valuable to small and medium-sized companies.

A company's management, including its board of directors, and shareholders find that the significant benefits discussed above make the financial statement audit valuable.

LIMITATIONS OF AN AUDIT

A financial statement audit is subject to a number of inherent limitations. One constraint is that the auditor works within fairly restrictive economic limits. Following are two important economic limitations.

- **Reasonable Cost.** A limitation on the cost of an audit results in selective testing, or sampling, of the accounting records and supporting data. In addition, the auditor may choose to test internal controls and may obtain assurance from a well-functioning system of internal controls.
- **Reasonable Length of Time.** The auditor's report on many public companies is usually issued three to five weeks after the balance sheet date. This time constraint may affect the amount of evidence that can be obtained concerning events and transactions after the balance sheet date that may have an effect on the financial statements. Moreover, there is a relatively short time period available for resolving uncertainties existing at the statement date.

Another significant limitation is the established accounting framework for preparing financial statements. Following are two important limitations associated with the established accounting framework.

- **Alternative Accounting Principles.** Alternative accounting principles are permitted under GAAP. Financial statement users must be knowledgeable about a company's accounting choices and their effect on financial statements.
- **Accounting Estimates.** Estimates are an inherent part of the accounting process, and no one, including auditors, can foresee the outcome of uncertainties. Estimates range from the allowance for doubtful accounts and an inventory obsolescence reserve to impairment tests for fixed assets and goodwill. An audit cannot add exactness and certainty to financial statements when these factors do not exist.

Despite these limitations, a financial statement audit adds credibility to the financial statements.

[LEARNING CHECK

1-8   Explain the historical development of the demand for financial statement audits.
1-9   Cite four factors that contribute to the need for a financial statement audit.
1-10 Explain four economic benefits of a financial statement audit.
1-11 Describe four the inherent limitations of a financial statement audit.

[KEY TERMS

Access to capital markets, p. 21
Accounting estimates, p. 22
Alternative accounting principles,
  p. 22
Complexity, p. 21
Conflict of interest, p. 20
Consequence, p. 20
Control and operational
  improvements, p. 21

Deterrent to inefficiency and fraud,
  p. 21
Information risk, p. 21
Lower cost of capital, p. 21
Reasonable cost, p. 22
Reasonable length of time, p. 22
Remoteness, p. 21

[ORGANIZATIONS ASSOCIATED WITH THE PUBLIC ACCOUNTING PROFESSION]

The modern profession of public accounting is influenced by a number of professional and regulatory organizations that either function within the profession itself or directly influence the profession through their standard-setting and regulatory activities. These organizations, representing both the private and public sectors, are identified in Figure 1-5.

Auditor Knowledge 9

■ Know the public sector and private sector organizations associated with auditing and assurance services.

PUBLIC SECTOR ORGANIZATIONS

Securities and Exchange Commission

The **Securities and Exchange Commission (SEC)** is a federal government agency that was created under the 1934 Securities Exchange Act to regulate the distribution of securities offered for public sale and subsequent trading of securities on stock exchanges and over-the-counter markets. Under the provisions of this Act, the SEC has the authority to establish GAAP for companies under its jurisdiction. Throughout its history, the SEC has, with few exceptions, delegated this authority to the private sector, and it currently recognizes the pronouncements of the FASB

Figure 1-5 ■ Organizations Associated with the Public Accounting Profession

Public Sector Organizations	Private Sector Organizations
Securities and Exchange Commission	Public Companies Accounting Oversight Board
State boards of accountancy	American Institute of Certified Public Accountants
U.S. General Accounting Office	State societies of certified public accountants
Internal Revenue Service	Practice units (CPA firms)
State and federal courts	Accounting standards setting bodies: FASB and GASB
U.S. Congress	

as constituting GAAP in the filing of financial statements with the agency. In some instances, however, the SEC's disclosure requirements exceed GAAP.

The SEC also exerts considerable influence over auditing and the public accounting profession. The Sarbanes-Oxley Act of 2002 established a private sector Public Companies Accounting Oversight Board (see p. 25) to oversee the audit of public companies that are subject to securities laws. The PCAOB's rulemaking process results in proposals that do not take effect until the SEC approves them. Over the years, the SEC has not been reluctant to use this authority. Further consideration is given in Chapter 4 to the independent auditor's responsibilities in filings with the SEC.

State Boards of Accountancy

There are 54 boards of accountancy (one in each state, one in the District of Columbia, and one in each U.S. territory). The primary functions of the **state boards of accountancy** are issuing licenses to practice as a CPA, renewing licenses, and suspending or revoking licenses to practice. State boards usually consist of five to seven CPAs and at least one public member, who are generally appointed by the governor. A full-time administrator and a small (five to ten) administrative staff are common. Each board administers its state accountancy laws, which set forth the conditions for licensing of CPAs, codes of professional ethics, and, in most cases, mandatory continuing professional education requirements. State boards are also becoming more active in positive enforcement programs aimed at maintaining high quality in audit practice.

U.S. General Accounting Office

The **General Accounting Office (GAO)** is the nonpartisan, federal audit agency of the U.S. Congress. Headed by the Comptroller General of the United States, the GAO has the authority to issue standards pertaining to the audit of governmental organizations, programs, activities, and functions. Its standards have been published in a booklet called *Government Auditing Standards,* also known as the "yellow book" after the color of its cover. These standards apply not only to government auditors, but to CPAs who perform audits of federal agencies and other entities that receive federal financial assistance, including state and local governments, institutions of higher education, and certain nonprofit organizations and contractors.

Internal Revenue Service

The Internal Revenue Service (IRS) is the division of the U.S. Treasury Department responsible for administration and enforcement of the federal tax laws. A publication that has a major influence on CPAs who perform tax services is the IRS's Circular 230, *Rules Governing the Practice of Attorneys and Agents Before the Internal Revenue Service.* CPAs who depart from these rules are subject to fines and other penalties that can be imposed by the IRS.

State and Federal Courts

Occasionally, CPA firms are sued for alleged substandard work in performing audits or other services. In reaching a judgment in a particular case, generally the courts have looked to the standards of performance established by the profession itself. But occasionally, the courts have ruled that the profession's standards were not adequate for the protection of the public. Following trends of such court decisions, the profession has responded by raising existing practice standards. Examples include mandating the use of particular auditing procedures pertaining to accounts receivable, inventories, related-party transactions, and the discovery of subsequent events.

U.S. Congress

Following a number of widely publicized audit failures, congressional committees have undertaken several investigations of the accounting profession over the past two decades. The investigations have focused on such matters as the independence of CPA firms, their effectiveness in auditing publicly held companies, and their responsibilities for detecting and reporting fraud and illegal client acts (whistleblowing). The financial frauds at Enron and WorldCom prompted an inquiry into whether the profession's regulatory system is adequate to protect the public. In response, Congress passed the Sarbanes-Oxley Act of 2002 that created the PCAOB which sets independence, auditing, quality control, and ethics standards for auditors of public companies.

PRIVATE SECTOR ORGANIZATIONS

Public Companies Accounting Oversight Board

The **Public Companies Accounting Oversight Board (PCAOB)** describes itself as a private sector, nonprofit corporation, created by the Sarbanes-Oxley Act of 2002, to oversee the auditors of public companies in order to protect the interests of investors and further the public interest in the preparation of informative, fair, and independent audit reports. The PCAOB was given authority in five major areas:

1. Registering public accounting firms that audit the financial statements of public companies.
2. Setting quality control standards for peer review of auditors of public companies and conducting inspections of registered public accounting firms.
3. Setting auditing standards for audits of public companies.
4. Setting independence and ethics rules for auditors of public companies.
5. Performing other duties or functions to promote high professional standards for public company audits, and enforce compliance with the Sarbanes-Oxley Act of 2002.

The PCAOB has enforcement authority and can prohibit CPA, or accounting firms, from auditing public companies. The PCAOB's rulemaking process results in the adoption of rules that are then submitted to the SEC for approval. PCAOB rules do not take effect unless approved by the SEC.

American Institute of Certified Public Accountants

The public accounting profession's national professional organization is the **American Institute of Certified Public Accountants (AICPA).** As stated in its annual report, the mission of the AICPA is to act on behalf of its members and provide necessary support to assure that CPAs serve the public interest in performing quality professional services. Membership in the AICPA is voluntary. Currently, there are over 300,000 members of whom 45 percent are in public accounting, 40 percent in business and industry, and the remainder in education, government, or retired.

The AICPA provides a broad range of services to its members. In addition, the AICPA develops and distributes continuing professional education (CPE) materials and courses, provides technical accounting and auditing assistance through a technical information hotline and an extensive library of technical references, and publishes a variety of books, studies, and surveys, as well as three periodicals—the *Journal of Accountancy, The Tax Advisor,* and *The CPA Letter.*

Through its senior technical committees, members participate in establishing a variety of professional standards for CPAs who provide services to private companies. Three AICPA divisions or teams have a direct impact on auditing.

1. The AICPA Practice Monitoring Program is responsible for quality control standards and peer reviews of firms that provide assurance services to private companies.
2. The Auditing and Attest Standards Team sets auditing and attest standards for audit, accounting, and review services provided to private companies.
3. The Professional Ethics Division is responsible for setting and enforcing the AICPA Code of Professional Conduct.

State Societies of Certified Public Accountants

CPAs within each state have formed a state society (or association) of CPAs. As in the AICPA, membership in a state society is voluntary and many CPAs are members of both the AICPA and a state society. State societies function through small full-time staffs and committees composed of their members. Although state societies are autonomous, they usually cooperate with each other and the AICPA in areas of mutual interest, such as continuing professional education, quality control, and ethics.

Practice Units (CPA Firms)

A CPA may practice as a sole practitioner or as a member of a firm. A CPA firm may be organized as a proprietorship, limited liability partnership, professional corporation, or any other form of organization permitted by state law or regulation. There are approximately 45,000 practice units in the United States. These firms are often classified into four groups—the Big Four, second-tier, regional, and local firms.

The four largest firms in the United States are referred to as the Big Four. Together, their clients include over 95 percent of the Fortune 500 companies and thousands of smaller clients. The combined U.S. revenues of the Big Four exceeded $20 billion in 2003, or about one-quarter of the total revenues of the U.S. profession. Each of these firms had worldwide affiliations with partnerships in many countries. With offices in the principal cities of the United States as well as major cities throughout the world, these are truly international firms. The competitive environment is changing as some of the largest accounting firms are not CPA firms. Names like H&R Block, Century Business Services, and

American Express are on the list. Selected additional data for these and several other practice units are presented in Figure 1-6. In 1999 each of the Big Four firms earned less than 50 percent of its revenues from accounting and auditing services. These firms have now sold off significant portions of their consulting practices, and the pendulum has swung back to a point where the majority of these firms earn over 60 percent of their revenues from accounting and auditing services.

As the figure shows, distinct gaps in the size of revenues separate the second-tier firms from both the Big Four and smaller firms. Although the international reach of these firms is significantly less than that of the Big Four, the domestic practice of each is national in scope. Thus, these firms provide competition for the Big Four in serving large, publicly held companies as well as other clients of all sizes.

Figure 1-6 also includes three examples of regional firms. The offices of these firms tend to be concentrated in a more limited geographical area such as the East, Midwest, or West. Although these firms serve some publicly owned companies, their clients tend to be smaller than those of the Big Four and second-tier firms.

Local firms may have one or several offices within a state. The local firm is by far the most common form of practice unit. Although some local firms serve public companies, their clients are primarily smaller businesses and individuals. Some of the smallest local firms decline to perform audit services because of the high cost of maintaining competence and the increased exposure to legal liability.

To remain competitive, many smaller and midsized firms join an association of CPA firms. There are more than two dozen associations in the United States with as few as 6 and as many as 60 practice unit members. Associations vary widely in the services provided to members, but most offer staff training programs, a directory of experts in member firms available for consultation with other member firms about their areas of expertise, assistance in recruiting personnel, and client referral services.

Accounting Standard-Setting Bodies

The Financial Accounting Standards Board (FASB) and Governmental Accounting Standards Board (GASB) are independent private sector standard-setting bodies whose primary functions are the development of generally accepted accounting principles for business and not-for-profit entities, and state and local governmental entities, respectively. The statements and interpretations issued by both boards have been officially recognized by the AICPA as constituting GAAP.

The FASB consists of seven full-time members who are assisted by a research staff and an advisory council. Before its Statements of Financial Accounting Standards (SFASs) are issued, a due process is followed including issuing exposure drafts for public comment and, in some cases, holding public hearings. The GASB follows a similar process in issuing its Statements of Governmental Accounting Standards (SGASs).

Figure 1-6 ■ Select Accounting Firm Data

Rank by Revenue	Firm	U.S. Revenue ($Mil)	No. of U.S. Offices	No. of Partners	Prof. Staff	Revenues Sources (%) Actg/ Audit	Tax	MCS/ Other
Big Four								
1	Deloitte & Touche	6,511.0	91	2,613	20,487	39%	25%	27%
2	Ernst & Young	5,260.0	86	2,000	14,400	62%	35%	3%
3	PricewaterhouseCoopers	4,850.0	125	2,000	21,000	62%	33%	5%
4	KPMG	3,793.0	94	1,622	11,529	67%	33%	0%
		20,414.0						
Second Tier								
5	H&R Block	3,694.7	10,000	n.a.	n.a.	0%	58%	42%
6	RSM McGladrey	595.9	91	498	2,701	39%	42%	19%
7	Grant Thornton	484.8	48	328	2,217	52%	33%	15%
8	Jackson Hewitt Tax Inc.	397.3	4,225	n.a.	129	0%	100%	0%
9	American Express Tax and Business Services	367.5	50	330	1,650	36%	32%	32%
10	Century Business Services Inc.	354.0	146	n.a.	1,475	40%	40%	20%
11	BDO Seidman	350.0	36	281	1,243	46%	37%	17%
Regional								
12	Crowe Group LLP	247.3	16	153	925	24%	19%	57%
13	BKD	215.7	27	194	952	42%	36%	22%
14	Moss Adams	181.0	23	185	825	36%	38%	26%
Local								
23	Eisner	71.9	3	65	234	53%	27%	20%
25	Berdon	64.0	2	39	245	38%	36%	26%

Source: Accounting Today Special Report: Top 100 Firms Study 2000, March 2004.

[LEARNING CHECK

1-12 Identify six public sector organizations and five private sector organizations associated with the auditing profession.

1-13 Explain the authority of the SEC and state boards of accountancy with respect to auditors and the auditing profession.

1-14 a. Explain the authority given to the PCAOB.

b. Identify three important AICPA divisions or teams that have a direct impact on auditors.

1-15 a. In what form of business may a CPA firm be organized?
b. In what four groups are CPA firms often classified?

[KEY TERMS

American Institute of Certified
  Public Accountants (AICPA), p. 25
General Accounting Office, p. 24
Public Companies Accounting
  Oversight Board (PCAOB), p. 25

Securities and Exchange Commission
  (SEC), p. 23
State boards of accountancy, p. 24

[REGULATORY FRAMEWORK FOR ENSURING HIGH-QUALITY SERVICES]

Auditor Knowledge 10

■ Know the four components of the auditing profession's multilevel regulatory framework.

Every profession is concerned about the quality of its services, and the public accounting profession is no exception. Quality services are essential to ensure that the profession meets its responsibilities to the general public, clients, and regulators.

To help assure quality in the performance of audits and other professional services, the profession has developed a multilevel regulatory framework. This framework encompasses many activities of the private and public sector organizations associated with the profession that were described in previous sections of this chapter. For purposes of describing the multilevel framework, these activities may be organized into four components as follows:

■ **Standard setting.** The private and public sectors establish standards for accounting, professional services, ethics, and quality control to govern the conduct of CPAs and CPA firms.

■ **Firm regulation.** Each CPA firm adopts policies and procedures to assure that practicing accountants adhere to professional standards.

■ **Inspection and peer review.** The PCAOB and the AICPA have implemented a comprehensive program of inspection of audits by PCAOB staff and peers in other accounting firms.

■ **Government regulation.** Only qualified professionals are licensed to practice, and auditor conduct is monitored and regulated by the PCAOB, state boards of accountancy, and the courts.

Each component is discussed further in the following sections.

STANDARD SETTING

When performing auditing and assurance services CPAs must follow a variety of professional standards. Those standards are set differently for services performed for public companies and for private companies. Figure 1-7 outlines the various professional organizations that set relevant professional standards.

The focus of this discussion relates to the standards that influence the performance of high-quality audits. This book addresses **standard setting** that influences

Figure 1-7 ■ Standard-Setting Organizations in the United States

	Public Companies	Private Companies
Accounting: Generally accepted standards followed when preparing financial statements.	FASB/GASB/SEC	FASB/GASB
Auditing: Generally accepted standards for performing audits and reporting on financial statements.	PCAOB	AICPA
Quality Control: Standards for quality of practice that provide the basis for inspection and peer review.	PCAOB	AICPA
Ethics and Professional Conduct: Standards for ethical conduct.	PCAOB	AICPA
Other Attest and Assurance Services: Standards for performing other attest engagements or other assurance services.	AICPA	AICPA

the performance of high-quality audits and other assurance services—for example, professional standards associated with auditing standards, quality control standards, ethical standards, and standards for other attest and assurance services. In April 2003 the PCAOB adopted existing auditing and quality control standards that had previously been developed by the AICPA. The auditing standards that are common to the audits of both public and private companies are discussed throughout this book, along with discussion of additional standards that pertain to the audits of public companies. Quality control standards are examined below. When this book went to press, the quality control standards were the same for public and private companies. Standards for ethical conduct are discussed in Chapter 3. Once again, ethical standards that are common for auditors of public and private companies are discussed, along with how independence standards differ for auditors of public and private companies. Other attest and assurance services are discussed in Part 5 of this book.

Quality Control Standards

Statement on Quality Control Standards (SQCS) No. 1, System of Quality Control for a CPA Firm, mandates that a CPA firm shall have a system of quality control. SQCS No. 2 identifies five quality control elements that should be considered by a firm in adopting quality control policies and procedures to provide reasonable assurance of conforming with professional standards in performing auditing and accounting and review services. Their application to other services such as tax and consulting is voluntary. The five elements and their purposes are shown in Figure 1-8.

Quality control standards are important because they provide the basis for conducting peer reviews and inspections of the quality of work performed by CPA firms. The five elements of quality control can be summarized as follows:

Independence, Integrity, and Objectivity

Independence, integrity, and objectivity address whether a firm has no appearance of a vested interest in the client for whom it is performing attest services, and whether the firm performs professional services without subordi-

Auditor Knowledge 11

■ Know the elements of a system of quality control for a CPA firm's attest practice.

Figure 1-8 ■ Quality Control Elements (SQCS No. 2)

Element	Purpose
Independence, Integrity, and Objectivity	A firm should establish policies and procedures to assure that personnel: ■ Are independent of clients when performing attest services. ■ Perform all professional responsibilities with integrity and maintain objectivity while performing those responsibilities.
Personnel Management	The firm's policies and procedures related to personnel management should provide it with reasonable assurance that: ■ Personnel hired have the characteristics needed to perform competently. ■ Work is assigned to personnel who have the technical training and proficiency required for the assignment. ■ Personnel selected for advancement have the qualifications needed to perform the responsibilities they will be called on to assume. ■ Personnel participate in general and industry-specific continuing professional education and other professional development activities that enable them to fulfill their assigned responsibilities and the requirements of the AICPA and regulatory agencies.
Acceptance and Continuance of Clients and Engagements	In general, a firm should establish policies and procedures that minimize the likelihood of being associated with a client whose management lacks integrity. In addition, the firm must establish policies and procedures that: ■ Provide reasonable assurance that it will accept only engagements it can complete with due professional competence. ■ Facilitate an understanding with the client about the nature, scope, and limitations of the services to be performed.
Engagement Performance	A firm should establish policies and procedures for: ■ Planning, performing, supervising, reviewing, documenting, and communicating the results of each engagement. ■ Assuring that personnel consult with other professionals and seek assistance from persons having appropriate expertise, judgment, and authority, when appropriate, and on a timely basis.
Monitoring	Monitoring is an ongoing process of evaluating the firm's system of quality control. Inspection is a measure of the system of quality control at a point in time. A firm must establish policies and procedures that provide an ongoing consideration and evaluation of: ■ Relevance and adequacy of its policies and procedures. ■ Appropriateness of its guidance materials and any practice aids. ■ Effectiveness of professional development activities. ■ Compliance with its policies and procedures.

nating judgment and in a way that is free of conflicts of interest. For example, an international firm may have professional staff report their investments on a regular basis so that they make sure that professionals are independent of the clients in cases where they might influence the outcome of an audit. In addition, the tone communicated from the highest levels of a CPA firm should encourage CPAs to act with integrity and objectivity. These concepts are discussed in more depth in Chapter 3.

Personnel Management

Personnel management addresses a variety of procedures within a CPA firm for hiring, promoting, and firing accounting professionals. An important aspect of performing an audit involves making sure that auditors have adequate training, experience, and supervision to perform assigned tasks. Audit firms need to have procedures in place so that they hire employees with sufficient technical competence, they give individuals the training to allow for their advancement, and they ensure that work assignments and promotions are consistent with an individual's technical training and proficiency. Many firms evaluate work performance after work is completed for each client as a basis for effective personnel management.

Acceptance and Continuance of Clients and Engagements

Auditors have several concerns about **acceptance and continuance of clients and engagements.** First, the audit process relies on management's cooperation, and the process can break down if the client lacks honesty and integrity. CPA firms want to take steps to minimize the likelihood of being associated with a client that lacks integrity. Second, auditors also need to ensure that they can reasonably expect to complete an engagement with professional competence. It is common for some smaller audit firms to decline the audit of public companies or to decline engagements of clients in industries where they do not have sufficient expertise.

Engagement Performance

Engagement performance is about the policies and practices that ensure an audit is carried out appropriately with due professional care. For example, many key audit decisions require significant professional judgment. Many firms will therefore have several professionals review the work of others to ensure that professionals concur on key issues and that the working papers document compliance with professional standards.

Monitoring

Monitoring is an ongoing process whereby a firm evaluates the effectiveness of the other four elements of quality control. Most firms perform internal inspections in which a team from other offices actually inspects audit working papers, evidence of compliance with independence policies, personnel management decisions, and client acceptance and continuance decisions. In this way the firm monitors compliance with its own policies.

As a firm considers how it will administer a system of quality control, it should consider three key issues. First, responsibility should be assigned within the firm to appropriate individuals for the design and maintenance of its quality control policies. Second, it should communicate its quality control policies and procedures to its personnel on a timely basis in a manner that provides reasonable assurance that they are understood and complied with. Finally, it should document compliance with its quality control policies and procedures. The form and content of the documentation is a matter of professional judgment and depends on such factors as firm size, number of offices, degree of authority allowed personnel and offices, the nature and complexity of the accounting and attest practice, firm organization, and cost-benefit considerations.

FIRM REGULATION

Firm regulation occurs within a CPA firm. A prime example is implementing a system of quality control as mandated by the quality control standards discussed in the preceding section. This means that the firm's day-to-day actions will comply with the policies and procedures pertaining to the quality control elements. For example, to assist staff in meeting professional standards, firms provide on-the-job training and require their professionals to participate in continuing professional education courses. Personnel who adhere to standards for professional services and show growth and progression in their skills often receive pay raises and promotions. Personnel whose work is identified as substandard may be terminated if rapid improvement is not forthcoming.

A CPA firm is motivated by numerous incentives to do good work, including pride, professionalism, and a desire to be competitive with other firms. Additional motivation results from the desire to avoid the expense and damage to the firm's reputation that accompanies litigation and other actions brought against it for alleged noncompliance with professional standards.

INSPECTION AND PEER REVIEW

Quality control standards provide the basis for firm regulation and the performance of high-quality audit and attest services. **Inspection and peer review** provide an external review of whether a firm is in fact meeting quality control standards. The following discussion outlines both the PCAOB's inspection program of accounting firms that audit public companies and the AICPA's practice monitoring (peer review) program of accounting firms that perform audit and attest services for private companies.

PCAOB Inspection Program

The Sarbanes-Oxley Act of 2002 instructs the PCAOB to conduct a continuing program of inspections to assess the degree of compliance of each accounting firm registered to audit public companies with the rules of the PCAOB, the SEC, and other professional standards in connection with its performance of audits, issuance of audit reports, and related matters. In conducting inspections, the Sarbanes-Oxley Act of 2002 states that the PCAOB should:

- Inspect and review selected audit and review engagements of the firm.
- Evaluate the sufficiency of the firm's quality control systems and the firm's documentation and communication of that system.
- Perform such other testing of the audit, supervisory, and quality control procedures of the firm as are necessary or appropriate in light of the purpose of the inspection and the responsibilities of the board.

The PCAOB conducts annual inspections of firms that regularly provide audit reports for over 100 public companies. The PCAOB inspects the quality control activities of firms that provide audit reports for 100 or fewer public companies every three years.

Finally, the Sarbanes-Oxley Act of 2002 states that a written report of the Board's findings for each inspection shall be transmitted to the SEC and to each appropriate state regulatory authority, accompanied by any letter of response from the registered public accounting firm, and shall be made available in appropriate detail to the public.

AICPA Practice Monitoring (Peer Review) Program

Since the early 1980s the AICPA has sponsored a practice monitoring program through which a CPA firm would submit its accounting and auditing practice to a review by independent peers every three years. Participation is required for all members of the AICPA, and many state boards of accountancy require that auditors of private companies undergo a form of peer review equivalent to the AICPA program. Recall that auditors of public companies are inspected by the PCAOB.

The purpose of a peer review is to determine whether:

■ The reviewed firm's system of quality control for its accounting and auditing practice has been designed in accordance with quality control standards established by the AICPA.
■ The reviewed firm's quality control policies and procedures were being complied with to provide the firm with reasonable assurance of conforming with professional standards.
■ The reviewed firm has demonstrated the knowledge, skills, and abilities necessary to perform accounting, auditing, and attestation engagements in accordance with professional standards, in all material respects.

At the end of the peer review, the independent peer review team will issue a report on the firm's compliance with quality control standards and, if applicable, a letter of comment with recommendations for improvement. The firm may then file the report with the state board of accountancy, and clients can ask to see the results of a firm's peer review.

GOVERNMENT REGULATION

Government regulates the auditing profession primarily through the activities of state boards of accountancy (which have the authority to issue and revoke CPA licenses), the SEC, and state and federal courts as discussed in previous sections.

Recently, the U.S. Congress enacted the Sarbanes-Oxley Act of 2002 with regulatory legislation to be administered by the SEC and the PCAOB. The SEC plays an important role in linking private sector and public sector regulation; it does so through its authority over the PCAOB, a private sector organization. It is the SEC that puts significant teeth in the standard-setting, inspection, and enforcement authority of the PCAOB.

State boards of accountancy regularly ask firms to submit their peer review letters as part of obtaining a license for the firm to perform audit and attest services. Although peer reviews are performed as part of the self-regulation of the CPAs performing services for private companies, it is the state board of accountancy that has the authority to grant or revoke a CPA's, or CPA firm's, license to practice.

[LEARNING CHECK

1-16 a. What is the purpose of the profession's multilevel regulatory framework?
b. Describe the four components of the multilevel regulatory framework.

1-17 State the five elements of a system of quality control for a CPA firm.

1-18 a. Describe the key elements of the PCAOB inspection program.
b. Describe the purpose of the AICPA practice monitoring (peer review) program.

[KEY TERMS

Acceptance and continuance of
   clients and engagements, p. 32
Engagement performance, p. 32
Firm regulation, p. 29, 33
Government regulation, p. 29, 34
Independence, integrity, and
   objectivity, p. 30

Inspection and peer review, p. 29, 33
Monitoring, p. 32
Personnel management, p. 32
Standard setting, p.29

[FOCUS ON AUDITOR KNOWLEDGE]

This chapter introduces some basic knowledge about auditing and assurance services, presents the organizations associated with the public accounting profession, and provides an overview of the regulatory framework associated with ensuring high-quality audit and attest services. Figure 1-9 summarizes the key components of auditor knowledge discussed in this chapter and provides page references to where these decisions are discussed in more detail.

Figure 1-9 ■ Summary of Auditor Knowledge Discussed in Chapter 1

Auditor Knowledge	Summary	Chapter References
K1. Know the common attributes of activities defined as auditing.	The Report of the Committee on Basic Auditing Concepts of the American Accounting Association defines **auditing** as "a *systematic process* of *objectively obtaining and evaluating evidence* regarding *assertions about economic actions and events* to ascertain *the degree of correspondence* between those assertions and *established criteria* and *communicating the results* to *interested users*." The common attributes auditing activities are identified in the preceding italics.	pp. 6–7
K2. Know the differences between the different types of audits and auditors.	This chapter distinguishes between financial statement audits, compliance audits, and operational audits. Figure 1-2 provides a useful summary of the difference between these types of audits. The chapter also discusses the differences between independent auditors, internal auditors, and government auditors.	pp. 8–11
K3. Know the common attributes of assurance services.	The AICPA Special Committee on Assurance Services defines assurance services as "*independent professional services* that *improve the quality of information, or its context,* for *decision makers*." The common attributes of assurance services are identified in the preceding italics.	pp. 11–12
		(table continues)

Figure 1-9 ■ (Continued)

Auditor Knowledge	Summary	Chapter References
K4. Know the variety of services and levels of assurance in the universe of assurance services.	Figure 1-3 describes the universe of assurance services, which includes audit engagements, attest engagements, accounting and compilation engagements, and other assurance engagements. CPAs can provide a variety of levels of assurance when performing these engagements including reasonable assurance, negative assurance, assurance that varies with the nature of agreed-upon procedures, and engagements with no assurance.	pp. 12–15
K5. Know the value of the audit and other assurance services.	Decision makers need credible and reliable information to support their decisions. The purpose of the audit is to provide reasonable assurance that information used by investors, creditors, and others is, in fact, reliable. Figure 1-4 demonstrates that the information captured about business events is the foundation for many business decisions. If this foundation is weak, every step that builds on that foundation is also weak. The value of the audit can be seen in the losses suffered by investors in WorldCom who made investment decisions based on unreliable information about the company's profitability and liquidity and solvency risks.	pp. 15–17
K6. Know a historical perspective of the demand for auditing.	The chapter provides a historical prospective that looks back on the last 120 years and the events that have influenced the demand for auditing. In general, the demand for auditing has been significantly influenced by professional managers who misled investors by materially misstating their company's financial performance in financial statements prepared for owners and other investors. Auditors add credibility to management's assertions by reducing information risk for financial statement users.	pp. 18–20
K7. Know the factors that influence the need for financial statement audits.	The need for financial statement audits has been influenced by an inherent *conflict of interest* between management and owners, by the *consequence* and importance of financial statement information to investors, by the *complexity* inherent in the preparation of financial statements, and by the *remoteness* of investors from management of the firms they invest in.	pp. 20–21
K8. Know the economic benefits and inherent limitations associated with a financial statement audit.	The economic benefits of an audit to a company and its owners include (1) access to capital markets, (2) lower cost of capital, (3) the audit as a deterrent to inefficiency and fraud, and (4) control and operational improvements that are often suggested by auditors. The inherent limitations of an audit include the fact that audits must be performed (1) at a reasonable cost and (2) in a reasonable length of time. There are also two important inherent limitations associated with our established accounting framework: (1) alternative accounting principles are often accepted and (2) the accounting process involves making significant accounting estimates.	pp. 21–22

(table continues)

Figure 1-9 ■ (Continued)

Auditor Knowledge	Summary	Chapter References
K9. Know the public sector and private sector organizations associated with auditing and assurance services.	Figure 1-5 summarizes a number of public sector and private sector organizations that are associated with the public accounting profession. The chapter explains their role in accounting and auditing.	pp. 23–28
K10. Know the four components of the auditing profession's multilevel regulatory framework.	The four components of the auditing profession's multilevel regulatory framework are (1) standard setting (see Figure 1-7), (2) firm regulation, (3) inspection and peer review, and (4) government regulation.	pp. 29–30
K11. Know the elements of a system of quality control for a CPA firm's attest practice.	The five elements of quality control are (1) independence, integrity, and objectivity, (2) personnel management, (3) acceptance and continuance of clients and engagements, (4) engagement performance, and (5) monitoring. Each of these elements is explained further in Figure 1-8. The system of quality control provides the standards by which the profession evaluates an audit firm's quality of practice when performing peer reviews.	pp. 30–34

objective questions

Objective questions are available for the students at www.wiley.com/college/boynton

comprehensive questions

1-19   **(Types of audits and auditors)** J. Cowan, an engineer, is the president of Arco Engineering. At a meeting of the board of directors, Cowan was asked to explain why audits of the company are made by (1) internal auditors, (2) independent auditors, and (3) government auditors. One board member suggested that the company's total audit expense might be lower if all auditing was done by internal auditors. J. Cowan was unable to distinguish between the three types of auditors or to satisfactorily respond to the board member's suggestion.

Required

a. Explain the different kinds of audits made by each type of auditor.

b. Identify the sources of practice standards applicable to each type of auditor.

c. Comment on the board member's suggestion to have all auditing done by internal auditors.

1-20   **(Types of audits and auditors)** After performing an audit, the auditor determines that

1. The financial statements of a corporation are presented fairly.

2. A company's receiving department is inefficient.

3. A company's tax return does not conform with IRS regulations.

4. A government supply depot is not meeting planned program objectives.

5. The financial statements of a physician are properly prepared on a cash basis.

6. A foreman is not carrying out his assigned responsibilities.

7. The IRS is in violation of an established government employment practice.

8. A company is meeting the terms of a government contract.

9. A municipality's financial statements correctly show actual cash receipts and disbursements.

10. The postal service in midtown is inefficient.

11. A company is meeting the terms of a bond contract.

12. A department is not meeting the company's prescribed policies concerning overtime work.

Required

a. Indicate the type of audit that is involved: (1) financial, (2) compliance, or (3) operational.

b. Identify the type of auditor that is involved: (1) independent, (2) internal, (3) government—GAO, or (4) government—IRS.

c. Identify the primary recipient(s) of the audit report: stockholders, management, Congress, and so on. Use the following format for your answers:

TYPE OF AUDIT	TYPE OF AUDITOR(S)	PRIMARY RECIPIENT(S)

1-21   **(Accountant value chain and the value of the audit)** You have just completed an audit for a small business client. In the process of performing the audit you found that the client turns its receivables, on average, every 58 days (this is after the client increased its provision for doubtful accounts based on your audit). You also discover that the median collection period for the industry is 45 days and the upper quartile is 59 days. Answer the following questions using this information.

Required

a. Explain each step of the account's value chain in the context of this information and knowledge.

b. Explain the value of the audit in the context of whether the financial statements are compiled versus being audited.

1-22   **(Benefits and limitations of an audit)** A fellow business student questions the benefits of an audit as follows. "Why should a company hire auditors? As far as I can tell auditors of public companies charge millions of dollars in audit fees, and it is not clear to me that management receives any benefit for this expenditure. It is just money down the drain. It is also not clear to me that auditors accomplish anything. We have seen a number of material restatements of financial statements. Why should a company pay for audits that are ineffective? I think auditors are just a drain on society."

Required

a. Explain the economic benefits provided by a financial statement audit.

b. Explain the inherent limitations that might prevent auditors from finding every potential material misstatement in financial statements.

1-23 **(Organizations associated with the public accounting profession)** Several private and public sector organizations are associated with the profession. Listed below are activities pertaining to these organizations.

1. License individuals to practice as CPAs.

2. Promulgate GAAP.

3. Issue Statements on Auditing Standards.

4. Regulate the distribution and trading of securities offered for public sale.

5. Establish its own code of professional ethics.

6. Issue Statements of Financial Accounting Standards.

7. Impose mandatory continuing education as a requirement for renewal of license to practice as a CPA.

8. Issue disclosure requirements for companies under its jurisdiction that may exceed GAAP.

9. Issue auditing interpretations.

10. Cooperate with the AICPA in areas of mutual interest such as continuing professional education and ethics enforcement.

11. Take punitive action against an independent auditor.

12. Establish accounting principles for state and local governmental entities.

13. Establish GAAS.

14. Suspend or revoke a CPA's license to practice.

15. Establish quality control standards.

16. Operate as proprietorships, partnerships, or professional corporations.

17. Issue government auditing standards.

18. Administer federal tax laws.

Required

Indicate the organization or organizations associated with each activity.

1-24 **(Regulatory framework)** The accounting profession's commitment to achieving high quality in rendering professional services is demonstrated by the breadth and effectiveness of its multilevel regulatory framework.

Required

a. One component of this framework is standard setting which occurs primarily in the private sector. Identify four types of standards included in this component and the private sector bodies that establish them.

b. Identify and briefly describe the other three components of the regulatory framework.

1-25   **(Quality control elements)** The AICPA has established five elements of quality control. Listed below are specific policies and procedures adopted by the CPA firm of Baily, Brown & Co.:

1. Periodic evaluations are made of personnel.

2. Ongoing supervision is given to less experienced personnel.

3. An experienced CPA is designated as a public utility industry expert.

4. Rules on independence are communicated to the professional staff.

5. The scope and content of the firm's inspection program are defined.

6. All new employees must be college graduates.

7. Copies of Statements on Auditing Standards are provided for all professional staff.

8. A partner assigns personnel to engagements.

9. All new clients must be solvent at the time the engagement is accepted.

Required

a. Identify the quality control element that applies to each of the foregoing items.

b. For each element of quality control identified in (a) state the purpose of the element.

c. Indicate another policy or procedure that applies to the element. Use the following format for your answers:

POLICY/ PROCEDURE NUMBER	(A) QUALITY CONTROL ELEMENT	(B) PURPOSE OF POLICY/PROCEDURE	(C) ADDITIONAL PROCEDURE

1-26   **(Regulating audit quality)** The Public Companies Accounting Oversight Board and the AICPA's Practice Monitoring (Peer Review) Program play important roles in the profession's regulation of the quality of audit and assurance services.

Required

a. The activities of these two organizations are directed toward CPA firms. How, if at all, do these divisions have a direct impact on individual members?

b. Why do we have two organizations involved in peer review? Discuss the similarities in the objectives of the peer reviews and practice monitoring programs of the PCAOB and the AICPA.

c. Identify the similarities in the peer review objectives of the two organizations and the common responsibilities and functions of the peer review teams used by each.

d. What are the primary activities of the AICPA Practice Monitoring (Peer Review) Program?

professional simulation

Tom Meyers has a successful tax practice as a sole practitioner. Tom is a sole owner and he has 3 professional staff to assist him in tax research and tax return preparation. He has a number of clients that have small, and growing businesses. He has compiled financial statements for these businesses with no assurance. As a result, he has had minimal requirements for peer review. Now he has several clients who have grown to the point where they need audited financial statements for lenders. In order to better serve these clients, Tom is considering taking in Kenny Vaughn, an audit manager with a national CPA firm, as a partner to manage a new audit and assurance practice.

Tom and Kenny want to better understand what will be required in terms of how the combined practice will need to follow quality control standards. In particular, they are concerned about professional requirements for monitoring compliance with quality control standards. Research the professional standards and identify the quality control standards that:

1. Explain the monitoring procedures that should be performed by the firm.

2. Explain the factors that should be considered by small firms with a limited number of management individuals.

Do this by indicating in the box below the appropriate QC section paragraphs that responds to these questions.

1. QC Section _____

2. QC Section _____

Draft a report with your recommendations for specific monitoring procedures that should be performed by Meyers and Vaughn. Remember: Your response will be graded for both technical relevance and writing skills. For writing skills you should demonstrate an ability to develop your ideas, organize them, and express them clearly.

To: Tom Meyers and Kenny Vaughn

Re: Monitoring Procedures

From: CPA Candidate

AUDITOR RESPONSIBILITY FOR GOING CONCERN

An auditor has a responsibility to determine if substantial doubt exists at the date of the auditor's report about whether the audit client can continue as a going concern for the next year. The auditor bases this evaluation on the evidence obtained in performing the audit and considers the entity's financial position as of the balance sheet date.

Now consider the following information. As the auditor is completing the audit, the auditor notes the following circumstances.

- In the last year revenues have grown $2\frac{1}{2}$ times, but profitability has fallen from 2 percent to 1 percent of sales. Nevertheless, the company reports over $1 billion in net income.
- The entity's ratio of debt to equity has grown from 2.5:1 to 4.7:1.
- Fifty-two percent of pretax income is from noncash sources.
- Reported cash flow from operations increases from $1.2 billion to $4.7 billion; however, a significant portion of operating cash flows may not be recurring.
- The company had cash and cash equivalents of $1.3 billion at year-end.
- In the normal course of business, the company must retire debt in the coming year in the amount of about $2.1 billion.
- Prices for the company's products are at record highs, and the product is in high demand.
- The company's stock is near an all-time high, and the company has access to equity markets.
- The company has an investment grade credit rating, and it has over $2 billion in committed lines of credit.

If this is what you know about the company as you are completing your audit, take a moment and consider whether the auditor should have *substantial doubt* about whether the entity can continue as a going concern. Does *substantial doubt* exist? Is evaluating whether substantial doubt exists a clear-cut right or wrong issue? Yes or no?

This information was taken from Enron's financial statements as of December 31, 2000. On December 2, 2001, Enron filed for bankruptcy protection. Should Andersen have issued a going-concern opinion when its audit opinion was issued on February 23, 2001? Or did Enron fail primarily because of events that happened during 2001 and were not known in February 2001? Although Andersen was heavily criticized for its failure to find material misstatements in Enron's report on financial position and results of operations (debt to equity should have been 5.3:1, and net income should have been $847 million rather than $979 million), there have been few criticisms of the fact that it did not issue a going-concern opinion.

Read on in this chapter to better understand the auditor's responsibility, not just with respect to going concern, but other responsibilities as well.

Source: Enron Financial Statements as of December 31, 2000.

[PREVIEW OF CHAPTER 2]

If an audit firm performs a high-quality audit, what is the standard by which users should judge its responsibility to find material misstatements and fraud in financial statements? What is the auditor's responsibility to address such issues as whether an entity is a going concern or whether the entity has violated the law? What responsibility does an auditor have to evaluate an entity's system of internal control? Chapter 2 explains the auditor's basic responsibilities and discusses how the auditor communicates the primary findings of an audit in an auditor's report on the financial statements. The chapter also explains how the auditor communicates findings in an audit report on internal control over financial reporting in the audit of a public company. The following diagram provides an overview of the chapter organization and content.

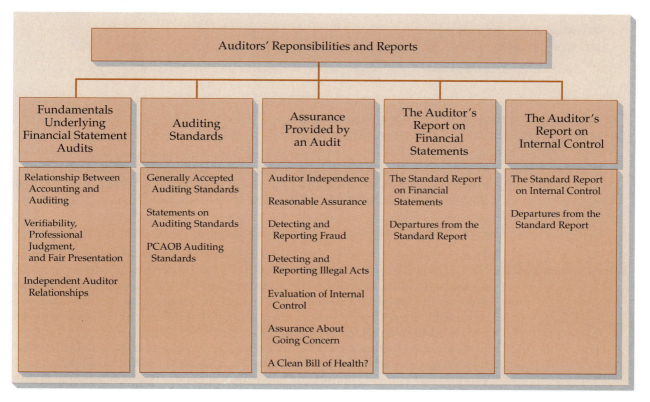

Chapter 2 addresses the following aspects of the auditor's knowledge and focuses on two important audit decisions addressed below.

focus on auditor knowledge

After studying this chapter you should understand the following aspects of an auditor's knowledge base:

K1. Know the relationship between accounting and auditing.

K2. Understand how the concept of verifiability relates to the concept of "fair presentation, in all material respects."

K3. Understand the auditor's relationship with management, the board of directors, the audit committee, and other groups.

K4. Know the 10 generally accepted auditing standards.

K5. Understand some important auditor's responsibilities that are implied by completing the audit.

K6. Understand the basic elements of the auditor's standard report on financial statements.

K7. Understand the basic elements of the auditor's standard report on internal controls over financial reporting.

---

focus on audit decisions

After studying this chapter you should understand the factors that influence the following audit decisions.

D1. When should the auditor use a nonstandard report on financial statements?

D2. When should the auditor use a nonstandard report on internal controls over financial reporting?

[FUNDAMENTALS UNDERLYING FINANCIAL STATEMENT AUDITS]

In this section, we examine the relationship between accounting and auditing. This section also explores the concept of verifiability in auditing and its relationship with the concept of reasonable assurance.

RELATIONSHIP BETWEEN ACCOUNTING AND AUDITING

Auditor Knowledge 1

■ **Know the relationship between accounting and auditing.**

There are significant differences in the methods, objectives, and parties responsible for the accounting process by which the financial statements are prepared and for the audit of the statements. Recall from Chapter 1 that management is responsible for the financial statements and related disclosures and that the auditor is responsible for obtaining reasonable assurance that those financial statements are presented fairly in all material respects.

Accounting methods involve identifying the events and transactions that affect the entity. Once identified, these items are measured, recorded, classified, and summarized in the accounting records. In addition, management should institute a system of internal control over that process to improve the reliability of financial reporting. The result of this process is the preparation and distribution of financial statements that are in conformity with generally accepted accounting principles (GAAP). The ultimate objective of accounting is the communication of relevant and reliable financial data that will be useful for decision making. Thus, accounting is a creative process. An entity's employees are involved in the accounting process, and ultimate responsibility for the financial statements lies with the entity's management.

The typical audit of financial statements involves performing risk assessment procedures to understand the entity's business and industry, including its system of internal control. This knowledge allows the auditor to develop a point of view regarding the risk of material misstatement. Armed with this knowledge, the auditor designs audit procedures to obtain evidence that are responsive to the assessed risks. The auditor uses this knowledgeable perspective to see if the risks are, in fact, present. Ultimately, the goal of a high-quality audit is to obtain reasonable assurance that the financial statements present fairly the entity's financial position, results of operations, and cash flows in conformity with GAAP.[1] Rather than creating new information, the primary objective of auditing is to add credibility to the financial statements prepared by management. Audits allow financial statement users to make decisions with knowledge about a high level of integrity (but not a guarantee) of the information that they are using to support their decisions.

The relationship between accounting and auditing in the financial reporting process is illustrated in Figure 2-1.

The current financial reporting model focuses on the measurement and reporting of transactions in financial statements. This process includes significant professional judgment involved in evaluating the reasonableness of accounting estimates. For example, today's financial reporting model expects management to estimate future cash flows from past transactions. Specifically, management must estimate current receivables that may not be collected in the future or examine whether the entity will sell the current inventory in the future at a price that is sufficient to recover its cost. The most significant challenge in today's audits comes from the prospective elements embedded in the current financial reporting model.

The majority of this book focuses on the audit of financial statements. However, audits of public companies are integrated audits in which the auditor audits (1) the financial statements, (2) management's assertion about the effectiveness of its internal control over financial reporting, and (3) the underlying effectiveness of the system of internal control. Although our primary focus is on the financial statement audit, in particular sections we will highlight the auditor's responsibility and communications with respect to auditing internal controls over financial reporting.

The auditor's understanding of the total business provides the context for many audit tests and positions the auditor to discuss a variety of accounting and financial performance issues with the audit committee or the board of directors. Furthermore, management may engage the auditor to provide other assurance services that build on the knowledge obtained while performing the audit.

VERIFIABILITY, PROFESSIONAL JUDGMENT, AND FAIR PRESENTATION

Auditor Knowledge 2

■ Understand how the concept of verifiability relates to the concept of "fair presentation, in all material respects."

Auditing is based on the assumption that financial statement data are verifiable. Data are verifiable when two or more qualified individuals, working independently, reach essentially similar conclusions from an examination of the data. Verifiability is primarily concerned with the availability of evidence attesting to the validity of the information being considered. In some disciplines, data are considered verifiable only if the examiners can prove beyond all doubt that the data are either true or false. This is not the case in accounting and auditing.

[1] In the case of public companies, the auditor should follow the standards of the Public Companies Accounting Oversight Board. In April 2003 the PCAOB adopted generally accepted auditing standards, and they will suggest modifications as appropriate for the audits of public companies.

Figure 2-1 ■ Relationship Between Accounting and Auditing

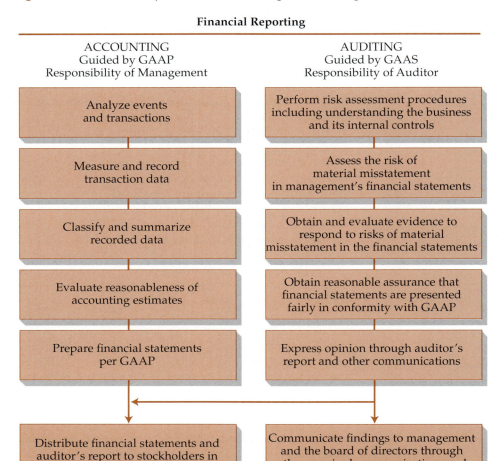

Financial Reporting

ACCOUNTING
Guided by GAAP
Responsibility of Management

AUDITING
Guided by GAAS
Responsibility of Auditor

ACCOUNTING	AUDITING
Analyze events and transactions	Perform risk assessment procedures including understanding the business and its internal controls
Measure and record transaction data	Assess the risk of material misstatement in management's financial statements
Classify and summarize recorded data	Obtain and evaluate evidence to respond to risks of material misstatement in the financial statements
Evaluate reasonableness of accounting estimates	Obtain reasonable assurance that financial statements are presented fairly in conformity with GAAP
Prepare financial statements per GAAP	Express opinion through auditor's report and other communications
Distribute financial statements and auditor's report to stockholders in annual report	Communicate findings to management and the board of directors through other required communications and assurance services

The concept of "**fair presentation** of financial position, results of operations, and cash flows, in all material respects" implies that there is a level of imprecision in accounting. Consider the following examples.

■ How precise is the balance for cash? In fact, it is fairly precise and is based on the amount of cash on deposit after accounting for deposits in transit, outstanding checks, and other reconciling items.

■ How precise is the balance for accounts receivable? Gross receivables can be fairly precise if it is based on actual shipment made and sales prices. However, revenue recognition practices in some industries (e.g., software, long-term contracts) require significant estimation. Moreover, the allowance for doubtful accounts adds an element of estimation and imprecision to the process of preparing financial statements.

■ How precise is the balance for inventory? How many different ways can a company compute the value of inventory? LIFO? dollar value LIFO? FIFO? the retail method? There may be a material difference in the valuation of inventory based on the choice of inventory methods. Furthermore, should variances from standard costs be included in inventory or directly expensed as part of cost of sales? Such questions must be answered to determine the cost of inventory, let alone considering the estimation involved in evaluating the net realizable value of inventory.

The imprecision in accounting leads to an imprecision in the ability to verify financial statement presentations. Accounting and auditing require the application of significant professional judgment. Hence, the auditor seeks only a reasonable basis for expressing an opinion on the fairness of the financial statements. In making an examination, the auditor obtains evidence for sound and well-grounded conclusions about the *fairness* and *representational faithfulness* of the accounting treatment of transactions, balances, and disclosures in the financial statements.

In addition, auditors must consider cost-benefit tradeoffs when performing an audit. Hence, an audit is only designed to look for misstatements in financial statements that are **material,** or significant, to financial statement users. Auditors may not attempt to verify items that are so small, or immaterial, that they have no significance for financial statement users. If various accounts included in accounts receivable are so small that they could not aggregate to an amount that would influence a financial statement user, the auditor will spend little time and effort verifying those accounts. In turn, the auditor does not perform a 100 percent audit. The auditor does, however, focus attention on those items that could aggregate to an amount that would be material, or significant, to a financial statement user. The concept of "fair presentation, in all material respects" implies that the auditor's involvement simply assures their reasonableness, not exactness.

INDEPENDENT AUDITOR RELATIONSHIPS

In a financial statement audit, the auditor maintains professional relationships with four important groups: (1) management, (2) the board of directors and audit committee, (3) internal auditors, and (4) stockholders.

Management

The term **management** refers collectively to individuals who actively plan, coordinate, and control the entity's operations and transactions. In an auditing context, management refers to the company officers, including its chief executive officer, its chief financial and operating officers, and key supervisory personnel. It is management that is responsible for fairly presenting financial position, results of operations, and cash flows in financial statements, not the auditor.

During the course of an audit, extensive interaction takes place between the auditor and management. To obtain the evidence needed in an audit, the auditor often requires confidential data about the entity. An adversary relationship will not work. Neither will a relationship in which management attempts to conceal evidence. It is imperative, therefore, to have a relationship based on mutual trust, respect, and a high degree of candor. Even with a high degree of mutual trust and respect, the typical approach the auditor should take toward management's assertions may be characterized as one of **professional skepticism.** This means that the auditor recognizes the need to objectively evaluate conditions observed and evidence obtained during the audit. The auditor should neither disbelieve management's assertions nor glibly accept them without underlying evidence.

Board of Directors and Audit Committee

The board of directors of a corporation is responsible for seeing that the corporation is operated in the best interests of the stockholders. The auditor's relationship with the directors depends largely on the composition of the board. In the case of many private companies, the board consists primarily of company officers (who often are also majority shareholders), and the auditor's relationship with the board and management is essentially one and the same. Many private companies do not have audit committees, in which case the auditor communicates required communications, such as weaknesses in internal controls or concerns about financial reporting, to the board as a whole. Even though management may own a majority of the shares of private companies, auditors should maintain an adequate degree of professional skepticism and consider the interests of minority shareholders.

Public companies usually have a number of independent, outside members on the board. Outside members may be owners in a company, but they are not officers or employees of the company and they usually only receive compensation from the company for their service as a director. (Compensation may be in the form of direct cash payments or stock options.) Public company **audit committees,** composed exclusively of outside, independent members of the board, serve as an intermediary between the auditor and management. Today public company audit committees must have individuals with significant accounting knowledge. The functions of an audit committee, as outlined in Section 301 of the Sarbanes-Oxley Act of 2002, is directly responsible for:

- Appointment, compensation, and oversight of the public accounting firm to conduct the annual audit.
- Establishing procedures for the receipt, retention, and treatment of complaints received by the public company regarding internal controls and auditing.

In addition, the audit committee shall have the authority to engage independent counsel or other advisors, as it determines necessary to carry out its duties.

An audit committee normally carries out these responsibilities by:

- Discussing the scope of the audit with the auditor.
- Inviting direct auditor communication on major problems encountered during the course of the audit.
- Reviewing the financial statements and discussing accounting principles, disclosures, and the auditor's report with the auditor on completion of the engagement.

In addition, the audit committee may be the primary check and balance over management discretion in financial reporting in smaller public companies. The auditor committee may review journal entries made by the CFO, accounting estimates, and the accounting for significant transactions. The audit committee also plays an important role in strengthening the auditor's ability to apply appropriate professional skepticism in an audit.

Internal Auditors

An independent auditor ordinarily has a close working relationship with the entity's internal auditors. Management, for example, may ask the independent auditor to review the internal auditors' planned activities for the year and report on the quality of their work. The independent auditor also has a direct interest in the work of internal auditors that pertains to the entity's system of internal control.

It is also permissible for the internal auditor to provide direct assistance to the independent auditor in performing a financial statement audit. The internal auditor's work cannot be used as a *substitute* for the independent auditor's work, but it can be an important *complement.* In determining the effect of such work on the audit, the independent auditor should (1) consider the competence and objectivity of the internal auditor and (2) evaluate the quality of the internal auditor's work. More is explained about this in Chapters 11 and 12.

Stockholders

Stockholders rely on audited financial statements for assurance that management has properly discharged its stewardship responsibility. The auditor therefore has an important responsibility to stockholders as the primary users of the audit report. During the course of an engagement, the auditor is not likely to have direct personal contact with stockholders who are not the entity's officers, key employees, or directors. Auditors may, however, attend the annual stockholders' meeting and may be asked to respond to stockholders' questions.

Who Is the Client?

In a public company the audit committee is responsible for selecting the auditor. However, the fact that the company pays the audit fee does not necessarily mean that the auditor should take the company's point of view. The auditor also needs to represent the interest of the public, of shareholders, and of potential shareholders, even though these individuals do not pay the audit fee. It is important for the auditor to be independent, neutral, and unbiased in performing an audit.

LEARNING CHECK

2-1   Contrast accounting and auditing as to objectives, methodology, applicable standards, and responsible parties.

2-2   Explain the relationship between verifiability and the concept of "fair presentation, in all material respects" in financial statements.

2-3   Explain the relationship between independent auditors and (1) management, (2) the board of directors and audit committee, (3) internal auditors, and (4) stockholders.

2-4   When performing an audit, who is the audit client?

KEY TERMS

Audit committees, p. 48	Material, p. 47
Fair presentation, p. 46	Professional skepticism, p. 47
Management, p. 47	

AUDITING STANDARDS

When the PCAOB was established in 2002, it was given authority to set auditing standards for auditors of public companies. In April 2003 the PCAOB adopted the generally accepted auditing standards that have been adopted by the Auditing Standards Board (ASB) of the AICPA. These 10 generally accepted auditing standards establish a framework for conducting audits, and they are not intended to provide detailed guidance for conducting audits. In may ways they are similar to the FASB Conceptual Framework that provides broad-based guidance for what should be included in financial statements, rather than specific rules or standards to be followed. The following discussion explains the 10 generally accepted auditing standards.

GENERALLY ACCEPTED AUDITING STANDARDS (GAAS)

Auditor Knowledge 4

■ Know the 10 generally accepted auditing standards.

The most widely recognized auditing standards associated with the public accounting profession are known as the 10 **generally accepted auditing standards (GAAS).** These standards were originally approved by the members of the AICPA in the late 1940s. They have since been incorporated into the Statements on Auditing Standards. All of the other standards contained in the SASs are sometimes referred to as interpretations or extensions of the 10 GAAS.

The 10 GAAS are presented in Figure 2-2, which also identifies the three categories into which they are grouped. Together they establish the quality of performance and the overall objectives to be achieved in a financial statement audit. Accordingly, peers and courts of law use GAAS in evaluating the auditor's work.

General Standards

The general standards relate to the qualifications of the auditor and to the quality of the auditor's work. As indicated in Figure 2-2, there are three general standards.

Adequate Technical Training and Proficiency

Every profession puts a premium on technical competence. The competency of the auditor is determined by three factors: (1) formal university education for entry into the profession, (2) practical training and experience in auditing, and (3) continuing professional education during the auditor's professional career. The importance of the first factor is highlighted by the fact that most states require candidates for the CPA Exam to earn the equivalent of 150 semester units of college credit. Continuing professional education requirements mandated by many state boards of accountancy, the AICPA, and state societies are discussed in Chapter 1.

Independence in Mental Attitude

Competency alone is not sufficient. The auditor must also be free of management's influence in performing the audit and in reporting the findings. The second general standard likens the auditor's role in an audit to the role of an arbitrator in a labor dispute or a judge in a legal case. The auditor must also meet the independence requirements in the AICPA's Code of Professional Conduct as discussed in the next chapter.

Figure 2-2 ■ Generally Accepted Auditing Standards

General Standards
1. The audit is to be performed by a person or persons having adequate technical training and proficiency as an auditor.
2. In all matters relating to the assignment, an independence in mental attitude is to be maintained by the auditor or auditors.
3. Due professional care is to be exercised in the performance of the audit and the preparation of the report.

Standards of Field Work
1. The work is to be adequately planned and assistants, if any, are to be properly supervised.
2. A sufficient understanding of the entity and its environment, including its internal control, should be obtained to assess the risk of material misstatement of the financial statements whether due to error or fraud, and to design the nature, timing and extent of further audit procedures.[a]
3. Sufficient competent audit evidence should be obtained through audit procedures performed to afford a reasonable basis for an opinion regarding the financial statements under audit.[b]

Standards of Reporting
1. The report shall state whether the financial statements are presented in accordance with generally accepted accounting principles.
2. The report shall identify those circumstances in which such principles have not been consistently observed in the current period in relation to the preceding period.
3. Informative disclosures in the financial statements are to be regarded as reasonably adequate unless otherwise stated in the report.
4. The report shall contain either an expression of opinion regarding the financial statements, taken as a whole, or an assertion to the effect that an opinion cannot be expressed. When an overall opinion cannot be expressed, the reasons therefore should be stated. In all cases where an auditor's name is associated with financial statements, the report should contain a clear-cut indication of the character of the auditor's work, if any, and the degree of responsibility the auditor is taking.

[a] The wording of the second field work standard was based on an Auditing Standards Board discussion draft of a proposed auditing standard dated November 2004.
[b] The wording of the third field work standard was based on an Auditing Standards Board discussion draft of a proposed auditing standard dated November 2004.

Source: AICPA Professional Standards.

Due Professional Care

Just as the physician is expected to be prudent and thorough in performing a physical examination and making a diagnosis, the auditor is expected to be diligent and careful in performing an audit and issuing a report on the findings. In meeting this standard, the experienced auditor should critically review the work done and the judgments exercised by less experienced personnel who participate in the audit. The standard of due care requires the auditor to act in good faith and not to be negligent in an audit.

Standards of Field Work

The field work standards are so named because they pertain primarily to the conduct of the audit at the entity's place of business, that is, in the field. Chapters 5 through 19 deal extensively with meeting the three standards of field work.

Adequate Planning and Proper Supervision

For the audit to be both effective and efficient, it must be adequately planned. Planning includes the development of audit strategies and the design of audit programs for the conduct of the audit. Proper supervision is essential in an audit because staff assistants with limited experience often execute major portions of the audit programs.

Understanding the Entity and Its Environment, Including Internal Control

A series of factors influence the risk of material misstatement, whether due to error or to fraud. This standard requires the auditor to understand:

- The entity's industry, regulatory, and other external factors.
- The nature of the entity, including its application of accounting policies.
- The entity's objectives and strategies and related business risks, as well as its risk assessment process.
- The entity's measurement and review of financial performance.
- The entity's system of internal control.

The auditor needs an understanding of the objectives, strategies, and business risks that are often correlated with the risk of material misstatement in financial statements. For example, if an entity is producing more than it is able to sell, it may have to write down inventory to its net realizable value. The entity's system of internal control is also an important factor in an audit. For example, effective internal controls should safeguard the entity's assets and produce reliable financial data. Conversely, ineffective controls may permit misappropriation of assets and result in unreliable financial information. It is essential, therefore, for the auditor to understand the entity and its environment, including its system of internal control to develop a perspective regarding the risk of material misstatement that will allow the auditor to plan an effective and efficient audit.

Sufficient Competent Audit Evidence

The ultimate objective of this field work standard is to require the auditor to have a reasonable basis for expressing an opinion on the entity's financial statements. Meeting this standard requires the exercise of professional judgment in determining both the amount (sufficiency) and the quality (competence) of evidence needed to support the auditor's opinion.

Standards of Reporting

In reporting the results of the audit, the auditor must meet four reporting standards.

Financial Statements Presented in Accordance with GAAP

The first reporting standard requires the auditor to identify GAAP as the established criteria used to evaluate management's financial statement assertions. As indicated earlier, generally accepted accounting principles include the pronouncements of authoritative bodies such as the FASB and the GASB. Special provisions for meeting this standard when a company uses a comprehensive basis of accounting other than GAAP are discussed in Chapter 20.

Consistency in the Application of GAAP

Meeting this standard requires the auditor to explicitly refer in the auditor's report to any circumstance where GAAP have not been consistently followed in the current period in relation to the preceding period. This standard is designed to enhance the comparability of financial statements from period to period. Under this standard, when GAAP have been consistently applied there is no reference to consistency in the auditor's report.

Adequacy of Informative Disclosures

This standard relates to the adequacy of the notes to the financial statements and other supplemental forms of disclosure. The standard has an impact on the auditor's report only when management's disclosures are inadequate. In most such cases, the auditor is required to include the necessary disclosures in the auditor's report.

Expression of Opinion

The final reporting standard requires the auditor either to express an opinion on the financial statements taken as a whole or to state that an opinion cannot be expressed. In most audits, it is possible for the auditor to express one of several types of opinions. The different types of opinion that may be expressed are briefly explained later in this chapter and illustrated in the Appendix to Chapter 2.

International Auditing and Assurance Standards Board (IAASB)

In 1977, 63 accountancy bodies (including the AICPA) representing 49 countries signed an agreement creating the International Federation of Accountants (IFAC). The broad objective of IFAC is "the development of a worldwide coordinated accountancy profession with harmonized standards." Toward this end, IFAC has established, as a standing subcommittee, the International Auditing and Assurance Standards Board (IAASB) with the responsibility and authority to issue International Standards on Auditing. The mission of the IAASB is to establish high-quality auditing, assurance, quality control, and related services standards and to improve the uniformity of practice by professional accountants throughout the world, thereby strengthening public confidence in the global auditing profession and serving the public interest.

Today some countries adopt IAASB standards as their own. In other countries, compliance with the international standards is voluntary, and they do not override local standards (e.g., the SASs in the United States). Where differences exist between the international standards and local standards, the local member body (e.g., the AICPA's Auditing Standards Board) is expected to give prompt consideration to such differences with a view to achieving harmonization. In recent years the U.S. Auditing Standards Board and the IAASB have worked jointly in creating auditing standards that have global acceptance. Most of the auditing principles and practices discussed in this text are consistent with IAASB standards.

Applicability of Generally Accepted Auditing Standards

Generally accepted auditing standards are applicable in each financial statement audit made by an independent auditor regardless of the entity's size, form of business organization, type of industry, or whether the entity is for profit or not-for-profit. In April 2003 the PCAOB adopted GAAS that were in effect at that time. Thus, the standards apply equally to the audit of the financial statements of an unincorporated corner grocery store, a school district, and a large corporation such as Exxon or General Motors.

STATEMENTS ON AUDITING STANDARDS (SAS)

Statements on Auditing Standards (SASs) are interpretations of generally accepted auditing standards. The Auditing and Attest Standards Team of the AICPA is responsible for establishing auditing standards for the financial statement audits of private companies. One arm of this team is the **Auditing Standards Board (ASB),** which has been designated as the senior technical body of the AICPA to issue pronouncements on auditing standards. The ASB also is responsible for providing auditors with guidance for implementing its pronouncements by approving interpretations and audit guides prepared by the staff of the Auditing Standards Division. The ASB's 19 members represent small and large practice units, state boards of accountancy, academia, government, and the public.

Before an SAS is issued, an exposure draft of the proposed statement is widely circulated for comment to CPA firms, accounting educators, and others. The proposed statement and comments received on it are then further deliberated by the board in open meetings prior to adoption. The approval of two-thirds of the ASB members is required for issuance of an SAS. SASs explain the nature and extent of an auditor's responsibility and offer guidance to an auditor in performing the audit. Compliance with SASs is mandatory for AICPA members who must be prepared to justify any departures from such statements.

When issued, SASs and all related auditing interpretations are codified by auditing section (AU) number. Codifying SASs by AU number permits new SASs to be inserted by topic rather than in chronological order. They are then incorporated into the AICPA's looseleaf service entitled Professional Standards. Volume 1 is available in both hard copy and an electronic version on compact disks. A list of all SASs in effect when this text went to press, together with the corresponding AU section numbers, is provided on the inside back cover of this text.

PCAOB AUDITING STANDARDS

Section 103 of the Sarbanes-Oxley Act directs the PCAOB to establish, among other things, auditing and related attestation standards to be followed by public accounting firms when auditing public companies. The **Public Companies Accounting Oversight Board (PCAOB)** is a five-member board of financially literate members. Two of those members must be (or have been) CPAs, and the remaining three members cannot be (or cannot have been) CPAs. The PCAOB's rulemaking process results in the adoption of rules that are then submitted to the Securities and Exchange Commission for approval. PCAOB rules do not take effect unless approved by the Commission. The following link provides the status of PCAOB rules as of the present time: http://www.pcaobus.org/pcaob_rulemaking.asp.

Today there is a significant overlap between the rules of the PCAOB and the Statements on Auditing Standards. To date, the PCAOB has indicated that it reserves the right to set new auditing standards for public companies. Yet until such time as the PCAOB promulgates new auditing standards, auditors are to follow existing SASs. As a result, this text focuses on the Statements on Auditing Standards and highlights different rules that are in place for auditors of public companies. Our concern through most of this book is with generally accepted auditing standards promulgated by the AICPA for audits of private company financial statements, with appropriate modifications for the standards of the PCAOB for the audits of public company financial statements.

[LEARNING CHECK

2-5 What is the ASB, with what organization is it affiliated, and what is its composition?

2-6 What are SASs, and what is the process for their issuance?

2-7 What is the authority of the PCAOB with respect to setting auditing standards, and what is the process for their issuance?

2-8 a. Identify the three categories of generally accepted auditing standards.
  b. Briefly indicate the subject matter of each of the 10 generally accepted auditing standards.
  c. Does the PCAOB recognize the 10 generally accepted auditing standards?

[KEY TERMS

Auditing Standards Board (ASB), p. 54

Generally accepted auditing standards (GAAS), p. 50

Public Companies Accounting Oversight Board (PCAOB), p. 54

Statements on Auditing Standards (SAS), p. 54

[ASSURANCE PROVIDED BY AN AUDIT]

Users of audited financial statements expect auditors to:

Auditor Knowledge 5

■ Understand some important auditor's responsibilities that are implied by completing the audit.

■ Perform the audit with technical competence, integrity, independence, and objectivity.

■ Search for and detect material misstatements, whether intentional or unintentional.

■ Prevent the issuance of misleading financial statements.[2]

The following discussion explains some important assurances that are provided to every financial statement user when the auditor uses the standard audit

---

[2] Report of the National Commission on Fraudulent Financial Reporting, 1987, p. 49.

Figure 2-3 ■ Key Issues Associated with the Assurance Provided by an Audit

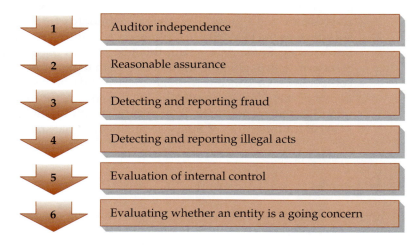

1	Auditor independence
2	Reasonable assurance
3	Detecting and reporting fraud
4	Detecting and reporting illegal acts
5	Evaluation of internal control
6	Evaluating whether an entity is a going concern

report. Figure 2-3 provides an overview of some key issues that financial statement users should understand about the assurance provided by an audit.

AUDITOR INDEPENDENCE

Independence is the cornerstone of the auditing profession. It means that the auditor is neutral about the entity and, therefore, objective. The public can place faith in the audit function because an auditor is impartial and recognizes an obligation for fairness.

Although the entity pays the auditor's fee, the CPA has a significant responsibility to known users of the auditor's report. The auditor must not subordinate his or her judgment to any specific group. The auditor's independence, integrity, and objectivity are the qualities that allow the audit to add credibility to management's assertions in the financial statements.

REASONABLE ASSURANCE

Auditors are responsible for planning and performing an audit to obtain reasonable assurance that the financial statements are free of material misstatement. The concept of reasonable assurance, however, does not *guarantee* the accuracy of the financial statements.

The concept of **reasonable assurance** implies that audits involve tests. Auditors rarely examine 100 percent of the items in an account or transactions class. Instead, they select a portion of those items and apply procedures to them to form an opinion on the financial statements. The auditor exercises skill and judgment in deciding what evidence to look at, when to look at it, how much to look at, and who to assign to the task of collecting and evaluating particular evidence, as well as in interpreting and evaluating the results. If no evidence of material misstatement is found in these tests, the auditor concludes that the financial statements are presented fairly in accordance with GAAP.

The concept of reasonable assurance also implies that management's financial statements include accounting estimates and are not exact. GAAP requires managers to make more and more estimates of fair value. For example, managers must estimate the allowance for doubtful accounts, the net realizable value of inventory, and managers must perform impairment tests on both fixed assets and goodwill. Management and auditors must also use judgment in determining how to apply generally accepted accounting principles. The application of dollar value LIFO, for example, requires significant professional judgment. GAAP is inherently imprecise. Hence, an audit cannot guarantee financial statement accuracy, and an audit cannot increase the precision of an accounting estimate. Audits can only provide a high level of assurance, reasonable assurance, that financial statements are presented fairly in all material respects.

DETECTING AND REPORTING FRAUD

Financial statement users expect auditors to search for and detect fraud. Fraud, however, is a broad legal concept. AU 316, *Consideration of Fraud in a Financial Statement Audit* (SAS No. 99), states that the auditor's interest specifically relates to "fraudulent acts that cause a material misstatement of the financial statements." AU 316 recognizes two types of misstatements associated with fraud: (1) misstatements arising from fraudulent financial reporting and (2) misstatements arising from misappropriation of assets.

Fraudulent financial reporting may involve acts such as:

- Manipulation, falsification, or alteration of accounting records or supporting documents from which financial statements are prepared.
- Misrepresentation in, or intentional omission from, the financial statements of events, transactions, or other significant information.
- Intentional misapplication of accounting principles relating to amounts, classification, manner of presentation, or disclosure.

Fraudulent financial reporting need not be the result of a grand plan or conspiracy. It may be that management rationalizes the appropriateness of a material misstatement, for example, as an aggressive rather than indefensible interpretation of complex accounting rules, or as a temporary misstatement of financial statements, including interim statements, expected to be corrected later when operational results improve.

Misappropriation of assets involves the theft of an entity's assets where the effect of the theft causes the financial statements not to be presented in conformity with generally accepted accounting principles. Misappropriation can be accomplished in various ways including:

- Embezzling cash or other liquid assets.
- Stealing assets.
- Causing an entity to pay for goods or services not received.

Misappropriation of assets may also be accompanied by false or misleading records or documents.

Responsibility to Detect Fraud

The auditor's responsibility for detecting fraud is the same as the auditor's responsibility for detecting unintentional errors. First, the auditor must specifically assess the risk of fraud in every audit, both fraudulent financial reporting and misappropriation of assets, in order to develop a knowledgeable perspective about the likely causes of fraud. The assessment of risk of material misstatement due to fraud is a cumulative process that includes a consideration of risk factors individually and in combination. The audit team will conduct a brainstorming session to evaluate the risk of material fraud, including (1) incentives and motives for fraud, (2) the opportunity to commit fraud, and (3) rationalizations that might allow someone to commit fraud. This process is discussed in more detail in Chapter 9.

Second, the auditor must plan and perform an audit to respond to identified risks and to obtain reasonable assurance about whether the financial statements are free of material misstatements, whether caused by error or fraud. AU 316 specifically provides guidance on how the auditor responds to the risk assessment in contemplating subsequent steps in the audit and in evaluating audit test results as they relate to the risk of misstatements due to fraud.

Third, an auditor should conduct the audit with due professional care and an attitude of professional skepticism. Auditors should approach audits with a mindset that recognizes the possibility that material fraud might be present, regardless of any past experience with the entity and regardless of the auditor's belief about the integrity and honesty of management. The auditor must objectively evaluate all evidence and conditions observed during the audit. If the auditor observes indicators that are associated with a higher risk of fraud, the auditor should ensure that he or she approaches the audit with an appropriate degree of professional skepticism and collects evidence that is responsive to the risk factors observed.

Responsibility to Report Fraud

When the auditor concludes that the financial statements are materially misstated and the financial statements are not prepared in accordance with GAAP, the auditor should insist that the financial statements be revised by management. When management agrees to make appropriate changes, the auditor can issue a standard audit report and express an unqualified opinion on the financial statements. However, if the financial statements are not revised, the auditor should appropriately modify the standard report for a departure from GAAP and disclose all substantive reasons in the audit report.

The auditor also has responsibilities for communicating the discovery of fraud to management and possibly to others. The auditor's key responsibilities for communicating the discovery of fraud are as follows:

- Whenever the auditor determines that there is evidence that even a minor fraud exists, the matter should be brought to the attention of management, generally at least one level higher than the level at which the fraud occurred.
- Any fraud involving senior management, and fraud perpetrated at any level that causes a material misstatement of the financial statements, should be reported by the auditor directly to the audit committee or board of directors.
- The auditor is generally precluded by ethical and legal obligations from disclosing fraud outside the entity. However, the auditor may be required to do so:
  - In response to a court subpoena.
  - In response to the SEC when the auditor has withdrawn or been dismissed from the engagement, or when the auditor has reported fraud or illegal acts

(defined below) to the audit committee or board of directors and the committee or board fails to take appropriate action.

■ To a successor auditor who makes inquiries in accordance with professional standards.

■ To a funding or other agency in accordance with audit requirements for entities that receive governmental financial assistance.

DETECTING AND REPORTING ILLEGAL ACTS

An illegal act refers to such acts as the payment of bribes, the making of illegal political contributions, and the violation of other specific laws and governmental regulations. All U.S. companies are subject to the illegal payments provisions of the Foreign Corrupt Practices Act, which prohibits payments to foreign government officials for the purpose of obtaining or retaining business in a foreign country.

Responsibility to Detect Illegal Acts

Two characteristics of illegal acts influence the auditor's responsibility for detection.

■ The determination of whether an act is illegal is dependent on legal judgment that normally is beyond the auditor's professional competence.

■ Illegal acts vary considerably in their relation to financial statements. Some laws and regulations such as income tax law have a *direct and material* effect on the provision for income tax expense and related liabilities in the financial statements. However, other laws such as those pertaining to occupations, safety, and health and to environmental protection usually have only an *indirect* effect on the financial statements (i.e., contingent liabilities).

The auditor has a different level of responsibility for two different types of illegal acts. First, AU 317.05, *Illegal Acts by Clients* (SAS 54), indicates that the auditor's responsibility for misstatements resulting from **illegal acts having a direct and material effect on the determination of financial statement amounts** is the same as that for errors or fraud. For example, a violation of tax law that results in a material misstatement of tax expense and tax liabilities would have a direct effect on the financial statements. That is, the auditor should plan an audit to detect such illegal acts that are material to the financial statements and implement the plan with due professional care. For these acts, the auditor should apply auditing procedures to ascertain whether any direct and material illegal acts have occurred. The audit should provide reasonable assurance that the financial statements are free of material misstatement owing to direct and material illegal acts.

Second, the auditor has a lower level of responsibility for **illegal acts that have an indirect effect on the financial statements.** These are all other illegal acts, and the auditor's responsibility is restricted to information that comes to the auditor's attention. Illegal acts that have an indirect effect on the financial statements, such as violating environmental law or other state or federal laws, affect the financial statements only to the degree that they result in loss contingencies. For example, if a lawsuit has been brought against an audit client, the auditor evaluates that lawsuit in the context of the accounting required by SFAS No. 5 (e.g., probability of material loss). Because of the foregoing characteristics of indirect effect illegal acts, an audit made in accordance with GAAS provides no assurance that all such illegal acts will be detected.

Auditors develop audit plans based on risk indicators. The following indicators may indicate an increased risk of illegal acts: (1) unauthorized transactions, (2) investigations by governmental agencies, and (3) failure to file tax returns. When the auditor suspects that an illegal act has been committed, he or she should discuss the matter with an appropriate level of the entity's management and consult with the entity's legal counsel. If necessary, the auditor should also apply additional procedures to obtain an understanding of the act and its effects on the financial statements.

Responsibility to Report Illegal Acts

The auditor's primary responsibility is for fair presentation in the financial statements. When an illegal act having a material effect on the financial statements is not properly disclosed, the auditor should insist that management revise the financial statements. If the financial statements are not appropriately revised, the auditor has a responsibility to inform financial statement users through a qualified or adverse opinion that the financial statements are not in accordance with GAAP. If the auditor is unable to obtain sufficient evidence about an illegal act, he or she should communicate this information through a qualified opinion or a disclaimer explaining the nature of the scope limitation. If management refuses to accept the auditor's report, the auditor should withdraw from the engagement and indicate the reasons to the audit committee in writing.

The auditor's responsibilities for disclosing illegal client acts to outside parties are the same as those for material fraud. In addition, the Private Securities Litigation Reform Act of 1995 imposes a requirement under certain circumstances on independent auditors of publicly held companies subject to the Securities Exchange Act of 1934. The Private Securities Litigation Reform Act of 1995 amended the 1934 Act to require the following:

■ When the audit committee or board of directors of a publicly held company has been adequately informed with respect to illegal acts detected in the audit, and the auditor determines that the illegal acts have a material effect on the financial statements, and senior management or the board of directors has not taken appropriate remedial actions with respect to such illegal acts, and the failure to take remedial actions is reasonably expected to warrant departure from a standard audit report or warrant resignation by the auditor, then the auditor shall report these conclusions to the public company's board of directors.

■ A public company whose board of directors receives the report referred to above must so inform the SEC not later than one business day after the receipt of such report and furnish the independent auditor with a copy of the notice provided to the SEC.

■ If the independent auditor fails to receive a copy of the public company's notice to the SEC before the expiration of the required one business day period, the auditor shall, within one additional day, furnish to the SEC a copy of the report previously provided to the public company's board of directors. In such case the auditor may also wish to consider resigning from the engagement.

The amended 1934 Act further provides that no auditor shall be liable in a private action for any finding, conclusions, or statement expressed in a report made to the SEC pursuant to the above requirement. SEC rules further provide that such reports are exempt from disclosure under the Freedom of Information Act to the same extent as are other SEC investigative records.

EVALUATION OF INTERNAL CONTROL

The auditor's responsibility for (1) evaluating internal control over financial reporting and (2) reporting this evaluation to the shareholders and other users of financial statements is different for public companies versus private companies. The auditor of a private company reports only on the financial statements. The reader of a private company financial statement obtains *no* assurance about the system of internal control over financial reporting. A private company may have a poor system of internal control and inadequate segregation of duties, and the auditor might find material misstatements in the underlying financial records. If management adjusts the financial statements for the misstatements found by the auditor, and the revised financial statements present fairly the company's financial position, results of operations, and cash flows in all material respects, the company will receive an unqualified opinion on its financial statements.

The public company auditor has a very different responsibility. The public company auditor must perform an integrated audit that results in (1) an opinion on the financial statements, (2) an opinion on management's assessment of internal control over financial reporting, and (3) an opinion on the effectiveness of the system of internal control over financial reporting. The auditor's report on internal control over financial reporting that goes to the public must report material weaknesses in internal control. These are weaknesses in internal control that have more than a remote possibility of resulting in a material misstatement of quarterly or annual financial statements. As explained later in this chapter, if a company has a sound system of internal control in many aspects, but has one material weakness (e.g., inadequate control over disclosures regarding pension plans or derivative financial instruments), it will receive an adverse opinion that it does not have an adequate system of internal control over financial reporting. In addition, auditors must report to the audit committee significant deficiencies in internal control. A significant deficiency in internal control is a weakness in internal control that has more than a remote possibility that a misstatement of more than an inconsequential amount may occur in quarterly or annual financial statements, which is a relatively low threshold. The concept of material weaknesses and significant deficiencies is illustrated later in this chapter in Figure 2-6.

Because the auditor of a public company is now responsible for issuing three opinions, one on the financial statements and two on internal controls, this only underscores the importance of performing a high-quality audit.

ASSURANCE ABOUT A GOING CONCERN

The primary purpose of the audit is to provide reasonable assurance that the financial statements are fairly presented in accordance with GAAP. Financial statement users must use the financial statements in making their own decisions about the risk of doing business with a company or making an investment in a company. Fair presentation is not a guarantee that an entity will continue as a going concern. Thus, the fact that an entity becomes bankrupt subsequent to the issuance of a standard audit report does not, in itself, indicate a substandard performance or audit failure by the auditor.

Nevertheless, no independent professional understands an entity's business circumstances better than the auditor. AU 341, The Auditor's Consideration of an Entity's Ability to Continue as a Going Concern (SAS 59), provides that the auditor has a responsibility to evaluate whether there is substantial doubt about the entity's ability to continue as a **going concern** for a reasonable period of time, not to exceed one year beyond the date of the financial statements being audited. The concept of **substantial doubt about an entity's ability to continue as a going concern** is not mere doubt. Professional standards say that the auditor may conclude that there is substantial doubt if, for example, an entity has suffered recurring net losses and negative cash flow from operations and has defaulted on loan contracts. The audit procedures performed to evaluate a going concern are discussed in more detail in Chapter 19.

When the auditor concludes that there is substantial doubt about the entity's ability to continue as a going concern during the year following the date of the financial statements, she or he should state this conclusion in the audit report. If management includes adequate disclosures in the financial statements concerning the entity's ability to continue as a going concern, the auditor will issue an unqualified opinion on the financial statements with an additional paragraph explaining the going-concern uncertainty. If management's disclosures are considered inadequate, there is a departure from GAAP and the auditor should appropriately modify the standard report for a departure from GAAP and should therefore disclose all substantive reasons in the audit report.

Consider the following two cases. First, review the information about Enron provided in the opening vignette for Chapter 2. Although there might have been doubt about Enron's ability to continue as a going concern, the company had access to significant debt and equity markets when the auditor issued an opinion on the financial statements. Given the economic conditions at the time of the auditor's report, Andersen LLP concluded that there was not substantial doubt about Enron's ability to continue as a going concern. A significant portion of Enron's subsequent collapse was its inability to generate operating cash flow in 2001, something that was not known at the auditor's report date. Although Andersen was significantly criticized for its failure to find material misstatements in Enron's report financial position and results of operations, there have been few criticisms of the fact that it did not issue a going-concern opinion.

In a second case, Radin, Glass & Co., LLP issued a going-concern opinion on the Financial Statements of U.S. Technologies, Inc. (see Appendix 2A, p. 85, for this audit opinion) in April of 2002. At December 31, 2001, U.S. Technologies reported a $10.8 million loss on revenues of only $2.2 million, with cash outflow from operations of $6.2 million. In spite of contributed capital amounting to $59.4 million, total liabilities exceeded total assets by $7.6 million. Note 2 to the company's financial statements addressed the going-concern issue, the capital raised during 2001, and the need to raise additional equity capital during 2002 to continue as a going concern. In this case, the auditor reached a conclusion that raised substantial doubt about the entity's ability to continue as a going concern, and management addressed the situation in a note to the financial statements. In the end, U.S. Technologies, Inc., did not make it through 2002.

A CLEAN BILL OF HEALTH?

Some financial statement users and reporters in the media consider an auditor's standard report to constitute a clean "bill of health." For example, some users believe that an audit endorses an entity's policy decisions, its use of resources, or the adequacy of its internal controls. This is not the case. The auditor's opinion on the financial statement does not pertain to these matters. It only pertains to whether the financial statements present fairly the entity's financial position, results of operations, and cash flows, in all material respects. A private company might have poor internal controls, and the auditor might propose audit adjustments, which management accepts, to reach the position where the financial statements fairly present financial position, results of operations and cash flows, and the company receives an unqualified opinion on its financial statements.

Other financial statement users feel that an audit provides positive assurance that a business is a safe investment and will not fail. As previously discussed, the absence of reference to substantial doubt in the auditor's report should not be viewed as providing assurance about an entity's ability to continue as a going concern.

A financial statement audit only enhances users' confidence that financial statements do not contain material misstatements because the auditor is an independent and objective expert who is also knowledgeable of the entity's business and financial reporting requirements. In the case of public companies, an audit of internal controls is also intended to enhance the user's confidence that financial statements are free of material misstatement. A public company may have financial difficulties, those difficulties may be disclosed in the financial statements, and the company may also have good internal controls over financial reporting. As a result, it might receive unqualified opinions on the financial statement and on its system of internal control over financial reporting, and yet face economic difficulties.

[LEARNING CHECK

2-9 a. What is implied by the concept of reasonable assurance that the financial statements are free of material misstatement?

b. Explain several important limitations associated with the concept of reasonable assurance.

2-10 a. What is the auditor's responsibility for detecting fraud while performing a financial statement audit?

b. What is the auditor's responsibility for reporting fraud discovered during the audit to management? to the board of directors? to parties outside the entity?

2-11 a. What is the auditor's responsibility for detecting illegal acts while performing a financial statement audit?

b. What is the auditor's responsibility for reporting illegal acts discovered during the audit to management? to the board of directors? to parties outside the entity?

c. What is the auditor's potential liability to clients for reporting illegal acts to the SEC in accordance with the Private Securities Litigation Reform Act of 1995?

2-12 a. Explain the auditor's responsibility to evaluate the system of internal control over financial reporting for a public company.

b. How does this differ from the auditor's responsibility to evaluate internal control for a private company?

2-13 What is the auditor's responsibility to report to financial statement users about an entity's ability to continue as a going concern?

2-14 Is an unqualified audit opinion equivalent to a "clean bill of health" for the audit client?

KEY TERMS

Fraudulent financial reporting, p. 57
Going concern, p. 62
Independence, p. 56
Illegal acts having a direct and material effect on determination of financial statement amounts, p. 59

Illegal acts that have an indirect effect on the financial statements, p. 59
Misappropriation of assets, p. 57
Reasonable assurance, p. 56
Substantial doubt about the an entity's ability to continue as a going concern, p. 62

THE AUDITOR'S REPORT ON FINANCIAL STATEMENTS

The audit report is the auditor's formal means of communicating with financial statement users a conclusion about the audited financial statements. In issuing an audit report, the auditor must meet the four generally accepted auditing standards of reporting. The following discussion explains the audit report, important variations of the audit report, and the assurances that are communicated to financial statement users.

THE STANDARD REPORT ON FINANCIAL STATEMENTS

Auditor Knowledge 6

■ Understand the basic elements of the auditor's standard report on financial statements.

A *standard report* is the most common report issued. It contains an **unqualified opinion** stating that the financial statements present fairly, in all material respects, the financial position, results of operations, and cash flows of the entity in conformity with generally accepted accounting principles. This conclusion may be expressed only when the auditor has formed such an opinion on the basis of an audit performed in accordance with GAAS.

Because of its importance in a financial statement audit, a basic understanding of the form and content of the standard report is essential. The ASB last changed the form and content of the standard report in 1988 by issuing SAS No. 58, *Reports on Audited Financial Statements* (AU 508). This report, which has stood the test of time, was designed to better communicate to users of audited financial statements the work done by the auditor and the character and limitations of an audit. A second objective was to clearly differentiate between the responsibilities of management and the independent auditor in the financial statement audit.

An example of a standard report on comparative financial statements is presented in Figure 2-3. To the right of the sample report is a listing of the basic elements of the report. Each of these elements is prescribed in AU 508. It should be noted that the standard report has three paragraphs, which are referred to as the introductory, scope, and opinion paragraphs. Each of these paragraphs is explained in the following sections.

Figure 2-3 ■ Auditor's Standard Report on Financial Statements

REPORT OF ERNST & YOUNG LLP,
INDEPENDENT AUDITORS

To the Board of Directors and Stockholders, Intel
Corporation:

We have audited the accompanying consolidated
balance sheets of Intel Corporation as of December
25, 2004 and December 27, 2003, and the related
consolidated statements of income, stockholders'
equity and cash flows for each of the three years in
the period ended December 25, 2004. Our audits
also included the financial statement schedule listed
in the Index at Part IV, Item 15. These financial statements and schedule are the responsibility of the
company's management. Our responsibility is to
express an opinion on these financial statements
based on our audits.

   We conducted our audits in accordance with the
standards of the Public Companies Accounting
Oversight Board (United States). Those standards
require that we plan and perform the audit to obtain
reasonable assurance about whether the financial
statements are free of material misstatement. An
audit includes examining, on a test basis, evidence
supporting the amounts and disclosures in the
financial statements. An audit also includes assessing the accounting principles used and significant
estimates made by management, as well as evaluating the overall financial statement presentation. We
believe that our audits provide a reasonable basis
for our opinion.

   In our opinion, such consolidated financial statements present fairly, in all material respects, the consolidated financial position of Intel Corporation as
of December 25, 2004 and December 27, 2003, and
the consolidated results of their operations and their
cash flows for each of the three years in the period
ended December 25, 2004 in conformity with
accounting principles generally accepted in the
United States of America. Also, in our opinion, the
related financial statement schedule, when considered in relation to the basic financial statements
taken as a whole, presents fairly in all material
respect the information set forth therein.

   We also have audited, in accordance with the
standards of the Public Company Accounting Oversight Board (United States), the effectiveness of
Intel Corporation's internal control over financial
reporting as of December 25, 2004, based on criteria
established in Internal Control–Integrated Framework issued by the Committee of Sponsoring Organizations of the Treadway Commission and our
report dated February 15, 2005 expressed an
unqualified opinion thereon.

/s/   Ernst and Young LLP

San Jose, California

February 15, 2005

Basic Elements of the Auditor's Standard Report

Title	Includes the word "Independent"
Addressee	The Report is addressed to the Board of Direc-tors and Stockholders of the entity.
Introductory Paragraph	Identifies: • Type of service performed ("We have audited") • Financial statements and schedule audited • Entity audited • Dates of the statements • Management's responsibility for the finan-cial statements • Auditor's responsibility for the opinion
Scope Paragraph	States: • The audits were conducted in accordance with the standards of the Public Companies Accounting Oversight Board. With a private company this would refer to conducting an audit in accordance with auditing standards generally accepted in the United States. These standards require: • Planning and performing an audit to obtain reasonable assurance that the finan-cial statements are free of material misstate-ment • Examining evidence on a test basis • Assessing accounting principles used and sig-nificant estimates made by management • Evaluating overall financial statement pres-entation • Auditor's belief that the audit provides a reasonable basis for opinion
Opinion Paragraph	Expresses auditor's opinion as to whether financial statements and schedule: • Present fairly, in all material respects, • The company's financial position as of bal-ance sheet date • The results of operations and cash flows for the period • In conformity with U.S. GAAP
Additional Explanatory Wording	Refers to the audit opinion on internal controls over financial reporting that was completed simultaneously with the audit of the financial statements.
Firm's Signature	Manual or printed signature
Date	Last day of field work

Title and Address

Similar to the auditor's report on financial statements, the auditor's report on internal controls over financial reporting contains a title, *Report of Ernst & Young LLP, Independent Auditors,* which indicates that the auditor is independent of the company being audited. In this case the report is addressed to the board of directors and stockholders of Intel Corporation.

Introductory Paragraph

The **introductory paragraph** of the report contains three factual statements. A primary objective of this paragraph is to clearly distinguish between the responsibility of management and the auditor. The wording of this paragraph is presented below:

> We have audited the ... balance sheets ... of the X Company ... for the years then ended.

This sentence states that the auditor has audited specific financial statements of a designated company. Each of the financial statements is identified, together with the dates appropriate to each statement.

> These financial statements are the responsibility of management.

This wording acknowledges that responsibility for the financial statements rests with management. Conversely, this sentence is intended to refute the notion that the auditor develops the representations underlying the financial statements.

> Our responsibility is to express an opinion ... based on our audits.

This sentence specifically indicates the auditor's responsibility. The auditor's role is to conduct an audit and to express an opinion based on the findings. When read in conjunction with the second sentence, there is a clear differentiation between the responsibility of management and the responsibility of the auditor.

Scope Paragraph

As its name suggests, the **scope paragraph** describes the nature and scope of the audit. It satisfies the portion of the fourth reporting standard that requires the auditor to give a clear-cut indication of the character of the audit. The scope paragraph also identifies several limitations of an audit. The wording of this paragraph is:

> We conducted our audits in accordance with the standards of the Public Companies Accounting Oversight Board (United States).

In the report of a private company, this would refer to conducting an audit in accordance with generally accepted auditing standards. In this context, these standards include the 10 GAAS, all applicable SASs, and applicable standards of the PCAOB. This sentence asserts that the auditor has met these standards.

> These standards require that we ... audit to obtain reasonable assurance ... financial statements are free of material misstatement.

This sentence identifies two significant inherent limitations of an audit. First is the acknowledgment that the auditor seeks only reasonable, rather than absolute, assurance. Thus, the reader is informed that there is some risk in an audit. Second, the concept of materiality is introduced. An audit is planned and performed to discover material, but not all, misstatements in the financial statements.

> An audit includes examining, on a test basis, evidence supporting ... the financial statements.

This wording further explains another inherent limitation of an audit. The words "test basis" indicate that less than 100 percent of the evidence was examined. Furthermore, a test basis implies that there is a risk that evidence not examined may be important in assessing the fairness of the overall financial statement presentation and disclosures.

> An audit also includes assessing the accounting principles ... significant estimates ... evaluating the overall financial statement presentation.

This sentence provides further insight into the character of the audit. It states that the auditor exercises judgment in assessing and evaluating management's financial statement representations. Reference to significant estimates by management means that the financial statements are inherently imprecise.

> We believe that our audits provide a reasonable basis for our opinion.

This sentence identifies another limitation of an audit by stating that only a reasonable basis is needed for an opinion. The concept of a reasonable, rather than a conclusive or absolute, basis is consistent with the concepts of test basis and reasonable assurance stated earlier in the paragraph. This sentence also contains an assertion that the auditor has formed a positive conclusion about the scope of the audit work performed.

Opinion Paragraph

The **opinion paragraph** satisfies the four reporting standards, as explained below.

> In our opinion, the financial statements referred to above...

In interpreting the meaning and significance of this clause, it is proper to conclude that the opinion is being expressed by a professional, experienced, and expert person or persons. It is incorrect, however, to conclude that this phrase says, *"We certify," "We guarantee,"* or *"We are certain (or positive)."* The second part of this clause makes reference to the financial statements identified in the introductory paragraph; the titles of the individual statements are not repeated. The expression of an opinion satisfies the fourth standard of reporting.

> ...present fairly, in all material respects ... financial position ... results of their operations and their cash flows...

The intended connotation of the words *present fairly* is that the financial statements are presented reasonably and without bias or distortion. An auditor does not use the words *accurately, truly, factually, correctly,* or *exactly* because of the existence of estimates in the financial statements. The auditor's opinion on fairness pertains to the financial statement taken as a whole. It does not apply to the accuracy or correctness of individual accounts or components of each financial statement. An unqualified opinion expresses the auditor's belief that the financial statements accomplish their stated purpose by presenting fairly the entity's financial position (balance sheet), results of operations (income and retained earnings statements), and cash flows (statement of cash flows). An unqualified opinion also means that any differences between management and the auditor on material accounting matters have been resolved to the auditor's satisfaction.

The phrase *in all material respects* informs users that the auditor's opinion does not attest to the absolute accuracy of the financial statements. This limitation is stated because of the test basis of an audit and the inclusion of significant estimates in the financial statements.

...in conformity with generally accepted accounting principles...

This clause satisfies the first standard of reporting that states the report shall indicate whether the financial statements are prepared in accordance with GAAP. The term *generally accepted accounting principles* provides the criteria for the auditor's judgment as to the fairness of the financial statements. Independent auditors agree on the existence of a body of U.S. GAAP, and these sources of GAAP are detailed in AU 411.05, *The Meaning of Present Fairly in Conformity with Generally Accepted Accounting Principles in the Independent Auditor's Report.*

As stated earlier, the second and third standards of reporting require comment in the auditor's report only when there has been an inconsistency in applying GAAP or management has failed to make all required disclosures. Thus, in the absence of any comments on these matters in the auditor's report, the appropriate conclusion is that these two reporting standards have been met.

DEPARTURES FROM THE STANDARD REPORT

Audit Decision 1

■ **When should the auditor use a non-standard report on financial statements?**

Auditors must recognize when circumstances may arise where it is inappropriate for the auditor to issue a standard report. Departures from the standard report fall into the following categories:

■ Standard report with explanatory language.
■ Other types of opinions
    ■ Qualified opinion
    ■ Adverse opinion
    ■ Disclaimer of opinion

The following discussion explains when auditors should use these various auditor reports.

Standard Report with Explanatory Language

The distinguishing characteristic of this category of reports is that the opinion paragraph continues to express an unqualified opinion because the financial statements present fairly an entity's financial position, results of operations, and cash flows in conformity with GAAP. However, the following circumstances require the auditor to add an **explanatory paragraph** or other explanatory language to the standard report. The auditor should use this option when:

- An entity elects to make a change in accounting principles from one acceptable method to another (see p. 86).
- The auditor reaches a conclusion that substantial doubt exists about the entity's ability to continue as a going concern (see p. 85).
- The auditor wishes to emphasize information contained in the notes to the financial statements, such as a related party transaction (see p. 88).

In addition, the auditor will modify the language of the audit report when a significant aspect of the audit relies on the audit work and opinion of another auditor.

Although the explanatory information is usually provided in an explanatory paragraph following the opinion paragraph, in some cases it merely involves the addition of explanatory wording within the three standard paragraphs, and in rare cases an explanatory paragraph is added before the opinion paragraph. Examples of these reports that contain unqualified opinions on the financial statements are presented in Appendix 2A.

OTHER TYPES OF OPINIONS

The second category of departures results when either of the following circumstances occurs:

- The financial statements contain a material departure from GAAP.
- The auditor has been unable to obtain sufficient competent evidence regarding one or more of management's assertions and as a result does not have a reasonable basis for an unqualified opinion on the financial statements as a whole.

In these cases, the auditor will express one of the following types of opinions:

- A **qualified opinion,** which states that except for the effects of the matter(s) to which the qualification relates, the financial statements present fairly … in conformity with GAAP.
- An **adverse opinion,** which states that the financial statements do not present fairly … in conformity with GAAP.
- A **disclaimer of opinion,** which states that the auditor does not express an opinion on the financial statements.

Departures from GAAP include using accounting principles that are not generally accepted, misapplying GAAP, and failing to make disclosures required by GAAP. For example, an entity might misapply GAAP by making an accounting estimate that materially misstates an entity's financial position and results of operations. Alternatively, if an entity's financial statements reflect a change in accounting principles that was not made in accordance with APB Opinion No. 20, the statements contain a departure from GAAP. In these circumstances, the auditor will express a *qualified opinion* if there is a material departure from GAAP (see p. 89)or an *adverse opinion,* if in the auditor's judgment the departure from GAAP has an extremely material effect on the financial statements (see p. 91).

A **scope limitation** occurs when the auditor has been unable to obtain sufficient competent evidence to verify whether one or more assertions are in conformity with

GAAP. In these cases, the auditor will issue a *qualified opinion* when circumstances impose a material scope restriction (see p. 90). For example, an auditor might be engaged after the beginning of the year and is unable to observe the existence of beginning inventories that would impact a conclusion about financial position (beginning inventory) and results of operations (cost of goods sold). Alternatively an auditor engaged to audit only the balance sheet for a company being acquired might find that the company has inadequate records of the cost of fixed assets, but otherwise the auditor is able to obtain sufficient competent evidence about financial position.

An auditor will use a *disclaimer of opinion* when an entity imposes a material scope restriction (such as preventing the auditor from obtaining sufficient competent evidence related to one or more of management's assertions in the financial statements) or when a scope limitation pertains to matters that could have an extremely material effect on the statements (see p. 92).

Whenever one of these other types of opinions is expressed, the reason(s) for the opinion should be explained in one or more explanatory paragraphs immediately before the opinion paragraph. The opinion paragraph then begins with a reference to the explanatory paragraph(s), followed by wording appropriate to the type of opinion being expressed (qualified opinion, adverse opinion, or disclaimer of opinion).

A summary of the types of auditors' reports discussed in this chapter, the circumstances when each is appropriate, and a typical profile for each type of report is presented in Figure 2-4. It should be noted that this summary does not include all variations of audit reports. The page numbers in Figure 2-4 refer to illustrations of the types of reports in Appendix 2A. Illustrative examples of the reports, an explanation of what they mean, and a discussion of the auditor's criteria for using the report are provided.

LEARNING CHECK

2-15 a. What are the seven basic elements of the auditor's standard report?
b. What is the significance of the date of the auditor's standard report?

2-16 How is compliance with the four standards of reporting of GAAS indicated in the auditor's standard report?

2-17 a. Identify two categories of departures from the auditor's standard report.
b. Identify three types of circumstances that require a departure from the auditor's standard report and indicate the type or types of opinion appropriate for each.

2-18 State the wording in the opinion paragraph that differentiates each of the four types of opinions that may be expressed.

KEY TERMS

Adverse opinion, p. 69
Departures from GAAP, p. 69
Disclaimer of opinion, p. 69
Explanatory paragraph, p. 69
Introductory paragraph, p. 66

Opinion paragraph, p. 67
Qualified opinion, p. 69
Scope limitation, p. 69
Scope paragraph, p. 66
Unqualified opinion, p. 64

Figure 2-4 ■ Types of Auditors' Reports and Circumstances

Circumstance	Standard Report Unqualified Opinion	Departures from Standard Report				
		Standard Report with Explanatory Language Unqualified Opinion	Other Types of Opinions		
			Qualified	Adverse	Disclaimer
Financial statements conform to GAAP, audit completed in accordance with GAAS, and: • Circumstances requiring explanatory language do not exist.	✓ p. 65				
• Circumstances requiring explanatory language exist (e.g., accounting change or going concern).		✓ pp. 85–88			
Financial statements contain a **departure from GAAP>**			✓ Material p. 89	✓ Extremely material and pervasive p. 91	
Auditor unable to obtain sufficient competent evidence (**scope limitation**)			✓ Material p. 90		✓ Extremely material p. 92

Typical Report Profiles

TITLE	TITLE	TITLE
Addressee	Addressee	Addressee
Introductory paragraph	Introductory paragraph	Introductory paragraph
Scope paragraph	Scope paragraph	Scope paragraph[a]
Unqualified opinion paragraph	Unqualified opinion paragraph	Explanatory paragraph
Signature Date	Explanatory paragraph[b]	Qual. adverse or disclaimer of op.
	Signature Date	Signature Date

[a] Scope paragraph omitted for disclaimer of opinion.
[b] Explanatory paragraph located before opinion paragraph in rare cases.

THE AUDITOR'S REPORT ON INTERNAL CONTROL

The major difference between the audit of a privately held company and that of a public company is that auditors of public companies must perform a combined audit that results in two reports. First, public company auditors report on management's financial statements as discussed in the preceding section. Second, auditors report on internal control over financial reporting.

THE STANDARD REPORT

Auditor Knowledge 7

■ **Understand the basic elements of the auditor's standard report on internal controls over financial reporting.**

A *standard report* is the most common report issued. It contains an unqualified opinion stating that management's assertion about its system of internal control is fairly stated in all material respects. This conclusion may be expressed only when the auditor has identified no material weaknesses in internal control over financial reporting and when there have been no restrictions on the scope of the auditor's work. The auditor should form an opinion on the basis of an audit performed in accordance with the professional practice standards established by the PCAOB.

The standard report on internal control received by Intel Corporation is presented in Figure 2-5. To the right of the sample report is a listing of the basic elements of the report. Each of these elements is prescribed in the standards of the PCAOB. It should be noted that the standard report has five paragraphs, which are referred to as the introductory paragraph, definition, scope, inherent limitations, and opinion paragraphs as explained below.

Finally, Section 404 of the Sarbanes-Oxley Act of 2002 addresses reporting on internal controls only over financial reporting. A company may also have internal controls that relate to compliance with laws and regulations or effective and efficient utilization of assets. This report on internal controls only addresses internal control over financial reporting, and other controls are not covered by the scope of this audit. **Internal control over financial reporting** is defined in the definition paragraph of the auditor's report (see below).

Title and Address

Similar to the auditor's report on financial statements, the auditor's report on internal controls over financial reporting contains a title, *Report of Ernst & Young LLP, Independent Auditors,* which indicates that the auditor is independent of the company being audited. The report is usually addressed to the board of directors and stockholders.

Introductory Paragraph

The introductory paragraph of the report contains three factual statements. The primary objective of this paragraph is to identify what has been audited and to clearly distinguish between the responsibility of management and that of the auditor. The wording of this paragraph is presented below:

> We have audited management's assessment, included in the accompanying [title of management's report] that Intel Corporation maintained effective internal control over financial reporting as of December 25, 2004, based on criteria established in Internal Control—Integrated Framework issued by the Committee of Sponsoring Organizations of the Treadway Commission (COSO).

Figure 2-5 ■ Auditor's Standard Report on Internal Control over Financial Reporting

REPORT OF ERNST & YOUNG, LLP, INDEPENDENT AUDITORS

To the Board of Directors and Stockholders, Intel Corporation:

We have audited management's assessment, included in the accompanying Management Report on Internal Control over Financial Reporting that Intel Corporation maintained effective internal control over financial reporting as of December 25, 2005, based on criteria established in Internal Control-Integrated Framework issued by the Committee of Sponsoring Organizations of the Treadway Commission (the COSO criteria). Intel Corporation is responsible for maintaining effective internal control over financial reporting and for its assessment about the effectiveness of internal control over financial reporting. Our responsibility is to express an opinion on management's assessment and an opinion on the effectiveness of the company's internal control over financial reporting based on our audit.

We conducted our audit in accordance with the standards of the Public Companies Accounting Oversight Board (United States). Those standards require that we plan and perform the audit to obtain reasonable assurance about whether effective internal control over financial reporting was maintained in all material respects. Our audits included obtaining an understanding of internal control over financial reporting, testing and evaluating the design and operating effectiveness of internal control, and performing such other procedures as we considered necessary in the circumstances. We believe that our audit provides a reasonable basis for our opinion.

A company's internal control over financial reporting is a process designed to provide reasonable assurance regarding the reliability of financial reporting and the preparation of financial statements for external purposes in accordance with generally accepted accounting principles. A company's internal control over financial reporting includes those policies and procedures that (1) pertain to the maintenance of records that, in reasonable detail, accurately and fairly reflect the transactions and dispositions of the assets of the company; (2) provide reasonable assurance that transactions are recorded as necessary to permit preparation of financial statements in accordance with generally accepted accounting principles, and that receipts and expenditures of the company are being made only in accordance with authorizations of management and directors of the company; and (3) provide reasonable assurance regarding prevention or timely detection of unauthorized acquisition, use, or disposition of the company's assets that could have a material effect on the financial statements.

Because of its inherent limitations, internal control over financial reporting may not prevent or detect misstatements. Also, projections of any evaluation of effectiveness to future periods are subject to the risk that control may become inadequate because of changes in conditions, or that the degree of compliance with the policies or procedures may deteriorate.

In our opinion, management's assessment that Intel Corporation maintained effective internal control over financial reporting as of December 25, 2004, is fairly stated, in all material respects, based on the COSO criteria. Also in our opinion Intel Corporation maintained, in all material respects, effective internal control over financial reporting as of December 25, 2004 based on the COSO criteria .

We have also audited, in accordance with the standards of the Public Companies Accounting Oversight Board (United States), the 2004 consolidated financial statements of Intel Corporation and our report dated February 15, 2005 expressed an unqualified opinion on those financial statements.

/s/   Ernst and Young LLP

San Jose, California

February 15, 2005

Basic Elements of the Auditor's Standard Report

Title
Addressee
Includes the word "Independent"
The Report is addressed to the Board of Directors and Stockholder's of the entity.

Introductory Paragraph
Identifies:
- Type of service performed ("We have audited")
- Management's assertion that it maintained an effective system of internal control was audited
- Name of entity audited
- Dates of the assertion regarding internal control
- Management's responsibility for the assertion
- Reference to COSO criteria for internal control
- Auditor's responsibility for the two opinions

Scope Paragraph
States that the audit was conducted in accordance with the standards of the Public Companies Accounting Oversight Board. These standards require:
- Planning and performing an audit to obtain reasonable assurance about whether effective internal control over financial reporting was maintained, in all material respects
- Understanding the system of internal control over financial reporting
- Evaluating the effectiveness of its design
- Evaluating its effective operation
- Auditor's belief that the audit provides a reasonable basis for the opinion

Definition Paragraph
The purpose of internal control over financial reporting is to provide:
- Reasonable assurance
- Over the reliability of financial reporting and the preparation of financial statements in accordance with GAAP.

Three aspects of internal control over financial reporting:
1. Maintain records of transactions in reasonable detail
2. Provide reasonable assurance that transactions are recorded to permit preparation of financial statements in accordance with GAAP, and all receipts and expenditures are authorized
3. Provide reasonable assurance regarding prevention, or timely detection, of unauthorized acquisition, use or disposition of the company's assets that are material in the context of the financial statements.

Inherent Limitations Paragraph
Inherent limitations may prevent the system of internal control over financial reporting from being 100% effective.

Explains the risk that internal controls may not function in the future as they have in the past.

Opinion Paragraph
Expresses auditor's opinion as to whether *management's assertion* about internal controls over financial reporting financial statements:
- Present fairly, in all material respects,
- As of balance sheet date
- In conformity with COSO criteria
Also expresses the auditor's opinion that the company maintained effective internal control over financial reporting.

Explanatory Paragraph
States that the auditor also audited the financial statements of the company, identifies the financial statements, and states the opinion expressed on the financial statements.

Firm's Signature
Date
Manual Signature
City and State or Country
Last day of field work

This sentence states that the CPA firm has audited management's assessment of the effectiveness of internal control over financial reporting included in management's report as of December 25, 2004. Note that management is making an assertion that internal control was effective as of the last day of the fiscal year. Performing all of the testing on December 25, however, is neither practical nor appropriate. PCAOB standards suggest that auditors obtain evidence about operating effectiveness at different times throughout the year, provided that the auditor updates those tests or obtains other evidence that the controls continued to operate effectively at the end of the company's fiscal year. Also note that the criteria for judging the effectiveness of internal control are the criteria established in *Internal Control–Integrated Framework* issued by the Committee of Sponsoring Organizations of the Treadway Commission (COSO). These criteria are discussed further in Chapter 10.

> Intel Corporation is responsible for its assessment about the effectiveness of internal control over financial reporting.

This wording acknowledges that responsibility for the assessment of internal control over financial reporting rests with management. Conversely, this sentence is intended to refute the notion that the auditor develops the representations about internal control over financial reporting.

> Our responsibility is to express an opinion on management's assessment based on our audit.

This sentence specifically indicates the auditor's responsibility. The auditor's role is to make an audit and to express an opinion based on the findings. When read in conjunction with the second sentence, there is a clear differentiation between the responsibility of management and the responsibility of the auditor.

Scope Paragraph

As its name suggests, the scope paragraph describes the nature and scope of the audit and identifies several limitations of an audit. The wording of this paragraph is:

> We conducted our audit in accordance with auditing and related professional practice standards established by the standards of the Public Companies Accounting Oversight Board (United States).

This sentence asserts that the auditor has met the standards established by the PCAOB.

> Those standards require that we plan and perform the audit to obtain reasonable assurance about whether effective control over financial reporting was maintained in all material respects.

This sentence identifies two significant inherent limitations of an audit. First is the acknowledgment that the auditor seeks only reasonable, rather than absolute, assurance. Thus, the reader is informed that there is some risk in an audit. Second, the concept of materiality is introduced. An audit is planned and performed to discover deficiencies in internal control over financial reporting that could lead to material, but not all, misstatements in the financial statements.

> Our audits included obtaining an understanding of internal control over financial reporting, testing and evaluating the design and operating effectiveness of internal control, and performing such other procedures as we considered necessary in the circumstances.

This wording further explains another inherent limitation of an audit. The words *testing and evaluating* indicate that less than 100 percent of the possible evidence about internal control was examined. Furthermore, testing implies that there is a risk that evidence not examined may be important in assessing the fairness of the conclusion about internal control.

> We believe that our audit provides a reasonable basis for our opinion.

This sentence identifies another limitation of an audit by stating that only a reasonable basis is needed for an opinion. The concept of a reasonable, rather than a conclusive or absolute, basis is consistent with the concepts of test basis and reasonable assurance stated earlier in the paragraph. This sentence also contains an assertion that the auditor has formed a positive conclusion about the scope of the audit work performed.

Definition Paragraph

This paragraph defines internal control over financial reporting. The first sentence states the purpose of internal control over financial reporting.

> A company's internal control over financial reporting is a process designed to provide reasonable assurance regarding the reliability of financial reporting and the preparation of financial statements for external purposes in accordance with generally accepted accounting principles.

An important aspect of this definition is that it addresses the concept of reasonable assurance. When auditing either internal control or financial statements, the concept of reasonable, not absolute, assurance is central. A guarantee of the accuracy of management's assertion is not possible.

The paragraph then goes on to define internal control over financial reporting by three important goals. It represents policies and procedures that

1. Pertain to the maintenance of records that in reasonable detail accurately and fairly reflect the transactions and dispositions of the assets of the company.
2. Provide reasonable assurance that transactions are recorded as necessary to permit preparation of financial statements in accordance with generally accepted accounting principles; and that receipts and expenditure of the company are being made only in accordance with authorizations of management and directors of the company.
3. Provide reasonable assurance regarding prevention or timely detection of unauthorized acquisition, use, or disposition of the company's assets that could have a material effect on the financial statements.

Inherent Limitations Paragraph

The inherent limitations paragraph states:

> Because of its inherent limitations, internal control over financial reporting may not prevent or detect misstatements. Also, projections of any evaluation of effectiveness to future periods are subject to the risk that control may become inadequate because of changes in conditions, or that the degree of compliance with the policies or procedures may deteriorate.

The inherent limitations paragraph addresses the fact that the company's system of internal control may not always prevent or detect misstatements. Although not specifically stated in this paragraph, the types of inherent limitations that prevent internal control over financial reporting from being effective include:

- Mistakes in judgment when applying internal control.
- Breakdowns and fatigue. Many aspects of internal control are human processes that may function inconsistently over time. They may function at a very high level but not work perfectly.
- Collusion between individuals may cause segregation of duties to break down, and internal controls may appear to function when they are not.
- Management override. Senior management may have authority that would cause otherwise functioning internal controls to break down. Auditors must assess the risk of management override, but that risk might not be reduced to zero.

Because inherent limitations are known features of the financial reporting process, it is possible to design systems to reduce, but not eliminate, the risk associated with such limitations.

Finally, the paragraph clearly states that while internal control over financial reporting might have functioned effectively in the past, there is a very real risk that it may not function as effectively in the future, and the auditor's opinion does not address the likelihood of the system functioning in future periods as effectively as it did in the past.

Opinion Paragraph

The opinion paragraph provides the auditor's conclusion about management's assertion regarding internal control over financial reporting. It is structured similar to the opinion paragraph in the auditor's report on financial statements.

> In our opinion,...

In interpreting the meaning and significance of this clause, it is proper to conclude that the opinion is being expressed by a professional, experienced, and expert person or persons. It is incorrect, however, to conclude that this phrase says, *"We certify," "We guarantee,"* or *"We are certain (or positive)."*

> ...management's assertion that Intel Corporation maintained effective internal control over financial reporting as of December 25, 2004 is fairly stated, in all material respects, based on the criteria established in Internal Control–Integrated Framework issued by the Committee of Sponsoring Organizations of the Treadway Commission (COSO).

This clause makes reference to management's assessment about effective internal control over financial reporting. The intended connotation of the words *fairly stated* is that management's assertion is presented reasonably and without material bias or distortion. An auditor does not use the words *accurately, factually, correctly,* or *exactly* because of the inherent limitations of a system of internal control. The auditor's opinion on fairness pertains to management's assertion about the evaluation of internal control and to whether the auditor's agrees with management's assertion. Finally, the auditor's report makes reference to the established criteria for evaluating internal control over financial reporting, which is the COSO criteria published in *Internal Control–Integrated Framework.* This framework is discussed in detail in Chapter 10.

> Also, in our opinion, Intel Corporation maintained, in all material respects, effective internal control over financial reporting as of December 25, 2004, based on the criteria established in Internal Control–Integrated Framework issued by the Committee of Sponsoring Organizations of the Treadway Commission (COSO).

The auditor's opinion on internal control over financial reporting is a dual opinion. In this sentence, the auditor provides an opinion on the adequacy of the system of internal control itself. In order to receive an unqualified opinion, the auditor must conclude that there are no material weaknesses in the system of internal control over financial reporting. As discussed below, the company may have significant deficiencies in internal control over financial reporting, which are reported to the audit committee, and still receive an unqualified opinion on internal control. This is discussed further in the next section on departures from the standard report. This sentence expresses the auditor's opinion that Intel Corporation established an effective system of internal control over financial reporting.

Explanatory Paragraph

The explanatory paragraph describes the fact that the auditor performed both an audit of internal controls and an audit of the financial statements as stated below.

> We have also audited, in accordance with the standards of the Public Companies Accounting Oversight Board (United States), the balance sheet of Intel Corporation as of December 25, 2004 and December 27, 2003 and related statements of income, cash flows, and equity for the three years then ended, and our report dated January xx, 2005 expressed an unqualified opinion on those financial statements.

The paragraph identifies the financial statements that were audited, the date of the audit report, and the opinion that was issued. Normally, users would expect that the opinion would be an unqualified opinion and the date of the audit report would be the same as the date of the report on internal controls. This statement is important to users as they can infer that the opinion on internal controls was informed by the audit work that supported the opinion on the financial statements.

Signature and Date

The engagement partner should manually sign the auditor's report. The date, as with the date on the auditor's report, represents the date that the auditor completed the process of obtaining evidence to form an opinion about management's assertion regarding internal control over financial reporting. This is called the last day of field work.

DEPARTURES FROM THE STANDARD REPORT

Audit Decision 2

■ When should the auditor use a non-standard report on internal controls over financial reporting?

An auditor will depart from the standard report when a material weakness in internal control over financial reporting exists. Two important definitions are relevant here.

■ A **significant deficiency** is an internal control deficiency that adversely affects the company's ability to initiate, authorize, record, process, or report external financial data reliably in accordance with GAAP. A significant deficiency could be a single deficiency, or a combination of deficiencies, that results in more than a remote likelihood that a misstatement of the annual or interim financial statements that is more than inconsequential in amount will not be prevented or detected.

■ A **material weakness** is a significant deficiency that, by itself, or in combination with other significant deficiencies, results in more than a remote likelihood that a material misstatement of the annual or interim financial statements will not be prevented or detected.

The auditor should evaluate the significance of a deficiency in internal control over financial reporting by initially determining (1) the likelihood that a deficiency could result in a misstatement of an account balance or disclosure and (2) the magnitude of the potential misstatement resulting from the deficiency or deficiencies. The significance of a deficiency in internal control over financial reporting depends on the potential for a misstatement, not on whether a misstatement has actually occurred. Figure 2-6 provides an example of how an auditor might quantify the difference between a deficiency in internal control, a significant deficiency in internal control, and a material weakness. However, these differences are a matter of professional judgment, and auditors might use criteria that are different from those illustrated in this figure.

Figure 2-6 ■ Example Criteria for Evaluating a Deficiency in Internal Control

	Likelihood of Misstatement	Magnitude of Potential Misstatement
Internal Control Deficiency	Remote (less than a 5 to 10% chance[a])	Inconsequential (less than 0.5 to 1% of pretax income[a])
Significant Deficiency	More than remote (more than a 5 to 10% chance[a])	More than inconsequential (more than 0.5 to 1% of pretax income[a])
Material Weakness	More than remote (more than a 5 to 10% chance[a])	Material (more than 4 to 5% of pretax income[a])

[a] Quantifications are a matter of professional judgment, and auditors might use criteria that are different from those illustrated in this figure.

The PCAOB standards indicate that the following circumstances should be regarded as at least a significant deficiency and is a strong indicator that a material weakness in internal control over financial reporting exists.

■ Restatement of previously issued financial statements to reflect the correction of a misstatement.

■ Identification by the auditor of a material misstatement in financial statements in the current period that was not initially identified by the company's internal control over financial reporting. This is still a strong indicator of a material weakness, even if management subsequently corrects the misstatement.

■ Ineffective oversight of the company's external financial reporting and internal control over financial reporting by the company's audit committee.

■ For larger, more complex entities, an ineffective internal audit or risk assessment function.

■ For complex entities in highly regulated industries, an ineffective regulatory compliance function.

■ Identification of fraud of any magnitude on the part of senior management.

■ Significant deficiencies that have been communicated to management and the audit committee, remain uncorrected after a reasonable period of time.

Figure 2-7 identifies some common circumstances when an auditor should depart from the standard report on internal control over financial reporting, and the type of opinion that the auditor should use.

Material Weakness in Internal Control over Financial Reporting

If there are significant deficiencies that, individually or in combination, result in one or more material weaknesses, management is precluded from concluding that internal control over financial reporting is effective. In these circumstances, the auditor must express an adverse opinion on the effectiveness of the company's internal control over financial reporting. The key aspects of this report would describe the material weakness in internal control over financial reporting in an explanatory paragraph, and the auditor's opinion would state that the company has not maintained effective internal control over financial reporting. This is the case even if there is only one material weakness (e.g., inadequate internal control over disclosures about derivative financial instruments) and the balance of the system of internal control over financial reporting is considered to be effective.

Readers must also understand that it is possible for the auditor to render an adverse opinion on the effectiveness of internal control over financial reporting and issue an unqualified opinion on the financial statements. For example, the auditor might identify the possibility of a material misstatement due to inadequacies in internal control that results in a material weakness. However, in performing audit procedures the auditor determined that the financial statements were not materially misstated. Or perhaps material misstatement was found and corrected by the entity. If a material weakness in internal control existed, it would result in an adverse opinion on internal control, but since the financial statements were presented fairly the auditor can issue an unqualified opinion on the financial statements.

Figure 2-7 ■ Departures from the Standard Report on Internal Control over Financial Reporting

Circumstances	Opinion
A material weakness exists in internal controls. For example, the auditor may have identified a material misstatement in the financial statements in the current period that was not initially identified by the company's internal control over financial reporting. Users should also understand that a company may get an adverse opinion on the effectiveness of its system of internal control, even if it has only one material weakness.	Adverse opinion
A significant deficiency in internal controls exists. For example, the auditor might have identified a deficiency in internal controls over revenue recognition. In the auditor's opinion, the significant deficiency could result in more than a remote likelihood that a misstatement of the annual or interim financial statements that is more than inconsequential in amount (but less than material) will not be prevented or detected. The auditor reports this to management and the audit committee.	Unqualified opinion
Circumstance imposed scope limitation. For example, the auditor might have identified a material weakness at an interim date, and the entity implements new controls to correct the deficiency. However, if the new controls are placed in operation near year-end, the auditor may not have sufficient time to determine that they actually are operating effectively at fiscal year-end.	Withdraw or disclaim opinion or qualified opinion
Management imposes a scope limitation. For example, in a multi-location audit the entity imposes a restriction on visiting certain locations that are important to the scope of the audit.	Withdraw or disclaim opinion

Significant Deficiency in Internal Control over Financial Reporting

Auditors may find what they believe are significant deficiencies that do not result in one or more material weaknesses in the financial statements. Auditors have a responsibility to report all significant deficiencies, weaknesses that might result in misstatements that are more than inconsequential in amount, to management and the audit committee. If significant deficiencies do not aggregate to a level of material weaknesses, the auditor can make a statement that management has an effective system of internal control over financial reporting. Nevertheless, because of the responsibility to report all significant deficiencies to the audit committee, some auditors describe the auditor's responsibility for internal control as one where the auditor has a high responsibility for a low threshold of internal control weaknesses.

Scope Limitations

The auditor can express an unqualified opinion on internal control over financial reporting only if the auditor has been able to apply all the procedures necessary under the circumstances. If there are restrictions on the scope of the engagement imposed by the circumstance surrounding the audit, the auditor should choose among withdrawing from the engagement, disclaiming an opinion, or expressing a qualified opinion. The auditor's decision depends on his or her assessment of the importance of the omitted procedure(s) to his or her ability to form an opinion on the effectiveness of the company's internal control over financial reporting. Furthermore, the standards of the PCAOB state that when the restrictions are imposed by management, the auditor should withdraw from the engagement or disclaim an opinion on the effectiveness of internal control over financial reporting.

Figure 2-6 provides several examples of scope restrictions. A common scope restriction occurs when a material weakness is identified prior to the date specified in the report and management implements controls to correct the deficiency. In some cases the new control may be placed in operation for such a short period of time that the auditor cannot draw a conclusion about the effectiveness of operation of the control. In this case the auditor should modify the opinion because of a scope limitation.

Are Companies Ready for Audits of Their Internal Controls over Financial Reporting?

In 2003 the Financial Executives Institute surveyed CFOs and other senior financial executives about their readiness for audits of internal controls over financial reporting and the cost of complying with Sarbanes-Oxley Act Section 404 audits of internal control. According to the survey, only 25 percent of respondents said that they had deployed a permanent solution to Section 404 requirements. Many companies, particularly smaller public companies, are not ready. As a result, the PCAOB pushed back their effective dates beyond the proposed effective date in the standards that they originally exposed for comment. The new effective dates are such that generally, a company that has equity market capitalization over $75 million will have to comply with these rules for fiscal years ending after November 15, 2004. Smaller companies will not have to have audits of their system of internal control over financial reporting until their first year-end after July 15, 2005.

[LEARNING CHECK

2-19   a. What are the nine basic elements of the auditor's standard report on internal control over financial reporting?
   b. What is the significance of the date of the auditor's standard report?
   c. What are the professional standards that govern the audit of management's assertion regarding the effectiveness of internal control over financial reporting?

2-20   a. Define internal control over financial reporting.
   b. What aspects of a company's overall system of internal control are not included as part of internal control over financial reporting?

2-21   Describe the inherent limitations of internal control over financial reporting.

2-22 a. When should an auditor issue an adverse opinion on internal controls over financial reporting?

b. Provide an example of a scope limitation and explain the criteria an auditor should use when making a decision about when either to withdraw from an engagement or issue a disclaimer of opinion or a qualified opinion because of a scope limitation.

c. Explain why an auditor might issue an adverse opinion on internal controls over financial reporting and issue an unqualified opinion on the financial statements.

KEY TERMS

Internal control over financial reporting, p. 72, 75	Material weakness, p. 78
	Significant deficiency, p. 78

FOCUS ON AUDITOR KNOWLEDGE AND AUDIT DECISIONS

This chapter introduces some basic knowledge about the assurance provided by an audit. It also explains the reports used to communicate results to financial statement users. Figures 2-8 and 2-9 summarize the important components of auditor knowledge and key audit decisions discussed in this chapter. Page references to a detailed discussion of these issues are provided.

Figure 2-8 ■ Summary of Auditor Knowledge Discussed in Chapter 2

Auditor Knowledge	Summary	Chapter References
K1. Know the relationship between accounting and auditing.	Accounting involves the process of identifying, measuring, recording, classifying, summarizing, and reporting events that affect an entity in financial statements. Management is responsible for reporting and disclosing events and transactions in its financial statements. Auditing involves gathering evidence to obtain reasonable assurance that the financial statements are presented fairly in all material respects. Auditors are responsible for their report on fair presentation in the financial statements.	pp. 44–46
K2. Understand how the concept of verifiability relates to the concept of "fair presentation, in all material respects."	Accounting requires the application of significant professional judgment, and the imprecision in accounting leads to an imprecision in the ability to verify financial statement presentations. Hence, the auditor seeks only a reasonable basis for expressing an opinion on the fairness of the financial statements.	pp. 45–47

(table continues)

Figure 2-8 ■ (Continued)

Auditor Knowledge	Summary	Chapter References
K3. Understand the auditor's relationship with management, the board of directors, the audit committee, and other groups.	Auditors have differing relationships with management, the board of directors and audit committee, internal auditors, and stockholders. These relationships are explained in the chapter. The auditor must work particularly closely with management but must also approach this relationship with an appropriate level of professional skepticism.	pp. 47–49
K4. Know the 10 generally accepted auditing standards.	Generally accepted auditing standards are divided into three groups: general standards, field work standards, and reporting standards. The general standards address the auditor's (1) technical training and proficiency, (2) independence, and (3) use of due professional care. The field work standards address (1) audit planning, (2) evaluation of the entity and its environment, including internal controls, and (3) obtaining sufficient, competent evidence. The reporting standards address (1) whether the financial statements conform to GAAP, (2) whether accounting principles used are consistent with those used in the previous years, (3) the adequacy of disclosures, and (4) the expression of an opinion by the auditor.	pp. 50–55
K5. Understand some important auditor's responsibilities that are implied by completing the audit.	This section of the chapter explains the concept of reasonable assurance. Auditors must use professional judgment when making decisions regarding the selection of evidence to support an opinion on the financial statements. The section also discusses the auditor's responsibility for detecting and reporting both fraud and illegal acts. Finally, it addresses the auditor's annual responsibility for evaluating an entity's system of internal control and when substantial doubt may exist about whether an entity is a going concern.	pp. 55–63
K6. Understand the basic elements of the auditor's standard report on financial statements.	The standard audit report includes the following elements that are explained in detail in the chapter; (1) the title and addresses, (2) the introductory paragraph, (3) the scope paragraph, (4) the opinion paragraph, (5) and the firm's signature and report date.	pp. 64–68
K7. Understand the basic elements of the auditor's standard report on internal controls over financial reporting.	Auditors of public companies must perform a combined audit of the financial statements and of the entity's internal control over financial reporting. The standard audit report includes the following elements that are explained in detail in the chapter: (1) the title and addresses, (2) the introductory paragraph, (3) the definition paragraph, (4) the scope paragraph, (5) the inherent limitations paragraph, (6) the opinion paragraph, (7) and the firm's signature and report date.	pp. 72–78

Figure 2-9 ■ Summary of Audit Decisions Discussed in Chapter 2

Audit Decision	Factors that Influence the Audit Decision	Chapter References
D1. When should the auditor use a nonstandard report on financial statements?	Circumstances in which the auditor would use an unqualified opinion with additional explanatory wording. • The entity changes from one acceptable accounting principle to another. • The auditor has substantial doubt about the entity's ability to continue as a going concern. • The auditor wishes to emphasize information. • The auditor relies on the audit work and audit opinion of another auditor. Circumstances in which the auditor would use a qualified opinion. • The financial statements contain a material departure from GAAP. • Circumstances impose a material scope restriction. Circumstances in which the auditor would use an adverse opinion. • The financial statements contain such an extremely material departure from GAAP that the financial statements do not present fairly financial position, results of operations, or cash flows. Circumstances in which the auditor would use a disclaimer of opinion. • Circumstance imposes an extremely material scope restriction, or the client imposes a material scope restriction.	pp. 68–71
D2. When should the auditor use a nonstandard report on internal controls over financial reporting?	The auditor would issue an adverse opinion on internal controls over financial reporting if a material weakness in internal controls is identified. Client-imposed scope restriction may cause the auditor to disclaim opinion or withdraw from the engagement. Circumstance-imposed scope restriction might cause the auditor to issue a qualified opinion or disclaim opinion. If the circumstances are sufficiently severe, the auditor may consider withdrawing from the engagement.	pp. 78–81

appendix 2a

EXAMPLE DEPARTURES FROM THE STANDARD AUDIT REPORT

Following are a variety of examples of departures from the standard auditor's report. Each example is accompanied by an explanation of (1) what the report means for financial statement users and (2) the auditor's criteria for using the report.

Unqualified Opinion on the Financial Statements with Explanatory Language regarding Going Concern: The following opinion was issued by Radin, Glass & Co., LLP on April 10, 2002 with respect to the financial statements for U.S. Technologies, Inc. for the years ended December 31, 2001 and 2000. **Note: The portions of the auditor's report that differ from the standard, three-paragraph audit opinion are highlighted in bold.**

REPORT OF INDEPENDENT CERTIFIED PUBLIC ACCOUNTANTS

Board of Directors
U.S. Technologies Inc.
Washington, D.C.

We have audited the accompanying consolidated balance sheets of U.S. Technologies Inc. as of December 31, 2001 and 2000 and the related consolidated statements of operations, stockholders' equity (capital deficit), and cash flows for each of the two years in the period ended December 31, 2001. These financial statements are the responsibility of the Company's management. Our responsibility is to express an opinion on these financial statements based on our audits.

We conducted our audits in accordance with auditing standards generally accepted in the United States of America. Those standards require that we plan and perform the audit to obtain reasonable assurance about whether the financial statements and schedule are free of material misstatement. An audit includes examining, on a test basis, evidence supporting the amounts and disclosures in the financial statements and schedule. An audit also includes assessing the accounting principles used and significant estimates made by management, as well as evaluating the overall presentation of the financial statements and schedule. We believe that our audits provide a reasonable basis for our opinion.

In our opinion, the consolidated financial statements referred to above present fairly, in all material respects, the financial position of U.S. Technologies Inc. at December 31, 2001 and 2000, and the results of its operations and its cash flows for each of the two years in the period ended December 31, 2001 in conformity with accounting principles generally accepted in the United States of America.

The accompanying consolidated financial statements have been prepared assuming that the Company will continue as a going concern. As discussed in Note 2 to the consolidated financial statements, the Company has suffered recurring losses from operations and has a working capital and net capital deficiency that raise substantial doubt about its ability to continue as a going concern. Management's plans in regard to these matters are also described in Note 2. The financial statements do not include any adjustments that might result from the outcome of this uncertainty.

/s/ Radin, Glass & Co., LLP
Certified Public Accountants
New York, NY
April 10, 2002

What does the report mean for financial statement users?

This report contains the standard three paragraphs included in an unqualified opinion. The second paragraph is a standard paragraph that indicates the audit firm conducted its audit in accordance with generally accepted auditing standards (*this would now read in accordance with the standards of the Public Companies Accounting Oversight Board*) and there were no limitations to the scope of the auditor's work. In the third paragraph the auditor expresses an unqualified opinion, which concludes that the financial statements present fairly U.S. Technologies' financial position, results of operations and cash flows.

The final paragraph (in bold) indicates that the auditor reached a conclusion that there is "substantial doubt" about U.S. Technologies' ability to continue as a going concern, due to the company's recurring losses, its working capital deficiency, and net capital deficiency. In addition, the auditor points out that no adjustments have been made to the financial statements as a result of this uncertainty, such as classifying all assets and liabilities as current or valuing assets at liquidation value.

What are the auditor's criteria for using this type of report?

Professional standards require that auditors evaluate the entity's ability to continue as a going concern in every audit. The auditor's responsibility is to determine whether there is *substantial doubt* (not just doubt) about whether the entity can continue as a going concern for a period of one year from the date of the financial statements. The auditor evaluates whether there is substantial doubt about the entity's ability to continue as a going concern based on the results of normal audit procedures (risk assessment procedures and further audit procedures) performed to form an opinion on the financial statements. If the auditor believes there is substantial doubt about the entity's ability to continue as a going concern, he or she should take the following steps: (1) obtain information about management's plans that are intended to mitigate the effect of such conditions or events, and (2) assess the likelihood that such plans can be effectively implemented. This is discussed further in Chapter 19.

If the auditor determines that substantial doubt exists, the auditor will evaluate the adequacy of management's disclosure. If there is adequate disclosure, then the auditor will add a fourth paragraph expressing the firm's conclusion about going concern. If the auditor concludes that disclosure is inadequate, the auditor will issue a qualified opinion or an adverse opinion associated with a departure from GAAP.

Unqualified Opinion on the Financial Statements with Explanatory Language regarding a change in accounting principles accounted for in conformity with GAAP: The following opinion was issued by Ernst and Young., LLP on January 29, 2003 with respect to the financial statements for Verizon Communications, Inc. for the years ended December 31, 2002, 2001, and 2000. **Note: The portions of the auditor's report that differ from the standard, three-paragraph audit opinion are highlighted in bold.**

REPORT OF INDEPENDENT AUDITORS

To the Board of Directors and Shareowners of Verizon Communications Inc.:

We have audited the consolidated balance sheets of Verizon Communications Inc. and subsidiaries (Verizon) as of December 31, 2002 and 2001, and the related consolidated statements of income, cash flow and changes in shareowners' investment for each of the three years in the period ended December 31, 2002. These financial statements are the responsibility of Verizon's management. Our responsibility is to express an opinion on these financial statements based on our audits.

We conducted our audits in accordance with auditing standards generally accepted in the United States. Those standards require that we plan and perform the audit to obtain reasonable assurance about whether the financial statements are free of material misstatement. An audit includes examining, on a test basis, evidence supporting the amounts and disclosures in the financial statements. An audit also includes assessing the accounting principles used and significant estimates made by management, as well as evaluating the overall financial statement presentation. We believe that our audits provide a reasonable basis for our opinion.

In our opinion, the consolidated financial statements referred to above present fairly, in all material respects, the consolidated financial position of Verizon at December 31, 2002 and 2001 and the results of their operations and their cash flows for each of the three years in the period ended December 31, 2002 in conformity with accounting principles generally accepted in the United States.

As discussed in Note 2 to the consolidated financial statements, Verizon changed its method of accounting for goodwill and other intangible assets in accordance with Statement of Financial Accounting Standards (SFAS) No. 142 "Goodwill and Other Intangible Assets" effective January 1, 2002, and as discussed in Note 14 to the consolidated financial statements, Verizon changed its method of accounting for derivative instruments in accordance with SFAS No. 133, "Accounting for Derivative Instruments and Hedging Activities" and SFAS No. 138, "Accounting for Certain for Derivative Instruments and Certain Hedging Activities" effective January 1, 2001.

/s/ Ernst and Young LLP
Certified Public Accountants
[New York, NY]
January 29, 2003

What does the report mean for financial statement users?

This report contains the standard three paragraphs included in an unqualified opinion and then an explanatory paragraph after the opinion.

The second paragraph is a standard paragraph that indicates that the auditor conducted its audit in accordance with generally accepted auditing standards *(this would now read in accordance with the standards of the Public Companies Accounting Oversight Board)* and there were no limitations to the scope of the auditor's work. In the third paragraph the auditor expressed an unqualified opinion, which concludes that the financial statements present fairly Verizon's financial position, results of operations and cash flows.

The fourth paragraph describes the changes in accounting principles (the method of accounting for goodwill and other intangible assets and the method of accounting for derivative instruments) and refers to the notes (2 and 14) to the financial statements where GAAP disclosures regarding the accounting changes are explained.

What are the auditor's criteria for using this type of report?

Professional standards state that the consistency of financial statements is key to reporting. A change in accounting principle is made in conformity with GAAP when (1) the new principle is a generally accepted accounting principle, (2) the change is properly accounted for and disclosed in the financial statements, and (3) management can justify that the new principle is preferable. When an acceptable change in GAAP has occurred between accounting periods (material to the financial statements), the auditor adds an explanatory paragraph to describe the change and refer readers to the corresponding note to the financial statements where the effect of the accounting change is described.

These changes result in an unqualified opinion since the financial statements reflect a change from one acceptable generally accepted accounting principle to another, the method of change is acceptable, and the auditor determined that management was justified making the changes, which were driven by new pronouncements of the Financial Accounting Standards Board.

If the auditor concludes that disclosure is inadequate, the auditor will issue a qualified opinion or an adverse opinion associated with a departure from GAAP.

Note: If the change in GAAP is immaterial, a standard auditor's report is used.

Unqualified Opinion on the Financial Statements with Opinion based in part on report of another auditor where there is no scope limitation or nonconformity with GAAP: The following opinion is a fictitious opinion for a private company based on the guidance provided in generally accepted auditing standards, AU 508.13. **Note: The portions of the auditor's report that differ from the standard, three-paragraph audit opinion are highlighted in bold.**

INDEPENDENT AUDITOR'S REPORT

To the Board of Directors of MLJ Company

We have audited the accompanying balance sheets of MLJ Company as of December 31, 20x2 and 20x1, and the related statements of income, stockholders' equity and cash flows for the years then ended.These financial statements are the responsibility of the Company's management. Our responsibility is to express an opinion on these financial statements based on our audits. **We did not audit the financial statements of XYZ Company, a wholly owned subsidiary, which statements reflect total assets of $10 Million and $ 9 Million as of December 31, 20x2 and 20x1, respectively, and total revenues of $12 Million and $ 10 Million for the years then ended. Those statements were audited by other auditors whose report has been furnished to us, and our opinion, insofar as it relates to the amounts included for XYZ Company, is based solely on the report of the other auditors.**

We conducted our audits in accordance with auditing standards generally accepted in the United States. Those standards require that we plan and perform the audit to obtain reasonable assurance about whether the financial statements are free of material misstatement. An audit includes examining, on a test basis, evidence supporting the amounts and disclosures in the financial statements. An audit also includes assessing the accounting principles used and significant estimates made by management, as well as evaluating the overall financial statement presentation. We believe that our audits **and the report of other auditors** provide a reasonable basis for our opinion.

In our opinion, **based on our audits and the report of other auditors,** the financial statements referred to above present fairly, in all material respects, the financial position of MLJ Company as of December 31, 20x2 and 20x1 and the results of its operations and its cash flows for the years then ended in conformity with accounting principles generally accepted in the United States.

/s/ Reedy and Abel, LLP
Certified Public Accountants
Portland, Oregon
February 14, 20x3

What does the report mean for financial statement users?

Note that all three paragraphs are altered for this type of report to reflect shared scope. The introductory paragraph mentions another auditor and the principal auditor explains a division of responsibility. This paragraph explains the magnitude of the portion of the financial statements audited by other auditors.

The scope paragraph also mentions that the other auditor's report was an important basis for the principal auditor's opinion.

Finally, the opinion paragraph expresses an unqualified opinion on the financial statements, stating that in the auditors' opinion, they fairly present the entity's financial position, results of operations, and cash flows. The opinion paragraph mentions the work of the other auditor to explain a division of responsibility between the other auditor and the principal auditor regarding the basis for the unqualified opinion.

The name of the other auditor is not mentioned unless that auditor gives express permission to use the name and the report of that auditor is also presented.

What are the auditor's criteria for using this type of report?

Auditors use this report when another auditor has performed a material part of the audit examination and the principal auditor decides to explain the division of responsibility. The auditor may mention the other auditor if the work was not well known to the principal auditor such as work performed by a correspondent firm, if the work was not performed under the principal auditor's guidance and/or the principal auditor did not review the work of the other auditor.

Once the principal auditor has decided to mention the other auditor, he is required to make inquiries about the professional reputation and to obtain a representation from the audit firm that it is independent of the entity. In cases where the other firm's principal practice is in a foreign country, the principal auditor should also communicate with the other auditor to ascertain the auditor's familiarity with GAAS and GAAP in the United States.

If no reference is made to another auditor in the auditor's report the principal auditor has assumed responsibility for any work performed by another auditor, and a standard report will be issued.

Unqualified Opinion on the Financial Statements with Emphasis of a matter by the auditor: The following opinion is a fictitious opinion for a private company based on the guidance provided in generally accepted auditing standards, AU 508.19. **Note: The portions of the auditor's report that differ from the standard, three-paragraph audit opinion are highlighted in bold.**

INDEPENDENT AUDITOR'S REPORT

To the Board of Directors of MLJ Company:

We have audited the accompanying balance sheets of MLJ Company as of December 31, 20x5 and 20x4, and the related statements of income, stockholders' equity and cash flows for the years then ended. These financial statements are the responsibility of the Company's management. Our responsibility is to express an opinion on these financial statements based on our audits.

We conducted our audits in accordance with auditing standards generally accepted in the United States. Those standards require that we plan and perform the audit to obtain reasonable assurance about whether the financial statements are free of material misstatement. An audit includes examining, on a test basis, evidence supporting the amounts and disclosures in the financial statements. An audit also includes assessing the accounting principles used and significant estimates made by management, as well as evaluating the overall financial statement presentation. We believe that our audits provide a reasonable basis for our opinion.

In our opinion, the financial statements referred to above present fairly, in all material respects, the financial position of MLJ Company as of December 31, 20x5 and 20x4 and the results of its operations and its cash flows for each of the years then ended in conformity with accounting principles generally accepted in the United States.

As discussed in note 8 to the financial statements, the Company has had numerous dealings with businesses controlled by, and people who are related to, the officers of the Company.

/s/ Reedy and Abel, LLP
Certified Public Accountants
Portland, Oregon
February 14, 20x6

What does the report mean for financial statement users?

First, this report contains the standard three paragraphs included in an unqualified opinion. The second paragraph is a standard paragraph that indicates that the auditor conducted their audit in accordance with generally accepted auditing standards *(reports on the audits of public companies would refer to the standards of the PCAOB)* and there were no limitations to the scope of the auditor's work. In the third paragraph the auditor expresses an unqualified opinion, which concludes that the financial statements present fairly MLJ Company's financial position, results of operations and cash flows.

Second, the auditor includes a fourth paragraph to emphasize a matter that the auditor feels warrants some additional explanatory language, while still expressing an unqualified opinion. In this case the auditor wants to point the reader to note 8 that discusses related party transactions.

What are the auditor's criteria for using this type of report?

Emphasis paragraphs are not required. The auditor uses this type of report to emphasize a matter to the financial statement user. This is still an unqualified opinion, but the auditor feels that an issue should be emphasized to the financial statement user. Examples of matters the auditor may wish to emphasize are —
The entity is a component of a larger business enterprise.
The entity has had significant transactions with related parties.
The entity has unusually important subsequent events.

Phrases such as "with the foregoing [following] explanation" should not be used in the opinion paragraph as it could be misconstrued as a qualification of the auditor's opinion.

Qualified Opinion for Departure from GAAP: The following opinion is a fictitious opinion for a private company based on the guidance provided in generally accepted auditing standards, AU 508.35-.57. **Note: The portions of the auditor's report that differ from the standard, three-paragraph audit opinion are highlighted in bold.**

INDEPENDENT AUDITOR'S REPORT

To the Board of Directors of MLJ Company

We have audited the balance sheets of MLJ Company as of December 31, 20x7 and 20x6, and the related statements of income, stockholders' equity and cash flows for the years then ended. These financial statements are the responsibility of the Company's management. Our responsibility is to express an opinion on these financial statements based on our audits.

We conducted our audits in accordance with auditing standards generally accepted in the United States. Those standards require that we plan and perform the audit to obtain reasonable assurance about whether the financial statements are free of material misstatement. An audit includes examining, on a test basis, evidence supporting the amounts and disclosures in the financial statements. An audit also includes assessing the accounting principles used and significant estimates made by management, as well as evaluating the overall financial statement presentation. We believe that our audits provide a reasonable basis for our opinion.

The Company has excluded, from property and debt in the accompanying balance sheets, certain lease obligations that, in our opinion, should be capitalized in order to conform with generally accepted accounting principles. If these lease obligations were capitalized, property would be increased by $18 Million and $16 Million long-term debt by $19.5 Million and $18.8 Million, and retained earnings would be decreased by $1.5 Million and $2.8 Million as of December 31, 20x7 and 20x6, respectively. Additionally, net income would be decreased by $1.5 Million and $1.3 Million respectively, for the years then ended.

In our opinion, **except for the effects of not capitalizing certain lease obligations as discussed in the preceding paragraph,** the financial statements referred to above present fairly, in all material respects, the financial position of MLJ Company as of December 31, 20x7 and 20x6 and the results of their operations and their cash flows for the years then ended in conformity with accounting principles generally accepted in the United States.

//s/ Reedy and Abel, LLP
Certified Public Accountants
Portland, Oregon
February 14, 20x8

What does the report mean for financial statement users?

This report has a standard introductory and scope paragraph meaning that there were no scope restrictions and the auditor was able to perform an audit in accordance with generally accepted auditing standards. When performing the audit, the auditor determined that the financial statements contained a material departure from generally accepted accounting principles that management did not change. The financial statements are the responsibility of management, and in this case, management chose to treat capital leases as operating leases.

In the third paragraph the auditor explains the departures from GAAP in sufficient detail that financial statement users can modify the financial statement before analyzing their content.

The opinion paragraph states that "except for" the failure to treat capital leases in accordance with generally accepted accounting principles, the balance of the financial statements are presented fairly, in all material respects.

The fact that the auditor has the ability to issue this type of report often causes audit entities to make adjustments necessary to present financial statements in accordance with GAAP and earn an unqualified opinion from their auditors.

What are the auditor's criteria for using this type of report?

The auditor expresses this type of opinion after making a judgment that the financial statements contain a material departure from generally accepted accounting principles and the effect on the financial statements is material.

The decision about whether to express a qualified or an adverse opinion (see separate example of an adverse opinion) should be based on the materiality of the departure from generally accepted accounting principles, the pervasiveness of the departure from GAAP, and the significance of the items to the financial statements as a whole.

Departure from generally accepted accounting principles might include
- Inadequate disclosures in the notes to the financial statements.
- Inappropriate use of accounting principles.
- Unreasonable accounting estimates.

When it is practicable, the auditor will provide the disclosures, or quantify their effect on the financial statements in a middle paragraph preceding the opinion paragraph.

Note: If the departure from GAAP is not material the auditor may issue a standard report.

Qualified Opinion for Scope Limitation: The following opinion is a fictitious opinion for a private company based on the guidance provided in generally accepted auditing standards, AU 508.22-.34. **Note: The portions of the auditor's report that differ from the standard, three-paragraph audit opinion are highlighted in bold.**

INDEPENDENT AUDITOR'S REPORT

To the Board of Directors of MLJ Company

We have audited the accompanying balance sheets of MLJ Company as of December 31, 20x8 and 20x7, and the related statements of income, stockholders' equity and cash flows for the years then ended. These financial statements are the responsibility of the Company's management. Our responsibility is to express an opinion on these financial statements based on our audits.

Except as discussed in the following paragraph, we conducted our audits in accordance with auditing standards generally accepted in the United States. Those standards require that we plan and perform the audit to obtain reasonable assurance about whether the financial statements are free of material misstatement. An audit includes examining, on a test basis, evidence supporting the amounts and disclosures in the financial statements. An audit also includes assessing the accounting principles used and significant estimates made by management, as well as evaluating the overall financial statement presentation. We believe that our audits provide a reasonable basis for our opinion.

We were unable to obtain audited financial statements supporting the Company's investment in a foreign affiliate stated at $10 Million and $9.5 Million at December 31, 20x8 and 20x7, respectively, or its equity in earnings of that affiliate of $500,000 and $ 350,000, which is included in net income for the two years then ended and described in Note 12 to the financial statements; nor were we able to satisfy ourselves as to the carrying value of the investment in the foreign affiliate or the equity in its earnings by other auditing procedures.

In our opinion, **except for the effects of such adjustments, if any, as might have been determined to be necessary had we been able to examine evidence regarding the foreign affiliate investment and earnings,** the financial statements referred to above present fairly, in all material respects, the financial position of MLJ Company as of December 31, 20x8 and 20x7 and the results of its operations and its cash flows for the years then ended in conformity with accounting principles generally accepted in the United States.

/s/ Reedy and Abel, LLP
Certified Public Accountants
Portland, Oregon
February 14, 20x9

What does the report mean for financial statement users?

Note that the second paragraph refers the reader to a third paragraph that explains why the auditor was not able to fully perform an audit in accordance with generally accepted auditing standards. Other than the one exception noted, the auditor performed an audit in accordance with generally accepted auditing standards.

The explanatory paragraph describes the magnitude of not being able to audit the financial statements of a foreign affiliate, both in terms of the investment reported on the balance sheet and the earnings from the foreign affiliate reported on the income statement. This paragraph states that the auditor has not obtained satisfactory evidence for these items to support an unqualified opinion.

The auditor's qualified opinion tells the user that the auditor was not able to fully complete the audit due to scope limitations. In this example, the user obtains no assurance regarding the investment in the foreign affiliate or earnings of that foreign affiliate. However, other than this one exception, the auditor was able to perform an audit in accordance with generally accepted auditing standards and the auditor issues an unqualified opinion on all other aspects of the financial statements.

What are the auditor's criteria for using this type of report?

If a scope limitation exists, the auditor must chose between a qualified opinion and a disclaimer of opinion (see separate example of a disclaimer of opinion). The auditor's decision to qualify his or her opinion or disclaim an opinion because of a scope limitation depends on his or her assessment of the importance of the omitted procedure(s) to his or her ability to form an opinion on the financial statements being audited. Auditors normally make this judgment by considering the significance of the omitted procedure(s) relative to the financial statements.

For example, the auditor might issue a qualified opinion: When the auditor cannot obtain audited financial statements to support an investment in an affiliated company. When the audit firm is engaged after the beginning of the year and the auditor is unable to observe beginning inventories.

When the entity has inadequate accounting records, such as with an initial audit of fixed assets where assets have been owned for many years.

These are scope limitations imposed by the circumstances of the engagement and they do not have a pervasive effect on the financial statements.

Adverse Opinion for Departure from GAAP: The following opinion is a fictitious opinion for a private company based on the guidance provided in generally accepted auditing standards, AU 508.58-.60. **Note: The portions of the auditor's report that differ from the standard, three-paragraph audit opinion are highlighted in bold.**

INDEPENDENT AUDITOR'S REPORT

To the Board of Directors of MLJ Company:

We have audited the balance sheets of MLJ Company as of December 31, 20x3 and 20x2, and the related statements of income, stockholders' equity and cash flows for each of the years then ended. These financial statements are the responsibility of the Company's management. Our responsibility is to express an opinion on these financial statements based on our audits.

We conducted our audits in accordance with auditing standards generally accepted in the United States. Those standards require that we plan and perform the audit to obtain reasonable assurance about whether the financial statements are free of material misstatement. An audit includes examining, on a test basis, evidence supporting the amounts and disclosures in the financial statements. An audit also includes assessing the accounting principles used and significant estimates made by management, as well as evaluating the overall financial statement presentation. We believe that our audits provide a reasonable basis for our opinion.

As discussed in Note 6 to the financial statements, the Company carries its property, plant and equipment accounts at appraisal values, and provides depreciation on the basis of such values. Further, the Company does not provide for income taxes with respect to differences between financial income and taxable income arising because of the use, for income tax purposes, of the installment method of reporting gross profit from certain types of sales. Generally accepted accounting principles require that property, plant and equipment be stated at an amount not in excess of cost, reduced by depreciation based on such amount, and that deferred income taxes be provided.

Because of the departures from generally accepted accounting principles identified above, as of December 31, 20x3 and 20x2, inventories have been increased $9 Million and $9 Million by inclusion in manufacturing overhead of depreciation in excess of that based on cost; property, plant and equipment, less accumulated depreciation, is carried at $10 Million and $12 Million in excess of an amount based on the cost to the Company; and deferred income taxes of $3 Million and $4 Million have not been recorded; resulting in an increase of $12 Million and $14 Million in retained earnings and in appraisal surplus of $10 Million and $12 Million, respectively. For the years ended December 31, 20x3 and 20x2, cost of goods sold has been increased $1 Million and $2 Million respectively, because of the effects of the depreciation accounting referred to above and deferred income taxes of $2 Million and $3.5 Million have not been provided, resulting in an increase in net income of $1 Million and $1.5 Million, respectively.

In our opinion, **because of the effects of the matters discussed in the preceding paragraphs, the financial statements referred to above do not present fairly, in conformity with accounting principles generally accepted in the United States, the financial position of MLJ Company as of December 31, 20x3 and 20x2, or the results of its operations or its cash flows for the years then ended.**

//s/ Reedy and Abel, LLP
Certified Public Accountants
Portland, Oregon
February 14, 20x4

What does the report mean for financial statement users?

This report has a standard introductory and scope paragraph, meaning that there were no scope restrictions and the auditor was able to perform an audit in accordance with generally accepted auditing standards. When performing the audit, the auditor determined that the financial statements contained an extreme material departure from generally accepted accounting principles that management did not change. The financial statements are the responsibility of management, and in this case, management chose to value property, plant, and equipment at its fair value, to provide depreciation based on fair value, and to omit the provision for deferred income taxes.

The auditor carefully detailed the departures from generally accepted accounting principles in the middle paragraphs, but the auditor also determined that the departures were so material and so pervasive that the financial statement *did not* fairly present financial position or results of operations, or cash flows in accordance with generally accepted accounting principles.

The fact that the auditor has the ability to issue this type of report often causes audit entities to make adjustments necessary to present financial statements in accordance with GAAP and earn an unqualified opinion from their auditors.

What are the auditor's criteria for using this type of report?

The decision to express an adverse opinion rather than a qualified opinion is based on the materiality and the pervasiveness of the departure from generally accepted accounting principles, and the significance of the items to the financial statements as a whole. Auditors normally express this type of opinion on the financial statements when the departure from generally accepted accounting principles is extremely material and pervasive to the financial statements, and the financial statements are so misleading that they do not fairly present financial position, results of operations, or cash flows of the entity.

Disclaimer of Opinion for Scope Limitation: The following opinion is a fictitious opinion for a private company based on the guidance provided in generally accepted auditing standards, AU 508.22-.34.and AU 508.61-63. **Note: The portions of the auditor's report that differ from the standard, three-paragraph audit opinion are highlighted in bold.**

INDEPENDENT AUDITOR'S REPORT

To the Board of Directors of MLJ Company

We were engaged to audit the balance sheets of MLJ Company as of December 31, 20x4 and 20x3, and the related statements of income, stockholders' equity and cash flows for the years then ended. These financial statements are the responsibility of the Company's management. **[Omit last sentence of the introductory paragraph.]**

[Omit the scope paragraph.]

The Company did not make a count of its physical inventory in 20x4 or 20x3, stated in the accompanying financial statements at $6.5 Million as of December 31, 20x4, and at $7.1 Million as of December 31, 20x3. Further, evidence supporting the cost of property and equipment acquired prior to December 31, 20x3, is no longer available. The Company's records do not permit the application of other auditing procedures to inventories or property and equipment.

Since the Company did not take physical inventories and we were not able to apply other auditing procedures to satisfy ourselves as to inventory quantities and the cost of property and equipment, the scope of our work was not sufficient to enable us to express, and we do not express, an opinion on these financial statements.

/s/ Reedy and Abel, LLP
Certified Public Accountants
Portland, Oregon
February 14, 20x5

What does the report mean for financial statement users?

A disclaimer of opinion states that the auditor does not express an opinion on the financial statements. An auditor may decline to express an opinion whenever he or she is unable to form, or has not formed, an opinion as to the fairness of presentation of the financial statements in conformity with generally accepted accounting principles.

There are a number of signals that the auditor has not given an opinion on the financial statements. Note that the introductory paragraph says that the auditor was "engaged to audit" rather than "we have audited." The last sentence that normally states that the auditor's responsibility is to express an opinion on the financial statements is also omitted as the auditor has not formed an opinion on the financial statements.

The scope paragraph is omitted from the report because the scope limitation is so severe that the auditor is unable to comply with generally accepted auditing standards and therefore has not completed the scope of an audit.

The third paragraph provides all of the substantive reasons for the disclaimer and describes the potential effects on the financial statements of the items for which the auditor has not obtained satisfactory evidence to support an unqualified opinion. In the example to the left, the auditor specifies the amount of inventory that was not supported by an inventory observation.

Finally, the opinion paragraph explains that due to the severe scope limitations, the auditor is unable to express an opinion on the financial statements.

What are the auditor's criteria for using this type of report?

The auditor's decision to disclaim an opinion because of a scope limitation depends on his or her assessment of the importance of the omitted procedure(s) to his or her ability to form an opinion on the financial statements being audited.

A disclaimer is appropriate when the auditor has not performed an audit sufficient in scope to enable him or her to form an opinion on the financial statements. In addition, when the entity imposes significant scope restrictions, the auditor will usually disclaim an opinion on the financial statements. For example, the refusal of management to take responsibility for financial statements or sign a representation letter would normally lead to a disclaimer of opinion. In addition, if management prevented audit procedures that are significant to the financial statements, such as requesting confirmation of the existence and terms of receivables, the auditor should disclaim opinion on the financial statements.

Unqualified Opinion—Other Comprehensive Basis of Accounting: The following opinion is a fictitious opinion for a private company based on the guidance provided in generally accepted auditing standards, AU 623.02-.10. **Note: The portions of the auditor's report that differ from the standard, three-paragraph audit opinion are highlighted in bold.**

INDEPENDENT AUDITOR'S REPORT

To the Board of Directors of MLJ Company:

We have audited the accompanying **statements of assets, liabilities, and capital—income tax basis of MLJ Partnership as of December 31, 20x6 and 20x5, and the related statements of revenue and expenses—income tax basis and of changes in partners' capital accounts—income tax basis** for the years then ended. These financial statements are the responsibility of the Partnership's management. Our responsibility is to express an opinion on these financial statements based on our audits.

We conducted our audits in accordance with auditing standards generally accepted in the United States. Those standards require that we plan and perform the audit to obtain reasonable assurance about whether the financial statements are free of material misstatement. An audit includes examining, on a test basis, evidence supporting the amounts and disclosures in the financial statements. An audit also includes assessing the accounting principles used and significant estimates made by management, as well as evaluating the overall financial statement presentation. We believe that our audits provide a reasonable basis for our opinion.

As described in Note 1, these financial statements were prepared on the basis of accounting the Partnership uses for income tax purposes, which is a comprehensive basis of accounting other than generally accepted accounting principles.

In our opinion, the financial statements referred to above present fairly, in all material respects, **the assets, liabilities, and capital of MLJ Partnership as of December 31, 20x6 and 20x5, and its revenue and expenses and changes in partners' capital accounts for the years then ended, on the basis of accounting described in Note 1.**

//s/ Reedy and Abel, LLP
Certified Public Accountants
Portland, Oregon
February 14, 20x7

What does the report mean for financial statement users?

In some cases private companies will use a comprehensive basis of accounting other than generally accepted accounting principles. For example, many small business prepare financial statements using the same basis of accounting that they use for federal income tax purposes. These companies can engage the auditor to audit the financial statements prepared on an other comprehensive basis of accounting (OCBOA), and many times banks and other creditors will use those financial statements when making credit decisions.

The reader will notice an immediate difference in the introductory paragraph as the financial statement names reflect the basis of accounting. The terms balance sheet, income statement, and statement of cash flows, without modification, are reserved for generally accepted accounting principles.

The scope paragraph is the same as the standard report because the scope of the audit has not been limited.

There is an explanatory paragraph before the opinion, which states the basis of presentation and refers to the note to the financial statement that describes the comprehensive basis of accounting that was used to prepare the financial statements.

The opinion paragraph is slightly modified from the standard report to reflect the different financial statement titles and to state that the financial statements present fairly according to the accounting basis described in the note to the financial statements. If the auditor felt that the financial statements departed materially from the other comprehensive basis of accounting, the auditor would issue a qualified or adverse opinion.

What are the auditor's criteria for using this type of report?

The auditor should issue this type of report when the entity uses a basis of accounting other than GAAP. Many companies subject to regulatory bodies keep their books solely according to the method prescribed by the agency. Also, many small businesses and individual practitioners use the tax, cash, or modified cash basis of accounting.

There are four comprehensive bases of accounting other than GAAP that are recognized:

1. A basis used to comply with the requirements of a regulatory agency

2. The basis used to file the entity's income tax return

3. The cash receipts and disbursements basis of accounting

4. A basis that uses a definite set of criteria with substantial support such as the price-level basis of accounting

Objective questions are available for the students at www.wiley.com/college/boynton

comprehensive questions

2-23 **(Relationship between accounting and comprehensive auditing)** Listed below in alphabetical order are the steps that are included in preparing and completing a comprehensive audit, and distributing financial statements.

1. Analyze events and transactions.

2. Assess the risk of material misstatement in management's financial statements.

3. Classify and summarize recorded data.

4. Communicate findings to management and the board of directors through other required communications and assurance services.

5. Distribute financial statements and auditor's report to stockholders in annual report.

6. Evaluate reasonableness of accounting estimates.

7. Express opinion through auditor's report and other communications.

8. Measure and record transaction data.

9. Perform risk assessment procedures including understanding the business and its internal controls.

10. Prepare financial statements per GAAP.

11. Obtain and evaluate evidence to respond to risks of material misstatement in the financial statements.

12. Obtain reasonable assurance that financial statements are presented fairly in conformity with GAAP.

Required

a. Prepare a diagram of the relationship between accounting and auditing in the preparation and audit of financial statements. Show each of the steps in the proper sequence.

b. Management and the independent auditor share the responsibility for the assertions contained in financial statements. Evaluate and discuss the accuracy of this statement.

c. Public companies hire auditors because of a requirement to comply with the rules of the SEC. Evaluate and discuss the accuracy of this statement.

2-24 **(Financial statement audits)** The following two statements are representative of attitudes and opinions sometimes encountered by CPAs in their professional practices:

1. Today's audit consists of test checking. This is dangerous because test checking depends on the auditor's judgment, which may be defective. An audit can be relied on only if every transaction is verified.

2. An audit by a CPA is essentially negative and contributes to neither the gross national product nor the general well-being of society. The auditor does not create; he merely checks what someone else has done.

Required

Evaluate each of the above statements and indicate

a. Areas of agreement with the statement, if any.

b. Areas of misconception, incompleteness, or fallacious reasoning included in the statement, if any.

Complete your discussion of each statement (both parts a and b) before going on to the next statement.

AICPA (adapted)

2-25   **(Management and auditor responsibilities)** Footnotes are important in determining whether the financial statements are presented fairly in accordance with generally accepted accounting principles. Following are two sets of statements concerning footnotes.

1. Student A says that the primary responsibility for the adequacy of disclosure in the financial statements and footnotes rests with the auditor in charge of the audit field work. Student B says that the partner in charge of the engagement has the primary responsibility. Student C says that the staff person who drafts the statements and footnotes has the primary responsibility. Student D contends that it is the entity's responsibility.

Required

Which student is correct?

2. It is important to read the footnotes to financial statements, even though they often are presented in technical language and are incomprehensible. The auditor may reduce his exposure to third-party liability by stating something in the footnotes that contradicts completely what he has presented in the balance sheet or income statement.

Required

Evaluate the above statement and indicate:

a. Areas of agreement with the statement, if any.

b. Areas of misconception, incompleteness, or fallacious reasoning included in the statements, if any.

AICPA (adapted)

2-26   **(Generally accepted auditing standards)** There are 10 GAAS. Listed below are statements that relate to these standards.

1. The auditor is careful in doing the audit and writing the audit report.

2. A more experienced auditor supervises the work of an inexperienced auditor.

3. The auditor investigates and reaches conclusions about the entity and its environment including its internal controls.

4. A predesigned schedule is followed during the audit.

5. The auditor is an accounting graduate with several years of experience in auditing.

6. In the auditor's judgment, the financial statements conform to all FASB statements.

7. The auditor is objective and unbiased in performing the audit.

8. The entity used the same accounting principles this year as last year.

9. The audit produced all the evidence needed to reach a conclusion about the entity's financial statements.

10. The entity's notes to the financial statements contain all essential data.

11. The auditor expresses an opinion on the financial statements.

Required

a. Identify by category and number within each category the GAAS to which each statement relates (i.e., general standard no. 1, field work standard no. 2, etc.).

b. For each answer in (a) above, provide the full statement of the standard. Use the following format for your answers:

IDENTIFICATION OF STANDARD	STATEMENT OF STANDARD

2-27   **(Detection of misstatements including fraud)** Reed, CPA, accepted an engagement to audit the financial statements of Smith Company. Reed's discussions with Smith's new management and the predecessor auditor indicated the possibility that Smith's financial statements may be misstated due to the possible occurrence of errors, fraud, and illegal acts.

Required

a. Identify and describe Reed's responsibilities to detect Smith's errors and fraud. Do not identify specific audit procedures.

b. Identify and describe Reed's responsibility to report Smith's errors and fraud.

AICPA (adapted)

2-28   **(Illegal client acts)** During the year under audit, an entity may have committed an illegal act.

a. Define the term *illegal act*.

b. What characteristics of illegal acts influence the auditor's responsibilities?

c. The auditor's responsibility for illegal client acts is the same regardless of their effects on the financial statements. Do you agree? Explain.

d. What information during the course of an audit may be indicative of possible illegal acts? How should the auditor respond to this evidence?

e. What are the possible effects of illegal acts on the auditor's report? What other responsibilities does the auditor have to communicate illegal acts to others?

2-29   **(GAAP vs. GAAS)** The auditor's standard report contains the terms generally accepted auditing standards and generally accepted accounting principles.

Required

a. Indicate the paragraph(s) of the standard report in which each term appears.

b. Distinguish between the terms.

c. Why is it important that the auditor state that the audited financial statements are in conformity with GAAP?

d. What is the relationship, if any, between Statements on Auditing Standards and GAAS?

2-30 **(Auditor's standard report)** The auditor's standard report contains standardized wording. Listed below are the sentences in the standard report.

1. We conducted our audit in accordance with auditing standards generally accepted in the United States.

2. We believe that our audit provides a reasonable basis for our opinion.

3. In our opinion, the financial statements referred to above present fairly, in all material respects, the financial position of X Company as of December 31, 20x2 and 20x1, and the results of its operations and its cash flows for the years then ended in conformity with accounting principles generally accepted in the United States.

4. We have audited the accompanying balance sheets of X Company as of December 31, 20x2 and 20x1, and the related statements of income, retained earnings, and cash flows for the years then ended.

5. An audit includes examining, on a test basis, evidence supporting the amounts and disclosures in the financial statements.

6. Our responsibility is to express an opinion on these financial statements based on our audits.

7. Those standards require that we plan and perform the audit to obtain reasonable assurance about whether the financial statements are free of material misstatement.

8. An audit also includes assessing the accounting principles used and significant estimates made by management, as well as evaluating the overall financial statement presentation.

9. These financial statements are the responsibility of the company's management.

Required

a. Identify the paragraph in which each sentence appears. If there is more than one sentence in the paragraph, indicate the sequence of the sentence in the paragraph.

b. State the primary purpose of each paragraph in the standard report.

2-31 **(Departures from standard report)** Circumstances may necessitate a departure from the auditor's standard report.

Required

a. Indicate the two types of departures from the auditor's standard report.

b. Indicate the effects on the auditor's report when a company makes a change in an accounting principle in conformity with GAAP.

c. State the other types of opinions an auditor may express.

d. Indicate the effects on the auditor's report when the auditor wishes to express a qualified opinion because of nonconformity with GAAP.

2-32 **(Auditor's standard report on internal control)** The auditor's standard report contains standardized wording. Listed below are the sentences in the standard report.

1. X Company is responsible for its assessment about the effectiveness of internal control over financial reporting.

2. We believe that our audit provides a reasonable basis for our opinion.

3. Also, projections of any evaluation of effectiveness to future periods are subject to the risk that control may become inadequate because of changes in conditions, or that the degree of compliance with the policies or procedures may deteriorate.

4. Our responsibility is to express an opinion on management's assessment based on our audit.

5. Our audits included obtaining an understanding of internal control over financial reporting, testing and evaluating the design and operating effectiveness of internal control, and performing such other procedures as we considered necessary in the circumstances.

6. A company's internal control over financial reporting is a process designed to provide reasonable assurance regarding the reliability of financial reporting and the preparation of financial statements for external purposes in accordance with generally accepted accounting principles.

7. A company's internal control over financial reporting includes those policies and procedures that (1) pertain to the maintenance of records that in reasonable detail accurately and fairly reflect the transactions and dispositions of the assets of the company; (2) provide reasonable assurance that transactions are recorded as necessary to permit preparation of financial statements in accordance with generally accepted accounting principles; and (3) provide reasonable assurance regarding prevention or timely detection of unauthorized acquisition, use, or disposition of the company's assets that could have a material effect on the financial statements.

8. Those standards require that we plan and perform the audit to obtain reasonable assurance about whether effective control over financial reporting was maintained in all material respects.

9. In our opinion, management's assertion that ABC Corporation and subsidiaries maintained effective internal control over financial reporting as of June 30, 2004, is fairly stated, in all material respects, based on the criteria established in Internal Control–Integrated Framework issued by the Committee of Sponsoring Organizations of the Treadway Commission (COSO).

10. Because of its inherent limitations, internal control over financial reporting may not prevent or detect misstatements.

Required

a. Identify the paragraph in which each sentence appears. If there is more than one sentence in the paragraph indicate the sequence of the sentence in the paragraph.

b. State the primary purpose of each paragraph in the standard report.

---

cases

2-33   **(Generally accepted auditing standards)** Ray, the owner of a small company, asked Holmes, CPA, to conduct an audit of the company's records. Ray told Holmes that an audit is to be completed in time to submit audited financial statements to a bank as part of a loan application. Holmes immediately accepted the engagement and agreed to provide an auditor's report within three weeks. Ray agreed to pay Holmes a fixed fee plus a bonus if the loan was granted.

Holmes hired two accounting students to conduct the audit and spent several hours telling them exactly what to do. Holmes told the students not to spend time reviewing the controls, but instead to concentrate on proving the mathematical accuracy of the ledger accounts and summarizing the data in the accounting records that support Ray's financial statements. The students followed Holmes's instructions and after two weeks gave Holmes the financial statements that did not include footnotes. Holmes reviewed the statements and prepared an unqualified auditor's report. The report, however, did not refer to generally accepted accounting principles or to the year-to-year application of such principles.

Required

Briefly describe each of the generally accepted auditing standards and indicate how the action(s) of Holmes resulted in a failure to comply with each standard. Organize your answer as follows:

BRIEF DESCRIPTION OF GENERALLY ACCEPTED AUDITING STANDARDS	HOLMES'S ACTIONS RESULTING IN FAILURE TO COMPLY WITH GENERALLY ACCEPTED AUDITING STANDARDS

2-34 **(Detection of fraud)** Several years ago, Dale Holden organized Holden Family Restaurants. Holden started with one restaurant that catered to the family trade. Holden's first restaurant became very popular because the quality of the food and service was excellent, the restaurant was attractive yet modest, and the prices were reasonable.

The success with his first restaurant encouraged Dale Holden to expand by opening additional Holden Family Restaurants in other metropolitan locations throughout the state. Holden has opened at least one new restaurant each year for the last five years, and there are now a total of eight restaurants. All of the restaurants are successful because Holden has been able to maintain the same high standards that were achieved with the original restaurant.

With the rapid expansion of business, Holden has hired a controller and supporting staff. The financial operations of the restaurants are managed by the controller and his department. This allows Holden to focus his attention on the restaurant operations and plan for future locations.

Holden has applied to the bank for additional financing to open another restaurant this year. For the first time ever, the bank asked him to provide financial statements audited by a CPA. The bank assured Holden that the certified statements were not being required because it doubted his integrity or thought him to be a poor credit risk. The loan officer explained that bank policy required all businesses over a certain size to supply audited statements with loan applications, and Holden's business had reached that size.

Holden was not surprised by the bank's requirement. He had ruled out an audit previously because he has great respect for his controller's ability, and he wanted to avoid the fee associated with the first audit as long as possible. However, the growth of his business and the increased number of restaurant locations make an audit a sound business requirement. He also believes that an additional benefit of the independent audit will be the probable detection of any fraud that may be occurring at his restaurants.

To fulfill the bank request for audited statements, Dale Holden has hired Hill & Associates, CPAs.

Required

a. Hill & Associates has been hired to perform an audit leading to the expression of an opinion on Holden Family Restaurants' financial statements. Discuss Hill & Associates' responsibility for the detection of fraud in a general-purpose audit.

b. What effect, if any, would the detection of fraud during the audit of Holden Family Restaurants by Hill & Associates have on their expression of an opinion on the financial statements? Give the reasons for your answer.

CMA (adapted)

You are working on the ToyCo audit for the year ended December 31, 20X2. Assume that each of the two sections of this question are unrelated.

During the year ended December 31, 20X2 ToyCo acquired a 30% investment in an unconsolidated foreign subsidiary, ForCo that sells raw materials to the company and others. As of February 2, 20X3 management had received only unaudited financial statements from ForCo, which it used to book its investment and the equity in the earnings of the foreign affiliate. The unaudited financial statements are the only information that you can obtain regarding the material investment in ForCo. The partner in charge of the engagement has reached a conclusion that it is likely that no additional evidence will be available to support the investment in ForCo and she would like to know the potential impact on the audit report. Research the issue of the potential lack of evidence about ForCo on the auditor's report. Cut and paste the standard sections that apply to this issue.

Your audit firm was first engaged to audit ToyCo on April 1, 20X0. The company's first audit was for the year ended December 31, 20X0. Your firm was unable to audit inventories on January 1, 20X0. You are now completing the audit of comparative balance sheets as of December 31, 20X2 and 20X1, and related statements of income, retained earnings, and cash flows for the years then ended. Draft the auditor report on the comparative financial statements for the two years ended December 31, 20X2.

INDEPENDENCE AND NONAUDIT SERVICES

In August 2000 the Panel on Audit Effectiveness of the Public Oversight Board[1] addressed the important issue of the effect of nonaudit services on independence. The Panel on Audit Effectiveness reported the following shift in revenues of the then Big 5 CPA firms.

	1990 All Clients	1990 SEC Clients	1999 All Clients	1999 SEC Clients
Accounting and Auditing	53%	71%	34%	48%
Tax	27%	17%	22%	20%
Consulting	20%	12%	44%	32%
Total	100%	100%	100%	100%

During this nine-year period of time, the ratio of accounting and auditing fees to consulting fees for SEC clients changed from 6 to 1 to 1.5 to 1. This change led then SEC chairman Arthur Levitt to testify before the Panel on Audit Effectiveness as follows: "Is the audit merely a conduit to the cross-selling of other, more lucrative firm services? ... I have grave concerns that the audit process, long rooted in independence and forged through professionalism, may be diminished—perhaps even sacrificed—in the name of more financial and commercial opportunities."

At the other end of the spectrum, Dan Goldwasser, a member of the American Bar Association's law and accounting committee, stated that "Nonaudit services allow a firm to gain greater understanding of a company. The more an auditor knows about the company, the better."

Staff for the Panel on Audit Effectiveness performed its own in-depth review of the quality of audit work performed in a sample of 126 audits performed for public companies. Of these 126 audit engagements, 37 also included significant consulting engagements for the client. The staff did not identify any engagements in which providing nonaudit services had a negative effect on the audit, and they concluded that in about a quarter of these engagements the performance on nonaudit services had a positive impact on the audit. Based on its findings and testimony before the panel, they agreed that:

· Independence is essential for promoting public confidence in the audit process and must be monitored continuously.

· As long as auditors provide nonaudit services to audit clients, there will be at least an issue with respect to the appearance of independence.

---

[1] Students can learn more about the Public Oversight Board (POB) at http://www.publicoversightboard.org/about.htm. The POB was formed in 1977 to oversee the SEC Practice Section of the AICPA and functioned as an important component of the accounting self-regulatory structure until it was dissolved in 2002.

- There has been an explosive growth in nonaudit services in recent years, to the point where many large firms' revenues from these services exceed their audit revenues.
- In their zeal to emphasize the array of services that CPAs offer, audit firms and the AICPA scarcely acknowledge auditing services in the public images that they portray. This serves to exacerbate the independence issue and to downplay the importance of auditing.

However, the Panel was split in its final conclusions about whether auditors of SEC registrants should be prohibited from performing nonaudit services. Readers can view the entire report and its arguments at www.pobauditpanel.org. The debate was partially resolved when the Sarbanes-Oxley Act of 2002 prohibited auditors of public companies from performing various nonaudit services. This matter is discussed further in this chapter in the section "Independence" and "Nonattest Services."

[PREVIEW OF CHAPTER 3]

One of the distinguishing characteristics of any profession is the existence of a code of professional conduct or ethics for its members. Ethical behavior requires consideration of more than a few results of conduct and regulatory activities. No professional code of ethics or regulatory framework can anticipate all the situations that might arise requiring professional judgments about ethical behavior. Accordingly, we begin this chapter with a brief discussion of general ethics before moving on to the subject of professional ethics. We then examine the AICPA's *Code of Professional Conduct* in considerable detail. The following diagram provides an overview of the chapter organization and content.

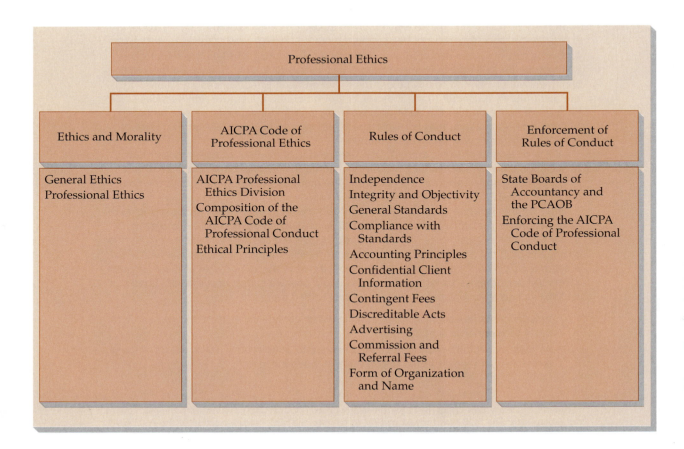

Chapter 3 addresses the following aspects of the auditor's knowledge and focuses on several important audit decisions related to a CPA Code of Professional Ethics.

focus on auditor knowledge

After studying this chapter you should understand the following aspects of an auditor's knowledge base:

K1. Know the nature of general ethics.

K2. Understand the purpose of professional ethics.

K3. Know the components of the AICPA Code of Professional Conduct and related pronouncements.

K4. Understand the essence of the Code's six ethical principles.

K5. Know the organizations and procedures involved in enforcing the Rules of Conduct.

focus on audit decisions

After studying this chapter you should understand the factors that influence the following audit decisions.

D1. What must a CPA do to comply with the Rules of Conduct regarding independence, integrity, and objectivity?

D2. What must a CPA do to comply with the Rules of Conduct regarding general standards and accounting principles?

D3. What must a CPA do to comply with the Rules of Conduct regarding responsibilities to clients?

D4. What must a CPA do to comply with the Rules of Conduct regarding other professional responsibilities and practices?

ETHICS AND MORALITY

Ethics is derived from the Greek word *ethos,* meaning "character." Another term for ethics is **morality,** which comes from the Latin *mores,* meaning "custom." Morality focuses on the "right" and "wrong" of human behavior. Thus, ethics deals with questions about how people act toward one another. Philosophers and ethicists have developed numerous theories of ethical conduct.

GENERAL ETHICS

Auditor Knowledge 1

■ **Know the nature of general ethics.**

People are constantly confronted with the need to make choices that have consequences for both themselves and others. Too often, an **ethical dilemma** arises where what is good for one party affected by a choice is not good for another party affected by the same choice. In some cases, individuals are confronted by competing ethical values. It has been said that in such situations, individuals should ask two questions: "What good do I seek?" and "What is my obligation in this circumstance?"

General ethics attempts to deal with these questions by defining what is good for the individual and society, and by trying to establish the nature of obligations or duties that individuals owe themselves and each other. But the inability to agree on what constitutes that "good" and "obligation" has led philosophers to divide into two groups. One group, the *ethical absolutists*, maintain that there are universal standards that do not change over time and that apply to everyone. The other group, the *ethical relativists*, says that people's ethical judgments are determined by the changing customs and traditions of the society in which they live. Some argue that both groups are right—that every individual makes numerous life choices that must be guided by unchanging universal standards, and many other choices that are subject to the changing mores of society.

Because no universal set of standards or changing codes of ethics can clearly point to the correct choice of behavior in all situations, some ethicists have worked on developing frameworks for general ethical decision making. Following is one such six-step framework.

1. Obtain the facts relevant to the decision.
2. Identify the ethical issues from the facts.
3. Determine who will be affected by the decision and how.
4. Identify the decision maker's alternatives.
5. Identify the consequences of each alternative.
6. Make the ethical choice.

This framework is particularly helpful when clear choices are not available such as when ethical rules of conduct or the application of accounting principles require significant professional judgment, or in situations where there may be competing ethical values.

PROFESSIONAL ETHICS

Professional ethics represent a commitment by a profession to ethical principles and rules of conduct. A commitment to ethical behavior is a key element that separates recognized professions from other occupations. They usually represent standards of behavior that are both idealistic and practical in purposes. Although codes of ethics may be designed in part to encourage ideal behavior, they must also be both practical and enforceable. To be meaningful they must strike a balance of being above the law but below the ideal.

States often grant professions exclusive rights to practice a professional activity. In most states CPAs are the only professionals that can sign an audit report. In return for this monopoly, professionals have an obligation to act in the public interest. A profession imposes professional ethics on its members who voluntarily accept standards of professional behavior that are more rigorous than those required by law. In many states, state boards of accountancy impose similar ethical standards. A code of ethics significantly affects the reputation of a profession and the confidence in which it is held.

In 1999 the forward-looking CPA Vision Project acknowledged that the profession must be recognized more for its values than for its services. The CPA Vision Project identified the following five core values associated with the CPA profession.

■ Integrity
■ Objectivity

- Competence
- Continuing education and lifelong learning
- Attuned to broad business issues

In aggregate, these values are important to earning the public's trust. Auditors deliver value to shareholders and other investors when they have the competence to identify potential material misstatements in financial statements, and they also have the integrity to expect the client to revise the financial statements or receive a qualified opinion on those statements.

LEARNING CHECK

3-1 How do general ethics guide human behavior?

3-2 What is the difference between the ethical absolutists and ethical relativists schools of thought?

3-3 a. What are the six steps in the general framework for ethical decision making?

b. Develop an example of when these six steps would be helpful to CPAs.

3-4 a. What is the purpose of professional ethics?

b. How are professional ethics imposed?

3-5 a. State the core values identified in the CPA Vision Project.

b. Explain why each of these values is important to the public's confidence in the public accounting profession.

KEY TERMS

Ethical dilemma, p. 103
Ethics, p. 103
General ethics, p. 103

Morality, p. 103
Professional ethics, p. 104

AICPA CODE OF PROFESSIONAL ETHICS

We now turn our attention to the AICPA's Code of Professional Conduct, which governs AICPA members and is administered by the AICPA Professional Ethics Team. Students should be particularly aware that many state boards of accountancy have adopted their own code of ethics that applies to all CPAs who hold a license from the state board. Most state boards of accountancy have adopted rules that are similar to the AICPA code, but they may differ in unique respects. If an auditor is auditing a public company, he or she must also must conform to SEC and PCAOB regulations and rules that are discussed later in this chapter. The AICPA Code is discussed here as it governs over 350,000 members in every state and jurisdiction in the United States.

AICPA PROFESSIONAL ETHICS DIVISION

Professional ethics are so important to the accounting profession that the bylaws of the AICPA provide that there shall be a Professional Ethics Division. The mission of the Professional Ethics Division is to (a) develop and maintain standards of ethics and effectively enforce such standards, thereby ensuring that the public interest is protected, (b) increase the public awareness of the value of the CPA; and (c) provide timely and quality guidance to enable members to be the premier value providers in their field. The division consists of a relatively small full-time staff, active volunteer members, and ad hoc investigatory volunteers, as needed. The Professional Ethics Division performs the following major functions to accomplish its mission.

- **Standard setting:** The Professional Ethics Executive Committee interprets the AICPA Code of Professional Conduct and proposes amendments to the code of conduct.
- **Ethics enforcement:** The Professional Ethics Team investigates complaints of potential disciplinary matters involving members of the AICPA and state CPA societies through the Joint Ethics Enforcement Program (JEEP).
- **Technical inquiry services ("ethics hotline"):** The professional Ethics Team educates members and promotes the understanding of ethical standards contained in the AICPA Code of Professional Conduct by responding to member inquiries on the application of the AICPA Code of Professional Conduct to specific areas of practice.

The Professional Ethics Division also publishes a quarterly newsletter. You can learn more about the AICPA Professional Ethics Division at http://www.aicpa.org/members/div/ethics/index.htm.

COMPOSITION OF THE AICPA CODE OF PROFESSIONAL CONDUCT

Auditor Knowledge 3

■ Know the components of the CPA's Code of Professional Conduct and related pronouncements.

The **AICPA's Code of Professional Conduct (the Code)** defines the ethical responsibilities for AICPA members. In 1988 the AICPA members adopted two sections of the AICPA's Code of Professional Conduct:

- **Principles** that express the basic tenets of ethical conduct and provide the framework for the Rules.
- **Rules of Conduct** that establish minimum standards of acceptable conduct in the performance of professional services.

As expressions of the ideals of professional conduct, the Principles are not set forth as enforceable standards. In contrast, the Rules of Conduct establish minimum standards of acceptable conduct and are enforceable.

In addition to these two sections of the Code, the Professional Ethics Division's Executive Committee issues the following pronouncements:

- **Interpretations of the Rules of Conduct** that provide guidelines about the scope and applicability of specific rules.
- **Ethical Rulings** that indicate the applicability of the Rules of Conduct and Interpretations to a particular set of factual circumstances.

Figure 3-1 ■ AICPA Code of Professional Conduct Sections and Related Pronouncements

	Component	Nature	Enforceable?
Code Section:	Principles	Express the basic tenets of ethical conduct and provide a framework for the Rules.	No
	Rules of Conduct	Establish minimum standards of acceptable conduct in the performance of professional services.	Yes
Related Pronouncement:	Interpretations of Rules of Conduct	Provide guidelines about the scope and applicability of specific rules.	The CPA must be prepared to justify any departures.
	Ethical Rulings	Indicate the applicability of the rules and interpretations to particular factual circumstances.	The CPA must be prepared to justify any departures.

Members who depart from the interpretations or ethical rulings must justify such departures in disciplinary hearings. A summary of the Code sections and related pronouncements is presented in Figure 3-1.

ETHICAL PRINCIPLES

> **Auditor Knowledge 4**
>
> ■ **Understand the essence of the Code's six ethical principles.**

In the code of Professional Conduct, the following six principles express the basic tenets of ethical conduct and provide the framework for the Rules of Conduct:

- Responsibilities
- The public interest
- Integrity
- Objectivity and independence
- Due care
- Scope and nature of services

Responsibilities

In carrying out their **responsibilities** as professionals, members should exercise sensitive professional and moral judgments in all their activities.[2]

CPAs render important and essential services in our free enterprise system. All members have responsibilities to those who use their professional services. In addition, members have an ongoing responsibility to cooperate with other members to (1) improve the art of accounting, (2) maintain the public's confidence in

---

[2] All definitions of principles and rules are from applicable ethics sections of the *AICPA Professional Standards*, Volume 2 (New York: AICPA, 2005).

the profession, and (3) carry out the self-regulatory activities described in this chapter. The overall objective in meeting this principle is to maintain and enhance the stature of the public accounting profession.

The Public Interest

> Members should accept the obligation to act in a way that will serve **the public interest,** honor the public trust, and demonstrate commitment to professionalism.

The **public interest** is defined as the collective well-being of the community of people and institutions that CPAs serve. The CPA's public interest includes clients, creditor grantors, governmental agencies, employees, stockholders, and the general public. A distinguishing mark of any profession is acceptance of its responsibility to the public.

CPAs are expected to meet professional standards in all engagements. In serving the public interest, members should conduct themselves in a manner that shows a level of professionalism consistent with the principles of the code.

Integrity

> To maintain and broaden public confidence, members should perform all professional responsibilities with the highest sense of integrity.

Integrity is a personal characteristic that is indispensable in a CPA. It is the benchmark by which members must ultimately judge all decisions made in an engagement. **Integrity** is measured in terms of what is right and just. Integrity requires a member to be, among other things, honest and candid within the constraints of client confidentiality. Moreover, integrity requires that service and the public trust should not be subordinated to personal gain and advantage. Integrity can permit inadvertent error and the honest difference of opinion; however, it cannot tolerate intentional distortion of facts or subordination of judgment. Integrity requires a member to observe both the form and the spirit of technical and ethical standards; circumvention of those standards constitutes subordination of judgment.

Objectivity and Independence

> A member should maintain objectivity and be free of conflicts of interest in discharging professional responsibilities. A member in public practice should be independent in fact and appearance when providing auditing and other attestation services.

Objectivity is a state of mind. Although this principle is not precisely measurable, it nevertheless is held up to members as an imperative. **Objectivity** means being impartial and unbiased in all professional matters. CPAs often serve multiple interests in many different capacities and must demonstrate their objectivity in varying circumstances. CPAs in public practice render attest, tax, and management advisory services. Some CPAs also prepare financial statements in the role of CFO or Controller, and other CPAs work as internal auditors. Regardless of service or capacity, CPAs should protect the integrity of their work, maintain objectivity, and avoid any subordination of their judgment. Irrespective of whether a CPA is an auditor or a member of management, CPAs owe a duty of remaining impartial and unbiased.

Independence precludes relationships that may appear to impair a member's objectivity in rendering attestation services. For example, a CPA's objectivity may be impaired if the auditor's spouse has an ownership interest in an audit client. No matter how competent CPAs may be in performing auditing and other attest services, their opinions will be of little value to those who rely on their reports unless they are independent. In rendering attest services, members must be **independent in fact;** this means that members should act with integrity and objectivity. Members must also be **independent in appearance.** To meet this test, members should not have a financial interest or a key business relationship with a client. For example, CPAs who perform attest engagements should not be part of management or serve on the client's board of directors. Members in public practice should continuously assess their relationship with clients to avoid situations that may appear to, or in fact, impair their independence.

Due Care

A member should observe the profession's technical and ethical standards, strive continually to improve competence and the quality of services, and discharge professional responsibility to the best of the member's ability.

The principle of due care is at the center of the profession's ongoing quest for excellence in the performance of professional services. **Due care** requires each member to discharge his or her professional responsibilities with competence and diligence.

Competence is the product of education and experience. Education begins with preparation for entry to the profession. It extends to continuing professional education throughout a member's career. Experience involves on-the-job training and acceptance of increased responsibilities during a member's professional life.

Diligence involves steady, earnest, and energetic application and effort in performing professional services. It also means that a member should (1) be thorough in his or her work, (2) observe applicable technical and ethical standards, and (3) complete the service promptly.

Due care extends to the planning and supervision of engagements for which a member is responsible. For example, each member is expected to properly supervise any assistants participating in an engagement.

Scope and Nature of Services

A member in public practice should observe the Principles of the Code of Professional Conduct in determining the scope and nature of services to be provided.

This principle applies only to a member who renders services to the public. In deciding whether to provide specific services in a given situation, a member should consider all of the preceding principles. If any principle cannot be met, the engagement should be declined. In addition, a member should:

- Practice only in a firm that has implemented internal quality control procedures.
- Determine whether the scope and nature of other services requested by an audit client would create a conflict of interest in providing audit services for that client.
- Assess whether the requested service is consistent with the role of a professional.

⌈LEARNING CHECK

3-6 What are the major functions of the AICPA's Professional Ethics Division?

3-7 a. Identify the two sections of the AICPA's Code of Professional Conduct and the two types of pronouncements related to them.

   b. Explain the enforceability of each of the section and related pronouncements.

3-8 a. What is the significance of the Principles of the AICPA's Code of Professional Conduct?

   b. Explain the essence of the six principles in the Code.

⌈KEY TERMS

Code of Professional Conduct, p. 106
Due care, p. 109
Ethical rulings, p. 106
Ethics enforcement, p. 106
Independent in appearance, p. 109
Independent in fact, p. 109
Integrity, p. 108
Interpretations of the Rules of Conduct, p. 106

Objectivity, p. 108
Principles, p. 106
Public interest, p. 108
Responsibilities, p. 107
Rules of Conduct, p. 106
Standard setting, p. 106
Technical inquiry services, p. 106
The public interest, p. 108

⌈RULES OF CONDUCT⌉

The AICPA Rules of Conduct guide a CPA in determining the appropriate professional behavior. For example, when a CPA finds financial fraud, who should be told? Management? The Board of Directors? The SEC? Shareholders? Creditors? Or what would be the impact on independence if an auditor's parents owned shares in an audit client? Can a consulting partner help the owner of a private company sell his business and take a fee as a percentage of the sales price? These are the types of issues the Rules of Conduct are intended to sort out.

The Rules of Conduct consist of 11 enforceable rules, as categorized in Figure 3-2. In formulating the rules, the AICPA strives to serve the best interests of the public, the profession, and its members. The rules are modified from time to time to recognize evolving norms of ethical conduct and other influences such as changes mandated by government agencies. For example, the independence Rules of Conduct and interpretations were modernized in 2002 to meet the public and SEC expectations regarding nonaudit services and to address challenges associated with having many professionals in international accounting firms that do not influence audits. The new rules also address many of the challenges of dual-career families where a spouse might earn compensation in an employee stock option or stock purchase plan from an audit client.

The AICPA's bylaws require that members adhere to the Rules of Conduct. The rules are applicable to all members (in public practice and in industry) and to all professional services performed (attest, tax, etc.) except when (1) the wording indicates otherwise (several rules indicate that they apply only to members in

Figure 3-2 ■ AICPA Rules of Conduct

Section	Rule	Applicability	
		All Members	Members in Public Practice
Section 100	Independence, Integrity, and Objectivity		
101	Independence		✓
102	Integrity and objectivity	✓	
Section 200	General Standards and Accounting Principles		
201	General standards	✓	
202	Compliance with standards	✓	
203	Accounting principles	✓	
Section 300	Responsibilities to Clients		
301	Confidential client information		✓
302	Contingent fees		✓
Section 400	Responsibilities to Colleagues		
	(No currently effective rules in this section.)		
Section 500	Other Responsibilities and Practices		
501	Acts discreditable	✓	
502	Advertising and other forms of solicitation		✓
503	Commission and referral fees		✓
505	Form of organization and name		✓

public practice) and (2) a member is practicing outside the United States and conforms to the host country's rules of the organized accounting profession. CPAs must also adhere to relevant state and SEC ethical rules.

A member in public practice may be held responsible for compliance with the rules of all persons under the member's supervision or those who are the member's partners or shareholders in the practice. In addition, a member cannot permit others to carry out acts on his or her behalf that, if carried out by the member, would violate the rules.

The following discussion states each rule and explains essential features of the rules.

RULE 101—INDEPENDENCE

> **Rule 101—Independence.** A member in public practice shall be independent in the performance of professional services as required by standards promulgated by bodies designated by Council.

Audit Decision 1

■ **What must a CPA do to comply with the Rules of Conduct regarding independence, integrity, and objectivity?**

Independence is the cornerstone of the auditing profession. It is so important that every auditor's report is entitled "Independent Auditor's Report." Financial statement users need to know that auditors are independent of the entities that they audit.

Auditors frequently think about independence in two ways; independence in fact and the appearance of independence. These facets of independence are depicted in Figure 3-3. Being **independent in fact** can be defined as acting with integrity and objectivity. Independence in fact is about being honest, about not subordinating the public trust to personal gain and advantages, and about being unbiased and impartial when performing attest services. Independence in fact is difficult for others to observe, but it is nevertheless the cornerstone upon which audit services provide value.

Being **independent in appearance** addresses a number of potential conflicts of interest that can be observed. An auditor's (or immediate family member's) having ownership interest in an audit client, participating in a joint venture with an attest client, having litigation threatened by an attest client, or having a loan from

Figure 3-3 ■ Independence in Fact vs. Appearance

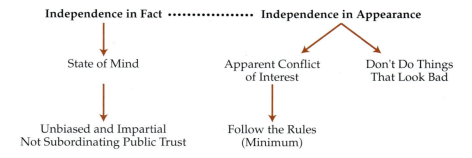

an audit client are examples of the types of activities that impair the appearance of independence for an audit firm.

Independence in fact is a state of mind, and it is impossible to observe what a CPA is thinking when performing attest services. In spite of the fact that it is difficult to observe independence in fact, *it is essential that the auditor approach every audit decision in an unbiased fashion.* The *appearance of independence* is observable and subject to enforcement under the Rules of Conduct. Rule 101 specifies a number of circumstances that can impair the appearance of independence to guide members in observable aspects of ethical conduct. The common factor of the issues raised in Rule 101 is that they are targeted at situations where CPAs appear to have a conflict of interest, such as having loans from clients or providing certain consulting services to clients. In addition, CPAs must use their common sense and avoid situations that look bad to the public, which relies on the CPAs independence.

Rule 101 incorporates into the Code, by reference, the independence requirements in technical standards issued by the AICPA. The bodies that have issued standards that include a requirement that the CPA be independent are the Auditing Standards Board and the Accounting and Review Services Committee. For example, a member must be independent in performing attest services such as a financial statement audit, an examination of prospective financial statements, and a review of the financial statements of a nonpublic entity. A member is not required to be independent in rendering nonattest services such as accounting, tax, and consulting services.

General Independence Rules

In November 2000 the SEC adopted the first changes in its independence rules since 1983, and the AICPA adopted similar rules in 2001. This discussion addresses the underlying drivers that caused the SEC and the AICPA to amend their independence rules, followed by a discussion of the new AICPA interpretations of the independence rules.

The accounting industry changed dramatically in the 1990s following the consolidation of many international CPA firms, the increasing globalization of accounting firms, and these firms' offerings of a wide range of multidisciplinary services. Today CPA firms have many professionals all over the globe, along with their family members, who have no influence over an audit. CPA firms have also seen an increase in the number of dual-career families who potentially have independence problems when an accounting professional's spouse receives compensation through stock options or other stock ownership schemes from an employer who is also an audit client. The growth of nonaudit services raises questions about the ability of CPA firms to remain independent while providing services that may result in professional fees that are larger than those provided by the independent audit. The following discussion addresses the independence rules as they apply to members of an accounting firm's professional staff and their family members. The discussion of interpretation 101-3 addresses the AICPA rules regarding nonaudit services.

An Engagement-Based Approach

The new independence rules follow an engagement-based approach and define a level of accounting professional—a covered member—who is a person in a position to potentially influence audit decisions or the outcome of an audit. The independence rules are particularly strict for a professional who falls under the *covered member* rules. These key independence terms are summarized in Figure 3-4. **Covered members** are defined as:

■ Members of the engagement team, including any professional who spends even a few minutes performing work on an attest engagement.

■ Partners and managers with consultation, oversight, or review responsibilities related to the engagement. These could be regional audit partners with review responsibilities for all the audit engagements in their region, or partners with industry specialization who regularly consult with other partners on audit matters.

■ Direct supervisors of the engagement partner, including all successive senior levels. This would include any direct supervisor of the engagement partner, all the way up to the senior partner in the accounting firm.

■ Professionals who perform (or expect to perform) more than 10 hours of nonattest services for the client. For example, a professional who performs only 8 hours of tax services would not be considered someone who could influence the audit. However, once a tax or consulting professional delivers 10 or more hours of professional services to an audit client, he or she is considered to be a covered member.

■ Partners who are in the same office as the lead partner on the engagement. Other partners in an office may have influence over compensation issues or other management decisions in the office, and hence they may be in a position to influence the audit even though they are not on the audit team. They therefore need to be independent of all audit engagements associated with the office. The term *office* is also broadly defined and represents the substance of work relationships, not just a physical location.

■ The firm, its benefit plans, and entities controlled by covered members. Hence, the firm or its benefit plan cannot invest in an audit client. Furthermore, a covered member cannot control an entity that invests in an audit client.

■ Those who evaluate partners' performance and compensation, including members of compensation committees. This means other partners who have significant influence over the lead partner on an audit engagement.

■ Individuals who consult with the audit team regarding technical or industry-related issues that are specific to the engagement. This is intended to include individuals who are authorized to give advice to the audit team and there is no minimum hours test. This will usually include partners and managers who may be called upon for specialized accounting or auditing advice.

■ Individuals who participate in quality control activities for the firm. These are usually partners and managers who conduct internal peer reviews and evaluate audit quality.

The *covered member* standard is one that includes a wide variety of individuals in an accounting firm who are in a position to influence audit decisions. However, it does not result in every professional in the firm having to meet the same standard.

Prohibited Activities

In order to preserve the appearance of independence, covered members are prohibited from the following activities. A *covered member* cannot:

■ Have a direct, or material indirect, investment in the audit client. Hence, a covered member cannot have any direct investment in an audit client. A

Figure 3-4 ■ Key Independence Terms

Covered Members

- Any member of the engagement team
- Partners and managers with consultation, oversight, or review responsibilities related to the engagement.
- Direct supervisors of the engagement partner, including all successive senior levels
- Professionals who perform (or expect to perform) more than 10 hours of nonattest services for the client.[a]
- Partners who are in the same office as the lead partner on the engagement.[a]
- The firm, its benefit plans, and entities controlled by covered members
- Those who evaluate partners' performance and compensations, including members of compensation committees
- Individuals who consult with the audit team regarding technical or industry-related issues specific to the engagement. This is intended to include individuals who are authorized to give advice to the audit team, and there is no hours test.
- Individuals who participate in quality control activities for the firm.

Prohibited Activities

- Cannot have a direct, or a material indirect, investment in the audit client.
- Cannot be a trustee or a trust or executor of an estate who invests directly in an audit client. (The AICPA and SEC permit an exception for a trustee who lacks authority to make investment decisions.)
- Cannot have a joint, closely held investment that is material to the covered member.
- Cannot have loans to or from the audit client. (There are some very limited exceptions.)

Covered Members' Immediate Family

- Spouse
- Spousal equivalent
- Dependents

Prohibited Activities

- Exactly the same as for a covered member.
- Cannot be employed in a "key position" with an audit client.
  - In a position to exercise influence over the financial statement, such as CEO, CFO, member of the board of directors, or treasurer.
  - Prepares, or supervises others who prepare, (1) the financial statements or (2) material accounting records.
  - Involved in accounting decision making.

Covered Members Close Relatives

- Parents
- Nondependent children
- Brothers and sisters

Prohibited Activities

- May not hold a key position with an audit client.
- May not hold a material financial interest in an audit client, or have significant influence over an audit client (APB 18).

All Other Professional Employees and Their Immediate Family Members

Prohibited Activities

- Cannot have a direct investment of 5% or more in an audit client.
- Cannot have a business or key position employment relationship with an audit client.
- Cannot be a trustee, director or officer of an audit client, or a client's pension or profit-sharing trust.

[a] Certain covered members, nonattest partners and managers, and other partners in the office of the lead engagement partners may have an immediate family member who works for an audit client as long as they are not in a "key position." Immediate family members may participate in an employee benefit plan that includes employee stock ownership plans or employee stock option plans as long as benefits are offered equitably to all similar employees.

covered member can, however, own shares in a mutual fund that owns shares in the audit client, as long as the investment is immaterial to the covered member.

■ Be a trustee of a trust or executor of an estate who invests directly in an audit client. Both the AICPA and SEC permit an exception for a trustee who lacks authority to make investment decisions.

■ Have a joint, closely held investment that is material to the covered member. Hence, a covered member cannot form a joint business venture with an audit client. A covered member also cannot form such business ventures with officers and directors of audit clients.

■ Cannot have loans to or from the audit client. There are some very limited exceptions to this rule, but the general rule is that a covered person cannot accept a loan from an audit client or loan money to an audit client. The limited exceptions allow for some loans that were permitted prior to the existing rules to remain in place. The exceptions to the rule also allow for automobile loans and leases collateralized by the automobile; loans fully collateralized by the cash surrender value of an insurance policy; loans fully collateralized by cash deposits at the same financial institution (e.g., "passbook loans"); and credit cards and cash advances where the aggregate outstanding balance on the current statement is reduced to $5,000 or less by the payment due date.

Immediate Family Members

An **immediate family member** of a covered member would be the covered member's spouse, spousal equivalent, or dependent. A dependent could be a child, a parent, or another person who is dependent upon the covered person. An immediate family member is prohibited from the same activities that are prohibited for a covered member. The relationship is considered to be so close that any relationship between an immediate family member and an audit client is equivalent to the relationship between a covered member and the audit client.

In addition, an audit client cannot employ an immediate family member in what is defined as a **key position.** A key position would include a position where an immediate family member could exercise influence over the financial statement, such as CEO, CFO, member of the board of directors, or treasurer. In addition, a key person would be someone who prepares, or supervises others who prepare, (1) the financial statements or (2) material accounting records, or is involved in accounting decision making. Hence, an immediate family member could hold a position in marketing or management for an audit client, as long as that person was not in a position to exercise influence over the preparation of the financial statements.

An important issue for many spouses is their ability to participate in stock compensation plans. Today, it is common for many employees to be compensated with equity securities in addition to cash. A spouse of an accounting firm professional who is not a covered member can participate in an employee benefit plans that include employee stock ownership plans or employee stock option plans as long as the benefits are offered equitably to all similar employees. The same benefits are also extended to a limited group of covered members, nonattest partners and managers, and other partners in the office of the lead engagement partners may have an immediate family member who works for an audit client as long as they are not in a *key position.*

Close Relatives

A **close relative** of a covered member is defined as parents, nondependent children, and bothers and sisters. Independence is impaired for an audit firm if a close family member of a covered member (1) holds a key position with an audit client, or (2) holds a direct investment in the audit client that is material to the close relative, or (3) holds an investment that enables a close family member to have significant influence over an audit client.

Other Professionals and Their Immediate Family Members

A number of professionals (particularly tax and management advisory professionals) in an accounting firm are not considered covered members with respect to an audit engagement under the new standards. These professionals who are not in a position to influence the outcome of an audit, and their immediate family members, are allowed to have a direct investment in an audit client as long as the investment does not exceed 5 percent of the outstanding equity securities. For example, a tax partner in Cleveland, or her spouse, may have an investment in an audit client in San Francisco as long as the tax partner does not spend more than 10 hours a year performing nonaudit services for the client. Remember, independence would be impaired if the tax partner performed even one hour of audit services for the client. In addition, other professionals cannot have a business or an employment relationship with an audit client, and they cannot be a trustee, director, or officer of an audit client or a client's pension or profit-sharing trust.

Independence Interpretations

Since independence is critical to a variety of attest services, the AICPA has published 14 interpretations pertaining to Rule 101. These are summarized in Figure 3-5. A link to the actual ethical interpretations can be found at http://www.aicpa.org/about/code/index.htm. Several themes run through these interpretations. These include the effect of employment relationships with an attest client, nonaudit services, litigation, and unpaid fees for professional services on independence.

Employment or Association with an Attest Client

When a partner or professional employee of a CPA firm leaves the firm and is subsequently employed by an audit client, independence can be impaired inasmuch as the partner or professional employee may have continuing relationships, such as the payout of a pension plan, with the CPA firm. Furthermore, if a professional employee goes to work for an audit client, that employee may be familiar with the audit plan and/or staff working on the engagement, and there is a risk that the former employee could influence the engagement. These are important risks that may impair an audit firm's independence.

The rules are different for public and for private companies. With respect to public companies, Section 206 of the Sarbanes-Oxley Act of 2002 states that the CEO, Controller, CFO, Chief Accounting Officer, or person in an equivalent position cannot have been employed by the company's audit firm during the one-year period preceding the audit.

Figure 3-5 ■ Interpretations of Rule 101 on Independence

101-1—Interpretation of Rule 101: This interpretation defines a covered person and addresses financial interests and other relationships that impair independence.

101-2—Employment or association with attest clients: Addresses circumstances in which the partner or professional employee leaves a firm and subsequently becomes employed by or associated with an audit client, and specifies the conditions that must exist to maintain independence.

101-3—Performance of nonattest services: Often members assist clients by providing nonattest services including bookkeeping and financial statement preparation. This interpretation outlines important responsibilities that the client's management must take responsibility for in order to preserve independence, and it identifies activities that impair independence.

101-4—Honorary directorships and trusteeships of not-for-profit organization: Provides guidance when a member is asked to serve as an honorary director or trustee for an attest client.

101-5—Loans from financial institution clients and related terminology: A member's independence would normally be impaired if the covered member has any loan to or from an audit client or any officer, director, or principal stockholder of the client. This interpretation explains some specific exceptions to this general rule.

101-6—The effect of actual or threatened litigation on independence. Explains circumstances in which independence may be considered to be impaired as a result of litigation or the expressed intention to commence litigation.

[101-7]—[Deleted]

101-8—Effect on independence of financial interests in nonclients having investor or investee relationships with a member's client: Explains various ways in which a financial interest in a nonclient that has a significant influence on a client may impair independence with respect to a client.

[101-9]—[Deleted]

101-10—The effect on independence of relationships with entities included in the governmental financial statements: In general, a member issuing a report on a governmental client's general-purpose financial statements must be independent of the client. However, independence is not required with respect to a related organization if the client is not financially accountable for the organization and the required disclosure does not include financial information (for example, the ability to appoint or the appointment of governing board members).

101-11—Modified application of Rule 101 for certain engagements to issue restricted-use reports under the Statements on Standards for Attestation Engagements: Provides guidance on independence for engagements that are restricted for use only by identified parties.

101-12—Independence and cooperative arrangements with clients. In general, independence will be considered to be impaired if, during the period of a professional engagement or at the time of expressing an opinion, a member's firm had any joint business activity with the client that was material to the CPA's firm or to the client.

101-13—[Deleted].

101-14—The effect of alternative practice structures on the applicability of independence rules: Because of changes in the manner in which CPAs are structuring their practices, this interpretation provides guidance on how various alternatives to "traditional structures" affect independence.

With respect to private companies, a firm's independence will be considered impaired with respect to a client if a partner or professional employee leaves the firm and is subsequently employed by the client in a key position, unless all of the following conditions are met.

1. Amounts due to the former partner or professional employee for his or her previous interest in the firm and for unfunded, vested retirement benefits are not material to the audit firm, and the underlying formula used to calculate the payments remains fixed during the payout period. Retirement benefits may also be adjusted for inflation, and interest may be paid on amounts due.

2. The former partner or professional employee is not in a position to influence the accounting firm's operations or financial policies.

3. The former partner or professional employee does not participate or appear to participate in, and is not associated with the firm, whether or not compensated for such participation or association, once employment or association with the client begins. An appearance of participation or association results from such actions as:

   - The individual provides consultation to the firm.
   - The firm provides the individual with an office and related amenities (for example, secretarial and telephone services).
   - The individual's name is included in the firm's office directory.
   - The individual's name is included as a member of the firm in other membership lists of business, professional, or civic organizations, unless the individual is clearly designated as retired.

4. The ongoing attest engagement team considers the appropriateness or necessity of modifying the engagement procedures to adjust for the risk that, by virtue of the former partner or professional employee's prior knowledge of the audit plan, audit effectiveness could be reduced.

5. The firm assesses whether existing attest engagement team members have the appropriate experience and stature to effectively deal with the former partner or professional employee and his or her work, when that person will have significant interaction with the attest engagement team.

6. The subsequent attest engagement is reviewed to determine whether the engagement team members maintained the appropriate level of skepticism when evaluating the representations and work of the former partner or professional employee, when the person joins the client in a key position within one year of disassociating from the firm and has significant interaction with the attest engagement team. The review should be performed by a professional with appropriate stature, expertise, and objectivity and should be tailored based on the position assumed at the client, the position he or she held at the firm, the nature of the services he or she provided to the client, and other relevant facts and circumstances. Appropriate actions, as deemed necessary, should be taken based on the results of the review.

A partner or a professional employee merely seeking employment with an audit client may also impair independence. Rule 101-2 states that when a member of the attest engagement team or an individual in a position to influence the attest engagement intends to seek or discuss potential employment or association with an attest client, or is in receipt of a specific offer of employment from an attest client, independence will be impaired with respect to the client unless the person promptly reports such consideration or offer to an appropriate person in the firm, and removes himself or herself from the engagement until the employment offer is rejected or employment is no longer being sought. The purpose of this rule is to avoid situations where a person's integrity or objectivity might be compromised. If a professional is seeking a job from an audit client, it is important to avoid a situation where the person might be tempted to take an aggressive stance in favor of the client on a matter of professional judgment while seeking the favor of a client by way of a job offer.

When a covered member becomes aware that a member of the attest engagement team or an individual in a position to influence the attest engagement is considering employment or association with a client, the covered member should notify an appropriate person in the audit firm. Furthermore, the appropriate person should consider what additional procedures may be necessary to provide reasonable assurance that any work performed for the client by that person was performed with objectivity and integrity as required under Rule 102.

Nonattest Services

A major issue that the auditing profession has faced in the last decade is whether the performance of **nonattest services** (such as accounting services or financial statement design and implementation) impairs an auditor's integrity and objec-

PCAOB
Public Companies
Accounting Oversight Board

PCAOB, public companies and nonattest services

The Sarbanes-Oxley Act of 2002 makes it "unlawful" to perform audit services for a public company and also perform the following **nonattest services:**

- Bookkeeping or other services related to the accounting records or financial statements of the audit client.
- Financial information systems design and implementation.
- Appraisal or valuation services, fairness opinions, or contribution-in-kind reports.
- Actuarial services.
- Internal audit outsourcing services.
- Management functions or human resources.
- Broker or dealer, investment advisor, or investment banking services.
- Legal services and expert services unrelated to the audit.
- Any other service that the PCAOB determines, by regulation, is impermissible.

Many of these services put the auditor in a position where they might have to audit their own work, thereby creating the potential to impair independence. In addition, the audit committee of a public company must preapprove other nonattest services provided to public companies, and those services must be disclosed in periodic reports to investors.

tivity. Critics wonder whether an auditor can be objective with respect to audit issues when fees from nonattest services exceed fees from attest services. Can an auditor objectively evaluate the design and operation of internal controls when the auditor received substantial fees for information system design and implementation?

When an auditor considers the rules related to nonattest services and independence, he or she needs to understand that a different set of rules applies to auditors of public companies and auditors of private companies. Both the SEC and the Sarbanes-Oxley Act of 2002 set out the public company guidelines. The AICPA and state boards of accountancy have rules appropriate to private companies. The AICPA and many state boards of accountancy allow activities for private companies that are not allowed for public companies because many private companies (e.g., owner-managed business and small not-for-profit organizations that require audits) do not have the resources to internalize services that are often performed within public companies. The rules for public companies are presented on p. 120. The following discussion outlines the appropriate rules for nonattest services as they relate to private companies.

Private Companies

AICPA Rule 101-3 allows a member of his or her firm to perform nonattest services for attest clients under certain conditions. In each case the CPA must evaluate the effect of nonattest services on independence. In general, a CPA should not perform management functions or make management decisions for the attest client. However, the member may provide advice, research materials, and recommendations to assist the client's management in performing its functions and making decisions. In addition, the client must agree to perform the following functions in connection with the engagement to perform nonattest services:

- Make all management decisions and perform all management functions.
- Designate a competent employee, preferably within senior management, to oversee the services.
- Evaluate the adequacy and results of the services performed.
- Accept responsibility for the results of the services.
- Establish and maintain internal controls, including monitoring ongoing activities.

Rule 101-3 indicates that before performing nonattest services, the member should establish, and document in writing, an understanding with the client regarding (1) the objectives of the engagement, (2) the services to be performed, (3) the client's acceptance of its responsibilities, (4) the CPA's responsibilities, and (5) any limitations of the engagement. It is preferable that this understanding be documented in an engagement letter. In addition, the member should be satisfied that the client is in a position to have an informed judgment on the results of the nonattest services.

The purpose of the AICPA rule is to allow CPAs to assist many small business clients who may not have within the company a CPA, or a person with important expertise that may reside within a CPA firm. These businesses often need outside professional expertise that the CPA firm can provide. Nevertheless, a number of general activities would be considered to impair a CPAs firm's independence when auditing nonpublic companies. These include:

- Authorizing, executing, or consummating a transaction, or otherwise exercising authority on behalf of a client or having the authority to do so.
- Preparing source documents or originating data, in electronic or other form, evidencing the occurrence of a transaction (for example, purchase orders, payroll time records, and customer orders).
- Having custody of client assets.
- Supervising client employees in the performance of their normal recurring activities.
- Determining which recommendations of the member should be implemented.
- Reporting to the board of directors on behalf of management.
- Serving as a client's stock transfer or escrow agent, registrar, general counsel, or its equivalent.

Figure 3-6 provides examples of how the performance of these general activities would impair a CPA firm's independence, or how the client could take appropriate responsibilities to allow the CPA firm to assist the client without impairing independence.

Interpretation 101-3 provides a number of specific examples of activities that would or would not impair independence. For example, CPAs can perform various accounting and bookkeeping services for a client. Independence would be impaired if a CPA firm determined or changed journal entries, account codings or classification for transactions, or other accounting records without obtaining client approval; authorized or approved transactions; prepared source documents; or made changes to source documents without client approval. Independence would not be impaired if the CPA recorded transactions for which management had determined or approved the appropriate account classification, posted coded transactions to a client's general ledger, prepared financial statements based on information in the trial balance, posted client-approved entries to a client's trial balance, or proposed standard, adjusting, or correcting journal entries or other changes affecting the financial statements of the client. The client should review the entries and the member should be satisfied that management understands the nature of the proposed entries and the impact of the entries on the financial statements. Students can read the actual interpretation for additional discussion related to payroll and other disbursements, benefit plan administration, investment-advisory services, corporate finance-consulting and advisory services, executive or employee search, business risk consulting, or information systems design, implementation, or integration.

Litigation

Litigation involving CPAs and their clients raises questions about a member's independence. In general, independence is impaired whenever the existence or expressed threat of litigation has significantly altered, or is expected to materially change, the normal relationship between a client and a CPA. Litigation that results in an adversary position between a client and a CPA, or that links management and the CPA as co-conspirators in withholding information from stockholders, would impair the CPA's independence. In contrast, litigation brought by stockholders against a CPA would not necessarily affect independence.

Figure 3-6 ■ Independence and Nonaudit Services for Nonpublic Clients

Examples Where Independence Is Impaired	General Activities That Will Impair Independence	Examples Where Independence Is Not Impaired
A CPA may not accept responsibility to authorize payment of client funds, or accept responsibility to sign or cosign client checks, even if only in emergency situations. In a consulting engagement, a CPA may not act as a promoter, underwriter, broker-dealer, or guarantor of client securities, or distributor of private placement memoranda or offering documents.	**Authorizing, executing, or consummating a transaction, or otherwise exercising authority on behalf of a client or having the authority to do so**	When assisting a small business client with payroll using payroll time records provided and approved by the client, the CPA can generate unsigned checks or process the client's payroll. In a consulting engagement, a CPA may assist in identifying or introducing the client to possible sources of capital that meet the client's specifications or criteria.
In an accounting service engagement for a nonpublic client, a CPA may not determine or change journal entries, account codings or classification for transactions, or other accounting records without obtaining client approval. A CPA may not prepare source documents or originate data or make changes to source documents without client approval.	**Preparing source documents or originating data, in electronic or other form, evidencing the occurrence of a transaction (for example, purchase orders, payroll time records, and customer orders)**	In an accounting service engagement for a nonpublic client, a CPA may record transactions for which management has determined or approved the appropriate account classification, or post coded transactions to a client's general ledger and prepare financial statements based on information in the trial balance.
When performing payroll services, benefit plan administration, or other financial advisory services, a CPA may not have custody of client assets or maintain custody of client securities.	**Having custody of client assets**	No examples are relevant.
In an information system engagement, a CPA may not supervise client personnel in the daily operation of a client's information system.	**Supervising client employees in the performance of their normal recurring activities**	In an information system engagement, a CPA may design, install, or integrate a client's information system, provided the client makes all management decisions.
In an investment advisory engagement with an attest and tax client, a CPA cannot make investment decisions on behalf of client management or otherwise have discretionary authority over a client's investments.	**Determining which recommendations of the member should be implemented**	In an investment advisory engagement with an attest and tax client, a CPA can recommend the allocation of funds that a client should invest in various asset classes, depending upon the client's desired rate of return, risk tolerance, and so on.
In a consulting engagement, present business proposals to the board on the behalf of management.	**Reporting to the board of directors on behalf of management.**	In an assurance engagement, provide recommendations for improving the system for monitoring business risks.
In an investment advisory engagement, a CPA may not execute a transaction to buy or sell a client's investment or have custody of client assets, such as taking temporary possession of securities purchased by a client.	**Serving as a client's stock transfer or escrow agent, registrar, general counsel, or its equivalent**	In an investment advisory engagement, a CPA may review the manner in which a client's portfolio is being managed by investment account managers, including determining whether the managers are (1) following the guidelines of the client's investment policy statement; (2) meeting the client's investment objectives; and (3) conforming to the client's stated investment styles.

Unpaid Fees

The existence of unpaid fees for professional services has been deemed to assume the characteristics of a loan from the member to the client within the meaning of Rule 101 and its interpretations. Therefore, independence of the member's firm is considered to be impaired if, when the CPA's report on the client's current year is issued, fees remain unpaid, whether billed or unbilled, for professional services provided more than one year prior to the date of the report. This ruling does not apply to fees outstanding from a client in bankruptcy.

Examples of additional circumstances dealt with in other interpretations and ethics rulings on independence are presented in Figure 3-5.

RULE 102—INTEGRITY AND OBJECTIVITY

> **Rule 102—Integrity and objectivity.** In the performance of any professional service, a member shall maintain objectivity and integrity, shall be free of conflicts of interest, and shall not knowingly misrepresent facts or subordinate his or her judgment to others.

Rule 102 is a wide sweeping rule regarding integrity and objectivity that extends to all professional services (attest services, taxation, and financial planning services, etc.) and to all members (CPAs who are employed, for example, as CFOs, controllers, or internal auditors as well as CPAs in public practice). For example, in dealing with his or her employer's external accountant, a member in industry must be candid and not knowingly misrepresent facts or knowingly fail to disclose material facts. Furthermore, if a member in industry or in public practice has a disagreement or dispute with a supervisor relating to an accounting or auditing issue that is of significance to the financial statements or auditor's report, the member should take steps to ensure that the situation does not constitute a subordination of judgment. Such steps should include determining whether the supervisor's position represents an acceptable alternative under GAAP. If so, the member need do nothing further; if not, the member should bring the matter to the attention of someone at a higher level in the organization, such as the supervisor's superior. Ultimately, if the disagreement is not resolved satisfactorily to the member, he or she should consider (1) documenting the situation and (2) whether to continue his or her relationship with the employer. In addition, a member in public practice should not subordinate his or her judgments concerning the application of technical standards to the directives of clients. The public expects auditors to form their own independent judgments. Finally, a member performing a professional service for a client or employer should not have a significant relationship with another person, entity, product, or service that could be viewed as impairing the member's objectivity.

RULE 201—GENERAL STANDARDS

> **Rule 201—General standards.** A member shall comply with the following standards and with any interpretations thereof by bodies designated by Council.
> **A.** *Professional Competence.* Undertake only those professional services that the member or the member's firm can reasonably expect to be completed with professional competence.

B. *Due Professional Care.* Exercise due professional care in the performance of professional services.

C. *Planning and Supervision.* Adequately plan and supervise the performance of professional services.

D. *Sufficient Relevant Data.* Obtain sufficient relevant data to afford a reasonable basis for conclusions or recommendations in relation to any professional services performed.

Audit Decision 2

■ What must a CPA do to comply with the Rules of Conduct regarding general standards and accounting principles?

These general standards should not be confused with the three general standards of GAAS introduced in the last chapter. The four general standards in Rule 201 apply to all members, including those not in public practice, and to all types of professional services, not just to audits.

Rule 201A, Professional Competence, involves not only the technical qualifications of the member and the member's staff, but also the CPA's ability to supervise and evaluate the quality of the work performed by others. This part of Rule 201 is specifically directed at the member's decision-making process when the CPA is deciding whether to accept or decline an engagement. If, on the basis of facts known at the time, the CPA believes he or she has the capability to complete the assignment in accordance with professional standards, it is ethically permissible to accept the engagement. However, if, for example, neither the CPA nor the firm has the computer expertise required to audit a client with a sophisticated electronic data processing system and cannot acquire the necessary knowledge, it is not ethical to accept the engagement.

Due professional care, planning and supervision, and sufficient relevant data codify practices that must be followed in performing any service. Adherence to these requirements contributes to the quality of performance of professional engagements for the benefit of the public and the profession.

RULE 202—COMPLIANCE WITH STANDARDS

Rule 202—Compliance with standards. A member who performs auditing, review, compilation, management consulting, tax, or other professional services shall comply with standards promulgated by bodies designated by AICPA Council.

Currently, the technical standards that fall under this rule are those issued by the Auditing Standards Board, the Accounting and Review Services Committee, the Management Consulting Services Executive Committee, and the Tax Executive Committee. In addition, for purposes of this rule, Council has designated three bodies to promulgate standards of disclosure for financial information. They are the PCAOB, the FASB, the GASB, and the Federal Accounting Standards Advisory Board (FASAB).

RULE 203—ACCOUNTING PRINCIPLES

Rule 203—Accounting principles. A member shall not (1) express an opinion or state affirmatively that the financial statements or other financial data of any entity are presented in conformity with generally accepted accounting principles or (2) state that he or she is not aware of any material modifications that should be made to such statements or data in order for them to

(continues)

be in conformity with generally accepted accounting principles, if such statements or data contain any departure from an accounting principle promulgated by bodies designated by Council to establish such principles that has a material effect on the statements or data taken as a whole. If, however, the statements or data contain such a departure and the member can demonstrate that due to unusual circumstances the financial statements or data would otherwise have been misleading, the member can comply with the rule by describing the departure, its approximate effects, if practicable, and the reasons why compliance with the principle would result in a misleading statement.

What were the ethical requirements for CPAs who prepared the financial statements for Enron and WorldCom when it came to applying the rules of generally accepted accounting principles? Rule 203 of the Code of Conduct applies to all members, whether or not in public practice, who perform the acts described. Such acts will occur, for example, in (1) preparing or auditing financial statements, (2) performing an examination of prospective financial statements, or (3) reviewing interim financial information. The rule covers all services for which standards have been promulgated regarding GAAP, including engagements to report on a comprehensive basis other than GAAP. As noted above, Council has designated three groups to promulgate accounting principles: (1) the GASB for state and local government entities, (2) the FASAB for federal governmental entities, and (3) the FASB for all other entities.

RULE 301—CONFIDENTIAL CLIENT INFORMATION

Rule 301—Confidential client information. A member in public practice shall not disclose any confidential client information without the specific consent of the client.

This rule shall not be construed (1) to relieve a member of his or her professional obligations under rules 202 [ET section 202.01] and 203 [ET section 203.01], (2) to affect in any way the member's obligation to comply with a validly issued and enforceable subpoena or summons, or to prohibit a member's compliance with applicable laws and government regulations, (3) to prohibit review of a member's professional practice under AICPA or state CPA society or board of accountancy authorization, or (4) to preclude a member from initiating a complaint with, or responding to any inquiry made by, the professional ethics division or trial board of the Institute or a duly constituted investigative or disciplinary body of a state CPA society or board of accountancy.

Members of any of the bodies identified in (4) above and members involved with professional practice reviews identified in (3) above shall not use to their own advantage or disclose any member's confidential client information that comes to their attention in carrying out those activities. This prohibition shall not restrict members' exchange of information in connection with the investigative or disciplinary proceedings described in (4) above or the professional practice reviews described in (3) above.

Audit Decision 3

■ What must a CPA do to comply with the Rules of Conduct regarding responsibilities to clients?

It is fundamental that a CPA in public practice hold in strict confidence all information about a client's business affairs. Confidentiality is indispensable in establishing a basis of mutual trust between CPA and client.

Rule 301 requires the member to obtain the specific consent of the client before disclosing confidential client information. Preferably, the consent should be in writing. Consent is not required when any of the four exceptions stated in the rule are applicable.

The exceptions to Rule 301 enable the member to fulfill both professional and legal responsibilities. For example, in issuing an audit report, the member may disclose information required under GAAP that is not included in the financial statements.

The Rule 301 requirement to maintain confidentiality should be distinguished from the legal concept of **privileged communication.** Federal and state statutes grant privileged communication in certain relationships such as those between attorney and client, doctor and patient, and priest and parishioner. In these cases, communications between the professional and the client cannot be revealed even to a court unless the client waives privilege. No federal statute extends privileged communication status to CPA–client relationships. However, state statutes related to privileged CPA–client communication exist in 18 states.[3]

Rule 301 is the source of a number of ethical dilemmas for CPAs. For example, suppose in auditing Client A, an auditor discovers A is overcharging Client B for inventory purchases.[4] In addition, in the absence of a legislative or regulatory mandate, whistleblowing by auditors in cases involving illegal client acts runs counter to Rule 301.

RULE 302—CONTINGENT FEES

Rule 302—Contingent fees. A member in public practice shall not
(1) Perform for a contingent fee any professional services for, or receive such a fee from a client for whom the member or the member's firm performs,
   (a) an audit or review of a financial statement; or
   (b) a compilation of a financial statement when the member expects, or reasonably might expect, that a third party will use the financial statement and the member's compilation report does not disclose a lack of independence; or
   (c) an examination of prospective financial information;
or
(2) Prepare an original or amended tax return or claim for a tax refund for a contingent fee for any client.

The prohibition in (1) above applies during the period in which the member or the member's firm is engaged to perform any of the services listed above and the period covered by any historical financial statements involved in any such listed services.

Except as stated in the next sentence, a **contingent fee** is a fee established for the performance of any service pursuant to an arrangement in which no fee will be charged unless a specified finding or result is attained, or in which the amount of the fee is otherwise dependent upon the finding or result of such service. Solely for purposes of this rule, fees are not regarded as being contingent if fixed by courts or other public authorities, or, in tax matters, if determined based on the results of judicial proceedings or the findings of governmental agencies.

A member's fees may vary depending, for example, on the complexity of services rendered.

---

[3] The states with CPA–client privileged communication statutes are Arizona, Colorado, Florida, Georgia, Illinois, Indiana, Iowa, Kentucky, Louisiana, Maryland, Michigan, Missouri, Montana, Nevada, New Mexico, Pennsylvania, Tennessee, and Texas. Puerto Rico also has such a statute.
[4] For an actual case of this type, see write-up of *Fund of Funds, Ltd. V. Arthur Andersen & Co.* in Chapter 4.

Consider the following three situations:

1. Can a CPA perform an audit for a stated fee, but where no fee is received unless the client receives a bank loan using the financial statements?
2. Can a CPA in a management advisory service practice help a client sell a business for a stated fee, but where no fee is received unless the business is sold?
3. Can a CPA in a tax practice prepare an amended tax return for a new client, where the fee is a percentage of the refund received by the client?

Prior to being amended in 1990, this rule contained a general prohibition against members accepting contingent fees in connection with any service for any client. In 1990, the AICPA changed the rule to comply with an order from the U.S. Federal Trade Commission (FTC), which deemed the former rule to be in restraint of trade. In its current form, the rule represents a compromise between the AICPA, which wanted to retain the general prohibition, and the FTC, which wanted the rule eliminated in its entirety.

The rule does not prohibit a member from charging a fee based on the complexity or number of hours or days needed to complete the service. A member may also elect to lower per diem billing rates for a financially troubled client or perform services without charge for a charitable organization.

In response to the three situations discussed above, contingent fee engagements impair independence, so none of these engagements can be performed for a client where the CPA also performs attest services. However, the second case involving the sale of a business could be performed for a business that was not an attest client. In the third case, a CPA cannot prepare an amended tax return for a contingent fee for any client, irrespective of whether the CPA performs attest services for the client.

RULE 501—ACTS DISCREDITABLE

Rule 501—Acts discreditable. A member shall not commit an act discreditable to the profession.

Audit Decision 4

■ **What must a CPA do to comply with the Rules of Conduct regarding other responsibilities and practices?**

Under Rule 501, **acts discreditable** are actions by a member that may damage or otherwise impinge on the reputation and integrity of the profession. This rule enables disciplinary action to be taken against a member for unethical acts not specifically covered by other rules. Discreditable acts generally include acts committed in a person's professional capacity. In interpretations, the following acts are designated as discreditable: (1) retention of client records and auditor working papers, such as adjusting entries, necessary to complete the client's records; (2) discrimination and harassment in employment practices; (3) failure to follow standards and/or other procedures or other requirements in governmental audits; (4) negligence in the preparation of financial statements or records; (5) failure to follow requirements of governmental bodies, commissions, or other regulatory agencies in performing attest or other similar services; (6) solicitation or disclosure of CPA examination questions and answers; and (7) failure to file a tax return or pay a tax liability. Failure to file a personal tax return or pay a personal tax liability is also considered discreditable act. A member who commits a discreditable act usually is suspended or expelled from the AICPA.

RULE 502—ADVERTISING AND OTHER FORMS OF SOLICITATION

Rule 502—Advertising and other forms of solicitation. A member in public practice shall not seek to obtain clients by advertising or other forms of solicitation in a manner that is false, misleading, or deceptive. Solicitation by the use of coercion, over-reaching, or harassing conduct is prohibited.

The rules on advertising were modified significantly in 1990 to comply with a Federal Trade Commission order. The rule on advertising is enforced to prevent members from engaging in falsehood or deception. The rule cannot be used to prevent or discourage members from (1) soliciting potential clients by any means, including direct solicitation, and (2) using advertising that includes self-laudatory or comparative claims, testimonials, or endorsements.

Interpretation 502-5 points out that members are often asked to render professional services to clients of third parties who may have obtained the clients as the result of their own advertising and solicitation efforts. Members are permitted to enter into such engagements. However, the member has the responsibility to ascertain that all promotional efforts are within the bounds of the Rules of Conduct. In short, members must not do through others what they are prohibited from doing themselves by the Rules of Conduct.

Some state boards of accountancy have rules against direct solicitation of clients and some forms of advertising.

RULE 503—COMMISSIONS AND REFERRAL FEES

Rule 503—Commissions and referral fees.

A. *Prohibited commissions.* A member in public practice shall not for a commission recommend or refer to a client any product or service, or for a commission recommend or refer any product or service to be supplied by a client, or receive a commission, when the member or the member's firm also performs for that client

(a) an audit or review of a financial statement; or

(b) a compilation of a financial statement when the member expects, or reasonably might expect, that a third party will use the financial statement and the member's compilation report does not disclose a lack of independence; or

(c) an examination of prospective financial information.

This prohibition applies during the period in which the member is engaged to perform any of the services listed above and the period covered by any historical financial statements involved in such listed services.

B. *Disclosure of permitted commissions.* A member in public practice who is not prohibited by this rule from performing services for or receiving a commission and who is paid or expects to be paid a commission shall disclose that fact to any person or entity to whom the member recommends or refers a product or service to which the commission relates.

C. *Referral fees.* Any member who accepts a referral fee for recommending or referring any service of a CPA to any person or entity or who pays a referral fee to obtain a client shall disclose such acceptance or payment to the client.

This rule was also modified significantly in 1990 to comply with a FTC order. The former rule contained a general prohibition against members accepting any commission, even when disclosed to, and approved by, the client. The FTC deemed the former rule to be in restraint of trade.

When the FTC order leading to the amendment of Rule 503 was imposed in 1990, CPAs in 50 of the 54 jurisdictions nonetheless remained subject to state statutes or state board of accountancy regulations that barred them from accepting contingent fees and commissions. Now, most of these jurisdictions have eliminated or reduced limits on these arrangements for nonattest services. However, students should be aware that some states may bar contingent fees and commissions either through state board regulations or through state statutes. Some states may permit contingent fees but not commissions, or they may permit CPAs to accept, but not pay, commissions and referral fees.

Under the current rule, a CPA may accept a disclosed commission. For example, a CPA may accept a disclosed commission from a computer manufacturer based on equipment purchased by a client on the CPA's recommendation, except when the CPA performs any of the services described in the rule for the same client. Payments by a CPA to obtain a client are now permitted provided disclosure is made to the client.

RULE 505—FORM OF ORGANIZATION AND NAME

Rule 505—Form of organization and name. A member may practice public accounting only in a form of organization permitted by law or regulation whose characteristics conform to resolutions of Council.

A member shall not practice public accounting under a firm name that is misleading. Names of one or more past owners may be included in the firm name of a successor organization.

A firm may not designate itself as "Members of the American Institute of Certified Public Accountants" unless all of its CPA owners are members of the Institute.

Prior to being amended in 1997, Rule 505 mandated that members practice public accounting only in the form of a proprietorship, partnership, or professional corporation. The rule also closely regulated the name of the member's practice. Today accounting firms can take advantage of any form of organization permitted by state law or regulation and as the organization's characteristics conform to resolutions of Council. One important resolution of Council includes a requirement that CPAs own the majority (greater than 50 percent) of the financial interests in an attest firm.

Interpretation 505-3 states that the overriding focus of the AICPA Council Resolution was that CPAs remain responsible, financially and otherwise, for the attest work performed to protect the public interest. Interpretation 505-3 requires:

■ Compliance with all aspects of applicable state law or regulation.
■ Enrollment in an AICPA-approved practice-monitoring program.
■ Membership in the SEC Practice Section if the attest work is for SEC clients (as defined by Council).
■ Compliance with the independence rules prescribed by Rule 101, Independence.

■ Compliance with applicable standards promulgated by Council-designated bodies (Rule 202, Compliance with Standards [ET section 202.01]) and all other provisions of the Code of Conduct.

LEARNING CHECK

3-9 a. What authority underlies the Rules of the Code of Conduct?
  b. To whom, and in what circumstances, do the Rules apply?

3-10 What trends influenced the adoption of an engagement-based approach to independence by the SEC and the AICPA?

3-11 a. What individuals would be "covered persons" under Rule 101-1, and what activities impair independence for "covered persons?"
  b. What individuals would be "immediate family members" under Rule 101-1, and what activities impair independence for "immediate family members?"
  c. What individuals would be "close relatives" under Rule 101-1, and what activities impair independence for "close relatives?"
  d. What individuals would be "other professionals employees" under Rule 101-1, and what activities impair independence for "other professional employees?"

3-12 a. Explain the circumstances under which a partner or professional employee of an audit firm could accept a job with a public company audit client for the firm.
  b. Explain the circumstances under which a partner or professional employee of an audit firm could accept a job with a private company audit client for the firm.

3-13 a. Identify the nonattest services that impair independence for a public company audit client.
  b. Identify the general activities that impair independence when performing nonattest services for a private company audit client.

3-14 What are the AICPA ethical standards that apply to a CPA who is a CFO for a company?

3-15 a. State the essence of Rule 201—General Standards.
  b. Enumerate the four subcategories of this rule.

3-16 a. Explain five circumstances when a CPA could ethically disclose confidential client information.
  b. Explain the circumstances in which contingent fee arrangements are prohibited under Rule 302.

3-17 Explain the acts that are prohibited under:
  a. Rule 501—Acts Discreditable.
  b. Rule 502—Advertising and Other Forms of Solicitation.
  c. Rule 503—Commissions and Referral Fees.

3-18 a. Identify the forms of organization or practice units permitted under Rule 505.
  b. What requirements must be met for a CPA to practice in any of these forms?

KEY TERMS

ENFORCEMENT OF THE RULES OF CONDUCT

STATE BOARDS OF ACCOUNTANCY AND PUBLIC COMPANIES ACCOUNTING OVERSIGHT BOARD

Auditor Knowledge 5

■ Know the organizations and procedures involved in enforcing the Rules of Conduct.

Many states have written ethical rules into state accountancy statutes or state accountancy laws. In most cases these rules are similar to the AICPA Code of Conduct. Violation of the ethical statutes or rules is usually evaluated through due process provided by the board of accountancy. The sanctions available to many boards of accountancy are significant and can range from requiring continuing professional education to suspension or revocation of a license to practice as a CPA. A CPA must be aware of how the state accountancy law addresses ethical matters.

The Public Companies Accounting Oversight Board (PCAOB) has authority over audit firms that audit public companies and their professionals. The authority of the PCAOB is particularly relevant in the context of their rules regarding nonattest services. The PCAOB, through the SEC, has the authority to levy fines against firms and prohibit firms or individuals from auditing public companies.

ENFORCING THE AICPA CODE OF PROFESSIONAL CONDUCT

An AICPA member can only be charged with a violation of the Rules of the Code of Professional Conduct. However, in the event of an alleged violation of a rule, a member may have to justify any departures from applicable Interpretations of the Rules of Conduct and Ethics Rulings. Enforcement actions may be initiated as a result of (1) complaints by members and nonmembers, (2) review of newspapers and publications, such as the SEC *Docket* and the *IRS Bulletin*, by personnel in the Professional Ethics Division, and (3) transmittal of possible violations to the AICPA by state and federal agencies.

Enforcement of the Rules rests with two groups: the AICPA and state societies of CPAs. Both have the authority to undertake investigations of complaints, conduct hearings, and impose sanctions on those who have violated the Rules.

The AICPA's enforcement machinery resides in its Professional Ethics Division and a **joint trial board.** The maximum sanction that the AICPA can impose is to expel the member from the Institute.

State society enforcement is achieved through each state's Ethics Committee and the joint trial board. As in the case of the AICPA, the most severe sanction to be imposed by a state society is loss of membership in the society.

Joint Ethics Enforcement Procedures

In an effort to make enforcement of the Rules of Conduct more effective and disciplinary action more uniform, the AICPA has developed a **Joint Ethics Enforcement Program (JEEP).** Under JEEP, complaints against a member may be filed with either the AICPA or the state society. Normally, the AICPA has jurisdiction over cases involving (1) more than one state, (2) litigation, and (3) issues of broad national concern. The jurisdictional groups may act independently or jointly.

JEEP also provides for increased liaison between the AICPA and state society ethics committees. The Professional Ethics Division holds frequent meetings with state societies in an effort to improve the overall handling of ethics matters and to consult with the states on ways to increase the amount of resources devoted to ethics enforcement. The Professional Ethics Division reports semiannually to the membership of the AICPA on ethics cases processed under JEEP.

Joint Trial Board Procedures

There is a single **joint trial board** consisting of at least 36 AICPA members elected by Council from present or former Council members. The trial board becomes involved only when earlier enforcement procedures have found the complaint to be serious or the member involved has refused to cooperate. Trial board hearings are generally held by subboards comprised of at least five board members appointed to maximize representation from the general area in which the member resides. A member may request the full trial board to review the subboard's decision.

The joint trial board may take one of the following **disciplinary actions:**

- Admonish the member.
- Suspend the member for a period of no more than two years.
- Expel the member.

When the deficiency is attributable to a departure from the profession's technical standards, the trial board has the authority to impose additional requirements. For example, the board may require the member to complete specified professional development courses and report to the trial board upon their completion. The joint trial board must notify the Professional Ethics Division of its decision in each case.

Automatic Disciplinary Provisions

The bylaws (BL 7.3.1) of the AICPA include **automatic disciplinary provisions** that mandate suspension or termination of membership without a hearing in certain situations. Suspension results when the Secretary of the Institute is notified that a judgment or conviction has been imposed on a member for

- A crime punishable by imprisonment for more than one year.
- Willful failure to file any income tax return that the member, as an individual taxpayer, is required by law to file.

■ The filing of a false or fraudulent income tax return on the member's or a client's behalf.

■ Willful aiding in the preparation and presentation of a false and fraudulent income tax return of a client.

Termination of membership occurs when the member has exhausted all legal appeals on the judgment or conviction.

Under the automatic disciplinary provisions of the bylaws, membership in the AICPA shall be terminated without a hearing should a member's certificate as a CPA be revoked, withdrawn, or canceled as a disciplinary measure by any governmental agency. This provision also applies when a member's last or only certificate is revoked by a state board of accountancy for failing to meet continuing professional education requirements, unless the member is retired or disabled.

LEARNING CHECK

3-19 What is the possible role of a state board of accountancy in ethical matters? What rules would a state board of accountancy use when evaluating ethical behavior, and what is the maximum sanction that a state board of accountancy might be able to take against a CPA?

3-20 What is the possible role of the PCAOB in ethical matters? What rules would a PCAOB use when evaluating ethical behavior, and what sanctions are available for the PCAOB to take against a CPA or a CPA firm?

3-21 Identify the two groups that are responsible for enforcement of the AICPA Rules of Conduct and indicate the maximum sanction that can be imposed by each.

3-22 What is the purpose of the Joint Ethics Enforcement Program, and how does it operate?

3-23 What is the composition of the joint trial board, when does it become involved, and what disciplinary actions can it take?

3-24 Explain the automatic disciplinary provision of the AICPA and the action by members that results in application of the provisions.

KEY TERMS

Automatic disciplinary provisions, p. 133
Disciplinary actions, p. 133

Joint Ethics Enforcement Program (JEEP), p. 133
Joint trial board, p. 132

FOCUS ON AUDITOR KNOWLEDGE AND AUDIT DECISIONS

This chapter discusses professional ethics for CPAs. Figures 3-7 and 3-8 summarize the important components of auditor knowledge and key audit decisions discussed in this chapter. Page references are provided to where these issues are discussed in more detail.

Figure 3-7 ■ Summary of Auditor Knowledge Discussed in Chapter 3

Auditor Knowledge	Summary	Chapter References
K1. Know the nature of general ethics.	General ethics attempts to deal with these questions by defining what is good for the individual and society, and by trying to establish the nature of obligations or duties that individuals owe themselves and each other. The book suggests a six-step framework for dealing with ethical dilemmas, which includes the following: (1) obtain the facts relevant to the decision, (2) identify the ethical issues from the facts, (3) determine who will be affected by the decision and how, (4) identify the decision maker's alternatives, (5) identify the consequences of each alternative, and (6) make the ethical choice.	pp. 103–104
K2. Understand the purpose of professional ethics.	Professional ethics represent a commitment by a profession to ethical principles and rules of conduct. A commitment to ethical behavior is a key element that separates recognized professions from other occupations. In most states CPAs are the only professionals that can sign an audit report. In return for this monopoly, CPAs have an obligation to act in the public interest. The willingness of CPAs to voluntarily subscribe to the Code has contributed significantly to the stature and reputation of the profession.	pp. 104–105
K3. Know the components of the AICPA Code of Professional Conduct and related pronouncements.	The AICPA Code of Professional Conduct is divided into four major components: (1) principles that express the basic tenets of ethical conduct and provide the conceptual framework for the rules, (2) Rules of Conduct that establish minimum standards of acceptable conduct in the performance of professional services, (3) Interpretations of the Rules of Conduct that provide guidelines about the scope and applicability of specific rules, and (4) ethical rulings that indicate the applicability of the Rules of Conduct and interpretations to a particular set of factual circumstances. Figure 3-1 summarizes the nature and enforceability of each component of the Code of Professional Conduct.	pp. 106–107
K4. Understand the essence of the Code's six ethical principles.	The following six principles express the basic tenets of ethical conduct and provide the framework for the Rules of Conduct: (1) responsibilities, (2) the public interest, (3) integrity, (4) objectivity and independence, (5) due care, and (6) scope and nature of services. The essence of these six ethical principles is discussed in detail in the chapter.	pp. 107–110
K5. Know the organizations and procedures involved in enforcing the Rules of Conduct.	The AICPA and state societies of CPAs cooperate in a Joint Ethics Enforcement Program that provides mechanisms for investigating complaints of unethical conduct, and imposing sanctions on members who violate the Rules of Conduct. CPAs should also be aware of how state boards of accountancy may enforce ethical rules that are part of state accountancy laws, and how the PCAOB and SEC may enforce its own ethical rules.	pp. 132–134

Figure 3-8 ■ Summary of Audit Decisions Discussed in Chapter 3

Audit Decision	Factors that Influence the Audit Decision	Chapter References
D1. What must a CPA do to comply with the Rules of Conduct regarding independence, integrity, and objectivity?	Being independent in fact can be defined as acting with integrity and objectivity, which refers to being free of conflicts of interest, not knowingly misrepresenting facts, and not subordinating judgment. The AICPA independence rules follow an engagement-based approach. The rules identify a number of individuals who might be in a position to influence the outcome of an attest engagement who must be strictly independent from an attest client. Figure 3-4 summarizes the general guidance regarding important decisions about auditor independence. Figure 3-6 summarizes some important criteria for remaining independent while performing nonattest services for private company clients. It should be noted that the issues surrounding independence are so important that the SEC and the Sarbanes-Oxley Act of 2002 have established higher standards for auditors of public companies than the AICPA rules that are applicable to private companies.	pp. 112–124
D2. What must a CPA do to comply with the Rules of Conduct regarding general standards and accounting principles?	The general standards are important because they apply to all CPAs, not just CPAs in public practice. They also apply to CPAs who perform a variety of professional services in addition to audit services. The rules on general standards address four general standards of behavior (professional competence, due professional care, planning and supervision, and sufficient relevant data) that guide a CPA's work. The rules on compliance with standards outline a variety of AICPA standards that should be followed when performing professional service engagements. The accounting principle standards outline the accounting standards that should be followed in professional practice.	pp. 124–126
D3. What must a CPA do to comply with the Rules of Conduct regarding responsibilities to clients?	Responsibilities to clients relate to a CPA's responsibility with respect to confidential client information and to contingent fee arrangements. In general, CPAs should not disclose confidential information without the client's permission. Contingent fee arrangements reflect situations where no fee is charged unless a specific finding or result is obtained. A CPA cannot perform services for a contingent fee and remain independent with respect to the client nor can a CPA prepare a tax return for a contingent fee.	pp. 126–128
D4. What must a CPA do to comply with the Rules of Conduct regarding other professional responsibilities?	Other responsibilities address issues of discreditable acts (Rule 501), advertising and other forms of solicitation (Rule 502), commission and referral fees (Rule 503), and the form of organization and name (Rule 505). The essence of each rule is discussed in detail in the chapter.	pp. 128–131

objective questions

Objective questions are available for the students at www.wiley.com/college/boynton

comprehensive questions

3-25   **(General and professional ethics)** The membership of the AICPA has adopted the Code of Professional Conduct that is administered by the Institute's Professional Ethics Division.

Required

a. With the many general theories of ethics developed by philosophers and ethicists, why is it necessary or desirable for the profession to adopt such a Code?

b. In what respects, if any, does the AICPA's Code reflect the ethical absolutist and the ethical relativist schools of thought?

c. Identify an ethical dilemma that an auditor might face where answers to the questions "What good do I seek?" and "What is my obligation in this circumstance?" would be relevant.

d. According to the Preamble to the AICPA's Code, to what three groups does the CPA have obligations or responsibilities?

3-26   **(Framework for ethical decision making)** Assume that you are the audit partner on an engagement for a client that has had a string of operating losses. The company still has a positive net worth, but you are worried that the company might have to close down within the next year or so. When you tell the client's management that it should make full disclosure in the footnotes concerning substantial doubt about the entity's ability to continue as a going concern, management says, "Hogwash! There's no substantial doubt. The probability of our having to close down is remote. We'll make no such disclosure. To do so would only make our customers and creditors nervous, possibly making such a disclosure a self-fulfilling prophecy. Our competitors are as bad off as we are, and their auditors aren't making them send out a distress signal." You agree that the determination of "substantial doubt" is a judgment call.

Required

Apply the six-step general framework for ethical decision making to this dilemma.

3-27   **(Sections of the Code)** Ethical standards for the profession have been published in the form of the AICPA's Code of Professional Conduct.

Required

a. Identify and distinguish between the two sections of the Code.

b. Are both sections enforceable? Explain.

c. State each principle of the Code.

d. For each principle, identify two courses of action that will enable the member to meet the principle.

e. Explain the applicability of the Rules to the members of the AICPA.

3-28   **(Independence)** An auditor must not only appear to be independent; he or she must also be independent in fact.

Required

a. Explain the concept of an "auditor's independence" as it applies to third-party reliance on financial statements.

b. 1. What determines whether or not an auditor is independent in fact?

2. What determines whether or not an auditor appears to be independent?

c. Explain how an auditor may be independent in fact but not appear to be independent.

d. Would a CPA be considered independent for an audit of the financial statements of a:

1. Church for which he or she is serving as treasurer without compensation? Explain.

2. Country club for which his or her spouse is serving as treasurer-bookkeeper if he or she is not to receive a fee for the audit? Explain.

AICPA (adapted)

3-29 **(Independence)** The attribute of independence has been traditionally associated with the CPA's function of auditing and expressing opinions on financial statements.

Required

a. What is meant by "independence" as applied to the CPA's function of auditing and expressing opinions on financial statements? Discuss.

b. CPAs have imposed on themselves certain rules of professional conduct that induce their members to remain independent and to strengthen public confidence in their independence. Which of the Rules of Conduct are concerned with the CPA's independence? Discuss.

c. The Wallydrug Company is indebted to a CPA for unpaid fees and has offered to issue to the CPA unsecured interest-bearing notes. Would acceptance of these notes have any bearing on the CPA's independence with respect to Wallydrug Company? Discuss.

d. The Rocky Hill Corporation was formed on October 1, 20X0, and its fiscal year will end on September 30, 20X1. You audited the corporation's opening balance sheet and rendered an unqualified opinion on it. A month after rendering your report, you are offered the position of secretary of the company because of the need for a complete set of officers and for convenience in signing various documents. You will have no financial interest in the company through stock ownership or otherwise, will receive no salary, will not keep the books, and will not have any influence on its financial matters other than occasional advice on income tax matters and similar advice normally given a client by a CPA.

1. Assume that you accept the offer but plan to resign the position prior to conducting your annual audit with the intention of again assuming the office after rendering an opinion on the statements. Can you render an independent opinion on the financial statements? Discuss.

2. Assume that you accept the offer on a temporary basis until the corporation has gotten under way and can employ a secretary. In any event, you would permanently resign the position before conducting your annual audit. Can you render an independent opinion on the financial statements? Discuss.

AICPA

3-30 **(Rules of conduct)** There currently are 11 rules in the Code of Professional Conduct. Listed below are circumstances pertaining to these rules.

1. A member shall not express an opinion that the financial statements are presented in conformity with GAAP unless the pronouncements of the FASB have been followed.

2. A member shall not discriminate in employment of assistants.

3. A member shall not include self-laudatory statements that are not based on verifiable facts in advertisements.

4. A member shall not accept a commission for a referral to a client of products or services of others.

5. A member's fees may vary depending on the complexity of the service rendered.

6. A member is not precluded from responding to an inquiry by a trial board of the AICPA.

7. A member may not serve as a trustee for any pension trust of the client during the period covered by the financial statements.

8. A member shall adequately plan and supervise an engagement.

9. A member may not have or be committed to acquire any direct financial interest in the client.

10. A member shall not practice under a misleading firm name.

11. A member shall not knowingly subordinate his or her judgment to others.

12. A member shall follow the technical standards of the Auditing Standards Board in an audit engagement.

13. A member bases the fee on the findings determined by the IRS in a tax audit case.

14. A member discloses confidential information in a peer review of the firm's practice.

15. A member issues an unqualified opinion when a client departs from GAAP because of a conceptual disagreement with the FASB.

Required

a. Identify the rule to which each circumstance relates.

b. Indicate one other circumstance that pertains to each rule identified in (a) above.

3-31   **(Rules of conduct)** In the practice of public accounting, an auditor who is a member of the AICPA is expected to comply with the rules of the Code of Professional Conduct. Listed below are circumstances that raise a question about an auditor's ethical conduct.

1. The auditor has a bank loan with a bank that is an audit client.

2. An unqualified opinion is expressed when the financial statements of a county are prepared in conformity with principles established by the Governmental Accounting Standards Board.

3. An auditor retains the client's records as a means of enforcing payment of an overdue audit fee.

4. The auditor makes retirement payments to individuals who formerly were members of his firm.

5. An auditor sells her shares of stock in a client company in April prior to beginning work on the audit for the year ending December 31.

6. An auditor accepts an engagement knowing that he does not have the expertise to do the audit.

7. The auditor quotes a client an audit fee but also states that the actual fee will be contingent on the amount of work done.

8. The auditor's firm states in a newspaper advertisement that it has had fewer lawsuits than its principal competitors.

9. The auditor resigns her position as treasurer of the client on May 1, prior to beginning the audit for the year ending December 31.

10. The auditor discloses confidential information about a client to a successor auditor.

11. The auditor accepts an audit engagement when he has a conflict of interest.

12. An auditor prepares a small brochure containing testimonials from existing clients that he mails to prospective clients.

13. An auditor complies with the technical standards of the Accounting and Review Services Committee in reviewing the financial statements of a nonpublic entity.

14. An auditor examines the financial statements of a local bank and also serves on the bank's committee that approves loans.

15. An auditor pays a commission to an attorney to obtain a client.

Required

a. Identify the rule of the Code of Professional Conduct that applies to each circumstance.

b. Indicate for each circumstance whether the effect on the rule is (1) a violation, (2) not a violation, or (3) indeterminate. Give the reason(s) for your answer.

cases

3-32   **(Framework for ethical decision making)** Michael Harper is an audit partner in a local CPA firm who has a number of retail, wholesale, and manufacturing clients. In November of 20X6 Michael is nearing the completion of the audit of EFW, Inc., a wholesaler of exercise equipment who has a September 30th year-end. You are also performing planning and interim work for Sports and Fitness (S&F), a retailer of fitness equipment that has a January 31st year-end. S&F is a significant customer for EFW, Inc. In performing planning work on S&F, you discover that it is having financial difficulties and may not be able to pay its payable to the EFW from which it purchases product.

Required

a. What is your ethical dilemma?

b. Are there competing ethical rules here? If so, identify the rules and explain the conflict.

c. If you were the partner, how would you resolve the ethical dilemma? Apply the six-step general framework for ethical decision making to this dilemma and support your reasoning.

3-33   **(Independence)** Jones and Jones, CPA, has a manufacturing client, Widgit Technologies, Inc. (WTI), that is a small, owner-managed business with annual revenues of approximately $8 million. WTI employs a bookkeeper but is not large enough to employ a CPA in-house. WTI regularly asks Margaret Jones, the partner on the engagement, for advice on accounting issues, and Jones and Jones drafts the financial statements for the company. The client reviews the financial statements before they are printed by Jones and Jones with an audit opinion attached.

During the current year WTI asked Jones and Jones to assist the company by rendering a business valuation service. WTI is asking Jones and Jones to (1) estimate the value of WTI and (2) consult with WTI in the form of making recommendations on steps that WTI can take that will grow the value of the business.

Required

    a. Since Jones and Jones is preparing the financial statements for WTI, is Jones and Jones independent with respect to WTI? What conditions, if any, must Jones and Jones meet in order to be independent with respect to WTI?

    b. Would your answer to (a) be the same if WTI was a public company subject to SEC rules and regulations?

    c. Can Jones and Jones take on the business valuation services and consulting engagement and remain independent with respect to WTI? Explain your reasoning.

    d. Would your answer to (c) be the same if WTI was a public company subject to SEC rules and regulations?

3-34   **(Ethical issues)** Gilbert and Bradley formed a corporation called Financial Services, Inc., each taking 50 percent of the authorized common stock. Gilbert is a CPA and a member of the American Institute of CPAs. Bradley is a CPCU (Chartered Property Casualty Under-writer). The corporation performs auditing and tax services under Gilbert's direction and insurance services under Bradley's supervision. The opening of the corporation's office was announced by a three-inch, two-column ad in the local newspaper.

    One of the corporation's first audit clients was the Grandtime Company. Grandtime had total assets of $600,000 and total liabilities of $270,000. In the course of the audit, Gilbert found that Grandtime's building with a book value of $240,000 was pledged as security for a 10-year term note in the amount of $200,000. The client's statements did not mention that the building was pledged as a security for the note. However, as the failure to disclose the lien did not affect either the value of the assets or the amount of the liabilities and the audit was satisfactory in all other respects, Gilbert rendered an unqualified opinion on Grand-time's financial statements. About two months after the date of the opinion, Gilbert learned that an insurance company was planning a loan to Grandtime of $150,000 in the form of a first-mortgage note on the building. Realizing that the insurance company was unaware of the existing lien on the building, Gilbert had Bradley notify the insurance company of the fact that Grandtime's building was pledged as security for the term note.

    Shortly after the events described above, Gilbert was charged with a violation of professional ethics.

Required

Identify and discuss the ethical implication of those acts by Gilbert that were in violation of the AICPA Code of Professional Conduct.

3-35   **(Ethical issues)** The following situations involve Herb Standard, staff accountant with the regional CPA firm of Cash & Green:

    1. The bookkeeper of Ethical Manufacturing Company resigned two months ago and has not yet been replaced. As a result, Ethical's transactions have not been recorded and the books are not up to date. To comply with terms of a loan agreement, Ethical needs to pre-pare interim financial statements but cannot do so until the books are posted. Ethical looks to Cash & Green, its independent auditors, for help and wants to borrow Herb Standard to perform the work. Ethical wants Herb because he did its audit last year.

    2. Herb Standard discovered that his client, Ethical Manufacturing Company, materially understated net income on last year's tax return. Herb informs his supervisor about this, and the client is asked to prepare an amended return. The client is unwilling to take cor-rective measures. Herb informs the Internal Revenue Service.

    3. While observing the year-end inventory of Ethical Manufacturing Company, the plant manager offers Herb Standard a fishing rod, which Ethical manufactures, in apprecia-tion for a job well done.

4. Herb Standard's acquaintance, Joe Lender, is chief loan officer at Local Bank, an audit client of Cash & Green. Herb approaches Joe for an unsecured loan from Local Bank and Joe approves the loan.

5. Herb Standard is a member of a local investment club composed of college fraternity brothers. The club invests in listed stocks and is fairly active in trading. Last week the club purchased the stock of Leverage Corp., a client of another Cash & Green office. Herb has no contact with the members of this office.

Required

For each situation, (a) identify the ethical issues that are involved and (b) discuss whether there has or has not been any violation of ethical conduct. Support your answers by reference to the rules of the Code of Professional Conduct.

professional simulation

Sharon Langdale is the audit partner in a large Midwest office of a national accounting firm. She has just delivered a proposal to the audit committee of EquipCo, a large, privately held manufacturing company to perform the company's annual audit. The company is considering going public in the next 2-3 years and now wants a large CPA firm to perform their audit. EquipCo has multiple locations that will involve several offices around the world in the annual audit.

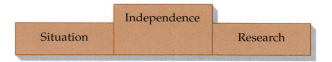

In planning for the audit, Langdale instructed Robert Benson, an assistant on the engagement, to draft a list of individuals who would need to be independent so that they could be assigned to the engagement. Indicate whether the following individuals would cause independence problems if they owned stock in EquipCo.

	Independence Problem?
1. A tax partner in Sharon Langdale's office.	○
2. A consulting partner in another office where work on the EquipCo audit is performed. However, the partner performed no work for EquipCo.	○
3. The spouse of a staff accountant who works on the EquipCo audit works as a financial analyst for EquipCo.	○
4. The audit firm's benefit plan owns EquipCo stock.	○
5. A manager in another office who regularly is involved in internal quality control functions.	○
6. A parent of a staff accountant who works on the EquipCo audit, holds an immaterial investment in EquipCo.	○

7. The spouse of an audit partner in an office that performs work for EquipCo (the audit partner does not perform any work for EquipCo and is not in the chain of command for the audit). ○

8. A tax manager in an office that performs work for EquipCo performs five hours of work on the audit of the tax accrual. ○

9. The Midwest regional audit partner who performs no work on the EquipCo audit. ○

10. An audit manager in Asia who performs no work on the EquipCo audit. ○

11. An audit partner in Sharon's office finds that a mutual fund that he owns in his investment portfolio has an immaterial investment in EquipCo. ○

Situation	Independence	Research

While EquipCo is still a private company, it approaches Monica Lee, a tax manager in Sharon Langdale's office an offers her a job in EquipCo's tax department. Cut and paste the AICPA ethical standard sections that apply to Monica's situation.

[4] AUDITOR'S LEGAL LIABILITY

THE COST OF MALPRACTICE

The Baptist Foundation of Arizona (BFA) sold different types of investments and savings accounts, most of which were supposedly backed by collateral. Investors were told that the accounts paid interest greater than most banks and that some of the profit would benefit Baptist causes. There are two key aspects to this case. First, the BFA invested heavily in real estate, a high-risk investment strategy, and problems began for BFA when the Arizona real estate market took a downturn. In order to show a profit, BFA officials allegedly entered into a number of transactions in which properties were sold at inflated prices to entities that borrowed funds from the foundation (and were unlikely to pay for the properties unless the real estate market turned around). Second, in what was in economic substance a "Ponsi scheme," BFA officials took money from new investors to fund the cash flow needed to pay returns to existing investors.

Investors brought a lawsuit against BFA's auditors, Arthur Andersen, LLP, alleging that the firm issued false and misleading audit reports (unqualified opinions) on the BFA's financial statements that allowed BFA to perpetuate the fraud. Dan Guy, a former director of the Auditing Standards Division of the AICPA, served as an expert witness for the plaintiffs. Bob Allen of the Associated Baptist Press summarized Dan Guy's comments as follows:

> Dan Guy, a director of the American Institute of Certified Public Accountants, accused Andersen of an "unpardonable" breach of accounting standards. A 1997 audit report of foundation account "falls below the minimum accounting standards" and "never should have been released," he testified.
>
> Guy, who studied Andersen case files in the audit, said an audit team failed to investigate charges of misconduct, issuing a clean bill of health. At the least, he said, auditors should have tested the foundation's ability to operate as a going concern, which likely would have disclosed its shaky finances.
>
> He said Andersen missed red flags, including warning by one of its own accountants, an anonymous call to its Chicago office and a series of investigative newspaper articles quoting former foundation employees.

In the end, Arthur Andersen, LLP, settled the malpractice lawsuit out of court for $217 million without admitting any wrongdoing. The settlement included revoking CPA licenses for two partners (a former partner and a current partner) who worked on the foundation's audit.

Sources: The Arizona Corporate Commission web site

Bob Allen, "Arthur Andersen settles, yet again, with Arizona foundation investors," Associated Baptist Press, May 7, 2001.

[PREVIEW OF CHAPTER 4]

As a matter of perspective, the public accounting profession has had an extremely low percentage of alleged audit failures compared to the total number of audits conducted. However, audit failures are like nuclear accidents: they rarely happen, but when they do they have enormous consequences. The consequences of audit failures impact investors, creditors, and every audit firm. Although many auditors never experience an audit failure in an entire career, they nevertheless must pay significant amounts for professional liability insurance coverage. It is important for all auditors to understand their legal obligations to clients and the third-party investors who rely on their reports. The following diagram provides an overview of the chapter organization and content.

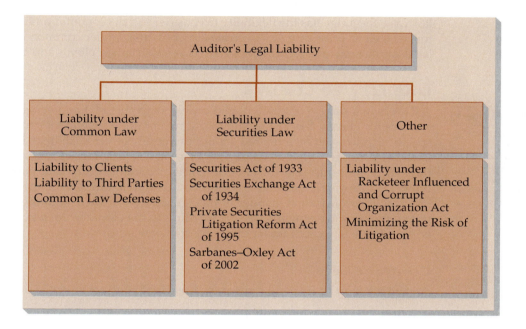

focus on auditor knowledge

Chapter 4 addresses the following aspects of the auditor's general knowledge related to auditor's legal liability. After studying this chapter you should understand the following aspects of an auditor's knowledge base:

K1. Know the auditor's legal liability to clients under common law and understand the consequences of important cases under common law.

K2. Know the auditor's legal liability to third parties under common law and understand the consequences of important cases under common law.

K3. Know the common law defenses available to the auditor.

K4. Understand and distinguish the auditor's liability under the securities acts of 1933 and 1934 and understand the consequences of important cases under these acts.

K5. Know how the Private Securities Litigation Reform Act of 1995 affects the auditor's liability under statutory law.

K6. Understand how the auditing environment has changed because of the Sarbanes-Oxley Act of 2002.

K7. Know the auditor's liability under the Racketeer Influenced and Corrupt Organization Act.

K8. Understand the precautions a CPA can take to minimize the risk of litigation.

[LIABILITY UNDER COMMON LAW]

Common law is frequently referred to as unwritten law. It is based on judicial precedent rather than legislative enactment. **Common law** is derived from principles based on justice, reason, and common sense rather than absolute, fixed, or inflexible rules. The principles of common law are determined by the social needs of the community. Hence, common law changes in response to society's needs. In a specific case, the accountant's liability is determined by a state or federal court that attempts to apply case law precedents that it feels are controlling. Because there are 51 such independent jurisdictions in the United States, different decisions may result with respect to relatively similar factual circumstances.[1] In a common law case, the judge has the flexibility to consider social, economic, and political factors as well as prior case law doctrines (precedents). Under common law, a CPA's legal liability extends principally to two classes of parties: clients and third parties.

LIABILITY TO CLIENTS

Auditor Knowledge 1

■ Know the auditor's legal liability to clients under common law and understand the consequences of important cases under common law.

A CPA is in a direct contractual relationship with clients. In agreeing to perform services for clients, the CPA assumes the role of an independent contractor. The specific service(s) to be rendered should preferably be set forth in an engagement letter, as described in Chapter 7. The term **privity of contract** refers to the contractual relationship that exists between two or more contracting parties. In the typical auditing engagement, it is assumed that the audit is to be made in accordance with professional standards (i.e., generally accepted auditing standards) unless the contract contains specific wording to the contrary. An accountant may be held liable to a client under either contract law or tort law.

Contract Law

An auditor may be liable to a client for **breach of contract** when he or she:

■ Issues a standard audit report when he or she has not made an audit in accordance with GAAS.
■ Does not deliver the audit report by the agreed-upon date.
■ Violates the client's confidential relationship.

A CPA's liability for breach of contract extends to subrogees. A **subrogee** is a party who has acquired the rights of another by substitution. For example, the bonding of employees is considered an important part of a company's internal control environment. When an embezzlement occurs, the bonding company reimburses the insured for its losses. Then, under the right of subrogation to the insured's contractual claim, it can bring suit against the CPA for failing to discover the fraud.

When a breach of contract occurs, the plaintiff usually seeks one or more of the following remedies: (1) specific performance of the contract by the defendant, (2) direct monetary damages for losses incurred due to the breach, or (3) incidental and consequential damages that are an indirect result of nonperformance.

---

[1] The 50 states and the District of Columbia constitute the 51 jurisdictions.

Tort Law

A CPA may also be liable to a client under tort law. A **tort** is a wrongful act that injures another person's property, body, or reputation. A tort action may be based on any one of the following causes:

- **Ordinary negligence.** Failure to exercise the degree of care a person of ordinary prudence (a reasonable person) would exercise under the same circumstances.
- **Gross negligence.** Failure to use even slight care in the circumstances.
- **Fraud.** Intentional deception, such as the misrepresentation, concealment, or nondisclosure of a material fact, that results in injury to another.[2]

Under tort law, the injured party normally seeks monetary damages. The auditor's working papers are vital in refuting charges for breach of contract and breach of duty in a tort action. In many cases, the plaintiff has the option to sue under either contract or tort law. The best course of action in a given case involves legal technicalities that are beyond the scope of this book.

Cases Illustrating Liability to Clients

Two cases pertaining to liability to clients are considered below. The first case involves negligence, and the second relates to breach of contract.

The *1136 Tenants'* case has frequently been used to demonstrate the importance of having a written contract (engagement letter) for each professional engagement. A written contract is important, but it was not the only issue in this case. The critical issue was the CPA's failure to inform the client of employee wrongdoing, regardless of the type of service rendered.

The second case is *Fund of Funds, Ltd.* v. *Arthur Andersen & Co.*[3] In this case, the plaintiff sued the auditors for breach of contract because the auditors failed to disclose fraud to the client when the auditors' engagement letter contained a specific representation that any fraud would be revealed. The fraud, totaling over $120 million, resulted from overcharges on a contract between the plaintiff and King Resources, both audited by Andersen. Andersen admitted discovery of the violation of the contract in auditing King but declined to disclose the fraud to Fund of Funds because of the AICPA's Ethics Rule 301 that prohibits disclosure of confidential information. The court ruled for the plaintiff on the grounds that the defendants failed to comply with the terms of their engagement letter. Further consideration is also given to other issues in this particular case later in the chapter.

LIABILITY TO THIRD PARTIES

The common law liability of the auditor to third parties is important in any discussion of the auditor's legal liability. A **third party** may be defined as an individual who is not in privity with the parties to a contract. From a legal standpoint, there are two classes of third parties: (1) a primary beneficiary and (2) other beneficiaries. A **primary beneficiary** is anyone identified to the auditor by name prior to the audit who is to be the primary recipient of the auditor's report. For exam-

---

[2] In some cases, a distinction is made between fraud and **constructive fraud.** The latter may be inferred from gross negligence or reckless disregard for the truth.

[3] *Fund of Funds* v. *Arthur Andersen & Co.,* 545F Supp. 1314 (S.D.N.Y. 1982).

1136 Tenants' Corp. v. Max Rothenberg & Co. (1971) liability to client for negligence[4]

The plaintiff, a corporation owning a cooperative apartment house, sued the defendant, a CPA firm, for damages resulting from the failure of the defendant to discover the embezzlement of over $110,000 by the plaintiff's managing agent, Riker. Riker had orally engaged Rothenberg at an annual fee of $600.

The plaintiff maintained that Rothenberg had been engaged to perform all necessary accounting and auditing services. The defendant claimed he was only engaged to do write-up work and prepare financial statements and related tax returns. As evidence of their respective contentions, the plaintiff booked the accountant's fee as auditing expenses, and the defendant marked each page of the financial statements as unaudited. In addition, the accountant in a letter of transmittal to the financial statements stated that (1) the statements were prepared from the books and records of the corporation and (2) no independent verifications were undertaken thereon. The trial court found that the defendant was engaged to perform an audit because Rothenberg admitted that he had performed some limited auditing procedures such as examining bank statements, invoices, and bills. In fact, the CPA's working papers included one entitled "Missing Invoices," which showed over $40,000 of disbursements that did not have supporting documentation. The CPA did not inform the plaintiff of these invoices, and no effort was made to find them. The trial court also found that the CPA was negligent in the performance of the service and awarded damages totaling $237,000. The appellate court affirmed saying:

- Regardless of whether the CPA was making an audit or performing write-up work, there was a duty to inform the client of known wrongdoing or other suspicious actions by the client's employees.
- Defendant's work sheets indicate that the defendant did perform some audit procedures.
- The record shows that the defendant was engaged to audit the books and records and that the procedures performed by the defendant were "incomplete, inadequate, and improperly performed."

Auditor Knowledge 2

■ Know the auditor's legal liability to third parties under common law and understand the consequences of important cases under common law.

ple, if at the time the engagement letter is signed, the client informs the auditor that the report is to be used to obtain a loan at the City National Bank, the bank becomes a primary beneficiary. In contrast, **other beneficiaries** are unnamed third parties, such as creditors, stockholders, and potential investors.

The auditor is liable to all third parties for gross negligence and fraud under tort law. In contrast, the auditor's liability for ordinary negligence has traditionally been different between the two classes of third parties.

Liability to Primary Beneficiaries

The privity of contract doctrine extends to the primary beneficiary of the auditor's work. The landmark case, *Ultramares Corp.* v. *Touche* (now Deloitte), upheld the privity of contract doctrine under which third parties cannot sue auditors for ordinary negligence. However, Judge Cardozo's decision extended to primary benefi-

---

[4] *1136 Tenants' Corp.* v. *Max Rothenberg & Co.* (36A2d 30 NY 2nd 804), 319 NYS2d 1007 (1971).

> ### *Ultramares Corp.* v. *Touche* (1931)
> ### liability for third party negligence[5]
>
> The defendant auditors, Touche, failed to discover fictitious transactions that overstated assets and stockholders equity by $700,000 in the audit of Fred Stern & Co. On receiving the audited financial statements, Ultramares loaned Stern large sums of money that Stern was unable to repay because it was actually insolvent. Ultramares sued the CPA firm for negligence and fraud.
>
> The court found the auditors guilty of negligence but ruled that accountants should not be liable to any third party for negligence except to a primary beneficiary. Judge Cardozo said:
>
> > If liability for negligence exists, a thoughtless slip or blunder, the failure to detect a theft or forgery beneath the cover of deceptive entries may expose accountants to a liability in indeterminate amounts, for an indeterminate time, to an indeterminate class. The hazards of a business conducted on these terms are so extreme as to enkindle doubt whether a flaw may not exist in the implication of a duty that exposes to these consequences.
>
> The court also ruled that the finding on negligence does not emancipate accountants from the consequences of fraud. It concluded that gross negligence may constitute fraud.

ciaries the rights of one in privity of contract. Hence, Ultramares as a primary beneficiary could sue and recover for losses suffered because of the auditor's ordinary negligence.

An analysis of the decision reveals several significant environmental factors that are particularly interesting in view of the current legal environment described earlier in this chapter. First, the judge recognized that extending liability for ordinary negligence to any third party might discourage individuals from entering the accounting and auditing profession, thus depriving society of a valuable service. Second, he feared the impact that a broader encroachment on the privity doctrine might have on other professionals such as lawyers and doctors. Third, the decision reaffirmed the auditor's liability to any third party for gross negligence or fraud.

Liability to Other Beneficiaries

The *Ultramares* decision remained virtually unchallenged for 37 years, and it still is followed today in many jurisdictions. However, since 1968, several court decisions have served to extend the auditor's liability for ordinary negligence beyond the privity of contract doctrine. The following environmental factors contributed to this development:

- The concept of liability evolved significantly to include consumer protection from the wrongdoing of both manufacturers (product liability) and professionals (service liability).

[5] *Ultramares Corp.* v. *Touche,* 255 N.Y. 170, 174 N.E. 441 (1931).

- Businesses and accounting firms grew in size, making them better able to shoulder the new threshold of responsibility.
- The number of individuals and groups relying on audited financial statements grew steadily.

Court decisions have recognized two categories of other third-party beneficiaries: (1) foreseen class and (2) foreseeable parties.

A Foreseen Class

The first shift away from *Ultramares* occurred in the form of judicial acceptance of the specifically **foreseen class** concept. This concept is explained in *Restatement (Second) of Torts* § 552 as follows.

Restatement (Second) of Torts § 552 (1977)

(1) One who, in the course of his (her) business, profession, or employment, or any other transactions in which he (she) has a pecuniary interest, supplies false information for the guidance of others in their business transactions, is subject to liability for pecuniary loss caused to them by their justifiable reliance upon the information, if he(she) fails to exercise reasonable care of competence in obtaining or communicating the information.
(2) Except as stated in Subsection 3, the liability stated in Subsection (1) is limited to loss suffered
  (a) by a person or one of a limited group of persons for whose benefit and guidance he (she) intends to supply the information or knows that the recipient intends to supply it; and
  (b) through reliance upon it in a transaction that he (she) intends the information to influence or knows that the receipt so intends or in a substantially similar transaction.
(3) The liability of one who is under a public duty to give the information extends to loss suffered by any of the class of persons for whose benefit the duty is created, in any of the transactions in which it is intended to protect them.

Subsection (2) extends the auditor's liability to "a limited group of persons for whose benefit the CPA intends to supply the information." Thus, if the client informs the CPA that the audit report is to be used to obtain a bank loan, all banks are foreseen parties, but trade creditors and potential stockholders would not be part of the foreseen class. The liability is limited to losses suffered through reliance on the information in a transaction known by the auditor or a similar transaction. In the above instance, this means that the accountant would not be liable if the audit report was used by a bank to invest capital in the client's business in exchange for common stock instead of granting a loan.

The foreseen class concept does not extend to all present and future investors, stockholders, or creditors. Court decisions have not required that the injured party be specifically identified, but the class of persons to which the party belonged had to be limited and known at the time the auditor provided the information.

Foreseeable Parties

Foreseeable parties are individuals or entities whom the auditor either knew or should have known would rely on the audit report in making business and investment decisions. This concept extends the auditor's duty of due care to any foreseeable party who suffers a pecuniary loss from relying on the auditor's representation. Foreseeable parties include all creditors, stockholders, and present and future investors. The courts use foreseeability extensively in cases involving physical injury. For example, foreseeability is almost universally used in product liability cases when the manufacturer's negligence causes the physical injury. This concept was first applied in an audit negligence case in the early 1980s.

Cases Illustrating Liability to Other Beneficiaries

The leading cases that extended the accountant's liability for ordinary negligence to foreseen parties and to foreseeable parties are shown below. The finding in Rusch Factors Inc., which provides the same liability exposure as the *Restatement (second) of Torts* adopted in 1977, was the prevailing rule of law in most jurisdictions until 1983, when *Rosenblum* v. *Adler* occurred (see page 152).

In reaching its decision in *Rosenblum,* the New Jersey Supreme Court cited the following public policy factors that appear, in part, aimed at countering Judge Cardozo's arguments in upholding the privity doctrine in *Ultramares:* (1) insurance is available to accountants to cover these risks, (2) the CPA has a moral responsibility to anyone relying on his or her opinion, and (3) more rigid standards will cause accountants to do better work.

The foreseeability standard was subsequently embraced by similar rulings in Wisconsin, California, and Mississippi. Several recent developments have begun to reverse the trend toward unlimited liability exposure for accountants under the common law.

In 1985, the New York Court of Appeals expressly rejected the foreseeability standard in *Credit Alliance Corp.* v. *Arthur Andersen & Co.* Instead, the court reverted to a "near privity rule," establishing three criteria for determining whether a plaintiff can bring a claim against an auditor for ordinary negligence: (1) the plaintiff did in fact rely on the auditor's report, (2) the auditor knew that the plaintiff intended to rely on the report, and (3) the auditor, *through some actions on his or her own part, evidenced understanding of the plaintiff's intended reliance.*

Rusch Factors Inc. v. *Levin* (1968)
liability to foreseen parties[6]

The plaintiff had asked the defendant accountant to audit the financial statements of a corporation seeking a loan. The certified statements indicated that the potential borrower was solvent when, in fact, it was insolvent. Rusch Factors sued the auditor for damages resulting from its reliance on negligent and fraudulent misrepresentations in the financial statements. The defendant asked for dismissal on the basis of lack of privity of contract.

The court ruled in favor of the plaintiff. While the decision could have been decided on the basis of the primary benefit rule set forth in *Ultramares,* the court instead said

The accountant should be liable in negligence for careless financial misrepresentation relied upon by *actually foreseen and limited classes of persons.* In this case, the defendant knew that his certification was to be used for *potential financiers of the ... corporation* (emphasis added).

---

[6]*Rusch Factors, Inc.* v. *Levin,* 284 F. Supp. 85 (D.C.R.I. 1986)

Rosenblum v. Adler (1983) liability to foreseeable parties[7]

The plaintiffs, Harry and Barry Rosenblum, acquired common stock of Giant Stores Corporation, a publicly traded corporation, in conjunction with the sale of their business to Giant. The stock subsequently proved to be worthless after Giant's audited financial statements were found to be fraudulent. The defendant, Adler, was a partner in Touche Ross & Co. (now Deloitte) that audited the Giant financial statements.

Plaintiffs claimed negligence in the conduct of the audit and stated that the auditor's negligence was a proximate cause of their loss. Defendants argued for dismissal of the suit because plaintiffs were not in privity with the auditors and they were not a foreseen party.

The Supreme Court of New Jersey denied dismissal, stating

- When the independent auditor furnishes an opinion with no limitation in the certificate regarding to whom the company (audited) may disseminate the financial statements, he has a duty to all those whom that auditor should reasonably foresee as recipients from the company of the statements for its proper business purposes, provided that the recipients rely on the statements pursuant to those business purposes.
- Certified financial statements have become the benchmark for various reasonably foreseeable business purposes, and accountants have been engaged to satisfy these ends. In such circumstances, accounting firms should no longer be permitted to hide within the citadel of privity and avoid liability for their malpractice. The public interest will be served by the rule we promulgate this day.
- Regardless of whether the defendants had actual knowledge of Giant's proposed use of the audited financial statements in connection with the merger, it was reasonably foreseeable that Giant would use the statements in connection with the merger and its consummation.

In 1992, in yet another landmark case known as *Bily* v. *Arthur Young & Co.*, the California Supreme Court ended the foreseeability standard in that state. After perhaps the most thorough analysis by any court of the purpose and effects of audits and audit reports, and following a thorough review of approaches taken by other courts as well as the basic principles of tort liability announced in the California court's own prior cases, it stated:

> We conclude that an auditor owes no general duty of care regarding the conduct of an audit to persons other than the client. An auditor may, however, be held liable for negligent misrepresentations in an audit report to those persons who act in reliance upon those misrepresentations in a transaction which the auditor intended to influence, in accordance with the rule of section 552 of the Restatement Second of Torts. . . . Finally, an auditor may also be held liable to reasonably foreseeable third persons for intentional fraud in the preparation and dissemination of an audit report.[8]

A summary of the auditor's liability under common law is presented in Figure 4-1. Although the extent of the auditor's exposure to liability to third parties for

[7] *H. Rosenblum Inc.* v. *Adler,* 461 A 2d 138 (N.J. 1983)

[8] *Robert R. Bily* v. *Arthur Young & Co.,* 11 Cal. Rptr. 2d 51 (Cal. 1992). In a footnote to its decision, the court also noted that "express third party beneficiaries" may under appropriate circumstances be the practical and legal equivalents of clients, but there was no such party in the *Bily* Case.

Figure 4-1 ■ Liability Under the Common Law

Liability to Clients:

Under contract law   - for **breach of contract**

Under tort law   - for **fraud, gross negligence,** and **ordinary negligence**

Liability to Third Parties:

Under tort law   - to all third parties for **fraud** and **gross negligence**

                      - to designated parties for **ordinary negligence** as follows:

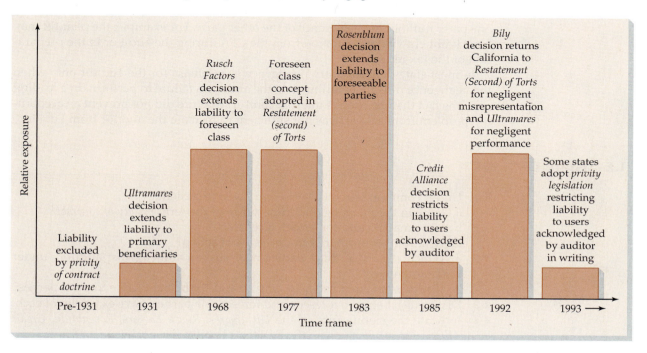

ordinary negligence has been subject to the whims of the courts, it now appears that in all but three states (Mississippi, New Jersey, and Wisconsin) either the rule embraced in the *Restatement (Second) of Torts,* or the stricter *Credit Alliance* or privity legislation rules, prevail.

COMMON LAW DEFENSES

The auditor generally must use due care as a defense in breach of contract suits involving charges of negligence. In tort actions, the primary defenses are due care or contributory negligence.

When using the **due care defense** in a suit pertaining to an audit engagement, the auditor attempts to show that the audit was made in accordance with GAAS. The auditor's working papers are critical in this defense. In addition, the auditor hopes to convince the court that there are inherent limitations in the audit process. Thus, because of selective testing, there is a risk that material errors or irregularities, if they exist, may not be detected.

The *Restatement (Second) of Torts* Section 465 (1965) defines **contributory negligence** as

> (C)onduct on the part of the plaintiff which falls below the standard to which he (she) should conform his (her) own protection, and which is a legally contributing cause cooperating with the negligence of the defendant in bringing about the plaintiff's harm.

Thus, if a plaintiff has contributed to his or her own injury (loss) by his or her own negligence, the law considers him or her to be as responsible as the defendant for the injury. In such a case, there is no basis for recovery because the negligence of one party nullifies the negligence of the other party. For example, the plaintiff may have withheld vital information from the CPA during the audit or in the preparation of the tax return.

In most states, contributory negligence is a defense for the auditor only when the negligence directly contributes to the auditor's failure to perform. In a leading case, the fact that the client's internal control structure did not prevent an accounting problem from arising was not sufficient to insulate the auditor from liability.[9]

LEARNING CHECK

4-1 Under common law, a CPA may be liable to a client.
    a. Explain the meaning and importance of the term *privity of contract.*
    b. How may an auditor breach a contract?
    c. What causes ordinarily underlie a tort action?

4-2 a. Which classes of third parties may sustain suits against auditors under common law?
    b. Under what circumstances may an auditor be held liable to third parties?

4-3 Distinguish between foreseen and foreseeable parties. Give examples of each.

4-4 Indicate the significance of the *Ultramares, Rusch Factors, Rosenblum, Credit Alliance,* and *Bily* cases on the auditor's liability for negligence.

4-5 a. What are the accountant's primary defenses in tort actions?
    b. Define contributory negligence.
    c. When does contributory negligence ordinarily represent a valid defense?

KEY TERMS

Breach of contract, p. 146
Common law, p. 146
Contributory negligence, p. 154
Due care defense, p. 153
Foreseeable parties, p. 150
Foreseen class, p. 150
Fraud, p. 147
Gross negligence, p. 147

Ordinary negligence, p. 147
Other beneficiaries, p. 148
Primary beneficiary, p. 147
Privity of contract, p. 146
Subrogee, p. 146
Third party, p. 147
Tort, p. 147

---

[9] *National Security Corp. v. Lybrand,* 256 AD226, 9 NYS 2d 554 (1939).

LIABILITY UNDER SECURITIES LAW

Auditor Knowledge 4

■ Understand and distinguish the auditor's liability under the securities acts of 1933 and 1934 and understand the consequences of important cases under these acts.

Securities laws fall under **statutory law,** which is established by state and federal legislative bodies that specifically address auditor's liability under certain circumstances. Most states also have **blue sky laws** for the purpose of regulating the issuing and trading of securities within a state. Usually, these statutes require that audited financial statements be filed with a designated regulatory agency. The two most important federal statutes affecting auditors are the Securities Act of 1933 and the Securities Exchange Act of 1934, which are administered by the Securities and Exchange Commission (SEC). The 1933 Act requires audited financial statements to be included in registration statements filed with the SEC when nonexempt entities initially offer securities for sale to the public. The 1934 Act requires public companies with assets in excess of $5 million and more than 300 stockholders to file annual reports with the SEC, including audited financial statements.

Two factors contribute to a broader exposure to legal liability under the securities laws than under common law: (1) the 1933 Act grants certain unnamed third parties rights against auditors for ordinary negligence, and (2) criminal indictments may be brought against auditors under both the 1933 and 1934 Acts. In the following sections, in-depth consideration is given to the auditor's legal liability under federal securities laws.

SECURITIES ACT OF 1933

The 1933 Act is known as the *Truth in Securities Act.* It is designed to regulate security offerings to the public through the mails or in interstate commerce. Suits against auditors under this Act are usually based on Section 11, Civil Liabilities on Account of False Registration Statement, which states, in part:

In case any part of the registration statement, which such part became effective, contained an untrue statement of a material fact or omitted to state a material fact required to be stated therein or necessary to make the statements therein not misleading, any person acquiring such security (unless it is proved that at the time of the acquisition he know of such untruth or omission) may … sue…

It should be noted that "any person" purchasing or otherwise acquiring the securities may sue. This includes unnamed third parties. The act makes the auditor liable for losses to third parties resulting from ordinary negligence, as well as from fraud and gross negligence, to the effective date of the registration statement, which may be 20 working days after the statement is filed with the agency.

Section 11 includes two key terms: a **material fact** and **misleading financial statement.** These terms are defined by the SEC as follows:

The term *material*, when used to qualify a requirement for the furnishing of information as to any subject, limits the information required to those matters about which an average prudent investor ought reasonable to be informed.[10]

(continues)

---

[10] SEC, Rule 1-102, regulation S-X.

> Financial statements are presumed to be misleading or inaccurate when a material matter is presented in a financial statement in accordance with an accounting principle that has no authoritative support, or has authoritative support but where the SEC has ruled against its use.[11]

Under the civil provisions of the 1933 Act, monetary damages recoverable by a plaintiff are limited to the difference between (1) the amount the investor paid for the security and (2) the market or sales price at the time of the suit. If the security has been sold, the amount recoverable is the difference between the amount paid and the sales price. Criminal penalties are provided under Sections 17 and 24. For example, Section 24 provides for penalties on conviction of no more than $10,000 in fines or imprisonment of not more than five years, or both, for *willfully* making an untrue statement or omitting a material fact in a registration statement.

Bringing Suit under the 1933 Act

The principal effects of this Act on the parties involved in a suit may be summarized as follows:

Plaintiff

- May be any person acquiring securities described in the registration statement, whether or not he or she is a client of the auditor.
- Must base the claim on an alleged material false or misleading financial statement contained in the registration statement.
- Does not have to prove reliance on the false or misleading statement or that the loss suffered was the proximate result of the statement if purchase was made before the issuance of an income statement covering a period of at least 12 months following the effective date of the registration statement.
- Does not have to prove that the auditors were negligent or fraudulent in certifying the financial statements involved.

Defendant

- Has the burden of establishing freedom from negligence by proving that he (or she) had made a reasonable investigation and accordingly had reasonable ground to believe, and did believe, that the statements certified were true at the date of the statements and as of the time the registration statement became effective, or
- Must establish, by way of defense, that the plaintiff's loss resulted in whole or in part from causes other than the false or misleading statements.

The reasonable investigation concept is often referred to as the **due diligence defense.** Section 11(c) states that the standard of reasonableness is the care

---

[11] SEC, Financial Reporting Release No. 1, Section 101 (1982).

required of a prudent person in the management of his (or her) own property. For an auditor, the basis for a reasonable investigation of audited financial statements is GAAS.

Cases Brought Under the 1933 Act

A major civil case under the Securities Act of 1933 is the *BarChris* case. The auditing issues in this case are described below.

Escott v. BarChris Construction Corp. (1968) civil liability under Securities Act of 1933[12]

BarChris was a company that was in constant need of cash. Purchasers of debentures filed suit under Section 11 when the company filed for bankruptcy, alleging that the registration statement pertaining to the sale of the bonds contained material false statements and material omissions. One of the defendants was a national public accounting firm, Peat, Marwick, Mitchell & Co. (now KPMG), which pleaded the due diligence defense.

In certifying the registration statement that preceded the bankruptcy by 17 months, the accounting firm performed a subsequent events review, called an S-1 review by the SEC. The purpose of the review was to ascertain whether, subsequent to the certified balance sheet, any material changes had occurred that needed to be disclosed to prevent the balance sheet from being misleading.

The court concluded that Peat Marwick's written audit program for the review was in conformity with generally accepted auditing standards. However, it also found that the work done by a senior who was performing his first S-1 review was unsatisfactory. In ruling that the accounting firm had not established a due diligence defense, the court said

- The senior's review was useless because it failed to discover a material change for the worse in BarChris's financial position that required disclosure to prevent the balance sheet from being misleading.
- The senior did not meet the standards of the profession because he did not take some of the steps prescribed in the written program.
- The senior did not spend an adequate amount of time on a task of this magnitude, and, most important of all, he was too easily satisfied with glib answers.
- There were enough danger signals in the materials examined to require some further investigation.

As a result of this case, an SAS was issued on subsequent events that includes specific review procedures, as explained in Chapter 19.

A major criminal case brought under Section 24 of the 1933 Act is described next.

---

[12] *Escott* v. *BarChris Construction Corp.*, 283 F. Supp 643 (S.D.N.Y. 1986).

This case, also called the *Continental Vending* case, involved loans made by Continental Vending to its affiliated company, Valley Commercial Corporation, which subsequently lent the money to the president of Continental (Roth). The loans to Roth were secured primarily by the pledging of Continental common stock owned by Roth. Valley, in turn, pledged this stock as collateral against the loans from Continental. The auditor for Continental did not audit Valley. The defendants (a senior partner, a junior partner, and an audit senior of an international accounting firm) approved the following note to the financial statements:

> The amount receivable from Valley Commercial Corp. (an affiliated company of which Mr. Harold Roth is an officer, director, and stockholder) bears interest at 12% a year. Such amount, less the balance of the notes payable to that company, is secured by the assignment to the Company of Valley's equity in certain marketable securities. As of February 15, 1963, the amount of such equity at current market quotations exceeded the net amount receivable.

The government argued that the note should have said

> The amount receivable from Valley Commercial Corp. (an affiliated company of which Mr. Harold Roth is an officer, director, and stockholder), which bears interest at 12% a year, was uncollectible at September 30, 1962, since Valley had loaned approximately the same amount to Mr. Roth, who was unable to pay. Since that date, Mr. Roth and others have pledged as security for the repayment of his obligation to Valley and its obligation to Continental (now $3,900,000 against which Continental's liability to Valley cannot be offset) securities which, as of February 14, 1963, had a market value of $2,978,000. Approximately 80 percent of such securities are stock and convertible debentures of the Company.

Specifically, the government charged that the defendant's note was false and misleading because

- Continental's footnote did not show that Roth obtained the money.
- The nature of the collateral was not disclosed even though 80 percent of it consisted of unregistered securities issued by Continental.
- The net amount of the Valley receivables was improper because the Valley payable that had been offset represented notes discounted with outsiders.
- Reference to the secured position in February did not disclose the significant increase in the Valley receivables at that date.

The defendants, supported by the testimony of eight leaders in the accounting profession, contended that their note was in conformity with GAAP and that such compliance was a conclusive defense against criminal charges of misrepresentation. However, the trial judge rejected this argument and instructed the jury that the "critical test" was whether the balance sheet fairly presented financial position without reference to generally accepted accounting principles. The jury concluded that the balance sheet did not present fairly, and the three defendants were convicted of the criminal charges. The U.S. Court of Appeals refused to reverse the decision and held that

> We do not think the jury was … required to accept the accountants' evaluation whether a given fact was material to overall fair presentation, at least not when the accountant's testimony was not based on specific rules and prohibitions to which they could point, but only on the need for the auditor to make an honest judgment and their conclusion that nothing in the financial statements themselves negated the conclusion that an honest judgment had been made. Such evidence may be highly persuasive, but it is not conclusive, and so the trial judge correctly charged.

The defendants were found guilty. They were fined $17,000 and their licenses to practice as CPAs were revoked.

---

[13] *United States* v. *Simon* [425 F 2d 796 (2d Cir. 1969)].

As a result of this case, a SAS was issued on the meaning of "present fairly." A major conclusion of this SAS was that the auditor's judgment on fairness should be applied within the framework of GAAP. In addition, a SAS was published on the auditor's responsibilities for related party transactions. These SASs are discussed in later chapters.

SECURITIES EXCHANGE ACT OF 1934

Congress passed this Act to regulate the public trading of securities. The 1934 Act requires companies included under the Act to (1) file a registration statement when the securities are publicly traded on a national exchange or over the counter for the first time and (2) keep the registration statement current through the filing of annual reports, quarterly reports, and other information with the SEC. Certain financial information, including the financial statements, must be audited by independent public accountants. Because of the recurring reporting requirements with the SEC, the Act is often referred to as the Continuous Disclosure Act. The principal liability provisions of the 1934 Act are set forth in Sections 18, 10, and 32.

Section 18 Liability

Under Section 18(a)

> Any person who shall make or cause to be made any statement in any application, report, or document filed pursuant to this title … which … was made false or misleading with respect to any material fact, shall be liable to any person (not knowing that such statement was false or misleading) who, in reliance upon such statement, shall have purchased or sold a security at a price which was affected by such statement, for damages caused by such reliance, unless the person sued shall prove that he acted in good faith and had no knowledge that such statement was false or misleading.

Section 18 liability is relatively narrow in scope because it relates only to a false or misleading statement in documents "filed" with the SEC under the Act.

Section 10 Liability

Section 10(b) provides that

> It shall be unlawful for any person, directly or indirectly, by the use of any means or instrumentality of interstate commerce or of the mails, or of any facility of any national securities exchange to use or employ, in connection with the purchase or sale of any security registered on a national securities exchange or any security not so registered, any manipulative or deceptive device or contrivance in contravention of such rules and regulations as the Commission may prescribe as necessary or appropriate in the public interest or for the protection of investors.

Under this section, the SEC promulgated Rule 10b-5, which states that it is unlawful for any person, directly or indirectly, to

- Employ any device, scheme, or artifice to *defraud.*
- Make *any untrue statement* of a material fact or *omit* to state a material fact necessary to make the statements made, in the light of the circumstances under which they were made, not misleading.

- Engage in any act, practice, or course of business that operates, or would operate, as a *fraud* or *deceit* on any person in connection with the purchase or sale of any security.

Section 10(b) and Rule 10b-5 are often referred to as the antifraud provisions of the 1934 Act. Section 10 is broad in scope because it applies to both the public and private trading of securities.

Section 32 Liability

Section 32(a) establishes criminal liability for "willfully" and "knowingly" making false or misleading statements in reports filed under the 1934 Act. This section also provides for criminal penalties for violating the antifraud provisions of Section 10(b) consisting of fines of not more than $100,000 or imprisonment for not more than five years, or both.

Bringing Suit Under the 1934 Act

There are similarities and differences in the effects of Sections 10 and 18 on the parties involved. Under both sections, the plaintiff (1) may be any person buying or selling the securities, (2) must prove the existence of a material false or misleading statement, and (3) must prove reliance on such statement and damage resulting from such reliance. However, the responsibility of the plaintiff differs under the two sections in terms of proof of auditor fraud. Under Section 18, the plaintiff does not have to prove that the auditor acted fraudulently, but in a Section 10, Rule 10b-5 action, such proof is required.

The defendant in a Section 18 suit must prove that he or she (1) acted in good faith and (2) had no knowledge of the false or misleading statement. This means that the minimum basis for liability is gross negligence. Accordingly, the auditor's position under Section 18 is the same as under the common law doctrine of *Ultramares* in which he or she may also be held liable to third parties for gross negligence. An injured plaintiff in a Section 18 action is allowed to recover "out-of-pocket" losses, which are determined by the difference between the contract price and the real or actual value on the transaction date. The latter is generally established by the market price when the misrepresentation or omission occurred.

Differences Between the 1933 and 1934 Acts

The securities acts apply to different situations. The 1933 Act applies to the initial distribution of securities (capital stock and bonds) to the public by the issuing corporation, whereas the 1934 Act applies to the initial sale and trading of securities for national security markets. Differences between Section 11 of the 1933 Act and Sections 10 and 18 of the 1934 Act exist as to (1) the plaintiff, (2) proof of reliance on the false or misleading financial statements, and (3) the auditor's liability for ordinary negligence. These differences are summarized in Figure 4-2. Many more cases have been brought against auditors under the 1934 Act than the 1933 Act because the 1934 Act applies to annual filings as well as certain registration statements.

Cases Brought under the 1934 Act

Lawsuits against auditors under the 1934 Act are usually based on Section 10(b) and Rule 10b-5. During the decade of the mid-1960s to the mid-1970s, plaintiffs

Figure 4-2 ■ Summary of Key Differences in Key Sections of the 1933 and 1934 Acts

Item	1933 Act	1934 Act
Plaintiff	Any person acquiring the security	Either the buyer or the seller of the security
Plaintiff must prove reliance	No	Yes
Defendant liability for ordinary negligence	Yes	No

were able to obtain a number of judgments against CPA firms for ordinary negligence under these provisions. A 1976 decision by the U.S. Supreme Court in *Ernst & Ernst* (now Ernst & Young) v. *Hochfelder* marked the end of the accountant's liability for ordinary negligence under Section 10 of the 1934 Act. This landmark case is explained next.

Ernst & Ernst v. *Hochfelder* (1976)
civil liability for negligence under Rule 10b-5 of 1934 Act[14]

The plaintiffs (Hochfelder) were investors in an escrow account allegedly kept by the president (Lester K. Nay) of First Securities Co., a small brokerage firm, audited by the defendant CPA firm (now Ernst & Young).

The escrow account, in which a high rate of return was promised, was a ruse perpetrated by Nay. To prevent detection, all investors were instructed to make their checks payable to Nay and to mail them directly to him at First Securities. Within the brokerage house, Nay imposed a "mail rule" that such mail was to be opened only by himself. The escrow account was not recorded on First Securities' books. The fraud was uncovered in Nay's suicide note.

Plaintiffs sued Ernst for damages under Rule 10b-5 for aiding and abetting the embezzlement. They based their claim entirely on the premise that the accountants were negligent in their audit because they had not challenged or investigated the "mail rule."

Following conflicting lower court decisions, the U.S. Supreme Court ruled in favor of the defendants, saying:

> When a statute speaks so specifically in terms of manipulation and deception, and of implementing devices and contrivances—the commonly understood terminology of intentional wrongdoing—and when its history reflects no more expansive intent, we are quite unwilling to extend the scope of the statute to negligent conduct.

The Supreme Court failed to rule on whether reckless behavior is sufficient for liability under Rule 10b-5.

Based on this decision, an auditor is no longer liable to third parties under Section 10(b) and Rule 10b-5 of the 1934 Act for ordinary negligence. That is, the

---

[14] *Ernst & Ernst* v. *Hochfelder*, 425 US 185, 96 S Ct 1375, 47 L Ed 2nd 688 (1976).

auditor has no liability in the absence of any intent to deceive or defraud (legally called **scienter**).[15]

The following case dealt with several legal issues and elaborated on the requisite scienter under Rule 10b-5.

The Fund of Funds Limited v. *Arthur Andersen & Co.* (1982)
civil liability under 1934 Act, common law fraud, and breach of contract[16]

The Fund of Funds Limited (FOF), a mutual investment fund, entered into an oral contract as part of a diversification program to purchase oil and gas properties from King Resources Corporation (KRC) at prices no less favorable than the seller received from other customers.

Arthur Andersen & Co. (AA) was the auditor for both companies, and the same key audit personnel participated in both engagements. In its engagement letter to FOF, AA made the specific representation that any irregularities discovered by the accounting firm would be revealed to the client. In auditing KRC, AA discovered that FOF was being billed at prices that were significantly higher than other customers. AA, however, failed to inform FOF because it did not wish to breach the rule of confidential client information. Plaintiff claimed that AA was required to disclose the overcharge or to resign at least one of the two accounts.

As an open-ended mutual fund, FOF was required to value its investment portfolio, which included its investments in natural resources, on a daily basis. The daily share value was used for redeeming investor shares. In its December 31, 1969, financial statements, FOF booked a significant upward revaluation in certain natural resource interests. Their evaluation was based in part on nonarm's length non-bona fide sales of small portions of the same interests by KRC. These sales did not satisfy the guidelines established by AA for issuing an unqualified opinion on KRC's financial, but such an opinion was nevertheless issued. AA claimed that their report on KRC was not the cause of FOF's revaluation and that they had no knowledge of the non-bona fide sales prior to issuing their report.

The jury found AA liable for aiding and abetting violations of securities laws (Rule 10b-5) and common law fraud because of their failure to disclose their knowledge of KRC's wrongdoings to FOF. In addition, the jury found the accounting firm guilty of breach of contract because they did not comply with the specific representation in their engagement letter. Plaintiff was awarded damages of $81 million. The judge in the case subsequently reduced the damages to an undisclosed amount.

The decision also included a finding on reckless behavior. The jury found that the requisite of scienter was met through the accountant's recklessness. It said:

■ A reckless misrepresentation, or reckless omission to state information necessary to make that which is stated not misleading, is one that disregards the truth or falsity of the information disclosed in light of a known danger or patently obvious danger.

---

[15] Scienter may be established by proof of either (1) actual knowledge of the falsity of the representation of (2) a reckless disregard for the truth or falsity of the representation.

[16] *Fund of Funds* v. *Arthur Andersen & Co.,* 545F Supp. 1314 (S.D.N.Y. 1982).

- The accountants acted with requisite scienter in disregarding known and obvious risks to FOF in issuing its unqualified opinion.
- We also find support for a finding of gross recklessness as the auditors conspicuously failed to test the arm's length nature of the transactions.

Following is an example of a criminal case brought under Section 32 of the 1934 Act.

United States v. Natelli (1975) criminal liability[17]

In this case, commonly known as the *National Student Marketing Corporation* case, two auditors were convicted of criminal liability for failing to properly disclose the writeoff of uncollectible accounts. In the financial statements of the current year (1969), uncollectible accounts pertaining to 1968 regular sales on advertising contracts, which had only been verified by telephone, were reported in part as a retroactive adjustment against sales acquired by pooling in 1968. The accompanying footnote failed to state that regular sales for 1968 were overstated 20 percent and that actual net earnings were only 46 percent of reported earnings. The court concluded that

- The treatment of the retroactive adjustment was done intentionally to conceal errors in the 1968 statements.
- A professional cannot escape criminal liability on a plea of ignorance when they have shut their eyes to what was plainly to be seen.

Aiding-and-Abetting

Many of the growing body of abusive securities suits mentioned at the beginning of this chapter have been brought under Section 10(b) of the 1934 Act. Accountants and other professionals such as attorneys and underwriters have frequently been cited under this section for aiding-and-abetting securities fraud. **Aiding-and-abetting** means an indirect involvement or tangential role in purported wrongdoing. In a 1994 decision in the case of *Central Bank of Denver N.A.* v. *First Interstate Bank of Denver N.A.*, the U.S. Supreme Court ruled that professionals cannot be sued under that section for mere aiding-and-abetting.[18] The decision, which directly involved private suits, did not clarify whether the SEC can continue to bring aiding-and-abetting actions under Section 10(b).

PRIVATE SECURITIES LITIGATION REFORM ACT OF 1995

Auditor Knowledge 5

- Know how the Private Securities Litigation Reform Act of 1995 affects the auditor's liability under statutory law.

Congress passed the Private Securities Litigation Reform Act of 1995 to reduce frivolous litigation risk for auditors, publicly traded companies, and those parties affiliated with security issuers, such as officers, directors, and other professional advisors (e.g., underwriters and lawyers). The Reform Act substantially revised the Securities Act of 1933 and the Securities Exchange Act of 1934. Specific provisions of the Act are discussed below.

---

[17] *United States* v. *Natelli,* 527 F.2d 311 (1975).
[18] "Justices Deal Investors a Blow in Certain Suits," *Wall Street Journal,* April 20, 1994, p. A3.

Proportionate Liability

The Reform Act instituted a system of **proportionate liability** under which defendants who are not found to have "knowingly committed a violation" of securities laws are liable based on the defendant's percentage of responsibility. This is intended to reduce the coercive pressure for innocent parties to settle meritless claims out of court rather than risk exposing themselves to liability for a grossly disproportionate share of the damages in a case. Defendants who "knowingly committed a violation" continue to be jointly and severally liable for all damages that may be assessed.

If a defendant does not knowingly commit a violation of the securities acts, the Reform Act also places a cap on the proportionate share of damages that cannot be collected from other defendants. If another defendant's share cannot be collected from that defendant, or from jointly and severally liable defendants, each proportionately liable defendant is then liable for a proportionate share of the uncollectible amount, only up to an amount equal to an additional 50 percent of such defendant's initial share.

Cap on Actual Damages

The Reform Act also caps the actual damages under the securities acts based on an investor purchase price of a security and the mean trading price during a 90-day period following the date on which information is released that corrects the misstatement or omission in the financial statements. For example, assume that an investor purchases a security at $20 per share. On the day of the release of the information that corrects the misstatement, the closing price for the security falls to $10. During the following 90-day period, the security returns to a closing price of $15 per share with an average for the period of $13 per share. Actual damages would be capped at $7 per share.

Responsibility to Report Illegal Acts

The Reform Act imposed new reporting requirements on auditors who detect or otherwise become aware of illegal acts by issuers of securities. This was discussed in Chapter 2 but bears repeating here. If an auditor concludes that an illegal act has a direct and material effect on the financial statements, senior management has not taken appropriate action, and the failure warrants a departure from a standard report or a resignation from the engagement, the auditor should report these conclusions directly to the board of directors. The board should then notify the SEC within one day. If the board does not file a timely report with the SEC, the auditor should make a report to the SEC. The Reform Act explicitly states that the auditor will not be held liable in a private action for any finding, conclusions, or statements made in such reports.

Other Changes Provided by the Reform Act

The Reform Act also provides other relief that was sought by the accounting profession. The Act:

■ Requires plaintiffs to pay defendants reasonable attorney's fees and expenses directly related to litigation found by the court to be frivolous and unwarranted.

- Provides for a stay of discovery during the period a motion to dismiss is pending, thereby reducing a cost that often forces innocent parties to settle frivolous class action suits.

- Limits punitive damages by eliminating securities fraud as a basis for bringing action under the Racketeer Influenced and Corrupt Organization Act, which provides for treble damages (discussed later in this chapter).

- Places limits on the rights of third parties to sue by limiting the number of times a plaintiff can be a lead plaintiff to no more than five class actions in any three-year period and by imposing stricter pleading standards to be met by plaintiffs.

- Changes the manner in which the court appoints lead plaintiffs in class actions to favor institutional investors likely to have the largest financial stake in the relief sought and to mitigate the "race to the courthouse by professional plaintiffs" who hold minimal ownership interests.

These federal legislative reforms have provided the profession with significant relief under statutory law.

SARBANES-OXLEY ACT OF 2002

Auditor Knowledge 6

■ Understand how the auditing environment has changed because of the Sarbanes-Oxley Act of 2002.

The Sarbanes-Oxley Act of 2002 had a number of provisions that influenced the auditing environment. For auditors the Sarbanes-Oxley Act of 2002 made it illegal to provide certain nonattest services to clients and changed the regulation of the auditing profession. It also changed the audit environment by imposing increased penalties for management of public companies who engage in fraudulent financial reporting. The changes for auditor's and for management are discussed below.

Changes for Auditors

The Sarbanes-Oxley Act of 2002 makes it "unlawful" to perform audit services for a public company and also perform the following nonattest services for audit clients:

- Bookkeeping or other services related to the accounting records or financial statements of the audit client
- Financial information systems design and implementation
- Appraisal or valuation services, fairness opinions, or contribution-in-kind reports
- Actuarial services
- Internal audit outsourcing services
- Management functions or human resources
- Broker or dealer, investment adviser, or investment banking services
- Legal services and expert services unrelated to the audit
- Any other service that the PCAOB determines, by regulation, is impermissible

The provision of nonattest services was discussed in more detail in Chapter 3.

The Sarbanes-Oxley Act of 2002 also changed the regulatory environment. The Act gave the PCAOB authority to establish auditing standards, quality control standards, and independence standards for auditors of public companies; and to inspect the work of public company auditors. Prior to the Sarbanes-Oxley Act of 2002 the professional auditors were responsible for these functions through the self-regulatory functions of the American Institute of CPAs.

Changes for Management of Public Companies

The Sarbanes-Oxley Act of 2002 strengthened penalties imposed on management of public companies who are found responsible for false and misleading financial statements. Following is an overview of key provisions of the Act that affect managements of public companies.

Section 302 requires a public company's CEO and CFO to prepare a statement to accompany the audit report to certify the "appropriateness of the financial statements and disclosures contained in the periodic report, and that those financial statements and disclosures fairly present, in all material respects, the operations and financial condition of the issuer." It also creates a liability for the CEO and CFO who knowingly and intentionally make false certifications.

Section 303 makes it unlawful for any officer or director of an issuer to take any action to fraudulently influence, coerce, manipulate, or mislead any auditor engaged in the performance of an audit for the purpose of rendering the financial statements materially misleading.

Section 305 requires the CEO and CFO of a company that restates financial statements due to "material noncompliance" with financial reporting requirements to "reimburse the company for any bonus or other incentive-based or equity-based compensation received" during the 12 months following the issuance or filing of the noncompliant document and "any profits realized from the sale of securities of the issuer" during that period. Furthermore, this section of the Act authorizes the federal courts to "grant any equitable relief that may be appropriate or necessary for the benefit of investors" for any action brought by the SEC for violation of the securities laws.

Title VIII of the Act, the *Corporate and Criminal Fraud Accountability Act of 2002:*

- Makes it is a felony to "knowingly" destroy or create documents to "impede, obstruct or influence" any existing or contemplated federal investigation.
- Requires auditors required to maintain "all audit or review work papers" for five years.
- Extends the statute of limitations on securities fraud claims to the earlier of five years from the fraud, or two years after the fraud was discovered.
- Extends "whistleblower protection" to employees of public companies and their auditors that would prohibit the employer from taking certain actions against employees who lawfully disclose private employer information to, among others, parties in a judicial proceeding involving a fraud claim. Whistleblowers are also granted a remedy of special damages and attorney's fees.
- Creates a new crime for securities fraud that has penalties of fines and up to 10 years imprisonment.

Title IX of the Act enhances penalties for white-collar crimes as follows:

- The maximum penalty for mail and wire fraud is increased from 5 to 10 years.

■ Financial Statements filed with the SEC must be certified by the CEO and CFO. The certification must state that the financial statements and disclosures fully comply with provisions of the Securities Exchange Act and that they fairly present, in all material respects, the operations and financial condition of the issuer. Maximum penalties for willful and knowing violations of this section are a fine of not more than $500,000 and/or imprisonment of up to five years.

In addition, the SEC was given authority to seek a court freeze of extraordinary payments to directors, offices, partners, controlling persons, and agents of employees and to prohibit anyone convicted of securities fraud from being an officer or director of any publicly traded company. Finally, Title IX creates a crime for tampering with a record or otherwise impeding any official proceeding and asks the U.S. Sentencing Commission to review sentencing guidelines for securities and accounting fraud.

[LEARNING CHECK

4-6 a. Who may bring suit under the 1933 Securities Act?
     b. What is the basis for such action?

4-7 What are the responsibilities of the plaintiff and the defendant in a 1933 Act suit?

4-8 State the issues and the court's conclusions in the *BarChris* case.

4-9 a. Who may bring suit under the 1934 Securities Exchange Act?
     b. Is the basis for action the same as in a 1933 Act suit? Explain.

4-10 Explain the conditions associated with liability under Rule 10b-5 of the 1934 Act.

4-11 What are the responsibilities of the plaintiff and the defendant in a 1934 Act suit?

4-12 a. What was the basis for the *Hochfelder* case?
     b. What is the significance of the decision in the case?

4-13 a. Indicate the jury's findings in the *Fund of Funds* case.
     b. State the accounting issue and the jury's findings in the *Continental Vending* case.

4-14 a. What is proportionate liability defined by the Private Securities Reform Act of 1995? What finding is important for a defendant to obtain the benefits of proportionate liability?
     b. How does the concept of proportionate liability change the auditor's legal liability under statutory law?

4-15 Identify five other ways in which the Private Securities Reform Act of 1995 will potentially change auditors' legal liability. Explain how each is of potential benefit to the auditor.

4-16 Explain a new responsibility that the Private Securities Litigation Reform Act of 1995 imposed on auditors.

4-17 a. Identify how the Sarbanes-Oxley Act of 2002 changed the audit environment for auditors.
     b. Identify and explain new liabilities for managements of public companies created by the Sarbanes-Oxley Act of 2002.

KEY TERMS

Aiding-and-abetting, p. 163
Blue sky laws, p. 155
Due diligence defense, p. 156
Material fact, p. 155

Misleading financial statement, p. 155
Proportionate liability, p. 164
Scienter, p. 162
Statutory law, p. 155

OTHER CONSIDERATIONS

Although the majority of suits against auditors under statutory law cite violations of the securities laws discussed in the preceding sections, the 1980s and early 1990s saw a groundswell of activity under RICO, another fraud statute.

LIABILITY UNDER RACKETEER INFLUENCED AND CORRUPT ORGANIZATIONS ACT (RICO)

Auditor Knowledge 7

■ Know the auditor's liability under Racketeer Influenced and Corrupt Organization Act.

RICO was originally drafted as part of the 1970 Organized Crime Control Act to curtail the inroads of organized crime into legitimate business. RICO contains civil provisions that permit all private persons victimized by a "pattern of racketeering activity" to sue for treble damages and attorneys' fees. Despite its focus on organized crime, the provisions of RICO have been extended to losses suffered from fraudulent securities offerings and failures of legitimate businesses. CPAs have often been named as codefendants on the theory that their involvement with the issuance of materially false financial statements for a minimum of 2 years out of a 10-year period constitutes a pattern of racketeering activity. The possibility of treble damages and the transfer of plaintiff's attorneys' fees to losing defendants served as powerful incentives for plaintiffs to bring actions against auditors under RICO whenever possible and for auditors to feel coerced to settle out of court.

In 1993 the U.S. Supreme Court heard a case known as *Reves* v. *Ernst & Young.* In this case, which involved investor losses related to a farmers' cooperative that went bankrupt, the Court ruled that RICO "requires some participation in the operation or management of the enterprise itself." It further concluded that the auditor's provision of unqualified audit reports for two consecutive years on the co-op's alleged misleading financial statements did not meet the participation test.

It should be noted, however, that auditors may remain culpable under RICO if a court concludes the auditor's relationship with a client went beyond the traditional role of auditing. In *ESM Government Securities* v. *Alexander Grant & Co.* the management of ESM devised a scheme of fictitious transactions to conceal operating losses from 1977 through 1984. The defendant's partner in charge of the audits beginning with the 1978 audit was advised by management subsequent to the 1978–1979 audits that the Grant audit team had failed to detect the fraud. Faced with potential damage to his career, the partner agreed to forgo disclosure of the fraud to give management one year to make up the losses. Management failed to do so, but the partner continued to cover up the scheme until the company collapsed in 1985. Alexander Grant was reported to have reached out-of-court settlements approaching $50 million.

MINIMIZING THE RISK OF LITIGATION

Auditor Knowledge 8

■ **Understand the pre-cautions a CPA can take to minimize the risk of litigation.**

CPAs are currently practicing in a climate where national public policy is emphasizing protection for the consumer (general public) from substandard work by professionals. An analysis of court cases involving CPAs reveals the following precautions that a CPA may take to minimize the risk of becoming involved in litigation.

■ *Use engagement letters for all professional services.* Such letters provide the basis for the contractual arrangements and minimize the risk of misunderstanding about the services that have been agreed on.

■ *Make a thorough investigation of prospective clients.* The purpose of an investigation is to minimize the likelihood that the CPA will be associated with a client whose management lacks integrity.

■ *Emphasize quality of service rather than growth.* The ability of a firm to properly staff an engagement is vital to the quality of the work that will result. Acceptance of new business that will likely lead to excessive overtime, abnormally heavy workloads, and limited supervision by experienced professionals should be resisted.

■ *Comply fully with professional pronouncements.* Strict adherence to Statements on Auditing Standards is essential. An auditor must be able to justify any material departures from established guidelines.

■ *Recognize the limitations of professional pronouncements.* Professional guidelines are not all-encompassing. In addition, it should be recognized that judges, juries, and regulatory agencies will use subjective tests of reasonableness and fairness in judging the auditor's work. The auditor must use sound professional judgment during the audit and in the issuance of the audit report.

■ *Establish and maintain high standards of quality control.* As suggested in Chapter 1, both the CPA firm and individual auditors have clearly established responsibilities for quality control. Outside peer reviews provide important independent assurance of the quality and the continued effectiveness of prescribed procedures.

■ *Exercise caution in engagements involving clients in financial difficulty.* The impending threat of insolvency or bankruptcy may lead to intentional misrepresentations in the financial statements. Many lawsuits against auditors have resulted from the bankruptcies of companies following the issuance of the auditor's report. The auditor should carefully weigh the sufficiency and competency of the evidence obtained in audits of such companies.

■ *Audit risk alerts.* Periodically, the AICPA staff, in consultation with the Auditing Standards Board, issues audit risk alerts. These audit risk alerts contain important information about economic or regulatory developments in particular industries that may influence the auditor's exercise of professional judgment. Audit risk alerts are helpful in assessing the reasonableness and fairness of financial statements for a client in a particular industry.

[LEARNING CHECK

4-18 a. Contrast the original intent of the Racketeer Influenced and Corrupt Organization Act (RICO) with the courts' interpretations of its provisions.

b. What advantages does a plaintiff have in a RICO suit compared with a suit brought under the federal securities acts?

c. How may accountants be involved in a RICO suit?

4-19 Identify actions the auditor may take to minimize the risk of litigation.

[KEY TERM

RICO, p. 168

[SUMMARY]

Although the proportion of audit failures to all audits is very low, the consequences of even a few large audit failures can be significant for investors, creditors, and other market participants, as well as for auditors. In order to meet their public responsibility auditors must exercise due care and conduct audits that are free of negligence. Figure 4-3 provides a summary of the various laws that address the auditor's liability to clients and third parties.

Figure 4-3 ■ Summary of Auditor's Civil Liability

AUDITOR'S LIABILITY TO CLIENTS			
Law	**Who can sue?**	**For What**	**Key Cases**
Contract Law	A client or the client's subrogee may sue for a breach of contract.	Ordinary negligence	*1136 Tenants* v. *Max Rothenberg & Co.*
Tort Law	A client or the client's subrogee may sue for a wrongful act that injures the client's property, body, or reputation.	Ordinary negligence Gross negligence Fraud	

AUDITOR'S LIABILITY TO THIRD PARTIES WHO RELY ON FINANCIAL STATEMENTS			
Law	**Who can sue?**	**For What**	**Key Cases**
Tort Law: Primary Beneficiaries Doctrine	A primary beneficiary of the audit who is identified to the auditor by name prior to the audit.	Ordinary negligence Gross negligence Fraud	*Ultramares* v. *Touche* *Credit Alliance Corp.* v. *Arthur Andersen & Co.*

(continues)

Figure 4-3 ■ (Continued)

Law	Who can sue?	For What	Key Cases
Auditor's Liability to Third Parties Who Rely on Financial Statements			
Tort Law: Restatements of Torts	A limited group of persons for whose benefit the CPA intends to supply an audit report on financial statements.	Ordinary negligence Gross negligence Fraud	Rusch Factors Inc. v. Levin Bily v. Arthur Young & Co.
Tort Law: Foreseeable Third Parties Doctrine	Persons whom the auditor either knew or should have known would rely on the audit report in making business and investment decisions.	Ordinary negligence Gross negligence Fraud	Rosenblum v. Alder
SEC Act of 1933[a]	Any person who purchased or otherwise acquired a new issue of securities covered by a registration statement that included a material misstatement of fact in the financial statements.	Ordinary negligence Gross negligence Fraud	Escott v. BarChris Construction Corp.
SEC Act of 1934[a]	A purchaser or seller of traded securities that can prove the existence of a material misstatement and can show that reliance on that misstatement caused damages.	Gross negligence Fraud	Ernst & Ernst v. Hochfelder Fund of Funds v. Arthur Andersen & Co.
Racketeer Influenced and Corrupt Organizations Act	Persons who suffered losses from fraudulent securities offerings and failures of legitimate businesses.	Requires participation in the operation or management of the enterprise itself. Auditors may be liable if the auditor's relationship with the client goes beyond the traditional role of auditing.	Reves v. Ernst & Young

[a]The Private Securities Litigation Reform Act of 1995 instituted a system of proportionate liability and a cap on actual damages along with other changes to the federal securities laws.

FOCUS ON AUDITOR KNOWLEDGE

This chapter introduces some basic knowledge about the auditor's legal liability. Figure 4-4 summarizes the key components of auditor knowledge discussed in Chapter 4 and provides page references to where these decisions are discussed in more detail.

Figure 4-4 ■ Summary of Auditor Knowledge Discussed in Chapter 4

Auditor Knowledge	Summary	Chapter References
K1. Know the auditor's legal liability to clients under common law and understand the consequences of important cases under common law.	Under common law auditors may be liable for ordinary negligence associated with either breach of contract or tort actions.	pp.146–147
K2. Know the auditor's legal liability to third parties under common law and understand the consequences of important cases under common law.	Common law varies from state to state. Three important doctrines that address common law to third parties are (1) the primary beneficiaries doctrine, (2) the restatement of torts doctrine, and (3) the foreseeable third parties doctrine. These doctrines explain when an auditor would be liable to third parties for ordinary negligence. Figure 4-1 identifies important cases discussed in the chapter that address liability to third parties under common law.	pp. 147–153
K3. Know the common law defenses available to the auditor.	The primary defense under common law is the due care defense, where the auditor attempts to show that an audit was performed in accordance with GAAS. The auditor's working papers are critical to this defense. At times, the auditor might also be able to use a contributory negligence defense when third parties legally contribute to the cause of the damages.	pp. 153–154
K4. Understand and distinguish the auditor's liability under the securities acts of 1933 and 1934 and understand the consequences of important cases under these acts.	The auditor's liability to financial statement users under the securities acts of 1933 and 1934 are significantly different as summarized in Figure 4-2 and 4-3. Under the 1933 Securities Act auditors are liable for their negligence to persons who purchased or otherwise acquired a new issue of securities covered by a registration statement that included a material misstatement of fact in the financial statements. The 1934 Securities Act governs the trading of securities. Under the 1934 Act the auditor must be found to intend to deceive or defraud or be guilty of gross negligence to be found liable. Today, investors who suffer damages due to material misstatements in financial statements often find it easier to sue auditors under common law than under the 1934 Securities Act. Figure 4-3 identifies important cases related to civil liability under these securities laws. Auditors can also be found criminally liable under the securities laws. Key cases discussed in the chapter related to auditor's criminal liability include *United States* v. *Simon and United States* v. *Natelli*.	pp. 155–163

(continues)

Figure 4-4 ■ (Continued)

Auditor Knowledge	Summary	Chapter References
K5. Know how the Private Securities Litigation Reform Act of 1995 affects the auditor's liability under statutory law.	The two most important reforms under the Private Securities Litigation Reform Act of 1995 include instituting a system of proportionate liability and a cap on damages into the federal securities laws. In addition, the law imposed new reporting requirements on auditors who detect or otherwise become aware of illegal acts that have a material effect on the financial statements by issuers of securities. The law also instituted a number of other reforms that made it difficult to bring frivolous lawsuits against auditors.	pp. 163–165
K6. Understand how the auditing environment has changed because of the Sarbanes-Oxley Act of 2002.	The Sarbanes-Oxley Act of 2002 changed the audit environment for both auditors and management. This section of the chapter discusses both nonattest services that are now unlawful for auditors to perform for audit clients, and the PCAOB's new responsibility for setting auditing standards, quality control standards, and independence standards for auditors of public companies. In addition, the section describes the legal liability of management, particularly the CEO and CFO. Knowing and willful violation of the Sarbanes-Oxley Act of 2002 can result in fines and imprisonment. Finally, improved systems of internal control will improve the audit environment.	pp. 165–167
K7. Know the auditor's liability under the Racketeer Influenced and Corrupt Organization Act.	For a number of years the Racketeer Influenced and Corrupt Organization Act (RICO) was a serious concern for auditor because of the possibility of treble damages and the transfer of plaintiff's attorneys' fees to losing defendants. In 1993 the U.S. Supreme Court found in *Reves* v. *Ernst & Young* that RICO "requires some participation in the operation or management of the enterprise itself." It further concluded that the auditor's provision of unqualified audit reports associated with alleged misleading financial statements did not meet the participation test. However, auditors may remain culpable under RICO if a court concludes the auditor's relationship with a client went beyond the traditional role of auditing.	p. 168
K8. Understand the precautions a CPA can take to minimize the risk of litigation.	Auditors can take a number of steps to minimize litigation including the (1) use of engagement letters for all professional services, (2) making a thorough investigation of prospective clients, (3) emphasizing quality of service rather than firm growth, (4) complying fully with professional pronouncements, (5) recognizing the limitations of professional pronouncements, (6) establishing and maintaining high standards of quality control, and (7) exercising caution in engagements involving clients in financial difficulty.	p. 169

objective questions

objective questions

Objective questions are available for the students at www.wiley.com/college/boynton

comprehensive questions

4-20 **(Common law—constructive fraud, negligence)** Astor Inc. purchased the assets of Bell Corp. A condition of the purchase agreement required Bell to retain a CPA to audit Bell's financial statements. The purpose of the audit was to determine whether the unaudited financial statements furnished to Astor fairly presented Bell's financial position. Bell retained Winston & Co., CPAs, to perform the audit.

While performing the audit, Winston discovered that Bell's bookkeeper had embezzled $500. Winston had some evidence of other embezzlements by the bookkeeper. However, Winston decided that the $500 was immaterial and that the other suspected embezzlements did not require further investigation. Winston did not discuss the matter with Bell's management. Unknown to Winston, the bookkeeper had, in fact, embezzled large sums of cash from Bell. In addition, the accounts receivable were significantly overstated. Winston did not detect the overstatement because of Winston's inadvertent failure to follow its audit program.

Despite the foregoing, Winston issued an unqualified opinion on Bell's financial statements and furnished a copy of the audited financial statements to Astor. Unknown to Winston, Astor required financing to purchase Bell's assets and furnished a copy of Bell's audited financial statements to City Bank to obtain approval of the loan. Based on Bell's audited financial statements, City loaned Astor $600,000.

Astor paid Bell $750,000 to purchase Bell's assets. Within six months, Astor began experiencing financial difficulties resulting from the undiscovered embezzlements and overstated accounts receivable. Astor later defaulted on the City loan.

City has commenced a lawsuit against Winston based on the following causes of action:

- Constructive fraud
- Negligence

Required

In separate paragraphs, discuss whether City is likely to prevail on the causes of action it has raised, setting forth reasons for each conclusion.

AICPA

4-21 **(Common law—negligence, fraud)** Tyler Corp. is insolvent. It has defaulted on the payment of its debts and does not have assets sufficient to satisfy its unsecured creditors. Slade, a supplier of raw materials, is Tyler's largest unsecured creditor and is suing Tyler's auditors, Field & Co., CPAs. Slade had extended $2 million of credit to Tyler based on the strength of Tyler's audited financial statements. Slade's complaint alleges that the auditors were either (1) negligent in failing to discover and disclose fictitious accounts receivable created by management or (2) committed fraud in connection therewith. Field believes that Tyler's financial statements were prepared in accordance with GAAP and, therefore, its opinion was proper. Slade has established that:

- The accounts receivable were overstated by $10 million.
- Total assets were reported as $24 million, of which accounts receivable were $16 million.
- The auditors did not follow their own audit program, which required that confirmation requests be sent to an audit sample representing 80 percent of the total dollar amount of outstanding receivables. Confirmation requests were sent to only 45 percent.
- The responses that were received represented only 20 percent of the total dollar amount of outstanding receivables. This was the poorest response in the history of the firm, the

next lowest being 60 percent. The manager in charge of the engagement concluded that further inquiry was necessary. This recommendation was rejected by the partner in charge.

■ Field had determined that a $300,000 account receivable from Dion Corp. was nonexistent. Tyler's explanation was that Dion had reneged on a purchase contract before any products had been shipped. At Field's request, Tyler made a reversing entry to eliminate this overstatement. However, Field accepted Tyler's explanation as to this and several similar discrepancies without further inquiry.

Slade asserts that Field is liable:

■ As a result of negligence in conducting the audit.

■ As a result of fraud in conducting the audit.

Required

Discuss Slade's assertions and the defenses that might be raised by Field, setting forth reasons for any conclusions stated.

AICPA

4-22   **(Common law—privity defense)** Perfect Products Co. applied for a substantial bank loan from Capitol City Bank. In connection with its application, Perfect engaged William & Co., CPAs, to audit its financial statements. William completed the audit and rendered an unqualified opinion. On the basis of the financial statements and William's opinion, Capitol granted Perfect a loan of $500,000.

Within three months after the loan was granted, Perfect filed for bankruptcy. Capitol promptly brought suit against William for damages, claiming that it had relied to its detriment on misleading financial statements and the unqualified opinion of William.

William's audit workpapers reveal negligence and possible other misconduct in the performance of the audit. Nevertheless, William believes it can defend against liability to Capitol based on the privity defense.

Required

Answer the following, setting forth reasons for any conclusions stated.

a. Explain the privity defense and evaluate its application to William.

b. What exceptions to the privity defense might Capitol argue?

AICPA

4-23   **(Statutory law—1933 Act)** The Dandy Container Corporation engaged the accounting firm of Adams and Adams to audit financial statements to be used in connection with a public offering of securities. The audit was completed, and an unqualified opinion was expressed on the financial statements that were submitted to the Securities and Exchange Commission along with the registration statement. Two hundred thousand shares of Dandy Container common stock were offered to the public at $11 a share. Eight months later, the stock fell to $2 a share when it was disclosed that several large loans to two "paper" corporations owned by one of the directors were worthless. The loans were secured by the stock of the borrowing corporation that was owned by the director. These facts were not disclosed in the financial report. The director involved and the two corporations are insolvent.

1. The Securities Act of 1933 applies to the above-described public offering of securities in interstate commerce.

2. The accounting firm has potential liability to any person who acquired the stock in reliance on the registration statement.

3. An investor who bought shares in Dandy Container would make a prima facie case if he

alleged that the failure to explain the nature of the loans in question constituted a false statement or misleading omission in the financial statements.

4. The accountants could avoid liability if they could show they were neither negligent nor fraudulent.

5. The accountants could avoid or reduce the damages asserted against them if they could establish that the drop in price was due in whole or in part to other causes.

6. The Dandy investors would have to institute suit within one year after discovery of the alleged untrue statements or omissions.

7. The SEC would defend any action brought against the accountants in that the SEC examined and approved the registration statement.

8. Although Adams and Adams knew of the loans, and related collateral, and concluded that they did not need to be disclosed, they can still sustain the claim that they are only proportionally liable for any damages suffered by shareholders because the financial statements are management's responsibility.

Required

Indicate whether each of the above statements is true or false under statutory law. Give the reason(s) for your answer.

AICPA

4-24   **(Statutory law—1934 Act; common law—negligence)** To expand its operations, Dark Corp. raised $4 million by making a private interstate offering of $2 million in common stock and negotiating a $2 million loan from Safe Bank. The common stock was properly offered pursuant to the Securities Act of 1933.

In connection with this financing, Dark engaged Crea & Co., CPAs, to audit Dark's financial statements. Crea knew that the sole purpose for the audit was so that Dark would have audited financial statements to provide to Safe and the purchasers of the common stock. Although Crea conducted the audit in conformity with its audit program, Crea failed to detect material acts of embezzlement committed by Dark's president. Crea did not detect the embezzlement because of its inadvertent failure to exercise due care in designing its audit program for this engagement.

After completing the audit, Crea rendered an unqualified opinion on Dark's financial statements. The purchasers of the common stock relied on the financial statements in deciding to purchase the shares. In addition, Safe approved the loan to Dark based on the audited financial statements.

Within 60 days after the sale of the common stock and the making of the loan by Safe, Dark was involuntarily petitioned into bankruptcy. Because of the president's embezzlement, Dark became insolvent and defaulted on its loan to Safe. Its common stock became virtually worthless. Actions have been commenced against Crea by:

- The purchasers of the common stock who have asserted that Crea is liable for damages under Section 10(b) and Rule 10b-5 of the Securities Exchange Act of 1934.

- Safe, based on Crea's negligence.

Required

In separate paragraphs, discuss the merits of the actions commenced against Crea, indicating the likely outcomes and the reasons therefore.

AICPA (adapted)

4-25   **(Statutory law—1934 Act; common law)** The following information applies to both Parts I and II: James Danforth, CPA, audited the financial statements of the Blair Corporation for the year ended December 31, 20X1. Danforth rendered an unqualified opinion on February 6, 20X2. The financial statements were incorporated into Form 10-K and filed with the Securities and Exchange Commission. Blair's financial statements included as an asset a previously sold certificate of deposit (CD) in the amount of $250,000. Blair had purchased the CD on December 29, 20X1, and sold it on December 30, 20X1, to a third party, who paid Blair that day. Blair did not deliver the CD to the buyer until January 8, 20X1. Blair deliberately recorded the sale as an increase in cash and other revenue, thereby significantly overstating working capital, stockholders' equity, and net income. Danforth confirmed Blair's purchase of the CD with the seller and physically observed the CD on January 5, 20X2.

PART I: Assume that on January 18, 20X2, while auditing other revenue, Danforth discovered that the CD had been sold. Further assume that Danforth agreed that in exchange for an additional audit fee of $20,000, he would render an unqualified opinion on Blair's financial statements (including the previously sold CD).

Required

Answer the following, setting forth reasons for any conclusions stated:

a. The SEC charges Danforth with criminal violations of the Securities Exchange Act of 1934. Will the SEC prevail? Include in your discussion what the SEC must establish in this action.

b. Assume the SEC discovers and makes immediate public disclosure of Blair's action, with the result that no one relies to his detriment on the audit report and financial statements. Under these circumstances, will the SEC prevail in its criminal action against Danforth?

PART II: Assume that Danforth performed his audit in accordance with generally accepted auditing standards (GAAS) and exercised due professional care, but did not discover Blair's sale of the CD. Two weeks after issuing the unqualified opinion, Danforth discovered that the CD had been sold. The day following this discovery, at Blair's request, Danforth delivered a copy of the audit report, along with the financial statements, to a bank that in reliance thereon made a loan to Blair that ultimately proved uncollectible. Danforth did not advise the bank of his discovery.

Required

Answer the following question, setting forth reasons for any conclusions stated: If the bank sues Danforth for the losses it sustains in connection with the loan, will it prevail?

AICPA

---

case

4-26   **(Statutory law; common law)**

PART I: The common stock of Wilson, Inc. is owned by 20 stockholders who live in several states. Wilson's financial statements as of December 31, 20X5, were audited by Doe & Co., CPAs, who rendered an unqualified opinion on the financial statements. In reliance on Wilson's financial statements, which showed net income for 20X5 of $1.5 million, Peters, on April 10, 20X6, purchased 10,000 shares of Wilson stock for $200,000. The purchase was from a shareholder who lived in another state. Wilson's financial statements contained material misstatements. Because Doe did not carefully follow GAAS, it did not discover that the statements failed to reflect unrecorded expenses that reduced Wilson's actual net income to $800,000. After disclosure of the corrected financial statements, Peters sold his shares for $100,000, which was the highest price he could obtain.

Peters has brought an action against Doe under federal securities law and state common law.

Required

Answer the following, setting forth reasons for any conclusions stated:

a. Will Peters prevail on his federal securities law claims?

b. Will Peters prevail on his state common law claims?

PART II: Able Corporation decided to make a public offering of bonds to raise needed capital. On June 30, 20X6, it publicly sold $2.5 million of 12 percent debentures in accordance with the registration requirements of the Securities Act of 1933.

The financial statements filed with the registration statement contained the unqualified opinion of Baker & Co., CPAs. The statements overstated Able's net income and net worth. Through negligence Baker did not detect the overstatements. As a result, the bonds, which originally sold for $1,000 per bond, have dropped in value to $700.

Ira is an investor who purchased $10,000 of the bonds. He promptly brought an action against Baker under the Securities Act of 1933.

Required

Answer the following question, setting forth reasons for any conclusions stated:

Will Ira prevail on his claim under the Securities Act of 1933?

AICPA

professional simulation

Astor Electronics, Inc. is engaged in the business of marketing a wide variety of computer-related products throughout the United States. Its shares are widely traded on a recognized exchange. In connection with the trading of securities, Astor engaged Apple & Co., CPAs, to audit Astor's 20X8, 20X7, and 20X6 financial statements. The audited financial statements were made available on Astor's web site, including Apple's unqualified opinion. On Astor's financial statements, certain inventory items were reported at a cost of $930,000 when, in fact, they had a fair market value of less than $100,000 because of technological obsolescence. Apple accepted the assurances of Astor's controller that cost was the appropriate valuation, despite the fact that Apple was aware of ongoing sales of the products at prices substantially less than cost. All of this was thoroughly documented in Apple's working papers.

Musk purchased 10,000 shares of Astor's common stock after the release of the annual report at a total price of $300,000. In deciding to make the purchase, Musk had reviewed the audited financial statements of Astor and Musk was impressed by Astor's apparent financial strength. By mid 20X9 Astor's management discovered that the audited financial statements reflected the materially overstated valuation of the company's inventory. Astor advised the SEC and its shareholders of the problem and restated its financial statements. Musk, on receiving notice from Astor of the overstated inventory amount, became very upset because the stock value was now substantially less than what it would have been had the financial statements been accurate. After disclosure the stock price fell to $20 per share, and 90 days later the share price had only recovered to $24 per share. The average trading price during that 90-day period was $21 per share. Musk has commenced an action against Apple, alleging that Apple is liable to Musk based on the following causes of action: (1) negligence under common law, and (2) a violation of Section 10(b) and Rule 10b-5 of the Securities Exchange Act of 1934.

The state law applicable to this action follows the Restatement of Tort doctrine with respect to accountants' liability to third parties for negligence or fraud.

Apple has also asserted that the actions should be dismissed because of the absence of any contractual relationship between Apple and Musk, i.e., a lack of privity.

Draft a memo to the working papers with your analysis of the auditor's legal liability under common law. Your memo should explain (1) the standard of care that the courts generally use to evaluate negligence in conducting an audit, and (2) whether Musk would be able to recover damages from the auditor for negligence under the Restatement of Torts doctrine, and (3) whether Musk would be able to recover damages under Section 10(b) and Rule 10b-5 of the Securities Exchange Act of 1934.

To: Audit File

Re: Liability for Negligence Under Common Law and under Section 10(b) and Rule 10b-5 of the Securities Exchange Act of 1934.

From: CPA Candidate

[2] AUDIT PLANNING

HOW MUCH OF WHAT DO I AUDIT?

Assume for a moment that you just found yourself responsible for organizing the audit of the Adolph Coors Company, a public company headquartered in Golden, Colorado. Here is your challenge. For the year ended December 28, 2003, the company produced 32.7 million barrels of beer and other malt beverages in its operations in the United States, Canada, United States Territories, the United Kingdom, and the Republic of Ireland. The company generated $2.4 billion in sales from its American business segment and $1.6 billion in sales from its European business segment. Net earnings amounted to $174 million, and cash flow from operations totaled $544 million. The company had total assets of approximately $4.4 billion, including $621 million in trade receivable and $209 million in inventory, $1.4 billion in properties and production facilities, and $1.2 billion in goodwill and other intangibles. The company had approximately $3.2 billion in total debt and $1.2 billion of total equity.

You can't audit everything. So how much do you need to audit to obtain reasonable assurance that the financial statements, including 38 pages of footnotes, are presented fairly in all material respects? How many locations need to be visited? How much of the inventory do you want to observe? Will you observe inventory at an interim date or at year-end? How should audit time and energies be allocated between accounts receivable, inventory, property and equipment, goodwill and intangibles, accounts payable, notes payable, current and deferred taxes payable, the financial statement disclosures, and the list goes on and on.

Assume that you are assigned to the audit of Adolph Coors Company and you have to make audit decisions about how to allocate limited audit resources. You want to complete a high-quality audit that will allow investors to use your opinion with a very high level of assurance (reasonable assurance) that the financial statements are free of material misstatement. Chapter 5 provides an overview of the process that guides auditors, like you, in making these decisions.

[PREVIEW OF CHAPTER 5]

The purpose of a financial statement audit[1] is to obtain reasonable assurance that the financial statements are free of material misstatements. The auditor cannot economically

---

[1] Auditors of public companies perform a dual-purpose audit to obtain reasonable assurance about (1) the fairness of presentation of amounts and disclosures in the financial statements and (2) the effectiveness of the entity's system of internal control. This chapter focuses primarily on obtaining reasonable assurance about fair presentation in the entity's financial statements.

audit every transaction supporting the financial statements. Hence, the auditor needs to make a variety of decisions that influence the evidence that is obtained and as a result, the evidence that is not obtained. The following diagram provides an overview of the chapter organization and content.

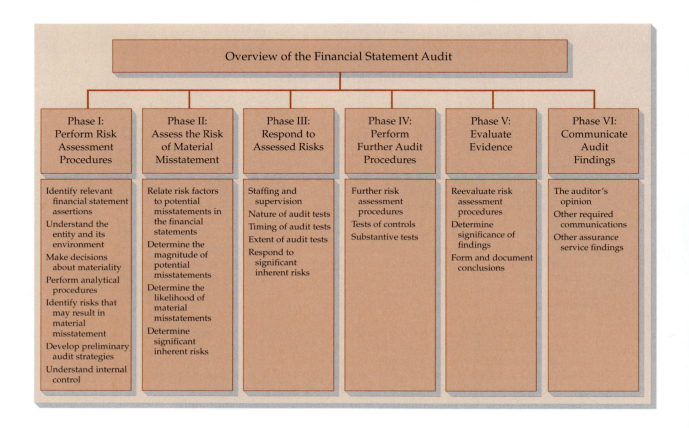

Chapter 5 provides an overview of the audit process. After studying this chapter you should understand the following aspects of an auditor's knowledge base:

K1. Understand the six phases that provide an overview of the audit process.

K2. Understand the auditor's risk assessment procedures.

K3. Understand the four steps in assessing the risk of material misstatement.

K4. Understand how the auditor responds to assessed risks of material misstatement.

K5. Understand the three classifications of further audit procedures.

K6. Understand the auditor's considerations when evaluating audit evidence.

K7. Understand three ways in which the auditor communicates audit findings.

OVERVIEW OF THE AUDIT PROCESS

Auditor Knowledge 1

■ Understand the six phases that provide an overview of the audit process.

The overall objective of a financial statement audit is the expression of an opinion on whether the client's financial statements are presented fairly, in all material respects, in conformity with GAAP. The diagnostic process of making judgments about the accounts likely to contain material misstatement and obtaining reasonable assurance about fair presentation in the financial statements involves six distinct phases.

1. Perform risk assessment procedures.
2. Assess the risk of material misstatement.
3. Respond to assessed risks.
4. Perform further audit procedures.
5. Evaluate audit evidence.
6. Communicate audit findings.

These phases of the audit are depicted in Figure 5-1. The remainder of the chapter provides an overview of each phase of the audit process and explains its importance to the audit process.

PHASE I: PERFORM RISK ASSESSMENT PROCEDURES

Auditor Knowledge 2

■ Understand the auditor's risk assessment procedures.

Chapter 2 pointed out that the auditor has a responsibility to assess the risk of material misstatement and then design audit procedures and tests that respond to the risk of material misstatement. Fully understanding the risk of material misstatement involves seven broad steps:

1. Identify relevant financial statement assertions.
2. Understand the entity and its environment.
3. Make decisions about materiality.
4. Perform analytical procedures.
5. Identify risks that may result in material misstatements, including the risk of fraud.
6. Develop preliminary audit strategies.
7. Understand internal control.

Financial statement assertions assist the auditor in understanding how financial statements might be misstated. This understanding also assists the auditor in understanding relevant aspects of the business. Simultaneously, understanding the business and industry helps the auditor identify important business risks where there is an increased risk of financial statement misstatement. It is also important to understand that an audit is a continuous process of gathering, updating, and analyzing information about the risk of material misstatement in the financial statements. Auditors often cycle through various risk assessment procedures many times as they obtain evidence that better informs decisions previously made. The following discussion provides an overview of the importance of each of these seven broad steps.

Figure 5-1 ■ Overview of the Audit Process

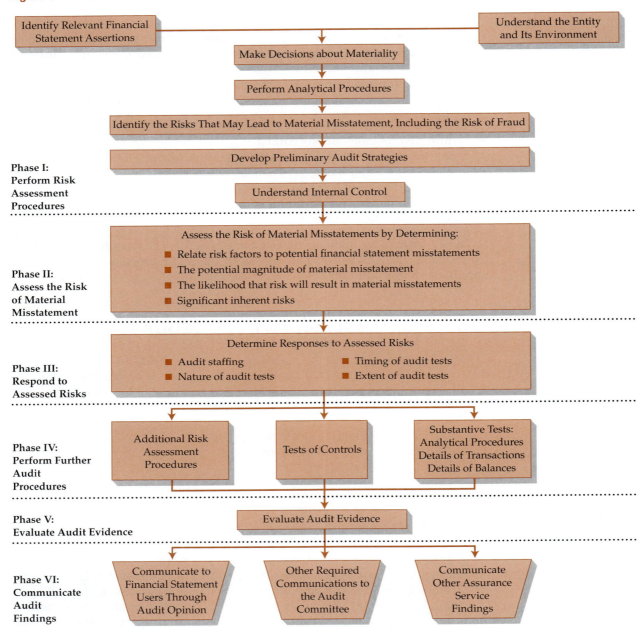

IDENTIFY RELEVANT FINANCIAL STATEMENT ASSERTIONS

The overall objective of a financial statement audit is the expression of an opinion on whether the client's financial statements are presented fairly, in all material respects, in conformity with GAAP. To meet this objective, it is customary in the audit to identify specific audit assertions for each account reported in the financial statements. Assertions are important because they assist the auditor in understanding how financial statements might be misstated and guide auditors in the collection of evidence. Hence, the auditor uses assertions to (1) make decisions about the assessment of risk by considering the types of potential misstatements that may occur, and (2) design audit procedures that are appropriate to the assertion and to the risk assessment. For example, consider the following balance sheet component:

Current Assets:
Inventory (note 4) $40,252,900

In reporting this item in the balance sheet, management makes the following two explicit assertions: (1) the inventory exists and (2) the correct amount of inventory, including considerations of net realizable value, is $40,252,900. Management also makes the following three implicit assertions: (1) all inventory that should be reported has been included, (2) all the reported inventory is owned by the entity, and (3) all appropriate disclosures regarding inventory is included in the notes to the financial statements. If any of these assertions are materially misstated, the financial statements are materially misstated.

Similar assertions underlie all of the asset, liability, equity, revenue, and expense components of financial statements. Accordingly, the Auditing Standards Board in AU 326.03 (SAS 31) *Evidential Matter,* has recognized the following five broad categories of financial statement assertions:

- Existence or occurrence
- Completeness
- Rights and obligations
- Valuation or allocation
- Presentation and disclosure

The following sections explain each of the basic five assertion, followed by examples of each assertion.

Existence or Occurrence

Assertions about **existence or occurrence** deal with whether the assets or liabilities of the entity exist at a given date and whether recorded transactions have occurred during a given period.

Management's assertions about existence extend to assets with physical substance, such as cash and inventories, as well as to accounts without physical substance, such as accounts receivable and accounts payable. In the example cited above, the existence assertion pertains to whether items included in inventory are valid (i.e., they exist). This assertion does not extend to whether $40,252,900 is the correct amount for these items. The latter relates to the valuation or allocation assertion, as explained later.

Under the existence or occurrence assertion, management also asserts that the revenues and expenses shown in the income statement, and cash flows shown on the statement of cash flows, are the results of transactions and events that occurred during the reporting period. Again, this assertion extends only to whether transactions and events occurred, not to whether the amounts reported are correct. A misrepresentation of the existence and occurrence assertion would result if fictitious transactions associated with the costs of sales are reported in the financial statements.

The auditor's concern about this category of assertions relates primarily to the overstatement of financial statement components through the inclusion of items that do not exist or the effects of transactions that did not occur.

Completeness

Assertions about **completeness** deal with whether all transactions and accounts that should be presented in the financial statements are indeed included.

For each financial statement account, management implicitly asserts that all related transactions and events have been included. For example, management asserts that the inventory balance of $40,252,900 includes all inventories that are owned by the company. A misrepresentation of the completeness assertion for inventory would result if the effects of some inventory purchases, manufacturing costs, or provision for obsolete inventory were omitted.

The auditor's concern about the completeness assertion relates primarily to the possible understatement of financial statement components through the omission of items that exist, or cutoff problems that result in inappropriately recording transactions in the wrong accounting period. If omissions are identified, the issue of the correct dollar amounts at which they should be included relates to the valuation or allocation assertion.

The completeness assertion is particularly important in determining whether an entity is auditable. If the auditor concludes that there is not sufficient evidence to determine that all transactions have been recorded, frequently the auditor must disclaim opinion on the financial statements. Once the auditor has determined that all transactions for a particular transaction class have been recorded, he or she can then proceed to audit the remaining assertions.

Rights and Obligations

Assertions about **rights and obligations** deal with whether assets are the rights of the entity and liabilities are the obligations of the entity at a given date.

The rights and obligations assertion is unique because it deals only with assets and liabilities, and pertains only to the balance sheet, while each of the other assertions pertains to all of the financial statements. This assertion normally refers to ownership rights and legal obligations. For example, management implicitly asserts that it owns its cash, receivables, inventory, and other assets reported in the balance sheet, and that accounts payable and other liabilities are the legal obligations of the reporting entity. In the case of inventory an entity asserts that it owns the inventory, that it has not recorded consignment inventory as if it was its own, and that any obligations such as pledging inventory as collateral for a loan have been disclosed.

Valuation or Allocation

Assertions about **valuation or allocation** deal with whether asset, liability, revenue, and expense components have been included in the financial statement at the appropriate amounts.

The reporting of a financial statement component at an appropriate amount means that the amount (1) has been determined to be in conformity with GAAP and (2) is clerically and mathematically accurate.

Determining whether amounts are in conformity with GAAP addresses the proper measurement of assets, liabilities, revenues, and expenses, which includes all of the following:

- Proper application of valuation principles such as cost, net realizable value, market value, and present value
- Proper application of the matching principle
- The reasonableness of management's accounting estimates
- Consistency in the application of accounting principles

Thus, for example, inventory would be misstated if an inventory valuation method was improperly applied, or if current inventories were not fairly presented at their net realizable value. Accounting estimates such as the estimation of net realizable value of inventory, should be reasonable and the estimation process should be consistently followed from period to period. Finally, the entity's accounting principles should be consistently applied across periods, except when a change is justified.

Clerical accuracy refers to such matters as accuracy in entering details on source documents, in recording journal entries, in posting to ledgers, and in maintaining agreement between control accounts and subsidiary ledgers. Mathematical accuracy refers to such matters as determining arithmetically correct totals for invoices, journals, and account balances, as well as to the correctness of computations for such items as accruals and depreciation. Continuing our previous inventory receivable illustration, a misstatement in the valuation or allocation assertion would result from clerical errors in attaching values to individual inventory items, or errors in determining the cost of manufactured inventory.

Presentation and Disclosure

Assertions about **presentation and disclosure** deal with whether particular components of the financial statements are properly classified, described, and disclosed.

In the financial statements, management implicitly asserts that the components are properly presented and that accompanying disclosures are adequate.

---

valuation is not existence

Auditors disclaimed an opinion on a client's financial statements citing the following reason:

> Additions to fixed assets were found to include principally warehouse improvements. … Unfortunately, complete detailed cost records were not kept and no exact determination could be made as to the actual cost of said improvements.

In reality there were no warehouse improvements. The courts concluded that the disclaimer was misleading because it referred only to the valuation assertion and not to the existence assertion. Thus, the auditors were found guilty of negligence in doing the audit.

Source: Rhode Island Hospital Trust National Bank v. Swartz, Bresenhoff, Yavner & Jacobs, 482 F. 2nd 1000 (4th Cir. 1973).

Presentation and disclosure often include the following aspects, which are illustrated in the context of inventory.

- **Occurrence and Rights and Obligations.** Disclosed events and transactions have occurred and pertain to the entity. For example, disclosed information about inventory is factual.
- **Completeness.** All disclosures that should have been included in the financial statements have been included. For example, all disclosures regarding inventory are disclosed.
- **Classifications and Understandability.** Inventory is properly classified as raw materials, work-in-process, and finished goods. Financial information is appropriately presented and clearly expressed.[2]
- **Accuracy and Valuation.** Financial and other information is disclosed accurately and at appropriate amounts. For example, disclosed information about the value of raw material, work-in-progress, finished goods, or LIFO reserves is accurate and at appropriate amounts.

The five basic financial statement assertions are important because they provide a roadmap to the process of collecting evidence about fair presentation in the financial statements. Financial statement assertions allow the auditor to divide and conquer audit challenges by focusing on individual assertions in the financial statements. The auditor needs to collect evidence to evaluate management's assertions for each material account balance and transaction class. Different assertions require different evidence. Chapter 6 explains how the auditor develops specific audit objectives to guide the collection of audit evidence for these assertions. When the auditor has sufficient, competent evidence for each assertion in a material account balance or transaction class, he or she has completed that portion of the audit and moves on to the next task.

UNDERSTAND THE ENTITY AND ITS ENVIRONMENT

In order to render an opinion about whether an entity's financial statements are presented fairly in accordance with GAAP, an auditor must understand the underlying economic substance of the entity's business and its environment. Hence, it is important for the audit team to understand the entity's competitive environment in which it sells products or services, the entity's cost structure, its investments in productive capacity, and its decisions about financing investments through the use of debt, leases, or equity.

Generally accepted auditing standards[3] require that an auditor obtain an understanding of the audit entity and its environment. The auditor should obtain an understanding of:

1. An entity's industry, regulatory environment, and other external factors.
2. The nature of the entity, including the entity's selection and application of accounting policies.

---

[2] FASB Concept Statement No. 2, *Qualitative Characteristics of Accounting Information,* defines understandability as "the quality of information that allows users to perceive its significance."

[3] The following discussion of understanding an entity and its environment is based on an *Auditing Standards Board Exposure Draft* dated December 2, 2002. A similar requirement was adopted by the International Auditing and Assurance Standards Board on October 31, 2003.

3. Objectives, strategies, and related business risks that may result in material misstatements.
4. Management and review of the entity's financial performance.

The auditor uses this information and knowledge to (a) develop expectations about the financial statements, and (b) assess the risk of material misstatement.

Industry, Regulatory Environment, and Other External Factors

Understanding an **entity's industry, regulatory environment and other external factors** includes obtaining knowledge about the entity's industry condition, such as the competitive environment, supplier and customer relationships, and technological developments; the regulatory environment including relevant accounting pronouncements, and the legal and political environment, and factors such as general economic conditions. For example, assume that an audit client has lost technological advantage to competitors who have introduced products that make the client's products obsolete. An auditor might use this knowledge in audit planning to identify an increased risk that inventory might not be stated at the lower of cost or market, or that the entity might have to make concessions to customers who currently hold the product but cannot sell the product to the end consumer. The latter might influence the need to provide for sales allowances or for doubtful accounts if customers are unable to sell inventory to the end consumer. Both represent problems associated with the valuation and allocation assertion when valuing assets on the balance sheet.

The Nature of the Entity, Including Its Selection and Applications of Accounting Policies

Generally accepted auditing standards describe the **nature of the entity** as "the entity's operations, its ownership, the types of investments that it is making and plans to make, and the way the entity is structured and how it is financed." For example, understanding the high fixed cost nature a hotel chain's operations makes auditing the utilization of capacity a critical aspect of the audit. Alternatively, if an auditor finds that the entity uses special purpose entities (SPEs) in financing investments, there is an increased risk of material misstatement associated with whether the SPEs should be consolidated (completeness assertion). Furthermore, if the client is a construction company with long-term construction contracts that require use of the percentage of completion method, the auditor faces an increased risk associated with revenue recognition (existence and occurrence assertion) or with the value of various receivables and payables on the balance sheet (valuation and allocation assertion).

The auditor will usually understand how the entity creates value. This would usually include understanding the entity's products and services, customers, its supply chain and manufacturing processes, the importance of innovation and branding, and the entity's cost structure. For example, some manufacturers are only successful if a certain percentage of revenue comes from new products. If the revenues from new products decline, the auditor might also expect gross margins to decline as well. This step assists the auditor in developing an expectation regarding financial statement amounts and disclosures. Further, if reported amounts and disclosures are inconsistent with the auditor's expectations, then the risk of misstatement in the financial statements is increased.

In addition, the auditor should understand the **entity's selection and application of accounting policies.** The selection and application of accounting policy is a critical aspect of management's discretion in financial reporting. This may include, for example, decisions about whether to consolidate special purpose entities or decisions about the application of revenue recognition principles. The auditor should pay particular attention to accounting for significant and unusual transactions or the effect of significant accounting policies in controversial or emerging areas where there is a lack of authorative guidance or consensus.

Objectives, Strategies, and Related Business Risks That May Result in Material Misstatements

Objectives, strategies, and business risks may be defined as follows:[4]

- An **entity's objectives** are the overall plans for the entity as defined by those charged with governance and management
- **Strategies** are the operational approaches by which management intends to achieve its objectives
- **Business risks** result from significant conditions, events, circumstances, or actions, that could adversely affect the entity's ability to achieve its objectives and execute its strategies.

Understanding an entity's objectives, strategies, and business risks are important because the risk of material misstatement is often associated with an entity's business risk. Following are several examples of how an entity's business risks may be associated with the risk of material misstatement in the financial statements.

- If an entity is unable to accomplish a strategy associated with obtaining a significant percent of revenues from new products (such as obtaining FDA approval for new drugs developed by research and development), there may be an increased risk associated with revenue recognition (the existence and occurrence assertion) or with the impairment of development costs that may have been capitalized (valuation and allocation assertion).
- If an entity is planning to go private and to repurchase a significant portion of equity from existing owners, management may have an incentive to understate earnings. In this case the auditor might be concerned that all sales are recorded (the completeness or revenues) or that all recorded expenses are appropriate (the occurrence of expenses).

Management and Review of the Entity's Financial Performance

The auditor should also obtain an understanding of the process of managing and reviewing financial results. Management often uses internal measures to obtain information about progress toward meeting the entity's objectives. Internally gen-

---

[4] The following definitions are based on an *Auditing Standards Board Exposure Draft* dated December 2, 2002, and subsequent drafts discussed by the ASB. The International Auditing and Assurance Standards Board adopted a similar requirement on October 31, 2003.

erated information used by management may include financial or nonfinancial performance indicators, budgets, variance analysis, or other reports. Such measures may highlight unexpected results or trends requiring management's inquiry of others. A deviation in performance measures from expected results (based on the current internal and external environment) may enable management to detect material misstatements and correct them on a timely basis. Such deviations may also alert auditors to the risk of material misstatement.

Earnings management is a significant concern for auditors. Earnings management may range from appropriate activities such as cutting back expenses during times of reduced cash flows, to inappropriate activities such as misusing accounting for revenue recognition (the existence and occurrence assertion) to report sales and earnings that meet or exceed targets. The pressure to engage in inappropriate earnings management may be increased when the client uses performance-based bonuses or incentive compensation packages based on sales or earnings.

MAKE DECISIONS ABOUT MATERIALITY

An auditor's unqualified opinion states that the financial statements present fairly, in all material respects, the company's financial position, results of operations, and cash flows in accordance with GAAP. The Financial Accounting Standards Board's Concept Statement No. 2 defines **materiality** as "the magnitude of an omission or misstatement of accounting information, that in light of surrounding circumstances, makes it probable that the judgment of a reasonable person relying on the information would have been changed or influenced by the omission or misstatement." The concept recognizes that some accounting issues are important for fair presentation and some are not based on the auditor's understanding of financial statement users.

How does the concept of materiality influence the audit process? First, the auditor makes a judgment about materiality while planning the engagement in order to make important decisions about the scope of the audit. The auditor need not plan an audit to find omissions or misstatements that either individually, or in aggregate, are immaterial. It takes more evidence to obtain reasonable assurance that any misstatement in recorded inventory, for example, does not exceed $500,000 than it does to be assured that the misstatement does not exceed $1 million.

Second, the concept of materiality guides the auditor when evaluating audit findings. Once auditors collect audit evidence, they must assess the significance of audit findings. When sampling is used, auditors must project known misstatements on the population as a whole. These projected misstatements must then be evaluated to determine whether, in the auditor's judgment, they would influence the decisions of a reasonable financial statement user.

Chapter 8 discusses materiality judgments in more detail and provides examples of how auditors make materiality decisions. The materiality decision is a key element of the audit as it guides the auditor in a variety of subsequent decisions about what is important or unimportant in forming an opinion on the financial statements.

PERFORM ANALYTICAL PROCEDURES

Analytical procedures are evaluations of financial information made by a study of plausible relationships among both financial and nonfinancial data. Generally accepted auditing standards require the analytical procedures to be preformed as part of audit planning because they are effective at identifying accounts that may contain financial statement misstatements. Analytical procedures often involve comparing the relationship between unaudited financial data from the current year with similar audited data from the prior year, or with industry statistics. The auditor might also compare unaudited information with budgets or forecasts or with relevant nonfinancial information.

For example, the auditor might calculate accounts receivable turn days for a client. If an entity has a history of collecting receivables approximately every 35 days, and receivable turn days for the first four quarters are calculated at 33, 35, 34, and 46 respectively, this is preliminary evidence that the entity might have revenue recognition problems (existence and occurrence assertion) and that revenues might be overstated in the fourth quarter. Alternatively, if gross margins increase significantly, accompanied by an increase in inventory turn days, this is an indication that costs that should have been included in cost of sales might have been capitalized and included in inventory balances (valuation assertion).

IDENTIFY THE RISKS THAT MAY LEAD TO MATERIAL MISSTATEMENT, INCLUDING THE RISK OF FRAUD

The standard audit report explains that the audit is designed to obtain reasonable—not absolute—assurance that the financial statements are free of material misstatement. Since the audit does not guarantee that the financial statements are free of material misstatement, some degree of risk exists that the financial statements may contain misstatements that go undetected by the auditor. Statement on Auditing Standards AU 312.02 (SAS 47), *Audit Risk and Materiality in Conducting the Audit*, defines **audit risk** as "the risk that the auditor may unknowingly fail to appropriately modify his or her opinion on the financial statements that contain a material misstatement."

If the auditor interprets reasonable assurance as a 98 percent level of certainty that the financial statements are free of material misstatement, then audit risk is 2 percent. Auditors cannot, within reasonable cost, examine all possible evidence regarding every assertion for every account balance and transaction class. The audit risk model guides auditors making decisions about the collection of audit evidence, so that the auditor achieves the desired level of reasonable assurance.

Audit Risk Model

A common audit tool for considering the risk of material misstatement is the audit risk model. Auditors describe audit risk as being a function of the following: inherent risk, control risk, and detection risk as depicted in Figure 5-2. The following discussion briefly explains these key factors associated with the audit risk model.

Inherent Risk

Generally accepted auditing standards (AU 312) defines **inherent risk** as "the susceptibility of an assertion to a material misstatement, assuming that there are no related internal controls." Inherent risk is a client situation that the auditor tries to understand by obtaining evidence through risk assessment procedures. The assessment of inherent risk involves evaluating evidence about the factors that

Figure 5-2 ■ Summary of Audit Risk Components

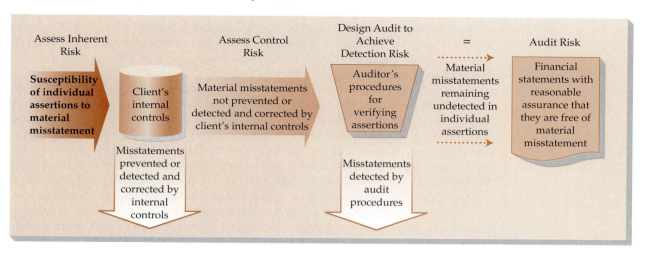

may cause misstatements in an assertion. For example, valuations requiring complex calculations are more likely to be misstated than simple calculations. The need to meet reported earnings targets may cause management to use accounting techniques to improve reported earnings. When the auditor considers the risk of fraud, the auditor considers inherent risk factors such as incentives or pressures to commit fraud as well as an employee's willingness to rationalize fraud.

Ultimately, the auditor is trying to understand the risk that an assertion will be misstated before considering the client's system of internal control. For example, if the auditor is auditing an assertion that requires a complex calculation, such as the percentage of completion method for construction company, the auditor might assess inherent risk as high or at the maximum. This means that there is a very high probability that a material misstatement might occur prior to considering the client's system of internal control. If the auditor is auditing an assertion that involves a simple calculation, such as the amortization of prepaid expenses, the auditor might assess the risk as moderate or low, meaning that, in the auditor's judgment, there is a moderate or low probability that a material misstatement will occur before considering the client's system of internal control. Various inherent risk factors and specific inherent risk factors associated with fraud are discussed in Chapter 9.

Control Risk

Generally accepted auditing standards (AU 312) defines **control risk** as "the risk that a material misstatement that could occur in an assertion will not be prevented or detected on a timely basis by the entity's internal controls." Management often recognizes the inherent risk of misstatement, such as the risk associated with theft of gold as a raw material, and it designs internal controls to prevent, or detect and correct such problems. Today's business environment usually relies on computerized internal controls to identify potential misstatements such as recorded sales that are not supported by shipped goods, or inventory that is valued incorrectly. Control risk is also a client situation that, in every audit, the auditor tries to understand by obtaining evidence through risk assessment procedures. If internal controls appear to be effective, the auditor will often perform tests of controls to obtain evidence to support this conclusion.

Furthermore, a sound system of internal control is a good way to decrease the risk of fraud. A good system of internal control has sufficient checks and balances that minimize the opportunity to commit fraud. Without the opportunity, the fraud triangle breaks down (see Figure 5-4).

A low control risk assessment means that internal controls are effective and that there is a low risk that the system of internal control will fail to prevent, or detect and correct, a material misstatement. In order to assess control risk as low the auditor needs evidence that controls are effectively designed and that they operate effectively throughout the period. The auditor does this by obtaining an understanding of internal controls and by performing tests of controls. It is possible that an entity may have effective controls for some assertions and ineffective controls for other assertions. As a result, the auditor might assess control risk as low for some assertions and as high or maximum for other assertions. A high or maximum control risk assessment means that there is a high or maximum probability that the system of internal control will fail to prevent, or detect and correct, a material misstatement related to a financial statement assertion.

Detection Risk

Generally accepted auditing standards (AU 312) defines **detection risk** as "the risk that the auditor will not detect a material misstatement that exists in an assertion." Once the auditor has made decisions about overall audit risk, and has obtained evidence about the client's inherent and control risks, he or she uses the audit risk model to guide decisions about the audit evidence that is needed to restrict detection risk to an appropriately low level. A low detection risk means that there is a low probability that the auditor's direct test of an assertion will fail to detect a material misstatement. For example, if the auditor determines that inherent risk should be assessed at the maximum and internal controls are ineffective, the auditor needs to set detection risk at a low level in order to achieve a sufficiently low level of audit risk. This logic says that the auditor needs to design significant audit procedures to ensure that the auditor obtains reasonable assurance of finding any material misstatements that might be present. Alternatively, if inherent risk is assessed at the maximum, but the auditor has persuasive evidence that the system of internal controls would prevent or detect material misstatements, the auditor might perform less extensive tests when auditing an assertion. The auditor controls detection risk by using professional judgment to make decisions about:

- Which audit procedures to perform.
- When to perform audit procedures.
- The extensiveness of audit procedures.
- Who should perform audit procedures.

Relationship Between Audit Risk and Evidence

Consider the audit risk model presented in Figure 5-2. The auditor uses this logic over and over for each assertion in the financial statements. In every case the auditor sets audit risk at a sufficiently low level to ensure that reasonable assurance is obtained that each assertion is free of material misstatement. Second, the auditor

Figure 5-3 ■ Example Risk Assessments

	Audit Risk	Inherent Risk	Control Risk	Detection Risk
Assertion 1: Existence of Inventory	2%	100%	7%	29%
Assertion 2: Valuation and Allocation of Inventory	2%	100%	50%	4%

assesses the risk that a material misstatement will occur in an assertion (i.e., inherent risk). Third, the auditor gains an understanding of the entity's internal controls relevant to an assertion and may perform tests of the effectiveness of those controls (i.e., control risk). After considering inherent and control risks, the auditor makes a judgment about the risk of material misstatement in the financial information about the assertion that is presented for audit and sets the scope of audit procedures accordingly (i.e., set detection risk to achieve the appropriate level of audit risk). For example, consider the two sets of quantitative risk assessments identified in Figure 5-3.

In the first instance the auditor might be auditing a large assembler and retailer of computer equipment with a significant supply chain management system. Inventory is very material to the financial statements, and if inventory is overstated, gross profit will be overstated as well. Given a large volume of inventory transactions, the auditor might assess inherent risk at the maximum. However, the client might also maintain a perpetual inventory and regularly compares inventory on hand with inventory per the perpetual records. In order to support the low control risk assessment, the auditor collects evidence that the controls are in fact effective through tests of controls. On the basis of this evidence, the auditor assesses control risk as having only a 7 percent chance of failing to detect a material misstatement. The combined inherent and control risk assessment results in a low risk that a material misstatement would happen in this assertion. As a result of the competent evidence obtained through tests of controls, the auditor might accept a 29 percent risk that direct audit tests of the assertion might not detect a material misstatement. For example, the auditor might accept a smaller sample size when observing the existence of inventory. In this case the auditor also plans to achieve a very low level of audit risk (a 2 percent chance that combined audit procedures will fail to detect a material misstatement). However, because of the evidence obtained about the effectiveness of internal controls, the auditor can accept a higher level of detection risk to achieve the desired results.

Now consider the valuation of inventory. A critical component of the valuation of inventory is the net realizable value and technical obsolescence of inventory. Technology has been changing rapidly enough that the company regularly has to write down the value of inventory near the end of each item's product life cycle. This issue involves significant management discretion, and the controller normally makes the annual adjustment and the chief financial officer reviews the adjustment. Inherent risk is at the maximum due to the subjectivity and complexity involved in making the accounting estimate. Although the CFO review provides some level of control over the accounting estimate, the auditor is also concerned about the risk of management override and the possibility that controller and CFO share a motivation to manage earnings. As a result, the auditor feels that there is a 50 percent chance that internal controls might fail to correctly estimate the inventory obsolescence reserve. The combined inherent and control risks are high, and the auditor will want to respond to these risks by making sure that auditing procedures have a low risk that the auditor would fail to detect a material misstatement. The auditor examines slow-moving inventory and carefully looks at sales after year-end to determine the extent to which sale prices on older items are below cost. The auditor will set the scope of substantive tests so that they have only a 4 percent chance of failing to detect a material misstatement in the valuation and allocation assertion. The auditor has evaluated the client conditions represented by inherent and control risks, and has made decisions about audit procedures to set detection risk at a level that will ensure that the desired very low level of audit risk is achieved.

Auditors use the logic of the audit risk model over and over during the audit to plan an audit that is responsive to the risk of material misstatement. The concept of audit risk is also consistent with the fact that the audit is designed to provide reasonable assurance, not absolute assurance, that the financial statements are free of material misstatements. An audit does not guarantee that the financial statements are free of material misstatement.

Risk of Fraud

Recall from Chapter 2 that generally accepted auditing standards (AU 316, SAS 99) require auditors to assess the risk of material misstatement due to fraud. When auditors consider inherent risk and control risk, they must also consider the risk of fraud. Auditors usually consider the risk of material misstatement due to two types of fraud separately: fraudulent financial reporting and misappropriation of assets. The risks that may lead to fraudulent financial reporting (such as the overstatement of productive assets and understatement of expenses at WorldCom) are often quite different from the risks that lead to the embezzlement of assets. Figure 5-4 describes the "fraud triangle" that depicts the common aspects of all frauds. Fraud usually requires that the individual(s) committing fraud have:

1. The opportunity to commit fraud.
2. Incentives or pressures to engage in fraud.
3. The ability to rationalize fraud as being consistent with internal ethical values.

At early stages of an audit, the audit team engages in a brainstorming session to make sure every person on the audit team is cognizant of the potential risk factors that may increase the risk of fraud.

Figure 5-4 ■ The Fraud Triangle

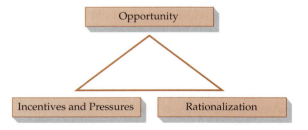

A common example of fraudulent financial reporting involves the overstatement of revenues. First, fraudulent financial reporting usually involves some level of management override of internal controls (control risk) that allows the opportunity for an accounting manager to misstate revenues. Second, these instances usually involve an incentive in the way of a bonus or a significant pressure from senior management to meet revenue targets (inherent risk). Finally, in these cases it is common for the accounting officers involved in overstating revenues to rationalize that it is necessary to be a "team player," or it is acceptable because they believe that other accountants also engage in improper revenue recognition.

Similarly, misappropriation of assets involves these same common fraud factors. Usually the misappropriation of assets is also accompanied by the opportunity that is created by poor segregation of duties and poor or ineffective internal controls (high control risk). Furthermore, an employee may have a personal pressure such as the need to pay for private school, college, excessive spending, or a gambling debt. Employees may rationalize the activity by believing that they are underpaid or that they are taking a temporary loan from the company. These are examples of the types of risk factors that an audit team considers in every audit. Generally accepted auditing standards also say that the auditor does not have to identify all three aspects of the fraud triangle in order to assess the risk of fraud as high. These factors are often difficult to observe, so identifying one or two aspects of the fraud triangle may be enough to cause the auditor to restrict detection risk to a low level.

DEVELOP PRELIMINARY AUDIT STRATEGIES

Auditors often make preliminary decisions about the components of the audit risk model and develop preliminary strategies for the collection of evidence. In a recurring audit, the auditor begins the audit with previous experience with the entity. After updating that knowledge for changes in the entity and its environment, and performing a few initial audit planning procedures, the auditor may begin to develop expectations of whether internal controls continue to function as expected, and whether other factors exist that might indicate a potential for misstatements. Auditors often develop preliminary audit strategies for auditing an assertion. A preliminary audit strategy might be expressed as a preliminary decision about the expected audit risks, such as those noted in Figure 5-3. Hence, for the existence of inventory, the auditor might plan to test internal controls. If evidence shows that internal controls are effective, the auditor might plan to observe inventory at an interim date, and the auditor might be able to observe a smaller proportion of exiting inventory. Alternatively, the auditor might develop a preliminary plan to directly obtain evidence about the valuation of inventory. If the auditor is concerned about the lower of cost or market issues with inventory, the auditor might obtain evidence about the entity's ability to sell inventory after year-end at prices that allow the entity to recover its costs. In developing preliminary audit strategies, the auditor is making initial decisions about the collection of evidence.

UNDERSTAND INTERNAL CONTROL

Auditors are required to obtain an understanding of the entity's system of internal control in every audit. The auditor uses this understanding to:

1. Identify types of potential misstatements.
2. Consider factors that affect the risks of material misstatement.
3. Design the nature, timing, and extent of further audit procedures.

First, the auditor uses the understanding of internal control to identify the types of potential misstatements that may occur. For example, consider a revenue system for a church that receives significant cash contributions. The nature of the entity's receipts creates a concern over the completeness of revenues. Or consider the challenges of a manufacturing jeweler in controlling raw material—gold. One ounce of gold is both small and quite valuable, making the existence and occurrence assertion related to the gold inventory an important concern. These examples show that understanding the nature of the transaction is very useful in understanding the types of potential misstatements that may occur for an organization.

Second, the auditor usually understands how the system of internal control would prevent, or detect and correct, potential misstatement for each financial statement assertion. A strong system of internal control reduces the potential for financial statement misstatement. Good segregation of duties and internal controls over the receipt of cash in the church will reduce the possibility of unrecorded revenues. Strong internal controls over the manufacturing jeweler's gold inventory that compare the gold used in production with the gold content of finished goods reduces the likelihood of theft or unauthorized use of inventory. A thorough understanding of the system of internal control assists the auditor not only in identifying potential types of misstatements but in understanding the risk that material misstatements may in fact occur. In the audit of a public company, a thorough understanding of the entity's system of internal control is necessary to audit that system and to express an opinion on the system of internal control over financial reporting.

Finally, the auditor uses the knowledge of the system of internal control to design further audit procedures to collect evidence. For example, the documentary or electronic audit trail is part of the system of internal control. It is essential to understand this system in order to identify the appropriate evidence to test financial statement assertions. In addition, if the auditor identifies a strong system of internal control related to an assertion, the auditor may choose to collect more evidence about the operating effectiveness of internal controls and less evidence about the financial statement transactions or balances influenced by the system of internal control over financial reporting.

Let's summarize some key concepts presented to this point in the chapter. The auditor performs a variety of risk assessment procedures to obtain an understanding of the factors that affect the risk of material misstatement. It is important to understand the financial statement assertions because they provide a roadmap that identifies the types of potential misstatements in a transaction class. The auditor also obtains an understanding of the entity and its environment as the risk of material misstatement is often associated with the financial consequences of the client's business risks. The auditor also makes a decision early in the audit about the magnitude of misstatement that individually, or in aggregate, would be material to the financial statements. At an early stage auditors perform analytical procedures on the unaudited data to identify assertions that might be misstated. The auditor then considers the risk of fraud and other inherent risks, and learns the system of internal control that responds to those risks. Understanding inherent risk and control risk, including the risk of fraud, prepares the auditor for the process of assessing the risk of material misstatement for various financial statement assertions.

LEARNING CHECK

5-1   a. What is the overall objective of the financial statement audit?

       b. Identify the six phases of a financial statement audit.

5-2   a. State the five categories of management's financial statement assertions and briefly explain each.

       b. What is the difference between a misstatement resulting from the existence or occurrence assertion and a misstatement resulting from the completeness assertion?

       c. Identify four aspects associated with the presentation and disclosure assertion.

5-3   a. Explain what is meant by understanding "the entity's industry, regulatory environment, and other factors" and explain how the auditor uses this knowledge in understanding the risk of material misstatement.

       b. Explain what is meant by understanding "the nature of the entity" and explain how the auditor uses this knowledge in understanding the risk of material misstatement.

       c. Explain what is meant by understanding the entity's "objectives, strategies, and related business risks" and explain how the auditor uses this knowledge in understanding the risk of material misstatement.

       d. Explain what is meant by understanding the entity's "management and review of the entity's financial performance" and explain how the auditor uses this knowledge in understanding the risk of material misstatement.

5-4   Explain the concept of materiality and describe two ways the concept of materiality is used in planning and performing the audit.

5-5   a. Define audit risk.

       b. Define the three components of audit risk.

       c. How do the fraud risk factors relate to the components of audit risk?

       d. Explain how the audit risk model is used to make decisions about audit evidence.

5-6   a. Explain the difference between fraudulent financial reporting and misappropriation of assets and give an example of each.

       b. Describe each of the three risk factors that are related to the risk of fraud.

5-7   Identify and explain three ways that the auditor uses his or her understanding of the entity's system of internal control.

KEY TERMS

Analytical procedures, p. 193

Audit risk, p. 194

Business risks, p. 192

Completeness, p. 188

Control risk, p. 195

Detection risk, p. 196

Entity's objectives, p. 192

Entity's industry, regulatory environment, and other external factors, p. 191

Entity's selection and application of accounting policies, p. 192

Existence or occurrence, p. 187

Inherent risk, p. 194

Materiality, p. 193

Nature of the entity, p. 191

Presentation and disclosure, p. 189

Rights and obligations, p. 188

Strategies, p. 192

Valuation or allocation, p. 188

PHASE II: ASSESS THE RISK OF MATERIAL MISSTATEMENT

Auditor Knowledge 3

■ Understand the four steps in assessing the risk of material misstatement.

At the conclusion of Phase I of the audit, the auditor has identified various risks of material misstatement. In the process of assessing the risk of material misstatement the auditor:

1. Relates risk factors to potential financial statement misstatements, either at the financial statement level or the assertion level.
2. Determines whether risks are of a magnitude that will result in a material misstatement in the financial statements.
3. Determines the likelihood that risks will result in material misstatements.
4. Determines the existence of significant inherent risks.

RELATE RISK FACTORS TO POTENTIAL FINANCIAL STATEMENT MISSTATEMENTS

Initially, the auditor must relate the risk factors identified while performing risk assessment procedures to the potential for misstatements in the financial statements. For example, the auditor needs to understand whether misstatements are likely in sales and receivables, or inventories, or in accounting for fixed assets. The auditor also needs to understand whether factors, such as a weak system of internal control, are present that would have a pervasive effect on the financial statements.

Assertion Level Risks

An **assertion level risk** is one that influences only one or a few assertions. For example, an audit client may have recently implemented a new accounting system in the revenue cycle that was not subjected to significant testing with test data. This could impact a variety of assertions related to revenue recognition and receivables, but it will not have an impact beyond the specific transaction cycle. Alternatively, the auditor might identify a business risk associated with the introduction of new technology that will compete with one of the company's major product lines. Furthermore, the division that will compete with this new product introduction was acquired a few years ago, with the company paying a substantial amount for goodwill. This risk may relate specifically to lower of cost or market issues with inventory or to whether there is an impairment in the value of goodwill (both valuation and allocation assertion issues). Similarly, the application of a new accounting pronouncement may have a very targeted impact on the financial statements.

Financial Statement Level Risks

A **financial statement level risk** is one in which the risk factor relates pervasively to the financial statements as a whole. For example, a weak control environment where management does not create an environment of control consciousness or does not hold middle management accountable for use of the entity's resources may affect many transaction classes, account balances, and assertions. In a similar way, if management lacks significant accounting knowledge, this could have a pervasive impact on multiple transactions classes and assertions. Some weaknesses in internal controls may have a pervasive impact on the financial statements. For example, weak computer general controls increase the risk of inappropriate access to multiple computer applications and data, and errors may be more likely in multiple transactions classes. Hence, when the auditor considers the potential for misstatements in financial statements, the auditor must consider whether risk factors have a pervasive impact on those financial statements or whether they have a specific impact on particular assertions.

DETERMINE THE MAGNITUDE OF POTENTIAL MISSTATEMENTS

When assessing inherent and control risks for an audit client, the auditor must determine the magnitude of potential misstatements related to those risk factors. For example, it is common for businesses to make cost-benefit considerations when implementing a system of internal control, and a business may feel that the cost of controlling small misstatements is greater than the benefit. The auditor needs to distinguish between risk factors associated with potential misstatements that might be clearly immaterial and risk factors associated with potential misstatements that could aggregate to a material amount. For example, it is more likely that revenue recognition issues will have a larger potential impact on the financial statements than prepaid expenses. Furthermore, the valuation of inventory is more likely to be significant for a paper manufacturer (which is capital intense and has a variety of manufacturing costs) than for a hotel or bank.

Every statement from the Financial Accounting Standards Board comes with a qualification that it need not be applied to immaterial items. In some cases management might account for immaterial transactions incorrectly because it is expedient. The auditor must apply professional judgment to distinguish between the risk factors related to items that might be immaterial and would not have a significant impact on the financial statements, and the risk factors associated with smaller items that might aggregate to a material amount. The auditor must also consider the risk that past immaterial transactions which were not accounted for in accordance with GAAP, have now risen to a level that is material to the financial statements.

DETERMINE THE LIKELIHOOD OF MATERIAL MISSTATEMENTS

In addition to examining the magnitude of potential risks, the auditor also needs to determine the likelihood that those risks will result in a material misstatement in the financial statements. It is common for auditors to identify risk factors associated with high inherent risks where the likelihood of material misstatement is reduced by the client's system of internal control. In making this assessment the auditor considers both inherent and control risks. For example, a construction company may have a high inherent risk due to the complexity of estimating long-term construction contracts. Many modest-size construction companies also have moderate to weak internal controls. The combination results in a high probability of material misstatement in the underlying financial data. As a result, the auditor needs to design sufficient and competent audit procedures to detect material misstatements.

Auditors also need to be vigilant to uncover material misstatements in the financial statements, even if they are low-probability events. Recent history has shown that only one or two percent of public companies have had to restate earnings in a given year. However, the bankruptcies of Enron and WorldCom, which were related in part to material misstatements in their financial statements, resulted in billions of dollars of losses for investors and the employees of those companies. High-quality audits are alert for low-probability events that may result in material misstatements of the financial statements that would influence the decisions of financial statement users.

DETERMINE SIGNIFICANT INHERENT RISKS

Generally accepted auditing standards[5] state that the auditor should determine which of the identified risks are, in the auditor's judgment, significant inherent risks that require special audit consideration. In the next phase of the audit, responding to assessed risks, the auditor needs to give particular attention to risks that are identified as significant inherent risks.

Significant inherent risks arise in most audits, but determining those risks is a matter of the auditor's professional judgment and excludes the auditor's consideration of internal control. In identifying significant inherent risks the auditor considers matters such as:

- Whether the risk is a risk of fraud. For example, a significant inherent risk might be identified if auditors felt that all three elements of the fraud triangle were present.
- Whether the risk is related to recent economic, accounting, or other developments that require special attention. For example, the auditor might identify a significant inherent risk associated with a new accounting pronouncement that would be implemented for the first time during the current audit.
- The complexity of the transactions that may give rise to the risk. For example, a client might engage in a sale and leaseback arrangement that has complex terms associated with the agreement.
- Whether the risk involves significant transactions with related parties. For example, significant transactions with affiliated companies, officers, or directors represent a significant inherent risk.
- The degree of subjectivity in the measurement of financial information related to the risk. For example, the application of the percentage of completion method for a construction company would represent a significant inherent risk.
- Whether the risk involves significant nonroutine transactions. Nonroutine transactions are transactions that are unusual, due either to size or to nature, and therefore occur infrequently. For example, the client might only evaluate the adequacy of the allowance for doubtful accounts once a year. A client's inattention to collection issues may represent a significant inherent risk.

---

[5] The following discussion of understanding an entity and its environment is based on an Auditing Standards Board Exposure Draft dated December 2, 2002. A similar requirement was adopted by the International Auditing and Assurance Standards Board on October 31, 2003.

- Whether the risk involves judgmental matters. For example, significant judgments that require the development of accounting estimates such as the judgment about fair value would represent a significant inherent risk.
- Significant business risks are often significant inherent risks. For example, an entity with high fixed costs such as an airline, telecommunications company, or hotel would have a significant inherent risk associated with the utilization of capacity. Underutilization of capacity could result in decreased profitability and cash flows compared to budgets or market expectations, and possible improper capitalization of excess capacity costs, that need special audit attention.

The auditor's response to significant audit risks is discussed next in Phase III of the audit.

LEARNING CHECK

5-8 Explain the four steps in assessing the risk of material misstatement.

5-9 Distinguish between the risk of material misstatement at the assertion level and the risk of material misstatement at the financial statement level. Provide an example of each.

5-10 You and a colleague are discussing the risk of material misstatement in the allowance for doubtful accounts for an audit client. The client's past track record shows that they very rarely write-off receivables and when they do they are never material in amount. The client also uses the direct write-off method of accounting for doubtful accounts. Your colleague believes that based on past experience the probability of material misstatement is low for the valuation of accounts receivable, and that this assertion does not need significant audit attention. How would you respond to this viewpoint?

5-11 What is meant by the term *significant inherent risk?* Provide two examples of significant inherent risks.

KEY TERMS

Assertion level risk, p. 202
Financial statement level risk, p. 202

Significant inherent risk, p. 204

PHASE III: RESPOND TO ASSESSED RISKS

Auditor Knowledge 4

- Understand how the auditor responds to assessed risks of material misstatement.

When the auditor identifies risks that may result in a material misstatement in the financial statements, he or she must develop appropriate responses to such risk to ensure that audit risk is maintained at an appropriately low level. In planning the audit, it is important to develop a clear link between the assessed risks of material misstatement and the auditor's planned response to obtain reasonable assurance that the financial statements are free of material misstatement. The auditor usually responds to assessed risks with a variation of four major responses. Common responses to assessed risks include decisions about the:

- Staffing and supervision of the audit.
- Nature of audit tests.
- Timing of audit tests.
- Extent of audit tests.

STAFFING AND SUPERVISION

It is common for auditors to respond to higher financial statement level risks through decisions about **staffing and supervision** by assigning more experienced professionals to the engagement, increasing the level of supervision of professional staff, or by using the work of a specialist. Recall that financial statement level risks usually have a pervasive impact on multiple transactions classes and assertions. If, for example, the auditor assesses that there is a high risk of misstatement owing to the fact that the company has a poor internal control environment and there is a low level of consciousness toward errors in interim financial statements, the auditor might respond either by assigning more experienced professionals to the engagement or by increasing the level of supervision of professional staff.

Selection of specialist or professional staff is also an appropriate way to respond to assertion level risks. For example, assume that the audit client imports and exports grain and feed. When observing inventory, the auditor might want to have a specialist present who can distinguish between different types of grain. The specialist might also be able to take samples to determine whether various grains are subject to disease or other factors that would impair the value of the commodity. It is also common to assign more experienced professionals, such as those with considerable experience with agricultural clients, to assertions that involve a high degree of complexity or subjectivity in determining financial statement values.

NATURE OF AUDIT TESTS

Decisions about the **nature of audit tests** are related to the auditor's choices about the type of evidence that they collect to support an opinion. There are three common types of audit procedures:

- **Risk assessment procedures** that are designed to help the auditor assess the risk of material misstatement in an assertion, whether performed early in the audit engagement or in response to new information. Recall that the auditor uses risk assessment procedures to obtain evidence about inherent risks and the risk of fraud.
- **Tests of control** that are designed to provide evidence about the operating effectiveness of various aspects of internal control. Tests of controls provide evidence to support control risk assessments below the maximum.
- **Substantive tests** that are designed to provide evidence about the fair presentation of management's assertions in the financial statements. Substantive tests include:
  - **Initial procedures** that involve understanding the economic substance of the account balance or transactions being audited and agreeing on detailed information about an account to the general ledger (such as comparing an accounts receivable subsidiary ledger to the general ledger).

- **Substantive analytic procedures** that involve the use of comparisons to assess the fairness of an assertion. For example, the auditor might evaluate sales per square foot of retail space in testing the reasonableness of revenues.
- **Tests of details of transactions** that involve examining documentary support for transactions. For example, an auditor might inspect sales orders and a bill of lading behind a recorded sales invoice.
- **Tests of details of balances** that involve examining support for a general ledger balance. For example, the auditor might send confirmations to customers to obtain evidence that they owe receivables.
- **Tests of details of accounting estimates** that involve obtaining evidence in support of the client's estimation process and ensuring that the estimation process is applied consistently from period to period.
- **Tests of details of disclosures** that involve examining support for financial statement disclosures. For example, the auditor might read a loan contract to ascertain the maturity schedule and debt covenants for the loan.

Substantive tests provide the evidence that allows the auditor to achieve the desired detection risk and ensure that overall audit risk is reduced to an appropriately low level.

Recall the risk assessments illustrated in Figure 5-3. For assertion 1, the existence of inventory, the nature of the auditor's evidence would include significant tests of controls (testing the effectiveness of the client's perpetual inventory system) as well as some limited substantive tests (direct observation of inventory). For assertion 2, the valuation of inventory, the auditor would perform few tests of controls because controls are not expected to be effective. However, the auditor would plan to obtain significant evidence by testing the pricing of inventory to underlying vendor's invoices (substantive tests of balances). In addition, the auditor would obtain evidence about sales prices after year-end to support a conclusion about the lower of cost or market objective (substantive test of an accounting estimate).

TIMING OF AUDIT TESTS

The auditor may choose to modify the **timing of audit tests** by choosing to perform tests of controls or substantive tests at an interim date. Again, recall the risk assessments illustrated in Figure 5-3. For assertion 1, the existence of inventory, the auditor will likely perform tests of controls at an interim date. If internal controls are found to be effective, the auditor will also likely perform substantive tests to observe inventory at a date one or two months prior to year-end. The auditor will usually change the timing of a substantive test to an interim date only when control risk is assessed as low. This reduces the risk that a material misstatement will happen between the date of the test and the balance sheet date. When the auditor performs audit tests at an interim period, the auditor is also required to obtain evidence of the remaining period to determine that conclusions draw at interim are still valid.

The auditor might also respond to financial statement level risk by adding an element of unannounced procedures or performing procedures at unpredictable times in the selection of further audit procedures. For example, the auditor might choose to show up unannounced for an inventory observation at a particular location. The auditor might also choose to perform tests of computer general controls at an unpredictable interim time in order to better assess the effectiveness of internal controls that are placed in operation.

EXTENT OF AUDIT TESTS

The auditor may choose to respond to assessed risks by making decisions about the **extent of audit tests** (sample size) of planned audit procedures. In general, the auditor can accept smaller sample sizes when detection risk is high, and the auditor should use larger sample sizes when detection risk is low. Again, recall the risk assessments illustrated in Figure 5-3. For assertion 1, the existence of inventory, the auditor will likely use smaller sample sizes for observing inventory because detection risk is relatively high. For assertion 2 however (the valuation of inventory), the auditor needs larger sample sizes when testing sales after year-end to obtain more sufficient evidence about the lower of cost or market assertions.

The auditor should be aware of two cautions regarding sample size. First, increasing sample size is an effective way to respond to risk only if the tests are relevant to the specific risk. For example, sending more confirmations to customers may not help the auditor to better assess the collectibility of receivables, for confirmations are not relevant to the net realizable value of receivables. Second, if the sample size is too small, there may be an unacceptable risk that the auditor's conclusion from the sample may be different from the conclusion reached if the entire population were to be subjected to the same audit procedure. Chapter 13 provides guidance on planning, performing, and evaluating audit samples.

RESPOND TO SIGNIFICANT INHERENT RISKS

Significant inherent risks arise in most audits, and they may range from risks of material misstatement resulting from the client's business risks to nonroutine or complex transactions, to a high assessed risk of fraud. There are some important considerations when designing effective responses to significant inherent risks.

First, the auditor should evaluate the effectiveness of the design of internal controls related to all significant inherent risks. Second, if the auditor plans on obtaining evidence from tests of controls to mitigate a significant inherent risk, the auditor should test the operating effectiveness of the relevant control in the current audit period (an issue related to the timing of audit tests).[6] Third, the auditor should perform substantive tests that are responsive to significant inherent risks. For example, if the auditor finds that management is under pressure to meet earning expectations, there may be a related risk that management is inflating sales by entering into sales agreements that include terms that preclude revenue recognition. In these circumstances, the auditor might design external confirmations not only to confirm the outstanding amount, but also to confirm the details of the sales agreements, including date, any rights of return, and delivery terms. Finally, it is unlikely that evidence obtained from substantive analytical procedures alone (a choice regarding the nature of audit tests) will represent sufficient competent evidence for assertions with significant inherent risks.

---

[6] In a public company audit, the auditor must always obtain evidence from tests of controls in the current period to support an opinion on the effectiveness of internal control over financial reporting.

[LEARNING CHECK

5-12 Describe several situations when staffing or increased supervision is an appropriate response to assessed risks.

5-13 Describe the purpose of (a) risk assessment procedures; (b) tests of controls; and (c) substantive tests.

5-14 Explain the purpose of six major types of substantive tests and provide an example of each.

5-15 Describe two different audit strategies that use a different nature of audit tests to audit the existence of inventory.

5-16 a. Explain what is meant by the timing of audit tests and provide an example of how the auditor would change the timing of confirming the existence of accounts receivable.

b. Under what conditions is the auditor likely to change the timing of audit tests to an interim date?

5-17 a. Explain what is meant by the extent of audit tests and provide an example in the context of testing the existence of inventory.

b. Identify two important cautions regarding the extent of audit procedures.

5-18 Explain three important considerations when responding to significant inherent risks.

[KEY TERMS

Extent of audit tests, p. 208
Initial procedures, p. 206
Nature of audit tests, p. 206
Risk assessment procedures, p. 206
Staffing and supervision, p. 206
Substantive analytic procedures, p. 207
Substantive tests, p. 206

Tests of control, p. 206
Tests of details of accounting estimates, p. 207
Tests of details of balances, p. 207
Tests of details of disclosures, p. 207
Tests of details of transactions, p. 207
Timing of audit tests, p. 207

[PHASE IV: PERFORM FURTHER AUDIT PROCEDURES]

Auditor Knowledge 5

■ Understand the three classifications of further audit procedures.

In general, the auditor's responsibility is to assess the risk of material misstatement, to develop an audit plan to respond to the risk of material misstatement and obtain reasonable assurance, and to execute that audit plan with due professional care. Phases I and II of the audit involve performing risk assessment procedures and assessing the risk of material misstatement. In Phase III the auditor designs an audit plan that is responsive to the assessed risk, and in Phase IV, the auditor performs further audit procedures to execute that plan with due professional care. Further audit procedures include performing:

■ Further risk assessment procedures.

■ Tests of controls.

■ Substantive tests.

FURTHER RISK ASSESSMENT PROCEDURES

The audit is a cumulative and iterative process. In the process of performing tests of controls, the auditor may obtain evidence that contradicts preliminary risk assessments or prior understandings of the system of internal control. In addition, the auditor might obtain evidence of misstatements when performing substantive tests that is inconsistent with previous risk assessments, based on the auditor's initial understanding of the entity and its environment. Either of these conditions might cause the auditor to perform additional risk assessment procedures to more fully understand the underlying risks within an entity. Using due professional care requires consistent evidence from risk assessment procedures, the results of tests of controls, and the results of substantive tests.

TESTS OF CONTROLS

The auditor performs tests of control to obtain evidence about the effective operations of internal controls relevant to an assertion. When planning the audit, the auditor usually weighs the tradeoff to obtain more evidence about fair presentation of an assertion based on the fact that internal controls function effectively and less evidence in the form of substantive tests of transactions, balances, and disclosures. Given that the auditor cannot evaluate 100 percent of the information supporting transactions, balances, and disclosures in the financial statements, the auditor needs to make choices about which type of evidence best fits the entity and the audit assertion.

For many assertions, the auditor may have a choice about whether or not to perform tests of controls.[7] In some instances the auditor might determine that it is efficient to perform only substantive tests of an assertion. However, in other instances the client may use information technology and programmed controls so extensively that the auditor must perform tests of controls in order to reduce audit risk to an appropriately low level. For example, when auditing a financial institution, information about transactions initiated at automated teller machines are captured electronically and provide little paper trail. The auditor may find it necessary to test the internal controls over these transactions in order to obtain reasonable assurance about their fair presentation in the financial statements.

An important aspect of exercising due professional care when performing tests of controls involves understanding how different aspects of internal control interact with each other. For example, the purpose of computer general controls is to control individual computer applications. If computer general controls are ineffective, the application controls may be subject to unauthorized changes or inadequate testing that may make the application ineffective. Most programmed application controls require some level of manual followup of exceptions. If the programmed application is effective but the manual followup is not, the control ultimately breaks down. Furthermore, if the overall control environment and the tone at the top of the entity does not encourage a high level of control consciousness, then there is a reduced likelihood that other control activities will be effective.

In summary, when performing tests of controls, the auditor cannot merely look at a specific control activity. The auditor must obtain sufficient competent evidence

---

[7] In a public company audit, the auditor will always perform test of controls in order to support an opinion on the effectiveness of internal control over financial reporting.

regarding the entire system of internal control and the effectiveness of how various control elements interact with each other. The system of internal controls will often only be as strong as its weakest link. Chapter 11 provides a detailed discussion of how the auditor makes decisions about the nature, timing, and extent of test of controls and the evidence needed to support a low control risk assessment.

SUBSTANTIVE TESTS

Once the auditor has performed risk assessment procedures and tests of controls, the auditor has a basis for determining the appropriate level of detection risk. The auditor then performs substantive tests such as analytical procedures and substantive tests of details of transactions, balances, and disclosures to reduce audit risk to an appropriately low level. Due professional care means that the auditor designs substantive tests with sufficient care to obtain reasonable assurance that each assertion is free of material misstatement.

In general, the higher the auditor's inherent and control risk assessments, and the lower the auditor's assessed level of detection risk, substantive evidence needs to be both more reliable and relevant to the assertion. For example, when the auditor assesses detection risk as low for the existence of receivables, the auditor is more likely to obtain evidence from confirmation with customers than from examination of internal documents related to the sales included in receivables. Moreover, when choosing among various types of substantive evidence, some procedures may be more appropriate than others. For example, when the auditor identifies significant inherent risks, it is unlikely that audit evidence obtained from substantive analytical procedures alone will be sufficient. Chapter 6 provides a detailed discussion of the factors that influence the sufficiency and competency of evidence.

When the auditor performs substantive tests at an interim date, the auditor must take steps to update those conclusions and obtain reasonable assurance that a material misstatement did not occur between the date of the auditor's initial conclusion and year-end. For example, if the auditor observes inventory one month prior to year-end, then the auditor will usually investigate inventory transactions that occurred during the last month of the year to obtain reasonable assurance about the fair presentation of inventory at year-end. Chapter 12 provides a detailed discussion about the auditor's decisions that ensure that designed substantive tests are responsive to assessed risks to ensure that the auditor obtains sufficient, competent evidence to achieve the planned level of assurance.

[LEARNING CHECK

5-19 Explain why the auditor would perform further risk assessment procedures later in the audit.

5-20 a. Explain the primary reason the auditor would consider for performing tests of controls?

b. In what instances would the auditor feel it was necessary to perform tests of controls?

5-21 How should an auditor respond to a low assessed level of detection risk?

[PHASE V: EVALUATE EVIDENCE]

Evaluating evidence can be categorized in three major steps.

1. Reevaluate risk assessment procedures.
2. Determine the significance of findings.
3. Form and document conclusions.

REEVALUATE RISK ASSESSMENT PROCEDURES

Auditor Knowledge 6

■ **Understand the auditor's considerations when evaluating audit evidence.**

As part of evaluating audit evidence, the auditor should determine whether the assessment of the risk of material misstatements at the assertion level remain appropriate. For example, the magnitude and extent of misstatements that the auditor detects by performing substantive procedures may alter the auditor's judgment about the risk assessments. Alternatively, analytical procedures performed at final review stages may indicate a previously unrecognized risk of material misstatement. In such circumstances, the auditor needs to reevaluate the planned audit procedures based on the revised consideration of assessed risks for some or all assertions.

DETERMINE THE SIGNIFICANCE OF FINDINGS

An auditor should evaluate both the significance of deviations of prescribed control procedures and the significance of errors or fraud discovered during the audit.

The concept of effectiveness of operation of internal controls recognizes that there may be some deviations in the way controls are applied. Deviations may be caused by changes in key personnel, significant seasonal fluctuations in the volume of transactions, or human error. When deviations in internal control are detected, the auditor needs to make inquiries and obtain evidence to understand these deviations and their potential consequences. For example, if the auditor finds errors in a computer program owing to inadequate testing of the program, the auditor needs to determine whether other programs are affected by this deviation from computer general control procedures. The auditor needs to make sure that the audit plan responds to significant deviations in internal controls with adequate substantive testing. The more pervasive the nature of the deviations from internal control policies, the more the auditor may need to consider significant revisions in the audit plan.

If the auditor finds instances of error or fraud when performing substantive tests, he or she cannot assume that known problems are isolated occurrences. Therefore, before a conclusion is reached, the auditor evaluates the nature of the misstatement, the significance of the projected misstatement that might exist in the population, and whether the nature, timing, or extent of audit procedures need to be reconsidered. For example, if an auditor determines that management has engaged in management override of normal inventory procedures to influence the valuation of inventory, the auditor must consider the implications for both inventory and other aspects of the audit, including the need to revise audit strategies for other transactions classes, account balances, or disclosures.

The purpose of a high-quality audit is to obtain reasonable assurance that the financial statements are free of material misstatement, so that financial statement users may use financial statements with an underlying belief in the soundness and integrity of the financial reporting system. This occurs only when the auditor carefully plans and executes an audit, and carefully evaluates audit findings. The auditor must conclude that evidence found in audit findings is representative of the unsampled portion of the population. Thus, the auditor's process of evaluating evidence includes both evaluating known evidence and projecting those results on the unsampled portions of audit populations.

FORM AND DOCUMENT CONCLUSIONS

Ultimately, the sufficiency and competency of audit evidence is a matter of professional judgment, influenced by such factors as the:

- Significance of the potential misstatement in an assertion and the likelihood of its having a material effect, individual or in aggregate, with other potential misstatements on the financial statements.
- Effectiveness of management's responses and controls to address the risks.
- Experience gained during previous audits with respect to similar potential misstatements.
- Results of audit procedures performed, including whether such audit procedures identify instances of fraud or error.
- Source and reliability of available information.
- Persuasiveness of the audit evidence.
- Understanding of the entity and its environment, including its internal control.

If the auditor has not obtained sufficient competent evidence, the auditor should obtain additional audit evidence, or express a qualified or disclaimer of opinion related to the scope limitation.

Finally, the audit team should document their work in the audit working papers. The auditor's documentation would normally include:

- The overall responses to the risks of misstatement at the financial statement level.
- The nature, timing, and extent of further audit procedures.
- The linkage of those procedures with the assessed risk at the assertion level.
- The results of the audit procedures.
- The nature and effect of aggregated misstatements.
- The auditor's conclusion as to whether the aggregated misstatements cause the financial statement to be materially misstated.
- The qualitative factors the auditor considered in evaluating whether misstatements were material and the audit conclusions.

The manner in which these matters are documented is based on the auditor's professional judgment.

[LEARNING CHECK

5-22 A colleague in your auditing class stated that it seems overwhelming for the auditor to reevaluate the risk assessment for *every* assertion in the financial statements as part of evaluating evidence at the end of the audit. Do you agree or disagree? State your reasons.

5-23 Explain the purpose of evaluating deviations from prescribed control procedures as part of evaluating audit evidence.

5-24 If the auditor finds only one instance of unintentional error during the audit, can the auditor assume that this is an isolated instance? Why or why not?

5-25 What should be documented as part of the auditor's working papers?

PHASE VI: COMMUNICATE AUDIT FINDINGS

Auditor Knowledge 7

■ Understand three ways in which the auditor communicates audit findings.

The final key element of the audit involves communication of findings. The audit, and other services performed as part of the audit, are of no value until they are communicated to management and others who use the audit. The communication of audit findings can be divided into three categories:

■ Communication on the financial statements through the auditor's report.
■ Other required communications with management and the board of directors.
■ Communication of other assurance service findings.

THE AUDITOR'S OPINION

The primary communication of audit findings is contained in the auditor's report on the financial statements. The fourth reporting standard of generally accepted auditing standards states that the auditor will issue a report that contains an expression of opinion regarding the financial statements, taken as a whole, or states that an opinion cannot be expressed on the financial statements. As outlined in Chapter 2, the auditor chooses among a variety of opinions including a(n):

■ Unqualified opinion.
■ Unqualified opinion with an additional explanatory paragraph.
■ Qualified opinion.
■ Disclaimer of opinion.
■ Adverse opinion.

AU 508 provides professional guidance on the facts and circumstances in which the auditor might choose among a variety of standard audit report wordings that communicate specific messages to those who use financial statements. Appendix 2A illustrates the variety of opinions that the auditor, may use depending on audit findings.

Recall from Chapter 2 that auditors of public companies will have to issue two additional opinions regarding management systems of internal control over financial reporting: (1) an opinion on management's assertion about the effectiveness of internal control and (2) an opinion on the operating effectiveness of the system of internal control. Figure 2-7 outlined the auditor's choices regarding the opinions on internal control and over financial reporting, which include a(n):

■ Unqualified opinion.
■ Qualified opinion (for scope).

- Disclaimer of opinion.
- Adverse opinion (a material weakness exists in the system of internal control).

Management of a public company may have a significant deficiency in internal controls, which would be reported to the audit committee, and receive an unqualified opinion on internal controls over financial reporting. PCAOB Auditing Standard No. 2 provides professional guidance on the facts and circumstances in which the auditor might choose among a variety of audit report wordings communicating specific messages to users of reports on internal controls.

OTHER REQUIRED COMMUNICATIONS

The auditor's opinion on the financial statements is not the only outcome of the audit. In addition to issuing a report on the financial statement, the auditor is required by professional standards to discuss certain matters with an audit committee, or with individuals possessing a level of authority and responsibility equivalent to that of an audit committee, such as a board of directors, board of trustees, or an owner in an owner-managed enterprise. These matters include the discussion of:

- Internal controls.
- Significant accounting policies.
- Management judgments and accounting estimates.
- Significant audit adjustments.
- Other information contained in audited financial statements.
- Disagreements with management.
- Consultation with other accountants.
- Difficulties encountered in performing the audit.

Required communications regarding internal controls are discussed further in Chapter 11, and other required communications are discussed in more detail in Chapter 19.

OTHER ASSURANCE SERVICE FINDINGS

CPAs who perform audits have earned public respect not only because of their ability to audit financial statements, but because of their overall business acumen. In order to effectively audit the financial statements of a company, the CPA must be able to:

- Apply ethical rules of the profession.
- Understand an entity's business risks, goals, and objectives and determine the degree to which those goals and objectives have been met.
- Understand the client's transaction streams and information systems and anticipate how transactions, when taken in aggregate, will impact an entity.
- Understand the company's internal controls and evaluate the degree to which they serve the client's needs.
- Assess risk, verify management's assertions, and document audit conclusions.
- Evaluate an entity's cash flow, profitability, liquidity, solvency, and operating cycle and its performance in an industry relative to its competitors.

In addition, the auditor enjoys unparalleled access as a professional to the client's books and records and operating facilities, as well as the client's plans and goals.

Many clients feel that the auditors have not shared what they know about the organization if they only receive an audit opinion from the auditors, along with other required communications. Did the client receive the full value of the knowledge of the audit team?

Consider for a moment the knowledge that is resident on an audit team. During a career most auditors develop an expertise in an industry. They often are familiar with key sources of industry data and understand the competitive factors in that industry. In addition, the audit team often includes individuals with expertise in information systems, and they understand how effective use of information systems support the key decision-making processes of the entity.

Following are some examples of additional assurance services that are based on the knowledge obtained during the audit. It is also important for the auditor to retain an advisory role and not make management decisions while performing these services to avoid independence problems.

Business Risk Assessment

Auditors obtain an understanding of an entity's competitive environment and business risks as part of planning the audit. Auditors do this because many important audit risks are associated with the financial consequences of client's business risks. The purpose of an assurance engagement on risk assessment might include any of the following types of services:

- Identification and assessment of primary potential risks faced by the entity
- Independent assessment of risks identified by the entity
- Evaluation of an entity's systems for identifying and limiting risks

Hence, the nature of the CPA service depends on the risk assessment practices that exist within the entity. Each of these services is built upon the CPA's understanding of the entity's business risks and on tailoring the assurance service to the decision maker's needs, usually management or the board of directors.

Performance Measurement

The auditor is often well positioned to benchmark company performance relative to others in the industry. Usually the auditor has access to industry statistics and information about the performance of the best companies in an industry. CPAs have good analytic skills and are well versed in comparing companies based on their profitability, ability to generate free cash, the length of their operating cycle, liquidity, and solvency. In addition, CPAs can use their knowledge of key competitiveness factors to ensure that a company's information system focuses management on key business management issues. CPAs often can assist management in the development of performance measurement systems that provide internal leading indicators related to the company's ability to generate earnings and cash flow.

Like the business risk assessment service, the customers of the performance measurement assurance service are usually management and the board of directors. The auditor can advise management and the board of directors on important leading indicators that they should be monitoring to better measure the entity's performance. However, auditors need to be careful not to become involved in design or implementation services that would impair audit independence.

These are but a few examples of the other assurance services provided by auditors. In each case these services extend beyond traditional services required in an audit. Other assurance services are discussed in more detail in Chapter 20.

[LEARNING CHECK

5-26 Identify the three basic categories of communication of audit findings. Provide two examples of the communications in each category.

[FOCUS ON AUDITOR KNOWLEDGE]

This chapter provides an overview of the audit process. Figure 5-5 summarizes the key components of auditor knowledge discussed in Chapter 5 and provides page references to where these decisions are discussed in more detail.

Figure 5-5 ■ Summary of Auditor Knowledge Discussed in Chapter 5

Auditor Knowledge	Summary	Chapter References
K1. Understand the six phases that provide an overview of the audit process.	The six phases of the audit are (1) performing risk assessment procedures, (2) assessing the risk of material misstatement, (3) responding to assessed risks, (4) performing further audit procedures, (5) evaluating audit evidence, and (6) communicating audit findings.	p. 185
K2. Understand the auditor's risk assessment procedures.	Fully understanding the risk of material misstatement involves seven broad steps: (1) identifying relevant financial statement assertions, (2) understanding the entity and its environment, (3) making decisions about materiality, (4) performing analytical procedures, (5) identifying risks that may result in material misstatements, including the risk of fraud, (6) developing preliminary audit strategies, and (7) understanding the entity's system of internal control.	pp. 185–200
K3. Understand the four steps in assessing the risk of material misstatement.	Once the auditor has identified various risks of material misstatement, the auditor needs to (1) specifically relate risks to potential misstatements in the financial statements, either at the financial statement level or the assertion level, (2) consider whether risks are of a magnitude that will result in a material misstatement in the financial statements, and (3) consider the likelihood that risks will result in material misstatements. Finally, the auditor needs to determine the existence of significant inherent risks.	pp. 202–205
K4. Understand how the auditor responds to assessed risks of material misstatement.	The auditor specifically responds to the risk of material misstatement through staffing and supervision and the choice of the nature, timing, and extent of audit procedures. In addition, the chapter described several specific responses to significant inherent risks.	pp. 205–208

(continues)

Figure 5-5 ■ (Continued)

Auditor Knowledge	Summary	Chapter References
K5. Understand the three classifications of further audit procedures.	Further audit procedures can be classified as (1) further risk assessment procedures, (2) tests of controls that are designed to test the operating effectiveness of internal control policies and procedures, or (3) substantive tests that are designed to directly test the fair presentation of assertions in the financial statements.	pp. 209–211
K6. Understand the auditor's considerations when evaluating audit evidence.	The process of evaluating evidence involves (1) reevaluating assessed risks based on audit findings, (2) evaluating the significance of deviations from prescribed internal controls and the significance of errors or fraud found during the audit, and (3) forming a conclusion about fair presentation of assertions in the financial statements and documenting those conclusions.	pp. 212–213
K7. Understand three ways in which the auditor communicates audit findings.	The auditor usually identifies a number of findings during a financial statement audit. The auditor reports on fair presentation in the financial statements through the auditor's report. In addition, the auditor communicates a number of findings such as the quality of accounting principles and deficiencies in internal controls to the audit committee. Finally, the auditor may also communicate the findings of other assurance services to various decision makers.	pp. 214–217

[FOCUS ON AUDIT DECISIONS]

This chapter provides an overview of the financial statement audit, and it presents introductory explanations of a number of important decisions that auditors need to make during an audit. Figure 5-6 summarizes these important audit decisions and provides a reference to where those decisions are discussed further in the remainder of the book.

Figure 5-6 ■ Summary of Important Audit Decisions

Phases of the Audit	Important Audit Decisions	Further Discussions
I. Perform risk assessment procedures	Identification of relevant assertions	Chapter 6
	Decisions about sufficiency and competency of evidence	Chapter 6
	Client acceptance and retention decisions	Chapter 7
	Using the understanding about the entity and its environment for audit planning	Chapter 7
	Decisions about materiality and tolerable misstatement	Chapter 8
	Decisions about the effectiveness of analytical procedures	Chapter 8
	How to use analytical procedures to identify potential misstatements	Chapter 8
	Decisions about the risk of fraud	Chapter 9
	Decisions about the assessment of inherent risk	Chapter 9
	Decisions about the identification of significant inherent risks	Chapter 9
	Decisions about preliminary audit strategy	Chapter 9
	Decisions about control risk	Chapters 10 and 11

(continues)

Figure 5-6 ■ (Continued)

Phases of the Audit	Important Audit Decisions	Further Discussions
II. Assess the risk of material misstatement	Relating risk factors to potential misstatements Assessing the magnitude of potential misstatements Assessing the likelihood of potential misstatements	Chapter 12 Chapter 12 Chapter 12
III. Respond to assessed risks	Decisions about the nature of audit tests Decisions about the timing of audit tests Decisions about the extent of audit tests Decisions about assigning staff to audit tests	Chapter 12 Chapter 12 Chapters 12 and 13 Chapter 12
IV. Perform further audit procedures	Auditing the revenue cycle Auditing the acquisitions cycle Auditing the production and inventory cycle Auditing the payroll cycle Auditing the investing and financing cycle Auditing investments and cash balances	Chapter 14 Chapter 15 Chapter 16 Chapter 16 Chapter 17 Chapter 18
V. Evaluate audit evidence	Evaluating the results of substantive tests Evaluating evidence about subsequent events, litigation, claims, and assessments and other evidence obtained at the conclusion of the audit Evaluating the cumulative effect of misstatements discovered during the audit Evaluating going concern	Chapters 14–18 Chapter 19 Chapter 19 Chapters 2 and 19
VI. Communicate audit findings	Communicating with financial statement users Communicating findings regarding internal controls Other required communications with management and the board of directors Communicating the findings of other assurance services	Chapters 2 and 20 Chapters 2, 11, 19, and 20 Chapter 19 Chapter 20

objective questions

Objective questions are available for students at www.wiley.com/college/boynton

comprehensive questions

5-27 **(Overview of the audit process)** A colleague of yours is trying to understand the existence of audit failures. As a user of financial statements, she asserts, there is a one-for-one correspondence between an entity's transactions and the way they are summarized and reported in the financial statements. "Isn't the audit process a matter of simply ensuring (1) that every transaction is recorded in the financial statements and (2) that every recorded transaction is correctly recorded? Why is the audit process more complicated than a simple two-step process?"

Required

Respond to your colleague's statement that the audit is merely a two-step process. Your response should:

a. Evaluate your colleague's view of the audit.

b. Provide an alternative overview of the audit process.

c. Explain how each step of the audit process supports the auditor's opinion on the financial statements.

d. Explain other benefits that accrue from a well-designed and well-performed audit.

5-28 **(Steps involved in planning the audit)** You are discussing the audit of accounts receivable with the senior on the audit of a manufacturing company. Discuss how the evidence you might collect to support an opinion on sales and accounts receivable would be affected by:

a. Knowledge of the business and industry

b. Assertions

c. Materiality

d. Performance of analytical procedures

e. Assess the risk of material misstatement, including the risk of fraud

f. Develop preliminary audit strategies

g. Understand the entity's system of internal control

Required

Using the following format, develop an example of how each relates to audit evidence.

KEY AUDIT PLANNING STEPS	DESCRIBE HOW AUDIT PLANNING STEP WOULD INFLUENCE COLLECTION OF AUDIT EVIDENCE
a. Knowledge of the entity and its environment	
b. Assertions	
c. Materiality	
d. Performance of analytical procedures	
e. The risk of material misstatement, including the risk of fraud	
f. Development of preliminary audit strategies	
g. The entity's internal control	

5-29 **(Assertions)** In planning the audit of a client's inventory, an auditor identified the following issues that need audit attention.

1. Inventories are properly stated at the lower of cost or market.

2. Inventories included in the balance sheet are present in the warehouse on the balance sheet date.

3. Inventory quantities include all products, materials, and supplies on hand.

4. Liens on the inventories are properly disclosed in notes to the financial statements.

5. The client has legal title to the inventories.

6. The financial statements disclose the amounts of raw materials, work in progress, and finished goods.

7. Inventories include all items purchased by the company that are in transit at the balance sheet date and that have been shipped to customers on consignment.

8. Inventories received on consignment from suppliers have been excluded from inventory.

9. Quantities times prices have been properly extended on the inventory listing, the listing is properly totaled, and the total agrees with the general ledger balance for inventories.

10. Slow-moving items included in inventory have been properly identified and priced.

11. Inventories are properly classified in the balance sheet as current assets.

Required

Identify the assertion for items 1 through 11 above.

5-30 **(Assertions)** In planning the audit of a client's financial statements, an auditor identified the following issues that need audit attention.

1. The allowance for doubtful accounts is fairly presented in amount.

2. All accounts payable owed as of the balance sheet date are included in the financial statements.

3. All purchase returns recorded in the general ledger are valid.

4. There is a risk that purchases made in the last week of the month might be recorded in the following period.

5. The client may have factored accounts receivable.

6. The client has used special-purpose entities to finance a building. Neither the building nor the debt is included in the financial statements.

7. A retail client values its inventory using the retail method of accounting.

8. A construction client uses the percentage of completion method for recognizing revenues.

9. A client has a defined benefit pension plan and does not have competent employees to write footnote disclosures.

10. A client acquired a subsidiary company and paid a high amount of goodwill when the stock market, and resulting values, were at all-time highs.

11. A client financed the acquisition of assets using preferred stock that pays a 3 percent dividend and must be redeemed from the shareholders next year.

Required

Identify the assertion for items 1 through 11 above.

5-31 **(Understanding the entity and its environment)** You are responsible for presenting a portion of your accounting firm's staff training program on the importance of understanding the business and industry. Explain how the following activities will help the auditor form an opinion on the fairness of presentation of the financial statements. Provide examples for each answer.

a. Industry, regulatory environment, and other factors

b. The nature of the entity

c. Objectives, strategies, and business risks

d. Management and review of the entity's financial performance

5-32 **(Materiality concepts)** Financial statements are materially misstated when they contain errors or irregularities whose effect, individually or in the aggregate, is important enough to prevent the statements from being presented fairly in conformity with GAAP.

Required

a. Financial statements may be misstated when they contain departures from facts. Identify two other types of circumstances that may cause the statements to be misstated.

b. In planning the audit, materiality should be assessed at two levels. Identify the two levels and state the reason for each.

c. Audit planning may occur in July for a client with a December 31 year-end. If data are available for the first six months of the year only, how can the auditor determine planning materiality for the annual audit?

d. The size of an account balance sets an upper limit on the amount of misstatement in the account. Is this statement correct? Explain.

e. Distinguish between the terms *material account balance* and *materiality* and state how each relates to the amount of evidence needed for an assertion.

5-33 **(Risk components and relationships)** Shown below are seven situations in which the auditor wishes to use the audit risk model to determine planned acceptable levels of detection risk and planned levels of evidence needed for specific financial statement assertions. The auditor has used judgment in arriving at the quantitative expressions for audit, inherent, and control risk.

ASSERTION	A	B	C	D	E	F	G
Desired audit risk	1%	1%	5%	5%	5%	5%	10%
Assessed inherent risk	20%	100%	20%	50%	100%	100%	50%
Planned assessed level of control risk	50%	7%	50%	40%	7%	80%	20%
Planned detection risk	_____	_____	_____	_____	_____	_____	_____
Planned evidence	_____	_____	_____	_____	_____	_____	_____

Required

a. Define the four types of risk listed above.

b. Using the audit risk model, calculate the planned detection risk for each of the situations above.

c. Rank the seven situations from most evidence required (1) to least evidence required (7).

d. What do the results obtained for situations (E) and (F) mean with respect to procedures to obtain evidence to achieve planned detection risk?

e. State how your answers to part (b) would be affected by a change in only one of the following factors, while the other two factors are held constant at the levels indicated in the table:
   1. Increase in desired audit risk.
   2. Decrease in assessed inherent risk.
   3. Increase in planned assessed level of control risk.

5-34 **(Risk of material misstatement)** Your client, a manufacturer of computer components, has experienced slowing demand for its product. Recently, it cut back from three shifts a day to two shifts a day, and the company has eliminated the backlog of orders that existed in prior years by providing financing to customers. Newspaper reports indicate that competition has taken significant business away from the client because a large investment in R&D has not resulted in improved products. Furthermore, a small handful of your client's customers are experiencing financial difficulties because of slowing demand for your client's products.

Required

a. Consider the implications of the above information for revenues. What assertions, if any, are likely to be misstated? As a result, what accounts are likely to be overstated or understated? Explain your reasoning.

b. Consider the implications of the above information for inventory. What assertions, if any, are likely to be misstated? As a result, what accounts are likely to be overstated or understated? Explain your reasoning.

5-35 **(Developing responses to assessed risks)** Your client, General Television, Inc. manufactures televisions and during the current year acquired Micro Engineering, Inc., which manufactured flat panel plasma screens for computers so that it could compete in the market for flat panel televisions. Following is a list of several risks that have been identified in the audit of this television manufacturer.

1. General Television has strong internal controls over the existence of inventory. It has a good perpetual inventory system and regularly compares inventory on hand with the perpetual records.

2. Prices have been changing rapidly in General Television's marketplace. Although the marketplace is relatively stable for traditional televisions, the prices on flat panel televisions have become much more competitive.

3. General Television had to pay a premium to acquire Micro Engineering. General Television had independent appraisals of the fair value of assets and has determined that about 35 percent of the purchase price should be allocated to goodwill.

Required

Answer the following questions for the risks described in 1, 2, and 3 above.

a. Identify the relevant assertion.

b. Does this assertion represent a significant inherent risk? Explain.

c. How might you respond to this risk in terms of staffing decisions?

d. How might you respond to this risk in terms of the nature of audit tests?

e. How might you respond to this risk in terms of the timing of audit tests?

f. How might you respond to this risk in terms of the extent of audit tests?

5-36 **(Nature of audit procedures)** Assume that you are auditing inventory for a clothing retailer. Following are eight general types of audit procedures used by auditors.

1. Further risk assessment procedures

2. Tests of controls

3. Initial procedures

4. Analytical procedures

5. Tests of details of transactions

6. Tests of details of balances

7. Tests of details of accounting estimates

8. Tests of details of disclosures

Required

Using the following table (1) provide an example of each procedure in the context of auditing inventory and (2) explain how each procedure would relate to an element of the audit risk model.

CATEGORY OF AUDIT PROCEDURE	EXAMPLE IN THE CONTEXT OF AUDITING INVENTORY	HOW WOULD THE PROCEDURE RELATE TO AN ELEMENT OF THE AUDIT RISK MODEL?
1. Further risk assessment procedures		
2. Tests of controls		
3. Initial procedures		
4. Analytical procedures		
5. Tests of details of transactions		
6. Tests of details of balances		
7. Tests of details of accounting estimates		
8. Tests of details of disclosures		

5-37   **(Evaluation of audit findings)** You are auditing cutoff for accounts payable of a company and you find three transactions that are of concern. The voucher is the document that the company uses to record accounts payable in the purchases journal.

a. Voucher # 50021, dated 1/5/X5, is supported by an underlying vendor's invoice in the amount of $20,000 dated December 30, 20X4 shipped FOB destination. The vendor's invoice matches the quantity on the receiving report (1,000 items) dated January 3, 20X5, and the price on the purchase order ($20) dated 12/15/X4.

b. Voucher # 50185, dated 1/5/X5, is supported by an underlying vendor's invoice in the amount of $100,000 dated December 27, 20X4, shipped FOB shipping point. The vendor's invoice matches the quantity on the receiving report (100,000 items) dated December 30, 20X4, and the price on the purchase order ($1) dated 12/05/X4.

c. Voucher # 50244, dated 1/12/X5, is supported by an underlying vendor's invoice in the amount of $70,000 dated January 2, 20X5, shipped FOB destination. The vendor's invoice matches the quantity on the receiving report (3,500 items) dated January 5, 20X5, but the price of $20 per unit on the voucher does not match the price of $22 per unit on the invoice or the price on the purchase order ($22) dated 12/23/X4.

Required

a. For each item, determine whether a cutoff error exists, and identify the amount of the error.

b. Assume that you took a sample of $1 million of transactions posted to the purchases journal in January, out of a population of $4 million. The three items above are the only items that you questioned. All other items in your sample were accurately recorded. If your results are representative of the unsampled items in the population, propose a journal entry to correct the projected misstatements that you believe exist in the population.

5-38 **(Communicating audit findings)** You are having lunch with a member of the board of directors of a prospective client. You have just explained how the audit opinion adds to the confidence of financial statement users by providing reasonable assurance that the financial statements are free of material misstatements. The director then asks what additional benefits the company might attain from the audit and your expertise in the business and industry.

Required

a. How would you respond to the director's questions regarding additional benefits that the company might attain from the audit and how they are communicated?

b. What precautions must the auditor take to ensure that he or she remains independent with respect to the audit engagement when providing value-added services?

professional simulation

Assume that you have just been promoted to the position of in-charge accountant on the audit of Alpha Corporation, a manufacturer of auto parts. Alpha Corporation is a private company that is wholly owned by George Alpha. Michelle Driscoll has been the partner on the engagement for 10 years, since the Alpha Corporation first needed an audit for bank financing. Michelle has an excellent knowledge of the business, its competitive environment, and is very knowledgeable about the entity's accounting systems and the situations that have given rise to audit adjustments in prior years.

Several of the auditors who previously worked on the Alpha Corporation audit have moved on in their careers. The former audit manager recently took a position as CFO for a start-up company. The in-charge accountant on the Alpha Corporation engagement moved to the tax department and is now working on Alpha Corporation's tax planning. Michelle finds that she has a completely new staff working on the audit engagement this year. As she considers the audit firm's responsibility to evaluate the risk of fraud in the Alpha Corporation engagement she feels that she is quite knowledgeable about the entity's fraud risks, but that everyone else on the engagement is approaching this audit for the first time. She has asked you to research the firm's professional responsibilities. Research U.S. generally accepted auditing standards to determine the professional responsibilities for discussion among engagement personnel regarding the risks of material misstatement due to fraud. Cut and paste the standard sections that apply to this issue.

```
                                    ┌──────────────────┐
                                    │  Draft Report    │
                    ┌───────────────┼───────────┐      │
                    │   Situation   │  Research │      │
                    └───────────────┴───────────┴──────┘
```

Michelle would also like to understand the firm's responsibility to identify and document fraud risk factors. Draft a memo that (1) outlines the responsibility of an audit firm to identify fraud risk factors, (2) provides some example fraud risk factors related to fraudulent financial reporting, and (3) outlines the professional requirements for documenting the auditor's consideration of fraud in the working papers.

To: Michelle Driscoll

Re: Fraud Risk Factors

From: CPA Candidate

[6] AUDIT EVIDENCE

SUNBEAM CORPORATION

During 1997 Sunbeam Corporation offered financial incentives to various customers to provide purchase orders substantially in advance of their actual need for the product. Sunbeam also offered to hold the merchandise in its warehouses until the normal time for delivery. For revenue recognition purposes, Sunbeam treated these transactions as "bill-and-hold" sales and recognized $14 million in sales revenue and over $6 million in net income.

The criteria for recognition of revenue on bill-and-hold sales requires that the following conditions for recognition of revenue be met: (1) the risks of ownership must pass to the buyer; (2) the customer must make a fixed commitment to purchase the goods, preferably reflected in written documentation; (3) the buyer, not the seller, must request that the transaction be on a bill-and-hold basis and must have a substantial business purpose for ordering the goods on a bill-and-hold basis; (4) there must be a fixed schedule for delivery of the goods that is reasonable and consistent with the buyer's business purpose; (5) the seller must not retain any specific performance obligations such that the earnings process is not complete; (6) the ordered goods must have been segregated from the seller's inventory and not be subject to being used to fill other orders; and (7) the equipment must be complete and ready for shipment.

In Accounting and Auditing Enforcement Release No. 1706, the Securities and Exchange Commission alleged that the audit engagement Partner, Phillip Harlow, CPA, failed to ensure that the audit team performed procedures adequate to obtain sufficient, competent audit evidence and verify that the company's bill-and-hold sales complied with GAAP requirements for revenue recognition. In particular, the team failed to obtain evidence that the buyer, not the seller, had a substantial business purpose for the bill-and-hold sale. Furthermore, Sunbeam's customers had not requested sales on a bill-and-hold basis. Without admitting or denying the Commission's findings, Phillip Harlow agreed to give up his privilege of appearing or practicing before the SEC as an accountant.

The key issue here revolves around obtaining sufficient competent audit evidence. Phillip Harlow could have performed a higher quality audit had he, and the engagement team under his supervision, obtained evidence from the buyer, as well as the seller (the client), to support a conclusion on the bill-and-hold sale. Failure to address this one aspect of the audit resulted in a material misstatement in the financial statements. This chapter provides a discussion of the requirements of generally accepted auditing standards regarding obtaining sufficient, competent audit evidence to support an opinion on the financial statements.

Source: SEC, Accounting and Auditing Enforcement Release No. 1706, January 27, 2003.

[PREVIEW OF CHAPTER 6]

The auditor begins planning the audit with the end in mind. Let's work our way backward for a moment. The overall objective of a high-quality financial statement audit is to obtain reasonable assurance that the client's financial statements are presented fairly, in all material respects, in conformity with GAAP. Stepping back one level, the auditor should obtain sufficient, competent evidential matter to afford a reasonable basis for his or her opinion. Regardless of whether evidence comes in the form of risk assessment procedures, tests of controls, or substantive tests, the auditor should follow some general rules that guide audit decisions about the quality of evidence. The following diagram provides an overview of the chapter organization and content.

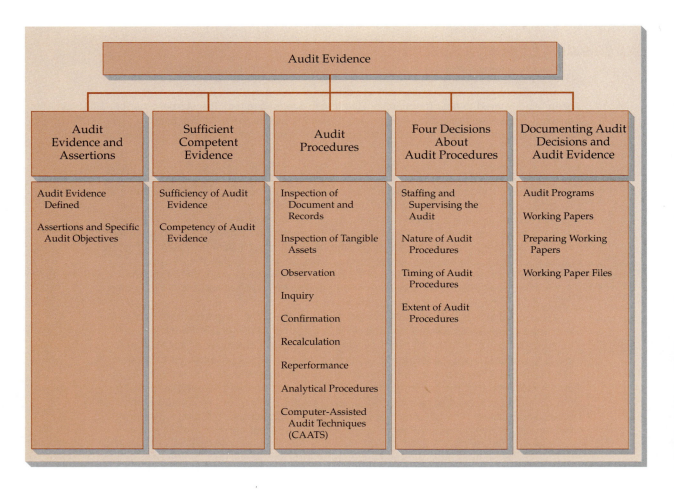

Chapter 6 focuses on audit evidence and documenting audit evidence and conclusions. This chapter addresses the following aspects of the auditor's knowledge and focuses on four important audit decisions.

[AUDIT EVIDENCE AND ASSERTIONS]

AUDIT EVIDENCE DEFINED

Auditor Knowledge 1

■ Know the definition of audit evidence and understand the difference between how accounting records and other information are used as audit evidence.

Audit evidence is all the information used by the auditor in arriving at the conclusion on which the audit opinion is based. Audit evidence includes (1) the accounting records underlying the financial statements and (2) other information that corroborates the accounting records and supports the auditor's logical reasoning about fair presentation in the financial statements. Audit evidence is cumulative in nature and includes audit evidence obtained from audit procedures performed during the course of the audit. It may include audit evidence obtained from other sources, such as from previous audits or from the firm's quality control procedures for the acceptance and continuance of clients.

The accounting student should already be familiar with the basic components of accounting records identified in Figure 6-1. **Accounting records** generally include the records of initial entries and supporting records. For example, accounting records would include:

■ Checks and records of electronic funds transfers.
■ Invoices.
■ Contracts.
■ The general and subsidiary ledgers.
■ Journal entries and other adjustments to the financial statement that are not reflected in formal journal entries.

Figure 6-1 ■ Types of Audit Evidence

Nature of Audit Evidence	Third Standard of Field Work
ACCOUNTING RECORDS (Accounting records alone do not provide sufficient evidence on which to base an audit opinion.)	
■ Checks and records of electronic funds transfers.	
■ Invoices	
■ Contracts	
■ The general and subsidiary ledgers	
■ Journal entries and other adjustments to the financial statement that are not reflected in formal journal entries	
■ Records such as worksheets and spreadsheets supporting cost allocations, computations, and reconciliations	
■ Disclosures	**Sufficient Competent Evidence**
OTHER INFORMATION	
■ Minutes of meetings	
■ Confirmation from third parties	
■ Analysts' reports	
■ Comparable data about competitors (benchmarking)	
■ Internal control manuals	
■ Information obtained through audit procedures such as inquiry, observation, or inspection of records or documents	
■ Information developed by the auditor that permits the auditor to reach a conclusion through valid logical reasoning	

■ Records such as worksheets and spreadsheets supporting cost allocations, computations, and reconciliations.

■ Disclosures.

The entries in the accounting records may be initiated, recorded, processed, and reported in electronic form. The accounting records may also be part of an integrated system that shares data to support the entity's financial reporting, operations, and compliance needs.

Management prepares the financial statements based on the accounting records of the entity. The auditor obtains some audit evidence by testing the accounting records. For example, the auditor might use generalized audit software to test the mathematical accuracy of supporting accounting records, to ensure that they are internally consistent and that they agree with the financial statement. Alternatively, the auditor might use computer-assisted audit techniques to reperform procedures performed in the financial reporting process. However, accounting records alone do not provide sufficient evidence on which to base an audit opinion on the financial statements. Hence, the auditor obtains other information to develop a persuasive package of audit evidence.

Other information that the auditor may use as audit evidence includes, for example:

- Minutes of meetings
- Confirmation from third parties
- Analysts' reports
- Comparable data about competitors (benchmarking)
- Internal control manuals
- Information obtained through audit procedures such as inquiry, observation, or inspection of records or documents
- Information developed by the auditor that permits the auditor to reach a conclusion through valid logical reasoning

In summary, audit evidence represents all the information that is obtained by performing risk assessment procedures, tests of controls, and substantive tests to support an opinion on the financial statements. The auditor uses a combination of tests of accounting records and other information to support that opinion.

ASSERTIONS AND SPECIFIC AUDIT OBJECTIVES

Audit Decision 1

■ How does an auditor determine specific audit objectives from the categories of assertions?

Recall from Chapter 5 that management's assertions in the financial statements guide the auditor in (1) assessing the risk of material misstatement in the financial statements and (2) planning the collection of audit evidence that is a response to those risks. The five management assertions outlined in generally accepted auditing standards are:

- Existence or occurrence
- Completeness
- Rights and obligations
- Valuation or allocation
- Presentation and disclosure

In obtaining evidence to support an opinion on the financial statements, the auditor develops specific audit objectives for each account balance and transaction class in the financial statements (e.g., revenue cycle, expenditure cycle, inventory cycle). Specific audit objectives are a refinement of assertions. They are important because each audit objective usually is affected by different risks and requires different evidence. Figure 6-2 presents a framework for developing specific audit objectives.

This framework is based on the results of a joint Auditing Standards Board and International Auditing and Assurance Standards Board project.[1] Using this framework, the auditor needs to identify the relevant transactions, account balances, and disclosures in the financial statements for a transaction cycle that is being audited. For illustration purposes, let's assume that the auditor is auditing the revenue cycle. The revenue cycle has three major transactions classes: (1) credit sales, (2) cash receipts, and (3) sales adjustments, which include sales returns and

---

[1] These specific audit objectives were included in an Auditing Standards Board Exposure Draft dated December 2, 2002. These were also adopted as assertions by the International Auditing and Assurance Standards Board on October 31, 2003.

Figure 6-2 ■ Framework for Developing Specific Audit Objectives

Specific Audit Objectives	E&O	C	R&O	V&A	P&D
TRANSACTION OBJECTIVES					
Occurrence. Transactions and events that have been recorded have occurred and pertain to the entity.	x				
Completeness. All transactions and events that should have been recorded are recorded.		x			
Accuracy. Amounts and other data related to recorded transactions and events have been recorded appropriately.				x	
Cutoff. Transactions and events have been recorded in the correct accounting period.	x	x			
Classification. Transactions and events have been recorded in the proper accounts.					x
BALANCE OBJECTIVES					
Existence. Assets, liabilities, and equity interests exist.	x				
Completeness. All assets, liabilities, and equity interests that should have been recorded are recorded.		x			
Rights and Obligations. The entity holds or controls rights to assets, and liabilities are the obligations of the entity.			x		
Valuation and Allocation. Assets, liabilities, and equity interests are included in the financial statements at the appropriate amounts, and any appropriate valuation adjustments are appropriately recorded.				x	
DISCLOSURE OBJECTIVES					
Occurrence and Rights and Obligations. Disclosed events and transactions have occurred and pertain to the entity.					x
Completeness. All disclosures that should have been included in the financial statements have been included.					x
Classification and Understandability. Financial information about revenues is appropriately presented, and information in disclosures is clearly expressed. For example, information about receivables from customers, affiliated companies, officers and directors, and from other related parties is appropriately classified and clearly disclosed.					x
Accuracy and Valuation. Financial and other information is disclosed fairly and at appropriate amounts.					x

allowance and write-offs of bad debts. The balance associated with the revenue cycle is accounts receivable. Finally, the auditor needs to consider the disclosures associated with revenues and receivables.

The auditor would then develop specific audit objectives as discussed in the following section.

Transaction Class Audit Objectives

In general, the auditor wants to cover the following five audit objectives for three transaction classes: (1) credit sales, (2) cash receipts, and (3) sales adjustments. Hence, the auditor's specific audit objectives associated with revenues transactions would be:

- **Occurrence.** All sales, cash receipts, and sales adjustments transactions that have been recorded actually occurred during the period. For example, the audit should determine whether recorded revenues meet GAAP criteria for revenue recognition.
- **Completeness.** All sales, cash receipts, and sales adjustments that occurred during the period have been recorded. For example, an audit should determine whether all sales returns have in fact been recorded.
- **Accuracy.** All sales, cash receipts, and sales adjustments have been recorded accurately. For example, sales are recorded in the correct amounts based on the number of items shipped and appropriate prices.
- **Cutoff.** All sales, cash receipts, and sales adjustments have been recorded in the correct accounting period. For example, sales transactions are recorded in the period in which title passes to goods or services.
- **Classification.** All sales, cash receipts, and sales adjustments have been recorded in the proper accounts. For example, trade receivables are segregated from receivables from affiliated companies, employees, or officers.

Using this framework, the auditor should evaluate risk and obtain evidence for each of the five specific audit objectives for sales transactions, cash receipt transactions, and for sales adjustment transactions.

Account Balance Audit Objectives

When planning an audit of the revenue cycle, the auditor would develop specific audit objectives for only one account balance—accounts receivable. These audit objectives would be:

- **Existence.** Accounts receivable represent valid amounts owed by customers at the balance sheet date. Recorded accounts receivable exist. For example, the auditor should determine that recorded receivables represent amounts actually owing from customers.
- **Completeness.** Accounts receivable include all claims on customers at the balance sheet date. For example, the auditor should determine that all receivables that should have been recorded are recorded.
- **Rights and Obligations.** Accounts receivable at the balance sheet date represent the legal claims of the entity on customers for payment. For example, the auditor should determine that recorded receivables represent receivables where the entity controls the right to the amount owed and does not represent receivables where the right has been factored or sold.
- **Valuation and Allocation.** Accounts receivable is properly recorded at its net realizable value. For example, the auditor should determine that accounts receivable are recorded at the correct gross amount and that appropriate allowances for doubtful accounts are recorded. Again, the auditor would use this framework to guide the evaluation of risk of material misstatement and to

obtain evidence for each of the four specific audit objectives for accounts receivable. Note, for example, that the evidence needed to evaluate the allowance for doubtful accounts is different from the evidence needed to evaluate the accuracy of sales and receivables even though both objectives are related to the valuation and allocation assertion.

Disclosure Audit Objectives

Finally, when planning an audit of the revenue cycle, the auditor would develop specific audit objectives for note disclosures. These audit objectives would be:

- **Occurrence and Rights and Obligations.** The disclosed revenue events and transactions have occurred and pertain to the entity. For example, the information that has been disclosed about revenue recognition policies or about pledged or factored receivables is factual.
- **Completeness.** All revenue and receivable disclosures that should have been included in the financial statements have been included. For example, all disclosures regarding the factoring of receivables are disclosed.
- **Classification and Understandability.** Financial information about revenues is appropriately presented and information in disclosures is clearly expressed. For example, information about receivables from customers or affiliated companies is appropriately classified and clearly disclosed.
- **Accuracy and Valuation.** Financial and other information about revenues and receivables is disclosed accurately and at appropriate amounts. For example, disclosed information about whether the amounts and collectibility of receivables are from related parties, employees, or officers are fairly presented.

These specific audit objectives identify several different facets associated with the presentation and disclosure assertion. The risks associated with understandability may be different from the risks associated with accuracy and valuation or with completeness of disclosures. As a result, the auditor will likely design different audit procedures for each specific audit objective.

A Few Examples

Consider a few examples of how auditors use the concepts of specific audit objectives when making decisions about audit evidence. Assume for a moment that an audit client manufactures various consumer and household appliances. You have determined that there is not a significant risk of fraud or other risks that might have a pervasive impact on the financial statements (such as management with weak accounting knowledge or experience). You also feel that management promotes a high level of control consciousness. However, you have noted that the client's production levels have exceeded its ability to make sales through the third quarter and that the client has seen a buildup in inventory levels. Management is actively working with its customers (wholesalers and large retailers) to find ways to promote sales to end consumers. Now consider two transaction-level audit objectives related to sales transactions, occurrence and accuracy.

With respect to the occurrence objective, the auditor might consider that the inherent risk is very high, particularly considering that management is actively working to increase the level of sales. In these circumstances auditors are often concerned about revenue recognition, especially if the company must make concessions about the right of return inventory in order to make sales. Next the auditor will want to consider internal controls related to the audit objective. For example, the client might use a programmed control to ensure that every sales invoice is matched with a bill of lading ensuring that goods are shipped before an invoice is recorded. However, it is rare for programmed controls to look at terms associated with the right to return goods that have been shipped, so again the auditor might assess control risk as a high risk of material misstatement due to right of return issues. When it comes to designing substantive tests, the auditor's greatest concern is with sales that have not yet been paid for, for example, the outstanding receivables. Because of the very high inherent and control risks, the auditor might decide to confirm both the existence of the receivable and the terms of the sale to address the inherent risk associated with rights of return. If the confirmations are returned from customers without exceptions and the sales were made without the right of return, the auditor has evidence about both the existence of the receivable and the occurrence of the sale.

The accuracy audit objective has less subjective elements and is usually a matter of quantity times price. As a result, the auditor might assess the inherent risk of misstatement for the accuracy assertion as moderate. Internal controls are often effective for routine transactions. Hence, programmed controls might pull prices from a master price list and compare quantities with both the quantity ordered and the quantity shipped. Let's assume further that the auditor performs tests of controls and concludes that programmed controls and manual followup of exceptions operated effectively during the current period. The evidence might support a decision to assess control risk as low. For substantive tests the confirmation related to occurrence and existence of sales will also provide evidence about accuracy. Hopefully, the confirmations from customers will disclose few exceptions and provide evidence that is consistent with the prior conclusion that internal controls function effectively.

Finally, consider the account balance specific audit objective associated with the collectibility of receivables. This specific audit objective is also related to the valuation and allocation assertion. However, the internal controls over this objective are different from the controls over the accuracy assertion (also related to the valuation and allocation assertion). In this case the control might relate to approval of customer credit. However, even customers with good credit ratings may have a difficult time paying receivables in a slow economy. The auditor might assess inherent risk and control risk at the maximum for this assertion and use generalized audit software to analyze the payment history of each customer and print a history of customers with past due balances. This might provide evidence to support an estimate of the allowance for doubtful accounts.

Note that in each case, the auditor considers the risk of misstatement for specific audit objectives and designs substantive tests to respond to the risk of misstatement for each specific audit objective. It is also important to note that some evidence satisfies more than one audit objective. Confirming receivables, for example, provides evidence about the occurrence of sales, the existence of receivables, and the accuracy of sales. Confirmations, however, do not provide evidence about the collectibility of receivables.

LEARNING CHECK

6-1 a. Define audit evidence.

b. Would information obtained while performing risk assessment procedures or information obtained during prior audits serve as audit evidence? Explain.

6-2 a. What is meant by the term *accounting records?*

b. In the context of sales and collections, provide some examples of what are considered to be accounting records.

c. Are accounting records alone usually considered to be enough to represent sufficient evidence for an opinion on the financial statements?

6-3 a. What is meant by the term *other information?*

b. In the context of sales and collections, provide some examples of other information used to support an opinion on the financial statements.

6-4 a. Define each of the five assertions for fixed assets.

b. Develop the transaction class audit objectives for fixed assets and provide an example of each.

c. Develop the account balance audit objectives and provide an example of each in the context of fixed assets.

d. Develop the four disclosure audit objectives and provide an example of each in the context of fixed assets.

KEY TERMS

Accounting records, p. 229
Accuracy, p. 233
Accuracy and valuation, p. 234
Audit evidence, p. 229
Classification, p. 233
Completeness, p. 233
Cutoff, p. 233
Existence, p. 233

Occurrence, p. 233
Occurrence and rights and
  obligations, p. 234
Other information, p. 231
Rights and obligations, p. 233
Valuation and allocation, p. 233
Understandability, p. 234

SUFFICIENT COMPETENT EVIDENCE

Audit evidence is so pervasive to the nature of audit work that it is embedded in the third field work standard of generally accepted auditing standards. The third field work standard states:

> "Sufficient competent audit evidence is to be obtained through audit procedures performed to afford a reasonable basis for an opinion regarding the financial statement under audit."
>
> *Source:* AU 326.01 exposure draft

The concept of **sufficient audit evidence** relates to the quantity of audit evidence, and the concept of **competent audit evidence** relates to the quality of audit

Audit Decision 2

■ **What factors affect the sufficiency and competency of audit evidence?**

evidence, in particular, its relevance and its reliability in providing support for the assertions reported in the financial statements.

SUFFICIENCY OF AUDIT EVIDENCE

Sufficiency of audit evidence is a measure of the quantity of audit evidence. Factors that may affect the auditor's judgment as to sufficiency include:

■ Materiality.
■ Risk of material misstatement.
■ Size and characteristics of the population.

These factors are discussed below and summarized in Figure 6-3.

Materiality

Materiality refers to the significance of transaction classes, account balances, and disclosures to financial statement users. In general, more evidence is needed for transaction classes, accounts and disclosures that are material to the financial statements than for transaction classes, and accounts and disclosures that are immaterial. Thus, in the audit of a manufacturing company the amount of audit evidence in support of the audit assertions for inventories will be more extensive than the evidence needed for the audit assertions for cash.

Risk of Material Misstatement

The **risk of material misstatement** refers to the inherent risks that an assertion might be misstated and the control risk that internal control will fail to prevent or detect a material misstatement in an assertion. More persuasive evidence is needed for assertions that have a high risk of material misstatement than for assertions that have a low risk of material misstatement. For example, an assertion that has low inherent risk (such as the completeness assertion for payroll costs) will need less evidence than an assertion that has high inherent risk (such as the occurrence of sales and revenue recognition). In addition, more substantive evidence will be needed when a company has poor internal controls than when a company has good internal controls.

Figure 6-3 ■ Factors That Influence Audit Decisions about the Sufficiency of Audit Evidence

Less Evidence Required	Factors Related to the Sufficiency of Audit Evidence	More Evidence Required
Assertions that are less material to financial statement users	**Materiality**	Assertions that are more material to financial statement users
Assertions that have a lower risk of material misstatement	**Risk of Material Misstatement**	Assertions that have a higher risk of material misstatement
Smaller, more homogeneous populations	**Size and Characteristics of the Population**	Larger, more heterogeneous populations

Size and Characteristics of the Population

The **size of a population** refers to the number of items contained in the population, such as the number of sales transactions in the sales journal. The size of the accounting populations underlying financial statement assertions makes sampling a necessity in gathering evidence. Generally, the larger the population, the larger the quantity of evidence required to obtain a reasonable basis for reaching a conclusion about it. The **characteristics of a population** generally refer to the nature of the items included in a population. Generally, a more homogeneous audit population, such as a lumber inventory, can be audited with smaller sample sizes than heterogeneous populations, such as the inventory of a large department store. The exact relationship between population size and population characteristics and sample size depends on the purpose and nature of the sampling plan being used, as explained in Chapter 13.

COMPETENCY OF AUDIT EVIDENCE

Competency is a measure of the quality, or reliability, of audit evidence. In order to be competent, evidence must be relevant to the assertion. In addition, a variety of generalizations relate to the reliability of evidence. The following discussion addresses both the relevance and reliability of audit evidence.

Relevance of Audit Evidence

Relevance means that evidence must be pertinent to management's assertions in the financial statements. Thus, if the auditor is examining the existence of inventory, the auditor can obtain evidence by observing the client's inventory-taking. However, such evidence might not be relevant in determining whether the goods are owned by the client (rights and obligations) or their cost (valuation and allocation). Evidence related to one assertion is not a substitute for obtaining audit evidence regarding another assertion. The auditor should be fully aware of the relationship between evidence and assertions, including how the evidence describes the underlying economic substance of the assertions. Unnecessary cost and time result when the auditor obtains irrelevant evidence or does not fully understand the economic substance revealed in evidence.

Other Factors Related to the Reliability of Audit Evidence

In addition to being relevant, audit evidence must be **reliable** and trustworthy. A variety of factors affect the reliability of audit evidence; these factors are summarized in Figure 6-4. Although these generalizations about the reliability of audit evidence are helpful, they must be used with caution. For example, evidence obtained from external sources may not be reliable if the source is not knowledgeable. With respect to the last factor, when the auditor obtains evidence from one source that is inconsistent with evidence from another source, the auditor needs to determine what additional audit procedures are necessary to resolve the inconsistency.

Documentary evidence is used extensively in auditing, and, depending on the circumstance, it may pertain to a specific assertion. An audit rarely involves the

Figure 6-4 ■ Factors That Influence Audit Decisions about the Reliability of Audit Evidence

Evidence Is Less Reliable	Factors Related to the Reliability of Audit Evidence	Evidence Is More Reliable
Evidence obtained from an internal source, such as documents obtained from management	Independence of the source	Evidence obtained from an independent outside source, such as a customer or bank
Evidence obtained indirectly or by inference, such as making an inquiry about the application of a control	Obtained directly by the auditor	Evidence obtained directly by the auditor, such as directly observing the application of a control
Evidence generated internally when it is produced by a system where internal controls are ineffective	Internal controls over internal information	Evidence generated internally when it is produced by a system where internal controls operate effectively
Evidence when it is not documented in a contemporaneous fashion, such as a subsequent oral representation	Written documents	Evidence in documentary form, such as a contemporaneously written record of analysis of variations from budgets
Evidence in the form of photocopies or facsimiles	Original documents	Evidence in the form of original documents
Corroborating evidence from an outside source is inconsistent with evidence obtained within the entity	Consistency of evidence from differing sources	Corroborating evidence from an outside source is consistent with evidence obtained within the entity

authentication of documentation, nor is the auditor trained to be an expert in such authentication. However, the auditor considers the reliability of documentary evidence. As noted in Figure 6-4, documents that are produced by a strong system of internal control are more reliable than those produced by a poor system of internal control. Documents also range from those that are created by an independent source to those that are created internally but contain outside signatures by an independent source to those that are created internally and do not circulate outside of the organization. The effects of circulation on the reliability of documentary evidence are summarized in Figure 6-5.

Professional Judgment

An auditor works within economic limits that dictate that sufficient audit evidence must be obtained within a reasonable time and at a reasonable cost. Thus, the auditor is frequently faced with a decision as to whether the additional time and cost will produce commensurate benefits in terms of the persuasiveness of the evidence obtained. For example, to verify the existence of a client's 25 petty cash funds, the auditor could personally count each fund. A less costly alternative is to personally count five of the funds and, upon finding that the funds agree with the

Figure 6-5 ■ Effects of Circulation on Reliability of Documentary Evidence

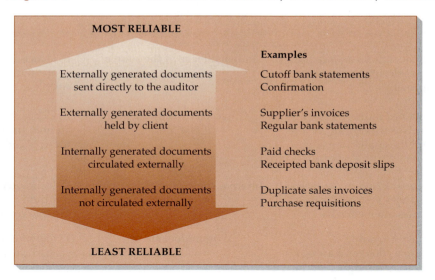

recorded amounts, rely on the reports of the client's internal auditors for the other 20. Although economic factors are a valid consideration in making decisions at the margin about gathering additional evidence, cost alone is never a valid basis for omitting an audit procedure for which there is not an alternative.

The auditor uses professional judgment in determining the quantity and quality of audit evidence. The auditor forms an opinion based on reasonable assurance that assertions in the financial statements are presented fairly in all material respect. The auditor is seldom convinced beyond all doubt with respect to the financial statement being audited. Ordinarily, the auditor finds it necessary to rely on audit evidence that is persuasive rather than conclusive. Nevertheless, reasonable assurance is not obtained when the auditor is not satisfied with audit evidence that is less than persuasive.

[LEARNING CHECK

6-5   Explain the factors that influence an auditor's decisions about the sufficiency of audit evidence.

6-6   Explain how the relevance of audit evidence bears on the auditor's decisions about the competency of audit evidence.

6-7   a. Identify six factors that influence the reliability of audit evidence.
      b. In the context of auditing sales and receivables, provide an example of how each factor influences the reliability of audit evidence.

6-8   a. Explain how the circulation of a document affects the reliability of documentary evidence.
      b. In the context of auditing sales and receivables, provide an example of a very reliable document and a document that would not be considered reliable.

[KEY TERMS

Characteristics of a population, p. 238
Competent audit evidence, p. 236
Materiality, p. 237
Relevance, p. 238

Reliable, p. 238
Risk of material misstatement, p. 237
Size of a population, p. 238
Sufficient audit evidence, p. 236

[AUDIT PROCEDURES]

Audit Decision 3

■ What types of audit procedures may be used in an audit?

Audit procedures are the methods or techniques the auditor uses to gather and evaluate audit evidence. The auditor performs audit procedures to accomplish the following objectives:

1. To obtain an understanding of the entity and its environment, including its internal control, to assess the risk of material misstatements at the financial statement level and at the assertion level (risk assessment procedures). The auditor *always* performs risk assessment procedures to provide a satisfactory basis for the assessed risks of material misstatement. However, risk assessment procedures by themselves do not provide sufficient competent evidence on which to base an audit opinion.
2. To test the operating effectiveness of controls in preventing or detecting material misstatements at the assertion level (tests of controls). Tests of controls are required when the auditor plans to assess control risk below the maximum and develop an audit strategy that assumes the operating effectiveness of internal controls. Tests of controls are also required when the client's accounting system is so information technology intense that substantive procedures alone do not provide sufficient, competent audit evidence.
3. To support an assertion or detect material misstatements at the assertion level (substantive tests). The auditor plans and performs substantive tests that are responsive to assessed risks. Furthermore, the auditor *always* performs substantive tests because of the inherent limitations of internal control and because risk assessment procedures are inherently judgmental.

Figure 6-6 identifies the basic choices of audit procedures that an auditor may elect to use when auditing an assertion or specific audit objective. The following discussion reviews nine basic types of procedures used by auditors to accomplish these goals. Part 4 of the book provides extensive examples of how auditors use each of these audit procedures in the context of auditing specific transaction cycles and related account balances.

INSPECTION OF DOCUMENTS AND RECORDS

Inspection of documents and records consist of examining records and documents, whether internal or external, in paper form, electronic form, or other media. This procedure is used extensively in auditing. Inspection of documents permits determination of the precise terms of invoices or contracts. At the same time the auditor often considers the implications of the evidence in the context of understanding the

Figure 6-6 ■ Potential Choices of Audit Procedures

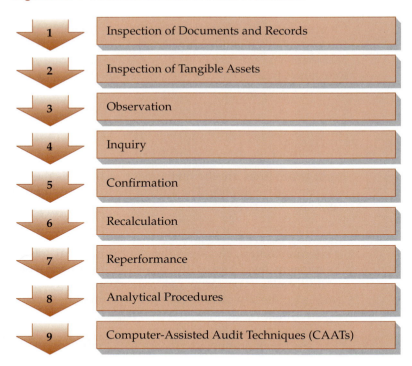

1. Inspection of Documents and Records
2. Inspection of Tangible Assets
3. Observation
4. Inquiry
5. Confirmation
6. Recalculation
7. Reperformance
8. Analytical Procedures
9. Computer-Assisted Audit Techniques (CAATs)

economic and competitive factors of an entity. For example, when the auditor inspects a lease contract, he or she verifies the appropriateness of the accounting for the lease, whether the lease is from a variable interest entity that should be consolidated, and evaluates how the lease impacts financing and investing activities of the entity. Furthermore, the auditor will consider how the lease will impact the entity's ability to generate additional revenues and how the entity's fixed cost structure may be impacted by the transactions.

Some documents represent direct audit evidence of the existence of an asset; for example, a document constituting a financial instrument such as a stock or bond. However, inspection of such documents may not necessarily provide audit evidence about ownership or value. Terms such as *reviewing, reading,* and *examining* are synonymous with inspecting documents and records. Inspecting documents may provide a means for evaluating documentary evidence. Thus, through inspection the auditor can assess the authenticity of documents, or perhaps detect the existence of alterations or questionable items. A derivation of inspecting is scanning, which involves less careful scrutiny of documents and records.

Two important audit terms associated with the inspection of documents are *vouching* and *tracing.* These audit procedures involve the inspection of documents in a specific fashion.

Vouching

Vouching involves (1) selecting entries in the accounting records and (2) obtaining and inspecting the documentation that served as the basis for the entries in order to determine the validity and accuracy of the recorded transactions. For example, when testing the occurrence of sales, the auditor might select transactions from the sales journal and vouch the transaction back to supporting documents, such as a bill of lading and customer order. Vouching is used extensively to detect overstatements in the accounting records. Thus, it is an important procedure in obtaining evidence pertaining to existence or occurrence assertions.

Tracing

In **tracing,** the auditor (1) selects documents created when transactions are executed and (2) determines that information from the documents is properly recorded in the accounting records (journals and ledgers). In tracing, the direction of testing is opposite to that used in vouching. The direction of testing is from the documents to the accounting records, thus retracing the original flow of the data through the accounting system. For example, when testing the completeness of sales, the auditor might select a sample of sales orders or bills of lading and trace the transaction to its recording in the sales journal and general ledger.

Because this procedure provides assurance that data from source documents were ultimately included in the accounts, it is especially useful for detecting understatements in the accounting records. Thus, it is an important procedure in obtaining evidence pertaining to completeness assertions. The effectiveness of the procedure is enhanced when the client uses serially prenumbered documents. Figure 6-7 shows the principal differences between vouching and tracing.

INSPECTION OF TANGIBLE ASSETS

Inspection of tangible assets consists of physical examination of the assets of an entity. Inspecting tangible resources provides the auditor with direct personal knowledge of their existence and physical condition. Although inspecting tangible assets, such as observing inventory, provides strong evidence about the existence assertion, it does not necessarily provide evidence about the entity's rights to the inventory. Inspecting physical inventory and noting its physical condition

Figure 6-7 ■ Inspection of Documents—Vouching vs. Tracing

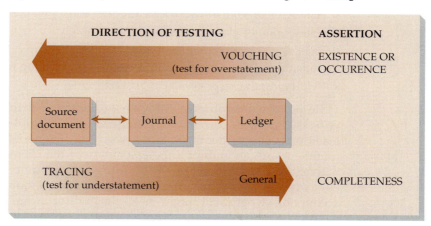

also may not provide sufficient, competent evidence about the valuation assertion. Inventory may be in good physical condition but be technologically obsolete.

OBSERVATION

Observation consists of looking at a process or procedure being performed by others. The activity may be the routine processing of a particular type of transaction such as cash receipts to see that employees are performing their assigned duties in accordance with company policies and procedures. Observation is particularly important when obtaining an understanding of internal controls. The auditor might also observe the care being taken by client employees in conducting the annual physical inventory, which provides an opportunity to distinguish between observing and inspecting tangible assets. That is, the auditor may observe the process of client employees taking the physical inventory. However, the auditor may also inspect or examine certain inventory items to make her or his own assessment of their condition. Thus, the subject matter of observing is personnel, procedures, and processes. From these observations, the auditor obtains direct personal knowledge related to the audit objective.

Auditors also need to use caution when assessing the reliability of audit evidence obtained through observation. Observation is limited to the point in time at which the observation takes place. For example, when observing the performance of an internal control, the evidence is limited to that point in time. Furthermore, auditors also understand that the act of being observed may affect how the process or procedure is performed. In the audit of a small business, the audit team may only be on the client's premises for two or three weeks during the year, and client personnel may be on their best behavior when the audit team is present.

INQUIRY

Inquiry consists of seeking information from knowledgeable persons, both financial and nonfinancial, throughout the entity or outside the entity. Inquiry is an audit procedure that is used extensively throughout the audit and often is complementary to performing other audit procedures. Inquiry involves:

- Considering the knowledge, objectivity, experience, responsibility, and qualifications of the individual to be questioned.
- Asking clear, concise, and relevant questions.
- Using open or closed questions appropriately.
- Listening actively and effectively.
- Considering the reactions and responses and asking followup questions.
- Evaluating the responses.

Responses to inquiry may provide the auditor with information not previously possessed or with corroborative evidence. For example, effective inquiry might lead the auditor to identify an unforeseen risk of material misstatement, or inquiry might confirm an auditor's understanding of the client's internal control. Alternatively, responses might provide information that differs significantly from other evidence the auditor has obtained. For example, inquiry of an employee in the accounting department might make the auditor aware of possible management override of internal controls, or it might make the auditor aware of incentives or rationalizations that influence the risk of fraud. In such cases, inquiries provide the basis for auditors to modify or perform additional audit procedures.

The reliability of audit evidence obtained from responses to inquiries is affected by the training, knowledge, and experience of the auditor performing the inquiry because the auditor analyzes and assesses responses while performing inquiry and refines subsequent inquiries according to the circumstances. The results of inquiry usually require corroborating evidence, for it is rarely considered objective or unbiased, and it usually comes from employees of the company rather than from an independent source. Inquiry alone ordinarily will not provide sufficient audit evidence to detect a material misstatement at the assertion level or to evaluate the design of a control and to determine whether it has been effectively implemented. Finally, in the case of inquiries about management's intent, the information available to support management's intent may be limited. In these cases, understanding management's past history of carrying out its stated intentions with respect to assets or liabilities, management's stated reasons for choosing a particular course of action, and management's ability to pursue a specific course of action may provide relevant information about management's intent.

CONFIRMATION

Confirmation, a specific type of inquiry, is the process of obtaining a representation of information or of an existing condition directly from a third party. In the usual case, the client makes the request of the outside party in writing, but the auditor controls the mailing of the inquiry. The request should include instructions requiring the recipient to send the response directly to the auditor. For example, the auditor might have management request that the customer confirm the balances of accounts receivable and terms or conditions of a sales contract (AU 330.05). Confirmation is also used to obtain audit evidence about the absence of certain conditions, for example, the absence of a "side agreement" that may influence revenue recognition. Confirmations are used in auditing because the evidence is usually objective and comes from an independent source.

RECALCULATION

Recalculation consists of checking the mathematical accuracy of documents or records. Auditors often use audit software to perform recalculations such as footing an accounts receivable file and agreeing the total to the general ledger. This is often an important initial procedure. For example, the auditor will want to make sure that the detail of an accounts receivable file agrees with the general ledger before the file is used to produce confirmations. Other examples include recalculating journal totals, depreciation expense, interest accruals and bond premiums or discounts, quantity times unit price extensions on inventory summary sheets, as well as the totals on supporting schedules and reconciliations.

REPERFORMANCE

Reperformance is the auditor's independent execution of procedures or controls that were originally performed as part of the entity's internal control. The auditor may use reperformance in a variety of ways. The auditor may reperform selected aspects of the processing of selected transactions to determine that the original processing conformed to prescribed internal controls. For example, the auditor may reperform the customer credit check for a sales transaction to determine that the customer did indeed have sufficient credit available at the time the transaction was processed. The auditor might use computer-assisted audit techniques to reperform programmed control procedures or use audit software to reperform the client's aging of accounts receivable. Finally, the auditor might reperform manual procedures such as the manual followup of items that appear on computer generated exception report.

ANALYTICAL PROCEDURES

Analytical procedures consist of evaluation of financial information made by a study of plausible relations among both financial and nonfinancial data. These procedures include the calculation and use of simple ratios, vertical analysis or common size statements, comparisons of actual amounts with historical data or budget expectations, and the use of mathematical and statistical models such as regression analysis. The models may involve the use of nonfinancial data (e.g., number of employees) as well as financial data. Analytical procedures often involve measuring the business activity underlying operations and comparing the measures of key economic business drivers with related financial results. Analytical procedures are generally used to develop an expectation for a financial statement account and to assess the reasonableness of the financial statements in that context. Analytical procedures are discussed further in Chapter 8.

COMPUTER-ASSISTED AUDIT TECHNIQUES

Computer-assisted audit techniques (CAATs) use audit software to accomplish a variety of audit procedures outlined above. When the client's accounting records are maintained on electronic media, the auditor may use CAATs to do the following:

- Perform the calculations and comparisons used in analytical procedures.
- Select a sample of accounts receivable for confirmation.
- Scan a file to determine that all documents in a series have been accounted for.
- Compare data elements in different files for agreement (such as the prices on sales invoices with a master file containing authorized prices).
- Submit test data to the client's programs to determine that computer aspects of internal controls are functioning.
- Reperform a variety of calculations such as totaling the accounts receivable subsidiary ledger or inventory file.

CAATs may be used as analytical procedures to develop an expectation for an account balance or transaction class, or they may be used to perform tests that confirm the auditor's expectation. Computer-assisted audit techniques are explained in greater detail in Chapters 10 and 11 as well as throughout Part 4 of this text.

[LEARNING CHECK

6-9 Identify nine types of audit procedures and provide an example of each in the context of auditing sales and accounts receivable.

6-10 What is the principal difference between vouching and tracing?

KEY TERMS

Analytical procedures, p. 246
Computer-assisted audit techniques
   (CAATs), p. 246
Confirmation, p. 245
Inquiry, p. 244
Inspection of documents and records,
   p. 241

Inspection of tangible assets, p. 243
Observation, p. 244
Recalculation, p. 245
Reperformance, p. 245
Tracing, p. 243
Vouching, p. 242

[FOUR DECISIONS ABOUT AUDIT PROCEDURES]

Audit Decision 4

■ What are the four critical audit decisions about audit procedures to be performed?

Recall from Chapter 5 that Phase III of the audit involves responding to assessed risks. The auditor considers four important audit decisions when responding to the assessed risk of material misstatement at the financial statement level and at the assertion level. The auditor must make decisions about:

■ Staffing and supervision the audit—who will perform what audit procedures?
■ Nature of audit tests—what audit procedures should be performed?
■ Timing of audit tests—when should audit procedures be performed?
■ Extent of audit tests—how much of a population should be audited?

Figure 6-8 provides a summary of how the assessed risk of material misstatement influences these decisions. The following section discusses these four decisions in more detail.

In addition, electronic data processing has important implications for the collection of audit evidence. In some cases, all the transactions that are recorded in electronic form are supported by documentary evidence. However, SAS No. 80, Amendment to Statement on Auditing Standards No. 31, *Evidential Matter* (AU 326.18), points out that in certain entities, some of the accounting data and corroborating evidential matter are available only in electronic form. Source documents such as purchase orders, bills of lading, invoices, and checks are replaced with electronic messages. Other entities may use electronic data interchange (EDI) or image processing systems. In EDI, the entity and its customers or suppliers use communication links to transact business electronically. Purchase, shipping, billing cash receipt, and cash disbursement transactions are often consummated entirely by the exchange of electronic messages between the parties. In image processing systems, documents are scanned and converted into electronic images to facilitate storage and reference, and the source documents may not be retained after conversion. Certain electronic evidence may exist at a certain point in time. However, such evidence may not be retrievable after a specified period of time if files are changed and if backup files do not exist.

When electronic records replace documentary evidence, the auditor needs to consider the audit implications. The auditor should consider whether client practices impact material account balances and transaction classes, and assess the resulting implications for staffing the audit as well as the nature, timing, and extent of audit procedures. The implications of the client's use of electronic files are discussed below.

Figure 6-8 ■ Factors that Influence Audit Decisions about Audit Procedures

Higher Risk of Material Misstatement	Decisions about Audit Procedures	Lower Risk of Material Misstatement
The audit team may include individuals with more audit experience, more experience in the industry, or may have increased levels of supervision.	**Staffing and supervision**	The audit team may include individuals with less audit experience and less experience in the industry, or may need decreased levels of supervision.
The auditor might choose to primarily obtain audit evidence with substantive tests.	**Nature of audit procedures**	The auditor might perform more tests of controls and fewer substantive tests.
The auditor might choose substantive audit procedures that provide more persuasive evidence regardless of the cost of obtaining evidence.		The auditor might choose substantive audit procedures that provide less persuasive evidence when considering benefits and costs.
The auditor will likely perform audit procedures at the balance sheet date.	**Timing of audit procedures**	The auditor may perform audit procedures at an interim date and update the conclusions for the remaining period.
The auditor will usually perform audit procedures on a larger proportion of the population.	**Extent of audit procedures**	The auditor might perform audit procedures on a smaller proportion of the population.

STAFFING AND SUPERVISING THE AUDIT

Recall that financial statement level risks usually have a pervasive impact on multiple transaction classes and assertions. For example, if the entity has a poor internal control environment and there is a high risk that management might override control activities, then the auditor might respond to this risk by assigning staff with an increased level of audit experience. The auditor might also assign staff with a higher level of industry experience to audit assertions that have a high degree of subjectivity or complexity, whereas the auditor might feel that it is appropriate to assign entry-level staff to audit assertions that are not complex.

A common member of today's audit team is a computer audit specialist. Computer audit specialists are trained in understanding the audit implications of the client's EDP systems and are knowledgeable of issues related to computer hardware and software. If a client has significant EDP issues, a computer specialist will usually be assigned to important aspects of understanding the entity and its internal control, performing tests of controls, or performing substantive tests.

NATURE OF AUDIT PROCEDURES

A common decision involves the choice of audit procedures. In general, when the risk of material misstatement is high, the auditor will attempt to obtain highly reliable evidence. For example, when auditing accounts receivable, the auditor will usually have customers confirm that they owe the amount of receivables shown in the client's accounting records. In some cases, however, customers may not be knowledgeable about what they owe. For example, consumers may not have a basis for knowing what the amount of their utility bill should be. In this case the auditor might consider an alternative test such as investigating the adequacy of internal controls and testing documentary evidence involving cash flows and the relationship between customer billings and subsequent cash receipts. The existence of significant audit risk also impacts the choice of audit procedures. For example, if a significant audit risk exists for an assertion (e.g., revenue recognition), it is unlikely that substantive analytical procedures alone will provide sufficient competent evidence.

If a client maintains important documentation and evidence in electronic form for a material account balance or transaction class, it will have several implications for the nature of audit tests. It may affect procedures used to obtain an understanding of the client, tests of controls, and substantive tests. The auditor will usually want to understand the files where data are stored and how to access the files. The auditor may perform a variety of tests of the client's control procedures that ensure the reliability and accuracy of the underlying data. Finally, the auditor might consider using computer-assisted audit techniques to directly access and test records maintained only in electronic form.

New opportunities and challenges are also posed by the impact of technology on traditional forms of evidence, such as the faxing of confirmations (documentary evidence sent electronically from a third party to the auditor). The auditor will usually consider controls related to the origination, transmission, and receipt of faxed information in assessing the reliability of the evidence.

TIMING OF AUDIT PROCEDURES

Decisions about the timing of audit procedures involve whether the audit procedure will be performed at an interim date or at fiscal year-end. When the auditor makes a preliminary assessment of control risk as low, the auditor will usually perform tests of controls at an interim date. If the auditor confirms that internal controls are effective, the risk that misstatements will occur between performing a substantive test, such as confirming receivables, at an interim date and year-end is reduced. Performing tests of balances at an interim date allows the auditor to reach an overall opinion soon after year-end. However, if internal controls are not effective, and the risk of misstatement in an assertion is high, the auditor will usually perform substantive tests as of the balance sheet date.

The auditor also considers the client's use of information technology when making decisions about the timing of tests. If a client uses an image processing system to scan documents and original documents are not retained, the auditor will want to consider the implications for the timing of procedures related to tests of transactions. If it is important to inspect original documentary evidence, then the auditor must plan the timing of tests consistent with the existence of appropriate documentary evidence.

EXTENT OF AUDIT PROCEDURES

Finally, the auditor must make a decision about how extensive audit procedures should be. Usually the auditor will perform more extensive audit procedures when the risk of material misstatement is high. For example, if internal controls over the counting of inventory are weak, the auditor may visit all of the client's locations and test count a higher proportion of the inventory on hand.

In some cases the auditor can cost-effectively perform extensive tests if a client maintains records in electronic form and the auditor can directly access the electronic records. For example, the auditor may be able to subject 100 percent of the transactions in a population to being screened by the computer for a particular characteristic or trait. The auditor may be able to use computer-assisted audit techniques to screen every cash disbursement and identify related-party transactions. Alternatively, the auditor may use the computer to segment an inventory population and perform extensive price tests on inventory where prices changed over 10 percent from the prior year, and minimal price tests where prices are similar to the prior year's prices. The auditor's application of computer-assisted audit techniques to electronic data files has allowed for audit strategies whereby the auditor can target procedures on high-risk subpopulations and perform less extensive procedures on subpopulations where errors are less likely.

[LEARNING CHECK

6-11   a. What is meant by the auditor's decisions about staffing and supervising the audit?
   b. Provide an example of these decisions in the context of the revenue cycle.
   c. Identify the factors that influence an auditor's decisions about staffing and supervision.
   d. Explain how decisions about staffing and supervision are influenced when the client's accounting records and corroborating evidence are available only in electronic form.

6-12   a. What is meant by the auditor's decisions about the nature of audit procedures?
   b. Provide an example of these decisions in the context of the revenue cycle.
   c. Identify the factors that influence an auditor's decisions about the nature of audit procedures.
   d. Explain how decisions about the nature of audit procedures are influenced when the client's accounting records and corroborating evidence are available only in electronic form.

6-13   a. What is meant by the auditor's decisions about the timing of audit procedures?
   b. Provide an example of these decisions in the context of the revenue cycle.
   c. Identify the factors that influence an auditor's decisions about the timing of audit procedures.
   d. Explain how decisions about the timing of audit procedures are influenced when the client's accounting records and corroborating evidence are available only in electronic form.

6-14   a. What is meant by the auditor's decisions about the extent of audit procedures?
   b. Provide an example of these decisions in the context of the revenue cycle.
   c. Identify the factors that influence an auditor's decisions about the extent of audit procedures.

d. Explain how decisions about the extent of audit procedures are influenced when the client's accounting records and corroborating evidence are available only in electronic form.

[DOCUMENTING AUDIT DECISIONS AND AUDIT EVIDENCE]

AUDIT PROGRAMS

> **Auditor Knowledge 2**
>
> ■ **Know the purpose of an audit program.**

Generally accepted auditing standards (AU 311.05) state that in planning the audit, the auditor should consider the nature, extent, and timing of work to be performed and should prepare a written audit program for every audit. The **audit program** documents decisions about the audit procedures that the auditor believes are necessary to obtain reasonable assurance that the financial statements are presented fairly in all material respects. The form of the audit program will vary with the circumstances of the audit and the practices and policies of an audit firm. However, normally an audit program will list procedures to be performed, identify who performed the procedures and the date that the procedures were performed, and provide a cross-reference to the working papers where the procedures are documented. Figure 6-9 provides an example of an audit program outlining substantive tests of accounts receivable. This example program does not address tests of controls.

Figure 6-9 ■ Substantive Audit Program for Accounts Receivable Assertions

Working Paper Reference	Substantive Audit Procedures	Auditor	Date
	Amalgamated Products, Inc. *Audit program for Substantive Tests of Accounts Receivable* Year Ending December 31, 20XX		

	Initial Procedures (1–2)
	1. Obtain an understanding of the client's products and services, markets, competition, customers, industry, and regulatory factors. Understand how these factors may affect the client's sales and revenue recognition.
	2. Perform initial procedures on accounts receivable balances and records that will be subjected to further testing.
	  a. Trace beginning balances for accounts receivable and related allowance to prior year's working papers.
	  b. Review activity in general ledger accounts for accounts receivable and related allowance and investigate entries that appear unusual in amount or source.
	  c. Obtain accounts receivable trial balance and determine that it accurately represents the underlying accounting records by:		

(continues)

Figure 6-9 ■ (Continued)

Working Paper Reference	Substantive Audit Procedures	Auditor	Date
	Amalgamated Products, Inc. *Audit program for Substantive Tests of Accounts Receivable* Year Ending December 31, 20XX		

Amalgamated Products, Inc.
Audit program for Substantive Tests of Accounts Receivable
Year Ending December 31, 20XX

Working Paper Reference	Substantive Audit Procedures	Auditor	Date

	i. Footing trial balance and determining agreement with (1) the total of the subsidiary ledger or accounts receivable master file and (2) the general ledger.
	ii. Testing agreement of customers and balances listed on trial balance with those included in subsidiary ledger or master file.
	3. Perform analytical procedures
	  a. Analyze results relative to expectations based on prior years, industry data, budgeted amounts, or other data.
	  b. Analyze results relative to expectations based on inventory purchased or produced.
	  c. Calculate ratios:
	    i. Accounts receivable turnover days
	    ii. Accounts receivable to total current assets
	    iii. Uncollectible accounts expense to net credit sales.
	    iv. Uncollectible accounts expense to write-offs of accounts receivable.
	
	Test details of revenue transactions (4–6).
	4. Vouch a sample of recorded receivable transactions to support documentation.
	  a. Vouch debits to supporting sales invoices, shipping documents, and sales orders.
	  b. Vouch credits to remittance advices or sales adjustments authorizations for sale returns and allowance or uncollectible account write-offs.
	5. Perform cutoff tests for sales and sales returns.
	  a. Select a sample of recorded sales transactions for several days before and after year-end and examine support sales invoices and shipping documents to determine that sales were recorded in the proper period.
	  b. Select sample of credit memos issued after year-end, examine supporting documentation such as dated receiving reports, and determine that returns were recorded in the proper period. Also, consider whether volume of sales returns after year-end suggests the possibility of unauthorized shipments before year-end.
	6. Perform cash receipts cutoff test.
	  a. Observe that all cash received through the close of business on the last day of the fiscal year is included in cash on hand or deposits in transit and that no receipts or the subsequent period are included, or
	  b. Review documentation such as daily cash summaries, duplicate deposits slips, and bank statements covering several days before and after the year-end data to determine proper cutoff.		

(continues)

Figure 6-9 ■ (Continued)

	Amalgamated Products, Inc. *Audit program for Substantive Tests of Accounts Receivable* Year Ending December 31, 20XX		
Working Paper Reference	**Substantive Audit Procedures**	**Auditor**	**Date**

	Tests of Details of Balances (7–8)
	7. Confirm accounts receivable.
	  a. Determine the form, timing, and extent of confirmation requests.
	  b. Select and execute a sample and investigate exceptions.
	  c. For positive confirmation requests for which no reply was received, perform alternative followup procedures:
	    i. Vouch to subsequent payments identifiable with items comprising account balance at confirmation date to supporting documentation as in step 4b above.
	    ii. Vouch items comprising balance at confirmation date to documentary support as in 4a above.
	  d. Summarize the results of confirmation and alternative followup procedures.
	8. Tests of factoring and pledging of receivables
	  a. Determine if any receivables have been factored or pledged as collateral and review related contracts.
	  b. Confirm agreements for factoring or pledging of receivables.
	9. Tests of Details of Accounting Estimates
	  a. Develop an expectation for the allowance for doubtful accounts and uncollectible account expense given industry trends, growth in sales, changes in credit policy, etc.
	  b. Foot the aged trial balance of receivables and agree total to the general ledger.
	  c. Test aging by vouching amounts in aging categories for a sample of accounts to supporting documents.
	  d. For past due accounts:
	    i. Examine evidence of collectibility such as correspondence with customers and outside collection agencies, credit reports, and customers' financial statements.
	    ii. Discuss collectibility of accounts with appropriate management personnel.
	  e. Evaluate adequacy of allowance component for each aging category and in the aggregate.
	10. Tests of Details of Disclosures
	  a. Determine that receivables are properly identified and classified as to type and expected period of realization.
	  b. Determine whether there are credit balances that are material in the aggregate and that should be reclassified as liabilities.
	  c. Determine the appropriateness of disclosures and accounting for related party, pledged, assigned, or factored receivables.
	  d. Evaluate the completeness of presentation and disclosures for inventories in drafts of financial statements and determine conformity with GAAP by reference to a disclosure checklist.
	  e. Read disclosures and independently evaluate their understandability.		

WORKING PAPERS

The audit team should document their work (audit decisions made and audit evidence obtained) in the audit working papers. The auditor's documentation would normally include:

■ The overall responses to the risks of misstatement at the financial statement level.

■ The nature, timing, and extent of the further audit procedures.

■ The linkage of those procedures with the assessed risk at the assertion level.

■ The results of the audit procedures.

■ The nature and effect of aggregated misstatements.

■ The auditor's conclusion as to whether the aggregated misstatements cause the financial statement to be materially misstated.

■ The qualitative factors the auditor considered in evaluating whether misstatements are material and the conclusion.

The manner in which these matters are documented is based on the auditor's professional judgment. The documentation of audit evidence is provided in working papers. Generally accepted auditing standards (AU 339.03, *Working Papers*) describe **working papers** as records kept by the auditor of the procedures applied, the tests performed, the information obtained, and the pertinent conclusion reached in the audit.

Types of Working Papers

Many types of working papers are prepared in an audit. These include (1) a working trial balance, (2) schedules and analyses, (3) audit memoranda and documentation of corroborating information, and (4) adjusting and reclassifying entries. Working papers are usually prepared using software developed for microcomputers. Figure 6-10 is an example of a microcomputer-generated working paper.

Working Trial Balance

The purpose of a **working trial balance** is to summarize the general ledger and any audit adjustment or reclassifying entries in a form that matches the financial statements. A partial working trial balance is illustrated in Figure 6-10. Note that inclusion of the final (audited) balances for the prior year facilitates the performance of certain analytical procedures.

A working trial balance is of paramount importance in an audit because it:

■ Serves as the connecting link between the client's general ledger accounts and the items reported in the financial statements.

■ Provides a basis for controlling all the individual working papers.

■ Identifies the specific working papers containing the audit evidence for each financial statement item.

For example, Figure 6-10 indicates that the amount reported in the financial statements for cash is supported by additional working papers with a working paper reference of A, the evidence supporting marketable securities can be found in a section of the working papers with a reference or index of B, and so on. The software used by many auditors to generate working papers will electronically link working papers AA-1, A, A-1, A-2, and AE-1 exhibited in Figure 6-11.

Figure 6-10 ■ Partial Working Trial Balance Working Paper

Omni, Inc.
Working Trial Balance—Balance Sheet
December 31, 20x1

W/P Ref: AA-1
Prepared By: GBC Date: 2/20/x2
Reviewed By: ARE Date: 2/15/x2

W/P REF	Acct. No.	Description	Final Balance 12/31/x0	Ledger Balance 12/31/x1	Adjustments AJE REF	Adjustments Debit (Credit)	Adjusted Balance 12/31/x1	Reclassifications RJE REF	Reclassifications Debit (Credit)	Final Balance 12/31/x1
		Current Assets								
A		Cash	392,000	427,000	(1)	50,000	477,000			477,000
B	150	Marketable Securities	52,200	62,200			62,000			62,200
C		Receivables (net)	1,601,400	1,715,000	(1)	(50,000)	1,665,000	(A)	10,000	1,675,000
D	170	Inventories	2,542,500	2,810,200	(2)	133,000	2,943,200			2,943,200
E		Prepaid Expenses	24,900	19,500			19,500			19,500
		Total Current	4,613,000	5,033,900		133,000	5,166,900		10,000	5,176,900
F	240	Long-term Investments	190,000	190,000			190,000			190,000
G		Property, Plant & Equipment (net)	3,146,500	3,310,900			3,310,900			3,310,900
		Total	7,759,500	8,534,800		133,000	8,667,800		10,000	8,677,800
		Liabilities and Stockholders' Equity								
		Current Liabilities								
M	400	Notes Payable	750,000	825,000			825,000			825,000
N	410	Accounts Payable	2,150,400	2,340,300	(2)	(133,000)	2,473,300	(A)	(10,000)	2,483,300
O	420	Accrued Payables	210,600	189,000			189,000			189,000
P	430	Income Taxes Payable	150,000	170,000			170,000			170,000
		Total Current	3,261,000	3,524,300		(133,000)	3,657,300		(10,000)	3,667,300
R	500	Bonds Payable	1,000,000	1,200,000			1,200,000			1,200,000
S	600	Common Stock	2,400,000	2,400,000			2,400,000			2,400,000
T	700	Retained Earnings	1,098,500	1,410,500			1,410,500			1,410,500
		Total	7,759,500	8,534,800		(133,000)	8,667,800		(10,000)	8,677,800

Figure 6-11 ■ Integrated Working Papers for Cash

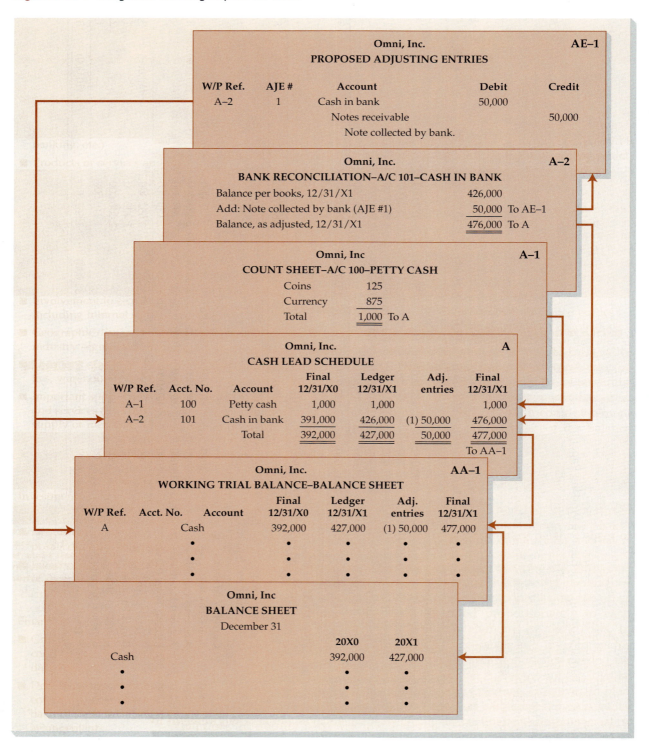

Schedules and Analyses

The terms **working paper schedule** and **working paper analysis** are used interchangeably to describe the individual working papers that contain the evidence supporting the items in the working trial balance. When several general ledger accounts are combined for reporting purposes, a **group schedule** (also called a lead schedule) should be prepared. In addition to showing the individual ledger accounts comprising the group, the **lead schedule** identifies the individual working paper schedules or analyses that contain the audit evidence obtained for each account comprising the group. The middle portion of Figure 6-11 illustrates the use of a cash lead schedule for Omni, Inc. (working paper A) and how it is linked both to the cash line of the working trial balance (working paper AA-1) and the supporting working papers for the two general ledger cash accounts listed on the lead schedule (i.e., working paper A-1 for A/C 100—Petty cash and working paper A-2 for A/C 101—Cash in bank).

Individual schedules or analyses often show the composition of an account balance at the balance sheet date (or another date of audit interest) as in working paper A-1 of Figure 6-11. Other examples would include a list of customer balances comprising the accounts receivable control account balance or a list of investments comprising the marketable securities account balance. Working paper schedules may also show the changes in one or more related account balances during the period covered by the financial statements as illustrated in Figure 6-12. In some cases, the auditor has the client prepare the schedule, which may be indicated by the letters **PBC** for "prepared by client." The auditor then performs the work indicated by the tick marks (or some other form of legend) and related explanations on the working paper as also illustrated in Figure 6-12.

Audit Memoranda and Corroborating Information

Audit memoranda refer to written data prepared by the auditor in narrative form. Memoranda may include comments on the performance of auditing procedures including (1) the scope of work, (2) findings, and (3) audit conclusions. For example, the auditor might write a memo summarizing the scope of confirmations, confirmations responses, findings, and audit conclusions based on the evidence.

In addition, the auditor might prepare audit memoranda to document corroborating information such as:

- Extracts of minutes of board of directors meetings.
- Written representations from management and outside experts.
- Copies of important contracts.

Adjusting and Reclassifying Entries

It is important to distinguish between adjusting entries and reclassifying entries. **Audit adjusting entries** are corrections of client errors or omission or misapplications of GAAP. Thus, if adjusting entries are ultimately deemed to be material, individually or in the aggregate, the client should record the adjustments in the general ledger and in the financial statements. In contrast, **reclassifying entries** pertain to the proper financial statement presentation of correct account bal-

Figure 6-12 ■ Notes Receivable and Interest Working Paper

Omni, Inc. Notes Receivable and Interest December 31, 20x1										Prepared By: ACE Reviewed By: PAR			W/P Ref: C-4 Date: 1/20/x2 Date: 2/4/x2
					Acts. 160,161,450								
	Notes Receivable	Interest											
Maker	Date Made	Due	Interest Rate	Face Amount	Balance 12/31/x0	Debits	Credits	Balance 12/31/x1		Accrued 12/31/x0	Earned 20x1	Collected 20x1	Accrued 12/31/x1
Coffman,Inc.	7/1/X0	6/30/X1	10%	25,000	25,000 ✗		25,000	—		1,250 ✗	1,250 γ	2,500 CR	—
Morrison Bros.	11/1/X0	10/31/X1	10%	30,000	30,000 ✗		30,000	—		500 ✗	2,500 γ	3,000 CR	—
Shirley and Son	4/1/X1	3/31/X2	12%	40,000 ✓	—	40,000		40,000 *v*		—	3,600 γ	—	3,600
Warner Corporation	10/1/X1	9/30/X2	12%	20,000 ✓	—	20,000		20,000 *v*		—	600γ	—	600
					55,000	60,000	55,000	60,000 ^		1,750	7,950	5,500	4,200 ^
					F	F	F	FF		F	F	F	FF
								To C					To C

✗ Agreed to 12/31/X0 working papers
v Confirmed with maker – no exceptions
✓ Examined note during cash count
F Footed
FF Footed and crossfooted
^ Traced to ledger balances
CR Traced collections to cash receipts and deposit slips
γ Verified computations

ances. For example, assume that the accounts receivable balance includes a material amount of customer accounts with credit balances pertaining to customer advances. Although it is not necessary for the client to record the reclassifying entry on its books, for reporting purposes the financial statements need to be adjusted and the auditor needs to have an audit trail. This is illustrated in Figure 6-10 and will result in the reclassification being reflected in the financial statements.

The summaries of adjusting and reclassifying entries are initially designated as "proposed" entries because the auditor's final judgment as to which entries must be made may not occur until the end of the audit and because the client must approve them. The disposition of each proposed entry should ultimately be recorded on the working papers. Of course, if the client declines to make adjusting or reclassifying entries that the auditor feels are necessary, the auditor's report must be appropriately modified.

PREPARING WORKING PAPERS

Auditor Knowledge 4

■ **Understand the essential techniques of good working paper presentation.**

A number of basic techniques or mechanics are widely used in preparing working papers. The following essential techniques of good working paper preparation should always be observed:

■ *Heading.* Each working paper should contain the name of the client, a descriptive title identifying the content of the working paper, such as Bank Reconciliation—City National Bank, and the balance sheet date or the period covered by the audit.

■ *Index number.* Each working paper is given an index or reference number, such as A-1, B-2, and so forth, for identification and filing purposes.

■ *Cross-referencing.* Data on a working paper that is taken from another working paper or that is carried forward to another working paper should be cross-referenced with the index numbers of those working papers as illustrated in Figure 6-11. Most software for preparing working papers allows them to be electronically cross-referenced and linked.

■ *Tick marks.* Tick marks are symbols, such as check marks, that are used on working papers to indicate that the auditor has performed some procedure on the item to which the tick mark is affixed, or that additional information about the item is available elsewhere on the working paper. A legend on the working paper should either explain the nature and extent of the work represented by each tick mark or provide additional information applicable to the items so marked.

■ *Signatures and dates.* Upon completing their respective tasks, both the preparer and reviewer of a working paper should initial and date it. This establishes responsibility for the work performed and the review.

Figure 6-12 illustrates all of the essential points described above.

Reviewing Working Papers

Reviewing working papers ensures that a high-quality audit has been performed and that its results are documented in the working papers. There are several levels in the review of working papers within a CPA firm. The first-level review is made by the preparer's supervisor, such as a senior or manager. This review occurs when the work on a specific segment of the audit has been completed. The reviewer is primarily interested in:

- The scope of work performed.
- The evidence and findings obtained.
- The audit judgment exercised.
- The conclusions reached by the auditor.

Other reviews are made of the working papers when all the field work has been completed. These reviews are explained in Chapter 19 under "Evaluating the Findings."

WORKING PAPER FILES

Working papers are generally filed under the following two categories: (1) a permanent file and (2) a current file. The **permanent file** contains data that are expected to be useful to the auditor on future engagements with the client. In contrast, the **current file** contains corroborating information pertaining to the execution of the current year's audit program. Items typically found in the permanent file are:

- Copies of the articles of incorporation and bylaws.
- Chart of accounts and procedure manuals.
- Organization charts.
- Plant layout, manufacturing processes, and principal products.
- Terms of capital stock and bond issues.
- Copies of long-term contracts, such as leases, pension plans, and profit-sharing and bonus agreements.
- Schedules for amortization of long-term debt and depreciation of plant assets.
- Summary of accounting principles used by the client.

are working papers really confidential?

After nine years of judicial proceedings, the U.S. Supreme Court ruled that an auditor's working papers used to determine a client's income tax liability are relevant to an Internal Revenue Service tax audit. The Court concluded that the audit working papers are not protected from disclosure in response to an IRS summons issued under the Internal Revenue Code even though they were not used in preparing the tax returns. Thus, in preparing working papers, an auditor should realize that they may be subjected to public scrutiny through courts of law even in situations when the auditor is not a litigant.

Source: United States v. *Arthur Young & Co., et al.,* U.S. Supreme Court, No. 82–687 (March 1984).

Ownership and Custody of Working Papers

Working papers belong to the auditor. The auditor's ownership rights, however, are subject to constraints imposed by the auditor's own profession. Rule 301 of the AICPA's Code of Professional Conduct stipulates that a CPA shall not disclose any confidential information obtained during the course of a professional engagement without the consent of the client, except for certain circumstances as stated in the rule.

Custody of the working papers rests with the auditor, and he or she is responsible for their safekeeping. Working papers included in the permanent file are retained indefinitely. Current working papers should be retained for as long as they are useful to the auditor in servicing a client or are needed to satisfy legal requirements for record retention. The Sarbanes-Oxley Act of 2002 and many state laws require the auditor to retain working papers for at least seven years.

[LEARNING CHECK

6-15 Explain the nature and purpose of audit working papers.

6-16 Identify four major types of working papers.

6-17 Describe five essential techniques of good working paper preparation.

6-18 Identify two categories of working paper files and differentiate the contents of each.

6-19 a. Who owns and maintains custody of working papers?

b. Is it ever appropriate for the auditor to disclose the contents of working papers to anyone other than the client?

[KEY TERMS

Audit adjusting entries, p. 257
Audit memoranda, p. 257
Audit program, p. 251
Current file, p. 260
Group schedule, p. 257
Lead schedule, p. 257
PBC (prepared by client), p. 257

Permanent file, p. 260
Reclassifying entries, p. 257
Working paper analysis, p. 257
Working paper schedule, p. 257
Working papers, p. 254
Working trial balance, p. 254

[FOCUS ON AUDITOR KNOWLEDGE AND AUDIT DECISIONS]

This chapter focuses on the purpose of audit evidence, financial statement assertions and how they guide audit evidence, important decisions about the collection of audit evidence, and the use of audit programs and audit working papers to document audit evidence. In making decisions to support high-quality audit work, the auditor must be able to use the knowledge summarized in Figure 6-13 and address the decisions summarized in Figure 6-14. Page references are provided to where these issues are discussed in more detail.

Figure 6-13 ■ Summary of Auditor Knowledge Discussed in Chapter 6

Auditor Knowledge	Summary	Chapter References
K1. Know the definition of audit evidence and understand the difference between how accounting records and other information are used as audit evidence.	Audit evidence is all the information used by the auditor in arriving at the conclusion on which the audit opinion is based. Accounting records underlying the financial statements such as check, invoices, journals, and general and subsidiary ledgers are helpful but do not provide sufficient evidence on which to base an audit opinion. The auditor must also obtain other information that corroborates the accounting records and supports the auditor's logical reasoning about fair presentation in the financial statements, such as confirmation from third parties, and information obtained through inquiry, observation, and inspection of documents.	pp. 229–231
K2. Know the purpose of an audit program.	The purpose of an audit program is to document the audit plan for an account balance or transaction class. An audit program contains the audit procedures that the auditor believes are necessary to obtain reasonable assurance that the account or transaction class is free of material misstatements.	pp. 251–253
K3. Understand the nature and purpose of audit working papers.	Working papers are records and documentation kept by the auditor of the audit procedures applied, the tests performed, the information obtained, and the pertinent conclusion reached in the audit. Working papers organize and document the auditor evidence and conclusion related to an account balance or transaction class.	pp. 254–259
K4. Understand the essential techniques of good working paper presentation.	Good working papers normally include the following: a clear heading describing the purpose of the working paper, an index number that allows for clear filing of the working paper, cross-referencing such that information taken from one working paper provides a clear audit trail to its source of information in the working papers, tick marks and legends that explain the audit work performed on various aspects of an account or group of transactions, and signatures and dates indicating who completed a task and when the work was completed.	pp. 259–261

Figure 6-14 ■ Summary of Audit Decisions Discussed in Chapter 6

Audit Decision	Factors That Influence the Audit Decision	Chapter References
D1. How does an auditor determine specific audit objectives from the categories of assertions?	Assertions assist the auditor in the development of specific audit objectives, which guide the collection of evidence. The auditor will usually develop five transaction class audit objectives (occurrence, completeness, accuracy, cutoff, and classification), four account balance audit objectives (existence, completeness, rights and obligations, and valuation and allocation), and four disclosure audit objectives (occurrence and rights and obligations, completeness, classification and understandability, and accuracy and valuation), for each material account balance and transaction class. Figure 6-2 explains the relationship between assertions and specific audit objectives.	pp. 231–235

(continues)

Figure 6-14 ■ (Continued)

Audit Decision	Factors that Influence the Audit Decision	Chapter References
D2. What factors affect the sufficiency and competency of audit evidence?	Sufficiency is a measure of the quantity of audit evidence. The factors that influence the sufficiency of audit evidence are (1) materiality, (2) risk of material misstatement, and (3) size and characteristics of the audit population. Figure 6-3 illustrates how these factors affect auditor's decisions about the amount of evidence that is needed for an assertion. Competency of evidence is a measure of the quality, or reliability, of audit evidence. The factors that influence the competency of audit evidence are (1) the independence of the source, (2) whether evidence is obtained directly by the auditor, (3) the internal controls over internal information, (4) whether evidence involves written documents, (5) whether the auditor can obtain original documents, and (6) the consistency of evidence from differing sources. Figure 6-4 illustrates the factors that affect the auditor's decisions about the quality of evidence.	pp. 236–240
D3. What types of audit procedures may be used in an audit?	The auditor may choose from the following types of audit procedures when obtaining evidence to support an assertion: (1) inspection of records or documents including vouching and tracing procedures, (2) inspection of tangible assets, (3) observation, (4) inquiry, (5) confirmation, (6) recalculation, (7) reperformance, (8) analytical procedures, and (9) computer-assisted audit techniques (CAATs). The chapter discussion explains these procedures and provides illustrative examples.	pp. 241–246
D4. What are the four critical audit decisions about audit procedures to be performed?	The four critical decisions about audit procedures include decisions about: (1) staffing and supervising the audit, (2) the nature of audit procedures (what audit procedures are to be performed), (3) the timing of audit procedures (when audit procedures are to be performed), and (4) the extent of audit procedures (how much of the audit population should be audited). Figure 6-8 illustrates how auditors consider these factors when planning the audit.	pp. 247–250

objective questions

Objective questions are available for students at www.wiley.com/college/boynton

comprehensive questions

6-20 **(Audit evidence)** The third GAAS of field work requires that the auditor obtain sufficient competent audit evidence to afford a reasonable basis for an opinion regarding the financial statements under audit. In considering what constitutes sufficient competent evidential matter, a distinction should be made between underlying accounting records and other information available to the auditor.

Required

a. Discuss the nature of audit evidence to be considered by the auditor in terms of the underlying accounting records, other corroborating information available to the auditor, and the methods by which the auditor tests or gathers competent evidence.

b. State the presumptions that can be made about the validity of audit evidence with respect to (1) other information and (2) underlying accounting records.

AICPA (adapted)

6-21   **(Audit evidence)** In an audit of financial statements, an auditor must judge the validity of the audit evidence obtained.

Required

a. In the course of an audit, the auditor asks many questions of client officers and employees.

   1. Describe the factors that the auditor should consider in evaluating inquiry and oral evidence provided by client officers and employees.

   2. Discuss the validity and limitations of inquiry and oral evidence.

b. An audit may include computation of various balance sheet and operating ratios for comparison to prior years and industry averages. Discuss the validity and limitations of ratio analysis in an audit.

c. In connection with his audit of the financial statements of a manufacturing company, an auditor is observing the physical inventory of finished goods, which consists of expensive, highly complex electronic equipment. Discuss the validity and limitations of the audit evidence provided by the procedure.

AICPA

6-22   **(Audit evidence)** During the course of an audit, the auditor examines a wide variety of documentation. Listed below are some forms of documentary evidence and the sources from which they are obtained.

1. Bank statement sent directly to the auditor by the bank.
2. Creditor monthly statement obtained from client's files.
3. Vouchers in client's unpaid voucher file.
4. Duplicate sales invoices in filled order file.
5. Time tickets filed in payroll department.
6. Credit memo in customer's file.
7. Material requisitions filed in storeroom.
8. Bank statement in client's files.
9. Management working papers in making accounting estimates.
10. Paid checks returned with bank statement in (1) above.
11. Letter in customer file from collection agency on collectibility of balance.
12. Memo in customer file from treasurer authorizing the write-off of the account.

Required

a. Classify the evidence by source into one of four categories: (1) directly from outsiders, (2) indirectly from outsiders, (3) internal but validated externally, and (4) entirely internal.

b. Comment on the reliability of the four sources of documentary evidence.

6-23 **(Sufficiency of audit evidence)** Making decisions about the sufficiency of audit evidence requires significant professional judgment. Explain how the following factors might impact the auditor's professional judgment regarding the sufficiency of audit evidence involved in the audit of inventory for a manufacturer:

a. Materiality

b. Risk of material misstatement

c. Size and characteristics of the population

6-24 **(Audit procedures and evidence)** A variety of specific audit procedures for obtaining audit evidence are as follows.

1. Inspect and count securities on hand.

2. Confirm inventories stored in public warehouses.

3. Obtain written report from a chemical engineer on grades of gasoline held as inventory by an oil company.

4. Recompute depreciation charges.

5. Learn about possible lawsuit in conversation with client's legal counsel during luncheon.

6. Compute and compare gross profit rates for the current and preceding years.

7. Examine certificates of title to delivery trucks purchased during the year.

8. Obtain letter from management on the pledging of assets under loan agreements.

9. Vouch sales journal entries to sales invoices.

10. Observe the client's count of cash on hand.

11. Trace "paid" checks to check register entries.

12. Use computer to scan file to determine that all documents in a numbered series have been accounted for.

Required

a. Indicate (1) the type of evidence obtained by each procedure and (2) the assertion or assertions to which it pertains.

b. List by number the types of evidence that are (1) obtained directly from the independent sources outside the enterprise and (2) obtained by the auditor's direct personal knowledge.

6-25 **(Substantive tests and audit evidence)** In meeting the third standard of field work, the auditor may perform the following types of substantive tests: (a) tests of details of transactions, (b) tests of details of balances, (c) tests of details of disclosures, and (d) analytical procedures. Below are listed specific audit procedures that fall within one of these categories.

1. Compare actual results with budget expectations.

2. Vouch entries in check register to "paid" checks.

3. Recalculate accrued interest payable.

4. Confirm customer balances.

5. Calculate inventory turnover ratios and compare with industry data.

6. Reconcile bank accounts at year-end.

7. Vouch sales journal entries to sales invoices.

8. Count office supplies on hand at year-end.

9. Examine deeds of ownership for land purchased during year.

10. Obtain representation letter from management.

11. Scan postings to repair expense for evidence of charges that should be capitalized.

12. Ask storeroom supervisor about obsolete items.

13. Examine a loan document to determine terms of the note and debt maturities.

Required

List the numbers of the foregoing procedures. For each procedure, indicate the type of substantive test and the type of audit procedure used by the auditor. Use the following format for your answers:

AUDIT PROCEDURE NO.	TYPE OF SUBSTANTIVE TEST	TYPE OF AUDIT PROCEDURE

6-26 **(Audit programs and assertions)** Assume that you are responsible for developing an audit program for a manufacturing client that sells to over 1,400 customers. You want to ensure your audit program addresses all relevant assertions for sales and accounts receivable. Address the following question in the context of the audit sales and receivables for this manufacturing client.

Required

a. What is the purpose of an audit program?

b. Explain why auditors translate audit assertions into specific audit objectives when developing an audit program.

c. If you are auditing the existence and occurrence assertion, what specific audit objectives should be accomplished by developing an audit program? Explain the purpose of each audit objective.

d. If you are auditing the valuation or allocation assertion, what specific audit objectives should be accomplished by developing an audit program? Explain the purpose of each audit objective.

6-27 **(Working papers)** The preparation of working papers is an integral part of a CPA's audit of financial statements. On a recurring engagement, a CPA reviews his audit programs and working papers from his prior audit while planning his current audit to determine their usefulness for the current engagement.

Required

a. 1. What are the purposes or functions of working papers?

   2. What records may be included in working papers?

b. What factors affect the CPA's judgment of the type and content of the working papers for a particular engagement?

c. To comply with GAAS, a CPA includes certain evidence in his working papers—for example, "evidence that the engagement was planned and work of assistants was supervised and reviewed." What other evidence would a CPA include in audit working papers to comply with generally accepted auditing standards?

AICPA (adapted)

6-28 **(Working papers)** Smith is the partner in charge of the audit of Blue Distributing Corporation, a wholesaler that owns one warehouse containing 80 percent of its inventory. Smith is reviewing the working papers that were prepared to support the firm's opinion on Blue's financial statements, and Smith wants to be certain essential audit records are well documented.

Required

What evidence should Smith find in the working papers to support the fact that the audit was adequately planned and the assistants were properly supervised?

AICPA (adapted)

6-29 **(Adjusting and reclassifying entries)** The accountant for the Brian Co. is preparing financial statements for the year-ended December 31. Your review of the accounting records discloses the need for the following adjusting and reclassifying entries:

1. Office Supplies has a balance of $2,400. An inventory at December 31 shows $1,700 of supplies on hand.

2. There are two insurance accounts in the trial balance, Prepaid Insurance—$9,200 and Insurance Expense—$2,800. Unexpired insurance at the statement date is $3,000.

3. All rent receipts ($25,000) were credited to rent income. At the end of the year, $5,000 of rentals are unearned.

4. The allowance for uncollectibles has a credit balance of $6,000. An aging schedule shows estimated uncollectibles of $14,000.

5. The balance in accounts payable is $122,400. Included in this amount is $10,400 of advance deposits made by Brian Co. on future purchases.

6. The ledger shows interest receivable of $3,200 at the beginning of the year. All interest collections have been credited to interest revenue. At December 31 of the current year, accrued interest receivable totals $3,800.

7. A capital expenditure of $6,000 was debited to repairs expense of October 1. The annual rate of depreciation on the machinery is 10 percent.

8. Freight-in of $5,000 was debited to freight-out.

9. Accounts receivable has a balance of $118,400. This balance is net of customers with credit balances of $15,000.

10. Bonds payable has a balance of $550,000. Bonds maturing within the next year total $50,000.

Required

Journalize the adjusting and reclassifying entries. Identify the adjustments by number and the reclassifications by letter.

6-30   **(Working papers)** The following schedule was prepared by staff accountant C. B. Sure on completing the verification of a December 31 client-prepared reconciliation of the City Bank General Account in the audit of Bold, Inc.

BOLD INC. #102 CITY BANK RECONCILIATION			A – 1 PREPARED BY: CLIENT REVIEWED BY: C. B. SURE
Per Bank			$ 62,765.18 v
Deposits in Transit			1,452.20 v
Outstanding Checks	87.10 v	619.75 v	
	232.90 v	1,100.00 v	
	17.20 v	472.19 v	(2,529.14)
Other (See AJEs 12 & 13 on cash lead Schedule A)			510.55
Reconciled Balance			$ 62,198.79 v

v = Verified

As a senior on the job, you discuss the work done with Sure and determine:

1. The balance per bank agreed with the amount shown on the bank confirmation received directly from the bank.

2. The deposit in transit was traced to the January bank statement.

3. All outstanding checks were traced to the December check register.

4. Adjusting entry 12 was for the collection of a $515 noninterest-bearing note by the bank; entry 13 was for December bank charges of $4.45.

5. The recorded balance per books at December 31 is $61,267.69.

6. In comparing "paid" checks with the check register, an error was discovered. Check number 2640 for $980 to a creditor was recorded by Bold, Inc., as $890. The bank paid the correct amount.

7. The final step, done on January 7, was to check the mathematical accuracy of the schedule.

Required

a. Prepare the bank reconciliation working paper in good form, showing adjusted balances per bank and per books.

b. Prepare the adjusting entries that presumably were made.

c. Prepare a cash lead schedule assuming (1) account number 101, Petty Cash $5,000 (working paper A-2, no adjustments) and (2) account number 103, City Bank—Payroll $20,000 (working paper A-3, no adjustment).

d. Show how cash will appear in the working trial balance.

professional simulation

Assume that you have just been promoted to the position of in-charge accountant on the audit of Lancer Corporation, which manufactures and wholesales consumer products. Lancer's customer base is represented by about 10% of the customers that represent 65% of sales and a very large number of smaller retailers that make up the other 35% of the company's sales. Last year Baker and Co. (Lancer's auditors) send positive confirmations to a sample of Lancer's customers. All of Lancer's larger customers responded to the positive confirmations, but many of the smaller customers did not.

As in-charge on the Lancer audit, you have discussed the low response rate from the smaller customers with the audit manager, Dustin Barker. You have suggested sending negative confirmations to the smaller customers. The Dustin wants you to research the guidance provided by the U.S. Auditing Standards about using negative confirmation. Specifically, cut and paste the standard section that explains the significance of the evidence provided by unreturned negative confirmations.

Dustin would also like you to research the U.S. auditing standards about the factors that influence the reliability of confirmation. Draft a memo that summarizes the factors that influence the reliability of confirmations as evidence about the existence and occurrence of receivables and sales.

To: Dustin Barker, Manager

Re: Factors that influence the reliability of confirmations

From: CPA Candidate

ZZZZ BEST: CLIENT ACCEPTANCE AND CLIENT RESIGNATION

How important are a CPA firm's client acceptance and retention procedures? Consider the following situation. ZZZZ Best Company, Inc., was a Southern California company that was in the insurance restoration business (carpet cleaning and repairing fire and smoke damage to buildings) that was preparing to go public with a $15 million initial public offering in 1986. A local CPA, George Greenspan, audited the company's financial statements until ZZZZ Best's investment bankers insisted that the company hire a "Big Eight" accounting firm to conduct the annual audits. ZZZZ Best hired Ernst and Whinney (E&W) to conduct a review of ZZZZ Best's financial statements for the three months ended July 31, 1986, that would be included in the registration statements, assist in preparing a registration statement to be filed with the SEC, provide a comfort letter to ZZZZ Best's underwriters, and audit the financial statements for the year ending April 30, 1987.

It is unclear what client acceptance procedures were performed to evaluate the integrity of management. Barry Minkow, then only 20 years old, headed ZZZZ Best. As a teenager he had been involved in writing bad checks and credit card forgery. There was conflicting congressional testimony about whether E&W contacted George Greenspan (the predecessor auditor) prior to accepting the ZZZZ Best engagement.

E&W issued an unqualified review report on the financial statements for the three months ended July 31, 1986, included in the registration statement. ZZZZ Best made its initial public offering, and the company's fortunes continued to soar as its market capitalization rose to an amount in excess of $200 million.

E&W never completed the full scope audit for the year ended April 30, 1987. ZZZZ Best made it difficult for the auditors to visit insurance restoration sites. Then, in May 1987 several events caused E&W to seriously question management's integrity. First, auditors paid attention to a *Los Angeles Times* article which revealed that Minkow had been involved in a series of credit card forgeries as a teenager. Then ZZZZ Best issued a press release that reported record profits and earnings without any discussion with E&W. Finally, E&W followed up on allegations made by a third party that ZZZZ Best's insurance restoration business was total fiction and uncovered some evidence supporting this allegation. Citing concerns about the integrity of management and the possible existence of fraud, E&W brought its concerns to the board of directors and resigned the engagement on June 2, 1987.

Does it matter how an auditor of a public company resigns? In this case it took 45 days (the maximum time allowed by law) before E&W made a filing with the SEC revealing its concern that ZZZZ Best's insurance contracts might be fraudulent. During this 45-day period, the board of directors was aware of allegations of fraud, but investors were not. Was it right to resign as an auditor because of concern about the integrity of management? Yes. Was it in the public interest to wait the maximum time to first reveal the possible existence of fraud to shareholders? Many members of Congress thought that waiting so long did not serve the public interest. Today the time necessary to report such issues has been shortened to two business days after a change in auditors.

This chapter discusses the process used by auditors to make decisions about client acceptance and retention. In addition, the chapter discusses the importance of understanding the business and industry. If E&W had obtained an understanding of the insurance restoration business, it would have realized that the unaudited revenues that ZZZZ Best reported for the year ended April 30, 1987 were larger than the entire national insurance reimbursements for fire restoration.

Sources: U.S. Congress, House, Subcommittee on Oversight and Investigations of the Committee on Energy and Commerce, *Failure of ZZZZ Best Co.* (Washington, DC: U.S. Government Printing Office, 1988) and D. Akst, *Wonder Boy, Barry Minkow—The Kid Who Swindled Wall Street* (New York: Scribner, 1990).

[PREVIEW OF CHAPTER 7]

This chapter has three major parts. First, the chapter explains the steps involved in client acceptance and retention decisions. Second, the steps involved in risk assessment procedures performed in the planning phase of the audit are identified. Finally, there is in-depth coverage of the first step in audit planning—obtaining an understanding of the entity and its environment. The following diagram provides an overview of the chapter organization and content.

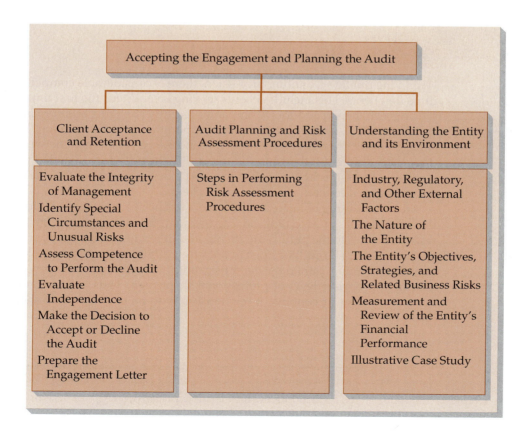

Chapter 7 focuses on decisions about client acceptance and retention, the steps involved in risk assessment, and how the auditor uses knowledge of the entity and its environment when planning the audit. This chapter addresses the following aspects of the auditor's knowledge and focuses on four important audit decisions addressed below.

---

focus on auditor knowledge

After studying this chapter you should understand the following aspects of an auditor's knowledge base:

K1. Understand the purpose and content of the engagement letter.

---

focus on audit decisions

After studying this chapter you should understand the factors that influence the following audit decisions.

D1. What steps should be followed in making a decision about client acceptance and retention?

D2. What steps should be performed in the risk assessment phase of the audit?

D3. How does the auditor use knowledge of the entity and its environment when planning an audit?

D4. Identify factors related to the entity and its environment that assist the auditor in (1) developing a knowledgeable perspective about the company and (2) assessing the risk of material misstatement.

[CLIENT ACCEPTANCE AND RETENTION]

Audit Decision 1

■ What steps should be followed in making a decision about client acceptance and retention?

Within the public accounting profession, there is considerable competition among firms for clients. This includes clients seeking an audit for the first time and clients seeking a change in auditors. Companies recently changing auditors include General Electric Co., Gateway, Inc., Sprint Corporation, and Adams Golf, Inc. Auditor changes result from a variety of factors including (1) mergers between corporations with different independent auditors, (2) the need for expanded professional services, (3) dissatisfaction with a firm, (4) a desire to reduce the audit fee, (5) or an audit firm's concern about the audit client.

An auditor is not obligated to perform a financial statement audit for any entity that requests it. In accepting an engagement, an auditor takes on professional responsibilities to the public, the client,[1] and other members of the public accounting profession. The auditor must maintain credibility with creditors, shareholders, and the investing public by demonstrating independence, integrity, objectivity, and an appropriate level of professional skepticism. Thus, a decision to accept a new audit client or continue a relationship with an existing client should not be taken lightly.

---

[1] Professional literature refers to the entity that hires the auditor as the audit client. However, auditors should keep in mind that shareholders, regulators, and all categories of financial statement users are also "clients" that benefit from the audit.

Figure 7-1 ■ Steps Associated with Client Acceptance and Retention

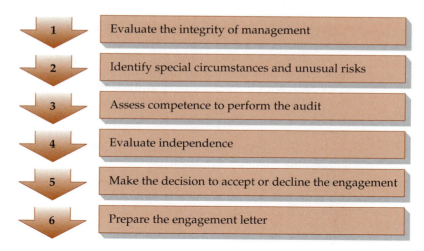

1	Evaluate the integrity of management
2	Identify special circumstances and unusual risks
3	Assess competence to perform the audit
4	Evaluate independence
5	Make the decision to accept or decline the engagement
6	Prepare the engagement letter

The importance of this decision is reflected in the inclusion of acceptance and continuation of clients as one of the quality control elements for CPA firms as previously discussed in Chapter 1. Figure 7-1 identifies the steps CPA firms should take to ensure acceptance of only those audit engagements that can be completed in accordance with all applicable professional standards. Each step is discussed below.

EVALUATE THE INTEGRITY OF MANAGEMENT

The primary purpose of a financial statement audit is to express an opinion on *management's* financial statements. Engagement performance depends on considerable client cooperation. Accordingly, the auditor should accept an audit engagement only when he or she believes that the client's management can be trusted. When management lacks integrity, there is an increased risk that material errors or fraud may occur. This was a significant problem for the auditors of Enron, WorldCom, and other companies that engaged in fraudulent financial reporting. Integrity of management may show up in the pressure that senior management may put on accounting personnel to use accounting techniques to accomplish earnings targets. Many executives place a premium on the representational faithfulness of financial statements, whereas others may be more concerned with how accounting techniques might be used to achieve specific goals. Problems with management integrity increase the risk that an unqualified opinion will be expressed when the financial statements are materially misstated.

For a new client, the auditor may obtain information about management's integrity by communicating with the predecessor auditor and by making inquiries of other third parties. For an existing client, the auditor's previous experience with the client's management should be considered.

Communicate with the Predecessor Auditor

For a client who has been audited, the knowledge of the client's management acquired by the predecessor auditor is essential information for a successor auditor. Before accepting the engagement, AU 315.03, *Communication Between Predecessor and Successor Auditors* (SAS 84), requires the **successor auditor** (who is considering accepting a new client) to take the initiative to communicate, either orally or in writing, with the **predecessor auditor** (the client's existing or former auditor). The communication should be made with the client's permission, and the client should authorize the predecessor to respond fully to the successor's inquiries. Authorization is required because the profession's code of ethics prohibits the predecessor auditor from disclosing confidential information obtained in an audit without the client's permission.

In the communication, the successor auditor should make specific and reasonable inquiries regarding matters that may affect the decision to accept an engagement, such as:

- Information that might bear on the integrity of management.
- Disagreements with management about accounting principles and auditing procedures, or other similarly significant matters.
- Communications to audit committees or others with equivalent authority and responsibility regarding fraud, illegal acts by clients, internal control related matters, and quality of accounting principles.
- The predecessor's understanding of the reasons for a change in auditors.

The predecessor auditor is expected to respond promptly and fully, assuming the client gives consent. If the client's consent is not given or the predecessor auditor does not respond fully, the successor auditor should consider the implications for deciding whether to accept the engagement.

Make Inquiries of Other Third Parties

Information about management's integrity may also be obtained from knowledgeable persons such as attorneys, bankers, and others in the financial and business community who have had business relationships with the prospective client. In some cases, making an inquiry of the local chamber of commerce and the Better Business Bureau may also be helpful.

Other potential sources of information include (1) reviewing news items on top management changes in the financial press, and (2) in the case of prospective SEC clients who have been previously audited, reviewing the report filed with the SEC concerning a change in auditors.

Review Previous Experience with Existing Clients

Before making a decision to continue an engagement with an audit client, the auditor should carefully consider prior experiences with the client's management. For example, the auditor should consider any material errors, fraud, or illegal acts discovered in prior audits. The auditor might also consider management's willingness to make suggested changes in internal control. During an audit, the auditor makes inquiries of management about such matters as the existence of contingencies, the completeness of all minutes of board of directors' meetings, and compliance with regulatory requirements. The truthfulness of management's responses to such inquiries in prior audits should be carefully considered in evaluating the integrity of management.

IDENTIFY SPECIAL CIRCUMSTANCES AND UNUSUAL RISKS

A key element of the audit involves assessing the risk of material misstatement in the financial statements. CPAs are also concerned about the **auditor's business risk** of being associated with companies having financial difficulties or going-concern problems. If an entity experiences financial or legal difficulties, and if plaintiffs can find any pretext for claiming reliance on the financial statements, it is widely recognized that litigation will likely involve the auditors, who are often thought to have "deep pockets." Matters pertaining to this step in accepting an engagement include identifying the intended users of the audited financial statements, making a preliminary assessment of the prospective client's legal and financial stability, identifying scope limitations, and evaluating the entity's auditability.

Identify Intended Users of Audited Statements

Chapter 4 points out that the auditor's legal responsibilities in an audit may vary based on the intended users of the statements. Thus, the auditor should consider any named beneficiaries or foreseen or foreseeable third parties regarding whom the potential for liability exists under the common law. The auditor should also consider whether a common set of audited statements will meet the needs of all intended users or whether any special reports will be required. For example, regulated companies may be required to furnish certain audited information not required by GAAP. Added reporting requirements may mean additional competency requirements, increased audit costs, and broaden the auditor's legal liability exposure.

Assess Prospective Client's Legal and Financial Stability

If an entity experiences legal difficulties, as discussed above, such litigation will likely involve the auditors, who are often thought to have "deep pockets." Thus, auditors may incur the financial and other costs of defending themselves no matter how professionally they perform their services.

For this reason, auditors should attempt to identify and reject prospective clients that pose a high risk of litigation. This might include companies whose operations or principal products are the subject of investigations by authorities or are the subject of material lawsuits, the outcome of which could adversely impact the viability of the business. It might also include companies already known to be experiencing financial instability such as inability to meet debt payments or raise needed capital. Even when there are no signs of current difficulties, consideration should be given to the likelihood of such matters as future write-downs associated with deteriorating business conditions. Procedures the auditor can use to identify such matters are inquiries of management, reviews of credit bureau reports, analysis of previously issued audited or unaudited financial statements, and, if applicable, previous filings with regulatory agencies.

Identify Scope Limitations

When considering whether to accept an engagement, the auditor should evaluate whether any scope limitations increase the risk that he or she may not be able to issue an unqualified opinion. The auditor should consider whether management has imposed any restrictions on performing audit procedures. If management prevents visits to certain locations that the auditor considers material, or restricts contacts with customers or suppliers, the auditor must consider whether such actions preclude the expression of an unqualified opinion. Alternatively, the auditor might be engaged after year-end, or other timing considerations might make it impracticable to apply auditing procedures considered necessary in the audit. The auditor should also consider the implications of accepting an engagement if the predecessor auditor's workpapers are not available for review. The inability to review the predecessor's workpapers makes it difficult to understand the details supporting the beginning audited balances. Any of these circumstances may impact the final decision regarding the nature of the auditor's opinion.

Evaluate the Entity's Financial Reporting Systems and Auditability

Before accepting an engagement, the auditor should evaluate whether other conditions exist that raise questions as to the prospective client's auditability. Such conditions might include the absence, or poor condition, of important accounting records, the absence of a sufficient audit trail, or management's disregard of its responsibility to maintain other elements of adequate internal controls. As companies increasingly rely on electronic data processing, the auditor must consider the implications of whether corroborating evidence exists in document form, or whether important evidence is available only in electronic form. If the auditor has sufficient concerns about the adequacy of accounting records or the audit trail, the engagement should be declined or there should be a clear understanding with the client of the possible effects of such conditions on the auditor's report.

ASSESS COMPETENCE TO PERFORM THE AUDIT

The first general standard of GAAS states:

> The audit is to be performed by a person or persons having adequate technical training and proficiency as an auditor.
>
> *Source:* AU 210.01.

Thus, before accepting an audit engagement, auditors should determine whether they have the professional competence to complete the engagement in accordance with GAAS. This generally involves identifying the key members of the audit team and considering the need to seek assistance from consultants and specialists during the course of the audit.

Services Desired

Most clients that need an audit also require additional services. Smaller organizations that do not have a CPA working within the organization may require a variety of accounting services, such as having the auditor perform key accounting work, make journal entries, or draft the financial statements.[2] The client may desire to have the CPA firm prepare tax returns, for both the organization and the key owners or managers. In a risk-based audit, the risk of misstatement in the financial statements is associated with the financial implications of client's business risks. As the auditor obtains an understanding of how the client manages business risks, she or he may also make recommendations on how to better manage those risks and improve the performance of the business. Finally, auditors have a high level of expertise in information systems and internal controls. The client may seek the auditor's recommendations about the adequacy of its business risk assessment process, improved performance measurement systems, or improved internal controls. The audit firm should consider whether it has the competence to perform the full range of services required by the audit engagement.

Identify the Audit Team

Chapter 6 describes audit staffing as one of four key decisions that the auditor must consider regarding the collection of audit evidence. Furthermore, assigning personnel to engagements is one of the five quality control elements. The objective is to ensure that the knowledge, skill, and ability of the audit team match the professional staffing needs of the engagement. In making assignments, the nature and extent of supervision to be provided should also be taken into account. Generally, the more able and experienced the personnel assigned to a particular engagement, the less is the need for direct supervision.

The typical **audit team** consists of:

- A partner, who has both overall and final responsibility for the engagement.
- One or more managers, who usually have significant expertise in the industry and who coordinate and supervise the execution of the audit program.
- One or more seniors, who may have responsibility for planning the audit, executing parts of the audit program, and supervising and reviewing the work of staff assistants.
- Staff assistants, who perform many of the required audit procedures.

In addition, the engagement may include a computer audit specialist who will assist in evaluating computer aspects of internal controls.

The key members of the audit team are generally identified prior to acceptance of the engagement to ensure their availability. In addition, when a prospective client has invited a firm to submit a proposal to obtain the engagement, it is common practice to include the resumes of the key members of the proposed audit team. This allows the prospective client to assess the credentials of the individuals who will be assigned to the engagement.

Consider Need for Consultation and the Use of Specialists

In determining whether to accept an engagement, it is appropriate for an auditor to consider using consultants and specialists to assist the audit team in perform-

---

[2] Recall from Chapter 3 that SEC rules on independence are more stringent than AICPA rules. If a client anticipates going public in the upcoming three years, the client and the auditor should plan on meeting the SEC guidelines, not merely the AICPA guidelines.

ing the audit. In fact, the quality control element of consultation states that firms should adopt policies and procedures to provide reasonable assurance that personnel will seek assistance, to the extent required, from persons having appropriate levels of knowledge, competence, judgment, and authority. Thus, for example, it may be anticipated that an audit team in a practice office may need to consult with a computer or industry expert in the firm's national office to deal with complex client issues that arise in the course of the audit.

Similarly, certain matters may require the use of a specialist outside the auditor's firm. An auditor is not expected to have the expertise of a person trained for, or qualified to engage in, the practice of another profession or occupation. AU 336, *Using the Work of a Specialist* (SAS 73), recognizes that the auditor may use the work of specialists to obtain competent evidential matter. Following are a few examples of an outside **specialist** that may be used in an audit:

- Appraisers to provide evidence about the valuation of assets such as art
- Engineers to determine the quantities of mineral reserves on hand
- Actuaries to determine amounts used in accounting for a pension plan
- Attorneys to assess the probable outcome of pending litigation
- Environmental consultants to determine the impact of environmental laws and regulations

Before using a specialist, the auditor is expected to become satisfied as to the professional qualifications, reputation, and objectivity of the specialist. For example, the auditor should consider: (1) whether the specialist has acquired the professional certification, license, or other recognition of competence appropriate in the specialist's field, (2) the results of inquiries of the specialist's peers and others familiar with his or her reputation and professional standing, and (3) whether the specialist has any relationship with the client that might impair his or her objectivity.

EVALUATE INDEPENDENCE

The second general standard of GAAS states:

> In all matters relating to the assignment, an independence in mental attitude is to be maintained by the auditor or auditors.
>
> *Source:* AU 220.01.

Independence on audit engagements is required by Rule 101 of the AICPA's Code of Professional Conduct and is one of the quality control elements. Furthermore, if the prospective client is required to file audited financial statements with the SEC, the auditor must comply with the PCAOB's requirements pertaining to independence.

Thus, before accepting a new audit client, the auditing firm must evaluate whether there are any circumstances that would impair its independence with respect to the client. One procedure is to circulate the name of a prospective client to all professional staff to identify any prohibited financial or business relationships. Many large firms ask all professional staff to report their equity interests in companies along with other information, and they maintain a database that allows them to flag potential independence problems. If it is concluded that the independence requirements cannot be met, the engagement should be declined. In addition, the firm should determine that acceptance of the client would not result in any conflicts of interest with other clients.

MAKING THE DECISION TO ACCEPT OR DECLINE THE AUDIT

In making a decision about accepting or declining an audit, the audit firm is managing its own business risks. Common reasons for refusing to accept an audit client include the items previously discussed, such as concern about the integrity of management, special risks such as scope limitations, audibility concerns or disagreements with predecessor auditors, problems associated with obtaining the necessary expertise for the audit, or independence problems. An important part of a firm's quality control revolves around internal procedures that bring these concerns to the surface and allow the firm to make appropriate decisions about accepting or continuing clients.

Figure 7-2 summarizes the key factors that may influence decisions about accepting or retaining clients. Circumstances that might cause a firm to withdraw from an audit might include:

- Concerns about the integrity of management or the withholding of evidence that surfaces during the audit.
- The client's refusal to correct material misstatements in the financial statements.
- The client's failure to take appropriate steps to remedy fraud or illegal acts discovered during the audit.

A CPA firm should address the acceptability and continuation of audit clients the same way it addresses the acceptance of new clients. Ideally, a CPA firm will make decisions about the continuation of audit clients before commencing the engagement. However, if there are concerns about the integrity of management, withholding evidence, or other auditability problems, they should be brought to a partner's attention. A CPA firm will usually consult with outside legal counsel when considering whether it should withdraw from an engagement in progress. If an engagement letter has been signed, the auditor may be responsible for a breach of contract. Often the auditor will give management a letter that outlines the auditor's concern and the actions that management needs to take in order for the audit to proceed. If management does not meet its obligations in an audit, the auditor may be in a better position to withdraw from an engagement that is in progress.

PREPARE THE ENGAGEMENT LETTER

Auditor Knowledge 1

■ Understand the purpose and content of the engagement letter.

As the final step in the acceptance phase, it is good professional practice to confirm the terms of each engagement in an engagement letter as illustrated in Figure 7-3. The form and content of **engagement letters** may vary for different clients, but they should generally include the following:

- Clear identification of the entity and the financial statements to be audited.
- The objective or purpose of the audit.

Figure 7-2 ■ Factors That Influence Client Acceptance and Retention

Positive Factors Regarding Client Acceptance and Retention	Factors That Influence Client Acceptance and Retention	Negative Factors Regarding Client Acceptance and Retention
Management shows integrity in business and accounting decisions. Management places a premium on representational faithfulness of accounting information.	**Integrity of management**	Concerns exist about the integrity of management in business and accounting decisions. Management is preoccupied with attaining specific accounting numbers.
Minimal regulatory reporting requirements The client is financially stable and profitable, with no significant concerns about debt covenants. No scope limitations exist. The entity has a strong accounting system with good internal controls.	**Special circumstance and unusual risks**	Significant regulatory reporting requirements with close monitoring by regulators. The client is experiencing profitability issues, weak cash flows, and is close to violation of debt covenants. The client voices significant concerns about the scope of audit work. The entity has a weak accounting system with few internal controls.
The firm has expertise to deliver services requested by the client or has access to specialists that can meet client needs.	**Competence issues**	The firm does not have expertise needed to provide the full scope of services requested by the client, or does not have affiliation with specialists to meet client needs.
No independence problems exist, or independence problems can be resolved prior to client acceptance.	**Independence issues**	Independence and conflict of interest issues exist that cannot be resolved prior to client acceptance.

- Reference to the professional standards (e.g., GAAS) to which the auditor will adhere (and, if applicable, to governing legislation or regulations, as when performing certain government-required audits).
- An explanation of the nature and scope of the audit and the auditor's responsibilities.
- A statement to the effect that a properly designed and executed audit may not detect all material fraud.
- A reminder to management that it is responsible for preparing the financial statements and for maintaining an adequate system of internal control.
- An indication that management will be asked to provide certain written representations to the auditor.
- A description of any auxiliary services to be provided by the auditor such as the preparation or review of tax returns.
- The basis on which fees will be computed and any billing arrangements.
- A request for the client to confirm the terms of the engagement by signing and returning a copy of the letter to the auditor.

Figure 7-3 ■ Engagement Letter

REDDY AND ABEL CERTIFIED PUBLIC ACCOUNTANTS

Mr. Thomas Thorp, President
Melville Co., Inc.
Route 32
Midtown, New York 11746

Dear Mr. Thorp:

We are pleased to confirm our understanding of the services we are to provide for Melville Co., Inc. for the year ending December 31, 20X1.

We will audit the balance sheet of Melville Co., Inc as of December 31, 20X1 and the related statements of income, retained earnings, and cash flow for the year then ended. The objective of our audit is the expression of an opinion about whether your financial statements are fairly presented, in all material respects, in conformity with generally accepted accounting principles. Our audit will be conducted in accordance with generally accepted auditing standards and will include tests of your accounting records and other procedures we consider necessary to enable us to express such an opinion. If we are unable to complete the audit, or are unable to form or have not formed an opinion, we may decline to express an opinion or to issue a report as a result of this engagement.

Our procedures will include tests of documentary evidence supporting the transactions recorded in the accounts, tests of the physical existence of inventories, and direct confirmation of receivables and certain other assets and liability by correspondence with selected customers, creditors, and banks. At the conclusion of the audit we will require certain written representations from you about the financial statements and related matters.

An audit includes examining, on a test basis, evidence supporting the amounts and disclosures in the financial statements; therefore, our audit will involve judgment about the number of transactions to be examined and the areas to be tested. Also, we will plan and perform the audit to obtain reasonable assurance about whether the financial statements are free of material misstatement. Because of the concept of reasonable assurance and because we will not perform a detailed examination of all transactions, there is a risk that material errors, fraud, or other illegal acts, may exist and not be detected by us. In addition, an audit is not designed to detect errors, fraud, or illegal acts that are immaterial to the financial statements. Our responsibility as auditors is limited to the period covered by our audit and does not extend to any later periods for which we are not engaged as auditors.

Our audit will include obtaining an understanding of internal control sufficient to plan the audit and to determine the nature, timing, and extent of audit procedures to be performed. An audit is not designed to provide assurance on internal control or to identify reportable conditions, that is, significant deficiencies in the design or operation of internal control. However, during the audit, if we become aware of such reportable conditions, we will communicate them to you.

We understand that you are responsible for making all financial records and related information available to us and that you are responsible for the accuracy and completeness of that information. We will advise you about appropriate accounting principles and their application and will assist in the preparation of your financial statements, but the responsibility for the financial statements remains with you. This responsibility includes the establishment and maintenance of adequate records and effective internal controls over financial reporting, the selection and application of accounting principles, and the safeguarding of assets. Management is also responsible for identifying and ensuring that the entity complies with applicable laws and regulations.

We understand that your employees will prepare all cash, accounts receivable, and other confirmations we request and will locate any documents selected by us for testing.

As part of our engagement, we will also prepare the federal and state income tax returns for your company for the year ended December 31, 20X1.

We expect to begin our audit on approximately September 15, 20X1 and to complete your tax returns and issue our report not later than March 1, 20X2. We will observe the counting of inventories on December 31, 20X1.

We estimate our fees for those services will range from $___ to $__ for the audit and $_____ to $__ for the tax return. You will also be billed for travel and other out-of-pocket costs such as report production, typing, postage, etc. Additional expenses are estimated to be $___. The fee estimate is based on anticipated cooperation from your personnel and the assumption that unexpected circumstance will not be encountered during the audit. If significant additional time is necessary, we will discuss it with you and arrive at a new fee estimate before we incur the additional costs. Our invoices for these fees will be rendered each month as work progresses and are payable on presentation. In accordance with our firm policies, work may be suspended if your account becomes 60 days or more overdue and will not be resumed until your account is paid in full. If we elect to terminate our services for nonpayment, you will be obligated to compensate us for all time expended and to reimburse us for all out-of-pocket expenditures through the date of termination.

We appreciate the opportunity to be of service to you and believe this letter accurately summarizes the significant terms of our engagement. If you have any questions, please let us know. If you agree with the terms of our engagement as described in this letter, please sign the enclosed copy and return it to us.

Your truly,

Reddy and Abel, Certified Public Accountants

This letter correctly sets forth the understanding of Melville Co., Inc.

_____   _____
Mr. Thomas Thorp, President   Date

To eliminate the need to prepare a new letter each year on recurring audits, a statement may be added to the initial letter to the effect that it will be effective for future years unless it is terminated, amended, or superseded. Of course, if there are any significant future changes in the terms of the engagement, the nature or size of the client's business, its management, or legal requirements, a revised letter should be prepared.

An engagement letter constitutes a legal contract between the auditor and the client and should be renewed each year. Clearly stating the nature of services to be performed and the responsibilities of the auditor, as noted in Chapter 4, may help the auditor to avoid becoming involved in litigation.

[LEARNING CHECK

7-1 a. State the steps involved in accepting an audit engagement.
   b. Contrast the manner in which the auditor can evaluate the integrity of management between a new and a recurring audit engagement.

7-2 a. Why is it considered necessary for a successor auditor to communicate with a predecessor audit?
   b. Identify three matters about which the successor auditor should direct inquiries to the predecessor auditor.

7-3 Before accepting an audit engagement, the auditor should identify special circumstances and unusual risks.
   a. Why is it important to identify the intended users of financial statements?
   b. Why should a prospective client's legal and financial stability be evaluated?
   c. Identify three conditions that raise questions as to a prospective client's auditability.

7-4 a. Why is it essential for auditors to determine whether they have the competence to complete an engagement before accepting it?
   b. What is involved in making this determination?

7-5 a. What is the composition of a typical audit team?
   b. Is it ever appropriate to accept an engagement in which the members of the proposed audit team do not possess all the expertise needed to complete the audit? Explain.

7-6 a. State four examples of situations in which an auditor might want to use the services of a specialist outside the auditor's firm.
   b. What should an auditor do before relying on the work of a specialist?

    c. Is it ever appropriate to use a specialist that has a relationship with the client? Explain.

7-7 a. Why is it important for an auditor to evaluate independence in deciding whether to accept a new client?

    b. What should an auditor do if he or she concludes that independence requirements cannot be met?

7-8 a. State three reasons that an auditor might choose not to accept a potential audit client.

    b. State three reasons that an auditor might choose to resign from a current audit client.

    c. Contrast the decision to accept an audit engagement with the decision to continue an audit engagement for an existing audit client.

7-9 a. What are the purposes of an engagement letter?

    b. Who prepares the engagement letter, to whom is it sent, and what is its disposition?

[KEY TERMS

Audit team, p. 277	Predecessor auditor, p. 274
Auditor's business risk, p. 275	Specialist, p. 278
Engagement letters, p. 279	Successor auditor, p. 274

[AUDIT PLANNING AND RISK ASSESSMENT PROCEDURES]

Audit planning is a critical aspect of an effective audit. Planning serves much the same purpose in auditing that it does in personal planning for college or in business planning for the development of a new product such as a personal computer. In each instance, planning results in an orderly arrangement of the parts or steps to achieve the desired objective. The first GAAS of field work states:

> The work is to be adequately planned, and assistants, if any, are to be properly supervised.
>
> *Source:* AU 310.01.

Audit planning involves performing risk assessment procedures, assessing the risk of material misstatement in the financial statements, and developing an overall audit strategy to respond to those risks. **Supervision** involves directing the assistants on the audit team who participate in completing the various phases of the audit. The extent of supervision required on an engagement depends on, among other factors, the qualifications of the persons performing the work. Thus, in planning the audit, provision should be made for more supervision when several members of the audit team are inexperienced than when they are all experienced.

An important first step in planning the audit is performing risk assessment procedures to identify factors that influence the risk of material misstatement in the financial statements. The auditor should approach risk assessment procedures with an attitude of professional skepticism about such matters as the integrity of management, errors and fraud, and illegal acts. The amount of risk assessment procedures required in an engagement will vary with the size and complexity of the entity. Also, considerably more effort is needed to perform risk assessment procedures in an initial audit than in a recurring audit.

STEPS IN PERFORMING RISK ASSESSMENT PROCEDURES

Audit Decision 2

■ What steps should be performed in the risk assessment phase of the audit?

Performing risk assessment procedures involves a number of key steps initially presented in Chapter 5. The key steps involved in performing risk assessment procedures are shown in Figure 7-4.

The process of identifying relevant financial statement assertions (Step 1) was discussed in Chapter 6. Obtaining an understanding of the entity and its environment (Step 2) is a critical risk assessment procedure that establishes the foundation for many other audit procedures. Understanding the business and industry particularly sets the foundation for making decisions about materiality (Step 3). The auditor uses this knowledge about what is significant to financial statement users to design and perform analytical procedures (Step 4) to identify potential risks of material misstatement. The auditor then performs additional risk assessment procedures to identify the risk of material misstatement for significant financial statement assertions, including making specific assessment of the risk that fraud might have a material impact on the financial statements (Step 5). The auditor is now in a position to make judgments about preliminary audit strategies (Step 6). Armed with this knowledge, the auditor then obtains an understanding of the system of internal control to ascertain that it appropriately responds to the risk of material misstatement (Step 7). The second step in performing risk assessment procedures is discussed in the remainder of this chapter. Decisions about

Figure 7-4 ■ Key Steps in Performing Risk Assessment Procedures

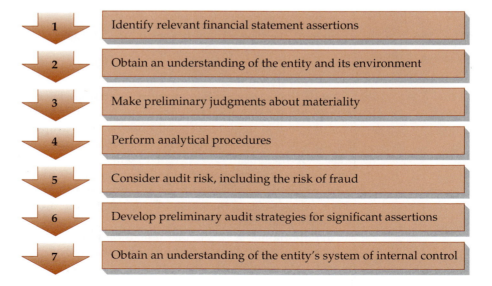

1. Identify relevant financial statement assertions
2. Obtain an understanding of the entity and its environment
3. Make preliminary judgments about materiality
4. Perform analytical procedures
5. Consider audit risk, including the risk of fraud
6. Develop preliminary audit strategies for significant assertions
7. Obtain an understanding of the entity's system of internal control

materiality and performing analytical procedures are discussed in Chapter 8. Steps 5 and 6 are discussed in Chapter 9, and step 7 in Chapter 10.

[UNDERSTANDING THE ENTITY AND ITS ENVIRONMENT]

Audit Decision 3

■ How does the auditor use knowledge of the entity and its environment when planning an audit?

As part of performing risk assessment procedures, generally accepted auditing standards require auditors to obtain an understanding of the entity and its environment.[3] Figure 7-5 provides an overview of the key steps in obtaining this understanding.

The auditor uses this information for two important purposes. First, the auditor wants to develop a knowledgeable perspective about the entity and its financial statements. In this step the auditor is attempting to develop expectations about amounts and disclosures that should be reported in the financial statements. If the information that is presented for audit differs significantly from the auditor's expectation, one possible explanation is that the information contains possible misstatements. For example, an auditor might develop an expectation of decreased sales owing to the fact that the company has a history of exporting a

Figure 7-5 ■ Key Steps in Understanding the Entity and Its Environment

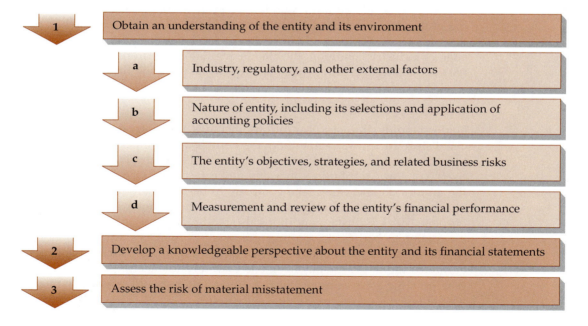

1   Obtain an understanding of the entity and its environment

    a   Industry, regulatory, and other external factors

    b   Nature of entity, including its selections and application of accounting policies

    c   The entity's objectives, strategies, and related business risks

    d   Measurement and review of the entity's financial performance

2   Develop a knowledgeable perspective about the entity and its financial statements

3   Assess the risk of material misstatement

---

[3] The following discussion of assertions is based on an Auditing Standards Board (ASB) Exposure Draft dated December 2, 2002, and subsequent updates presented to the ASB for discussion. A requirement to understand the entity and its environment was adopted by the International Auditing and Assurance Standards Board on October 31, 2003.

significant amount of product to a country that has imposed increased tariffs or trade restrictions on that product. In 2003, for example, Japan banned imports of beef from the United States following one known incident of mad cow disease. If the audit entity had a history of exporting beef to Japan, and yet revenues held constant or increased, the auditor would want to find evidence to determine whether the company found other markets for the product or whether there was an error in revenue recognition. Hence, the auditor is unable to develop a knowledgeable perspective about revenues without fully understanding the audit entity and its environment.

Second, knowledge of the entity and its environment will assist the auditor in assessing the risk of material misstatement. For example, the entity may have a significant line of business that involves long-term construction contracts. Accounting for these contracts involves both significant estimations of revenues and costs, and complex applications of GAAP. The opportunity for misestimation or misapplying GAAP is so significant that the auditor will usually recognize this as a significant inherent risk and assess inherent risk at the maximum.

Figure 7-6 provides examples of key factors associated with understanding the entity and its environment, along with (1) how the auditor uses this information to develop a knowledgeable perspective about the entity and (2) assesses the risk of material misstatement.

INDUSTRY, REGULATORY, AND OTHER EXTERNAL FACTORS

Generally accepted auditing standards require auditors to obtain an understanding of the client's industry, regulatory, and other external factors when planning the audit. The following discussion addresses how the auditor would use knowledge of industry condition, the client's regulatory environment, and other external factors affecting the client's business, when planning the audit.

Industry Conditions

Understanding **industry conditions** includes understanding the market for a client's products, the competition, the entity's and competitor's capacity relative to market conditions, and price competition. For example, if an entity has high fixed cost, low contributions margins, and is faced with intense price competition, the auditor should expect the company to be financially challenged. The introduction of a new technology by competitors might make an entity's technology obsolete. Weak industry conditions also tend to increase the level of stock market sensitivity to bad news, putting pressure on management to obtain targeted results. If projections cannot be obtained through solid earnings and cash flow, auditors might expect management to resort to meeting financial targets by manipulating accounting techniques. The auditor should respond to this list with a heightened level of professional skepticism.

Regulatory Environment

The auditor should also understand the entity's **regulatory environment,** including the degree to which the entity and its products or services are regulated by government or private agencies. For example, the pharmaceutical

Figure 7-6 ■ The Auditor's Understanding of the Entity and Its Environment

Knowledge of the Entity and Its Environment	Developing a Knowledgeable Perspective about the Entity and Its Financial Statements	Assessing the Risk of Material Misstatement
Industry, Regulatory, and Other External Factors		
Industry Conditions ■ The market and competition, including demand, capacity, and price competition ■ Cyclical or seasonal activity ■ Product technology relating to the entity's products	The auditor's understanding of industry conditions, such as the effects of an economic downturn and increases in capacity utilization is critical for estimating both revenues and costs. Further significant technology change may make a product obsolete, leading the auditor to an expectation of write-downs of inventory.	Weak industry conditions tend to create a sensitivity in capital markets to bad news. This may heighten pressure on management to meet short-term performance indicators such as earnings, revenue growth, or ratios tied to debt covenants. Such conditions usually affect multiple account balances and transaction classes. Auditors must approach these conditions with a heightened level of objectivity and professional skepticism.
Regulatory environment ■ Accounting principles and industry-specific practices ■ Regulatory framework in a regulated industry ■ Government policies currently affecting the conduct of the entity's business, such as tariffs and trade restrictions	Auditors must understand regulatory practices that require the application of specific industry GAAP. Furthermore, knowledge of increased tariffs or trade restrictions might cause the auditor to expect a decline in revenues of affected products (either prices or quantities).	The auditor should be aware that complex regulations may increase the risk of noncompliance, which in turn may result in an illegal act that has a direct and material effect on the financial statements.
Other external factors affecting the entity's business ■ General level of economic activity ■ Interest rates and availability of financing ■ Inflation and currency revaluation	Declines in economic activity, accompanied by declines in the stock market, often lead to restricting the availability of capital in equity and debt markets. The auditor might expect heightened attention to debt covenants.	Companies often hedge risks of foreign currency rates or changing interest rates with derivative financial instruments. Rapid changes in interest rates or currency revaluation in a foreign country may provide an increased risk of material misstatement in accounting for derivative financial instruments.

(continues)

Figure 7-6 ■ (Continued)

Knowledge of the Entity and Its Environment	Developing a Knowledgeable Perspective about the Entity and Its Financial Statements	Assessing the Risk of Material Misstatement

Nature of the Entity, Including Its Selection and Application of Accounting Policies

Business Operations

- Method of obtaining revenues (e.g., manufacturing, retailing, banking, etc.)
- Products or services and markets (e.g., major customer and contracts, market share or reputation of products)
- Conduct of operations (e.g., stages and methods of production, business segments)
- Alliances, joint ventures, and outsourcing activities
- Involvement in e-commerce, including Internet sales
- Geographic dispersion and industry segmentation
- Locations of production facilities, warehouses, and offices
- Important suppliers of goods and services (e.g., stability of supply or methods of delivery, such as just-in-time)
- Transactions with related parties

The auditor's knowledge of the entity's products and services assists the auditor in understanding (1) sources of revenues, (2) the nature of costs, and (3) the types of assets an entity might need. The auditor of a pharmaceutical company, for example, would need to be aware of new drugs that have received FDA approval in the year under audit to understand the potential for revenues. Knowledge of the product life cycle of various drugs will assist the auditor in understanding R&D costs as well as the viability of intangible assets.

Companies that enter into new markets (such as technology companies offering software products for the first time) will likely require the application of new accounting principles (revenue recognition for software).

Furthermore, knowledge of a product's life cycle, particularly in some technology industries with short product life cycles, may assist the auditor in estimating the useful lives of manufacturing equipment.

Transactions with related parties lack the independent negotiations as to structure and price that are present in transactions with unrelated parties, increasing the possibility that their legal form may differ from their economic substance.

Investments

- Capital investment activities
- Acquisitions, mergers, or disposals of business activities
- Investments and disposition of securities and loans

Knowledge of acquisitions or capital investments will alert the auditor to expect changes in the company's asset structure. As the mix of productive assets changes, the auditor should also expect related changes in sales and return on assets.

Expansion through merger may be necessary to achieve an entity's goals. However, it also may create challenges of integrating internal control processes or meeting expanded financing needs. Misstatements in financial reporting or liquidity crises may result.

Financing

- Group structure, including consolidated and nonconsolidated entities
- Debt structure, including covenants, guarantees and off-balance sheet financing arrangements
- Use of derivative financial instruments

Changes in long-term assets usually lead the auditor to expect changes in financing. Auditors also need to be alert to understanding how many companies use complex transactions, such as transferring assets and debt to variable interest entities, joint ventures, or partnerships while retaining substantially all the risks and rewards of ownership.

The use of new types of complex financial instruments or sophisticated business structures may increase the likelihood of misapplication of GAAP. Auditors need to consider whether variable interest entities need to be consolidated in an entity's financial statements.

(continues)

Figure 7-6 ■ (Continued)

Knowledge of the Entity and Its Environment	Developing a Knowledgeable Perspective about the Entity and Its Financial Statements	Assessing the Risk of Material Misstatement
Nature of the Entity (*continued*)		
		Auditors also need to be alert to violations of debt covenants or the triggering of guarantees that may cause substantial doubt about the entity's ability to continue as a going concern.
Financial Reporting ■ Accounting principles and industry-specific practices ■ Accounting for fair value ■ Industry-specific significant categories (e.g., research and development for pharmaceuticals)	The auditor's knowledge of industry-specific categories such as research and development for technology or pharmaceutical companies, or the importance of a loan loss reserve for banks, focuses the auditor's attention on items important to financial statement readers.	Complex accounting, such as accounting for long-term contracts, may increase the risk of incorrect estimations or misapplication of GAAP. Auditors should also be concerned that assumptions underlying the calculation of fair values of hard-to-value assets are reasonable and based on current information. Furthermore, disclosures should adequately portray the methods for calculating fair value and the related degree of uncertainty.
Entity's Objectives, Strategies, and Related Business Risk		
Entity objectives and strategies (*and related business risk*) ■ New products and services (*increased product liability*) ■ Expansion of the business (*demand has not been accurately estimated*) ■ Response to industry or regulatory requirements (*decreased industry demand or increased legal exposure due to regulations*)	The auditor's knowledge of the entity's objectives and strategies will assist in developing expectations of changes from prior year's performance. The auditor should also be alert to the financial consequences of not achieving planned business strategies such as decreased profitability and cash flows and potential violation of debt covenants.	Increased business risk often results in uncertainty in financial performance that may have implications for revenue recognition (the auditor should be alert to side arrangements or special terms), accounting estimates (net realizable value of assets), or other applications of GAAP (useful lives of assets).
Effects of implementing a strategy (*Incomplete or improper implementation*)	The auditor's knowledge of stage of development of new strategies may assist in determining whether costs should be capitalized or expensed.	Failure to fully implement a new strategy may provide the incentive for management to attempt to use accounting methods to obtain desired results.

(continues)

Figure 7-6 ■ (Continued)

Knowledge of the Entity and Its Environment	Developing a Knowledgeable Perspective about the Entity and Its Financial Statements	Assessing the Risk of Material Misstatement
Measurement and Review of the Entity's Financial Performance		
The entity may use the following tools to monitor or review its financial performance: ■ Key ratios and operating statistics ■ Key performance indicators ■ Use of forecasts, budgets, and variance analysis ■ Analyst reports and credit rating reports	The auditor's knowledge of industry standards for operating statistics may assist the auditor in developing expectations of financial statement amounts and disclosures. For example, an auditor might be able to compare a retail client's results with industry standards for sales per square foot of retail space or inventory turn days.	Significant differences of actual performance from budgets, forecasts, or expected amounts may indicate a possible misapplication of GAAP. A decline in rating of a public company by analysts may alert the auditor to potential business risks and their financial consequences. For example, specific knowledge obtained in an analyst's report may alert the auditor to credit or default risk of a significant customer, supplier, or trading partner.

industry is highly regulated. The economic consequences of being the first product to receive FDA approval of a new drug can be significant. Furthermore, governments impose various tariffs and other trade barriers that might have a material impact on a company. Auditors should be knowledgeable of regulations so that they can understand the economic consequences on the entities that they audit. If an audit client fails to obtain regulatory approval for a product, the auditor should consider the inherent risks associated with write-downs in the value of assets.

Some regulations have a direct impact on accounting practices. Parts of the energy industry are highly regulated, and many public utility commissions specify certain accounting practices. Moreover, GAAP is a form of regulation, and recent accounting rules such as SFAS No. 133, *Accounting for Derivative Instruments and Hedging Activities,* or SFAS No. 142, *Goodwill and Other Intangible Assets,* are highly technical. Failure to understand such technical rules is an example of how the regulatory environment affects the inherent risk of material misstatement in the financial statements.

Other External Factors Affecting the Entity's Business

Other external factors include the general level of economic activity, changes in interest rates, availability of financing, and other broad economic factors such as inflation or currency revaluation. During the economic downturn that began late in 2000, business operating cash flow and capital spending deteriorated while borrowing capacity dwindled.

Investor wealth declined by trillions of dollars as the stock market tumbled, making equity capital more difficult to obtain. Companies responded with employee layoffs, inventory liquidations, and voluntary and involuntary restructurings. Declining economic conditions often place an increased level of pressure on management, such as meeting earnings targets or financial ratios tied to debt covenants. Auditors must be alert to the implications of these pressures. In some cases declines in overall economic conditions may create circumstances that require write-offs of receivables, write-downs in the value of inventory, or material declines in the value of assets valued at fair value and increase the inherent risk of misstatements in financial statement assertions.

THE NATURE OF THE ENTITY, INCLUDING ITS SELECTION AND APPLICATION OF ACCOUNTING POLICIES

Auditors should also obtain an understanding of the nature of the audit client when planning the audit, including its selection and application of accounting policies. The following discussion addresses both what the auditor should understand and how the auditor would employ this knowledge in audit planning.

Business Operations

Knowledge of the entity's **business operations** includes understanding such matters as the entity's:

- Method of obtaining revenues (e.g., manufacturing, retailing, import-export trading, banking, utility, etc.).
- Products or services and markets (e.g., major customers and contracts, terms of payment, profit margins, market share, competitors, exports, pricing policies, reputation of products, warranties, back orders, marketing strategy, and objectives).
- Conduct of operations (e.g., stages and methods of productions, business segments, fixed vs. variables costs, details of declining or expanding operations).
- Location of production facilities, warehouses, and offices.
- Employment (e.g., wages levels, union contracts, postemployment benefits, incentive bonus programs and government regulation related to employment matters).
- Transactions with related parties.

An auditor usually expects differing financial positions, results of operations, and cash flows for manufacturers versus services companies. Companies in the airline or hotel industries, for example, have high fixed costs, and capacity utilization is an important aspect of the business. The auditor of the airline might focus on the relationship between fuel costs, employee compensation, and revenues. This type of information helps the auditor develop a knowledgeable perspective about financial amounts and disclosures that are specific to the entity.

Knowledge of the entity's business operations may influence the selection and application of accounting policies. For example, the terms and conditions of sales made in the normal course of business will influence revenue recognition principles. The extent to which an airline offers frequent flyer miles influences the application of accounting for frequent flyer liabilities. Finally, the expected product life cycle, which can be very short for some technology companies, will influence the useful life of related manufacturing equipment.

Auditors also use knowledge of the entity's operations to identify significant inherent risks. Auditors of manufacturing companies are usually concerned about the fairness of assertions related to receivables and inventories, where such assertions might not be significant for service companies. A bank auditor might focus on the fairness of the entity's loan loss reserves because of the centrality of business loans to the bank's business operations.

Another important aspect of understanding business operations involves obtaining knowledge of related party transactions. **Related party transactions** are transactions between a company and its management, principal owners, and their immediate family members, and or affiliated companies. These transactions represent high inherent risks because they may not have the economic substance of an arm's length transaction between two independent parties. AU 334, *Related Parties*, describes important audit procedures that should be performed in planning an audit. It is particularly important to identify the existence of related parties so that transactions with related parties can be identified throughout the audit. For example, the auditor might identify related parties by requesting information from management, reviewing filings with the SEC and other regulatory agencies, reviewing stockholder listings of closely held companies to identify principal stockholders, or reviewing prior years' working papers for the names of known related parties.

Investments

Knowledge of the entity's **investing activities** includes understanding the entity's:

- Capital investment activities, including investments in plant and equipment and technology, and any recent or planned changes.
- Acquisitions, mergers, or disposals of business activities (planned or recently executed).
- Investments and disposition of securities and loans.
- Investments in nonconsolidated entities, including partnerships, joint ventures, and special-purpose entities.

A crucial decision for any business is its investment in productive assets. A forest products company is usually concerned about its investments both in timber and timberlands and manufacturing capacity. The company's ability to generate revenues is dependent on these investments. Critical investments for technology and pharmaceutical companies are their investments in research and development. Software companies invest in people, and although this human capital cannot be capitalized on the balance sheet, it is nevertheless important to revenue generation. Understanding the nature of an entity's investments assists the auditor in developing expectations of financial statement amounts and disclosures.

In an environment where public companies are under significant pressure to perform, an auditor should understand the relationships between productive assets and a company's revenues and cost. It is essential for auditors to understand the economic drivers of financial results. For example, some technology companies might spend several billion dollars on a manufacturing line for a product that might have a useful life of 18 to 24 months. This understanding is critical for estimating depreciation expense and matching expenses with revenues.

Financing

Knowledge of the entity's **financing activities** includes understanding the entity's:

- Debt structure, including covenants, restrictions, guarantees, and off-balance sheet financing arrangements.
- Group structure—major subsidiaries and associated entities, including consolidated and nonconsolidated structures.
- Leasing of property, plant, and equipment for use in the business.
- Beneficial owners.
- Use of derivative financial instruments.

Decisions about the acquisition and financing of productive assets go hand in hand. Many companies now use complex transactions with related companies, along with intricate operating agreements to accomplish both specific financial reporting and operating objectives. The use of special-purpose entities or variable interest entities to structure the use of assets and keep debt of the balance sheet is a significant inherent risk for auditors of both public and private companies. Sophisticated financing structures may increase the risk of misapplication of GAAP.

During good economic times, companies might commit to financial guarantees that seem to be only a remote possibility. During an economic downturn, however, the need to make good on guarantees might become a reality. Auditors should be alert to the violation of debt covenants, or events that might trigger guarantees, for such events might raise substantial doubt about an entity's ability to continue as a going concern.

Financial Reporting

Knowledge of the entity's **financial reporting** activities includes understanding such matters as the entity's:

- Accounting principles and industry-specific practices.
- Revenue recognition practices.
- Accounting for fair values.
- Inventories (e.g., locations and quantities).
- Industry-specific significant accounts and transaction classes (e.g., loans and investments for banks, accounts receivable and inventory for manufacturers, research and development for pharmaceuticals).
- Accounting for unusual or complex transactions, including those in controversial or emerging areas, for example, accounting for stock-based transactions.
- Financial statement presentation and disclosure.

Auditors should be knowledgeable about industry-specific accounting practices. The airline industry, for example, has specific accounting practices for accounting for the liability associated with frequent flyer miles. The software industry has specific industry practices associated with the question of when the costs of developing software should be capitalized rather than expensed. This understanding is essential for developing a knowledgeable perspective about the entity's accounting practices and whether they present fairly in accordance with GAAP.

THE ENTITY'S OBJECTIVES, STRATEGIES, AND RELATED BUSINESS RISKS

Generally accepted auditing standards require auditors to obtain an understanding of an entity's objectives, strategies, and related business risks. These terms are defined as follows:

- An **entity's objectives** are the overall plans for the entity as defined by those charged with governance and management.
- An **entity's strategies** are the operational approaches by which management intends to achieve it objectives.
- **Business risks** result from significant conditions, events, circumstances, or actions that could adversely affect the entity's ability to achieve its objectives and execute its strategies.

The following discussion addresses both what the auditor should understand about an entity's objectives, strategies, and related business risks and how the auditor uses this knowledge in audit planning.

Objectives, Strategies, and Related Business Risks and the Effects of Implementing a Strategy

Knowledge of the entity's objectives, strategies, and related business risks and the effects of implementing strategy normally includes understanding:

- Industry developments (potential related business risk: the entity does not have the personnel or expertise to deal with the changes in the industry).
- New products and services (potential related business risk: increased product liability)
- New accounting requirements (potential related business risk: incomplete or improper implementation and increased costs).
- Regulatory requirements (potential related business risk: increased legal exposure).
- Current and prospective financing requirements (potential related business risk: loss of financing due to inability to meet requirements).
- Use of information technology (potential related business risk: systems and processes not compatible).
- The effects of implementing strategy, particularly any effects that will lead to new accounting requirements (potential related business risk: incomplete or improper implementation).

Significant inherent risks are often closely associated with an entity's business risks. If an audit client is unable to develop a product to compete with new technology introduced by competitors, the entity likely faces declines in profitability, cash flows, and the possible write-down of inventory. If an audit client expands business by acquiring another entity, and the client overestimates demand for the acquired company's product, it may need to write down the value of goodwill associated with the acquisition. If profitability and cash flow are insufficient to meet financing requirements, the entity may have to address going-concern issues. When business risks become a reality, auditors need to make sure the financial consequences of such risks are fairly presented and disclosed in the financial statements.

MEASUREMENT AND REVIEW OF THE ENTITY'S FINANCIAL PERFORMANCE

Generally accepted auditing standards also require auditors to obtain an understanding of the **measurement and review of the entity's financial performance**, including both internal and external measures. Such measures might include:

- Key ratios and operating statistics
- Key performance indicators
- Employee performance measures and incentive compensation plans
- Industry trends
- The use of forecasts, budgets, and variance analysis
- Analyst reports and credit rating reports

A company might use a variety of financial and nonfinancial measures to monitor performance. Today, many companies measure the efficiency of the manufacturing process by comparing the quantity of raw material used to the quantity of finished goods produced, the labor hours involved in producing finished goods, and material and labor variances. In addition, it might monitor the effectiveness of the manufacturing process using quality control statistics or measures of the amount of rework required to meet standards. This information is essential for developing a knowledgeable perspective about reported amounts for inventory and cost of sales.

Many performance measures, such as those described above, are produced by the entity's information system. If management assumes that data used for reviewing the entity's performance are accurate without having a basis for that assumption, errors may exist in the information, potentially leading management (or the auditor using the same information) to incorrect conclusions about performance. If the auditor uses management's performance measures to form an audit conclusion (e.g., in performing analytical procedures), he or she should consider the reliability of the information system that produces the measure and whether the measure is sufficiently precise to detect material misstatements.

Management and auditors use performance measure information in different ways. When reported measures differ from management's expectations, management may take corrective action to improve the entity's performance. For example, poor inventory turnover might cause a company to offer more attractive pricing in order to sell inventory. However, the auditor should consider whether a deviation in performance measures might indicate a risk of misstatement in underlying financial information. A decline in inventory turnover might mean that certain manufacturing costs are being capitalized as part of inventory rather than being expensed. Deviations from expected performance measures are critical when assessing the inherent risk associated with financial statement assertions.

ILLUSTRATIVE CASE STUDY

The following discussion illustrates each of the steps described above using hypothetical data for New Technology, Inc. (NTI), a continuing audit client. The financial statements for NTI are presented in Chapter 8. The following paragraph briefly explains NTI's business and its competitive environment.

New Technology, Inc.

New Technology, Inc. (NTI) was founded nine years ago by a group of engineers who were focused on entertainment applications of computer technology. These engineers left former employers with significant wealth and wanted to start their own business. Four founders plus the CFO hold various ownership interests in the company. NTI's initial years were difficult as the company spent most of the initial investment on research and development, but the company has produced a series of successful products that have received market acceptance in the last three years. The company has generated positive cash flow from operations for the last five years. An initial accumulated deficit has been eliminated as the company has experienced success in a niche market.

NTI produces hard drives (similar to computer hard drives) primarily for the audio and video industry. The company has nurtured relationships with manufacturers of MP3 players, personal video recorders, and digital video recording equipment. NTI's industry is very competitive, and the cost of its products has consistently fallen while offering more capacity to customers. The company has earned a market niche because of product quality, effective research and development, and pricing terms offered to assemblers who use NTI's product in their equipment. Sales growth had been driven by consumer demand for these new products, but sales have also been dependent upon pricing and sales terms. Consumer demand is growing rapidly, but the company also faces increasing competition from larger public companies. Furthermore, the company is experiencing much faster growth than is seen in the economy as a whole. Almost 70 percent of NTI's business is with audio and video equipment assemblers who enjoy substantial allowances depending on market conditions, and NTI bears significant risks associated with ownership until the product is resold to end consumers. Assemblers usually submit blanket purchase orders on a quarterly basis, and shipments are made based on an assembler's weekly authorization. The company grants its assemblers price protection, and certain assemblers have limited rights to return products.

In anticipation of going public, the company has followed SEC Staff Accounting Bulletin 101, *Revenue Recognition in Financial Statements*. A small portion of the company's revenues is from retail-packaged products sold through several electronic equipment wholesale companies and through the Internet at the company's web site. The company faces the usual business risks associated with competition from other companies and new products. Product profitability depends on initial acceptance of products into the marketplace. The company believes that it will have to make significant product improvements every year or two related to increasing the speed of accessing data as well as storage capacity.

NTI currently has only one research and manufacturing facility in North America, and it is about to sign a seven-year lease to open a second manufacturing location in Malaysia. Research and development expenditures are essential to continue presence in the market. The company allocates about 12 percent of sales to research and development of new products, and the company holds several patents that have allowed it to compete effectively for market share. NTI focuses its engineering on coordinating its product design and manufacturing processes in order to bring its products to market in a cost-effective and timely manner. NTI manufactures or purchases certain magnetic heads, media controllers, spindle motors, and other mechanical parts used in the head disk assembly. The assembly process occurs in a clean room environment, which demands skill in process engineering and efficient utilization of the clean room layout in order to reduce the high operation cost of this manufacturing equipment. NTI is subject to a variety of regulations in connection with its operations. It believes that it has obtained, or is in the process of obtaining, all necessary environmental permits for its operations. NTI warrants its new manufactured disk drives against defects in materials and workmanship for a period of one to five years from the date of sale.

NTI is primarily equity financed, but it also uses accounts payable and advances from customers as financing sources. In recent years the company has been able to limit capital spending to about $110 million a year on new manufacturing and clean room equipment. The company has financed the equipment out of operating cash flow. However, more extensive capital investment will be needed to set up clean rooms and manufacturing equipment in the facility planned for next year in Malaysia. The company has recently started to explore plans to finance growth with an initial public offering.

NTI develops an annual budget and usually completes the budgeting process about four months prior to the start of the fiscal year. However, changes in the competitive environment often force budget revisions during the year. The company prepares monthly financial statements by the end of the second week of the following month and regularly compares actual performance to adjusted budgets. The company also carefully monitors the research and development process time from beginning an R&D project to bringing products to market, and the period of time from releasing new technology to when competitors introduce competitive products.

Understanding New Technology, Inc. and Its Environment

Figure 7-7 illustrates the process of identifying important traits about an entity's business and its environment and how the auditor relates those traits to the potential risk of material misstatement in the financial statements. Before studying this figure, students should (1) identify significant factors noted earlier that assist in building a knowledgeable perspective about NTI and (2) determine how those factors might influence the risk of material misstatement in the financial statements.

[LEARNING CHECK

7-10 State the seven key steps involved in performing risk assessment procedures.

7-11 a. What are the general areas of knowledge of the entity's industry, regulatory environment, and other external factors that the auditor should understand?

b. Develop examples to illustrate two ways that the auditor would use this knowledge in planning the audit.

7-12 a. What are the general areas that should be covered when understanding the nature of the entity being audited?

b. Develop examples to illustrate two ways that the auditor would use this knowledge in planning the audit.

Figure 7-7 ■ New Technologies, Inc., an Illustrative Case Study

Required Knowledge of the Entity and Its Environment	A Knowledgeable Perspective about NTI	Risk of Material Misstatement
Industry, Regulatory, and Other External Factors		
Industry Conditions	NTI produces hard drives (similar to computer hard drives) primarily for MP3 players, personal video recorders, and digital video recording equipment. This is a very competitive industry, and the cost of product has consistently fallen while offering more capacity to customers. The company has earned a market niche because of product quality, effective research and development, and pricing terms offered to assemblers who use NTI's product in their equipment. Sales growth had been driven by consumer demand for these new products, but sales have also been dependent upon pricing and sales terms.	The company reports a 50 percent growth in revenues. Although the industry is growing rapidly, professional skepticism must be exercised with respect to revenue recognition (existence and occurrence), particularly given the company's generous sales terms.
■ The market and competition, including demand, capacity, and price competition		
■ Cyclical or seasonal activity		
■ Product technology relating to the entity's products		
Regulatory environment	SEC Staff Accounting Bulletin 101, *Revenue Recognition in Financial Statements*.	Although NTI is still a private company, it is considering an IPO. Therefore, it is important to make sure that it follows GAAP for public companies if financial statements will be included in a registration statement.
■ Accounting principles and industry-specific practices		
■ Regulatory framework in a regulated industry	NTI is subject to a variety of regulation in connection with its operations. It believes that it has obtained, or is in the process of obtaining, all necessary environmental permits for its operations.	Potential regulation issues represent indirect illegal acts that should be considered in the context of FASB No. 5 contingencies. Evaluate responses from the entity's lawyers at the end of the audit.
■ Government policies currently affecting the conduct of the entity's business, such as tariffs and trade restrictions		
Other external factors affecting the entity's business	Consumer demand is growing rapidly for the entity's product, and the company reports significant sale increases. The company is experiencing much faster growth than is seen in the economy as a whole.	Professional skepticism must be exercised to reconcile the rapid company growth with the modest growth evidenced in the economy as a whole (occurrence of revenues).
■ General level of economic activity		
■ Interest rates and availability of financing		
■ Inflation and currency revaluation		

(continues)

Nature of the Entity, Including Its Selection and Application of Accounting Policy

Business Operations

- Method of obtaining revenues (e.g., manufacturing, retailing, banking, etc.)

- Products or services and markets (e.g., major customers and contracts, market share, or reputation of products)

- Conduct of operations (e.g., stages and methods of production, business segments)

- Alliances, joint ventures, and outsourcing activities

- Involvement in e-commerce, including Internet sales

- Geographic dispersion and industry segmentation

- Locations of production facilities, warehouses, and offices

- Important suppliers of goods and services (e.g., stability of supply or methods of delivery, such as just-in-time)

- Transactions with related parties

Almost 70 percent of NTI's business is with audio and video equipment assemblers who enjoy substantial allowances depending on market conditions, and NTI bears significant risks associated with ownership until the product is resold to end consumers. Assemblers usually use blanket purchase orders on a quarterly basis, and shipments are made based on an assembler's weekly authorization. The company grants its assemblers price protection, and certain assemblers have limited rights to return products.

The remainder of the company represents retail-packaged products sold through several electronic equipment wholesale companies and through the Internet at the company's web site.

NTI currently has only one research and manufacturing facility in North America. Research and development expenditures are essential to continue presence in the market. The company plans expenditures at about 12 percent of sales to research and development of new products. NTI focuses its engineering on coordinating its product design and manufacturing processes in order to bring its products to market in a cost-effective and timely manner.

NTI manufactures or purchases certain magnetic heads, media controllers, spindle motors, and other mechanical parts used in the head disk assembly. The assembly process occurs in a clean room environment, which demands skill in process engineering and efficient utilization of the clean room layout in order to reduce the high operation cost of this manufacturing equipment.

NTI warrants its new manufactured disk drives against defects in materials and workmanship for a period of one to five years from the date of sale.

Revenue recognition represents a significant inherent risk in this audit. The economic substance of sales agreements that allow for price production while assemblers are holding inventory is similar to consignment sales. Confirmations should focus on both the existence of receivables and the occurrence of sales by confirming terms of sale and rights of return.

Most of the company's research and development expenses should be expensed. The company reports some other assets, and the existence and valuation of intangibles represents a significant inherent risk.

The cost of inventory, including the cost of clean rooms and other manufacturing costs, are significant. The valuation of manufactured inventory is a significant inherent risk, including the need to carefully audit overhead costs that might be capitalized as part of inventory.

The completeness and valuation of the warranty reserve included in accrued expenses represents a significant inherent risk.

(continues)

Figure 7-7 ■ (Continued)

Required Knowledge of the Entity and Its Environment	A Knowledgeable Perspective about NTI	Risk of Material Misstatement
Nature of the Entity (*continued*)		
Investments ■ Capital investment activities ■ Acquisitions, mergers, or disposals of business activities ■ Investments and disposition of securities and loans	NTI is about to sign a seven-year lease to open a second manufacturing location in Malaysia. In recent years the company has been able to limit capital spending to about $110 million a year on new manufacturing and clean room equipment. More extensive capital investment will be needed to set up clean rooms and manufacturing equipment in the facility planned for next year in Malaysia.	The audit needs to evaluate the lease in Malaysia to determine whether this is a capital lease or an operating lease (presentation and disclosure). If it qualifies as a capital lease, we need to consider whether there is a material subsequent event that requires disclosure.
Financing ■ NTI is primarily equity financed. ■ The company has received advances from customers as a source of financing.	NTI has been primarily equity financed from its inception. However, it has also regularly used accounts payable and advances from customers as financing sources. The company has financed the equipment through operating cash flow. The company is currently under discussion with various banks regarding financing these capital improvements.	Receipt of cash from customers may represent customer deposits, and not necessarily revenue that can be recognized in the current period. If the company acquires a material amount of debt or equity financing after balance sheet date, this represents a material subsequent event that will require disclosure. If the company proceeds with an initial public offering, additional review needs to be scheduled. We also need to determine whether the company will be prepared for an audit of its system of internal control.
Financial Reporting ■ Accounting principles and industry-specific practices ■ Accounting for fair value ■ Industry-specific significant categories (e.g., research and development for pharmaceuticals)	NTI includes significant manufacturing overheads associated with clean rooms as part of inventory. Most research and development expenditures are expensed.	The existence and valuation of manufacturing overhead included in inventory is a significant issue. Careful attention must be paid to the existence and valuation of patents and other intangible assets.

(*continues*)

Entity's Objectives, Strategies, and Related Business Risks

Entity objectives and strategies (*and related business risk*) ■ New products and services (*increased product liability*) ■ Expansion of the business (*demand has not been accurately estimated*) ■ Response to industry or regulatory requirements (*decreased industry demand or increased legal exposure due to regulations*)	The company faces the usual business risks associated with competition from other companies and new products. Product profitability depends on the initial acceptance of products into the marketplace. The company believes that it will have to make significant product changes every year or two related to increasing the speed of accessing data as well as storage capacity.	Due to possible obsolescence of inventory the auditor should pay careful attention to the net realizable value audit objective.
Effects of implementing a strategy (*incomplete or improper implementation*)	Incomplete or improper implementation of research and development or manufacturing quality control issues could cause the company to lose its competitive advantage.	If the company loses its technological advantage, it could lose customers, have to make additional pricing concessions, or possibly have to accept product returns from major customers. This may impact either revenue recognition or require an increased reserve for obsolete inventory.

Measurement and Review of the Entity's Financial Performance

The entity may use the following tools to monitor or review its financial performance: ■ Key ratios and operating statistics ■ Key performance indicators. Budgets may not be a reliable tool for analytical procedures due to the fact that mid-year budget revisions are common. ■ Use of forecasts, budgets, and variance analysis ■ Analyst reports and credit rating reports	NTI develops an annual budget and usually completes the budgeting process about four months prior to the start of the fiscal year. However, changes in the competitive environment often force revisions of budgets during the year. The company prepares monthly financial statements by the end of the second week of the following month and regularly compares actual performance to adjusted budgets. The company also carefully monitors the research and development time from beginning an R&D project to bringing products to market, and the period of time from releasing new technology to when competitors introduce competitive products.	Because changes in budgets have often been required by changing competitive forces, it is important to understand the economic drivers behind budget changes. Budgets may not be a reliable tool for analytical procedures due to the fact that mid-year budget revisions are common.

7-13 a. What are the general areas of knowledge of the entity's objectives, strategies, and related business risks that the auditor should understand?

b. Develop examples to illustrate two ways that the auditor would use this knowledge in planning the audit.

7-14 a. What are the general areas of knowledge of management and review of the entity's performance that the auditor should understand?

b. Develop examples to illustrate two ways that the auditor would use this knowledge in planning the audit.

7-15 Explain the procedures that an auditor would perform to obtain an understanding of the entity's business and its operating environment.

[KEY TERMS

Audit planning, p. 283
Business operations, p. 291
Business risks, p. 294
Entity's objectives, p. 294
Entity's strategies, p. 294
Financial reporting, p. 293
Financing activities, p. 293
Industry conditions, p. 286

Investing activities, p. 292
Measurement and review of the entity's financial performance, p. 295
Other external factors, p. 290
Regulatory environment, p. 286
Related party transactions, p. 292
Supervision, p. 283

[FOCUS ON AUDITOR KNOWLEDGE AND AUDIT DECISIONS]

This chapter focuses on client acceptance and retention decisions as well as initial risk assessment procedures performed in planning the audit. The chapter provides an overview of the steps involved in audit planning in Figure 7-4 and then discusses the knowledge that the auditor should obtain about the entity and its environment in Figure 7–5. In making decisions to support high-quality audit work, the auditor must be able to use the knowledge summarized in Figure 7-8 and address the decisions summarized in Figure 7-9. Page references are provided indicating where these issues are discussed in more detail.

Figure 7-8 ■ Summary of Auditor Knowledge Discussed in Chapter 7

Auditor Knowledge	Summary	Chapter References
K1: Understand the purpose and content of the engagement letter.	An engagement letter provides for a clear understanding with the client about the purpose of an audit engagement. Figure 7-3 provides a sample engagement letter that explains management's responsibilities, the auditor's responsibilities, as well as fee arrangements.	pp. 279–282

Figure 7-9 ■ Summary of Audit Decisions Discussed in Chapter 7

Audit Decision	Factors that Influence the Audit Decision	Chapter References
D1. What steps should be followed in making a decision about client acceptance and retention?	Client acceptance and retention involves the following steps that are discussed in detail in the chapter: (1) evaluating the integrity of management, (2) identifying special circumstances and unusual risks, (3) assessing competence to perform the audit, (4) evaluating independence, (5) making the decision to accept or decline the audit, and (6) preparing the engagement letter. Figure 7-2 provides a summary of how information obtained when performing these steps assists the auditor in making positive or negative decisions about client acceptance and retention.	pp. 272–279
D2. What steps should be performed in the risk assessment phase of the audit?	The steps associated with the auditor's risk assessment procedures are illustrated in Figure 7-4. Seven important risk assessment procedures are (1) identifying relevant financial statement assertions, (2) understanding the entity and its environment, (3) making materiality decisions, (4) performing analytical procedures, (5) considering audit risk, including the risk of fraud, (6) developing preliminary audit strategies for significant assertions, and (7) understanding the entity's system of internal control.	pp. 284–285
D3. How does the auditor use knowledge of the entity and its environment when planning an audit?	As part of planning the audit, the auditor should obtain an understanding of (1) the entity's industry, regulatory, and other external factors, (2) the nature of the entity including its selection and application of accounting policies, (3) the entity's objectives, strategies, and related business risks, and (4) the management and review of the entity's financial performance. The auditor uses this information to develop a knowledgeable perspective about the entity's financial performance and to identify potential risks of material misstatement. Figures 7-6 and 7-7 provide examples of what the auditor should learn about an audit client and how that knowledge is used.	pp. 285–295
D4. Identify factors related to the entity and its environment that assist the auditor in (1) developing a knowledgeable perspective about the company and (2) assessing the risk of material misstatement.	The last section of the chapter provides an example of how the auditor uses knowledge of a entity's business and its environment to assess the risk of material misstatement. This section explores a fictitious company, Net Technologies, Inc. Students should focus on the factors identified in Figure 7-7 and understand how the auditor uses this information to develop a knowledgeable perspective about the company and to identify potential risks of material misstatement in the financial statements.	pp. 296–297

objective questions

Objective questions are available for the student at www.wiley.com/college/boynton

comprehensive questions

7-16 **(Accepting the engagement)** Sunny Energy Applications Co. sells solar-powered swimming pool heaters. Sunny contracts 100 percent of the work to other companies. As Sunny is a new company, its balance sheet has total assets of $78,000, including $24,000 of "stock subscriptions receivable." The largest asset is $42,000 worth of "unrecovered development costs." The equity side of the balance sheet is made up of $78,000 of "Common Stock Subscribed."

The company is contemplating a public offering to raise $1 million. The shares to be sold to the public for the $1 million will represent 40 percent of the then issued and outstanding stock. There are two officer-employees of the company, Mike Whale and Willie Float, former officers of Canadian Brass Co. Float is being sued by the SEC for misusing funds raised by Canadian Brass in a public offering. The funds were used as compensatory balances for loans to a Physics Inc. Physics Inc. was controlled by Float and is the predecessor for Sunny Energy Applications.

Canadian Brass is being sued by the SEC for reporting improper (exaggerated) income. Float was chief executive at the time. Many organizations are engaged in researching the feasibility of using solar energy. Most of the organizations are considerably larger and financially stronger than Sunny Energy. The company has not been granted any patents that would serve to protect it from competitors.

Required

a. What potential risks may be present in this engagement?

b. What specific auditing and accounting problems appear to exist?

c. What additional information do you feel you need to know about the company?

d. Do you believe the engagement should be accepted or rejected? Why?

7-17 **(Communication with predecessor/engagement letter)** The audit committee of the board of directors of Unicorn Corp. asked Tish & Field, CPAs, to audit Unicorn's financial statements for the year ended December 31, 20X3. Tish & Field explained the need to make an inquiry of the predecessor auditor and requested permission to do so. Unicorn's management agreed and authorized the predecessor auditor to respond fully to Tish & Field's inquiries.

After a satisfactory communication with the predecessor auditor, Tish & Field drafted an engagement letter that was mailed to the audit committee of the board of directors of Unicorn Corp. The engagement letter clearly set forth arrangements concerning the involvement of the predecessor auditor and other matters.

Required

a. What information should Tish & Field have obtained during their inquiry of the predecessor auditor prior to acceptance of the engagement?

b. Describe what other matters Tish & Field would generally have included in the engagement letter.

7-18 **(Using work of a specialist)** Kent, CPA, is engaged in the audit of Davidson Corp.'s financial statements for the year ended December 31, 20XX. Kent is about to commence auditing Davidson's employee pension expense, but Kent's preliminary inquiries concerning Davidson's defined benefit pension plan led Kent to believe that some of the actuarial computations and assumptions are so complex that they are beyond the competence ordinarily required of an auditor. Kent is considering engaging Park, an actuary, to assist with this portion of the audit.

Required

a. What factors should Kent consider in the process of selecting Park?

b. What matters should be understood among Kent, Park, and Davison's management as to the nature of the work to be performed by Park?

AICPA (adapted)

7-19 **(Engagement letter)** The CPA firm of Test & Check has been appointed auditors for the XYZ Corporation by the company's audit committee. The engagement is limited to making an audit of the company's financial statements. The audit fee is to be at the firm's regular per diem rates plus travel costs. To confirm the arrangements, Test & Check sends the following engagement letter:

March 10, 20xx

Mr. D.R. Rand, Controller
XYZ Corporation
Maintown, ME. 03491

Dear Mr. Rand:

This will confirm our understanding of the arrangements for our examination of the financial statements of XYZ Corporation for the year ending December 31, 20XX.

We will examine the Company's balance sheet at December 31, 20XX, and the related statements of income, retained earnings, and cash flows for the year then ended, for the purpose of auditing them. Our audit will be in accordance with generally accepted auditing standards, which require that we plan and perform the audit to assure that the financial statements are correct.

Our audit will include examining, on a test basis, evidence supporting the financial statements. We will also assess the accounting methods used and significant estimates made by management. Because of the characteristics of irregularities, our audit cannot detect all material irregularities. We will, of course, report to you anything that appears to us during our audit that looks suspicious. Our fee for this audit will be on a cost-plus basis, including travel costs. Invoices will be rendered every two weeks and are payable on presentation.

We are pleased to have this opportunity to serve you. If this letter correctly expresses your understanding, please sign the enclosed copy and return it to us.

Very truly yours,   Approved By: _____

Test & Check, CPAs   Date:_____

M.E. Test

Partner

Required

List the deficiencies in the engagement letter. For each deficiency, indicate the proper wording. Use the following format for your answers—do not write a proper engagement letter:

DEFICIENCY	PROPER WORDING

7-20   **(Accepting the engagement)** Dodd, CPA, audited Adams Company's financial statements for the year ended December 31, 20X8. On November 1, 20X9 Adams notified Dodd that it was changing auditors and that Dodd's services were being terminated. On November 5, 20X9, Adams invited Hall, CPA, to make a proposal for an engagement to audit its financial statements for the year ended December 31, 20X9.

Required

a. What procedures concerning Dodd should Hall perform before accepting the engagement?

b. What additional procedures should Hall consider performing during the planning phase of this audit (after acceptance of the engagement) that would not be performed during the audit of a continuing client?

AICPA

7-21   **(Audit planning)** In late spring of 20X4, you are advised of a new assignment as the in-charge accountant of your CPA firm's recurring annual audit of the Lancer Company. You are given the engagement letter for the audit covering the calendar year December 31, 20X4, and a list of personnel assigned to this engagement. It is your responsibility to plan and supervise the fieldwork for the engagement.

Required

Discuss the necessary preparation and planning for the Lancer Company annual audit prior to the beginning fieldwork at the entity's office. In your discussion, include the sources you should consult, the type of information you should seek, the preliminary plans and preparation you should make for the fieldwork, and any actions you should take relative to the staff assigned to the engagement. Do not write an audit program.

AICPA

7-22   **(Understanding the entity and its environment)** You have just been assigned as in-charge accountant on HipStar, Inc. a new audit client in the recording industry. HipStar is an emerging growth company that finds new recording artists, records their music, and distributes the music directly to consumers exclusively over the Internet. The company does not produce CDs or tapes and does not distribute the artist's music through traditional distribution channels. In order to better understand HipStar, you have set out to understand the following:

1. Industry conditions

2. The regulatory environment

3. Other external factors affecting the business

4. The entity's business operations

5. The entity's investing activities and financing activities

6. The entity's financial reporting activities

7. The entity's objectives, strategies, and related business risks

8. How the entity measures and reviews its financial performance.

Required

For each of these eight categories (1) describe the knowledge and understanding you want to obtain about HipStar to develop a knowledgeable perspective about the entity and (2) identify how this knowledge might assist in assessing the risk of material misstatement. Use the following format:

KEY CATEGORIES	DESCRIBE THE KNOWLEDGE USED TO DEVELOP A KNOWLEDGEABLE PERSPECTIVE ABOUT HIPSTAR	IDENTIFY HOW THIS KNOWLEDGE MIGHT ASSIST IN ASSESSING THE RISK OF MATERIAL MISSTATEMENT
1. Industry conditions		
2. Regulatory environment		
3. Other external factors affecting the business		
4. The client's business operations		
5. The client's investing activities and financing activities		
6. The client's financial reporting activities		
7. The client's objectives, strategies, and related business risks		
8. How the client measures and reviews the entity's financial performance		

7-23 **(Procedures to understand the entity and its environment)** You have just been assigned to audit the annual audit of a small, independent college. Below is a list of audit procedures that you might perform to understand the entity and its environment. Describe how these audit procedures would assist you in planning and performing the audit using the following format.

AUDIT PROCEDURE	DESCRIBE HOW THESE AUDIT PROCEDURES WOULD ASSIST YOU IN PLANNING AND PERFORMING THE AUDIT
Review industry data	
Review key information about the entity	
Tour the entity's operations.	
Make inquiries of the audit committee	
Make inquiries of management.	
Review prior year's working papers	
Determine the existence of related parties	

7-24 **(Related parties)** Temple, CPA, is auditing the financial statements of Ford Lumber Yards, Inc., a privately held corporation with 300 employees and five stockholders, three of whom are active in management. Ford has been in business for many years but has never had its financial statements audited. Temple suspects that the substance of some of Ford's business transactions differs from their form because of the pervasiveness of related party relationships and transactions in the local building supplies industry.

Required

Research the professional auditing standards, AU 334 on *Related Parties*, and describe the audit procedures Temple should apply to identify related party relationships and transactions.

AICPA

cases

7-25 **(New Client Acceptance) Comprehensive Case: Mt. Hood Furniture, Inc.**
Company Background Information: Your employer, Reddy & Abel, LLP, Certified Public Accountants (who is registered with the PCAOB and audits public companies), has been approached by a prospective client, Mt. Hood Furniture, Inc., about your firm taking on their account. The firm has adopted procedures for the acceptance and retention of clients following the AICPA guidelines for quality control in an accounting practice. The firm requires that a partner interview all prospective clients to determine what services the client needs and the ability of the firm to provide those services. As the prospective senior on the engagement, you accompanied the partner on the interview. The following is a summary of your notes from the interviews with senior management.

Notes from Client Interview: Mt. Hood Furniture, Inc. is an Oregon corporation incorporated in 1961. The company is a regional manufacturer of office furniture and cabinetry. The product line includes desks, chairs, filing cabinets, bookcases, credenzas, and European-style cabinets. Approximately 80 percent of fiscal year 20X3 net sales were in office furniture and 20 percent in cabinetry. The cabinetry unit underwent major retooling commencing in 20X2, which approximated 85 percent of the capital expenditures that year. The retooling was financed with significant long-term debt. The improvements enabled the company to manufacture ready-to-assemble furniture products, and develop a modular ready-to-install cabinet line, which has resulted in an increase in sales. The company has developed new, award-winning designs in office furniture, designs that stress the efficient and ergonomic use of technology. Ample opportunity exists to expand sales of the existing product lines. Management estimates that the current physical plant can support up to $50 million in sales without significant additions of manufacturing and distribution capacity. Additional sales up to $50 million are expected to result in additional costs associated with the variable cost of production and variable overheads but should not require increases in fixed costs.

Office furniture is a highly competitive, multibillion-dollar annual market. With a strong economy the market has grown about 15 percent per year over the last two years; however, industry experts expect this growth to slow down in the years ahead. Mt. Hood does not have significant market share and competes with a number of nationally recognized companies. Mt. Hood's primary advantages are competitive pricing and consistently high-quality products. Its low-profit margins are part of a pricing strategy to build market share by undercutting the competition. The custom office cabinetry grants the company a wider profit margin and substantial sales growth potential. This is a unique product line; it offers a custom-built look that is not readily available from other manufacturers. Demand is steadily growing. The company plans to expand its marketing in this niche.

The company's manufacturing and executive offices are located in facilities leased from the founder, adjacent to shipping and transportation facilities in the Pacific Northwest. Two adjacent buildings house the corporation, with the offices located above the warehouse. The company purchases raw materials including coil steel, bar stock, hardware, laminated particleboard, casters, fabric, rubber and plastic products, and shipping cartons. Materials are delivered to the dock by common carriers or by suppliers' trucks. Finished products are shipped FOB from the warehouse or picked up by the customer. Mt. Hood has a delivery truck for smaller, local orders.

The company has 180 employees involved in manufacturing operations and 20 in the executive offices. The company's workforce is stable and highly skilled. Many of the employees have been with the company for more than 15 years. The company's work environment and solid reputation have allowed it to attract and keep employees in a tight marketplace. Mt. Hood offers both pension and profit-sharing plans; the plans have been in place for over 25 years.

The company distributes its products through a small network of approximately 150 office furniture dealers in major U.S. cities. Recently, the company placed its product with several national chains and warehouse-club chains. Most of the sales growth over the last two years is attributed to this new distribution channel; it represented 35 percent of year-20X3 sales. Their largest single customer accounts for 8 percent of sales. The company also produces a catalogue and has an information web site with an order link. The office cabinetry line offers custom orders for on-site installation. Customers include major hotels and professional and corporate offices. Today 20 percent of sales come from this line, and the chief operating officer would like to see this line grow to a total of $25 million in sales in the next three to five years. Individuals, which comprise about 5 percent of total sales, can order directly from Mt. Hood Furniture using the company's web site. A large showroom is maintained at the corporate offices; customers may also place orders at the showroom.

Mt. Hood Furniture is subject to a variety of federal, state, and local laws and regulations relating to the use, storage, handling, generation, transportation, treatment, emission, discharge, disposal and remediation of, and exposure to, hazardous and nonhazardous substances, materials, and wastes. In particular, the U.S. Environmental Protection Agency standards for the wood furniture manufacturing industry require reduction of emissions of certain volatile organic compounds found in the coatings, stains, and adhesives used by Mt. Hood. Company officers believe that Mt. Hood's operations are in substantial compliance with all environmental laws.

Mt. Hood Furniture, Inc. is family owned and not publicly traded; 1 million shares of $1 par common stock are authorized. Major stockholders include the founder, who recently retired as chairman of the board, Robert S. Saws. He holds 30 percent of the outstanding shares. Mr. Saws is 70 years old and until his retirement was closely involved in all major decisions affecting the company. He personally signed corporate checks and supervised the company's operations. He is very proud of his company's strong reputation for being ethical and for meeting its commitments and promises. His son, Conrad P. Saws, has worked in the business for the last 15 years, is the current president and chairman of the board, and under his father's guidance during the last 5 years, has assumed the responsibility of overseeing the business's day-to-day operations. Conrad is also a 30 percent owner. Other family members own an additional 30 percent of the business. The chief operating officer (COO) and chief financial officer (CFO) are the only nonfamily owners at 5 percent each.

Mt. Hood's senior management is comprised of Conrad Saws, the president and chairman of the board; James Doyle, the COO; and Julia Anderson, the CFO. Doyle joined the company two years ago after working for 13 years in the industry for a major office furniture manufacturer. Anderson has worked for the company for about 15 months. She was an audit manager with Reddy and Able prior to joining Mt. Hood Furniture, Inc.

The board of directors includes the retired chairman (Robert Saws), the president and current chairman (Conrad Saws), a family member with a business background in the retail residential furniture sector (Howard Saws), another family member trained in architecture and interior design (Catherine Saws), and the senior president of a large regional bank. During the on-site interview, you and Mr. Reddy met with Robert Saws privately for over two hours, then were introduced to and interviewed individually the other members of the senior management team. Each of these interviews extended beyond an hour and allowed Mr. Reddy the opportunity to explore the business goals driving the company.

Robert and Conrad Saws have been the driving force behind the company's success over its long history. They made it clear they know and understand the industry. In their view, succeeding in the increasingly competitive office furniture marketplace necessitates that the company focus its resources on taking calculated risks to increase its market share and name recognition. They also believe the company must specialize its product lines. They see the office cabinetry niche as one the company can develop more fully so that this product line will be able to cater to the growing preference for a customized office work environment at reasonable cost. They explained that Mt. Hood has two general directions in production. The fastest growing sales are in product lines marketed through warehouse outlets. In this market, price and availability are the overriding purchase determinates. The dynamics of the workplace dictate the other growing sales line: office furniture that caters to a technology-based work environment where increasing the productivity and flexibility of increasingly expensive office space is the driver. They are confident the company has assembled a management team capable of improving profitability and sales.

When asked about the change in accounting firms, Conrad Saws informed Mr. Reddy that the prior accountant was very skilled at completing the audit to meet debt covenants, but the company needed an accounting firm capable of helping Mt. Hood move beyond the present. This included assistance with financial planning (both personal and for the company), developing better performance measures for the company, and improving the incentive compensation plan for key employees. Beginning this year, the company put a bonus plan in place for key executives based on sales growth. They saw no reason for any scope limitations, and they expect the firm of Reddy & Abel to offer suggestions to facilitate the firm's desire to successfully negotiate the expansion. They also said that they would contact their previous auditor and grant them permission to talk candidly with Reddy and Abel about the potential change in auditors. Mr. Saws' banker and attorney separately recommended Reddy & Abel as a firm capable of understanding the forces driving business success, and capable of forming a mutually beneficial working relationship. Robert Saws also volunteered that his niece is a senior accountant with Reddy & Abel. She owns a few shares of Mt. Hood Furniture, and is also the executor of Mr. Saws' will.

The interview with the other senior management team members added details to the company's business position. The COO explained that the current information systems have been stressed by the company's growth over the past three years. Significant computer system improvements are in process (which represents major capital expenditures in 20X3). The timeline for completing the implementation of a new database system indicates that it should go on-line in the second quarter of year 20X4. The upgrade is a major capital expenditure and is seen as a vehicle for improving information throughput and providing timely information on the company's financial performance. The company expects to spend between $75,000 and $85,000 in 20X4 to complete the project. Maintaining the physical plant at its current production capacity is estimated to run $250,000 to $400,000 per year.

The CFO is concerned about improving cash flow from operations and speeding up the operating cycle, changes that could involve reassessing Mt. Hood's credit and payment terms. The COO is worried that tightening credit terms would hinder sales growth. The president is adamant about maintaining sufficient inventory to make sure orders can be shipped with minimal backorders. The CFO commented that the major reason for the audit is to satisfy a debt covenant of the lender and explained the company's debt maturities are accelerating, hampering cash flows available for investing to expand sales. In expanding capacity to grow sales beyond $50 million, the CFO suggests that the company consider venture capital to grow the company until it is ready for an IPO. In the past, the major lender has been the primary financial statement user, along with several creditors, but the CFO plans to show the financial statements and in-house projections to potential venture capitalists as well. Current planned expansion costs are estimated to require about $3 million in land, manufacturing, and distribution facilities, which could raise revenues to $100 million.

Other Information: After the interview, Mr. Reddy contacted the prior auditor, Mr. Will B. Dunn, CPA, regarding the potential change in auditor. Mr. Dunn was not surprised that Mt. Hood Furniture was considering a change in auditor. He had been Robert Saws' accountant for nearly 30 years. In recent years, Conrad had taken more responsibility and had been more aggressive about growing the company. Mt. Hood hired outside management for the first time in company history, and with the hiring of a CFO for the first time, he had expected this phone call. Mr. Dunn expressed no concern about the integrity of management. Several years ago, Mr. Dunn said that Conrad Saws had raised several questions with Mr. Dunn about revenue recognition on some possible "bill-and-hold" sales in advance of negotiating a sales agreement with a national office supply and furniture chain. No problems were noted in the subsequent audit. Mr. Dunn expressed concern about the current accounting system that was expected to be replaced in 20X4. Audit adjustments in the last few years resulted from cutoff problems, from an adjustment due to an error in counting inventory, and from discussions over bad debt reserves. Dunn noted that Ms. Anderson was challenged by an accounting staff that needed more training and an accounting system that was having difficulty keeping up with the company's recent trend associated with the increased volume of transactions. Finally, he noted that if Mr. Reddy's firm was selected as auditor, he would cooperate by allowing Mr. Reddy to review his working papers to the extent needed to prepare for the upcoming audit. Discussions with Mt. Hood Furniture's banker and outside legal counsel confirmed that company management had a reputation of acting with integrity and honesty.

Financial Information: Audited financial results for 20X1 and 20X2, along with unaudited financial information for 20X3 are included in Chapter 8 (Figure 8-15) as part of Problem 8-18 along with relevant industry statistics.

Required

a. Identify the professional guidance that would assist Reddy & Abel in making a decision about client acceptance. Outline the key issues that you believe should be addressed when making a decision about client acceptance. Prepare a working paper for the file using the following format.

LIST IMPORTANT ISSUES REGARDING CLIENT ACCEPTANCE	EXPLAIN POSITIVE INDICATORS	DESCRIBE POTENTIAL ISSUES OF CONCERN	SOLUTIONS OR POSSIBLE RESOLUTIONS FOR ISSUES OF CONCERN
1.			
2.			
Etc.			

At the bottom of the working paper, draw an overall conclusion regarding accepting or rejecting the client.

b. Draft an engagement letter for partner review. You may assume that the fee estimate for audit services will run between $20,000 and $25,000, and the fee for tax services is estimated between $7,500 and $10,000. Separate proposals may be presented at a later date for additional services based on audit findings.

7-26 **(Understanding the Entity and its Environment) Comprehensive Case: Mt. Hood Furniture, Inc.**

Required

At this stage the auditor obtains an understanding of the entity and its environment to anticipate account balances and assertions that are likely to be misstated. Outline the important aspects of understanding Mt. Hood Furniture and its external environment. Discuss the key issues that are present in the Mt. Hood case using the following format.

KNOWLEDGE OF MT. HOOD FURNITURE, INC. AND ITS EXTERNAL ENVIRONMENT	HOW THE KNOWLEDGE WILL ASSIST IN DEVELOPING A KNOWLEDGEABLE PERSPECTIVE ABOUT THE FINANCIAL STATEMENTS	HOW THE KNOWLEDGE INCREASES OR MITIGATES POTENTIAL RISKS OF MATERIAL MISSTATEMENT
Industry conditions		
Regulatory environment		
Other external factors affecting the business		
The client's business operations		
The client's investing activities and financing activities		
The client's financial reporting activities		
The client's objectives, strategies, and related business risks		
How the client measures and reviews the entity's financial performance		

professional simulation

Early in 20x4 Hawkins & Co., CPAs was approached about bidding on the audit of Big Dog Construction (BDC). BDC is a construction company that lays sewer and waste treatment pipe, and builds pipelines to transport oil and natural gas. BDC's major clients are cities, counties, and energy companies. BDC is privately owned. "Big Dog" Herman, and his three brothers own 100 percent of the company, which has grown to the size where sales hit $95 million dollars in the fiscal year 20x3.

The senior partner of Hawkins & Co., is preparing a bid for the 20x4 audit of BDC. He has asked you to assist him in the process. He is aware the professional standards require communication with the predecessor auditor, and he want you to research the relevant professional standards. Identify the auditing standards that explain the what should be discussed in the inquiry of the predecessor auditor. Do this by indicating in the space below the appropriate AU section paragraphs that identify what should be included in an inquiry of the predecessor auditor.

1. AU Section Paragraphs _____

Situation	Research	Inquiry of Predecessor	Draft Report

Identify the issues that should be discussed as part of the communication between the predecessor and successor auditors.

Included in Discussion with Predecessor Auditor

1. Information that might bear on the integrity of management. ○
2. Disagreements with management about accounting principles ○
3. The predecessor's understanding of the reasons for the change in auditors. ○
4. The extent of procedures performed in the prior year. ○
5. Communication with the audit committee about fraud or illegal acts. ○
6. Disagreements with management about auditing matters. ○
7. The predecessor's evaluation of internal control. ○
8. Communication with the audit committee about auditor independence. ○

Situation	Research	Inquiry of Predecessor	Draft Report

During inquiry of the predecessor auditor and other professionals the senior partner learns that BDC has just been engaged to construct an oil pipeline across environmentally sensitive land. The client is a major oil company, and all required permits have apparently been obtained. The partner wants to ensure that the audit complies with all professional standards on understanding the industry, regulatory, and other external factors. Draft a memo to Mr. Hawkins explaining what should be included in the auditor's understanding of industry, regulatory, and other external factors. For each key item, explain why the understanding is relevant to the audit.

To: Robert Hawkins, Senior Partner

Re: Factors that influence the reliability of confirmations

From: CPA Candidate

KEY ITEMS TO BE INCLUDED IN THE UNDERSTANDING OF THE INDUSTRY, REGULATORY, AND OTHER EXTERNAL FACTORS.	EXPLAIN HOW THE UNDERSTANDING IDENTIFIED TO THE LEFT IS RELEVANT TO THE AUDIT.

[8] MATERIALITY DECISIONS AND PERFORMING ANALYTICAL PROCEDURES

WHAT SIZE OF MISSTATEMENT IS MATERIAL?

Consider the following hypothetical situation. As an auditor you disagree with a client's revenue recognition procedures, and the magnitude of the misstatement overstates revenues by $\frac{1}{2}$ of 1 percent, overstates pretax income by 2 percent, and overstates earnings per share by four cents a share on EPS of $3.27. Your client is resistant to changes because a competitor recently missed its earnings per share target by two cents a share and the company lost $150 million in market capitalization. Are there clear guidelines to follow?

The U.S. Supreme Court has provided little help in this matter. In *TSC Industries* v. *Northway* the Court stated that "ideally it would be desirable to have absolute certainty in the application of the materiality concept," but it concluded that "such a goal is illusory and unrealistic … [t]he materiality concept is judgmental in nature and it is not possible to translate this into a numerical formula."

In 1999 Arthur Levitt, former chairman of the SEC, crystallized his concern about materiality decisions in a speech entitled *The Numbers Game,* where he stated: "some companies misuse the concept of materiality. They intentionally record errors within a defined percentage ceiling. Then they try to excuse that fib by arguing that the effect on the bottom line is too small to matters … When either management or the outside auditors are questioned about these clear violations of GAAP, they answer sheepishly. 'It doesn't matter. It's immaterial.'"

SEC Staff Accounting Bulletin (SAB) 99 subsequently addressed the materiality issue in several ways. First, SAB 99 states that the use of a percentage test alone to make materiality determinations is not acceptable. The SEC staff goes on to state that there are numerous instances in which misstatements below 5 percent of net income could well be material, and it recommended qualitative guidance, such as whether the misstatement or omission masks a change in earnings or sales trends, hides a failure to meet analysts' consensus expectations for the company, changes a loss into income or vice versa, or whether the misstatement has the effect of increasing management compensation, such as satisfying certain requirements for the award of bonuses or other incentive compensation. Second, it reminds registrants that intentional misstatements, even if they are immaterial, may violate the Securities Exchange Acts. In keeping adequate books and records, registrants should consider (1) the significance of the misstatement, (2) how the misstatement arose, (3) the cost of correcting the misstatement, and (4) the clarity of authoritative accounting guidance with respect to the misstatement.

SAB 99 primarily provides guidance to registrants and their auditor about how to evaluate known or possible misstatements. It does not address issues associated with materiality decisions made in planning the audit. Those decisions are addressed in this chapter.

Source: SEC Release on Materiality in Financial Disclosure by Cadwalader, Wickersham & Taft.

[PREVIEW OF CHAPTER 8]

Figure 7-4 describes seven key steps in performing risk assessment procedures. This chapter focuses on two of those steps: making preliminary judgments about materiality levels and performing analytical procedures. The following diagram provides an overview of the chapter organization and content.

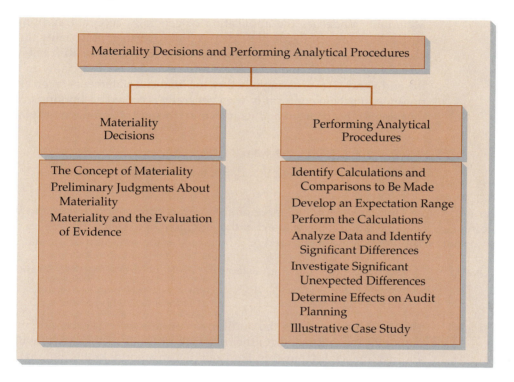

Chapter 8 focuses on making materiality decisions and using analytical procedures to identify accounts and assertions that are likely to contain misstatements. This chapter addresses the following aspects of the auditor's knowledge and focuses on thee important audit decisions addressed below.

focus on auditor knowledge

After studying this chapter you should understand the following aspects of an auditor's knowledge base:

K1. Understand the concept of materiality as it is used in auditing.

K2. Understand the relationship between materiality and audit evidence.

K3. Understand the role of analytical procedures in planning and performing the audit.

---

focus on audit decisions

After studying this chapter you should understand the factors that influence the following audit decisions.

D1. Make preliminary judgments about materiality at the financial statement level.

D2. Make preliminary judgments about materiality at the account balance level.

D3. Identify risks of material misstatement by using analytical procedures.

[MATERIALITY DECISIONS]

Materiality underlies the application of generally accepted auditing standards, particularly the standards of fieldwork and reporting. Materiality thus has a pervasive effect in a financial statement audit. AU 312, *Audit Risk and Materiality in Conducting an Audit,* requires the auditor to consider materiality in (1) planning the audit and (2) evaluating whether the financial statements taken as a whole are presented fairly in conformity with generally accepted accounting principles. The meaning of this concept and its relevance to audit planning are explained next.

THE CONCEPT OF MATERIALITY

The Financial Accounting Standards Board defines **materiality** as

The magnitude of an omission or misstatement of accounting information that, in the light of surrounding circumstance, makes it probable that the judgment of a reasonable person relying on the information would have been changed or influenced by the omission or misstatement.

Source: "Qualitative Characteristics of Accounting," Statement of Financial Accounting No. 2, Stamford, CT: Financial Accounting Standards Board, 1980, p. xv.

Auditor Knowledge 1

■ **Understand the concept of materiality as it is used in auditing.**

This definition requires the auditor to consider both (1) the circumstances pertaining to the entity and (2) the information needs of those who will rely on the audited financial statements. For example, an amount that is material to the financial statements of one entity may not be material to the financial statements of another entity of a different size or nature. Also, what is material to the financial statements of a particular entity might change from one period to another. Thus, the auditor may conclude that the materiality levels for working capital accounts should be lower for a company on the brink of bankruptcy than for a company with strong operating cash flows that can easily retire obligations as they come due, because of increased concerns by financial statement users about these operating accounts. In considering the information needs of users, it is usually appropriate to assume that the users will be reasonably informed investors.

Auditors make preliminary judgments about materiality for two purposes. First, they make preliminary judgments about materiality in order to make decisions about the scope of audit procedures. As a general rule, when an auditor expects that a small amount of misstatement will be material, the auditor will select a larger sample size to obtain reasonable assurance that an account is free of that small amount of misstatement. Second, the auditor makes judgments about materiality to evaluate whether known misstatements are significant enough to require the entity to adjust the financial statements, or the auditor will issue a qualified opinion. This chapter focuses on the first purpose of making preliminary judgments about materiality—determining materiality levels of audit planning.

PRELIMINARY JUDGMENTS ABOUT MATERIALITY

The auditor makes preliminary judgments about materiality levels in planning the audit. This assessment, often referred to as **planning materiality,** may ultimately differ from the materiality levels used at the conclusion of the audit in evaluating the audit findings because (1) the surrounding circumstances may change and (2) additional information about the entity will have been obtained during the course of the audit. For example, the entity may have obtained the financing needed to continue as a going concern that was in doubt when the audit was planned, and the audit may affirm that the company's short-term solvency has significantly improved during the year. In such cases, the materiality level used in evaluating the audit findings might be higher than planning materiality.

In planning an audit, the auditor should assess materiality at the following two levels:

- The *financial statement level* because the auditor's opinion on fairness extends to the financial statements taken as a whole.
- The *account balance level* because the auditor verifies account balances in reaching an overall conclusion on the fairness of the financial statements.

Factors that should be considered in making preliminary judgments of materiality at each level are explained in the following sections.

Materiality at the Financial Statement Level

Audit Decision 1

■ Make preliminary judgments about materiality at the financial statement level.

Financial statement materiality is the minimum aggregate misstatement in a financial statement that is important enough to prevent the statement from being presented fairly in conformity with GAAP. In this context, misstatements may result from misapplication of GAAP, departures from fact, or omissions of necessary information.

In audit planning, the auditor should recognize that there may be more than one level of materiality relating to the financial statements. Each statement, in fact, could have several levels. For the income statement, materiality could be related to total revenues, operating income, income before taxes, or net income. For the balance sheet, materiality could be based on total assets, current assets, working capital, or stockholders' equity.

In making a preliminary judgment about materiality, the auditor initially determines the aggregate (overall) level of materiality for each statement. For example, it may be estimated that errors totaling $100,000 for the income statement and $200,000 for the balance sheet alone would be material. It would be inappropriate in this case for the auditor to use balance sheet materiality in planning the audit because if balance sheet misstatements amounting to $200,000 also affect the income statement, the income statement will be materially misstated. For planning purposes, the auditor should use the smallest aggregate level of misstatements considered to be material to any one of the financial statements. This decision rule is appropriate because (1) the financial statements are interrelated and (2) many auditing procedures pertain to more than one statement. For instance, the auditing procedure to determine whether year-end credit sales are recorded in the proper period provides evidence about both accounts receivable (balance sheet) and sales (income statement).

The auditor's preliminary judgments about materiality are often made six to nine months before the balance sheet date. Thus, the judgments may be based on annualized interim financial statement data. Alternatively, they may be premised on the financial results of one or more prior years adjusted for current changes, such as the general condition of the economy and industry trends. Materiality judgments involve both quantitative and qualitative considerations.

Quantitative Guidelines

Currently, neither accounting nor auditing standards contain official guidelines on quantitative measures of materiality. The following illustrate some guidelines used in practice:

- 5 to 10 percent of net income before taxes (10 percent for smaller incomes, 5 percent for larger ones).
- ½ to 1 percent of total assets
- 1 percent of equity
- ½ to 1 percent of gross revenue
- A variable percentage based on the greater of total assets or revenue

An example of the last guideline is presented in Figure 8-1, which shows a table used by a Big Four accounting firm to calculate planning materiality. Applying this approach to an emerging business such as Net Technology, Inc. (presented

Figure 8-1 ■ Materiality Levels Based on a Variable Percentage of Total Assets or Revenues

If the Greater of Total Assets or Revenues is		Materiality Is	Of the Excess Over
Over	But Not Over		
$ 0	$ 30 thousand	$ 0 + .059	$ 0
30 thousand	100 thousand	1,780 + .031	30 thousand
100 thousand	300 thousand	3,970 + .0214	100 thousand
300 thousand	1 million	8,300 + .0145	300 thousand
1 million	3 million	18,400 + .0100	1 million
3 million	10 million	38,300 + .0067	3 million
10 million	30 million	85,500 + .0046	10 million
30 million	100 million	178,000 + .00313	30 million
100 million	300 million	397,000 + .00214	100 million
300 million	1 billion	856,000 + .00145	300 million
1 billion	3 billion	1,840,000 + .00100	1 billion
3 billion	10 billion	3,830,000 + .00067	3 billion
10 billion	30 billion	8,550,000 + .00046	10 billion
30 billion	100 billion	17,800,000 + .00031	30 billion
100 billion	300 billion	39,700,000 + .00021	100 billion
300 billion	—	82,600,000 + .00015	300 billion

empirical data in materiality rules of thumb

In a comparative study of materiality rules of thumb, researchers calculated five materiality measures for three companies considered representative of manufacturing, retail, and financial audit clients. Among the reported results are the following, which are based on 10-year averages (1977 to 1986) of actual financial data for the three companies:

Absolute Size of Materiality Measures and Ratios (000s Omitted)

	Concord Fabrics, Inc.	Mott's Supermarkets	Golden West Financial
Materiality measures			
1. 5% of average income	$150	$240	$35,560
2. Variable % of gross profit	$180	$ 510	N/A
3. 0.5% of total assets	$200	$ 220	$ 35,760
4. 1% of equity	$210	$ 240	$ 2,680
5. 0.5% of revenues	$470	$1,300	$ 3,730
Ratios			
Largest to smallest	3.1	6.0	13.3

The researchers observed, "The results of this 'small sample' study provide empirical evidence that among five commonly employed 'rules of thumb' definitions for materiality, sizable differences can occur depending on the industry of the audit client and the definition chosen. For example, for the financial company examined, the largest of the materiality measures was, on average, over 13 times bigger than the smallest measures. … Such large differences in materiality definitions would presumably lead to correspondingly large differences in audit scope decisions depending on which definition is chosen to quantify 'planning materiality.'" They further conclude, "While more evidence is needed, it appears that additional authoritative guidance would be helpful."

Source: Kurt Pany and Stephen Wheeler, "A Comparison of Various Materiality Rules of Thumb," *The CPA Journal* (June 1989), pp. 62–63.

later in Chapter 8), which shows total assets of $4,221,000 and total revenues of $5,638,000, results in planning materiality of approximately $60,000 (i.e., $38,300 + [(0.0067 × ($5,638,000 − $3,000,000)]). This amount was rounded to the nearest ten thousand dollars. Similarly, the table shows that planning materiality for Intel for the year ended December 27, 2003 would be approximately $23.1 million based on total assets of $47.1 billion and net revenues of $30.1 billion.

Qualitative Considerations

Qualitative considerations relate to the causes of misstatements. A misstatement that is quantitatively immaterial may be qualitatively material. This may occur, for instance, when the misstatement is attributable to an irregularity or an illegal act by the entity. Discovery of either occurrence might cause the auditor to conclude there is a significant risk of additional similar misstatements. AU 312.13 states that although the auditor should be alert for misstatements that could be qualitatively material, it ordinarily is not practical to design procedures to detect them.

Materiality at the Account Balance Level

Account balance materiality is the minimum misstatement that can exist in an account balance for it to be considered materially misstated. Misstatement up to that level is known as **tolerable misstatement.** The concept of materiality at the account balance level should not be confused with the term *material account balance*. The latter term refers to the *size of a recorded account balance*, whereas the concept of materiality pertains to the *amount of misstatement* that could affect a user's decision. The recorded balance of an account generally represents the upper limit on the amount by which an account can be overstated. Thus, accounts with balances much smaller than materiality are sometimes said to be immaterial in terms of the risk of overstatement. However, there is no limit on the amount by which an account with a very small recorded balance might be understated. Thus, it should be realized that accounts with seemingly immaterial balances may contain understatements that exceed materiality.

In making judgments about materiality at the account balance level, the auditor must consider the relationship between it and financial statement materiality. This consideration should lead the auditor to plan the audit to detect misstatements that may be immaterial individually, but that, when aggregated with misstatements in other account balances, may be material to the financial statements taken as a whole.

Allocating Financial Statement Materiality to Accounts

When the auditor's preliminary judgments about financial statement materiality are quantified, a preliminary estimate of materiality for each account may be obtained by allocating financial statement materiality to the individual accounts. The allocation may be made to both balance sheet and income statement accounts. However, because most balance sheet misstatements also affect income statement misstatements, many auditors make the allocation on the basis of the balance sheet accounts.

In making the allocation, the auditor should consider (1) the amount of misstatement that would influence a financial statement user and (2) the probable cost of verifying the account. For example, misstatements are more likely to exist in inventories than in plant assets, but it usually is more costly to audit inventories than plant assets.

To illustrate the allocation, consider the following summary balance sheet of New Technologies, Inc. in Figure 8-2.

The auditor anticipates few misstatements in cash, plant assets, and other current and noncurrent assets. Based on prior experience with the entity, the auditor expects that these accounts will be significantly less costly to audit than the other accounts. In plan A, materiality has been allocated proportionately to each account without regard to expected monetary misstatements or audit costs. In plan B, larger materiality allocations are made to receivables and inventories for which the costs of detection are higher. Thus, the amount of evidence needed for receivables and inventory is reduced, compared to plan A, because of the inverse relationship between account balance materiality and evidence. However, in plan B the auditor must be confident that a misstatement of 1.9 percent of receivables or inventory would not have a significant influence on financial statement users. If, for example, the amount allocated to receivables was approximately 10 percent of receivables, a 10 percent misstatement might influence the decisions of a rea-

Figure 8-2 ■ Materiality Allocation for New Technologies, Inc.

	Balance	%	Planned Tolerable Misstatement ($ 000 Omitted)				Plan B TM as a % of Acct. Bal.
			Plan A	%	Plan B	%	
Cash	$ 593	14%	$ 8.5	14%	$ 2.0	3%	0.3%
Accounts receivable	$ 1,335	32%	$ 19.3	32%	$ 25.0	42%	1.9%
Inventory	$ 1,327	31%	$ 18.8	31%	$ 25.0	42%	1.9%
Plant assets	$ 714	17%	$ 10.0	17%	$ 7.0	12%	1.0%
Other current and noncurrent assets	$ 252	6%	$ 3.5	6%	$ 1.0	2%	0.4%
	$ 4,221	100%	$ 60.0	100%	$ 60.0	100%	

sonable financial statement user. If this was the case, the auditor must bring tolerable misstatement down to a level that he or she believes would not influence a financial statement user.

In plan B the auditor is simply allowing for a greater proportion of the total allowable misstatements to remain in those accounts where it would be most expensive to detect the misstatements. Although the smaller materiality allocations for cash, plant assets, and other assets increase the amount of evidence needed for those accounts, compared to plan A, the fact that they are less costly to audit should result in an overall savings. The allocation of the preliminary estimate of materiality may be revised as the fieldwork is performed. For example, under plan B, if after auditing accounts receivable the maximum misstatement in that account is estimated to be $15,000, the $10,000 unused portion of materiality for that account can be reallocated to inventory. However, each decision about tolerable misstatement must first be viewed in the context of potential financial statement users.

Although the foregoing illustration suggests a certain degree of precision in allocating financial statement materiality to accounts, in the final analysis the process is heavily dependent on the subjective judgment of the auditor regarding the amount of error that would influence the decisions of a reasonable financial statement user. Figure 8-3 summarizes the factors that influence this subjective audit decision.

Figure 8-3 ■ Factors that Influence Planning Materiality Decisions

Primary Factor that Influences Decisions about Overall Materiality and Tolerable Misstatement	Determine the level of misstatement that will influence a reasonable person relying on the financial statements
Secondary Factors that Influence Decisions about Overall Materiality and Tolerable Misstatement	Cost-Benefit Considerations. Allocation of larger amounts of tolerable misstatement to accounts that are costly to audit (but not more than would influence reasonable persons relying on the financial statements).

Relationship Between Materiality and Audit Evidence

Auditor Knowledge 2

■ Understand the
relationship between
materiality and audit
evidence.

As noted in Chapter 6, materiality is one of the factors that affects the auditor's judgment about the sufficiency (quantity needed) of evidential matter. In making generalizations about this relationship, the distinction between the terms *materiality* and *material account balance* mentioned previously must be kept in mind. For example, it is generally correct to say that the lower the amount of tolerable misstatement, the greater the amount of evidence needed (inverse relationship) for an account balance or transaction class. This is the same as saying that it takes more evidence to obtain reasonable assurance that any misstatement in the recorded inventory balance does not exceed $100,000 than it does to be assured the misstatement does not exceed $200,000. It is also generally correct to say that the larger or more significant an account balance is, the greater the amount of evidence needed (direct relationship). This is the same as saying that more evidence is needed for inventory when it represents 30 percent of total assets than when it represents 10 percent.

MATERIALITY AND THE EVALUATION OF EVIDENCE

The concepts of financial statement materiality and tolerable misstatement also play an important role in the evaluation of evidence found during the audit. At the end of the audit, the auditor first reevaluates materiality at the financial statement level given new knowledge that may be obtained at the end of the audit. For example, auditors often make planning materiality decisions based on interim information, and year-end information may be different from what was projected at an interim date. The auditor will then consider tolerable misstatement and the amount of misstatements that might influence financial statement users at the account balance level.

Then the auditor needs to consider the evidence obtained during the audit. Often evidence is obtained through sampling plans, and when sampling is used the results of a sample need to be projected on the entire population. For example, if $500,000 worth of overstatements are found in a sample of $20 million out of an accounts receivable population of $50 million, a simple ratio projection would estimate that the population contains $1,250,000 of overstatements ($500,000 ÷ $20 million × $50 million). The auditor then needs to determine whether misstatements amounting to $1,250,000 would influence financial statement users. The auditor would consider the cause of the problem (e.g., intentional revenue recognition vs. unintentional cutoff problems), the magnitude of the misstatement compared with accounts receivable (3 percent), as well as the impact of the misstatement on total revenues, net income, and cash flow from operations. The auditor will both compare this projected amount with tolerable misstatement and use professional judgment in considering how the potential magnitude of the problem would influence financial statement users. The auditor will also consider how this individual misstatement might aggregate with other misstatements and whether the aggregate amount of misstatement is material, even if individual misstatements might not be material.

When evaluating the significance of known and projected misstatements, the auditor should also consider qualitative issues. For example, SEC Staff Accounting Bulletin 99 suggests that if a misstatement masks a change in an earnings or sales trend, hides a failure to meet financial analysts' consensus expectations for the company, of if the misstatement changes income into a loss, it might be qualitatively material, even if it is not quantitatively material. Hence, when evaluating evidence at the end of the audit, the auditor needs to consider both the quantitative and qualitative aspects of whether known and projected misstatements will influence financial statement users.

Sampling issues are discussed further in Chapter 13, and the evaluation of evidence at the end of the audit, in Chapter 19.

[LEARNING CHECK

8-1 a. Define materiality.
     b. What requirements does this definition impose on the auditor?

8-2 State the two levels at which preliminary judgments of materiality should be made in the planning phase and state the reason for each.

8-3 Why might planning materiality differ from the materiality level used in evaluating audit findings?

8-4 a. In audit planning, the auditor should recognize that there may be more than one level of materiality relating to the financial statements. Explain.
     b. What decision rule should be used when different materiality levels are identified for the balance sheet and income statement? Why?

8-5 a. What official quantitative guidelines exist for financial statement materiality?
     b. State five quantitative guidelines commonly used in practice.

8-6 a. How do qualitative considerations relate to making materiality judgments?
     b. A misstatement that is quantitatively immaterial may be qualitatively material. Explain.

8-7 a. Define materiality at the account balance level.
     b. What is another name for materiality at this level?
     c. Distinguish between the terms *material account balance* and *materiality*.

8-8 a. Identify two factors the auditor should consider in allocating financial statement materiality to accounts.
     b. If the amount of error found in an account is less than a tolerable misstatement, what effect might this have on the audit of other accounts?
     c. How are materiality and audit evidence related? Explain.

8-9 a. Explain how auditors evaluate the materiality of misstatements found in the process of collecting audit evidence.
     b. List three examples of situations that might be quantitatively immaterial but qualitatively material.

[KEY TERMS

Account balance materiality, p. 320
Financial statement materiality,
   p. 317

Materiality, p. 316
Planning materiality, p. 317
Tolerable misstatement, p. 320

[PERFORMING ANALYTICAL PROCEDURES]

AU 329.02, *Analytical Procedures* (SAS 56), defines **analytical procedures** as "evaluations of financial information made by a study of plausible relationships among
both financial and nonfinancial data." Such procedures range from simple comparisons to the use of complex mathematical and statistical models involving
many relationships and data elements.

Analytical procedures are used in auditing for the following purposes:

1. In the planning phase of the audit, to assist the auditor in planning the nature,
   timing, and extent of other auditing procedures.
2. In the testing phase, as a substantive test, to obtain evidential matter about particular assertions related to account balances or classes of transactions.
3. At the conclusion of the audit, in a final review of the overall reasonableness of
   the audited financial statements.

The first and third uses are required on all financial statement audits. The second use is optional. However, the authors recommend designing analytical procedures to obtain evidential matter about every material account balance or transaction class. Analytical procedures are usually very cost effective, and they
provide a balance between using the auditor's knowledge of the entity and its
environment and testing balances and transactions with other substantive tests
that test the audit trail. The remainder of this chapter focuses on using analytical
procedures for audit planning.

Analytical procedures can assist the auditor in planning by (1) enhancing the
auditor's understanding of the client's business, and (2) identifying unusual relationships and unexpected fluctuations in data that may indicate areas of greater
risk of misstatement. The second alternative is often described as the attention-
directing objective of analytical procedures.

The steps involved in performing analytical procedures are presented in Figure
8-4 and discussed next. A comprehensive case study is then presented to illustrate
the performance of each step.

Figure 8-4 ■ Steps Involved in Performing Analytical Procedures

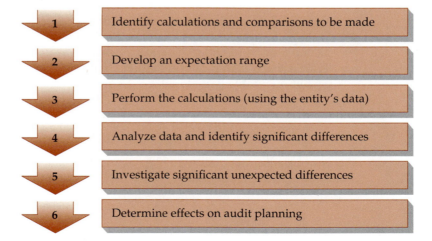

1. Identify calculations and comparisons to be made
2. Develop an expectation range
3. Perform the calculations (using the entity's data)
4. Analyze data and identify significant differences
5. Investigate significant unexpected differences
6. Determine effects on audit planning

IDENTIFY CALCULATIONS AND COMPARISONS TO BE MADE

The sophistication and extent of analytical procedures used in planning vary based on the size and complexity of the entity, the availability of data, and the auditor's judgment. The types of calculations and comparisons commonly used include the following:

- **Absolute data comparisons.** This procedure involves simply comparing a current amount, such as an account balance, with an expected or predicted amount.

- **Common-size financial statements.** Also known as vertical analysis, this technique involves calculating the percentage of a related total that a financial statement component represents (e.g., cash as a percentage of total assets, or gross margin as a percentage of sales). The percentage is then compared with an expected amount, such as industry data.

- **Ratio analysis.** Numerous ratios frequently used by management or financial analysts can be calculated and compared with expected values for the ratios. The calculated amounts can be analyzed individually or in related groups such as solvency, efficiency, and profitability ratios. (Appendix 8A explains the purpose, calculation, and interpretation of 16 common financial ratios used in analytical procedures.)

- **Trend analysis.** Trend analysis involves comparing certain data (absolute, common-size, or ratio) for more than two accounting periods to identify important changes that may not be obvious from comparisons limited to just the current and prior period.

- **Relationships of financial information with relevant nonfinancial information.** Nonfinancial data such as the number of employees, square footage of selling space, and volume of goods produced may be used in estimating related account balances such as payroll expense, sales, and cost of goods manufactured. Nonfinancial information is important because it is a measure of the underlying economic activity that drives financial outcomes. This type of information also must be tailor-made for industry and sometimes for each entity that has a unique niche in an industry.

Generally, analytical procedures performed in the planning phase use highly aggregated, organizationwide data based on year-to-date or projected annual data. However, for organizations with diverse operations, some disaggregation by product line or division may be necessary for the procedures to be effective. In other cases, such as when the entity's business is seasonal, it may be desirable to perform the analysis on monthly or quarterly data rather than year-to-date or annual data.

Effectiveness of Analytical Procedures

When developing expectations of financial statement amounts and relationships, the auditor should consider the factors that influence the effectiveness of analytical procedures. These factors are summarized in Figure 8-5.

Some analytical procedures are directly related to an assertion. For example, comparisons of aggregate salaries paid with the number of personnel may indicate unauthorized payments that may not be apparent from testing individual transactions. Alternatively, if an auditor compares gross margin for the current

did analytical procedures help WorldCom auditors?

On July 8, 2002, Melvin Dick, Arthur Andersen's former senior global managing partner, technology, media, and communications practice, testified before the House Committee on Financial Services:

> "We performed numerous analytical procedures at various financial statement line items, including line costs, revenues in, and plant and service, in order to determine if there were significant variations that required additional work. We also utilized sophisticated auditing software to study WorldCom's financial statement line items, which did not trigger any indication that there was a need for additional work."

Although the details of Andersen's analytical procedures have not been disclosed, Neal Hitzig, a partner retired from Ernst and Young, hypothesizes about why they may not have been effective. He compared 5 ratios for WorldCom, Sprint, AT&T, Nextel, Castel Crown, AmTelSat, U.S. Cellular, and Western Wireless. The ratios were Cost of Revenues to Revenues, Change in Cost of Revenues to Change in Revenues, Revenues to Plant and Equipment, Change in Cost of Revenues to Change in Plant and Equipment, and Cost of Revenues to Plant and Equipment. Hitzig points out that the last three ratios which were formulated with property plant and equipment in the denominator reveal grater volatility for WorldCom but normal values for the critical years of 2000 and 2001.

Neal Hitzig points out two weaknesses in analytical procedures. First, any audit procedure runs some risk of failing to detect material misstatements. This is a matter of audit risk. Second, improper specification of the relationship between the variables used in analytical procedures undermines their effectiveness. Misstatements in the data that are used to form the expectation are perhaps the most insidious source of bias, especially if they exist in data that the auditor assumes are accurate. This may very well be the case when comparing one set of financial numbers with another set because fraudulent financial reporting often reports numbers that appear to be reasonable when they should not appear reasonable. He further points out that if the underlying data are unaudited (whether or not they are from independent sources), the auditor has no basis for presuming that those data are materially correct.

Mr. Hitzig goes on to describe one situation in which analytical procedures may be more effective. In this case he compares nonfinancial data (sales floor area for various stores in a chain of retail stores) with financial data (such as the amount of inventory). If the auditor is able to apply statistical regression analysis to estimate a relationship between the two data sets, the auditor greatly increases the reliability of the underlying audit procedure.

Source: Neal B. Hitzig, "The Hidden Risk in Analytical Procedures: What WorldCom Revealed," *The CPA Journal*, February, 2004, pp. 33–35.

year with gross margin for the prior year, it is more difficult to relate comparisons to specific assertions that might be misstated.

The auditor should also consider the plausibility and predictability of the relationship being investigated. For example, comparing the current ratio for one year to another involves a number of different accounts that could vary in different ways, and it involves balance sheet data that represent only one point in time. Income statement and cash flow data capture transactions over a period of time that are more stable and predictable. Analytical procedures are often more effective at finding unintentional misstatement than intentional misstatements (fraud)

Figure 8-5 ■ Factors that Influence the Effectiveness of Analytical Procedures

Less Effective	Key Factors	More Effective
Analytical procedures may or may not specifically relate to the assertion.	**Nature of the assertion**	Analytical procedures specifically relate to the assertion.
Data that may not be related to each other may lead to erroneous conclusions. Relationships that are dynamic or unstable are less predictable.	**Plausibility and predictability of relationship**	Data that is related to each other will lead to more reliable conclusions. Relationships that are stable are also more predictable.
Data used is from sources inside the entity. Data was not developed under a reliable system of internal controls. The data has not been subjected to audit testing in the current or prior years. Expectations are developed using data from a single source.	**Availability of reliable data**	Data used is from independent sources outside the entity. Data was developed under a reliable system of internal controls. Data has been subjected to audit testing in the current or prior years. Expectations are developed using data from a variety of sources.
Imprecise models lead to a wider range of expectations. Imprecise models have multiple factors that affect the data being audited, and it is difficult to distinguish the factors that influence the outcome.	**Precision of the expectation**	Precise models lead to a narrower range of expectations. Precise models identify the factors that affect the data being audited.

because through fraudulent financial reporting, relationships have often been made to look reasonable.

A number of different sources influence the reliability of data used to develop expectations for analytical procedures. For example, audited prior-year entity data are considered more reliable than unaudited prior-year data. Internal information that is subjected to effective internal control procedures is more reliable than information that is not effectively controlled. The reliability of budget data depends on the continuing validity of the assumptions used in their preparation and the care used in compiling the budgeted amounts. The usefulness of industry data depends on the degree of similarity between an entity's operations and accounting methods and those of the industry. Thus, industry comparisons may be of limited value when, for example, entity data reflect the effects of operating in multiple industries, or when inventory or depreciation methods used by the entity differ from those typically used in an industry. As a result, analytical models that compare financial data with underlying nonfinancial data (e.g., sales per square foot of retail space) are often more effective than analytical models that compare this year's financial data with last year's financial data.

Finally, the auditor should consider the precision of the model used to develop expected amounts. The auditor's use of statistical analytical procedures often allows for developing very precise expectations of reported amounts. Alternatively, models that compare one ratio from one year with the same ratio from another year may be affected by multiple factors that offset one another, which leads to less effective analytical procedures. Analytical procedures that focus on individual product lines are often more precise than analytical procedures that aggregate multiple lines of business.

DEVELOP AN EXPECTATION RANGE

A basic premise underlying the use of analytical procedures in auditing is that relationships among data may be expected to continue in the absence of known conditions to the contrary. For example, the auditor might know of consistent relationships between client financial data and industry statistics. If the auditor is able to determine that there is a reliable pattern between client financial data and industry statistics, the auditor can assume that such a relationship will also exist in the audit period unless the auditor knows of particular conditions that make the prior relationships invalid. In addition, it is important for the auditor to independently develop expectations before performing the calculations on client data so that the eventual comparisons are unbiased. This premise is used in developing expectations from a variety of sources. These sources include both historical and future-oriented internal (client) data and external (industry) data.

- Client financial information for **comparable prior period(s)** giving consideration to known changes. Under this approach, in the absence of known conditions to the contrary, it is simply assumed that a current account balance, common-size percentage, ratio, or the relationship of financial and nonfinancial data should approximate the prior period amount. An example of giving consideration to a known change is expecting that total payroll costs will equal last year's amount adjusted for a predictable increase resulting from higher wage rates under a new union contract and/or higher payroll taxes.
- Anticipated results based on **formal budgets** and **forecasts.** This approach includes the use of client-prepared budgets and forecasts for the current period as well as auditor-prepared forecasts. The latter may include extrapolations from prior interim or annual data, or the results of other value-added services performed for the client.
- **Relationships among elements of financial information within the period.** This includes considering how changes in one account would be expected to affect other accounts. For example, an increase in the average amount of debt outstanding would lead to an expected increase in interest expense. Similarly, an increase in credit sales might lead to an expected increase in accounts receivable and in bad debt expense.
- **Industry data.** Common-size percentages, ratios, and trend data typical of companies within an industry are available for comparison purposes from sources such as Dun & Bradstreet, Robert Morris Associates, and Standard & Poor's. In some cases, only a broad industry average is published for a given data element. In other cases, three values are published for a data element, representing the upper-quartile, median, and lower-quartile values of the reporting companies. Auditors also look at specific financial data developed from competitors in the same industry.

Once the auditor has determined the relationship that will be used to develop an expectation of a financial statement amount or ratio, the auditor must also consider tolerable misstatement for the account and estimate the amount of difference from the auditor's expectation that would result in a material misstatement in the financial statements. In the NTI case discussed in the previous section, the auditor could tolerate a $25,000 misstatement in inventory. The current value for inventory turnover says that inventory turns approximately two times a year. A $25,000 change in inventory and cost of sales in either direction would say that expected inventory turnover should fall in a range of 1.9 to 2.1. If the auditor's expectation regarding inventory turn days fell outside of this range, then the auditor should investigate inventory further to determine the underlying cause for the difference between the auditor's expectation and the reported results.

Auditors who use statistical analytical procedures have a built-in tool that allows them to develop (1) a very precise expectation of reported amounts and (2) a statistical expectation range. If the reported amount falls within that range, then the numbers appear to be reasonable on the surface. If the reported amounts fall outside the statistical expectation range, then the auditor needs to determine the direction of difference between the expectation and the reported amount. If the reported amount appears to be overstated, the auditor may likely have an existence or occurrence, or a valuation and allocation problem. If the reported amount appears to be understated, then the auditor likely has a completeness problem.

PERFORM THE CALCULATIONS

This step includes accumulating the data to be used in calculating the absolute amount and percentage differences between current and prior-year amounts, calculating the common-size and ratio data, and so on. Because planning occurs several months before current year-end account balances are available, this step involves the use of actual year-to-date and/or projected year-end data. It also includes gathering the industry data for comparison purposes. Computer software is commonly used in making the calculations and comparisons, and may also be used in extracting information from organization and industry databases.

When trend analysis is performed, it is common practice to use carryforward schedules. As part of the permanent working paper file, these schedules are designed to permit the addition of a column each year for current-period data while avoiding having to recopy the prior-year data for comparison purposes.

ANALYZE DATA AND IDENTIFY SIGNIFICANT DIFFERENCES

Analysis of the calculations and comparisons should further the auditor's understanding of the entity's business. For example, analysis of appropriate ratio data facilitates the ongoing assessment of the entity's solvency, efficiency, and profitability relative to prior years and other companies in the industry. Similarly, comparison of the entity's prior- and current-year data may help the auditor to understand the effects of significant events or decisions on the entity's financial statements.

A key part of the analysis is identifying fluctuations in the data that are unexpected or the absence of expected fluctuations that may signal an increased risk of misstatements. These represent data points that fall outside of the auditor's expectation range. Some firms use statistical models to develop an expectation range and determine when a difference is large enough to warrant investigation. However, most firms continue to use simple rules of thumb to develop an expectation range. In these cases auditor might investigate differences in excess of (1) a predetermined dollar amount, (2) a percentage difference, or (3) a combination of both. The auditor should be aware that even a small percentage change between the prior-year and current-year amount of an account with a large balance such as sales could result in a much larger percentage change in net income. Also, even a large percentage change in an expense account with a small balance might involve an absolute difference so small as to have little impact on net income. Ultimately, the process of determining when a difference is significant involves the exercise of judgment about the concept of materiality.

INVESTIGATE SIGNIFICANT UNEXPECTED DIFFERENCES

Significant unexpected differences should be investigated. This step usually involves reconsidering the methods and factors used in developing the expectations and making inquiries of management. Sometimes new information will support revising the expectation, which in turn eliminates the significant difference. Before such action is taken based on management's responses to inquiries, the responses should ordinarily be corroborated with other evidential matter. Hence, significant differences should be considered when determining the impact on the audit plan and when evaluating audit evidence.

DETERMINE EFFECTS ON AUDIT PLANNING

Unexplained significant differences are ordinarily viewed as indicating an increased risk of misstatement in the account(s) involved in the calculation or comparison. In such a case, the auditor will usually plan to perform more detailed tests of the account(s). Analytic procedures often provide the auditor with clues about whether an account is more likely to be overstated or understated. By directing the auditor's attention to areas of greater risk, the analytical procedures may contribute to performing a more effective and efficient audit.

ILLUSTRATIVE CASE STUDY

Audit Decision 3

■ Identify risks of material misstatement by using analytical procedures.

Now we illustrate each of the steps described above using hypothetical data for New Technology, Inc. (NTI), a continuing audit client, which is presented in Figure 8-6. The NTI case was introduced in Chapter 7. NTI is a company that makes hard drives for audio and video laser equipment. The company's standard industry classification (SIC) code is 3599.

Identify Calculations and Comparisons to Be Made

NTI is a growth company that has experienced significant sales growth. As a result, comparisons of current-year data with prior-year data will show significant changes. Hence, this illustration focuses on the use of vertical analysis, ratio analysis, and comparisons with industry data, which are presented in Figure 8-7.

Figure 8-6 ■ Net Technology, Inc., Draft Financial Statements

	($000 Omitted) Current Year Unaudited		Prior Year Audited	
Assets				
Cash and cash equivalents	$ 593	14.0%	$ 428	13.2%
Accounts receivable, net	$ 1,335	31.6%	$ 837	25.8%
Inventory	$ 1,327	31.4%	$ 1,025	31.5%
Other current assets	$ 53	1.3%	$ 19	0.6%
Total current assets	$ 3,308	78.4%	$ 2,309	71.1%
Property plant and equipment at cost	$ 1,776	42.1%	$ 1,718	52.9%
Less accumulated depreciation	$ (1,062)	–25.2%	$ (958)	–29.5%
	$ 714	16.9%	$ 760	23.4%
Other assets	$ 199	4.7%	$ 180	5.5%
Total assets	$ 4,221	100.0%	$ 3,249	100.0%
Liabilities and Shareholders' Equity				
Accounts payable	$ 180	4.3%	$ 164	5.0%
Accrued expenses	$ 301	7.1%	$ 206	6.3%
Income taxes payable	$ 66	1.6%	$ –	0.0%
Deferred revenues	$ 114	2.7%	$ 10	0.3%
Current portion of long-term debt	$ 25	0.6%	$ 40	1.2%
Current liabilites	$ 686	16.3%	$ 420	12.9%
Other long-term liabilities	$ 56	1.3%	$ 39	1.2%
Total liabilties	$ 742	17.6%	$ 459	14.1%
Common stock	$ 1,151	27.3%	$ 1,151	35.4%
Retained earnings	$ 2,328	55.2%	$ 1,639	50.4%
Total shareholders' equity	$ 3,479	82.4%	$ 2,790	85.9%
Total liabilities and shareholders' equity	$ 4,221	100.0%	$ 3,249	100.0%
Income Statement				
Net sales	$ 5,638	100.0%	$ 3,780	100.0%
Cost of sales	$ 2,691	47.7%	$ 1,975	52.2%
Gross margin	$ 2,947	52.3%	$ 1,805	47.8%
Selling, general and administrative	$ 1,350	23.9%	$ 1,045	27.6%
Research, development and engineering	$ 683	12.1%	$ 429	11.3%
Total operating expenses	$ 2,033	36.1%	$ 1,474	39.0%
Operating income	$ 914	16.2%	$ 331	8.8%
Interest expense	$ (8)	–0.1%	$ (35)	–0.9%
Interest income	$ 40	0.7%	$ 6	0.2%
Income before taxes	$ 946	16.8%	$ 302	8.0%
Provision for income taxes	$ 257	4.6%	$ 108	2.9%
Net income	$ 689	12.2%	$ 194	5.1%

(continues)

Figure 8-6 ■ (Continued)

	($000 Omitted)	
	Current Year Unaudited	**Prior Year Audited**
Statement of Cash Flows		
Cash flow from operations		
Net income	$ 689	$ 194
Items included in net income that do not use (provide) cash		
Depreciaiton and amortization	$ 131	$ 117
(Gain) loss on the sale of property and equipment	$ (23)	$ 7
Changes in operating accounts		
(Increase) decease in trade receivables	$ (498)	$ (143)
(Increase) decease in inventories	$ (302)	$ (191)
(Increase) decease in other current assets	$ (34)	$ 1
Increase (decrease) in accounts payables	$ 16	$ 59
Increase (decrease) in other accrued liabilities	$ 161	$ 51
Increase (decrease) in deferred revenues	$ 104	$ 6
Cash flow from operations	$ 244	$ 101
Cash flow from investing activities		
Purchase of property plant, and equipment	$ (108)	$ (112)
Sale of property plant, and equipment	$ 46	$ 24
Increase in other assets	$ (19)	$ (5)
Cash flow from investing activities	$ (81)	$ (93)
Cash flow from financing activities		
Retirement of debt	$ (38)	$ (57)
Borrowing	$ 40	$ 36
Cash flow from financing activity	$ 2	$ (21)
Change in cash	$ 165	$ (13)
Cash at the beginning of the year	$ 428	$ 441
Cash at the end of the year	$ 593	$ 428

Develop an Expectation Range

The auditor in this case has two important ways to develop expectations about the financial statements. First, using the SIC code, the auditor can obtain industry information on comparable companies. Some of this information obtained from Robert Morris Associates is included in Figure 8-7. If the auditor uses industry data, the auditor needs to develop an expectation range within which the auditor might consider that the client data meets expectations. For example, consider

Figure 8-7 ■ New Technology, Inc., Ratio Analysis

	Current Year Unaudited		Prior Year Audited		
PROFITABILITY					
Asset turnover	1.34		1.16		
Profit margin	12.3%		5.7%		
Return on Assets	**16.5%**		**6.7%**		
Common earnings leverage	99%		90%		
Capital structure leverage	1.21		1.16		
Return on Common Equity	**19.8%**		**7.0%**		
OPERATING CYCLE					
Accounts receivable turnover (days)	86.4		80.8		
Inventory turnover (days)	180.0		189.4		
Gross operating cycle	266.4		270.3		
Accounts payable turnover	22.0		27.6		
Net operating cycle	244.5		242.6		
LIQUIDITY/SOLVENCY					
(Current portion of debt + dividends)/ Cash flow from operations	10%		40%		
Free cash flow	$ 117		$ (16)		
Current ratio	4.82		5.50		
Quick ratio	3.37		3.09		
Debt to equity	0.21		0.16		

Company Growth Rates	Sales	AR	CGS	Inv	AP
Current year growth	49%	59%	36%	29%	10%

Robert Morris Associates Comparables (SIC Code 3699)					Industry Median
Profitability					
Sales/total assets	1.34		1.16		2.0
% Profit before taxes/total assets	22.4%		9.3%		9%
% Profit before taxes/tangible net worth	28.8%		11.6%		27%
Gross profit as a % of sales	52.3%		47.8%		35.8%
Operating profit as a % of sales	16.2%		8.8%		8.1%
Profit before taxes as a % of sales	16.8%		8.0%		7.3%
Turnover					
Sales/Receivables	4.2		4.5		7.4
Cost of sales/Inventory	2.0		1.9		4.8
Cost of sales/Payables	15.0		12.0		10.6
Liquidity and Solvency					
Current ratio	4.8		5.5		1.6
Quick ratio	3.4		3.1		1.0
Debt/Worth	0.2		0.2		1.8

inventory turnover. Previously, we noted that if inventory was fairly stated our expectation for inventory turnover should fall within a range of 1.9 and 2.1 times a year. If we use industry median as an expectation, with a 4.8 median inventory turns, NTI's inventory and cost of sales values fall well outside the expectation range, indicating a possible problem with slow inventory turns and a possible inventory obsolescence problem.

Perform Calculations

After obtaining data from comparative companies, the auditor will perform calculations with client data. Figure 8-7 includes some ratios that might regularly be calculated by the auditor along with calculations used by Robert Morris Associates when their calculations differ from standard calculations used by the auditor.

Analyze Data and Identify Significant Differences

Once key calculations have been performed, the auditor must identify significant differences from expectations. At this point you should take a moment and study Figures 8-6 and 8-7 and identify what you believe are the top four or five issues with important audit implications.

Investigate Significant Unexpected Differences

Often the auditor will make an initial attempt to follow up on unexpected differences. The auditor is looking for indicators that fall outside of the auditor's expectation range. For purposes of example, Figure 8-8 identifies the audit implications as if the auditor was not able to obtain explanations for key differences.

At this stage the auditor should attempt to identify the direction of unexpected differences and link that understanding to possible assertions that might be misstated. Consider the previous discussion of inventory turnover. NTI's inventory turnover is substantially slower than the industry, indicating that inventory amounts are higher than what you would expect compared to the rest of the industry (relative to cost of sales). This would indicate a potential concern about either the existence of inventory or the valuation of inventory (inventory obsolescence problems).

NTI also appears to be paying off its accounts payable at a faster rate than in previous years. Accounts payable turnover has gone from 12 to 15 times a year, and the 15 times payable turns appear to be substantially faster than the industry median of 10. High accounts payable turnover ratios may be affected by accounts payable being understated, which would be a potential indicator of a completeness problem.

Determine Effects on Audit Planning

The primary reason for performing analytic procedures in audit planning is to identify accounts that may contain potential misstatements and to design an audit that will respond to the risk of material misstatement. Figure 8-8 summarizes several significant differences noted while performing analytical procedures, along with the related implications for subsequent audit tests. Note that Figure 8-8 focuses on specific assertions, not merely account balances, that need additional audit attention.

Figure 8-8 ■ New Technology Inc., Summary of Findings of Analytical Procedures

Significant Difference	Audit Implications
Sales have grown by nearly 50%. Receivables are growing faster than sales, and the company's AR turnover is slower than industry median.	The fast growth in sales combined with the slow accounts receivable turnover should cause the auditor to heighten professional skepticism with respect to revenue recognition (existence and occurrence), or the risk of significant sales returns after year-end. The auditor should also attend to the issue of valuation of receivables at their net realizable value (valuation and allocation).
The company's inventory turnover is significantly slower than the industry median.	Given the potential for obsolescence due to new technologies, combined with a very slow inventory turnover, the auditor should attend carefully to lower of cost or market issues with respect to inventory (valuation and allocation). Lower than expected inventory turnover indicates possible overstatements of inventory, which may be due to problems with the existence of inventory (existence and occurrence).
The company's profit margins are significantly stronger than the industry median. This is seen in strong gross profit margins, strong operating profit margins, and in a strong return on assets.	Given that the company's asset turnover measures are slower than industry, it will be particularly important to understand the economic drivers and competitive advantage that allows the company to realize higher profit margins. The auditor should be alert to the fact that strong margins might result from costs being capitalized and included in inventory rather than being expensed in the current period (classification aspect of presentation and disclosure).
Accounts payable is not growing as fast as cost of goods sold, and accounts payable turnover appear to be faster than industry average while receivables and inventory turnover is slower than average.	It is possible that there are unrecorded liabilities (completeness problems). The auditor should attend carefully to a search for unrecorded liabilities. This may also be the cause of unusually high profit margins.
The company appears to be quite liquid. It is generating free cash flow, and it does not have significant debt. Part of the strong cash position is due to significant increases in deferred revenues.	The auditor should confirm that the company is in fact in a strong cash position and is generating strong cash flow from operations. The auditor should attend to the existence of new deferred revenues (customer deposits). Although the company has strong financial resources, its potential for the future depends significantly on its ability to develop new product innovations. The company is in an industry that is dependent on both human and intangible resources.

[LEARNING CHECK

8-10 a. State three uses of analytical procedures in an audit engagement.
       b. Which uses are required in all audits?

8-11 a. How can analytic procedures assist the auditor in audit planning?
       b. List the steps involved in the effective use of analytical procedures in the planning phase.

8-12 a. Describe the types of calculations and comparisons commonly used in analytical procedures.
       b. What premise underlies the use of analytical procedures in auditing?

c. Identify four sources of information the auditor may use in developing expectations.

[KEY TERMS

Absolute data comparisons, p. 325
Analytical procedures, p. 324
Common-size financial statements, p. 325
Comparable prior periods, p. 328
Forecasts, p. 328
Formal budgets, p. 328
Industry data, p. 328

Ratio analysis, p. 325
Relationship of financial information with relevant nonfinancial information, p. 325
Relationship among elements of financial information within the period, p. 328
Trend analysis, p. 325

[FOCUS ON AUDITOR KNOWLEDGE AND AUDIT DECISIONS]

This chapter focuses on two critical aspects of audit planning: (1) Making preliminary decisions about overall materiality and tolerable misstatement and (2) performing analytical procedures. In making decisions to support high-quality audit work, the auditor must be able to use the knowledge summarized in Figure 8-9 and address the decisions summarized in Figure 8-10. Page references are provided indicating where these issues are discussed in more detail.

Figure 8-9 ■ Summary of Auditor Knowledge Discussed in Chapter 8

Auditor Knowledge	Summary	Chapter References
K1. Understand the concept of materiality as it is used in auditing.	The concept of materiality focuses on the amount of omission or a misstatement that would change the decision of a reasonable financial statement user. The auditor should consider both the circumstances pertaining to the entity and the information needs of those who will rely on the audited financial statements.	pp. 316–317
K2. Understand the relationship between materiality and audit evidence.	There is an inverse relationship between tolerable misstatement and the amount of evidence needed to obtain reasonable assurance that an account balance is free of material misstatement. For example, it takes more evidence to obtain reasonable assurance that any misstatement in the accounts receivables and revenues does not exceed $100,000 than it does to be assured the misstatement does not exceed $200,000.	pp. 322–323
K3. Understand the role of analytical procedures in planning and performing the audit.	Auditors are required to perform analytical procedures in planning the audit (to identify accounts likely to contain misstatements) and in the final stages of the audit (to evaluate the overall reasonableness of the audited financial statements). The auditor may also elect to perform analytical procedures as substantive test.	pp. 324–330

Figure 8-10 ■ Summary of Audit Decisions Discussed in Chapter 8

Audit Decision	Factors that Influence the Audit Decision	Chapter References
D1. Make preliminary judgments about materiality at the financial statement level.	The chapter describes some rules of thumb that an auditor might use when determining overall materiality at the financial statement level. Many auditors calculate multiple values (e.g., 5% pretax income or a variable percentage of the greater of total assets or total revenues) and then make a final determination based on their judgment about the amount of misstatement that would change the decisions of financial statement users. Figure 8-1 provides a common tool used to make decisions about materiality at the financial statement level based on a variable percentage of the greater of total assets or total revenues.	pp. 317–319
D2. Make preliminary judgments about materiality at the account balance level.	When planning the audit, auditors must determine the amount of misstatement that they can tolerate in an account balance or transaction class to determine the scope of audit procedures. This amount is called a tolerable misstatement. In making decisions about a tolerable misstatement, the auditor considers the following factors identified in Figure 8-3: ■ Primary Factor: What is the amount of misstatement that will influence a reasonable user of the financial statements? ■ Secondary Factors: Cost-benefit considerations	pp. 320–321
D3. Identify risks of material misstatement by using analytical procedures.	The chapter provides an illustrative case study that walks students through a six-step process to identify accounts that may contain material misstatements. When the auditor is considering the overall effectiveness of analytical procedures, the auditor should consider the following factors that are illustrated in Figure 8-5. ■ Nature of the Assertion ■ Plausibility and Predictability of Relationship ■ Availability of Reliable Data ■ Precision of the Expectation When the auditor develops an expectation range, the auditor will usually calculate a range around the expectation of plus or minus tolerable misstatement. Finally, when evaluating data, the auditor should determine the direction of the difference from the expectation. Overstatements represent possible existence or occurrence, or valuation and allocation problems. Understatements represent possible completeness problems.	pp. 330–335

KEY FINANCIAL RATIOS USED IN ANALYTICAL PROCEDURES

Users of financial statements can obtain valuable insights into a company's financial condition and performance through analysis of key financial ratios. The same analysis performed by auditors provides them with a better understanding of a client's business. Moreover, when ratios calculated on current data are compared with expectations developed from previous years' data, budgeted amounts, or industry norms, insights can be gained into areas with a high risk of misstatement. For example, when comparisons reveal unexpected fluctuations, or when expected fluctuations do not occur, the auditor will generally want to investigate whether the aberration is due to the misstatement of one or more variables used in calculating the ratio.

Figure 8-11 explains the calculation of the ratios commonly used for ratio analysis. In addition, comments are provided on the purpose of each ratio and how it is interpreted. The comments on interpretation are general in nature and would be tailored according to a particular client's circumstances such as its recent experience and the industry in which it operates.

Figure 8-11 ■ Ratios Commonly Used for Analytical Procedures

Ratio	Calculation	Purpose and Interpretation
Profitability		
Asset Turnover	$\dfrac{\text{Sales}}{\text{Total Assets}}$	Measures the relationship between sales and total assets. The larger the number, the more a company is able to generate sales with its asset base.
Profit Margin	$\dfrac{\text{Net Income} + (\text{Interest} *(1 - \text{Tax Rate}))}{\text{Sales}}$	Measures the profitability, independent of financing costs, as a percentage of sales. The larger the number, the higher the company's net profit margin (independent of financing costs).
Return on Assets	Assets Turnover × Profit Margin	Measures profitability in relation to the asset structure of the company. This is a good measure for comparing performance between companies as it is independent of financing decisions. The higher the number, the higher the rate of return on assets a company has generated.
Common Earnings Leverage	$\dfrac{\text{Net Income} - \text{Preferred Dividends}}{\text{Net Income} + (\text{Interest} *(1 - \text{Tax Rate}))}$	Measures the impact of financing decisions on earnings. It compares net income to common shareholders, after all financing costs (including the cost of preferred equity) as a percentage of prefinancing earnings. This number is less than or equal to one, and the higher the number the less prefinancing earnings are consumed by financing costs.

(continues)

Figure 8-11 ■ (Continued)

Ratio	Calculation	Purpose and Interpretation
Profitability (*cont.*)		
Capital Structure Leverage	$$\dfrac{\text{Total Assets}}{\text{Common Equity}}$$	Measures the impact of financing on the balance sheet. Common equity is defined as total equity less preferred equity. The larger the ratio, the more total assets are financed with debt.
Return on Common Equity	Return on Assets × Common Earnings Leverage × Capital Structure Leverage	Measures the rate of return after all financing costs are compared to common shareholder's equity. The larger the ratio, the more return the company has generated for common shareholders, after all financing costs are considered.
Operating Cycle		
Accounts Receivable Turnover (days)	$$\dfrac{\text{Accounts Rec., Net}}{\text{Sales}} \times 365$$	Estimate of the number of days it takes to collect accounts receivable. Smaller numbers represent faster collection times.
Inventory Turnover (days)	$$\dfrac{\text{Inventory}}{\text{Cost of Goods Sold}} \times 365$$	Estimate of the number of days a company holds inventory, from purchase to sale. Smaller numbers indicate shorter inventory holding periods.
Gross Operating Cycle	AR Turnover + Inv. Turnover	Estimate of the number of days from the time a company purchases inventory, sells it, and collects the receivable. Smaller numbers represent faster turnover of a company's operating assets.
Accounts Payable Turnover	$$\dfrac{\text{Purchases}}{\text{Accounts Payable}} \times 365$$	Estimate of the number of days a company takes to pay its payables. Larger numbers represent slower creditor payment periods.
Net Operating Cycle	Gross Operating Cycle – Accounts Payable Turnover	Recognizes that a company may use creditor financing to finance inventory purchases. This is an estimate of the time the company is out of cash while waiting to sell inventory and collect sales. Smaller numbers indicate faster turnover of operating assets.
Liquidity and Solvency		
Ability of Cash Flow from Operations to Cover Current Debt and Dividends	$$\dfrac{\text{Cash Flow from Operation}}{\text{Current Portion of Debt} + \text{Dividends}}$$	Estimate the company's ability to cover current debt maturities and dividends with operating cash flows. Larger numbers represent increased ability to cover current debt maturities and dividends with operating cash flows.
Free Cash Flow	Cash Flow from Operations – Capital Expenditures	Measures the cash flow remaining after covering cash outflows for operations and capital expenditures. Larger numbers indicate that a company has the capacity to finance operations and capital expenditures with operating cash flows.

(continues)

Figure 8A-1 ■ (Continued)

Ratio	Calculation	Purpose and Interpretation
Liquidity and Solvency *(cont.)*		
Current Ratio	$\dfrac{\text{Current Assets}}{\text{Current Liabilities}}$	Measures the degree to which current liabilities are covered by current assets. The larger the ratio, the greater the liquidity.
Quick Ratio	$\dfrac{\text{Current Monetary Assets}}{\text{Current Monetary Liabilities}}$	Estimates the protection afforded to short-term creditors by cash or near cash assets. The larger the ratio, the greater the liquidity.
Debt to Equity	$\dfrac{\text{Total Liabilities}}{\text{Shareholders' Equity}}$	Measures the extent to which a company is using its debt financing capacity. In general, this ratio should not exceed 100% because in such cases creditors will have more at stake than owners.

objective questions

Objective questions are available for the student at www.wiley.com/college/boynton

comprehensive questions

8-13   **(Planning materiality)** You have been assigned to plan the audit of Household, Inc., a retailer of household appliances. Summary financial statements for Household, Inc. for the year ended December 31, 20X6 and 20X5 are presented in Figure 8.12.

Required

a. Determine overall financial statement level materiality.

b. Allocate overall financial statement materiality to asset accounts.

8-14   **(Evaluating the significance of misstatements)** You are concluding the audit of Sun Island Apparel, Inc. as of December 31, 20x1. You believe that you can tolerate $675,000 in misstatements to pretax income. You have noted only three issues that may affect the financial statements based on evidence found during the audit. They are:

1. When auditing accounts receivable, you investigated every sales transaction between December 26th 20x1 and January 5th 20x2. You have problems with revenue recognition on two shipments that were ordered in December of 20x1, recorded in revenue as of December 31, 20x1 but the customer did not pick the items up until January 4, 20x2. These shipments had a retail value of $240,000 and a cost of $130,000. The inventory was held aside as the company expected customers to pick up the inventory prior to year-end, and it was not counted as part of inventory. These were the only sales cutoff problems discovered. Tolerable misstatement for accounts receivable and sales was $260,000.

2. When auditing inventory, you determined that the company still had $395,000 of last year's designs and inventory on hand. Based on past history you believe that the com-

Figure 8-12 ■ Household, Inc. Summary Financial Statements ($ 000 Omitted)

Income Statement	20x6	20x5
Sales	$ 3,513	$ 3,413
Cost of sales	$ 2,622	$ 2,475
Gross proft	$ 891	$ 938
Selling general and administrative expenses	$ 797	$ 781
Operating income	$ 94	$ 157
Other income and expense	$ (13)	$ (14)
Pretax income	$ 81	$ 143
Income tax expense	$ 32	$ 55
Net income	$ 49	$ 88
Balance Sheet		
Cash and cash equivalents	$ 208	$ 190
Accounts receivable	$ 89	$ 73
Inventories	$ 1,183	$ 1,179
Current assets	$ 1,480	$ 1,442
Property, plant and equipment	$ 630	$ 649
Goodwill	$ 96	$ 88
Total assets	$ 2,206	$ 2,179
Accounts payable	$ 565	$ 638
Accrued expenses	$ 401	$ 376
Taxes, including income taxes	$ 121	$ 93
Total current liabilities	$ 1,087	$ 1,107
Long-term debt	$ 150	$ 152
Total liabilities	$ 1,237	$ 1,259
Common stock	$ 661	$ 661
Retained earnings	$ 308	$ 259
Total equity	$ 969	$ 920
Total liabilities and equity	$ 2,206	$ 2,179
Summary Cash Flow Information		
Cash flow from operations	$ 127	$ 175
Cash flow from investing activities	$ (107)	$ (90)
Cash flow from financing activities	$ (2)	$ 10
Change in cash	$ 18	$ 95

pany can realize approximately $175,000 on the sale of this inventory. No other problems were noted associated with the not realizable value audit objective. Tolerable misstatement for inventory was $250,000.

3. In performing a search for unrecorded liabilities, you audited every cash purchase between January 2, 20x2 and January 20, 20x2. The only problems you noted are described as follows. You find $200,000 in invoices that were received from subcontractors who

manufacture apparel in mid-January. The invoices were dated December 21, 20x1. Inventory was shipped on December 27, 20x1 (FOB shipping point), received on December 31, 20x1, and was counted in inventory. In addition, you found one invoice in the amount of $150,000 for the purchase of new equipment that was dated December 29, 20x1 but was not received from the vendor until January 10, 20x2 when it was paid in cash. The goods were shipped FOB shipping point. No accrual was made for these invoices. Tolerable misstatement for accounts payable was $240,000.

Required

a. Propose adjusting journal entries for the three items noted above.

b. Make an overall determination about what journal entries you believe that the client should book in order for the financial statements to present fairly in all material respects.

8-15 **(Analytical procedures)** In audit planning the audit of Construction Industry Resources, Inc., a building supply company. You have completed analytic procedures relevant to purchases and inventory. The results of these procedures are included in Figure 8-13.

Required

Analytical procedures show that inventory turnover decreased from 31–34 days to 27 days, and gross margins declined to the lowest level in five years. What might this indicate about the risk of misstatement with respect to inventory and inventory purchases?

8-16 **(Analytical procedures)** In audit planning the audit of Circuits Technology, Inc. (CTI). CTI resells, installs, and provides computer networking products (client software, gateway hardware and software, and twinax hardware) to other businesses. Figure 8-14 provides some summary information from CTI's financial statements.

Required

a. Calculate purchases, gross margin, inventory turn days, accounts receivable turn days, and accounts payable turn days for the years ended 20x2, 20x3, 20x4, 20x5.

b. Describe the trends identified by performing analytical procedures in the gross operating cycle, the net operating cycle, and gross margin.

Figure 8-13 ■ Selected Financial Information ($000)

	X1	X2	X3	X4	X5
Building supply revenues	$ 90,100	$ 99,380	$ 117,468	$ 137,085	$ 160,800
Lumber brokerage revenues	$ —	$ —	$ 45,021	$ 63,480	$ 90,141
	$ 90,100	$ 99,380	$ 162,489	$ 200,564	$ 250,941
Inventory turn days					
Building supplies	32	34	31	33	27
Lumber brokerage			7	6	6
Gross margin					
Building supplies	20.1%	18.5%	18.6%	19.1%	18.0%
Lumber brokerage			3.9%	4.1%	4.2%

Figure 8-14 ■ CTI Selected Financial Information ($000)

	20x1	20x2	20x3	20x4	20x5
Accounts receivable, net	$ 837	$ 1,335	$ 1,121	$ 962	$ 822
Inventory	$ 1,025	$ 1,327	$ 1,099	$ 1,003	$ 1,027
Accounts payable	$ 164	$ 380	$ 225	$ 201	$ 175
Sales	$ 3,780	$ 5,638	$ 4,623	$ 4,022	$ 3,905
Cost of sales	$ 1,812	$ 2,691	$ 2,399	$ 2,095	$ 1,859
Gross margin	$ 1,968	$ 2,947	$ 2,224	$ 1,927	$ 2,046

c. If tolerable misstatement is $45,000 for inventory, develop an expectation range for inventory turn days.

d. With respect to inventory, what might these trends indicate about the potential misstatement in inventory?

comprehensive case

Figure 8-15 provides preliminary financial statement data for Mt. Hood Furniture, Inc. The data for 20x1 and 20x2 is audited, and the data for 20x3 is the unaudited data that has been completed immediately following the closing of the financial records.

8-17 **(Mt. Hood Furniture; materiality)** Complete the following requirements based on the information presented in Figure 8-15. A spreadsheet on the textbook website includes the raw data included in Figure 8-15 for the case along with accompanying industry data.

Required

Prepare a memo for the working papers outlining your preliminary judgments about materiality. This is the stage where the auditor makes preliminary decisions about what will be considered material when setting the scope of audit procedures. You should draw conclusions about (1) materiality at the financial statement level and (2) materiality at the account balance level where you allocate the overall financial statement materiality to appropriate balance sheet accounts. Discuss your consideration of both quantitative and qualitative factors in your discussion.

8-18 **(Mt. Hood Furniture; analytical procedures in audit planning)** Complete the following requirements based on the information on Mt. Hood Furniture provided in Figure 8-15. This is the stage where the auditor uses his or her understanding of the business and industry and the results of analytical procedures in audit planning to anticipate account balances and assertions that are likely to be misstated, and to plan initial audit responses.

a. Calculate the ratios on page 347 for Mt. Hood Furniture based on the information in Figure 8-15 and compare them with industry information for the same period. The raw data included in Figure 8-15 for the case, along with accompanying industry data, is available in an MS Excel file at www.wiley.com/college/boynton.

Figure 8-15 ∎

Mt. Hood Furniture, Inc. Balance Sheet December 31

	20X3 Unaudited	20X2 Audited	20X1 Audited	Industry Data 20X3	Industry Data 20X2	Industry Data 20X1
Assets						
Cash	$ 1,192,292	$ 1,767,692	$ 1,171,500	5.1%	9.3%	9.5%
Accounts receivable	$ 6,982,923	$ 5,380,712	$ 4,928,090			
Allowance for doubtful accounts	$ (51,000)	$ (46,500)	$ (47,850)			
	$ 6,931,923	$ 5,334,212	$ 4,880,240	32.9%	32.6%	28.6%
Inventory	$ 6,753,764	$ 4,368,626	$ 4,091,012	27.6%	24.2%	21.0%
Prepaid expenses	$ 562,824	$ 410,009	$ 464,786			
Total current assets	$ 15,440,802	$ 11,880,537	$ 10,607,537	68.4%	67.4%	61.7%
Property, plant & equipment	$ 12,318,474	$ 11,932,046	$ 9,155,408			
Accumulated depreciation	$ (4,780,586)	$ (4,334,936)	$ (4,044,896)			
Net fixed assets	$ 7,537,889	$ 7,597,110	$ 5,110,512	21.8%	25.1%	27.4%
Total assets	$ 22,978,691	$ 19,477,647	$ 15,718,049			
Liabilities and Shareholders' Equity						
Accounts payables	$ 4,052,336	$ 2,866,371	$ 2,556,827	17.3%	14.5%	10.2%
Accrued payroll and payroll taxes	$ 562,824	$ 318,597	$ 235,725			
Accrued expenses	$ 1,350,779	$ 983,642	$ 929,570			
Notes payable to banks	$ 1,801,038	$ 1,506,828	$ 2,014,068	13.7%	8.4%	10.8%
Current portion of long-term debt	$ 337,500	$ 300,000	$ 225,000	3.1%	6.5%	3.4%
Total current liabilities	$ 8,104,476	$ 5,975,438	$ 5,961,189	46.5%	38.7%	35.2%
Long-term debt	$ 6,941,957	$ 6,220,178	$ 2,794,551	11.8%	13.5%	19.3%
Deferred income taxes	$ 67,539	$ 53,349	$ 46,479			
Total liabilities	$ 15,113,972	$ 12,248,964	$ 8,802,219	63.4%	56.8%	59.1%
Common stock	$ 375,000	$ 262,500	$ 225,000			
Additional paid-in capital	$ 450,260	$ 348,786	$ 40,973			
Retained earnings	$ 7,039,460	$ 6,617,397	$ 6,649,857			
Total equity	$ 7,864,719	$ 7,228,683	$ 6,915,830	36.6%	43.2%	40.9%
Total liabilities and shareholders' equity	$ 22,978,691	$ 19,477,647	$ 15,718,049			

(continues)

Figure 8-15 ■ (Continued)

Mt. Hood Furniture, Inc. Income Statement & Statement of Changes in Retained Earnings
For the Year Ended December 31

	20X3 Unaudited	20X2 Audited	20X1 Audited	Industry Data 20X3	Industry Data 20X2	Industry Data 20X1
Net sales	$ 35,274,720	$ 27,558,375	$ 21,198,750	100.0%	100.0%	100.0%
Cost of goods sold	$ 25,397,798	$ 20,117,614	$ 15,263,100	72.3%	67.9%	67.6%
Gross profit	$ 9,876,922	$ 7,440,761	$ 5,935,650	27.7%	32.1%	32.4%
Depreciation	$ 445,650	$ 290,040	$ 201,389			
Selling expenses	$ 4,232,966	$ 3,582,589	$ 2,713,440			
General and administrative expenses	$ 3,527,472	$ 3,031,421	$ 2,247,068			
Other expenses	$ 282,198	$ 220,467	$ 169,590			
	$ 8,488,286	$ 7,124,517	$ 5,331,486			
Operating income	$ 1,388,635	$ 316,244	$ 604,164	24.2%	26.1%	26.7%
Interest expense	$ 654,398	$ 329,700	$ 133,572	3.5%	6.0%	5.7%
Interest income	$ (78,375)	$ (64,013)	$ (53,031)			
Other expense, net	$ 23,625	$ 26,981	$ 24,795			
	$ 599,648	$ 292,668	$ 105,336			
Income before taxes	$ 788,988	$ 23,576	$ 498,828	2.9%	5.2%	4.8%
Income taxes	$ 291,926	$ 3,536	$ 179,578			
Net income	$ 497,062	$ 20,040	$ 319,250			
Retained earnings at the beginning of the year	$ 6,617,397	$ 6,649,857	$ 6,375,608			
Dividends	$ (75,000)	$ (52,500)	$ (45,000)			
Retained earnings at the end of the year	$ 7,039,460	$ 6,617,397	$ 6,649,857			

(continues)

Figure 8-15 ■ (Continued)

Mt. Hood Furniture, Inc.
Statement of Cash Flows For the Year Ended December 31

	20X3 Unaudited	20X2 Audited	20X1 Audited
Cash Flow from Operations			
Net income	$ 497,062	$ 20,040	$ 319,250
Depreciation	$ 445,650	$ 290,040	$ 201,389
Deferred income taxes	$ 14,190	$ 6,870	$ 357
Change in operating assets and liabilities			
Accounts receivable	$ (1,597,712)	$ (453,972)	$ 116,319
Inventory	$ (2,385,138)	$ (277,614)	$ (370,497)
Prepaid expenses	$ (152,816)	$ 54,777	$ (264,923)
Accounts payable	$ 1,185,965	$ 309,545	$ 327,593
Accrued payroll and payroll taxes	$ 244,227	$ 82,872	$ 81,984
Accrued expenses	$ 367,137	$ 54,072	$ (346,475)
Cash flow provided by operations	$ (1,381,434)	$ 86,629	$ 64,997
Cash Flow from Investing Activities			
Acquisition of property, plant, and equipment	$ (386,429)	$ (2,915,313)	$ (238,473)
Proceeds from the sale of property, plant, and equipment	$ —	$ 138,675	$ —
Net cash used in investing activities	$ (386,429)	$ (2,776,638)	$ (238,473)
Cash Flow from Financing Activities			
Long-term borrowing	$ 1,059,279	$ 3,725,627	$ —
Retirement of long-term debt	$ (300,000)	$ (225,000)	$ (716,337)
Changes in notes payable to banks	$ 294,210	$ (507,240)	$ 722,651
Cash dividends paid	$ (75,000)	$ (52,500)	$ (45,000)
Issuance of common stock	$ 213,974	$ 345,314	$ —
Cash flow provided by financing activities	$ 1,192,463	$ 3,286,200	$ (38,687)
Net increase in cash	$ (575,400)	$ 596,191	$ (212,163)
Cash at the beginning of the year	$ 1,767,692	$ 1,171,500	$ 1,383,663
Cash at the end of the year	$ 1,192,292	$ 1,767,692	$ 1,171,500

Mt. Hood Furniture's debt maturities can be described as follows:

Debt maturities for each of the next 5 years as of December 31,	20X3 Unaudited	20X2 Audited	20X1 Audited
Maturities next year	$ 337,500	$ 300,000	$ 225,000
Maturities 2 years out	$ 375,000	$ 300,000	$ 262,500
Maturities 3 years out	$ 375,000	$ 337,500	$ 262,500
Maturities 4 years out	$ 525,000	$ 337,500	$ 300,000
Maturities 5 years out	$ 750,000	$ 450,000	$ 300,000

RATIO	20X3	20X2	20X1
a. Asset turnover (sales/total assets)			
b. Profit margin (% profit before taxes/sales)			
c. ROA (% profit before taxes/total assets)			
d. Capital structure leverage (total assets/total equity)			
e. Return on equity (% profit before taxes/tangible net worth)			
f. Sales/Net fixed assets			
g. AR turnover in days (AR/sales × 365)			
h. Inventory turnover in days (Inv./CGS × 365)			
i. Gross operating cycle			
j. AP turnover in days (AP/CGS × 365)			
k. Net operating cycle			
l. Current ratio			
m. Quick ratio			
n. Free cash flow			
o. Cash flow from operations to current debt + Dividends			
p. Debt/Worth			

b. Write a memo for the audit file with your conclusions regarding analytical procedures performed in audit planning. Use the columnar format outlined below where you (1) identify significant differences noted when performing analytical procedures, and (2) explain the audit implications of the significant differences noted (e.g., state whether analytical procedures indicate that account balances are likely to be overstated or understated and identify assertions that are likely to be misstated).

SIGNIFICANT DIFFERENCES	AUDIT IMPLICATIONS
1.	
2.	
Etc.	

professional simulation

During July of 20x9 Kingston & Co., CPAs was planning the audit for Heykamp Hardware, that has a December 31 year-end. Heykamp Hardware has been a recurring audit for Kingston for the last eight years. Heykamp has sixteen locations in rural areas and enjoys little competition. During preliminary discussions with the CEO of Heykamp Hardware, you learn that Heykamp is planning on opening one to three new locations before year-end. Treat the following questions as independent from one another.

You are the in-charge accountant on Heykamp Hardware and you need to make preliminary decisions about materiality for audit planning purposes. This is your first job as an in-charge accountant and you are discussing the process with another colleague in the office. You have interim financial statements for the first six months of the year, but you are concerned that year-end results might differ significantly from the first six months because the company can expand by adding one to three new locations before year-end. Your colleague is unconcerned. He states that it is common for the auditor's preliminary judgment about materiality to differ from the judgment about materiality used in evaluating the audit findings.

Is your colleague correct? What do the professional standards say about whether the auditor's preliminary judgment about materiality may differ from the judgement about materiality used in evaluating the audit findings?

1. Answer this question by indicating the appropriate AU section paragraph(s) that address this issue. AU Section Paragraph(s) _____

2. Answer the following question. If the auditor uses a judgment about materiality in evaluating audit findings that is significantly different from the judgment used in audit planning, what are the implications for the sufficiency of audit procedures already performed?

In planning the audit of Heykamp Hardware you obtain the following results when performing analytical procedures.

RATIO	UNAUDITED RATIO	AUDITOR'S EXPECTATION RANGE
Accounts Receivable Turn Days	39 days	28 days–34 days
Sales and Accounts Receivable	Sales Growth: 12%	Sales Growth: 12%–15%
Growth Rates	Accounts Receivable Growth: 21%	Accounts Receivable Growth: 12%–15%

Write a memo to the audit file explaining the planning implications associated with the audit findings above. Identify account balances are likely to be overstated or understated and identify assertions that are likely to be misstated.

To: Audit File

Re: Analysis of results of analytical procedures

From: CPA Candidate

FRAUD IS ON THE RISE: RESULTS OF THE KPMG FRAUD SURVEY 2003

In the spring of 2003, KPMG Forensic commissioned phone interviews with 459 executives of public companies with revenues of $250 million or more, as well as individuals from state and federal government agencies. They found that 75 percent of these organizations had experienced fraud in the last 12 months, a 13 percent increase over the results of their 1998 survey.

Following is a brief summary of the frequency and magnitude of the types of fraud discovered.

Type of Fraud	Percentage Experiencing Fraud in the Last 12 mo.	Average Annual Cost of Fraud ($000)
Fraudulent financial reporting	7%	$ 257,932[a]
Medical/Insurance fraud	12%	$ 33,709
Consumer fraud	32%	$ 2,705
Vendor related, third-party fraud	25%	$ 759
Misconduct	15%	$ 732
Employee fraud	60%	$ 464
Computer crime	18%	$ 67

[a] One company reported costs of financial reporting fraud of $4 billion.

Assessing the risk of fraud is challenging because the types of fraud that are least frequent, fraudulent financial reporting and medical and insurance fraud, are also the most expensive. As a result, auditors need to develop skills at separating the ordinary from the unusual.

The 2003 KPMG Fraud Survey reports surprisingly high percentage rates for the incidence of fraud. Fraud is not something that happens less than 1 percent of the time. Even fraudulent financial reporting does not appear to be a rare event. One in 14 of the companies surveyed reported that they had experienced fraudulent financial reporting in the last 12 months, and the cost of this type of fraud is very high.

In addition, the survey identified factors that contributed to the fraud in the organization. The frequency of reporting underlying factors from fraud surveys in 2003, 1998, and 1994 is as follows.

Factors Contributing to Fraud	2003	1998	1994
Collusion between employees and third parties	48%	31%	33%
Inadequate internal controls	39%	58%	59%
Management override of internal controls	31%	36%	36%
Collusion between employees and management	15%	19%	23%
Lack of control over management by directors	12%	11%	6%
Ineffective/Nonexistent ethics or compliance program	10%	8%	7%

The quality of procedures performed in the risk assessment process, including recognizing factors that are associated with the occurrence of fraud, has a significant influence on the effectiveness of audit tests in detecting material misstatements. Chapter 9 explores the audit risk model in more detail, including an emphasis on the risk of fraud.

Source: KPMG 2003 Fraud Survey.

[PREVIEW OF CHAPTER 9]

Figure 7-4 describes six key steps in performing risk assessment procedures. This chapter focuses on two of those steps: consider audit risk, including the risk of fraud, and develop preliminary audit strategies for significant financial statement assertions. The following diagram provides an overview of the chapter organization and content.

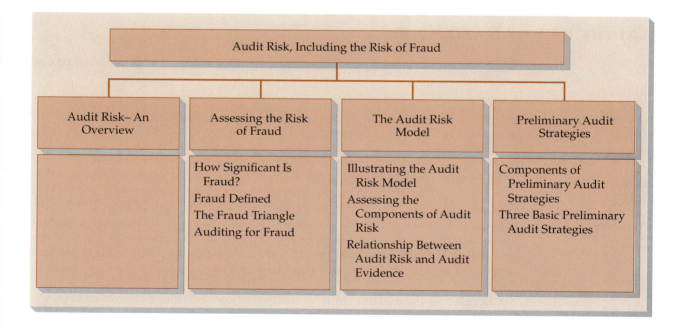

Chapter 9 focuses on risk assessment procedures associated with assessing the risk for fraud, other inherent risk, and using the audit risk model to develop preliminary audit strategies for various assertions. This chapter addresses the following aspects of the auditor's knowledge and the auditor's decision process.

focus on auditor knowledge

After studying this chapter you should understand the following aspects of an auditor's knowledge base:

K1. Know the importance of the concept of audit risk and its individual components.

K2. Know the definition of fraud and its two major components.

K3. Understand the relationship between inherent risk, control risk, analytical procedures risk, and test of details risk.

K4. Understand the relationship between detection risk and audit evidence.

focus on audit decisions

After studying this chapter you should understand the factors that influence the following audit decisions.

D1. What three conditions are generally present when fraud occurs?

D2. What risk assessment procedures should be used to assess the risk of fraud?

D3. What factors influence the auditor's assessment of inherent risk?

D4. How does an auditor develop a preliminary audit strategy for various assertions?

[AUDIT RISK—AN OVERVIEW]

Audit Risk and Materiality in Conducting an Audit, AU 312.02, defines audit risk as follows:

> **Audit risk** is the risk that the auditor may unknowingly fail to appropriately modify his or her opinion on financial statements that are materially misstated.

Auditor Knowledge 1

■ **Know the importance of the concept of audit risk and its individual components.**

The overall concept of audit risk is the inverse of the concept of reasonable assurance. The more certain the auditor wants to be of expressing the correct opinion, the lower will be the audit risk he or she is willing to accept. If 99 percent certainty is desired, audit risk is 1 percent, whereas if 95 percent certainty is considered satisfactory, audit risk is 5 percent. Usually professional judgments regarding reasonable assurance and the overall level of audit risk are set as a matter of audit firm policy, and audit risk will be comparable from one audit to another.

Recall that the auditor controls neither inherent risk nor control risk. Inherent risk and control risk are client-related factors. The auditor performs risk assessment procedures to develop a knowledgeable perspective about the risk factors that are present in a client's situation. Armed with this knowledge, the auditor then designs further audit procedures that are responsive to the client's risk factors.

What does the auditor need to know about the client to develop a knowledgeable perspective? The auditor needs to know enough so that he or she can:

- Relate risk to potential misstatements in the financial statements, either at the financial statement level (risks that have a pervasive effect on the financial statements) or the assertion level (risks that relate to particular assertions).
- Consider whether risks are of a magnitude that will result in a material misstatement in the financial statements.
- Consider the likelihood that risks will result in material misstatements.

The next sections of this chapter devote substantial attention to the risk assessment procedures associated with understanding the risk of fraud and the assessment of inherent risk. It then discusses the audit risk model in more detail and explains how the auditor makes a preliminary assessment of risk in order to make preliminary decisions about the collection of audit evidence.

ASSESSING THE RISK OF FRAUD

HOW SIGNIFICANT IS FRAUD?

Fraudulent financial reporting got everyone's attention with the collapse of Enron and WorldCom when investors lost approximately $66 billion and $176 billion respectively. The evidence shows that these were not isolated instances. The KPMG Fraud Survey reported that 7% of the companies surveyed had problems with fraudulent financial reporting. The GAO *Report on Financial Statement Restatement* identified 919 restatements of public company financial statements (approximately 6 percent of all public companies) between January 1997 and June 30, 2002. The *2004 Report to the Nation* by the Association of Certified Fraud Examiners reports on 508 individual fraud cases that resulted in over $761 million in losses. The victims of fraud reported in this study appeared in every segment of our economy; 42 percent in privately held companies, 30 percent in publicly traded companies, 16 percent in government, and 12 percent in not-for-profit organizations.

Generally accepted auditing standards recognize a responsibility for finding these types of material misstatements and state that the auditor has a responsibility to plan and perform the audit to obtain reasonable assurance about whether the financial statements are free of material misstatement, whether caused by error or fraud (AU 110.02). GAAS (AU 316–SAS 99) requires auditors to perform specific risk assessment procedures *in every audit* to assess the risk of fraud, both due to fraudulent financial reporting and misappropriation of assets. These responsibilities are explained in more detail in the following sections.

FRAUD DEFINED

Auditor Knowledge 2

- Know the definition of fraud and its two major components.

Fraud is a broad legal concept. Auditors are not lawyers and do not make legal decisions about the legal specifications of fraud. However, auditors are interested in acts that result in a material misstatement of the financial statements. From the auditor's perspective, the primary factor that distinguishes fraud from error is whether the underlying action that results in the misstatement of the financial statements is intentional or unintentional. Generally accepted auditing standards define fraud as follows:

Fraud is an intentional act that results in a material misstatement in financial statements that are the subject of an audit.

A footnote to this definition goes on to point out the difficulty of evaluating intent, "particularly in matters involving accounting estimates and the application of accounting principles. For example, unreasonable accounting estimates may be unintentional or may be the result of an intentional attempt to misstate the financial statements. Although an audit is not designed to determine intent, the auditor has a responsibility to plan and perform the audit to obtain reasonable assurance about whether the financial statements are free of material misstatement, whether the misstatement is intentional or not."

Source: AU 316.05.

Auditors are particularly concerned about two types of misstatements that are relevant to the auditor's consideration of fraud—misstatements arising from fraudulent financial reporting and misstatements arising from misappropriation of assets, which are defined as follows:

Misstatements arising from **fraudulent financial reporting** are intentional misstatements or omissions of amounts or disclosures in financial statements designed to deceive financial statement users where the effect causes the financial statements not to be presented, in all material respects, in conformity with generally accepted accounting principles (GAAP). Fraudulent financial reporting may be accomplished by the following:

- Manipulation, falsification, or alteration of accounting records or supporting documents from which financial statements are prepared
- Misrepresentation in or intentional omission from the financial statements of events, transactions, or other significant information
- Intentional misapplication of accounting principles relating to amounts, classification, manner of presentation, or disclosure

Fraudulent financial reporting need not be the result of a grand plan or conspiracy. It may be that management representatives rationalize the appropriateness of a material misstatement, for example, as an aggressive rather than indefensible interpretation of complex accounting rules, or as a temporary misstatement of financial statements, including interim statements, expected to be corrected later when operational results improve.

Misstatements arising from **misappropriation of assets** (sometimes referred to as theft or defalcation) involve the theft of an entity's assets where the effect of the theft causes the financial statements not to be presented, in all material respects, in conformity with GAAP. Misappropriation of assets can be accomplished in various ways, including embezzling receipts, stealing assets, or causing an entity to pay for goods or services that have not been received. Misappropriation of assets may be accompanied by false or misleading records or documents, possibly created by circumventing controls.

The standards go on to state that the auditor's primary concern is only with those misappropriations of assets for which the effect of the misappropriation causes the financial statements not to be fairly presented, in all material respects, in conformity with GAAP.

Source: AU 316.06.

Hence, when the auditor attempts to develop a knowledgeable perspective about the risk of fraud, the auditor is primarily concerned about intentional actions that cause the financial statements to be materially misstated. The auditor should be equally concerned about misstatements arising from fraudulent financial reporting and misappropriation of assets. It is essential that the auditor be alert to factors that increase the risk of material misstatement due to fraud. These risk factors are discussed in the next section.

THE FRAUD TRIANGLE

Audit Decision 1

■ **What three conditions are generally present when fraud occurs?**

In order to make decisions about the risk of fraud, the auditor should understand that three conditions are generally present when fraud occurs. These are known as the three corners of the "fraud triangle" depicted in Figure 9-1.

1. **Incentives/Pressures.** Management or other employees have an incentive or are under pressure, which provides a reason to commit fraud.
2. **Opportunity.** Existing circumstances provide an opportunity for fraud to be perpetrated, such as the ability of management to override controls, the absence of controls, or ineffective controls.
3. **Rationalization.** Those involved in committing fraud are able to rationalize the fraudulent behavior. In other words, some individuals possess an attitude, character, or set of ethical values that allow them to knowingly and intentionally commit a dishonest act.

These three characteristics also interact with each other. For example, individuals who might otherwise be honest might commit fraud and intentionally misstate financial information, in an environment that imposes sufficient pressure on them.

Fraudulent Financial Reporting

Fraudulent financial reporting is a serious problem for auditors of public companies and, in some cases, private companies. The problem goes beyond the few instances of WorldCom, Waste Management, and Enron. As previously noted, the 2003 KPMG Fraud Survey found that 7 percent of the respondents said that they experienced fraudulent financial reporting problems, and the GAO study found that nearly 6 percent of public companies reported restatements of previously reported earnings. The incentives and pressures on chief financial officers are sig-

Figure 9-1 ■ The Fraud Triangle

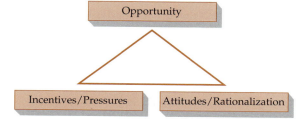

nificant. In a 1998 *Business Week* survey 67 percent of CFO's indicated that they had been asked to materially misstate earnings.[1] A similar survey by *CFO Magazine* found that 45 percent of CFOs indicated that they had been asked to materially misstate earnings.[2] These are extraordinarily high percentages. The incentives to achieve targets and attain bonuses, and the pressures associated with not meeting analysts estimates, are enormous in public companies. Auditors must be alert for the types of risk factors that are often associated with fraudulent financial reporting. Examples of these factors are presented in Figure 9-2.

The greatest opportunities for fraudulent financial reporting exist with complex transactions and accounting estimates that are difficult to corroborate. Perhaps the best way to mitigate the incentives and reduce the opportunity for fraud begins with the board of directors and its audit committee. Effective oversight of the financial reporting process by competent directors with significant financial reporting experience can create a tone at the top of the organization that expects representational faithfulness in financial reporting. This requires audit committee members who are capable of asking penetrating questions of management and auditors who are capable of identifying and understanding the economic substance of both complex transactions and accounting estimates. The opportunity is also reduced when senior management leads by example in making decisions that reinforce representational faithfulness in financial reporting. However, auditors must recognize that senior management is also in a position to make decisions that may not result in fair presentation in the financial statements, so this aspect of assessing the risk of fraudulent financial reporting needs careful review.

Finally, auditors should be alert to the signs of management attitudes or rationalizations that permit fraudulent financial reporting. This can reveal itself when nonfinancial management shows excessive participation in determining accounting results. When nonfinancial management shows an excessive preoccupation with the determination of accounting estimates, it may provide a signal that achieving earnings targets is more important than representational faithfulness in reporting results. Frauds rarely start with an original plot to materially misstate financial reports. Rather, there is significant evidence that fraudulent financial reporting begins with a series of immaterial misstatements that eventually result in bigger and bolder steps that lead to material misstated financial statement. When management feels that it is appropriate to justify marginal or inappropriate accounting based on the immateriality of items, it may signal a willingness to use accounting techniques (rather than underlying economic substance) to achieve financial goals. Figure 9-2 provides other examples of management attitudes or rationalizations that create situations allowing for fraudulent financial reporting.

Auditors must approach audits with a sufficient degree of professional skepticism and recognize the types of factors depicted in Figure 9-2. When even one or two of these factors are present, the auditor's knowledgeable perspective should lead to decisions to assess inherent risk or control risk at high levels.

---

[1] S. Shuster, "The Seventh Annual Business Week Forum of Chief Financial Officers," *Business Week*, July 13, 1998.
[2] S. Barr, "Misreporting Results," *CFO: The Magazine for Senior Financial Executives*, December, 1998, pp. 36–48.

Figure 9-2 ■ Risk Factors Associated with Fraudulent Financial Reporting

Risk Factors	Examples of High-Risk Conditions
Incentives/Pressures	Economic, Industry, and Operating Conditions ■ Low barriers to entry, high degree of competition combined with declining margins. ■ Vulnerability to technological change, product obsolescence, or interest rates. ■ Inability to generate operating cash flows. ■ Rapid growth in profitability compared to others in the industry. Pressure from third parties ■ There are optimistic or aggressive expectations regarding profitability, revenues, or other targets. ■ The company is close to debt covenants. Management's personal financial position is threatened by the entity's financial performance. ■ Management has significant financial interests in the entity. ■ A significant portion of management's compensation is based on bonuses tied to accounting numbers. Senior management places excessive pressure on other managers to meet financial targets.
Opportunity	The nature of the industry or the entity's operations provides opportunities to engage in fraudulent financial reporting that can arise from the following: ■ Significant related-party transactions not in the ordinary course of business or with related entities not audited or audited by another firm. ■ Assets, liabilities, revenues, or expenses based on significant estimates that involve subjective judgments or uncertainties that are difficult to corroborate. ■ Significant, unusual, or highly complex transactions, especially those close to period end that pose difficult "substance over form" questions. There is ineffective monitoring of management as a result of the following: ■ Domination of management by a single person or small group (in a nonowner-managed business) without compensating controls. ■ Ineffective board of directors or audit committee oversight over the financial reporting process. There is a complex or unstable organizational structure, as evidenced by the following: ■ Overly complex organizational structure involving unusual legal entities or managerial lines of authority. ■ High turnover of senior management, counsel, or board members. Internal control components are deficient as a result of the following: ■ Inadequate monitoring of controls, including automated controls. ■ High turnover rates or employment of ineffective accounting, internal audit, or information technology staff. ■ Ineffective accounting and information systems, including situations involving reportable conditions.

(continues)

Figure 9-2 ■ (Continued)

Risk Factors	Examples of High-Risk Conditions
Attitudes/Rationalization	■ Management and employees do not place a high priority on the entity's values or ethical standards. ■ Nonfinancial management shows excessive participation in, or preoccupation with, the selection of accounting principles or the determination of significant estimates. ■ Management shows an excessive interest in maintaining or increasing the entity's stock price or earnings trend. ■ Management is concerned about achieving commitments made to analysts, creditors, and other third parties regarding aggressive or unrealistic forecasts. ■ Management places a low priority on correcting known weaknesses in internal controls on a timely basis. ■ Management attempts to justify marginal or inappropriate accounting on the basis of materiality on a recurring basis.

Misappropriation of Assets

The KPMG 2003 Fraud Survey also shows a high frequency of problems such as vendor fraud (which usually involves collusion with employees), employee fraud, management and employee misconduct, and computer fraud. The goal of these behaviors is usually misappropriation of assets. Figure 9-3 provides examples of the types of risk factors that are often associated with misappropriation of assets.

The incentives and pressures that motivate employees to engage in fraud range from employees that have a grudge associated with management because an expected promotion or bonus was not earned, to those whose benefits or other compensation were lost, or who were exposed to the uncertainty associated with possible layoff. For example, a loyal bookkeeper denied a $100 monthly raise may find other ways to obtain the raise. Employees may have a variety of motivations that are difficult to identify, such as having to pay bills associated with gambling debts, sending children to private school, covering an investment loss, or living beyond one's means. Alternatively, an employee might invest in a business opportunity, the opportunity goes bust, and the employee makes up the loss by finding a way to embezzle assets from a company. Many of these motivations are not obvious, and the auditor often picks up clues by comments overheard in lunchrooms or in other casual conversations with employees.

Opportunity is the second, and critical, aspect of the fraud triangle. Employees involved in the misappropriation of assets usually have access to cash, inventory, or various assets that can be easily converted into cash. When employees see that internal controls are weak, it provides an opportunity for fraud. The *2002 Report to the Nation* by the Association of Certified Fraud Examiners reported that 86 percent of fraud cases were deemed to have insufficient internal control or to have allowed its controls to be ignored by its employees or management. For example, a purchasing agent might exploit weak controls to have assets shipped to a home rather than to the business and have the business pay the invoice. The opportunity for fraud can be mitigated by a strong system of internal control. The key

Figure 9-3 ■ Risk Factors Associated with Misappropriation of Assets

Risk Factors	Examples of High-Risk Conditions
Incentives/Pressures	Personal financial obligations may create pressure on management or employees with access to cash or other assets susceptible to theft to misappropriate those assets. Adverse relationships between the entity and employees with access to cash or other assets susceptible to theft may motivate those employees to misappropriate those assets. For example, adverse relationships may be created by the following: ■ Known or anticipated future employee layoffs. ■ Recent or anticipated changes to employee compensation or benefit plans. ■ Promotions, compensation, or other rewards inconsistent with expectations.
Opportunity	Certain characteristics or circumstances may increase the susceptibility of assets to misappropriation. For example, opportunities to misappropriate assets increase when there are the following: ■ Large amounts of cash on hand or processed. ■ Inventory items that are small in size, of high value, or in high demand. ■ Easily convertible assets, such as bearer bonds, diamonds, or computer chips. Inadequate internal control over assets may increase the susceptibility of misappropriation of those assets. For example, misappropriation of assets may occur because there is the following: ■ Inadequate segregation of duties or independent checks. ■ Inadequate recordkeeping with respect to assets. ■ Inadequate system of authorization and approval of transactions (for example, in purchasing). ■ Inadequate physical safeguards over cash, investments, inventory, or fixed assets. ■ Lack of complete and timely reconciliations of assets. Inadequate management understanding of information technology, which enables information technology employees to perpetrate a misappropriation such as inadequate access controls over automated records, including controls over and review of computer systems event logs.
Rationalization	■ Disregard for the need for monitoring or reducing risks related to misappropriations of assets. ■ Disregard for internal control over misappropriation of assets by overriding existing controls or by failing to correct known internal control deficiencies. ■ Behavior indicating displeasure or dissatisfaction with the company or its treatment of the employee. ■ Changes in behavior or lifestyle that may indicate assets have been misappropriated.

aspects of a good system of internal control are discussed in depth in the next chapter but (1) good segregation of duties, (2) appropriate authorization of transactions, and (3) accurate records that are regularly compared with assets minimize the opportunity for employee fraud.

When assets are misappropriated, individuals usually find ways to rationalize the behavior by putting their personal well-being ahead of their responsibilities to their employers. Sometimes individuals rationalize their behavior by believing that they are only doing what others have done. Sometimes individuals start by believing that the amount is small and they will pay it back. Soon they find that the small amount goes undetected, and they forget about paying it back and find themselves "hooked" on their new source of cash. In some cases employees feel that their talents have been overlooked, and they see fraud as a form of compensation. An individual's ability to rationalize fraudulent behavior is difficult to detect because an auditor cannot audit someone's thoughts. Auditors should be alert to clues that might show up in an individual's behavior, such as not taking vacations so that they can continue to cover up fraud or not cooperating in correcting known deficiencies in internal controls.

Finally, auditors should not assume that all three conditions (incentives/pressures, opportunity, and rationalization) must be observed before concluding that there are identified risks of fraud. Incentives and rationalization may be difficult to observe. Management or employees may actively try to hide some of the risk factors and cover up the existence of fraud. Professional standards are clear that, although the risk of material misstatement due to fraud may be greatest when all three fraud conditions are observed or evidenced, the auditor cannot assume that the inability to observe one or two of these conditions means that the risk of material misstatement due to fraud is low.

AUDITING FOR FRAUD

Risk Assessment Procedures

Audit Decision 2

■ What risk assessment procedures should be used to assess the risk of fraud?

What procedures should auditors perform to support a decision about the risk of material misstatement due to fraud? Professional standards on the *Consideration of Fraud in the Financial Statement Audit* (AU 316–SAS 99) suggest that auditors should perform the following procedures to identify the risk of material misstatement due to fraud.

■ Make inquiries of management and others within the entity to obtain their views about the risk of fraud and how it is addressed.

■ Consider any unusual or unexpected relationships that have been identified in performing analytical procedures in audit planning.

■ Consider other information obtained while planning the audit.

Auditors usually make a series of inquiries about management's views regarding the risk of fraud and policies that have been established to mitigate those risks. For example, auditors should inquire of management about whether management has knowledge of any fraud, suspected fraud, or allegations of fraud affecting the entity. The auditor should also understand how management communicates to employees its views on business practices and ethical behavior. Auditors usually begin by making inquiries of management about their awareness of fraud risk and programs that have been put in place to prevent or detect fraud. Auditors should also make direct inquiries of the audit committee (or at least its chair) regarding the audit committee's view of the risk of fraud and the audit committee's oversight in this area. Finally, auditors usually find that it is helpful to conduct discussions with employees with varying levels of authority, including operating

how is fraud detected?
results of the KPMG Fraud Survey 2003

Companies discover fraud through a variety of means. For example, internal controls or anonymous tips might trigger an internal audit investigation. Good internal controls might create the opportunity for unusual transactions to be reported by vendors or customers. The following table summarizes a number of methods used to uncover fraud as reported in the KPMG Fraud Surveys of 2003, 1998, and 1994.

Methods of Uncovering Fraud	2003	1998	1994
Internal controls	77%	51%	52%
Internal audit	65%	43%	47%
Notification by employee	63%	58%	51%
Accident	54%	37%	28%
Anonymous tip	41%	35%	26%
Notification by customer	34%	41%	34%
Notification by regulator/law enforcement	19%	16%	8%
Notification by vendor	16%	11%	15%
External audit	12%	4%	5%

Companies regularly consider the types of policies and activities that they use to mitigate or prevent the occurrence of fraud. The following table summarizes a variety of fraud mitigation policies that companies instituted in the 12 months prior to the 2003 KPMG Fraud Survey.

Fraud Mitigation Policies Instituted in the Last 12 Months	%
Strengthened internal controls	75%
Instituted periodic compliance audits	44%
Created an employee hotline	42%
Appointed compliance personnel	41%
Established a code of conduct for all employees	40%
Conducted background checks for hires with budgetary responsibility	38%
Instituted fraud awareness training	28%
Tied employee evaluation to ethics or compliance objectives	24%
Other policies	19%

personnel not directly involved in the financial reporting process, and employees involved in initiating, recording, or processing complex or unusual transactions (e.g., sales transactions with multiple elements). Responses to inquiries might serve to corroborate management's representations, or they might provide information such as employees describing instances of management override of controls. When the auditor obtains inconsistent responses, he or she should obtain additional information to resolve the inconsistencies.

Analytical procedures performed in audit planning (discussed in the previous chapter) may be helpful in identifying accounts and assertions that are likely to contain misstatements. For example, an increase in gross margins combined with an increase in the number of inventory turn days may indicate that production costs have been capitalized that should be expensed. These results might also indicate problems with recording fictitious inventory. Furthermore, a comparison of revenues and sales returns by month during the year and shortly after year-end may indicate the existence of undisclosed side agreements with customers that preclude revenue recognition. However, the auditor should also be aware that analytical procedures that compare only financial numbers might be ineffective in finding fraudulent financial reporting. In the case of fraud, the numbers may have been made to look reasonable. As a result, auditors often attempt to compare financial results with nonfinancial measures of business activity, such as comparing inventory quantities and values with direct labor hours.

Finally, the auditor should consider other information obtained during audit planning. Auditors may, for example, pick up clues about the risk of fraud when performing client acceptance and retention procedures (Chapter 7), such as concerns about the integrity of management or challenges in recording complex transaction noted by the predecessor auditor. A continuing auditor might review the prior year's internal control letter to determine whether identified weaknesses in internal control have been corrected. Auditors might find that a company is very close to significant debt covenants when obtaining an understanding of the entity and its environment (Chapter 7). Finally, auditors have a professional requirement to understand the entity's system of internal control (discussed in Chapter 10). Weak internal controls provide the opportunity for fraud. The auditor should consider all the information acquired while performing risk assessment procedures in order to develop a knowledgeable perspective about the risk of fraud.

Brainstorming Session

GAAS (AU 316) requires the audit team members to discuss the risk of fraud as part of audit planning. This **brainstorming session** has several objectives. The brainstorming session should:

- Allow junior members of the audit team to benefit from more senior members' knowledge of the audit client and of how fraud might be perpetrated.
- Allow more seasoned personnel a fresh set of eyes that might identify risks that otherwise might be overlooked.
- Allows audit management to set the appropriate tone for the audit and to emphasize the importance of approaching the audit with a "questioning mind."
- Emphasize the possibility that fraud might exist in any audit.

The primary goal is to consider audit areas where the entity is most vulnerable to the risk that fraud could result in material misstatements in the financial statements. For example, the audit team might consider pressures faced by management to meet debt covenants or pressures from an owner-manager that expects certain levels of entity performance.

An important goal is to link the risk factors to specific account balances or assertions that are likely to be misstated. For example, one person's discussion with the purchasing agent, and a review of the purchases journal, may indicate that a high volume of business is directed to one vendor. However, another person's discussion with an owner-manager may provide no indication of establishing an exclusive supply relationship with a vendor. If there is a high volume of transactions that can be material to the financial statements, the audit team may want to design procedures to review the reasonableness of prices (the valuation and allocation assertion) in this aspect of the purchases cycle to evaluate the potential for vendor kickbacks to a purchasing agent. All three aspects of the fraud triangle may not be apparent. There may be valid business reasons for the situations. Nevertheless, the auditor needs to respond by assessing inherent or control risk as high, and by designing audit procedures that restrict detection risk to a low level.

Specific Risks

Fraudulent financial reporting often happens as a result of revenue misstatements (AU 316.41). Management may recognize revenue prematurely or record fictitious revenues in order to meet financial market expectations. Management may also understate revenues during periods of strong performance in order to shift sales to the subsequent period. As a result, auditors should approach the audit with a presumption that improper revenue recognition is a fraud risk.

Professional standards also state that even if the auditor does not identify specific fraud risks, there is a possibility that management override of internal controls could occur. Management is in a unique position to perpetrate fraud because of its ability to, directly or indirectly, manipulate accounting records and prepare fraudulent financial statements. As a result, auditors should perform certain procedures to address the risk of management override of controls. For example, auditors should examine journal entries and other adjustments for evidence of possible material misstatement due to fraud.

In summary, a significant aspect of developing a knowledge perspective about the risk involves explicit discussion and evaluation of fraud risk factors. Auditors should (1) perform procedures to understand the relevant aspect of the fraud triangle (see Figures 9-1, 9-2, and 9-3) so that they can make informed decisions about the risk of material misstatement due to fraud. Once specific risk factors are identified, the auditor should evaluate whether they are of a (2) magnitude and a (3) likelihood that they will result in material misstatements in the financial statements.

[LEARNING CHECK

9-1 Provide some of the evidence regarding the significance of fraud in the United States.

9-2 Define fraud and the two components of fraud that are relevant to the auditor's decisions about the risk of fraud in the financial statement audit.

9-3 a. What are the three elements of the fraud triangle?
  b. Develop an example of a high-risk situation related to fraudulent financial reporting where all three elements of the fraud triangle are present.
  c. Develop an example of a high-risk situation related to misappropriation of assets where all three elements of the fraud triangle are present. In parts (b) and (c) link your examples to specific risks at the financial statement level or the assertion level.

9-4   Describe the risk assessment procedures used by auditors to identify risks of material misstatements in the financial statements due to fraud.

9-5   Identify four objectives of the "brainstorming session" performed by the audit team in the risk assessment process.

9-6   Explain two specific risks of fraud that the auditor should always consider in every audit. How should the auditor respond to these risks when making decisions about the risk of material misstatement.

[KEY TERMS

Audit risk, 352
Brainstorming session, p. 362
Fraud, p. 354
Fraudulent financial reporting, p. 354

Incentives/Pressures, p. 355
Misappropriation of assets, p. 354
Opportunity, p. 355
Rationalization, p. 355

[THE AUDIT RISK MODEL]

Chapter 5 introduced the three components of audit risk as inherent risk, control risk, and detection risk. The audit risk concept is particularly important for several reasons. First, it provides a framework for making decisions about the risk of financial statement misstatement. Second, the audit risk model provides a framework for making decisions about the appropriate level of detection risk. For a specified level of audit risk, there is an inverse relationship between assessed levels of inherent and control risks and the level of detection risk that an auditor can accept for an assertion. Thus, the lower the assessments of inherent and control risks, the higher the acceptable level of detection risk.

ILLUSTRATING THE AUDIT RISK MODEL

Auditor Knowledge 3

■ Understand the relationship between inherent risk, control risk, analytical procedures risk, and test of details risk.

The **audit risk model** expresses the relationship among the audit risk components as follows:

$$AR = IR \times CR \times DR$$

The symbols represent audit, inherent, control, and detection risk, respectively. To illustrate the use of the model, assume that the auditor has made the following risk assessments for a particular assertion, such as the existence or occurrence assertion for inventories.

$$AR = 5\% \quad IR = 75\% \quad CR = 50\%$$

Detection risk can be determined as follows:

$$DR = \frac{AR}{IR \times CR} = \frac{0.05}{0.75 \times 0.50} = 13\%$$

A 13 percent detection risk means the auditor needs to plan substantive tests in such a way that there is an acceptable risk that they will have approximately a 13 percent chance of failing to detect material misstatements. This risk is acceptable if the auditor has evidence from risk assessment procedures and tests of controls to support the inherent and control risk assessments.

The Appendix to AU 350, *Audit Sampling* (SAS Nos. 39, 43, and 45), contains an expanded audit risk model that subdivides detection risk into two components: AP for analytical procedures risk and TD for the risk associated with substantive tests of details risk (tests of transactions and tests of balances). **Analytical procedures risk** is the risk that substantive analytical procedures will fail to detect material misstatements in the financial statements. **Test of details risk** is the risk that test of details of transactions and balances will fail to detect material misstatements in the financial statements. Hence, the relationship among audit risk components can be expressed as follows:

$$AR = IR \times CR \times AP \times TD$$

For purposes of illustration assume that the auditor has sufficient evidence to support the following risk assessments:

$$AR = 2\% \quad IR = 100\% \quad CR = 10\% \quad and \ AP = 50\%$$

Test of details risk can be determined as follows:

$$TD = \frac{AR}{IR \times CR \times AP} = \frac{0.02}{1.0 \times 0.10 \times 0.5} = 40\%$$

A 40 percent test of details risk means the auditor needs to plan tests of transactions and tests of balances in such a way that there is an acceptable risk that they will have approximately a 40 percent chance of failing to detect material misstatements. This risk is acceptable if the auditor has evidence from risk assessment procedures, tests of controls, and effective analytical procedures to support the inherent, control, and analytical procedures risk assessments. The expanded audit risk model provides the auditor with the tool to consider the assurance that is obtained by performing substantive analytical procedures. (The expanded audit risk model will be used throughout the remainder of the text.)

When the audit risk model is used in the planning phase to determine the planned detection risk for an assertion, CR is often based on the auditor's planned assessed level of control risk. If it is subsequently determined that the actual level of control risk for an assertion differs from the planned level, the model should be reapplied using the actual assessed level for CR. The revised detection risk is then used in finalizing the design of substantive tests of transactions or tests of balances.

In practice, many auditors do not attempt to quantify each of the risk components, making it impossible to mathematically solve the risk model. However, even when not solved mathematically, familiarity with the model makes the following relationships clear: to hold audit risk to a specified level, the higher the assessed levels of inherent, control, and analytical procedures risks, the lower will be the assessed levels of risk for tests of details.

Risk Components Matrix

Some auditors who use nonquantitative expressions for risk use a **risk components matrix** like the one shown in Figure 9-4. Study of the matrix indicates that

Figure 9-4 ■ Risk Components Matrix (Test of Details Risk in Bold)

Inherent Risk Assessment	Control Risk Assessment	Risk that Analytical Procedures Will Not Detect Material Misstatements			
		High	**Moderate**	**Low**	**Very Low**
Maximum	Maximum	Very low	Very low	Very low	Low
	High	Very low	Very low	Low	Moderate
	Moderate	Very low	Low	Moderate	High
	Low	Low	Moderate	High	X
High	Maximum	Very low	Very low	Low	Moderate
	High	Very low	Low	Moderate	High
	Moderate	Low	Moderate	High	X
	Low	Moderate	High	X	X
Moderate	Maximum	Very low	Low	Moderate	High
	High	Low	Moderate	High	a
	Moderate	Moderate	High	a	a
	Low	High	a	a	a
Low	Maximum	Low	Moderate	High	a
	High	Moderate	High	a	a
	Moderate	High	a	a	a
	Low	a	a	a	a

X—This strategy is not appropriate as it is unlikely that audit evidence from substantive analytical procedures alone will provide sufficient, competent evidence related to an assertion with significant inherent risks.
[a] Substantive tests of details may not be necessary.

it is consistent with the audit risk model in that the acceptable levels of test of details risk are inversely related to inherent, control, and analytical procedures risk assessments. The matrix assumes that audit risk is restricted to a low level. The matrix indicates, for example, that if inherent risk is assessed at the maximum, control risk at moderate, and analytical procedures risk at moderate, the acceptable level of detection risk for tests of details is low. If, however, inherent risk is assessed at moderate, control risk is assessed at low, and analytical procedures risk is assessed at low, other substantive tests may not be necessary. This assumes that sufficient, competent evidence is obtained by risk assessment procedures to support the auditor's risk assessments.

ASSESSING THE COMPONENTS OF AUDIT RISK

Figure 9-5 provides an overview of the steps involved in using the audit risk model. Before making decisions about the nature, timing, and extent of audit procedures, the auditor should develop a knowledgeable perspective about how misstatements in the financial statements might occur. The auditor does so by assessing inherent risk, control risk, and fraud risk. When considering the risk of fraud,

Figure 9-5 ■ Steps Involved in Using the Audit Risk Model

many auditors consider issues of incentives/pressures and rationalization as inherent risks, and evaluate opportunity as part of assessing control risks. Hence, it is important to consider the combined effect of both inherent and control risks before planning substantive audit procedures. The auditor then proceeds to make decisions about the appropriate use of substantive analytical procedures and tests of details.

Assessing Inherent Risk

Statements on Auditing Standards defines inherent risk as follows:

Inherent risk is the susceptibility of an assertion to a material misstatement, assuming that there are no controls.

Source: AU 312.27.

Audit Decision 3

■ What factors influence the auditor's assessment of inherent risk?

A significant aspect of developing a knowledgeable perspective includes understanding the susceptibility of an assertion to misstatement. In making a decision about inherent risk, the auditor should consider two types of risks; (1) risks that have a pervasive effect on the financial statements and may affect many accounts and assertions and (2) risks that may pertain only to a specific assertion for a specific account. Figure 9-6 provides some examples of each type of inherent risk. Once specific risk factors are identified, the auditor should evaluate whether they are of a (1) magnitude and a (2) likelihood that they will result in material misstatements in the financial statements. In addition, if significant inherent risks are identified, the auditor should respond by obtaining evidence about internal control during the current audit period and by obtaining significant evidence through tests of details of transactions and balances.

Figure 9-6 ■ Examples of Inherent Risk Factors

Examples of Pervasive Inherent Risk Factors	Influence on the Financial Statements
Low profitability of the entity relative to the industry or sensitivity of operating results to economic factors	If management is under pressure to deliver profitability in competitive economic conditions, management may consider ways to achieve profitability through a variety of uses of management discretion in financial reporting.
A company's experience of going-concern problems such as lack of working capital	Management often believes that receiving a going-concern opinion will be the last straw that causes a company to fail. Management may consider the use of management discretion in financial reporting to make financial reports appear better than the underlying financial position, results of operations, and cash flows of the entity in order to avoid a going-concern opinion.
The impact of technological developments on the company's operations and competitiveness	Changes that make a company's products less competitive may impact a variety of accounting estimates ranging from an inventory obsolescence reserve to a reserve for sales returns, to the allowance for doubtful accounts (because customers cannot resell inventory)
Management turnover, reputation, and accounting skills	If management has poor accounting skills, the auditor might expect multiple problems with the application of GAAP. If management is new to the entity, even if that management has strong accounting background, it often takes a period of time to understand the true underlying substance of the entity and accounting choices may be misapplied.

Examples of Assertion Specific Inherent Risk Factors	Influence on the Financial Statements
Difficult-to-audit accounts or transactions	A difficult to audit transaction might include the use of a special-purpose entity to lease property or to sell receivables. Inherent risk would be high related to those specific assertions that are affected by the transactions (including whether the entity should be consolidated).
Contentious or difficult accounting issues	The auditor might have a contentious accounting issue such as the content of disclosures for a related party transaction. This might affect the presentation and disclosures assertion only, or it might affect measurement issues with respect to the specific transaction.
Susceptibility to misappropriation	Inherent risk might be higher for the existence of a gold inventory than it would be for the existence of cut timber because the former might be easily misappropriated.
Complexity of calculations	The calculations associated with a dollar value LIFO valuation or the valuation of a large retail inventory using the retail method represents a significant inherent risk that is focused on the valuation assertion for inventory.

Pervasive inherent risk factors represent risk factors that affect multiple account balances and assertions. Many small-business audits, for example, involve situations where management does not have adequate accounting skills, and it is likely that management and employees may unintentionally misapply GAAP. The lack of adequate accounting skills could affect multiple transactions and multiple assertions in many accounts. There is also some evidence that the rate and magnitude of misstatements increases with the turnover of accounting employees. New employees have a start-up period during which they are acquiring an understanding of the relationship between the underlying economic substance of the entity and the entity's accounting issues. Finally, many of the factors that increase the incentives/pressures for fraudulent financial reporting affect the use of management's discretion in financial reporting throughout the financial statements.

On the other hand, other risk factors are account balance or assertion specific. For example, many inventories have unique valuation issues. If an auditor is auditing grain in a grain elevator, the auditor may need the assistance of an expert to (1) identify the specific grain held by the company and (2) run tests to determine whether the grain is subject to any disease or other problem that could affect its value. Long-term construction contacts often require significant estimates that affect the value of a few specific accounts related to the contract. The auditor might also be aware of specific problems that have recurred in prior audits where the client does not have the expertise in the company to properly account for particular transactions. Each of these represents account-specific problems that are unlikely to have a pervasive impact on the financial statements.

Identifying Significant Inherent Risks

Generally accepted auditing standards[3] state that the auditor should determine which of the identified risks are, in the auditor's judgment, significant inherent risks that require special audit consideration. Examples of **significant inherent risks** include the risk of fraud; recent economic, accounting, or other developments that require special attention; or a complex transaction (e.g., a client might engage in a sale and lease back arrangement with a related party that has complex terms associated with the agreement). A significant inherent risk is a matter of professional judgment. They usually involve significant accounting estimates, non-routine transactions, or the financial consequences of significant business risks. For example, underutilization of capacity could result in decreased profitability and cash flows compared to budgets or market expectations, and possible improper capitalization of excess capacity costs.

The auditor should identify significant inherent risks during audit planning, and the auditor should respond to significant inherent risks in ways that ensure that a high level of sufficient, competent evidence is obtained showing that these risks will not result in material misstatements in the financial statements. The auditor should respond to these significant inherent risks by (1) assessing inherent risk as maximum or high for relevant assertions, (2) obtaining evidence about

---

[3] The following discussion of significant inherent risks is based on an Auditing Standards Board Exposure Draft dated December 2, 2002 and recent exposure drafts that have been made public as part of the Auditing Standards Board agenda. A similar requirement was adopted by the International Auditing and Assurance Standards Board on October 31, 2003.

the effectiveness of design of internal controls related to the assertion, (3) ensuring that evidence about internal controls over significant inherent risks is obtained during the current audit period, and (4) obtaining significant evidence through tests of details of transactions and balances.

In addition, there may be some assertion where substantive tests alone will not reduce audit risk to a sufficiently low level. Increasingly, the initial information on a transaction is captured in electronic form. For example, banking transactions at automated teller machines (ATMs) do not leave a paper trail, and the only record that the bank has of the transaction is in electronic form. In these cases it is essential to test internal controls over the completeness and accuracy of ATM transactions.

Finally, inherent risks exist independently of the audit of financial statements. Thus, the auditor cannot change the actual level of inherent risk. Rather, the auditor performs risk assessment procedures to develop a knowledgeable perspective about the inherent risks that are present. The procedures performed to support the assessment of inherent risk include:

- Procedures associated with client acceptance and continuance decisions
- Procedures performed to understand the entity and its environment
- Analytical procedures
- Procedures performed to assess the risk of fraud
- Evidence obtained in performing previous audits
- Evaluation of other evidence obtained while performing the audit

In essence, the auditor uses all the information obtained while performing a variety of audit planning procedures to assess inherent risk.

Assessing Control Risk

Statements on Auditing Standards define control risk as follows:

> **Control risk** is the risk that a material misstatement that could occur in an assertion will not be prevented or detected on a timely basis by the entity's internal controls.
>
> *Source:* AU 312.27.

Making a decision about control risk is a function of the effectiveness of the client's internal controls. Effective internal controls over an assertion reduce control risk, whereas ineffective internal controls increase control risk. A good system of internal controls also has a significant effect on reducing the opportunity for fraud. Control risk can never be zero because internal controls cannot provide complete assurance that all material misstatements will be prevented or detected.

Although the auditor cannot change the actual level of control risk for an assertion, he or she can vary the assessed level of control risk by modifying (1) the procedures used to obtain an understanding of the internal controls related to the assertion and (2) the procedures used to perform tests of controls. The factors that influence the auditor's assessment of control risk are explained in detail in Chapters 10 and 11 of this text. Generally, a more extensive understanding and testing of internal controls are required when the auditor wishes to support a low assessed level of control risk.

Normally, auditors determine a **planned assessed level of control risk** for each assertion in the planning phase of the audit. Planned assessed levels are based on assumptions about the effectiveness of the design and operation of the client's internal controls. In repeat engagements, the planned assessed levels are often based on information in prior years' working papers. An **actual assessed level of control risk** is subsequently determined for each assertion based on evidence obtained from the study and evaluation of the client's system of internal control when performing further audit procedures in phase IV of the audit as explained in Chapter 5.

Assessing Detection Risk

Statements on Auditing Standards define detection risk as follows:

Detection risk is the risk that the auditor will not detect a material misstatement that exists in an assertion.

Source: AU 312.27.

Decisions about detection risk can be expressed as a combination of analytical procedures risk and test of details risk. Analytical procedures risk and tests of details risk are controlled by the effectiveness of auditing procedures and their application by the auditor. Unlike inherent and control risk, the actual level of analytical procedures risk or test of details risk can be changed by the auditor by varying the nature, timing, and extensiveness of substantive tests performed on an assertion. Recall from Chapter 6 the factors that influence the reliability of audit evidence. The use of more effective audit procedures results in a lower detection risk than is possible with less effective audit procedures. Similarly, substantive tests performed at or near the balance sheet date rather than at an interim date, or the use of a larger rather than smaller sample result in lower levels of detection risk.

In the planning phase of the audit, a **planned acceptable level of detection risk** for analytical procedures and for tests of details is determined for each significant assertion using the audit risk model discussed above. These planning decisions about the design of substantive tests are discussed extensively in Chapter 12. The planned levels of detection risk should be revised, when necessary, based on evidence obtained about the effectiveness of internal controls or specific audit findings.

It is not appropriate under GAAS for the auditor to conclude that inherent and control risks are so low that it is not necessary to perform any substantive tests for all of the assertions pertaining to an account. Some evidence must always be obtained from substantive tests for each material assertion in the financial statements.

RELATIONSHIP BETWEEN AUDIT RISK AND AUDIT EVIDENCE

Auditor Knowledge 4

■ **Understand the relationship between detection risk and audit evidence.**

The audit risk model is used to help the auditor develop a knowledgeable perspective about the risk of misstatement and make decisions about the sufficiency of evidential matter. In making generalizations about the audit risk model, care must be taken in specifying the risk term about which a generalization is being made.

Figure 9-7 ■ Interrelationship among Materiality, Detection Risk, and Substantive Audit Evidence

There is an inverse relationship between detection risk and the sufficiency and competency of evidence needed to support the auditor's opinion on the financial statements. That is, for a particular client, the lower the level of detection risk to be achieved, the greater the amount of evidence needed. For a particular assertion, the lower the acceptable level of analytical procedures risk or tests of details risk determined by the auditor, the greater the sufficiency and competency of substantive tests needed to restrict overall detection risk to that level.

Interrelationships among Materiality, Detection Risk, and Substantive Audit Evidence

In separate sections, we previously explained that there is an inverse relationship between materiality and audit evidence, and an inverse relationship between detection risk and the evidence obtained from substantive audit procedures. Figure 9-7 illustrates these relationships, as well as the interrelationships among all three concepts. For example, if in Figure 9-7, we hold detection risk constant and reduce the materiality level, more substantive audit evidence should be obtained. Similarly, if we hold the materiality level constant and increase detection risk (because of evidence obtained about low inherent risk or effective internal controls), less substantive audit evidence needs to be obtained. In general, if we wish to reduce detection risk, the auditor will normally obtain more persuasive evidence from substantive audit tests while holding the materiality level constant.

In addition, there is also an inverse relationship between the detection risk (or the combined assessments analytical procedures risk and test of details risk) and the sufficiency and competency of evidence needed to support a conclusion about an assertion. If the combined assessment of analytical procedures risk and tests of details risk results in a low risk that substantive tests will fail to detect a material misstatement, the auditor needs more sufficient and more competent evidence from analytical procedures and tests of details to support an audit conclusion about fair presentation of the assertion.

[LEARNING CHECK

9-7   Explain two distinct reasons why the audit risk concept is important.

9-8   a. Define inherent risk.

b. Explain the difference between pervasive inherent risk factors and account balance or assertion-specific inherent risk factors. Provide an example of each.

9-9 a. Define control risk.
   b. Can control risk be zero? Explain.
   c. What must the auditor do to support a control risk assessment below the maximum?

9-10 a. Define analytical procedures risk.
   b. What influences the planned assessed level of analytical procedures risk for an assertion?
   c. For assertions that represent significant inherent risks, can the auditor design effective analytical procedures that preclude the performance of tests of details of transactions?

9-11 a. Define test of details risk.
   b. What influences the planned assessed level of test of details risk for an assertion?

9-12 What is the relationship among the components of audit risk?

9-13 Generally, the auditor specifies an overall audit risk level for the financial statements as a whole and then uses the same level for each assertion. However, the levels of inherent risk, control risk, analytical procedures risk, and tests of details risk can vary by assertion. Explain.

9-14 Is it ever appropriate under GAAS for the auditor to conclude that inherent and control risks are so low that it is unnecessary to verify any assertion for a material account balance? Explain.

9-15 Explain the relationship between materiality, detection risk, and substantive audit evidence.

[KEY TERMS

Actual assessed level of control risk, p. 371
Analytical procedures risk, p. 365
Audit risk model, p. 364
Control risk, p. 370
Detection risk, p. 371
Inherent risk, p. 367

Planned acceptable level of detection risk, p. 371
Planned assessed level of control risk, p. 371
Risk components matrix, p. 365
Significant inherent risks, p. 369
Test of details risk, p. 365

[PRELIMINARY AUDIT STRATEGIES]

Audit Decision 4

■ How does an auditor develop a preliminary audit strategy for various assertions?

The auditor's ultimate objective is to perform a high-quality audit. He or she does so by collecting and evaluating evidence concerning the assertions contained in management's financial statements. Because of the interrelationships among materiality and the components of audit risk discussed earlier, the auditor may choose from among alternative preliminary audit strategies in planning the audit of individual assertions. In the remainder of this chapter, we identify the components of preliminary audit strategies, describe three alternative strategies, and explain their application in the context of long-term debt.

A **preliminary audit strategy** is not a detailed specification of audit procedures to be performed in completing the audit. Instead, it represents the auditor's preliminary decisions about an audit approach. In an initial audit, for example, the auditor is developing tentative conclusions about the relative emphasis to be given to various types of audit tests. In a repeat engagement, the specification of various components of a preliminary audit strategy might include a presumption by the auditor that risk assessments, analytical procedures, tests of controls, or tests of details used in the prior year will be appropriate for use in the current year as well. Final decisions on these matters are made as the audit progresses.

COMPONENTS OF PRELIMINARY AUDIT STRATEGIES

In developing preliminary audit strategies for assertions, the auditor specifies four components as follows:

1. The assessed level of inherent risk.
2. The planned assessed level of control risk considering:
   - The extent of understanding the internal controls to be obtained.
   - Tests of controls to be performed in assessing control risk.
3. The planned assessed level of analytical procedures risk considering:
   - The extent of the understanding of the business and industry to be obtained.
   - Analytical procedures to be performed that provide evidence about the fair presentation of an assertion.
4. The planned level of tests of details that, when combined with other procedures, reduces audit risk to an appropriately low level.

The manner in which the auditor specifies the four basic components of an audit strategy is explained in the following sections.

THREE BASIC PRELIMINARY AUDIT STRATEGIES

Figure 9-8 describes three common preliminary audit strategies in terms of the audit risk model. The following discussion illustrates each of these audit strategies for different assertions associated with the audit of long-term debt.

Figure 9-8 ■ Preliminary Audit Strategies and the Audit Risk Model

Audit Strategy	IR	CR	AP	TD
A response to lower inherent risk	Moderate or low	Moderate or low	Moderate or low	High or very high
A lower assessed level of control risk approach	Maximum	Low	Moderate, high, or maximum	Moderate or high
A primarily substantive approach	Maximum	High or maximum	Moderate, high, or maximum	Moderate to very low

Response to Lower Inherent Risk

Many assertions are not subject to complex calculations, misappropriation of assets, or accounting estimates. Consider the valuation assertion for long-term debt. The auditor is concerned about both the valuation of debt instruments (notes and bonds) and the valuation of interest expense. These calculations are not complex, and once the auditor is confident that all debt is recorded, the valuation assertion is relatively straightforward. This is not a high-inherent-risk assertion.

In this case, the auditor might attempt to emphasize the use of substantive analytical procedures in designing substantive tests. The emphasis on substantive analytical procedures assumes (1) reliable data is available for analytical procedures, (2) a reliable predictive model for estimating an account balance (e.g., interest expense is a function of interest rate, principle outstanding, and time outstanding), and (3) analytical procedures are less costly than other audit procedures. Hence, **a response to lower inherent risk** might specify the components of the audit strategy as follows:

- Assess inherent risk below the maximum for low-risk assertions.
- Use the knowledge of the entity and its environment to develop reliable analytical models that capture the underlying business drivers. For example, knowledge of the entity's need for external financing helps the auditor develop an expectation of outstanding principle amounts.
- Use a planned assessed level of analytical procedures risk that is as low as feasible. For example the auditor will often analytically test the reasonableness of interest expense by determining the average cost of financing.
- Use a planned assessed level of control risk that may be at moderate or low to provide assurance that the data used for analytical procedures is reliable. For example, the auditor may want to know that controls over the recording of principle outstanding are effective.
- Plan less extensive substantive tests of transactions and balances as a result of the risk reduction available from lower inherent risks, control risks, and effective analytical procedures.

The auditor might also use this strategy for lower inherent risk areas such as the valuation of prepaid expenses or accrued payroll liabilities. The auditor often obtains a significant understanding of the business and its underlying economic drivers when gaining an understanding of the entity and its environment. Auditors often use this information when developing expectations regarding account balances. For example, an auditor might have developed an analytical model from examining the relationship between nonfinancial measures of the volume of business activity, gross payroll, and accrued payroll taxes. If gross payroll and payroll taxes are consistent with expectations, the auditor may appropriately restrict the level of substantive tests of details.

A Lower Assessed Level of Control Risk Approach

Many audit assertions represent significant inherent risks. In this circumstance it is not appropriate for an auditor to consider an audit strategy that relies primarily on analytical procedures. Most public companies also have strong systems of internal control, and the auditor will usually plan to test those controls. If the controls are effective, the auditor will use the evidence obtained from tests of controls to modify the nature, timing, or extent of substantive tests. In this case the auditor will often follow a lower assessed level of the control risk approach.

Through **a lower assessed level of control risk approach,** the auditor specifies the components of the audit strategy as follows:

- Use a planned assessed level of control risk at moderate or low.
- Plan to obtain an extensive understanding of relevant portions of internal controls, particularly control activities.
- Plan tests of controls, probably testing computer controls embedded in the client's system.
- Plan restricted substantive tests of transactions or balances based on a moderate or high planned acceptable level of detection risk.

For example, companies often have strong controls over the existence of various debt instruments. Usually someone in the treasury function ensures that recorded debt instruments are the obligations of the entity. When debt is added to most financial statements, directors often want to know the underlying reason for the debt. As a result, controls are often strong in this area. As a result, the auditor will usually perform tests of controls to obtain evidence that controls are in fact effective. With evidence that internal controls are strong for an assertion, the auditor is justified in moving the timing of substantive tests to an interim date and reducing the extensiveness of substantive tests.

The auditor might choose this strategy anytime when he or she believes that controls related to an assertion are well designed and highly effective. This strategy usually means that the auditor will understand internal controls in considerable depth, including the effectiveness of computer general controls, and the specific characteristics of programmed control procedures. This will often be the case for assertions pertaining to accounts that are affected by a high volume of routine transactions such as sales, accounts receivable, inventory, purchases, accounts payable, and payroll expenses.

PCAOB
Public Companies
Accounting Oversight Board

audit strategies for public companies

Auditors of public companies must perform a dual-purpose audit. They must perform an audit that will allow them to issue opinions on both the entity's financial statements and its system of internal control. Hence, the auditor must obtain a thorough understanding of internal controls as they relate to every material assertion in the financial statements. Furthermore, the auditor must test the operating effectiveness of controls related to each assertion in the financial statements. This positions the auditor to follow a lower assessed level of control risk approach for most financial statements assertions. This is particularly true for assertions associated with the processing of routine transactions. However, the auditor might still follow a primarily substantive approach when auditing accounting estimates or assertions that involve a high level of complexity, such as determining whether special-purpose entities should be consolidated in the company's financial statements, in spite of the fact that the auditor has tested controls related to that assertion. In these cases, the auditor might choose to follow a primarily substantive approach in order to obtain sufficient evidence that the assertions are free of material misstatement.

A Primarily Substantive Approach

In many audits of small businesses, internal controls may not be sufficiently effective to allow for the effective use of a lower assessed level of control risk approach. The auditor may know in advance, perhaps from prior experience dealing with the client, that internal controls related to the assertion do not exist or are ineffective. In other cases, there may be such a significant inherent risk that the auditor might choose to emphasize substantive testing. For example, the primary risk with respect to most liabilities is a risk that liabilities are understated. With respect to long-term debt, the auditor is often concerned about the appropriateness of off-balance sheet financing, whether the debt and assets in special-purpose entities should be consolidated, and whether all debt is in fact recorded. As a result, the auditor may plan a primarily substantive approach. Under **a primarily substantive approach,** the auditor specifies the components of the audit strategy as follows:

- Use a planned assessed level of control risk at a high level (or at the maximum).
- Plan to obtain a minimum understanding of relevant portions of internal controls that is sufficient to plan an audit.
- Plan few, if any, tests of controls.
- Plan extensive substantive tests based on a low planned acceptable level of detection risk.

With respect to long-term debt, the auditor might confirm the outstanding balances on notes payable, even when a note has been paid off and reduced to zero. This is often a cost-effective means of testing for understatement.

A primarily substantive approach is usually chosen when the auditor concludes that the costs of performing additional procedures to obtain a more extensive understanding of internal controls and tests of controls to support a lower assessed level of control risk would exceed the cost of performing more extensive substantive tests. The auditor might also use this approach when auditing assertions that are affected by a high degree of subjectivity or involve highly complex transactions. Nevertheless, the auditor should still obtain a sufficient understanding of internal control to be able to identify the potential for material misstatement. In some cases, the auditor may feel more confident in the results of the audit by directly testing assertions with substantive tests, even if the client has designed internal controls related to those assertions. These circumstances might pertain to assertions for accounts that have relatively small populations or infrequent transactions, such as plant assets or capital stock. The primarily substantive approach may also be used for more assertions in initial audits than in recurring audits.

A primarily substantive approach emphasizing tests of details and a lower assessed level of control risk approach are on opposite ends of a continuum of possible decisions about:

- The planned assessed level of control risk
- The extent of understanding of internal controls
- The assurance desired from tests of controls (e.g., the sufficiency and competency of evidence obtained from tests of controls)
- The planned level of substantive tests to be performed to reduce audit risk to an appropriately low level

Figure 9-9 ■ Two Common Preliminary Audit Strategies

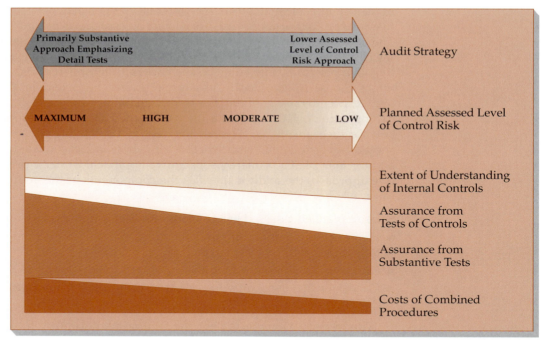

The contrast between these two approaches is depicted in Figure 9-9, which provides a graphic overview of the varying degrees of emphasis given to different components of these two audit strategies. The bottom segment of the figure indicates the potential for cost savings under the lower assessed level of control risk approach.

In the next three chapters, we explain in greater detail how auditors apply these basic audit strategies in planning and organizing the audit within the transaction cycle framework. Chapter 10 focuses on obtaining the understanding of internal controls required under each approach. Chapter 11 explains the methodology for testing controls, usually computer controls, and how the information is used in determining control risk assessments for specific assertions. Chapter 12 explains how those assessments affect the determination of detection risk and the design of substantive tests. The general framework developed in these chapters is then applied to each of the cycles and transaction classes in the chapters comprising Part 4 of this text.

LEARNING CHECK

9-16 What is the auditor's ultimate objective in planning and performing the audit?

9-17 a. What is a preliminary audit strategy?

b. Identify the four components of audit strategies.

9-18 a. Identify three audit strategies.

b. Explain the relative cost and effectiveness of each audit strategy.

9-19 Why may a common strategy be used for a group of assertions affected by the same transaction class?

[KEY TERMS

A lower assessed level of control risk approach, p. 376

A primarily substantive approach, p. 377

A response to lower inherent risk, p. 375

Preliminary audit strategy, p. 374

[FOCUS ON AUDITOR KNOWLEDGE AND AUDIT DECISIONS]

This chapter focuses on several critical aspects of audit planning: (1) assessing inherent risk, including the risk of fraud, and (2) using the audit risk model, and (3) developing preliminary audit strategies. In making decisions to support high-quality audit work, the auditor must be able to use the knowledge summarized in Figure 9-10 and address the decisions summarized in Figure 9-11. Page references are provided indicating where these issues are discussed in more detail.

Figure 9-10 ■ Summary of Auditor Knowledge Discussed in Chapter 9

Auditor Knowledge	Summary	Chapter References
K1. Know the importance of the concept of audit risk and its individual components.	The audit risk model provides a practical way for auditors to think about the combined inherent and control risks that a material misstatement will affect the financial statements being audited. Auditors use the audit risk model to (1) relate specific risks to potential misstatements in the financial statements and consider whether specific risks are of a (2) magnitude and a (3) likelihood that they will result in material misstatements in the financial statements. The auditor uses this knowledge of inherent risk and control risk to determine detection risk and to design audit procedures to ensure that overall audit risk is reduced to an appropriately low level.	pp. 352–353
K2. Know the definition of fraud and its two major components.	Auditors define fraud as an intentional act that results in a material misstatement in financial statements that are the subject of an audit. The two major components of fraud are (1) fraudulent financial reporting, which represents intentional misstatements or omissions of amounts or disclosures in financial statements designed to deceive financial statement users, and (2) misappropriation of assets that involves the theft of an entity's assets where the effect of the theft cause misstatements of financial statements.	pp. 353–355

(continues)

Figure 9-10 ■ (Continued)

Auditor Knowledge	Summary	Chapter References
K3. Understand the relationship between inherent risk, control risk, analytical procedures risk, and test of details risk.	The chapter provides a discussion of an expanded audit risk model where detection risk is divided into two components; (1) analytical procedures risk and (2) test of details risk. Figure 9-4 provides a risk components matrix that explains the relationship between the four elements of the audit risk model. In general, as inherent and control risks increase, the auditor must design analytical procedures and substantive tests that have a lower combined risk of failing to detect a material misstatement in the financial statements.	pp. 364–366
K4. Understand the relationship between detection risk and audit evidence.	There is an inverse relationship between detection risk and the amount of evidence needed to support an opinion on the financial statements. The lower the level of detection risk to be achieved, the greater the amount of evidence is needed. The lower the acceptable level of analytical procedures risk or test of details risk determined by the auditor, the greater the sufficiency and competency of substantive tests needed to restrict audit risk to an appropriate level.	pp. 371–372

Figure 9-11 ■ Summary of Audit Decisions Discussed in Chapter 9

Audit Decision	Factors that Influence the Audit Decision	Chapter References
D1. What three conditions are generally present when fraud occurs?	The three conditions that are generally present when fraud occurs are known as the three points of the fraud triangle. They are (1) incentives and pressures that provide the reason to commit fraud, (2) the opportunity to commit fraud, such as the ability of management override controls or the absence of effective controls, and (3) the ability to rationalize the fraudulent behavior. Figures 9-2 and 9-3 provide numerous examples of these factors as they relate to both fraudulent financial reporting and misappropriation of assets. Finally, because some of these conditions are difficult to observe, auditors should not assume that all three conditions must be observed before concluding that there are identified risks of fraud.	pp. 355–360
D2. What risk assessment procedures should be used to assess the risk of fraud?	The major audit procedures used to assess the risk of fraud include (1) inquiries of management and others within the entity, (2) analytical procedures, and (3) other risk assessment procedures such as client acceptance and retention procedures or procedures used to understand the entity and its environment. In every audit the audit team should engage in a brainstorming session to consider various possible risks of fraud. This often lets more junior staff obtain the experience and wisdom of more seasoned members of the audit team, and people who are new to the engagement may identify items that other staff members might overlook. The chapter provides a number of examples of how this information can be used to assess the risk of fraud.	pp. 360–363

(continues)

Figure 9-11 ■ (Continued)

Audit Decision	Factors that Influence the Audit Decision	Chapter References
D3. What factors influence the auditor's assessment of inherent risk?	An important aspect of developing a knowledgeable perspective regarding the risk of material misstatement involves assessing the inherent risk that a misstatement will occur in an assertion, before considering the system of internal control. Figure 9-6 outlines the factors that influence the inherent risk of misstatement in an assertion, both (1) risks that have a pervasive effect on the financial statements and (2) risks that are assertion specific. This chapter also provides guidance on identifying significant inherent risks that require particular audit responses.	pp. 367–370
D4. How does an auditor develop a preliminary audit strategy for various assertions?	A preliminary audit strategy represents the auditor's preliminary decisions about an audit approach for various assertions being audited. Three preliminary audit strategies are discussed and illustrated in the chapter: (1) an approach that responds to lower inherent risks, (2) a lower assessed level of control risk approach, and (3) a primarily substantive approach. Figure 9-8 relates all three approaches to the audit risk model, and Figure 9-9 explains the difference between the second and third approaches (where inherent risk is often assessed at or near the maximum).	pp. 373–378

objective questions

Objective questions are available for the student at www.wiley.com/college/boynton

comprehensive questions

9-20   **(Risk of fraud)** Following are a number of factors recognized by the auditor as having an effect on the risk of fraud.

1. Personal financial obligations may create pressure on management or employees with access to cash or other assets susceptible to theft to misappropriate those assets.

2. A company has significant, unusual, or highly complex transactions, especially those close to period end that pose difficult "substance over form" questions.

3. A company experiences rapid growth or unusual profitability, especially compared to that of other companies in the same industry.

4. A company has an inadequate system of authorization and approval of transactions (for example, in purchasing).

5. Employees show disregard for the need to monitor or reduce risks related to misappropriations of assets.

6. Personal financial obligations may create pressure on management or employees with access to cash or other assets susceptible to theft to misappropriate those assets.

7. There is excessive pressure on management or operating personnel to meet financial targets set up by the board of directors or management, including sales or profitability incentive goals.

8. Assets, liabilities, revenues, or expenses based on significant estimates that involve subjective judgments or uncertainties are difficult to corroborate.

9. Nonfinancial management shows an excessive participation in or preoccupation with the selection of accounting principles or the determination of significant estimates.

10. Management shows a domineering behavior in dealing with the auditor, especially involving attempts to influence the scope of the auditor's work or the selection or continuance of personnel assigned to or consulted on the audit engagement.

11. Employees anticipate future layoffs.

12. An employee's behavior indicates displeasure or dissatisfaction with the company or its treatment of the employee.

13. A company has significant related-party transactions not in the ordinary course of business or related entities not audited or audited by another firm.

Required

For each of the foregoing risk factors, use the following codes to identify the risk component that is most directly related to (a) fraudulent financial reporting or misappropriation of assets and (b) incentives/pressures, opportunity, or rationalization.

FFR = Fraudulent Financial Reporting	I/P = Incentives/Pressures
MA = Misappropriation of Assets	O = Opportunity
	R = Rationalization

9-21 **(Fraud risk)** Consider the following situation. Company A is a public company that competes in the highly competitive market for manufactured household products. The company is dominated by Rob Bigbucks, the chairman and chief executive officer who has guided the company since it was a private company and has extensive influence on all aspects of company operations. Rob is known to have a short temper and in the past has threatened individuals in the accounting department with the lack of pay raises if they failed to assist him in achieving company goals. Furthermore, the company has extended its influence over customers and has dictated terms of sale to ensure that customers are able to obtain desired quantities of their most popular products. Bonuses based on sales are a significant component of the compensation package for individual product sales managers. Sales managers who do not meet sales targets three quarters in a row are often replaced. The company has performed well up until a recent recession, but now the company is having difficulty moving inventory in most product lines as retailers have difficulty selling in a down economy.

Required

1. Identify the fraud risk factors that are present in the case above.

2. Identify the accounts and assertions that are most likely to be misstated based on the fraud risk factors noted in the case.

9-22 **(Detection risk and audit evidence)** Shown below are seven situations in which the auditor wishes to determine planned acceptable levels of detection risk and the planned levels of evidence needed for specific financial statement assertions. The auditor has used judgment in arriving at the quantitative expressions for various risk factors.

SITUATION

	A	B	C	D	E	F	G
Desired audit risk	1%	1%	5%	5%	5%	5%	10%
Assessed inherent risk	20%	50%	20%	100%	100%	50%	50%
Planned assessed level of control risk	50%	50%	80%	10%	80%	25%	25%
Planned assessed level of analytical procedures	50%	50%	25%	75%	15%	50%	50%
Planned assessed level of tests of details risk							
Planned evidence							

Required

a. Using the audit risk models, determine the acceptable level of tests of details risk for each situation.

b. Rank the seven situations from the most evidence required from substantive tests (1) to least evidence required from substantive tests (5). You may have ties.

c. What do the results obtained for situations C and G mean with respect to procedures designed to obtain evidence to achieve the planned assessed level of test of details risk?

d. Is situation E an acceptable audit strategy? Explain your answer.

e. Identify two alternative audit strategies, assuming that inherent risk is at the maximum. What level of understanding is important to each of these audit strategies?

9-23   **(Detection risk and audit evidence)** Shown below are five situations in which the auditor wishes to determine planned acceptable levels of detection risk and the planned levels of evidence needed for specific financial statement assertions. The auditor has used judgment in arriving at the nonquantitative expressions for various risk factors.

SITUATION

	A	B	C	D	E
Desired audit risk	Very low	Very low	Very low	Very low	Very low
Assessed inherent risk	Maximum	High	Moderate	Low	Maximum
Planned assessed level of control risk	Low	High	High	Moderate	High
Planned assessed level of analytical procedures	Moderate	Moderate	Low	Low	High
Planned assessed level of tests of details risk					
Planned evidence					

Required

a. Using the risk components matrix in Figure 9-4, determine the acceptable level of tests of details risk for each situation.

b. Rank the five situations from the most evidence required from substantive tests (1) to the least evidence required from substantive tests (5). You may have ties.

c. Explain your ranking of situation D.

9-24   **(Inherent risk)** Following are 10 pairs of assertions:

1. a. Existence or occurrence of inventory.
   b. Existence or occurrence of building.

2. a. Valuation or allocation of cash.
   b. Valuation or allocation of deferred income taxes.

3. a. Existence or occurrence of accounts payable.
   b. Completeness of accounts payable.

4. a. Rights and obligations of accrued wages payable.
   b. Rights and obligations of liability under warranties.

5. a. Presentation and disclosure of repairs and maintenance expense.
   b. Presentation and disclosure of telephone expense.

6. a. Valuation or allocation of long-term investments.
   b. Valuation or allocation of land.

7. a. Existence or occurrence of accounts receivable.
   b. Completeness of accounts receivable.

8. a. Existence or occurrence of cash.
   b. Valuation or allocation of cash.

9. a. Valuation or allocation of bad debts expense.
   b. Valuation or allocation of depreciation expense.

10. a. Valuation or allocation of receivable due from affiliate.
    b. Valuation or allocation of note payable to bank.

Required

a. For each pair of assertions, indicate whether (a) or (b) would typically have the higher inherent risk and state why.

b. In addition to factors that affect individual assertions, the assessment of inherent risk requires consideration of matters that may have a pervasive effect on many or all accounts or assertions in an entity's financial statements. State five examples of matters that may have such pervasive effects.

9-25   **(Inherent risk)** Following are examples of inherent risk factors:

1. The original CFO for a company in the entertainment industry just retired, and a new CFO, with modest industry experience, was hired from a CPA firm.

2. During the last year the company's most profitable product has experienced significant competition, and inventory quantities are building.

3. A software company has recently changed its product and is now selling a site license bundled with consulting services to tailor the software to the client's needs.

4. Financial difficulties during a recent economic slowdown have put the company in a position where it is close to violation of debt covenants.

5. A larger diversified retailer has just made a decision to put a high-end jewelry line in its stores.

6. A pharmaceutical company recently invested $500 million in research and development over the last five years in a product that failed to receive FDA approval.

Required

Evaluate the inherent risks noted above using the following framework.

INHERENT RISK FACTOR	PERVASIVE EFFECT (YES/NO)	ACCOUNTS AFFECTED	ASSERTIONS AFFECTED
1.			
2.			
Etc.			

9-26 **(Risk components)** Following are a number of factors recognized by the auditor as having an effect on one or another of the components of audit risk for one or more of management's financial statement assertions:

1. Manufactured equipment is leased to customers under a variety of lease terms tailored to the customers' needs.

2. The company's control policies and procedures for receiving and depositing cash are ineffective.

3. The company's management is under intense pressure to meet projected annual growth in revenues of 20 percent.

4. The availability of external nonfinancial data that are highly correlated with the company's sales causes the auditor to believe that analytical procedures will be effective in determining whether revenue is misstated.

5. The company has experienced high turnover in key management positions.

6. The auditor decides to confirm accounts receivable at the balance sheet date rather than at an interim date.

7. The company suffers from inadequate working capital.

8. High levels of overtime experienced by clerical employees have resulted in numerous errors in processing accounting information due to fatigue and carelessness.

9. To ensure that audit risk is kept to an acceptably low level, the auditor plans to make extensive use of tests of details of balances.

10. The company's primary activities are in the field of genetic engineering.

Required

Using the following codes, identify the risk component that is directly affected by each of the foregoing factors:

IR = Inherent Risk   AP = Analytical Procedures Risk

CR = Control Risk   TD = Test of Details Risk

9-27 **(Preliminary audit strategies)** A major part of audit planning is selecting an appropriate audit strategy for obtaining sufficient competent evidence for each significant financial statement assertion. These strategies are based on the interrelationship among evidence, materiality, and the components of audit risk.

Required

a. Define the term *preliminary audit strategy.*

b. What components should be specified in developing a preliminary audit strategy? How do they relate to the audit risk model?

c. Identify two alternative strategies, assuming that inherent risk is at the maximum. What level of understanding is important to each of these audit strategies?

d. State the circumstances that favor the use of each strategy, including how cost considerations affect the choice of a strategy.

9-28   **(Preliminary audit strategies)** Several significant financial statement assertions and related circumstances (not necessarily for a single client) are listed below:

1. Occurrence of sales revenue—the client operates a chain of music video stores.

2. Valuation or allocation of property, plant, and equipment—the client had only two acquisitions and two disposals during the year.

3. Occurrence of sales revenues—all the client's revenues are based on a flat per diem rate for each person receiving service daily, in monthly billings to a government agency under one large account. The client systems carefully track the number of individuals receiving service.

4. Accuracy of sales revenues—all the client's revenues are based on a flat per diem rate for each person receiving service daily, in monthly billings to a government agency under one large account.

5. Completeness of cash disbursements—the company processes approximately 2,000 checks per month for payments to vendors based on approved vouchers.

6. Existence of long-term investments—for the past eight years, the company has owned a 30 percent interest in two subsidiary companies.

7. Valuation or allocation of liability under warranties—all of the company's products are warranted for 12 months.

8. Occurrence of salaries and wages expense—the client is a university that hires 90 percent of its faculty on annual contracts, many with tenure.

9. Valuation or allocation of deferred income taxes—timing differences relate primarily to differences in depreciation and inventory costing methods used for book and tax purposes.

10. Valuation or allocation of common stock—the company had a significant number of stock transactions, but the auditor believes it will not be cost effective to perform tests of controls.

Required

Based on the limited information given, indicate the preliminary audit strategy that the auditor would likely choose for each of the foregoing assertions.

---

cases

Refer to the information presented in Chapter 7 associated with Cases 7-25 and 7-26. This information will be used with Case 9-29. This case is part of a set of cases related to the audit of Mt. Hood Furniture, Inc., which is coordinated with a number of chapters in the book.

9-29   **(Mt. Hood Furniture: inherent risk)** Complete the following requirements based on the information presented at the end of Chapter 7 related to Mt. Hood Furniture as part of Case 7-25.

Required

Prepare a memo for the working papers that summarizes the key conclusions regarding inherent risks. Use the following the format in your summary.

INHERENT RISK FACTOR	PERVASIVE EFFECT (YES/NO)	ACCOUNTS AFFECTED	ASSERTIONS AFFECTED
1. Management's goal to increase sales to $50 M	No	Sales, Accounts Receivable	Existence or occurrence
2.			
Etc.			

professional simulation

You are auditing the financial statements of Queen Manufacturing, Inc. (QMI). QMI has been a client for a number of years, the entity has a sound system of internal controls, and management has been cooperative in the audit process. The company has had a series of years with solid growth in both revenues and earnings. Due to a recent recession, performance in the fourth quarter is critical to whether QMI will report a profit or a loss.

You have been discussing the auditor's responsibility to design audit procedures to look for fraud with a colleague. Your colleague states that an audit must assume that management is honest. The firm's clients are screened annually as part of the firm's client acceptance and retention policies, which should provide the auditor with assurance that management is honest. Further, an audit relies on the cooperation of management, to provide evidence in the form of documents retained as part of the accounting system.

Is your colleague correct? Can the auditor assume that management is honest? What do the professional standards say about the auditor's responsibility to evaluate management? Cut and paste the standard sections that apply to this issue.

You have been asked by the engagement partner to participate in the "brainstorming session" as part of audit planning and the discussion of the risk of fraud in the audit of QMI. In particular, the partner has asked you to prepare a presentation for the audit team on the professional standards regarding professional skepticism. You should address two specific issues. First, how do the auditing standards define professional skepticism? Second, assume that you have completed the brainstorming session and that you have identified few significant fraud risks. The firm believes that in many audit areas you will plan on testing internal controls so that you might modify the nature, timing, and extent of audit tests accordingly. What do professional standards require in terms of exercising professional skepticism, even if the auditor has assessed detection risk as high in an given audit area. Include relevant citations in a memo to the audit team.

To: Audit Team

Re: Professional Skepticism

From: CPA Candidate

Situation	Research	Professional Skepticism	Fraud Risk

Following is list of various fraud risks. Identify whether the following situations represent incentives/pressures, opportunity, or attitudes/rationalizations.

	Incentive/ Pressure	Opportunity	Attitude/ Rationalization
1. Assets, liabilities, revenues, or expenses based on significant estimates that involve subjective judgments or uncertainties that are difficult to corroborate	○	○	○
2. Excessive interest by management in maintaining or increasing the entity's stock price or earnings trend	○	○	○
3. Lack of complete and timely reconciliations of assets	○	○	○
4. High vulnerability to rapid changes, such as changes in technology, product obsolescence, or interest rates	○	○	○
5. Adverse relationships between the entity and employees with access to cash or other assets susceptible to theft	○	○	○
6. Behavior indicating displeasure or dissatisfaction with the company or its treatment of the employee	○	○	○
7. Significant, unusual, or highly complex transactions, especially those close to period end that pose difficult "substance over form" questions	○	○	○
8. A practice by management of committing to analysts, creditors, and other third parties to achieve aggressive or unrealistic forecasts	○	○	○

10 UNDERSTANDING INTERNAL CONTROL

THE IMPORTANCE OF INTERNAL CONTROL

The importance of internal control to management and independent auditors has been recognized in the professional literature for many years. A 1947 publication by the AICPA entitled *Internal Control* cited the following factors as contributing to the expanding recognition of the significance of internal control:

- The scope and size of the business entity have become so complex and widespread that management must rely on numerous reports and analyses to effectively control operations.
- The check and review inherent in a good system of internal control affords protection against human weaknesses and reduces the possibility that errors or irregularities will occur.
- It is impracticable for auditors to make audits of most companies within economic fee limitations without relying on the client's system of internal control.

During the five decades following this publication, management, independent auditors, and, external parties, such as investors and regulators, have placed even greater importance on internal control.

In 1977, Congress passed the Foreign Corrupt Practices Act (FCPA). Under this Act, management and directors of companies subject to reporting requirements of the Securities Exchange Act of 1934 are required to comply with antibribery and accounting standards provisions and maintain a satisfactory system of internal control. The FCPA is administered by the Securities and Exchange Commission (SEC), and management and directors who do not comply with its provisions are subject to fines, penalties, and/or imprisonment.

Ten years later, the National Commission on Fraudulent Financial Reporting (Treadway Commission) reemphasized the importance of internal control in reducing the incidence of fraudulent financial reporting. The commission's final report, issued in October 1987, included the following:

- Of overriding importance in preventing fraudulent financial reporting is the "tone set by top management" that influences the corporate environment within which financial reporting occurs.
- All public companies should maintain internal control that will provide reasonable assurance that fraudulent financial reporting will be prevented or subject to early detection.
- The organizations sponsoring the Commission, including the Auditing Standards Board (ASB), should cooperate in developing additional guidance on internal control systems.

In 1988, the ASB issued SAS 55, *Consideration of the Internal Control Structure in a Financial Statement Audit* (AU 319). The SAS significantly expanded both the meaning of internal control and the auditor's responsibilities in meeting the second standard of field-work. In 1990, the AICPA issued a 263-page audit guide with the same title as the SAS to assist auditors in applying SAS 55.

Finally, following up on the last recommendation of the Treadway Commission referred to previously, in 1992 the Committee of Sponsoring Organizations (COSO) of the Treadway Commission issued a report entitled *Internal Control—Integrated Framework*. According to COSO, the two principal purposes of its efforts were to:

■ Establish a common definition of internal control serving the needs of different parties.
■ Provide a standard against which business and other entities can assess their control systems and determine how to improve them.

Then the ASB issued Statements and Standards for Attestation Engagements No. 2, which allowed auditors to conduct an audit and report on a client's system of internal control over financial reporting. Then in 1995 the ASB amended AU 319 with SAS 78, *Consideration of Internal Control in a Financial Statement Audit,* to conform professional standards to the framework and language used in the COSO Report.

Financial statement users have questioned whether it is more important to have assurance on the financial statements themselves or assurance over the system that produces an entity's financial statements. About a decade after the ASB created the first standards for attest engagement on internal controls, the U.S. Congress passed the Sarbanes–Oxley Act of 2002. Section 404 of this Act and PCAOB Standard No. 2 require managements of public companies to assess the adequacy of internal controls over financial reporting, and their auditors must audit both management's assessment of internal controls over financial reporting and the actual effectiveness of the system of internal controls over financial reporting (in addition to auditing the financial statements themselves).

[PREVIEW OF CHAPTER 10]

Chapter 10 continues the discussion of important audit planning and risk assessment procedures and addresses one major issue: understanding the entity's system of internal control. The following diagram provides an overview of the chapter organization and content.

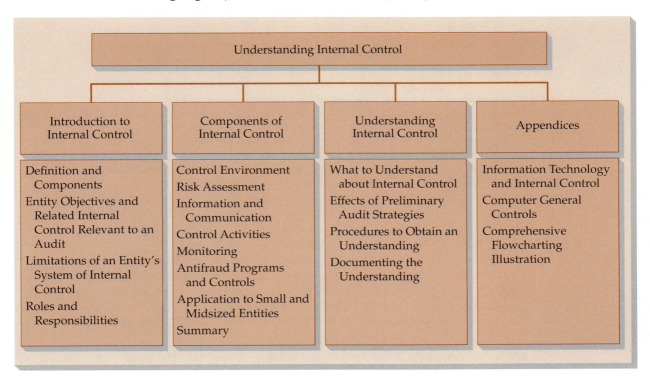

Chapter 10 focuses on the elements of a strong system of internal control. This chapter addresses the following aspects of the auditor's knowledge and the auditor's decision process.

After studying this chapter you should understand the following aspects of an auditor's knowledge base:

K1. Know the definitions of internal control and the five interrelated components of internal control.

K2. Know the inherent limitations of internal control and explain the roles and responsibilities of various parties for an entity's internal controls.

K3. Know the purpose of understanding internal control needed to plan an audit and how that understanding is used.

focus on audit decisions

After studying this chapter you should understand the factors that influence the following audit decisions.

D1. What are the key components of a strong control environment, including relevant IT aspects?

D2. What are the key components of strong risk assessment activities, including relevant IT aspects?

D3. What are the key components of an effective information and communication system, including relevant IT aspects?

D4. What are the key components of strong control activities, including relevant IT aspects?

D5. What are the key components of strong monitoring activities, including relevant IT aspects?

D6. What are the key components of a strong antifraud program and controls?

D7. What audit procedures are used to obtain an understanding of internal controls?

D8. What are the requirements and alternative methods for documenting the understanding of internal control?

INTRODUCTION TO INTERNAL CONTROL

In this section, we examine the contemporary definition of internal control and five interrelated components of internal control. In addition, we consider which entity objectives addressed by internal control are relevant to a financial statement audit, briefly describe the components of internal control, acknowledge certain inherent limitations of internal control, and specify the roles and responsibilities of various parties for an entity's internal control.

DEFINITION AND COMPONENTS

The COSO report defines internal control as follows:

Internal control is a process, effected by an entity's board of directors, management, and other personnel, designed to provide reasonable assurance regarding the achievement of objectives in the following categories:

- Reliability of financial reporting
- Compliance with applicable laws and regulations
- Effectiveness and efficiency of operations

Source: Committee of Sponsoring Organizations of the Treadway Commission, *Internal Control—Integrated Framework* (Jersey City, NJ; American Institute of Certified Public Accountants, 1992).

Auditor Knowledge 1

■ Know the definitions of internal control and the five interrelated components of internal control.

The COSO report also emphasized that the following **fundamental concepts** are embodied in the foregoing definition:

■ Internal control is a process that is integrated with, not added onto, an entity's infrastructure. It is a means to an end, not an end in itself.
■ People implement internal control. It is not merely a policy manual and forms, but people at every level of an organization.
■ Internal control can be expected to provide only reasonable assurance, not absolute assurance, because of its inherent limitations.
■ Internal control is geared to the achievement of objectives in the overlapping categories of financial reporting, compliance, and operations.

Implicit in the last bullet is the assumption that management and the board do in fact formulate and periodically update entity objectives in each of the three categories.

To provide a structure for considering the many possible controls related to the achievement of an entity's objectives, the COSO report (and AU 319.07) identifies five interrelated **components of internal control:**

■ **Control environment** sets the tone of an organization, influencing the control consciousness of its people. It is the foundation for all other components of internal control, providing discipline and structure.
■ **Risk assessment** is the entity's identification and analysis of relevant risks to achievement of its objectives, forming a basis for determining how the risks should be managed.
■ **Control activities** are the policies and procedures that help ensure that management directives are carried out.
■ **Information and communication** are the identification, capture, and exchange of information in a form and time frame that enable people to carry out their responsibilities.
■ **Monitoring** is a process that assesses the quality of internal control performance over time.

These five components are described in detail in later sections of this chapter.

ENTITY OBJECTIVES AND RELATED INTERNAL CONTROL RELEVANT TO AN AUDIT

As previously noted, management adopts internal control to provide reasonable assurance of achieving three categories of objectives: (1) reliability of financial information, (2) compliance with applicable laws and regulations, and (3) effectiveness and efficiency of operations. Because not all of those objectives and related controls are relevant to an audit of financial statements, one of the auditor's first tasks in meeting the second standard of fieldwork is to identify those objectives and controls that are relevant. Generally, this includes those that pertain directly to the first category—reliability of financial reporting. In addition, Section 404 of the Sarbanes–Oxley Act of 2002 only focuses on internal control over financial reporting.

Other objectives and related controls may also be relevant if they pertain to data the auditor uses in applying audit procedures. Examples include objectives and related controls that pertain to:

- Nonfinancial data used in analytical procedures, such as the number of employees, the entity's manufacturing capacity and volume of goods manufactured, and other production and marketing statistics.
- Certain financial data developed primarily for internal purposes, such as budgets and performance data, used by the auditor to obtain evidence about the amounts reported in the financial statements.

Chapter 2 of this text explained the auditor's responsibilities for detecting errors and irregularities, including management and employee fraud, and for detecting certain illegal acts. Thus, an entity's objectives and controls related to these matters are also relevant to the auditor. In particular, objectives and controls in the category of compliance with applicable laws and regulations are relevant when they could have a direct and material effect on the financial statements.

LIMITATIONS OF AN ENTITY'S SYSTEM OF INTERNAL CONTROL

Auditor Knowledge 2

■ Know the inherent limitations of internal control and explain the roles and responsibilities of various parties for an entity's internal controls.

One of the fundamental concepts identified earlier in the chapter is that internal control can provide only reasonable assurance to management and the board of directors regarding the achievement of an entity's objectives. AU 319.16-18, *Consideration of Internal Control in a Financial Statement Audit,* identifies the following **inherent limitations** that explain why internal control, no matter how well designed and operated, can provide only reasonable assurance regarding achievement of an entity's control objectives.

- *Mistakes in judgment.* Occasionally, management and other personnel may exercise poor judgment in making business decisions or in performing routine duties because of inadequate information, time constraints, or other procedures.
- *Breakdowns.* Breakdowns in established control may occur when personnel misunderstand instructions or make errors owing to carelessness, distractions, or fatigue. Temporary or permanent changes in personnel or in systems or procedures may also contribute to breakdowns.
- *Collusion.* Individuals acting together, such as an employee who performs an important control acting with another employee, customer, or supplier, may be able to perpetrate and conceal fraud so as to prevent its detection by internal control (e.g., collusion among three employees from personnel, manufacturing, and payroll departments to initiate payments to fictitious employees, or kickback schemes between an employee in the purchasing department and a supplier or between an employee in the sales department and a customer).
- *Management override.* Management can overrule prescribed policies or procedures for illegitimate purposes such as personal gain or enhanced presentation of an entity's financial condition or compliance status (e.g., inflating reported earnings to increase a bonus payout or the market value of the entity's stock, or to hide violations of debt covenant agreements or noncompliance with laws and regulations). Override practices include making deliberate misrepresentations to auditors and others such as by issuing false documents to support the recording of fictitious sales transactions.
- *Cost versus benefits.* The cost of an entity's internal control should not exceed the benefits that are expected to ensue. Because precise measurement of both

costs and benefits usually is not possible, management must make both quantitative and qualitative estimates and judgments in evaluating the cost-benefit relationship.[1]

For example, an entity could eliminate losses from bad checks by accepting only
certified or cashier's checks from customers. However, because of the possible
adverse effects of such a policy on sales, most companies believe that requiring
identification from the check writer offers reasonable assurance against this type
of loss.

ROLES AND RESPONSIBILITIES

The COSO report concludes that everyone in an organization has some responsibility for, and is actually a part of, the organization's internal control. In addition,
several external parties, such as independent auditors and regulators, may contribute information useful to an organization in effecting control, but they are not
responsible for the effectiveness of internal control. Several responsible parties
and their roles are as follows:

- *Management.* It is management's responsibility to establish effective internal
  control. In particular, senior management should set the "tone at the top" for
  control consciousness throughout the organization and see that all the components of internal control are in place. Senior management in charge of organizational units (divisions, etc.) should be accountable for the resource in their
  units. The CEO and CFO of public companies must also make an assessment of
  the adequacy of internal controls over financial reporting.
- *Board of directors and audit committee.* Board members, as part of their general
  governance and oversight responsibilities, should determine that management
  meets its responsibilities for establishing and maintaining internal control. The
  audit committee (or in its absence, the board itself) has an important oversight
  role in the financial reporting process.
- *Internal auditors.* Internal auditors should periodically examine and evaluate the
  adequacy of an entity's internal control and make recommendations for
  improvements. They are part of the monitoring component of internal control,
  and active monitoring by internal auditors may improve the overall control
  environment.
- *Other entity personnel.* The roles and responsibilities of all other personnel who
  provide information to, or use information provided by, systems that include
  internal control should understand that they have a responsibility to communicate any problems with noncompliance with controls or illegal acts of which
  they become aware to a higher level in the organization.
- *Independent auditors.* When performing risk assessment procedures, an independent auditor may discover deficiencies in internal control that he or she
  communicates to management and the audit committee, together with recommendations for improvements. This applies primarily to financial reporting
  controls, and to a lesser extent to compliance and operations controls. If the

---

[1] The PCAOB has taken the position that cost-benefit is not a valid reason not to have adequate internal controls over financial reporting relating to assertions that could have a material effect on the financial statements.

management's responsibilities in an audit of internal control over financial reporting

Managements of public companies are responsible for *both* fair presentation in the financial statement and maintenance of an effective system of internal control over financial reporting. The PCAOB Auditing Standard No. 2 establishes the following responsibility for management with respect to the company's internal control. Management must:

- Accept responsibility for the effectiveness of the company's internal control over financial reporting.
- Evaluate the effectiveness of the company's internal control over financial reporting using suitable criteria (generally COSO).
- Support its evaluation with sufficient evidence, including documentation.
- Present a written assessment of the effectiveness of the company's internal control over financial reporting as of the end of the company's most recent fiscal year.

PCAOB
Public Companies
Accounting Oversight Board

auditor of a private company follows a primarily substantive approach, he or she may learn enough to understand the specific risks of misstatement, but may not evaluate the effectiveness of many control procedures. A private company audit in accordance with GAAS is performed primarily to enable the auditor to properly plan the audit. Neither does it result in the expression of an opinion on the effectiveness of internal control, nor can it be relied upon to identify all or necessarily even most significant weaknesses in internal control.

- *Other external parties.* Legislators and regulators set minimum statutory and regulatory requirements for establishing internal controls by certain entities. The Sarbanes–Oxley Act of 2002 is an example. Another example is the Federal Deposit Insurance Corporation Improvement Act of 1991, which requires that certain banks report on the effectiveness of their internal control over financial reporting and that such reports be accompanied by an independent accountant's attestation report on management's assertions about effectiveness.

[LEARNING CHECK

(The following questions draw from the opening vignette as well as from the chapter material.)

10-1 a. Who administers the Foreign Corrupt Practices Act of 1977, and to whom does it pertain?
      b. What provisions of the Act relate to internal control and how?

10-2 a. What recommendations did the National Commission on Fraudulent Financial Reporting make regarding internal control?
      b. What is COSO? What were the two principal purposes of its efforts regarding internal control, and why did it undertake these efforts?

10-3 a. State the COSO definition of internal control.
      b. Identify five interrelated components of internal control.
      c. Which entity objectives and related internal controls are of primary relevance in a financial statement audit?

10-4   Identify and briefly describe several inherent limitations of internal control.

10-5   Identify several parties that have roles and responsibilities related to an entity's internal control and briefly describe their roles and responsibilities.

KEY TERMS

Components of internal control, p. 392
Control activities, p. 392
Control environment, p. 392
Fundaments concepts, p. 392
Information and communication, p. 392

Inherent limitations, p. 393
Internal control, p. 391
Monitoring, p. 392
Risk assessment, p. 392

COMPONENTS OF INTERNAL CONTROL

The COSO report and AU 319, *Consideration of Internal Control in the Financial Statement Audit* (SAS 78), identifies five interrelated components of internal control as listed in Figure 10-1. Each of the five components includes numerous control policies and procedures that are needed to achieve entity objectives in each of the three categories of objectives previously identified—financial reporting, compliance, and operations. We have identified a sixth category, antifraud programs and controls. PCAOB Standard No. 2 considers antifraud programs and controls to be an integral aspect of internal controls. We discuss these controls separately because they affect all other aspects of internal control.

Each component is explained in a following section. These explanations focus on the relationship of each component to those entity objectives and related internal control in each category that are of greatest relevance to the financial statement

Figure 10-1 ■ Components of Internal Control

1	Control Environment
2	Risk Assessment
3	Information and Communication
4	Control Activities
5	Monitoring
**	Antifraud Programs and Controls

audit—namely, those that are designed to prevent or detect material misstatements in the financial statements.

CONTROL ENVIRONMENT

The **control environment** represents the tone set by management of an organization that influences the control consciousness of its people. It is the foundation for all other components of internal control, providing discipline and structure.

Audit Decision 1

■ What are the key components of a strong control environment, including relevant IT aspects?

A strong control environment comprises numerous factors that work together to enhance the control consciousness of people who implement controls throughout an entity. Among these are the following (AU 319.25):

- Integrity and ethical values
- Commitment to competence
- Board of directors and audit committee
- Management's philosophy and operating style
- Organizational structure
- Assignment of authority and responsibility
- Human resource policies and practices

The extent to which each factor is formally addressed by an entity will vary based on such considerations as its size and maturity. These factors constitute a major part of an entity's culture. Brief discussion of each of these control environment factors follows.

Integrity and Ethical Values

The COSO report notes that managers of well-run entities have increasingly accepted the view that "ethics pay—that ethical behavior is good business." In order to emphasize the importance of **integrity and ethical values** among all personnel of an organization, the CEO and other members of top management should:

- *Set the tone by example,* by consistently demonstrating integrity and practicing high standards of ethical behavior.
- *Communicate* to all employees, verbally and through written policy statements and codes of conduct, that the same is expected of them, that each employee has a responsibility to report known or suspected violations to a higher level in the organization, and that the violations will result in penalties.
- *Provide moral guidance* to any employees whose poor moral backgrounds have made them ignorant of what is right and wrong.
- *Reduce or eliminate incentives and temptations* that might lead individuals to engage in dishonest, illegal, or unethical acts. Examples of incentives for negative behavior include placing undue emphasis on short-term results or meeting unrealistic performance targets, or bonus and profit-sharing plans with terms that might elicit fraudulent financial reporting practices. A strong control environment encourages employees to stay well away from questionable accounting practices and it places a strong emphasis on representational faithfulness in financial reporting.

Commitment to Competence

To achieve entity objectives, personnel at every level in the organization must possess the requisite knowledge and skills needed to perform their jobs effectively. **Commitment to competence** includes management's consideration of the knowledge and skills needed, and the mix of intelligence, training, and experience required to develop that competence. For example, meeting financial reporting objectives in a large publicly held company generally requires higher levels of competence on the part of the chief financial officer and accounting personnel than would be the case for a small privately held company. It is also important for senior management to attend to the competence and training of individuals who develop or work with IT.

Board of Directors and Audit Committee

The composition of the **board of directors and audit committee** and the manner in which they exercise their governance and oversight responsibilities have a major impact on the control environment. Factors that impact the effectiveness of the board and audit committee include their independence from management; the accounting knowledge, experience and stature of their members; the extent of their involvement and scrutiny of management's activities; the appropriateness of their actions (e.g., the degree to which they raise and pursue difficult questions with management). An effective audit committee can enhance the independence and professional skepticism of an external auditor. The lack of an audit committee in a private company may not be a weakness if the board as a whole can carry out the audit committee's responsibilities.

Management's Philosophy and Operating Style

Many characteristics may form a part of management's philosophy and operating style and have an impact on the control environment. The characteristics of **management's philosophy and operating style** include:

- Approach to taking and monitoring business risks.
- Reliance on informal face-to-face contacts with key managers versus a formal system of written policies, performance indicators, and exception reports.
- Attitudes and actions toward financial reporting.
- Conservative or aggressive selection from available accounting principles.
- Conscientiousness and conservatism in developing accounting estimates.
- Conscientiousness and understanding of the risks associated with IT.

The last four characteristics are of particular significance in assessing the control environment over financial reporting. For example, if management is aggressive in making judgments about accounting estimates (e.g., provision for bad debts, obsolete inventory, or depreciation expense) in ways that shift expenses from one period to another, earnings may be materially misstated.

Organizational Structure

An **organizational structure** contributes to an entity's ability to meet its objectives by providing an overall framework for planning, executing, controlling, and mon-

external auditor evaluation of audit committees

A company's audit committee plays an important role within the control environment and monitoring components of internal control over financial reporting. An effective audit committee helps set a positive tone at the top. The company's board of directors is primarily responsible for evaluating audit committee effectiveness. However, PCAOB Standard No. 2 also states that the auditor should evaluate the effectiveness of the auditor committee as part of understanding the control environment and monitoring. The external auditor should focus on the audit committee's oversight of the company's external financial reporting and internal control over financial reporting. When making this evaluation, the auditor might consider:

- The independence of the audit committee from management.
- The clarity with which the audit committee's responsibilities are articulated.
- How well the audit committee and management understand those responsibilities.
- The audit committee's involvement and interaction with the independent auditor.
- The audit committee's interaction with key members of financial management.
- Whether the right questions are raised and pursued with management and the auditor.
- Whether questions indicate an understanding of the critical accounting policies and judgmental accounting estimates.
- The audit committee's responsiveness to issues raised by the auditor.

Ineffective oversight by the audit committee of the company's external financial reporting should be regarded as at least a significant deficiency and is a strong indicator of a material weakness in internal control over financial reporting.

PCAOB
Public Companies
Accounting Oversight Board

itoring an entity's activity. Developing an organizational structure for an entity involves determining the key areas of authority and responsibility and the appropriate line of reporting. These will depend in part on the entity's size and the nature of its activities. An entity's organizational structure is usually depicted in an organization chart that should accurately reflect lines of authority and reporting relationships. Management should attend not only to the structure of the entity's operations, but also to the organizational structure of information technology and accounting information systems (see the discussion of segregation of duties regarding IT on p. 447). An auditor needs to understand these relationships to properly assess the control environment and how it may impact the effectiveness of particular controls.

Assignment of Authority and Responsibility

The **assignment of authority and responsibility** includes the particulars of how and to whom authority and responsibility for all entity activities are assigned, and should enable each individual to know (1) how his or her actions interrelate with those of others in contributing to the achievement of the entity's objectives and (2) for what each individual will be held accountable. This factor also includes policies dealing with appropriate business practices, knowledge and experience of key personnel, and resources provided for carrying out duties.

Often when individuals or managers are not held accountable for their responsibilities, little attention is given to the accounting system and the completeness and accuracy of information that flows from the accounting system. If a manager is not held accountable for the results of his or her operating unit, there is little incentive to correct errors in accounting for transactions. Although written job descriptions should delineate specific duties and reporting relationships, it is important to understand informal structures that may exist and how individuals are held accountable for their responsibilities.

The auditor should also be aware of how management assigns authority and responsibility for IT. This includes methods of assigning authority and responsibility over computer systems documentation, and the procedures for authorizing and approving system changes. A lack of accountability over making changes in programmed control procedures creates an environment that is conducive to utilizing IT to cover employee fraud.

Human Resource Policies and Practices

A fundamental concept of internal control previously stated is that it is implemented by people. Thus, for internal control to be effective, it is critical that **human resource policies and procedures** be employed that will ensure that the entity's personnel possess the expected levels of integrity, ethical values, and competence. Such practices include well-developed recruiting policies and screening processes in hiring; orientation of new personnel to the entity's culture and operating style; training policies that communicate prospective roles and responsibilities; disciplinary actions for violations of expected behavior; evaluation, counseling, and promotion of people based on periodic performance appraisals; and compensation programs that motivate and reward superior performance while avoiding disincentives to ethical behavior.

Summary of Control Environment

The control environment is critical because it has a pervasive effect on the other four components of internal control. For example, if senior management does not hire competent individuals and fails to underscore the importance of ethics and competence in the performance of work that supports the accounting system, employees may not perform other control procedures with adequate professional care. If top management, in assigning authority and responsibility, does not hold other managers accountable for their use of resources, there is little incentive to effectively implement the remaining components of internal control. If, however, top management emphasizes the importance of internal control and the need for reliable information for decision making, it increases the likelihood that other aspects of internal control will operate effectively. Top management can also take steps that minimize the incentives to engage in fraud, whether fraudulent financial reporting or misappropriation of assets. Figure 10-2 summarizes some of the factors that can strengthen other aspects of internal control and lower the risk of material misstatement or weaken other aspects of internal control and increase the risk of material misstatement.

Figure 10-2 ■ Summary of Control Environment Factors

Higher Risk of Material Misstatement	Control Environment Factors	Lower Risk of Material Misstatement
■ Top management may engage in questionable business practices. ■ Top management places a premium on achieving short-term results. ■ Top management may encourage structuring transactions to meet GAAP requirements that do not match underlying economic substance. ■ Top management sets unrealistic targets to attain bonuses.	Integrity and ethical values	■ Demonstrates high standards of ethical behavior. ■ Top management emphasizes the importance of reporting known or suspected ethical violations ■ Top management emphasizes the importance of ethical business practices and representational faithfulness in financial reporting. ■ Top management minimizes incentives for fraud.
■ Budgets constrain management, and some aspects of the organization may not have fully competent personnel. ■ Operating positions have a priority over accounting or IT positions when it comes to obtaining competent personnel.	Commitment to competence	■ Top management seeks out competent personnel at every level of the organization. ■ Top management seeks out competent personnel with accounting and IT skills for relevant positions
■ The board of directors is more passive in its governance roles and relies heavily on management. ■ The auditor committee does not have members who are knowledgeable of accounting and auditing issues.	Board of directors and audit committee	■ The board of directors and the audit committee are active in their governance roles. ■ The audit committee has competent members who are knowledgeable of accounting and auditing issues.
■ Top management is aggressive about taking business risks and may not monitor the impact of prior investment decisions. ■ Top management emphasizes sales and operations issues and does not devote sufficient attention to risk associated with IT and the use of management discretion in financial reporting. ■ Top management is concerned about reporting financial results that meet sales and earnings targets.	Management's philosophy and operating style	■ Top management is thoughtful about taking business risks, and appropriate monitoring systems are in place. ■ Top management is conscientious in understanding the risks associated with IT and the use of management discretion in financial reporting. ■ Top management emphasizes the importance of representational faithfulness in financial reporting.
■ The organization structure is strained and may not fully support effective planning, executing, controlling, and monitoring the entity's activities. ■ The smaller size of the organization may not allow for adequate segregation of duties in IT and in other areas.	Organizational structure	■ Organizational structure supports effective planning, executing, controlling, and monitoring the entity's activities. ■ Organizational structure allows for adequate segregation of duties in IT and in other areas.

(continues)

Figure 10-2 ■ (Continued)

Higher Risk of Material Misstatement	Control Environment Factors	Lower Risk of Material Misstatement
■ Inadequate communication of authority and responsibility hinders lower levels of management from coordinating their actions with others to achieve organizational objectives. ■ Focus on immediate goals may not allow for appropriate monitoring of and accountability for organizational resources. ■ Constraints limit assigning authority and responsibility in IT or in accounting in ways that would allow for appropriate segregation of duties and checks and balances.	Assignment of authority and responsibility	■ Authority and responsibility is assigned so that lower levels of management know how their actions interrelate with others in contributing to organizational objectives. ■ Authority and responsibility is assigned with appropriate monitoring of and accountability for organizational resources. ■ Top management assigns authority and responsibility in IT and in accounting in ways that allow for appropriate segregation of duties and checks and balances.
■ Budget constraints limit HR policies and practices, and entity personnel may not possess a high level of integrity, ethical values, or competence.	Human resource policies and practices	■ HR policies and practices ensure that entity personnel possess the expected level of integrity, ethical values, and competence.

RISK ASSESSMENT

Risk assessment for financial reporting purposes is an entity's identification, analysis, and management of risk relevant to the preparation of financial statements that are fairly presented in conformity with generally accepted accounting principles.

Source: AU 319.28.

Audit Decision 2

■ What are the key components of strong risk assessment activities, including relevant IT aspects?

Management's risk assessment process is depicted in Figure 10-3. Management's purpose is to (1) identify risk and (2) place effective controls in operation to control those risks. Management needs to seek a balance such that the higher the risk of misstatement in the financial statements, the more effective the controls should be to prevent misstatements, or detect and correct them on a timely basis. In a strong risk assessment system, management should consider:

■ The entity's business risks and their financial consequences.
■ The inherent risks of misstatement in financial statement assertions.
■ The risk of fraud and its financial consequences.

To the extent that management appropriately identifies risks and successfully initiates control activities to address those risks, the auditor's combined assessment of inherent and control risks for related assertions will be lower. In some cases,

Figure 10-3 ■ Management's Risk Assessment Process

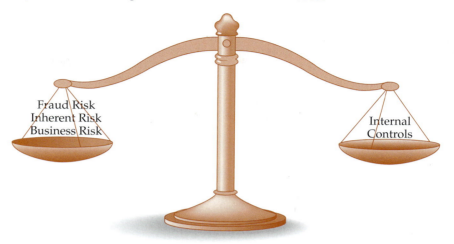

however, management may simply decide to accept some level of risk without imposing controls because of cost or other considerations.

Management's risk assessment should include consideration of the risks associated with IT discussed in Appendix 10A. For example, management should design information and controls systems that mitigate the problems associated with the impact of IT in reducing the traditional segregation of duties. If management designs and implements a good system of computer general controls, many of these overall risks will be reduced to a manageable level.

In a strong risk assessment system, management should also include special consideration of the risks that can arise from changed circumstances described in AU 319.29:

■ Changes in operating environment
■ New personnel
■ New or revamped information systems
■ Rapid growth
■ New technology
■ New lines, products, or activities
■ Corporate restructurings
■ Foreign operations
■ New accounting pronouncements

To the extent that these risks are present, management should put controls in place to control these risks. For example, when management develops a new information system for a segment of the organization, user departments should be involved in developing the specifications of the system, there should be significant testing of the system with test data, and users should be involved in the final tests to ensure that the new system accomplishes its goals. These are important control activities that need to respond to the risk that a new information system may not function as desired.

INFORMATION AND COMMUNICATION

The **information and communication system** relevant to financial reporting objectives, which includes the **accounting system,** consists of the methods and records established to identify, assemble, analyze, classify, record, and report entity transactions (as well as events and conditions) and to maintain accountability for the related assets and liabilities. *Communication* involves providing a clear understanding of individual roles and responsibilities pertaining to internal control over financial reporting.

Source: AU 319.34.

Audit Decision 3

■ **What are the key components of an effective information and communication system, including relevant IT aspects?**

As noted in the foregoing, a major focus of the accounting system is on transactions. **Transactions** consist of exchanges of assets and services between an entity and outside parties, as well as the transfer or use of assets and services within an entity. It follows that a major focus of control policies and procedures related to the accounting system is that transactions be handled in a way that supports representational faithfulness and the application of GAAP in the financial statements. Thus, an effective accounting system should:

■ Identify and record only the valid transactions of the entity that occurred in the current period (existence and occurrence assertion).

■ Identify and record all valid transactions of the entity that occurred in the current period (completeness assertion).

■ Ensure that recorded assets and liabilities are the result of transactions that produced entity rights to, or obligations for, those items (rights and obligations assertions).

■ Measure the value of transactions in a manner that permits recording their proper monetary value in the financial statements (valuation or allocation assertion).

■ Capture sufficient detail of all transactions to permit their proper presentation in the financial statements, including proper classification and required disclosures (presentation and disclosure assertion).

An effective accounting system should provide a complete audit trail or transaction trail for each transaction. An **audit trail** or **transaction trail** is a chain of evidence from initiating a transaction to its recording in the general ledger and financial statements provided by coding, cross-reference, and documentation connecting account balances and other summary results with original transaction data. Transaction trails are essential both to management and to auditors. Management uses the trail in responding to inquiries from customers or suppliers concerning account balances. It is particularly important for management to ensure a clear transaction trail in IT systems where documentary evidence may be retained for only a short period of time. Computer systems that use on-line processing should create a unique transaction number that can be used to establish such a transaction trail. Auditors use the trail in tracing and vouching transactions as explained in Chapter 6.

Documents and records represent an aspect of the information and communication system that provides important audit evidence. *Documents* provide evidence of the occurrence of transactions and the price, nature, and terms of the transactions. Invoices, checks, contracts, and time tickets are illustrative of common types of documents. When duly signed or stamped, documents also provide a basis for establishing responsibility for executing and recording transactions. *Records* include employee earnings records, which show cumulative payroll data for each employee, and perpetual inventory records. Another type of record is daily summaries of documents issued, such as sales invoices and checks. The summaries are then independently compared with the sum of corresponding daily entries to determine whether all transactions have been recorded. In modern accounting systems, records are usually in electronic format, and entities may create printed copies for ease of use.

Communication includes making sure that personnel involved in the financial reporting system understand how their activities relate to the work of others both inside and outside the organization. This includes the role of the system in reporting exceptions for followup as well as reporting unusual exceptions to higher levels within the entity. Policy manuals, accounting and financial reporting manuals, a chart of accounts, and memoranda also constitute part of the information and communication component of internal control.

CONTROL ACTIVITIES

Control activities are those policies and procedures that help ensure that management directives are carried out. They help ensure that necessary actions are taken to address risks to achievement of the entity's objectives. Control activities have various objectives and are applied at various organization and functional levels.

Source: AU 319.32.

A strong system of control activities contains a number of elements that need to be placed in operation for the control activities to be effective. Figure 10-4 describes one way that control activities relevant to a financial statement audit can be described.

1. Authorization Controls

Audit Decision 4

■ What are the key components of strong control activities, including relevant IT aspects?

A major purpose of **proper authorization** procedures is to ensure that every transaction is authorized by management personnel acting within the scope of their authority. Each transaction entry should be properly authorized and approved in accordance with management's general or specific authorization. General authorization relates to the general conditions under which transactions are authorized, such as standard price lists for products and credit policies for charge sales. Specific authorization relates to the granting of the authorization on a case-by-case basis. When transactions are individually processed, authorization is usually provided in the form of a signature or stamp on the source document or in the form of electronic authorization that leaves a computerized audit trail.

Proper authorization procedures often have a direct effect on control risk for existence and occurrence assertions, and in some cases, valuation or allocation assertions, such as the authorization of an expenditure or the authorization of a customer's credit limit. The board of directors may authorize capital expenditures at a designated amount. Expenditures in excess of that amount might indicate

Figure 10-4 ■ Control Activities

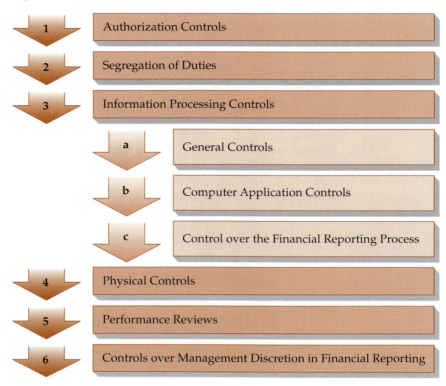

1 Authorization Controls

2 Segregation of Duties

3 Information Processing Controls

a General Controls

b Computer Application Controls

c Control over the Financial Reporting Process

4 Physical Controls

5 Performance Reviews

6 Controls over Management Discretion in Financial Reporting

existence problems (an invalid transaction) or presentation and disclosure problems (expenses classified as assets).

2. Segregation of Duties

Strong **segregation of duties** involves segregating (1) transaction authorization, (2) maintaining custody of assets, and (3) maintaining recorded accountability in the accounting records. Figure 10-5 depicts the traditional segregation of duties. Failure to maintain strong segregation of duties makes it possible for an individual to commit an error or fraud and then be in a position to conceal it in the normal course of his or her duties. For example, an individual who processes cash remittances from customers (has access to the custody of assets) should not also have authority to approve and record credits to customers' accounts for sales returns and allowances or write-offs (authorize transactions). In such a case, the individual could steal a cash remittance and cover the theft by recording a sales return or allowance or bad-debt write-off.

Sound segregation of duties also involves comparing recorded accountability with assets on hand. For example, sound internal control involves independent bank reconciliations comparing bank balances with book balances for each bank account. Perpetual inventory records should also be periodically compared with inventory on hand.

Proper segregation of duties, should also be maintained within the IT department and between IT and user departments. Several functions within IT—systems develop-

Figure 10-5 ■ Traditional Segregation of Duties

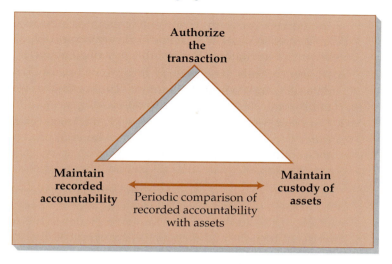

ment, operations, data controls, and securities administration—should be segregated (see Figure 10-21). In addition, IT should not correct data submitted by user departments and should be organizationally independent from user departments. Segregation of duties within IT is so important that it is considered a critical aspect of general controls (see the discussion of organization and operation control on p. 447).

3. Information Processing Controls

Information processing controls address risks related to the authorization, completeness, and accuracy of transactions. These controls are particularly relevant to the financial statement audit. Most entities, regardless of size, now use computers for information processing in general and for accounting systems in particular. In such cases, it is useful to further categorize information processing controls as general controls and application controls, which are discussed below.

3a. General Controls

The purpose of **general controls** is to control program development, program changes, and computer operations, and to secure access to programs and data. The following five types of general controls are widely recognized:

■ **Organization and operation controls** address the segregation of duties within the IT department and between IT and user departments. A critical component is segregating access to programs from access to data files. Weakness in these controls usually affects all IT applications.

■ **Systems development and documentation controls** relate to (1) review, testing, and approval of new systems and program changes, and (2) controls over documentation.

■ **Hardware and systems software controls** are an important factor that contributes to the high degree of reliability of today's information technology.

Hardware and software controls are designed to detect any malfunctioning of the equipment. To achieve maximum benefit from these controls, (1) there should be a program of preventive maintenance on all hardware, and (2) controls over changes to systems software should parallel the systems development and documentation controls described above.

- **Access controls** are designed to prevent unauthorized use of IT equipment, data files, and computer programs. The specific controls include a combination of physical, software, and procedural safeguards.

- **Data and procedural controls** provide a framework for controlling daily computer operations, minimizing the likelihood of processing errors, and assuring the continuity of operations in the event of a physical disaster or computer failure through adequate file backup and other controls.

Computer general controls pertain to the IT environment and all IT activities as opposed to a single IT application. Because of the pervasive character of general controls, if the auditor is able to obtain evidence that general controls function effectively, then the auditor also has important assurance that individual applications may be properly designed and operate consistently during the period under audit. For example, strong computer general controls involve regular testing and review of individual programs that process sales, cash receipts, payroll, and many other transactions. Alternatively, deficiencies in general controls may affect many applications and may prevent the auditor from assessing control risk below the maximum for many applications and transaction cycles. Students not familiar with the details of computer general controls should study the in-depth discussion in Appendix 10B.

3b. Computer Application Controls

The purpose of **application controls** is to use the power of information technology to control transactions in individual transaction cycles. Hence, applications controls will differ for each transaction cycle (e.g., sale vs. cash receipts). The following three groups of application controls are widely recognized:

- Input controls
- Processing controls
- Output controls

These controls are designed to provide reasonable assurance that the recording, processing, and reporting of data by IT are properly performed for specific applications. Thus, the auditor must consider these controls separately for each significant accounting application, such as billing customers or preparing payroll checks.

In today's IT environment, application controls execute the function of **independent checks** by (1) using programmed application controls to identify transactions that contain possible misstatements and (2) having people follow up and correct items noted on exception reports. The following discussion explains how programmed controls may be used to identify items that should be included on various exception reports.

Input Controls   Input controls are program controls designed to detect and report errors in data that are input for processing. They are of vital importance in IT systems because most of the errors occur at this point. Input controls are designed to provide reasonable assurance that data received for processing have been properly authorized and converted into machine-sensible form. These controls also include the people who follow up on the rejection, correction, and resubmission of data that were initially incorrect.

Controls over the conversion of data into machine-sensible form are intended to ensure that the data are correctly entered and converted data are valid. Specific controls include:

- *Verification controls.* These controls often compare data input for computer processing with information contained on computer master files, or other data independently entered at earlier stages of a transaction.
- *Computer editing.* These are computer routines intended to detect incomplete, incorrect, or unreasonable data. They include:
  - *Missing data check* to ensure that all required data fields have been completed and no blanks are present.
  - *Valid character check* to verify that only alphabetical, numerical, or other special characters appear as required in data fields.
  - *Limit (reasonableness) check* to determine that only data falling within predetermined limits are entered (e.g., time cards exceeding a designated number of hours per week may be rejected).
  - *Valid sign check* to determine that the sign of the data, if applicable, is correct (e.g., a valid sign test would ensure that the net book value of an asset was positive and that assets are not overdepreciated).
  - *Valid code check* to match the classification (i.e., expense account number) or transaction code (i.e., cash receipts entry) against the master list of codes permitted for the type of transaction to be processed.
  - *Check digit* to determine that an account, employee, or other identification number has been correctly entered by applying a specific arithmetic operation to the identification number and comparing the result with a check digit embedded within the number.

The correction and resubmission of incorrect data are vital to the accuracy of the accounting records. If the processing of a valid sales invoice is stopped because of an error, both accounts receivable and sales will be understated until the error is eliminated and the processing completed. Misstatements should be corrected by those responsible for the mistake. Furthermore, strong controls create a log of potential misstatements, and the data control group periodically reviews their disposition.

Processing Controls Processing controls are designed to provide reasonable assurance that the computer processing has been performed as intended for the particular application. Thus, these controls should preclude data from being lost, added, duplicated, or altered during processing.

Processing controls take many forms, but the most common ones are programmed controls incorporated into the individual applications software. They include the following:

- *Control totals.* Provision for accumulating control totals is written into the computer program to facilitate the balancing of input totals with processing totals for each run. Similarly, run-to-run totals are accumulated to verify processing performed in stages.

- *File identification labels.* External labels are physically attached to magnetic tape or disks to permit visual identification of a file. Internal labels are in machine-sensible form and are matched electronically with specified operator instructions (or commands) incorporated into the computer program before processing can begin or be successfully completed.

- *Limit and reasonableness checks.* A limit or reasonableness test would compare computed data with an expected limit (e.g., the product of payroll rates times hours worked would be included on an exception report and not processed if it exceeded an predetermined limit).

- *Before-and-after report.* This report shows a summary of the contents of a master file before and after each update.

- *Sequence tests.* If transactions are given identification numbers, the transaction file can be tested for sequence (e.g., an exception report would include missing numbers or duplicate numbers in a sequence of sales invoices).

- *Process tracing data.* This control involves a printout of specific data for visual inspection to determine whether the processing is correct. For evaluating changes in critical data items, tracing data may include the contents before and after the processing (e.g., information from shipping data with information on sales invoices).

Output Controls   **Output controls** are designed to ensure that the processing results are correct and that only authorized personnel receive the output. The accuracy of the processing results includes both updated machine-sensible files and printed output. This objective is met by the following:

- *Reconciliation of totals.* Output totals that are generated by the computer programs are reconciled to input and processing totals by the data control group or user departments.

- *Comparison to source documents.* Output data are subject to detailed comparison with source documents.

- *Visual scanning.* The output is reviewed for completeness and apparent reasonableness. Actual results may be compared with estimated results.

The data control group usually controls who can have access to data in a database and maintains control over any centrally produced reports for the distribution of output. This group should exercise special care over the access to, or distribution of, confidential output. To facilitate control over the disposition of output, systems documentation should include reports of who has access to various aspects of a database or some form of a report distribution sheet.

3c. Controls over the Financial Reporting Process

Figure 10-6 provides an overview of the financial reporting process in many businesses. In many cases, computer application controls provide a strong control over the information that is included in a computer database. When the time comes to prepare financial statements, a structured query language (SQL) is used to access the database and download information into a spreadsheet. However, once the data is in a spreadsheet, it may be subject to little or no controls. Data in

Figure 10-6 ■ Overview of the Financial Reporting Process

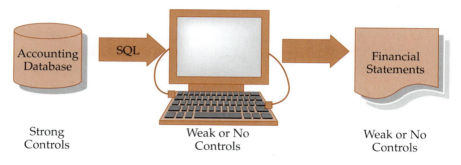

Accounting Database | SQL | Financial Statements

Strong Controls   Weak or No Controls   Weak or No Controls

spreadsheets can be easily accessed and manipulated without leaving an audit trail. If a macro is written incorrectly, it might inadvertently omit information from particular general ledger account, or otherwise lose critical financial statement information. Furthermore, a significant amount of information included in footnote disclosures is often maintained or summarized in spreadsheets. The sum of the controls over the information included in spreadsheets is only as strong as the weakest link in the control chain.

Many companies summarize a significant amount of financial statement information using spreadsheets. As part of a sound system of internal control companies should limit access to spreadsheets. Furthermore, good controls include testing the completeness of accuracy of inputs, and controlling the accuracy of output (e.g., testing spreadsheets with test data). Some companies perform an independent, manual check on the logic of each spreadsheet and the data that is summarized with spreadsheets. Companies should also maintain an inventory of spreadsheets used in the financial reporting process and keep clear documentation of the function accomplished by each spreadsheet. Without these controls the benefits obtained from strong computer application controls can be lost by having inadequate controls over the processing of financial statement information in spreadsheets, or other financial statement preparation software, prior to the preparation of the financial statements.

4. Physical Controls

Physical controls are concerned with limiting the following two types of access to assets and important records: (1) direct physical access and (2) indirect access through the preparation or processing of documents such as sales orders and disbursement vouchers that authorize the use or disposition of assets. Physical controls pertain primarily to security devices and measures used for the safekeeping of assets, documents, records, and computer programs or files. Security devices include on-site safeguards such as fireproof safes and locked storerooms, and off-site safeguards such as bank deposit vaults and certified public warehouses. Security measures also include limiting access to storage areas to authorized personnel. Such controls reduce the risk of theft and are thus relevant in assessing control risk for existence or occurrence assertions.

Physical controls also involve the use of mechanical and electronic equipment in executing transactions. For example, cash registers help to assure that all cash receipt transactions are rung up, and they provide locked-in summaries of daily receipts. Such controls are relevant in assessing control risk for completeness assertions.

When IT equipment is used, access to the computer, computer records, data files, and programs should be restricted to authorized personnel. The use of passwords, keys, and identification badges provides means of controlling access. When such safeguards are in place, control risk may be reduced for various existence or occurrence, completeness, and valuation or allocation assertions related to transaction classes and accounts processed by IT.

Finally, physical control activities include periodic counts of assets and comparison with amounts shown on control records. Examples include petty cash counts and physical inventories. These activities may be relevant in assessing existence or occurrence, completeness, and valuation or allocation assertions as discussed further in Part 4 of the text in the context of specific transaction cycles.

5. Performance Reviews

Examples of **performance reviews** include management review and analysis of

- Reports that summarize the detail of account balances such as an aged trial balance of accounts, reports of cash disbursements by department, or reports of sales activity and gross profit by customer or region, salesperson, or product line.
- Actual performance versus budgets, forecasts, or prior-period amounts.
- The relationship of different sets of data such as nonfinancial operating data and financial data (for example, comparison of hotel occupancy statistics with revenue data).

Management's use of reports that drill down and summarize the transactions that make up sales or cash disbursements may provide an independent check on the accuracy of the accounting information. For example, a university department chair might review the details of the payroll that was charged to his or her department on a monthly basis. The quality of this review may provide control over the occurrence, completeness, and valuation of payroll transactions. Management's analysis of operating performance may serve another purpose similar to the auditor's use of analytical procedures in audit planning. That is, management may develop nonfinancial performance measures that correlate highly with financial outcomes, and may allow it to detect accounts that might be misstated. Such misstatements might involve existence or occurrence, completeness, valuation or allocation, or presentation and disclosure assertions.

6. Controls over Management Discretion in Financial Reporting

The PCAOB in Auditing Standard No. 2, *An Audit of Internal Control over Financial Reporting Performed in Conjunction with an Audit of Financial Statements,* expects public companies to establish internal controls in the three following areas:

1. Controls over significant nonroutine and nonsystematic transactions, such as assertions involving judgments and estimates.
2. Controls over the selection and application of GAAP.
3. Controls over disclosures.

In these circumstances it is rare to find good internal controls in private companies. Private companies may have solid internal control over routine transactions that are high in volume, and internal controls are often very cost-effective. However, the circumstances identified above often involve significant management discretion, and the size and nature of the company are such that the auditor is the primary check and balance over these issues. Public companies with more resources are now establishing internal controls over all aspects of financial statement disclosure. As a general rule, key decisions about accounting for individual transactions, accounting policy, or disclosures should not rest with one individual. It is important that such critical decisions represent the consensus of a knowledgeable group.

Internal **controls over nonroutine and nonsystematic transactions,** such as assertions involving accounting estimates, often have two layers of control. The first stage is control over the data used to make the judgmental computation, and the second stage is the concurrent review process. For example, if management makes an estimate of the allowance for doubtful accounts, the auditor should determine that the data used in making the assessment should be appropriately controlled. An accounting estimate can be no more reliable than the data used to develop the accounting estimate. The data should come from a system that is relevant to the estimate. Second, there should also be a review process that allows for a followup process that reviews prior accounting estimates with hindsight. In addition, there should be an internal process involving individuals who understand the business issues related to the accounting estimates that focuses on ensuring consistent estimates. The independent review process should focus on the consistency of the estimation process. The goal is to avoid the abuses where management has developed accounting estimates that tend to overestimate expenses in good years and underestimate expenses in years of poor fiscal performance.

Some companies are also developing **disclosure committees** to provide an independent review of the appropriateness of selection of choices of accounting principles, accounting for unusual and nonrecurring transactions, the reasonableness of accounting estimates, and the overall level of disclosure in the financial statements. These committees are often staffed with both (1) individuals who have strong accounting backgrounds and (2) members of operational management who are familiar with the company's operations and transactions. Disclosure committees, and then the audit committee, generally review these critical elements of the financial statements before they are released to the auditor. These committees are most effective when they are staffed by knowledgeable individuals who provide an independent check on the initial decisions made by a controller, chief accounting officer, or a chief financial officer.

MONITORING

Monitoring is a process that assesses the quality of internal control performance over time. It involves assessing the design and operation of controls on a timely basis and taking necessary corrective actions.

Source: AU 319.38.

Audit Decision 5

■ What are the key components of strong monitoring activities, including relevant IT aspects?

Effective monitoring activities usually involve (1) ongoing monitoring programs, (2) separate evaluations, and (3) an element of reporting deficiencies to the audit committee.

Ongoing monitoring activities might take a variety of forms. An active internal audit function that regularly performs tests of controls using an integrated test facility or internal auditors may regularly rotate tests of different aspects of the system of internal control. In addition, controls may be designed with various self-monitoring processes. For example, problems with internal control may come to management's attention through complaints received from customers about billing errors or from suppliers about payment problems, or from alert managers who receive reports with information that differs significantly from their first-hand knowledge of operations.

Monitoring also occurs through separate periodic evaluations. Managements of public companies must perform periodic evaluations of internal controls in order to support an assertion about the effectiveness of the system of internal control. Furthermore, management and the audit committee should be conscious of IT risks and perform separate evaluations of computer general controls because of their pervasive effect on various programmed application controls. The audit committee also might charge internal audit with periodic reviews of IT risks and controls. Finally, management may receive information from the separate evaluation of regulators, such as bank examiners.

The final element of sound monitoring controls involves the reporting of deficiencies to the audit committee (or full board of directors). Deficiencies that surface through ongoing monitoring programs or separate evaluations should be regularly brought to the audit committee for discussion and decisions about corrective actions.

ANTIFRAUD PROGRAMS AND CONTROLS

Antifraud programs and controls are policies and procedures put in place to help ensure that management's antifraud directives are carried out. An effective antifraud program should impact every aspect of the system of internal control. Figure 10-7 summarizes a variety of common aspects of strong antifraud programs and controls.

Figure 10-7 ■ Antifraud Programs and Controls

Control Environment
- Code of conduct/ethical company culture
- Ethics hotline
- Audit committee oversight
- Hiring and promotion

Fraud Risk Assessment
- Systematic assessment of fraud risks
- Evaluation of likelihood and magnitude of potential misstatement

Information and Communication
- Adequacy of the audit trail
- Antifraud training

Control Activities
- Adequate segregation of duties
- Linking controls to fraud risks

Monitoring
- Developing an effective oversight process
- "After the fact" evaluations by internal audit

Audit Decision 6

■ What are the key components of strong antifraud programs and controls?

Creating an ethical company culture is an aspect of the control environment that has a pervasive impact on other aspects of internal controls. Implementing an ethical company culture includes setting a tone at the top of the organization, establishing a code of conduct, creating a positive workplace environment, hiring and promoting ethical employees, providing ethics training, and disciplining and prosecuting violators. For example, in 2002 Genesco, Inc., found evidence of improper revenue recognition when it asked employees to sign an ethics statement. It then launched an internal investigation, and when it found evidence that the divisional president, CFO, and controller booked sales for goods that had not been shipped, the employees were dismissed. This activity sent a strong statement about the importance of ethics in accounting and business practices. The code of conduct should also address conflicts of interest, related party transactions, illegal acts, and monitoring of the code by management and the audit committee or board. Many corporations have established ethics hotlines for accepting confidential submissions of concerns about fraud and questionable accounting matters. It is essential that these hotlines be directed to internal auditors or an independent outside company, which will then anonymously report issues raised through the hotline to management and the audit committee.

A specific aspect of management's risk assessment process should concern itself with the risk of fraud. Management should address both the risk of misappropriation of assets and the risk of fraudulent financial reporting. An important first step in responding to fraud risk is for management to consider a regular program of antifraud training, which is part of the information and communication system. Management should also make sure that there is an adequate audit trail to allow control activities to function effectively.

As noted in Figure 10-3, it is essential that management institute sufficient controls to offset the fraud risks present in an organization. A strong system of internal control can limit the opportunity for fraud. If adequate segregation of duties exists, and information processing controls (both general controls and specific application controls) are designed to prevent or detect and correct misstatements, the opportunity for fraud is reduced. An audit committee must provide an oversight role in implementing controls over management discretion in financial reporting.

Finally, effective monitoring is necessary to ensure that other antifraud programs work effectively. The audit committee and management must regularly monitor the effectiveness of the control environment, risk assessment, information and communication, and control activities in preventing or detecting fraud. The audit committee should receive separate "after the fact" reports from internal auditors regarding issues reported through the ethics hotline. If monitoring activities become ineffective, it may not be long before other antifraud controls begin to deteriorate.

APPLICATIONS OF COMPONENTS TO SMALL AND MIDSIZED ENTITIES

All five components of internal control are applicable to entities of all sizes. However, the degree of formality and the specifics of how the components are implemented may vary considerably for practical and sound reasons. AU 319.15 identifies the following factors to be considered in deciding on how to implement each of the five components:

- The entity's size
- Its organization and ownership characteristics
- The nature of its business
- The diversity and complexity of its operation
- Its methods of processing data
- Its applicable legal and regulatory requirements

Following are some of the differences typical of smaller versus larger entities. Smaller entities are less likely to have written codes of conduct, outsider directors, formal policy manuals, sufficient personnel to provide for optimal segregation of duties, or internal auditors. However, they can mitigate these conditions by developing a culture that places an emphasis on integrity, ethical values, and competence. In addition, owner-managers can assume responsibility for certain critical tasks, such as approving credit, signing checks, reviewing bank statements and bank reconciliations, monitoring customer balances, and approving the write-off of uncollectible accounts. Moreover, the familiarity that managers of smaller entities can have with all critical areas of operations, and the simpler and shorter lines of communication, can obviate the need for numerous other formalized control activities essential in larger entities.

SUMMARY

This concludes the discussion of the components of internal control. Two summary tables are presented to capture key issues from the preceding discussion. Figure 10-8 provides a list of questions that address many of the key issues that the auditor should understand about the client's system of internal control. A summary of the components is presented in Figure 10-9, including important IT components.

Figure 10-8 ■ Key Questions Regarding a Client's System of Internal Control

Component of Internal Control	Key Questions
Control Environment	
Integrity and ethical values	Does everyone at the client embrace standards of proper behavior?
Commitment to competence	Does the client hire the best people?
Board of directors and audit committee	Does the board actively monitor the way management manages the business?
	How involved is the audit committee in the financial reporting function?
	What is the collective effect of the board's and audit committee's actions regarding internal control?
Management's philosophy and operating style	Does management philosophy about business risks support a strong system of internal control?
	What is the collective effect of management's actions regarding internal control?

(continues)

Figure 10-8 ■ (Continued)

Component of Internal Control	Key Questions
Control Environment *(continued)*	
Organizational structure	Does management have the right people in the right roles to achieve its objectives?
	Did management consider IT risks when thinking about the organizational structure of IT?
Assignment of authority and responsibility	Does the organization support a high level of accountability for the accomplishment of organizational objectives and ownership of controls?
Human resource policies and practices	Are HR supports in place to emphasize the importance of controls?
Risk Assessment	How does management identify, and continually monitor, relevant business risks, inherent risks, and fraud risks?
	Are control objectives aligned with actual business processes and risks? Is there a shared understanding of accountability for objectives, risks, and controls?
Information and Communication	For each significant transaction cycle, how does the accounting system identify, assemble, analyze, classify, record, and report the entity's transactions? Is a clear understanding of individual roles and responsibilities communicated?
Control Activities	
Authorization	Is there a method of specific authorization for each significant transaction cycle?
Segregation of duties	Is there appropriate segregation of duties within each transaction cycle?
Information processing controls	
General controls	Are effective controls in place to segregate program development and design from IT operations?
	Are effective controls in place over program changes?
Application controls	Do effective input, processing, and output controls monitor transaction class assertions?
	Is manual followup of computer-identified exceptions effective?
Controls over the financial reporting process	Are procedures in place to control data that is downloaded into spreadsheets to ensure the completeness and accuracy of the financial reporting process?
Physical controls	Do physical controls adequately control access to the entity's assets and resources?
Performance reviews	Does management adequately review the performance of each key operating unit?
	Do unit managers adequately review transactions charged to their responsibility center?
Controls over management discretion in financial reporting	Are key accounting decisions centralized in one or a few key individuals?
	Are accounting estimates consistent and based on reliable data?
	Has the audit committee placed in operation effective controls over management discretion in financial reporting?

(continues)

Figure 10-8 ■ (Continued)

Component of Internal Control	Key Questions
Monitoring	Are there effective ways for customers and vendors to independently report concerns about information coming from the financial reporting system?
	Is management involved in monitoring the effectiveness of other aspects of internal control?
Antifraud Programs and Controls	Does the control environment set a tone at the top that encourages ethical conduct?
	Does the company offer an anonymous hotline or other opportunities for employees to report suspected fraud to individuals who are independent of management?
	Does management have an effective program for assessing fraud risks and for matching effective controls with assessed risks?
	Does management have an effective program for ongoing monitoring of fraud risk and for separate "after the fact" evaluation of fraud?

[LEARNING CHECK

10-6 a. Name the six components of internal control.
 b. In a financial statement audit, the auditor focuses on each component's relationship to entity objectives and related controls that are designed to do what?

10-7 a. List the factors that comprise the control environment.
 b. State four things the CEO and other members of top management should do to emphasize the importance of integrity and ethical values among the entity's personnel.
 c. Explain the important IT aspects of the control environment.

10-8 a. How is management's risk assessment for financial reporting purposes similar to, and different from, the auditor's risk assessment?
 b. Identify the key risks that management should be concerned about with respect to information technology and internal control.

10-9 a. In addition to its being a part of the information and communication component, how would you describe the accounting system?
 b. What are the attributes of an effective accounting system?
 c. Discuss how the attributes identified in (b) above relate to one or more of the five categories of financial statement assertions.
 d. Identify key IT aspects of the information and communication system.

10-10 a. What is the objective of segregation of duties?
 b. Describe two key aspects of segregation of duties.
 c. Describe important segregations of duties within the IT department.

10-11 a. Explain the purpose of computer general controls.
 b. If computer general controls are effective, what are the implications for other aspects of the audit?

Figure 10-9 ■ Components of Internal Controls

Component	Description Relative to Financial Reporting	Key Factors	Important IT Factors
Control Environment	Sets the tone for an organization; influences control consciousness of its people, is the foundation for all other components of internal controls.	Control environment factors: ■ Integrity and ethical values. ■ Commitment to competence. ■ Board of directors and audit committee. ■ Management's philosophy and operating style. ■ Organizational structure. ■ Assignment of authority and responsibility. ■ Human resource policies and practices.	■ Involvement of management in setting policies for developing, modifying, and using computer programs and data. ■ Form of organization structure of data processing. ■ Methods of assigning authority and responsibility over computer systems documentation, including procedures for authorizing transactions and approving systems changes.
Risk Assessment	Entity's identification, analysis, and management of risks relevant to the preparation of financial statements that are fairly presented in conformity to GAAP.	Process should consider: ■ Relationship of risks to specific financial statement assertions and the related activities of recording, processing, summarizing, and reporting financial data. ■ Internal and external events and circumstances. ■ Special consideration of changed circumstances. ■ Inherent risks.	Assessment of risk: ■ That transaction trail may be available for only a short period of time. ■ Of reduced documentary evidence of performance of controls. ■ Files and records usually cannot be read without a computer. ■ That decreased human involvement in computer processing can obscure errors that might be observed in manual systems. ■ Of IT system vulnerability to physical disaster, unauthorized manipulation, and mechanical malfunction. ■ That IT systems may reduce traditional segregation of duties. ■ That changes in systems are more difficult to implement and control.

(continues)

Figure 10-9 ■ (Continued)

Component	Description Relative to Financial Reporting	Key Factors	Important IT Factors
Information and Communication	The information systems include the *accounting system* and consist of the methods and records established to identify, assemble, analyze, classify, record, and report entity transactions, and maintain accountability for related assets and liabilities; *communication* involves providing a clear understanding of individual roles and responsibilities pertaining to internal controls over financial reporting.	Focus of accounting system is on transactions: ■ Effective accounting systems should result in handling of transactions in a way that prevents misstatements in management's financial statement assertions. ■ Systems should provide a complete *audit* or *transaction trail.* ■ Includes policy manuals, charts of accounts, and memoranda.	■ Transaction may be initiated by computer. ■ Audit trail may be in electronic form. ■ How data is converted from source documents to machine-sensible form. ■ How computer files are accessed and updated. ■ Computer processing involvement from initiation for transaction to inclusion in financial statements. ■ Computer involvement in reporting process used to prepare financial statements.

Control Activities	Policies and procedures that help ensure that management directives are carried out and that necessary actions are taken to address risks to achievement of entity objectives; have various objectives and are applied at various organizational and functional levels.	Categories:
		 ■ Authorization
		 ■ Segregation of Duties
		 ■ Information processing controls
		 • General controls
		 • Application controls
		 • Controls over the financial reporting process?
		 ■ Physical controls
		 ■ Performance reviews
		 ■ Controls over management discretion in financial reporting
			General controls
			   Organization and operation controls
			   Systems development and documentation controls
			   Hardware and system software controls
			   Access controls
			   Data and procedural controls
			 Application controls
			   Input
			   Processing
			   Output

Monitoring	Process by appropriate personnel that assess the quality of internal controls over time; includes assessment and design, whether operating as intended, and whether modified as appropriate for changed conditions.	Can occur through: ■ Ongoing activities ■ Separate period evaluations ■ May include input from: • Internal sources such as management and internal auditors • External sources such as a customers, suppliers, regulators, and independent auditors	IT may be monitored in a similar fashion to other internal controls
Antifraud Programs and Controls	Specific programs that help ensure that management's antifraud directives are carried out.	■ See Figure 10-7 for antifraud aspects of each element of the system of internal control.	

10-12 a. Indicate the purpose of each of the three types of applications controls.
b. Identify the categories of controls pertaining to the conversion of data.

10-13 a. Explain the risks associated with the financial reporting process and explain relevant controls that might prevent or detect misstatements in the financial reporting process.

10-14 a. Differentiate between independent checks, performance reviews, and monitoring.
b. Describe several situations in which performance reviews may provide control over financial statement assertions.
c. Describe who should be involved in the monitoring, and discuss how an entity should monitor risks associated with information technology.

10-15 a. Describe the controls that a company might design to effectively control the development of an appropriate allowance for doubtful accounts.
b. Describe the controls that a company might design to effectively control nonroutine transactions.
c. Describe the controls that a company might design to effectively control the selection and application of GAAP.

10-16 Describe the controls a company might use as part of its antifraud programs and controls.

[KEY TERMS

Access controls, p. 408
Accounting system, p. 404
Antifraud programs and controls, p. 414
Application controls, p. 408
Assignment of authority and responsibility, p. 399
Audit trail, p. 404
Board of directors and audit committee, p. 398
Commitment to competence, p. 398
Control activities, p. 405
Control environment, p. 397
Controls over nonroutine and nonsystematic transactions, p. 413
Data and procedural controls, p. 408
Disclosure committees, p. 413
Documents and records, p. 404
General controls, p. 407
Hardware and systems software controls, p. 407
Human resource policies and procedures, p. 400
Independent checks, p. 408

Information processing controls, p. 407
Information and communication system, p. 404
Input controls, p. 408
Integrity and ethical values, p. 397
Management's philosophy and operating style, p. 398
Monitoring, p. 413
Organization and operation controls, p. 407
Organizational structure, p. 398
Output controls, p. 410
Performance reviews, p. 412
Physical controls, p. 411
Processing controls, p. 409
Proper authorization, p. 405
Risk assessment, p. 402
Segregation of duties, p. 406
Systems development and documentation controls, p. 407
Transaction trail, p. 404
Transactions, p. 404

[UNDERSTANDING INTERNAL CONTROL]

The auditor has two separate reasons for obtaining an understanding of internal control. The foundation needed for an audit of the financial statements requires that an auditor obtain an understanding of internal control that allows the auditor to plan the audit and make decisions about the nature, timing, extent, and staffing of audit tests. In addition, public company auditors must also obtain sufficient knowledge to plan an audit to express reasonable assurance about the effectiveness of internal control over financial reporting. Figure 10-10 provides a comparison of these two purposes.

WHAT TO UNDERSTAND ABOUT INTERNAL CONTROL

Auditor Knowledge 3

■ **Know the purpose of understanding internal control needed to plan an audit and how that understanding is used.**

A sufficient understanding of internal control is essential for an effective audit because it informs the auditor about where misstatements are likely to occur. In order to support an opinion on the financial statements (rather than an opinion on internal controls), auditors need a sufficient knowledge of internal control to plan a financial statement audit. **Obtaining an understanding** involves performing procedures to:

■ Understand the design of policies and procedures related to each component of internal control.

■ Determine whether the policies and procedures have been placed in operation.

The auditor uses this knowledge in three ways. The auditor should know enough to

1. Identify the types of potential misstatements that may occur.
2. Understand the factors that affect the risk of material misstatement.
3. Design further audit procedures.

Each of these three steps is discussed below.

Figure 10-10 ■ Understanding Internal Control in Private Company and Public Company Audits

Knowledge to Support an Opinion on the System of Internal Control

The auditor should have sufficient knowledge to plan and perform an audit to obtain reasonable assurance that material weaknesses in internal control are identified

Knowledge to Support an Opinion on Financial Statements

The auditor needs sufficient knowledge of internal control to:
■ Identify the types of potential misstatement that may occur.
■ Understand the factors that effect the risk of material misstatement
■ Design the nature, timing, and extent of further audit procedures

> **understanding of internal controls needed to support an opinion on internal controls**
>
> Auditors of public companies need to have sufficient knowledge to support *both* an opinion on the financial statement and an opinion on internal control over financial reporting (ICFR). The latter requires that the auditor understand the system of ICFR in sufficient detail that the auditor can determine that effective controls have been placed in operation to prevent or detect any material misstatement (individually or in aggregate) in the financial statements on a timely basis. Even if the auditor plans a primarily substantive approach for an assertion (e.g., the valuation of net receivables), the auditor needs to understand (and test) the client's system of internal controls over that assertion. For *each significant process*, the auditor of a public company should:
>
> - Understand the flow of transactions, including how transactions are initiated, authorized, recorded, processed, and reported.
> - Identify the points within the process at which a misstatement—including a misstatement due to fraud—related to each relevant financial statement assertion could arise.
> - Identify the controls that management has implemented to address these potential misstatements.
> - Identify the controls that management has implemented for the prevention or timely detection of unauthorized acquisition, use, or disposition of the company's assets.

PCAOB
Public Companies
Accounting Oversight Board

Identifying the Types of Potential Misstatements that May Occur

An important aspect of assessing the risk of material misstatement involves obtaining an understanding of the points at which errors or fraud could occur. Some internal control weaknesses have a pervasive effect on the financial statements. A poor control environment, or weak computer general controls, might increase the risk of material misstatement for most or all assertions in the financial statements. Other weaknesses are assertion specific. At some stage in the recording of a transaction, the change of information, or the addition of new information, may not be controlled. For example, an entity might record sales when an order is taken from a customer rather than when goods are shipped, resulting in potential cutoff errors. Perhaps a company has designed effective computer controls, but due to changes in personnel the company has hired someone who does not adequately understand the role that he or she plays in following up on items that appear on exception reports. This lack of knowledge and inappropriate manual followup may create potential for error or fraud. As a result, auditors usually consider how errors in each financial statement assertion might occur. Once this potential is understood, the auditor will identify potential controls that prevent or detect misstatements in each assertion.

Understanding the Factors that Affect the Risk of Material Misstatement

Once the auditor understands the types of potential misstatements that may occur, the auditor must assess the risk of material misstatement. When considering the factors that affect the risk of material misstatement, the auditor usually considers:

- The magnitude of the misstatement that might occur.
- The likelihood of misstatements in the financial statements.

For example, the magnitude of a revenue recognition problem is usually greater than the magnitude of a misstatement in the amortization of prepaid expenses. In addition, revenue recognition might be a more likely problem for a software company that is selling a group of bundled products and services than for a retailer who delivers goods at the point of sale. Every company might have a risk of a material misstatement if a hacker is able to gain unauthorized access to a company's computer system. The magnitude of potential misstatement might be very significant. However, the auditor must also assess the likelihood of such an event. If a company has good access controls, strong firewalls, and other controls that might detect attempts at unauthorized access to computer systems, the likelihood of unauthorized access is remote.

Designing Further Audit Procedures

The auditor uses the knowledge of internal control in three ways. At this stage the auditor has completed the risk assessment procedures outlined in Figure 7-4. First, the auditor needs to consider whether these procedures are adequate to allow the auditor to assess the risk of material misstatement for each significant financial statement assertion. If the auditor does not have adequate information, the auditor should perform additional risk assessment procedures.

Second, the auditor uses this knowledge to plan tests of controls. The design of tests of controls is discussed extensively in Chapter 11. Finally, the auditor needs to know the system of internal control in order to design substantive tests. Knowledge of the audit trail is essential in understanding the potential for error or fraud and for designing effective substantive tests. Chapter 12 discusses the important audit decisions about the design of substantive audit procedures.

Risks for Which Substantive Tests Alone Will Not Reduce Audit Risk to a Sufficiently Low Level

In some cases, the client's accounting system is sufficiently automated that substantive tests alone will not reduce audit risk to a sufficiently low level. Many businesses that take orders over the phone do not generate a paper trail for the transactions. For example, many airlines take reservations over the phone (or electronically over the Internet), record the reservation and transaction in electronic form, and then issue an electronic ticket. Some companies have purchase systems that never generate a paper purchase order, but have only an electronic trail of the transaction and provide the vendor with only an electronic purchase order in a business-to-business e-commerce system. In these cases the only way that the auditor can obtain reasonable assurance about the completeness and accuracy of the transactions in the transaction cycle is to test computer general controls, computer application controls, and manual followup procedures. In many charitable organizations, there is no way to ensure the completeness of donations without testing the internal controls over cash receipts. The understanding of the nature of the system of internal controls may dictate a lower assessed level of control risk audit strategy.

EFFECTS OF PRELIMINARY AUDIT STRATEGIES

In Chapter 9, three alternative preliminary audit strategies for planning the audit of significant financial statement assertions were identified and explained (see Figure 9-8). With a public company a deep understanding of internal control is needed regardless of which strategy is chosen because the auditor must issue an opinion on the effectiveness of the entity's system of internal control. However, private company auditors may plan to obtain a minimal understanding of internal control for assertions where a primarily substantive approach is efficient. Although the level of understanding of internal control sufficient to plan audit tests varies depending on the planned audit strategy, a greater understanding of internal control is needed under the lower assessed level of control risk approach than under a primarily substantive approach. This is particularly true of the control activities component as explained further in the following sections.

An important issue in a private company audit is understanding the minimum level of understanding of internal control that the auditor needs when performing primarily substantive approach. An auditor cannot assess control risk at the maximum without support. Following is a brief summary of the minimum knowledge that the auditor needs in order to understand the risk of misstatement and to plan a primarily substantive approach.

■ *Control Environment.* Because the control environment has such a pervasive influence on other aspects of internal control, as well as the risk of misstatement in the financial statements, the auditor should answer the questions about the control environment outlined in Figure 10-8. In every audit, the auditor needs to understand the control environment's collective effect on other aspects of internal control.

■ *Risk Assessment.* The auditor should understand how management has designed controls to offset business risks, inherent risks, and the risk of fraud. The questions in Figure 10-8 provide a common understanding about risk assessment that the auditor should obtain in any audit.

■ *Information and Communication.* Regardless of audit strategy, AU 319.36 indicates that the auditor should obtain sufficient knowledge of the information systems relevant to financial reporting to understand:

  ■ The classes of transactions in the entity's operations that are significant to the financial statements.

  ■ How those transactions are initiated.

  ■ The accounting records, supporting documents, and specific accounts in the financial statements involved in the processing and reporting of transactions.

  ■ The accounting processing involved from the initiation of a transaction to its inclusion in the financial statements, including electronic means (such as computer and electronic data interchange) used to transmit, process, maintain, and access information.

  ■ The financial reporting process used to prepare the entity's financial statements, including significant accounting estimates and disclosures.

The auditor needs to understand the information and communication system in sufficient detail to identify the points at which misstatements may occur in the accounting system and to be able to design effective substantive tests.

- *Control Activities.* Control activities are essential to reducing the opportunity for fraud. At a minimum, auditors should understand how transactions are authorized and the adequacy of segregation of duties. The degree to which auditors understand control activities is related to the extent to which the auditor plans to test those controls and change the nature, timing, or extent of substantive tests.

- *Monitoring.* It is important to understand the types of activities used by the entity, top management, accounting management, and internal auditors to monitor the effectiveness of internal control in meeting financial reporting objectives. Knowledge should also be obtained as to how corrective actions are initiated based on information gleaned from monitoring activities.

GAAS (AU 319.23) suggests several other factors that should be considered in reaching a judgment about the required level of understanding, as follows:

- Knowledge of the client from previous audits.
- Preliminary assessments of materiality and inherent risk (as explained in Chapters 8 and 9).
- An understanding of the entity and its environment (as explained in Chapter 7).
- The complexity and sophistication of the entity's operations and systems, including whether the method of controlling information processing is based on manual procedures independent of the computer or is highly dependent on computerized controls.

In addition, when significant inherent risks are identified, the auditor must understand the design of internal controls relevant to those assertions and whether the controls have been placed in operation.

When the auditor plans to audit an assertion following a lower assessed level of control risk approach, the auditor will normally understand the control activities aspect of the system of internal controls in much more depth. Under a lower assessed level of control risk approach, the auditor will usually understand information processing controls (general controls, application controls, and controls over the financial reporting process), manual followup procedures, and other controls (e.g., performance reviews) that may be relevant to the planned audit strategy.

PROCEDURES TO OBTAIN AN UNDERSTANDING

Audit Decision 7

■ What audit procedures are used to obtain an understanding of internal controls?

In obtaining an understanding of controls that are relevant to audit planning, the auditor should perform procedures to provide sufficient knowledge of the design of the relevant controls pertaining to each of the five internal control components and whether they have been placed in operation. AU 319.41 suggests that the **procedures to obtain an understanding** consist of:

- Reviewing previous experience with the client.
- Inquiring of appropriate management, supervisory, and staff personnel.
- Inspecting documents and records.
- Observing entity activities and operations.
- Tracing transactions through the information and communication system.

The nature and extent of the procedures performed generally vary from entity to entity and are influenced by the size and complexity of the entity, the auditor's

knowledge to plan an audit of internal controls over financial reporting

When planning an audit of internal controls over financial reporting, the auditor needs a comprehensive knowledge of the company. Some of that knowledge pertains directly to the entity's system of internal controls, including:

- Knowledge of the company's internal control over financial reporting obtained in other engagements.
- The extent of recent changes in internal control over financial reporting.
- Management's process for assessing the effectiveness of the company's internal control over financial reporting based on control criteria.
- Control deficiencies previously communicated to the audit committee or management.
- The type and extent of available evidence related to the effectiveness of the company's internal control over financial reporting.
- Preliminary judgments about the effectiveness of internal control over financial reporting.
- The number of significant business locations or units, including management's documentation and monitoring of controls over such locations or business units.

In addition, the auditor needs knowledge of the company and its environment. This knowledge might include:

- Matters affecting the industry in which the company operates, such as financial reporting practices, economic conditions, laws and regulations, and technological changes.
- Matters relating to the company's business, including its organization, operating characteristics, capital structure, and distribution methods.
- The extent of recent changes in the company's operations.
- Preliminary judgments about materiality, risk, and other factors related to the determination of a material weakness.
- Legal or regulatory matters of which the company is aware.

Hence, an understanding of the company and its environment that is obtained for an audit of the financial statements also sets the context for an audit of internal control over financial reporting.

PCAOB
Public Companies
Accounting Oversight Board

previous experience with the entity, the nature of the particular control, and the entity's documentation of specific controls.

When the auditor has previous experience with the client, the previous year's working papers should contain a great deal of information relevant to the current year's audit. The previous year's conclusions about strengths and weaknesses in internal control can be used as the starting point, with the auditor making inquiries about changes that may have occurred in the current year that would affect the previous conditions. The working papers should also contain information about the types of misstatements found in prior audits and their causes. The working papers might show whether prior misstatements resulted from (1) lack of adequate controls, (2) deliberate circumvention of prescribed controls, (3) unintentional noncompliance with prescribed controls by inexperienced personnel, or (4) differences in professional judgment about accounting estimates. The auditor can follow up on this information to determine whether corrective actions have been taken.

Relevant documents and records of the entity should be inspected. Examples include organization charts, policy manuals, the chart of accounts, accounting ledgers, journals, source documents, transaction flowcharts, and reports used by management in performance reviews such as comparative reports showing actual and budgeted data and variances. These inspections will inevitably lead to additional inquiries about specific controls and changes in conditions. Observation of the performance of some controls will be needed to determine that they have been placed in operation.

To reinforce the understanding of some aspects of the accounting system and certain control activities, some auditors perform a **transaction walkthrough review.** A transaction walkthrough allows the auditor to observe—firsthand—how controls actually work. A transaction walkthrough is a required step in performing an audit of internal controls over financial reporting. It provides the auditor with evidence to:

- Confirm the auditor's understanding of the process flow of transactions.
- Confirm the auditor's understanding of the design of controls identified for all five components of internal control over financial reporting, including those related to the prevention or detection of fraud.
- Confirm that the auditor's understanding of the process is complete by determining whether all points in the process at which misstatements related to each relevant financial statement assertion that could occur have been identified.
- Evaluate the effectiveness of the design of controls.
- Confirm whether controls have been placed in operation.

Transaction walkthroughs should include effective inquiry to ensure that employees fully understand how to effectively implement the controls that they are responsible for. Some auditing firms also provide special training for staff in interviewing skills used in administering questionnaires. For example, by being alert to nonverbal signals given by interviewees, such as the hesitancy to respond, apparent lack of familiarity with controls, or undue nervousness during interviews, the auditor's understanding can be significantly enhanced.

LEARNING CHECK

10-17 a. Explain the purpose of understanding internal control in a private entity audit.
b. Explain the purpose of understanding internal control in a public company audit.

10-18 a. Identify two matters that should be covered in obtaining an understanding of internal control.
b. Explain three ways in which the auditor uses knowledge of internal control. Provide an example of each.

10-19 a. What effect does the auditor's choice of preliminary audit strategy for an assertion have on the level of understanding needed for each element of internal control?

b. What other factors affect the auditor's judgment about the required level of understanding?

10-20 a. What should the auditor understand about the control environment component of internal control?

b. What aspects of the information system relevant to financial reporting should be included in the auditor's understanding?

10-21 a. What procedures can be used in obtaining an understanding of internal control?

b. What is a transaction walkthrough review?

10-22 Explain how the understanding of internal control for a public company differs from the understanding of internal control associated with the audit of a private entity in accordance with GAAS.

[KEY TERMS

Obtaining an understanding, p. 422
Procedures to obtain an
   understanding, p. 426

Transaction walkthrough review,
   p. 428

DOCUMENTING THE UNDERSTANDING

Audit Decision 8
■ **What are the requirements and alternative methods for documenting the understanding of internal control?**

Documenting the understanding of internal control is required in all audits. AU 319.44 states that the form and extent of documentation are influenced by the size and complexity of the entity, and the nature of the entity's internal control. Documentation in the working papers may take the form of completed questionnaires, flowcharts, decision tables (in a computerized accounting system), and narrative memoranda. In an audit of a large entity involving a combination of audit strategies, all four types of documentation may be used for different parts of the understanding. In an audit of a small entity where the primarily substantive approach predominates, a single memorandum may suffice to document the understanding of all the components.

The auditor may document the understanding concurrent with obtaining it. Auditors frequently record clients' responses to inquiries in questionnaires that become part of the working papers. Auditors can also document the understanding of the entity's accounting system and certain control activities by preparing flowcharts or including in the working papers flowcharts provided by the clients for the auditor's use. In a repeat engagement, it may only be necessary to update questionnaires, flowcharts, or narrative memoranda carried forward from the prior year's working papers. Documentation need pertain only to portions of internal control that are relevant to the audit. The following discussion explains four forms of documentation commonly used by auditors: questionnaires, flowcharts, decision tables, and narrative memoranda.

Questionnaires

A **questionnaire** consists of a series of questions about internal control that the auditor considers necessary to prevent material misstatements in the financial statements. The questions are usually phrased so that either a *Yes, No,* or *N/A* (not applicable) answer results, with a *Yes* answer indicating a favorable condition. Space is also provided for comments such as who performs a control procedure and how often. There are usually separate questions for each major transaction class (e.g., sales or cash disbursements). The auditor's software then analyzes the pattern of responses across related questions and guides the auditor through subsequent steps in assessing control risk and designing substantive tests for specific financial statement assertions.

Excerpts from two questionnaires are illustrated in Figures 10-11 and 10-12. These illustrations pertain to parts of the control environment and the control activities' internal control components. In Figure 10-12, it may be observed that the questions relate to several possible categories of control activities. For example, questions 1 and 4 pertain to authorization procedures, 2 and 6 to documents and records, 5, 8, and 9 to independent checks, 3 to physical controls, and 7a and b to segregation of duties. More importantly, the questions may be linked to financial statement assertions. For example, *No* answers to the questions listed below could signal the potential for misstatements in the indicated related assertions for cash disbursements:

Questions	Assertions
1,2, 6, or 7a	Existence and Occurrence
2, 3, 7b, 8, or 9	Completeness
5, 8, 9	Valuation and allocation
8, 9	Existence and Occurrence, Cutoff
5	Presentation and Disclosure

Note that some questions pertain to more than one assertion.

As a means of documenting the understanding, questionnaires offer a number of advantages. They are usually developed by very experienced professionals and provide excellent guidance to the less experienced staff. They are relatively easy to use, and they significantly reduce the possibility of overlooking important internal control structure matters.

Flowcharts

A **flowchart** is a schematic diagram using standardized symbols, interconnecting flow lines, and annotations that portray the steps involved in processing information through the accounting system. Flowcharts vary in the extent of detail shown. A broad overview flowchart containing just a few symbols can be prepared for the accounting systems as a whole or for a particular transaction cycle such as a revenue cycle. In addition, very detailed flowcharts can be prepared depicting the processing of individual classes of transactions such as sales, cash receipts, purchases, cash disbursements, payroll, and manufacturing.

Many of the flowcharts shown in this text are designed to work with a narrative description that describes controls in additional detail. These flowcharts show:

- The flow of transactions from initiating the transaction to their summarization in the general ledger (that support the financial statements).
- The key functions included in the flowchart.
- The documentary audit trail.
- Key reports produced by the accounting system.

Figure 10-11 ■ Excerpts from Internal Control Questionnaire —Control Environment

Client	_Amalgamated Products, Inc._	Balance Sheet Date	_12/31/x1_
Completed by	_R&C_	Date _9/12/x1_	Reviewed by _g&j_ Date _9/29/x1_

Internal Control Questionnaire
Component: Control Environment

Question	Yes, No, N/A	Comments
Integrity and ethical values:		
1. Does management set the "tone at the top" by demonstrating a commitment to integrity and ethics through both its words and deeds?	_Yes_	_Management is conscious of setting an example. Entity does not have a formal code of conduct; expectations of_
2. Have appropriate entity policies regarding acceptable business practices, conflicts of interest, and codes of conduct been established and adequately communicated?	_Yes_	_employees included in a policy manual distributed to all employees. Profit_
3. Have incentives and temptations that might lead to unethical behavior been reduced or eliminated?	_Yes_	_sharing plan monitored by audit committee._
Board of directors and audit committee:		
1. Are there regular meetings of the board and are minutes prepared on a timely basis?	_Yes_	_Board consists of nine inside members, three of whom currently serve on audit_
2. Do board members have sufficient knowledge, experience, and time to serve effectively?	_Yes_	_committee._ _Consideration is being given to adding_
3. Is there an audit committee composed of outside directors?	_No_	_three outside members to board who would comprise the audit committee._
Management's philosophy and operating style:		
1. Are business risks carefully considered and adequately monitored?	_Yes_	_Management is conservative about business risks._
2. Is management's selection of accounting principles and development of accounting estimates consistent with objective and fair reporting?	_Yes_	_Management has readily accepted all proposed adjustments in prior audits._
3. Has management demonstrated a willingness to adjust the financial statements for material misstatements?	_Yes_	
Human resource policies and practices:		
1. Do existing personnel policies and procedures result in recruiting or developing competent and trustworthy people necessary to support an effective internal control structure?	_Yes_	
2. Do personnel understand the duties and procedures applicable to their jobs?	_Yes_	_Formal job descriptions are provided for all positions. Normal turnover._
3. Is the turnover of personnel in key positions at an acceptable level?	_Yes_	

Figure 10-12 ■ Excerpts from Internal Control Questionnaire—Control Activities

Client	_Amalgamated Products, Inc._			Balance Sheet Date	_12/31/x1_
Completed by	_R&C_	Date _9/12/x1_		Reviewed by _g&j_ Date	_10/29/x1_

Internal Control Questionnaire
Component: Control Activities

Question	Yes, No, N/A	Comments
Cash disbursements transactions:		
1. Is there an approved payment voucher with supporting documents for each check prepared?	_Yes_	
2. Are prenumbered checks used and accounted for?	_Yes_	_Safe in treasurer's office._
3. Are unused checks stored in a secure area?	_Yes_	_Only the treasurer and assistant treas-_
4. Are only authorized personnel permitted to sign checks?	_Yes_	_urer can sign checks._
5. Do check signers verify agreement of details of check and payment voucher before signing?	_Yes_	
6. Are vouchers and supporting documents cancelled after payment?	_Yes_	_Vouchers and all supporting documents are stamped "Paid."_
7. Is there segregation of duties for:		
a. Approving payment vouchers and signing checks?	_Yes_	
b. Signing checks and recording checks?	_Yes_	
8. Is there an independent check of agreement of daily summary of checks issued with entry to cash disbursements?	_No_	_Comparison currently made by assistant treasurer; will recommend comparison be performed by asst. controller._
9. Are there periodic independent reconciliations of checking accounts?	_Yes_	_Performed by assistant controller._

■ Computer programs and files where information is stored.

A detailed example of cash receipts is provided in Appendix 10c: Comprehensive Flowcharting Illustration.

Once a flowchart is obtained from the client or prepared by the auditor, many auditors perform a transaction walkthrough, as previously described, to test its accuracy and completeness. The flowchart should then be studied to identify and document strengths and weakness. Internal control strengths provide the potential for the auditor to perform tests of controls and support an audit strategy of a lower assessed level of control risk. Internal control weaknesses create situations where the auditor must determine whether there are mitigating strengths or whether there are significant risks of misstatement in assertions that must be addressed by a substantive audit strategy.

Flowcharts are easy to read and understand. They provide a quick overview of a system for an individual who is not familiar with that system. Today many audit firms develop flowcharts with computer software that allows the auditor to identify internal control strengths and weaknesses on the flowchart, describe the controls in detail, and cross-reference the strengths and weaknesses to subsequent audit tests.

Decision Tables

A **decision table** is a matrix used to document the logic of a computer program. Decision tables usually have three key components, (1) conditions related to accounting transactions, (2) actions taken by the computer program, and (3) decision rules that are used to like conditions with subsequent actions. Figure 10-13 provides an example of a decision table.

The *conditions* included in a decision table usually represent conditions related to control procedures that are relevant to the audit. Figure 10-13 provides two examples in the expenditure cycle. First, a computer program might compare the vendor number input to record a liability with vendor numbers that have previously been approved as part of a master vendor file. Second, the expenditure program might compare information from the vendor's invoice with information previously entered into the computer regarding goods that were received. Numerous examples of control procedures (conditions) are discussed in Part 4 of the text for the revenue cycle, the expenditure cycle, and the production and payroll cycles.

Actions represent the actions taken by the computer program when conditions are encountered. Continuing the example in Figure 10-13, we see that when the first condition is encountered, the computer program will process the transactions when the expected conditions are met. However, if the vendor number entered in accounts payable does not match a vendor on the approved vendor list, the transaction will not be processed and an exception will appear on the data entry screen. An alternative action is described in the second example. In this case, if the information on the vendor's invoice does not match the receiving information, the transaction is put in a suspense file and an exception report is printed for further investigation.

The combination of conditions and actions describe the program's decision rules. For example, if the conditions of the control procedures described in Figure 10-13 are met, the transaction is processed. Understanding the decision rules is critical to designing tests of controls. For example, the auditor might choose to submit test data to test each decision rule of audit interest. The decision rules in the decision table clearly describe the types of test data that would need to be designed and submitted to perform a test of controls.

Figure 10-13 ■ Example Decision Table Documentation

	Decision Rules		
	1	2	3
Conditions			
Does the vendor number match with the authorized vendor file?	Y	N	
Does receiving information match with information on the vendor's invoice?	Y		N
Actions			
Process transaction.	X		
Show exception on data entry screen and ask operator to reenter data.		X	
Move transaction to suspense file and print exception on exception report for further investigation.			X

Decision tables are particularly useful when understanding programmed application controls. The advantages of decision tables are that they are compact and easily understood, they provide a systematic approach for analyzing program logic, and it is easy to design tests of controls using decision tables.

Narrative Memoranda

A **narrative memorandum** consists of written comments concerning the auditor's consideration of internal controls. A memorandum may be used to supplement flowcharts or other forms of documentation by summarizing the auditor's overall understanding of internal control, individual components of internal control, or specific policies or procedures. In audits of small entities, a narrative memorandum may serve as the only documentation of the auditor's understanding. Figure 10-14 illustrates this type of documentation for a small owner-managed company. Narrative memoranda are cost-effective, easy to create, and descriptive of the internal controls used by an entity.

Figure 10-14 ■ Narrative Memorandum Documenting Understanding of Control Environment

CLIENT *Quinco, Inc.*		**BALANCE SHEET DATE** *12/31*	
Completed by: *m/w*	**Date:** *9/30/X5*	**Reviewed by:** *jp*	**Date:** *11/02/X5*
Updated by: *m/w*	**Date:** *9/15/X6*	**Reviewed by:** *jp*	**Date:** *10/29/X6*

Understanding of the Control Environment

The Company manufactures plastic fishing worms at one location and is managed by its sole owner, Ed Jones. Management of the company is dominated by Jones, who is responsible for marketing, purchasing, hiring, and approving major transactions. He has an understanding of the business and the industry in which it operates. Jones believes that hiring experienced personnel is particularly important because there are no layers of supervisory personnel and thus, because of limited segregation of duties, few independent checks of employees' work. Jones has a moderate-to-conservative attitude toward business risks. The business has demonstrated consistent profitability and, because Jones considers lower taxes to be as important as financial results, he has a conservative attitude toward accounting estimates.

Jones and Pat Willis, the bookkeeper, readily consult with our firm on routine accounting questions, including the preparation of accounting estimates (tax accrual, inventory obsolescence, or bad debts). Our firm also assists in assembling the financial statements.

The Company's board of directors is composed of family members. The board is not expected to monitor the business or the owner-manager's activities.

Most of the significant accounting functions are performed by Willis, the bookkeeper, and Jones's secretary, Chris Ross. Willis was hired by the company in 19X0, has a working knowledge of accounting fundamentals, and we have no reason to question her competence. Willis regularly consults with our firm on unusual transactions, and past history indicates that it is rare for adjustments to arise from errors in the processing of routine transactions.

Jones made the decision to purchase a microcomputer and a turnkey accounting software package. The source code is not available for this software. Access to the computer and computer files is limited to Willis, Ross, and Jones, who effectively have access to all computer files.

The owner-manager carefully reviews computer generated financial reports, such as reports on receivable aging, and compares revenues and expenses with prior years' performance. He also monitors the terms of the long-term debt agreement that requires certain ratios and compensating balances.

Source: AICPA Audit Guide, *Consideration of the Internal Control Structure in a Financial Statement Audit* (1990), p. 117–118.

management's documentation of internal control over financial reporting

Management of a public company is responsible for documenting internal controls over financial reporting. That documentation should include:

- The design of controls over all relevant assertions related to all significant accounts and disclosures in the financial statements. The documentation should include the five components of internal control over financial reporting and company-level controls such as:
  - Controls within the control environment.
  - Management's risk assessment process.
  - Centralized process and controls, including shared service environments.
  - Controls to monitor the results of operations.
  - Controls to monitor other controls, including activities of the internal audit function, the audit committee, and self-assessment programs.
  - The period-end financial reporting process.
  - Board-approved policies that address significant business control and risk management practices.
- Information about how significant transactions are initiated, authorized, recorded, processed, and reported.
- Sufficient information about the flow of transactions to identify the point at which material misstatements due to error or fraud could occur.
- Controls designed to prevent or detect fraud, including who performs controls and the related segregation of duties.
- Controls over the period-end financial reporting process.
- Controls over safeguarding of assets.
- The results of management's testing and evaluation.

Inadequate documentation could cause the independent auditor to conclude that there is a limitation on the scope of the engagement.

PCAOB
Public Companies
Accounting Oversight Board

[LEARNING CHECK

10-23 a. What methods can be used to document the auditor's understanding of internal control?
 b. Can documentation occur concurrently with obtaining an understanding? Explain.

10-24 a. What is the general nature of the questions included in internal control questionnaires?
 b. Identify several advantages of using questionnaires to document the auditor's understanding of internal control.

10-25 a. How may narrative memoranda supplement other forms of documentation?
 b. Would a narrative memorandum ever be appropriate as the sole documentation of the auditor's understanding of internal control? Explain.

10-26 a. What is a flowchart?

b. What essential components of a system should be displayed in a flowchart?

10-27 a. What is management's responsibility to document the system of internal control in a public company where the auditor is engaged to give an opinion on the system of internal control?

b. How should the auditor respond in an engagement to audit the system of internal control if management's documentation is deemed inadequate?

[KEY TERMS

Decision table, p. 433
Documenting the understanding, p. 429

Flowchart, p. 430
Narrative memorandum, p. 434
Questionnaire, p. 429

[FOCUS ON AUDITOR KNOWLEDGE AND AUDIT DECISIONS]

This chapter focuses on understanding the client's system of internal control. In making decisions to support high-quality audit work, the auditor must be able to use the knowledge summarized in Figure 10-15 and address the decisions summarized in Figure 10-16. Page references are provided indicating where these issues are discussed in more detail.

Figure 10-15 ■ Summary of Auditor Knowledge Discussed in Chapter 10

Auditor Knowledge	Summary	Chapter References
K1. Know the definitions of internal control and the five interrelated components of internal control.	Internal control is a process, effected by an entity's board of directors, management, and other personnel, designed to provide reasonable assurance regarding the achievement of objectives in the following categories: (1) reliability of financial reporting, (2) compliance with applicable laws and regulations, and (3) effectiveness and efficiency of operations. The auditor is primarily concerned with internal controls over financial reporting. The five interrelated components of internal control are (a) the control environment, (b) risk assessment, (c) information and communication, (d) control activities, and (e) monitoring.	pp. 392–393
K2. Know the inherent limitations of internal control and explain the roles and responsibilities of various parties for an entity's internal controls.	Inherent limitations of any system of internal control include mistakes in judgment, breakdowns, collusion, management override, and cost versus benefits (although this last limitation may not be relevant for public companies). This section also discusses the responsibilities of management, the board of directors and audit committee, internal auditors, other entity personnel, and independent auditors.	pp. 393–395

(continues)

Figure 10-15 ■ (Continued)

Auditor Knowledge	Summary	Chapter References
K3. Know the purpose of understanding internal control needed to plan an audit and how that understanding is used.	In a financial statement audit, the auditor needs sufficient knowledge of internal control to (1) identify the types of potential misstatements that may occur, (2) understand the factors that affect the risk of material misstatement, and (3) design the nature, timing, and extent of further audit procedures. When the auditor is engaged to express an opinion on internal controls over financial reporting, the auditor must obtain sufficient knowledge to plan and perform an audit to obtain reasonable assurance that deficiencies which, individually or in aggregate, would represent a material weakness in internal control, are identified.	pp. 422–428

Figure 10-16 ■ Summary of Audit Decisions Discussed in Chapter 10

Audit Decision	Factors that Influence the Audit Decision	Chapter References
D1. What are the key components of a strong control environment, including relevant IT aspects?	The control environment is a critical aspect of internal control because of its pervasive effect on other components of internal control. Key components of the control environment include integrity and ethical values, commitment to competence, board of directors and audit committee, management's philosophy and operating style, organizational structure, assignment of authority and responsibility, and human resource policies and practices. Important IT aspects of the control environment are summarized in Figure 10-9.	pp. 397–402
D2: What are the key components of strong risk assessment activities, including relevant IT aspects?	The risk assessment process is one in which management assesses the risk of misstatement in specific financial statement assertions related to the activities of recording, processing, summarizing, and reporting financial data. Management uses this risk assessment to guide the design of specific control activities. Important IT aspects of the risk assessment process are summarized in Figure 10-9.	pp. 402–403
D3. What are the key components of an effective information and communication system, including relevant IT aspects?	The information and communication system relevant to financial reporting objectives, which includes the accounting system, consists of the methods and records established to identify, assemble, analyze, classify, record and report entity transactions (as well as events and conditions) and to maintain accountability for the related assets and liabilities. *Communication* involves providing a clear understanding of individual roles and responsibilities pertaining to internal control over financial reporting. Important IT aspects of information and communication processes are summarized in Figure 10-9.	pp. 404–405

(continues)

Figure 10-16 ■ (Continued)

Audit Decision	Factors that Influence the Audit Decision	Chapter References
D4. What are the key components of strong control activities, including relevant IT aspects?	Important aspects of control activities include controls over authorization of transactions, segregation of duties, information processing controls including general and application controls, physical controls, performance reviews, controls over management discretion in financial reporting, and antifraud programs and controls. Important IT aspects of control activities are summarized in Figure 10-9.	pp. 405–413
D5: What are the key components of strong monitoring activities, including relevant IT aspects?	Monitoring is a process that assesses the quality of internal control performance over time. It involves assessing the design and operation of controls on a timely basis and taking necessary corrective actions. Important IT aspects of monitoring activities are summarized in Figure 10-9.	pp. 413–414
D6. What are the key components of a strong antifraud program and controls?	Effective antifraud programs and controls influence every aspect of the system of internal control through monitoring. Figure 10-9 provides an overview of the elements of an effective system of antifraud programs and controls.	pp. 414–415
D7. What audit procedures are used to obtain an understanding of internal controls?	An auditor normally uses the following procedures to obtain an understanding of the entity's system of internal control: reviewing previous experience with the client, inquiring of appropriate management, supervisory, and staff personnel, inspecting documents and records, observing entity activities and operations, and tracing transactions through the information and communication system.	pp. 426–428
D8. What are the requirements and alternative methods for documenting the understanding of internal control?	Auditors are required to document their understanding of the client's system of internal control in every audit. That documentation is flexible and may include the use of questionnaires, flowcharts, decision tables, and narrative memoranda. The text provides numerous examples of four forms of documentation.	pp. 429–435

appendix 10a

INFORMATION TECHNOLOGY AND INTERNAL CONTROL

Information technology (IT) was one of the most important developments of the second half of the twentieth century. Computer installations now range in size from microcomputers to minicomputers to large mainframe computers linked together in complex international communication networks. A company may elect to lease or own its computer system or to use outside, independent computer service organizations to process accounting data. Nearly all companies now use computers to some extent in their accounting systems.

Regardless of the extent of computerization or the methods of data processing used, management is responsible for establishing and maintaining an appropriate system of internal control. Similarly, the auditor has the responsibility to obtain an understanding of internal control sufficient to plan the audit. This appendix provides an introductory overview of some important IT concepts that are useful in understanding an entity's system of internal control.

Important IT Components

The auditor should be familiar with the following components of an IT system:

- Hardware
- Software
- Data organization and processing methods

Computer Hardware

Hardware is the physical equipment associated with the system. The basic hardware configuration consists of the central processing unit (CPU) and peripheral input and output devices. Figure 10-17 illustrates common types of computer hardware. The principal hardware component is the CPU, and it is composed of a

Figure 10-17 ■ Computer Hardware

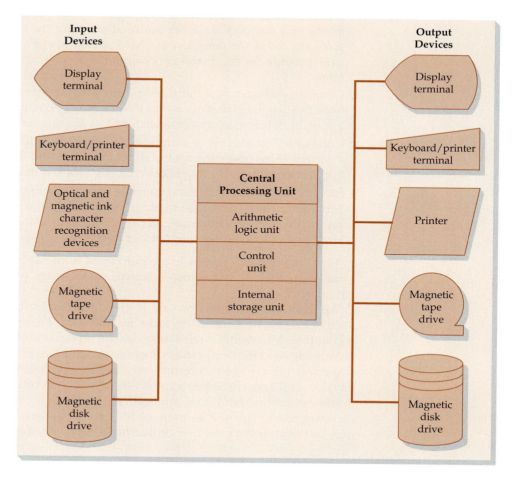

control unit, an internal storage unit, and an arithmetic-logic unit. The control unit directs and coordinates the entire system, including the entry and removal of information from storage, and the routing of the data between storage and the arithmetic-logic unit. The internal storage unit, or computer "memory" unit, is so named because it is capable of performing mathematical computations and certain logical operations. Peripheral to the CPU are input devices, output devices, and auxiliary storage devices. Peripheral equipment in direct communication with the CPU is considered to be on-line.

Computer Software

This component consists of the programs and routines that facilitate the programming and operation of the computer. There are several kinds of computer software. Of particular interest to auditors are the systems programs and applications programs.

Systems programs, sometimes called supervisory programs, perform general functions required for the operation of the computer as it executes specific tasks. Systems programs include the following:

- *Operating systems* direct the operation of the computer, including input and output devices, main storage, execution of programs, and management of files.
- *Utility programs* perform common data processing tasks, such as copying, reorganizing data in a file, sorting, merging, and printing. Other kinds of utility programs may be used to gather information about the use of the hardware and software, aid in the detection of unauthorized use or changes to programs and data, provide documentation of program logic, and facilitate testing of new systems.
- *Compilers and assemblers* translate specific programming languages into instructions in a language that can be understood by the computer. Each computer has a specific machine language determined by the engineers who designed it.
- Companies employing a computerized database utilize *database management* systems. These programs control the data records and files independently of the applications programs that allow changes in or use of the data.
- *Security programs* restrict and monitor access to programs and data. Security programs can restrict access to programs or data, allow read only access, or read and write access. Furthermore, security programs monitor and report unauthorized attempts to access programs or data.

Systems programs generally are purchased from hardware suppliers and software companies. They are then adapted, as necessary, by each user to suit individual needs.

Applications programs contain instructions that enable the computer to perform specific data processing tasks for the user. These tasks include financial accounting, budgeting, engineering design, and quality control. Within financial accounting, specific applications include general ledger accounting; sales order, shipping, billing, and accounts receivable; purchasing, receiving, vouchers payable, and cash disbursements; inventory; and payroll. In some cases, the programs operate as standalone applications. Increasingly, in modern systems, they are designed to operate as parts of integrated systems. Applications programs may be developed by the user or purchased from software vendors.

Data Organization and Processing Methods

The accounting function often involves recording, updating, retrieving, and reporting on large volumes of transaction data and related information. To understand how all this information is handled in an IT environment, the auditor must be familiar with the principal methods of data organization and data processing as explained in the following sections.

Data Organization Methods

The term **data organization methods** refers to the ways data are organized within a computer file. The two principal methods of data organization are the database method and the traditional file method.

The **database method** of data organization is the principal method used in many accounting applications. The method is based on the creation and maintenance of a single common direct access file for all applications using common data. Thus, each data element is stored only once but is accessible by all authorized application programs. In the case of the payroll and personnel applications mentioned earlier, the employee name, Social Security number, address, and pay rate data would be included in the file just once but would be usable in both application programs. Sophisticated database management systems software is designed to provide control over which users and applications can access and change specific data elements.

Once used only in very large systems, the database method has gained popularity in medium and smaller systems as well. Audit approaches to IT systems that utilize the database method are complex and specialized knowledge and the use of sophisticated software are often required. It is common for a computer specialist to be a member of the audit team in many audits today.

The **traditional file method** of data organization may be used in a few accounting applications. Under this method the following two types of files are maintained: (1) master files that contain up-to-date information about a given class of data such as the current balances of customers' accounts or the current quantities of inventory items and (2) transaction files that contain the details of individual transactions of the same class such as a day's credit sales or a day's cash disbursements.

These files are usually organized for direct access processing. In direct access files, neither the master nor related transaction file data need to be maintained in any particular order. Thus, the transaction file need not be sorted prior to processing. Under the traditional file method, separate master and transaction files are maintained for each application such as accounts receivable, inventory, payroll, and sales. Typically, the data in these files are accessible only by the single application program for which the files were created. Because of this, redundancy of data across files is common. For instance, a payroll file generally includes the following data elements among others: employee name, Social Security number, address, and pay rate. These same data elements are likely to be repeated in a separate personnel file. The creation and maintenance of the same data elements in several files is costly. The single program access and redundancy drawbacks of the traditional file method have made the database method more popular.

Data Processing Methods

The term **data processing methods** refers to the ways data are entered into and processed by the computer. The following sections explain the two widely used methods: (1) on-line entry/batch processing and (2) on-line entry/on-line processing.

Under the **on-line entry/batch processing** method of processing, individual transactions are entered directly into the computer via a terminal as they occur. A machine-readable validated transaction file is accumulated as the transactions are entered. This file is subsequently processed to update the master file. An advantage of this method is that the data are subjected to certain edit or validation checks by the computer program at the time of entry and error messages are communicated immediately to the terminal operator. For example, the programmed edit routine may detect missing, incomplete, or invalid data such as a nonexistent customer number. This permits immediate detection and correction of most data entry errors. The method also retains the control advantage of batch entry/batch processing—namely, batch control totals and batch reference numbers.

On-line entry/batch processing may be used either with reference access to the related master file or with no access. In reference access, the file may be read but not updated from the terminal. Reference access is necessary in cash receipts processing in which payments received from customers must be matched with open invoices in the customer's file. In contrast with no access, the related master file cannot be read when the transaction data are entered. Figure 10-18 illustrates on-

Figure 10-18 ■ On-Line Entry/Batch Processing

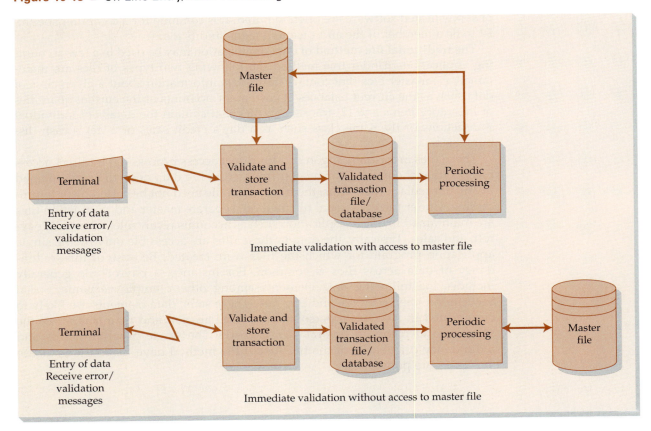

line entry/batch processing both with and without access. On-line entry/batch processing may also be used with a database system of file organization.

The **on-line entry/on-line processing** method differs from on-line entry/batch processing in the following two respects: (1) master files are updated concurrently with data entry and (2) a transaction log is produced that consists of a chronological record of all transactions. To provide a transaction trail, each transaction is assigned a unique identifying number by the computer program. On-line entry/on-line processing is used in airline and hotel reservations systems. A common accounting application is found in many retail stores where electronic cash registers immediately update inventory records when the sale is rung up.

The major disadvantages of this type of processing are the risk of errors in the master file from concurrent updating and the possible loss of part or all of the master files in case of hardware failure. To minimize these risks, some companies use memo updating of the master file at the time of data entry. This involves the use of a copy of the master file. The transaction log is then used to update the actual master file periodically. Figure 10-19 illustrates both immediate processing and memo updating of the master file under on-line processing.

Benefits and Risks of IT Systems

In order to understand internal control in a computer environment, it is important to understand the benefits and risks of IT systems. The major benefits of IT systems over manual systems include the following:

- IT systems can provide greater consistency in processing than manual systems because they uniformly subject all transactions to the same controls.
- More timely computer-generated accounting reports may provide management with more effective means of analyzing, supervising, and reviewing the operations of the company.
- IT systems enhance the ability to monitor the entity's performance and activities.

Important risks of IT systems over manual systems include the following:

- The IT system may produce a transaction trail that is available for audit for only a short period of time.
- There is often less documentary evidence of the performance of control procedures in computer systems.
- Files and records in IT systems are usually in machine-sensible form and cannot be read without a computer.
- The decrease of human involvement in computer processing can obscure errors that might be observed in manual systems.
- IT systems may be more vulnerable to physical disaster, unauthorized manipulation, and mechanical malfunction than information in manual systems.
- Various functions may be concentrated in IT systems, with a corresponding reduction in the traditional segregation of duties followed in manual systems.
- Changes in the system are often more difficult to implement and control in IT systems than in manual systems.
- IT systems are vulnerable to unauthorized changes in programs, systems, or data in master files.

Figure 10-19 ■ On-Line Entry/On-Line Processing

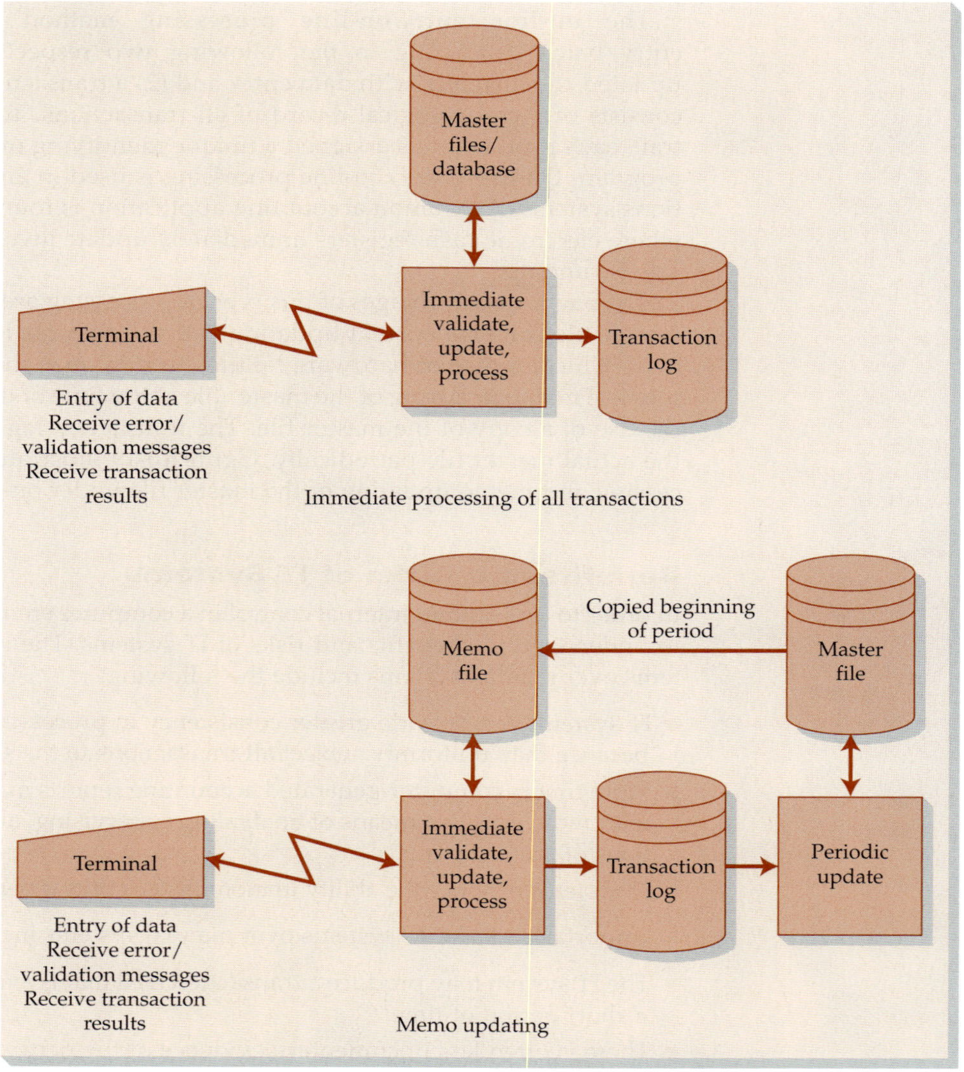

- Unauthorized access to data may result in the destruction of data or improper changes to data, including the recording of unauthorized or nonexistent transactions, or inaccurate recording of transactions.
- Reliance is placed on systems that process inaccurate data, process data inaccurately, or both.
- There may be inappropriate manual intervention.

Many of these risks are controlled by layering control procedures, such that one set of controls is designed to control the processing of transactions, whereas another set of controls is designed to control the systems and programs that con-

Figure 10-20 ■ On-Line Entry/On-Line Processing

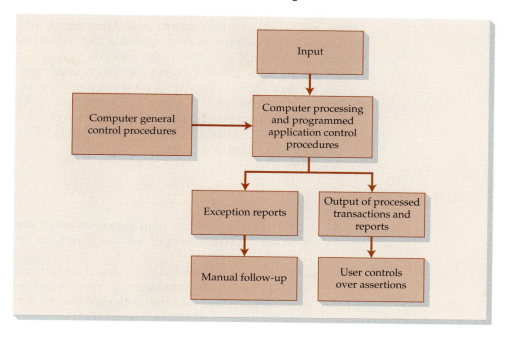

trol and process transactions. Figure 10-20 provides an important overview of control procedures in a computer environment. This figure describes how important controls function in IT systems, regardless of the methods of input, data organization, data processing, or output devices. The following paragraphs describe the control procedures depicted in Figure 10-20.

For purposes of illustration, consider the processing of a sales order. When a sales order is input, the computer program accepts the data and submits it to various edit checks and controls, such as the validity of the item number or customer number or whether the customer's credit limit has been reached. The controls are called computer application controls, which are designed to provide reasonable assurance that IT records, processes, and reports data properly for specific applications. Different applications controls will be custom made for applications such as sales, cash receipts, purchases, inventory control, or payroll.

The results of computer processing and application controls are usually twofold. First, the computer will output transactions and reports. In some systems, the processed transactions or reports will be subject to manual controls such as supervisory review. Second, the system generates exception reports. Some exception reports may appear on a screen, such as an edit check of the validity of a customer number. Some exception reports may result in printed reports, such as all transactions in a batch where customers exceeded their credit limit. In either case, people must follow up on the exceptions noted by the computer. The effectiveness of the control depends on the effectiveness of both the programmed application control and the manual followup.

Finally, an important set of controls is called general controls. Computer general controls control program development, program changes, computer operations, and access to programs and data. They represent a higher level of controls designed to provide reasonable assurance that individual computer applications operate consistently and effectively. Computer general controls are explained in depth in Appendix 10B. Since several levels of control are important to IT systems, this also allows for a variety of audit strategies when testing computer controls, which will be discussed in Chapter 11. Understanding this overview will make it easier to understand the computer aspects of each of the five components of internal control identified in the COSO report and AU 319, *Consideration of Internal Control in a Financial Statement Audit.*

[LEARNING CHECK

10A-1 a. What is the principal hardware component in an IT system?
　　　　b. What hardware components are peripheral to the principal hardware component?

10A-2 a. Explain the nature and functions of computer software.
　　　　b. Distinguish between systems programs and applications programs.

10A-3 a. Distinguish between the traditional file and database methods of organizing data.
　　　　b. Distinguish between sequential methods of data processing and direct access processing.

10A-4 For each of the two methods of data processing, indicate (a) their essential characteristics and (b) an advantage and a disadvantage.

10A-5 a. Describe several advantages of computer processing of accounting information over manual systems.
　　　　b. Describe the risks of computer processing of accounting information over manual systems.

10A-6 a. Develop a diagram that depicts the importance of internal control functions in computer systems, regardless of the methods of data input, data organization, or data processing.
　　　　b. In the context of the processing of a payroll transaction, describe each stage depicted in your diagram.

10A-7 a. Define computer applications controls and explain their purpose.
　　　　b. Define computer general controls and explain their purpose.

[KEY TERMS

Applications programs, p. 440
Data organization methods, p. 441
Data processing methods, p. 442
Database method, p. 441
On-line entry/batch processing,
　p. 442

On-line entry/on-line processing,
　p. 442
Systems programs, p. 440
Traditional file method, p. 441

COMPUTER GENERAL CONTROLS

The purpose of **general controls** is to control program development, program changes, computer operations, and to secure access to programs and data. The following five types of general controls are widely recognized:

- Organization and operation controls
- Systems development and documentation controls
- Hardware and system software controls
- Access controls
- Data and procedural controls

Computer general controls pertain to the IT environment and all IT activities as opposed to a single IT application. Thus, these controls are pervasive in their effect. If the auditor is able to obtain evidence that general controls function effectively, then the auditor also has assurance that individual applications may be properly designed and operate effectively. Alternatively, deficiencies in general controls may affect many applications and may prevent the auditor from assessing control risk below the maximum for many applications and transaction cycles. Each aspect of computer general controls is explained below.

Organization and Operation Controls

Organization and operation controls relate to the management philosophy and operating style and organizational structure control environment factors. In addition, these general controls pertain to the segregation of duties within the IT department and between IT and user departments. Weakness in these controls usually affects all IT applications.

The organizational structure shown in Figure 10-21 illustrates an arrangement that provides for clear-cut lines of authority and responsibility within the IT department.

Figure 10-21 ■ IT Functions Requiring Segregation of Duties

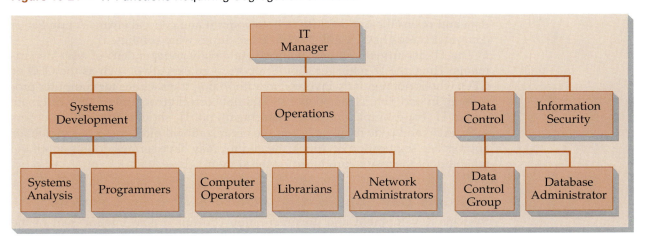

The primary responsibilities for each position are as follows:

POSITION	PRIMARY RESPONSIBILITIES
IT Manager	Exercises overall controls, develops short- and long-range plans, and approves systems.
Systems Development	
Systems Analysts	Evaluates existing systems, designs new systems, outlines the systems, and prepares specifications for programmers.
Programmer	Flowcharts logic of computer programs, develops and documents programs, and debugs programs.
IT Operations	
Computer Operator	Operates the computer hardware and executes the program according to operating instructions.
Librarian	Maintains custody of systems documentation, programs, and files.
Network Administrator	Plans and maintains networks linking programs and data files.
Data Control	
Data Control Group	Acts as liaison with user departments and monitors input, processing, and output.
Database Administrator	Designs content and organization of the database and controls access to and use of the database.
Information Security	
Security Administrator	Manages security of IT systems, including hardware and security software, monitors access to programs and data, and follows up on security breaches.

The fundamental duties that should always be segregated are systems development, operations, data control, and information security. In small organizations, the positions of systems analysts and programmers may be combined. However, the combining of systems development and operations duties results in incompatible duties. This would give an individual access to both programs and data and opens the opportunity to both commit and conceal errors. A number of computer frauds have resulted when these duties were combined.

The IT department should be organizationally independent of user departments. Thus, the IT manager should report to an executive, such as the CFO or CEO, who is not regularly involved in authorizing transactions for computer processing. In addition, IT personnel should not correct errors unless they originate within IT. For example, the sales department, not IT, should correct sales orders with an invalid code number. When the organizational plan does not provide for appropriate segregation of duties, the auditor may have serious doubts about the reliability of the results produced by the system.

Systems Development and Documentation Controls

Systems development and documentation controls are an integral part of the information and communication component of internal control. Systems development controls relate to (1) review, testing, and approval of new systems, (2) control of program changes, and (3) documentation procedures. The following procedures are helpful in providing the necessary controls:

- Systems design should include representatives of user departments and, as appropriate, the accounting department and internal auditors.
- Each system should have written specifications that are reviewed and approved by management and the user department.
- Systems testing should be a cooperative effort of users and IT personnel.
- The IT manager, the database administrator, user personnel, and the appropriate level of management should give final approval to a new system before it is placed in normal operation.
- Program changes should be approved before implementation to determine whether they have been authorized, tested, and documented.

Documentation controls pertain to the documents and records maintained by a company to describe computer processing activities. Documentation allows management to (1) review the system, (2) train new personnel, and (3) maintain and revise existing systems and programs. Documentation provides the auditor with the primary source of information about the flow of transactions through the system and related accounting controls. Documentation includes:

- Descriptions and flowcharts of the systems and programs
- Operating instructions for computer operators
- Control procedures to be followed by operators and users
- Descriptions and samples of required inputs and outputs

In database management systems, an important documentation control is the data dictionary/directory. The directory is software that keeps track of the definitions and locations of data elements in the database.

Hardware and Systems Software Controls

Hardware and systems software controls are an important factor that contributes to the high degree of reliability of today's information technology. Hardware and software controls are designed to detect any malfunctioning of the equipment. This category of controls includes the following:

- *Dual read.* Input data are read twice, and the two readings are compared.
- *Parity check.* Data are processed by the computer in arrays of bits (binary digits of 0 or 1). In addition to bits necessary to represent the numeric or alphabetic characters, a parity bit is added, when necessary, to make the sum of all the 1 bits even or odd. As data are entered and ultimately transferred within the computer, the parity check is applied by the computer to assure that bits are not lost during the process.
- *Echo check.* The echo check involves transmitting data received by an output device back to the source unit for comparison with the original data.
- *Read after write.* The computer reads back the data after they have been recorded, either in storage or in the output device, and verifies the data by comparison with their original source.

To achieve maximum benefit from these controls, (1) there should be a program of preventive maintenance on all hardware, and (2) controls over changes to systems software should parallel the systems development and documentation controls described above.

Access Controls

Access controls should prevent unauthorized use of IT equipment, data files, and computer programs. The specific controls include physical, software, and procedural safeguards.

Access to computer hardware should be limited to authorized individuals, such as computer operators. Physical safeguards include the housing of equipment in an area that is separate from user departments. Security guards, door locks, or special keys should restrict access to the computer areas.

Access to data files and programs should be designed to prevent unauthorized use of both data and programs. Physical controls exist in the form of a library and a librarian. Access to program documentation and data files should be limited to individuals authorized to process, maintain, or modify particular systems. Ordinarily, the librarian keeps a log of the use of files and programs. Alternatively, under the database method of filing, the data dictionary software provides an automated log of access to programs and data elements.

In systems with on-line entry of data, many users have direct access to the CPU through remote input devices. Access often extends beyond company employees to outside agents and even to customers who have special keys, such as magnetic cards issued by banks, which activate the computer. To provide the necessary control, each user of a remote input device is given a key, code, or card that identifies the holder as an authorized user. Other access controls are (1) computer callback procedures when the telephone is used to dial the computer and (2) passwords that are checked by the computer before a person can enter a transaction.

Procedural and software safeguards should involve management review of computer utilization reports. Security software that limits access to programs and data files, and keeps a log of programs and files that have been accessed, should be reviewed by IT security administration. IT security administrators both manage security software and follow up on security violations.

Data and Procedural Controls

Data and procedural controls provide a framework for controlling daily computer operations, minimizing the likelihood of processing errors, and assuring the continuity of operations in the event of a physical disaster or computer failure.

The first two objectives are achieved through a control function performed by individuals or departments that are organizationally independent of computer operations. The data control group within IT usually assumes this responsibility. The control function involves:

- Accounting for all input data
- Following up on processing errors
- Verifying the proper distribution of output

The ability to maintain the continuity of computer operations involves (1) the use of off-premise storage for important files, programs, and documentation; (2) physical protection against environmental hazards; (3) formal record retention and recovery plans for data; and (4) arrangements for the use of backup facilities at another location.

The ability to reconstruct data files is equally important. When sequential processing is used, a common method of record reconstruction is the **grandfather-father-son concept** illustrated in the top panel of Figure 10-22 Under this concept the new updated master file is the son. The master file utilized in the updating run that produced the son is the father, and the previous master file is the grandfather. To update those earlier master files, records of the transactions for the current and prior periods must be retained. In the event that the current computer master file is destroyed, the system then has the capability to replace it. Ideally, the three generations of master files and the transaction files should be stored in separate locations to minimize the risk of losing all the files at one time. When direct access processing is used, the master file and transaction logs should be dumped, or copied, periodically to a movable disk. In the event the on-line files are destroyed or damaged, these disks may be used with a special recovery program to reconstruct the master file as illustrated in the lower panel of Figure 10-22.

[LEARNING CHECK

10B-1 a. Information and processing controls is one category of control activities. What risks do these controls address?
       b. Name two subcategories of information and processing controls in a computerized system.
       c. Identify five types of general controls and state their common attribute.

10B-2 a. What are documentation controls in an IT department?
       b. Why is documentation important to management and the auditor?
       c. What items should be included in IT documentation?

10B-3 a. Explain the purposes and nature of access controls.
       b. Enumerate the access controls that may be used in an on-line entry system.

10B-4 a. Indicate the scope of data and procedural controls.
       b. Describe the activities of a data control group.

[KEY TERMS

Access controls, p. 450

Data and procedural controls, p. 450

General controls, p. 447

Grandfather-father-son concept, p. 451

Hardware and systems software controls, p. 449

Organization and operation controls, p. 447

Systems development and documentation controls, p. 448

Figure 10-22 ■ Reconstruction of Data Files

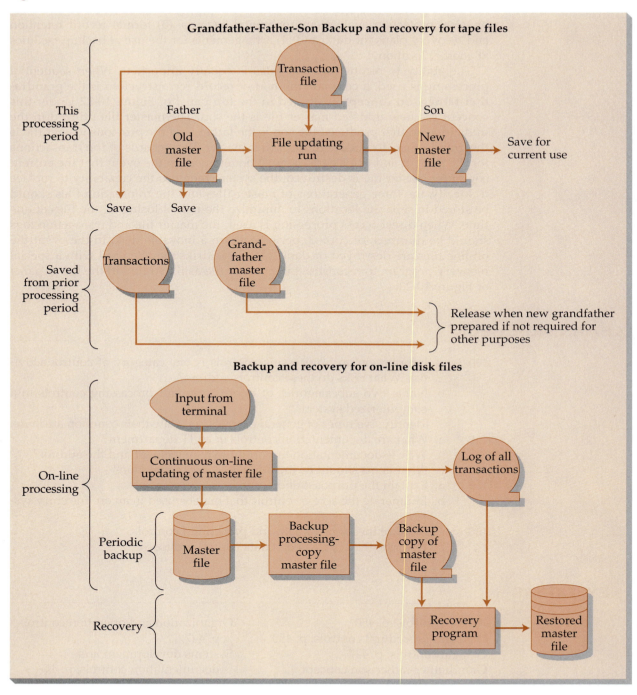

COMPREHENSIVE FLOWCHARTING ILLUSTRATION

Flowcharting is a creative task, making it unlikely that any two people would draw flowcharts exactly alike for any given system. The more commonly used flowcharting symbols are shown in Figure 10-23. Some firms supplement these basic symbols with more extensive sets of special-purpose symbols.

Figure 10-23 ■ Flowcharting Symbols

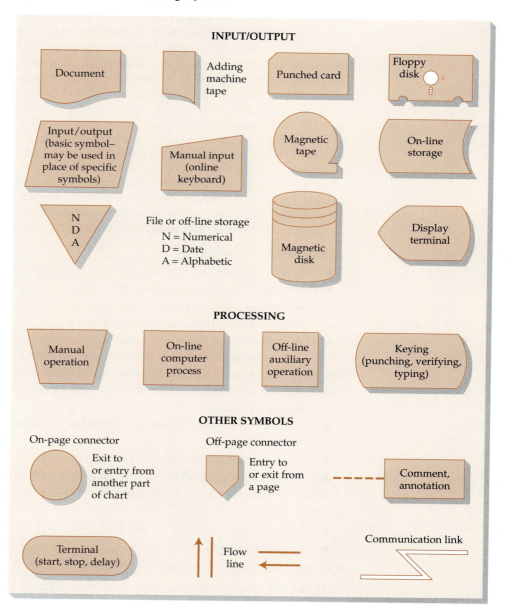

Most auditors prepare flowcharts for each material class of transactions. Flowcharts generally include:

- The flow of transactions from initiating the transaction to their summarization in the general ledger (that supports the financial statements).
- The key functions included in the flowchart.
- The documentary audit trail.
- Key reports produced by the accounting system.
- Computer programs and files where information is stored.

This information is important, for it assists the auditor in identifying where new information is added or where information changes form (from documents to electronic form and back to documents) from initiating the transaction to the general ledger. This is where the risk of misstatement is the highest. The flowchart does not document every copy of every document that the client might use, but it does show the critical path from initiating the transaction to the general ledger. The flowchart is designed as an overview of the transaction flow and is supplemented by the following narrative discussion obtained through inquiries of the client personnel, observations, and review of documents.

A flowchart is a means to an end, not an end in itself. Besides enabling the auditor to follow the transaction from initiating the transaction to the general ledger, it should also allow the auditor to see the relationships that exist between controls and to facilitate the identification of key controls related to specific financial statement assertions. Because many important controls are programmed controls, an accompanying narrative is often necessary to describe the role information technology plays in detecting potential misstatements and reporting exceptions for followup. The combined flowchart and narrative are useful in identifying the following:

- Documents and records
  - The use of remittance advices returned by customers with payments.
  - Preparation of prelist of cash receipts for use in subsequent control.
  - Retention of validated deposit slips for use in subsequent control.
  - Computer files where information is stored.
  - The generation of exception reports, the cash receipts journal, the aged trial balance, and report of cash transactions and balances.
- Segregation of handling cash (mailroom and cashier) from recorded accountability (accounts receivable), from following up on exception reports (office of CFO).
- Independent checks
  - Computer compares deposit information with independent information from prelist.
  - Run-to-run comparisons by the computer.
  - Computer comparison of subsidiary ledger with general ledger.
  - Independent bank reconciliation.
- Other controls
  - Restrictive endorsement of checks immediately upon receipt.
  - Deposit of receipts intact daily.
- Management reviews of cash transactions and overall cash balances.

Figure 10-24 provides an illustrative flowchart of the cash receipts system described below. Figure 14-6 illustrates how sales might be initiated and how goods are delivered and billed to customers.

Figure 10-24 ■ System Flowchart—Cash Receipts Transactions

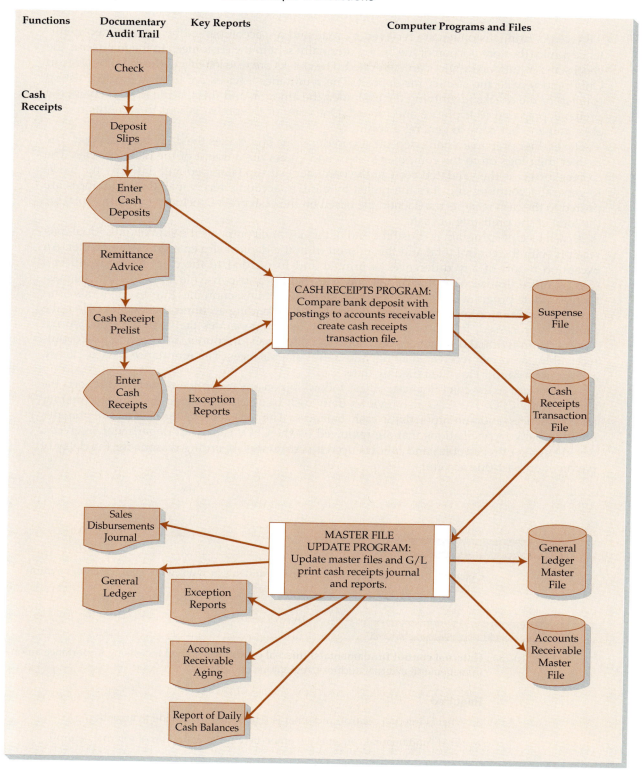

example system of cash receipts

All receipts from customers are received by mail and are accompanied by a preprinted remittance advice (bottom portion of the billing originally sent to the customer). In the mailroom, the checks and remittance advices are separated. The checks are restrictively endorsed (For Deposit Only) and sent to the cashier for deposit. The remittance advices are used to create a listing (prelist) of the checks identifying the customer, the amount, and the specific invoices paid; the prelist is prepared in triplicate and totaled. One copy of the prelist is sent to accounts receivable, and another copy to general accounting.

The cashier prepares a bank deposit slip in duplicate and makes the daily bank deposit. The cashier then logs on to the computer system and enters the amount of the daily deposit. The cashier forwards the validated copy of the bank deposit slip (stamped and dated by the bank) to general accounting and files the prelist by date. In accounts receivable, the remittances are posted to the cash receipts transaction file based on the cash prelist, including a control total for the total of the prelisting of cash.

A cash receipts program is run at the end of the day and compares the sum of individual cash receipts with the control total and the amount from the deposit slip entered by the cashier. An exception report of any differences is printed and forwarded to the chief financial officer's (CFO's) office. Transactions that do not match are held in a suspense file for followup. The master file update program then processes the cash receipts transaction file. Run-to-run totals compare the beginning receivables, plus cash receipts, with ending accounts receivables before the routine is processed. It also updates the general ledger, generates the Cash Receipts Journal (shows the individual transactions and daily totals for cash, discounts, and posting to accounts receivable), accounts receivable aging, and daily cash balances. The remittance advice, prelist, and summary report are then filed by date.

An assistant to the chief financial officer follows up on any exception reports and reports the results to the CFO. The CFO also reviews daily cash transactions (including cash receipts) for reasonableness and monitors daily cash balances. The assistant to the CFO also prepares monthly bank reconciliations that are reviewed by the CFO. The credit department receives a weekly aging of receivables and follows up with customers regarding reasons for the delay of payment on past-due accounts.

objective questions

Objective questions are available for the students at www.wiley.com/college/boynton

comprehensive questions

10-28 **(Internal control fundamentals)** Internal control has gained increasing importance among management, external auditors, regulators, and others.

Required

a. What is internal control, and what is it intended to provide to an entity?

b. What fundamental concepts are embodied in the definition of internal control?

c. List the five components of an internal control structure.

d. When considering the effectiveness of an internal control structure, what inherent limitations should be considered?

e. Identify six parties who have a role or responsibility regarding an entity's ICS and briefly state the role or responsibility of each.

10-29 **(Obtaining an understanding)** In meeting the second generally accepted auditing standard of fieldwork, the auditor is required to obtain sufficient understanding of each component of an entity's internal controls to plan the audit of the entity's financial statements.

Required

a. What knowledge should be obtained about the control components in obtaining an understanding of it?

b. How does the auditor obtain the understanding?

c. Is it necessary in all cases to document the understanding?

d. Briefly discuss the alternative methods available for documenting the understanding and comment on the relative advantages or disadvantages of each.

10-30 **(Control environment)** Peterson, CPA, is auditing the financial statements of the publicly held manufacturing company, Amalgamated Products, Inc. In complying with the second standard of fieldwork, Peterson seeks to obtain an understanding of Amalgamated's control environment.

Required

a. Identify the control environment factors that can affect the effectiveness of specific policies and procedures related to the other components of an internal control structure.

b. What should the auditor understand about the control environment and the factors that comprise it to have sufficient knowledge of this component?

c. What effect may the preliminary audit strategy have on the required level of understanding of the control environment factors?

10-31 **(Components of internal control)** The chapter identified five components of internal control. Listed below are specific control policies and procedures prescribed by Suntron Company.

1. Management gives careful consideration to the requisite knowledge and skills personnel need at all levels of the organization.

2. General controls and application controls are established in the electronic data processing department.

3. Management acts to reduce or eliminate incentives and temptations that might lead individuals to engage in dishonest or illegal acts.

4. Management is alert to complaints received from customers about billing errors.

5. Management gives special consideration to the risks that can arise from the use of information technology in the accounting system.

6. Employees' responsibilities are assigned so as to avoid any individual's being in a position to both commit an error or irregularity and then conceal it.

7. IT management has designed controls to prevent unauthorized use of IT equipment, data files, and computer programs.

8. The processing of payroll includes a check on the total number of hours submitted. If

more than 65 hours are reported in a weekly pay period, the transaction is printed on an exception report and put in a suspense file for additional review or additional authorization.

9. Suntron's internal audit staff periodically assesses the effectiveness of various ICS components.

10. Policy manuals, accounting and financial reporting manuals, and a chart of accounts have been developed and implemented.

Required

a. Identify the components of internal control to which each policy or procedure relates.

b. For each item, identify one other policy or procedure for that internal control component that is not on the preceding list.

10-32 **(Components of internal control)** Internal controls can be categorized using the following framework.

1. Control environment
2. Risk assessment
3. Information and communication
4. Control activities
    4.1. Authorization
    4.2. Segregation of duties
    4.3. Information processing controls
        4.3.1. Computer general controls
        4.3.2. Computer application controls
        4.3.3. Controls over the financial reporting process
    4.4. Physical controls
    4.5. Performance reviews
    4.6. Controls over management discretion in financial reporting
5. Monitoring
6. Antifraud programs and controls

Following is a list of controls prescribed by Waterfront, Inc.

a. Management has established a code of conduct that includes rules regarding conflicts of interest for purchasing agents.

b. Waterfront has established a disclosure committee to review the selection of new accounting policies.

c. Any computer program revision must be approved by user departments after testing the entire program with test data.

d. The managers of each of Waterfront's manufacturing departments must review all expenditures charged to their responsibility center weekly.

e. The CEO, CFO, and controller review the financial consequences of business risks annually to ensure that controls are in place to address significant business risks.

f. Human resources focuses on ensuring that accounting personnel have adequate qualifications for work performed in billing and accounts receivable.

g. Security software limits access to programs and data files, and keeps a log of programs and files that have been accessed, which is then reviewed by the security manager daily.

h. A computer program prints a daily report of all shipments that have not yet been billed to customers.

i. The controller reviews sales and collections bimonthly.

j. The computer compares the information on the sales invoice with underlying shipping information.

k. Customer billing complaints are directed to internal audit for followup and resolution.

l. The documentary transaction trail for all credit sales is documented in company policy manuals.

m. A committee of the board of directors evaluates and monitors business risks.

n. Access to spreadsheets used in the financial reporting process is limited and spreadsheets are tested with test data on a quarterly basis.

Required

a. Indicate the category of internal control applicable to each procedure using the framework above.

b. Identify an assertion to which each procedure pertains (some procedures may have a pervasive impact on multiple assertions).

10-33 **(Segregation of duties)** The Richmond Company, a client of your firm, has come to you with the following problem. It has three clerical employees who must perform the following functions:

1. Maintain general ledger.
2. Maintain accounts payable ledger.
3. Maintain accounts receivable ledger.
4. Prepare checks for signature.
5. Maintain disbursements journal.
6. Issue credits on returns and allowances.
7. Reconcile the bank account.
8. Handle and deposit cash receipts.

Required

Assuming there is no problem as to the ability of any of the employees, the company requests your advice on assigning the above functions to the three employees in such a manner as to achieve the highest degree of internal control. It may be assumed that these employees will perform no other accounting functions than the ones listed.

a. State how you would recommend distributing the above functions among the three employees. Assume that, with the exception of the nominal jobs of the bank reconciliation and the issuance of credits on returns and allowances, all functions require an equal amount of time. (*Hint:* Give each employee a job title.)

b. List four possible unsatisfactory combinations of the above-listed functions.

AICPA (adapted)

10-34 **(Control activities and related assertions)** Several categories of control activities are identified in the chapter using the following framework.

a. Authorization

b. Segregation of duties

    c. Information processing controls

        1. General controls

        2. Application controls

        3. Controls over the financial reporting process

    d. Physical controls

    e. Performance reviews

    f. Control over management discretion in financial reporting

Following are specific control procedures prescribed by Trusty Company.

1. The computer must match information from a vendor's invoices with information from receiving and information from the purchase order before a check is issued.

2. A knowledgeable audit committee reviews and approves new applications of GAAP.

3. Two authorized signatures are required on every check over $100,000.

4. Each month management carefully reviews the aged trial balance of accounts receivable to identify past-due balances and follows up for collection.

5. A supervisor must approve overtime work.

6. The computer assigns sequential numbers to sales invoices used in the billing system.

7. The computer verifies the mathematical accuracy of each voucher and prints an exception report for items with mathematical errors.

8. Employee payroll records are kept on a computer file that can only be accessed by certain terminals and are password protected.

9. Internal auditors review journal entries periodically for reasonableness of account classifications.

10. The chairman of the audit committee directly accepts confidential e-mails or other submissions concerning questionable accounting and auditing matters.

11. Checks received from customers and related remittance advices are separated in the mailroom and subsequently processed by different individuals.

12. All vouchers must be stamped "paid" on payment.

13. Department managers review accounting for warranty claims on a weekly basis.

14. On a quarterly basis, warranty expenses are compared with actual warranty claims.

15. Only computer operators are allowed in the computer room.

16. The computer will not complete the processing of a batch when the accounts receivable control account does not match the total of the subsidiary ledgers.

Required

a. Indicate the category of control activities applicable to each procedure using the framework above.

b. Identify an assertion to which each procedure pertains.

10-35   **(Control procedures for cash receipts)** At the Main Street Theater, the cashier, located in a box office at the entrance, receives cash from customers and operates a machine that ejects serially numbered tickets. To gain admission to the theater, a customer hands the ticket to a doorperson stationed some 50 feet from the box office at the entrance to the theater lobby. The doorperson tears the ticket in half, opens the door, and returns the stub to the customer. The other half of the ticket is dropped by the doorperson into a locked box.

Required

a. What internal controls are present in this phase of handling cash receipts?

b. What steps should be taken regularly by the manager or other supervisor to give maximum effectiveness to these controls?

c. Assume that the cashier and doorperson decided to collaborate in an effort to abstract cash receipts. What action might they take?

d. Continuing the assumption made in (c) above of collusion between the cashier and doorperson, what features of the control procedures would be likely to disclose the embezzlement?

AICPA

cases

10-36   **(Identifying control strengths and weaknesses)** Brown Company provides office services for more than 100 small clients. These services consist of

1. Supplying temporary personnel
2. Providing monthly bookkeeping services
3. Designing and printing small brochures
4. Copying and reproduction services
5. Preparing tax reports

Some clients pay for these services on a cash basis; others use 30-day charge accounts; and still others operate on a contractual basis with quarterly payments. Brown's new office manager was concerned about the effectiveness of controls over sales and cash flow. At the manager's request, the process was reviewed and disclosed the following:

1. Contracts were written by account executives and then passed to the accounts receivable department where they were filed. Contracts had a limitation (ceiling) as to the types of services and the amount of work covered. Contracts were payable quarterly, in advance.

2. Client periodic payments on contracts were identified to the contract, and a payment receipt was placed in the contract file. Accounting records showed Credit Revenue; Debit Cash.

3. Periodically, a clerk reviewed the contract files to determine their status.

4. Work orders relating to contract services were placed in the contract file. Accounting records showed Debit Cost of Services; Credit Cash or Accounts Payable or Accrued Payroll.

5. Monthly bookkeeping services were usually paid for when the work was complete. If not paid in cash, a copy of the invoice marked "Unpaid $_____" was put into a cash pending file. It was removed when cash was received, and accounting records showed Debit Cash; Credit Revenue.

6. Design and printing work was handled like bookkeeping. However, a design and printing order form was used to accumulate costs and to compute the charge to be made to the client. A copy of the order form served as a billing to the client and when cash was received as a remittance advice.

7. Reproduction (copy) work was generally a cash transaction that was rung up on a cash register and balanced at the end of the day. Some reproduction work was charged to open accounts. A billing form was given to the client with the work, and a copy was put in an open file. It was removed when paid. In both cases, when cash was received, the accounting entry was Debit Cash; Credit Revenue.

8. Tax work was handled like the bookkeeping services.

9. Cash from cash sales was deposited daily. Cash from receipts on account or quarterly payments on contracts were deposited after being matched with evidence of the receivable.

10. Bank reconciliations were performed using the deposit slips as original data for the deposits on the bank statements.

11. A cash log was maintained of all cash received in the mail. This log was retained and used for reference purposes when a payment was disputed.

12. Monthly comparisons were made of the costs and revenues of printing, design, bookkeeping, and tax service. Unusual variations between revenues and costs were investigated. However, the handling of deferred payments made this analysis difficult.

Required

a. List eight examples of poor internal control that are evident.

b. List six examples of good internal control that are in effect.

10-37 **(Flowcharting: key controls)** SummerVoice, Inc., a distributor of music CDs to retailers and a new audit client of yours, processes sales in the following manner:

As orders are received, sales order clerks use on-line terminals and an order program to determine that the customer has been approved and that the order will not cause the customer's balance to exceed the customer's authorized credit limit. If the customer is a new one, the order is transferred to the credit department who checks credit and enters customer information on the customer master file for approved customers. The program also checks the inventory master file to determine that goods are on hand to fill the order, and it prices the sales order based on information in an approved master price file. If the order is accepted, the computer enters it into an open order file and a copy of the sales order form is produced on a printer in the sales order department and sent to the customer. When an order is not accepted, a message is displayed on the terminal indicating the reason for the rejection.

The approved sales order is electronically forwarded to the warehouse as authorization to release goods to shipping. The warehouse completes a packing slip and forwards goods to shipping. In shipping, personnel first make an independent check on agreement of the goods received with the accompanying sales order form. They then use their on-line terminals and a shipping program to retrieve the corresponding sales order from the open order file and add appropriate shipping data. The perpetual inventory system is also updated for the shipment of goods. Next the computer transfers the transaction from the open order file to a shipping file and produces a prenumbered shipping document on the printer in the shipping department. A report is generated daily of unfilled orders and back orders for the sales department.

Sales invoices are automatically generated based on shipped goods. The computer rechecks vendor information and data on goods shipped against data entered in sales and shipping. The computer prices the information based on information on the sales order and checks the numerical accuracy of the sales invoice. The computer also checks dates shipped with dates on the sales invoice. As each billing is completed, the computer enters it into a sales transaction file. After all the transactions in the batch have been processed, the billing program compares the total invoices with the total shipments for the day.

The transaction file is processed and posted to the sales transaction file, the accounts receivable master file, and the general ledger master file. Run-to-run totals compare beginning balances plus processed transactions with ending balances immediately prior to posting the transactions. Exceptions are printed on an exception report, and these transactions are held in a suspense file to be cleared by the billing supervisor.

The program also produces monthly statements. All customer inquiries on monthly statements are directed to the controller's office for followup. A separate program also prints daily sales reports with sales, gross margins, and inventory-on-hand by product for management review. Management must also coordinate followup on all past-due receivables with the credit department.

Required

a. Prepare a flowchart of the system described above.

b. For each financial statement assertion related to credit sales, identify internal control that may provide reasonable assurance of preventing misstatements or detecting and correcting misstatements on a timely basis.

professional simulation

You have been assigned to the audit of Alpha Corporation, a manufacturer of auto parts. Alpha Corporation is a private company that is wholly owned by George Alpha, that has only one manufacturing location. The auto parts that Alpha manufactures are shipped to approximately 25 manufacturing plants in the United States. During the current year Alpha Corporation upgraded its accounting system. The system upgrade involved changing software and implementing a totally new accounting package related to purchases, inventory and inventory control, and expenditures. Accounting personnel in the company have been upgraded to support the new system.

In the past the audit approach for inventory has followed a primarily substantive approach. It has been cost effective to directly observe inventory at year-end and perform price testing on the inventory after year-end. The partner on the engagement, Michelle Driscoll, believes that it will continue to be cost effective to follow a primarily substantive approach. Michelle knows that professional standards require the auditor to understand internal controls in every audit. Even though the audit will follow a primarily substantive approach, what guidance do the professional standards provide about the understanding of the new accounting system and related internal controls that is necessary to plan the audit. Cut and paste the standard sections that apply to this issue.

Situation	Research	Communication	Internal Controls

You are helping Michelle prepare for a planning meeting with Alpha's audit committee. Michelle knows that a discussion of the new system of internal controls will come up. In particular she want to brief the audit committee on the inherent limitations of any system of internal control. Prepare a memo outlining the inherent limitations of a system of internal control. Support your memo with guidance provided by relevant professional standards.

To: Michelle Driscoll, Partner

Re: Inherent Limitations of an Entity's Internal Control

From: CPA Candidate

Situation	Research	Communication	Internal Controls

Following is a list of various control activities that might be found in Alpha's system of internal control. For each control identify the assertion that might be controlled by the Alpha's policy or procedure using the following coding:

a. Existence and occurrence
b. Completeness
c. Rights and obligations
d. Valuation and allocation
e. Presentation and disclosure

	a.	b.	c.	d.	e.
1. The computer verifies an employee authorization code in order to enter a purchase order.	○	○	○	○	○
2. The computer produces a report of all receiving reports that have not resulted in a voucher.	○	○	○	○	○
3. The computer matches information on the voucher regarding quantities and prices of goods purchased with underlying receiving reports and purchase orders.	○	○	○	○	○
4. The computer compares the account coding on a voucher with the account coding on the purchase order.	○	○	○	○	○
5. The computer checks the mathematical accuracy of the voucher and supporting vendor's invoice.	○	○	○	○	○
6. The computer has a unique account coding for the receipt and acquisition of consignment inventory.	○	○	○	○	○
7. The computer matches each voucher with an underlying receiving report and cancels the related vendor's invoice to prevent duplicate payment.	○	○	○	○	○

[3] AUDIT TESTING METHODOLOGY

[11] AUDIT PROCEDURES IN RESPONSE TO ASSESSED RISKS: TESTS OF CONTROLS

INTERNAL CONTROLS AT ENRON

On February 23, 2001, Arthur Andersen, LLP issued an opinion that "management's assertion that the system of internal control at Enron Corp., and its subsidiaries, as of December 31, 2000, 1999 and 1998 was adequate to provide reasonable assurance as to the reliability of the financial statements and the protection of assets from unauthorized acquisition, use, or disposition, is fairly stated, in all material respects, based on current standards of control criteria." This report was based on AICPA Attestation Standards on reporting on internal control and would have used the COSO components of internal control as the criteria for reporting on internal control.

Arthur Andersen, LLP would have needed to perform tests of controls to support this opinion. With the benefit of hindsight, what have we learned about the internal controls at Enron and the possible effectiveness of tests of controls?

1. We know that Enron's board of directors waived its own conflicts of interest policy and allowed Andrew Fastow, its CFO, to negotiate for Enron with companies where the CFO had ownership interests. Ultimately, Fastow earned approximately $31 million for himself on these deals. However, from Andersen's perspective the board of directors approved these transactions.

2. Enron had a corporate code of ethics. It said the right things. But was the code followed? In order for an internal control to be effective, it must be well designed, placed in operation, and operate effectively. In this case it was well designed but largely ignored. Senior management failed to set a tone at the top about the importance of ethics.

3. Internal controls start with the tone at the top of the organization. In addition to the problem with ethics, senior management placed significant pressures on other managers regarding the importance of meeting earning targets. Enron officers received millions of dollars in executive bonuses based on "hitting the numbers." At the end of 1999 Enron executives arranged a transaction with Merrill Lynch and paid a $17 million fee for a late fourth-quarter transaction that allowed Enron to recognize $50 million in earnings and meet their earnings targets and pay bonuses. (See SEC Litigation release No. 18515.) This is exactly the type of pressure that SAS 99 refers to in terms of incentives for fraudulent financial reporting.

4. Enron established a Risk Management and Control department to review significant transactions at Enron. However, the traders and deal-makers at Enron were also in a position to review the performance of and have input on the promotions and bonuses of the Risk Management and Control officials who reviewed their deals. Risk Manage-

ment and Controls was not independent, and as a result the group often tempered its conclusions. In other instances, senior management ignored their risk assessments in order to book deals and earnings, even if the venture was high risk. This was one more control that was placed in operations but was not always effective.

5. A company's first line of defense is its employees. Yet the concerns raised by Sharon Watkins, Margaret Ceconi, and other Enron employees were ignored and not taken seriously.

So what should an auditor obtain in the way of evidence about the effective operation of internal controls? This is the topic of discussion in Chapter 11.

[PREVIEW OF CHAPTER 11]

Chapter 11 begins with phases II and III of the audit, assessing the risk of material misstatement and responding to assessed risks. An auditor will normally plan to perform tests of controls if he or she determines that effective internal controls have been placed in operation to prevent or detect and correct misstatements in financial statement assertions. Public company auditors must test controls related to all significant financial statement assertions in order to render an opinion on internal controls. Private company auditors will perform tests of controls when following a lower assessed level of control risk approach. The following diagram provides an overview of the chapter organization and content.

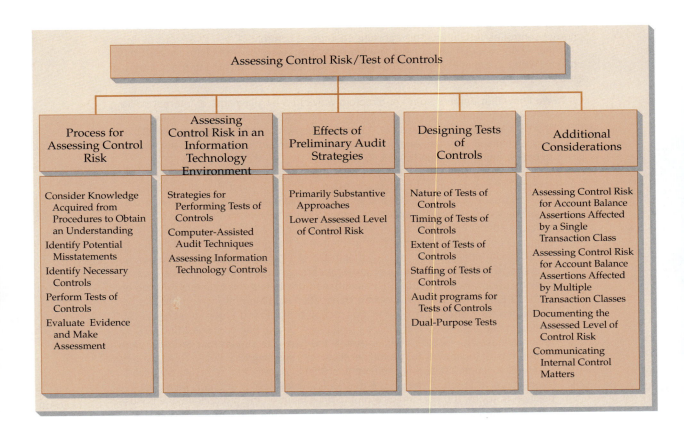

Assessing Control Risk/Test of Controls				
Process for Assessing Control Risk	Assessing Control Risk in an Information Technology Environment	Effects of Preliminary Audit Strategies	Designing Tests of Controls	Additional Considerations
Consider Knowledge Acquired from Procedures to Obtain an Understanding Identify Potential Misstatements Identify Necessary Controls Perform Tests of Controls Evaluate Evidence and Make Assessment	Strategies for Performing Tests of Controls Computer-Assisted Audit Techniques Assessing Information Technology Controls	Primarily Substantive Approaches Lower Assessed Level of Control Risk	Nature of Tests of Controls Timing of Tests of Controls Extent of Tests of Controls Staffing of Tests of Controls Audit programs for Tests of Controls Dual-Purpose Tests	Assessing Control Risk for Account Balance Assertions Affected by a Single Transaction Class Assessing Control Risk for Account Balance Assertions Affected by Multiple Transaction Classes Documenting the Assessed Level of Control Risk Communicating Internal Control Matters

Chapter 11 focuses on the process of testing controls and assessing control risk. This chapter addresses the following aspects of the auditor's knowledge and the auditor's decision process.

focus on auditor knowledge

After studying this chapter you should understand the following aspects of an auditor's knowledge base:

K1. Know the steps in assessing control risk.

K2. Know the difference between assessing control risk under two major preliminary audit strategies.

focus on audit decisions

After studying this chapter you should understand the factors that influence the following audit decisions.

D1. What three basic audit strategies can be used for testing controls in the IT environment?

D2. What types of computer-assisted audit techniques can be used in performing tests of controls?

D3. What factors bear on the degree of assurance provided by tests of controls?

D4. What is the process of assessing control risk for account balance assertions affected by single and multiple transaction classes?

D5. What are the requirements for documenting the control risk assessment?

D6. What are the auditor's requirements for communicating internal control matters to the audit committee?

[PROCESS FOR ASSESSING CONTROL RISK]

Assessing control risk is the process of evaluating the effectiveness of an entity's internal control in preventing or detecting material misstatement in the financial statements.

Source: AU 319.47.

Auditor Knowledge 1

■ Know the steps in assessing control risk.

The purpose of assessing control risk is to assist the auditor in making a judgment about the risk of material misstatement in financial statement assertions. Assessing control risk involves evaluating the effectiveness of:

■ the design of internal controls, and

■ the operation of internal controls.

Assessing control risk also helps the auditor make decisions about the nature, timing, and extent of audit procedures. Ultimately, tests of controls provide evidential matter as part of the reasonable basis of the auditor's opinion.

Control risk, like other components of the audit risk model, is assessed in terms of individual financial statement assertions. Many controls prevent misstatements in assertions when transactions are recorded. It is important to keep in mind that

Figure 11-1 ■ Steps to Assessing Control Risk

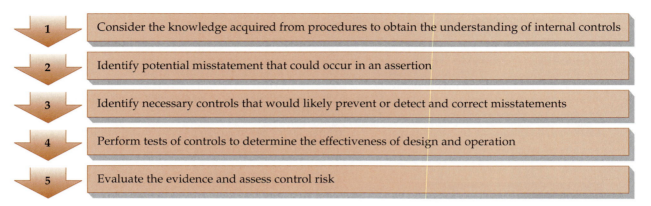

1	Consider the knowledge acquired from procedures to obtain the understanding of internal controls
2	Identify potential misstatement that could occur in an assertion
3	Identify necessary controls that would likely prevent or detect and correct misstatements
4	Perform tests of controls to determine the effectiveness of design and operation
5	Evaluate the evidence and assess control risk

control risk assessments are made for individual assertions, not for internal controls as a whole, individual internal control components, or individual policies or procedures.

In making an assessment of control risk for an assertion, an auditor usually follows the steps outlined in Figure 11-1. The fourth step, performing tests of controls, is not required for private companies when control risk is assessed at the maximum. Each of these steps in the assessment process is discussed in a following section.

CONSIDER KNOWLEDGE ACQUIRED FROM PROCEDURES TO OBTAIN AN UNDERSTANDING

The auditor performs **procedures to obtain an understanding** of internal controls for significant financial statement assertions, as explained in Chapter 10. He or she documents the understanding in the form of completed internal control questionnaires, flowcharts, and/or narrative memoranda. Analysis of this documentation is the starting point for assessing control risk. In particular, AU 319.25 states the understanding that is to be used by the auditor to (1) identify types of potential misstatements, (2) consider factors that affect the risk of material misstatements, and (3) design tests of controls, when applicable. Thus, for policies and procedures relevant to particular assertions, the auditor carefully considers the Yes, No, and N/A responses and written comments in the questionnaires and the strengths and weaknesses noted in flowcharts and narrative memoranda.

As the auditor obtains an understanding of internal control, he or she will usually make inquiries, observe the performance of duties and controls, and inspect documents. In the process the auditor may obtain evidence about how the control actually operates that may allow him or her to assess control risk below the maximum. Usually the evidence is not extensive enough to allow the auditor to assess control risk at a low level, but it may be sufficient to support a control risk assessment as high. The auditor may base an assessment of control risk on the evidence collected while obtaining an understanding of internal controls.

IDENTIFY POTENTIAL MISSTATEMENTS

Identifying potential misstatements is a process whereby the auditor considers the points at which errors or fraud could occur, for assertions pertaining to each major class of transactions, account balance, and related disclosures in the financial statements. Some auditing firms use computer software that links responses to specific questions in computerized questionnaires to potential misstatements for particular assertions. Nevertheless, it is important for any auditor to understand the logic that computerized decision support systems use to evaluate whether an assertion is adequately controlled. For example, potential misstatements may be identified for cash disbursement assertions and for the two primary account balances affected by cash disbursements—cash and accounts payable. Examples of potential misstatements for several assertions pertaining to cash disbursement transactions are shown in the first column in Figure 11-2. It is the understanding of assertions that guides an auditor's understanding of potential misstatements.

IDENTIFY NECESSARY CONTROLS

An auditor may identify **necessary controls** that would likely prevent or detect and correct specific potential misstatements in an assertion by using computer software that processes internal control questionnaire responses or by manually using checklists. When identifying necessary controls the auditor will usually ascertain:

- The nature of controls that would prevent or detect and correct misstatements in an assertion.
- The nature of controls that have been implemented by management.
- The significance of each control. In some cases more than one control may relate to an assertion, and the auditor will usually want to identify **key controls** (e.g., the controls that the auditor believes are most effective at preventing or detecting and correcting misstatements).
- The risk that designed controls may not operate effectively.

The second column in Figure 11-2 illustrates potential controls for specific financial statement assertions. Note that many controls are designed to identify a specific potential misstatement. In other cases, a single control may pertain to more than one type of potential misstatement. The control periodic independent bank reconciliation, shown at the bottom of the second column, may detect checks recorded in the cash disbursements journal at an incorrect amount (valuation and allocation assertion), and it may also detect unrecorded checks (completeness assertion).

Many internal controls have a common design. Every transaction has four basic functions; (1) initiation of the transaction, (2) delivery or receipt of goods or services, (3) recording of the transaction, and (4) consideration, as depicted in Figure 11-3.

The following discussion examines how a company might design internal controls to control the completeness, existence and occurrence, valuation and allocation (accuracy), and presentation and disclosure (classification) assertions, regardless of the transaction cycle that is being controlled.

Internal controls over the completeness assertion generally start by capturing information about a transaction when it is initiated and then follow the transaction forward through each function. It is common to use prenumbered documents, account for the prenumbering of documents, and then develop a one-for-one

Figure 11-2 ■ Potential Misstatements, Necessary Controls, and Tests of Controls—Cash Disbursement Transactions

Potential Misstatement (Assertion)	Necessary Control	Test of Control
A cash disbursement may be made for unauthorized purpose (existence and occurrence).	The computer matches the check information with information supporting the voucher and accounts payable for each disbursement transaction.	Use computer-assisted audit techniques such as test data to test computer application control.
	Only authorized personnel are permitted to run the program and handle checks where the computer prints and signs checks.	Observe individuals handling cash disbursements and compare them with list of authorized personnel.
	There are separate duties for approving payment vouchers and signing checks.	Observe segregation of duties.
A voucher may be paid twice (existence and occurrence).	The computer electronically cancels voucher and supporting information when check is issued.	Use computer-assisted audit techniques such as test data to test computer application control.
	Payment voucher and supporting documents are stamped "Paid" when check is issued.	Observe documents being stamped and/or inspect sample of paid documents for presence of "Paid" stamp.
A check may be issued for the wrong amount, or it may be recorded in the wrong amount (valuation).	The computer matches the check information with information supporting the voucher and accounts payable for each disbursement transaction.	Use computer-assisted audit techniques such as test data to test computer application control.
	The computer compares the sum of checks issued with the entry to cash disbursements.	Use computer-assisted audit techniques such as test data to test computer application control.
	Periodic independent bank reconciliations are made.	Observe performance of bank reconciliations and/or inspect bank reconciliations.

Figure 11-3 ■ Transaction Functions and the Design of Internal Controls

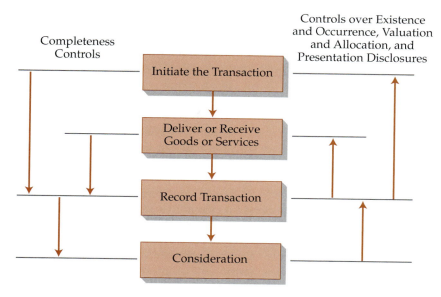

match of initiated transactions with the delivery or receipt of goods or services and with the recording of the transaction. For example, a system may generate reports of all sales orders that have not been shipped and of all shipments that have not resulted in sales invoices. Companies also usually reconcile the recorded sales with the eventual cash receipt or generate reports of past due receivables to determine why cash has not been received.

Internal controls over the existence and occurrence assertion generally work just the opposite of those designed for the completeness assertion. Controls over the occurrence of sales normally compare information associated with the recording of transactions with information associated with the passage of title, which is normally captured during the delivery or receipt of goods and services. For example, a company might compare information input for a sales invoice with information previously captured during the shipment of goods or the delivery of services (information about both quantities recorded vs. quantities shipped and information about accounting period when the transaction is recorded vs. the accounting period when goods were shipped). Controls over the occurrence of cash receipts or disbursements are normally compared with information about the existence of receivables or payables.

Internal controls over the valuation and allocation assertion are similar to those for the existence and occurrence assertion. Controls over valuation (accuracy) normally compare information associated with the recording of transactions with information obtained both with the delivery or receipt of goods and services and information associated with the initiation of the transaction. For example, it is common to compare information input for a sales invoice with information previously captured during the shipment of goods or the delivery of services as well as information that was captured when the transaction was initiated. Controls over the valuation of cash receipts or disbursements are normally compared with accounts receivable or accounts payable information.

Internal controls over the presentation and disclosure assertion (classification) normally compare information associated with the recording of transactions with information created when the transaction is initiated. These controls normally compare general ledger account numbers associated with the recording of transactions with account numbers that are assigned when the transaction is initiated. For example, is it common to compare information input for a sales invoice with account codes on sales orders.

Understanding necessary controls also requires consideration of circumstances and judgment. For example, in cases of a very high volume of cash disbursement transactions, an independent check of the agreement of the daily summary of checks issued with the entry in the cash disbursements journal, thus permitting timely detection of misstatements, may be critical. When the volume of cash disbursements is light and timely detection of misstatements is not as essential, periodic independent bank reconciliations may adequately compensate for the lack of a daily independent check. In such a circumstance, the bank reconciliation might be referred to as a **compensating control.**

The necessary controls shown in Figure 11-2, whether programmed application controls or manual controls, may all be classified as belonging to the control activities component of internal controls. The auditor should be aware that certain controls pertaining to other internal control components may simultaneously affect the risk of potential misstatement in assertions pertaining to several transactions classes or account balances. For example, control environment issues such as the competency and trustworthiness of certain managers and employees involved in the processing of cash disbursement transactions can affect any of the assertions for that transaction class. In fact, the lack of competence and trustworthiness in key managers or employees can negate the effectiveness of other control activities. Thus, the auditor must assimilate information about each element of the system of internal control when considering the risk of potential misstatements in particular assertions. This concept may be represented graphically as follows:

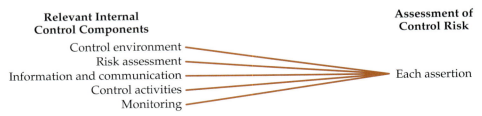

The auditor can make a preliminary assessment of control risk based on a thorough understanding of the design of controls and whether they have been placed in operation. However, this knowledge will only permit the auditor to assess control risk at the maximum. To arrive at an assessment of control risk below the maximum, *evidence* must be obtained about the *operating effectiveness* of the necessary controls.

PERFORM TESTS OF CONTROLS

The third column of Figure 11-2 lists a possible test of control for each of the necessary controls specified in the second column. The tests described include computer-assisted audit techniques, inspecting documentary evidence, inquiring of client personnel, and observing client personnel performing controls. The results of each of the **tests of controls** should provide evidence about the effectiveness of the design and operation of the related necessary control. For example, by using computer-assisted audit techniques to test that the computer compares the sum of checks issued with the entry to cash disbursements, the auditor obtains evidence about the operating effectiveness of controls over the recording of cash disbursement transactions.

In determining the tests to be performed, the auditor considers the type of evidence that will be provided and the cost of performing the test. Once the tests to be performed have been selected, it is customary for the auditor to prepare a formal written audit program for the planned tests of controls. Additional information on planning and performing tests of controls is provided in a later section of this chapter.

EVALUATE EVIDENCE AND MAKE ASSESSMENT

The final assessment of control risk for a financial statement assertion is based on evaluating the evidence gained from (1) procedures to obtain an understanding of internal controls and (2) related tests of controls. Determining the assessed level of control risk is a matter of professional judgment. Auditors should consider the nature, timing, and extent of tests of controls when making that judgment. These judgments are discussed later in the chapter.

If the auditor identifies internal control strengths related to an assertion, he or she should determine whether it is cost effective to test the operating effectiveness of internal controls and modify the nature, timing, or extent of substantive testing. If the auditor identifies deficiencies in internal control related to an assertion, he or she should consider the likelihood (frequency of deviations) and magnitude of potential misstatements (see Figure 2-6) when determining whether the deficiency is a significant deficiency or a material weakness in internal controls.

Finally, as noted in Chapter 9, control risk assessments may be expressed in quantitative terms (such as there is a 5 percent risk that relevant controls will not prevent or detect and correct the particular type of misstatement) or qualitative terms (such as there is a low risk that relevant controls will not prevent or detect and correct the particular type of misstatement). It should also be recalled that assessing control risk for an assertion is a critical factor in determining the acceptable level of detection risk for that assertion. If control risk is assessed too low, detection risk may be set too high and the auditor may not perform sufficient substantive tests, resulting in an ineffective audit. Conversely, if control risk is set too high, more substantive testing may be done than necessary, resulting in an inefficient audit.

[LEARNING CHECK

11-1 a. What is meant by the term *assessing control risk?*
      b. Control risk is assessed in terms of what?

11-2 Enumerate five steps involved in the process of assessing control risk.

11-3 a. How are potential misstatements and necessary controls identified in a typical audit? Explain four steps involved in identifying necessary controls.

      b. Explain how the completeness assertion is normally controlled for most transactions.

      c. Explain how the occurrence, accuracy, cutoff, and classification objectives are normally controlled for most transactions.

11-4 a. Explain the role of evidence obtained from *procedures to obtain an understanding* in assessing control risk.

      b. Explain the role of evidence obtained from *tests of controls* in assessing control risk.

11-5 If a client has a deficiency in internal controls related to revenue recognition, how should the auditor evaluate the significance of such a deficiency?

[KEY TERMS

Assessing control risk, p. 469
Compensating control, p. 474
Identifying potential misstatements, p. 470
Key controls, p. 471

Necessary controls, p. 471
Procedures to obtain an understanding, p. 470
Tests of controls, p. 475

[ASSESSING CONTROL RISK IN AN INFORMATION TECHNOLOGY ENVIRONMENT]

Recall from Chapter 10 that information processing controls include both general control procedures and application control procedures. In addition, the auditor should be cognizant of manual followup procedures for the transactions identified by application controls and the possibility of user controls directly related to an assertion. These procedures are summarized in Figure 11-4. This figure will be helpful in understanding three important audit strategies for performing tests of controls when accounting and control systems make extensive use of information technology (IT).

STRATEGIES FOR PERFORMING TESTS OF CONTROLS

Audit Decision 1

■ What three basic audit strategies can be used for testing controls in the IT environment?

The auditor should choose among the following three strategies when assessing control risk:

1. Assessing control risk based on user controls.
2. Planning for a low control risk assessment based on application controls.
3. Planning for a high control risk assessment based on general controls and manual followup.

Each strategy is explained further below.

User Controls

In many cases, the client may design manual procedures to test the completeness and accuracy of transactions processed by the computer. For example, managers who are familiar with transactions that they have authorized may review a list of

Figure 11-4 ■ Overview of Computer Controls

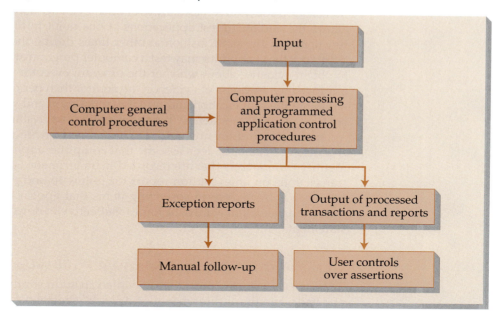

purchases that have been charged to their responsibility center. Alternatively, an individual in a user department may compare computer-generated output with source documents supporting the transaction. Although both of these controls may detect and correct misstatements, the latter may be performed with a greater level of detail and may provide a higher level of assurance that misstatements are detected and corrected.

If user controls exist, the auditor can test the controls directly, similar to testing other human controls. This is also known as **auditing around the computer.** The advantage of this strategy for testing controls is that there is no need to test the complexities of computer programs.

Application Controls

Many auditors take advantage of automated controls and plan strategies for assessing control risk at a low level based on computer application controls. In order to execute this strategy, the auditor should

■ Test the computer application controls.
■ Test computer general controls.
■ Test the manual followup of exceptions noted by application controls.

The effectiveness of all three levels of controls is important to a low control risk assessment. First, the auditor should test computer application controls using some form of computer-assisted audit techniques (CAATs). The purpose is to determine that the application control properly identifies exceptions.

Second, computer general controls must also be tested. General controls provide assurance that application controls are properly designed and tested, and any changes are authorized. In essence, they provide increased assurance that application controls function consistently over time. Evidence about strong general controls allows the auditor to test applications at one point in time and believe that they functioned in the same fashion at other times during the audit period. AU319.96 points out that an auditor may test a computer program at a particular point in time to obtain evidence about whether the program executes the control effectively. To improve the timeliness of evidence, the auditor then performs tests of controls pertaining to the modification and use of that program and whether the programmed control operated consistently during the period (i.e., testing general controls).

Finally, the auditor must also test the effectiveness of manual followup procedures. For example, let's assume that computer application controls correctly identify transactions that are recorded in an erroneous amount and report these transactions on an exception report for followup and correction. If the manual followup is ineffective in correcting items that appear on the exception report, then the application control becomes ineffective in detecting and correcting misstatements.

General Controls and Manual Followup Procedures

For some assertions, the auditor may plan an audit strategy that emphasizes tests of details, and the auditor may plan a "high" control risk assessment for an assertion. The *AICPA Internal Control Audit Guide* presents an audit strategy that allows the auditor to accomplish this task based on evidence about the effectiveness of general controls and manual followup procedures. When the auditor tests general controls, he or she will usually learn about the effectiveness of the design and testing of application controls. In addition, the auditor may be able to make inferences about the effectiveness of application controls in identifying exceptions through inquiry of knowledgeable individuals who perform manual followup procedures. For example, individuals who follow up on exceptions might understand the transaction stream in sufficient detail that they can anticipate transactions that should appear on exception reports. When such transactions do appear on exception reports, the auditor may be able to draw an inference about the programmed control. This evidence may be sufficient to allow the auditor to assess control risk at a high level, but the auditor should test programs directly with computer-assisted audit techniques if he or she wants to assess control risk as moderate or low.

COMPUTER-ASSISTED AUDIT TECHNIQUES

Audit Decision 2

■ What types of computer-assisted audit techniques can be used in performing tests of controls?

Computer-assisted audit techniques (CAATs) involve using the computer to directly test application controls. This is also known as **auditing through the computer.** These tests are used extensively in testing input validation routines (computer editing) and programmed processing controls. The auditor may find that using the computer in tests of controls is advantageous when

■ A significant part of the internal controls is imbedded in a computer program.
■ There are significant gaps in the visible audit trail.
■ There are large volumes of records to be tested.

Using CAATS requires that a member of the audit team have computer knowledge and skills, and it may require the possible disruption of the client's IT operations while the auditor uses its IT equipment, programs, and files. Finally, CAATs provide an effective means of testing computer application controls. The auditor must also test the operating effectiveness of manual followup procedures in order to draw a conclusion about the overall effectiveness of the control activities related to an assertion.

When developing an audit strategy for testing computer controls, the auditor should choose from among the following CAATs to test the operation of specific programmed application controls: (1) parallel simulation, (2) test data, (3) integrated test facility, and (4) continuous monitoring of on-line real-time systems.

Parallel Simulation

In **parallel simulation,** actual company data are reprocessed using an auditor-controlled software program. This method is so named because the software is designed to reproduce or simulate the client's processing of real data. A graphic portrayal of this approach is shown in the left half of Figure 11-5.

Parallel simulation may be performed at different times during the year under audit, and it may also be applied to the reprocessing of the historical data. This approach does not contaminate client files, and it may be conducted at an independent computer facility.

This approach has the following advantages:

■ Because real data are used, the auditor can verify the transactions by tracing them to source documents and approvals.

■ The size of the sample can be greatly expanded at relatively little additional cost.

■ The auditor can run the test independently.

Figure 11-5 ■ Parallel Simulation versus Test Data Approach

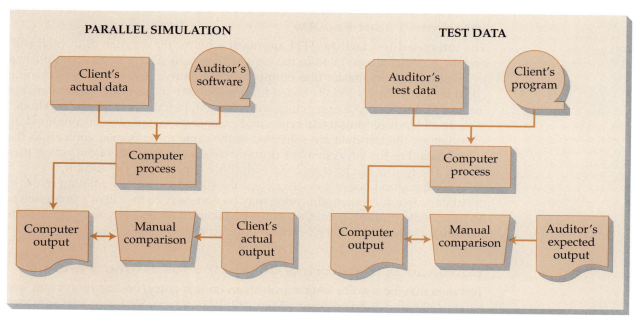

If the auditor decides to use parallel simulation, care must be taken to determine that the data selected for simulations are representative of actual client transactions. It is also possible that the client's system may perform operations that are beyond the capacity of the auditor's software.

Test Data

Under the **test data approach,** dummy transactions are prepared by the auditor and processed under auditor control by the client's computer program. The test data consist of one transaction for each valid and invalid condition the auditor wishes to test. Test data for a payroll test might include both a valid and an invalid overtime pay condition. The output from processing the test data is then compared with the auditor's expected output to determine whether the controls are operating effectively. This approach to testing is relatively simple, quick, and inexpensive. Decision tables used to document programmed control can be helpful in identifying the conditions to be tested with the test data. However, the method has the following deficiencies:

- The client's program is tested only at a specific point in time rather than throughout the period.
- The method is a test of only the presence and functioning of the controls in the program tested.
- There is no examination of documentation actually processed by the system.
- Computer operators know that test data are being run, which could reduce the validity of the output.
- The scope of the test is limited by the auditor's imagination and knowledge of the controls within the application.

A graphic portrayal of the test data approach is shown in the right half of Figure 11-5.

Integrated Test Facility

The **integrated test facility (ITF) approach** requires the creation of a small subsystem (a minicompany) within the regular IT system. This may be accomplished by creating dummy master files or appending dummy master records to existing client files. Test data, specially coded to correspond to the dummy master files, are introduced into the system together with actual transactions. The test data should include all kinds of transaction errors and exceptions that may be encountered. In this manner, the test data are subjected to the same programmed controls as the actual data. For the subsystem, or dummy files, a separate set of outputs is produced. The results can be compared with those expected by the auditor.

The ITF method has as a disadvantage the risk of potentially creating errors in client data. In addition, modification may be necessary to the client's programs to accommodate dummy data. Care must be taken to reverse any test transactions that are included in the client's accounting records.

Continuous Monitoring of On-Line Real-Time Systems

Test data may be used to test controls in an on-line entry/on-line processing system (also known as an on-line real-time [OLRT] system). However, this approach is not widely used by auditors because of the contamination of file data and the difficulty of reversing the hypothetical data. Parallel simulation may also be used, but the availability of generalized audit software that can be used to simulate OLRT processing is very limited.

In lieu of traditional testing, the auditor often arranges for **continuous monitoring** of the system. Under this technique, an audit routine is added to the client's processing programs. Transactions entering the system are sampled at random intervals, and the output from the routine is used in testing the controls.

To provide for the integration of audit software into an OLRT processing system, **audit hook** capabilities must be built into the client's computer programs—both the operating and application programs—at the time they are created. Audit hooks are points in a program that allow audit modules, or programs, to be integrated into the system's normal processing activities. These audit modules provide the auditor with a means of selecting transactions possessing characteristics of interest to the auditor, such as a transaction of a certain kind or an amount greater or lesser than a given value. Once a particular transaction has been identified as being of interest, a record of it can be retained by one of several methods. Two of these methods are tagging transactions and audit logs.

Tagging Transactions

The **tagging transactions** method involves placing an indicator, or tag, on selected transactions. The presence of this tag enables a transaction to be traced through the system as it is being processed. The system must be programmed to provide for the creation of a hardcopy printout of all paths followed by the transaction. Data with which the tagged transaction interacts at designated steps in the processing can be captured as well.

Audit Log

An **audit log,** sometimes called a **systems control audit review file (SCARF),** is a record of certain processing activities. The log is used to record events that meet auditor-specified criteria as they occur at designated points in the system. Identified transactions or events are written onto a file available only to the auditor. The auditor can later print or use other techniques to analyze the file and make further tests as appropriate.

ASSESSING INFORMATION TECHNOLOGY CONTROLS

The process of assessing control risk is the same whether the client uses manual controls, controls that take advantage of information technology, or both. Thus, it is necessary to (1) consider the knowledge acquired from procedures to obtain an understanding, (2) identify potential misstatements that may occur in assertions, (3) identify controls necessary to prevent or detect and correct such misstatements, (4) perform tests of controls, and (5) evaluate the evidence and make the control risk assessment.

Figure 11-6 and 11-7 show representative listings of potential misstatements and necessary controls for general controls and application controls, respectively. Figure 11-7 provides a general way of thinking about input, processing, and output controls that may facilitate thinking about testing application controls. However, the auditor will normally identify potential misstatements relevant to spe-

Figure 11-6 ■ Control Risk Assessment Considerations for Computer General Controls

Potential Misstatement	Necessary Control	Test of Control
Organizational and Operational Controls		
Computer operators may modify programs to bypass programmed controls.	Segregation of duties within IT for computer programming and computer operations.	Observe segregation of duties within IT.
IT personnel may initiate and process unauthorized transactions.	Segregation of duties between user departments and IT for initiating and processing transactions.	Observe segregation of duties between user departments and EDP.
System Development and Documentation Controls		
System design may not meet the needs of user departments or auditors.	Participation of personnel from user departments and internal audit in design and approving new systems.	Inquire about participants involved in designing new systems; examine evidence for approval of new system.
Unauthorized program changes may result in unanticipated processing errors.	Internal verification of proper authorization, testing, and documentation of program changes before implementation.	Examine evidence of internal verification; trace selected program changes to supporting documentation.
Hardware and System Controls		
Equipment malfunction may result in processing errors.	Built-in hardware and system software controls to detect malfunctions.	Examine hardware and system software specifications.
Unauthorized changes in system software may result in processing errors.	Approval and documentation of all system software changes.	Examine evidence of approval and documentation changes.
Access Controls		
Unauthorized users may gain access to IT equipment.	Physical security of IT facilities; management review of utilization reports.	Inspect security arrangements and utilization reports.
Data files and programs may be processed or altered by unauthorized users.	Use of library, librarian, and logs to restrict access and monitor usage.	Inspect facilities and logs.
Data and Procedural Controls		
Errors may be made in inputting or processing data or distributing output.	Use of data control group responsible for maintaining control over data input, processing, and output.	Observe operation of data control group.
Continuity of operations may be disrupted by disaster such as fire or flood.	Contingency plan including arrangements for use of off-premise backup facilities.	Examine contingency plan.
Data files and programs may be damaged or lost.	Storage of backup files and programs off premises; provision for reconstruction of data files.	Examine storage facilities; evaluate file reconstruction capability.

Figure 11-7 ■ Control Risk Assessment Considerations for Computer Application Controls

Potential Misstatement	Necessary Control	Test of Control
Input Controls		
Data for unauthorized transactions may be submitted for processing	Authorization and approval of data in user departments; application controls compares data with previous authorization.	Examine source documents and batch transmittals for evidence of approval; test application control with CAATs and test manual follow-up.
Valid data may be incorrectly converted to machine-sensible form.	Verification (rekeying); computer editing, control totals.	Observe data verification procedures; use CAATs to test edit routines and test manual followup; examine control total reconciliations.
Errors on source documents may not be corrected and resubmitted.	Maintenance of error logs; return to user department for correction; manual followup.	Inspect error logs and evidence of followup.
Processing Controls		
Wrong files may be processed and updated.	Use of external and internal file labels.	Observe use of external file labels; examine documentation for internal file labels.
Data may be lost, added, duplicated, or altered during processing.	Use of control totals, limit and reasonableness checks, and sequence tests.	Examine evidence of control total reconciliations, use CAATs to test computer checks and test manual followup.
Output Controls		
Output may be incorrect.	Reconciliation of totals by data control group or user department.	Examine evidence of reconciliations.
Output may be distributed to unauthorized users.	Use of report distribution control sheets; data control group monitoring.	Inspect report distribution control sheets, observe data control group monitoring.

cific assertions of audit interest, then identify the potential controls (including application controls) that exist, and finally design appropriate tests of controls.

Recall that tests of controls are performed to obtain evidence about the effectiveness of the design or operation of the control. The auditor performs such tests when there is reason to believe that the evidence will permit a further reduction in the assessed level of control risk. The third column of Figures 11-6 and 11-7 shows possible tests of controls. Tests of computer general controls involve the observations of segregation of duties and inspection of documentation showing that computer general controls were performed. Tests of computer application controls involve some form of CAATs and testing of manual followup procedures.

In a computerized system, controls may or may not produce visible evidence. When the computer produces visible evidence to verify that procedures were in operation and to evaluate the propriety of performance, tests of IT controls may include inspection of documentation. However, if such evidence is not generated by the computer, the tests of controls must include CAATs as discussed above.

[LEARNING CHECK

11-6 a. Briefly describe three strategies for testing internal controls when information technology is used for significant accounting processing.
  b. Identify two strategies that might be used to support a low control risk assessment. Discuss the difference between the two strategies.
  c. Discuss a third audit strategy that might be used to assess control risk at a high level. Explain why this strategy will not support a low control risk assessment.

11-7 a. Under what circumstances might it be an advantage to test controls with the computer?
  b. What are the disadvantages of auditing through the computer?

11-8 What are the advantages and disadvantages of the computer-assisted audit technique known as parallel simulation?

11-9 a. What is the difference between the conventional test data approach and the integrated test facility approach?
  b. In lieu of traditional testing, what approaches can be used in on-line entry/on-line processing systems?

[KEY TERMS

Audit hook, p. 481
Audit log, p. 481
Auditing around the computer, p. 477
Auditing through the computer, p. 478
Computer-assisted audit techniques (CAATS), p. 478

Continuous monitoring, p. 481
Integrated test facility (ITF) approach, p. 480
Parallel simulation, p. 479
Systems control audit review file (SCARF), p. 481
Tagging transactions, p. 481
Test data approach, p. 480

[EFFECTS OF PRELIMINARY AUDIT STRATEGIES]

Regardless of the preliminary audit strategy chosen for a particular part of the audit, the auditor is required to identify types of potential misstatements in assertions. However, the manner in which the auditor considers factors that affect the risk of misstatements and assesses the risk can vary in several respects based on the audit strategy chosen. Figure 11-8 highlights the differences in the two approaches to meeting the second standard of fieldwork.

PRIMARILY SUBSTANTIVE APPROACHES

Recall from the discussions in Chapters 9 and 10 that when an auditor chooses a primarily substantive approach, he or she should have sufficient knowledge of the

Figure 11-8 ■ Methodologies for Meeting the Second Standard of Fieldwork

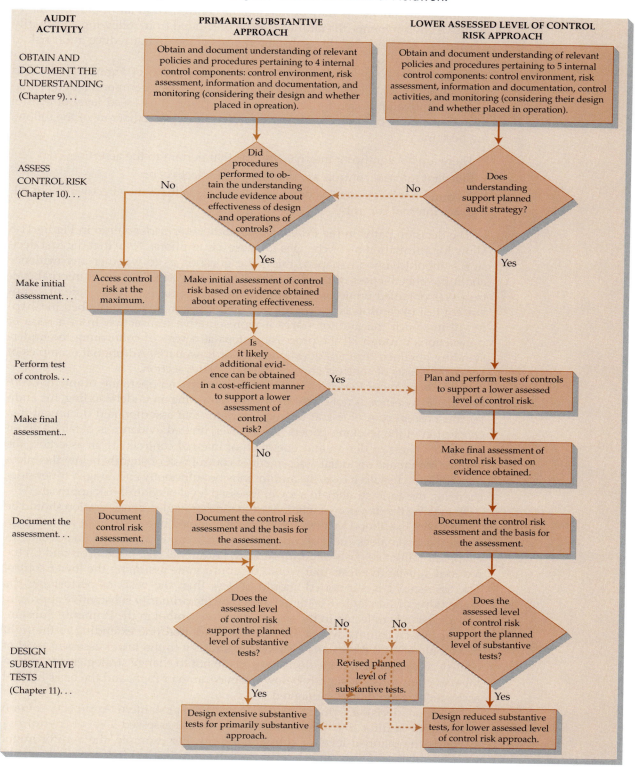

system of internal control to understand the potential causes of misstatements and how those misstatements may or may not be controlled. In addition, in some IT intensive environments, the auditor may be precluded from following a primarily substantive approach because substantive tests alone do not reduce audit risk to an appropriately low level.

A number of differences may be noted in the portion of Figure 11-8 labeled Assess Control Risk. First, as discussed in Chapter 9, one component of a primarily substantive approach for an assertion is a planned assessed level of control risk of maximum or high. This is based on the assumption that one of the following pertains:

■ There are no significant internal controls that pertain to the assertion,
■ Relevant internal controls are unlikely to be effective, or
■ It would not be efficient to obtain evidence to evaluate the effectiveness of relevant internal controls.

The decision paths in the *Primarily Substantive Approach* column in Figure 11-8 allow for affirmation of, or changes to, these assumptions. Note that the first decision symbol (diamond shaped) raises the question as to whether any evidence about the effectiveness of the design and operating effectiveness of internal controls was obtained while understanding internal controls. An example of a concurrent test of controls is the transaction walkthrough review described in Chapter 10 in which the auditor traces a representative transaction from a class of transactions through all the processing steps as a way of confirming the understanding obtained through questionnaires or flowcharts. Additional examples of concurrent tests of controls are explained in a later section.

If evidence about the effectiveness of the design and operation of internal controls for an assertion is not established while obtaining an understanding, the auditor must assess control risk at the maximum for that assertion and document that conclusion in the working papers. If, however, limited evidence is obtained about the effectiveness of design and operation of internal controls for an assertion, the auditor may make an initial assessment of control risk of slightly below the maximum or high. In such a case, the auditor may be sufficiently encouraged to consider changing the audit strategy to a lower assessed level of control risk approach.

In making the decision of whether to change strategies, consideration should be given to the likelihood that evidence can be obtained in a cost-efficient manner to support a lower assessment of control risk such as moderate or low. To be cost-efficient, the combined costs of performing (1) additional tests of controls and (2) the reduced substantive tests that would be appropriate assuming the lower control risk assessment is supported should be less than the costs of performing the higher level of substantive testing required by the primarily substantive approach. This decision is reflected in the second decision symbol in the Primarily Substantive Approach column where the Yes branch (dotted line extending to the right from that symbol) represents a change in strategy to the lower assessed level of control risk approach. If the decision is made not to change strategies, the assessment of control risk at slightly below the maximum or high, and the basis for that assessment, should be documented.

The final decision symbol in the Primarily Substantive Approach column requires the auditor to consider whether the actual assessed level of control risk supports the planned level of substantive tests. For example, the auditor might have originally specified the planned level of control risk at the maximum, resulting in the highest planned level of substantive tests. But if the evidence acquired while obtaining the required understanding supports an actual assessment of control risk as high, revision of the planned level of substantive tests to a lower level would be appropriate. The auditor then proceeds with the detailed design of the appropriate level of substantive tests.

LOWER ASSESSED LEVEL OF CONTROL RISK

In some cases a lower assessed level of control risk approach is planned because the client has effective internal controls and the auditor plans to test those controls, reduce control risk, and modify the nature, timing, or extent of substantive tests accordingly. This is often the case with audits of public companies. The auditor sometimes plans a lower assessed level of control risk approach because substantive tests alone will not reduce audit risk to a sufficiently low level.

A more extensive understanding and documentation of relevant internal controls, particularly the control activities component of internal controls, is ordinarily appropriate in order to support the auditor's planned level of control risk of moderate or low for an assertion. Conceivably, on the basis of a system walkthrough, the auditor might find that contrary to expectations the control appears to be ineffective. In such a case, it is appropriate to change the strategy to a primarily substantive approach. In Figure 11-8, this is reflected in the No branch extending to the left from the first decision symbol in the *Lower Assessed Level of Control Risk Approach* column.

If the auditor continues with the lower assessed level of control risk approach, he or she plans and performs the additional tests of controls. The evidence obtained from the tests of controls is then evaluated to make the **final or actual assessment of control risk.** The final assessment and the basis for that assessment are then documented in the working papers.

The final decision symbol in the Lower Assessed Level of Control Risk Approach column in Figure 11-8 requires the auditor to consider whether the actual assessed level of control risk supports the planned level of substantive tests, and if not, to revise the planned substantive tests. For example, the auditor might have originally specified a planned low assessed level of control risk, resulting in the lowest planned level of substantive tests. But if evidence from tests of controls leads to an actual assessed level of control risk of moderate, revision of the planned substantive tests to support a lower level of detection risk would be appropriate. Or, if contrary to expectations the controls are found to be highly ineffective (control risk is assessed at high or maximum), the auditor would need to revise the planned level of substantive tests to reflect a change to a primarily substantive approach. This is represented by the dotted line slanting downward to the left in the revised planned level of substantive tests block near the bottom of Figure 11-8. In either case, this figure depicts the iterative nature of the audit process, and the final step involves designing the detailed substantive tests appropriate for the circumstances.

DESIGNING TESTS OF CONTROLS

The purpose of assessing control risk is to assist the auditor in making a judgment about the risk of material misstatement in financial statement assertions. To

Audit Decision 3

■ What factors bear on the degree of assurance provided by tests of controls?

accomplish this task, the auditor must evaluate the effectiveness of both the design and operation of relevant controls.

Tests of controls that are designed to evaluate the operating effectiveness of a control are concerned with (1) how the control was applied, (2) the consistency with which it was applied during the period, and (3) by whom it was applied. The assurance obtained by tests of controls is influenced by making decisions about the nature, timing, and extent of tests of controls.

NATURE OF TESTS OF CONTROLS

The **nature of tests of controls** relates to the type of evidence obtained. Tests of controls normally include:

■ Inquiries of appropriate entity personnel
■ Inspection of documents, reports, or electronic files, indicating performance of the control
■ Observation of the application of the control
■ Reperformance of the application of the control by the auditor, including the use of computer-assisted audit techniques (CAATs).

The more assurance that the auditor desires from tests of controls, the more reliable the evidence needs to be. Auditors often use a combination of the above types of tests of controls to obtain evidence about a control's effective design and operation.

Inquiry is designed to determine (1) an employee's understanding of computer controls, (2) an employee's understanding of his or her duties, (3) the individual's performance of those duties, and (4) the frequency, causes, and disposition of deviation. For example, employees who work closely with transactions may be in a position to know whether transactions should appear on an exception report. Inquiry of the employee may help the auditor understand the employee's skill and competency in performing a control, along with the employee's knowledge of both the computer control and the purpose of manual follow-up. Inquiry might also uncover information about transactions that should appear on an exception report, such as a report of goods that have been ordered but not shipped, and whether transactions that were expected to appear on the report did not show up. The auditor should also consider that unsatisfactory answers from an employee might indicate improper application of a control. However, inquiry alone does not provide sufficient, competent evidence to allow for an assessment of control risk below the maximum. Inquiry should be supplemented with observation, inspecting documents, or reperforming controls.

Ideally, observation should be performed without the employee's knowledge or on a surprise basis. Inquiring and observing are especially useful in obtaining evidence about appropriate use of segregation of duties. The limitation of observation is that it only applies to the time at which it is performed.

Inspecting documents and records is applicable when there is a transaction trail of performance in the form of notations on exception reports, signatures, or validations stamps that indicate whether the control was performed and identify the individual who performed it. For example, the auditor may inspect notations left by employees on exception reports or those notations left by management who reviews reports summarizing business transactions. The inspection of records may provide reliable evidence about the actions performed by employees or management to follow up on issues raised by control activities. However, a signature on a document, such as a voucher package or a management report, to indicate that the signer approved it does not necessarily mean that the person carefully reviewed the package before signing. Hence, the auditor usually reperfoms the control to evaluate how carefully a control is performed.

In reperforming the control, the auditor performs the same procedures that would be performed in implementing the control. For example, if a manager reviews a week's worth of sale transactions to ascertain that they were made to customers with appropriate credit risks, the auditor should review the list signed by the manager and evaluate whether each customer met the companies credit risk criteria. If an employee performs follow-up procedures on all checks exceeding the limit for machine-signed checks, the auditor needs to review the exception list and ascertain the subsequent disposition of items on the exception report. If the manual follow-up was not consistent with company policy, then the auditor must conclude some evidence of ineffectiveness of control was obtained. The auditor then needs to consider the probability that a material misstatement in an assertion could occur due to this weakness.

Ultimately, the nature of the control influences the type of audit procedure that is performed. For example, when testing manual followup procedures, the auditor needs to evaluate both the accuracy of the report (often by testing both computer general controls and by testing the programmed controls over the accuracy of the report) and the effectiveness of the followup procedures. Testing controls over an accounting estimate often involves testing the accuracy of the data used to develop the estimate and manual controls over the reliability and consistency of the estimation process.

Finally, the absence of misstatements does not necessarily mean that a control is effective. However, if misstatements are found during the audit, the auditor should consider such misstatements when evaluating the effectiveness of internal controls.

TIMING OF TESTS OF CONTROLS

The **timing of tests of controls** determines the period of reliance on tests of controls. If the auditor tests controls only at a particular point in time, then the auditor only obtains evidence that the control operated effectively at that point in time. If the auditor tests controls throughout the period, then the auditor obtains evidence about operating effectiveness during that period of time.

For example, observation pertains only to the point in time at which it was applied. Hence, it may be insufficient to evaluate the effectiveness for periods not subjected to the test. The use of CAATs, such as test data, provide a conclusion about a computer program only at the point in time at which it was applied. In order to improve the timeliness of the evidence, the auditor will also apply tests of computer general controls over the modification and the use of that computer program during the audit period to obtain evidence about whether the programmed control operated consistently during the audit period. The combination of evidence about effective computer general controls allows the auditor to extend the conclusion about application controls to a greater portion of the audit period than just the period when the computer applications were tested directly.

When the auditor obtains evidence about the design or operation of controls during an interim period, he or she should determine what additional evidential matter should be obtained for the remaining period. The auditor should consider the following factors when considering the evidence that needs to be obtained during the remaining period:

- The significance of the assertion involved
- The specific controls that were evaluated during the interim period
- The degree to which the effective design and operation of those controls were evaluated
- The results of the tests of controls used to make that evaluation
- The length of the remaining period
- The evidential matter about design or operation that may result from tests of monitoring controls on the part of the client and substantive test performed in the remaining period.

In addition, the auditor should obtain evidential matter about the nature and extent of any significant changes in internal control, including its policies, procedures, and personnel that occur subsequent to the interim period.

For example, let's assume that the auditor performs tests of control over the existence and occurrence and valuation of recorded sales (and receivables), assesses control risk as low, and plans on performing substantive tests by sending confirmations several months prior to year-end. Prior to sending confirmations, and again at year-end, the auditor should update his or her conclusion regarding a low control risk assessment. If the relevant control procedures are programmed control procedures, the auditor will usually make inquiries about program changes and changes in the manual followup procedures. If there are significant changes in IT personnel, the auditor might perform additional tests of computer general controls and consider the need for additional tests of the computer applications. If there are changes in personnel performing manual followup procedures, the auditor might perform additional tests of the effectiveness of manual followup of items appearing on exception reports. The goal is to determine whether the earlier conclusion regarding tests of controls is still valid, prior to performing substantive tests.

An issue of continuing controversy relates to whether the auditor may consider evidence obtained during prior audits about the effective design or operation of controls in assessing control risk in the current audit. The number of computer applications may be so significant that auditors consider rotating tests of specific application controls. Generally accepted auditing standards allow auditors to rotate tests of controls for private companies such that controls are tested at least every three years. However, if the control relates a significant inherent risk, then the control should be tested during the current audit period. Furthermore, rotation of tests of controls from year to year is not appropriate when the auditor is issuing an opinion on internal controls.

If the auditor plans to use audit evidence about the effectiveness of controls from prior audits, the auditor should obtain evidence about whether changes have been made since the control was last tested. The auditor would normally use a combination of inquiry, observation, and inspection to confirm the understanding of the effectiveness of design of the control and to verify that it has still been placed in operation. For example, in the case of an automated control, the auditor might make inquiries and inspect logs that contain information about changes in

timing of tests of controls when reporting on the effectiveness of internal controls

The period of time over which the auditor performs tests of controls varies with the nature of the controls being tested and with the frequency with which specific controls operate. Some controls operate continuously (for example, controls over sales). Others operate only at certain times (for example, controls over the count of physical inventories or controls over the preparation of financial statements).

When the auditor reports on the effectiveness of controls "as of" a specific date and obtains evidence about the operating effectiveness of controls at an interim date, he or she should determine what additional evidence should be obtained concerning the operation of the control for the remaining period. In making that determination, the auditor should evaluate:

- The specific controls tests prior to the "as of" date and the results of those tests.
- The degree to which evidence about the operating effectiveness of those controls was obtained.
- The length of the remaining period.
- The possibility that significant changes were made in internal control over financial reporting subsequent to the interim date.

For controls over significant nonroutine transactions, controls over accounts or processes with a high degree of subjectivity or judgment in measurement, or controls over the recording of period-end adjustment, the auditor should perform tests of controls closer to, or at, the "as of" date.

PCAOB
Public Companies
Accounting Oversight Board

programmed controls. If the control has changed since it was tested in a prior period, the evidence gathered then may no longer be relevant.

EXTENT OF TESTS OF CONTROLS

Generally, the lower the planned assessed level of control risk, the greater the extent of tests of controls. In the case of an audit of internal controls over financial reporting, the auditor must obtain evidence about the effectiveness of control for all relevant assertions related to all significant accounts and disclosures in the financial statements.

In making an assessment about the **extent of tests of controls,** the auditor should consider the following factors:

- *The nature of the control.* The auditor should subject manual controls to more extensive testing than automated controls. A single test of each condition of a programmed control may be sufficient to obtain a high level of assurance that the control operated effectively if general controls are also operating effectively. However, manual controls usually require more extensive testing. In general, as the level of complexity and the level of judgment in the application of a control increase, the extent of the auditor's testing should also increase. If the level of competency of the person performing the control decreases, the extent of testing should also increase.

- *Frequency of operation.* Generally, the more frequent the operation of a manual control, the more operations of the control the auditor should test. Some controls operate less frequently, such as monthly account reconciliations, and the auditor would usually test fewer operations of these controls than controls that operate daily or on every transaction.
- *Importance of the control.* Controls that are more important should be tested more extensively. Some controls such as the control environment or computer general controls have a pervasive impact on other controls. The more that the auditor plans to assess control risk below the maximum based on these controls, or report on their effective operation, then the more extensive the auditor's test needs to be.

Chapter 13 provides an extensive discussion of factors that influence sample size for tests of controls.

STAFFING TESTS OF CONTROLS

A final audit decision involves the **staffing of tests of controls,** or who should perform tests of controls. For example, an audit team will usually include a computer audit specialist to evaluate computer general control procedures and to perform computer-assisted audit techniques. If the client has designed controls to control particular business risks, such as the risk of incorrect Medicare billing, the auditor may want to have staff who are familiar with specific government regulations perform tests of these controls. In many cases, an entry-level staff accountant can be assigned to perform tests of controls over routine transactions such as sales, expenditures, and payroll.

AUDIT PROGRAMS FOR TESTS OF CONTROLS

The auditor's decisions regarding the nature, extent, and timing of tests of controls along with audit staffing should be documented in an audit program and related working papers. A sample audit program for tests of controls of cash disbursement transactions is illustrated in Figure 11-9. Note that the program lists the procedures to be used in performing the tests pertaining to the indicated assertions and provides columns to indicate (1) cross-references to the working papers where the results of the tests are documented, (2) who performed the tests, and (3) the date the tests were completed. Details concerning the extent and timing of the tests may be indicated in the audit program or in the cross-referenced working papers as assumed in this illustration. The preparation of working papers showing the details of samples and the results of tests is explained in Chapter 13 of this text, which covers attribute sampling for tests of controls. It may be noted that the tests listed in the formal audit program in Figure 11-9 are derived from the possible tests of controls listed in the third column of Figure 11-2. Some of the tests have been rearranged and combined, however, to make their performance more efficient.

DUAL-PURPOSE TESTS

In most audits, tests of controls are performed primarily during interim work, and substantive tests of balances are performed primarily during year-end work.

Figure 11-9 ■ Illustrative Partial Audit Program for Tests of Controls

Prepared By: _____ Date: _____			
Reviewed By: _____ Date: _____			

Amalgamated Products, Inc.
Planned Tests of Controls–Cash Distribution Transactions
Year Ending December 31, 20XX

Working Paper Reference	Assertion/Tests of Controls	Auditor	Date
	1. Arrange to use the client's computer facilities to test programmed application controls using test data.		
	Occurrence		

	2. Submit test data to ascertain that the program properly identifies exceptions for:
	  a. Transactions where the voucher information does not match with underlying supporting information. (*Note:* This also tests controls over valuation.)
	  b. Transactions that are submitted twice.		

	3. Inspect exception reports issued by the computer in the normal course of business and evaluate the effectiveness of manual followup procedures.		
	4. Observe that only authorized personnel are permitted to handle checks when the computer signs checks.		
	5. Observe segregation of duties between approving vouchers for payment and the handling of signed checks.		
	6. Inspect documents to ascertain that payment vouchers and supporting documents are stamped "paid" when the check is issued.		
	Completeness		

	7. Submit test data to ascertain that the program properly identifies exceptions for:
	  a. Breaks in the sequence of prenumbered checks.
	  b. Mismatches between the sum of checks issued and the total posting to cash disbursements. (*Note:* This also tests controls over valuation.)		

	8. Observe handling and storage of unused checks.		
	9. Make inquires about any cash disbursements paid by a method other than by check.		
	10. Inspect independent bank reconciliations and evaluate the effectiveness of this controls (*Note:* This control also tests controls over existence and occurrence and valuation.)		

However, it is permissible under GAAS to perform substantive tests of details of transactions to detect monetary errors in the accounts during interim work. When this occurs, the auditor may simultaneously perform tests of controls on the same transactions. For instance, the auditor may examine exception reports associated with the recording of expenditures. At the same time, the auditor may tabulate the monetary errors in the vouchers.

Tests that simultaneously test internal controls and provide substantive evidence are referred to as **dual-purpose testing.** When this type of testing is done, the auditor should exercise care in designing the tests to ensure that evidence is obtained as to both the effectiveness of controls and monetary errors in transactions. Some firms use dual-purpose testing because it may be more cost-efficient to perform the tests simultaneously rather than separately.

[LEARNING CHECK

11-10 Explain several differences in the methodologies for meeting the second standard of fieldwork under a primarily substantive approach versus the lower assessed level of control risk approach.

11-11 Identify three issues that the auditor should evaluate when making a decision about the effectiveness of internal controls.

11-12 Identify four different types of audit procedures that the auditor might use when performing tests of controls. Explain the reliability of each different audit procedure.

11-13 a. What is meant by the timing of tests of controls?
b. If the auditor performs tests of controls at an interim period, what factors should he or she consider in determining whether to obtain additional evidence during the remainder of the audit period?
c. May the auditor use evidence about the effectiveness of internal control obtained in a prior audit to support a conclusion about the effectiveness of internal control in the current audit? If yes, what steps should the auditor take to evaluate the continuing reliability of evidence from the prior audit in the context of the current audit?

11-14 a. In general, how does the extent of tests of controls relate to planned assessed level of control risk?
b. Identify the factors that bear on the auditor's decisions about the extent of tests of controls. Provide an example of how each factor influences the extent of tests of controls.

11-15 Provide two examples of circumstances where it would be appropriate to use audit staff with special qualifications in performing tests of controls. When is it most appropriate to use entry-level staff to perform tests of controls?

11-16 What are dual-purpose tests?

[KEY TERMS

Dual-purpose testing, p. 494
Extent of tests of controls, p. 491
Final or actual assessment of control risk, p. 487

Nature of tests of controls, p. 488
Staffing for tests of controls, p. 492
Timing of tests of controls, p. 489

[ADDITIONAL CONSIDERATIONS]

ASSESSING CONTROL RISK FOR ACCOUNT BALANCE ASSERTIONS AFFECTED BY A SINGLE TRANSACTION CLASS

Audit Decision 4

■ What is the process of assessing control risk for account balance assertions affected by single and multiple transaction classes?

The process of assessing control risk for account balance assertions is straightforward for accounts that are affected by a single transaction class. This is the case for most income statement accounts. For example, sales are increased by credits for sales transactions in the revenue cycle, and many expense accounts are increased by debits for purchase transactions in the expenditure cycle. In these cases, the auditor's control risk assessment for each account balance assertion is the same as the control risk assessment for the same transaction class assertion. For example, the control risk assessment for the existence & occurrence assertion for the sales account balance should be the same as that for the existence and occurrence assertion for sales transactions. Similarly, the control risk assessment for the valuation and allocation assertion for many expenses should be the same as that for the valuation and allocation assertion for purchase transactions.

ASSESSING CONTROL RISK FOR ACCOUNT BALANCE ASSERTIONS AFFECTED BY MULTIPLE TRANSACTION CLASSES

Many balance sheet accounts are significantly affected by more than one transaction class. For example, the accounts receivable balance is increased by sales transactions in the revenue cycle and decreased by cash receipts or by sales returns and allowances. In these cases, assessing control risk for an account balance assertion requires consideration of the relevant control risk assessments for each transaction class that significantly affects the balance.

The existence and occurrence of accounts receivable (which results in an overstatement of accounts receivable) is affected by three transactions: (1) the existence and occurrence of sales, (2) the completeness of cash receipts, and (3) the completeness of sales returns and allowances. Hence, if a sale is recognized that should not have been, it results in an existence problem for accounts receivable. Similarly, if there is a completeness problem with cash receipts or with sale returns, it will also result in an overstatement of accounts receivable (an existence problem). It is important to understand that failure to record a cash receipt from a customer (the completeness problem) results in an existence misstatement for accounts receivable.

The completeness of accounts receivable (which results in an understatement of accounts receivable) is also affected by three transactions: (1) the completeness of sales, (2) the existence and occurrence of cash receipts, and (3) the existence and occurrence of sales returns and allowances. Hence, if a sale goes unrecorded, it results in an completeness problem for accounts receivable. Similarly, if there is an occurrence problem with cash receipts or with sale returns, the result will be an understatement of accounts receivable (a completeness problem). Figure 11-10 provides several examples of the types of transactions that increase or decrease an account balance.

Figure 11-10 ■ Summary of Relationships Between Account Balance Assertions and Transaction Class Assertions

	Account Balance Assertion	Transaction Class Assertions that Increase the Account Balance	Transaction Class Assertions that Decrease the Account Balance
Example 1	Existence of accounts receivable	Existence and occurrence of sales	Completeness of cash receipts
			Completeness of sale returns and allowances
Example 2	Completeness of accounts payable	Completeness of purchases	Existence and occurrence of cash disbursements
			Existence and occurrence of purchase returns

The following general rules explain the relationship between transaction class assertions and account balance assertions.

■ The control risk assessment for the existence and occurrence assertion for an account balance is related to the existence and occurrence assertion for the transactions that increase the account balance as well as the completeness assertions for the transactions that decrease the account balance.

■ The control risk assessment for the completeness assertion for an account balance is related to the completeness assertion for the transactions that increase the account balance as well as the existence and occurrence assertion for the transactions that decrease the account balance.

■ The rights and obligations assertion for an account balance is related to the rights and obligations assertions for transactions that both increase and decrease the account balance.

■ The valuation and allocation assertion for an account balance is related to the valuation and allocation assertions for transactions that both increase and decrease the account balance.

■ The presentation and disclosure assertion for an account balance is related to the presentation and disclosure assertions for transactions that both increase and decrease the account balance.

This relationship is depicted in Figure 11-11.

COMBINING DIFFERENT CONTROL RISK ASSESSMENTS

Referring to the example 1 in Figure 11-10, suppose the auditor obtained the following control risk assessments from the working papers based on his or her understanding of relevant portions of internal control based on tests of controls:

ASSERTION	CONTROL RISK ASSESSMENT
Existence and occurrence of sales	Low
Completeness of cash receipts	Low
Completeness of sales returns and allowance	Moderate

Figure 11-11 ■ Summary of Relationship between Account Balance Assertions and Transaction Class Assertions

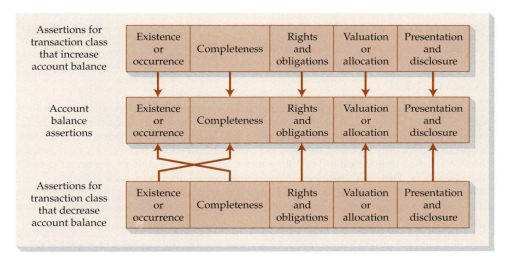

When the control risk assessments for the relevant transaction class assertions differ, the auditor may judgmentally weigh the significance of each assessment in arriving at a combined assessment. Alternatively, some firms elect to use the most conservative (highest) of the relevant assessments. Hence, the control risk assessment for the existence of accounts receivable should be "moderate" unless sales returns and allowances are immaterial.

Once control risk for the account balance assertion has been determined, it should be compared with the planned assessed level of control risk. When the planned level is supported, the auditor can proceed to design substantive tests based on the preliminary audit strategy. If the planned assessed level of control risk is not supported, the planned level of substantive tests and related audit tests should be revised to obtain the desired level of audit risk.

DOCUMENTING THE ASSESSED LEVEL OF CONTROL RISK

Audit Decision 5

■ What are the requirements for documenting the control risk assessment?

The auditor's working papers should include **documentation of the control risk assessment.** The requirements are as follows:

■ Control risk is assessed at the maximum: Only this conclusion needs to be documented.

■ Control risk is assessed at below the maximum: The basis for the assessment must be documented.

AU 319 does not illustrate or offer guidance on the form of the documentation. In practice, a common approach is to use narrative memoranda organized by financial statement assertions. This approach is illustrated in Figure 11-12, which documents the control risk assessments for selected sales transaction assertions. Note that the basis for the assessment below the maximum for the completeness

Figure 11-12 ■ Partial Documentation for Control Risk Assessment

---

Client: Young Fashions, Inc.   **Balance Sheet Date:** 9/30/X5

Completed by: CRS   **Date:** 5/19/X5   **Reviewed by:** EMT   **Date:** 5/28/X5

Control risk assessment for: Sales Transactions

COMPLETENESS

Client internal controls relevant to completeness relate primarily to the computer listing of unmatched sales orders, bills of lading, packing slips, and sales invoices. Based on discussions with accounts receivable personnel on 5/11/X5 and with selected shipping personnel at Texas and California locations on 4/18/X5 and 5/8/X5, respectively, it normally can take up to two weeks between the placing of a sales order and shipment. It is rare, however, for an unmatched bill of lading or packing slip to remain on the unmatched documents report for more than two days. This was corroborated by examining the unmatched documents report for selected days (see W/P XX-4-2 [not illustrated here]) where the longest period a bill of lading or packing slip was outstanding was two days. Selected transactions on these reports were traced to underlying documents with no exceptions.

Based on this examination of evidential matter, combined with the results of discussions with accounts receivable and shipping personnel, and corroborating observations, control risk is assessed at moderate.

VALUATION AND ALLOCATION

Control risk is assessed at the maximum.

Source: AICPA Audit Guide: Consideration of Internal Control in the Financial Statement Audit (1990), p. 145. (Adapted)

---

assertion is given, whereas only the conclusion is stated when the assessment is at the maximum, as indicated for the accuracy assertion.

COMMUNICATING INTERNAL CONTROL MATTERS

The auditor is required to identify and report to the audit committee, or other entity personnel with equivalent authority and responsibility, certain conditions that relate to an entity's internal control observed during an audit of the financial statements. Generally accepted auditing standards and the PCAOB define a significant deficiency as follows:[1]

A **significant deficiency** is a control deficiency, or combination of control deficiencies, that adversely affects the company's ability to initiate, authorize, record, process, or report external financial data reliably in accordance with generally accepted accounting principles such that there is more than a remote likelihood that a misstatement of the company's annual or interim financial statement that is more than inconsequential will not be prevented or detected.

---

[1] The definitions are from PCAOB Auditing Standards No. 2, *An Audit of Internal Control over Financial Reporting Performed in Conjunction with an Audit of Financial Statements*. At the time the book went to print the Auditing Standards Board was considering adoption of similar definitions.

Audit Decision 6

■ **What are the auditor's requirements for communicating internal control matters to the audit committee?**

The term *remote likelihood* is used in the same context as used in FASB No. 5 that addresses terms such as probably, reasonably possible, and remote. Hence, *remote likelihood* means that the chance of a future event or events occurring is slight. A misstatement is *inconsequential* if a reasonable person would conclude after considering the possibility of further undetected misstatements that the misstatement, either individually or when aggregated with other misstatements, would *clearly* be immaterial to the financial statements. If a reasonable person could not reach such a conclusion regarding a particular misstatement, that misstatement is more than inconsequential.

A material weakness is defined as follows:

> A **material weakness** is a significant deficiency, or combination of significant deficiencies, that results in more than a remote likelihood that a material misstatement of the annual or interim financial statements will not be prevented or detected.

Hence, the auditor must make a professional judgment about a deficiency in internal control and whether it rises to a level of (1) a significant deficiency or (2) a material weakness. This judgment is made based on a combination of the likelihood of the misstatement and the potential magnitude of the misstatement that might occur owing to the deficiency in internal control. One possible view of a quantitative framework in making this evaluation is depicted in Figure 11-13.

If a material weakness in internal controls over financial reporting exists in a public company, an auditor communicates this to both management and the audit committee, and will issue an adverse report on the effectiveness of internal controls. In addition, auditors are required to communicate all significant deficiencies in internal control to management and the audit committee. Reporting items that are more than inconsequential in amount to the audit committee sets a relatively low threshold for items that reach the audit committee of the board of directors.

Communication of internal control-related matters is an important outcome of the financial statement audit. This is particularly important knowledge for the

Figure 11-13 ■ Example Criteria for Evaluating a Deficiency in Internal Control

Type of Deficiency	Likelihood of Misstatement	Magnitude of Potential Misstatement
Internal Control Deficiency	Remote (Less than a 5% to 10% chance)[a]	Inconsequential (Less than 0.5% to 1% of pretax income)[a]
Significant Deficiency	More than remote (More than a 5% to 10% chance)[a]	More than inconsequential (More than 0.5% to 1% of pretax income)[a]
Material Weakness	More than remote (More than a 5% to 10% chance)[a]	Material (More than 4% to 5% of pretax income)[a]

[a] Quantifications are a matter of professional judgment, and auditors might use criteria that are different from those illustrated in this figure

audit committee, for good internal controls are important to reducing the opportunity for fraud. Auditors will normally evaluate whether the client has sufficient controls to address problems that are created by an entity's business risks, inherent risk, and fraud risks. For example, in an effort to manage a just-in-time inventory system, the client may design a system that uses electronic data interchange to communicate inventory quantities to the vendor and order goods when inventory falls below predetermined levels. The client's internal control should provide reasonable assurance that such orders are properly authorized and accounted for. Additional information about the communication of internal control matters is presented in Chapter 19.

[LEARNING CHECK

11-17 Explain the process for assessing control risk for:
   a. Account balance assertions affected by a single transaction class.
   b. Account balance assertions affected by multiple transaction classes.
11-18 How may the auditor assess the level of control risk for an account balance assertion when the assessed levels of control risk for multiple related transaction class assertions are not all the same?
11-19 a. What are the requirements for documenting the assessed level of control risk for an assertion?
   b. What form does the documentation often take in practice?
11-20 a. What responsibility does the auditor have for communicating internal control-related matters?
   b. Differentiate the terms *significant deficiency* and *material weaknesses*.

[KEY TERMS

Documentation of the control risk
   assessment, p. 497

Material weakness, p. 499
Significant deficiency, p. 498

[FOCUS ON AUDITOR KNOWLEDGE AND AUDIT DECISIONS]

This chapter focuses on understanding the client's system of internal control. In making decisions to support high-quality audit work, the auditor must be able to use the knowledge summarized in Figure 11-14 and address the decisions summarized in Figure 11-15. The page references indicate where these issues are discussed in more detail.

Figure 11-14 ■ Summary of Auditor Knowledge Discussed in Chapter 11

Auditor Knowledge	Summary	Chapter References
K1. Know the steps in assessing control risk.	The steps involved in assessing control risk include: (1) considering the knowledge acquired from procedures to obtain an understanding about whether controls pertaining to the assertion have been designed and placed in operation by the entity's management, (2) identifying potential misstatements that could occur in an assertion, (3) identifying the necessary controls that would likely prevent or detect and correct the misstatements, (4) performing tests of controls on the necessary controls to determine the effectiveness of their design and operation, and (5) evaluating the evidence and making the assessment.	pp. 465–475
K2. Know the difference between assessing control risk under two major preliminary audit strategies.	Figure 11-8 illustrates the differences between the two major preliminary audit strategies. If the auditor is planning a primarily substantive approach for an assertion, then he or she will often use the knowledge about the effectiveness of internal controls that is obtained while obtaining the understanding of internal controls, and then proceed to appropriate substantive tests that reduce detection risk to an appropriately low level. If the auditor is following a lower assessed level of control risk approach, then the auditor plans more extensive tests of controls that will allow for a modification of the nature, timing, or extent of planned substantive tests.	pp. 484–487

Figure 11-15 ■ Summary of Audit Decisions Discussed in Chapter 11

Audit Decision	Factors that Influence the Audit Decision	Chapter References
D1. What three basic audit strategies can be used for testing controls in the IT environment?	The three basic audit strategies for testing controls in the IT environment are: (1) testing user controls, (2) testing computer application controls, computer general controls, and manual followup procedures and (3) testing only computer general controls and manual followup procedures. (This final strategy does not provide sufficient, competent evidence to allow for a control risk assessment of moderate or low.)	pp. 476–478
D2. What types of computer-assisted audit techniques can be used in performing tests of controls?	The computer-assisted audit techniques that can be used for testing computer application controls include (1) parallel simulation, (2) test data, (3) an integrated test facilities (ITF), or (4) computer monitoring of on-line, real-time systems, including tagging transactions or using a system control audit review file. The chapter explains how to implement each form of CAATs.	pp. 478–484

(continues)

Figure 11-15 ■ (Continued)

Audit Decision	Factors that Influence the Audit Decision	Chapter References
D3. What factors bear on the degree of assurance provided by tests of controls?	The more assurance that the auditor desires from tests of controls, the more the auditor needs sufficient and competent evidence from tests of controls. This section of the chapter discusses audit decisions about the nature (competency of evidence), timing (when evidence is collected during the period), extent (sample size), and staffing (who collects and evaluates the evidence) of tests of controls and how they influence the sufficiency and competency of evidence from tests of controls.	pp. 487–494
D4: What is the process of assessing control risk for account balance assertions affected by single and multiple transaction classes?	The determination of control risk for income statement balances is not complex. For example, the occurrence of sales is directly related to the occurrence assertion. However, balance sheet accounts are more complex, for these balances are affected by multiple transactions. Hence, the existence & occurrence of a balance sheet account is related to the existence and occurrence assertion for those transactions that increase the account balance, and is related to the completeness assertion for those transactions that decrease the account balance. Likewise, the completeness of a balance sheet account is related to the completeness assertion for those transactions that increase the account balance, and is related to the existence and occurrence assertion for those transactions that decrease the account balance.	pp. 495–497
D5. What are the requirements for documenting the control risk assessment?	If control risk is assessed at the maximum, the auditor need only document this conclusion. If control risk is assessed below the maximum, then the auditor needs to document the basis for the assessment.	pp. 497–498
D6. What are the auditor's requirements for communicating internal control matters to the audit committee?	Auditors must communicate all *significant deficiencies* in internal control to management and the board of directors. In addition, auditors need to identify for management and the audit committee any deficiency in internal controls that is so significant that it should be considered a *material weakness*. In the case of a public company, the existence of a material weakness in internal control over financial reporting will result in an adverse report to the public on the effectiveness of internal control over financial reporting.	pp. 498–500

objective questions

Objective questions are available for the student at www.wiley.com/college/boynton

comprehensive questions

11-21 **(Assessing control risk)** An auditor is required to obtain a sufficient understanding of each of the components of an entity's system of internal control to plan the audit of the entity's financial statements and to assess control risk for the assertions embodied in the account balance, transaction class, and disclosure components of the financial statements.

Required

a. Explain the reasons an auditor may assess control risk at the maximum level for one or more assertions embodied in an account balance.

b. What must an auditor do to support assessing control risk at less than the maximum level when the auditor has determined that controls have been placed in operation?

c. What should an auditor consider when seeking a further reduction in the planned assessed level of control risk?

d. What are an auditor's documentation requirements concerning an entity's system of internal control and the assessed level of control risk?

AICPA (adapted)

11-22 **(Assessing control risk for programmed application controls)** Your client controls the existence and occurrence of sales by having the computer program match the information supporting sales invoices with underlying shipping documents before a sales invoice is recorded. The customer information is matched with customer information on a bill of lading, the quantities billed are matched with packing slip information, prices are matched with the sales order, and the invoice date is matched with the accounting period in which goods are shipped. If the transaction does not exactly match the underlying information it is printed on an exception report and not processed.

Required

Explain the tests of controls that need to be performed to assess control risk at a low level based on the programmed controls described above.

11-23 **(Effects of audit strategies on assessing control risk)** As an audit manager at Gung & Ho, CPAs, you have been scheduled to serve as the discussion leader for an in-office training session on consideration of internal control in a financial statement audit.

Required

Prepare an outline of comments you plan to make to indicate similarities and differences in how each of the following items is handled under a primarily substantive approach.

a. Obtaining and documenting the understanding.

b. Performing concurrent tests of controls.

c. Making an initial assessment of control risk.

d. Performing additional or planned tests of controls.

e. Making a final assessment of control risk.

f. Documenting the control risk assessment.

g. Designing substantive tests.

IIA (adapted)

11-24 **(General controls, potential misstatements, and tests of controls)** In considering the internal control for the Aliva Company, Joan Davies, CPA, develops an internal control questionnaire for EDP general controls that includes the following questions:

1. Is there adequate segregation of duties between programmers and computer operators?

2. Is access to computer facilities restricted to authorized personnel?

3. Are systems software changes properly authorized, tested, and documented?

4. Is there a disaster contingency plan?

5. Is there a data control function to control input and output processing?

6. Is the initiation and authorization of transactions done outside the EDP department?

7. Are there proper authorization, testing, and documentation for systems and program changes?

8. Is access to data files and programs restricted to authorized users?

9. Are hardware and systems software controls adequate to detect equipment malfunctions?

10. Is there adequate participation by users and internal auditors in new systems development?

11. Is the correction of source documents done by user departments?

12. Is there off-premises storage of backup files and programs?

Required

a. Identify the category of general controls to which each question pertains.

b. Indicate a possible misstatement that could occur, assuming a *No* answer to each question.

c. Identify a possible test of controls, assuming a *Yes* answer to each question. (Present your answers in tabular form using a separate column for each part.)

11-25 **(Potential misstatements and tests of controls)** Your firm has been engaged to audit the financial statements of the Haven Company. In obtaining an understanding of internal control pertaining to cash disbursement transactions, the following questionnaire is used:

1. Are there periodic independent bank reconciliations of bank accounts?

2. Is a daily summary of checks prepared and agreed to checks issued?

3. Are supporting documents stamped "paid" or otherwise canceled after payment?

4. Are unused checks stored in a secure area with access limited to authorized personnel?

5. Are checks prenumbered and accounted for?

6. Is there supervisory approval of account classification when entering transactions?

7. Is a check protection device used to imprint check amounts?

8. Is there segregation of duties between journalizing and posting?

9. Is there an independent check of daily check summary amounts with check register entries?

Required

a. Identify a potential misstatement that could occur, assuming a *No* answer to each question.

b. For each question, would you expect the control procedure to be a computer control or a manual control?

c. Identify a possible test of controls for the control procedure, assuming a *Yes* answer to each question.

Present your answer in tabular form with separate columns for parts a, b, and c.

11-26 **(Potential misstatements and tests of controls)** Your firm has been engaged to audit the financial statements of the Haven Company. In obtaining an understanding of internal control pertaining to credit sales, the following questionnaire is used:

1. Does the company evaluate the customer's credit history, and is amount of available credit checked before a sale is authorized?

2. Is there adequate segregation of duties between authorizing sales, shipping goods, and recording sales?

3. Does management compare all shipments with recorded sales to ensure that all sales are recorded?

4. Is every recorded sale checked against shipping records for appropriateness of revenue recognition?

5. Are there adequate controls over the accuracy of the sales invoice?

6. Are there adequate controls to ensure that the sales invoices are recorded in the correct time period?

7. Are there adequate controls to ensure that the proper customer is billed for shipments?

8. Does management review all sales that are recorded on a weekly basis?

9. Do adequate controls exist to review company accounting policies regarding revenue recognition?

10. Do adequate controls exist to review the consistency of the estimation of the provision for doubtful accounts?

Required

a. Identify a potential misstatement that could occur, assuming a *No* answer to each question.

b. For each question, would you expect the control procedure to be a computer control or a manual control?

c. Identify a possible test of controls for the control procedure, assuming a *Yes* answer to each question.

Present your answer in tabular form with separate columns for parts a, b, and c.

11-27 **(Necessary application controls/tests of controls)** In auditing the financial statements of the Marshall Company, you discover the following misstatements in the application controls of the company's EDP system:

1. Valid data were incorrectly converted to machine-sensible form.

2. Output data did not agree with original source documents.

3. Processing errors were made on valid input data.

4. The wrong file was processed and updated.

5. Output was distributed to unauthorized users.

6. Erroneous input data from a user department were corrected and processed by the EDP department.

7. Input data were processed twice during handling.

8. Unauthorized input data were processed.

9. Erroneous input data from a user department were returned for correction but were not resubmitted for processing.

Required

a. Identify the application control function (input, processing, or output) that is relevant to each error or irregularity.

    b. Identify a control that could have prevented each misstatement.

    c. Identify a possible test of controls for each necessary control identified in part b. (Present your answers in tabular form using separate columns for each part.)

11-28 **(Necessary application controls/tests of controls)** In auditing the financial statements of the The Lively Trout Company, you discover the following internal controls associated with the company's EDP system:

1. Computer generates prenumbered control over requisitions and purchase orders and checks numerical sequence.

2. Computer compares account distribution on the voucher with account distribution on purchase requisition or purchase order.

3. Computer checks batch totals and run-to-run totals to ensure that all transactions are processed.

4. Computer matches of voucher information regarding vendor, type of good, quantity of goods, and dollar amount against authorized purchase order and receiving report.

5. Computer checks for a valid purchase order in order to initiate receiving report.

6. Computer verification of employee authorization code to enter requisition or purchase order.

7. Computer performs limit test on requisitions and purchase orders. Necessary approvals tied to limit test.

8. Computer checks the mathematical accuracy of the voucher and supporting documents.

9. Computer compares vendor on purchase order to master vendor file.

10. Computer checks for goods ordered and not received within a reasonable period of time.

11. Computer checks for goods received but not recorded as a liability within a reasonable period of time. In the case of services, the computer checks for services ordered but not recorded as a liability within a reasonable period of time.

12. Computer compares accounting period in which the voucher is recorded with the accounting period received.

13. Computer checks the mathematical accuracy of the voucher and supporting documents.

14. Computer compares sum of subsidiary ledger accounts with general ledger control account.

Required

Identify the assertion that is controlled by each of the control procedures identified above.

11-29 **(Auditing around versus through the computer)** CPAs may audit "around" or "through" computers in examining financial statements of clients who use computers to process accounting data.

Required

    a. Describe the auditing approach referred to as auditing around the computer.

    b. Under what conditions does the CPA decide to audit through the computer instead of around the computer?

c. In auditing through the computer, the CPA may use test data.
   1. What are test data?
   2. Why does the CPA use test data?

d. How can the CPA become satisfied that the computer program tapes presented by the client are actually being used to process its accounting data?

AICPA

11-30 **(Controls in an on-line real-time system)** You have been engaged by Central Savings and Loan Association to audit its financial statements for the year ended December 31, 20X1. The CPA who audited the financial statements at December 31, 20X0, rendered an unqualified opinion.

In January 20X1, the Association installed an on-line real-time computer system. Each teller in the association's main office and seven branch offices has an on-line input-output terminal. The customer's mortgage payments and savings account deposits and withdrawals are recorded in the accounts by the computer from data input by the teller at the time of the transaction. The teller keys the proper account by account number and enters the information in the terminal keyboard to record the transaction. The accounting department at the main office also has direct access to the computer via on-line terminals. The computer is housed at the main office.

In addition to servicing its own mortgage loans, the association acts as a mortgage servicing agency for three life insurance companies. In this latter activity, the association maintains mortgage records and serves as the collection and escrow agent for the mortgagees (the insurance companies), who pay a fee to the association for these services.

Required

You would expect the association to have certain internal controls in effect because an on-line real-time computer system is employed. List the internal controls that should be in effect solely because this EDP system is employed, classifying them as

a. Those controls pertaining to input of information.

b. All other types of computer controls.

AICPA (adapted)

11-31 **(Assessing control risk for account balance assertions)** After completion of interim work, Jan Jackson, manager of the Melville Company audit, makes the following control risk assessments for transaction classes:

	EXISTENCE OR OCCURRENCE	COMPLETENESS	VALUATION OR ALLOCATION
Revenue cycle			
Credit sales	Low	Low	Low
Collections from customers	Low	Moderate	Low
Sales returns and allowances	Low	Moderate	Moderate
Expenditure cycle			
Purchases	Low	High	Low
Cash disbursements	Low	Low	Low
Purchase returns	Low	Moderate	Low

All sales and purchase transactions of the Melville Company are made on account.

Jan takes a conservative approach to risk assessments. Before finalizing the design of substantive tests, she realizes that she must determine control risk assessment for the existence and occurrence, completeness, and valuation or allocation account balance assertions for the following accounts:

Cash	Accounts Payable
Accounts Receivable	Sales

She assesses control risk at the maximum for the rights and obligations and presentation and disclosure account balance assertions for each account where applicable.

Required

Identify the transaction class or classes that affect each account balance. Then determine the appropriate control risk assessment for the indicated account balance assertions. Use the following format for your solution:

	TRANSACTION CLASS THAT		ACCOUNT BALANCE CONTROL RISK ASSESSMENT		
ACCOUNT	INCREASES ACCOUNT	DECREASES ACCOUNT	EXISTENCE AND OCCURRENCE	COMPLETENESS	VALUATION OR ALLOCATION

---

cases

11-32 **(Evaluation of EDP controls)** You have been assigned to the annual audit of Explosives, Inc. You contact the senior, Bob Good, as instructed and arrange a date to discuss the client and the current year's audit.

At your meeting with Good, the company and the current year's audit were discussed. During the discussion, Good emphasized that he wanted to take a good look at the data processing (DP) department. He had attended the firm's one-week course on computer auditing and felt strongly about the need for such review.

On the eighth day of the job, Bob received word that his immediate attention was needed on another job. He had performed most of the work on the DP department and wants you to complete it. Good left the following working papers to help you:

General Background

The DP department has evolved from a strictly batch entry/batch processing operation and now currently uses a mix of tape and on-line disk processing methods. The department is under the supervision of Gus Sampson, who has worked in it since its inception. He reports to the controller.

The department is located on the third floor of the east office wing. It shares office space with the research department and the general accounting department. The machines, however, are physically separated from the other departments by glass doors. The chemical mixing department is located just below on the second floor. The first floor houses the plant personnel department, various conference rooms, and other administrative offices.

The DP department services corporate accounting, the local plant, and three other plant locations elsewhere in the country. The department recently upgraded its computer. Within the DP department, there are three groups, each with specific duties:

1. Data entry

2. Systems analysis

3. Programming and operations

Each group has its own supervisor who reports to the DP manager.

Computer Room Operations

All the machine operators know the jobs they run quite well and have the knowledge to make changes in the operating procedures and programs when they encounter difficulties. This has greatly increased efficiency as less time is lost due to machine halts caused by program interruptions. Gus stated that because of the operators' familiarity with the various jobs, he does not have to devote much time to supervising them.

When asked about operating manuals for the operators, Gus replied that it would be a waste of time to prepare them because the operators are so familiar with the programs and jobs. If a problem develops, an operator can simply look at a source program listing and make the necessary correction. Gus said he seldom reviewed any console sheets because of the confidence he had in his operators. He complained, however, about the accounting people always giving him bad data and then complaining about the output. "GIGO is the rule," he said.

During the tour of the computer room with Gus, you noticed that various disks, some with labels and some without, were in file racks, on tables, on top of equipment, and in the corner of the floor. In another corner, you noticed open boxes of various forms and payroll checks. You had expected to see only two or three operators in the computer room, but there were five or six people in it. When you asked Gus about these conditions, he said he had read all the books and publications on controlling the computer room and felt that most of the alleged dangers were exaggerated. He trusted his employees and believed his shop was one of the best in the area. As for the additional people, he felt that too many people are mystified by the computer. Consequently, he maintains an open door policy so people can come in and see "what the monster is all about."

Programming Group

Information about this group was obtained from Betty James, the head programmer, who reports to Gus Sampson. The members of this group mainly write new programs and maintain current programs, about 75 percent of which were written years ago using an earlier generation programming language. These programs are currently being rewritten in a more modern and efficient language for use on the upgraded computer.

Documentation for the old programs and some of the new ones consists of source listings. The old programs were written by Gus, Betty, and a fellow who has left the company. Because Gus and Betty are still around, there has not been any need to prepare additional documentation. Betty said, however, that Gus has been thinking about developing documentation standards for all programs.

Betty mentioned numerous problems have arisen lately due to an operator or programmer making an undocumented "patch" in a program so the job can be run. Sometimes, the change causes other errors to occur. Gus has attempted to stop the operators from making changes, but with the programs being accessible to everyone, it has been impossible to enforce.

Required

a. Draw an organization chart of the EDP department.

b. For each of the eight EDP controls mentioned in the chapter, discuss (1) the weaknesses in the internal controls of Explosives, Inc., and (2) your recommendations for improvement.

11-33   **(Mt. Hood Furniture assessing control risk)** Complete the following requirements based on (1) the information presented at the end of Chapter 7 related to Mt. Hood Furniture and (2) the following additional information.

Inquiries and observations associated with understanding internal controls revealed the following. Robert Saws and his son Conrad have always placed a premium on the values of integrity and ethics. For years, business was conducted on a handshake, and commitments made by the company were always honored. Integrity and ethics are also valued in employees, and this quality has been evidenced in any employee who has been with the company for more than a year or two. In recent years, as the company has directed resources to a new product line, and company revenues have grown, the company has actively sought out competent employees to fill out the management team by bringing in a new chief operating officer and a new chief financial officer (CFO).

Many accounting and information systems issues have been delegated to the CFO, who has responsibility for the company's financing needs, accounting, and information systems. Julia Anderson almost immediately initiated a project to upgrade the company's computerized accounting system. A new director of IT, Jay Harris, reports directly to Julia and oversees data control and systems security. Key positions within IT include a director of computer operations and a programming director. Julia was hired because of her familiarity with benefits and risks of enterprise resource planning systems, and she reviews progress on the new system installation with the IT manager monthly. The IT manager is also responsible for managing the current system until the new system has been tested and is ready to use. Furthermore, Julia recently hired Harry Alston to act as an internal auditor. Harry reports directly to the CFO. Currently, the internal auditor is reconciling all bank accounts. The board of directors approved the hiring of an internal auditor, and, in the absence of an audit committee, Julia plans to discuss internal audit findings with the board of directors on an annual basis.

Julia is currently under pressure to produce financial statements within ten days after the end of the month. Both Robert and Conrad Saws believe that this is essential to good business management. Once the financials are produced they are closely reviewed with managers of day-to-day operations to ensure that managers are held accountable for the resources with which they are entrusted.

Other procedures performed to obtain an understanding of internal control revealed the following information.

1. Mt. Hood has identified a small group of office furniture dealers whose operations have deteriorated to the point that their ability to repay the company is doubtful. The company has decided to make additional shipments to these dealers on a C.O.D. basis. It is anticipated that a large provision for doubtful accounts may be necessary to reduce these accounts to estimated realizable value.

2. The tool inventory consists of a conglomeration of miscellaneous items, most of which are small quantities with very minor unit prices. This inventory totals $42,395.89, which is an insignificant portion of the total inventories.

3. The purchased parts stockroom is segregated from the production areas by a wire fence. While visiting the plant, you noted that the gate was left open all day and access to the stockroom (which contains many valuable and easily concealed items) was available to any employee. The stockroom's perpetual inventory records were formerly checked by an employee who made periodic test counts. This employee has retired and not been replaced. As a result, such counting has ceased. You expanded your tests in view of these situations and are satisfied that the perpetual records reasonably reflect the quantities on hand.

4. The board of directors just adopted a policy that will allow the company to invest excess funds in short-term securities. The CFO will have sole authority for purchase and sale of

the investments. Securities purchased will be credited to a company account at a local brokerage house. The securities are held in the company's name. All correspondence related to the investments is sent directly to the CFO. She, in turn, forwards brokerage advices to her assistant for recording in the accounts.

5. A complete physical inventory of the company's office furniture has recently been taken.

Required

a. Identify the control environment factors that impact the company's internal control.

b. List the strengths and weaknesses in Mt. Hood's internal control.

c. Indicate your suggestions for improving the weaknesses identified in (b) above.

d. For the accounts receivable and inventory accounts identify one assertion for which you would assess control risk at the maximum or slightly below the maximum. Explain your logic.

professional simulation

You have been assigned to the audit of Alpha Corporation, a manufacturer of auto parts. Alpha Corporation is a private company that is wholly owned by George Alpha, that has only one manufacturing location. The auto parts that Alpha manufactures are shipped too approximately 25 manufacturing plants in the United States. During the current year Alpha Corporation upgraded its accounting system. The system upgrade involved changing software and implementing a totally new accounting package related to purchases, inventory and inventory control, and expenditures. Accounting personnel in the company have been upgraded to support the new system.

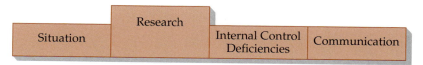

You have concluded that it may be cost effective to perform tests of controls over purchases and expenditures. The client's new system has significant programmed application controls and you intend to test programmed controls to match each vendor's invoice with information from underlying purchase orders and receiving reports. Based on a system walkthrough you believe transactions that are reported on exception reports are cleared in one or two days. The partner on the engagement, Michelle Driscoll, wants to make sure that the audit team has identified all the controls that are relevant to the assertions. In particular, she would like you to research what professional standards say about identifying and testing computer general controls. Cut and paste the standard sections that apply to this issue.

George Alpha has made an inquiry about the system of internal control at his company. You have been engaged only to audit the financial statements. In some areas your firm has developed an audit strategy where you plan to test internal controls and modify the nature, timing, and extent of audit procedures. However, for a substantial portion of the audit your firm plans to follow a primarily substantive approach. You know that professional standards require that you communicate significant deficiencies in internal controls to management and the board of directors (or its audit committee). What is the auditor's responsibility for identifying significant deficiencies in internal control as part of a financial statement audit? Compare and contrast the likelihood that the auditor will identify significant deficiencies in audit areas where the auditor follows a lower assessed level of control risk approach vs. audit areas where you follow a primarily substantive approach.

Situation	Research	Internal Control Deficiencies	Communication

When obtaining an understanding of internal control in the expenditure cycle you find that there are reasonable controls to ensure that items recorded as accounts payable are valid, but you do not find controls to ensure that either goods ordered are received, or that goods received are recorded as accounts payable in the proper period. Prepare a letter to George Alpha, president of Alpha Corporation, explaining this one weakness and recommending improvements in the system of internal control. Use the appropriate form and content for the report that is recommended in professional standards.

AUDIT PROCEDURES IN RESPONSE TO ASSESSED RISKS: SUBSTANTIVE TESTS

THE IMPORTANCE OF RISK ASSESSMENT PROCEDURES AND AUDIT PROGRAMS

On October 15, 2001, Gas and Oil Technologies, Inc., filed a registration statement on Form S-1, seeking to raise up to $60 million from the sale of its common stock in an initial public offering. The most significant asset reportings in the Gas and Oil Technologies financial statements were patents in the amount of $21.75 million. The assets, however, were totally fictitious, and the company had neither evidence of their costs at the date of acquisition nor evidence of the patents' fair value to support an impairment test.

The financial statements were audited by Kent D. Saliger, a licensed CPA in the state of Nevada. In an SEC investigation into the audit of the financial statements included in the S-1, the SEC found the following:

- Saliger failed to obtain an understanding of internal controls sufficient to determine the nature, timing, and extent of substantive tests needed for the audit.
- Saliger failed to conduct audit risk assessments.
- Saliger failed to prepare audit programs.
- Saliger failed to obtain sufficient competent evidential matter upon which to base an opinion, specifically as it related to the valuation and recording of patents on the financial statements.

As a result, Saliger issued unqualified audit reports certifying that Gas & Oil's financial statements fairly presented its financial condition in conformity with GAAP, when in fact they did not.

Because of his reckless and improper professional conduct, Kent D. Saliger was denied the privilege of appearing or practicing before the SEC as an accountant.

Chapter 12 focuses on many of the issues that are addressed in this case. The chapter examines an auditor's responsibilities for:

- Assessing the risk of material misstatement in the financial statements.
- Linking risk assessments to audit decisions about the nature, timing, and extent of audit procedures.
- Responsibilities for documenting those procedures in the form of an audit program.

Source: Accounting and Auditing Enforcement Release No. 1615.

[PREVIEW OF CHAPTER 12]

Chapter 12 focuses on the second and third phase of the audit. In Phase II the auditor assesses the risk of material misstatement. In Phase III the auditor plans further audit procedures. The following diagram provides an overview of the chapter organization and content.

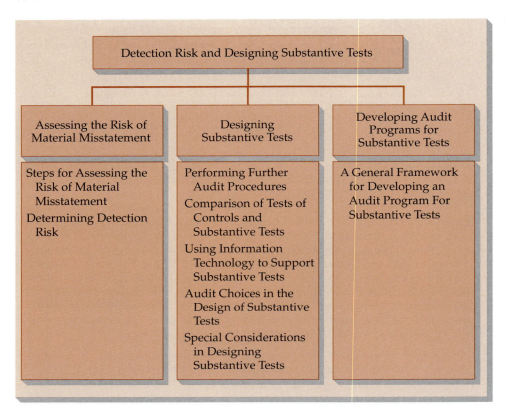

Chapter 12 focuses on the process of designing substantive tests. This chapter addresses the following aspects of the auditor's knowledge and the auditor's decision process.

focus on auditor knowledge

After studying this chapter you should understand the following aspects of an auditor's knowledge base:

K1. Know the difference between tests of controls and substantive tests.

K2. Understand the general framework for developing audit programs for substantive tests.

focus on audit decisions

After studying this chapter you should understand the factors that influence the following audit decisions.

D1. What key steps should be performed in the process of assessing the risk of material misstatement in the financial statements?

D2. How do various risk factors relate to the type of potential misstatement?

D3. What is the process for evaluating the planned level of substantive tests as specified in the preliminary audit strategy?

D4. How can the auditor use information technology to support various substantive tests?

D5. How are the nature, timing, extent, and staffing of substantive tests varied to achieve an acceptable level of detection risk?

D6. What special considerations should be addressed in designing substantive tests for selected types of accounts?

ASSESSING THE RISK OF MATERIAL MISSTATEMENT

Audit Decision 1

■ **What key steps should be performed in the process of assessing the risk of material misstatement in the financial statements?**

STEPS FOR ASSESSING THE RISK OF MATERIAL MISSTATEMENT

Phase II of the audit involves using the knowledge obtained when performing risk assessment procedures to assess the risk of material misstatement. Reaching a conclusion about the risk of material misstatement involves the three critical steps listed in Figure 12-1. The following discussion explores each of these steps.

The Type of Potential Misstatement

Audit Decision 2

■ **How do various risk factors relate to the type of potential misstatement?**

A critical aspect of the audit process involves recognizing risk factors and then linking those risks factors to assertions that are likely to be misstated. Risk factors can affect the potential for misstatements in the financial statements in two ways. Some risks have a pervasive effect on the financial statements and influence multiple account balances and assertions (e.g., financial statement level risks). Other risks factors are assertion specific (e.g., assertion level risks). Figure 12-2 provides a series of ten examples of how the auditor would use the knowledge obtained while performing risk assessment procedures to evaluate potential misstatements in the financial statements.

Examples 1, 5, 8, and 10 represent risk factors that may have a pervasive impact on many or all assertions in the financial statements. This should heighten the auditor's concern about the risk of material misstatement throughout the financial statements. Example 10, weak computer general controls, might impact multiple

Figure 12-1 ■ Steps for Assessing the Risk of Material Misstatement

1. Evaluate the Type of Potential Misstatements that May Occur
2. Evaluate the Magnitude of Potential Misstatements
3. Evaluate the Likelihood of Potential Misstatements

Figure 12-2 ■ Examples of Risk Assessment Procedures and the Type of Potential Misstatement that May Occur

Risk Assessment Procedure	Example Risk Factor	Type of Potential Misstatement
1. Understand the Entity and Its Environment	The company is in an industry that is experiencing economic difficulty and intense price competition.	Weak industry conditions tend to create a sensitivity in capital markets to bad news. This may heighten pressure on management to meet short-term performance indicators (e.g., earnings or revenue growth). This would have a pervasive impact on many financial statement assertions.
2. Understand the Entity and Its Environment	The company has recently changed the nature of its product and is bundling software with other services to customize and implement software and related controls.	The change in business product combined with the bundling of products may create new problems associated with revenue recognition (existence and occurrence). It is likely that cash has been received in advance of revenue recognition and the company should record unearned revenues (completeness).
3. Analytical Procedures	Analytical procedures for a manufacturer show a significant increase in both profit margins and inventory turn days.	It is possible that inventory is overstated. The auditor should be alert to problems with the existence and occurrence or valuation and allocation of inventory.
4. Analytical Procedures	Analytical procedures for a retailer show significant decreases in both profit margins and inventory turn days.	It is possible that the retailer is experiencing problems with inventory shrinkage. This heightens the risk of fraud due to misappropriation of assets (e.g., assets taken from inventory without recording sales).
5. Consider the Risk of Fraud	Senior management has sent a very strong message, and offered increased incentives, to middle managers to meet financial targets.	Management may have the incentive to engage in fraudulent financial reporting (FFR). Management has the opportunity to utilize its discretion in a variety of ways and may rationalize FFR to obtain incentives offered to meet targets. Furthermore, the control environment may be weak, which may have a pervasive impact on many assertions.
6. Consider the Risk of Fraud	An employee in a small to medium-sized business responsible for cash disbursements did not receive an expected promotion and pay increase.	There is an increased risk of employee fraud. An employee may have both the incentive for fraud (not receiving expected promotion and pay increase) and the opportunity to commit fraud with authority to disburse cash. The auditor should be alert for problems with the existence and occurrence of cash disbursements.
7. Consider Other Inherent Risk Factors	A construction industry client uses the percentage of completion method to recognize revenues and expenses on current projects.	Significant revenues, expenses, assets, and liabilities arise from the use of the percentage of completion method, which is dependent on a significant accounting estimate. The auditor should be alert for problems with the valuation and allocation assertion.
8. Consider Other Inherent Risk Factors	A company is experiencing working capital and going-concern problems.	Potential going-concern problems could have a pervasive impact on financial statements.
9. Understand the Entity's System of Internal Control	The client has a strong control environment and good controls over the existence of inventory.	The risk of misstatement in the existence assertion is minimized by strong internal controls.
10. Understand the Entity's System of Internal Control	The client has weak computer general controls, including poor controls over the approval of system changes.	The risk of unauthorized changes to computer programs, or inadequate testing of new programs, increases the risk that programmed application controls may not function as designed.

account balances and transaction classes, and the auditor should be alert to problems in either routine or nonroutine transactions. Example 5, strong incentives offered by management to meet financial targets, might affect assertions that are associated with nonroutine transactions, end-of-quarter transactions, the choice of new accounting principles, or accounting estimates. In addition, the auditor should also be alert to problems with routine transactions, such as revenue recognition.

Examples 2,3,4, 6, and 7 provide examples of risk factors that are assertion specific. Example number 2 represents a situation where a software company changes its practices from just selling software licenses to bundling software licenses with other services to customize and implement new computer programs. The likely types of misstatements are (1) problems with the existence and occurrence assertion and premature revenue recognition, and (2) problems with the completeness assertion and the failure to recognize unearned revenues when cash is received in advance of recognizing revenues. An important audit skill is the auditor's ability to recognize risk factors and then link risk factors to specific assertions that might be misstated.

Example 9 presents a situation where the client has strong internal controls, and as a result the likelihood of material misstatement is reduced rather than increased. When these situations are present, the auditor will usually perform tests of controls to obtain sufficient, competent evidence that controls operate effectively, which will allow the auditor to accept a higher level of detection risk. Students should study each of the ten examples and their relationship with the type of misstatements that may occur.

The Magnitude of Potential Misstatements

Some potential misstatements are more significant than others. Following are some examples of how the auditor might consider the magnitude of potential misstatement in the financial statements.

- The existence of inventory is more significant for a manufacturer than for a hotel or many other service companies.
- Inventory is more susceptible to theft for a jeweler than for a lumber company.
- The depreciation of fixed assets is more significant for a paper manufacturer than for an advertising agency.
- The completeness of unearned revenues is more significant for a software company than for a point of sale retailer.

Audit time and resources are limited. Auditors need to allocate more audit attention to the assertions that can have a potential material effect, individually or in aggregate, on the financial statements.

Likelihood of Material Misstatement

Once the auditor has identified risks of possible material misstatements, the auditor must also consider how likely they are. Once the auditor has identified various business risks, inherent risks, and fraud risks that might affect the financial statements, he or she should consider the adequacy of the system of internal controls. For example, a retail jewelry store often shows items in store windows and displays that are highly valuable. Because of the increased risk of theft, these items are often displayed in locked showcases during store hours, and they are usually put in a safe when the store is closed. Other retailers, with less valuable items in store windows and displays, will leave those items in the store window during hours when the store is closed due to the small risk of theft. The greater the effectiveness of controls that a company puts in place, the less the likelihood of material misstatement.

Internal controls are costly, however. Many private companies have few, if any, controls over management's discretion in financial reporting or over financial statement disclosures. Some private companies feel that they are so resource constrained that they hire accounting staff with inadequate skills, and there is a weak control environment. As a result, these entities are often audited with a heavy emphasis on substantive tests because the likelihood of material misstatement is so high. Public companies may have controls related to most, or all, financial statement assertions, and the auditor will test these controls as part of issuing an opinion on internal controls over financial reporting. As a general rule, the higher the likelihood of material misstatement (after considering inherent risk and control risk), the more the auditor should respond with substantive tests to obtain reasonable assurance that the auditor is able to detect and correct any material misstatements.

DETERMINING DETECTION RISK

Audit Decision 3

■ What is the process for evaluating the planned level of substantive tests as specified in the preliminary audit strategy?

The auditor uses the audit risk model to link the evidence obtained from risk assessment procedures about inherent risk and control risk, including the risk of fraud, to decisions about detection risk. Recall that detection risk is the risk that the auditor will not detect a material misstatement that exists in an assertion. Chapter 9 explains that a planned acceptable level of detection risk is specified for each significant financial statement assertion. Furthermore, recall that regardless of whether the auditor chooses to use quantitative or nonquantitative expressions of the risk levels, planned detection risk is determined based on the relationships expressed in the following model:

$$DR = AP \times TD = \frac{AR}{IR \times CR}$$

The model shows that for a given level of audit risk (AR) specified by the auditor, detection risk (DR) is inversely related to the assessed levels of inherent risk (IR) and control risk (CR) that are determined by risk assessment procedures. Planned detection risk is the basis for the planned level of substantive tests. Furthermore, detection risk can be broken down into analytical procedures risk and tests of details risk as discussed in Chapter 9. Ultimately, the auditor should plan and perform a combination of analytical procedures and tests of details to restrict detection risk to an appropriate level. Figure 12-3 summarizes the relationships among preliminary audit strategies, planned detection risk, and planned levels of substantive tests that are explained in Chapter 9. Before making decisions about substantive tests, the auditor must determine whether the planned level of substantive tests and associated planned detection risk needs to be revised.

Students should recall that the audit is a dynamic process. The auditor should compare the actual or final level of assurance obtained from risk assessment pro-

Figure 12-3 ■ Preliminary Audit Strategy, Planned Detection Risk, and Planned Emphasis on Audit Tests

Preliminary Audit Strategy	Planned Detection Risk	Planned Assurance Obtained From
Lower inherent risk and analytical procedures	Moderate or high	Evidence regarding moderate or low inherent risk and analytical procedures using reliable data
A lower assessed level of control risk	Moderate or high	More extensive tests of controls and less extensive tests of details of transactions and balances performed at a date one or two months prior to year-end
A primarily substantive approach	Low or very low	More extensive tests of details of transactions and balances performed at year-end

cedures with the planned assessed levels of inherent risk and control risk. If the final assessed level of risk is the same as the planned assessed level of risk, the auditor may proceed to design specific substantive tests based on the preliminary audit strategy. Otherwise, the level of substantive tests must be revised before designing specific substantive tests to accommodate a revised acceptable level of detection risk. For example, assume the preliminary audit strategy was based on the lower assessed level of control risk approach and included a planned assessed level of control risk at a low level, and the auditor planned less extensive substantive tests at an interim date. If the final assessed level of control risk was moderate or high, the auditor would need to move substantive tests from interim to year-end and increase the extent of tests of details in order to accommodate a lower acceptable level of detection risk.

[LEARNING CHECK

12-1 Explain the three steps associated with assessing the risk of material misstatement.

12-2 How would the auditor change the audit strategy if a risk is a financial statement level risk versus an assertion level risk?

12-3 Develop an example of a risk of material misstatement that might be found during each of the following risk assessment procedures.
  a. Understanding the entity and its environment
  b. Performing analytical procedures
  c. Understanding the risk of fraud
  d. Understanding inherent risks
  e. Understanding the entity's system of internal control

12-4 For each of the preliminary audit strategies state (1) the appropriate level of planned detection risk, (2) the planned audit procedures that provide the auditor with significant assurance, and (3) whether a higher or lower level of assurance is needed from substantive tests.

12-5 When and how does an auditor determine a revised or final acceptable level of detection risk for an assertion?

[DESIGNING SUBSTANTIVE TESTS]

PERFORMING FURTHER AUDIT PROCEDURES

Phase III of the audit involves performing further audit procedures. This might include performing further risk assessment procedures, tests of controls, and substantive tests. The auditor is likely to perform further risk assessment procedures when evidence obtained during the audit does not confirm earlier risk assessments. Tests of controls are normally performed when the client has placed effective controls in operation (see Chapter 11). This chapter focuses on the design of substantive tests. The following sections discuss:

1. The difference between tests of controls and substantive tests.
2. How information technology and generalized audit software might be used to support substantive tests.
3. Audit choices in the design of substantive tests.
4. Special considerations in the design of substantive tests.

COMPARISON OF TESTS OF CONTROLS AND SUBSTANTIVE TESTS

Auditor Knowledge 1
■ Know the difference between tests of controls and substantive tests.

Two important aspects of performing further audit procedures in the collection of audit evidence include making decisions about the mix of tests of controls and substantive tests. Audit choices regarding test of controls were discussed in depth in Chapter 11. This chapter focuses on audit choices regarding substantive tests. Figure 12-4 provides a comparison of the differences between tests of controls and substantive tests. Following this section, the remainder of the chapter examines audit choices regarding substantive tests.

USING INFORMATION TECHNOLOGY TO SUPPORT SUBSTANTIVE TESTS

Audit Decision 4
■ How can the auditor use information technology to support various substantive tests?

When the client uses information technology for significant accounting applications, the auditor has an opportunity to use audit software packages to make the audit more effective and more efficient. In addition to using computer-assisted audit techniques for tests of controls (see Chapter 11), audit software has been developed for a wide variety of substantive testing applications. The following section explains generalized audit software and describes various ways in which this software can be used in performing substantive tests.

Generalized Audit Software

Generalized audit software is the auditor's software that can be used for analyzing and testing clients' computer files. Thus, it is transportable from one client to another. These packages are available at moderate cost from software vendors (e.g., Idea and ACL), the AICPA, and CPA firms that use their own internally developed packages. Generalized audit software enables the auditor to deal effectively with large quantities of data. It also permits the auditor to place less reliance on the client's IT personnel. The auditor may be able to sort large files such as a purchases file and select transactions of interest for further examination. Only the

Figure 12-4 ■ A Comparison of Tests of Controls and Substantive Tests

	Tests of Controls	Substantive Tests
Purpose	To determine effectiveness of design and operation of internal controls	To determine fairness of significant financial statement assertions
Types	Tests of the control environment	Initial procedures
	Tests of the client's risk assessment system	Analytical procedures
	Tests of the information and communication system	Tests of details of transactions
	Tests of control activities	Tests of details of balances
	Tests of the monitoring system	Tests of details of accounting estimates
	Tests of antifraud programs and controls	Substantive tests required by GAAS
		Tests of details of disclosures
Nature of test measurement	Frequency of deviations from designed controls	Monetary errors in transactions and balances
Applicable audit procedures	Inquiring, observing, inspecting, reperforming, and computer-assisted audit techniques	Same as tests of controls, plus analytical procedures, counting, confirming, tracing, and vouching
Timing	Primarily interim work[a]	At balance sheet date or one or two months prior to year-end[b]
Audit risk component	Control risk	Detection risk
Primary fieldwork standard	Second	Third
Required by GAAS	When audit risk cannot be reduced to a sufficiently low level by substantive tests alone	Yes

[a] Concurrent tests of controls are performed in audit planning with risk assessment procedures to understand the system of internal control. Additional tests of controls are performed during interim fieldwork.
[b] Tests of details of transactions may also be performed with tests of controls as *dual-purpose tests* during fieldwork.

availability of client data files and the auditor's ingenuity limit the use of generalized audit software in auditing. The software may be designed to perform nearly all of the auditing procedures that an auditor might perform manually. Some examples of substantive testing applications are explained in the following sections. Chapters 13 and 14 include case assignments where generalized audit software can be used to perform audit tests on sample audit populations.

Reconcile Detail Audit Data with the General Ledger

An important first step involves obtaining detailed records from a client and testing the data to make sure that the supporting data matches the general ledger. Auditors often obtain files such as an accounts receivable file or an inventory file for the client in electronic form. The first step that should be performed is to ensure that the underlying detail matches the accounting records. Auditors often obtain accounts receivable subsidiary files from a client that the auditor uses to prepare confirmations. If the file has a date other than month-end, which does not match the client's month end general ledger, it is likely that the auditor will send confirmations in erroneous amounts. This may result in customers confirming that balances include errors, when they do not. Hence, an important first step involves using generalized audit software to total the detailed information and to compare control totals to the general ledger (at an interim date) or to financial statement amounts (at year-end).

Selecting and Printing Audit Samples

The computer can be programmed to select audit samples according to criteria specified by the auditor. These samples can be used for a variety of purposes. Individual customer accounts receivable may be selected for confirmation, or the auditor may be interested in obtaining a listing of all items over a certain dollar amount. In the case of confirmation requests, the computer may also be used to print the confirmation letter as well as the envelope. A more comprehensive discussion of the use of confirmation in performing substantive tests of accounts receivable is presented in Chapter 14. The auditor might also use generalized audit software to sample items that are likely to contain errors. For example, when auditing the cost of manufactured inventory the auditor might sample costs that have changed by more than 10 percent from the previous audit. Prices that have changed significantly may have a higher risk of error than prices that are stable.

Testing Calculations and Making Computations

Another common use of the computer is to test the accuracy of computations in machine-readable data files. Tests of extensions, footing, or other computations may be performed. Inventory quantities may be extended by a unit cost and the amount of the inventory recalculated. An auditor might be able to use the client's data to recalculate the accounts receivable aging. Because of the speed of computer processing, these types of recomputations can easily be performed on an entire audit population.

Testing the Entire Population

Generalized audit software allows auditors to screen an entire population rather than rely on a sampling procedure. An auditor might test the allowance for doubtful accounts by using generalized audit software to develop a payment history for each customer. Generalized audit software allows an auditor to quickly develop a record for time from shipment to receipt of payment for each sales transaction. In a similar fashion, an auditor can scan a perpetual inventory file to search for slow-moving inventory. This type of information can be quite helpful when testing accounting estimates.

Summarizing Data and Performing Analyses

The auditor frequently desires to have the client data reorganized in a manner that will suit a special purpose. For instance, the auditor may want to determine slow-moving inventory items, debit balances in accounts payable, or past due accounts receivable. Similarly, in performing analytical procedures, the auditor may utilize the computer to compute desired ratios, extract nonfinancial data from the client's database for comparison with financial data, or perform statistical regression analysis and an analytical procedure.

AUDIT CHOICES IN THE DESIGN OF SUBSTANTIVE TESTS

Audit Decision 5

■ How are the nature, timing, extent, and staffing of substantive tests varied to achieve an acceptable level of detection risk?

Substantive tests are an important part of the process of obtaining sufficient competent evidential matter as required by the third standard of fieldwork. Substantive tests provide evidence about the fairness of each significant financial statement assertion, or they may reveal monetary errors or misstatements in the recording or reporting of transactions and balances. The auditor must make decisions about the nature, timing, extent, and staffing of substantive tests in order to have a reasonable basis for an opinion on the client's financial statements. Each of these choices is discussed here, including how the assessment of inherent and control risks affects these choices.

Nature of Substantive Tests

The **nature of substantive tests** refers to the type and effectiveness of the auditing procedures to be performed. When the acceptable level of detection risk is low, the auditor must use more effective procedures. When the acceptable level of detection risk is high, less effective and less costly procedures can be used. Figure 12-5 identifies six types of substantive tests that are discussed in the following sections.

1. Initial Procedures

Several types of **initial procedures** are performed before proceeding to other substantive tests. First, the auditor must have an understanding of the economic substance of the transactions that are subject to audit. For example, when auditing receivables and revenues, it is important to understand the nature of the products

Figure 12-5 ■ Nature of Substantive Tests

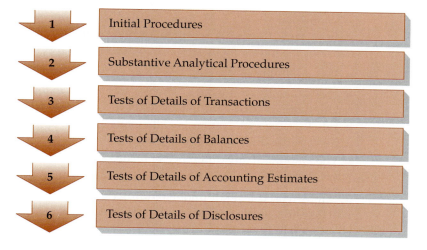

1. Initial Procedures
2. Substantive Analytical Procedures
3. Tests of Details of Transactions
4. Tests of Details of Balances
5. Tests of Details of Accounting Estimates
6. Tests of Details of Disclosures

that are being sold. It may be a simple matter of selling goods. At the same time, the auditor needs to be alert for signs of transactions that are effectively consignment sales. However, in software organizations the sale may be a combination of selling a license agreement and consulting services associated with tailoring the product to the customer's needs. In this case it is likely that all revenue cannot be recognized at once. Similarly, the client might issue redeemable preferred stock that is legally an equity transaction, but in economic substance it is a debt transaction and should be reported as debt on the balance sheet.

Another important initial procedure involves tracing beginning balances in the general ledger to the audited balances in the prior year's financial statements. This is important to testing the completeness and accuracy of the data underlying the accounting records. Furthermore, an auditor will usually obtain detailed, electronic information about an account balance such as an accounts receivable subsidiary ledger, a perpetual inventory, or an accounts payable subsidiary ledger. It is essential that these detail balances be summed and agreed to the general ledger before proceeding with other audit work. Otherwise, the auditor may be auditing erroneous information.

Two initial procedures that require special consideration in a first-time audit are (1) determining the propriety of the account balances at the beginning of the period being audited, and (2) ascertaining the accounting principles used in the preceding period as a basis for determining the consistency of application of such principles in the current period. These procedures are normally accomplished by reference to the working papers of a predecessor auditor. In a continuing engagement, these procedures can be accomplished by reference to the prior year's working papers.

2. Substantive Analytical Procedures

The use of analytical procedures in audit planning to identify areas of greater risk of misstatement is explained in Chapters 5 and 8. Analytical procedures may also be used in the testing phase of the audit as a substantive test to obtain evidence about a particular assertion. In some cases, they are used as a supplement to tests of details. Analytical procedures may be used as the primary substantive test when inherent risk is moderate or low. However, substantive analytical procedures should not be used as the primary test for assertions with significant inherent risks.

For many assertions, **substantive analytical procedures** that compare plausible relationships among both financial and nonfinancial data may be effective substantive tests. Generally accepted auditing standards state that the auditor should consider the following matters when designing substantive analytical procedures:

- The suitability of the substantive analytical procedure given the assertion.
- The reliability of the data, whether internal or external, from which the expectation of recorded amounts or ratios is developed.
- Whether the expectation is sufficiently precise to identify a material misstatement at the desired level of assurance.
- The amount of any difference of recorded amounts from expected values that is acceptable.

An increased level of understanding of the entity and its environment usually will help the auditor design analytical procedures with more predictable relationships that, in turn, provide more effective evidence.

For high inherent risk assertions, substantive analytical procedures are considered less effective than tests of details. In other cases, however, the opposite may be true. For example, comparisons of aggregate payments to suppliers with goods received may indicate excessive payments that may be more difficult to detect by testing individual transactions. Similarly, comparisons of aggregate salaries with the number of personnel employed may more readily indicate unauthorized payments than is possible with tests of transactions.

In some cases where substantive analytical procedures are effective, they may also add to the efficiency of the audit. For example, for public utilities and cable companies, relatively small amounts of revenue are billed to and collected from many thousands of customers each month. Tests of details of these high-volume, low-value revenue transactions would be very tedious and costly. On the other hand, revenues in such cases can often be estimated with a fair degree of precision using independent variables such as number of subscribers, billing rates for various types of services, and temperature data (for electric and gas utilities). For a cable company client, the auditor could multiply data about the average number of subscribers for each type of service offered by the monthly fee for that service times 12 to estimate total revenues for the year. The auditor's estimated balance for revenues can then be compared with the reported balance as part of the evidence used in determining whether revenues are fairly stated. In other cases, the expected relationship of one account balance to another might be used. For example, total sales commissions expense could normally be estimated from total sales revenues rather than by examining the details of entries to sales commissions. Following are a few additional examples of how analytical procedures might be effective in auditing income statements accounts. Note that in each of these cases the auditor needs reliable data about the underlying business activity.

Account	Analytical Procedure
Hotel room revenue	Number of rooms × Occupancy rate × Average room rate
Tuition revenue	Number of equivalent fulltime students × Tuition rate for a fulltime student
Wages expense	Average number of employees per pay period × Average pay per period × Number of pay periods
Gasoline expense	Number of miles driven ÷ Average miles per gallon × Average per gallon cost

When the results of the substantive analytical procedures conform to expectations, and the acceptable level of detection risk for the assertion is high, it may not be necessary to perform tests of details. Thus, consideration should be given to the extent to which these procedures can contribute to achieving the acceptable level of detection risk before selecting tests of details. When evaluating overall detection risk, it is often cost efficient to obtain a final assessment for analytical procedures risk before performing tests of details.

3. Tests of Details of Transactions

Tests of details of transactions primarily involve tracing and vouching. The details of transactions might be traced from source documents (such as a sales

efficacy of analytical procedures

How effective are analytical procedures in detecting misstatements? In a study of 281 misstatements requiring financial statement adjustments in 152 audits, researchers found the following: Auditors' expectations of errors based on prior audits of the client and their discussions with client personnel led to the detection of 19 percent of all errors, 24 percent of the 82 largest errors, and 27 percent of the 26 extremely large errors. After analytical procedures were applied, 45.6 percent of all errors, 54.9 percent of the 82 largest errors, and 69 percent of the extremely large errors were signaled. The authors concluded that increased utilization of these procedures "might improve the auditor's effectiveness and/or efficiency in detecting errors, and also allow a 'fine tuning' of substantive tests of details."

Source: R. E. Hylas and R. H. Ashton, "Audit Detection of Financial Statement Errors," *Accounting Review* (October 1982), pp. 751–765.

order and a bill of lading) to the recording of sales invoices in the sales journal to test the completeness assertion. Or the details of entries in the cash disbursements journal and perpetual inventory records can be vouched to supporting documents such as canceled checks and vendors' invoices to test the existence and occurrence and valuation assertions. The auditor's focus in performing these substantive tests is on finding monetary errors.

In these tests, the auditor uses evidence obtained about some (a sample) or all of the individual transactions in an account to reach a conclusion about the account balance. These tests generally use documents available in client files. The effectiveness of the tests depends on the particular procedure and documents used. For example, it will be recalled that externally generated documents (vendor's invoices) and internally generated documents that are circulated externally (canceled checks) are more reliable than internally generated documents that have not been circulated externally (purchase requisitions).

Tests of details of transactions can be particularly effective when they are targeted at potential errors. For example, computer-assisted audit strategies may allow the auditor to identify and select payroll transactions where the employee worked an unexpectedly large number of hours, or to select purchase transactions in excess of expected amounts. The auditor may use continuous monitoring to tag such transactions, or may use generalized audit software to sort transactions and identify transactions for testing. The thoughtful use of generalized audit software can greatly enhance substantive tests of details.

The cost efficiency of tests of details of transactions may also be enhanced when performed concurrently with tests of controls as a dual-purpose test. The auditor might simultaneously evaluate the client's controls over the allowance for doubtful accounts and draw an independent conclusion about the reasonableness of the allowance at the same time.

The auditor might obtain a substantial amount of evidence about transaction class assertions by using analytical procedures and by learning about transactions when auditing account balances (e.g., an overstatement of inventory represents an understatement of cost of sales). When the evidence obtained from analytical procedures and from tests of details of related balance sheet accounts that also provide evidence about transaction class assertions do not reduce detection risk to an acceptably low level, direct tests of details of assertions pertaining to income statement accounts are necessary. This may be the case when:

- Inherent risk is high. This may occur in the case of assertions affected by non-routine transactions and management's judgments and estimates. This may also occur for significant inherent risk such as revenue recognition.
- Control risk is high. This situation may occur when (1) related internal controls for nonroutine and routine transactions are ineffective or (2) the auditor elects not to test the internal controls.
- Analytical procedures reveal unusual relationships and unexpected fluctuations. These circumstances are explained in a preceding section.
- The account requires analysis. Analysis is usually required for accounts that (1) require special disclosure in the income statement, (2) contain information needed in preparing tax returns and reports for regulatory agencies such as the SEC, and (3) have general account titles that suggest the likelihood of misclassifications and errors.

Accounts that usually require separate analysis using tests of details of transactions generally include:

Legal expense and professional fees	Taxes, licenses, and fees
Maintenance and repairs	Rents and royalties
Travel and entertainment	Contributions
Officers' salaries and expenses	Advertising

4. Tests of Details of Balances

Tests of details of balances focus on obtaining evidence directly about an account balance rather than the individual debits and credits comprising the balance. For example, the auditor may request banks to confirm cash balances and customers to confirm accounts receivable balances. The auditor may also inspect plant assets, observe the client's inventory taking, and perform pricing tests of the ending inventory.

The effectiveness of these tests depends on the particular procedure performed and the type of evidence obtained. The following illustrates how the effectiveness of tests of balances can be tailored to meet different detection risk levels for the valuation or allocation assertion for cash in bank:

DETECTION RISK	TESTS OF DETAILS OF BALANCES
High	Scan client-prepared bank reconciliation and verify mathematical accuracy of reconciliation.
Moderate	Review client-prepared bank reconciliation and verify major reconciling items and mathematical accuracy of reconciliation.
Low	Prepare bank reconciliation using bank statement obtained from client and verify major reconciling items and mathematical accuracy.
Very low	Obtain bank statement directly from bank, prepare bank reconciliation, and verify all reconciling items and mathematical accuracy.

Note in this illustration that when detection risk is high, the auditor may use internally prepared documentation and perform limited auditing procedures. In contrast, when detection risk is very low, the auditor uses documentation obtained directly from the bank and performs extensive auditing procedures.

Tests of details of balances often involve the use of external documentation and/or the direct personal knowledge of the auditor such as the confirmation of receivables or the observation of inventory. Therefore, they can be very effective. They also tend to be the most time consuming and costly to perform.

5. Tests of Details of Accounting Estimates

An accounting estimate is an approximation of a financial statement element, item, or account in the absence of exact measurement. Examples of accounting estimates include periodic depreciation, the provision for bad debts, and warranty expense. Tests of accounting estimates usually require unique evidence. For example, confirmation of accounts receivable may provide evidence that a customer owes a receivable and the amount owed to the company. It does not, however, provide evidence that the receivable is collectable. Rather the auditor needs to develop evidence about customer payment histories.

Accounting estimates usually involve a significant prospective element, for example, whether receivables will be collected in the future or what warranties costs will be paid in the future. Management is responsible for establishing the process and controls for preparing accounting estimates. Auditors should use professional skepticism when evaluating accounting estimates and be alert to inconsistent estimates where management over-reserves during good economic times (building "cookie jar" reserves) so that they might under-reserve during poor economic times.

AU 342.07, *Auditing Accounting Estimates* (SAS 57), states that the auditor's objective in performing **tests of details of accounting estimates** is to obtain sufficient competent evidential matter to provide reasonable assurance that

- All accounting estimates that could be material to the financial statements have been developed.
- The accounting estimates are reasonable in the circumstances.
- The accounting estimates are presented in conformity with applicable accounting principles and are properly disclosed.

In determining whether all necessary estimates have been made, the auditor should consider the industry in which the entity operates, its methods of conducting business, and new accounting pronouncements.

An entity's system of internal control may reduce the likelihood of material misstatements of accounting estimates and thereby reduce the extent of substantive tests. With public companies the auditor should evaluate the internal controls over the accuracy of the data used to develop accounting estimates and the controls over the consistency of the estimation process.

Evidence of the reasonableness of an estimate may be obtained by the auditor from one or a combination of the following approaches:

- Perform procedures to review and test management's process in making the estimate. For example, the auditor might review the data used by management in developing an allowance for doubtful accounts. The auditor might review the client's evaluations of customer credit and a disclosure committee's review of customers with past due receivables. With a public company the auditor might simultaneously test controls over the allowance for doubtful accounts and substantively test the reasonableness of the allowance.

- Prepare an independent expectation of the estimate. Many private companies do not have adequate controls over accounting estimates. A controller might estimate the allowance for doubtful accounts, and the only review is the auditor's tests. In this case the auditor might use generalized audit software to test the client's aging of receivables and to calculate payments histories for clients with past due receivables. Based on this detail, the auditor might develop his or her own estimate of the allowance.

- Review subsequent transactions and events occurring prior to completing the audit that pertain to the estimate. An effective means of evaluating an accounting estimate involves the use of hindsight. The auditor might review the client's collection history during the first 45 days of the year before drawing a final conclusion about the allowance for doubtful accounts. If a public company develops estimates of the allowance at the end of every quarter, the auditor can use hindsight to review the estimates from the prior year-end, and the estimates for the first three quarters, to evaluate the accuracy of the client's estimation process.

6. Tests of Details of Disclosures

Tests of details of disclosures are tests to evaluate the completeness, existence and rights and obligations, valuation and allocation, and classification understandability of disclosures (see Figure 6-2). Most auditors will test the completeness of disclosures with a decision aid such as a disclosure checklist. These disclosure checklists are usually organized by account balance or financial reporting topic and provide a detailed summary of the types of disclosures that are required by GAAP. In the process of completing the audit, individuals on the audit team must complete the disclosure checklist and compare existing disclosures to the potential for needed disclosures in the financial statements.

Testing the existence and rights and obligations, the valuation and allocation, and the classification assertions related to financial statement disclosures usually involves direct tests of the disclosures, such as reading contracts, vouching information to underlying transaction information, confirming information with outside third parties, and reperforming calculations. In some cases, such as the disclosures related to defined benefit pension plans, the auditor might use the report of a specialist (an actuary) to obtain sufficient, competent evidence. Auditors will usually evaluate the understandability of disclosures using professional judgment to evaluate the clarity of the disclosures and how the disclosures compare with other similar disclosures in other financial statements.

Responding to Significant Inherent Risks

When the auditor identifies a risk as a significant inherent risk, the auditor must respond with tests of details of transactions and/or balances. Auditors can also combine tests of details of transactions or balances with analytical procedures that are specifically responsive to the risk. If the auditor is relying on internal controls to modify the nature, timing, or extent of audit tests, then the auditor must obtain evidence about the effective operation of internal controls during the current audit period. Hence, the auditor would normally audit revenue recognition by performing tests of transactions to evaluate the appropriateness of revenue recognition given the specific details of the transaction. The auditor would probably focus more attention on revenue recognition for complex transactions with multiple deliverables than on a simple transaction associated with the shipment of goods.

Timing of Substantive Tests

The acceptable level of detection risk may affect the timing of substantive tests. The choice about **timing of substantive tests** is about what whether or not to perform substantive tests of balances as of balance sheet date, or a date prior to balance sheet date. If control risk is low and detection risk is high, the tests may be performed several months before the end of the year. In contrast, when detection risk for an assertion is low, the substantive tests will ordinarily be performed at or near the balance sheet date.

Substantive Tests Prior to Balance Sheet Date

An auditor may apply substantive tests to the details of an account at an interim date. The decision to perform the tests prior to the balance sheet date should be based on whether the auditor can control the added audit risk that material misstatements existing in the account at the balance sheet date will not be detected by the auditor. This risk becomes greater as the time period remaining between the date of the interim tests and the balance sheet date is lengthened.

The potential added audit risk can be controlled if substantive tests for the remaining period can provide a reasonable basis for extending the audit conclusions from the tests performed at the interim date to the balance sheet date. AU 313, *Substantive Tests Prior to Balance Sheet Date* (SAS No. 45), states the conditions contributing to the control of this risk: (1) internal control during the remaining period is effective, (2) there are no conditions or circumstances that might predispose management to misstate the financial statements in the remaining period, (3) the year-end balances of the accounts examined at the interim date are reasonably predictable as to amount, relative significance, and composition, and (4) the client's accounting system will provide information concerning significant unusual transactions and significant fluctuations that may occur in the remaining period. If these conditions do not exist, the account should be examined at the balance sheet date.

In practice, early substantive testing of account balances is not done unless tests of controls have provided convincing evidence that internal control is operating effectively. Moreover, it is unlikely that the auditor will perform substantive tests prior to the balance sheet date on all assertions pertaining to an account. For example, the auditor might observe the client's inventory taking on an early date in meeting the existence or occurrence and completeness assertions. However, the auditor would obtain market value quotations subsequent to the balance sheet date in meeting the valuation or allocation assertion.

Substantive tests prior to the balance sheet date do not eliminate the need for substantive tests at the balance sheet date. Tests for the remaining period ordinarily should include:

■ Comparison of the account balances at the two dates to identify amounts that appear to be unusual and investigation of such amounts.

- Other analytical procedures or other substantive tests of details to provide a reasonable basis for extending the interim audit conclusions to the balance sheet date.

When properly planned and executed, the combination of substantive tests prior to the balance sheet date and substantive tests for the remaining period should provide the auditor with sufficient competent evidential matter to have a reasonable basis for an opinion on the client's financial statements.

Extent of Substantive Tests

The acceptable level of detection risk will also affect the **extent of substantive tests.** If detection risk is high, less extensive tests may be performed. In contrast, when detection risk for an assertion is low, the substantive tests will ordinarily be more extensive. Extent is used in practice to mean the number of items or sample size to which a particular test or procedure is applied. Thus, more extensive substantive tests are being performed when the auditor confirms 200 accounts receivable rather than 100 accounts, or vouches 100 sales journal entries to supporting documents rather than 50 entries.

The appropriate sample size for a particular test is a matter of professional judgment. Figure 12-6 summarizes the factors that influence the auditor's decisions about sample size and describes the influence of each factor on sample size. Statistical sampling for substantive tests may be used to assist the auditor in determining the sample size needed to achieve a specified level of detection risk. The topic of audit sampling is discussed in detail in Chapter 13.

However, the auditor should take note that increasing the extent of tests is only helpful when the test is relevant to the assertion being tested. In addition, the auditor can increase the extensiveness of tests by using generalized audit software. This tool can allow the auditor to scan 100 percent of a population of transactions or balances with particular characteristics.

Figure 12-6 ■ Factors that Influence Sample Size for Substantive Tests

Larger Samples	Factor (Relationship to Sample Size)	Smaller Samples
Larger populations with higher book values should result in a larger sample size.	Book value of the population (direct)	Smaller populations with lower book values should result in a smaller sample size.
The more heterogeneous the population, the larger the sample size.	Variation in the population (direct)	The more homogeneous the population, the smaller the sample size.
The smaller the amount of misstatement that the auditor can tolerate, the larger the sample size.	Tolerable misstatement (inverse)	The larger the amount of misstatement that the auditor can tolerate, the smaller the sample size.
Smaller amounts of sampling risk should result in larger sample size.	Tests of details risk (inverse)	Larger amounts of sampling risk should result in smaller sample size.

Staffing Substantive Tests

AU 230, *Due Professional Care in the Performance of Work* (SAS No. 1), states that auditors should be assigned to tasks and supervised commensurate with their level of knowledge, skill, and ability so that they can evaluate the audit evidence they are examining. SAS No. 99, *Consideration of Fraud in a Financial Statement Audit* (AU 316.50), states that the auditor may respond to the risk of material misstatement due to fraud by the assignment of personnel. A task such as evaluating the obsolescence of inventory may require a greater level of industry expertise and experience than observing the existence of inventory. Substantive tests should be assigned to personnel with the requisite skill, ability, and experience.

Summary of Relationships among Audit Risk Components and the Nature, Timing, and Extent of Substantive Tests

A graphic summary of several important relationships among the audit risk components and the nature, timing, and extent of substantive tests is presented in Figure 12-7.

   As noted at the beginning of this part of the chapter, designing substantive tests involves determining the nature, timing, and extent of substantive tests for each significant financial statement assertion. In the next section, we consider how the auditor relates assertions and substantive tests in developing written audit programs for substantive tests.

Figure 12-7 ■ Relationship among Audit Risk Components and the Nature, Timing, Extent, and Staffing of Substantive Tests

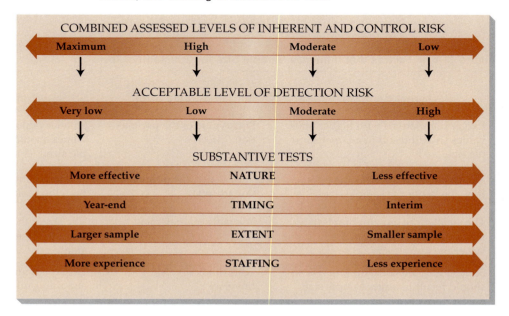

SPECIAL CONSIDERATIONS IN DESIGNING SUBSTANTIVE TESTS

Audit Decision 6

■ What special considerations should be addressed in designing substantive tests for selected types of accounts?

When making audit decisions about the design of substantive tests, auditors must determine whether some special considerations are relevant to designing substantive tests for selected types of accounts. The following discussion focuses on two special considerations: (1) the relationship between auditing balance sheet and income statement accounts, and (2) the implications of related party transactions.

Auditing Balance Sheet and Income Statement Accounts

Traditionally, account balance assertions focus on the balance sheet, and transaction assertions focus on the income statement and statement of cash flows. However, when performing tests of account balance assertions, the auditor often learns about the fair presentation of transactions. Auditors learn about the occurrence of sales when testing the existence of accounts receivables. Following are examples of accounts that are linked together. When the auditor audits the account balance assertions, the auditor also obtains information about the transaction class assertions for these accounts.

Balance Sheet Account	Related Income Statement Account
Accounts receivable	Sales
Inventories	Cost of sales
Prepaid expenses	Various related expenses
Investments	Investment income
Plant assets	Depreciation expense
Accrued payable and accrued expenses	Various related expenses
Interest-bearing liabilities	Interest expense

Accounts Involving Related Party Transactions

Generally accepted auditing standards (AU 334) state that auditors should identify related party transactions in audit planning. Examples of **related party transactions** include transactions with affiliated companies, entities for which investments are accounted for on the equity method, principal owners, and management. These types of transactions are a concern to the auditor because they may not be executed on an arms-length basis. For example, some of the material misstatements in Enron's financial statements related to accounting for transactions where Andrew Fastow, the CFO, negotiated both sides of the transaction.

The auditor's objective in auditing related party transactions is to obtain evidential matter as to the purpose, nature, and extent of these transactions and their effect on the financial statements. The evidence should extend beyond inquiry of management. AU 334.09, *Related Parties*, indicates that substantive tests should:

- Obtain an understanding of the business purpose of the transaction.
- Examine invoices, executed copies of agreements, contracts, and other pertinent documents, such as receiving reports and shipping documents.
- Determine whether the transaction has been approved by the board of directors or other appropriate officials.
- Test for reasonableness the compilation of amounts to be disclosed, or considered for disclosure, in the financial statements.
- Arrange for the audits of intercompany account balances to be performed as of concurrent dates, even if the fiscal years differ, and for the examination of specified, important, and representative related party transactions by the auditors for each of the parties, with appropriate exchange of relevant information.
- Inspect or confirm and obtain satisfaction concerning the transferability and value of collateral.

In auditing identified related party transactions, the auditor is not expected to determine whether a particular transaction would have occurred if the parties had not been related or what the exchange price and terms would have been. The auditor is required, however, to determine the economic substance of the related party transactions and their effects on the financial statements.

[LEARNING CHECK

12-6   Contrast tests of controls and substantive tests as to (a) types, (b) purpose, (c) nature of test measurement, (d) applicable audit procedures, (e) timing, (f) audit risk component, (g) primary fieldwork standard, and (h) whether required by GAAS.

12-7   a. What is the purpose of substantive tests?
        b. What is the relationship between the acceptable level of detection risk and the nature of substantive tests?

12-8   Explain the purpose of initial procedures and explain the special concerns that the auditor has in a first-year audit.

12-9   a. What are the advantages and disadvantages of using analytical procedures as substantive tests?
        b. What factors affect the expected effectiveness and efficiency of analytical procedures as substantive tests?
        c. The role of analytical procedures relative to tests of details may be greater for income statement accounts than balance sheet accounts. Why?

12-10   a. What are the primary audit procedures used in performing tests of details of transactions?
        b. How does the cost of tests of details of transactions compare with the cost of the other three types of substantive tests? How might they be made more cost efficient?
        c. Explain the circumstances that usually result in applying tests of details directly to income statement accounts.

12-11   a. Contrast the focus of tests of details of balances versus tests of details of transactions.
        b. What is the relative effectiveness and costliness of tests of details of balances?

12-12 a. What is the auditor's objective in auditing accounting estimates?

b. Indicate the factors to be considered in evaluating the reasonableness of accounting estimates.

12-13 a. What is the relationship between the acceptable level of detection risk and the timing of substantive tests?

b. What factors should the auditor consider in deciding whether to perform substantive tests prior to the balance sheet date?

c. How may the auditor control the potential added audit risk for the period from the date of testing to the balance sheet date?

12-14 What is the relationship between the acceptable level of detection risk and the extent of substantive tests?

12-15 Explain how an auditor may obtain evidence about transaction class assertions when performing tests of balance sheet accounts. Provide an example.

12-16 a. What are the auditor's objectives in auditing related party transactions?

b. Identify the substantive tests that may be used in auditing related party transactions.

[KEY TERMS

Extent of substantive tests, p. 531
Generalized audit software, p. 520
Initial procedures, p. 523
Nature of substantive tests, p. 523
Related party transactions, p. 533
Substantive analytical procedures, p. 524

Tests of details of accounting estimates, p. 528
Tests of details of balances, p. 527
Tests of details of disclosures, p. 529
Tests of details of transactions, p. 525
Timing of substantive tests, p. 530

[DEVELOPING AUDIT PROGRAMS FOR SUBSTANTIVE TESTS]

A GENERAL FRAMEWORK FOR DEVELOPING AN AUDIT PROGRAM FOR SUBSTANTIVE TESTS

Auditor Knowledge 2

■ Understand the general framework for developing audit programs for substantive tests.

The auditor's decisions regarding the design of substantive tests are required to be documented in the working papers in the form of written audit programs (AU 311.09). An audit program is a list of audit procedures to be performed. The general framework for developing an audit program must accomplish two tasks.

1. It should describe the nature of procedures to be performed.
2. It should ensure that audit evidence is obtained for all financial statement assertions (audit objectives).

The Nature of Procedures to be Performed

Audit programs normally disclose the nature of audit tests. Decisions about the timing, extent, and staffing of audit procedures are normally documented in the audit working papers themselves. The purpose of an audit program is to show the nature of tests performed. The substantive audit programs throughout the remainder of this text are organized according to the nature of the substantive test, which is as follows:

1. Initial procedures
2. Substantive analytical procedures
3. Tests of details of transactions
4. Tests of details of balances
5. Tests of detail of accounting estimates
6. Tests of details of disclosures

In addition to listing audit procedures, an audit program should have columns for (1) a cross-reference to other working papers containing the evidence obtained from each procedure, (2) the initials of the auditor who performed each procedure, and (3) the date performance of the procedure was completed. Figure 12-8 shows an audit program in this format.

In practice, auditors hold different views on the extent of detail to be shown in an audit program. For example, certain details of the sample design, including sample size, for the various tests can be shown on the audit program itself or, as presumed in Figure 12-8, in the supporting working papers that are cross-referenced on the audit program. In any case, audit programs should be sufficiently detailed to provide

- An outline of the work to be done
- A basis for coordinating, supervising, and controlling the audit
- A record of the work performed

The audit program in Figure 12-8 is presented at this time solely to illustrate the format of audit programs for substantive tests and how they can be developed. The application of the substantive tests shown in the figure is explained further in Chapter 16, which includes coverage of inventories as part of the audit of an entity's production cycle.

Addressing All Assertions

Finally, it is essential that every substantive audit program cover all relevant financial statements assertions. Figure 12-9 illustrates the audit objective framework introduced in Chapter 6 (Figure 6-2). The audit objectives are helpful because different audit objectives usually need different tests. This framework also ensures that the auditor plans audit tests for every assertion in the financial statements. Figure 12-9 also provides a cross-reference between the example substantive tests in Figure 12-8 and how they relate to specific audit objectives.

[LEARNING CHECK

12-17 a. What is an audit program?
      b. Identify two tasks that need to be accomplished in the framework for developing an audit program.
      c. What essential information is generally documented in an audit program?

12-18 a. List six types of substantive audit procedures that are normally included in a substantive audit program.
      b. Explain the relationship between audit programs and audit assertions.

Figure 12-8 ■ Illustrative Audit Program for Substantive Tests on Inventories

Prepared By: _____ Date: _____			
Reviewed By: _____ Date: _____			

Amalgamated Products, Inc.
Audit program for substantive tests of inventories
Year Ending December 31, 20XX

Working Paper Reference	Assertion/Tests of Controls	Auditor	Date
	Initial Procedures (1–2)		
	1. Obtain an understanding of the entity and its environment and determine:		
	a. The significance of inventory and cost of sales to the entity.		
	b. Key economic drivers that influence the entity's cost of sales, product costing for inventory, as well as lower cost or market issue.		
	c. Make inquiries about terms of sale of inventory and determine if terms are equivalent to consignment sales.		
	2. Verify totals and agreement of inventory balances and records that will be subjected to further testing.		
	a. Trace beginning inventory to prior year's working papers.		
	b. Review activity in inventory accounts and investigate unusual items.		
	c. Verify totals of perpetual records and other inventory schedules and their agreement with ending general ledger balances.		
	3. Perform analytical procedures		
	a. Review industry experience and trends.		
	b. Examine analysis of inventory turnover.		
	c. Review relationship of inventory balances to recent purchasing production and sales activities.		
	d. Compare the growth in the inventory balance to the growth in sales volume.		
	4. Test details of inventory transactions.		
	a. Vouch additions to inventory records to vendor's invoices (raw materials), manufacturing cost records (work in process), and completed production reports (finished goods).		
	b. Trace data from purchases, manufacturing, and completed production records to inventory records.		
	c. Test cutoff of purchases (receiving), movement of goods through manufacturing, and sales (shipping).		
	Tests of Details of Balances (5–9)		
	5. Observe client's physical inventory count.		
	a. Make test counts from physical inventory to recorded inventory and vice versa.		
	b. Look for indications of slow-moving, damaged, or obsolete inventory.		

(continues)

Figure 12-8 ■ (Continued)

Working Paper Reference	Assertion/Tests of Controls	Auditor	Date
	c. Account for all inventory tags and count sheets used in physical counts.		
	d. Make inquiries about and observe any consignment inventory.		
	6. Confirm inventories at locations outside the entity.		
	7. Test clerical accuracy of inventory records.		
	a. Trace test counts to records.		
	b. Recalculate extension of quantities times unit prices.		
	c. Vouch items on inventory listings to inventory tags and count sheets.		
	d. Trace items on inventory tags and count sheets to inventory listing.		
	e. Reconcile physical counts to perpetual records and general ledger balances.		
	8. Test inventory pricing.		
	a. Examine vendor's paid invoices for purchased inventory.		
	b. Examine propriety of direct labor and overhead rates, standard costs, and variances pertaining to manufactured inventory.		
	c. Obtain sales prices after year-end and evaluate the net realized value of inventory.		
	d. Review perpetual inventory records, production records, and purchasing records for indications of current activity.		
	e. Compare inventories with current sales catalogues and sales reports.		
	9. Tests of consignment inventory		
	a. Examine consignment agreements and contracts.		
	b. Confirm agreements for assignment and pledging of inventories.		
	10. Tests of Details of Accounting Estimates		
	a. Inquire about slow-moving, excess, or obsolete inventories and determine need for write-downs.		
	b. Evaluate the existence of slow-moving inventory using generalized audit software.		
	c. Determine the net realizable value of inventory by looking at subsequent sale prices and the direct costs of selling inventory during a period following year-end.		
	11. Tests of Details of Disclosures		
	a. Compare disclosure related to the existence and rights and obligations of inventory to the results of tests performed above.		
	b. Evaluate the completeness of presentation and disclosures for inventories in drafts of financial statements and determine conformity with GAAP by reference to a disclosure checklist.		
	c. Read disclosures and independently evaluate their classification and understandability.		
	d. Vouch the accuracy of inventory disclosures to tests performed above.		

Figure 12-9 ■ Inventory Audit Objectives and Example Substantive Tests

Specific Audit Objectives	Example of Substantive Tests [Reference to Figure 12-8 in Brackets]
Transaction Class Audit Objectives	
Occurrence	Review activity in inventory accounts and investigate unusual items [2b].
	Vouch additions to inventory records to vendor's invoices (raw materials) manufacturing cost records (work in process), and completed production reports (finished goods) [4a].
	Make inquiries about terms of sale of inventory and determine if terms are equivalent to consignment sales [1c].
Completeness	Trace data from purchases, manufacturing, and completed production records to inventory records [4b].
Accuracy	Trace beginning inventory to prior year's working papers [2a].
	Review activity in inventory accounts and investigate unusual items [2b].
	Vouch additions to inventory records to vendor's invoices (raw materials), manufacturing cost records (work in process), and completed production reports (finished goods) [4a].
Cutoff	Review activity in inventory accounts and investigate unusual items [2b].
	Test cutoff of purchases (receiving), movement of goods through manufacturing, and sales (shipping) [4c].
Classification	Vouch additions to inventory records to vendor's invoices (raw materials), manufacturing cost records (work in process), and completed production reports (finished goods) [4a].
Account Balance Audit Objectives	
Existence	Observe client's physical inventory count and make test counts from counted inventory to physical inventory [5a].
	Trace test counts to records [7a].
	Account for all inventory tags and count sheets used in physical counts [5c].
	Vouch items on inventory listings to inventory tags and count sheets [7c].
	Reconcile physical counts to perpetual records and general ledger balances [7e].
	Confirm inventories at locations outside entity [6].
Completeness	Verify totals of perpetual records and other inventory schedules and their agreement with ending general ledger balances [2c].
	Observe client's physical inventory count and make test counts from physical inventory to counted inventory [5a].
	Trace test counts to records [7a].
	Account for all inventory tags and count sheets used in physical counts [5c].
	Trace items on inventory tags and count sheets to the final inventory listing [7d].
	Reconcile physical counts to perpetual records and general ledger balances [7e].
	Confirm inventories at locations outside the entity [6].
Rights and Obligations	Make inquiries about terms of sale of inventory and determine if terms are equivalent to consignment sales [1c].
	Make inquiries about and observe any consignment inventory [5d].
	Examine consignment agreements and contracts [9a].
	Confirm agreements for assignment and pledging of inventories [9b].

(continues)

Figure 12-9 ■ (Continued)

Specific Audit Objectives	Example of Substantive Tests [Reference to Figure 12-8 in Brackets]
Valuation and Allocation	Verify totals of perpetual records and other inventory schedules and their agreement with ending general ledger balances [2c].
	Look for indications of slow-moving, damaged, or obsolete inventory [5b].
	Recalculate extension of quantities times unit prices [7b].
	Examine vendor's paid invoices for purchased inventory [8a].
	Examine propriety of direct labor and overhead rates, standard costs, and variances pertaining to manufactured inventory [8b].
	Obtain sales prices after year-end and evaluate the net realized value of inventory [8c].
	Review perpetual inventory records, production records, and purchasing records for indications of current activity [8d].
	Compare inventories with current sales catalogues and sales reports [8e].
	Inquire about slow-moving, excess, or obsolete inventories and determine need for write-downs [10a].
	Evaluate the existence of slow-moving inventory using generalized audit software [10b].
	Determine the net realizable value of inventory by looking at subsequent sales prices and the direct costs of selling inventory during a period following year-end [10c]
Disclosure Audit Objectives	
Occurrence and rights and obligations	Confirm agreements for assignment and pledging of inventories [9b].
	Compare disclosure related to the existence and right and obligations of inventory to the results of tests performed above [11a].
Completeness	Evaluate the completeness of presentation and disclosures for inventories in drafts of financial statements and determine conformity with GAAP by reference to a disclosure checklist [11b].
Classification and Understandability	Read disclosures and independently evaluate their classification and understandability [11c].
Accuracy and valuation	Vouch the accuracy of inventory disclosures to tests performed above [11d].
Procedures that relate to many audit objectives	Obtain an understanding of the entity and its environment and determine (a) the significance of inventory and cost of sales to the entity, and (b) the key economic drivers that influence the entity's cost of sales, product costing for inventory, as well as lower of cost or market issues [1].
	Perform analytical procedures: (a) reviewing industry experience and trends (b) examining analysis of inventory turnover, (b) reviewing relationship of inventory balances to recent purchasing production and sales activities and (d) comparing the growth in the inventory balance to the growth in sales volume [3].

[FOCUS ON AUDITOR KNOWLEDGE AND AUDIT DECISIONS]

This chapter focuses on designing substantive tests. In making decisions to support high-quality audit work, the auditor must be able to use the knowledge summarized in Figure 12-10 and address the decisions summarized in Figure 12-11. The page references provided indicate where these issues are discussed in more detail.

Figure 12-10 ■ Summary of Auditor Knowledge Discussed in Chapter 12

Auditor Knowledge	Summary	Chapter References
K1. Know the difference between tests of controls and substantive tests.	Tests of controls are designed to support a conclusion about the effectiveness of design and operations of internal controls. Substantive tests are designed to support a conclusion about the fair presentation of various financial statement assertions. Figure 12-4 provides a comparison of tests of controls and substantive tests, as well as a variety of comparisons that distinguish between the two forms of audit evidence.	p. 520
K2. Understand the general framework for developing audit programs for substantive tests.	The final section of the chapter explains a framework for developing an audit program for substantive tests. Within this framework the auditor should determine the role of (1) initial procedures, (2) substantive analytical procedures, (3) tests of details of transactions, (4) tests of details of balances, (5) tests of details of accounting estimates, and (6) tests of details of disclosures in supporting an audit opinion. A second essential aspect of the framework for developing audit programs is to ensure that substantive tests address all specific audit objectives (assertions) related to the transaction class being tested. The chapter illustrates this process in the context of auditing inventory.	pp. 535–540

Figure 12-11 ■ Summary of Audit Decisions Discussed in Chapter 12

Audit Decision	Factors that Influence the Audit Decision	Chapter References
D1. What key steps should be performed in the process of assessing the risk of material misstatement in the financial statements?	Assessing the risk of material misstatement involves accomplishing three goals: (1) relating risks to type of potential misstatements in the financial statements, either at the financial statement level or the assertion level, (2) considering whether risks are of a magnitude that will result in a material misstatement in the financial statements, and (3) considering the likelihood that risks will result in material misstatements.	p. 515
D2. How do various risk factors relate to the type of potential misstatement?	A critical aspect of the audit process involves identifying potential risk factors and relating them to the types of potential misstatements that can occur. Figure 12-2 provides a series of examples of how the various risk factors discussed in previous chapters, relating each example to the type of potential misstatement, might occur in the financial statements.	pp. 515–518
D3. What is the process for evaluating the planned level of substantive tests as specified in the preliminary audit strategy?	The book discusses three important preliminary audit strategies: (1) lower inherent risk and analytical procedures, (2) a lower assessed level of control risk approach, and (3) a primarily substantive approach. The chapter reviews the impact of each audit strategy on substantive tests. The discussion is summarized in Figure 12-3.	pp. 518–519

(continues)

Figure 12-11 ■ (Continued)

Audit Decision	Factors that Influence the Audit Decision	Chapter References
D4. How can the auditor use information technology to support various substantive tests?	Generalized audit software is an important audit tool. This section of the chapter describes how generalized audit software can be used to (1) reconcile detail audit data with the client's general ledger, (2) select and print samples, (3) test calculations and make computations, (4) test an entire audit population, and (5) summarize data and perform analyses.	pp. 520–523
D5. How are the nature, timing, extent and staffing of substantive tests varied to achieve an acceptable level of detection risk?	This chapter section discusses an auditor's choices about the nature of audit procedures, including the role of (1) initial procedures, (2) substantive analytical procedures, (3) tests of details of transactions, (4) tests of details of balances, (5) tests of details of accounting estimates, and (6) tests of details of disclosures in supporting an audit opinion. This section also discusses the auditor's choices about the timing of audit procedures and important steps that the auditor needs to take to (1) update evidence obtained at an interim date and (2) assess the risk that misstatements could occur between obtaining evidence at an interim date and year-end. The extent of substantive tests (see Figure 12-6) is related to: (1) the book value of the population, (2) the variability of the population being sampled, (3) tolerable misstatement, and (4) tests of details risk (sampling risk). The staffing of substantive tests is related to the skill needed to evaluate the audit evidence.	pp. 523–532
D6. What special considerations should be addressed in designing substantive tests for selected types of accounts?	This final section explains how tests of balances also provide information about transactions that are included in those balances and provides an explanation of how evidence about many balance sheet accounts also provides evidence about income statement accounts. It also explains the audit procedures that should be performed to identify and audit related party transactions.	pp. 533–534

objective questions

Objective questions are available for the student at www.wiley.com/college/boynton

comprehensive questions

12-19   **(Risk factors and preliminary audit strategies)** Figure 12-2 provides a number of examples of risk factors noted while performing risk assessment procedures and relates these factors to the types of potential misstatements that can occur. These are:

1. The company is in an industry that is experiencing economic difficulty and intense price competition.

2. The company has recently changed the nature of its product and is bundling software with other services to customize and implement software and related controls.

3. Analytical procedures for a manufacturer show a significant increase in both profit margins and inventory turn days.

4. Analytical procedures for a retailer show significant decreases in both profit margins and inventory turn days.

5. Senior management has sent a very strong message, and offered increased incentives, to middle managers to meet financial targets.

6. An employee in a small to medium-sized business responsible for cash disbursements did not receive an expected promotion and pay increase.

7. A construction industry client uses the percentage of completion method to recognize revenues and expenses on current projects.

8. A company is experiencing working capital and going-concern problems.

9. The client has a strong control environment and good controls over the existence of inventory.

10. The client has weak computer general controls, including poor controls over the approval of system changes.

Required

Take a moment and study the types of potential misstatements identified for each risk factor in Figure 12.-2. Then explain an appropriate preliminary audit strategy for each risk factor. Use the following format.

EXAMPLE RISK FACTOR	AUDIT STRATEGY
(Use number)	

12-20   **(Risk assessments and audit strategies)** The following risk factors were identified by various audit teams during the audit of their clients.

1. The client has a strong control environment and good controls over the existence of inventory.

2. The client is in an industry that has both significant regulatory oversight and complex regulations.

3. The client has recently experienced turnover in its information technology group, resulting in decreased segregation of duties and a deterioration of computer general controls.

4. The client is a private university with primarily full-time students, a small amount of receivables at year-end, and good internal controls over revenues.

5. A company's business plans are dependent on the success of entering new foreign markets with existing products.

6. The client has used significant borrowing to fund expansion in a competitive industry and has a narrow tolerance range regarding debt covenants.

7. Analytical procedures for a manufacturer show significant increases in both profit margins and inventory turn days.

8. Inventory items are small in size and high in value.

9. The telecommunications client is in a capital-intensive industry, and fixed assets additions involve complex accounting issues.

10. The audit team has experienced several attempts by management to justify marginal or inappropriate accounting on the basis of immateriality.

11. Analytical procedures for a manufacturer show significant increases in both revenue growth and accounts receivable turn days.

Required

For each risk factor (a) identify the type of misstatement that can occur and (b) an audit strategy that is relevant to the risk factor.

EXAMPLE RISK FACTOR	TYPE OF POTENTIAL MISSTATEMENT	AUDIT STRATEGY
(Use number)		

12-21   **(Determining detection risk)** All of the internal control work in the audit of the Hurst Corporation has been completed, and the final assessed levels of control risk have been compared with the planned assessed levels of control risk for specified assertions. The auditor's preliminary audit strategy for these assertions was the lower assessed level of control risk approach.

Required

a. What should the auditor do next before designing specific substantive tests?

b. If it is necessary to determine a revised acceptable level of detection risk for some assertions, how can that be done?

c. When multiple substantive tests are designed for the same assertion, must the same acceptable level of detection risk be specified for each test? Explain.

12-22   **(Designing substantive tests)** Final acceptable levels of detection risk have been determined for several assertions. The auditor is prepared to proceed with designing specific substantive tests.

Required

a. What is the purpose of substantive tests?

b. What factors pertaining to substantive tests can be varied to accommodate different acceptable levels of detection risk? Explain how each factor is varied to accommodate a low versus a high acceptable level of detection risk.

c. Indicate the six types of substantive tests and the relative effectiveness and cost of each.

12-23   **(Audit programs)** After determining the acceptable level of detection risk for specified assertions for a new audit client and completing all other preliminary planning steps, the auditor develops an audit program for substantive tests.

Required

a. Describe the basic features and purposes of audit programs for substantive tests.

b. Describe a general framework for developing an audit program for substantive tests for a group of assertions, assuming all preliminary planning steps have been completed.

c. Contrast the preparation of audit programs for an initial versus a recurring audit engagement.

12-24 **(Financial statement assertions)** In designing the audit program for substantive tests of accounts receivable and plant assets in the Abbott Company, the auditor identified the following audit objectives:

1. Accounts receivable include all claims on customers at the balance sheet date.

2. Recorded plant assets represent assets that are in use at the balance sheet date.

3. Accounts receivable are properly identified and classified in the balance sheet.

4. Plant assets are stated at cost less accumulated depreciation.

5. The allowance for uncollectible accounts is a reasonable estimate of future bad debts.

6. The entity has ownership rights to all plant assets at the balance sheet date.

7. Accounts receivable represent legal claims on customers for payment.

8. Plant asset balances include the effects of all transactions and events that occurred during the period.

9. Accounts receivable represent claims on customers at the balance sheet date.

10. Depreciation methods used by the client are adequately disclosed in the notes to the financial statements.

11. The accounts receivable balance represents gross claims on customers and agrees with the sum of the accounts receivable subsidiary ledger.

12. Capital lease agreements are disclosed in accordance with GAAP.

13. Appropriate disclosures are made about accounts receivable that are assigned or pledged at the balance sheet date.

14. Plant assets are properly identified and classified in the balance sheet.

Required

Identify the financial statement assertion to which each objective relates. Use the following format for your answers:

OBJECTIVE	ASSERTION
(Use number)	

12-25 **(Types of substantive tests and audit objectives)** Audit procedures used in performing substantive tests during the audit of the Harris Company are as follows:

1. Count cash on hand.

2. Confirm accounts receivable.

3. Vouch plant asset additions to purchase documents.

4. Recalculate accrued interest on notes payable.

5. Inquire of management about pledging of plant assets as security for long-term debt.

6. Compute inventory turnover ratio.

7. Vouch ending inventory pricing to purchase invoices.

8. Review client-prepared bank reconciliation.

9. Verify accuracy of accounts receivable balance and agreement with subsidiary ledger.

10. Obtain details of accounts receivable subsidiary ledger and reconcile to the general ledger.

11. Compare statement disclosures for leases with GAAP.

12. Review adequacy of client's provision for uncollectable accounts.

13. Examine certificates of title for delivery equipment.

14. Confirm receivables.

15. Trace bad-debt write-off authorizations to accounts receivable.

16. Observe client's inventory taking.

17. Trace unpaid vendors' invoices to accounts payable at year-end.

18. Compare pension disclosures to a disclosure checklist.

Required

For each of the audit procedures, identify (a) the type of substantive test (1—initial procedures, 2—analytical procedure, 3—test of details of transactions, 4—test of details of balances, 5—tests of accounting estimates, or 6—tests of details of disclosures), and (b) one audit objective to which the test relates. Present your answer in columnar form using the following headings:

AUDIT PROCEDURE	TYPE OF SUBSTANTIVE TEST	AUDIT OBJECTIVE
(Use number)		

12-26 **(Misstatements/assertions/substantive tests)** The following misstatements were detected by the auditor in performing substantive tests of inventories during the audit of Wixon Company.

1. Slow-moving, defective, and obsolete items are included in the inventory but not properly identified.

2. Inventory quantities do not include all goods on hand.

3. Some items are not held for sale or used in the normal course of business.

4. Inventories are stated at cost even when market value is lower.

5. The major categories of inventories are not disclosed in the balance sheet.

6. All inventories included in the balance sheet do not physically exist.

7. The entity does not have legal title to all inventories.

8. Inventories pledged as collateral are not disclosed in the financial statements.

9. Inventory quantities do not include all items stored at outside locations.

10. Inventories include items billed to customers and owned by others.

11. Inventory listings of quantities do not include all tag numbers.

12. The bases of inventory valuation are not disclosed in the financial statements.

13. Purchased goods in transit at the balance sheet date shipped F.O.B. shipping point are not included in inventories.

14. Some manufacturing inventories are classified in the balance sheet as a noncurrent asset.

15. Inventories are stated at the higher of cost or current replacement cost.

The auditor used the following substantive tests:
a. Observe physical inventory counts.
b. Confirm inventories at locations outside the entity.
c. Review perpetual inventory records for current activity.
d. Compare inventories with current sales catalogue.
e. Test shipping and receiving cutoff procedures.
f. Account for all inventory tags.
g. Test clerical accuracy of inventory listings.
h. Examine consignment agreements and contracts.
i. Examine paid vendors' invoices.
j. Compute inventory turnover.
k. Obtain current market value quotations.
l. Review drafts of the financial statements.
m. Inquire about inventories pledged under loan contracts.

Required

For each misstatement, indicate (a) the financial statement assertion that is relevant and (b) the substantive test(s) that was (were) used for the discovery. Present your answer in tabular form with the following column headings:

MISSTATEMENT	ASSERTION	SUBSTANTIVE TEST
(Use number)		Use letter(s)

Note: A substantive test may apply to more than one misstatement, and more than one test may have been used.

12-27 **(Timing of substantive tests)** Cook, CPA, has been engaged to audit the financial statements of General Department Stores, Inc., a continuing audit client, which is a chain of medium-sized retail stores. General's fiscal year will end on June 30, 20X6, and General's management has asked Cook to issue the auditor's report by August 1, 20X6. Cook will not have sufficient time to perform all of the necessary fieldwork in July 20X6, but will have time to perform most of the fieldwork as of an interim date, April 30, 20X6.

For the accounts to be tested at the interim date, Cook will also perform substantive tests covering the transactions of the final two months of the year. This will be necessary to extend Cook's conclusions to the balance sheet date.

Required

a. Describe the factors Cook should consider before applying principal substantive tests to General's balance sheet accounts at April 30, 20X6.

b. For accounts tested at April 30, 20X6, describe how Cook should design the substantive tests covering the balances as of June 30, 20X6, and the transactions of the final two months of the year.

(AICPA adapted)

12-28 **(Nature and timing of substantive tests)** Tina Thomas is participating in her first audit engagement. As a manager on the audit, you have the responsibility of briefing Tina on the firm's policies about substantive tests.

Required

Explain to Tina

a. The circumstances that may permit substantive tests prior to the balance sheet date.

b. How the auditor may control the potential audit risk from such testing for the remainder of the year under audit.

c. The nature of substantive testing for the remainder of the year.

d. How substantive tests are typically applied to income statement account balances.

e. How analytical procedures may be applied to income statement accounts.

f. The circumstances that may necessitate performing tests of details to income statement accounts.

12-29 **(Related party transactions/accounting estimates)** Don Drake has had limited auditing experience. Prior to beginning a new audit engagement, Don asks you, as audit manager, questions about auditing related party transactions and accounting estimates.

Required

Answer the following questions:

a. What are the audit objectives for these two types of special accounts?

b. What audit procedures may be used to obtain evidence for each type of account?

c. Are there any restrictions or constraints in auditing related party transactions?

d. How do the responsibilities of management and the auditor differ for accounting estimates?

e. What are the key factors that should be considered in evaluating the reasonableness of accounting estimates?

f. What are the principal sources of evidence concerning the reasonableness of accounting estimates?

12-30 **(General framework for developing audit program for substantive tests)** Apex Manufacturing Company was formed ten years ago. At that time it took out a 30-year mortgage to purchase land and a factory building that continues to house all of its manufacturing, warehousing, and office facilities. It also owns various manufacturing and office equipment acquired at various dates. It is in the process of self-constructing an addition to the factory building to provide more warehouse space. The addition is approximately 50 percent complete and should be completed during the next fiscal year. The general ledger for Apex includes the following accounts for plant assets: Land, Factory Building, Manufacturing Equipment, Office Equipment, and related accumulated depreciation control accounts for each of the last three accounts. The details of the cost and accumulated depreciation for each item of manufacturing and office equipment are maintained in separate sections of a plant ledger. There is also a Construction-in-Progress account for the accumulated costs of the warehouse addition.

Apex is a new audit client that has never been audited before. You have completed the preliminary planning for the audit of plant assets and are about to design substantive tests. Under the circumstances, you have assessed both inherent and control risk as high for all plant asset assertions.

Required

a. Using only your general knowledge of accounting for plant assets and the general framework for developing an audit program for substantive tests described in the chapter, develop an audit program for your first audit of the plant asset accounts of Apex Manufacturing Company.

b. Following each procedure in your audit program, indicate the assertion or assertions to which it applies by using the following letters. Transaction class audit objectives: Occurrence (EO1), Completeness (C1), Accuracy (VA1), Cutoff (EO2/C2), Classification (PD1); Account balance audit objectives: Existence (EO3), Completeness (C2), Rights and Obligations (RO1), Valuation and Allocation (VA2); Disclosure audit objectives: Existence and Rights and Obligations (PD2), Completeness (PD3), Classification and Understandability (PD4), and Accuracy and Valuation (PD5).

professional simulation

You have just been assigned to the audit of a new manufacturing client, Carroll Manufacturing Inc. (CMI). Russell Carroll owns 60 percent of CMI, one of CMI's major supplier of raw materials (SteelCo) owns 25 percent percent of CMI, and two family members own the other 15 percent of CMI. Russell's brother, Frederick Carroll, owns the majority of the shares of SteelCo. CMI manufactures engines that are sold to several automotive manufacturers. In the normal course of business CMI must provide seven-to-ten year warranties on the engines. CMI major manufacturing facility is adjacent to SteelCo's facility. CMI leases the manufacturing facility from a real estate investment trust that is jointly owned by Russell and Frederick Carroll.

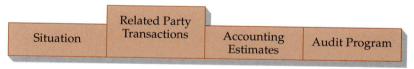

Since this is a first year audit it is clear that related party transactions will be a significant portion of this audit. The engagement partner has asked you to research the firm's responsibilities with respect to related party transactions. Cut and paste the auditing standard sections that explain the general procedures that should be performed to (1) determine the existence of related parties and (2) identify transactions with related parties.

A material issue in the CMI audit is going to be the adequacy of the provision for warranties. While CMI is a new client for your firm, CMI has been manufacturing automotive engines for over 15 years. The firm carefully monitors its quality control statistics and manufacturing has developed extensive statistics on warranty costs for each model of engine that it has ever produced. Cut and paste the auditing standard sections that explain the general procedures that should be performed in evaluating the reasonableness of the provision for warranties.

Situation	Related Party Transactions	Accounting Estimates	Audit Program

Draft an audit program for the audit of the revenue cycle including procedure to audit both revenues and accounts receivable.

[13] AUDIT SAMPLING

WHAT IS AN APPROPRIATE SAMPLE SIZE?

The issue of sufficiency of audit evidence addresses the quantity of audit evidence to be obtained. Auditors have a variety of professional literature that provide guidance about what to consider when making decisions about the quantity of audit evidence, and a few cases may give us some clues about what not to do in an audit. Consider the following.

Fine Host Corporation (FHC) was a Connecticut-based company that provided food and beverage concession, catering, and other services in approximately 400 facilities in 38 states. It conducted an initial public offering in June 1996. We now know that FHC engaged in a financial fraud that, when detected, resulted in the collapse of its stock price and eventually the end of its existence as a public company.

FHC improperly capitalized expenses as assets. In the 1995 financial statements that represented the most current annual statements included in the registration statement, FHC capitalized contract acquisition costs. When a contract was signed to provide food and beverage services to sports arenas, convention centers, and other facilities, the costs attributed to those contracts were transferred to a "contract rights" account and were capitalized to be amortized over the term of the contract. This practice is permissible under GAAP only to the extent that the costs are directly related to the acquisition of assets with a future economic benefit. However, FHC capitalized costs such as airfare, lodging, food, flowers, and color illustrations for proposals.

In its 1995 financial statements, FHC capitalized a total of $4.6 million in contract acquisition costs. Several years later when FHC restated its earnings, it wrote off almost $4.3 million of these capitalized costs (approximately 113 percent of pretax income).

During the audit of the 1995 financial statements, the engagement team under the supervision of John Bacsik, the engagement partner, and Barbara Horvath, the engagement manager, sampled only nine items, totaling $9,332 of the $4.6 million in contract acquisition costs.

The SEC found that the engagement team, under the supervision of Bacsik and Horvath, failed to collect sufficient, competent evidence to support an opinion on the financial statements. The SEC also found that Bacsik and Horvath failed to properly plan and supervise audit procedures necessary to support a reasonable basis for an audit opinion. Bacsik was denied the privilege of appearing or practicing before the SEC as an accountant, and Horvath was censured by the SEC.

A critical issue in this case was a sample size that was considered to be too small. This chapter explores the professional literature associated with audit sampling, including AU 350, *Audit Sampling* (SAS 39), and the AICPA audit and accounting guide entitled *Audit Sampling* (hereinafter referred to as the *Audit Sampling Guide*) that was published to assist auditors in implementing the SAS.

Sources: SEC Accounting and Auditing Enforcement Releases 1482 and 1483.

[PREVIEW OF CHAPTER 13]

Chapter 13 focuses on the use of audit sampling when performing further audit procedures (phase IV in figure 5-1). The chapter addresses audit sampling for both tests of controls and substantive tests. The following diagram provides an overview of the chapter organization and content.

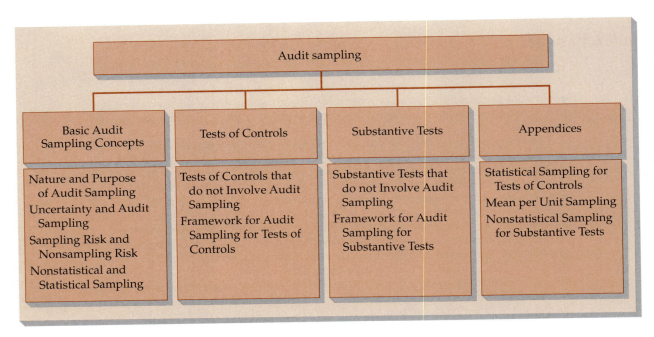

Chapter 13 focuses on audit sampling. This chapter addresses the following aspects of the auditor's knowledge and the auditor's decision process.

focus on auditor knowledge

After studying this chapter you should understand the following aspects of an auditor's knowledge base:

K1. Know the definition of audit sampling and when it applies.

K2. Understand the relationship of generally accepted auditing standards to audit sampling.

K3. Understand the difference between sampling and nonsampling risk and know the four types of sampling risk.

K4. Know the similarities and differences between nonstatistical and statistical sampling.

[BASIC AUDIT SAMPLING CONCEPTS]

NATURE AND PURPOSE OF AUDIT SAMPLING

Auditor Knowledge 1

■ Know the definition of audit sampling and when it applies.

Generally accepted auditing standards (AU 350.01) defines **audit sampling** as the application of an audit procedure to less than 100 percent of the items within an account balance or class of transactions for the purpose of evaluating some characteristics of the entire balance or class.

Audit sampling is applicable to both tests of controls and substantive tests. However, it is not equally applicable to all the auditing procedures that may be used in performing these tests. For example, audit sampling is widely used in vouching, confirming, and tracing, but it is ordinarily not used in inquiring, observing, and analytical procedures.

UNCERTAINTY AND AUDIT SAMPLING

Auditor Knowledge 2

■ Understand the relationship of generally accepted auditing standards to audit sampling.

Both the second and third standards of fieldwork contain an element of uncertainty. In meeting the evidential matter standard, the auditor is required only to have a reasonable basis for an opinion. The auditor is justified in accepting some uncertainty when the cost and time required to make a 100 percent examination of the data are, in his or her judgment, greater than the adverse consequences of possibly expressing an erroneous opinion from examining only a sample of the data. Because this is normally the case, sampling is widely used in auditing.

The uncertainties inherent in audit sampling are collectively referred to as audit risk. The uncertainty associated with audit sampling applies to two components of audit risk: (1) control risk and (2) test of details risk. This chapter discusses how the auditor addresses the uncertainty associated with audit sampling for both tests of controls and substantive tests of details.

SAMPLING RISK AND NONSAMPLING RISK

Auditor Knowledge 3

■ Understand the difference between sampling and non-sampling risk and know the four types of sampling risk.

When sampling is used in meeting the second and third standards of fieldwork, it should be recognized that uncertainties may result from factors (1) associated directly with the use of sampling (sampling risk) and (2) unrelated to sampling (nonsampling risk).

Sampling Risk

Sampling risk relates to the possibility that a properly drawn sample may not be representative of the population. Thus, the auditor's conclusion about internal controls or the details of transactions and balances based on the sample may be different from the conclusion that would result from the examination of the entire population. In performing tests of controls and substantive tests, the following types of sampling risk may occur:

---

tests of controls

The risk of assessing control risk too low is the risk that the assessed level of control risk based on the sample supports the planned assessed level of control risk when the true operating effectiveness of the internal control, if known, would not be considered adequate to support the planned assessed level.

The risk of assessing control risk too high is the risk that the assessed level of control risk based on the sample does not support the planned assessed level of control risk when the true operating effectiveness of the internal control, if known, would be considered adequate to support the planned assessed level.

---

substantive tests

The **risk of incorrect acceptance** is the risk that the sample supports the conclusion that the recorded account balance is not materially misstated when it is materially misstated.

The **risk of incorrect rejection** is the risk that the sample supports the conclusion that the recorded account balance is materially misstated when it is not materially misstated.

These risks have a significant impact on both the effectiveness and efficiency of the audit. The risk of assessing control risk too low and the risk of incorrect acceptance relate to audit effectiveness. When the auditor reaches either of these erroneous conclusions, the auditor's combined procedures may not be sufficient to detect material misstatements, and he or she may not have a reasonable basis for an opinion.

In contrast, the risk of assessing control risk too high and the risk of incorrect rejection relate to the efficiency of the audit. When either of these erroneous conclusions is reached, the auditor will increase substantive tests unnecessarily. However, such effort will ordinarily lead ultimately to a correct conclusion, and the audit will nevertheless be effective.

The types of sampling risks for tests of controls and substantive tests and their effects on the audit are summarized in Figure 13-1.

Nonsampling Risk

Nonsampling risk refers to the portion of audit risk that is not due to examining only a portion of the data. Sources of nonsampling risk include (1) human mistakes, such as failing to recognize errors in documents, (2) applying auditing procedures inappropriate to the audit objective, (3) misinterpreting the results of a sample, and (4) relying on erroneous information received from another party, such as an erroneous confirmation response. Nonsampling risk can never be mathematically measured. However, proper planning and supervision and adher-

Figure 13-1 ■ Sampling Risks for Tests of Controls and Substantive Tests

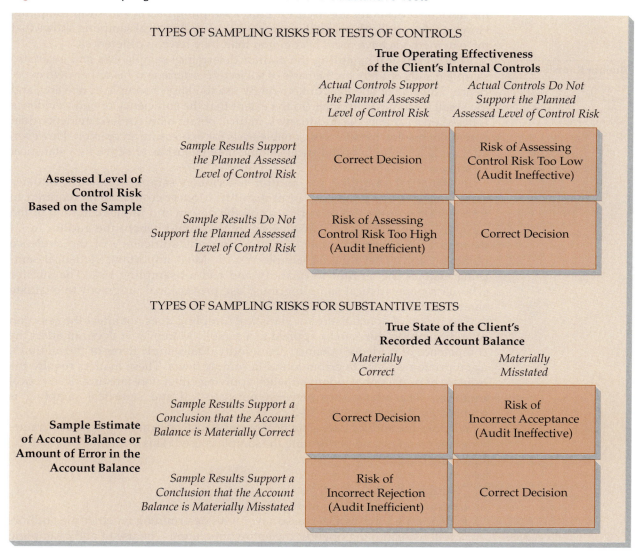

ence to the quality control standards described in Chapter 1 can hold nonsampling risk held to a negligible level.

NONSTATISTICAL AND STATISTICAL SAMPLING

In performing audit tests in accordance with GAAS, the auditor may use either nonstatistical sampling or statistical sampling, or both. Both types of sampling require the exercise of judgment in planning and executing the sampling plan and in evaluating the results. Moreover, both types of sampling can provide sufficient evidential matter as required by the third standard of fieldwork. Both types of audit sampling are also subject to either sampling or nonsampling risk. The critical difference between the statistical sampling and nonstatistical sampling is that the laws of probability are used to control sampling risk in statistical sampling. However, the application of either nonstatistical or statistical sampling shows that the two methods have more in common than they have in differences.

In **nonstatistical sampling** the auditor determines sample size and evaluates sample results entirely on the basis of subjective criteria and his or her own experience. Thus, he or she may unknowingly use too large a sample in one area and too small a sample in another. To the extent that the sufficiency of audit evidence is based on a sample, the auditor may, in turn, obtain more (or less) evidence than is actually needed to have a reasonable basis for expressing an opinion. However, a properly designed nonstatistical sample may be just as effective as a statistical sample.

In **statistical sampling** the auditor determines sample size and evaluates sample results using the laws of probability. Modest costs may be required to train auditors in the use of statistics and the design and implementation of the sampling plan. However, statistical sampling should benefit the auditor in (1) designing an efficient sample, (2) measuring the sufficiency of the evidence obtained, and (3) evaluating sample results. Most important, statistical sampling enables the auditor to quantify and control sampling risk. The auditor who uses nonstatistical sampling must use professional judgment to evaluate sampling risk.

The choice of nonstatistical or statistical sampling does not affect the selection of auditing procedures to be applied to a sample. Moreover, it does not affect the competence of evidence obtained about individual sample items or the auditor's appropriate response to errors found in sample items. These matters require the exercise of professional judgment when applying either nonstatistical or statistical sampling. The relationship between nonstatistical and statistical sampling is graphically shown in Figure 13-2.

Whether the auditor uses statistical or nonstatistical sampling, a similar framework for planning and performing the sample is used. This technique involves the following steps.

1. Determine the test objectives.
2. Determine procedures to meet objectives.
   - Figure 13-2 shows a step associated with determining whether the auditors will use sampling or audit the entire population. The use of audit sampling is assumed in the remainder of the chapter.
3. Make a decision about the audit sampling technique.
4. Define the population and sampling unit.
5. Determine the sample size.
6. Select a representative sample.
7. Apply audit procedures.
8. Evaluate the sample results.
9. Document conclusions.

These nine steps will be illustrated in the next two sections on audit sampling for tests of controls and audit sampling for substantive tests.

The essential differences between sampling for tests of controls and sampling for substantive tests can be summarized as follows.

<aside>
Auditor Knowledge 4

- Know the similarities and differences between nonstatistical and statistical sampling.
</aside>

Figure 13-2 ■ Steps in Statistical or Nonstatistical Sampling

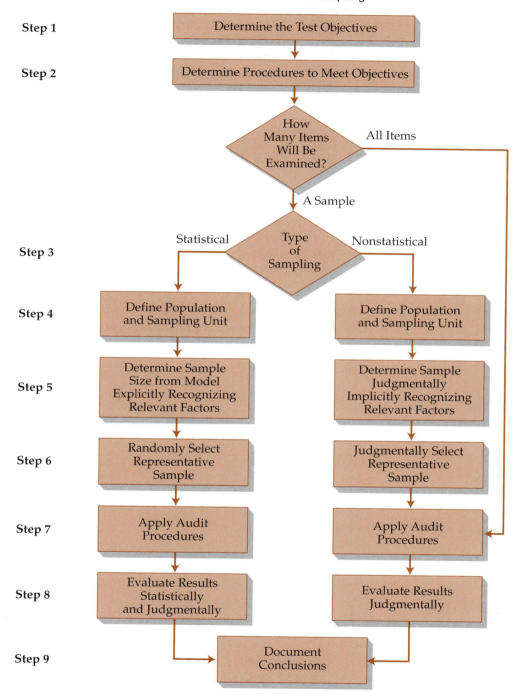

Type of Test	Purpose
Test of controls	To estimate the rate of deviations from prescribed controls in a population
Substantive test	To estimate the total dollar amount of a population or the dollar amount of error in a population

LEARNING CHECK

13-1 Warren Boyd, a beginning staff accountant, believes that audit sampling applies only to tests of controls but may be used with all auditing procedures relating to tests of controls. Is Warren correct? Explain.

13-2 a. Distinguish between sampling risk and nonsampling risk.
b. Explain the types of sampling risk that may occur in auditing and their potential effects on the audit.

13-3 a. What are the basic similarities and differences between statistical and nonstatistical sampling?
b. Identify the benefits to the auditor in using statistical sampling.

13-4 a. Indicate the types of statistical sampling techniques that may be used in auditing.
b. Explain the essential differences between the techniques.

13-5 a. Explain the primary purpose of sampling for tests of controls. Provide an example.
b. Explain the primary purpose of sampling for substantive tests. Provide an example.

KEY TERMS

Audit sampling, p. 553
Nonsampling risk, p. 554
Nonstatistical sampling, p. 556
Risk of assessing control risk too high, p. 554
Risk of assessing control risk too low, p. 554

Risk of incorrect acceptance, p. 554
Risk of incorrect rejection, p. 554
Sampling risk, p. 553
Statistical sampling, p. 556

TESTS OF CONTROLS

TESTS OF CONTROLS THAT DO NOT INVOLVE AUDIT SAMPLING

Audit Decision 1

■ When do the concepts of audit sampling not apply to tests of controls?

Auditors must recognize when the logic behind audit sampling may not apply to tests of controls. The concepts associated with audit sampling do not apply to:

■ Tests that rely primarily on inquiry and observation (e.g., many tests of the control environment, tests of segregation of duties, or observation of physical controls).

■ Tests of computer application controls because they can test a programmed decision point with only two elements of test data (one test to determine that the control appropriately accepts transactions that meet the control criteria and one to see that it appropriately rejects transactions that fail to meet control criteria).

■ Tests of computer application controls that may show exceptions on a computer screen and prevent further processing of a transaction (tested with inquiry and observation, and by submitting transactions that may generate expected error messages).

These are all examples of when audit sampling may not apply to tests of controls. The following discussion focuses on controls where audit sampling applies, whether it involves nonstatistical sampling or statistical sampling.

FRAMEWORK FOR AUDIT SAMPLING FOR TESTS OF CONTROLS

Audit Decision 2

■ What are the important audit judgments in applying audit sampling to tests of controls?

The following discussion applies the framework described in Figure 13-2 to nonstatistical sampling for tests of controls. Particular attention is given to the important audit judgments involved in each step of the process.

Step 1. Determine the Objectives of the Test of Controls

The overall objective of a test of controls is to estimate the rate of deviations from prescribed controls in a population. When auditing an assertion, the auditor will normally attempt to identify key controls that will allow the auditor to change the nature, timing, or extent of substantive tests for that assertion. The following discussion focuses on the use of nonstatistical sampling, which is often used to test small populations (e.g., populations of exception reports, management review of weekly or monthly transactions, or other controls that happen only monthly or quarterly). Many auditors will use some form of statistical sampling to test manual controls over individual transactions because this is a larger population of control activities. The key aspects of using statistical sampling for tests of controls are discussed in Appendix 13A.

When the auditor plans a test of controls, he or she should have determined that controls are well designed and placed in operation. This is usually accomplished during a system walkthrough. The primary purpose of audit sampling for tests of controls is to determine the consistency of application of the controls throughout the audit period. Hence, the auditor will normally select a sample to estimate the rate of deviation from prescribed control procedures. Following are several examples of the objective of various tests of controls.

■ To determine the rate of deviation from expected control environment or risk assessment procedures.

■ To determine the rate of deviation from computer general controls related to system documentation and documentation of system changes.

■ To determine the rate of deviation from prescribed manual followup procedures where individuals clear items appearing on exception reports.

■ To determine the rate of deviation from prescribed performance reviews.

■ To determine the rate of deviation from prescribed controls over management discretion in financial reporting.

- To determine the rate of deviation from prescribed antifraud programs and controls.
- To determine the rate of deviation from prescribed monitoring activities.

Step 2. Determine Procedures to Evaluate Internal Controls

The audit procedures that are used to evaluate the controls discussed above include inquiry of a variety of individuals, observation of people in the performance of their duties, inspection of documents, reports, and electronic files, and reperformance of the control by the auditor. Most of the controls we have described leave a documentary audit trail. For example, the auditor might obtain exception reports that have been reviewed by an employee and then reperform the control to determine that exceptions were properly followed up and corrected in an appropriate manner. Testing this documentary evidence of manual followup procedures, combined with evidence from the use of computer-assisted audit techniques to test programmed controls and tests of general controls, might allow the auditor to assess control risk as low for an assertion. The decisions made at this stage are about the nature and timing of audit procedures. Extensive audit procedures that are not relevant to internal controls over an assertion are of no audit value.

Step 3. Make a Decision about the Audit Sampling Technique

The major decision for the auditor is to determine whether to use nonstatistical sampling or statistical attribute sampling. In a system of internal controls population sizes are often small, the auditor might consider a nonstatistical sample. Following are a series of examples where the auditor might find it more effective to use nonstatistical sampling for tests of controls.

- Some tests of computer general controls such as inspecting logs that document program changes may be such that the auditor wants to review the entire population of logs documenting program changes and the auditor might use nonstatistical sampling to investigate individual changes to specific computer programs.
- Computer-programmed control procedures usually flag exceptions for manual followup. If exceptions are printed on daily or weekly exception reports for followup and correction, and employees make notations on printed exception reports, nonstatistical sampling may be an appropriate way to select exception reports to test the effectiveness of the manual followup procedure.
- Many performance reviews involve having management review various reports of financial and business performance. Revenue cycle reports may rank-order customers by profitability, report new customers, report customers with no activity in the last quarter, or show the volume of activity, sales prices, and margins by product. Payroll cycle reports may show the individual employees whose pay was charged to a responsibility center during a given pay period. These controls expect management to review and approve the completeness, accuracy, and reasonableness of the period's transactions. The auditor might obtain 100 percent of the reports reviewed by a given manager and use nonsta-

tistical sampling to select individual reports to test the effectiveness of management's performance review.

■ Controls over management discretion in financial reporting may occur infrequently, such as at the end of a quarter. If the control only functions at the end of the month or the end of the quarter, nonstatistical sampling is probably the most efficient way to determine how often the auditor wants to test the effectiveness of the control. If the auditor is sampling daily or weekly reports, he or she will want to use professional judgment to select a sample that is representative of the entire population.

Statistical attribute sampling is most effective for larger populations. If the auditor wants to test the effectiveness of a large population of manual controls, such as the manual approval of purchases, statistical attribute sampling (discussed in Appendix 13A) might be appropriate. However, nonstatistical sampling is becoming the norm for tests of controls in an era when most controls are programmed controls.

Step 4. Define the Population and Sampling Unit

The **population** is defined by the internal control of interest and represents all situations when the control should be performed. The **sampling unit** represents the way the auditor identifies the performance of internal controls of interest. For example, the auditor might want to examine the population of all program changes during the year to test general controls over program changes. In this example, the individual sampling unit would be a program change. Alternatively, the auditor might want to test a population of all management reports in the expenditure cycle where management is asked to review and approve all payroll expenditures charged to their responsibility center. The population would represent all reports sent to management for review and approval, and the individual sampling unit would be an individual payroll report sent to a manager. Even though the report may contain information about a number of transactions, the report is the sampling unit because it is the report that management responds to in controlling the transactions.

Where there are multiple client locations, such as branches or divisions, the auditor may elect to regard each segment as a separate population. This choice would clearly be warranted when there are significantly different controls at each location. However, when the controls are similar throughout the organization and consolidated statements are prepared, one population for all locations may be sufficient.

Step 5. Use Professional Judgment to Determine Sample Size

Whether the auditor uses nonstatistical sampling or statistical sampling, the same basic factors should be considered when determining sample size. In nonstatistical sampling it is not necessary for the auditor to quantify these factors explicitly in determining sample size. However, the auditor must recognize the following effects on sample size of a change in one factor when the other factors are held constant. Figure 13-3 explains the factors that influence sample size for a test of controls.

Figure 13-3 ■ Factors that Influence Sample Size for Tests of Controls

Larger Samples	Factor (Relationship to Sample Size)	Smaller Samples
Manual controls should be tested with larger sample sizes. Manual controls are subject to less consistency in application than automated controls.	**The nature of the control**	The auditor may use smaller sample sizes for automated controls because of the consistency of operation of automated controls.
The more frequent the operation of the control (e.g., on every transaction), the more operations of the control the auditor should test.	**Frequency of operation (Direct)**	The less frequent the operation of the control (e.g., monthly or quarterly) the fewer operations of the control the auditor can test.
Tests that are more important to the auditor's audit strategy should be tested more extensively.	**Importance of the control (Direct)**	Tests that are less important to the auditor's audit strategy should be tested less extensively.
Smaller amounts of sampling risk should result in larger sample size.	**Risk of assessing control risk too low (Inverse)**	Larger amounts of sampling risk should result in smaller sample size.
The smaller the rate of deviation from the prescribed control procedure that the auditor can tolerate, the larger the sample size.	**Tolerable deviation rate (Inverse)**	The larger the rate of deviation from the prescribed control procedure that the auditor can tolerate, the smaller the sample size.
The closer tolerable deviation rate and expected deviation rate are to each other, the larger the sample size.	**Expected population deviation rate (Direct)**	The greater the amount between tolerable deviation rate and expected deviation rate, the smaller the sample size.
The larger the population, the larger the sample size.	**Population size below 5,000 (Direct)**	The smaller the population, the smaller the sample size.
Population size does not affect sample size.	**Population size below 5,000 (No Effect)**	Population size does not affect sample size.

The Nature of the Control

The **nature of the control** refers to whether a control is manual or automated. It also refers to whether a control in place affects the consistency of operation of other controls. Automated controls that operate in an environment of strong computer general controls should be expected to operate consistently over time. As a result, they do not need repetitive testing by the auditor. Alternatively, various manual controls are subject to human fatigue and mistakes, so the effectiveness of their operation should be tested more extensively to determine the consistency of their operation over time.

Frequency of Operation

The **frequency of operation** refers to how often the control operates. Some controls operate on every transaction, such as various authorization controls. Alternatively, some controls operate only at month-end, with month-end reviews of accounting information by management. Some controls may operate only quarterly, such as some controls over management's discretion in financial reporting.

The more frequent the operation of a control, the larger the sample size should be. However, for manual controls that operate on each transaction, once the population size approaches 5,000, population size no longer has a significant effect on sample size (see discussion of population size below).

Importance of the Control

The **importance of the control** relates to the importance of the control to the auditor's audit strategy. For example, controls like the control environment and computer general controls have a pervasive impact on other controls and are very important to an audit strategy that relies on those other controls. As a result, controls that have a pervasive impact on the other controls should be tested more extensively than controls that are less central to the auditor's reliance on internal controls. In many transaction cycles the client may have built in redundant controls. The auditor does not need to test every one. The auditor might identify a few "key" controls that are very important to an assertion and test only those controls. Hence, the more important the control to the auditor's control risk assessment, the more extensively the auditor should test the controls.

Risk of Assessing Control Risk Too Low

Two types of sampling risk are associated with tests of controls: (1) the risk of assessing control risk too high, which relates to the efficiency of the audit, and (2) the risk of assessing control risk too low, which relates to the effectiveness of the audit. Because of the potentially serious consequences associated with an ineffective audit, the auditor desires to keep the risk of assessing control risk too low at a low level. In attribute sampling, the **risk of assessing control risk too low** must be stated explicitly.[1] Many auditors specify one level of this risk, such as 5 percent, for all tests of controls. Alternatively, other auditors vary the risk level directly with planned control risk, as illustrated below.

PLANNED CONTROL RISK	RISK OF ASSESSING CONTROL RISK TOO LOW
Low	5%
Moderate	10%
High	15%

Tolerable and Expected Deviation Rates

Tolerable deviation rate is the maximum rate of deviation from a control that an auditor is willing to accept and still use the planned control risk. The AICPA *Audit Sampling Guide* includes the following guidelines for quantifying an acceptable range for the tolerable deviation rate:

PLANNED CONTROL RISK	RANGE OF TOLERABLE DEVIATION RATE
Low	2%–7%
Moderate	6%–12%
High	11%–20%

---

[1] The factor reliability or confidence level is sometimes used in attribute sampling. This factor is the complement of the risk of assessing control risk too low. Thus, specifying 95 percent reliability is the equivalent of a 5 percent risk of assessing control risk too low.

The auditor should estimate the **expected population deviation rate,** which is the auditor's best guess of the actual deviation rate in the population. When there is a significant difference between tolerable and expected deviation rates, the sample size is relatively small. The AICPA *Audit Sampling Guide* (p. 58) illustrates the following effects of changes in expected population deviation rate on sample size assuming a 5 percent risk of assessing control risk too low:

TOLERABLE ERROR RATE	EXPECTED POPULATION DEVIATION RATE	SAMPLE SIZE
5%	0%	60
5%	10%	73
5%	20%	92
5%	30%	120
5%	40%	162

Population Size

When planning a test of controls, **population size** has little or no effect on sample size. The AICPA *Audit Sampling Guide* (p. 35) illustrates the following effects of changes in population size on sample size, assuming a 5 percent risk of assessing control risk too low, a 5 percent tolerable deviation rate, and a 1 percent expected population deviation rate:

POPULATION SIZE	SAMPLE SIZE	POPULATION SIZE	SAMPLE SIZE
100	64	2,000	92
500	87	5,000	93
1,000	90	100,000	93

As the tabulation shows, there is little difference in the sample size needed from a population of 500 units versus 5,000 units, and no difference between 5,000 units and 100,000 units.

Step 6. Select a Representative Sample

The process of selecting a sample should be unbiased, and the auditor should attempt to obtain a representative sample of the application of the control throughout the period being tested. Since tests of controls are often performed at an interim period, the auditor should select a representative sample of the control from the beginning of the year though the interim date. If the auditor is using nonstatistical sampling to test a documented control, the auditor should use professional judgment to select a sample that is representative of the operation of the control during the period being tested. If the auditor is using statistical attribute sampling, the auditor will normally use a random sampling technique to randomly select a sample out of the population being tested (e.g., a random sample of all purchase orders). In some cases an auditor will use the computer to randomly select transactions for further testing.

Step 7. Apply Audit Procedures

Once the auditor selects a sample, the auditor should apply audit procedures to determine whether the control has been consistently applied and the degree to which it operates effectively. In Step 2 the auditor determined the evidence that would support the fact that a control operates effectively. At this step the auditor evaluates the evidence that is obtained from the sample. For example, if the auditor is evaluating a manual control, the auditor will normally find evidence that (1) the person actually performed the control (e.g., initials or other documentation) and then (2) the auditor will reperform the control to determine that the person performed the control with requisite care and that it operated effectively. With a test of controls the auditor is seeking evidence of whether the control was effectively performed, not whether there are monetary misstatements in the sample. Generally accepted auditing standards are clear that the absence of monetary misstatements does not necessarily imply that controls are effective.

Step 8. Evaluate the Sample Results

Deviations from prescribed control procedures should be tabulated, summarized, and evaluated. Professional judgment is required in the evaluation of quantitative and qualitative results. When evaluating quantitative results, the auditor should compare evidence regarding the deviation rate in the sample to the tolerable deviation rate determined when planning the nonstatistical sample. The auditor who uses nonstatistical sampling should judgmentally consider whether there is an adequate allowance for sampling risk. If the quantitative deviation rate in the sample (e.g., 6 percent) is close to the tolerable deviation rate (e.g., 7 percent), then it is possible that the auditor is incorrectly concluding that control risk is low. However, if the sample deviation rate (e.g., 1 percent) has a greater deviation from the tolerable rate (e.g., 7 percent), then it is more likely that the auditor is correctly concluding that control risk is low.

If a test of programmed controls fails (e.g., the program does not reject a test transaction that is over a preset limit), then the programmed control is ineffective for that particular attribute (in this example, a control over valuation). The auditor then needs to consider whether there are other controls related to the same attribute or whether control risk should be assessed at the maximum. If user departments, or other appropriate levels of management, do not document approved program changes, the auditor needs to consider whether the evidence exceeds the tolerable rate and whether she or he needs to change the planned assessed level of control risk or assess control risk at the maximum. Tests of general controls are particularly important as they have a pervasive effect on all control systems that use information technology. Ultimately, the auditor needs to determine whether there is sufficient competent evidence to support a control risk assessment for the relevant audit objective of low, moderate, or high, or whether control risk needs to be assessed at the maximum.

Figure 13-15 in Appendix 13A provides a table that can be used to project sample results on the population using statistical attribute sampling once the results of individual deviations from prescribed control procedures have been determined.

The auditor's qualitative considerations would include (1) the nature and cause of the deviation, such as whether the deviation was due to error or fraud; and (2) the possible relationship of the deviation to other phases of the audit, such as whether the deviation is in a procedure that has a pervasive impact on other controls. The discovery of fraud ordinarily requires broader consideration of the evidence for other aspects of the audit than does the discovery of unintentional error.

Step 9. Document Conclusions

Once the auditor has completed the sampling process, the auditor should document the results of tests of controls in his or her working papers. This was discussed previously in Chapter 11. If the auditor assesses control risk below the maximum, the auditor needs to document the control risk assessment either quantitatively (e.g., 7 percent or 20 percent) or qualitatively (e.g., low, moderate, high, or maximum) and the basis for the conclusion (the results of tests of controls) should be included in the working papers.

[LEARNING CHECK

13-6 Explain several situations where the concepts of audit sampling do not apply to tests of controls.

13-7 a. Describe five types of control procedures where the auditor is likely to use a nonstatistical sample to test the effectiveness of control procedures.

   b. Explain why two test transactions should be sufficient to test a programmed control procedure.

   c. If the auditor wants to support a low control risk assessment for an audit objective based on tests of a programmed control procedure, what other controls must be tested to support the low control risk assessment?

13-8 List the steps involved in selecting and evaluating a nonstatistical or a statistical sample for tests of controls. Identify the professional judgments that must be made associated with each step.

13-9 List the seven factors that influence sample size for a test of controls. Assume that management reviews and approves a weekly expenditure report of all expenditures charged to a responsibility center. Explain how each factor would influence the number of reports selected for review and testing by the auditor.

[KEY TERMS

Expected population deviation rate, p. 564
Frequency of operation, p. 562
Importance of the control, p. 563
Nature of the control, p. 562
Population, p. 561

Population size, p. 564
Risk of assessing control risk too low, p. 563
Sampling unit, p. 561
Tolerable deviation rate, p. 563

[SUBSTANTIVE TESTS]

SUBSTANTIVE TESTS THAT DO NOT INVOLVE AUDIT SAMPLING

As with tests of controls, the auditor must recognize when the concepts associated with audit sampling apply, or do not apply, to substantive tests. In a few instances,

Audit Decision 3

■ When do the concepts of audit sampling not apply to substantive tests?

the logic behind audit sampling does not apply to substantive tests. For example, audit sampling does not apply to initial procedures, substantive analytical procedures, and many tests of details of accounting estimates and tests of details of disclosures. An auditor might audit the allowance for doubtful accounts by using generalized audit software to identify every customer that has had a history of having receivables more than 30 or 60 days past due. In so doing, the auditor is trying to investigate the entire population of slow paying customers.

Another situation where audit sampling does not apply is when the auditor selects all but an immaterial portion of the population. In this case the auditor might be able to assume that the unsampled items are in error and still conclude, with certainty, that the population is materially correct. However, if the auditor leaves a material portion of the population unsampled, then the auditor has some level of uncertainty in his or her conclusion. Furthermore, the auditor must project the results of the sample on the unsampled portion of the population.

The following discussion explains the basic framework for sampling for substantive tests. The discussion also addresses the concepts of sampling in the context of statistical probability proportionate to size (PPS) sampling. Appendix 13B addresses the same methodology with respect to the use of statistical mean per unit estimation, and Appendix 13C focuses on the use of nonstatistical sampling for substantive tests.

FRAMEWORK FOR AUDIT SAMPLING FOR SUBSTANTIVE TESTS

Audit Decision 4

■ What are the important audit judgments in applying probability proportionate to size sampling for substantive tests?

The following discussion applies the framework described in Figure 13-2 to probability proportionate to size (PPS) sampling for substantive tests. The discussion includes a particular focus on the audit judgments involved in applying PPS sampling for substantive tests. Students should focus on the important audit judgments involved in each step of the process.

Step 1. Determine the Objectives of the Substantive Test

The ultimate purpose of a substantive test is to obtain reasonable assurance that an assertion is presented fairly in all material respects. The auditor can use audit sampling for this goal by either (1) estimating the total dollar amount of a population or (2) estimating the dollar amount of misstatement in a population. For example, the auditor might use a sampling tool that allows the auditor to develop an estimate of total accounts receivable or total inventory. If this estimate is within a range of the book value of the account balance plus or minus tolerable misstatement, then the auditor can conclude that the population is materially correct. This method might be particularly appropriate if the client is attempting to determine the value of inventory based on a sample rather than counting the entire population.

Alternatively the auditor might estimate the amount of misstatement that might be present in an audit population. If this estimate is less than tolerable misstatement for the account, then the auditor can conclude that the account balance is materially correct. Probability proportionate to size (PPS) sampling is useful for this purpose. The methodology for applying PPS sampling to draw a conclusion about the maximum amount of misstatement that might exist in a population is discussed below.

Step 2. Determine the Substantive Audit Procedures to Perform

Important substantive procedures include tests of details of transactions and tests of details of balances. These are the most common procedures where the auditor would use audit sampling for substantive tests. For example, the auditor might audit the existence of accounts receivable by sending confirmations or audit the existence of inventory by observing inventory. The auditor might focus audit procedures related to the existence of property, plant, and equipment (PP&E) on additions to PP&E and test the additions by vouching to the documentation underlying the transaction. Chapter 12 explained how auditors develop substantive audit programs. It is important to make sure that the evidence obtained is relevant to the assertion. More extensive audit procedures are of no audit value if the evidence is not relevant to the assertion being tested.

Step 3. Make a Decision about the Audit Sampling Technique

PPS sampling is an approach that uses attribute sampling theory to express a conclusion in dollar amounts rather than as a rate of deviations. This form of sampling may be used in substantive tests of both transactions and balances. The PPS sampling approach illustrated in this chapter is based on the PPS sampling model described in the AICPA's *Audit Sampling Guide*. The model in the *Audit Sampling Guide* is primarily applicable in testing transactions and balances for overstatement. It may be especially useful in tests of:

- Receivables when unapplied credits to customer accounts are insignificant
- Investment securities
- Inventory price tests when few differences are anticipated
- Plant asset additions

PPS sampling may not be the most cost-effective approach for receivables and inventories when the foregoing conditions are not met and where the primary objective is to independently estimate the value of a class of transactions or balances.

The AICPA's *Audit Sampling Guide* (pp. 68–69) identifies several advantages and disadvantages of PPS sampling. The advantages of PPS sampling are:

- It is generally easier to use than classical variables sampling because the auditor can calculate sample sizes and evaluate sample results by hand or with the assistance of tables.
- The size of a PPS sample is not based on any measure of the estimated variation of audit values.
- PPS sampling automatically results in a stratified sample because items are selected in proportion to their dollar values.
- PPS systematic sample selection automatically identifies any item that is individually significant if its value exceeds an upper monetary cutoff.
- If the auditor expects no misstatements, PPS sampling will usually result in a smaller sample size than under classical variables sampling.
- A PPS sample can be designed more easily, and sample selection may begin before the complete population is available.

In contrast, PPS sampling has the following disadvantages:

- It includes an assumption that the audit value of a sampling unit should not be less than zero or greater than book value. When understatements or audit values of less than zero are anticipated, special design considerations may be required.
- If understatements are identified in the sample, the evaluation of the sample may require special considerations.
- The selection of zero balances or balances of a different sign (e.g., credit balances) requires special consideration.
- PPS evaluation may overstate the allowance for sampling risk (ASR) when misstatements are found in the sample. As a result, the auditor may be more likely to reject an acceptable book value for the population.
- As the expected number of misstatements increases, the appropriate sample size increases. Thus, a larger sample size may result than under classical variables sampling.

The auditor should exercise professional judgment in determining the appropriateness of this approach in a given audit circumstance. Most generalized audit software, such as *Idea* or *ACL,* allows for the easy use of statistical sampling, provided that the auditor understands the logic behind the statistics being used.

Step 4. Define the Population and Sampling Unit

The **population** consists of the class of transactions or the account balance to be tested. For each population, the auditor should decide whether all the items should be included. For example, four populations are possible when the population is based on account balances in the accounts receivable ledger, that is, (1) all balances, (2) only debit balances, (3) only credit balances, and (4) zero balances.

The **sampling unit** in PPS sampling is the individual dollar, and the population is considered a *number* of dollars equal to the total dollar amount of the population. Each dollar in the population is given an equal chance of being selected in the sample. Although individual dollars are the basis for sample selection, the auditor does not actually examine individual dollars in the population. Rather, he or she examines the account, transaction, document, or line item associated with the dollar selected. Individual dollars selected for a sample are sometimes thought of as *hooks* that, on selection, snag or bring in the entire item with which they are associated. The item snagged (account, document, etc.) is known as a logical sampling unit.

It is this feature that gives PPS sampling its name. The more dollars associated with a logical unit, the greater its chance of being snagged. Thus, the likelihood of selection is proportional to its size. This feature is also responsible for two limitations of PPS sampling. In testing assets, zero and negative balances should be excluded from the population because such balances have no chance of being selected in the sample.

PPS sampling is not suitable in testing liabilities for understatement because the more an item is understated, the less is its chance of being included in the sample. PPS sampling is biased against selecting very small items that should, in fact, be very large. As a result, many auditors using PPS sampling think about how to identify a **reciprocal population** that will be overstated if the account balance of interest is understated. For example, if accounts payable at year-end is understated, the voucher register for the period subsequent to year-end will likely be overstated because liabilities that are unrecorded at year-end are normally recorded in the subsequent period.

The item snagged (e.g., account or document) is known as the **logical sampling unit.** The auditor chooses a logical sampling unit compatible with the nature of the auditing procedures to be performed. Accordingly, if the auditor intends to seek confirmation of customer account balances, he or she would ordinarily choose the customer account as the logical unit. Alternatively, the auditor might choose to seek confirmation of specific transactions with customers. In that case, the auditor might choose sales invoices as the logical unit. The auditor then selects the sample items from a physical representation of the population, such as a computer printout of customer balances, or computer audit software may be used to select the sample items directly from a machine-readable form of the physical representation. Before selecting the sample, the auditor should determine that the physical representation is complete. Using the computer to reconcile a machine-readable file to a control total usually accomplishes this task.

In the following discussion we will develop an example for the Harris Company where (1) the population is defined as customer accounts with debit balances, (2) the aggregate book value of these accounts is $600,000, (3) the customer account is defined as the logical sampling unit, and (4) the printout from which the accounts are to be selected has been reconciled to the control account balance of $600,000 referred to above.

Step 5. Use Professional Judgment and Statistical Methods to Determine Sample Size

Whether the auditor uses nonstatistical sampling or statistical sampling, the same basic factors should be considered when determining sample size. Figure 13-4 provides an overview of the factors that influence sample size for PPS sampling. Once the auditor has made professional judgments about these factors, the following formula is used to determine sample size in PPS sampling:

$$n = \frac{BV \times RF}{TM - (AM \times EF)}$$

where

BV = book value of population tested
RF = reliability factor for the specified risk of incorrect acceptance
TM = tolerable misstatement
AM = anticipated misstatement
EF = expansion factor for anticipated misstatement

Each of these factors is explained below.

Book Value of Population Tested

The book value specified in determining sample size must relate precisely to the definition of the population as described in the preceding section. The amount of

Figure 13-4 ■ Factors that Influence Sample Size for PPS Sampling

Larger Samples	Factor (Relationship to Sample Size)	Smaller Samples
Larger populations with higher book values should result in a larger sample size.	**Book value of the population (Direct)**	Smaller populations with lower book values should result in a smaller sample size.
Smaller amounts of sampling risk should result in larger sample size.	**Risk of incorrect acceptance (Inverse)**	Larger amounts of sampling risk should result in smaller sample size.
The smaller the amount of misstatement that the auditor can tolerate, the larger the sample size.	**Tolerable misstatement (Inverse)**	The larger the amount of misstatement that the auditor can tolerate, the smaller the sample size.
The closer tolerable misstatement and expected misstatement are to each other, the larger the sample size.	**Anticipated misstatement (Direct)**	The greater the difference between tolerable misstatement and expected misstatement, the smaller the sample size.

the book value has a direct effect on sample size—the larger the book value being tested, the larger the sample size.

Reliability Factor for Specified Risk of Incorrect Acceptance

In specifying an acceptable level of risk of incorrect acceptance, the auditor should consider (1) the level of audit risk that he or she is willing to take that a material misstatement in the account will go undetected, (2) the assessed levels of inherent and control risks, and (3) the results of other tests of details and substantive analytical procedures that are relevant to the assertion. Hence, the **risk of incorrect acceptance** is determined using the audit risk model as shown below.

$$TD = \frac{AR}{IR \times CR \times AP}$$

For example, if the auditor concludes that inherent risk is at the maximum, control risk is low, and if other auditing procedures provide some assurance that the book value being tested is not materially misstated, he or she will be willing to accept a higher risk of incorrect acceptance for the PPS sample, perhaps up to 30 percent. If control risk is high, and if other substantive procedures provide little assurance about the account being tested, then greater assurance must be obtained from the test and the auditor will specify a low risk of incorrect acceptance, perhaps as low as 5 percent. The audit risk model, experience, and professional judgment must be used in making these determinations. The risk of incorrect acceptance has an inverse effect on sample size—the lower the specified risk, the larger the sample size.

The **reliability factor (RF)** for this risk is obtained from Figure 13-5. It is based on the risk of incorrect acceptance specified by the auditor and zero number of misstatements, regardless of the number of misstatements anticipated. In the Harris Company, the auditor specifies a 5 percent risk of incorrect acceptance. Thus, the reliability factor is 3.0.

Figure 13-5 ■ Reliability Factors for Determining PPS Sample Sizes

| | Reliability Factors for Zero Overstatements | | | | | | | |
| | Risk of Incorrect Acceptance | | | | | | | |
	1%	5%	10%	15%	20%	25%	30%	37%
Reliability Factors	4.61	3.00	2.31	1.90	1.61	1.39	1.21	1.00

Source: AICPA *Audit and Accounting Guide: Audit Sampling.*

Tolerable Misstatement

Tolerable misstatement (TM) is the maximum misstatement that can exist in an account before it is considered materially misstated. Some auditors use the term *materiality* (or *material amount*) as an alternative to TM. In specifying this factor, the auditor should realize that misstatements in individual accounts, when aggregated with misstatements in other accounts, may cause the financial statements as a whole to be materially misstated.

TM has an inverse effect on sample size—the smaller the TM, the larger the sample size. For the Harris Company, the auditor specifies a TM equal to 5 percent of book value, or $30,000.

Anticipated Misstatement and Expansion Factor

In PPS sampling, the auditor does not quantify the risk of incorrect rejection. This risk is controlled indirectly, however, by specifying the anticipated misstatement (AM) that is inversely related to the risk of incorrect rejection and directly related to sample size. **Anticipated misstatement (AM)** is the amount of misstatement that the auditor expects to occur in the population. The auditor uses prior experience and knowledge of the client and professional judgment in determining an amount for AM. The auditor must bear in mind that an excessively high amount will unnecessarily increase sample size, whereas too low an estimate will result in a high risk of incorrect rejection. For the Harris Company, the auditor specifies AM of $6,000 based on prior experience with the entity.

The **expansion factor (EF)** is required only when misstatements are anticipated. It is obtained from Figure 13-6, using the auditor's specified risk of incorrect acceptance. The smaller the specified risk of incorrect acceptance, the larger the EF. Like anticipated misstatement, the EF has a direct effect on sample size. In the Harris case study, the EF for anticipated misstatement is 1.6. The combined effect

Figure 13-6 ■ Expansion Factors for PPS Sampling

| | Expansion Factors for Anticipated Misstatements | | | | | | | |
| | Risk of Incorrect Acceptance | | | | | | | |
	1%	5%	10%	15%	20%	25%	30%	37%
Expansion Factors	1.90	1.60	1.50	1.40	1.30	1.25	1.20	1.15

Source: AICPA *Audit and Accounting Guide: Audit Sampling.*

of anticipated misstatement and EF is then subtracted from tolerable misstatement in determining sample size.

Calculation of Sample Size

The factors for determining sample size in the Harris Company are BV = $600,000; RF = 3.0; TM = $30,000; AM = $6,000; and EF = 1.6. Thus, sample size is 88, computed as follows:

$$n = \frac{\$600{,}000 \times 3.0}{\$30{,}000 - (\$6{,}000 \times 1.6)} = 88$$

Step 6. Select a Representative Sample

The process of selecting a sample should be unbiased, and the auditor should attempt to obtain a representative sample of the items in the balance or transaction class being sampled. The auditor can never be certain that a representative sample has been achieved. The concept of **sampling risk** (risk of incorrect acceptance) is a measure of whether or not the sample is representative. The auditor's best opportunity to obtain a representative sample is to select a random sample. Furthermore, many auditors will take steps to obtain a high proportion of the large dollars in the population. This is appropriate if the auditor is concerned about a risk of overstatement of the population. The following discussion explains the methodology for selecting a random sample using PPS sampling.

Calculate Sampling Interval

The most common selection method used in PPS sampling is systematic selection. This method divides the total population of dollars into equal intervals of dollars. A logical unit is then systematically selected from each interval. Thus, a **sampling interval (SI)** must be calculated as follows:

$$SI = \frac{BV}{n}$$

In the Harris Company, the sampling interval is $6,818 ($600,000 ÷ 88).

Select Random Sample

The initial step in the selection process is to pick a starting random number between 1 and 6,818. The sample will then include each logical unit that contains every 6,818th dollar thereafter in the population. In the selection process, it is necessary to determine the cumulative balance of the book values of the logical units to determine which logical units are "hooked" or "snagged" by the individu~~ dollar units selected. The process is illustrated for the Harris Company in ~~ 13-7, where (1) the customer account number is used to identify the l~~ and (2) the starting random number is 5,000. Note that the amoun~~ as unit selected column represent every 6,818th dollar after 5,0~~ selected causes the entire book value of the related logi~~ included in the sample. It is important to note that th~~ in the selection of all logical units with book v~~ sampling interval ($6,818 in this case). Thes~~ the auditor can draw a conclusion about th~~

Figure 13-7 ■ Systematic Selection Process

Logical Unit (Customer Number)	Book Value	Cumulative Balance	Dollar Unit Selected	Book Value of "Hooked" Sample Item
			Random start	
01001	$1,200	$1,200	↓	
01025	6,043	7,243 ←	5,000	→ $6,043
01075	2,190	9,433	+6,818	
01140	3,275	12,708 ←	11,818	→ 3,275
01219	980	13,688	+6,818	
01365	1,647	15,335		
01431	4,260	19,595 ←	18,636	→ 4,260
01592	480	20,075	+6,818	
01667	7,150	27,225 ←	25,454	→ 7,150
	•	•	•	•
	•	•	•	•
	•	•	•	•
Total	$600,000			

the auditor will audit every dollar in the sampling interval. Most auditors use generalized audit software to accomplish this task.

Step 7. Apply Audit Procedures

Once the auditor selects a sample, the auditor should apply audit procedures to determine the magnitude of misstatement in the items selected for auditing. In Step 2 the auditor determined the evidence that would support a conclusion about whether the account balance or transaction class was correct or contained a misstatement. If the auditor is sending confirmations, the auditor must use professional judgment to evaluate each confirmation.

Consider the following two example results from sending confirmations at an interim date, 11/30/X5. You confirmed the balance for Customer A with an accounts receivable balance of $30,000 on 11/30/X5, and Customer A confirms that the balance should have been zero. Further investigation shows that Customer A mailed a check on 11/29/X5 that was received by the audit client on 12/3/X5. In other words the check was in the mail, and the audit client had not received it yet. In this case the client's balance of $30,000 is correct. Now consider Customer B who has a $50,000 balance at 11/30/X5 and who confirmed the balance as being $40,000 on their records. Customer B claims that they returned goods worth $10,000 on 11/20/X5. Further investigation shows that the goods were received by the audit client on 11/28/X5 and that the client issued a credit memo on 12/4/X5. This is evidence of a misstatement because the balance as of the confirmation date, 11/31/X5, was misstated. These are examples of how the auditor must use professional judgment in evaluating audit evidence.

In the Harris Company example the auditor has chosen to send confirmations of accounts receivable to 88 customers. As we continue this example, assume that the confirmation of receivables reveals the following misstatements.

CUSTOMER NUMBER	BOOK VALUE (BV)	AUDIT VALUE (AV)
02745	$950	$855
03313	$2,500	$1,250
03922	$7,650	$6,885
04214	$5,300	$5,035
05869	$8,000	$—

Step 8. Evaluate the Sample Results

In evaluating the results of the sample, the auditor calculates an upper misstatement limit (UML) from the sample data and compares it with the tolerable misstatement specified in designing the sample. If UML is less than or equal to tolerable misstatement, the sample results support the conclusion that the population book value is not misstated by more than TM at the specified risk of incorrect acceptance.

The **upper misstatement limit (UML)** is calculated as follows:

$$UML = PM + ASR$$

where

PM = total projected misstatement in the population
ASR = allowance for sampling risk

No Misstatements Found in the Sample

The results of the sample are used to estimate the total **projected misstatement (PM)** in the population. When no misstatements are discovered in the sample, the PM factor in the formula above is zero dollars.

In the case of no misstatements, the **allowance for sampling risk (ASR)** factor consists of one component sometimes referred to as **basic precision (BP)**, which is the amount of estimated misstatement in the population, even if no misstatements are detected in the sample. The amount is obtained by multiplying the reliability factor (RF) for zero misstatements at the specified risk of incorrect acceptance times the sampling interval (SI). Ordinarily, the auditor uses the same risk of incorrect acceptance in this calculation that was specified in determining sample size. Thus, in the Harris Company, basic precision is $20,454, computed as follows:

$$BP = RF_0 \times SI$$
$$= 3.0 \times \$6,818$$
$$= \$20,454$$

Because PM is zero (no misstatements were found in the sample), UML is equal to ASR of $20,454, which is less than the $30,000 TM specified in the sample design. Thus, when no misstatements are found but some were anticipated, the auditor can conclude, without making additional computations, that the book value of the population is not overstated by more than TM. If the auditor chooses to make the above calculation, he or she may state the more precise conclusion that the book value of the population is not overstated by more than $20,454 at a 5 percent risk of incorrect acceptance.

Some Misstatements Found in the Sample

If misstatements are found in the sample, the auditor must calculate both the total projected misstatements in the population and the allowance for sampling risk to determine the upper misstatement limit for overstatements. The UML is then compared with TM.

A projected misstatement (PM) amount is calculated for each logical unit containing a misstatement. These amounts are then summed to arrive at PM for the entire population. The projected misstatement is calculated differently for (1) logical units with book value less than the sampling interval and (2) logical units with book value equal to or greater than the sampling interval.

For each logical unit with a book value less than the sampling interval that contains a misstatement, a tainting percentage (TP) and projected misstatement are calculated as follows:

$$\text{Tainting percentage} = (\text{book value} - \text{audit value}) \div \text{book value}$$
$$\text{Projected misstatement} = \text{tainting percentage} \times \text{sampling interval}$$

The calculations recognize that each logical unit included in the sample represents one sampling interval of the dollars in the population book value. Thus, the degree to which a logical unit is "tainted" with misstatement is projected to all of the dollars in the sampling interval it represents.

For each logical unit for which the book value is equal to or greater than the sampling interval, the projected misstatement is the amount of misstatement found in the unit (book value − audit value). Because the logical unit itself is equal to or greater than the sampling interval, a tainting percentage to project the misstatement to the interval is unnecessary. Rather, the actual amounts of such misstatements are used in arriving at PM for the population as a whole.

To illustrate, assume the PPS sample of the Harris Company's accounts receivable reveals the following misstatements:

BOOK VALUE (BV)	AUDIT VALUE (AV)	TAINTING PERCENTAGE [(BV − AV)/BV]	SAMPLING INTERVAL (SI)	PROJECTED MISSTATEMENT TP × SI OR (BV − AV)
$950	$855	10%	$6,818	$682
$2,500	$1,250	50%	$6,818	$3,409
$7,650	$6,885	N/A*	N/A*	$765
$5,300	$5,035	5%	$6,818	$341
$8,000	—	N/A*	N/A*	$8,000
				$13,197

* Logical unit is greater than sampling interval; therefore, projected misstatement equals actual misstatement (*BV − AV*).

Note that the first, second, and fourth logical units containing misstatements have book values less than the sampling interval. Accordingly, TPs have been calculated and used to determine the projected misstatements. The third and fifth units have book values greater than the sampling interval. Therefore, the projected misstatement for each is the difference between the book value and the audit value. The total misstatement in the sample is $10,375 ($24,400 − $14,025), and the total PM in the population is $13,197.

The allowance for sampling risk (ASR) for samples containing misstatements has two components, as indicated in the following formula:

$$ASR = BP + IA$$

where

   BP = basic precision

   IA = incremental allowance for sampling risk

The calculation of BP is the same whether or not there are misstatements found in the sample. Thus, in the Harris Company, this component is again $20,454, based on the RF of 3.0 (for zero errors and a 5 percent risk of incorrect acceptance) times the SI of $6,818.

To calculate the incremental allowance for sampling risk (IA), the auditor must consider separately the logical units with book values less than the sampling interval and those with book values equal to or greater than the sampling interval. Because all logical units equal to or greater than the sampling interval will have been examined 100 percent, and the auditor can draw a conclusion about these sampling intervals with certainty, there is no sampling risk associated with them. Consequently, the calculation of IA involves only misstatements related to logical units with book values less than the sampling interval.

The calculation of IA involves the following steps:

- Determine the appropriate incremental change in reliability factors.
- Rank the projected misstatements for logical units less than the sampling interval from highest to lowest.
- Multiply the ranked projected misstatements by the appropriate factor and sum the products.

The following tabulation illustrates the first step:

		5% RISK OF INCORRECT ACCEPTANCE	
NUMBER OF OVERSTATEMENTS	RELIABILITY FACTOR	INCREMENTAL CHANGE IN RELIABILITY FACTOR	INCREMENTAL CHANGE IN RELIABILITY FACTOR MINUS ONE
0	3.00	—	—
1	4.75	1.75	0.75
2	6.30	1.55	0.55
3	7.76	1.46	0.46
4	9.16	1.40	0.40

The data in the first two columns above are taken from Figure 13-8 for the specified risk of incorrect acceptance (5 percent in this illustration). Each entry in the third column is the reliability factor on the same line less the reliability factor on the previous line. The column 4 factors are obtained by subtracting one from each of the column 3 factors.

Figure 13-8 ■ Reliability Factors for Evaluating PPS Samples

Number of Overstatements	Reliability Factors for Overstatements								
	Risk of Incorrect Acceptance								
	1%	5%	10%	13%	15%	20%	25%	30%	37%
0	4.61	3.00	2.31	2.00	1.90	1.16	1.39	1.21	1.0
1	6.64	4.75	3.89	3.56	3.38	3.00	2.70	2.44	2.1
2	8.41	6.30	5.33	4.94	4.72	4.28	3.93	3.62	3.2
3	10.05	7.76	6.69	6.25	6.02	5.52	5.11	4.77	4.3
4	11.61	9.16	8.00	7.53	7.27	6.73	6.28	5.90	5.4
5	13.11	10.52	9.28	8.77	8.50	7.91	7.43	7.01	6.4
6	14.57	11.85	10.54	10.00	9.71	9.08	8.56	8.12	7.5
7	16.00	13.15	11.78	11.21	10.90	10.24	9.69	9.21	8.6
8	17.41	14.44	13.00	12.41	12.08	11.38	10.81	10.31	9.6
9	18.79	15.71	14.21	13.59	13.25	12.52	11.92	11.39	10.7
10	20.15	16.97	15.41	14.77	14.42	13.66	13.02	12.47	11.7

Source: AICPA *Audit and Accounting Guide: Audit Sampling.*

The second and third steps are illustrated below.

RANKED PROJECTED MISSTATEMENTS	INCREMENTAL CHANGE IN RELIABILITY FACTOR MINUS ONE	INCREMENTAL ALLOWANCE
$3,409	0.75	$2,557
682	0.55	375
341	0.46	157
		$3,089

Observe that (1) only the projected misstatements from the tabulation on page 576 for logical units with book values less than the sampling interval are ranked and (2) the appropriate reliability factor is obtained from column 4 of the tabulation illustrated above. The incremental allowances for the projected misstatements are then added to determine the total incremental allowance of $3,089. Thus, the total allowance for sampling risk in the Harris Company is $23,543, computed as follows:

BP	$20,454
IA	$3,089
ASR	$23,543

The UML equals the sum of PM and ASR. For the Harris sample, the UML is:

PM	$13,197
ASR	$23,543
UML	$36,740

Thus, the auditor may conclude (a quantitative conclusion) that the book value is not overstated by more than $36,740 at a 5 percent risk of incorrect acceptance. In the Harris sample, the UML exceeds the TM of $30,000 specified in designing the sample. When this occurs, the auditor should consider several possible reasons and alternative courses of action. These matters are discussed further below.

Qualitative Considerations

Whether UML is less than, equal to, or greater than TM, certain qualitative considerations should be made prior to reaching an overall conclusion. Misstatements may be due to (1) differences in principle or application or (2) errors or (3) fraud. Consideration should also be given to the relationship of the misstatements to other phases of the audit. For example, if misstatements are discovered in substantive tests in amounts or frequency greater than implied by the assessed level of control risk used in arriving at the risk of incorrect acceptance specified for the sample, the auditor should consider whether that assessment is still appropriate. If it is not appropriate, the auditor should redesign the sampling plan. If the auditor detects fraud in the sample, the auditor may want to perform additional procedures, even if the amount of the UML is less than tolerable misstatement. The nature of the fraud, particularly evidence of management fraud, may cause the auditor to change the scope of audit procedure for other aspects of the audit.

The auditor uses professional judgment in combining evidence from several sources to reach an overall conclusion about whether an account balance is free from material misstatement. When (1) the results of a PPS sample reveal the UML to be less than or equal to TM, (2) the results of other substantive tests do not contradict this finding, and (3) analysis of the qualitative considerations reveals no evidence of fraud, the auditor can generally conclude that the population is not materially misstated. When any of these conditions do not hold, further evaluation of the circumstances is necessary.

For example, if the UML is greater than TM, the auditor should consider the following possible reasons and actions:

- The sample is not representative of the population. The auditor might suspect this is the case when the sample contains immaterial misstatements that result in a projected UML that exceeds tolerable misstatement. In this case, the auditor might examine additional sampling units or perform alternative procedures to determine whether the population is misstated.[2]

- The amount of anticipated misstatement specified in designing the sample may not have been large enough relative to tolerable misstatement to adequately limit the allowance for sampling risk. That is, the population may not be misstated by more than TM, but because the amount of misstatement in the population is greater than anticipated, more precise information is needed from the sample. In this situation, the auditor may examine additional sampling units and reevaluate or perform alternative auditing procedures to determine whether the population is misstated by more than TM.

---

[2] A simple way to expand the sample is to divide the sampling interval in half. This will produce a sample containing all the units in the original sample plus an equal number of additional units. Other methods of expanding the sample size are beyond the scope of this text.

■ The population may be misstated by more than TM. The auditor may request that the client investigate the misstatements and, if appropriate, adjust the book value.

As a result of any of these courses of action, the client's book value might be adjusted. If the UML after adjustment is less than TM, the sample results would support the conclusion that the population, as adjusted, is not misstated by more than TM at the specified risk of incorrect acceptance. For example, in the Harris sample, one receivable with a book value of $8,000 was found to have an audit value of zero. If this account were written off, the PM for the population would be reduced by $8,000 to $5,197. The allowance for sampling risk would remain the same at $23,543, and UML would become $28,740 ($36,740 − $8,000), which is less than the $30,000 TM specified in designing the sample.

Step 9. Document Conclusions

Figure 13-9 illustrates how the application of PPS sampling in the audit of Harris Company's receivables may be documented. This example shows how the sample was designed, the specific audit evidence that was obtained, and the conclusions that were reached about the account balance. The working papers also make cross references to other working papers where important audit planning decisions, or other audit evidence, is documented.

[LEARNING CHECK

13-10 Explain several situations where the concepts of audit sampling do not apply to substantive tests.

13-11 List the steps involved in selecting and evaluating a nonstatistical or a statistical sample for substantive tests. Identify the professional judgment that must be made in each step.

13-12 Assume that you are auditing a client with a warehouse and three retail stores.
a. Explain two different ways that you might define the population.
b. Explain two different ways that you might define the sampling unit.

13-13 Explain the advantages and disadvantages associated with PPS sampling.

13-14 a. Distinguish between the sampling unit and the logical sampling unit in a PPS sample.
b. Why do units with zero balances and credit balances require special consideration in PPS sampling?

13-15 a. Give the formula for calculating sample size in PPS sampling.
b. Explain what each element in the formula represents and how a change in that element, other things constant, affects sample size.

13-16 What role does the specification of anticipated misstatement play in designing a PPS sample?

13-17 What three factors are considered in evaluating a PPS sample?

13-18 What are the two components of the allowance for sampling risk for PPS samples?

13-19 Explain the terms *tainting percentage* and *projected misstatement* as they pertain to individual items in a PPS sample.

Figure 13-9 ■ PPS Sampling Plan Working Paper

Harris Company
PPS Sample – Accounts Receivable
December 31, 20X1

W/P Ref. B-2
Prepared By: *W.C.B.*   Date: *1/22/X2*
Reviewed By: *R.E.Z.*   Date: *1/25/X2*

Objective: To obtain evidence that the aggregate book value of customer accounts with debit balances as of 12/31/X1 was not materially misstated.

Population and Sampling Unit: Total book value of accounts receivable with debit balances per master file. Logical sampling unit is the customer account.

Sample Size:

Book Value of the Population		$ 600,000 (BV)	
Risk of Incorrect Acceptance	*GF ~ 8*	5%	RF = 3.00
Tolerable Misstatement	*GF ~ 4*	$ 30,000 (TM)	
Anticipated Misstatement		$ 6,000 (AM)	EF = 1.60
Samples Size		88 (n)	

Sample Selection:

Sampling Interval = BV/n $ 6,818
Random Start $ 5,000
Logical sampling Sampling Units Selected Listed on W/P   B ~ 3

Evaluation of Sampling Plan:

Audit Procedures Applied Listed on W/P   *B ~ 1*
Book and Audit Values for Sample Items with Misstatements Listed Below

Evaluation of Sample Results

Projected Misstatement:

	Book Value BV	Audit Value AV	Tainting (BV – AV)/BV	Sampling Interval (SI)	Projected Misstatement TP * SI or (BV – AV)
1	$ 950	$ 855	10.0%	$ 6,818	$ 682
2	$ 2,500	$ 1,250	50.0%	$ 6,818	$ 3,409
3	$ 7,650	$ 6,885	10.0%	N/A	$ 765
4	$ 5,300	$ 5,035	5.0%	$ 6,818	$ 341
5	$ 8,000	$ –	100.0%	N/A	$ 8,000
					$ 13,197 (PM)

Allowance for Sampling Risk:
Basic Precision = RF * SI $ 20,454 (BP)

Incremental Allowance for Sampling Risk:

	Ranked Projected Misstatements	Incremental Change in Reliability Factor Minus One	
1	$ 3,409	0.75	$ 2,557
2	$ 682	0.55	$ 375
3	$ 341	0.46	$ 157
4	$ –	0.40	$ –
5	$ –	0.36	$ –
			$3,089 (IA)

Upper Misstatement Limit (PM + BP + IA) $ 36,739 (UML > TM)

Conclusion: *The UML of $36,740 exceeds TM of 30,000. Client subsequently agreed to write off one account with a book value of $8,000 and an audit value of zero. This reduces both PM and UML by $8,000, making UML $28,740 which is less than TM. See adjusting entry on w/p AE-1. After the client adjustment the results support a conclusion that the aggregate book value of customer accounts with debit balances, as adjusted, is materially correct.*

KEY TERMS

Allowance for sampling risk (ASR),
  p. 575
Anticipated misstatement (AM),
  p. 512
Basic precision (BP), p. 575
Expansion factor (EF), p. 572
Logical sampling unit, p. 570
Population, p. 569
PPS sampling, p. 568
Projected misstatement (PM), p. 575

Reciprocal population, p. 570
Reliability factor (RF), p. 571
Risk of incorrect acceptance, p. 571
Sampling interval (SI), p. 573
Sampling risk, p. 573
Sampling unit, p. 569
Tolerable misstatement (TM), p. 572
Upper misstatement limit (UML),
  p. 575

SUMMARY

Figure 13-10 summarizes the key steps in audit sampling for both tests of controls and for substantive tests. The body of the chapter explains these steps as they apply to nonstatistical sampling for tests of controls and to probability proportionate to size sampling. Additional applications of audit sampling are discussed in the appendices to this chapter, including the uses of statistical tests of controls (Appendix 13A), statistical mean per unit sampling (Appendix 13B) and nonstatistical sampling for substantive tests (Appendix 13C).

Figure 13-10 ■ Summary of the Steps Involved in Tests of Controls in Substantive Tests

	Tests of Controls (Nonstatistical)	Substantive Tests (Using PPS Sampling)
Step 1: Determine Audit Objectives	The purpose of a test of controls is to estimate the rate of deviations from prescribed controls in a population. At this stage the auditor should test key controls that allow the auditor to modify the nature, timing, or extent of substantive tests (see pp. 559).	A substantive test may be used either to estimate the dollar amount of a population or the dollar amount of misstatement in a population. PPS sampling is used for the later objective (see p. 567).
Step 2: Determine Procedures to Meet Audit Objectives	The auditor must use professional judgment to determine the procedures that will provide evidence about the operating effectiveness of key controls (see p. 560).	The auditor must use professional judgment to determine the procedures that will provide evidence about whether items in the population contain misstatements (see p. 568).
Step 3: Determine Type of Sampling to Be Used	Nonstatistical sampling for tests of controls is most appropriate where population sizes are small, such as when testing manual followup procedures (see pp. 560–561).	PPS sampling is an effective statistical tool to estimate the amount of misstatement in the population. The advantages and disadvantage of various sampling methods are discussed on the following pages. • PPS Sampling (p. 568) • Statistical MPU Estimation (p. 594) • Nonstatistical sampling (p. 604)

(continues)

Figure 13-10 ■ (Continued)

	Tests of Controls (Nonstatistical)	Substantive Tests (Using PPS Sampling)
Step 4: Define the Population and Sampling Unit	The population is defined by the internal control of interest and represents all situations when the control should be performed. The sampling unit usually identifies individual instances of the control being performed (see p. 561).	The account balance or class of transaction to be tested defines the population. A detailed discussion of how PPS sampling defines a logical sampling unit is provided on p. 569.
Step 5: Determine Sample Size	Sample size is influenced by the auditor's judgments about (see pp. 561–564): • The nature of the control • The frequency of operation of the control. • The importance of the control. • The risk of assessing control risk too low • The tolerable deviation rate • The expected deviation rate • Population size for small populations (below 5,000)	Sample size is influenced by the auditor's judgments about (see p. 571): • The book value of the population • The risk of incorrect acceptance • Tolerable misstatement • Anticipated misstatement
Step 6: Select Representative Sample	The auditor should use professional judgment to select a representative sample of the operation of the control (see p. 564).	The auditor should obtain an unbiased sample using a random sampling plan. A detailed discussion of how PPS sampling selects logical sampling units is provided on pp. 573–574).
Step 7: Apply Audit Procedures	The auditor should apply the audit procedures determined in step 2 (see pp. 564–565).	The auditor should apply the audit procedures determined in step 2 (see pp. 574–575).
Step 8: Evaluate Results	Evaluating results involves estimating the deviation rate based on sample evidence and comparing it with the tolerable rate (see p. 565).	Evaluating results involves estimating the amount of misstatement in the population based on sample evidence and comparing it with tolerable misstatement (see pp. 575–580).
Step 9: Document Conclusions	The auditor's working papers should document the auditor's conclusion about the level of control risk and the basis for that conclusion (see p. 566).	The auditor's working papers should document the auditor's conclusion about the estimated amount of misstatement in the population. An example is provided in Figure 13-9 (see p. 581).

[FOCUS ON AUDITOR KNOWLEDGE AND AUDIT DECISIONS]

This chapter focuses on audit sampling. In making decisions to support high-quality audit work, the auditor must be able to use the knowledge summarized in Figure 13-11 and address the decisions summarized in Figure 13-12. Page references indicate where these issues are discussed in more detail.

Figure 13-11 ■ Summary of Auditor Knowledge Discussed in Chapter 13

Auditor Knowledge	Summary	Chapter References
K1. Know the definition of audit sampling and when it applies.	Audit sampling refers to the application of audit procedures to less than 100 percent of the items in an account balance or transaction class for the purpose of evaluating some characteristic of the entire class. The risk associated with audit sampling is part of the inherent uncertainty associated with overall audit risk.	p. 553
K2. Understand the relationship of generally accepted auditing standards to audit sampling.	Both the second and the third fieldwork standards contain an element of uncertainty. In drawing a conclusion about control risk or detection risk, the auditor is only required to have a reasonable basis for an opinion.	p. 553
K3. Understand the difference between sampling and nonsampling risk and know the four types of sampling risk.	Sampling risk relates to the possibility that a properly drawn sample may not be representative of the population. Nonsampling risk refers to the portion of audit risk that is not due to examining only a portion of the data, including human mistakes, applying auditing procedures inappropriate to the audit objective, misinterpreting the results of a sample, and relying on erroneous information. The two types of sampling risk related to tests of controls are the risk of assessing control risk too low (which relates to audit effectiveness) and the risk of assessing control risk too high (which relates to audit efficiency). The two types of sampling risk related to substantive tests are the risk of incorrect acceptance (which relates to audit effectiveness) and the risk of incorrect rejection (which relates to audit efficiency).	pp. 553–555
K4. Know the similarities and differences between nonstatistical and statistical sampling.	Both statistical and nonstatistical sampling are subject to both sampling risk and nonsampling risk. The methodologies are similar in either approach, and the auditor should consider the same judgments when planning and performing an audit sample. However, when the auditor uses statistical sampling, the auditor has the benefit of using the laws of probability to determine an efficient sample size and to project sample results on the population.	pp. 555–558

Figure 13-12 ■ Summary of Audit Decisions Discussed in Chapter 13

Audit Decision	Factors that Influence the Audit Decision	Chapter References
D1. When do the concepts of audit sampling not apply to tests of controls?	When performing tests of controls, the concepts associated with audit sampling generally do not apply when the auditor uses inquiry and observation and when the auditor tests computer application controls. Many tests of computer application controls can be tested with only two tests of each programmed decision (one to see that the program properly processes transaction and one to see that it properly rejects a transaction). In addition, the concepts associated with inquiry and observation apply to application controls that produce error messages on computer screens.	pp. 558–559

(continues)

Figure 13-12 ■ (Continued)

Audit Decision	Factors that Influence the Audit Decision	Chapter References
D2. What are the important audit judgments in applying audit sampling to tests of controls?	Figure 13-10 summarizes the steps in applying audit sampling to tests of controls, including the key audit judgments that must be made in implementing a sampling plan for tests of controls.	pp. 559–560
D3. When do the concepts of audit sampling not apply to substantive tests?	Audit sampling may not apply to initial procedures, substantive analytical procedures, tests of details of accounting estimates, and tests of details of disclosures. In these cases the auditor is usually not auditing less than 100 percent of a population for the purpose of drawing a conclusion about the population.	pp. 566–567
D4. What are the important audit judgments in applying probability proportionate to size sampling for substantive tests?	Figure 13-10 summarizes the steps in applying audit sampling to probability proportionate to size sampling, including the key audit judgments that must be made in implementing this sampling plan for substantive tests.	pp. 567–581

appendix 13a

STATISTICAL ATTRIBUTE SAMPLING FOR TESTS OF CONTROLS

Chapter 13 introduced a method for selecting and evaluating audit samples for tests of controls that include the following steps.

1. Determine the test objectives.
2. Determine procedures to meet objectives, including evidence that the control was effective or ineffective.
3. Make a decision about the audit sampling technique.
4. Define the population and sampling unit.
5. Determine the sample size.
6. Select a representative sample.
7. Apply audit procedures.
8. Evaluate the sample results.
9. Document conclusions.

These steps were discussed on page 557. If, in step 3, the auditor determines that it is appropriate to test manual controls with statistical attribute sampling, the auditor may use statistics in step 5 to determine sample size and use statistics again in step 8 to evaluate sample results.

Assume that the client has manual controls as described in Figure 13-13. The following discussion will focus on step 5, determination of sample size; step 8, evaluation of sample results; and step 9, documentation of conclusions.

Figure 13-13 ■ Attributes to Be Tested

Attribute	Description of Attribute
1.	Approval of credit by authorized credit department personnel.
2.	Authorization of sale by appropriate sales order department personnel.
3.	Shipping department verification of goods shipped with sales order.

Step 5. Determine the Sample Size

In order to determine a sample size for each attribute or control to be tested, the auditor must specify a numerical value for each of the following factors:

- Risk of assessing control risk too low
- Tolerable deviation rate
- Expected population deviation rate

In addition, when sampling from a small population (fewer than 5,000 units), the population size must be approximated as explained further in a later section.

These factors influence sample size in the following way. As explained earlier, two types of sampling risk are associated with tests of controls: (1) the risk of assessing control risk too high, which relates to the efficiency of the audit, and (2) the risk of assessing control risk too low, which relates to the effectiveness of the audit. Because of the potentially serious consequences associated with an ineffective audit, the auditor desires to keep the risk of assessing control risk too low at a low level. In attribute sampling, the **risk of assessing control risk too low** must be stated explicitly.[3] Many auditors specify one level of this risk, such as 5 percent, for all tests of controls. Alternatively, other auditors vary the risk level directly with planned control risk as illustrated below.

PLANNED CONTROL RISK	RISK OF ASSESSING CONTROL RISK TOO LOW
Low	5 %
Moderate	10 %
High	15 %

Another important decision is the auditor's decision about **tolerable deviation rate,** which is the maximum rate of deviation from a control that an auditor is willing to accept and still use the planned control risk. The AICPA *Audit Sam-*

---

[3] The factor reliability or confidence level is sometimes used in attribute sampling. This factor is the complement of the risk of assessing control risk to low. Thus, specifying 95 percent reliability is the equivalent of a 5 percent risk of assessing control risk too low.

pling Guide includes the following guidelines for quantifying an acceptable range for the tolerable deviation rate:

Planned Control Risk	Range of Tolerable Deviation Rate
Low	2%–7%
Moderate	6%–12%
High	11%–20%

The auditor should estimate the **expected population deviation rate,** which is the auditor's best guess of the actual deviation rate in the population.

The following discussion examines the mechanical process of using tables to determine sample size based on the three factors listed above. We will then consider how the auditor determines a value for each of the factors, and explore how a change in the value of each factor affects sample size when the other factors are held constant.

Sample Size Tables

Figure 13-14 illustrates one type of table the auditor can use to determine sample size. Notice that the figure contains two tables: Table 1 for a 5 percent risk of assessing control risk too low and Table 2 for a 10 percent risk of assessing control risk too low. To use the tables, it is necessary to

- Select the table that corresponds to the specified risk of assessing control risk too low.
- Locate the column that pertains to the specified tolerable deviation rate.
- Locate the row that contains the expected population deviation rate.
- Read the sample size from the intersection of the column and row determined in steps two and three.

For practice in using the tables, the student should verify the sample sizes shown in column 4 of the following tabulation by looking up the values of the factors specified in columns 1 to 3:

Risk of Assessing Control Risk Too Low (%)	Tolerable Deviation Rate (%)	Expected Population Deviation Rate (%)	Sample Size
5	5	1.0	93
5	5	0.0	59
10	7	1.0	55
10	7	0.0	32

Tables for additional values of the risk of assessing control risk too low are available. Many auditors now enter the values for the factors that determine sample size into personal computer software to determine the appropriate sample size instead of using printed tables.

Figure 13-14 ■ Sample Size Tables for Statistical Attribute Sampling

Statistical sample sizes for tests of controls (for populations > 5,000 units)

Table 1. 5% risk of assessing control risk too low

Expected population deviation rate %	Tolerable deviation rate								
	2%	3%	4%	5%	6%	7%	8%	9%	10%
0.00	149	99	74	59	49	42	36	32	29
0.50	*	157	117	93	78	66	58	51	46
1.00	*	*	156	93	78	66	58	51	46
1.50	*	*	192	124	103	66	58	51	46
2.00	*	*	*	181	127	88	77	68	46
2.50	*	*	*	*	150	109	77	68	61
3.00	*	*	*	*	195	129	95	84	61
4.00	*	*	*	*	*	*	146	100	89
5.00	*	*	*	*	*	*	*	158	116
6.00	*	*	*	*	*	*	*	*	179

Table 2. 10% risk of assessing control risk too low

Expected population deviation rate %	Tolerable deviation rate								
	2%	3%	4%	5%	6%	7%	8%	9%	10%
0.00	114	76	57	45	38	32	28	25	22
0.50	194	129	96	77	64	55	48	42	38
1.00	*	176	96	77	64	55	48	42	38
1.50	*	*	132	105	64	55	48	42	38
2.00	*	*	198	132	88	75	48	42	38
2.50	*	*	*	158	110	75	65	58	38
3.00	*	*	*	*	132	94	65	58	52
4.00	*	*	*	*	*	149	98	73	65
5.00	*	*	*	*	*	*	160	115	78
6.00	*	*	*	*	*	*	*	182	116

* Sample size is too large to be cost-effective for most audit applications
Source AICPA, *Audit and Accounting Guide: Audit Sampling*, pp. 106–107. (adapted)

Step 8. Evaluate the Sample Results

Deviations found in the sample must be tabulated, summarized, and evaluated. Professional judgment is required in the evaluation of the following factors leading to an overall conclusion.

Calculate the Sample Deviation Rate

A **sample deviation rate** for each control tested is calculated by dividing the number of deviations found by the sample size examined. This rate is the auditor's estimate of the deviation rate in the population based on sample results.

Determine the Upper Deviation Limit

The **upper deviation limit** indicates the maximum deviation rate in the population based on the number of deviations discovered in the sample. The upper limit is expressed as a percentage, which is sometimes alternately referred to as the achieved upper precision limit or maximum population deviation rate.

The upper deviation limit is determined from evaluation tables like those shown in Figure 13-15. To use the tables, it is necessary for the auditor to:

- Select the table that corresponds to the risk of assessing control risk too low.
- Locate the column that contains the actual number of deviations (not the deviation rate) found in the sample.
- Locate the row that contains the sample size used.
- Read the upper deviation limit from the intersection of the column and row determined in steps 2 and 3.[4]

Illustrative upper deviation limits are as follows:

RISK OF ASSESSING CONTROL RISK TOO LOW (%)	NUMBER OF DEVIATIONS	SAMPLE SIZE	UPPER DEVIATION LIMIT (%)
5	1	100	4.7
5	2	150	4.1
10	3	120	5.5
10	4	200	4.0

When the sample size used does not appear in the evaluation tables, the auditor may (1) use the largest sample size in the table, not exceeding the actual sample size used, (2) interpolate, (3) obtain more extensive tables, or (4) use a computer program that will produce an upper limit for any sample size. The upper deviation limit determined from tables implicitly includes an allowance for sampling risk. Thus, the upper deviation limit can be used to determine whether a sample supports planned control risk. If the upper deviation limit is less than or

---

[4] It may be observed that both the evaluation tables in Figure 13-15 and the sample size tables are based on a one-tailed rather than two-tailed statistical test. This is because the auditor is not concerned about the lower bound on the population deviation rate. Instead, the auditor is concerned only that the actual population deviation rate does not exceed an upper bound defined as the tolerable deviation rate.

equal to the tolerable deviation rate specified in designing the sample, the results support planned control risk. Otherwise, the results do not support planned control risk.

Determine the Allowance for Sampling Risk

It will be recalled that sampling risk relates to the possibility that a properly drawn sample may nonetheless not be representative of the population. As indicated above, the evaluation of a sample can be made without explicitly calculating the allowance for sampling risk. However, knowing how the allowance can be determined is helpful in the evaluation process. The allowance for sampling risk is added to the sample deviation rate to produce an upper deviation limit that will exceed the true population deviation rate a known proportion of the time. When evaluation tables are used, the **allowance for sampling risk** is determined by subtracting the sample deviation rate from the upper deviation limit. Thus, in the first case above, the sample deviation rate is 1 percent (1/100) and the allowance is 3.7 percent (4.7% – 1.0%).[5] If three deviations had been found in the sample of 100, the upper deviation limit would be 7.6 percent, the sample deviation rate would be 3 percent (3/100), and the allowance for sampling risk would be 4.6 percent (7.6% – 3.0%).

The allowance for sampling risk is directly related to the number of deviations found in the sample as illustrated by the increase from 3.7 to 4.6 percent in this example. It follows, in statistical sampling, that when the sample deviation rate exceeds the expected population deviation rate, the allowance for sampling risk will be large enough to cause the upper deviation limit to exceed the tolerable deviation rate specified in designing the sample. Thus, the following generalizations can be stated:

■ Whenever the sample deviation rate exceeds the expected population deviation rate used to determine sample size, the upper deviation limit will exceed the tolerable deviation rate at the specified risk of assessing control risk too low and the sample results will not support planned control risk.

■ Conversely, whenever the sample deviation rate is less than or equal to the expected population deviation rate, the upper deviation limit will be less than or equal to the tolerable deviation rate at the specified risk of assessing control risk too low and the sample results will support planned control risk.

Step 9. Document Conclusions

The basis for the auditor's evaluation should be documented in the working papers. The working paper in Figure 13-16 permits an evaluation using either the upper deviation limit or the sample deviation rate. Recall that when the auditor assesses control risk below the maximum the auditor should document both the conclusion about control risk and the basis for the conclusion. Note that the working paper in Figure 13-16 states the basis for the conclusion by showing the results of the sample. It also states a conclusion about control risk. Control risk is assessed

---

[5] The allowance for sampling risk can also be computed directly using binomial probability distribution theory.

Figure 13-15 ■ Statistical Attribute Sampling Evaluation Tables

Statistical Sample Results Evaluation Table for Tests of Controls Upper Deviation Limit (Popn. > 5,000 units)

Table 3.   5% risk of assessing control risk too low

Sample Size	Actual Number of Deviations Found								
	0	1	2	3	4	5	6	7	8
25	11.3	17.6	*	*	*	*	*	*	*
30	9.5	14.9	19.5	*	*	*	*	*	*
35	8.2	12.9	16.9	*	*	*	*	*	*
40	7.2	11.3	14.9	18.3	*	*	*	*	*
45	6.4	10.3	13.3	16.3	19.2	*	*	*	*
50	5.8	9.1	12.1	14.8	17.4	19.9	*	*	*
55	5.3	8.3	11.0	13.5	15.9	18.1	*	*	*
60	4.9	7.7	10.1	12.4	14.6	16.7	18.8	*	*
65	4.5	7.1	9.4	11.5	13.5	15.5	17.4	19.3	*
70	4.2	6.6	8.7	10.7	12.6	14.4	16.2	18.0	19.7
75	3.9	6.2	8.2	10.0	11.8	13.5	15.2	16.9	18.4
80	3.7	5.8	7.7	9.4	11.1	12.7	14.3	15.8	17.3
90	3.3	5.2	6.8	8.4	9.1	11.3	12.7	14.1	15.5
100	3.0	4.7	6.2	7.6	8.9	10.2	11.5	12.7	14.0
125	2.4	3.7	4.9	6.1	7.2	8.2	9.3	10.3	11.3
150	2.0	3.1	4.1	5.1	6.0	6.9	7.7	8.6	9.4
200	1.5	2.3	3.1	3.8	4.5	5.2	5.8	6.5	7.1

Table 4.   10% risk of assessing control risk too low

Sample Size	Actual Number of Deviations Found								
	0	1	2	3	4	5	6	7	8
20	10.9	18.1	*	*	*	*	*	*	*
25	8.8	14.7	19.9	*	*	*	*	*	*
30	7.4	12.4	16.8	*	*	*	*	*	*
35	6.4	10.7	14.5	18.1	*	*	*	*	*
40	5.6	9.4	12.8	15.9	19.0	*	*	*	*
45	5.0	8.4	11.4	14.2	17.0	19.6	*	*	*
50	4.5	7.6	10.3	12.9	15.4	17.8	*	*	*
55	4.1	6.9	9.4	11.7	14.0	16.2	18.4	*	*
60	3.8	6.3	8.6	10.8	12.9	14.9	16.9	18.8	*
70	3.2	5.4	7.4	9.3	11.1	12.8	14.6	16.2	17.9
80	2.8	4.8	6.5	8.3	9.7	11.3	12.8	14.3	15.7
90	2.5	4.3	5.8	7.3	8.7	10.1	11.4	12.7	14.0
100	2.3	3.8	5.2	6.6	7.8	9.1	10.3	11.5	12.7
120	1.9	3.2	4.4	5.5	6.6	7.6	8.6	9.6	10.6
160	1.4	2.4	3.3	4.1	4.9	5.7	6.5	7.2	8.0
200	1.1	1.9	2.6	3.3	4.0	4.6	5.2	5.8	6.4

* Over 20%.
Source: AICPA, *Audit and Accounting Guide: Audit Sampling*, pp. 108–109 (adapted).

Figure 13-16 ■ Attribute Sampling Plan Working Paper

W/P Ref. H – 2

Prepared By: C.J.G.   Date: 10/6/x4

Reviewed By: R.C.P.   Date: 10/6/x4

Amalgamated Products, Inc.
Attribute Sampling – Sales Transactions
Year Ending December 31, 20X4

Objective: To test effectiveness of controls related to authorization controls and existence of sales.

Sampling Unit: The line item in the sales journal.

Selection Method: Random; Computer Generated List

(1) Attribute Description	(2) Risk of Assessing CR Too Low	(3) Tolerable Deviation Rate	(4) Exptd. Popn. Deviation Rate	(5) Sample Size per Table	(7) Number of Deviations	(8) Sample Deviation Limit	(9) Upper Deviation Limit	(10) Allowance for Sampling Risk	(11) Test UDL <= TDR
Approval of credit by authorized credit department personnel	5	7	0.5	66	2	3.0	9.7	6.7	NO
Authorization of sale by appropriate sales order department personnel	5	7	0.5	66	0	0.0	4.6	4.6	YES
Shipping department verification of goods shipped with sales order	5	7	0.5	66	0	0.0	4.6	4.6	YES

Conclusion: *Planned control risk assessment of low is supported for all controls except approval of credit (where control risk is assessed at moderate). Effect on planned control risk, detection risk, and substantive tests is documented on W/P H-4.*

Management Communication: *Deviations related to approval of credit represent a significant deficiency in internal control, which is included in draft management letter comment on W/P GF – 10. This will be communicated to both management and the audit committee.*

at low for two attributes and at moderate for one attribute. The working paper makes cross-references to W/P H-4 where the relationship between control risk and detection risk is discussed. This working paper also makes cross-reference to the general file where management letter comments are collected about significant deficiencies in internal control.

LEARNING CHECK

13A-1 a. Describe the factors that influence sample size when using statistical attribute sampling for tests of controls.

b. Explain two ways that an auditor might determine the risk of assessing control risk too low.

c. If the auditor wants to achieve a low control risk assessment, what is an appropriate tolerable deviation rate?

d. Explain the logic behind using a sample size of 59 for a statistical attribute sample.

13A-2 a. Identify the three steps involved in quantitatively evaluating sample results.

b. Indicate the steps involved in using sample evaluation tables.

c. If an auditor uses a sample size of 59 and finds one deviation from the prescribed control procedure, what can the auditor conclude?

13A-3 a. What factors should be considered in qualitatively evaluating sample results?

b. What alternative courses of action should be considered when sample results do not support the auditor's planned control risk?

KEY TERMS

Allowance for sampling risk, p. 590
Expected population deviation rate,
  p. 587
Risk of assessing control risk too low,
  p. 586

Tolerable deviation rate, p. 586
Sample deviation rate, p. 589
Upper deviation limit, p. 589

---

appendix 13b

CLASSICAL VARIABLES SAMPLING MEAN-PER-UNIT ESTIMATION

The auditor may use a classical variables sampling approach in substantive testing. Under this approach, normal distribution theory is used in evaluating the characteristics of a population based on the results of a sample drawn from the population.

MPU estimation sampling involves determining an audit value for each item in the sample. An average of these audit values is then calculated and multiplied by the number of units in the population to obtain an estimate of the total population value. An allowance for sampling risk associated with this estimate is also calculated for use in evaluating the sample results.

Steps 1 and 2. Determine the Audit Objectives and Audit Procedures

The objective of an MPU sampling plan may be to (1) obtain evidence that a recorded account balance is not materially misstated or (2) develop an independent estimate of an amount when no recorded book value is available. For illustrative purposes, it is assumed that the auditor seeks to obtain evidence that the recorded account balance for loans receivable in the Ace Finance Company is materially correct. The auditor might audit the existence and valuation at historical cost of loans receivable by sending confirmations to borrowers.

Step 3. Determine the Sampling Technique

Mean-per-unit estimation is most effective when the auditor does not have the book value of individual items in the sample, and the auditor wants to estimate the value of the total population. Classical variables sampling may be useful to the auditor when the audit objective relates to either the possible under- or overstatement of an account balance and other circumstances when PPS sampling is not appropriate or cost effective. The auditor may also choose to apply this technique when book values are available, although this is not a requirement for the statistical test.

Step 4. Define the Population and Sampling Unit

In defining the **population,** the auditor should consider the nature of the items comprising the population and whether all items should be eligible for inclusion in the sample. It is not necessary, however, to verify that the book values for the individual items sum to the total recorded book value of the population because the individual book values are not a variable in MPU calculations.

The **sampling unit** should be compatible with the audit objective and the auditing procedures to be performed. For example, if the objective is to determine that the recorded balance for accounts receivable is not materially misstated, and evidence is to be obtained by seeking confirmation of account balances from customers, the customer account should be the sampling unit. Alternatively, if the objective is to determine that the sales account is not materially misstated, and evidence is to be obtained by examining documents supporting recorded sales transactions, then line entries in the sales journal would be an appropriate sampling unit. A physical representation of all units comprising the population, such as a list of customer accounts, facilitates the process of selecting units for the sample.

For the Ace Finance Company, (1) the population is defined as 3,000 small loans receivable, (2) the recorded book value of these receivables is $1,340,000, (3) individual loans are defined as the sampling unit, and (4) the physical representation from which sample items are selected is a computer printout listing all loans receivable.

Step 5. Determine the Sample Size

Figure 13-17 summarizes the factors that influence sample size. Each of these factors is discussed below.

Population Size

It is critical to have accurate knowledge of the number of units in the population because this factor enters into the calculation of both the sample size and sample results. Population size directly affects sample size—that is, the larger the popu-

Figure 13-17 ■ Factors that Influence Sample Size for MPU Estimation

Larger Samples	Factor (Relationship to sample size)	Smaller Samples
Larger populations with larger numbers of units should result in a larger sample size.	**Population size in number of units (Direct)**	Smaller populations with fewer number of units should result in a smaller sample size.
The larger the standard deviation in the population, the larger the sample size.	**Estimated population standard deviation (Direct)**	The smaller the standard deviation in the population, the smaller the sample size.
The smaller the amount of misstatement that the auditor can tolerate, the larger the sample size.	**Tolerable misstatement (Inverse)**	The larger the amount of misstatement that the auditor can tolerate, the smaller the sample size.
Smaller amounts of sampling risk should result in larger sample size. The risk of incorrect rejection influences sample size, through the planned allowance for sampling risk.	**Risk of incorrect rejection (Inverse)**	Larger amounts of sampling risk should result in smaller sample size. The risk of incorrect rejection influences sample size, through the planned allowance for sampling risk.
Smaller amounts of sampling risk should result in larger sample size. The risk of incorrect acceptance influences sample size, through the planned allowance for sampling risk.	**Risk of incorrect acceptance (Inverse)**	Larger amounts of sampling risk should result in smaller sample size. The risk of incorrect acceptance influences sample size, through the planned allowance for sampling risk.
The more precise the estimate, the larger the sample size.	**Planned allowance for sampling risk (Inverse)**	The less precise the estimate, the smaller the sample size.

lation, the larger the sample size. As noted above, the population for the Ace Finance Company consists of 3,000 loans receivable.

Estimated Population Standard Deviation

In MPU estimation, the sample size required to achieve specified statistical objectives is related directly to the variability of the values of the population items. The measure of variability used is the **standard deviation.** Because an audit value is not obtained for every population item, the standard deviation of the audit values for the items in the sample is used as an estimate of the population standard deviation. But because the sample standard deviation is not known before the sample is selected, it also must be estimated.

There are three ways of estimating this factor. First, in a recurring engagement, the standard deviation found in the preceding audit may be used to estimate the standard deviation for the current year. Second, the standard deviation can be estimated from available book values. Third, the auditor can take a small presample of 30 to 50 items and base the estimate of the current year's population standard deviation on the audit values of these sample items. When this is done, the presample may be made a part of the final sample. Computer programs for MPU estimation sampling include a routine to calculate the estimated standard deviation.

The formula for calculating the standard deviation is

$$S_{x_j} = \sqrt{\sum_{j=1}^{n} \frac{(x_j - \bar{x})^2}{n-1}}$$

where

$\sum_{j=1}^{n}$ = sum of sample values; $j = 1$ means the summary should begin with the first item and n means that the summary should end with the last item in the sample

x_j = audit values of individual sample items

$\bar{x}$ = mean of the audit values of sample items

n = number of items audited

A primary concern of the auditor in MPU sampling is whether the population should be stratified. **Stratified sampling** involves dividing the population into relatively homogeneous groups or strata. A homogeneous group in this context is one that has little variability in the values of the items comprising the group or stratum. Sampling is performed separately on each stratum, and sample results for each stratum are subsequently combined to evaluate the total sample.

Stratification may be advantageous because the combined sample size often will be significantly less than a single sample size based on an unstratified population. This follows from the fact that sample size decreases as the variability of the population decreases. In fact, a change in the variability of a population affects sample size by the square of the relative change. Consequently, when the variation in the population changes from 200 to 100 (i.e., halved), the sample size required to meet the same statistical objectives is decreased by a factor of 4 (one-half squared equals one-fourth).

The optimal number of strata depends on the pattern of variation in the population values and the additional costs associated with designing, executing, and evaluating each stratified sample. Because of the complexity of the procedure, stratification is generally used only when appropriate computer software is available. To simplify subsequent illustrations in this chapter, unstratified samples are used.

The Ace Finance Company limits loans to a maximum of $500 per customer. Thus, variability is low, and the auditor concludes there is no need to stratify the population. Based on last year's audit, the auditor estimates a standard deviation of $100.

Tolerable Misstatement

The considerations applicable to **tolerable misstatement (TM)** are the same in MPU sampling as in PPS sampling. TM has an inverse effect on sample size. For the Ace Finance Company, the auditor specifies a TM of $60,000.

Risk of Incorrect Rejection

The **risk of incorrect rejection** permits the auditor to control the risk that the sample results will support the conclusion that the recorded account balance is materially misstated when it is not. The principal consequence of this risk is the potential incurrence of additional costs associated with expanded audit procedures following the initial rejection. However, the additional auditing procedures should ultimately result in the conclusion that the balance is not materially misstated.

In contrast to PPS sampling, the auditor must quantify the risk of incorrect rejection in MPU sampling as well as the risk of incorrect acceptance. The risk of incorrect rejection has an inverse effect on sample size. If the auditor specifies a very low risk of incorrect rejection, the size and cost of performing the initial sample will be larger. Therefore, the auditor's experience and knowledge of the client should be used to specify an appropriate risk of incorrect rejection to balance the costs associated with the initial sample and the potential costs of later expanding the sample.

In some computer software programs, the auditor inputs the risk of incorrect rejection directly as a percentage figure. Other programs require the auditor to input a confidence or reliability level, which is the complement of the risk of incorrect rejection. In either case, the computer then converts the percentage into an appropriate standard normal deviate, or U_R **factor**, for use in calculating the sample size. If the sample size is being calculated manually, a U_R factor for the specified risk of incorrect rejection is obtained from a table like the one illustrated in Figure 13-18.

The auditor decides to specify a 5 percent risk of incorrect rejection in the Ace Finance Company. Thus, the U_R factor is 1.96.

Risk of Incorrect Acceptance

The factors to be considered in specifying this risk are the same as in PPS sampling. The **risk of incorrect acceptance** of a materially misstated balance is ordinarily specified in the range from 5 to 30 percent, depending on the auditor's assessed level of control risk and the results of other substantive tests. The risk of incorrect acceptance has an inverse effect on sample size—the lower the specified risk, the larger the sample size. In Ace Finance, the auditor specifies a 20 percent risk of incorrect acceptance.

Figure 13-18 ■ Selected Risk of Incorrect Rejection Percentages and Corresponding Standards Normal Deviates or U_R Factors

Risk of Incorrect Rejection	Standard Normal Deviate (U_R Factor)	Corresponding Confidence or Reliability Level
0.30	± 1.04	0.70
0.25	± 1.15	0.75
0.20	± 1.28	0.80
0.15	± 1.44	0.85
0.10	± 1.64	0.90
0.05	± 1.96	0.95
0.01	± 2.58	0.99

Planned Allowance for Sampling Risk

The **planned allowance for sampling risk** (sometimes referred to as "desired precision") is derived from the following formula:

$$A = R \times TM$$

where

A = desired or planned allowance for sampling risk
R = ratio of desired allowance for sampling risk to tolerable misstatement
TM = tolerable misstatement

The ratio for the R factor is based on the specified risks of incorrect acceptance and incorrect rejection. The amount of the ratio is obtained from the table shown in Figure 13-19. For example, if the aforementioned risks are set at 20 and 10 percent, respectively, the R factor is 0.661. In the Ace Finance Company, the foregoing risks have been specified at 20 and 5 percent. Thus, the R factor is 0.70. This factor is then multiplied by the TM of $60,000 to produce an allowance for sampling risk of $42,000.

Sample Size Formula

The following formula is used to determine sample size for an MPU estimation sample:

$$n = \left(\frac{N \cdot U_R \cdot S_{x_j}}{A} \right)^2$$

Figure 13-19 ■ Ratio of Desired Allowance for Sampling Risk to Tolerable Misstatement

Risk of Incorrect Acceptance	Risk of Incorrect Rejection			
	0.20	0.10	0.05	0.01
0.01	0.355	0.413	0.457	0.525
0.025	0.395	0.456	0.500	0.568
0.05	0.437	0.500	0.543	0.609
0.075	0.471	0.532	0.576	0.641
0.10	0.500	0.561	0.605	0.668
0.15	0.511	0.612	0.653	0.712
0.20	0.603	0.661	0.700	0.753
0.25	0.563	0.708	0.742	0.791
0.30	0.707	0.756	0.787	0.829
0.35	0.766	0.808	0.834	0.868
0.40	0.831	0.863	0.883	0.908
0.45	0.907	0.926	0.937	0.952
0.50	1.000	1.000	1.000	1.000

where

N = population size

U_R = the standard normal deviate for the desired risk of incorrect rejection

S_{xj} = estimated population standard deviation

A = desired or planned allowance for sampling risk

In the Ace Finance Company, these four factors are 3,000, 1.96, $100, and $42,000, respectively. Thus, the sample size is 196, computed as follows:

$$n = \left(\frac{3000 \times 1.96 \times \$100}{42,000} \right)^2 = 196$$

This formula assumes sampling with replacement (i.e., an item once selected is put back into the population and is eligible for selection again). When sampling without replacement, a **finite correction factor** is recommended when the relationship between n (sample size) and N (population size) is greater than 0.05. The adjusted sample size (n') is determined as follows:

$$n' = \frac{n}{1 + \dfrac{n}{N}}$$

Because n/N is greater than 0.05 (196 ÷ 3,000 = 0.065) in Ace Finance, the adjusted sample size is

$$n' = \frac{196}{1 + \dfrac{196}{3000}} = 184$$

Step 6. Select a Representative Sample

Either the simple random number selection method or the systematic selection method may be used in selecting the sample under the MPU technique. In the Ace Finance Company, the auditor decides to use generalized audit software to randomly identify the 184 loans receivable to be examined.

Step 7. Apply Audit Procedures

The execution phase of an MPU estimation sampling plan includes the following steps:

- Perform appropriate auditing procedures to determine an audit value for each sample item
- Calculate the following statistics based on the sample data:
  - the average of the sample audit values ($\bar{x}$)
  - the standard deviation of the sample audit values (S_{xj})

The average and standard deviation statistics for the sample may be computed manually or by a computer.

For the Ace Finance sample, the sum of the audit values is assumed to be $81,328, resulting in an average audit value of $442 ($81,328 ÷ 184). The standard deviation of the audit values is assumed to be $90.

Step 8. Evaluate the Sample Results

Evaluating sample results involves making both a quantitative and a qualitative assessment of the results in order to reach an overall conclusion.

Quantitative Assessment

In making this evaluation in an MPU sampling plan, the auditor calculates

- The estimated total population value
- The achieved allowance for sampling risk, sometimes referred to as achieved precision
- A range for the estimated total population value, sometimes referred to as the precision interval

The **estimated total population value ($\hat{X}$)** is calculated as follows:

$$\hat{X} = N \cdot \bar{x}$$

Thus, the estimated total population value for Ace Finance Company's 3,000 loans receivable is:

$$\hat{X} = 3,000 \times \$442 = \$1,326,000$$

The basic formula for calculating the **achieved allowance for sampling risk (A′)** is:

$$A' = N \cdot U_R \cdot \frac{S_{x_j}}{\sqrt{n}}$$

where S_{x_j} is the standard deviation of the sample audit values. Note that the value for S_{x_j} is not the value for S_{x_j} used in determining sample size.

When the finite correction factor has been used in determining sample size, the formula is modified as follows:

$$A' = N \cdot U_R \cdot \frac{S_{x_j} \cdot \sqrt{1 - \frac{n'}{N}}}{\sqrt{n'}}$$

Therefore, the achieved allowance for sampling risk for Ace Finance is:

$$A' = 3,000 \times 1.96 \times \frac{\$90\sqrt{1 - \frac{184}{3,000}}}{\sqrt{184}} = \$37,798$$

The **range for the estimated total population value** is derived from the estimated total population value and the achieved allowance for sampling risk. The range is:

$$\hat{X} \pm A'$$

In Ace Finance Company, the calculation is as follows:

$$\hat{X} = \$1,326,000 \pm \$37,798$$
$$= \$1,288,202 \text{ to } \$1,363,798$$

If the book value falls within this range, the sample results support the conclusion that the book value is not materially misstated. This conclusion is valid in the case study as the book value of $1,340,000 falls within the range.

It should be recognized that the sample results may support the conclusion that the book value is not materially misstated, but not within the level of risk of incorrect acceptance specified by the auditor. To stay within the desired risk, achieved allowance for sampling risk (A') must be equal to or less than planned allowance for sampling risk (A). A' will be greater than A whenever the standard deviation of audit values is greater than the estimated population standard deviation used in determining sample size. For example, if the standard deviation of audit values in the Harris Company had been $110, A' would have been $46,197, which is greater than the $42,000 specified for A. In such a case, the auditor computes the **adjusted achieved allowance for sampling risk (A'')** by the following formula where TM is the tolerable misstatement specified in the sampling plan:

$$A'' = A' + TM\left(1 - \frac{A'}{A}\right)$$

A'' is $40,197, computed as follows:

$$A'' = \$46,197 + \$60,000\left(1 - \frac{\$46,197}{\$42,000}\right) = 40,197$$

Note that A'', $40,197, is less than A, $42,000. A'' is then substituted for A' in the formula used to calculate the range for the estimated population value. Using A'', we find that the estimated population range is $1,326,000 ± $40,197 or $1,285,803 to $1,366,197. Because the book value of $1,340,000 falls within the range, the sample results indicate that the book value is not materially misstated at the planned risk of incorrect acceptance.

The book value may fall outside the range because the achieved allowance for sampling risk is significantly smaller than the planned allowance. When this occurs, the auditor (1) calculates the difference between the book value and the far end of the range and (2) compares the difference to TM. If the difference is equal to or less than TM, the sample results indicate that the book value is not materially misstated. For example, if the achieved allowance in Ace Finance Company is $12,000, the range becomes $1,314,000 to $1,338,000 and the book value ($1,340,000) falls outside the precision interval. The difference between the book value and the far end of the range is $26,000 ($1,340,000 − $1,314,000). Because this is less than the TM of $60,000, the book value is supported.

Qualitative Assessment

Prior to reaching an overall conclusion, the auditor should consider the qualitative aspects of the sample results. These considerations are the same in MPU sampling as in PPS sampling.

Reaching an Overall Conclusion

When either the auditor's quantitative (statistical) or qualitative assessments of sample results support the conclusion that the population is materially misstated, professional judgment should be used in deciding on an appropriate course of action. The possible causes and actions are as follows:

CAUSES	ACTIONS
1. The sample is not representative of the population.	1. Expand the sample and reevaluate the results.
2. The achieved allowance for sampling risk may be larger than the desired allowance because the samples size was too small.	2. Expand the sample and reevaluate the results.
3. The population book value may be misstated by more than a tolerable amount.	3. Have client investigate and, if warranted, adjust the book value and reevaluate the sample results.

Step 9. Document Conclusions

Figure 13-20 summarizes the steps performed in designing, executing, and evaluating the MPU sampling plan to test the book value of Ace Finance Company's loans receivable and illustrates how these steps can be documented in a working paper.

LEARNING CHECK

13B-1 a. Give the formula for determining sample size in a mean-per-unit sampling plan.
b. Explain what each element in the formula represents.

13B-2 a. How is the risk of incorrect acceptance controlled in classical variables sampling plans?
b. Explain three ways of estimating the standard deviation for a mean-per-unit sampling plan.

13B-3 Explain the role of each of the following in mean-per-unit estimation:
a. Planned allowance for sampling risk.
b. Achieved allowance for sampling risk.
c. Adjusted achieved allowance for sampling risk.

13B-4 What alternatives exist when sample results do not support the book value?

KEY TERMS

Achieved allowance for sampling risk (A'), p. 600
Adjusted achieved allowance for sampling risk (A''), p. 601
Estimated total population value ($\hat{X}$), p. 600
Finite correction factor, p. 599
MPU estimation sampling, p. 593

Figure 13-20 ■ Mean-per-Unit Sampling Plan Working Paper

Ace Finance Company

W/P Ref. $B-4$

MPU Sample – Loans Receivable

December 31, 20X1

Prepared By: *W. C. B.*   Date: *1/22/X2*

Reviewed By: *R. E. Z.*   Date: *1/25/X2*

Objective: To obtain evidence that the aggregate book value of loans receivable as of 12/31/X1 was not materially misstated.

Population and Sampling Unit: 3,000 loans on computer listing prepared from master file. The sampling was the individual loan receivable.

Sample size:			
	Population Size	3,000	(N)
	Estimated Standard Deviation	100	(S_{x_j})
	Tolerable Misstatement	60,000	(TM)
	Risk of Incorrect Rejection	5%	$U_R = 1.96$
	Risk of Incorrect Acceptance	20%	
	Ratio of Desired Allowance for Sampling Risk	0.700	(R)
	Desired Allowance for Sampling Risk $= R \times TM$	42,000	(A)
	$n = (N \cdot U_R \cdot S_{x_j})/A)^2$	196	(n)
	$n' = n/(1 + (n/N))$	184	(n')

Sample Selection:	Simple random using computer-generated random numbers list to correspond to loan numbers. Sampling units selected are listed on W/P.	$B-5$

Execution of Sampling Plan	Audit Procedures Applied Listed on W/P	$B-1$	
	Audit Values of Sample Items Shown on W/P	$B-5$	
	Sum of Sample Audit Values	81,328	
	Average of Sample Audit Values	442.00	$\bar{x}$
	Standards Deviation of Sample Audit Values	90.00	S_{x_j}

Evaluation of Sample Results	Estimated Total Population Value $\hat{X} = N * \bar{x}$	1,326,000	$\hat{X}$
	Achieved Allowance for Sampling Risk $A'' = N * U_R * (S_{x_j} * \sqrt{1 - (n'/N)}/\sqrt{n'})$	37,798	A'
	Range: $\hat{X} \pm A'$	1,288,202 to 1,363,798	

Conclusion	*The total book value of $1,340,000 falls within the calculated range for the estimated total population value. Sample results support the conclusion that the loans receivable are materially correct.*

appendix 13c

NONSTATISTICAL SAMPLING FOR SUBSTANTIVE TESTS

Chapter 13 introduced a method for selecting and evaluating audit samples for tests of controls that include the following steps.

1. Determine the audit objectives.
2. Determine procedures to meet objectives about whether an account balance was materially correct or was materially misstated.
3. Make a decision about the audit sampling technique.
4. Define the population and sampling unit.
5. Determine the sample size.
6. Select a representative sample.
7. Apply audit procedures.
8. Evaluate the sample results.
9. Document conclusions.

These steps were discussed on page 557 in the context of probability proportionate to size sampling. As explained earlier, the auditor may choose to use nonstatistical sampling in certain substantive testing applications. The major differences between statistical and nonstatistical sampling are in the steps for determining sample size and evaluating sample results. These steps are often perceived as being more objective or rigorous in statistical sampling and more subjective and judgmental in nonstatistical samples. However, judgment is also required in statistical applications, and certain relationships considered explicitly in statistical samples may be helpful in designing and evaluating nonstatistical samples. The following discussion focuses on the unique aspects of nonstatistical sampling for substantive tests.

Step 5. Use Professional Judgment to Determine Sample Size

Whether the auditor uses nonstatistical or statistical sampling, the same factors should be considered when determining sample size. In nonstatistical sampling it is not necessary for the auditor to quantify these factors explicitly in determining sample size. However, the auditor must recognize the following effects on sample size of a change in one factor when the other factors are held constant. Figure 13-21 identifies the factors that influence sample size for a substantive test.

Four major factors influence sample size. The first is the book value of the population.

Figure 13-21 ■ Factors that Influence Sample Size for a Substantive Tests

Larger Samples	Factor (Relationship to sample Size)	Smaller Samples
Larger populations with higher book values should result in a larger sample size.	Book value of the population (Direct)	Smaller populations with lower book values should result in a smaller sample size.
The more heterogeneous the population, the larger the sample size	Variation in the population (Direct)	The more homogeneous the population the smaller the sample size.
The smaller the amount of misstatement that the auditor can tolerate, the larger the sample size.	Tolerable misstatement (Inverse)	The larger the amount of misstatement that the auditor can tolerate, the smaller the sample size.
Smaller amounts of sampling risk should result in larger sample size.	Risk of incorrect acceptance (Inverse)	Larger amounts of sampling risk should result in smaller sample size.

The **book value of the population** refers to the dollar amount of the account (or subaccount) being audited. In two different audits, one has accounts receivable of $4 billion and the other has accounts receivable of $10 billion. The auditor should select a larger sample from the $10 billion account balance. It is appropriate to think of the sample in terms of the proportion of the population being sampled. If in each case the auditor evaluates 75 percent of the dollars, the auditor is auditing a larger amount with 75 percent of the $10 billion receivables balance.

The second factor that influences sample size is the variation in the population. **Variation in the population** addresses the issue of how homogeneous or heterogeneous the population being sampled is. As an example consider two inventory populations. One inventory is a lumber inventory that is relatively homogeneous in quantity and pricing of the inventory. The second inventory is that of a large retailer that sells everything from food to clothing, to nursery items, to large appliances. Even if the two inventories were similar in book value, the auditor should select a larger sample for the retailer, with a very heterogeneous inventory, than for the lumberyard.

The third factor that influences sample size is **tolerable misstatement** which represents the dollar amount of misstatement that the auditor can tolerate in an account and still conclude that the account balance or transaction class is presented fairly in all material respects. Holding everything else constant, as the amount of misstatement that the auditors can tolerate increases, sample size will decrease.

The fourth factor that influences sample size is a measure of sampling risk, the risk of incorrect acceptance. Recall from Figure 13-1 that the risk of incorrect acceptance is related to the effectiveness of the audit, while the risk of incorrect rejection is related to the efficiency of the audit. The auditor normally determines the **risk of incorrect acceptance** by using the audit risk model and solving for tests of details risk. Remember, the risk of incorrect acceptance is not related to audit risk, but it is related to test of details risk. Hence, it is influenced by previous decisions about inherent risk and control risk. The risk of incorrect acceptance can be determined quantitatively by using the formula below, or it may be determined qualitatively by using a table similar to Figure 9-4.

$$TD = \frac{AR}{IR \times CR \times AP}$$

Step 6. Select a Representative Sample

The process of selecting a sample should be unbiased, and the auditor should attempt to obtain a representative sample of the items in the balance or transaction class being sampled. The auditor can never be certain that a representative sample has been achieved. The concept of **sampling risk** is a measure of whether the sample is representative. Usually, the auditor's best opportunity to obtain a representative sample is to select a random sample. In selecting a sample, many auditors will stratify a sample such that they take a high proportion of the large dollars in the population. This is appropriate if the auditor is concerned about a risk of overstatement of the population. Stratifying the population also allows for more homogeneous groupings, which makes for a more efficient sample. Consider the following stratification of an accounts receivable population with a total book value of $7.5 million. Assume that the auditor set tolerable misstatement for this population at $350,000.

STRATA	DOLLAR VALUE OF RECEIVABLES	BOOK VALUE OF THE POPULATION		N		n		BOOK VALUE OF THE SAMPLE	
1	Greater than $150,000	$ 1,750,000	23%	10	2%	10	33%	$ 1,750,000	62%
2	$15,000 – $150,000	$ 3,000,000	40%	90	18%	15	25%	$ 910,000	32%
3	Less than $15,000	$ 2,750,000	37%	400	80%	25	42%	$ 170,000	6%
		$ 7,500,000	100%	500	100%	50	100%	$ 2,830,000	100%
						10%		38%	

This is a typical audit population that has a lot of dollars in a few items (stratum 1) and a few dollars in a lot of items (stratum 3). In the first stratum the auditor selects everything over $150,000. This selection captures only 2 percent of the items in the population but 23 percent of the dollars in the population. Also, note that because the auditor audits 100 percent of the first stratum, the auditor can draw a conclusion about this stratum with certainty. Hence, this first stratum does not involve sampling. The auditors want to randomly, or haphazardly, select a representative and unbiased sample out of stratum 2 and stratum 3. In total the auditor audits only 10 percent of the items and 38 percent of the dollars of the population.

Step 7. Apply Audit Procedures

Applying audit procedures is the same for statistical and for nonstatistical sampling. For purposes of continuing the example discussed above, the following table shows the audited values for the sample selected from strata 1, 2, and 3.

STRATA	DOLLAR VALUE OF RECEIVABLES	BOOK VALUE OF THE POPULATION	n	BOOK VALUE OF THE SAMPLE	AUDITED VALUE OF THE SAMPLE
1	Greater than $150,000	$ 1,750,000	10	$ 1,750,000	$ 1,735,000
2	$15,000 – $150,000	$ 3,000,000	15	$ 910,000	$ 895,000
3	Less than $15,000	$ 2,750,000	25	$ 170,000	$ 155,000

Step 8. Evaluate the Sample Results

When evaluating sample results, the auditor should (1) project misstatement found in the sample to the audit population, and (2) consider sampling risk when evaluating sample results. Two acceptable methods of projecting misstatements in nonstatistical sampling are:

- A ratio method where the auditor estimates the audited value of the population based on a ratio of the audited value of the sample divided by the book value of the sample.
- A difference method where the auditor estimates the audited value of the population by adding (or subtracting) the projected difference between audited value and book value from the book value of the population.

To illustrate, the following discussion continues with the data discussed immediately above.

Under the **ratio method** the auditor would determine the audited value of *each stratum* using the following formula (as illustrated for the second stratum).

$$AV_i = \frac{AV_{ni} \times BV_i}{BV_{ni}} = \frac{\$895,000 \times \$3,000,000}{\$910,000} = \$2,950,549$$

The estimated audited value for each stratum using the ratio method is summarized as follows:

STRATA	DOLLAR VALUE OF RECEIVABLES	BOOK VALUE OF THE POPULATION	BOOK VALUE OF THE SAMPLE	AUDITED VALUE OF THE SAMPLE	ESTIMATED VALUE OF THE STRATA	ESTIMATED OVER-STATEMENT
1	Greater than $150,000	$ 1,750,000	$ 1,750,000	$ 1,735,000	$ 1,735,000	$ 15,000
2	$15,000 – $150,000	$ 3,000,000	$ 910,000	$ 895,000	$ 2,950,549	$ 49,451
3	Less than $15,000	$ 2,750,000	$ 170,000	$ 155,000	$ 2,507,353	$ 242,647
		$ 7,500,000	$ 2,830,000	$ 2,785,000	$ 7,192,902	$ 307,098

Under the **difference method** the auditor would determine the audited value of *each stratum* using the following formula (as illustrated for the second stratum).

$$AV_i = BV_i - D_i$$

where

$$D_i = \frac{AV_{ni} - BV_{ni}}{n_i} \times N_i$$

$$= \$3,000,000 + \left[\frac{(\$895,000 - \$910,000)}{15} \times 90 \right] = \$2,910,000$$

STRATA	DOLLAR VALUE OF RECEIVABLES	BOOK VALUE OF THE POPULATION	N	n	BOOK VALUE OF THE SAMPLE	AUDITED VALUE OF THE SAMPLE	ESTIMATED VALUE OF THE STRATUM	ESTIMATED OVER-STATEMENT
1	Greater than $150,000	$ 1,750,000	10	10	$ 1,750,000	$ 1,735,000	1,735,000	$ 15,000
2	$15,000 – $150,000	$ 3,000,000	90	15	$ 910,000	$ 895,000	2,910,000	$ 90,000
3	Less than $15,000	$ 2,750,000	400	25	$ 170,000	$ 155,000	2,510,000	$ 240,000
		$ 7,500,000	500	50	$ 2,830,000	$ 2,785,000	$ 7,155,000	$ 345,000

These examples were prepared so that each stratum had $15,000 of misstatement. Stratum 1 was audited 100 percent so that the projected misstatement under each method was $15,000. Under both the ratio and difference methods, the $15,000 misstatement in stratum 2 projects to a smaller estimated misstatement than in stratum 3 because a higher proportion of stratum 2 is sampled and the auditor is projecting the misstatement on a smaller unsampled portion of the stratum. Finally, the difference method projects a larger estimated amount of misstatement because the auditor selected a smaller proportion of total items (upon which the difference method is based) than total dollars (upon which the ratio method is based).

In nonstatistical samples, the auditor cannot calculate an **allowance for sampling risk** for a specific measurable level of risk of incorrect acceptance. However, the difference between projected misstatement (or estimated overstatement in this case) and tolerable misstatement may be viewed as an allowance for sampling risk. If tolerable misstatement exceeds projected misstatement by a large amount, the auditor may be reasonably assured that there is an acceptable low sampling risk that the actual misstatement exceeds tolerable misstatement. In the above two examples, tolerable misstatement exceeds projected misstatement by $42,902 and by $5,000, respectively. Most auditors would conclude that even though the estimated overstatement of $345,000 is less than the tolerable misstatement of $350,000 the amount is so close that it does not allow for a reasonable allowance for sampling risk. In this case the auditor is likely to extend the sample size and to perform additional audit procedures to a higher level of certainty (lower level of sampling risk) into the auditor's conclusion.

The number and size of misstatements found in the sample relative to expected misstatements are also helpful in assessing sampling risk. When the sample has been carefully designed and the number and size of misstatements found do not exceed the auditor's expectations, he or she can generally conclude that there is an acceptably low risk that actual misstatement exceeds tolerable misstatement.

When the results of a nonstatistical sample do not appear to support the book value, the auditor may (1) examine additional sample units and reevaluate, (2) apply alternative auditing procedures and reevaluate, or (3) ask the client to investigate and, if appropriate, make an adjustment.

In audit sampling, prior to reaching an overall conclusions, consideration should be given to the qualitative characteristics of the misstatements. If evidence of fraud is found, the auditor must not only consider the implications for the account balance and transaction class being audited, but the auditor should also consider whether the auditor needs to reconsider audit strategy for other account balances and transaction classes. In addition, the auditor should consider whether the evidence is consistent with previous assessments of inherent and control risks. For example, if the auditor assesses control risk as low, but finds multiple misstatements when performing substantive tests, the auditor should reassess control risk, and increase the degree of substantive testing accordingly.

Step 9. Document Conclusions

Once the auditor has completed the sampling process, it is important that the auditor document the results of substantive tests in his or her working papers. The auditor might prepare a working paper similar to the one illustrated in Figure 13-20.

[LEARNING CHECK

13C-1 How does the process of determining sample size differ in a statistical versus a nonstatistical sampling plan for a substantive test?

13C-2 Describe two acceptable methods for projecting misstatements found in nonstatistical samples.

13C-3 What may be viewed as the allowance for sampling risk in nonstatistical samples? Explain.

[KEY TERMS

Allowance for sampling risk, p. 608
Book value of the population, p. 605
Difference method, p. 607
Ratio method, p. 607

Risk of incorrect acceptance, p. 605
Sampling risk, p. 606
Tolerable misstatement, p. 605
Variation in the population, p. 605

objective questions

Objective questions are available for the student at www.wiley.com/college/boynton

comprehensive questions

13-20 **(Sampling for attributes—statistical and nonstatistical)** Sampling for attributes is often used to allow an auditor to reach a conclusion concerning a rate of occurrence in a population. A common use in auditing is to test the rate of deviation from a prescribed internal control procedure to obtain support for a planned level of control risk.

Required

a. When an auditor samples for attributes, identify the factors that should influence the auditor's judgment concerning the determination of
   1. Acceptable level of risk of assessing control risk too low,
   2. Tolerable deviation rate, and
   3. Expected population deviation rate.

b. State the effect on sample size of an increase in each of the following factors, assuming all other factors are held constant:
   1. Acceptable level of risk of assessing control risk too low,
   2. Tolerable deviation rate, and
   3. Expected population deviation rate.

c. Assuming nonstatistical sampling is used, evaluate the sample results of a test for attributes if authorizations are found missing on 7 check requests out of a sample of 100 tested. The population consists of 2,500 check requests, the tolerable deviation rate is 8 percent, and the risk of assessing control risk too low should be held to a low level.

d. How may the use of statistical sampling assist the auditor in evaluating the sample results described in (c), above?

AICPA (adapted)

13-21   **(Uncertainties in audit sampling)** One of the generally accepted auditing standards states that sufficient competent evidential matter is to be obtained through inspection, observation, inquiries, and confirmation to afford a reasonable basis for an opinion regarding the financial statements under examination. Some degree of uncertainty is implicit in the concept of "a reasonable basis for an opinion," because the concept of sampling is well established in auditing practice.

Required

a. Explain the auditor's justification for accepting the uncertainties that are inherent in the sampling process.

b. Discuss the uncertainties that collectively embody the concept of audit risk.

c. Discuss the nature of sampling risk and nonsampling risk. Include the effect of sampling risk on tests of controls in the auditor's study and evaluation of the internal control structure.

AICPA (adapted)

13-22   **(Nonstatistical sampling)** Assume that you are planning a test of management control procedures. Senior management has established a sound control environment and expects managers to be accountable for the resources they use. Each manager is asked to review a report of weekly expenditures and determine that the transactions actually occurred, that they are reasonably valued, and that they should be charged to his or her responsibility center. The company has three major divisions, and each division generates weekly reports for seven, nine, and ten managers, respectively.

Required

a. Develop a nonstatistical sampling plan to test this control assuming that you want to assess control risk as moderate. Carefully describe each step in developing the sampling plan.

b. What types of evidence might represent deviations from the prescribed control procedure?

c. Describe how many deviations from the prescribed control procedure you can tolerate and still assess control risk as moderate.

13-23   **(Judgment in statistical sampling)** The use of statistical sampling techniques in an audit of financial statements does not eliminate judgmental decisions.

Required

a. Identify and explain four areas in which judgment may be exercised by a CPA in planning a statistical sampling test.

b. Assume that a CPA's sample shows an unacceptable deviation rate. Describe the various actions that he or she may take based on this finding.

c. A nonstratified sample of 80 accounts payable vouchers is to be selected from a population of 3,200. The vouchers are numbered consecutively from 1 to 3,200 and are listed, 40 to a page, in the voucher register. Describe two different techniques for selecting a sample of vouchers for tests of controls.

AICPA (adapted)

13-24   **(PPS sampling)** Edwards has decided to use probability-proportional-to-size (PPS) sampling, sometimes called dollar-unit sampling, in the audit of a client's accounts receivable balance. Few, if any, errors of overstatement are expected.

Edwards plans to use the following PPS sampling table:

5% RELIABILITY FACTORS FOR OVERSTATEMENTS

NUMBER OF OVERSTATEMENTS	RISK OF INCORRECT ACCEPTANC				
	1%	5%	10%	15%	20%
0	4.61	3.00	2.31	1.90	1.61
1	6.64	4.75	3.89	3.38	3.00
2	8.41	6.30	5.33	4.72	4.28
3	10.05	7.76	6.69	6.02	5.52
4	11.61	9.16	8.00	7.27	6.73

Required

a. Identify the advantages of using PPS sampling over classical variables sampling.

Note: Requirements (b) and (c) are not related.

b. Calculate the sampling interval and the sample size Edwards should use, given the following information:

Tolerable misstatement	$15,000
Risk of incorrect acceptance	5%
Number of misstatements allowed	0
Recorded amount of accounts receivable	$300,000

c. Calculate total projected misstatement if the following three misstatements were discovered in a PPS sample:

	RECORDED AMOUNT	AUDIT AMOUNT	SAMPLING INTERVAL
1st misstatement	$400	$320	$1,000
2nd misstatement	500	0	1,000
3rd misstatement	3,000	2,500	1,000

AICPA

13-25 **(PPS sampling)** In the December 31, 20X1, audit of Lark Corporation, an auditor employs monetary-unit (probability-proportional-to-size) sampling in testing the valuation of physical inventory. The book value of inventory is $500,000 and represents the cumulative value of 2,000 vouchers. The maximum tolerable misstatement (or level of materiality) is determined to be $25,000 and the auditor decides on a 10 percent risk of incorrect acceptance. This completes the auditor's design specifications for the sample.

The test revealed one voucher that was on the books at $500 but had an audit value of $400. No other misstatements were found.

Required

a. What sample size and sampling interval were used by the auditor?

b. Under the assumption that the auditor wrote a conclusion based on the data presented, what would the conclusion state?

c. Critique the auditor's sampling plan and describe what actions the auditor might take given the sample results.

d. What are the advantages of using monetary-unit (probability-proportional-to-size) sampling as an audit tool?

IIA (adapted)

13-26 **(Evaluating a PPS sample)** Assume the following misstatements were found in a PPS sample:

SAMPLE ITEM	BOOK VALUE	AUDIT VALUE
1	$ 650	$ 585
2	540	0
3	1,900	0
4	2,200	1,650
5	2,800	2,660

Required

a. Calculate the projected misstatement assuming
   1. The sampling interval was $1,800.
   2. The sampling interval was $2,000.

b. If a risk of incorrect acceptance of 15 percent was specified in the sample design, the sampling interval was $2,000, and five misstatements were found as enumerated above, calculate
   1. Basic precision.
   2. The incremental allowance for sampling risk.
   3. The upper misstatement limit.

c. If tolerable misstatement was $50,000 and anticipated misstatement was $10,000, what conclusion would you reach based on your results in (b) above?

13-27 **(PPS sampling)** You decide to use statistical sampling to test the reasonableness of the recorded book value of the Key West Company's accounts receivable. Because the company's internal control procedures over accounts receivable have been evaluated by you as excellent and you believe few misstatements will be found, you decide to use probability-proportional-to-size sampling. The company has 4,000 customer accounts with a total book value of $3,000,000. You decide $150,000 is the maximum tolerable misstatement and anticipate that there may be $30,000 of misstatement in the population. You wish to limit the risk of incorrect acceptance to 10%. It is your intention to seek positive confirmation of accounts included in your sample and to apply alternative procedures to accounts for which no reply is received.

Required

a. Compute the sample size.

b. Compute the sampling interval.

c. Assume the following misstatements were found in the sample:

SAMPLE ITEM	BOOK VALUE	AUDIT VALUE
1	$800	$0
2	1,500	1,350
3	13,000	0
4	15,000	14,250

Calculate
   1. Projected misstatement.
   2. Allowance for sampling risk.
   3. Upper misstatement limit.

d. State your conclusion based on the results in (c).

13-28 **(Mean-per-unit sampling)** A contractor has 1,520 homes in various states of construction. From a random presample of 50 homes, you determine that the estimated population standard deviation is $2,000. On the basis of audit risk and other factors, you set the desired allowance for sampling risk at $250,000 and the desired risk of incorrect rejection at 10 percent.

Required

a. Determine sample size, assuming mean-per-unit sampling with replacement.

b. What would sample size be if the standard deviation was increased to $2,500?

c. Assume the auditor elects to limit sample size to 325 in the interest of cost efficiencies. What risk of incorrect rejection can be achieved if desired allowance for sampling risk remains at $250,000 and the standard deviation remains at $2,000?

d. What allowance for sampling risk results if the risk of incorrect rejection is held at 10 percent and sample size is 325?

e. Redo part (a) above assuming sampling without replacement.

13-29 **(Mean-per-unit sampling)** Data relative to three MPU sampling plans are presented below.

	1	2	3
Tolerable misstatement	$110,000	$140,000	$170,000
Size of population	5,000	6,000	8,000
Risk of incorrect rejection	10%	5%	10%
Estimated population standard deviation	$80	$105	$125
Risks that misstatements accumulating to greater than tolerable misstatements will not be detected by:			
Internal control	50%	40%	40%
Analytical and other substantive procedures (excluding this test of details)	25%	50%	85%
Desired overall audit risk	5%	5%	5%
Inherent risk	100%	100%	100%

Required

a. Using the audit risk model, determine an appropriate risk of incorrect acceptance for each population.

b. Calculate sample size in each of the plans. Show computations.

13-30 **(Mean-per-unit sampling)** Data relevant to the December 31, 20X1 audit of accounts receivable in two of your clients is presented in the tabulation below.

	COMPANY X	COMPANY Y
Client's book value	$90,000	$200,000
Population size	1,000	2,000
Desired risk of incorrect acceptance	20%	30%
Desired risk of incorrect rejection	10%	5%
Tolerable misstatement	$9,000	$ 10,000
Estimated standard deviation	$50	$25

Required

a. Determine sample size for each company using MPU estimation sampling.

b. Assume the total audited value of the Company X sample is $13,600 and the standard deviation is $52. Evaluate the sample results.

c. Assume the average of the sample audit values in the Company Y sample is $90 and the standard deviation is $30. Evaluate the sample results.

13-31 **(Nonstatistical sampling)** Wheeler and Jones, CPAs, are examining the December 31, 20X1, inventory of Better Parts, Inc., a distributor of electronic parts. They have already performed procedures to satisfy themselves that (1) a computer printout listing inventory at year-end in ascending sequence by stock number and lot number is complete, (2) the quantities shown thereon are correct, (3) the extensions of quantity times price are accurate, (4) the listing is properly footed, and (5) the total agrees to the general ledger ending inventory account balance.

As the next step, Wheeler and Jones decide to use a nonstatistical sample to test the pricing of the inventory. They plan to perform this test by checking prices to (1) vendor's invoices and (2) current price lists provided by vendors. The ending inventory consists of 3,000 stock items with a total recorded value of $1.9 million. A perpetual inventory record is maintained for each stock item. In addition, an inventory tag showing the quantity on hand at year-end is on file for each item.

Wheeler and Jones agree that a misstatement of $85,000 or more in the inventory balance, when combined with misstatements in other accounts, might result in material misstatement of the financial statements.

Required

a. To what component of audit risk does the inventory pricing test relate?

b. What factors should influence Wheeler and Jones's determination of sample size?

c. What should the sampling unit be and how should the sample items be selected?

d. Assume that a sample of the pricing of 100 stock items was examined. The total recorded value for these items was $75,000. Eight of the items in the sample had pricing errors resulting in those items being overstated by $4,800. How should Wheeler and Jones interpret the sample results?

13-32 **(Determining sample size for statistical attribute sampling)** This problem focuses on the determination of sample sizes.

Required

a. Given the constraints of an 8 percent tolerable deviation rate and an expected population deviation rate from 1 percent to 5 percent, indicate the specific combinations of these factors at both 5 percent and 10 percent levels of risk of assessing control risk too low that will result in sample sizes that will not be less than 125 or more than 200.

b. At a 5 percent risk of assessing control risk too low, a 5 percent tolerable deviation rate, and a 2 percent expected population deviation rate; sample size is 181. Compute the new sample size for each of the following changes, assuming other factors are held constant at the amounts stated above:
   1. Increase tolerable deviation rate to 7 percent.
   2. Decrease tolerable deviation rate to 4 percent.
   3. Decrease expected population deviation rate to 1 percent.
   4. Increase expected population deviation rate to 3 percent.
   5. Increase risk of assessing control risk too low to 10 percent.

13-33 **(Designing and evaluating an attribute sample)** In the audit of the Joan Company, the auditor specifies 10 attributes of interest. The statistical parameters for each condition and the number of deviations found in the sample are as follows:

ATTRIBUTE	TOLERABLE DEVIATION RATE (%)	RISK OF ASSESSING CONTROL RISK TOO LOW (%)	EXPECTED POPULATION DEVIATION RATE (%)	NUMBER OF SAMPLE DEVIATIONS
1	4	5	1.5	1
2	3	5	0.5	0
3	6	5	2.0	4
4	6	5	2.5	5
5	8	5	3.0	2
6	3	10	1.0	0
7	4	10	1.5	2
8	5	10	2.0	4
9	6	10	2.0	1
10	7	10	3.0	4

Required

a. Assuming a large population, determine the sample size for each attribute.

b. Rounding sample size down to the nearest sample size in the tables in Figure 13-14, determine the upper deviation limit for each attribute.

c. Determine the allowance for sampling risk for each attribute.

d. Identify the controls that support the auditor's planned control risk.

e. Identify the controls that do not support the auditor's planned control risk.

13-34 **(Designing and evaluating an attribute sample)** The audit team has obtained an understanding of the internal control structure of Yates Company and has determined that it is cost beneficial to perform tests of controls related to the expenditure cycle. The tests will be restricted to inventory purchases. The results will affect the nature, timing, and extent of the substantive test work related to the valuation or allocation assertion for inventory.

The audit team has determined that they are willing to accept a 5 percent risk of assessing control risk too low. The audit team has had favorable results in performing this test in prior years, but the client has experienced a significant number of personnel changes this past year.

The audit team has asked you to provide them with a number of alternative sampling plans from which they could make a selection.

Required

a. Assuming that the number of deviations expected is 2 percent, what is (1) the minimum sample size based on a low planned control risk and (2) the maximum sample size based on moderate planned control risk?

b. Based on the assumptions stated in (1) above, what conclusions can the auditor make if the sample results show (1) one deviation and (2) three deviations?

c. One of the attributes tested is "evidence of management approval of vendor's invoice." In your testing, you discover the following:
1. The manager's initials are not present, although you observed the manager reviewing the documentation. There were no errors in information contained on the documents or in the invoice extensions.
2. Management reviewed and approved the invoice and initialed the documents. However, the supporting documentation shows a difference in quantities received compared with the invoice, and no correction has been made.

3. The invoice was reviewed and approved by management prior to payment. The manager's initials are present, and the auditor reviewed the steps performed and found no exceptions. Which of the foregoing, if any, represent a deviation from the control procedure?

13-35   **(Critique of attribute sample application)** Baker, CPA, was engaged to audit Mill Company's financial statements for the year ended September 30, 20X1. After obtaining an understanding of Mill's internal control structure, Baker decided to obtain evidential matter about the effectiveness of both the design and operation of the policies and procedures that may support a low assessed level of control risk concerning Mill's shipping and billing functions. During the prior years' audits Baker used nonstatistical sampling, but for the current year Baker used a statistical sample in the tests of controls to eliminate the need for judgment.

Baker wanted to assess control risk at a low level, so a tolerable rate of deviation or acceptable upper precision limit (UPL) of 20 percent was established. To estimate the population deviation rate and the achieved UPL, Baker decided to apply a discovery sampling technique of attribute sampling that would use a population expected error rate of 3 percent for the 8,000 shipping documents, and decided to defer consideration of allowable risk of assessing control risk too low (risk of overreliance) until evaluating the sample results. Baker used the tolerable rate, the population size, and the expected population error rate to determine that a sample size of 80 would be sufficient. When it was subsequently determined that the actual population was about 10,000 shipping documents, Baker increased the sample size to 100.

Baker's objective was to ascertain whether Mill's shipments had been properly billed. Baker took a sample of 100 invoices by selecting the first 25 invoices from the first month of each quarter. Baker then compared the invoices to the corresponding prenumbered shipping documents.

When Baker tested the sample, eight errors were discovered. In addition, one shipment that should have been billed at $10,443 was actually billed at $10,434. Baker considered this $9 to be immaterial and did not count it as an error.

In evaluating the sample results, Baker made the initial determination that a reliability level of 95 percent (risk of assessing control risk too low 5 percent) was desired and, using the appropriate statistical sampling table, determined that for eight observed deviations from a sample size of 100, the achieved UPL was 14 percent. Baker then calculated the allowance for sampling risk to be 5 percent, the difference between the actual sample deviation rate (8 percent) and the expected error rate (3 percent). Baker reasoned that the actual sample deviation rate (8 percent) plus the allowance for sampling risk (5 percent) was less than the achieved UPL (14 percent); therefore, the sample supported a low level of control risk.

Required

Describe each incorrect assumption, statement, and inappropriate application of attribute sampling in Baker's procedures.

(AICPA)

cases

13-36   **(Mt. Hood Furniture—PPS sampling problem)** You have been assigned the task of testing the accuracy of the final inventory compilation for Mt. Hood Furniture. You may assume that you have separately observed the inventory and that you are satisfied that the inventory was accurately counted. However, you need to test that quantities were accurately transcribed to the final accumulation and valuation of inventory and that the inventory is correctly priced and accumulated. The table beginning on page 617 presents the audited values associated with Mt. Hood's pricing and accumulation of all items in inventory.

The book values will be given to you by your professor. You may assume that you have performed the tests to determine the proper pricing for raw materials, work in process, and finished goods. The student should understand that the auditor will normally obtain this information only for the items included in the sample.

Required

1. Identify the audit objectives that are accomplished by this test.

2. Determine sample size based on the following audit judgments.
   a. Tolerable misstatement is assessed at $325,000.
   b. The risk of incorrect acceptance is assessed at 37 percent.
   c. Anticipated misstatement is assessed at $100,000.

3. Develop a scenario that is consistent with setting the risk of incorrect acceptance at 37 percent.

4. Select a PPS sample of the above inventory population using the sample size determined in (2) above.

5. Explain the tests that you would perform to test the correctness of pricing of raw materials, work in progress, and finished goods. (The student may wish to consult Chapter 16.)

6. Determine the amount of projected population misstatement based on your sample.

7. Considering your quantitative and qualitative results, develop a statistical conclusion and an audit conclusion based on your sample.

Stock Number	Audited Quantity	Audited Price	Audited Amount	Stock Number	Audited Quantity	Audited Price	Audited Amount
Finished Goods							
10001	13	$ 250.00	$ 3,250.00	10201	11	$ 250.00	$ 2,750.00
10002	12	$ 275.00	$ 3,300.00	10202	11	$ 275.00	$3,025.00
10003	15	$ 270.00	$ 4,050.00	10203	16	$ 270.00	$ 4,320.00
10004	11	$ 200.00	$ 2,200.00	10204	11	$ 200.00	$ 2,200.00
10005	10	$ 400.00	$ 4,000.00	10205	9	$ 400.00	$ 3,600.00
10006	10	$ 410.00	$ 4,100.00	10206	12	$ 410.00	$ 4,920.00
10007	8	$ 400.00	$ 3,200.00	10207	10	$ 400.00	$ 4,000.00
10008	9	$ 410.00	$ 3,690.00	10208	9	$ 410.00	$ 3,690.00
10009	20	$ 750.00	$ 15,000.00	10209	16	$ 750.00	$ 12,000.00
10010	9	$ 750.00	$ 6,750.00	10210	13	$ 750.00	$ 9,750.00
10011	12	$ 800.00	$ 9,600.00	10211	14	$ 800.00	$ 11,200.00
10012	14	$ 800.00	$ 11,200.00	10212	8	$ 800.00	$ 6,400.00
10013	8	$ 750.00	$ 6,000.00	10213	2	$ 745.00	$ 1,490.00
10014	11	$ 750.00	$ 8,250.00	10214	4	$ 750.00	$ 3,000.00
10015	6	$ 800.00	$ 4,800.00	10215	5	$ 800.00	$ 4,000.00
10016	10	$ 800.00	$ 8,000.00	10216	7	$ 800.00	$ 5,600.00
10017	3	$ 900.00	$ 2,700.00	10217	8	$ 900.00	$ 7,200.00
10018	11	$ 900.00	$ 9,900.00	10218	9	$ 900.00	$ 8,100.00
10019	5	$ 1,000.00	$ 5,000.00	10219	11	$ 1,000.00	$ 11,000.00
10020	8	$ 1,000.00	$ 8,000.00	10220	5	$ 1,000.00	$ 5,000.00
10021	4	$ 1,250.00	$ 5,000.00	10221	4	$ 1,250.00	$ 5,000.00
10022	4	$ 1,250.00	$ 5,000.00	10222	6	$ 1,250.00	$ 7,500.00

Stock Number	Audited Quantity	Audited Price	Audited Amount	Stock Number	Audited Quantity	Audited Price	Audited Amount
10023	2	$ 1,250.00	$ 2,500.00	10223	7	$ 1,250.00	$ 8,750.00
10024	5	$ 1,275.00	$ 6,375.00	10224	5	$ 1,275.00	$ 6,375.00
10025	2	$ 1,300.00	$ 2,600.00	10225	4	$ 1,300.00	$ 5,200.00
10101	8	$ 250.00	$ 2,000.00	10301	15	$ 250.00	$ 3,750.00
10102	8	$ 275.00	$ 2,200.00	10302	16	$ 275.00	$4,400.00
10103	12	$ 270.00	$ 3,240.00	10303	18	$ 270.00	$ 4,860.00
10104	15	$ 200.00	$ 3,000.00	10304	11	$ 200.00	$ 2,200.00
10105	12	$ 400.00	$ 4,800.00	10305	13	$ 400.00	$ 5,200.00
10106	12	$ 410.00	$ 4,920.00	10306	13	$ 410.00	$ 5,330.00
10107	11	$ 400.00	$ 4,400.00	10307	17	$ 400.00	$ 6,800.00
10108	9	$ 410.00	$ 3,690.00	10308	14	$ 410.00	$ 5,740.00
10109	10	$ 750.00	$ 7,500.00	10309	22	$ 750.00	$ 16,500.00
10110	8	$ 750.00	$ 6,000.00	10310	16	$ 750.00	$ 12,000.00
10111	8	$ 800.00	$ 6,400.00	10311	12	$ 800.00	$ 9,600.00
10112	8	$ 800.00	$ 6,400.00	10312	14	$ 800.00	$ 11,200.00
10113	6	$ 750.00	$ 4,500.00	10313	18	$ 750.00	$ 13,500.00
10114	12	$ 750.00	$ 9,000.00	10314	17	$ 750.00	$ 12,750.00
10115	8	$ 800.00	$ 6,400.00	10315	12	$ 800.00	$ 9,600.00
10116	9	$ 800.00	$ 7,200.00	10316	14	$ 800.00	$ 11,200.00
10117	5	$ 900.00	$ 4,500.00	10317	14	$ 900.00	$ 12,600.00
10118	7	$ 900.00	$ 6,300.00	10318	17	$ 900.00	$ 15,300.00
10119	4	$ 1,000.00	$ 4,000.00	10319	10	$ 1,000.00	$ 10,000.00
10120	4	$ 1,000.00	$ 4,000.00	10320	12	$ 1,000.00	$ 12,000.00
10121	7	$ 1,250.00	$ 8,750.00	10321	19	$ 1,250.00	$ 23,750.00
10122	6	$ 1,250.00	$ 7,500.00	10322	15	$ 1,250.00	$ 18,750.00
10123	4	$ 1,250.00	$ 5,000.00	10323	13	$ 1,250.00	$ 16,250.00
10124	7	$ 1,275.00	$ 8,925.00	10324	12	$ 1,275.00	$ 15,300.00
10125	5	$ 1,300.00	$ 6,500.00	10325	15	$ 1,300.00	$ 19,500.00
10401	15	$250.00	$3,750.00	10601	13	$250.00	$3,250.00
10402	14	$275.00	$3,850.00	10602	12	$275.00	$3,300.00
10403	13	$270.00	$3,510.00	10603	17	$270.00	$4,590.00
10404	9	$200.00	$1,800.00	10604	11	$200.00	$2,200.00
10405	12	$400.00	$4,800.00	10605	10	$400.00	$4,000.00
10406	9	$410.00	$3,690.00	10606	15	$410.00	$6,150.00
10407	15	$400.00	$6,000.00	10607	12	$400.00	$4,800.00
10408	12	$410.00	$4,920.00	10608	12	$410.00	$4,920.00
10409	17	$750.00	$12,750.00	10609	6	$750.00	$4,500.00
10410	12	$750.00	$9,000.00	10610	4	$750.00	$3,000.00
10411	12	$800.00	$9,600.00	10611	9	$800.00	$7,200.00
10412	12	$800.00	$9,600.00	10612	9	$800.00	$7,200.00
10413	17	$750.00	$12,750.00	10613	8	$750.00	$6,000.00
10414	15	$750.00	$11,250.00	10614	2	$750.00	$1,500.00
10415	11	$800.00	$8,800.00	10615	9	$800.00	$7,200.00
10416	13	$800.00	$10,400.00	10616	9	$800.00	$7,200.00
10417	12	$900.00	$10,800.00	10617	6	$900.00	$5,400.00

Stock Number	Audited Quantity	Audited Price	Audited Amount	Stock Number	Audited Quantity	Audited Price	Audited Amount
10418	15	$900.00	$13,500.00	10618	7	$900.00	$6,300.00
10419	9	$1,000.00	$9,000.00	10619	4	$1,000.00	$4,000.00
10420	11	$1,000.00	$11,000.00	10620	6	$1,000.00	$6,000.00
10421	16	$1,250.00	$20,000.00	10621	4	$1,250.00	$5,000.00
10422	15	$1,250.00	$18,750.00	10622	4	$1,250.00	$5,000.00
10423	12	$1,250.00	$15,000.00	10623	4	$1,250.00	$5,000.00
10424	10	$1,275.00	$12,750.00	10624	5	$1,275.00	$6,375.00
10425	12	$1,300.00	$15,600.00	10625	4	$1,300.00	$5,200.00
10501	8	$250.00	$2,000.00	10701	6	$400.00	$2,400.00
10502	6	$275.00	$1,650.00	10702	5	$450.00	$2,250.00
10503	9	$270.00	$2,430.00	10703	6	$470.00	$2,820.00
10504	11	$200.00	$2,200.00	10704	6	$470.00	$2,820.00
10505	12	$400.00	$4,800.00	10705	4	$600.00	$2,400.00
10506	11	$410.00	$4,510.00	10706	8	$610.00	$4,880.00
10507	7	$400.00	$2,800.00	10707	2	$600.00	$1,200.00
10508	9	$410.00	$3,690.00	10708	6	$610.00	$3,660.00
10509	14	$750.00	$10,500.00	10709	8	$800.00	$6,400.00
10510	16	$750.00	$12,000.00	10710	8	$800.00	$6,400.00
10511	14	$800.00	$11,200.00	10711	2	$900.00	$1,800.00
10512	12	$800.00	$9,600.00	10712	8	$900.00	$7,200.00
10513	18	$750.00	$13,500.00	10713	6	$950.00	$5,700.00
10514	19	$750.00	$14,250.00	10714	5	$950.00	$4,750.00
10515	7	$800.00	$5,600.00	10715	10	$950.00	$9,500.00
10516	7	$800.00	$5,600.00	10716	5	$975.00	$4,875.00
10517	4	$900.00	$3,600.00	10717	9	$975.00	$8,775.00
10518	4	$900.00	$3,600.00	10718	7	$1,050.00	$7,350.00
10519	8	$1,000.00	$8,000.00	10719	2	$1,050.00	$2,100.00
10520	8	$1,000.00	$8,000.00	10720	9	$1,050.00	$9,450.00
10521	4	$1,250.00	$5,000.00	10721	4	$1,175.00	$4,700.00
10522	4	$1,250.00	$5,000.00	10722	5	$1,175.00	$5,875.00
10523	4	$1,250.00	$5,000.00	10723	6	$1,300.00	$7,800.00
10524	5	$1,275.00	$6,375.00	10724	2	$1,405.00	$2,810.00
10525	4	$1,300.00	$5,200.00	10725	3	$1,500.00	$4,500.00
10801	5	$400.00	$2,000.00	11001	13	$400.00	$5,200.00
10802	5	$450.00	$2,250.00	11002	14	$450.00	$6,300.00
10803	6	$470.00	$2,820.00	11003	18	$470.00	$8,460.00
10804	7	$470.00	$3,290.00	11004	19	$470.00	$8,930.00
10805	8	$600.00	$4,800.00	11005	25	$600.00	$15,000.00
10806	3	$610.00	$1,830.00	11006	23	$610.00	$14,030.00
10807	4	$600.00	$2,400.00	11007	17	$600.00	$10,200.00
10808	8	$610.00	$4,880.00	11008	16	$610.00	$9,760.00
10809	6	$800.00	$4,800.00	11009	14	$800.00	$11,200.00
10810	3	$800.00	$2,400.00	11010	19	$800.00	$15,200.00
10811	9	$900.00	$8,100.00	11011	15	$900.00	$13,500.00
10812	8	$900.00	$7,200.00	11012	14	$900.00	$12,600.00

Stock Number	Audited Quantity	Audited Price	Audited Amount	Stock Number	Audited Quantity	Audited Price	Audited Amount
10813	4	$950.00	$3,800.00	11013	19	$950.00	$18,050.00
10814	6	$950.00	$5,700.00	11014	22	$950.00	$20,900.00
10815	4	$950.00	$3,800.00	11015	24	$950.00	$22,800.00
10816	5	$975.00	$4,875.00	11016	22	$975.00	$21,450.00
10817	8	$975.00	$7,800.00	11017	17	$975.00	$16,575.00
10818	8	$1,050.00	$8,400.00	11018	15	$1,050.00	$15,750.00
10819	6	$1,050.00	$6,300.00	11019	10	$1,050.00	$10,500.00
10820	6	$1,050.00	$6,300.00	11020	13	$1,050.00	$13,650.00
10821	7	$1,175.00	$8,225.00	11021	10	$1,175.00	$11,750.00
10822	5	$1,175.00	$5,875.00	11022	14	$1,175.00	$16,450.00
10823	4	$1,300.00	$5,200.00	11023	18	$1,300.00	$23,400.00
10824	8	$1,400.00	$11,200.00	11024	18	$1,400.00	$25,200.00
10825	5	$1,500.00	$7,500.00	11025	11	$1,500.00	$16,500.00
10901	9	$400.00	$3,600.00	11201	4	$400.00	$1,600.00
10902	9	$450.00	$4,050.00	11202	3	$450.00	$1,350.00
10903	11	$470.00	$5,170.00	11203	2	$470.00	$940.00
10904	11	$470.00	$5,170.00	11204	3	$470.00	$1,410.00
10905	7	$600.00	$4,200.00	11205	4	$600.00	$2,400.00
10906	11	$610.00	$6,710.00	11206	5	$610.00	$3,050.00
10907	8	$600.00	$4,800.00	11207	7	$600.00	$4,200.00
10908	12	$610.00	$7,320.00	11208	9	$610.00	$5,490.00
10909	7	$800.00	$5,600.00	11209	8	$800.00	$6,400.00
10910	7	$800.00	$5,600.00	11210	10	$800.00	$8,000.00
10911	4	$900.00	$3,600.00	11211	6	$900.00	$5,400.00
10912	9	$900.00	$8,100.00	11212	5	$900.00	$4,500.00
10913	10	$950.00	$9,500.00	11213	8	$950.00	$7,600.00
10914	11	$950.00	$10,450.00	11214	3	$950.00	$2,850.00
10915	13	$950.00	$12,350.00	11215	8	$950.00	$7,600.00
10916	9	$975.00	$8,775.00	11216	2	$975.00	$1,950.00
10917	12	$975.00	$11,700.00	11217	7	$975.00	$6,825.00
10918	10	$1,050.00	$10,500.00	11218	5	$1,050.00	$5,250.00
10919	6	$1,050.00	$6,300.00	11219	5	$1,050.00	$5,250.00
10920	10	$1,050.00	$10,500.00	11220	5	$1,050.00	$5,250.00
10921	9	$1,175.00	$10,575.00	11221	6	$1,175.00	$7,050.00
10922	12	$1,175.00	$14,100.00	11222	5	$1,175.00	$5,875.00
10923	8	$1,300.00	$10,400.00	11223	4	$1,300.00	$5,200.00
10924	8	$1,400.00	$11,200.00	11224	5	$1,400.00	$7,000.00
10925	6	$1,500.00	$9,000.00	11225	1	$1,500.00	$1,500.00
11301	14	$400.00	$5,600.00	11501	11	$800.00	$8,800.00
11302	16	$450.00	$7,200.00	11502	18	$800.00	$14,400.00
11303	17	$470.00	$7,990.00	11503	12	$875.00	$10,500.00
11304	18	$470.00	$8,460.00	11504	14	$875.00	$12,250.00
11305	17	$600.00	$10,200.00	11505	11	$900.00	$9,900.00
11306	18	$610.00	$10,980.00	11506	14	$900.00	$12,600.00
11307	13	$600.00	$7,800.00	11507	12	$900.00	$10,800.00

Stock Number	Audited Quantity	Audited Price	Audited Amount	Stock Number	Audited Quantity	Audited Price	Audited Amount
11308	14	$610.00	$8,540.00	11508	13	$900.00	$11,700.00
11309	12	$800.00	$9,600.00	11509	15	$1,100.00	$16,500.00
11310	18	$800.00	$14,400.00	11510	11	$1,100.00	$12,100.00
11311	11	$900.00	$9,900.00	11511	14	$1,100.00	$15,400.00
11312	13	$900.00	$11,700.00	11512	13	$1,100.00	$14,300.00
11313	13	$950.00	$12,350.00	11513	10	$1,100.00	$11,000.00
11314	14	$950.00	$13,300.00	11514	15	$1,250.00	$18,750.00
11315	11	$950.00	$10,450.00	11515	10	$1,250.00	$12,500.00
11316	12	$975.00	$11,700.00	11516	14	$1,250.00	$17,500.00
11317	15	$975.00	$14,625.00	11517	11	$1,250.00	$13,750.00
11318	15	$1,050.00	$15,750.00	11518	13	$1,250.00	$16,250.00
11319	11	$1,050.00	$11,550.00	11519	10	$1,400.00	$14,000.00
11320	12	$1,050.00	$12,600.00	11520	12	$1,400.00	$16,800.00
11321	10	$1,175.00	$11,750.00	11521	10	$2,000.00	$20,000.00
11322	9	$1,175.00	$10,575.00	11522	8	$2,000.00	$16,000.00
11323	9	$1,300.00	$11,700.00	11523	7	$3,250.00	$22,750.00
11324	10	$1,400.00	$14,000.00	11524	7	$3,250.00	$22,750.00
11325	5	$1,500.00	$7,500.00	11525	8	$2,500.00	$20,000.00
11401	5	$800.00	$4,000.00	11601	6	$800.00	$4,800.00
11402	8	$800.00	$6,400.00	11602	6	$800.00	$4,800.00
11403	3	$875.00	$2,625.00	11603	8	$875.00	$7,000.00
11404	4	$875.00	$3,500.00	11604	7	$875.00	$6,125.00
11405	8	$900.00	$7,200.00	11605	11	$900.00	$9,900.00
11406	10	$900.00	$9,000.00	11606	8	$900.00	$7,200.00
11407	6	$900.00	$5,400.00	11607	5	$900.00	$4,500.00
11408	7	$900.00	$6,300.00	11608	7	$900.00	$6,300.00
11409	5	$1,100.00	$5,500.00	11609	6	$1,100.00	$6,600.00
11410	8	$1,100.00	$8,800.00	11610	9	$1,100.00	$9,900.00
11411	9	$1,100.00	$9,900.00	11611	7	$1,100.00	$7,700.00
11412	7	$1,100.00	$7,700.00	11612	3	$1,100.00	$3,300.00
11413	11	$1,100.00	$12,100.00	11613	4	$1,100.00	$4,400.00
11414	15	$1,250.00	$18,750.00	11614	10	$1,250.00	$12,500.00
11415	10	$1,250.00	$12,500.00	11615	7	$1,250.00	$8,750.00
11416	9	$1,250.00	$11,250.00	11616	6	$1,250.00	$7,500.00
11417	13	$1,250.00	$16,250.00	11617	11	$1,250.00	$13,750.00
11418	11	$1,250.00	$13,750.00	11618	9	$1,250.00	$11,250.00
11419	9	$1,400.00	$12,600.00	11619	13	$1,400.00	$18,200.00
11420	5	$1,400.00	$7,000.00	11620	10	$1,400.00	$14,000.00
11421	5	$2,000.00	$10,000.00	11621	7	$2,000.00	$14,000.00
11422	7	$2,000.00	$14,000.00	11622	9	$2,000.00	$18,000.00
11423	6	$3,250.00	$19,500.00	11623	7	$3,250.00	$22,750.00
11424	5	$3,250.00	$16,250.00	11624	5	$3,250.00	$16,250.00
11425	6	$2,500.00	$15,000.00	11625	4	$2,500.00	$10,000.00
11701	3	$800.00	$2,400.00	11901	7	$600.00	$4,200.00
11702	9	$800.00	$7,200.00	11902	6	$600.00	$3,600.00

Stock Number	Audited Quantity	Audited Price	Audited Amount	Stock Number	Audited Quantity	Audited Price	Audited Amount
11703	6	$875.00	$5,250.00	11903	10	$700.00	$7,000.00
11704	6	$875.00	$5,250.00	11904	6	$700.00	$4,200.00
11705	10	$1,100.00	$11,000.00	11905	7	$900.00	$6,300.00
11706	12	$1,100.00	$13,200.00	11906	5	$900.00	$4,500.00
11707	8	$1,100.00	$8,800.00	11907	4	$1,525.00	$6,100.00
11708	7	$1,100.00	$7,700.00	11908	7	$1,525.00	$10,675.00
11709	7	$1,500.00	$10,500.00	11909	6	$1,525.00	$9,150.00
11710	7	$1,500.00	$10,500.00	11910	5	$1,525.00	$7,625.00
11711	8	$1,600.00	$12,800.00	11911	6	$1,525.00	$9,150.00
11712	6	$1,600.00	$9,600.00	11912	5	$1,525.00	$7,625.00
11713	5	$1,450.00	$7,250.00	11913	6	$1,525.00	$9,150.00
11714	4	$1,450.00	$5,800.00	11914	8	$1,525.00	$12,200.00
11715	3	$1,700.00	$5,100.00	11915	6	$2,475.00	$14,850.00
11716	5	$1,700.00	$8,500.00	11916	8	$2,475.00	$19,800.00
11717	2	$1,800.00	$3,600.00	11917	5	$2,475.00	$12,375.00
11718	4	$1,800.00	$7,200.00	11918	8	$2,475.00	$19,800.00
11719	6	$1,400.00	$8,400.00	11919	6	$2,475.00	$14,850.00
11720	4	$1,400.00	$5,600.00	11920	8	$2,475.00	$19,800.00
11721	4	$2,000.00	$8,000.00	11921	6	$2,475.00	$14,850.00
11722	5	$2,000.00	$10,000.00	11922	7	$2,475.00	$17,325.00
11723	5	$3,250.00	$16,250.00	11923	4	$2,500.00	$10,000.00
11724	6	$3,250.00	$19,500.00	11924	5	$2,500.00	$12,500.00
11725	1	$5,500.00	$5,500.00	11925	5	$3,500.00	$17,500.00
11801	6	$600.00	$3,600.00	12001	9	$600.00	$5,400.00
11802	5	$600.00	$3,000.00	12002	7	$600.00	$4,200.00
11803	11	$700.00	$7,700.00	12003	14	$700.00	$9,800.00
11804	5	$700.00	$3,500.00	12004	16	$700.00	$11,200.00
11805	8	$900.00	$7,200.00	12005	10	$900.00	$9,000.00
11806	7	$900.00	$6,300.00	12006	10	$900.00	$9,000.00
11807	6	$1,525.00	$9,150.00	12007	8	$1,525.00	$12,200.00
11808	7	$1,525.00	$10,675.00	12008	9	$1,525.00	$13,725.00
11809	3	$1,525.00	$4,575.00	12009	3	$1,525.00	$4,575.00
11810	2	$1,525.00	$3,050.00	12010	6	$1,525.00	$9,150.00
11811	5	$1,525.00	$7,625.00	12011	7	$1,525.00	$10,675.00
11812	8	$1,525.00	$12,200.00	12012	9	$1,525.00	$13,725.00
11813	7	$1,525.00	$10,675.00	12013	5	$1,525.00	$7,625.00
11814	4	$1,525.00	$6,100.00	12014	7	$1,525.00	$10,675.00
11815	8	$2,475.00	$19,800.00	12015	11	$2,475.00	$27,225.00
11816	9	$2,475.00	$22,275.00	12016	8	$2,475.00	$19,800.00
11817	6	$2,475.00	$14,850.00	12017	8	$2,475.00	$19,800.00
11818	4	$2,475.00	$9,900.00	12018	6	$2,475.00	$14,850.00
11819	4	$2,475.00	$9,900.00	12019	8	$2,475.00	$19,800.00
11820	5	$2,475.00	$12,375.00	12020	5	$2,475.00	$12,375.00
11821	7	$2,475.00	$17,325.00	12021	5	$2,475.00	$12,375.00
11822	4	$2,475.00	$9,900.00	12022	9	$2,475.00	$22,275.00

STOCK NUMBER	AUDITED QUANTITY	AUDITED PRICE	AUDITED AMOUNT	STOCK NUMBER	AUDITED QUANTITY	AUDITED PRICE	AUDITED AMOUNT
11823	8	$2,500.00	$20,000.00	12023	7	$2,500.00	$17,500.00
11824	3	$2,500.00	$7,500.00	12024	5	$2,500.00	$12,500.00
11825	2	$3,500.00	$7,000.00	12025	5	$3,500.00	$17,500.00

Raw Materials				Work in Progress			
20001	2056	$12.80	$26,316.80	10005	10	$350.00	$3,500.00
20002	5090	$15.20	$77,368.00	10006	10	$350.00	$3,500.00
20003	6344	$10.50	$66,612.00	10007	10	$300.00	$3,000.00
20004	10052	$12.95	$130,173.40	10008	10	$310.00	$3,100.00
20005	9900	$10.95	$108,405.00	11201	10	$350.00	$3,500.00
20006	1233	$43.00	$53,019.00	11202	10	$350.00	$3,500.00
20007	1145	$43.00	$49,235.00	11203	10	$370.00	$3,700.00
20008	1130	$43.00	$48,590.00	11204	10	$370.00	$3,700.00
20009	1030	$43.00	$44,290.00	11205	10	$450.00	$4,500.00
20010	1288	$43.00	$55,384.00	11206	10	$460.00	$4,600.00
20011	10066	$5.85	$58,886.10	11207	10	$450.00	$4,500.00
20012	18300	$5.85	$107,055.00	11208	10	$460.00	$4,600.00
20013	18587	$5.85	$108,733.95	11209	10	$600.00	$6,000.00
20014	19525	$5.85	$114,221.25	11210	10	$600.00	$6,000.00
20015	13222	$5.85	$77,348.70	11211	10	$700.00	$7,000.00
20016	3606	$25.30	$91,231.80	11212	10	$700.00	$7,000.00
20017	4723	$25.30	$119,491.90	11213	10	$700.00	$7,000.00
20018	1434	$25.30	$36,280.20	11214	10	$700.00	$7,000.00
20019	6782	$25.30	$171,584.60	11215	10	$700.00	$7,000.00
20020	2644	$25.30	$66,893.20	11216	10	$700.00	$7,000.00
20021	4833	$27.30	$131,940.90	11217	10	$700.00	$7,000.00
20022	4521	$27.30	$123,423.30	11218	10	$825.00	$8,250.00
20023	3640	$27.30	$99,372.00	11219	10	$825.00	$8,250.00
20024	5703	$27.30	$155,691.90	11220	10	$825.00	$8,250.00
				11221	10	$875.00	$8,750.00
Small Tools Inventory			$37,989.00	11222	10	$875.00	$8,750.00
				11223	10	$900.00	$9,000.00
				11224	5	$1,000.00	$5,000.00
				11225	5	$1,100.00	$5,500.00

professional simulation

Research

Situation	Nonstatistical Audit Sampling	Audit Conclusions

You have been assigned to the audit of Astor Electronics, Inc. Astor is engaged in the business of marketing a wide variety of consumer electronic products throughout the United

States. Astor has over 100 stores in the United States that retail directly to consumers and four regional warehouses. Approximately 40 percent of Astor's inventory is in the company's four regional warehouses. You have been assigned to observe inventory in the warehouse for Astor's western region. What factors do professional standards identify that should be considered when planning a sample for substantive tests of details? Cut and paste the standard sections that apply to this issue.

```
                    ┌─────────────┐
                    │  Situation  │
 ┌──────────────────┤             ├──────────────────────────────────┐
 │    Research      │             │  Nonstatistical  │     Audit      │
 │                  │             │ Audit Sampling   │  Conclusions   │
 └──────────────────┴─────────────┴──────────────────┴────────────────┘
```

You have selected a nonstatistical sample for the western region warehouse for Astor Electronics, Inc. as follows:

STRATA	BOOK VALUE POPULATION		NUMBER OF ITEMS		SAMPLE SIZE		BOOK VALUE SAMPLE		AUDITED VALUE SAMPLE
1	$ 1,750,000	23%	350	5%	10	20%	$ 52,500	55%	$ 51,000
2	$ 3,000,000	40%	1,500	20%	15	30%	$ 30,500	32%	$ 30,500
3	$ 2,750,000	37%	5,500	75%	25	50%	$ 12,250	13%	$ 10,000
	$ 7,500,000	100%	7,350	100%	50	100%	$ 95,250	100%	$ 91,500

You have set tolerable misstatement for the inventory at $350,000.

```
                                       ┌──────────────────┐
                                       │  Nonstatistical  │
 ┌──────────────────┬─────────────────┤  Audit Sampling  ├─────────────┐
 │    Research      │    Situation    │                  │    Audit    │
 │                  │                 │                  │ Conclusions │
 └──────────────────┴─────────────────┴──────────────────┴─────────────┘
```

1. What is your estimate of the audited value of the population using nonstatistical ratio estimation?

2. What is your estimate of the audited value of the population using nonstatistical difference estimation?

```
                                                    ┌─────────────┐
                                                    │    Audit    │
 ┌──────────────────┬─────────────────┬────────────┤ Conclusions │
 │    Research      │    Situation    │ Nonstatistical            │
 │                  │                 │ Audit Sampling            │
 └──────────────────┴─────────────────┴───────────────────────────┘
```

Draft a memo with your conclusions about whether the book value of inventory in the western region warehouse is fairly presented in all material respects. Outline the reasoning behind your conclusions.

To: Audit File

Re: Results of Audit Sampling of Western Region Warehouse for Astor Electronics, Inc.

From: CPA Candidate

PART

[4]

AUDITING THE TRANSACTION CYCLES

WHAT IS THE MOST FREQUENT CAUSE OF FINANCIAL STATEMENT RESTATEMENTS?

In October 2002 the U.S. General Accounting Office released its report on *Financial Statement Restatement,* and revenue recognition problems topped the list of financial statement improprieties. Here is a sample of just how significant revenue recognition problems were:

- Thirty-eight percent of restatements between 1997 and June 30, 2002 involved revenue recognition issues.
- Revenue recognition issues were the primary reason for restatements in each year.
- Approximately 50 percent of the SEC's enforcement cases involved revenue recognition issues.
- Eight out of the top ten losses in market capitalization in 2000 related to improper revenue recognition. The top three lost nearly $20 billion in market value in just three days after reporting restatements of revenue recognition.

Auditors should be alert for the following types of problems.

Consignment Sales. Sale arrangements that have the characteristics of a consignment sale include giving the buyer a lengthy right of return, substantial payment is made upon the resale of the product, and sellers are required to repurchase inventory at a specified price, or the buyer does not assume risks of ownership due to future pricing concessions. For example, if a manufacturer promises a wholesaler future price concession based upon holding and financing costs for the length of time between purchase and sale, the sale should be accounted for as a consignment sale and revenue should be deferred.

Refund Rights. When rights of return exist, or are likely to be accepted, a reasonable estimate of refunds should be made before revenue is recognized. In determining the amount of the estimated refunds, management should consider competition, obsolescence, and the length of time over which the product can be returned.

Bill and Hold Transactions. These are transactions where a company bills customers without shipping goods (see the discussion of the Sunbeam Corporation in the introduction to Chapter 6). For example, assume that a manufacturer leases a portion of its facility to a customer and records revenue on sales to this customer when products are delivered to the customer's portion of the facility. Revenue recognition is appropriate only if the manufacturer has no rights or risk associated with the product once they were delivered to the customer's space.

Gross Sales. Top-line revenues may be very important. Companies may award bonuses based on total revenues, and companies have been valued based on multiples of revenues. Consider the hotel chain that manages properties that it does not own. It should not record revenues from managed properties in a similar fashion to owned properties and then record related expenses of property management. Rather, it should only record its management fee as revenues.

Round-Trip Transactions. Auditors should be alert to situations such as the fraud at Homestore, Inc. Homestore paid inflated sums to various vendors for services or products, the vendors used these funds to buy advertising from two media companies, and the media companies bought advertising from Homestore. Homestore then improperly recorded the money it received from the sale of the advertising as revenue in its financial statements. The SEC viewed these transactions as a circular flow of money where Homestore recognized its own cash as revenue.

Each of these situations represents important risks of material misstatement in the financial statements. Read on in the chapter to better understand how the auditor assesses the risk of such material misstatements and how the auditor should address revenue recognition when considering the risk of fraud.

Source: D. Paul Regan, "Revenue Recognition: Now, Later or Never?," *California CPA,* September 2003.

[PREVIEW OF CHAPTER 14]

Chapter 14 focuses on specific aspects of auditing the revenue cycle. It begins with a discussion of planning activities related to the revenue cycle. It then focuses on specific controls commonly seen in the revenue cycle as well as specific substantive tests related to the revenue cycle. The following diagram provides an overview of the chapter organization and content.

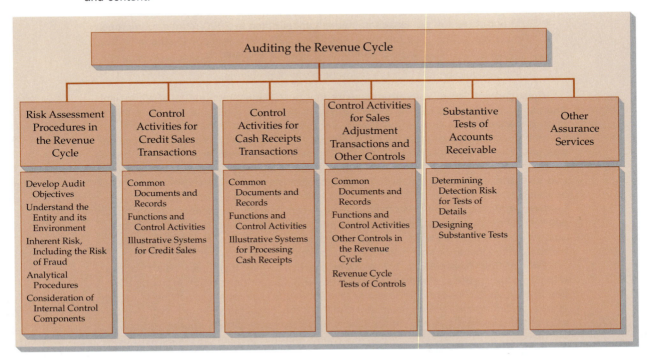

Chapter 14 focuses on the following aspects of the auditor's decision process associated with auditing the revenue cycle.

After studying this chapter you should understand the factors that influence the following audit decisions.

D1. What is the nature of the revenue cycle, and how are specific audit objectives developed for the revenue cycle?

D2. How does understanding the entity and its environment affect audit planning decisions in the revenue cycle?

D3. What are the important inherent risks in the revenue cycle?

D4. How does the auditor determine analytical procedures that would be effective in identifying potential misstatements in the revenue cycle?

D5. What are the relevant aspects of internal control components for the revenue cycle?

D6. What should be considered in evaluating control activities for credit sales transactions?

D7. What should be considered in evaluating control activities for cash receipts?

D8. What should be considered in evaluating control activities for sales adjustment transactions?

D9. What are the relevant aspects of tests of controls when the auditor plans to assess control risk below the maximum for the revenue cycle?

D10. What are the factors involved in determining an acceptable level of tests of details risk for accounts receivable assertions?

D11. How does the auditor determine the elements of an audit program for substantive tests to achieve specific audit objectives for accounts receivable?

D12. How are confirmation procedures used in auditing accounts receivable?

D13. How does the auditor use the knowledge obtained during the audit of the revenue cycle to support other assurance services?

RISK ASSESSMENT PROCEDURES IN THE REVENUE CYCLE

Audit Decision 1

■ What is the nature of the revenue cycle, and how are specific audit objectives developed for the revenue cycle?

An entity's **revenue cycle** consists of activities related to the exchange of goods and services with customers and to the collection of the revenue in cash. For a merchandising company, the classes of transactions in the revenue cycle include (1) **credit sales** (sales made on accounts), (2) **cash receipts** (collections on accounts and cash sales), and (3) **sales adjustments** (discounts, sales returns and allowances, and uncollectable accounts provisions and write-offs). These transactions affect the accounts depicted in Figure 14-1. Three of these accounts—cost of goods sold, inventory, and cash—are also affected by transaction classes in other cycles. Coverage of the audit of these accounts is deferred to later chapters.

DEVELOP AUDIT OBJECTIVES

The audit objectives for the revenue cycle relate to obtaining sufficient competent evidence about each significant financial statement assertion that pertains to revenue cycle transactions and balances. Recall from Chapter 6 (see Figure 6-2) that specific audit objectives are derived from five categories of management's assertions. Specific audit objectives are developed for transactions, balances, and disclosures related to a specific transaction cycle. These audit objectives for the rev-

Figure 14-1 ■ The Revenue Cycle

Revenue Transaction	Debit	Credit
Credit Sale	Accounts Receivable	Sales
	Cost of Goods Sold	Inventory
Cash Receipt	Cash	Accounts Receivable
	Sales Discounts	
Sales Returns and Allowances	Sales Returns and Allowances	Accounts Receivable
Provision for Bad Debts	Bad Debt Expense	Allowance for Doubtful Accounts
Write-off of Bad Debts	Allowance for Doubtful Accounts	Accounts Receivable

enue cycle are shown in Figure 14-2. Specific revenue cycle transactions are keyed to numbered audit objectives (C1 … C4, EO1 … EO4, and so on) that are used throughout Chapter 14.

UNDERSTAND THE ENTITY AND ITS ENVIRONMENT

Audit Decision 2

■ How does understanding the entity and its environment affect audit planning decisions in the revenue cycle?

Chapter 7 explained how the auditor uses an understanding of the entity and its environment to develop a knowledgeable perspective about the entity and its financial statements and to assess the risk of material misstatement. Understanding the entity and its environment assists the auditor in:

■ Developing an expectation of total revenues by understanding the client's capacity, marketplace, and clients.

■ Developing an expectation of gross margin by understanding the client's market share and competitive advantage in the marketplace.

■ Developing an expectation of net receivables based on the average collection period for the client and industry.

In addition, the process of generating revenues drives many expenses (e.g., cost of goods sold or selling expenses). Thus, understanding the revenue cycle assists in developing expectations of an entity's expenditures associated with other transaction cycles and assessing the risk that unaudited earnings contain material misstatements.

Figure 14-3 illustrates the importance of understanding the revenue cycle for five different entities, which are discussed throughout Part 4 of the text. These include a manufacturer of construction machinery and equipment (SIC 3531), a manufacturer of electronic computers (SIC 3571), a retail grocer (SIC 5411), a hotel (SIC 7011), and a local school district (SIC 8211). These examples define a wide spectrum of underlying business practices and an equally wide spectrum of risk for the auditor. The auditor would normally obtain this understanding though previous experience with the entity, obtaining information from trade associations, reading business periodicals and newspapers, and consulting with publications of industry information such as Robert Morris Associates or Value Line.

Figure 14-2 ■ Specific Audit Objectives for the Revenue Cycle

Specific Audit Objectives

Transaction Objectives

Occurrence. Recorded sales transactions represent goods shipped or services provided during the period **(EO1).**

Recorded cash receipt transactions represent cash received during the period **(EO2).**

Recorded sales adjustment transactions during the period represent authorized discounts, returns and allowances, and uncollectable accounts **(E03).**

Completeness. All sales **(C1)**, cash receipts **(C2)**, and sales adjustments **(C3)** made during the period were recorded.

Accuracy. All sales **(VA1)**, cash receipts **(VA2)**, and sales adjustments **(VA3)** are accurately valued using GAAP and correctly journalized, summarized and posted.

Cutoff. All sales **(EO1 or C1)**, cash receipts **(EO2 or C2)**, and sales adjustments **(EO3 or C3)** have been recorded in the correct accounting period.

Classification. All sales **(PD1)**, cash receipts **(PD2)**, and sales adjustments **(PD3)** have been recorded in the proper accounts.

Balance Objectives

Existence. Accounts receivable representing amounts owed by customers exists at the balance sheet date **(EO4).**

Completeness. Accounts receivable include all claims on customers at the balance sheet date **(C4).**

Rights and Obligations. Accounts receivable at the balance sheet date represent legal claims of the entity on customers for payment **(RO1).**

Valuation and Allocation. Accounts receivable represents gross claims on customers at the balance sheet date and agrees with the sum of the accounts receivable subsidiary ledger **(VA4).**

The allowance for uncollectable accounts represents a reasonable estimate of the difference between gross receivables and their net realizable value **(VA5).**

Disclosure Objectives

Occurrence and Rights and Obligations. Disclosed revenue cycle events and transactions have occurred and pertain to the entity **(PD4).**

Completeness. All revenue cycle disclosures that should have been included in the financial statements have been included **(PD5).**

Classification and Understandability. Revenue cycle information is appropriately presented and described and information in disclosures is clearly expressed **(PD6).**

Accuracy and Valuation. Revenue cycle information is disclosed accurately and at appropriate amounts **(PD7).**

Students should note that the manufacturers have the most significant issues with revenue recognition. The manufacturer of construction machinery and equipment may provide liberal terms of sale and may even finance the sale. The computer manufacturer may bundle products that have various conditions that must be met before revenue can be recognized. Revenue recognition is more straightforward for the retail grocer, hotel, and the school district. These last three industries also have very short collection periods and low credit risks.

Figure 14-3 ■ Understanding an Entity's Revenue Cycle

Example Industry Traits	Developing a Knowledgeable Perspective about the Entity's Financial Statements (Industry Median)	Assessing the Risk of Material Misstatement
Mfg. of Construction Machinery and Equipment • Sales dependent on level of construction spending • Companies may have a financing arm to finance sales of expensive equipment.	Sales to Total Assets: 2.0 Sales to Net Fixed Assets: 10.0 Median Gross Margin: 28.7% Median Collection Period. 45 days	• Concerns about terms of sale and revenue recognition. • Moderate collection risk • Loan loss reserve is important estimate in financing subsidiaries
Computer Mfg. • Sells products ranging from large computers and network servers to personal computers. • Consulting services may represent a significant component of revenues. • Margins depend on competing technologies.	Sales to Total Assets: 2.3 Sales to Net Fixed Assets: 25.7 Median Gross Margin: 34.4% Median Collection Period: 52 days	• Significant revenue recognition issues associated with bundled products. • Cash collection may precede revenue recognition, resulting in unearned revenues. • Competitive environment significantly affects selling prices and gross margins. • Normal concerns about collection risk.
Retail Grocer • Numerous products where product differentiation is difficult. • Companies are improving margins by leasing space to banks and coffee companies. • Intense competition from club stores and supercenters.	Sales to Total Assets: 5.0 Sales to Net Fixed Assets: 13.3 Median Gross Margin: 24.7% Median Collection Period: 2 days	• Do sales volumes cover fixed costs? • Gross margins related to product mix and space utilization.
Hotel • Importance of brand development. • Generates revenues from hotel occupancy and services (food and conferences), franchise fees, and property management.	Sales to Total Assets: 0.6 Sales to Net Fixed Assets: 0.7 Median Gross Margin: n/a Median Collection Period: 5 days	• Revenue recognition for property management in the hotel industry has changed as a result of EITF 97-2.[a] • Sales volumes, prices, and occupancy rates. • Major hotel companies that enter into management agreements experience a higher degree of collection risk.
Local School District • Tax levies are the major source of revenues. • Taxes may be distributed on headcount and student performance on exams.	Sales to Total Assets: 0.7 Sales to Net Fixed Assets: 1.2 Median Gross Margin: n/a Median Collection Period: 7 days	• What is the quality of the information system that reports student headcount? • Low collection risk. • Business risk associated with high fixed cost and enrollment declines.

a 1 EITF 97-2, "Application of FASB Statement No. 94 and APB Opinion No. 16 to Physician Practice Management Entities and Certain Other Entities with Contractual Management Agreements."

Audit Decision 3

■ **What are the important inherent risks in the revenue cycle?**

INHERENT RISK, INCLUDING THE RISK OF FRAUD

In assessing inherent risk for revenue cycle assertions, the auditor should consider pervasive factors that may affect assertions in several cycles, including the revenue cycle, as well as factors that may pertain only to specific assertions in the revenue cycle. These include factors that provide the incentive for management to misstate revenue cycle assertions and fraudulent financial reporting, such as:

■ Pressures to overstate revenues in order to report achieving announced revenue or profitability targets that were not achieved in reality owing to such factors as global, national, or regional economic conditions; the impact of technological developments on the entity's competitiveness; or poor management. Devices employed to overstate revenues are discussed in the opening vignette to this chapter.

■ Pressures to overstate cash and gross receivables or understate the allowance for doubtful accounts in order to report a higher level of working capital in the face of the need to meet debt covenants.

Other factors that contribute to misstatements in the revenue cycle include the following:

■ The volume of sales, cash receipts, and sales adjustment transactions is often high, resulting in numerous opportunities for errors to occur.

---

revenue recognition and cooking the books

Revenue is a critical driver of earnings and cash flows. If companies are trying to report good figures to Wall Street, they often must report sales growth. But what happens when a company does not achieve targeted sales growth? Most companies have the integrity to ensure that reported revenues are materially correct. However, this is not always the case. Following is a brief summary of five companies that *cooked the books.* Overstating revenues was a key part of the scheme to inflate revenues and earnings. Auditors are expected to uncover these types of financial statement problems.

As an aside, the chief executive officers of these companies were involved in the fraud, were convicted or pleaded guilty for their involvement in the accounting fraud, and spent time in jail.

COMPANY	WHAT THE COMPANY DID
Underwriters Financial Group	Reported nonexistent revenues to make a losing company look like a profit maker.
Donnkenny	Concocted false invoices and revenues to meet earnings goals.
California Micro Devices	Led staff to record sales for products not shipped or even manufactured.
Home Theater Products Int'l.	Invented customers and sales to show profits when red ink was the reality
FNN	Spun companies controlled by FNN into an elaborate plot that inflated FNN's sales.

Source: "Lies, Dammed Lies, and Managed Earnings," *Fortune,* August 2, 1999, p. 75.

- The timing and amount of revenue to be recognized may be contentious owing to factors such as ambiguous accounting standards, the need to make estimates, the complexity of the calculations involved, and purchasers' rights of return.
- When receivables are factored with recourse, the correct classification of the transaction, as a sale or a borrowing, may be contentious.
- Receivables may be misclassified as current or noncurrent owing to difficulties in estimating the likelihood of collection within the next year or the source of events on which collection is contingent.
- Cash receipt transactions generate liquid assets that are particularly susceptible to misappropriation.
- Sales adjustment transactions may be used to conceal thefts of cash received from customers by overstating discounts, recording fictitious sales returns, or writing off customers' balances as uncollectible.

Because of the variety and potential magnitude of the misstatements enumerated above that can occur in the absence of effective controls, the auditor must always give careful consideration to inherent risks in the revenue cycle. Risks associated with revenue recognition are such that the auditor should consider the existence and occurrence assertion to be a significant inherent risk. In many cases, management adopts extensive internal controls to address many of these issues attributable to their own risk assessment procedures.

ANALYTICAL PROCEDURES

Audit Decision 4
■ **How does the auditor determine analytical procedures that would be effective in identifying potential misstatements in the revenue cycle?**

Analytical procedures are cost effective, and they are often effective in identifying potential misstatements in the financial statements. The most effective analytical procedures use the auditor's knowledge of the business and industry. Some example analytical procedures that may apply to the revenue cycle are presented in Figure 14-4.

The first step in performing analytical procedures is obtaining an understanding of total revenues given (1) the client's capacity and (2) the client's marketplace for those products. The auditor should understand the **entity's capacity**—the maximum volume of sales that it could generate if it fully utilized its facilities and employees to manufacture and deliver products and services. Auditors should be sensitive to the volume of sales that an entity records given its maximum capacity, the number of shifts that an entity operates, and seasonal variations in the industry. It is generally more effective to evaluate total revenues against a measure of business activity than comparing current revenues with prior-year revenues. Hence, the auditor will often tailor analytical procedures to the client's industry that compare revenues with measures of the process that produces revenues. For example, the auditor might evaluate the following trends:

- Revenue per number of manufacturing employee labor hours, for a labor-intensive manufacturing process.
- Revenue to plant assets in a capital-intensive manufacturing process.
- Revenue per square foot of retail space for a grocer.
- Revenue compared to occupancy rates for industries such as hotels or airlines.
- Tax revenue per student for a school district.

Figure 14-4 ■ Analytical Procedures Commonly Used to Audit the Revenue Cycle

Ratio	Formula	Audit Significance
Sales to Capacity	Net Sales ÷ Nonfinancial Measure of Capacity	Helpful in assessing the reasonableness of total revenues.
Market Share	Client's Net Sales ÷ Net Sales of Industry	Helpful in assessing the reasonableness of both total revenues and gross margins. Larger market share is often associated with larger gross margins.
Sales to Total Assets	Sales ÷ Average Total Assets	This ratio is useful for manufacturing and other asset-based companies. Describes the relationship between assets and sales revenues.
Accounts Receivable Growth to Sales Growth	$((\text{Accounts Receivable}_t \div \text{Accounts Receivable}_{t-1}) - 1) \div ((\text{Sales}_t \div \text{Sales}_{t-1}) - 1)$	Ratios larger than 1.0 indicate that receivables are growing faster than sales. Large ratios may indicate possible collection problems.
Accounts Receivable Turn Days	Avg. Accounts Receivable ÷ Sales × 365	Useful in comparing with industry averages. Longer collection periods may indicate collection problems. Prior experience and current sales volumes may be useful in estimating current net receivables.
Uncollectable Accounts Expense to Net Credit Sales	Uncollectable Accounts Expense ÷ Net Sales	Useful in evaluating the reasonableness of uncollectable accounts expense. Smaller ratios may indicate an inadequate provision for uncollectable accounts.
Uncollectable Accounts Expense to Accounts Receivable Write-offs	Uncollectable Accounts $\text{Expense}_{t-1} \div \text{Actual Accounts Receivable Write-offs}_t$	Useful in evaluating the reasonableness of prior period's uncollectable accounts expense. Smaller ratios may indicate an inadequate estimation process.
New Product Revenues to Total Revenues	Revenues from New Products Introduced During the Year ÷ Total Revenues	Companies with a high proportion of revenues from new products may earn a premium gross margin due to ability to innovate.

When evaluating these figures, the auditor must also be sensitive to trends in the marketplace for the client's products. The auditor must be able to assess the reasonableness of revenue increases for a manufacturer of constructions equipment when road and government building construction is declining, or the reasonableness of occupancy rates and room prices for a hotel chain when new competitive properties have entered key markets.

Finally, it is important for the auditor to evaluate the client's accounts receivable turn days, or average collection period, and be able to compare the collection period with industry norms. Increases in the client's collection period are indicators that receivables are growing faster than sales volumes, which consumes operating cash flows and may lead to liquidity problems. It is particularly important for growth companies to monitor the entity's collection period because any growth in sales is usually accompanied by receivable growth that consumes operating cash. If receivables are growing faster than sales, it may be an indication that the company is accomplishing sales growth by taking on increased credit risk.

Other analytical procedures that the auditor might assess in the revenue cycle could include:

- Sales turnover, a ratio of sales to average total assets.
- Trends in gross margins compared with trends in market share.
- Estimates of accounts receivable given knowledge of the company's sales volumes, prices, and historical collection period.
- Comparison of accounts receivables to the receivables estimated in the company's cash budgets.
- Uncollectable accounts expense to net credit sales.
- Uncollectable accounts expense to actual uncollectable accounts written off.

CONSIDERATION OF INTERNAL CONTROL COMPONENTS

Audit Decision 5

■ What are the relevant aspects of internal control components for the revenue cycle?

In this section, we consider the applicability of four of the five internal control components to the revenue cycle—the control environment, risk assessment, information and communication (which includes the accounting system), and monitoring. An understanding of these components is required under either a primarily substantive audit strategy or a lower assessed level of control risk approach. The applicability of the fifth component, control activities, is discussed later in the chapter in separate sections for each of the three major transaction classes in the revenue cycle.

Recall from Chapter 10 that the auditor should obtain an understanding of the sales cycle that is sufficient to plan the audit. That is, the auditor needs to have a sufficient understanding to be able to (1) identify the types of potential misstatements, (2) consider factors that affect the risk of material misstatement, and (3) design substantive tests.

Control Environment

The control environment consists of several factors that may mitigate several of the inherent risks related to the revenue cycle discussed earlier in this chapter. In addition, these factors may enhance or negate the effectiveness of other internal control components in controlling the risk of misstatements in revenue cycle assertions.

A key control environment factor in reducing the risk of fraudulent financial reporting through the overstatement of revenues and receivables is management's adoption of, and adherence to, high standards of integrity and ethical values. Related aspects include eliminating incentives to dishonest reporting (e.g., undue emphasis on meeting unrealistic sales or profit targets) and the supporting activities of an effective board of directors and audit committee.

Several of the identified inherent risks related to contentious accounting issues, complex calculations, and accounting estimates that may pertain to revenue cycle assertions may be controlled if management has made the appropriate commitment to competence on the part of the chief financial officer and accounting personnel. In obtaining an understanding of this factor, in addition to current inquiries and observations of personnel, the auditor may consider prior experience with the client and may review personnel files.

Also relevant to mitigating several of the inherent risks discussed earlier is a characteristic of management's philosophy and operating style, which may be described as its attitudes and actions toward financial reporting. This characteristic includes management's conservative (or aggressive) selection from alternative accounting principles, and its conscientiousness and conservatism (or aggressiveness) in developing accounting estimates such as the allowances for uncollectable accounts and sales returns.

A number of special human resource policies and practices are often adopted for employees who handle cash receipts because of the susceptibility of cash to misappropriation. For example, many entities bond employees who handle cash. **Bonding** involves the purchase of a fidelity insurance policy against losses from the theft of cash and similar defalcations perpetrated by dishonest employees. Before the insurer issues a policy or adds an employee to an existing policy, it generally investigates the individual's honesty and integrity in previous positions. Bonding contributes to the control environment over cash receipts in two ways: (1) it may prevent the hiring or continued employment of dishonest individuals, and (2) it serves as a deterrent to dishonesty because employees know that the insurance company may vigorously investigate and prosecute any dishonest act. Additional practices include having employees who handle cash take mandatory vacations, and rotating employees' duties periodically. The thrust of these controls is to deter dishonesty by making employees aware that they may not be able to permanently conceal their misdeeds. Some embezzlements from banks and other entities, for example, have been traced to the seemingly dedicated employee who held the same job without taking a vacation for five or more years in order not to disrupt his or her routine of concealment.

Risk Assessment

Recall from Chapter 10 that management should assess business risks, inherent risks, and fraud risks and place controls to mitigate the implications of these risks. An important aspect of planning the audit involves obtaining an understanding of management's risk assessment procedures, risks identified, and management's responses in placing controls in operation. In particular, auditors should evaluate new controls associated with new product lines and new sources of revenues, management's response to new accounting standards for revenue transactions, and the impact on accounting and reporting of rapid growth in the revenue cycle and related changes in personnel.

Information and Communication (Accounting System)

Our primary concern with this component in this chapter pertains to the portion of the accounting system used in processing revenue cycle transactions and balances. An understanding of the revenue accounting system requires knowledge of how (1) sales are initiated, (2) goods and services are delivered, (3) receivables are recorded, (4) cash is received, and (5) sales adjustments are made, including the methods of data processing and the key documents and records used. Management should make appropriate provisions for documenting the processing and reporting on revenue cycle transactions and balances. This might include the chart of accounts, policy manuals, accounting and financial reporting manuals, and system flowcharts. The subsequent sections identify the key documents and records in the accounting system and provide illustrative examples of the system and related controls.

Monitoring

This component should provide management with feedback as to whether internal control pertaining to revenue cycle transactions and balances are operating as intended. The auditor should obtain an understanding of this feedback and whether management has initiated any corrective actions based on the information received from the monitoring activities. Possibilities include information received from (1) customers concerning billing errors, (2) regulatory agencies concerning disagreements on revenue recognition policies or related internal control matters, and (3) external auditors concerning reportable conditions or material weaknesses in relevant internal controls found in prior audits.

Initial Assessments of Control Risk and Preliminary Audit Strategy

If the client has a strong control environment, an effective risk assessment process, a sound system of information and communication, and effective monitoring, then the auditor will usually proceed to identify whether effective control activities have been placed in operation. Auditors often plan to follow a lower assessed level of control risk approach when auditing the revenue cycle, because of the high volume of revenue transactions. Control activities are usually effective in these circumstances. However, if significant weaknesses are noted in the control environment, which has a pervasive impact on other aspects of internal control, the auditor might choose to plan a primarily substantive approach. The control activities that would allow the auditor to assess control risk as low are discussed next for each of the three major transaction classes in the revenue cycle.

For revenue cycle assertions for which the auditor plans to assess control risk at high or maximum, he or she should have the knowledge needed to identify types of potential misstatements that could occur, assess the risk of material misstatement, and proceed with the design of substantive tests. The audit strategy may depend on the nature of the business and industry. When a client's revenues are concentrated within a few sources (such as a public school district's concentration of revenues collected by the state or county), the auditor may rely primarily on substantive tests of details.

[LEARNING CHECK

14-1   a. Describe the nature of the revenue cycle.

      b. Identify the major classes of transactions in the cycle for a merchandising company, and the primary accounts that are affected by these transactions.

14-2   a. How are specific audit objectives derived for the revenue cycle?

      b. State the specific audit objectives for credit sales transactions.

14-3   a. Explain how the auditor's knowledgeable expectation about the financial statements might be different for a computer manufacturer than for a hotel.

b. Explain why the auditor's assessment of the risk of material misstatement might be different for a computer manufacturer than for a hotel.

14-4 State two inherent risk factors that might motivate management to deliberately misstate revenues and receivables and two factors that might cause unintentional misstatements.

14-5 a. State an analytical procedure that an auditor might use to estimate total revenues for a household appliance manufacturer and for an airline.

b. State an analytical procedure that an auditor might use to estimate gross margin.

c. State two analytical procedures that an auditor might use to estimate net receivables and the allowance for doubtful accounts.

14-6 Identify elements of the control environment that are relevant to initiating and recording sales.

[KEY TERMS

Bonding, p. 637
Cash receipts, p. 629
Credit sales, p. 629

Entity's capacity, p. 634
Revenue cycle, p. 629
Sales adjustments, p. 629

[CONTROL ACTIVITIES FOR CREDIT SALES TRANSACTIONS]

Audit Decision 6

■ What should be considered in evaluating control activities for credit sales transactions?

Sales orders may be taken over-the-counter, or via telephone, mail order, traveling sales representatives, fax, or electronic data interchange. The goods may be picked up by the customer or shipped by the seller. Sales transactions are usually recorded using computer systems that may process transactions in either a real-time or batch processing mode. Control activities over sales transactions should be tailored to these varying circumstances.

Virtually every company that requires an audit has a computerized accounting system. Hence, this text focuses on how management would implement control activities using programmed control procedures. Recall from Chapters 10 and 11 that there are two types of computer controls:

■ General controls that relate to the computer environment and have a pervasive effect on computer applications.

■ Application controls that relate to the individual computerized accounting applications, such as the expenditure cycle.

Recall that if general controls are ineffective, reliance can rarely be placed on the application controls. For purposes of discussion, this chapter will assume that general controls are effective, as are the followup procedures that the entity uses to investigate issues that are triggered by application controls.

When evaluating internal controls over credit sales, it is important to understand the common documents, records, and the controls associated with the credit sale functions. The following discussion outlines the necessary controls that are relevant to the audit objectives identified at the outset of the chapter.

COMMON DOCUMENTS AND RECORDS

The numerous documents and records used by large companies in processing credit sales transactions often include the following:

- **Customer order.** Request for merchandise by a customer received directly from the customer or through a salesperson. May be a form furnished by the seller or the buyer's purchase order form.
- **Sales order.** Form showing the description, quantity, and other data pertaining to a customer order. It serves as the basis for initiating the transaction and internal processing of the customer order by the seller.
- **Shipping document.** Form used to show the details and date of each shipment. It may be in the form of a **bill of lading,** which serves as a formal acknowledgment of the receipt of goods for delivery by a freight carrier. Other shipping documents may include a **packing slip** with details on the items included in a shipment.
- **Sales invoice.** Form stating the particulars of a sale, including the amount owed, terms, and date of sale. It is used to bill customers, and it provides the basis for recording the sale.
- **Authorized price list.** Listing or computer master file containing authorized prices for goods offered for sale.
- **Sales transactions file.** Computer file of completed sales transactions. Used to print the sales invoices and sales journal, and to update the accounts receivable, inventory, and general ledger master files.
- **Sales journal.** Journal listing completed sales transactions.
- **Customer master file.** Contains the customer's shipping and billing information, and the customer's credit limit.
- **Accounts receivable master file.** Contains information on transactions with, and the balance due from, each customer. Serves as the basis for the **accounts receivable subsidiary ledger.**
- **Customer monthly statement.** Report sent to each customer showing the beginning balance, transactions during the month, and the ending balance.

FUNCTIONS AND CONTROL ACTIVITIES

The processing of revenue transactions involves the following revenue functions:

- **Authorizing sales.** The request by an entity for a sales transaction with another entity, including:
  - Accepting customer orders
  - Approving credit
- **Delivery of goods and services.** The physical shipment or delivery of a good or service, including:
  - Filling sales orders
  - Shipping sales orders
- **Recording sales.** The formal recognition of revenue by an entity. Each of these major functions should be assigned to a different individual or department, providing for adequate segregation of duties. The functions, applicable control activities, and relevant assertions and specific audit objectives are explained in the following sections. Figure 14-5 summarizes examples of programmed control procedures related to each of these functions.

Figure 14-5 ■ Control Risk Considerations—Credit Sale Transactions

Function	Potential Misstatement	Computer Control[a] (Manual Controls in Italics)	C1	EO1	VA1 VA5	PD1
Initiating Credit Sales	Sales may be made to unauthorized customers.	Only the credit department can add new customers to the customer master file.		P		
		The computer matches customer on sales order with customer master file.		P		
	Sales may be made without credit approval.	The computer matches amount of sales order with credit authorization on customer master file.			P	
Delivering Goods and Services	Goods may be released from warehouse for unauthorized orders.	Computer matches all goods pulled from inventory (perpetual inventory) to approved sales order.		P		
	Goods shipped may not agree with goods ordered.	Independent check by shipping clerk of agreement of goods received from warehouse with approved sales order.		D		
	Unauthorized shipments may be made.	Computer matches prenumbered shipping documents with approved sales order for each shipment.		D		
	Ordered goods may not be shipped.	Computer prints a report of all unfilled sales orders.	D			
Recording Sales	Some shipments may not be billed.	Computer prints a report of all goods shipped but not billed.	D			
		Accounting for all prenumbered sales invoices.	D			
		Comparison of control totals for shipping documents with corresponding totals for sales invoices.	D			
	Billings may be made for fictitious transactions, or duplicate billings may be made.	Sales are recorded only on the basis of sales invoices.		P		
		Computer matches sales invoice information with underlying shipping information.		D		
		Comparison of control totals for shipping documents with corresponding totals for sales invoices.	D	D		
	Sales invoices may be recorded in the incorrect accounting period.	Comparison of invoice date with the accounting period when goods were shipped.	D	D		
	Sales invoices may have incorrect prices.	Computer matches sales prices with authorized price list and sales order.			D	
	Invoices may not be journalized or posted to customer accounts.	Computer checks run-to-run total of beginning accounts receivable balances, plus sales transactions with the sum of ending accounts receivable balances.			D	
	Invoices may be posted to wrong customer accounts.	Computer matches customer number on sales invoice with customer number on sales order.				D
	Errors may be made in recording sales invoices.	*Mailing of monthly statements to customers with independent followup on customer complaints.*	D	D	D	D
		Management Control				
All Functions	Sales may be made to unauthorized customers or sales may not be collected.	An appropriate level of management reviews sales and collections on a regular basis.	D	D	D	D

[a] All computer controls assume that exceptions are either printed on an exception report for followup or an error message appears during input and the transaction cannot be processed without correction and acceptance.

P = potential control to prevent misstatement or unauthorized use of resources.

D = potential control to detect misstatement or unauthorized use of resources.

Authorizing Sales

Accepting Customer Orders

Sales orders from customers should be accepted only in accordance with management's authorized criteria. The criteria generally provide for specific approval of the order in the sales order department using a computer terminal to determine that the customer exists in a customer master file with approved credit limits. If the customer is not listed, approval by a credit department supervisor is usually required.

In many companies, the next step is preparing a prenumbered sales order form. The prenumbered sales order form permits following each transaction from initiation to delivery of goods or service, to recording the sale, to receipt of final consideration. The sales order represents the start of the transaction trail of documentary evidence. Information on open (unfilled) and filled sales orders is usually maintained in appropriate computer files.

Approving Credit

The process of approving credit is particularly important in the context of minimizing credit risk and ensuring that goods shipped are paid for on a timely basis. Well-managed entities take actions that ensure strong operating cash flows. The credit department gives credit approval in accordance with management's credit policies and authorized credit limits for each customer. Usually the computer can be programmed to compare a customer's outstanding receivable balance, plus the anticipated sale, with the customer's credit limit in the approved customer master file. Segregating responsibility for initiating a sale and approving credit prevents sales personnel from subjecting the company to undue credit risks to boost sales.

A credit check should be made for all new customers, which may include obtaining a credit report from a rating agency such as Dun & Bradstreet. Approval or nonapproval of credit is indicated by an authorized credit employee following prescribed procedures in having the new customer and credit information added to the accounts receivable master file.

Controls over approving credit are designed to reduce the risk of initially recording an individual revenue transaction at an amount in excess of the amount of cash expected to be realized from the transaction. Thus, they relate to the valuation or allocation assertion for sales transactions (VA1). Of course, the expectations of realizability for some of these amounts will change over time, resulting in the need for an allowance for uncollectable accounts. Controls over approving credit will enable management to make a more reliable estimate of the size of the allowance needed. Thus, these controls also relate to the valuation or allocation assertion for the allowance for uncollectable accounts (VA5).

Delivery of Goods or Services

Delivery of goods or services is the economic event that represents change in title and establishes the right to a receivable.

Filling Sales Orders

Company policy generally prohibits the release of any goods from the warehouse without an approved sales order. Furthermore, the computer may be programmed to match items taken from the perpetual inventory with items on an approved sales order. This control procedure is designed to prevent the unauthorized removal of items from inventory. The warehouse may receive an electronic copy of the approved sales order as authorization to fill the order and release the goods to the shipping department. When goods are pulled from inventory, a packing slip is normally produced to detail the items that will be shipped to the customer.

Shipping Sales Orders

Segregating the responsibility for shipping from approving and filling orders helps to prevent shipping clerks from making unauthorized shipments. In addition, an important manual control requires that shipping clerks make independent checks to determine (1) that goods received from the warehouse are accompanied by appropriate authorization and (2) that the order was properly filled (goods received agree with the details of the sales order) (EO1).

The shipping function also involves preparing multicopy shipping documents or bills of lading. Shipping documents can be prepared manually on prenumbered forms. Alternatively, the documents can be produced with the computer by using order information already in the computer and adding appropriate shipping data such as quantities shipped, carrier, and freight charges.

Daily computer checks to account for all shipping documents and to determine that all sales orders result in shipments and that a sales invoice was subsequently prepared for each shipping document provide an important control for the completeness assertion (C1).

Recording Sales

The process of recording sales involves preparing and sending prenumbered sales invoices to customers (billing customers) and recording sales invoices accurately and in the proper accounting period (recording sales). The auditor's primary concerns pertaining to this function are that the sales invoices are recorded accurately and in the proper period. The latter pertains to when the revenue is earned, which is usually when the goods are shipped.

The auditor's major concerns regarding billing are that customers are billed (1) for all shipments, (2) only for actual shipments (no duplicate billings or fictitious transactions), and (3) at authorized prices. Programmed application controls that reduce the risk of misstatement in the billing and recording process (and related specific audit objectives) include the following:

- Computer matching of sales invoice information with sales order and shipping information (EO1).
- Computer matching of sales prices on the sale invoice with an authorized price list and sales order prices in preparing the sales invoices (VA1).
- Computer-programmed checks on the mathematical accuracy of sales invoices (VA1).
- Comparison of control totals for shipping documents with corresponding totals for sales invoices (EO1 and C1).
- Computer comparison of date for recording the sales invoices with the time period in which the goods were shipped (EO1 and C1).
- Computer comparison of the customer number on the sales invoice with the account number on the sales order, which should have previously been compared with the master customer file (PD1).

- Run-to-run totals match the sum of beginning receivables balances, plus posted sales, with ending receivables balances (C1, EO1, VA1).

File copies of the sales invoices may be maintained in the billing department. A computer record of the billings is maintained in a sales transactions file.

Two important manual controls should also be in place in a system of well-designed internal control:

- Monthly statements should be mailed to customers with instructions to report any exceptions to a designated accounting supervisor not otherwise involved in the execution or recording of revenue cycle transactions (all revenue cycle objectives).
- The entity should establish an appropriate level of regular review and accountability by sales executives for sales analyses by product, division, salesperson, or region, and comparisons with budgets (all sales transaction objectives). Sales executives should also be held accountable for gross margins and subsequent collection of sales and accounts receivable writeoffs (VA4).

As an exercise, it is suggested that the student consider the rationale for the linkage of the above controls to the specific audit objectives indicated for each.

ILLUSTRATIVE SYSTEM FOR CREDIT SALES

In practice, there are many variations in the systems used to perform the functions involved in processing credit sales transactions. Figure 14-6 shows a flowchart of an on-line, batch-entry processing system that incorporates most of the controls discussed in the preceding sections. This figure summarizes the following information that is important to documenting the auditor's understanding of internal control: (1) key functions, (2) the documentary audit trail, (3) key reports produced by the system, and (4) the computer programs and files involved in the accounting system. Not every copy of every document is documented in the flowchart, inasmuch as the auditor needs only an understanding sufficient to plan the audit. The flowchart also follows the path that the transaction follows from initiating the transaction to recording in the general ledger, which support the financial statements. The auditor should also document important activities or control procedures, which may be accomplished by a brief written summary similar to the one that follows.

illustrative system for credit sales transactions

In the illustrative system, as orders are received sales order clerks use on-line terminals and an order program to determine that the customer has been approved and that the order will not cause the customer's balance to exceed the customer's authorized credit limit. If the customer is a new one, the order is transferred to the credit department, which checks credit and enters customer information on the customer master file for approved customers. The program also checks the inventory master file to determine that goods are on hand to fill the order and prices the sales order based on information in an approved master price file. If the order is accepted,

(continues)

Figure 14-6 ■ System Flowchart – Credit Sales Transactions

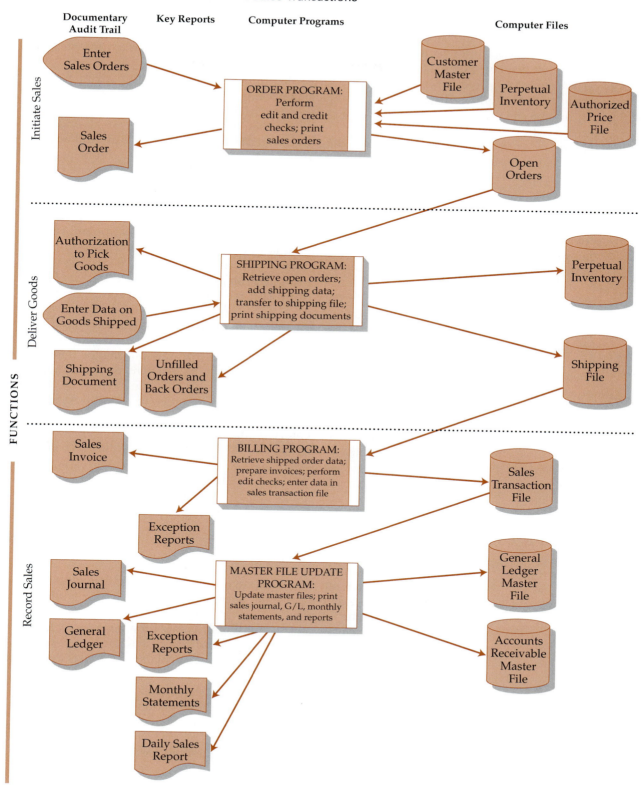

---

illustrative system for credit sales transactions *(continued)*

the computer enters it into an open order file and a copy of the sales order form is produced on a printer in the sales order department and sent to the customer. When an order is not accepted, a message is displayed on the terminal indicating the reason for the rejection.

The approved sales order is electronically forwarded to the warehouse as authorization to release goods to shipping. The warehouse completes a packing slip and forwards goods to shipping. In shipping, personnel first make an independent check on agreement of the goods received with the accompanying sales order form. They then use their on-line terminals and a shipping program to retrieve the corresponding sales order from the open order file and add appropriate shipping data. The perpetual inventory system is also updated for the shipment of goods. Next the computer transfers the transaction from the open order file to a shipping file and produces a prenumbered shipping document on the printer in the shipping department. A report of unfilled orders and back orders is generated daily.

Sales invoices are automatically generated based on shipped goods. The computer checks vendor information and data on goods shipped against data entered in sales and shipping. The computer prices the sales invoice based on information on the sales order and checks the numerical accuracy of the sales invoice. The computer also checks dates shipped with dates on the sales invoice. As each billing is completed, the computer enters it into a sales transaction file. After all the transactions in the batch have been processed, the billing program compares the total invoices with the total shipments for the day.

The transaction file is processed and posted to the sales transaction file, the accounts receivable master file, and the general ledger master file. Run-to-run totals compare beginning balances plus processed transactions with ending balances immediately prior to posting the transactions. Exceptions are printed on an exception report, and these transactions are held in a suspense file to be cleared by the billing supervisor.

The program also produces monthly statements. All customer inquiries on monthly statements are directed to the controller's office for followup. A separate program also prints daily sales reports with sales, gross margins, and inventory-on-hand by product for management review. Management must also coordinate followup on all past-due receivables with the credit department.

[LEARNING CHECK

14-7 a. State the functions that apply to sales transactions.

b. For each sales function, indicate (1) the department that performs the function, and (2) the principal document or record, if any, produced in performing the function.

14-8 If the auditor plans to assess control risk as low for a revenue cycle assertion based on programmed control procedures, discuss three types of controls that should be tested by the auditor and explain why each is important to the control risk assessment.

14-9 For each of the following potential misstatements for sales transactions, indicate a potential programmed control procedure and a possible computer-assisted audit technique to test the control:

a. Sales invoices may not be recorded.

b. Sales invoices may be recorded in the wrong accounting period.

    c. A fictitious sales invoice, or a sales transaction for which revenue should not be recognized, is recorded.

    d. Sales are made without credit approval.

    e. A sales invoice has incorrect quantities or prices.

    f. Sales invoices may not be posted or may be journalized.

    g. Sales invoices may be posted to the wrong customer accounts.

    h. Sales invoices may be recorded in the wrong time period.

14-10 Discuss several management controls that may help ensure that all sales transactions are properly recorded.

[KEY TERMS

Accounts receivable master file, p. 640

Accounts receivable subsidiary ledger, p. 640

Authorized price list, p. 640

Authorizing sales, p. 640

Bill of lading, p. 640

Customer master file, p. 640

Customer monthly statement, p. 640

Customer order, p. 640

Delivery of goods and services, p. 640

Packing slip, p. 640

Recording sales, p. 640

Sales invoice, p. 640

Sales journal, p. 640

Sales order, p. 640

Sales transactions file, p. 640

Shipping document, p. 640

[CONTROL ACTIVITIES FOR CASH RECEIPTS TRANSACTIONS]

Audit Decision 7

■ What should be considered in evaluating control activities for cash receipts?

Cash receipts result from a variety of activities. For example, cash is received from revenue transactions, short- and long-term borrowings, the issuance of capital stock, and the sale of marketable securities, long-term investments, and other assets. The scope of this section is limited to cash receipts from cash sales and collections from customers on credit sales. Other sources of cash receipts are discussed in the investing and financing cycles in Chapter 17, and audit strategy and procedures for cash balances are presented in Chapter 18. When evaluating internal controls over cash receipts, it is important to understand the common documents and records and the controls associated with the cash receipts functions. The following discussion outlines the necessary controls that are relevant to the audit objectives identified at the outset of the chapter.

COMMON DOCUMENTS AND RECORDS

Important documents and records used in processing cash receipts include the following:

■ **Remittance advice.** Document mailed to the customer with the sales invoices to be returned with the payment showing the customer's name and account number, invoice number, and amount owed (e.g., the portion of a telephone bill returned with payment).

■ **Prelist.** Listing of cash receipts received through the mail.

- **Cash count sheets.** Listing of cash and checks in a cash register. Used in reconciling total receipts with the total printed by the cash register.
- **Daily cash summary.** Report showing total over-the-counter and mail receipts received by the cashier for deposit.
- **Validated deposit slip.** Listing prepared by the depositor and stamped by the bank showing the date and total of a deposit accepted by the bank and the detail of receipts comprising the deposit.
- **Cash receipts transactions file.** Computer file of validated cash receipts transactions accepted for processing; used to update the accounts receivable master file.
- **Cash receipts journal.** Journal listing cash receipts from cash sales and collections on accounts receivable.

Reference is made to each of the above in the following sections.

FUNCTIONS AND CONTROL ACTIVITIES

The **cash receipts function**, which includes the processing of receipts from cash and credit sales, involves the following subfunctions:

- Receiving cash receipts
- Depositing cash in bank
- Recording the receipts

As in the case of credit sales transactions, segregation of duties in performing these functions is an important internal control activity. The functions, applicable control activities, and relevant assertions and specific audit objectives are explained in the following sections. Many of the controls related to receiving and depositing cash involve manual checks and balances rather than computer checks and balances. Computer controls are most effective in controlling the recording subfunction. Figure 14-7 summarizes example control procedures related to the cash receipts function.

Receiving Cash Receipts

A major risk in processing cash receipts transactions is the possible theft of cash before or after a record of the receipt is made. Thus, control procedures should provide reasonable assurance that documentation establishing accountability is created at the moment cash is received and that the cash is subsequently safeguarded.

Over-the-Counter Receipts

For over-the-counter receipts, the use of a cash register or point-of-sale terminal is indispensable. These devices provide:

- Immediate visual display for the customer of the amount of the cash sale and the cash tendered
- A printed receipt for the customer and an internal record of the transaction on a computer file or a tape locked inside the register
- Printed control totals of the day's receipts processed on the device

Figure 14-7 ■ Control Risk Considerations—Cash Receipt Transactions

Function	Potential Misstatement	Computer Control[a] (Manual Controls in Italics)	C2	EO2	VA2	PD2
Cash Receipts Function	Cash sales may not be registered.	*Use of cash registers or point-of-sale devices.*	P			
		Periodic surveillance of cash sales procedures.	D			
	Mail receipts may be lost or misappropriated after receipt.	*Restrictive endorsement of checks immediately on receipt.*	P			
		Immediate preparation of prelist of mail receipts.	P	P	P	
	Cash and checks received for deposit may not agree with the cash count sheets and prelist.	*Independent check of agreement of cash and checks with cash count sheets and prelist.*	D	D	D	
	Cash may not be deposited intact daily.	*Independent check of agreement of validated deposit slip with daily cash summary.*	D	D	D	
	Remittance advices may not agree with the prelist.	*Independent check of agreement of remittance advices with prelist.*	D	D	D	
	Some receipts may not be recorded.	Computer agreement of amounts journalized and posted with daily cash summary.	D		D	
	Errors may be made in journalizing receipts.	*Preparation of periodic independent bank reconciliations.*	D	D	D	D
	Receipts may be posted to the wrong customer account.	*Mailing of statements to customers.*	D	D	D	D
	Errors may be made in recording the check.	Computer comparison of information on check summary with recorded cash receipt.		D	D	D
		Independent bank reconciliation.	D	D	D	D
		Management Control				
	Cash receipts may not be recorded or may be posted to the wrong accounts.	An appropriate level of management monitors cash daily, including cash receipts, the reasonableness of the amounts, and the amount of credit to accounts receivable.	D	D	D	
		Management actively follows up on past due receivables.	D	D	D	

[a] All computer controls assume that exceptions are either printed on an exception report for followup, or an error message appears during input and the transaction cannot be processed without correction and acceptance.
P = potential control to prevent misstatement or unauthorized use of resources.
D = potential control to detect misstatement or unauthorized use of resources.

The customer's expectation of a printed receipt and supervisory surveillance of over-the-counter sales transactions helps to ensure that all cash sales are processed through the cash registers or terminals (C2). In addition, supervisors may be assigned responsibility for performing independent checks on the accuracy of cash count sheets and verifying agreement of cash on hand with the totals printed by the register or terminal (EO2, VA2). The cash, count sheets, and register or terminal-printed totals are then forwarded to the cashier's department for further processing and inclusion in the bank deposit (EO2, C2, VA2).

Mail Receipts

To minimize the likelihood of diversion of mail receipts, most companies request customers to pay by check. Some companies with a large volume of mail receipts use a **lockbox system.** A lockbox is a post office box that is controlled by the company's bank. The bank picks up the mail daily, credits the company for the cash, and sends the remittance advices and a prelisting of cash receipts to the company for use in updating accounts receivable. This system expedites the depositing of checks, permits the company to receive credit for the receipts sooner, and provides external evidence of the existence of the transactions (EO2). It also eliminates the risk of diversion of the receipts by company employees and failure to record the receipts (C2).

In companies that process their own mail receipts, mailroom clerks should (1) immediately restrictively endorse checks for deposit only (C2—increases likelihood receipts will be deposited and recorded) and (2) list the checks on a multicopy prelist. The latter may be done manually or on a computer terminal. Immediate preparation of the prelist establishes accountability for the receipts (EO2) and provides a batch or control total for use in independent checks on the completeness (C2) and accuracy (VA2) of processing. Remittance advices received with the checks, and a copy of the prelisting of cash receipts, are forwarded to accounts receivable accounting for use in updating customer accounts.

Depositing Cash in Bank

Proper physical controls over cash require that all cash receipts be **deposited intact daily.** Intact means all receipts should be deposited. This control reduces the risk that receipts will not be recorded (C2), and the resulting bank deposit record establishes the existence or occurrence of the transactions (EO2).

When the cashier receives over-the-counter and mail receipts, an independent check should be made to determine their agreement with the accompanying cash count sheets and prelist, respectively (EO2, C2, VA2). The totals for each are then entered on a daily cash summary, and the deposit is prepared. After making the deposit, the daily cash summary and validated deposit slip should be forwarded to general accounting.

Recording the Receipts

This function involves journalizing over-the-counter and mail receipts and posting mail receipts to customer accounts. Controls should ensure that only valid receipts are entered (EO2) and that all actual receipts are entered (C2) at the correct amounts (VA2).

To ensure that only valid transactions are entered, physical access to the accounting records or computer terminals used in recording should be restricted to authorized personnel. Over-the-counter receipts are generally recorded in general accounting based on the daily cash summary received from the cashier.

It is common for accounts receivable clerks to use a terminal to enter mail receipts into a cash receipts transactions file, which is subsequently used in updating both the accounts receivable and general ledger master files. To ensure the completeness (C2), accuracy (VA2), and proper classification (PD2) of recording mail receipts, the computer can check the agreement of the amounts journalized and posted with the control totals of the amounts shown on the prelists received from the mailroom or the daily cash summary and validated deposit slip received from the cashier. In addition, periodic bank reconciliations should be performed by an employee not otherwise involved in executing or recording cash transactions.

ILLUSTRATIVE SYSTEM FOR CASH RECEIPTS

As noted previously for credit sales systems, there are also many variations in systems for processing receipts. A flowchart for an illustrative system for processing mail receipts is presented in Figure 10-24 on page 455. It is suggested that the flowchart and the accompanying narrative be reviewed at this time.

CONTROL ACTIVITIES FOR SALES ADJUSTMENT TRANSACTIONS AND OTHER CONTROLS

COMMON DOCUMENTS AND RECORDS

Important documents and records used in processing sales adjustments include the following:

| **Audit Decision 8** |

■ What should be considered in evaluating control activities for sales adjustment transactions?

- **Sales return authorization.** Form showing the description, quantity, and other data pertaining to the goods that the customer is authorized to return. It serves as the basis for initiating the sales return and internal processing of the customer returns by the seller.
- **Authorization for accounts receivable write-off.** A form showing the procedures taken to attempt collection and document authorization of accounts receivable write-off.
- **Receiving report.** Report prepared on the receipt of goods from customers showing the kinds and quantities of goods received.
- **Credit memo.** Form stating the particulars of a credit to accounts receivable, including the specific items returned, prices, and amount credited. It provides the basis for recording the sales return.
- **Journal entry.** A document used to record adjustments such as an accounts receivable write-off in the general ledger.

Reference is made to each of the above in the following sections.

FUNCTIONS AND CONTROL ACTIVITIES

Sales adjustment transactions involve the following sales adjustment transactions:

- Granting cash discounts
- Granting sales returns and allowances
- Determining uncollectible accounts

In many companies, the number and dollar value of these transactions is immaterial. However, in some companies, the potential for misstatements resulting from errors and fraud in the processing of these transactions is considerable.

Granting Cash Discounts

Cash discounts are commonly granted for timely receipt of payments from customers, such as a 1 percent discount granted if cash is received within 10 days of the invoice date. Trade terms are often stated on the invoice, and the computer can test the existence and occurrence (EO3) as well as the accuracy of the discount (VA3) by comparing cash receipts date with the invoice date and recomputing the cash discount. The accuracy of total cash discounts (VA3) can be tested by comparing cash received plus the cash discount to the amount credited to accounts receivable.

Granting Sales Returns and Allowances

The possibility of recording fictitious sales adjustment transactions is a primary concern because it may be used to conceal fraud in processing cash receipts. For example, an employee might misappropriate cash received from a customer and cover up the fraud by writing a credit memo to reduce the receivable from the customer. Accordingly, control activities useful in reducing the risk of fraud focus on establishing the existence or occurrence of such transactions (EO3) and include the following:

■ All sales returns should be authorized by sales management (EO3).
■ Goods should be received only with a proper sales return authorization, and an independent count of goods returned should be recorded on a receiving report (EO3).
■ The computer should match credit memo information with the sales order, authorization of sale return, and the receiving report (EO3) and (VA3).
■ The computer should print daily reports of authorized sales returns that have not been received in the receiving department, and receivings that have not resulted in the recording of a credit memo (C2).

Furthermore, there should be adequate segregation of duties for authorizing sales returns, receiving goods, and recording credit memos. Usually management that is held accountable for financial results in a department will have the responsibility of authorizing sales adjustment transactions.

When there is the potential for material misstatements from sales adjustments transactions, the auditor should obtain an understanding of all relevant aspects of the internal control structure components and consider the factors that affect the risk of such misstatements. If sales adjustments are estimated at quarter end, management should establish controls to ensure that adjustments are made based on reliable information and that adjustments are consistent from quarter to quarter. A disclosure committee should review these estimates if they can aggregate with other adjustments to an amount material to the financial statements.

Determining Uncollectable Accounts

Good internal controls over the write-off of uncollectable accounts is important to prevent write-offs from being used to conceal fraud in processing cash receipts.

For example, an employee might misappropriate cash received from a customer and cover up the fraud by writing the customer's account off against the allowance for uncollectable accounts.

Good internal controls include:

- Authorization of all write-offs of uncollectable accounts by the treasurer's office and supported by documentation, such as correspondence with the customer or collection agencies (EO3 and VA3).
- Appropriate review of journal entries to ensure the appropriateness of the transaction (EO3, VA3, and PD3).

In addition, management should establish controls over accounting estimates such as the provision for bad debt expense. Management should ordinarily establish a process for monitoring aging and the collectability of receivables. Hindsight should be used to evaluate the adequacy of prior provisions for bad debt expense compared with subsequent receivables that go bad. It is essential that the data used to develop a provision for bad debt expense (the history of accounts written off) be reliable. In addition, a qualified and independent disclosure committee should review the allowance on a regular basis. These controls are necessary to determine the adequacy of the allowance (C3, VA5).

OTHER CONTROLS IN THE REVENUE CYCLE

The previous discussion focused on controls over transactions. It is also important to control balances and disclosures.

The primary account balance in the revenue cycle is accounts receivable. If good controls exist over credit sales, cash receipts, and sales adjustments, the accounts receivable balance should also be controlled, as it is the product of recording these transactions. Most companies control the completeness (C4), existence (EO4), and valuation of receivables at historical cost (VA4) by sending monthly statements to customers. It is important to recognize that the function of following up on issues raised by customers should be independent of accounts receivable.

Controls over the rights and obligations assertion relate to whether the company has legal claim to receivables. A company normally gives up claims to receivables when it sells the receivables or it pledges receivables as collateral. These transactions may not exist in many entities. However, if an entity sells its receivables, it should keep a documentary record of receivables that have been sold. This record should be compared with monthly statements sent by a bank or factoring company. This provides an independent check on the accuracy of the company's records (RO1).

Finally, management should establish controls over the occurrence and rights and obligations of disclosures (PD4), the completeness of disclosures (PD5), the classification and understandability of disclosures (PD6) and the accuracy and valuation of information included in disclosures (PD7). Public companies normally accomplish this task through the workings of a disclosure committee that is independent of the CFO or controller who prepares the disclosures, and includes individuals who are knowledgeable about GAAP and the transactions and disclosures relevant to the revenue cycle. If management uses spreadsheets to summarize disclosures (e.g., sales by geographic region or product line, or receivables classified as trade, related parties, or from employees) standard controls over the use of spreadsheets discussed in Chapter 10 should be in place (PD5, PD7).

REVENUE CYCLE TESTS OF CONTROLS

Audit Decision 9

■ What are the relevant aspects of tests of controls when the auditor plans to assess control risk below the maximum for the revenue cycle.

Most auditors plan to test controls that are effectively designed in the revenue cycle because of the high volume of routine transactions in this cycle. Public company auditors test controls to support an opinion on internal controls. Private company auditors will test controls that appear to be effective because of the audit efficiencies that exist with this strategy.

If the auditor plans to assess control risk as low for revenue cycle assertions covered by computer controls, he or she will usually have to:

■ Test the effectiveness of general controls.
■ Use computer-assisted audit techniques (CAATs) to evaluate the effectiveness of programmed controls.
■ Test the effectiveness of procedures to follow up on exceptions identified by programmed controls.

For example, the auditor might use test data to determine whether expected results appear on exception reports when he or she submits

■ A missing or invalid customer code.
■ An invalid product code.
■ An order that exceeds a customer's credit limit.
■ Transactions reporting shipments in quantities different from the amount ordered (both over and under).
■ Prices, vendor numbers, or other information on sales invoices that do not match information on the sales order.
■ Invoice quantities that do not match quantities on shipping documents.

The auditor might also use generalized audit software or a utility program to perform sequence checks and print lists of sales orders, shipping documents, or sales invoices whose numbers are missing in designated computer files.

[LEARNING CHECK

14-11　What subfunctions are involved in the processing of cash receipts transactions?

14-12　a. Describe two important controls pertaining to cash sales and indicate the transaction class audit objective(s) to which they relate.
　　　　b. Describe two important controls pertaining to the initial handling of mail receipts for companies that process their own receipts.

14-13　a. What is a lockbox system, and how can it affect control risk for cash receipts transactions?
　　　　b. What is the meaning of deposited intact daily, and how does this control affect control risk for cash receipts transactions?

14-14　Identify four controls that can aid in preventing or detecting errors or fraud in recording cash receipts. For each control discuss the tests of controls you would perform to assess its operating effectiveness.

14-15　a. Identify the functions pertaining to sales adjustment transactions.
　　　　b. State three types of controls pertaining to sales adjustment transactions and identify their common focus.

14-16　a. Explain why controls over revenue cycle transactions should also control the accounts receivable balance.

b. Explain the primary control over the accounts receivable balance itself.

c. How is the rights and obligations assertion controlled for accounts receivable?

d. How are disclosures controlled for accounts receivable?

14-17 Using the information in Figures 14-5 and 14-7, develop a test of controls for each assertion related to credit sales and to cash receipts.

KEY TERMS

Authorization for accounts receivable write-off, p. 651
Cash count sheets, p. 648
Cash receipts function, p. 648
Cash receipts journal, p. 648
Cash receipts transactions file, p. 648
Credit memo, p. 651
Daily cash summary, p. 648
Deposited intact daily, p. 650

Journal entry, p. 651
Lockbox system, p. 650
Prelist, p. 647
Receiving report, p. 651
Remittance advice, p. 647
Sales adjustment transactions, p. 651
Sales return authorization, p. 651
Validated deposit slip, p. 648

SUBSTANTIVE TESTS OF ACCOUNTS RECEIVABLE

Accounts receivable represent the primary balance in the revenue cycle. Receivables include amounts due from customers, employees, and affiliates on open accounts, notes, and loans, and accrued interest on such balances. Our consideration here is directed at gross receivables due from customers on credit sales transactions and the related contra account, the allowance for uncollectible accounts. It is important to recall that by auditing accounts receivable the auditor audits the related sales. In general, the sales that are most likely to represent potential misstatements are the uncollected sales. However, in certain industries it is common to receive cash before revenue is recognized. In these situations revenue recognition problems may be associated with transactions that should have been recorded as unearned revenue. As discussed in Chapter 12, the auditor should (1) assess the risk of material misstatement (determine the appropriate level of detection risk) and (2) design substantive tests that are responsive to those risks. The following discussion illustrates how the auditor accomplishes this goal in the revenue cycle.

DETERMINING DETECTION RISK

Audit Decision 10

■ What are the factors involved in determining acceptable level of tests of details risk for accounts receivable assertions?

An example risk matrix for the revenue cycle and accounts receivable assertions is presented in Figure 14-8. The following discussion explains the development of preliminary audit strategies that are consistent with this example risk matrix.

Existence and Occurrence

The existence and occurrence assertion for sales and accounts receivable represents a significant inherent risk because of the potential for revenue recognition problems. As a result, inherent risk is assessed at the maximum for this assertion.

Figure 14-8 ■ Example Risk Matrix for Accounts Receivable Assertions

Risk Component	Existence or Occurrence	Complete-ness	Rights and Obligations	Valuation or Allocation	Presentation and Disclosure
Audit Risk	Very low	Very low	Very low	Very low	Very low
Inherent Risk	Max	Moderate	Moderate	Max	High
Control Risk—Credit Sales Transactions	Low	Low	Moderate	Moderate	Moderate
Control Risk—Cash Receipt Transactions	Low	Low	Moderate	Low	Moderate
Control Risk—Sales Adjustment Transactions	Moderate	Low	Moderate	Moderate	Moderate
Combined Control Risk for Accounts Receivable Tests	Low	Moderate	Moderate	Moderate	Moderate
Analytical Procedures Risk	Moderate	Low	High	High	High
Acceptable Test of Details Risk	Moderate	Very high	Moderate	Very low	Low

Recall from Chapter 11 that the combined control risk assessment for accounts receivable is a function of internal controls over the occurrence related to credit sales (low) and the completeness of cash receipts (low) and sales adjustment transactions (low). As a result, the combined risk assessment for the existence of accounts receivable would be low. A common internal control over the occurrence of sales would be having the computer match sales invoice information with bill of lading and packing slip information input during the shipment of goods. An example of internal control over the completeness of cash receipts would include strong internal controls over the opening of mail and creation of a prelist of cash receipts, and subsequent comparison of the recording of cash receipts with the prelist and the deposit slip. Internal controls over the completeness of sales returns might include a comparison of all authorized sales returns with the generation of credit memos.

Since the existence of accounts receivable represents a significant inherent risk, the auditor should not plan to obtain substantial assurance from analytical procedures. The auditor might perform analytical procedures similar to those explained in Figure 14-4. The comparison of financial numbers with other financial numbers, investigation of capacity compared to sales, and an understanding of the entity's market share and other operating statistics might result in an assessment of analytical procedures risk as moderate. If the auditor simply compares current year with the prior year, without obtaining information about underlying business activity, analytical procedures risk should probably be assessed as high.

As a result, the appropriate level of detection risk for test of details is moderate. The primary test of details would involve the sending of confirmations (see subsequent discussion). Based on the combined control risk assessment as low, the auditor might send confirmations at an interim date. Confirmations will only need to be moderately extensive owing to the need to accomplish a moderate test of details risk.

Completeness

The auditor might assess inherent risk for the completeness assertion as moderate. In most cases there is a greater risk of overstatement of receivables and sales than of understatement of receivables and sales.

When considering the combined control risk assessment for the completeness of receivables, the auditor should evaluate the completeness assertions related to credit sales (low in this example) with the existence and occurrence assertion for cash receipts (low) and for sales adjustments (moderate). In this example, the conservative combined control risk assessment would be moderate. Internal controls over the completeness of sales would usually include daily followup on items shipped that had not resulted in sales invoices. Controls over the occurrence of cash receipts would include comparison of recorded cash receipts with the underlying prelisting of cash. Finally, controls over the occurrence of sales returns would include matching of credit memo information with underlying receiving reports.

Analytical procedures related to the completeness of sales and receivables would involve a comparison of sales to the underlying physical business such as a comparison of sales to capacity, sales to production levels, development of a deep understanding of the entity's market share, and a comparison of sales to total assets or sales to fixed assets. If these tests show that all sales appear to be recorded, the auditor can reduce the extensiveness of other substantive tests. In this example the auditor assesses test of details risk as very high. The auditor might assess the information about the completeness of sales obtained from sending confirmations, and perform cutoff tests on the recording of sales transactions at the end of the year.

Rights and Obligations

The assessment of inherent risk for the rights and obligations assertions depends on the entity's performance. Entities with strong operating cash flows rarely need to sell or factor receivables. Entities with weak operating cash flows, however, are more likely to sell receivables or pledge receivables as collateral.

If receivables have been factored, it is common to keep records of receivables that have been sold and to compare those records with monthly statements from the factoring company. Analytical procedures are not particularly effective at identifying the sale of rights to receivables, so the auditor usually plans to obtain most assurance from substantive tests of details.

Auditors often use generalized audit software to scan the cash receipts journal for large cash receipts. Receivables are usually sold in larger batches, and this might provide evidence of selling receivables. If inquiry or other evidence shows that the company has sold receivables, the auditor will confirm the sale or pledging of receivable with the entity to which the receivables were sold. It is ineffective to confirm the pledging of receivables with customers because they rarely know if their receivables have been sold.

Valuation and Allocation

The assessment of inherent risk for the valuation and allocation assertion is often set at high or maximum for accounts receivable because of the subjective nature of the allowance for doubtful accounts.

Controls over the valuation and allocation assertion with respect to historical cost involve the controls over the valuation of sales, cash receipts, and sales adjustments. These might include computer comparison of prices on sales invoices with the master price list, comparison of recorded cash receipts with the cash prelist, or comparison of prices on credit memos with sales invoice prices. Controls over the allowance for doubtful accounts include controls over the granting of credit, comparison of balances plus orders to credit limits, the follow-up on past due receivables, controls over the accuracy of receivables aging, and the quality of work of a disclosure committee that reviews the allowance for doubtful accounts. Control risk might be set at moderate because of the complex nature of the work of the disclosure committee in evaluating the adequacy of the allowance.

Analytical procedures usually involve computing the entity's accounts receivable turn days. This is a rather blunt tool for careful analysis of valuation issues, so analytical procedures risk is often set at high or maximum.

In this example, test of details risk is set at very low as a result of subjectivity of the assertion. The auditor can often test valuation at historical cost by sending confirmations to customers. Confirmations, however, do not provide valid evidence about the collectability of receivables. The auditor will often test the allowance by using generalized audit software to recalculate client aging, to identify customers with past due balances, and to determine credit histories for customers with past due balances. Auditors pay particular attention to customers that demonstrate deteriorating payment history as the year progresses.

Presentation and Disclosure

In developing a preliminary audit strategy for the presentation and disclosures assertion the auditor will usually plan a primarily substantive approach. Inherent risk associated with disclosures is often set at high or maximum. The disclosures related to receivables are often not complex, so it is appropriate to set inherent risk as high. Controls usually involve the work of a disclosure committee. Because analytical procedures are rarely effective for testing disclosures, the auditor will usually place significant emphasis on tests of details of disclosures. These tests are discussed in detail in a subsequent section of the chapter.

DESIGNING SUBSTANTIVE TESTS

Audit Decision 11
■ How does the auditor determine the elements of an audit program for substantive tests to achieve specific audit objectives for accounts receivable?

The next step is to finalize the audit program to achieve the specific audit objectives for the revenue cycle. The specific objectives addressed here are the ones listed in Figure 14-2. In Chapter 12, we introduced a general framework for developing audit programs for substantive tests. Examples of that framework are illustrated if Figures 12-8 and 12-9. That framework is followed here in developing an audit program for substantive tests for the revenue cycle which are presented in Figure 14-9. Each of these tests is discussed in more detail below.

Figure 14-9 ■ Possible Substantive Tests of Accounts Receivable Assertions

Category	Substantive Test	Specific Audit Objectives

Initial Procedures	1. Obtain an understanding of the business and industry and determine:
	  a. The significance of revenues and accounts receivable to the entity.
	  b. Key economic drivers that influence the entity's sales, margins, and collections.
	  c. Standard trade terms in the industry, including seasonal dating, collections period, etc.
	  d. The extent of concentration of activity with customers.
		All

	2. Perform initial procedures accounts payable balance and records that will be subjected to further testing.	
	a. Trace beginning balance for accounts receivable to prior year's working papers.	VA4
	b. Review activity in general ledger account for accounts receivable and investigate entries that appear unusual in amount or source.	RO1, EO1, EO4
	c. Obtain accounts receivable trial balance and determine that it accurately represents the underlying accounting records by:	
	i. Footing the trial balance and determining agreement with (1) the total of the subsidiary ledger or accounts receivable master file, and (2) the general ledger balance.	VA4
	ii. Testing agreement of customer and balances listed on the trial balance with those included in the subsidiary ledger or master file.	VA4

Analytical Procedures	3. Perform analytical procedures:
	  a. Develop an expectation for accounts receivable using knowledge of the entity's business activity, market share, normal trade terms, and its history of accounts receivable turn days.
	  b. Calculate ratios:
	    i. Compare sales to the entity's capacity.
	    ii. Compare sales growth and receivable growth.
	    iii. Accounts receivable turn days.
	    iv. Uncollectable accounts expense to net credit sales.
	    v. Uncollectable accounts expense to accounts receivable write-offs.
	  c. Analyze ratio results relative to expectations based on prior years, industry data, budgeted amounts, or other data.
		All

Tests of Details of Transactions	4. Vouch a sample of recorded revenue cycle transactions to supporting documentation.	
	a. Vouch receivable debits to supporting sales invoices, shipping documents, and sales orders.	EO1, PD1, EO4, VA1
	b. Vouch receivable credits to supporting cash receipts and cash prelists.	EO2, PD2, EO4, VA2
	c. Vouch receivable credits to remittance advices or sales adjustment authorizations for sales returns and allowance or uncollectible account write-offs.	EO3, PD3, EO4, VA3
	5. Trace a sample of revenue transactions from shipments to recording in the sales journal. Also trace a sample of cash receipts and sales returns to their recording in the accounting records.	C1, C2, C3
	6. Perform cutoff test for sales and sales returns.	
	a. Select a sample of recorded sales transactions from several days before and after year-end and examine supporting sales invoices and shipping documents to determine sales were recorded in the proper period.	EO1, C1, EO4, VA1
	b. Select sample of credit memos issued after year-end, examine supporting documentation such as dated receiving reports, and determine that returns were recorded in the proper period. Also consider whether volume of sales returns after year-end suggest possibility of unauthorized shipments before year-end.	EO3, C3, EO4, VA3

(continues)

Figure 14-9 ■ (Continued)

Category	Substantive Test	Specific Audit Objectives

	7. Perform cash receipts cutoff test.
	  a. Observe that all cash received through the close of business on the last day of the fiscal year is included in cash on hand or deposits in transit and that no receipts of the subsequent period are included, or
	  b. Review documentation such as daily cash summaries, duplicate deposit slips, and bank statements covering several days before and after year-end for proper cutoff.
		EO2, C2, EO4, VA2

Tests of Details of Balances	8. Confirm accounts receivable.
	  a. Determine the form, timing, and extent of confirmation requests.
	  b. Select and execute sample and investigate exceptions.
	  c. For positive confirmation requests for which no reply was received, perform alternative followup procedures:
	    • Vouch subsequent cash receipts identifiable with items comprising account balance at confirmation date to supporting documentation.
	    • Vouch items comprising balance at confirmation date to documentary support such as sale orders and shipping documents.
	9. a. Make inquiries about the sale, factoring, or pledging of accounts receivable.
	  b. Send confirmations to entities that have purchased accounts receivable or hold accounts receivable as collateral.
		EO4, C4, VA4, PD4
		EO4, C4, VA4, PD4
		EO4, C4, VA4, PD4
		
		RO1
		RO1

Tests of Details of Balances: Accounting Estimates	10. Evaluate adequacy of allowance component for each aging category and in the aggregate.
	  a. Foot and crossfoot the aged trial balance of receivables and agree total to the general ledger.
	  b. Test aging by vouching amounts in aging categories for sample of accounts to supporting documents.
	  c. For past-due accounts:
	    • Examine evidence of collectability such as correspondence with customers and outside collection agencies, credit reports, and customers' financial statements.
	    • Discuss collectability of accounts with appropriate management personnel.
	  d. Evaluate management's process for estimating the allowance for doubtful accounts using hindsight.
	  e. Evaluate the adequacy of the allowance given information about
	    • Industry trends.
	    • Aging trends.
	    • Collection history for specific customers.
		VA4
		
		VA5
		
		VA5
		
		VA5
		
		VA5

Required Procedures	11. Confirmation of receivable included in step 8 above.	EO4, C4, VA4, PD4

Tests of Details of Presentation and Disclosure	12. Compare statement presentation with GAAP.
	  a. Compare disclosures related to existence and rights and obligations of receivables to the results of tests performed above.
	  b. Determine that receivables are properly identified and classified as to type and expected period of realization.
	  c. Determine whether there are credit balances that are significant in the aggregate and that should be reclassified as liabilities.
	  d. Determine the appropriateness of disclosures and accounting for related party, pledged, assigned, or factored receivables.
	  e. Determine the need for disclosures regarding significant customers or sales by line of business.
	  f. Evaluate the completeness of presentation and disclosures for receivables in drafts of financial statements to determine conformity to GAAP by reference to disclosure checklist.
	  g. Read disclosures and independently evaluate their classification and understandability.
	  h. Vouch the accuracy of receivable disclosures to tests performed above.
		PD4
		
		PD4
		
		PD4
		
		PD4
		
		PD5
		
		PD5
		
		PD6
		
		PD7

Initial Procedures

The starting point for every audit test is to obtain an understanding of the business and industry. As previously discussed, it is important to understand the entity's policies regarding revenue recognition, as well as the entity's underlying economic drivers that impact total revenues and gross margin. The auditor should also understand standard trade terms, industry and client collection experience, seasonal aspects of the industry, and the extent of concentration of business with particular customers. This knowledge provides the context for evaluating the results of analytical procedures, tests of controls, and substantive tests. For example, the evidence obtained when performing detail tests of transactions and balances, such as invoice prices or the value of receivables for particular customers, should be consistent with expectations about industry competitiveness, the entity's productive time capacity, and the existence of major customers.

An important initial procedure for verifying accounts receivable and the related allowance account is tracing the current period's beginning balances to the ending audited balances in the prior year's working papers (when applicable). Next, the current period's activity in the general ledger control account and related allowance account should be reviewed for any significant entries that are unusual in nature or amount and that require special investigation. For example, the auditor should investigate any receivables and revenues that are not booked by way of recording sales invoices in the sales journal. In addition, a listing of all customer balances, called an **accounts receivable trial balance,** is obtained (usually in digital form). The auditor usually uses generalized audit software to foot the accounts receivable trial balance, and the total should be compared with (1) the total of the subsidiary ledger or master file from which it was prepared and (2) the general ledger control account. The auditor should also compare a sample of the customer's balance shown on the trial balance with that in the subsidiary ledger and vice versa to determine that the trial balance is an accurate and complete representation of the underlying accounting records. It can then serve as the physical representation of the population of accounts receivable to be subjected to further substantive testing.

Alternatively, the auditor can produce the accounts receivable trial balance directly from the client's master file using audit software. If the auditor can obtain the client's records in machine-readable form, he or she can also use generalized audit software to identify significant customers, analyze the volume of transactions with customers, and identify unusual transactions or a high volume of transactions near year-end.

An example of a working paper for an aged trial balance of receivables is presented in Figure 14-10. This working paper not only provides evidence of performance of the initial procedures just described, but several of the other substantive tests as discussed in subsequent sections. The initial procedures in verifying the accuracy of the trial balance and determining its agreement with the general ledger balance relate primarily to the posting and summarization component of the valuation or allocation assertion.

Analytical Procedures

The importance of analytical procedures was discussed earlier in this chapter. The auditor's goal is to develop expectations of the accounts receivable balance, of the relationship of accounts receivable to sales, and of the entity's gross margins. Sev-

Figure 14-10 ■ Aged Trial Balance Working Paper

Bates Company
Aged Trial Balance - Accounts Receivable - Trade
December 31, 20X1
(PBC)

Acct. 120

W/P Ref: B-1
Prepared By: QCE   Date: 1/15/x2
Reviewed By: PQR   Date: 1/20/x2

Account Name	Past Due Over 90 Days	Past Due Over 60 Days	Past Due Over 30 Days	Current	Balance Per Books 12/31/X1	Adjustments	Balance Per Audit 12/31/X1
Ace Engineering		2,529.04	2,016.14	11,875.90	16,421.08 ✓		16,421.08 C₁
ø Applied Devices	1,088.92 ท		15,938.89 ท	27,901.11 ท	43,840.00 ✓		43,840.00 C₂
ø Barry Manufacturing		743.12 ท	3,176.22 ท	8,993.01 ท	14,001.27 ✓		14,001.27 C₃
ø Brandt Electronics	501.10 ท	7,309.50 ท	30,948.01 ท	24,441.25 ท	63,199.86 ✓		63,199.86
Cermetrics, Inc.			3,813.76	8,617.30	12,431.06 ✓		12,431.06
ø Columbia Components				4,321.18 ✓	4,321.18		4,321.18
Drake Manufacturing			739.57	2,953.88	3,693.45 ✓		3,693.45
EMC		1,261.01	1,048.23	16,194.76	18,504.00 ✓		18,504.00
ø Groton Electric		7,799.36 ท	20,006.63 ท	89,017.15 ท	116,823.14 ✓		116,823.14 C₄
Harvey Industries		1,709.16	6,111.25	18,247.31	26,067.72 ✓		26,067.72
ø Jed Inc.	2,615.87 ท	12,098.00 ท	15,434.46 ท	56,536.88 ท	86,685.21 ✓	(9,416.96)	77,268.25 C₅
Jericho Electric		1,198.72	13,123.14		14,321.86 ✓		14,321.86
	• • • • • • •	• • • • • • •	• • • • • • •	• • • • • • •	• • • • • • •	• • • • • • •	• • • • • • •
ø W & M Manufacturing Corp.	814.98	1,904.65 ท	2,166.78 ท	28,389.69 ท	32,461.12 ✓		32,461.12 C₆₀
Yancey Corp.		2,861.05	9,874.13	13,561.80	27,111.96 ✓		27,111.96
	10,157.46	56,705.59	160,537.28	392,136.41	619,536.74 ✓	(9,416.96)	610,119.78
	✓	✓	✓	✓	B	B	B

√   Footed or crossfooted

ø   Customer name and balance per books agreed to subsidiary ledger

ท   Aging verified by examining transaction/dates of related unpaid sales invoices in subsidiary ledger

C#   Account selected for confirmation - see W/P B-2

eral analytical procedures that can be performed to provide evidence about accounts payable are shown in Figure 14-4. The auditor should pay particular attention to unexpected increases in revenues or receivables.

Tests of Details of Transactions

Tests of details of transactions may be performed during interim work along with tests of controls in the form of dual-purpose tests. This includes the test described in the next section. The cutoff tests described in subsequent sections are always performed as part of year-end work.

Vouch Revenue Transactions

The customer account file maintained by the client should contain such documents as customer orders, sales orders, shipping documents, sales invoices, credit memoranda, and correspondence. In performing this test, a sample of debits to customers' accounts can be vouched to supporting sales invoices and matching documents to provide evidence pertaining to the existence or occurrence, rights and obligations, and valuation or allocation assertions. Credits can be vouched to remittance advices and sales adjustment authorizations. Evidence that these reductions in customer balances are legitimate pertains to the completeness assertion for accounts receivable. These tests may be performed more extensively when the applicable level of detection risk to be achieved is low, when confirmation procedures are not practicable, or when it becomes necessary to supplement confirmation procedures.

Trace Revenue Transactions

In order to test the completeness assertion, the auditor should trace a sample of sales, cash receipts, and sales adjustment transactions to their recording in the accounting records. For sales, the auditor should start with a sample of shipments and trace transactions to the sales journal. For cash receipts the auditor would sample items off the prelisting of cash and trace them forward to the cash receipts journal. For sales returns the auditor would normally start with the sale returns authorization, and trace forward to the receiving report and the entry in accounting records.

Perform Cutoff Tests for Sales and Sales Returns

The **sales cutoff test** is designed to obtain reasonable assurance that (1) sales and accounts receivable are recorded in the accounting period in which the transactions occurred and (2) the corresponding entries for inventories and cost of goods sold are made in the same period.

Sales should be recorded in the period in which legal title to the goods passes to the buyer. The sales cutoff test is made as of the balance sheet date. For sales of goods from inventory, the test involves comparison of a sample of recorded sales from the last few days of the current period and the first few days of the next period with shipping documents to determine whether the transactions were recorded in the proper period. When prenumbered shipping documents are issued in sequence and the auditor is on hand to observe the number of the last shipping document used in the current period, he or she can then determine that each sales transaction recorded prior to year-end is supported by a shipping document with a number issued in the current period and that each sales transaction recorded after year-end is supported by a shipping document with a number issued in the subsequent period. For a calendar-year client, if January sales are recorded in December, there is a misstatement of the existence or occurrence assertion. Conversely, if December sales are not recorded until January, there is a misstatement of the completeness assertion.

The **sales return cutoff test** is similar and is particularly directed toward the possibility that returns made prior to year-end are not recorded until after year-end, resulting in the overstatement of receivables and sales. The correct timing can be determined by examining dated receiving reports for returned merchandise and correspondence with customers. The auditor should also be alert to the possibility that an unusually heavy volume of sales returns after year-end (perhaps up to the end of fieldwork and report date) could signal unauthorized shipments before year-end to inflate recorded sales and receivables.

Perform Cash Receipts Cutoff Test

The **cash receipts cutoff test** is designed to obtain reasonable assurance that cash receipts are recorded in the accounting period in which received. A proper cutoff at the balance sheet date is essential to the correct presentation of both cash and accounts receivable. For example, if December collections from customers are not recorded until January, accounts receivable will be overstated and cash will be understated at the balance sheet date. Conversely, if January collections from customers are recorded in December, cash will be overstated and accounts receivable will be understated. Thus, this test relates to the existence or occurrence and completeness assertions for both cash and accounts receivable.

Personal observation or a review of documentation can provide evidence concerning the promptness of the cutoff. If the auditor can be present at the year-end date, he or she can observe that all collections received prior to the close of business are included in cash on hand or in deposits in transit and are credited to accounts receivable. An alternative to personal observation is to review supporting documentation such as the daily cash summary and validated deposit slip for the last day of the year. The objective of the review is to determine that the deposit slip total agrees with the receipts shown on the daily cash summary. In addition, the auditor should determine that the receipts were recorded on the closing date.

Tests of Details of Balances

Two primary sets of procedures in this category of substantive tests for accounts receivable are discussed in the following sections: (1) confirmation of receivables and the related followup procedures and (2) procedures for evaluating the adequacy of the allowance for uncollectable accounts.

Audit Decision 12

■ How are confirma-
tion procedures used
in auditing accounts
receivable?

Confirm Receivables

Confirmation of accounts receivable involves direct written communication between individual customers and the auditor. The confirmation of receivables is a generally accepted audit procedure. AU 330, *The Confirmation Process* (SAS 67), states that there is a presumption that the auditor will request the confirmation of receivables during an audit unless:

■ Accounts receivable are immaterial to the financial statements.
■ The use of confirmations would be ineffective as an audit procedure.

■ The auditor's combined assessment of inherent risk and control risk is low, and that assessment, in conjunction with evidence expected to be provided by analytical procedures or other substantive tests of details, is sufficient to reduce audit risk to an acceptably low level for the applicable financial statement assertions. In many situations, both confirmation of accounts receivable and other substantive tests of details are necessary to reduce audit risk to an acceptably low level of the applicable financial statement assertions.

An auditor who does not request confirmation of receivables should document in the working papers how he or she overcame the presumption that confirmations should be requested. For example, the auditor might state the conclusion that based on the prior year's audit experience on that engagement, it is expected that the responses would be unreliable or the response rates would be inadequate in the current year. Also, in some cases, debtors may be unable to confirm balances if they use voucher systems that show the amount owed on individual transactions, but not the total amount owed to one creditor. This is generally true of governmental agencies. The auditor may be able to overcome this problem by confirming individual transactions rather than balances.

Occasionally, clients have prohibited auditors from confirming any or certain accounts receivable. Complete prohibition represents a serious limitation on the scope of the audit that generally results in a disclaimer of opinion on the financial statements. The effect of partial prohibition should be evaluated on the basis of management's reasons therefore, and whether the auditor can obtain sufficient evidence from other auditing procedures.

Forms of Confirmation

There are two forms of confirmation request: (1) the **positive confirmation,** which requires the debtor to respond whether or not the balance shown is correct, and (2) the **negative confirmation,** which requires the debtor to respond only when the amount shown is incorrect. The two forms are illustrated in Figure 14-11. The positive confirmation request is usually made in the form of a separate letter, but it may be in the form of a stamp on the customer's monthly statement. In contrast, the negative request is usually in the form of a stamp. The positive form generally produces the better evidence because under the negative form, the failure to receive a response can only lead to a presumption that the balance is correct, whereas the customer may have overlooked the request or neglected to return an exception.

A variation of the positive form is "the blank form," so named because the customer's balance is not stated. Instead, the customer is asked to fill in the balance. The use of this form provides a high degree of assurance about the information confirmed. However, the extra work required of the respondent may significantly reduce the response rate.

The selection of the form of the confirmation request rests with the auditor. In making the decision, the auditor considers the applicable level of detection risk and the composition of the customer balances. The positive form is used when detection risk is low or individual customer balances are relatively large. AU 330.20 indicates that the negative form should be used only when all three of the following conditions apply:

■ The acceptable level of detection risk for the related assertions is moderate or high.

Figure 14-11 ■ Confirmation Request Forms

BATES COMPANY
P.O. Box 1922 Sandusky, Ohio 44870

Ace Engineering Service
Box 131
Indiana, Pennsylvania 15701

This request is being sent to you to enable our independent auditors to confirm the correctness of our records. It is not a request for payment.

Our records on <u>December 31, 20X1</u> showed an amount of <u>$16,421.08</u> receivable from you. Please confirm whether this agrees with your records on that date by signing and returning this form directly to our auditors. An addressed envelope is enclosed for this purpose. If you find any difference please report details direct to our auditors in the space provided below.

_____

Controller _____

The above amount is correct ☐ .

The above amount is incorrect for the following reasons:

_____

_____

_____

_____

_____

(Individual or Company Name) _____

By: _____

Please examine this monthly statement carefully and advise our auditors

Reddy & Abel
Certified Public Accountants
465 City Center Bldg.
Marian, New York 11748

as to any exceptions.

A self-addressed envelope is enclosed for your convenience.

THIS IS NOT A REQUEST FOR PAYMENT

- A large number of small balances is involved.
- The auditor has no reason to believe that the recipients of the requests are unlikely to give them consideration.

Frequently, a combination of the two forms is used in a single engagement. For example, in the audit of a public utility, the auditor may elect to use the negative form for residential customers and the positive form for commercial customers. When the positive form is used, the auditor should generally follow up with a second and sometimes an additional request to those debtors that fail to reply.

Timing and Extent of Requests

When the applicable level of detection risk is low, the auditor ordinarily requests confirmation of receivables as of the balance sheet date. If the auditor follows a lower assessed level of control risk approach and is able to support a low control risk assessment, the confirmation date may be one or two months earlier. In such a case, the auditor is expected to vouch material changes between the confirmation date and balance sheet date and may elect to reconfirm accounts with unusual changes.

The extent of request, or sample size, is related to the factors discussed in Chapter 12 (see Figure 12-6). Negative confirmation requests require larger sample sizes than positive requests. Stratification may also affect sample size. For example, auditors frequently seek confirmation of all accounts in excess of a certain dollar (less than or equal to tolerable misstatement) balance or in excess of a certain age, and select a random sample of all other accounts. Sample size may be determined judgmentally or with the aid of a statistical sampling plan as explained in Chapter 13.

Controlling the Requests

The auditor must control every step in the confirmation process.
This means:

- Ascertaining that the amount, name, and address on the confirmation agree with the corresponding data in the customer's account.
- Maintaining custody of the confirmations until they are mailed.
- Using the firm's own return address envelopes for the confirmations.
- Personally depositing the requests in the mail.
- Insisting that the returns be sent directly to the auditor.

Client assistance can be used in the preparation of the requests, provided the foregoing controls are observed.

A working paper should indicate each account selected for confirmation, the results obtained from each request, and cross-references to the actual confirmation responses. A confirmation control working paper is illustrated in Figure 14-12. The actual confirmation responses should also be retained in the working papers.

Disposition of Exceptions

Confirmation responses will inevitably contain some exceptions. Exceptions may be attributed to goods in transit from the client to the customers, returned goods, or payments in transit from the customer to the client, items in dispute, errors, and irregularities. All exceptions should be investigated by the auditor and their reso-

Figure 14-12 ■ Confirmation Control Working Paper

Bates Company
Accounts Receivable Confirmation Control—Acct. 120
December 31, 20X1

W/P Ref: *B-2*
Prepared By: *a.C.E.* Date: *1/28/X2*
Reviewed By: *P.a.R* Date: *1/31/X2*

Conf. No.	Customer	Book Value	Confirmed Value ⱷ	Audited Value	(Over) Under Statement	Subsequent Collections Examined Thru 1-28-X2
1	Applied Devices	43,840.00	43,480.00	43,480.00		
2	Barry Mfg.	14,001.27	*ᑎR*	14,001.27		14,001.27 √
3	Brandt Electronics	63,199.96	63,199.96	63,199.96		
4	Groton Electric	116,823.14	116,823.14	116,823.14		
5	Jed Inc.	86,685.21	77,268.25	77,268.25	(9,416.96) ⓧ1	
60	W & M Mfg. Corp.	32,461.12	*ᑎR*	32,461.12 ᴎ		4,071.43 √
	Totals	470,847.92	414,968.57	461,430.96	(9,416.96)	

Response Recap:	# Items	$ Value
Confirmations mailed	60	470,847.92
Confirmations received	58	414,968.57
Response %	97	88

Summary of Results:	# Items	$ Value
Account total	300	619,536.74
Book value of confirmation sample	60	470,847.92
% Coverage of book value		76
Audited value of sample	60	461,430.96
Ratio of audited to book value of sample		98

ⱷ   *Signed confirmation response attached for confirmed values.*
ᑎR   *Nonresponse-alternative procedures performed.*
√   *Examined entries in cash receipts journal and related remittance advices for total collections indicated.*
ᴎ   *Examined supporting documentation for portion of book value remaining uncollected as of 1/28/X2.*
ⓧ1   *Credit memo issued 1/12/X2 for merchandise returned 12/28/X1. Adjusting entry:*
    Dr. Sales Returns   9,416.96
    Cr. Accounts Receivable   9,416.96 } See W/P B-1 and aE-1

lution indicated in the working papers as illustrated in Figure 14-12. For example, an auditor might vouch payments in transit to subsequent cash receipts.

Alternative Procedures for Dealing with Nonresponses

When no response has been received after the second or third positive confirmation request to a customer, alternative procedures should ordinarily be performed. AU 330.31 acknowledges that the omission of such procedures may be acceptable when both of the following conditions apply:

■ There are no unusual qualitative factors or systematic characteristics related to the nonresponses, such as that all nonresponses pertain to year-end transactions.

■ The nonresponses, projected as 100 percent misstatements to the populations and added to the sum of all other unadjusted differences, would not affect the auditor's decision about whether the financial statements are materially correct.

The two main alternative procedures are examining subsequent collections and vouching open invoices comprising customer balances.

The best evidence of existence and collectability is the receipt of payment from the customer. Before the conclusion of the audit fieldwork, the client will receive payments from many customers on amounts owed at the confirmation date. The matching of such collections back to open (unpaid) invoices comprising the customers' balances at the confirmation date establishes the existence and collectability of the accounts.

In performing this test, the auditor should recognize the possible adverse implications of collections that cannot be matched to specific transactions or balances. For example, a round sum amount may, on investigation, reveal items in dispute, and token payments on large balances may indicate financial instability on the part of the customer.

If the customer has not paid the receivable, the auditor can vouch the receivable to underlying customer orders and shipping documentation.

Summarizing and Evaluating Results

The auditor's working papers should contain a summary of the results from confirming accounts receivable. The summary should provide, as a minimum, statistical data on:

■ The number and dollar value of confirmations sent and responses received
■ The proportion of the population total covered by the sample
■ The relationship between the audited and book values of items included in the sample

The lower portion of Figure 14-12 illustrates how such data might be presented. Statistical and nonstatistical procedures may be used to project misstatements found in the sample to the population as explained in Chapter 13.

The combined evidence from the confirmations, alternative procedures performed on nonresponses, and other tests of details and analytical procedures is evaluated to determine whether sufficient evidence has been obtained to support management's assertions about gross accounts receivable. When numerous exceptions are found, or insufficient responses are received from confirmation requests and the auditor is unable to obtain sufficient competent evidence from other substantive tests, he or she will be unable to issue a standard auditor's report.

Applicability to Assertions

The confirmation of accounts receivable is the primary source of evidence in meeting the existence or occurrence assertion. Acknowledgment of the debt by the customer in the response confirms that the client has a legal claim on the customer. Thus, this test also provides evidence concerning the rights and obligations assertion. The confirmation of accounts receivable is not a request for payment. Thus, it does not provide evidence as to the collectability of the balance due. However, the responses may reveal previously paid items or disputed items that affect the proper valuation of the amount due. In this sense, confirmation of accounts receivable relates only to the valuation or allocation assertion for gross accounts receivable. When a customer's response indicates agreement with the book balance, there is evidence that the balance is complete. However, the evidence about the completeness assertion is limited because (1) unrecorded receivables cannot be confirmed and (2) customers are more likely to report errors of overstatement than errors of understatement.

Tests of Details of Accounting Estimates

The key accounting estimate involved in the revenue cycle is the allowance for doubtful accounts. Audit tests of this accounting estimate include:

- Using generalized audit software to foot and crossfoot the **aged trial balance** of accounts receivable and agreeing the total to the general ledger balance.
- Testing the aging of the amounts shown in the aging categories on the aged trial balance.
- Considering evidence concerning the collectability of past-due amounts by, for example, reading correspondence from customers.
- Identifying customers with past-due balances, and calculating credit histories for customers with past-due balances.
- Evaluating prior estimates of uncollectable accounts with subsequent experience and the benefit of hindsight.
- Using the evidence obtained above to assess the reasonableness of the percentages used to compute the allowance component required for each aging category and the adequacy of the overall allowance.

Refer to the example of an aged trial balance presented in Figure 14-10. The auditor can use generalized audit software to generate an aging of the client's master file. Alternatively, the aging of a customer's balance can be tested by vouching the amounts shown in each aging category to the subsidiary ledger or master file and determining the length of time between the dates the unpaid sales invoices were recorded and the trial balance date.

In considering the collectability of past-due amounts, the auditor will pay particular attention to customers that demonstrate deteriorating payment history as the year progresses. They may examine correspondence with customers and outside collection agencies, review customers' credit reports and financial statements, and discuss the collectability of specific accounts with appropriate management personnel.

The allowance for uncollectable accounts is an accounting estimate made by management that involves both objective and subjective considerations. In essence, it is a prospective estimate of receivables that will not be collected in the future. The auditor's responsibility is to judge the reasonableness of the allowance and related provision for uncollectable accounts expense. From the aging data, information about collectability, and analysis of the client's prior experience with uncollectable accounts, the auditor can assess the reasonableness of the percentages used to compute the allowance component required for each aging category and the adequacy of the overall allowance. An important aspect of evaluating prior experience with the entity involves using hindsight to evaluate prior estimates of the allowance and subsequent experience in collecting receivables outstanding at the date of the estimate. When the client's controls over (1) granting credit and (2) writing off uncollectable accounts are strong, less evidence will be required in making this assessment than when controls are weak.

Tests of Details of Disclosures

Figure 14-9 describes a number of tests of disclosures for the revenue cycle. The auditor must be knowledgeable about the statement presentation and disclosure requirements for accounts receivable and sales under GAAP. The requirements include proper identification and classification for receivables. A review of the accounts receivable trial balance may indicate receivables from employees, officers, affiliated companies, and other related parties that should be reclassified or separately disclosed, if material. The same source may reveal receivables with credit balances that, if significant in the aggregate, should be reclassified as current liabilities. GAAP also requires proper classification of receivables as current and noncurrent, and disclosures concerning the pledging, assigning, or factoring of receivables. Disclosures may be required regarding significant customers, or sales by significant lines of business. Evidence relevant to these matters should be obtainable by inquiring of management and reviewing minutes of board of directors' meetings and loan agreements. Evidence is also obtained through the audit procedures performed to test other assertions. Management's representations on these matters should be obtained in writing in a client representation letter as one of the final steps in the audit, as explained in Chapter 19.

[LEARNING CHECK

14-18 a. Identify the transaction classes that should be considered in assessing control risk for accounts receivable assertions.
    b. Which transaction class control risk assessments should be considered in assessing control risk for the existence of accounts receivable?
    c. When is it necessary to determine a revised acceptable level of detection risk and a revised level of tests of details risk?

14-19 Develop preliminary audit strategies for each financial statement assertion.

14-20 What is involved in vouching recorded receivables transactions to supporting documentation, and to what specific account balance audit objectives does the evidence pertain?

14-21 What cutoff tests are performed for accounts receivable, how are they performed, and to what account audit objectives does the evidence pertain?

14-22 a. Under what circumstance might it not be necessary to confirm accounts receivable?
    b. What factors should be considered in determining the form of the confirmation request?
    c. When positive confirmation requests are used, how does the auditor deal with nonresponses?

14-23 a. What roles does an aged trial balance play in an audit?
    b. What procedures should be applied to the aged trial balance?
    c. What steps should the auditor perform when auditing the accounting estimate associated with the allowance for doubtful accounts?
    d. If the auditor is auditing the allowance for doubtful accounts at year-end, why is it useful to evaluate prior accounting estimates using hindsight?

14-24 What disclosures for accounts receivable are required by GAAP?

KEY TERMS

Accounts receivable trail balance,
   p. 661
Aged trial balance, p. 670
Cash receipts cutoff tests, p. 664

Negative confirmation, p. 665
Positive confirmation, p. 665
Sales cutoff test, p. 663
Sales return cutoff test, p. 664

OTHER ASSURANCE SERVICES

Audit Decision 13

■ How does the auditor use the knowledge obtained during the audit of the revenue cycle to support other assurance services?

Generally accepted auditing standards do not require that the auditor perform other assurance services. However, many auditors develop industry specializations so that they can understand industry trends and better identify risks associated with financial statements not presenting fairly financial position, results of operations, or cash flows. The client and its board of directors usually want to take full advantage of the auditor's knowledge. In the process of performing the audit, the auditor may benchmark company performance against others in the industry. The auditor might address, for example, whether:

■ The company is effectively utilizing assets to generate sales based on a ratio of sales to total assets.
■ Receivables are growing faster than sales, thereby consuming valuable cash flows.
■ The company has appropriately addressed risks associated with a changing or maturing marketplace.
■ The company is bringing successful new product innovations to market and is enjoying a high percentage of revenues from new products, relative to the competition.

As an auditor completes the audit of the sales cycle, he or she should summarize key issues that might support other assurance service and client recommendations.

   To illustrate further, consider the information contained in Figure 8-7 regarding Net Technology, Inc. The collection period of 87 days (4.2 turns) is substantially longer than the industry median of 49 days (7.4 turns), and the ratio of sales to total assets of 1.34 is substantially below the industry median of 2.0. The auditor might recommend that the client consider encouraging a faster turn with cash discounts, possibly implement a policy of charging interest on past-due receivables, or revise its credit policy to speed up cash collections. The auditor might use knowledge obtained in other aspects of the audit to determine whether the poor utilization of total assets is due to receivable problems, inventory problems, or poor utilization of fixed assets. In this way the CPA uses the knowledge obtained during the audit to assist the client in identifying opportunities for improved business performance.

FOCUS ON AUDIT DECISIONS

This chapter focuses on the practical aspects of auditing the revenue cycle. The chapter pays particular attention to audit planning concerns related to the revenue cycle, specific internal controls that are tailored to the revenue cycle, and substantive tests for the revenue cycle. Figure 14-13 summarizes the audit decisions discussed in Chapter 14 and provides page references indicating where these decisions are discussed in more detail.

Figure 14-13 ■ Summary of Audit Decisions Discussed in Chapter 14

Audit Decision	Factors that Influence the Audit Decision	Chapter References
D1. What is the nature of the revenue cycle, and how are specific audit objectives developed for the revenue cycle?	The revenue cycle includes three major classes of transactions: (1) credit sales, (2) cash receipts, and (3) sales adjustments. The primary balance in the revenue cycle is accounts receivable, net of the allowance for doubtful accounts. Figure 14-2 develops specific audit objectives for the audit of the revenue cycle.	pp. 629–630
D2. How does understanding the entity and its environment affect audit planning decisions in the revenue cycle?	Different companies in different industries experience various risks associated with the revenue cycle. Revenue recognition is more problematic in some industries, and some industries have significant transactions that result in cash collection in advance of earning revenues. Figure 14-3 provides examples of five different industries and how knowledge of the entity and its environment can be used to develop expectations of the financial statements and to assess the risk of material misstatement. The chapter also discusses common inherent risks associated with the revenue cycle.	pp. 630–632
D3. What are the important inherent risks in the revenue cycle?	Auditors commonly encounter three significant inherent risks in the revenue cycle. First, revenue recognition issues are the most significant cause of financial statement restatements. Second, cash receipts present an opportunity for misappropriation of assets. Third, the allowance for doubtful accounts represents a significant accounting estimate associated with the revenue cycle. Additional inherent risk factors are also discussed in this chapter section.	pp. 633–634
D4. How does the auditor determine analytical procedures that would be effective in identifying potential misstatements in the revenue cycle?	Analytical procedures are cost effective, and they often identify assertions that need audit attention. Figure 14-4 explains a number of analytical procedures that are helpful in identifying potential misstatements in the revenue cycle. Additional analytical procedures that use nonfinancial data are also explained in the chapter discussion.	pp. 634–636
D5. What are the relevant aspects of internal control components for the revenue cycle?	This section of the chapter reviews important aspects of the control environment, risk assessment, information and communication, and monitoring that are relevant to the revenue cycle.	pp. 636–638
D6. What should be considered in evaluating control activities for credit sales transactions?	Making credit sales involves authorizing the sale, delivering goods or services, and recording the sale. It is essential for the auditor to understand the audit trail and common documents and records used in recording credit sales. These are discussed in detail in the chapter. Figure 14-5 provides a series of example control activities that are commonly used to control assertions related to credit sales.	pp. 639–646
D7. What should be considered in evaluating control activities for cash receipts?	Cash receipt functions include receiving cash, depositing cash, and recording cash receipts. This section explains the documents and records involved in recording cash receipts, and Figure 14-7 provides a series of examples of commonly used control activities that control assertions related to cash receipts.	pp. 647–651

(continues)

Figure 14-13 ■ (Continued)

Audit Decision	Factors that Influence the Audit Decision	Chapter References
D8. What should be considered in evaluating control activities for sales adjustment transactions?	Sales adjustments functions include granting cash discounts, granting sales returns and allowance, and determining uncollectable accounts. This section explains the documents and records involved in recording sale adjustments and provides a series of example control activities that control assertions related to each sales adjustment function.	pp. 651–653
D9. What are the relevant aspects of tests of controls when the auditor plans to assess control risk below the maximum for the revenue cycle?	Many of the control activities in the revenue cycle involve programmed controls. In order for the auditor to assess control risk as low, the auditor needs to (1) test computer general controls, (2) test the computer application itself, and (3) test the effectiveness of manual followup activities. Examples of tests of computer application controls are provided in this chapter discussion.	p. 654
D10. What are the factors involved in determining an acceptable level of tests of details risk for accounts receivable assertions?	Once the auditor has completed risk assessment procedures, the auditor can develop a preliminary audit strategy for each assertion. In determining the appropriate level of test of details risk, the auditor should consider inherent risk, control risk, and analytical procedures risk. This section examines common issues involved in assessing these risks, and example preliminary audit strategies are developed for each of the five basic financial statement assertions.	pp. 655–658
D11. How does the auditor determine the elements of an audit program for substantive tests to achieve specific audit objectives for accounts receivable?	This section of the chapter uses the framework developed in Chapter 12 to design substantive tests for the revenue cycle. Figure 14-9 focuses on the nature of substantive tests for the revenue cycle. It summarizes the initial procedures, analytical procedures, tests of details of transactions, tests of details of balances, tests of details of accounting estimates, and tests of details of disclosures relevant to the revenue cycle. The chapter discussion explores these tests in more detail.	pp. 658–664
D12: How are confirmation procedures used in auditing accounts receivable?	Confirmations are an important procedure for testing the existence and valuation of receivables at historic cost. The chapter discussion explains the use of positive and negative confirmations. In addition, it discusses important audit evidence that is needed when customers do not respond to confirmations.	pp. 664–671
D13: How does the auditor use the knowledge obtained during the audit of the revenue cycle to support other assurance services?	Once the auditor has completed an audit of the revenue cycle, the auditor should have information that supports an audit opinion as well as recommendations related to improvements in internal controls. In addition, the auditor probably has obtained knowledge that may be relevant to other assurance services such as risk assessment or performance measurement services. This final section of the chapter provides examples of how knowledge obtained while auditing the revenue cycle can be used to support other assurance services.	p. 672

objective questions

Objective questions are available for the student at www.wiley.com/college/boynton

comprehensive questions

14-25 **(Knowledge of the entity and its environment)** Your client is a regional motel chain. It owns 27 properties in your region and manages another 40 properties for absentee owners. All the motels located are on interstate freeways and achieve at least 60 percent of capacity on a regular basis. Many motels are fully booked during the summer travel season; however, during the balance of the year price competition is significant.

Required

Explain how your knowledge of the business and industry would impact your audit of total revenues and accounts receivable for the client.

14-26 **(Analytical procedures)** The following data was taken from the production and accounting records for Casuccio Manufacturing, Inc.

	UNAUDITED 20X9	AUDITED 20X8	AUDITED 20X7
Operating Data			
Capacity in Units	450,000	450,000	450,000
Production in Units	450,000	400,000	300,000
Inventory in Units	32,000	28,000	21,000
Financial Data ($000)			
Total Revenues	$ 35,200	$ 27,500	$ 21,200
Total Assets	$ 23,000	$ 19,500	$ 15,700
Accounts Receivable, Net	$ 5,900	$ 4,300	$ 3,900
Bad Debt Expense	$ 175	$ 135	$ 105
Accounts Receivable Written Off	$ 165	$ 125	$ 100

Required

1. Calculate the following ratios for 20x9, 20x8 and 20x7:
   a. Sales to total assets
   b. Sales to production
   c. Revenue per unit sold
   d. Accounts receivable growth to sales growth
   e. Uncollectable accounts expense to net credit sales
   f. Uncollectable accounts expense to accounts receivable written off
   g. Accounts receivable turn days

2. a. Describe the implications of the resulting ratios for the auditor's audit strategy for year 20x9.
   b. What specific audit objectives are likely to be misstated?
   c. How should the auditor respond in terms of potential audit tests?

14-27 **(Internal control questionnaire—cash receipts)** Harris, CPA, has been engaged to audit the financial statements of the Spartan Drug Store, Inc. Spartan is a medium-sized retail outlet that sells a wide variety of consumer goods. All sales are for cash or check. Cashiers utilize cash registers to process these transactions. There are no receipts by mail, and there are no credit card or charge sales.

Required

Construct the "Processing Cash Collections" segment of the internal control questionnaire on "Cash Receipts" to be used in the evaluation of the internal control structure for the Spartan Drug Store, Inc. Each question should elicit either a *Yes* or *No* response.

AICPA (adapted)

14-28   **(Controls over cash receipts processing at a church)** You have been asked by the board of trustees of a local church to review its accounting procedures. As a part of this review, you have prepared the following comments relating to the collections made at weekly services and recordkeeping for members' contributions:

1. The church's board of trustees has delegated responsibility for financial management and audit of the financial records to the finance committee. This group prepares the annual budget and approves major disbursements but is not involved in collections or recordkeeping. No audit has been considered necessary in recent years because the same trusted employee has kept church records and served as financial secretary for 15 years.

2. The collection at the weekly service is taken by a team of ushers. The head usher counts the collection in the church following each service. He then places the collection and a notation of the amount counted in the church safe. Next morning the financial secretary opens the safe and counts the collection again. She withholds about $100 to meet cash expenditures during the coming week and deposits the remainder of the collection intact. To facilitate the deposit, members who contribute by check are asked to draw their checks to "cash."

Required

Describe the weaknesses and recommend improvements in procedures for collections made at weekly services. Organize your answer using the following format:

WEAKNESS	RECOMMENDED IMPROVEMENT(S)

AICPA (adapted)

14-29   **(Flowcharting and evaluating on-line computer processing of cash receipts)** Until recently, Consolidated Electricity Company employed a batch processing system for recording the receipt of customer payments. The following narrative describes the procedures involved in this system.

The customer's payment and the remittance advice (a punch card) are received in the treasurer's office. An accounts receivable clerk in the treasurer's office keypunches the cash receipt into the remittance advice and forwards the card to the EDP department. The cash receipt is added to a control tape listing and then filed for deposit later in the day. When the deposit slips are received from EDP later in the day (approximately 2:30 P.M. each day), the cash receipts are removed from the file and deposited with the original deposit slip. The second copy of the deposit slip and the control tape are compared for accuracy before the deposit is made and then filed together.

In the EDP department, the remittance advices received from the treasurer's office are held until 2:00 P.M. daily. At that time, the customer payments are processed to update the records on magnetic tape and prepare a deposit slip in triplicate. During the update process, data are read, nondestructively, from the master accounts receivable tape, processed, and then recorded on a new master tape. The original and second copy of the deposit slip are forwarded to the treasurer's office. The old master tape (former accounts receivable file), the remittance advices (in customer number order), and the third copy of the deposit slip are filed and stored in a secure place. The updated accounts receivable master tape is maintained in the system for processing the next day.

Consolidated Electricity Company has revised and redesigned its computer system so that it has on-line capabilities. The new cash receipts procedures, described below, are designed to take advantage of the new system.

The customer's payment and remittance advice are received in the treasurer's office as before. A cathode ray tube terminal is located in the treasurer's office to enter the cash receipts. An operator keys in the customer's number and payment from the remittance advice and checks. The cash receipt is entered into the system once the operator has confirmed that the proper account and amount are displayed on the screen. The payment is then processed on-line against the accounts receivable file maintained on magnetic disk. The cash receipts are filed for deposit later in the day. The remittance advices are filed in the order they are processed; these cards will be kept until the next working day and then destroyed. The computer prints out a deposit slip in duplicate at 2:00 P.M. for all cash receipts since the last deposit. The deposit slips are forwarded to the treasurer's office. The cash receipts are removed from the file and deposited with the original deposit slip; the duplicate deposit slip is filed for further reference. At the close of business hours (5:00 P.M.) each day, the EDP department prepares a record of the current day's cash receipts activity on a magnetic tape. This tape is then stored in a secure place in the event of a systems malfunction; after 10 working days, the tape is released for further use.

Required

a. Prepare a systems flowchart for the company's new on-line cash receipts procedures.

b. Have the new cash receipts procedures as designed and implemented by Consolidated Electricity Company created any internal control structure problems for the company? Explain your answer.

ICMA (adapted)

14-30 **(Substantive tests of accounts receivable)** The following situations were not discovered by an inexperienced staff auditor in the audit of the Parson Company.

1. Several accounts were incorrectly aged in the client's aging schedule.
2. The accounts receivable turnover ratio was far below expected results.
3. Goods billed were not shipped.
4. Some year-end sales were recorded in the wrong accounting period.
5. Several sales were posted for the correct amount but to the wrong customers in the accounts receivable ledger.
6. The allowance for uncollectable accounts was understated.
7. Several sales were entered and posted at incorrect amounts.
8. Mathematical errors were made in totaling the accounts receivable ledger.
9. An unrecorded sale at the balance sheet date was collected in the next month.
10. Several fictitious sales were recorded.
11. The pledging of some customer accounts as security for a loan was not reported in the balance sheet.
12. Some year-end cash receipts were recorded in the wrong accounting period.

Required

a. Identify the substantive test that should have detected each error.

b. For each substantive test identified in (a), indicate the account balance audit objective to which it pertains.

c. Indicate the type of evidence obtained (i.e., physical, confirmations, documentary, written representations, mathematical, oral, or analytical) from each substantive test.

(Use a tabular format for your answers with one column for each part.)

14-31   **(Sales cutoff test)** You are engaged to perform an audit for the Wilcox Corporation for the year ended December 31, 20X0. Only merchandise shipped by the Wilcox Corporation to customers up to and including December 31, 20X0, has been eliminated from inventory. The inventory, as determined by physical inventory count, has been recorded on the books by the company's controller. No perpetual inventory records are maintained. All sales are made on an FOB shipping point basis. You are to assume that all purchase invoices have been correctly recorded.

The following lists of sales invoices are entered in the sales journal for the months of December 20X0 and January 20X1, respectively.

	SALES INVOICE AMOUNT	SALES INVOICE DATE	COST OF MERCHANDISE SOLD	DATE SHIPPED
December				
a.	$3,000	Dec. 21	$2,000	Dec. 31
b.	2,000	Dec. 31	800	Nov. 3
c.	1,000	Dec. 29	600	Dec. 30
d.	4,000	Dec. 31	2,400	Jan. 3
e.	10,000	Dec. 30	5,600	Dec. 29 (shipped to consignee)
January				
f.	$6,000	Dec. 31	$4,000	Dec. 30
g.	4,000	Jan. 2	2,300	Jan. 2
h.	8,000	Jan. 3	5,500	Dec. 31

Required

Based on a sales cutoff analysis, record necessary adjusting journal entries at December 31, in connection with the foregoing data.

AICPA

14-32   **(Confirmation procedures)** King, CPA, is auditing the financial statements of Cycle Co., an entity that has receivables from customers, which have arisen from the sale of goods in the normal course of business. King is aware that the confirmation of accounts receivable is a generally accepted auditing procedure.

Required

a. Under what circumstances could King justify omitting the confirmation of Cycle's accounts receivable?

b. In designing confirmation requests, what factors are likely to affect King's assessment of the reliability of confirmations that King sends?

c. What alternative procedures would King consider performing when replies to positive confirmation requests are not received?

14-33   The following information was taken from the accounting records for Aurora Manufacturing, Inc.

	YEAR 5 UNAUDITED	YEAR 4 AUDITED	YEAR 3 AUDITED	YEAR 2 AUDITED	YEAR 1 AUDITED
Accounts Receivable Gross	$535,000	$295,000	$265,000	$207,500	$175,000
Allowance for Uncollectible Accounts	($14,150)	($6,400)	($5,275)	($5,900)	($5,400)
Total Assets	$2,200,000	$1,800,000	$1,500,000	$1,200,000	$1,000,000
Total Revenues	$2,700,000	$2,050,000	$1,750,000	$1,400,000	$1,200,000
Uncollectable Account Expense	$33,750	$25,625	$21,875	$17,500	$15,000
Write-off of Accounts Receivable	$26,000	$24,500	$22,500	$17,000	$14,000
Industry Median					
Sales to Total Assets	1.25	1.23	1.29	1.26	
Accounts Receivable Collection Period	47	48	47	47	
Uncollectable Account Expense to Net Credit Sales	1.50%	1.30%	1.25%	1.25%	

Required

a. Calculate the following ratios for years 2, 3, 4, and 5:
- Sales to total assets
- AR growth to sales growth
- AR collection period
- Uncollectable account expense to net credit sales
- Uncollectable account expense to bad debt write-offs

b. Describe the implications of the resulting ratios for the auditor's audit strategy for year 5. What specific audit objectives are likely to be misstated? How should the auditor respond in terms of potential audit tests?

The following information is designed to be used with cases 14-34 and 14-36. These cases continue audit tests related to the audit of the Mt. Hood Furniture, Inc., which is coordinated with a number of chapters in this book.

Mt. Hood Furniture Sales Cycle Information

Computer Aspects of Accounting System

Mt. Hood Furniture, Inc. owns its own computer and computer software for sales, inventory management, purchases, payroll, general ledger, and other accounting applications. None of the accounting processing is outsourced. Mt. Hood's computer operations are headed by Jay Harris, the IT manager, who is relatively new to Mt. Hood. Jay also has taken on the responsibility for security administration. Mr. Harris recently hired Julie Macbeth as head of Systems Development. Ms. Macbeth has focused most of her attention on the development of a new system which will be implemented next year, and has kept changes to existing systems to a minimum. John Rufner is head of computer operations and is responsible for the day-to-day operations of existing computer systems, as well as installing hardware and operating system software associated with the new system which will come on-line in 20x4. Keith Brown serves as an assistant to the CFO and also is responsible for the data control function. Keith reconciles computer output every morning and is responsible for following-up on exception reports generated by the computer system.

Mt. Hood's accounting and inventory management are supported by a network of personal computers (PCs) with units at locations in the offices and warehouse and a central server to handle all accounting and inventory files. Printers are located in areas in which printed documents or records are routinely needed. The computer is used to control and process most transactions, to print documents, prepare accounting records, and prepare periodic financial statements. The company uses a network housed on a HP 9000 server. Access is controlled by passwords. However, passwords are not changed regularly and are controlled informally. Only employees with jobs requiring computer data entry or access to file information and reports are given passwords. Passwords are required to enter the system and specific applications within the system. Once logged on to the application, employees have access to most programs and can enter relevant data. All entered data are processed by batch processing at the end of the day. Data is stored on transaction files in a traditional file system of organization. Normal data entry takes place via the software, which subjects any input to various logical and numerical tests. Most input is backed up by paper trails of source documents and other business papers. The client has strong backup capabilities, and no hardware malfunctions have resulted in the loss of data.

Initiating Sales and Delivering Goods

The company sells its office furniture products to independent dealers in major U.S. cities, several national chains, and warehouse-club chains. The office cabinetry line offers custom orders for on-site installation. Customers include major hotels, professional, and corporate offices. The company also produces a catalogue and has an information web site with an order link. Most sales orders are taken by company sales staff that visits the dealers and buyers for national chains (with the exception of orders that are taken from the order link on the company's web site).

Approved prices are modified quarterly based on quantities in inventory, recent production costs, and competitive forces in the marketplace. Prices are determined at a meeting involving Conrad Saws, James Doyle, and Julia Anderson. Julia Anderson is responsible for updating the master price file, which is reviewed by the entire team once new prices have been entered into the computer.

Finished products are shipped FOB from the warehouse or picked up by the customer. Sales terms on all office furniture and custom cabinetry are FOB net 30, and interest is charged on all receivables over 30 days at a rate of prime plus 1 percent. The company does not ship any inventory on consignment, but office furniture inventory has been shipped to new dealers with terms on an initial shipment of net 120 days, before interest is charged.

When orders are received, they are routed directly to the warehouse, where prospective customers are compared with an approved customer list. If the customer is not on the approved customer list, the order is routed to Keith Brown, assistant to the CFO, who reviews the prospective customer's credit background and prepares a report for Julia Anderson. Julia puts her written approval or disapproval on the credit report. If credit is not approved, Mr. Brown contacts the company directly and asks if the company is prepared to accept goods shipped C.O.D. If they will accept goods shipped C.O.D., the customer is put on the approved customer list with notation to ship only on a C.O.D. basis. If credit is approved, the customer is added to the approved customer list and the warehouse is notified so that it can ship goods. Julia Anderson and Keith Brown are the only individuals with authority to update the approved customer master file, which includes information on whether goods can be shipped on credit or C.O.D.

The warehouse prepares a shipment for customers that are on the approved order list, and goods are shipped the same day or the next day for goods that are in stock. Goods not in stock are put on a back-order list that is shared with production. Using the computer, a warehouse clerk prepares printed copies of both packing slips and bills of lading. The computer does not allow the preparation of a packing slip or a bill of lading for companies not on the approved customer list. At the end of every day, packages of packing slips and bills of lading, signed by the freight carrier or customer, are sent to accounting.

Recording Sales

Sales invoices are prepared every night based on the information entered in shipping. The computer calculates an invoice based on the customer information, the information on goods shipped, and the pricing information from the master price file. The company also grants a 1 percent discount to dealers for orders over $50,000. Once the transaction file is updated, it is merged with the accounts receivable master file. The computer performs the following control procedures:

- The computer program checks internal file labels to ascertain that it is processing the current sales transaction file.

- The computer checks to see that the following fields have appropriate alpha or numeric information before the invoice is processed:

  - Customer information

  - Quantities ordered for each stock number

  - Quantities shipped for each stock number

  - Prices checked against the master price list

  - Bill of lading number

- The computer performs a reasonableness test on the amount of the sale invoice based on the customer number and customer sales history. A transaction is not processed without further approval if the calculated sales invoice is greater than 120 percent of the largest sale to the customer in the last two years.

Transactions that result in an error report are not processed and are printed on an error report. Keith Brown is responsible for clearing all exceptions the next day, including approving sales that exceed the reasonableness test.

When the transaction file is merged with the accounts receivable master file, the following computer controls are performed:

- A total of customer numbers is checked to ascertain that the complete master file is about to be processed.

- Run-to-run totals are calculated for total receivables comparing beginning receivables, plus sales, with the new receivable balance.

If these controls surface errors, the routine is not processed and Keith Brown needs to follow up and determine the errors and ensure that the run is correctly processed the next day. A report is also run comparing the number of items shipped with the number of items billed. This report also goes to Keith Brown for review and followup if necessary.

Cash Collections

All cash receipts are routed to the cashier, Megan Rogers, who prepares a prelisting of cash receipts and the bank deposit. She is also responsible for depositing cash and returning the validated deposit slip to Julia Anderson, the CFO. The prelisting of cash receipts is forwarded to Erin Riley in accounts receivable. She is responsible for entering cash receipts in the computer.

The cash receipts program is run every evening. When the transaction file is processed, the computer checks for appropriate alpha or numeric information in customer number and cash receipt fields before the cash receipt is processed. If these controls find errors, the routine is not processed. Keith Brown needs to follow up and make a determination on the errors and needs to ensure that the run is correctly processed the next day. A report is also run preparing a listing of cash received, which is forwarded to Julia Anderson for comparison with the bank deposit. When the transaction file is merged with the accounts receivable master file, the following computer controls are performed:

- A hash total of customer numbers is checked to ascertain that the complete master file is about to be processed.

- Run-to-run totals are calculated for total receivables comparing beginning receivables, less cash receipts, with the new receivable balance.

If these controls find errors, the routine is not processed. Keith Brown needs to follow up and determine the errors and ensure that the run is correctly processed the next day. In addition, a reasonableness test compares the cash receipts with the balance due. A separate report is printed of all customers whose balance results in a credit balance in accounts receivable. This report also goes to Keith Brown for review and followup if necessary.

Other Procedures

Keith Brown prepares a monthly bank reconciliation which is reviewed by Julia Anderson by the 10th of every month. Julia Anderson reviews an aging of accounts receivable weekly. She and Keith Brown follow up on past-due accounts. Julia Anderson prepares any journal entries to write off accounts receivable. These reports are reviewed and approved by Conrad Saws.

14-34 **(Mt. Hood Furniture, Inc., Review of Internal Controls in the Sales Cycle)** Complete the following requirements based on the information on Mt. Hood Manufacturing provided above.

Required

a. Prepare a flowchart for sales and cash receipt transactions for Mt. Hood Furniture, Inc.

b. Evaluate the strengths and weaknesses in the sales cycle for Mt. Hood Furniture, Inc. using the following format. Organize your evaluation by audit objective. For each audit objective, describe the relevant internal control strength or weakness, and cross-reference to the flowchart. For each strength, describe how you would test the control and then discuss the audit implications for other tests if the tests of controls show that the control is strong. For each weakness, discuss the implications of the weakness and recommend an appropriate improvement in internal controls. Use the following format.

AUDIT OBJECTIVE	DESCRIBE STRENGTH OR WEAKNESS	FLOWCHART REFERENCE	DESCRIBE TESTS OF CONTROL FOR STRENGTHS OR DESCRIBE IMPLICATIONS OF WEAKNESSES	DESCRIBE INFLUENCE OF STRENGTH ON AUDIT STRATEGY OR DESCRIBE RECOMMENDED IMPROVEMENT FOR WEAKNESSES
Occurrence				
Etc.				

14-35 **(Mt. Hood Furniture, Inc., Accounts Receivable Confirmations)** Complete the following requirements related to the confirmation of receivables for Mt. Hood Manufacturing based on previous work and the following information.

Required

a. Determine the sample size using PPS sampling that you want to use for sending accounts receivable confirmations. Use the materiality level that you allocated to accounts receivable in Chapter 8. Use an audit risk of 5 percent. You may assume that control risk for the relevant assertions is low. Make your own judgments about inherent risk and analytical procedures risk based on the evaluations you made in Chapters 7 and 8. You confirmed receivables at November 30, 20X3 when the book value of accounts receivable was $6,741,725.

b. You may assume that except for the following, you received confirmations from customers that showed no exceptions. Mt. Hood ships goods FOB shipping point. Determine whether the following conditions represent errors for purposes of your evaluation. Based on your evaluation of the following information and the parameters of the sample you designed above, evaluate the result of confirming accounts receivable.

1. Dealer No. 129 disputed receivables in the amount of $30,500, as they were not received until December 2, 20x3. Further investigation showed that the dealer ordered the goods on November 30, 20x3, and they were not counted in inventory when the inventory was taken on that date. The freight carrier came by late in the day and picked up the goods, even through the warehouse was normally shut down for inventory on November 30, 20x3. Cash in the amount of $30,500 was received on December 29, 20x3. The book value of the receivable for dealer No. 129 at November 30, 20x3 was $30,500.

2. Dealer No. 65 disputed receivables in the amount of $25,750, as it had been paid on November 30, 20x3. A check from dealer No. 65 was received and deposited on December 1, 20x3. The book value of the receivable for dealer No. 65 at November 30, 20x3 was $25,750.

3. No response was received from dealer No. 41. Goods amounting to $44,000 were shipped on November 29, 20x3. A review of the cash receipts journal showed that a check for $44,000 was deposited on December 24, 20x3. The book value of the receivable for dealer No. 41 at November 30, 20x3 was $44,000.

4. Dealer No. 78 disputed receivables in the amount of $755 claiming that they did not receive an appropriate volume discount on purchases over $50,000. The book value of the receivables for dealer No. 78 at November 30, 20x3 was $75,500.

5. Dealer No. 130 disputed the price on stock number 11205, which was priced at $1,500 per unit and should have been priced at $1,200 per unit on three units. Mt. Hood furniture issued a credit memo for $900 on December 7, 20x3. The book value of the receivable for dealer No. 130 at November 30, 20x3 was $30,500.

6. No response was received from custom cabinet customer No. 29. A review of the cash receipts journal showed that a check for $30,250 was deposited on December 16, 20x3. The book value of the receivable for dealer No. 29 at November 30, 20x3 was $30,250.

7. Discount Chain No. 501 disputed the price on stock number 10609, which was priced at $1,485 per unit and should have been priced at $1,188 per unit on 10 units. Mt. Hood Furniture issued a credit memo for $2,970 on December 10, 20x3. The book value of the receivable for Discount Chain No. 501 at November 30, 20x3 was $457,800.

8. Dealer No. 85 disputed the balance on the confirmation of $35,700 in its entirety. Further investigation showed that the balance was charged to the wrong customer. Goods were shipped to dealer No. 58. On December 3, 20x3 the error was discovered. A credit memo was issued to dealer No. 85 and an invoice was sent to dealer No. 58, which was paid in full on December 27, 20x3.

14-36   **(Mt. Hood Furniture, Inc., Allowance for Doubtful Accounts)**

Required

Evaluate the fair presentation of the allowance for doubtful accounts based on the following information.

Following is a summary of the activity in accounts receivable and in the allowance for doubtful accounts for the last two years. Also included below is the aging of accounts receivable at 12/31/x3. Discussion with Julia Anderson indicates that the company has followed a practice of providing for bad debts at a rate of approximately one-half of 1 percent of sales. The company has aggressively pushed to increase sales in the last few years. An important aspect of recent sales growth has been the addition of two discount chains as customers. The company's profit margins have been reduced by selling to these customers, but they have been faithful about paying on time. Julia also made the following comments about specific dealers:

- Dealers No. 29 and No. 49 are notoriously slow payers, but the company has not had to write off receivables from these dealers in the past. If the economy slows down, that could be a different story.

- Dealer No. 55 is having financial difficulty, and the company may have to write off its receivable.

- Dealer No. 122 has been turned over to a collection agency.

- Customer No. 4 is relatively new to the company and has been very slow to pay.

	ACCOUNTS RECEIVABLE	ALLOWANCE
Balance 12/31/x1	$4,928,089.50	($47,850.00)
Sales	$27,558,375.00	
Provision of Doubtful Accounts		$136,450.00
Write-off of Accounts Receivable	($137,800.00)	($137,800.00)
Cash Collections	($26,697,953.00)	
Balance 12/31/x2	$5,380,711.50	($46.500.00)
Sales	$35,274,720.00	
Provision for Doubtful Accounts		$180,000.00
Write-Off of Accounts Receivable	($176,000.00)	($176,000.00)
Cash Collections	($33,496,508.50)	
Balance 12/31/x3	$6,982,923.00	($51,000.00)

Data related to the annual sales, cash receipts, and sales adjustment transactions is available from the professor. This data can be used to evaluate the allowance for doubtful accounts using IDEA software.

professional simulations

Situation				
	Analytical Procedures	Internal Controls	Risk Assessment	Audit Procedures

You have just been assigned to the audit of a new manufacturing client, Carroll Manufacturing Inc. (CMI) and the in-charge accountant on the engagement. CMI manufactures automobile engines which are sold to several automotive companies. CMI has a few significant customers which represent the majority of its business.

| Situation | Analytical Procedures | Internal Controls | Risk Assessment | Audit Procedures |

RATIO	UNAUDITED RATIO	AUDITOR'S EXPECTATION RANGE
Accounts Receivable Turn Days	54 days	42 days–48 days
Sales and Accounts Receivable Growth Rates	Sales Growth: 7%	Sales Growth: 6%–9%
	Accounts Receivable Growth: 14%	Accounts Receivable Growth: 6%–9%
Sales to Net Fixed Assets	10.0	6.0–8.0

Write a memo to the audit file explaining the planning implications associated with the audit findings above. Identify assertions that are likely to be overstated or understated.

To: Audit File

Re: Analytical procedures

From: CPA Candidate

| Situation | Analytical Procedures | Internal Controls | Risk Assessment | Audit Procedures |

Assertion

A. Existence and Occurrence

B. Completeness

C. Rights and Obligations

D. Valuation or Allocation

E. Presentation and Disclosure

Identify the appropriate assertion for each of the following internal controls. Check all that apply.

Internal Control	(A)	(B)	(C)	(D)	(E)
1. The computer prints a report of all shipments that have not resulted in a sales invoice.	○	○	○	○	○
2. The computer matches the date on the bill of lading with the accounting period when the sales invoice is recorded.	○	○	○	○	○
3. The computer matches prices on the sale invoice with prices on the master price list.	○	○	○	○	○
4. The computer matches the customer number on the sales invoice with the customer number on the master customer file.	○	○	○	○	○
5. The computer compares control totals on shipping documents with corresponding control totals	○	○	○	○	○

| Situation | Analytical Procedures | Internal Controls | Risk Assessment | Audit Procedures |

Following is a brief summary of the results of tests of controls.

CONTROL	CONTROL RISK ASSESSMENT
The computer matches sales invoice information with underlying shipping information.	Low
The computer matches sales prices with the authorized price list.	Low
A prelist is prepared for cash receipts and compared with deposit slips.	Moderate
The computer prepares a daily report of authorized sales returns that have not resulted in a receiving report or a credit memo.	Low

Prepare a brief memo explaining how you would assess control risk in preparation for accounts receivable confirmations.

To: Audit File

Re: Control Risk Assessment

From: CPA Candidate

| Situation | Analytical Procedures | Internal Controls | Risk Assessment | Audit Procedures |

Audit procedure

A. Select a sample of recorded sales transactions from several days before and after year-end and examine supporting sale invoices and shipping documents to determine that sales were recorded in the proper period.

B. Trace beginning balance for accounts receivable to the prior year's working papers.

C. Send positive confirmations for accounts receivable and follow-up on disputed confirmations.

D. Trace a sample of revenue transactions from shipments to recorded sales invoices in the sale journal.

E. Determine whether there are credit balances that are significant in the aggregate that should be reclassified as liabilities.

F. Send confirmations to entities that have purchased accounts receivable.

G. Compare uncollectable accounts expense to net credit sales.

H. Review activity in the general ledger account for accounts receivable and investigate entries that appear unusual in amount or source.

I. Use generalized audit software to recompute the aging of accounts receivable and investigate the credit history of accounts that are over 60 days past due.

J. Observe that all cash received through the close of business on the last day of the fiscal year is included in cash on hand or deposits in transit and that no receipts of the subsequent period are included.

Determine the audit procedure that best addresses the following risks.

Risk	(A)	(B)	(C)	(D)	(E)	(F)	(G)	(H)	(I)	(J)
1. Recorded sales may not represent goods shipped during the year.	○	○	○	○	○	○	○	○	○	○
2. The allowance for doubtful accounts may not reasonably estimate the difference between gross receivables and their net realizable value.	○	○	○	○	○	○	○	○	○	○
3. All sales during the period may not be recorded.	○	○	○	○	○	○	○	○	○	○
4. All legal claims on accounts receivable are adequately disclosed.	○	○	○	○	○	○	○	○	○	○
5. Accounts receivable information may not be appropriately classified and presented in the financial statements.	○	○	○	○	○	○	○	○	○	○

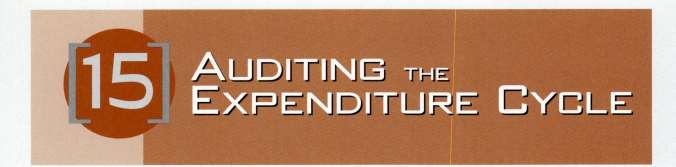

[15] AUDITING THE EXPENDITURE CYCLE

POOR INTERNAL CONTROLS RESULT IN A MATERIAL UNDERSTATEMENT OF ACCOUNTS PAYABLE AND NET INCOME

TruServ is a hardware store buying cooperative. On March 31, 2000, it reported a loss of more than $131 million for the fiscal year 1999, which included expenses it failed to report during fiscal years 1997 and 1998. The misstatements in TruServ's financial statements came to light when the entity's accounting staff closed its books for fiscal year 1999. The largest component of the previously unreported loss represented increases in cost of sales and accounts payable in the amount of $74.5 million.

A significant component of the problem represented a year-end accrual for unbilled merchandise. TruServ routinely made an accrual for merchandise it had received but for which it had not yet been billed. TruServ estimated the amount of the accrual for merchandise payable by using a report called the "open receiver file." However, the "open receiver file" was not accurate. Distribution center and warehouse employees were not keeping accurate records of the merchandise that was received. As a result, accounts payable was understated by approximately $36.9 million. Furthermore, because inventory was based on a physical count, cost of goods sold was also understated, resulting in an overstatement of net income.

In addition, TruServ claimed approximately $20 million in reductions in accounts payable related to claims for returned merchandise and allowances. If merchandise returned from a member could not be resold due to damage, or some other reason, the merchandise should have been removed from inventory and charged to cost of goods sold. Instead, TruServ removed the merchandise from inventory and reduced the amount of its merchandise payable by the same amount. However, it never received authorization to return merchandise to its vendors. As a result, accounts payable and cost of goods sold were understated, overstating net income.

Finally, in 1999 TruServ wrote off approximately $16.6 million in inventory adjustments for lost inventory, damaged goods, and the closing of distribution centers. TruServ should have reduced inventory and increased cost of goods sold. However, warehouse personnel did not correctly use inventory adjustment codes. As a result, TruServ wrote off the inventory and reduced its accounts payable by the same amount.

Each of these represented misstatements related to the expenditure cycle, ultimately resulting in a material understatement of accounts payable and expenses. Chapter 15 addresses the types of internal controls that would normally control these types of transactions. In addition, the chapter presents substantive audit procedures that should be performed by the auditor to identify these same types of misstatements.

Sources: SEC Accounting and Auditing Enforcement Releases 1727 and 1728, March 4, 2003.

[PREVIEW OF CHAPTER 15]

Chapter 15 focuses on specific aspects of auditing the expenditure cycle. It begins with a discussion of planning activities related to the expenditure cycle. It then focuses on specific controls commonly seen in the expenditure cycle as well as specific substantive tests related to the expenditure cycle. The following diagram provides an overview of the chapter organization and content.

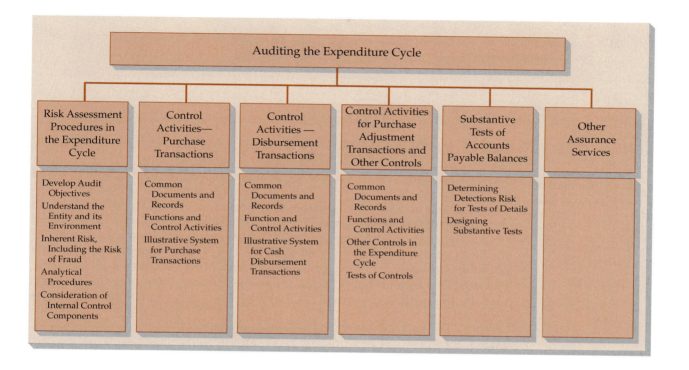

Chapter 15 focuses on the following aspects of the auditor's decision process associated with auditing the expenditure cycle.

focus on audit decisions

After studying this chapter you should understand the factors that influence the following audit decisions.

D1. What is the nature of the expenditure cycle, and how are specific audit objectives developed for the expenditure cycle?

D2. How does understanding the entity and its environment affect audit planning decisions in the expenditure cycle?

D3. What are important inherent risks in the expenditure cycle?

D4. How might the results of analytical procedures indicate potential misstatements in the expenditure cycle?

D5. What are the relevant aspects of internal control components for the expenditure cycle?

D6. What should be considered in evaluating control activities for purchase transactions?

D7. What should be considered in evaluating control activities for cash disbursements transactions?

D8. What should be considered in evaluating control activities for purchase adjustments?

D9. What are the relevant aspects of tests of controls when the auditor plans to assess control risk below the maximum for expenditure cycle transactions?

D10. What are the factors involved in determining the acceptable level of tests of details risk for accounts payable assertions?

D11. How does the auditor determine the elements of an audit program for substantive tests to achieve specific audit objectives for accounts payable?

D12. How does the auditor use the knowledge obtained during the audit of the expenditure cycle to support other assurance services?

[RISK ASSESSMENT PROCEDURES IN THE EXPENDITURE CYCLE]

Audit Decision 1

■ **What is the nature of the expenditure cycle, and how are specific audit objectives developed for the expenditure cycle?**

The **expenditure cycle** consists of the activities related to the acquisition of and payment for goods and services. The core expenditure cycle activities are (1) purchasing goods and services—**purchase transactions,** (2) making payments—**cash disbursement transactions,** and (3) **purchase adjustments** (purchase returns and price adjustements). Purchases and cash disbursements have a pervasive effect on the financial statements as depicted in Figure 15-1. This chapter focuses primarily on these transactions, internal controls related to purchases, cash disbursements, purchase returns, and tests of accounts payable balances. Internal controls are particularly important as purchase cycle transactions affect so many general ledger accounts.

This cycle does not include payroll transactions, which are covered in the personnel services cycle in Chapter 16. Tests of balances for long-term assets are covered in Chapter 17 on financing and investing activities. Chapter 18 covers tests of balances of investment securities and cash balances. This chapter focuses on the internal controls in the expenditure cycle that affect each of these other audit areas.

Figure 15-1 ■ Expenditure Cycle

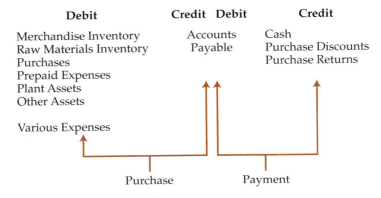

DEVELOP AUDIT OBJECTIVES

Auditors should obtain sufficient, competent evidence for each audit objective pertaining to purchase cycle transactions. Recall from Chapter 6 (see Figure 6-2) that specific audit objectives are derived from five categories of management's assertions. Specific audit objectives are developed for transactions, balances, and disclosures related to a specific transaction cycle. These audit objectives for the expenditure cycle are shown in Figure 15-2. Specific expenditure cycle transactions are keyed to numbered audit objectives (C1 … C4, EO1 … EO4, and so on) that are used throughout Chapter 15.

UNDERSTAND THE ENTITY AND ITS ENVIRONMENT

An important aspect of audit planning includes understanding the entity and its environment, the external market forces driving the business sector, and how these forces impact the entity's expenditure cycle. Every business faces different

Figure 15-2 ■ Specific Audit Objectives for the Expenditure Cycle

Specific Audit Objectives
Transaction Objectives **Occurrence.** Recorded purchase transactions represent goods or services received during the period **(EO1)**. Recorded cash disbursement transactions represent cash received during the period **(EO2)**. Recorded purchase returns represent goods returned during the period **(EO3)**. **Completeness.** All purchases **(C1)**, cash disbursements **(C2)** and purchase returns **(C3)** made during the period were recorded. **Accuracy.** All purchases **(VA1)**, cash disbursements **(VA2)**, and purchase returns **(VA3)** are accurately valued using GAAP and correctly journalized, summarized, and posted. **Cutoff.** All purchases **(EO1 or C1)**, cash disbursements **(EO2 or C2)**, and purchase returns **(EO3 or C3)** have been recorded in the correct accounting period. **Classification.** All purchases **(PD1)**, cash disbursements **(PD2)**, and purchase returns **(PD3)** have been recorded in the proper accounts. **Balance Objectives** **Existence.** Accounts payable represent amounts owed to vendors at the balance sheet date **(EO4)**. **Completeness.** Accounts payable includes all payments owing to vendors at the balance sheet date **(C4)**. **Rights and Obligations.** Accounts payable are obligations of the entity at the balance sheet date **(RO1)**. **Valuation and Allocation.** Accounts payable are correctly stated at the amounts owed **(VA4)**. **Disclosure Objectives** **Occurrence and Rights and Obligations.** Disclosed purchase cycle events and transactions have occurred and pertain to the entity **(PD4)**. **Completeness.** All purchase cycle disclosures that should have been included in the financial statements have been included **(PD5)**. **Classification and Understandability.** Revenue cycle information is appropriately presented and described and information in disclosures is clearly expressed **(PD6)**. **Accuracy and Valuation.** Purchase cycle information is disclosed accurately and at appropriate amounts **(PD7)**.

market forces that place differing demands on the company's cash flow. Recall that an entity's net operating cycle represents the time from using cash to purchase goods or services to collecting cash from the sale of goods or services. For a manufacturer the gross operating cycle is estimated by the average number of days it takes to turn inventory and collect receivables. The net operating cycle represents the gross operating cycle reduced by accounts payable turn days, the amount of time that an entity's suppliers will let it use trade credit before requiring payment for goods and services. Understanding the economic drivers in the expenditure cycle is usually critical for audits of manufacturers, wholesalers, retailers, and some service companies.

Figure 15-3 illustrates the importance of understanding the expenditure cycle for five different entities, which are discussed throughout Part 4 of the text. This chapter continues the discussion of five industries introduced in Chapter 14: a manufacturer of construction machinery and equipment (SIC 3531) a manufacturer of electronic computers (SIC 3571), a retail grocer (SIC 5411), a hotel (SIC 7011), and a local school district (SIC 8211). These examples define a wide spectrum of underlying business practices and an equally wide spectrum of risk for the auditor. The auditor would normally obtain this understanding through previous experience with the entity, obtaining information from trade associations, reading business periodicals and newspapers, and consulting publications of industry information such as Robert Morris Associates or Value Line.

Audit Decision 2
■ **How does understanding the entity and its environment affect audit planning decisions in the expenditure cycle?**

Audit Decision 3
■ **What are important inherent risks in the expenditure cycle?**

INHERENT RISK, INCLUDING THE RISK OF FRAUD

In assessing inherent risk for expenditure cycle assertions, the auditor should consider pervasive factors that may affect assertions throughout financial statements as well as factors pertaining only to specific assertions in the expenditure cycle.

accounts payable trends

A number of companies have reported problems with making duplicate payments. As a result, many companies outsource the process of invoice review. One company that reviewed its last three years' invoices discovered that it had made five quarterly state income tax payments, not four. After collecting interest for three years, the state of Texas cheerfully refunded the $2 million. RECAP, Inc. reports that typically one in 500 invoices that companies have already paid includes overcharges or was a duplicate payment.

Other recent trends in the accounts payable area include:

■ Installing or increasing the use of EDI, ERS, and electronic invoicing.
■ Improving efficiency, timeliness, and processes.
■ Installing or increases the use of imaging.
■ Improving customer services
■ Installing or increasing the use of electronic payments.
■ Cleaning up vendor files.

Source: www.recapinc.com.

Figure 15-3 ■ Understanding an Entity's Expenditure Cycle

Example Industry Traits	Developing a Knowledgeable Perspective about the Entity's Financial Statements (Industry Median)	Assessing the Risk of Material Misstatement
Mfg. of Construction Machinery and Equipment • Significant spending for raw materials. • Purchases is a core process that influences gross margins.	Net Operating Cycle: 97 days Accounts Payable Turn Days: 33 days Accounts Payable to Total Assets: 15.2% Current Ratio: 1.7 Quick Ratio: 0.7	• Concerns about purchase cutoff at year-end. • Concerns about potential unrecorded liabilities.
Computer Mfg. • Purchases must be managed aggressively to minimize inventory obsolescence.	Net Operating Cycle: 72 days Accounts Payable Turn Days: 40 days Accounts Payable to Total Assets: 19.4% Current Ratio: 1.6 Quick Ratio: 0.9	• Vendors often offer price concessions or terms such that goods do not have to be paid for until manufactured product is resold, leading to concerns about consignment traits of inventory. • Concerns about purchases cutoff at month-end. • Concerns about potential unrecorded liabilities.
Retail Grocer • Purchases a wide array of products including products with perishable characteristics. • Purchasing and supply chain management is an important aspect of profitability. • Wide variety of vendors.	Net Operating Cycle: 9 days Accounts Payable Turn Days: 15 days Accounts Payable to Total Assets: 3.4% Current Ratio: 1.2 Quick Ratio: 0.4	• Concerns about accounting for advertising allowances and other price concessions to stock merchandise. • Concerns about purchases cutoff at month-end. • Concerns about potential unrecorded liabilities.
Hotel • Purchases include food for restaurant and convention business. • Purchases are a less significant operating cost compared to retailer or manufacturer.	Net Operating Cycle: n/a Accounts Payable Turn Days: n/a Accounts Payable to Total Assets: 3.4% Current Ratio: 0.7 Quick Ratio: 0.6	• Purchases and accounts payable are less central to core business, resulting in reduced potential for unrecorded liabilities. • It is common to have significant unearned income.
Local School District • Purchases are incidental to the core product, educating students. • Core process may not be significantly affected by price increases.	Net Operating Cycle: n/a Accounts Payable Turn Days: n/a Accounts Payable to Total Assets: 3% Current Ratio: 1.8 Quick Ratio: 1.5	• Purchases and accounts payable are not central to core business, resulting in reduced potential for unrecorded liabilities.

Pervasive factors that might motivate management to misstate expenditure cycle assertions include:

- Pressures to understate expenses in order to report achieving announced profitability targets or industry norms, which were not achieved in reality owing to factors such as global, national, or regional economic conditions that affect operating costs, the impact of technological developments on the entity's productivity, or poor management.
- Pressures to understate payables in order to report a higher level of working capital when the entity is experiencing liquidity problems or going-concern doubts.
- Vendors may be tardy in sending invoices resulting in cutoff problems in recording payables.

These factors lead to a greater risk of understatement than overstatement of expenditures and payables.

The auditor should also consider the industry-related factors of the availability and price volatility of the raw materials and products needed by the entity to remain in business. For example, a grocer deals with numerous vendors and prices; intense market competition tends to stabilize prices. A shortage or price increase of an individual item has little effect on industry operation. Customers readily substitute green apples for red apples. This industry has limited exposure to the risk of raw material shortages or sudden price swings affecting their financial results. This may not be the case for the computer assembler, who may be dependent on a single vendor for a unique component critical to the assembled product. Should the vendor be unable to supply the part, the computer manufacturer's production is stalled, shipment of finished product is delayed, and the cash cycle is impaired. Industries whose core products cannot be substituted for other products are extremely vulnerable to price swings and shortages. Fuel for the airline industry is a good example of such a product. The auditor's knowledge of industry-related factors is particularly important to assessing the risk of misstatement in the financial statements.

The expenditure cycle is especially prone to a risk of employee fraud through unauthorized disbursement of cash. Other factors that may contribute to misstatements in the expenditure cycle assertions include the following:

- There is usually a high volume of transactions.
- Unauthorized purchases and cash disbursements may be made.
- Purchased assets may be misappropriated.
- There may be duplicate payment of vendor's invoices.
- Contentious accounting issues may arise concerning such matters as whether a cost should be capitalized or expensed (e.g., the treatment of repairs and maintenance costs or the classification of a lease as an operating or capital lease).

The auditor should consider each of these factors when assessing inherent risk for the expenditure cycle.

Finally, a growing trend in purchasing systems is the use of Electronic Data Interchange (EDI) or image processing systems. In EDI, the entity and its suppliers use communication links to transact business electronically. Purchases and cash disbursements may be consummated entirely by the exchange of electronic messages between the parties. In image processing systems, documents are scanned and converted into electronic images to facilitate storage and reference, and the source documents may not be retained after conversion. In image processing systems hard copy documents may only be available for a limited length of time. In addition, electronic evidence may not be retrievable after a specified period of time if files are changed and if backup files do not exist. Therefore, the auditor should consider the time during which information exists or is available in planning the audit and making decisions about the nature, timing, and extent of tests of controls (if relevant) and substantive tests.

ANALYTICAL PROCEDURES

Audit Decision 4
■ **How might the results of analytical procedures indicate potential misstatements in the expenditure cycle?**

Analytical tests are effective in identifying expenditure cycle accounts that are misstated. Analytical procedures risk is the element of detection risk that analytical procedures will fail to detect material errors. As previously stated, analytical procedures are extremely cost effective. Some example analytical procedures that may apply to the expenditure cycle are presented in Figure 15-4.

Many analytical procedures focus on the relationship between purchases and accounts payable. If a company is growing, it is common to expect purchases, inventory, and accounts payable to grow at consistent rates. The auditor's knowledge of the volume of purchases, combined with prior experience in terms of **accounts payable turn days** (the average number of days it takes to retire payables), is useful in estimating current year's payables. While ratios like the current ratio are easy to calculate, they may fluctuate based on influences from cycles other than the expenditure cycle, such as sales or investments.

Figure 15-4 ■ Analytical Procedures Commonly Used to Audit the Expenditure Cycle

Ratio	Formula	Audit Significance
Accounts Payable Turn Days	Avg. Accounts Payable ÷ Purchases × 365	Prior experience in accounts payable turn days combined with knowledge of current purchases can be useful in estimating current payables. A shortening of the period may indicate completeness problems.
Cost of Goods Sold to Accounts Payable	Cost of Goods Sold ÷ Accounts Payable	Unless the company has changed its payment policy, these amounts should change by approximately the same percentage from year to year.
Payables as a % of Total Assets	Accounts Payable ÷ Total Assets	Common sized balances in accounts payable are useful in comparing with industry data. A significant decline in this ratio may indicate completeness problems.
Current Ratio	Current Assets ÷ Current Liabilities	A significant increase in the current ratio compared to prior year's experience may indicate a completeness problem. However, this ratio may also be influenced by changes in asset accounts.
Quick Ratio	Current Monetary Assets ÷ Current Monetary Liabilities	A significant increase in the current ratio compared to prior year's experience may indicate a completeness problem. However, this ratio may also be influenced by changes in asset accounts.

CONSIDERATION OF INTERNAL CONTROL COMPONENTS

Audit Decision 5

■ What are the relevant aspects of internal control components for the expenditure cycle?

The auditor's required understanding of internal controls applicable to the expenditure cycle extends to all five internal control components. Four of the components are discussed in the following subsections. The control activities component is discussed later in the chapter in separate sections for purchases, cash disbursements, and purchase adjustments.

Control Environment

The expenditure cycle offers numerous opportunities for employee fraud in processing purchase and cash disbursements transactions. Purchasing agents may be subjected to pressures from solicitous vendors, including offers of "kickbacks" for transacting more business with those vendors. A strong tone at the top of the organization, and a control environment that emphasizes integrity and ethical values is extremely important in the expenditure cycle.

Management's commitment to competence should be reflected in the hiring, assignment, and training of personnel involved in processing purchase and cash disbursement transactions, maintaining custody of purchased assets, and reporting on expenditure cycle activities. Management may also require that employees involved in processing cash disbursements or maintaining custody of purchased assets be bonded.

The client's organizational structure and management's assignment of authority and responsibility over expenditure cycle activities should be clearly communicated and provide for clear lines of authority, responsibility, and reporting relationships. If management is held too rigidly to delivering targeted earnings, it may cause the incentive to misstate the financial statements through the management of purchases cutoff of other steps that result in unrecorded liabilities. On the other hand, if management is not held accountable for the use of the entity's resources, it is unlikely that entity personnel will take internal controls seriously. When understanding how management is held accountable for resources it is helpful to determine:

■ The reports used by management to evaluate the entity's performance review.
■ How often and how quickly management reports are reviewed.
■ The decisions that are based on the reports.
■ The entity's policies for following up on issues raised by key reports.

Risk Assessment

Management risk assessments related to expenditure cycle activities include consideration of such matters as:

■ The risk of purchasing kickbacks.
■ The risk of employee fraud through fraudulent purchases or cash disbursements.
■ The entity's ability to meet cash flow requirements for purchase transactions.
■ Loss contingencies associated with purchase commitments.

- The continued availability of important supplies and the stability of important suppliers.
- The effect of cost increases on the entity.
- The risks associated with the use of electronic data interchange and image processing systems.

If management demonstrates appropriate consideration of these risks, together with balancing control activities that mitigate these risks, the likelihood of misstatements associated with these circumstances is reduced.

Information and Communication (Accounting System)

An understanding of the accounting system requires knowledge of the methods of data processing and key documents and records used in processing expenditure cycle transactions. It is important to understand the flow of transactions through the accounting system from initiating the transaction to its recording in the general ledger and eventual summarization in the financial statements. Key information the auditor should understand includes:

- How purchases, payments, and returns are initiated.
- How purchase transactions are accounted for as goods and services are received or goods are returned.
- What accounting records, documents, accounts, and computer files are involved in accounting for the various stages of each purchase cycle transaction.
- The process by which an entity initiates payment for goods and services.

Figure 15-5 is an overview flowchart showing the basic features of a computerized system for processing purchases and cash disbursement transactions. Note that the flowchart supposes the receipt and entry of third-party documents. With the instant transfer of information via electronic data interchange, these documents may not be available. The flowchart is not intended to show every document, record, process, or account involved.

Variations in accounting systems include the use of either a purchases journal or a voucher register for recording purchases. A voucher system is assumed in this chapter. The key accounting records shown in the flowchart are the voucher register for recording purchases from suppliers and the cash disbursements journal or check register for recording payments to suppliers.

Monitoring

Several types of ongoing and periodic monitoring activities may provide management with information concerning the effectiveness of the other internal control components in reducing the risk of misstatements. Monitoring activities about which the auditor should obtain knowledge include (1) ongoing feedback from the entity's suppliers concerning any payment problems or future delivery problems, (2) communications from external auditors regarding reportable conditions or material weakness in relevant internal controls found in prior audits, and (3) periodic assessments by internal auditors of control policies and procedures related to the expenditure cycle.

Figure 15-5 ■ System Flowchart—Purchase Transactions

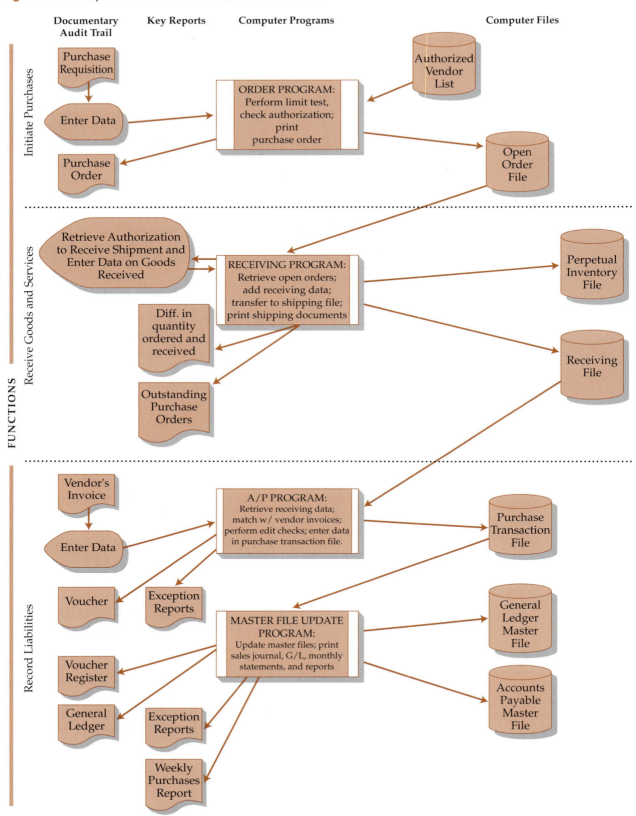

[LEARNING CHECK

15-1 Describe the nature of the expenditure cycles and identify the major classes of transactions in the cycle.

15-2 State the audit objectives for expenditure cycle transactions and balances that relate to each financial statement assertion category.

15-3 Describe the nature of one entity where the expenditure is significant to its financial statements and one entity where it is not. Explain the differences between the two. How would these difference affect audit strategy?

15-4 Explain several factors that the auditor should consider when allocating materiality to the audit of the expenditure cycle.

15-5 a. Identify several pervasive factors that might motivate management to misstate assertions in the expenditure cycle.

b. Identify several industry-related factors that might influence the risk of material misstatement in the expenditure cycle.

c. What other factor might influence the risk of material misstatement in the expenditure cycle?

d. Why are auditors more concerned about the understatement of liabilities than the overstatement of liabilities?

15-6 a. Identify several analytical procedures that the auditor might use to assess the likelihood that a material misstatement exists in the expenditure cycle.

b. Why would the analysis of accounts payable turnover provide for more accurate analysis of accounts payable than analyzing the current ratio?

15-7 Identify elements of the control environment that are relevant to initiating and recording purchases.

[KEY TERMS

Accounts payable turn days, p. 695
Cash disbursement transactions,
    p. 690

Expenditure cycle, p. 690
Purchase adjustments, p. 690
Purchase transactions, p. 690

[CONTROL ACTIVITIES—PURCHASE TRANSACTIONS]

Audit Decision 6

■ What should be considered in evaluating control activities for purchase transactions?

In this section, we consider control activities of an entity that are relevant to the specific audit objectives for purchase transactions. We begin by identifying some of the key documents and records used in processing transactions for purchases on account. Next, the major functions involved in executing and recording purchases of goods and services are identified and explained. The discussion of the functions includes how control procedures are interwoven to reduce the risk of misstatements in the financial statement assertions that are affected by purchase transactions. Among the control activities considered are segregation of duties, physical controls, management controls, and computer application controls.

Virtually every company that requires an audit has a computerized accounting system. Hence, this text focuses on how management would implement control activities using programmed control procedures. Recall from Chapter 10 that there are two types of computer controls:

- *General controls*, which relate to the computer environment and have a pervasive effect on computer applications.
- *Application controls*, which relate to the individual computerized accounting applications, such as the expenditure cycle.

If general controls are ineffective, reliance can rarely be placed on the application controls. For purposes of discussion, this chapter will assume that general controls are effective, as are the followup procedures that the entity uses to investigate issues that are triggered by application controls.

COMMON DOCUMENTS AND RECORDS

Several common documents and records involved in the expenditure cycle are discussed briefly below. The particulars of an EDP system may change the form of these documents or files. For example, the file structure discussed below is a more traditional one. For companies that use a database system, transaction records are stored in a database, and it is important for the auditor to understand the key tables that drive access to information in this system, and how those tables link together. Nevertheless, the following documents and records are found in most accounting systems:

- **Purchase requisition.** Written request for goods or services by an authorized individual or department to the purchasing department.
- **Purchase order.** Written offer from the purchasing department to a vendor or supplier to purchase goods or services specified in the order.
- **Approved vendor master file.** Computer file containing pertinent information on vendors and suppliers that have been approved to purchase services from and make payments to.
- **Open purchase order file.** Computer file of purchase orders submitted to vendors for which the goods or services have not been received.
- **Receiving report.** Report prepared on the receipt of goods showing the kinds and quantities of goods received from vendors.
- **Receiving file.** Computer file with receiving information on quantities of inventory received from vendors.
- **Vendor invoice.** The bill from the vendor stating the items shipped or services rendered, the amount due, the payment terms, and the date billed.
- **Voucher.** An internal form indicating the vendor, the amount due, and payment date for purchases received. It is used to authorize recording and paying a liability. Many purchase systems require a complete voucher packet before approving payment. The voucher packet usually contains a copy of the appropriate purchase requisition, purchase order, receiving report, vendor invoice, and voucher—all the documentation supporting the purchase transaction.
- **Exception reports.** Reports with information about transactions identified for further investigation by computer application controls.
- **Voucher summary.** Report of total vouchers processed in a batch or during a day.
- **Voucher register.** Formal accounting record of recorded liabilities approved for payment.

- **Purchase transactions file.** Computer file containing data for approved vouchers for purchases that have been received. Used to print the voucher register and update the accounts payable, inventory, and general ledger files.
- **Accounts payable master file.** Computer file containing data on approved unpaid vouchers. The file may be organized by vendor. It should sum to the balance in the accounts payable control account.
- **Suspense files.** Computer files that hold transactions that have not been processed because they have been rejected by computer application controls.

FUNCTIONS AND CONTROL ACTIVITIES

The processing of purchase transactions involves the following purchasing functions:

- **Initiating purchases.** The request by an entity for a transaction with another entity, including:
  - Placing vendors on an authorized vendor list
  - Requisitioning goods and services
  - Preparing purchase orders
- **Receipt of goods and services.** The physical receipt or shipment of a product or service, including:
  - Receiving the goods
  - Storing goods received for inventory
  - Returning goods to vendor
- **Recording liabilities** including preparing the payment voucher.

Each of these major functions should be assigned to a different individual or department. This provides classical segregation of duties by segregating authorization of transactions, custody of assets, and recording transactions. With this structure, the work of one employee or department can provide an independent check on the accuracy of the work of another. The functions, applicable control activities, and relevant assertions and related specific audit objectives are explained in the following sections. Figure 15-6 summarizes example control procedures related to each of these functions.

Initiating Purchases

In general, initiating a transaction represents the process of agreeing to a transaction with an independent third party. Many entities separate the following subfunctions for transactions above a specified dollar amount. For smaller transactions a department may have more latitude in requisitioning and ordering goods. When an entity grants greater latitude to a department in initiating transactions, the entity usually attempts to establish strong budget and accountability controls over a department's expenditures.

Placing Vendors on an Authorized Vendor List

The process of approving vendors for the delivery of goods and services is an important control, particularly in accounting systems that rely on computer controls. If management, typically the purchasing department, establishes strong controls over putting authorized vendors on an authorized vendor list, it is difficult for employees to initiate transactions with fictitious vendors.

Figure 15-6 ■ Control Risk Considerations—Purchase Transactions

Function	Potential Misstatement	Computer Control[a] *(Manual Controls in Italics)*	C1	EO1	VA1	PD1
Initiating Purchases	Potential lack of control over purchases and unrecorded liabilities.	Computer generates prenumbered control over requisitions and purchase orders and checks numerical sequence.	P			
	Purchases may be made for unauthorized purposes.	Computer verification of employee authorization code to enter requisition or purchase order.		P		
	Purchases may be made for unauthorized purposes or quantities.	Computer-performed limit test on requisitions and purchase orders. Necessary approvals tied to limit test.		P		
	Employees may create fictitious vendor and bill for services not received.	Computer compares vendor on purchase order to master vendor file. *Only a limited number of employees can add a vendor to the master vendor file.*		P		
Receiving Goods and Services	Goods may be received but not recorded.	Computer checks for goods ordered and not received within a reasonable period of time.	D			
	Receiving may accept goods that were not ordered or authorized.	Computer checks for a valid purchase order in order to initiate receiving report.		P		
Recording Liabilities	Goods or services may be received, but the appropriate liability may not be recorded.	Computer checks for goods received but not recorded as a liability within a reasonable period of time. In the case of services, the computer checks for services ordered but not recorded as a liability within a reasonable period of time.	D			
	Goods or services may be received, but the appropriate liability may not be recorded.	Computer checks batch totals and run-to-run totals to ensure that all transactions are processed.	D			
	Liabilities may be recorded for goods or services not received or may be recorded at an incorrect amount.	Computer matches voucher information regarding vendor, type of good, quantity of goods, and dollar amount against authorized purchase order and receiving report.		D		
	Submitting the same vendor's invoice twice for payment.	Computer reviews the vendor's invoice field for prior recording of the vendor's invoice number.		P		
		Manual controls require that supporting information is canceled and a voucher cannot be issued without original supporting documents.		P		
	Purchases may be recorded in the wrong accounting period.	Computer compares accounting period in which the voucher is recorded with the accounting period received.	D	D		
	Mathematical misstatements may be made while processing vouchers.	Computer checks the mathematical accuracy of the voucher and supporting documents.			D	
	Purchases may be incorrectly posted or summarized.	Computer compares sum of subsidiary ledger accounts with general ledger control account.			D	
	Purchases may be posted to the wrong accounts.	Computer compares account distribution on the voucher with account distribution on purchase requisition or purchase order.				D

(continues)

Figure 15-6 ■ (Continued)

Function	Potential Misstatement	Computer Control[a] (Manual Controls in Italics)	C1	EO1	VA1	PD1
		Management Control				
	Purchases may be recorded for goods or services not received, they may be posted to the wrong account, or in the wrong amount.	An appropriate level of management reviews all purchases charged to their responsibility center on a timely basis reviewing vendors, amounts, and accounts charged.		D	D	D

[a] All computer controls assume that exceptions are either printed on an exception report for followup or an error message appears during input and the transaction cannot be processed without correction and acceptance.

P = potential control to prevent misstatement or unauthorized use of resources.

D = potential control to detect misstatement or unauthorized use of resources.

Requisitioning Goods and Services

The purchase requisition represents the start of the transaction trail of documentary evidence in support of management's assertion as to the existence or occurrence of purchase transactions. Thus, it provides evidence about the specific audit objective (EO1) in Figure 15-2. Purchase requisitions usually are initiated from stores (the warehouse) for inventoried items or any department for items not inventoried. The important control consideration is that all requisitions meet the authorization policy established by the entity. Most companies permit general authorizations for regular operating needs for items included in a department's operating budget. The permitted dollar amount is often tied to the employee's level in the entity. In contrast, company policy frequently requires specific authorizations for capital expenditures and lease contracts. Purchases that are less routine and higher in dollar amount usually require a higher level of authorization than routine and less significant purchases.

Purchase requisition forms may be prepared manually or electronically. The supervisor who has budgetary responsibility for the purchase should approve each request (manually or electronically). In a computerized system a unique, sequentially numbered system should be used in numbering documents regardless of the originating department. Computer-prepared requisition orders should require entry of a valid employee number, which the computer would use to check if the requisition was within the authorization limit set for that employee. The computer would also screen the input fields for errors such as negative numbers, characters in a numeric field, and so on. Rejected data would produce an error report to be dealt with immediately in on-line systems, or to be corrected by the user department and resubmitted if the requisition was valid. A report of missing or out-of-sequence requisitions should be routinely produced, and any exceptions promptly investigated.

Preparing Purchase Orders

The purchasing department should have the authority to issue purchase orders only on the receipt of properly approved purchase requisitions. Preparing the purchase order continues the process of initiating a transaction. The role of purchases is to ascertain the best source of supply and, for major items, to obtain competitive bids. A computerized system would have an approved master vendor list and current price lists for items normally purchased. The purchase order would be completed with information from these lists.

Purchase orders should contain a precise description of the goods and services desired, quantities, price, and vendor name and address. Purchase orders should be prenumbered and accounted for. Prenumbered purchase orders allow for the ability to follow each transaction from initiation to receipt of goods or services, to recording the purchase, to payment of final consideration (C1), and purchase orders should be signed by an authorized purchasing agent (or authorized individual if purchase orders are generated in a department). The original is sent to the vendor, and copies are distributed internally to the receiving department (usually without quantity information), the accounts payable department, and the department that submitted the requisition. The quantity ordered is generally obliterated on the receiving department copy, so that receiving clerks will make careful counts when the goods are received. Depending on the extent of the computerized system, the only hard copy document generated would be the purchase order that is sent to the vendor. Some companies eliminate this as well by using EDI computer links with their suppliers.

Receipt of Goods and Services

Preparing a Receiving Report

A valid purchase order represents the authorization for the receiving department to accept goods delivered by vendors. The receipt of a good or service usually evidences the completion of a transaction and the establishment of a liability. Receiving department personnel should compare the goods received with the description of the goods on the purchase order, count the goods, and inspect the goods for damage. A prenumbered receiving report should be prepared for each order received to document that goods have been received and that a liability should be established. In computerized systems, the receiving report may be prepared by using information already in the computer and adding the appropriate receiving data such as quantities received. The computer system should compare the quantity ordered to that received and generate an exception report for appropriate followup.

The receiving report is an important document in supporting the existence or occurrence assertion for purchase transactions (EO1). In addition, most companies prepare daily reports of all receivings that have not resulted in vouchers to control the completeness assertion for purchases and accounts payable (C1). The information on the receiving report is forwarded to accounts payable, via a copy of the receiving report or electronically. Receiving reports are rarely prepared for the receipt of services (utility bills, rent, accounting services, etc.). In these cases management usually documents receipt of a service by approving a copy of the vendor's invoice for payment.

Storing Goods Received for Inventory

Upon delivery of goods to stores or other requisitioning departments, receiving clerks should obtain a signed receipt. Obtaining initials on a copy of the receiving report serves this purpose and provides further evidence for the existence or occurrence assertion for the purchase transaction (EO1). The signed receipt also establishes subsequent accountability for the purchased goods. Separating custody of goods received for inventory from other functions involved in purchasing reduces the risk of unauthorized purchases and the misappropriation of goods. An entity should keep the goods in secure storage with limited access and proper surveillance. Most computerized perpetual inventory systems allow warehouse management to keep track of inventory by specific location in the warehouse.

Recording Liabilities

The receipt of a good or service usually establishes an obligation for an entity to complete a transaction. Accrual accounting requires the recording of a liability. Many companies create a voucher, an internal document, to recognize the liability and record it in the purchases journal or voucher register. Usually, the accounts payable department is responsible for ensuring that purchases are accurately recorded. Many important controls, as seen in Figure 15-6, occur at the time of recording purchases. Controls over the recording of a liability, and the specific audit objectives to which they can relate, include the following:

- Computer prepares a report of all goods received that have not resulted in a voucher (C1).
- Computer agreement of the details of the voucher with the vendors' invoices and the related receiving reports and purchase orders (EO1, VA1).
- Computer comparison of the receiving report date with the accounting period when the voucher is recorded. They should be in the same accounting period (EO1, C1).
- Computer check of the mathematical accuracy of each voucher and supporting vendors' invoices (VA1).
- Computer comparison of run-to-run totals to determine that all vouchers are properly posted and summarized in the accounting records (VA1).
- Computer comparison of the coding of account distributions with the purchase order, indicating the asset or expense accounts to be debited, on the vouchers (PD1).
- The supporting documents should be stamped, perforated, or otherwise canceled to prevent resubmission for duplicate payment (EO1). Making duplicate payments is a significant inherent risk in the expenditure cycle.

Discrepancies should be addressed by responding to error messages at the terminal or through exception reports. The variances should be investigated and corrected on a timely basis.

Information about unpaid vouchers is usually maintained in an unpaid voucher file, or accounts payable subsidiary ledger file, pending their subsequent payment. The computer can regularly compare the balance in the general ledger control account with the sum of the account payable subsidiary ledger. In addition, monthly statements received from vendors can be reconciled with the recorded vendor balances (EO1, C1, VA1).

Finally, management should establish a system of accountability for use of the entity's resources. Department managers should regularly be asked to review the transactions that have been charged to their accounts. These managers should be familiar with the underlying business reasons for the transactions and review such reports to ensure that transactions are valid, are the obligation of the entity, are correctly valued, and should be charged to their accounts. If management has not established controls over accountability for the use of resources, it is evidence of a weakened control consciousness in the organization, and reduces the likelihood that other controls will function effectively.

ILLUSTRATIVE SYSTEM FOR PURCHASE TRANSACTIONS

A flowchart of an illustrative system for processing purchase transactions is shown in Figure 15-5. This figure summarizes the following information that is important to documenting the auditor's understanding of internal controls: (1) key functions, (2) the documentary audit trail, (3) key reports produced by the system, and (4) the computer programs and files involved in the accounting system. Every copy of every document is not documented in the flowchart, as the auditor needs only an understanding sufficient to plan the audit. The flowchart also shows the path that the transaction follows from initiating the transaction in the general ledger, which supports the financial statements. The auditor should also document important activities or control procedures, which may be accomplished by a brief written summary similar to the one that follows.

illustrative purchases system

The illustrative system of purchase transactions documented in Figure 15-6 initiates the transaction with a purchase requisition. Upon electronic receipt of a purchase requisition, purchase orders are prepared using on-line terminals. The computer checks the vendors against an authorized vendor list and performs a limit test based on the appropriate authorization and prints an exception report to be reviewed by the purchasing department manager. A copy of the purchase order is printed and sent to vendors. Receiving, stores, and accounts payable have access to appropriate open purchase order information on-line.

When goods arrive in the receiving department, receiving authorization is obtained by reference to the open purchase order file. The goods are then counted and inspected, and receiving clerks use their computer terminals to record the goods received, updating both a receiving file and the perpetual inventory. A daily report is produced for followup on (1) the differences between quantities ordered and quantities received and (2) purchase orders over two weeks old that have not been received. Receiving, stores, and accounts payable can access appropriate receiving information.

Processing the transaction continues upon the arrival of the vendor's invoice. Invoices are processed in batches of 25 and batch totals are entered into the computer. An accounts payable clerk enters invoice information, and the computer checks the mathematical accuracy of the invoice and compares the information (item, quantity, and accounting period) against the receiving report.

Vendor and account distribution data are compared with the purchase order. Batches that do not match the batch total cannot be processed, and input must be immediately reviewed. A daily report documents all exceptions, and related transactions are held in a suspense file to be cleared by the accounts payable supervisor. A report of open receiving reports that have not resulted in a voucher is produced weekly and daily during the last days of the month.

The master file update performs a run-to-run check by checking beginning accounts payable, plus new vouchers, which should equal ending accounts payable. The transaction file is used

(continues)

to update the accounts payable and general ledger master files. The total of the subsidiary ledger is also checked against the general ledger control account. A voucher is printed and supporting documents are canceled, attached to the voucher, and filed in accounts payable. As vendor statements are received, they are compared with the accounts payable subsidiary ledger, and followup is initiated for discrepancies.

At the end of every week a report is given to each manager of the purchases that have been charged to his or her account. Managers must review the report for accuracy, initial the report, and return it to the controller's office.

LEARNING CHECK

15-8 a. State the functions that apply to purchase transactions.

b. For each purchasing function, indicate (1) the department that performs the function, and (2) the principal document or record, if any, produced in performing the function.

15-9 For each of the following potential misstatements for purchase transactions, indicate a potential control procedure and a possible test of controls:

a. Vouchers may not be recorded for goods received.
b. Vouchers may be prepared for goods not ordered or received.
c. Goods may be taken from storage areas.
d. Goods received may not have been ordered.
e. Vouchers are recorded in the wrong accounting period.
f. Vouchers are recorded in the wrong amount.
g. Vouchers are charged to the wrong account.

KEY TERMS

Accounts payable master file, p. 701
Approved vendor master file, p. 700
Exception reports, p. 700
Initiating purchases, p. 701
Open purchase order file, p. 700
Purchase order, p. 700
Purchase requisition, p. 700
Purchase transactions file, p. 701
Receipt of goods and services, p. 701

Receiving file, p. 700
Receiving report, p. 700
Recording liabilities, p. 701
Suspense files, p. 701
Vendor invoice, p. 700
Voucher, p. 700
Voucher register, p. 700
Voucher summary, p. 700

CONTROL ACTIVITIES—CASH DISBURSEMENT TRANSACTIONS

In this section, we consider the common functions and control activities for cash disbursement transactions.

COMMON DOCUMENTS AND RECORDS

Audit Decision 7

■ What should be
considered in evaluat-
ing control activities
for cash disburse-
ments transactions?

Important documents and records used in processing cash disbursement transactions include the following:

- **Check.** Formal order to a bank to pay the payee the amount indicated on demand.
- **Check summary.** Report of all checks issued in a batch or during a day.
- **Cash disbursements transaction file.** Information on payments by check to vendors and others. Used for posting to the accounts payable and general ledger master files.
- **Cash disbursements journal or check register.** Formal accounting record of check issued to vendors and others.

FUNCTIONS AND CONTROL ACTIVITIES

The **cash disbursements function** is the process by which a company provides consideration for the receipt of goods and services. The cash disbursement function usually involves simultaneously paying the liability and recording the cash disbursement. The functions, applicable control activities, and relevant assertions/specific audit objectives are explained in the following sections. Example control procedures are summarized in Figure 15-7.

Paying the Liability and Recording the Disbursement

Usually, a treasury or cash management function is responsible for determining that unpaid vouchers are processed for payment on their due dates. All payments should be by check. The computer can be programmed to extract the vouchers due on each day from the accounts payable master file, and this report is reviewed to determine which payables should be paid, considering the company's cash position.

Once certain vouchers are identified for payment, the computer matches the check information against supporting information, performs programmed application controls, sets a flag that identifies that the voucher has been paid (to prevent duplicate payment), and the payment is recorded. Checks below a certain dollar amount may be machine signed, with larger checks requiring a manual signature from an authorized individual. Controls over the preparation and signing of the checks and related specific audit objectives include the following:

- Authorized personnel in the treasurer's department should be responsible for signing larger checks (EO2).
- Programmed controls check to determine that each check is matched with a properly approved unpaid voucher and that the name of the payee and the amount on the check agree with the voucher (EO2, VA2).
- Programmed controls cancel voucher number once it has been paid, and review paid voucher file to ensure that a voucher is not paid twice (EO2).
- To reduce the risk of theft or alterations, the department controlling the production of checks should control the mailing of the checks (EO2).
- No check should be made payable to "cash" or "bearer," and no blank checks should be issued (EO2, VA2, PD2).

Figure 15-7 ■ Control Risk Considerations—Cash Disbursement Transactions

Function	Potential Misstatement	Computer Control[a] (Manual Controls in Italics)	C2	EO2	VA2	PD2
Cash Disbursement	A check may not be recorded.	Computer accounts for prenumbered check series.	D			
		The computer compares the total on the check summary with the total vouchers submitted for payment.	P			
		Access to blank check and signature plates is controlled.	P			
	A check may not be recorded promptly.	Computer prints report of checks due but not yet paid.	D			
		Run-to-run totals compare beginning cash, less cash disbursements, with ending cash balance as well as beginning accounts payable less disbursements with ending accounts payable.	D			
	Checks may be issued for unauthorized purchases.	Computer compares check information with purchase order and receiving information or other authorization.		D		
		Computer performs a limit test on large disbursement, and these checks must be manually signed.		P		
	A voucher may be paid twice.	The computer has a field that identifies that a voucher has been paid and the voucher number cannot be reused.		D		
	A check may be issued for the wrong amount.	Computer comparison of check amount with related voucher amount.			D	
	A check may be altered after being signed.	*Manual control requires that check signers mail checks.*			P	
		Independent bank reconciliation.			D	
	Errors may be made in recording the check.	Computer comparison of information on check summary with related voucher information.		D	D	D
		Independent bank reconciliation.	D	D	D	D
	Management Control					
	Cash disbursements may be made for unauthorized purchases, or they may be made in the wrong amount.	An appropriate level of management monitors cash daily, including the amount of checks written daily, the reasonableness of the amounts, and the amount of debits to accounts payable daily.		D	D	

[a] All computer controls assume that exceptions are either printed on an exception report for followup or an error message appears during input and the transaction cannot be processed without correction and acceptance.
P = potential control to prevent misstatement or unauthorized use of resources.
D = potential control to detect misstatement or unauthorized use of resources.

- Prenumbered checks should be used and accounted for (C2).
- Access to blank checks and to signature plates should be limited to authorized personnel (C2).

In manual systems it is important that checks are matched with vouchers and underlying supporting documents, and that the vouchers are canceled to prevent duplicate payment.

The cash disbursements transaction file created when checks are prepared is used to update the accounts payable master file and general ledger accounts. The update program also produces the cash disbursement journal and a general ledger summary that are forwarded to accounting. Controls over cash disbursements include the following:

- Run-to-run totals comparing the beginning balance of the disbursement files plus transactions, with the expected ending balance of updated cash disbursement transaction files and the accounts payable master file.
- An independent check of the agreement of the total of the checks issued (usually reported on a check summary) with a batch total of the vouchers processed for payment (EO2, C2, VA2).
- An independent check by an accounting supervisor of the agreement of the amounts journalized and posted to accounts payable with the check summary received from the treasurer (EO2, C2, VA2).
- Independent bank reconciliations (EO2, C2, VA2).

Disbursement checks generally include a stub, similar to a payroll check stub, which identifies the vendor invoice number and the invoice(s) being paid. A copy of each check should be filed with the supporting voucher in the paid voucher file.

ILLUSTRATIVE SYSTEM FOR CASH DISBURSEMENT TRANSACTIONS

An illustrative system for processing cash disbursement transactions is shown in Figure 15-8. The flowchart continues the path documented in Figure 15-5 that expenditure transactions follow from initiating the transaction, through the consideration process, to the general ledger, which supports the financial statements. Not every copy of every document is documented in the flowchart, as the auditor needs only an understanding sufficient to plan the audit. The auditor should also supplement the flowchart with documentation of important activities or control procedures, which may be accomplished by a brief written summary similar to the one that follows.

The computer runs a daily report of vouchers that are due. The controller reviews the report, evaluates the company's cash position, and determines (and notes on the report) which vouchers should be paid.

An assistant in the controller's office enters the vouchers to be paid, and the cash disbursements program subjects each transaction to programmed controls and prepares prenumbered checks based on the information on the accounts payable master file. Programmed application controls compare the check information with the information on the accounts payable file and

(continues)

Figure 15-8 ■ System Flowchart—Cash Disbursement Transactions

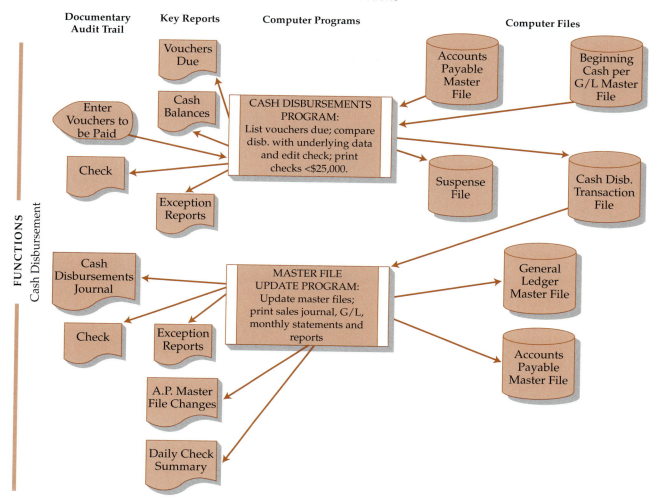

check to see that the voucher has not previously been paid. In addition, the program enters the payment data in a cash disbursements transaction file, performs a run-to-run total, and produces a check summary that is compared with the batch total prepared in accounts payable. Exceptions are put in a suspense file, and a daily exception report is printed for daily review and followup in the controller's office. Disbursements for vouchers in excess of $25,000 appear on a special report, and these checks must be personally signed by the chief financial officer or controller. The master file update program is then used to update the accounts payable and general ledger master files based on data in the cash disbursements transaction file. This program also produces the cash disbursement journal and a general ledger summary showing the totals posted to general ledger accounts. The daily check summary is compared with the total debits to accounts payable by the controller's office and then checks are mailed. An accountant in the office of the chief financial officer performs independent bank reconciliations.

LEARNING CHECK

15-10 Most computer systems simultaneously pay the liability and record the check. Discuss how cash disbursements are authorized and describe independent checks that are appropriate.

15-11 For each of the following control procedures pertaining to cash disbursement transactions, indicate the potential misstatement and possible tests of controls.

a. Checks are prenumbered and accounted for.

b. Check signers mail checks.

c. Computer compares check information with supporting voucher information.

d. Run-to-run totals compare beginning cash, less cash disbursements, with the ending cash balance.

e. Computer performs a limit test on large disbursements, which must be manually signed.

f. An appropriate level of management monitors cash daily, including the amount of checks written daily, the reasonableness of such amounts, and the amount of debits to accounts payable daily.

KEY TERMS

Cash disbursements function, p. 708

Cash disbursements journal or check register, p. 708

Cash disbursements transaction file, p. 708

Check, p. 708

Check summary, p. 708

CONTROL ACTIVITIES FOR PURCHASE ADJUSTMENT TRANSACTIONS AND OTHER CONTROLS

COMMON DOCUMENTS AND RECORDS

Audit Decision 8

■ What should be considered in evaluating control activities for purchase adjustments?

Important documents and records used in processing purchase adjustments include the following:

■ **Purchase Return Authorization.** Form showing the description, quantity, and other data pertaining to the goods that the vendor has authorized to return. It serves as the basis for initiating the purchase return.

■ **Shipping Report.** Report prepared on the shipment of goods to vendors showing the kinds and quantities of goods shipped.

■ **Debit Memo.** Form stating the particulars of a debit to accounts payable, including the specific items returned, prices, and amount credited. It provides the basis for recording the purchase return.

Reference is made to each of the above in the following discussion.

FUNCTIONS AND CONTROL ACTIVITIES

Purchase Returns and Allowances

Purchase adjustment transactions involve the recording of purchase returns and allowances. On occasion, goods received from vendors are defective and must be returned. In addition, vendors offer a number of inducements to purchase inventory. In some cases, vendors will agree to reduce the price for goods rather than have goods returned. On other cases they may agree to pay holding costs for a specific holding period. In many companies, the number and dollar value of these transactions is immaterial. However, in some companies, the potential for misstatements could reach a material amount.

Each of these transactions results in reducing payables and expenses and in improving reported liquidity and earnings. Sound financial reporting needs to establish adequate controls over these transactions to prevent their abuse in earnings management activities. Accordingly, control activities useful in reducing the risk of misstatements focus on establishing the existence or occurrence of such transactions (EO3) and include the following:

- All purchase returns should be authorized by the vendor (EO3).
- Goods should be retuned only with a proper purchase return authorization, and an independent count of goods returned should be recorded on shipping documents such as packing slips and bills of lading (EO3).
- The computer should match debit memo information with the authorization for purchase return and the shipping documents (EO3, VA3).
- The computer generates a report of all authorized purchase returns that have not been shipped or have not resulted in a debit memo (C3).

Furthermore, there should be adequate segregation of duties between obtaining authorization for purchase returns, shipping goods, and recording debit memos.

When there is the potential for material misstatements from purchase adjustments transactions, the auditor should obtain an understanding of all relevant aspects of the internal control structure components and consider the factors that affect the risk of such misstatements. If purchase adjustments are estimated at quarter end, management should establish controls to ensure that adjustments are made based on reliable information and that adjustments are consistent from quarter to quarter. A disclosure committee should review these estimates if they could aggregate with other adjustments to an amount that is material to the financial statements (VA4, PD7).

OTHER CONTROLS IN THE EXPENDITURE CYCLE

The previous discussion focused on controls over transactions. It is also important to control balances and disclosures.

The primary account balance in the expenditure cycle is accounts payable. If good controls exist over purchases, cash disbursements, and purchase adjustments, accounts payable should also be controlled. Most companies control the completeness (C4), existence (EO4), and valuation of receivables at historical cost (VA4) by reconciling the accounts payable subsidiary ledgers with vendor statements.

Controls over the rights and obligations assertion relate to whether the payables are the obligation of the entity. This is usually controlled when the liability is recorded by matching the voucher information with supporting data (RO1).

Finally, management should establish controls over the occurrence and rights and obligations of disclosures (PD4), the completeness of disclosures (PD5), the understandability of disclosures (PD6), and the accuracy and valuation of information included in disclosures (PD7). Public companies normally accomplish this task through the workings of a disclosure committee that is independent of the CFO or controller, and includes individuals who are knowledgeable about GAAP and the transactions and disclosures relevant to the expenditure cycle.

TEST OF CONTROLS

<table>
<tr><td>

Audit Decision 9

■ What are the relevant aspects of tests of controls when the auditor plans to assess control risk below the maximum for expenditure cycle transactions?

</td></tr>
</table>

Many auditors plan to test controls in the purchases cycle because of the high volume of routine transactions in this cycle. Public company auditors test controls to support an opinion on internal controls. Private company auditors will test controls that appear to be effective because of the audit efficiencies that exist with this strategy.

If the auditor plans to assess control risk as low for expenditure cycle assertions, he or she will usually have to:

- Test the effectiveness of general controls.
- Use computer-assisted audit techniques (CAATs) to evaluate the effectiveness of programmed controls.
- Test the effectiveness of procedures to follow up on exceptions identified by programmed controls.

For example, the auditor might use test data to determine whether expected results appear on exception reports when he or she submits

- Missing or invalid vendor code.
- Transactions reporting receivings in quantities different from the amount ordered (both over and under).
- Prices, vendor numbers, account numbers, or other information on vouchers that do not match information on the purchase order.
- Voucher quantities that do not match quantities on receiving reports.

The auditor might also use generalized audit software or a utility program to perform sequence checks and print lists of purchase orders, receiving documents, or vouchers whose numbers are missing in designated computer files.

[LEARNING CHECK

15-12 a. Explain the economic substance of purchase adjustments.
    b. State three types of controls pertaining to purchase adjustment transactions and identify their common focus.

15-13 a. Explain why controls over expenditure cycle transactions should also control the accounts payable balance.
    b. Explain the primary control over the accounts payable balance itself.
    c. How is the rights and obligations assertion controlled for accounts payable?
    d. How are disclosures controlled for accounts payable?

15-14 Using the information in Figures 15-6 and 15-7 develop a test of controls for each assertion related to purchases and cash disbursements.

KEY TERMS

Debit memo, p. 712
Purchase return authorization, p. 712

Shipping report, p. 712

SUBSTANTIVE TESTS OF ACCOUNTS PAYABLE BALANCES

Accounts payable is usually the largest current liability in a balance sheet and a significant factor in evaluating an entity's short-term solvency. Like accounts receivable, it is typically affected by a high volume of transactions and thus is susceptible to misstatements. However, as compared with the audit of asset balances, the audit of payables places greater emphasis on the completeness assertion relative to the existence or occurrence assertion. The reason for this is that if management were motivated to misrepresent payables, it would likely be to understate them in order to report a more favorable financial position. In addition, there is an inherent risk that vendor's invoices may not be received on a timely basis and payables may be recorded in a period after the receipt of goods or services.

Our attention here is focused on trade payables arising from expenditure cycle transactions. Other payables, such as wages and payroll taxes and various noncurrent liabilities, are covered in other cycle chapters.

DETERMINING DETECTION RISK FOR TESTS OF DETAILS

An example risk matrix for the purchases cycle and accounts payable assertions is presented in Figure 15-9. The following explains the development of preliminary audit strategies for assertions that are consistent with this example risk matrix.

Audit Decision 10

■ What are the factors involved in determining the acceptable level of tests of details risk for accounts payable assertions?

Existence and Occurrence

The existence and occurrence assertion for purchases and accounts payable represents a significant inherent risk because of the potential for employee fraud and misappropriation of assets. As a result, inherent risk is assessed at high for this assertion.

Recall from Chapter 11 that the combined control risk assessment for accounts payable is a function of internal controls over the occurrence of purchases (low) and the completeness of cash disbursements (low) and purchase adjustments (moderate). As a result, a conservative combined risk assessment for the existence of accounts payable would be moderate. A common internal control over the occurrence of purchases would be having the computer match sales voucher information with information from the receiving report. An example internal control over the completeness of disbursements would include a computer report of payments due to vendors but not yet paid. This control also depends on strong controls over the completeness of vouchers payable. Internal controls over the completeness of purchase returns might include a regular report of all authorized

Figure 15-9 ■ Example Risk Matrix for Accounts Payable Assertions

Risk Component	Existence or Occurrence	Complete- ness	Rights and Obligations	Valuation or Allocation	Presentation and Disclosure
Audit Risk	Very low	Very low	Very low	Very low	Very low
Inherent Risk	High	Max	Moderate	High	Max
Control Risk—Purchase Transactions	Low	Low	Moderate	Low	Moderate
Control Risk—Cash Disbursement Transactions	Low	Low	Moderate	Low	Moderate
Control Risk—Purchase Adjustment Transactions	Low	Moderate	Moderate	Low	Moderate
Combined Control Risk for Accounts Payable Tests	Moderate	Low	Moderate	Low	Moderate
Analytical Procedures Risk	High	High	High	High	High
Acceptable Test of Details Risk	Low	Low	Moderate	Moderate	Low

purchase returns that have not resulted in the generation of debit memos. The moderate control risk assessment for purchase returns is related to the challenge of obtaining control over the population of authorized returns.

The auditor might perform analytical procedures similar to those explained in Figure 15-4. As a result, the appropriate level of detection risk for test of details is low. The primary test of details would involve the vouching transactions to underlying receiving reports and approved vendor's invoices. Based on the combined control risk assessment of moderate, the auditor might perform tests of transactions at an interim date. Some level of vouching or confirming payables at year-end also provides evidence regarding the validity of this assertion.

Completeness

The auditor will likely assess inherent risk for the completeness assertion as maximum because of the risk of unrecorded liabilities.

When considering the combined control risk assessment for the completeness of receivables, the auditor should evaluate the completeness assertions for purchases (low in this example) with the existence and occurrence assertion for cash disbursements (low) and for purchase adjustments (low). Internal controls over the completeness of purchases would usually include daily followup on items received that had not resulted in vouchers. Controls over the occurrence of cash disbursements would include comparison of recorded cash disbursement with the underlying voucher. This control depends on controls over the existence of recorded purchases. Finally controls over the occurrence of purchase returns would include matching of debit memo information with underlying shipping information.

Analytical procedures related to the completeness of purchases and payables would involve a comparison of purchases to the underlying physical business such as a comparison of purchases to production levels, and being alert to a current ratio that just looks too good. Focusing on significant decreases in accounts payable turn days is a rather blunt tool, so analytical procedures risk is often set at high.

In this situation the auditor assesses test of details risk as low. The auditor often performs substantive tests by taking a sample of purchases after the end of the year to determine if they should have been recorded in the prior period. With a low test of details risk assessment the auditor would perform extensive tests after year-end to test the accuracy of purchases cutoff.

Rights and Obligations

The rights and obligations assertion addresses the issue of whether accounts payable are obligations of the entity at the balance sheet date. A consolidated entity needs to ensure that the recorded obligations are the obligations of the consolidated entity. This is a moderate inherent risk as entities rarely record obligations that they do not owe. Owner-managed companies need to make sure that they do not record obligations of the owner as obligations of the company. Rights and obligations is often controlled at the transaction level by ensuring that only the obligations of the entity are recorded in the books of original entry as payables.

Analytical procedures are a fairly blunt tool for auditing this objective. They would have to provide evidence that payables appear to be significantly overstated. Hence, auditors often rely on direct tests of transactions, vouching transactions to underlying source documents, to obtain competent evidence regarding the rights and obligations assertion.

Valuation or Allocation

The assessment of inherent risk for the valuation or allocation assertion is often set at high just because of the high volume of transactions that flow through accounts payable.

Controls over the valuation or allocation assertion involve the controls over the valuation of purchases, cash disbursements, and purchase adjustments. These might include computer comparison of prices on voucher invoices with underlying vendor's invoices and the purchase order, comparison of recorded cash disbursements with the recorded voucher, and comparison of prices on debit memo with the voucher and the vendor's invoice. These are routine transactions that can be effectively controlled, so a strong system of internal control should be able to restrict control risk to a low level.

Analytical procedures usually involve computing the entity's accounts payable turn days. This is a rather blunt tool for careful analysis of valuation issues, so analytical procedures risk is often set at high.

The valuation of payables is often tested simultaneously with the existence of payables. Auditors normally use a combination of vouching transactions to underlying vendor's invoices during tests of transactions at an interim date and some level of vouching or confirming payables at year-end.

Presentation and Disclosure

The greatest risk associated with presentation and disclosure is the risk of misclassification of expenses as capital assets. The GAO Report on Financial Statement Restatements showed that misclassification of costs and expenses was the second most common cause of restatements after revenue recognition problems. As a result, inherent risk is often set at maximum for this assertion. This problem focuses more on the debit side of the purchase, rather than the credit to accounts payable.

Internal controls over the classification of expenditures must be implemented at early stages of a transaction. The first assignment of account classifications usually happens with the purchase requisition or purchase order, and the recording of the transaction is compared with this information. Often account classifications are assigned to the individual who initiates a purchase requisition to minimize the risk of classification errors. Hence, if a particular manager initiates a purchase requisition, the transaction must be charged to that individual's responsibility center. In our example control risk is assessed at moderate because of the degree of subjectivity in this process.

Analytical procedures might focus on amount of certain expenses (repair and maintenance) from year to year, but this is not a precise test. Earning management activities often ensure that these relationships look reasonable. Hence, the auditor must devote significant attention to auditing the classification of transactions substantively to restrict test of details risk to a low level. This involves vouching transactions to underlying vendor's invoices during tests of transactions at an interim date and again at year-end, and reevaluating the appropriateness of account classifications assigned to the transactions. In addition, the auditor often performs tests associated with investing and financing activities to specifically evaluate issues associated with the classification of assets. These other tests are discussed in Chapter 17.

DESIGNING SUBSTANTIVE TESTS

Audit Decision 11

■ How does the auditor determine the elements of an audit program for substantive tests to achieve specific audit objectives for accounts payable?

Recall that the acceptable level of detection risk for each significant financial statement assertion is achieved by gathering evidence from appropriately designed substantive tests. The general framework for developing audit programs for substantive tests that was explained in Chapter 12 and illustrated in Chapter 14 for accounts receivable can also be used in designing substantive tests for accounts payable. A listing of possible substantive tests that might be included in an audit program developed on this basis appears in Figure 15-10. Note that each of the tests in the figure is keyed to one or more of the specific account balance audit objectives for accounts payable from Figure 15-2. Also note that multiple tests are keyed to each account balance audit objective. Each of the tests is explained below, including comments on how some tests can be tailored based on the applicable acceptable level of detection risk to be achieved.

Initial Procedures

The starting point for every audit test is obtaining an understanding of the business and industry. Understanding the significance of the purchase cycle to the entity provides a context for important risk assessments. Understanding the company's economic drivers, standard trade terms, and the extent of concentration of

Figure 15-10 ■ Possible Substantive Tests of Accounts Payable Assertions

Category	Substantive Test	Specific Audit Objectives

Initial Procedures	1. Obtain an understanding of the business and industry and determine:
	  a. The significance of purchases and accounts payable to the entity.
	  b. Key economic drivers that influence the entity's purchases and resultant account payables.
	  c. Standard trade terms in the industry, including seasonal dating, etc.
	  d. The extent of concentration of activity with suppliers and related purchase commitments.
	2. Perform initial procedures on the accounts payable balance and records that will be subjected to further testing.
	  a. Trace beginning balance for accounts payable to prior year's working papers.
	  b. Review activity in general ledger account for accounts payable and investigate entries that appear unusual in amount or source.
	  c. Obtain listing of accounts payable at balance sheet date and determine that it accurately represents the underlying accounting records by:
	    i. Footing the listing and determining agreement with (1) the total of the unpaid voucher file, subsidiary ledger, or accounts payable master file, and (2) the general ledger control account balance.
	    ii. Testing agreement of vendors and balance on listing with those included in the underlying accounting records.
		All
		
		VA4
		
		PD1, PD2, PD3, EO1, EO2, EO3
		
		VA4
		
		VA4

Analytical Procedures	3. Perform analytical procedures:
	  a. Develop an expectation for accounts payable using knowledge of the entity's business activity, normal trade terms, and its history of accounts payable turnover.
	  b. Calculate ratios:
	    i. Accounts payable turnover (purchases ÷ accounts payable).
	    ii. Accounts payable to total current liabilities.
	  c. Analyze ratio results relative to expectations based on prior years, industry data, budgeted amounts, or other data.
	  d. Compare expense balance to prior year or budgeted amounts for indications of possible understatement related to unrecorded payables.
		All

Tests of Details of Transactions	4. Vouch a sample of recorded expenditure cycle transactions to supporting documentation.
	  a. Vouch accounts payable credits to supporting vouchers, vendor invoices, receiving reports, and purchase orders and other supporting information.
	  b. Vouch accounts payable debits to cash disbursements or purchase returns memoranda.
	5. Perform purchases cutoff test.
	  a. Select a sample of recorded purchase transactions from several days before and after year-end and examine supporting vouchers, vendor invoices, and receiving reports to determine that purchases were recorded in the proper period, or
	  b. Observe the number of the last receiving report issued on the last business day of the audit period and trace sample of lower and higher numbered receiving reports to related purchase documents and determine that transactions were recorded in the proper period.
	6. Perform cash disbursements cutoff test.
	  a. Observe the number of the last check issued and mailed on the last day of the audit period and trace to the accounting records to verify accuracy of cutoff, or
	  b. Trace dates of "paid" checks returned with year-end cutoff bank statements to dates recorded.
		
		EO1, PD1, VA1, EO4
		
		EO2, PD2, VA2, EO4, EO3, PD3, VA3
		
		EO1, C1
		
		EO1, C1
		
		EO2, C2

(continues)

Figure 15-10 ■ (Continued)

Category	Substantive Test	Specific Audit Objectives
	7. Purchase return cutoff test. a. Determine purchase returns shipped back to vendors for a period of several days before and after year-end and determine that transactions are recorded in the proper period. b. Vouch the last purchase returns recorded in the books of original entry to vendor's authorization and shipping reports.	EO3, C3
	8. Perform search for unrecorded liabilities. a. Examine subsequent payments between balance sheet date and end of fieldwork, and when related documentation indicates payment was for obligation in existence at balance sheet date, trace to accounts payable listing. b. Examine documentation for payables recorded at year-end that are still unpaid at end of fieldwork. c. Investigate unmatched purchase orders, receiving reports, and vendor invoices at year-end. d. Inquire of accounting and purchasing personnel about unrecorded payables. e. Review capital budgets, work orders, and construction contracts for evidence of unrecorded payables.	C4, RO1
Tests of Details of Balances	9. Confirm accounts payable. a. Identify major vendors by reviewing voucher register or accounts payable subsidiary ledger or master file and send confirmation requests to vendors with large balances, unusual activity, small or zero balances, and debit balances. b. Investigate and reconcile differences.	EO4, VA4, RO1
	10. Reconcile unconfirmed payable to monthly statements received by client from vendors.	EO4, VA4, RO1
Presentation and Disclosure	11. Compare statement presentation with GAAP. a. Determine that payables are properly identified and classified as to type and expected period of payment.	PD4, PD7
	b. Determine whether there are debit balances that are significant in the aggregate and that should be reclassified.	PD4, PD7
	c. Determine the appropriateness of disclosures pertaining to related party or collateralized payables.	PD4, PD7
	d. Inquire of management about existence of undisclosed commitments or contingent liabilities.	PD4, PD7
	e. Evaluate the completeness of presentation and disclosures for payables in drafts of financial statements to determine conformity to GAAP by reference to disclosure checklist.	PD5
	f. Read disclosures and independently evaluate their classification and understandability.	PD6

business with certain suppliers provides the context for evaluating the results of analytical procedures, tests of controls, and substantive tests. Procedures performed to obtain this understanding were discussed earlier in the chapter.

Another initial procedure for substantive tests of accounts payable is tracing the beginning balance to the prior year's working papers, and using generalized audit software to scan the general ledger account for any unusual entries and to develop a listing of amounts owed at the balance sheet date. Ordinarily, the client provides a listing of the unpaid voucher file, the accounts payable subsidiary ledger, or master file in electronic form. The auditor can also use generalized audit software to determine the mathematical accuracy of the listing by refooting the total and by verifying that it agrees with the general ledger account balance.

Analytical Procedures

The importance of analytical procedures was discussed earlier in the chapter. The auditor's goal is to develop an expectation of payable account balances and the relationship between accounts payable and other key accounts such as purchases or inventory. Several analytical procedures that can be performed to provide evidence about accounts payable are shown in Figure 15-4. An abnormal decrease in the accounts payable turnover ratio or unexpected increases in the current ratio may provide indicators of understated liabilities. Analytical procedures are performed in final stages of the engagement to ensure that the evidence evaluated in details tests is consistent with the overall picture reported in the financial statements.

Tests of Details of Transactions

There are five major substantive tests of details of accounts payable transactions as shown in Figure 15-10 and as discussed in the following subsections. Recall that in performing these tests, the auditor is primarily concerned with detecting understatements of recorded payables as well as unrecorded payables. The extent to which each test is performed varies based on the acceptable levels of detection risk specified for the related assertions.

Vouch Recorded Payables to Supporting Documentation

In this test, credit entries to accounts payable are vouched to supporting documentation in the client's file such as vouchers, vendor invoices, receiving reports, and purchase orders. Debits to accounts payable are vouched to documentation of cash disbursement transactions, such as paid checks, or memoranda from vendors pertaining to purchase returns and allowances. Some vouching may have been performed during interim work, such as parts of dual-purpose tests along with tracings from source documents to accounting records. The extent of vouching is directly related to the auditor's conclusions about inherent risk, analytical procedures risk, and control risk. This test primarily provides evidence for the specific audit objectives related to four of the five assertions, excluding completeness. The applicability to the completeness assertion is limited because, whereas the improper reduction of recorded payables through invalid debits may be detected, the test will not detect payables that have never been recorded.

Perform Cutoff Test

The **purchases cutoff tests** involves determining that purchase transactions occurring near the balance sheet date are recorded in the proper period. This may be done by tracing dated receiving reports to voucher register entries and vouching recorded entries to supporting documentation. The test usually covers a period of five to ten business days before and after the balance sheet date. Evidence from the test pertains to the existence or occurrence and completeness assertions for accounts payable.

In examining documentation as part of this test, special consideration must be given to goods in transit at the balance sheet date. Goods shipped FOB (free on board) shipping point should be included in the inventory and accounts payable of the buyer. In contrast, goods in transit shipped FOB destination should remain in the inventory of the seller and be excluded from the buyer's inventory and accounts payable until arrival at the buyer's receiving department. In performing this test, the auditor should determine that a proper cutoff is achieved in the taking of the physical inventory, as explained further in Chapter 16, as well as in the recording of the purchase transactions.

A proper cutoff of cash disbursement transactions at the end of the year is essential to the correct presentation of cash and accounts payable at the balance sheet date. As in the case of the cash receipts cutoff test described in the preceding chapter, evidence for the **cash disbursement cutoff test** may be obtained by personal observation and review of internal documentation. When the auditor can be present at the balance sheet date, he or she can personally determine the last check written and mailed by the client. Subsequent tracing of this evidence to the accounting records will verify the accuracy of the cutoff. Alternatively, the auditor can trace "paid" checks dated within a period of several days before and after the balance sheet date to the dates the checks were recorded. Evidence from this test also pertains to the existence or occurrence and completeness assertions for accounts payable.

Purchase return cutoff tests are similar to other cutoff tests. First, the auditor should start with the shipping records for a period of five to ten days before an after year-end to ensure that purchase returns are accurately recorded in the accounting records. Then the auditor should go from the accounting records back to evidence in the shipping records to verify the accuracy of the last purchase returns recorded by the entity.

Perform Search for Unrecorded Payables

The **search for unrecorded accounts payable** consists of procedures designed specifically to detect significant unrecorded obligations at the balance sheet date. Thus, it relates to the completeness assertion for accounts payable.

A common procedure involves examining **subsequent payments,** which consists of examining the documentation for checks issued or vouchers paid after the balance sheet date. When the documentation indicates the payment is for an obligation that existed at the balance sheet date, it is traced to the accounts payable listing to determine whether it was included. This test is performed toward the end of fieldwork to enhance the opportunity of obtaining evidence concerning payables that were intentionally or inadvertently excluded from the listing of payables at the statement date. Thus, the test extends beyond the periods used in the cutoff tests described earlier.

Usually vendors will seek payment, even if a liability is not recorded at the balance sheet date. Hence, this may be an effective search for unrecorded liabilities. The auditor can also search this subsequent period looking for overstatements of subsequent payments and may focus on larger transactions.

Documentation supporting payables recorded but remaining unpaid through the end of fieldwork should also be examined on a test basis. This may also reveal obligations that existed but that were unrecorded as of the balance sheet date. Other procedures that may reveal unrecorded payables include (1) investigating unmatched purchase orders, receiving reports, and vendor invoices at year-end, (2) inquiring of accounting and purchasing personnel about unrecorded payables, and (3) reviewing capital budgets, work orders, and construction contracts for evidence for unrecorded payables.

Tests of Details of Balances

Two tests included in this category are (1) confirming accounts payable and (2) reconciling unconfirmed payables to monthly statements received by the client from vendors.

Accounts Payable Confirmations

Unlike the confirmation of accounts receivable, there is no presumption made about the **confirmation of accounts payable.** This procedure is optional because (1) confirmation offers no assurance that unrecorded payables will be discovered and (2) external evidence in the form of invoices and vendor monthly statements should be available to substantiate the balances. Confirmation of accounts payable is recommended when the detection risk is low, there are individual creditors with relatively large balances, or a company is experiencing difficulties in meeting its obligations. As in the case of confirming accounts receivable, the auditor must control the preparation and mailing of the request and should receive the responses directly from the respondent.

When the confirmation is to be undertaken, accounts with zero or small balances should be among those selected for confirmation because they may be more understated than accounts with large balances. In addition, confirmations should be sent to major vendors who (1) were used in the prior year but not in the current year and (2) do not send monthly statements. The positive form should be used in making the confirmation request as illustrated in Figure 15-11. It may be observed that the confirmation does not specify the amount due. In confirming a payable, the auditor prefers to have the creditor indicate the amount due because that is the amount to be reconciled to the client's records. Note that information is also requested regarding purchase commitments of the client and any collateral for the payable.

This test produces evidence for all accounts payable assertions. However, the evidence provided for the completeness assertion is limited because of the possible failure to identify and send confirmation requests to vendors with whom the client has unrecorded obligations.

Reconcile Unconfirmed Payables to Vendor Statements

In many cases, vendors provide monthly statements that are available in client files. In such cases, amounts owed to vendors per the client's listing of payables can be reconciled to those statements. The evidence from this procedure applies to the same assertions as confirmations, but is less reliable because the vendors' statements were sent to the client rather than directly to the auditor. In addition, statements may not be available from certain vendors.

Tests of Details of Disclosures

Figure 15-10 describes a number of tests of disclosures for the expenditure cycle. The auditor must be knowledgeable about the statement presentation and disclosure requirements for accounts receivable and sales under GAAP. Accounts payable should be properly identified and classified as a current liability. If the accounts payable balance includes material advance payments to some vendors for future delivery of goods and services, such amounts should be reclassified as advances to suppliers and included as assets. In addition, disclosures may be

Figure 15-11 ■ Accounts Payable Confirmation

Highlift Company
P.O. Box 1777
Cleveland, Ohio 39087

January 4, 20X1

Supplier, Inc.
2001 Lakeview Drive
Cleveland, Ohio 39098

Dear Sir or Madam:

Will you please send directly to our auditors, Reddy & Abel, Certified Public Accountants, an itemized statement of the amount owed to you by us at the close of business on December 31, 20X0? Will you please also supply the following information:

Amount not yet due $ _____

Amount past due $ _____

Amount of purchase commitments $ _____

Description of any collateral held:

A business reply envelope addressed to our auditors is enclosed. A prompt reply will be very much appreciated.

Very truly yours.

D. R. Owens

Controller
Highlift Company

required for collateralized and related-party payables, purchase commitments, and contingent liabilities. Thus, management's presentation and disclosures must be compared with these GAAP requirements. Evidence relevant to these matters should be obtainable by inquiring of management and reviewing minutes of board of directors' meetings and loan agreements. Evidence is also obtained through the audit procedures performed to test other assertions. Management's representations on these matters should be obtained in writing in a client representation letter as one of the final steps in the audit, as explained in Chapter 19.

OTHER ASSURANCE SERVICES

Audit Decision 12

■ How does the auditor use the knowledge obtained during the audit of the expenditure cycle to support other assurance services?

Generally accepted auditing standards do not require that the auditor perform other assurance services. However, many auditors develop industry specializations so that they can understand industry trends and better identify risks associated with financial statements not presenting fairly financial position, results of operations, or cash flows. The client and its board of directors usually want to take full advantage of the auditor's knowledge.

Consider the following example regarding a not-for-profit agency that performed services for a state agency. While completing an audit of the expenditure cycle the auditor recognized a change in business practices. Previously the state subcontracted with the agency for certain services and had a practice of paying a flat monthly fee at the beginning of the month for the delivery of services. Furthermore, the state obtained no reporting from the not-for-profit on the number of individuals who received service from the subcontractor. The not-for-profit entity had a built-in fixed cost with little accountability. When it came time to renegotiate the contract, the state negotiated a contract where the not-for-profit was reimbursed at the end of the month based on the number of persons served. This resulted in a significant cash outflow for the not-for-profit agency. Now cash was going out before it was reimbursed for services. Managers, who were focused on delivering a social need, paid little attention to preparing billing for services performed. They had not had to do this in the past. Based on recommendations from the auditor, the entity discovered that it had to more carefully monitor its performance of services to make sure that it served a sufficient number of individuals to cover its costs. It also had to ensure that billings were sent on a timely basis. Based on audit recommendations, the entity was also able to negotiate a cash advance from the state to address the cash flow problems that were created. This is one example of how the auditor might use the knowledge obtained during the audit, to deliver additional high-value services to audit clients.

Consider the following example relating to performance measurement services. In the process of performing the audit, the auditor may benchmark an entity's expenditures against others in the industry. For example, for the year ending January 28, 2000, Dell Computer took an average of 6 days to turn its inventory, 34 days to turn its receivables, and 43 days to clear its payables, resulting in obtaining 3 days of operating cash flow before it had to settle its liabilities. No cash was needed to fund the operating cycle. An important service offered by CPAs is helping their clients anticipate this type of opportunity and helping them develop the vision of how to make this type of positive cash flow a reality.

LEARNING CHECK

15-15 a. Which assertion is of primary importance to the auditor in auditing accounts payable? Why?

b. Indicate the relationship of control risk assessments for expenditure cycle transactions to the completeness assertion for accounts payable.

15-16 a. Identify the substantive tests that apply to the completeness assertion for accounts payable.

b. For each of the foregoing tests, indicate the other assertions to which they may relate.

15-17 Chris Cole believes the auditor's responsibilities for confirming accounts payable are the same as those for accounts receivable. Do you agree with Chris? Explain.

15-18 a. How does the auditor perform (1) a purchases cutoff test and (2) a cash disbursement cutoff test?

b. What assertions are affected by these tests?

15-19 Distinguish among the following tests and indicate the assertion to which each test pertains.

a. Vouch recorded payables to supporting documentation.

b. Examine subsequent payments.

c. Determine that payables are properly identified and classified.

15-20 Develop several examples of how the auditor might use his or her knowledge of the expenditure cycle to deliver other assurance services to an audit client.

KEY TERMS

Cash disbursement cutoff test, p. 722
Confirmation of accounts payable,
  p. 723
Purchases cutoff tests, p. 721

Purchase return cutoff tests, p. 722
Search for unrecorded accounts
  payable, p. 722
Subsequent payments, p. 722

FOCUS ON AUDIT DECISIONS

This chapter focuses on the practical aspects of auditing the expenditure cycle. The chapter pays particular attention to audit planning concerns related to the expenditure cycle, specific internal controls that are tailored to the expenditure cycle, and substantive tests for the expenditure cycle. Figure 15-12 summarizes the audit decisions discussed in Chapter 15 and provides page references indicating where these decisions are discussed in more detail.

Figure 15-12 ■ Summary of Audit Decisions Discussed in Chapter 15

Audit Decision	Factors that Influence the Audit Decision	Chapter References
D1. What is the nature of the expenditure cycle, and how are specific audit objectives developed for the expenditure cycle?	The expenditure cycle includes three major classes of transactions: (1) purchases, (2) cash disbursements, and (3) purchase adjustments. The primary balance in the expenditure cycle is accounts payable. Figure 15-2 develops specific audit objectives for the audit of the expenditure cycle.	pp. 690–691
D2. How does understanding the entity and its environment affect audit planning decisions in the expenditure cycle?	Different companies in different industries experience various risks associated with the expenditure cycle. Figure 15-3 provides examples of five different industries and how knowledge of the entity and its environment can be used to develop expectations of the financial statements and to assess the risk of material misstatement. The chapter also discusses common inherent risks associated with the expenditure cycle. The most significant inherent risk is associated with unrecorded liabilities. Cash disbursements present an opportunity for misappropriation of assets. Additional inherent risk factors are discussed in the chapter.	pp. 691–692
D3. What are important inherent risks in the expenditure cycle?	Common inherent risks in the expenditure cycle include pressures to understate payables and expenses (completeness problems), vendors may be tardy in sending invoices (completeness problems), and the double payment of invoices (existence problems). In addition, the auditor may have to modify audit strategies to accommodate the client's use of electronic data interchange or electronic imaging systems.	pp. 692–695
D4. How might the results of analytical procedures indicate potential misstatements in the expenditure cycle?	Analytical procedures are both cost effective and often identify assertions that need audit attention. Figure 15-4 explains a number of analytical procedures that can be used in the expenditure cycle. Additional analytical procedures that use nonfinancial data are also explained in the chapter discussion.	p. 695
D5. What are the relevant aspects of internal control components for the expenditure cycle?	This section of the chapter reviews important aspects of the control environment, risk assessment, information and communication, and monitoring that are relevant to the expenditure cycle. It is important for students to understand the documents found in the information and communication system as these represent the audit trail. Figure 15-5 provides a flowchart depiction of the recording of purchases.	pp. 696–698
D6. What should be considered in evaluating control activities for purchase transactions?	Making a purchase involves initiating the purchase, receiving goods or services, and recording the purchase. This section explains the documents and records involved in recording credit sales. Figure 15-6 provides a series of example control activities that control each assertion related to recording purchases.	pp. 699–707

(continues)

Figure 15-12 ■ (Continued)

Audit Decision	Factors that Influence the Audit Decision	Chapter References
D7. What should be considered in evaluating control activities for cash disbursements transactions?	Figure 15-8 provides a flowchart depiction of the recording of cash disbursement in the consideration stage of a purchase transaction. Figure 15-7 provides a series of example control activities that control assertions related to cash disbursements.	pp. 707–711
D8. What should be considered in evaluating control activities for purchase adjustments?	Purchase adjustments are less frequent than purchases or cash disbursements, but may be material to the financial statement. The chapter discussion explains the documents and records involved in recording purchase adjustments and provides a series of example control activities that control assertions related to purchase adjustment transactions.	pp. 712–714
D9. What are the relevant aspects of tests of controls when the auditor plans to assess control risk below the maximum for expenditure cycle transactions?	Many of the control activities in the expenditure cycle involve programmed controls. In order for the auditor to assess control risk as low, the auditor needs to (1) test computer general controls, (2) test the computer application itself, and (3) test the effectiveness of manual followup activities. Examples of tests of computer application controls are provided in this chapter discussion.	p. 714
D10. What are the factors involved in determining acceptable level of tests of details risk for accounts payable assertions?	In determining the appropriate level of test of details risk, the auditor should consider inherent risk, control risk, and analytical procedures risk. This chapter discussion provides example discussions of each of these risk assessments, Figure 15-9, and the auditor's response in terms of preliminary audit strategy for each of the five basic financial statement assertions.	pp. 715–718
D11. How does the auditor determine the elements of an audit program for substantive tests to achieve specific audit objectives for accounts payable?	The development of an audit program for accounts payable uses the framework developed in Chapter 12 to design substantive tests for the expenditure cycle. Figure 15-10 focuses on the nature of substantive tests for the expenditure cycle. It summarizes the initial procedures, analytical procedures, tests of details of transactions, tests of details of balances, and tests of details of disclosures relevant to the expenditure cycle. The chapter discussion explores these tests in more detail.	pp. 718–725
D12. How does the auditor use the knowledge obtained during the audit of the expenditure cycle to support other assurance services?	Once the auditor has completed an audit of the expenditure cycle, the auditor should have information that supports an audit opinion as well as recommendations related to improvements in internal controls. In addition, the auditor probably has obtained knowledge that may be relevant to other assurance services. This final section of the chapter provides examples of how knowledge obtained while auditing the expenditure cycle can be used to support other assurance services.	pp. 725–726

objective questions

Objective questions are available for the student at www.wiley.com/college/boynton

comprehensive questions

15-21 **(Knowledge of the entity and its environment)** Your client is a local independent grocer with five stores who competes with a number of large grocery chains. It purchases goods from several large grocery supply chains as well as from various vendors that sell directly to the store. Some vendors offer various advertising rebates or other price concession for stocking goods.

Required

Explain how your knowledge of the business and industry would impact your audit of total purchases and accounts payable for the client.

15-22 **(Analytical Procedures)** In planning the audit of Construction Industry Resources, Inc., a building supply company, you have completed analytic procedures relevant to purchases and inventory. The results of these procedures are included in Exhibit 15-22.

EXHIBIT 15-22 SELECTED FINANCIAL INFORMATION ($000)

	X1	X2	X3	X4	X5
Building Supply Revenues	$ 90,100	$ 99,380	$ 117,468	$ 137,085	$ 160,800
Lumber Brokerage Revenues	$ –	$ –	$ 45,021	$ 63,480	$ 90,141
	$ 90,100	$ 99,380	$ 162,489	$ 200,564	$ 250,941
Inventory Turn Days					
Building Supplies	32	34	31	33	27
Lumber Brokerage			7	6	6
Gross Margin					
Building Supplies	20.1%	18.5%	18.6%	19.1%	18.0%
Lumber Brokerage			3.9%	4.1%	4.2%

Required

Analytical procedures show that inventory turnover decreased from 31–34 days to 27 days, and gross margins declined to the lowest level in five years. What might this indicate about the risk of misstatement with respect to inventory and inventory purchases?

15-23 The following information was taken from the accounting records for Aurora Manufacturing, Inc.:

	YEAR 5 UNAUDITED	YEAR 4 AUDITED	YEAR 3 AUDITED	YEAR 2 AUDITED	YEAR 1 AUDITED
Inventory	$ 525,000	$ 460,000	$ 390,000	$ 310,000	$ 225,000
Current Assets	$ 1,350,000	$ 1,175,000	$ 950,000	$ 750,000	$ 600,000
Accounts Payable	$ 115,000	$ 113,000	$ 97,500	$ 850,000	$ 70,000
Current Liabilities	$ 545,000	$ 535,000	$ 440,000	$ 380,000	$ 320,000
Sales	$ 2,700,000	$ 2,050,000	$ 1,750,000	$ 1,400,000	$ 1,200,000
Cost of Goods Sold	$ 1,650,000	$ 1,225,000	$ 1,025,000	$ 850,000	$ 725,000
Industry Median					
Accounts Payable Turn Days	31	30	29	30	
Cost of Goods Sold to Accounts Payable	10.7	11.2	10.9	11.1	
Current Asset to Current Liabilities	1.9	2.2	2.3	2.1	

Required

a. Calculate the following information and ratios for years 2, 3, 4, and 5:
- Purchases
- Accounts payable turn days
- Cost of goods sold to accounts payable
- Current ratio

b. Describe the implications of the resulting ratios for the auditor's audit strategy in year 5. What specific audit objectives are likely to be misstated? How should the auditor respond in terms of potential audit tests?

15-24   **(Internal control questionnaire—purchasing functions)** Green, CPA, has been engaged to audit the financial statements of Star Manufacturing, Inc. Star is a medium-sized entity that produces a wide variety of household goods. All acquisitions of materials are processed through the purchasing, receiving, accounts payable, and treasury functions.

Required

Prepare the purchase order and receiving segments of the internal control questionnaire to be used in the evaluation of Star's internal control structure. Each question should elicit either a *Yes* or *No* response.

Do not prepare segments of the internal control questionnaire for other functions.

Do not discuss the internal controls over purchases.

AICPA (adapted)

15-25   **(Internal control evaluation—receiving function)** Dunbar Camera Manufacturing, Inc. is a manufacturer of high-priced precision motion picture cameras in which the specifications of component parts are vital to the manufacturing process. Dunbar buys valuable camera lenses and large quantities of sheetmetal and screws. Screws and lenses are ordered by Dunbar and are billed by the vendors on a unit basis. Sheetmetal is ordered by Dunbar and billed by the vendors on the basis of weight. The receiving clerk is responsible for documenting the quality and quantity of merchandise received.

Your understanding of the internal control structure indicates that the following procedures are being followed:

1. *Receiving.* Information from properly approved purchase orders, which are prenumbered, is stored in the computer. The receiving clerk has access to all the information on the purchase order sent to the vendor. The receiving clerk records receipts of merchandise on a computer form that matches the purchase order.

2. *Sheetmetal.* The company receives sheetmetal by railroad. The railroad independently weighs the sheetmetal and reports the weight and date of receipt on a bill of lading (waybill), which accompanies all deliveries. The receiving clerk only checks the weight on the waybill against purchase order information in the computer.

3. *Screws.* The receiving clerk opens cartons containing screws, then inspects and weighs the contents. The weight is converted to number of units by means of conversion charts. The receiving clerk then compares the computed quantity to the purchase order information in the computer.

4. *Camera lenses.* Each camera lens is delivered in a separate corrugated carton. Cartons are counted as they are received by the receiving clerk, and the number of cartons is compared to purchase order information in the computer.

Required

a. Explain why the internal control procedures as they apply individually to receiving reports and the receipts of sheetmetal, screws, and camera lenses are adequate or inadequate. Do not discuss recommendations for improvements.

b. For inadequacies in internal controls describe the financial statement misstatements that may arise, and describe how they may occur.

AICPA (adapted)

15-26   **(Internal control evaluation—purchasing and cash disbursements)** In 20X4 XY Company purchased over $10 million of office equipment under its "special" ordering systems, with individual orders ranging from $5,000 to $30,000. "Special" orders entail low-volume items that have been included in an authorized user's budget. Department heads include in their annual budget requests the types and dollar amounts of office equipment and their estimated cost. The budget, which limits the types and dollar amounts of office equipment a department head can requisition, is approved at the beginning of the year by the board of directors. Department heads prepare a purchase requisition form for equipment and forward the requisition to the purchasing department. XY's "special" ordering system functions as follows:

Purchasing: Upon receiving a purchase requisition, one of five buyers verifies that the person requesting the equipment is a department head. The buyer then selects the appropriate vendor by searching the various vendor catalogues on file. The buyer then phones the vendor, requesting a price quotation, and gives the vendor a verbal order. A prenumbered purchase order is then processed with the original sent to the vendor, and the purchase order information is stored in the computer and can be accessed by purchasing, receiving, and accounts payable. When the goods are received, the order is electronically transferred from the unfilled order file to the filled order file. Once a month the buyer reviews the unfilled order file to follow up and expedite open orders.

Receiving. The receiving department can access a copy of the purchase order. When equipment is received, the receiving clerk accesses the purchase order electronically and changes the purchase order for any difference between quantity on the purchase order and quantity received, which upon submission electronically becomes the receiving file. The computer system notifies the requisitioning department and purchasing department of the receipt.

Accounts Payable. The computer system maintains an open purchase order file. When a vendor's invoice is received, the invoice is entered into the computer, matched with the applicable purchase order, and a payable is set up by debiting the equipment account of the department requesting the items. Unpaid invoices are electronically stored in an open invoice file that includes information on due dates. Daily a report is run of payables due by date, and at the due date a check is prepared. The vendor's invoice is then filed with the purchase order in purchase order number in a paid invoice file, and the check is forwarded to the treasurer for signature.

Treasurer. Checks received daily from the accounts payable department are sorted into two groups—those greater than $10,000 and those $10,000 and less. Checks for $10,000 and less are machine signed. The cashier maintains the key and signature plate to the check-signing machines, and maintains a record of usage of the check-signing machine. All checks over $10,000 are signed by the treasurer or the controller.

Required

Describe the internal control weaknesses relating to the purchases and payments of "special" orders of XY Company for each of the following functions:

a. Purchasing

b. Receiving

c. Accounts payable

d. Cash disbursements

15-27   **(Internal control evaluation—cash disbursements)** Management has requested a review of internal control over cash disbursements for parts and supplies purchased at manufacturing plants. Cash disbursements are centrally processed at corporate headquarters based on disbursement vouchers prepared and approved at the manufacturing plants. Each manufacturing plant purchases parts and supplies for its own production needs.

In response to management's request, a thorough evaluation of internal control over disbursements for manufacturing plant purchases of parts and supplies is being planned. As a preliminary step in planning the engagement, each plant manager has been requested to provide a written description of his or her plant's procedures for processing disbursement vouchers for parts and supplies. Presented below are some excerpts from one of the written descriptions.

1. The purchasing department acts on purchase requisitions issued by the stores department.

2. A computer system generates prenumbered purchase orders based on information submitted by buyers in purchasing.

3. Receiving has complete access to purchase order information in the computer.

4. When goods are received, the receiving department logs the shipment in the computer by indicating that the purchase order was received and forwards this electronically to accounts payable.

5. When the vendor invoice is received, it is entered into the computer and matched electronically with purchase order and receiving information. Discrepancies are printed on an exception report for followup by accounts payable personnel.

6. The computer checks the clerical accuracy of information on vendor invoices. Discrepancies are printed on an exception report for followup by accounts payable personnel.

7. A prenumbered disbursement is prepared and forwarded along with supporting documentation to the plant controller, who reviews and approves the voucher.

8. Supporting documents are returned to accounts payable for filing, and approved disbursement vouchers are forwarded to corporate headquarters for payment.

9. A report listing checks issued by corporate headquarters is received and promptly filed by accounts payable.

Required

For each of the disbursement system procedures listed above, state whether the procedure is consistent with good internal control and describe how each procedure strengthens or weakens internal control.

CONSISTENT/ INCONSISTENT	STRENGTHENS OR WEAKENS
1. (Example) Consistent	Purchase requisitions provide the authorization for purchasing to order.

15-28 **(Accounts payable assertions/confirmations)** Mincin, CPA, is the auditor of the Raleigh Corporation. Mincin is considering the audit work to be performed in the accounts payable area for the current year's engagement. The prior year's papers show that confirmation requests were mailed to 100 of Raleigh's 1,000 suppliers. The selected suppliers were based on Mincin's sample that was designed to select accounts with large dollar balances. A substantial number of hours were spent by Raleigh and Mincin resolving relatively minor differences between the confirmation replies and Raleigh's accounting records. Alternative auditing procedures were used for those suppliers who did not respond to the confirmation requests.

Required

a. Identify the accounts payable assertions that Mincin must consider in determining the substantive tests to be followed.

b. Identify situations when Mincin should use accounts payable confirmations and discuss whether Mincin is required to use them.

c. Discuss why the use of large dollar balances as the basis for selecting accounts payable for confirmation might not be the most efficient approach and indicate what more efficient procedures could be followed when selecting accounts payable for confirmation.

AICPA (adapted)

15-29   **(Search for unrecorded liabilities)** You were in the final stages of your audit of the financial statements of Ozine Corporation for the year ended December 31, 20X0, when you were consulted by the corporation's president, who believes there is no point in your examining the 20X1 voucher register and testing data in support of 20X1 entries. He stated that (a) bills pertaining to 20X0 that were received too late to be included in the December voucher register were recorded as of the year-end by the corporation by journal entry, (b) the internal auditor made tests after the year-end, and (c) he would furnish you with a letter certifying that there were no unrecorded liabilities.

Required

a. Should a CPA's test for unrecorded liabilities be affected by the fact that the client made a journal entry to record 20X0 bills that were received late? Explain.

b. Should a CPA's test for unrecorded liabilities be affected by the fact that a letter is obtained in which a responsible management official certifies that to the best of his knowledge all liabilities have been recorded? Explain.

c. Should a CPA's test for unrecorded liabilities be eliminated or reduced because of the internal audit tests? Explain.

d. Assume that the corporation, which handled some government contracts, had no internal auditor but that an auditor for a federal agency spent three weeks auditing the records and was just completing his work at this time. How would the CPA's unrecorded liability test be affected by the work of the auditor for a federal agency?

e. What sources in addition to the 20X1 voucher register should the CPA consider to locate possible unrecorded liabilities?

AICPA

15-30   **(Substantive tests for accounts payable)** Taylor CPA is engaged in the audit of Rex Wholesaling for the year ended December 31, 20X2. Taylor performed a proper study of the internal control structure relating to the purchasing, receiving, trade accounts payable, and cash disbursement cycles, and has decided not to proceed with tests of controls. Based on analytical review procedures, Taylor believes that the trade accounts payable balance on the balance sheet as of December 31, 20X2 may be understated. Taylor requested and obtained a client-prepared trade accounts payable schedule listing the total amount owed to each vendor.

Required

What additional substantive auditing procedures should Taylor apply in auditing the trade accounts payable?

AICPA

15-31   **(Understanding Internal Controls, Fraud Risk Assessment, and Substantive Tests)**

Phase I

Company Background

Construction Industry Resources, Inc. (CIRI), a C Corporation, supplies building material to contractors and construction sites in a major metropolitan area. Today, CIRI has approximately $60 million in total assets and generates approximately $250 million in annual revenues. Les Browning, the majority shareholder, purchased CIRI five years ago when sales were approximately $90 million per year and it was only in the building supply business. Les Browning owns 70 percent of CIRI, a business associate who is not active in the operation of the business owns 10 percent of the business, and two family members (Les Browning's father and his brother) own 10 percent each. The other shareholders hold management positions in other businesses (not in the construction industry) and are not active in day-to-day management. Five years ago Les owned only 55 percent of the business, and he purchased 5 percent from each of the other shareholders based on an independent valuation of the business two years ago. Eventually Les plans to purchase 100 percent of the common stock outstanding, sometime in the next five years. Les has prided himself on his ability to grow sales and profits of the company, and he looks forward to another 10 to 15 years of running the company, and enjoying the benefits of ownership, before considering an exit strategy and retirement.

The board of directors is composed of the four shareholders, a representative of CIRI's major lender, the corporation's attorney, and its controller, Craig Ferris. The board of directors meets semiannually to review the company's performance and make decisions regarding officer bonuses and dividends. Unlike public companies, CIRI does not have an audit committee. An audit is needed for the bank and other creditors, and the auditor meets annually with the board as a whole.

CIRI is composed of two major divisions; one division is involved in the purchase and sale of lumber, building materials, hardware, and related products. The other division is a lumber brokerage business. The building supply division competes in a very competitive business environment where business must be earned on both price competitiveness and on quality of service. The building supply division has three retail/wholesale outlets in a major metropolitan area of approximately 2 million people. The lumber brokerage business is also extremely price competitive. As a result, the company operates on relatively high ratios of sales to total assets (high asset turnover), and profit margins are low.

When Les Browning came to CIRI, he had a strong sales background and he focused first on customer relations and building sales in the building supply business, paying attention to CIRI's relationships with the major general contractors and builders in the community. Les knew that profit margins were going to be thin, so he focused his energies on growing sales volume. Then three years ago he decided to launch the lumber brokerage division, which allowed CIRI direct access to lumber markets as well as allowing the company to continue a strong growth trend in total revenues.

Craig Ferris has been CIRI's controller for 30 years, and he continued with the company when Les Browning and his other shareholders acquired it. Les Browning is comfortable with Craig's skills and knows that he will have to increase the salary for the position to hire a replacement when Craig retires. Craig, while not a CPA, has a competent understanding of GAAP and knows many of the suppliers and general contractors in the construction business. In addition to completing monthly income statements and balance sheets for the company, Craig has paid a great deal of attention in recent years to the lumber brokerage business, particularly understanding and attempting to control the business risks associated with price volatility in the lumber markets.

Craig also reviews each store's overall performance when the financial statements are prepared each month, but the company does not have sufficient staff or time to develop budgets. Accountability for store performance is very informal. Store managers are paid competitive salaries, but they receive no bonuses. Hence, accounting numbers do not play in the determination of store managers' compensation packages. Furthermore, Craig Ferris and Les Browning feel that it would be too time consuming to develop budgets that reflect the seasonal nature of the business, and they feel that interim financial statements are sufficient to control the business.

You have been assigned to the audit of the building supplies division, specifically the purchases cycle, which consists primarily of the acquisition of inventories (many of which are delivered directly to building sites), the inventory cycle, and accounts payable.

Analytical Procedures

The information needed for analytical procedures is provided in Question 15-22.

Information and Communication and Control Activities

With respect to the accounting system and control activities, Les Browning has been rather hands off, focusing his attention on sales growth and lumber brokerage. He has been satisfied with Craig Ferris's ability to produce income numbers within 15 to 20 days after month-end, and he has relied on the annual audit to ensure that the accounting system is working correctly. In past audits, Les and Craig have accepted auditor-proposed journal entries related to the allowance for doubtful accounts and inventory shrinkage (a perpetual problem in the construction industry), but routine transactions have not resulted in significant audit problems. Three ongoing issues have been raised in prior management letters:

1. There is a segregation of duties problem in cash disbursements as Craig Ferris has access to the supply of unused checks, he signs checks, and performs the monthly bank reconciliations.

2. A similar segregation of duties issue has been raised regarding the activities of Wendy Roberts who authorizes credit, maintains accounts receivable records, and follows up on bad debts. However, Craig Ferris has responsibility for writing off bad debts.

3. There is no formal system and review associated with adding new vendors or new customers to master vendor and customer files.

Les Browning and other owners have not taken action on these issues because no significant audit adjustments have been proposed related to these problems. The owners have viewed the audit adjustments to the allowance for doubtful accounts as an issue where they welcome the oversight provided by outside auditors regarding an important accounting estimate.

The major change in the accounting system was planned last year and implemented at the beginning of the current year (20X5) when one of CIRI's major suppliers, Contractors Wholesale Supply (CWS), approached CIRI about implementing a purchasing system with electronic data interchange (EDI). Les Browning was eager to move forward with the system as it would keep CIRI on the cutting edge. In general, the EDI system allows CIRI to order goods electronically, CWS sends electronic sales invoices, and CIRI makes weekly payments by electronic funds transfer. Les Browning sees that the process will expedite shipments to customers, and CIRI would receive a 1 percent discount on all shipments ordered through the system. Craig Ferris was also willing to make the change since only modest computer programming changes were necessary at CIRI and a significant portion of the operating system was resident on the supplier's system.

Craig delegated implementation of the EDI system to Dennis Brewer. Dennis has been with the company for several years and has demonstrated strong technology skills. He was also responsible for accounts payable and accounting for inventories. Dennis looked at the systems project as a real opportunity to demonstrate his skills. Disappointed that he had not advanced faster in the organization, he had commented to colleagues about his frustration that most of his college friends had achieved management roles in their jobs, and they were earning good salaries and bonuses. Dennis has several children in private school and felt that this was his opportunity to earn advancement, status, and the salary he wanted and needed.

Following is a brief description of how the new EDI purchasing system functions at CIRI:

Initiating Purchases. Several buyers are responsible for purchasing inventory, managing store inventories, and making sales to general contractors and the larger builders in the metropolitan area. The buyers determine inventory to order based on their review of inventory on hand and requests from customers. Based on perceived inventory needs, the buyer can log onto the CSW/CIRI system using passwords and electronically place a CIRI prenumbered purchase order directly with CWS on an on-line, real-time basis. CWS confirms the order electronically, and an electronic sales order is sent from CWS to Dennis Brewer. Dennis Brewer receives exception reports each morning of any mismatches between CIRI purchase orders and CWS sales orders. (CWS writes sales orders based on inventory that they have in stock.) Dennis tracks all purchases based on the prenumbered purchase orders. Buyers have restricted access to only the order side of the system (buyers can also monitor all inventory quantities). Receiving access has been given only to the warehouse clerks at each store. Dennis Brewer has full access to the system.

Receiving Goods. When shipments are received from CWS, they are counted by the warehouse clerk at each of CIRI's three stores. The clerk then logs into the CWS/CIRI and enters quantities received in the electronic equivalent of a prenumbered receiving report. The electronic receiving report is sent from each store to Dennis Brewer. Furthermore, approximately 35 percent of purchases are drop shipped directly to customer locations. In other words, a building contractor will call a CIRI buyer, who will order the goods from CWS and have them shipped directly to the building site. The warehouse clerk at each store has responsibility for following up on drop shipments with customers and filing electronic receiving reports for drop shipments. Experience shows that this is a low priority for these warehouse clerks, and it often takes nagging by Dennis Brewer each week to get these reports filed. This was a problem in the manual system in that on-site project managers were not good about signing delivery reports. When the warehouse clerk at the responsible store files an electronic receiving report for drop shipments, the clerk also has responsibility for filing a shipping report to initiate CIRI's customer billing process.

The receiving information updates the perpetual inventory records for all items received at one of the three stores. The perpetual inventory is not updated for drop shipments. The buyers informally review the accuracy of the perpetual inventory for reasonableness. A full physical inventory is done at year-end, and the stores are closed for that event.

Recording Payables. When CWS ships goods, an invoice is electronically sent to Dennis Brewer. Each day Dennis receives a computer-generated report of items that have been ordered from CWS, a report of items ordered that have not been received, and a list of all billings that have not been matched with prenumbered receiving reports. Dennis pays the most attention to these reports on Wednesdays and Thursdays so that all billings are cleared for electronic payment on Friday. He particularly follows up on items where electronic invoices have been received from CWS that have not yet been matched with receiving reports sent from the stores. He then files these exception reports by date with his notations on the various reports. Once the electronic receiving report is electronically matched with the sales invoice, a payable is established and Dennis Brewer approves payment of the invoice.

Electronic Funds Transfer. Every Friday, the total of approved invoices is paid via electronic funds transfer from CIRI to CWS. Craig Ferris is responsible for reviewing and approving a list of cash disbursements before they are run. With respect to the EDI system, Craig performs an overall reasonableness check on the volume of activity with CWS.

Craig Ferris feels that the system has greatly reduced the paperwork, made the office more efficient, and allowed the company to maintain margins in a very competitive marketplace. Dennis Brewer was happy to work on the project and was pleased to be given the increased responsibility. However, Dennis was overheard in the lunchroom to have been disappointed that neither pay nor promotion advances were received as he expected, and that he is not earning what he deserves. Dennis expressed frustration that his career was going nowhere and that Craig Ferris and Les Browning were too tight fisted with promotion and recognition for the transition to go smoothly.

Required

1. Evaluate the effectiveness of the CIRI's control environment. You may evaluate each individual component of the control environment, but then develop an overall conclusion regarding the control environment and its influence on other aspects of internal control.

2. Analytical procedures show that inventory turnover decreased from 31–34 days to 27 days, and gross margins declined to the lowest level in five years. What might this indicate about the risk of misstatement with respect to inventory and inventory purchases?

3. a. Using the table below, evaluate the factors associated with the risk of fraud and the effectiveness of control activities with respect to the existence and occurrence assertion associated with the EDI purchasing system.

FRAUD RISK FACTORS

ASSERTION	INCENTIVES/ PRESSURES	OPPORTUNITY	ATTITUDE & RATIONALIZATION	CONTROL ACTIVITIES	POSSIBLE MISSTATEMENTS
Existence and occurrence of purchases and payables					

   b. Identify reportable conditions that you might identify in the EDI purchasing system.

4. Prepare a letter with the two most important internal control recommendations that you have for management. Each specific recommendation should describe the current system, explain the risk involved, and make specific recommendations for improvement. Focus on issues raised by the new system and not on issues that have been raised in prior audits.

Phase II

When obtaining an understanding of the accounting system, you looked at the file containing the exception reports reviewed by Dennis Brewer (e.g, for items billed but not received). While these reports are printed daily, often only three or four reports would be present for a given week. Dennis said that he really pays attention to the reports primarily on Wednesday and Thursday and that he often does not keep the reports from earlier in the week.

   Subsequently, you pulled a sample of 30 transactions from the EDI system to perform substantive tests of transactions and test the accuracy of recording transactions that are processed through the system. Of the 30 transactions selected at random, 19 represented transactions shipped directly to stores, and 11 represented drop shipments. The following exhibit summarizes the nature of this sample of 30.

SUMMARY INFORMATION REGARDING SUBSTANTIVE TESTS OF TRANSACTIONS

	$ BV OF POPN.	# OF TRANSACTIONS	SAMPLE SIZE	$ BV OF SAMPLE
Drop Shipments	$ 5,756,077	1,391	11	$ 80,530
Shipped to Stores	$ 10,615,018	1,737	19	$ 188,455
Purchases through the EDI System	$ 16,371,095	3,128	30	$ 268,985

You noted the following issues among the 30 transactions.

■ You find one item that shipped directly to the stores with an invoice total of $9,775 where one of the items on the invoice had a price per the purchase order of $67 per unit and it was billed at $76 per unit. The company purchased 100 units of the SKU number on that invoice and paid the invoice in full as billed.

■ The company was closed from Thursday June 30, 20X5 through Monday, July 4, 20X5. Inventory was taken on Thursday, June 30, 20X5. During the inventory count, a truck came in with a shipment from BCWSC. The value of the invoice was $9,875. The units were segregated from the rest of the inventory and not counted. At the end of the inventory, the shipment was added to the overall value of the inventory. During the closing of the books after July 4, the purchase was recorded as an accounts payable in the amount of $9,875 with a date of June 30, 20X5.

■ Auditing drop shipments has been a problem in past audits, as CIRI has not always had receiving documents to support deliveries to construction sites. However, your firm has been able to verify that shipments had been billed to customers, and subsequently cash was received associated with these deliveries. In the current year not only did you verify that the item was supported by electronic receiving reports, but you also followed up to find that they were billed to customers who paid for the goods. All 11 of the electronic invoices from BCWSC for drop shipments included in the sample were supported by electronic receiving reports, and they were paid in the correct amounts and on time. However, Dennis Brewer could not show where one transaction with an invoice amount of $4,323 had been billed to, and had been paid by, customers. He suggested two possibilities. First, he suggested that some customers had prepaid for the shipments. Second, he complained that he often had to follow up with the stores about filing receiving reports because someone at the store level failed to file a shipping report. However, his primary responsibility was only for the purchasing system, not the billing system and ensuring that vendors were paid on time. He could not verify what caused the problem with this transaction. Further followup failed to identify the underlying sales invoice for this transaction.

Required

5. What concerns, if any, are raised by the evidence noted above? Assuming that the problems found in the sample are representative of problems in the population, determine any relevant amount of projected misstatement based on your finding assuming that the ratio of misstatements to book value found in the strata from which they were selected are representative of the entire strata. After considering your findings, what additional audit procedures should be performed, if any?

6. What issues do you want to discuss with management? Draft the issues that you want to discuss with company management, including who in management discussions should be held with.

professional simulations

You have just been assigned to the audit of a new manufacturing client, Carroll Manufacturing Inc. (CMI) and the in-charge accountant on the engagement. CMI manufactures automobile engines which are sold to several automotive companies. CMI purchases raw steel and cast iron. CMI does its own tool and die work, but it still purchases a number of parts related to carburetion and ignition systems.

RATIO	UNAUDITED RATIO	AUDITOR'S EXPECTATION RANGE
Accounts Payable Turn Days	27 days	32 days – 38 days
Inventory Turn Days	55 days	58 days – 64 days
Gross Margin	48%	42% – 46%
Sales and Accounts Payable	Sales Growth: 7%	Sales Growth: 6% – 9%
Growth Rates	Accounts Payable Growth: 4%	Accounts Payable Growth: 6%–9%

The table above provides some preliminary information obtained during audit planning for CMI. Write a memo to the audit file explaining the planning implications associated with the audit findings above. Identify assertions that are likely to be overstated or understated.

To: Audit File

Re: Analytical procedures

From: CPA Candidate

Assertion

A. Existence and Occurrence

B. Completeness

C. Rights and Obligations

D. Valuation or Allocation

E. Presentation and Disclosure

Identify the appropriate assertion for each of the following internal controls. Check all that apply.

Internal Control	(A)	(B)	(C)	(D)	(E)
1. The computer matches the customer number on the voucher with the customer number on the master customer file.	○	○	○	○	○
2. Only the controller and the assistant controller have the authority to add a new vendor to the vendor master file.	○	○	○	○	○
3. The computer checks batch totals and run-to-run totals to ensure that all transactions are processed.	○	○	○	○	○

	Internal Control	(A)	(B)	(C)	(D)	(E)
4.	The manager of engine production reviews all purchases charged to his responsibility center on a weekly basis, reviewing vendors, amounts, and accounts charged.	○	○	○	○	○
5.	The computer matches the date on the receiving report with the accounting period when the voucher is recorded.	○	○	○	○	○
6.	The computer prints a report of all purchase orders that have not been received and receivings that have not resulted in the recording of a voucher.	○	○	○	○	○

Situation	Analytical Procedures	Internal Controls	Audit Procedures

Audit procedure

A. Vouch accounts payable credits to supporting vouchers, vendor invoices, receiving reports, and purchase orders and other supporting information.

B. Obtain an understanding of the business and industry and determine the significance of purchases and accounts payable to the entity.

C. Inquire of management about existence of undisclosed commitments or contingent liabilities.

D. Trace a sample of cash receipts transactions from cash receipts journal to the general ledger.

E. Vouch debit memos to underlying shipping reports and vendor's authorizations.

F. Obtain listing of accounts payable at balance sheet date and determine that it accurately represents the underlying accounting records by footing the listing and determining agreement with (1) the total of the unpaid voucher file, subsidiary ledger, or accounts payable master file, and (2) the general ledger control account balance.

G. Observe the number of the last receiving report issued on the last business day of the audit period and trace sample of lower and higher numbered receiving reports to related purchase documents and determine that transactions were recorded in the proper period.

H. Trace dates of "paid" checks returned with year-end cut-off bank statements to dates recorded.

I. Determine that payables are properly identified and classified as to type and expected period of payment.

J. Examine subsequent payments between balance sheet date and end of field work, and when related documentation indicates payment was for obligation in existence at balance sheet date, trace to accounts payable listing.

Determine the audit procedure that best addresses the following risks.

Risk	(A)	(B)	(C)	(D)	(E)	(F)	(G)	(H)	(I)	(J)
1. Recorded purchases may not represent goods received during the year.	O	O	O	O	O	O	O	O	O	O
2. Cash disbursements may not be recorded in the proper time period.	O	O	O	O	O	O	O	O	O	O
3. All purchases (and payables) during the period may not be recorded.	O	O	O	O	O	O	O	O	O	O
4. Accounts payable might be understated due to the recording of invalid purchase returns.	O	O	O	O	O	O	O	O	O	O
5. The auditor may not have complete information about individual accounts payable that make up the general ledger balance.	O	O	O	O	O	O	O	O	O	O

[16] AUDITING THE PRODUCTION AND PERSONNEL SERVICES CYCLES

OVERSTATING INVENTORY AND PROFITS

Auditing history abounds with stories of companies that have made material overstatements of inventory and profits. In the 1930s McKesson and Robbins materially overstated its salad oil inventory. This accounting fraud was so significant that generally accepted auditing standards were changed to require inventory observations. Nevertheless, inventory problems have continued.

In recent years, Phar-Mor intentionally overstated its inventory by reallocating losses into inventory. Company employees created fake invoices for merchandise purchases, made unsupported journal entries to increase inventory and decrease cost of goods sold, and overcounted and double-counted merchandise. When this fraud unraveled, the CFO was sentenced to 33 months in prison, the CEO went to jail for five years, and the auditors paid millions to shareholders.

Not all overstatements of inventories are intentional. In November of 2000 the senior management of NCI Building Systems, Inc., began to question its Components Division about high levels of inventory. The purchasing department was instructed to halt steel purchases, and yet inventory levels did not decrease as expected. Ultimately, errors stemmed from a new accounting system that was not adequately tested before being placed in operation and from poor internal controls. In an attempt to "fix" known errors in the accounting system, an employee made unsupported journal entries that resulted in increases in inventory accounts. Then the corporate controller booked a $2.6 million journal entry to increase inventory and decrease cost of goods sold based on representations from an account manager. The inventory was further overstated owing to inaccurate standard costs that capitalized waste scrap metal as inventory costs rather than expensing costs that were never associated with inventory production. This resulted in inventory being overstated by another $7.6 million of inventory. In total, internal control breakdowns resulted in restating earnings by approximately $18 million.

Chapter 16 discusses important audit planning procedures related to inventory audits, the components of a sound system of internal controls over inventory, and steps that should be taken by auditors to audit inventory. In addition, this chapter also explores issues related to the personnel services cycle, which are often an important component of manufactured inventory.

Sources: Joseph T. Wells, "Ghost Goods: How to Spot Phantom Inventory," *Journal of Accountancy,* June 2001, and Accounting and Auditing Enforcement Release 1892, October 9, 2003.

[PREVIEW OF CHAPTER 16]

Chapter 16 continues the discussion of operating activities by focusing on the production process. It first discusses audit planning, internal controls, and substantive tests related to the production of inventory. This is followed by a discussion of payroll costs. The following diagram provides an overview of the chapter organization and content.

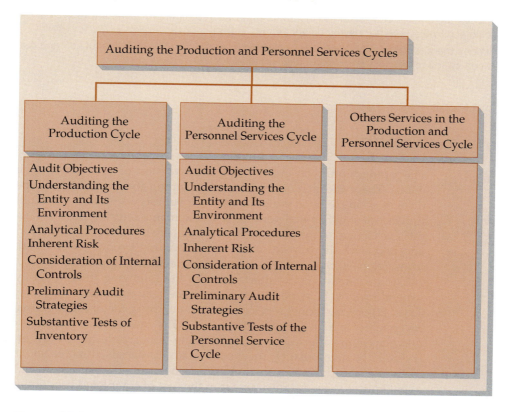

Chapter 16 focuses on the following aspects of the auditor's decision process associated with the production and personnel services cycles.

focus on audit decisions

After studying this chapter you should understand the factors that influence the following audit decisions.

D1. What is the nature of the production cycle, and how are specific audit objectives developed for the production cycle?

D2. What audit planning decisions should be made when developing an audit program for the production cycle?

D3. What should be considered in evaluating control activities for the production cycle transactions?

D4. What factors are involved in determining an acceptable level of tests of details risk for inventory assertions?

D5. How does the auditor determine the elements of an audit program for substantive tests to achieve specific audit objectives for inventory?

D6. What is the nature of the personnel services cycle, and how are specific audit objectives developed for the personnel services cycle?

D7. What audit planning decisions should be made when developing an audit program for the personnel services cycle?

D8. What should be considered in evaluating control activities for personnel services cycle transactions?

D9. What factors are involved in determining an acceptable level of tests of details risk for payroll balance assertions?

D10. How does the auditor determine the elements of an audit program for substantive tests to achieve specific audit objectives for payroll balances?

D11. How does the auditor use the knowledge obtained during the audit of the production and personnel services cycles to support other assurance services?

AUDITING THE PRODUCTION CYCLE

Audit Decision 1

■ **What is the nature of the production cycle, and how are specific audit objectives developed for the production cycle?**

The **production cycle** relates to the conversion of raw materials into finished goods. This cycle includes production planning and control of the types and quantities of goods to be manufactured, the inventory levels to be maintained, and the transactions and events pertaining to the manufacturing process. Transactions in this cycle begin at the point where raw materials are requisitioned for production, and end with the transfer of the manufactured product to finished goods. The transactions in this cycle are called **manufacturing transactions.**

The production cycle interfaces with the following three other cycles: (1) the expenditure cycle in purchasing raw materials and incurring various overhead costs, (2) the personnel services cycle in incurring factory labor costs, and (3) the revenue cycle in selling finished goods. The interaction of these cycles and the major accounts affected by manufacturing transactions are shown in Figure 16-1. It should be noted that (1) the credits to raw materials, direct labor, and manufacturing overhead; (2) the debits to work-in-process inventory; and (3) the subsequent entries to record the transfer of the cost of completed production from work in process to finished goods, result from manufacturing transactions in the production cycle. Finally, although usually considered a revenue cycle transaction, the transfer of costs from manufactured finished goods to cost of goods sold is based on cost data accumulated in the production cycle.

AUDIT OBJECTIVES

The specific audit objectives for the audit of the production cycle are presented in Figure 16-2. Each objective is derived from management's implicit or explicit assertions about investing cycle transactions as they relate to the production of inventory. These objectives are the primary ones for this cycle in most audits. They are not intended to be all-inclusive for all client situations.

Two groups of audit objectives are addressed in this section: (1) transaction class audit objectives pertaining to manufacturing transactions and cost of sales and (2) account balance audit objectives pertaining to inventory. To avoid redundancy, discussion of account balance audit objectives and related audit procedures for purchased inventories was deferred in the expenditure cycle in favor of joint coverage in this chapter with manufactured inventories. Similarly, discussion of audit objectives and related audit procedures for cost of goods sold was deferred

Figure 16-1 ■ Interface of Production Cycle with Other Cycles

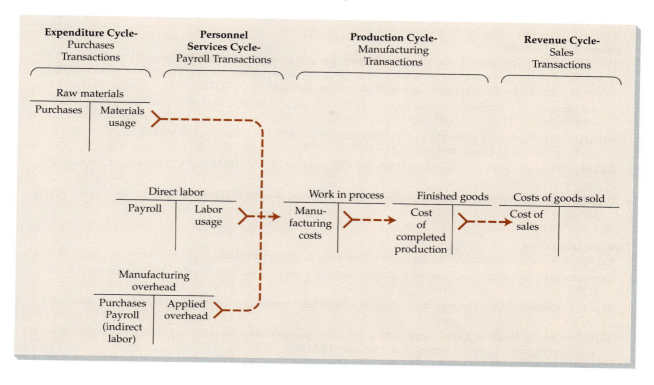

in the revenue cycle chapter pending coverage of the origin of such costs through purchases transactions in the expenditure cycle chapter and manufacturing transactions in this chapter. Thus, some of the evidence obtained in connection with objectives related to purchases and sales transactions in Chapters 15 and 14, respectively, is relevant to meeting the account balance audit objectives identified in Figure 16-2.

UNDERSTANDING THE ENTITY AND ITS ENVIRONMENT

Audit Decision 2

■ What audit planning decisions should be made when developing an audit program for the production cycle?

Understanding the business and industry assists in developing a knowledgeable perspective about the entity that is used to design an effective and efficient audit program. For many companies manufacturing inventory is a core process, and the ability of the entity to generate earnings and cash flows depends on how well the manufacturing process is managed. For many distribution and retailing companies, the management of inventory and its supply chain is critical to successful performance.

Throughout Part 4 of the text we have followed five industries and the importance of each cycle to the industry. Inventories are immaterial to two of these industries, the hotel industry and the school district. These are service industries, and the audit of inventory is usually insignificant to overall audit strategy for companies in either industry. However, in the audit of the retail grocer, the manufacturer of construction machinery and equipment, and the computer manufacturer, the audit of inventory is a core process that is both material and crucial to

Figure 16-2 ■ Selected Specific Audit Objectives for Inventory

Specific Audit Objectives

Transaction Objectives

Occurrence. Recorded manufacturing transactions represent material, labor, and overhead transferred to production and the movement to completed production to finished goods during the current period **(EO1)**. Recorded cost of sales represent the sale of inventory during the year **(EO2)**.

Completeness. All manufacturing transactions **(C1)** and cost of sales **(C2)** that occurred during the period were recorded.

Accuracy. Manufacturing transactions **(VA1)** and cost of sales **(VA2)** are accurately valued using GAAP and correctly journalized, summarized, and posted.

Cutoff. All manufacturing transactions **(EO1 and C1)** and cost of sales **(EO2 and C2)** have been recorded in the correct accounting period.

Classification. All manufacturing transactions **(PD1)** and cost of sales **(PD2)** have been recorded in the proper accounts.

Balance Objectives

Existence. Inventories included in the balance sheet physically exist **(EO3)**.

Completeness. Inventories include all materials, products, and supplies on hand at the balance sheet date **(C3)**.

Rights and Obligations. The reporting entity has legal title to recorded inventories at the balance sheet date **(RO1)**.

Valuation and Allocation. Inventories costing assumptions have been properly applied **(VA3),** and inventories are properly stated at the lower of cost or market **(VA4)**.

Disclosure Objectives

Occurrence and Rights and Obligations. Disclosed inventory transactions and balances have occurred and pertain to the entity **(PD3)**.

Completeness. All inventory disclosures that should have been included in the financial statements have been included **(PD4)**.

Classification and Understandability. Production cycle information is appropriately presented and described and information in disclosures is clearly expressed **(PD5)**.

Accuracy and Valuation. Inventory information is disclosed accurately and at appropriate amounts **(PD6)**.

the entity's success. When auditing a manufacturing company, the auditor will usually want to understand the capital intensiveness of the manufacturing process, as well as the mix of raw materials and labor that are needed in the manufacturing process. A particularly capital-intensive process, such as the manufacturing of construction equipment, will usually have a significant fixed cost that needs sufficient volume to ensure profitability. Figure 16-3 summarizes some key data for these industries.

ANALYTICAL PROCEDURES

Analytical procedures are cost effective and may alert the auditor to potential misstatements. If the financial statements presented for audit show a trend of increased profit margin combined with an increase in the number of inventory turn days, inventory may be overstated. This will alert the auditor to pay careful

Figure 16-3 ■ Understanding an Entity's Production Cycle

Example Industry Traits	Developing a Knowledgeable Perspective about the Entity's Financial Statements (Industry Median)	Assessing the Risk of Material Misstatement
Mfg. of Construction Machinery and Equipment • Relatively slow inventory turn. • Significant fixed costs are involved in the manufacturing process.	Inventory as a % of Total Assets: 35% Inventory Turn Days: 85 days Gross Margin: 28.7%	• The existence of inventory is a significant risk. • Products are not subject to significant obsolescence risk.
Computer Mfg. • Moderate inventory turn. • Gross margins depend on the technological superiority of products. • Companies outsource significant aspects of production and assemble more than manufacture products.	Inventory as a % of Total Assets: 25.3% Inventory Turn Days: 60 days Gross Margin: 34.4%	• Some inventory on hand may, in economic substance, be consignment inventory due to pricing terms. • The existence of inventory is a significant inherent risk. • The valuation of inventory is a significant inherent risk due to the technical obsolescence issue.
Retail Grocer • Very competitive environment and one product may be substituted easily for other products.	Inventory as a % of Total Assets: 27.9% Inventory Turn Days: 22 days Gross Margin: 24.7%	• The existence of inventory is a significant inherent risk. • The valuation of inventory is a significant inherent risk due to the complexity of applying the retail method and the risk associated with perishable inventories.
Hotel • Inventory is generally insignificant for this industry.	Inventory as a % of Total Assets: less than 1% Inventory Turn Days: N/A Gross Margin: N/A	• The risk of material misstatement is low due to the immateriality of inventory for this industry.
Local School District • Inventory is generally insignificant for this industry.	Inventory as a % of Total Assets: less than 1% Inventory Turn Days: N/A Gross Margin: N/A	• The risk of material misstatement is low due to the immateriality of inventory for this industry.

attention to the existence and valuation of inventory. The auditor might also be alert to cutoff problems that might have resulted in overstating inventory. A trend of decreased inventory turn days and decreased gross margin may indicate a problem with inventory shrinkage. Figure 16-4 presents some example analytical procedures along with an explanation of the problems that they might identify.

Figure 16-4 ■ Analytical Procedures Commonly Used to Audit the Production Cycle

Ratio	Formula	Audit Significance
Inventory Turn Days	Avg. Inventory Payable ÷ Cost of Goods Sold × 365	Prior experience in inventory turn days combined with knowledge of cost of sales can be useful in estimating current inventory levels. A lengthening of the period may indicate existence problems.
Inventory Growth to Cost of Sales Growth	$((\text{Inventory}_n \div \text{Inventory}_{n-1}) - 1) \div ((\text{Cost of Sales}_n \div \text{Cost of Sales}_{n-1}) - 1)$	Ratios larger than 1.0 indicate that inventories are growing faster than sales. Large ratios may indicate possible inventory obsolescence problems.
Finished Goods Produced to Raw Material Used	Finished Goods Quantities ÷ Raw Material Quantities	Useful in estimating the efficiency of the manufacturing process. May be helpful in evaluating the reasonableness of production costs.
Finished Goods Produced to Direct Labor	Finished Goods Quantities ÷ Direct Labor Hours	Useful in estimating the efficiency of the manufacturing process. May be helpful in evaluating the reasonableness of production costs.
Product Defects per Million	Number of Product Defects as a Percent of Each Million Produced	Useful in estimating the effectiveness of the manufacturing process. May be helpful in evaluating the reasonableness of production costs and warranty expenses.

When inventory is material to the financial statement audit, the auditor should not consider that analytical procedures are a substitute for other tests of details, but they may be very effective in focusing audit attention where misstatements are likely. In addition, Figure 16-4 suggests several comparisons of financial measures with underlying measures of business activity; raw materials used, and direct labor hours. If the auditor plans to use this type of data for a substantive analytical procedure, the auditor should test the control system that ensures the reliability of the data used to support an analytic conclusion.

INHERENT RISK

The inherent risk of misstatement in the financial statements arising from inventory transactions for the hotel chain or the school district is relatively low, for inventory is not a material part of the entity's core process. With a manufacturer, wholesaler, or retailer, however, inventory may be assessed at or near the maximum for the following reasons:

- The volume of purchases, manufacturing, and sales transactions that affects these accounts is generally high, increasing the opportunities for misstatements to occur.
- There are often contentious issues surrounding the identification, measurement, and allocation of inventoriable costs such as indirect materials, labor, and manufacturing overhead, joint product costs, and the disposition of cost variances, accounting for scrap, and other cost accounting issues.
- The wide diversity of inventory items sometimes requires the use of special procedures to determine inventory quantities, such as geometric volume of stockpiles, aerial photography, and estimation of quantities by experts.
- Inventories are often stored at multiple sites, adding to the difficulties associated with maintaining physical controls over theft and damages, and properly accounting for goods in transit between sites.
- The wide diversity of inventory items may present special problems in determining their quality and market value.
- Inventories are vulnerable to spoilage, obsolescence, and other factors such as general economic conditions that may affect demand and salability, and thus the proper valuation of the inventories.
- Inventory may be sold subject to right of return and repurchase agreements.

CONSIDERATION OF INTERNAL CONTROLS

Audit Decision 3

■ What should be considered in evaluating control activities for the production cycle transactions?

As in the case of the revenue and expenditure cycles, aspects of all five components of an entity's system of internal controls are applicable to manufacturing transactions in the production cycle. At this stage we assume that the entity has a strong control environment, sound risk assessment procedures, and effective monitoring of the system of internal control. The following discussion focuses on the accounting system aspects of the information and communication component, and on effective control activities. In addition, the discussion assumes that an entity has good segregation of duties and computer general controls are effective, so that the focus of the discussion is on programmed application control procedures.

Common Documents and Records

Following are some of the common documents, records, and computer files used in processing manufacturing transactions. An example accounting system that incorporates these documents is exhibited in Figure 16-5.

- **Production order.** Form indicating the quantity and kind of goods to be manufactured. An order may pertain to a job order or a continuous process.
- **Material requirements report.** Listing of raw materials and parts needed to fill a production order.
- **Materials issue slip.** Written authorization from a production department for stores to release materials for use on an approved production order.
- **Time ticket.** Record of time worked by an employee on a specific job.
- **Move ticket.** Notice authorizing the physical movement of work in process between production departments, and between work in process and finished goods.
- **Daily production report.** Report showing raw materials and labor used during the day.
- **Completed production report.** Report showing that work has been completed on a production order.
- **Standard cost master file.** A computer file containing standard costs.
- **Raw materials inventory master file.** A computer file with both the quantities of raw materials inventory on hand and actual cost of raw materials.
- **Work-in-process inventory master file.** A computer file with both the quantities of work-in-process inventory on hand, and actual cost of work in process.
- **Finished goods inventory master file.** A computer file with both the quantities of finished goods inventory on hand and actual cost of finished goods.

The use of each of these documents and records is explained in the following sections.

Functions and Related Controls

Executing and recording manufacturing transactions and safeguarding inventories involve the following manufacturing functions:

- Initiating production
  - Planning and controlling production
- Production of Inventory
  - Issuing raw materials
  - Processing goods in production
  - Transferring completed work to finished goods
  - Protecting inventories
- Recording manufacturing and inventory transactions
  - Determining and recording manufacturing costs
  - Maintaining correctness of inventory balances

The performance of these functions involves several departments such as production planning and control, stores (raw materials), the production departments,

Figure 16-5 ■ System Flowchart—Manufacturing Transactions

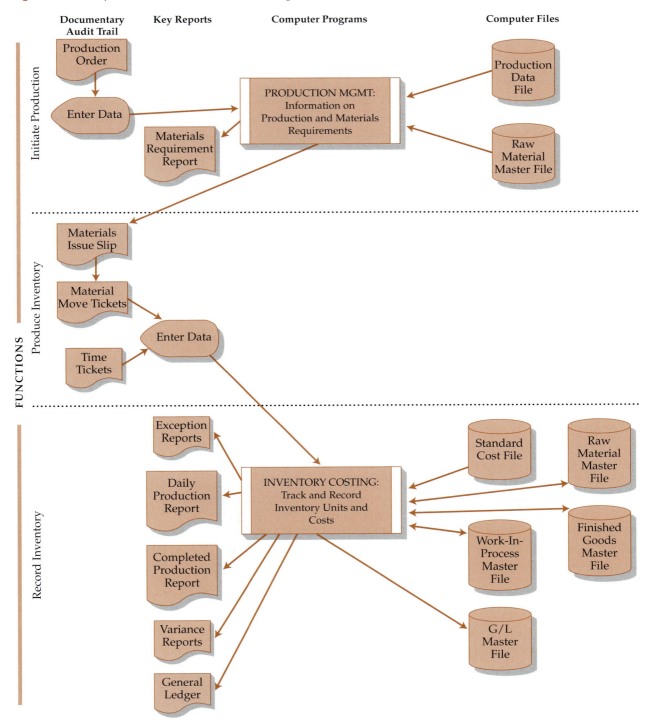

timekeeping, finished goods, IT, cost accounting, and general accounting. As with each of the other major transaction classes, there should be segregation of duties for executing and recording manufacturing transactions and maintaining custody of the manufacturing inventories. Controls pertaining to initiating production and the movement of goods are relevant in assessing control risk for the existence or occurrence and completeness assertions for manufacturing transactions and related inventories. Controls pertaining to recording inventory transactions are important in assessing control risk for the existence and occurrence, completeness, valuation or allocation, and presentation and disclosure assertions for manufacturing transactions and inventories. Figure 16-6 summarizes example control procedures related to each of these functions.

Initiating Production

Planning and Controlling Production

The authorization of production occurs in the production planning and control department based on orders received from customers or analysis of sales forecasts and inventory requirements. Documentation of the authorizations is provided by issuing prenumbered production orders (EO1). Information technology, or other means, should be used to account for all production orders issued and their eventual recording in manufacturing costs. A material requirements report is also prepared showing materials and parts needed and on hand. When orders must be placed with suppliers, a copy of this report is sent to purchasing (EO1).

Production planning and control is also responsible for monitoring materials and labor usage, and tracking the progress on production orders until they are completed and transferred to finished goods. The review of daily production activity reports and completed production reports is essential in meeting these responsibilities.

Produce Inventories

Issuing Raw Materials

Stores release raw materials to production on receipt of materials issue slips (or requisitions) authored by the production departments. The slips show the quantity and type of material requested and the production order number to be charged. Each slip should be signed by a supervisor or an authorized production worker. Information technology, or other means, should be used to match materials issue slips with production orders and their eventual recording in manufacturing costs (EO1, C1). A daily summary of materials usage is typically prepared as a component of the daily production activity report used in production planning and control (EO1, C1).

Processing Goods in Production

Labor incurred on specific production orders is recorded on time tickets; the timekeeping function may also be accomplished by having employees insert their badges in a computer terminal and key in the production order number whenever they start or stop work on a job. In either case, a daily summary of labor usage is typically prepared from the timekeeping data as a component of the daily production activity report (EO1, C1).

Figure 16-6 ■ Control Risk Considerations—Manufacturing Transactions

Function	Potential Misstatement	Computer Control[a] (Manual Controls in Italics)	C1	EO1	VA1	PD1
Initiating Production						
Planning and controlling production	Excessive production may be ordered.	*Approval of production orders in production planning and control.*		P		
Issuing raw materials	Use of raw materials is not authorized.	*Signed materials issue slips for approved production orders are required for all materials released to production.*		P		
		Computer accounts for prenumbered materials issues slips and reconciles slips with recording in daily production reports.	D	D		
Movement of Goods						
Processing goods in production	Direct labor hours may not be charged to production orders.	Computer compares production hours (or time tickets) to record direct labor hours on daily production reports.		P		
		Computer accounts for hours worked and hours charged to daily production reports.	D	D	D	D
Transferring completed work to finished goods inventory	Finished goods personnel may claim goods were not received from production.	*Signature of finished goods warehouse personnel on final move ticket on receipt of goods.*		P		
		Computer accounts for inventory move tickets and reconciles with recording on completed production report.	D	D	D	D
Protecting inventories	Inventories may be stolen from the warehouse.	*Use of locked warehouse with access restricted to authorized personnel only.*		P		
	Work in process may be stolen or misrouted during production.	*Use of plant surveillance personnel.*		P		
		Signed inventory move tickets to control movement of goods through production department, with tickets reconciled to daily production reports and completed production reports.	D	D		
Recording Manufacturing and Inventory Transactions						
Determining and recording manufacturing costs	Manufacturing costs may be recorded in incorrect amounts.	*Use of chart of accounts; timely reporting of manufacturing cost data for management performance reviews including budget comparisons.*			P	P
	Direct manufacturing costs allocated to work in process may not be recorded or may be recorded at incorrect amounts.	Computer compares daily production report data with underlying source documents (inventory move tickets and time cards).	D	D		
	Inappropriate overhead rates or standard costs may be used.	*Management approval of overhead rates and standard costs; timely reporting of manufacturing cost data for management performance reviews and investigation of variances.*			D	D
	Costs of completed production may not be transferred to completed goods or be transferred in incorrect amounts.	Computer compares completed production report data with underlying source documents (inventory move tickets and time cards).			D	D

(continues)

Figure 16-6 ■ (Continued)

Function	Potential Misstatement	Computer Control[a] (Manual Controls in Italics)	C1	EO1	VA1	PD1
Recording Manufacturing and Inventory Transactions (cont.)						
Maintaining the correctness of inventory balances.	Recorded inventory quantities may not agree with inventory owned quantities on hand.	*Periodic independent counts of inventories; comparison with records of amounts and ownership.*	D	D		D
	Inventory carrying values in subsidiary ledgers or master files may not agree with control accounts.	Computer checks on agreement of subsidiary records and control accounts.			D	
	Inventories may be carried at amounts in excess of market values.	*Periodic inspection of inventory condition; periodic inventory activity reports for management performance reviews.*			D	
		Management Controls				
	Management may not be held accountable for management of inventory resources, resulting in a variety of misstatements in the financial statements.	*An appropriate level of management monitors the level of production, and production costs, and the reasonableness of inventory levels relative to sales volume.*	D	D	D	D

[a] All computer controls assume that exceptions are either printed on an exception report for followup, or an error message appears during input and the transaction cannot be processed without correction and acceptance.
P = potential control to prevent misstatement or unauthorized use of resources.
D = potential control to detect misstatement or unauthorized use of resources.

When work on a production order is completed in one department and the goods have passed inspection, transfer to the next department is authorized by a move ticket that should be signed by the department receiving the goods. Information technology, or other means, should match time tickets and move tickets with the eventual recording in manufacturing costs (EO1, C1, VA1, PD1).

Transferring Completed Work to Finished Goods

When production of an order is complete and the goods have passed a final inspection, a completed production report is prepared. The goods are then forwarded to the finished goods warehouse, which accepts accountability for the goods by signing the final move ticket (EO1, C1).

Protecting Inventories

Manufacturing inventories are vulnerable to theft and damage. The storage of raw materials and finished goods inventories in locked storerooms with access restricted to authorized individuals is important in safeguarding these assets. The protection of work in process is facilitated through surveillance of production areas by supervisory and plant security employees, the tagging of goods, and the use of prenumbered move tickets to control the transfer of work in process through the plant (EO1, C1). In addition, the raw materials master file, work-in-progress master file, and finished goods master file should contain a perpetual inventory record in quantities. This recorded accountability should be regularly compared with the physical inventory on hand to ensure the accuracy of inventory records (EO1, C1).

Recording Manufacturing and Inventory Transactions

Determining and Recording Manufacturing Costs

This function involves the following:

- Charging direct materials and direct labor to work in process.
- Assigning manufacturing overhead to work in process.
- Transferring costs between production departments (in a process cost system).
- Transferring the cost of completed production to finished goods.

To ensure that manufacturing costs are properly recorded, the chart of accounts should provide for the many accounts needed to properly classify and track such costs. In addition, the timely reporting of cost data for use in management performance reviews of production activity and cost control provides a useful means of detecting misclassifications in recording manufacturing costs. Such reports normally include comparisons of actual and budgeted data by various cost classifications (EO1, C1, VA1, PD1).

Manufacturing costs may be assigned to work in process based on actual costs or standard costs. When the latter are used, they should be approved by management, and there should be timely reporting of variances from actual or budgeted amounts for investigation and followup as a part of the periodic performance reviews by management. Additional controls over the recording of manufacturing costs include:

- Independent checks on the agreement of entries for the allocation of manufacturing costs to work in process with data on materials and labor usage in daily production activity reports (EO1, VA1, PD1).
- Independent checks on the agreement of entries for the transfer of work in process to finished goods with data in completed production reports (EO1, VA1, PD1).
- A report of all material issue slips, time tickets, and inventory move tickets that are not included in a daily production report (C1).

Independent checks are often accomplished through programmed controls and independent follow-up of exceptions.

Maintaining Correctness of Inventory Balances

Maintaining correct inventory balances involves three activities. First, there should be periodic independent counts of inventory on hand and comparison with recorded quantities per the perpetual inventory records. These comparisons may reveal recorded quantities that no longer exist, incomplete records of quantities on hand, or inventory items that are misclassified in the records. This activity may occur just once a year in connection with the annual audit. However, strong controls result in counting inventory on a more frequent cyclical basis throughout the year. Second, there should be periodic independent checks on the agreement of the dollar carrying amounts for the raw materials, work in process, and finished goods inventory master files with their respective general ledger control accounts. Third, through periodic inspections of inventory condition and management review of inventory activity reports, adjustments to reduce inventory carrying values to market should be made when required (EO1, C1,VA1, VA4).

Management Controls

Management controls are often used to monitor each function described above. When management is held accountable for the use of resources at each stage of production, the likelihood of unintentional errors is decreased. As described above, management usually will closely monitor production orders, labor and materials used, the total accumulation of production costs, the existence of inventory, and the approval of standard costs (EO1, C1, VA1, PD1).

Additional Inventory Controls

Controls over cost of goods sold vary with the nature of the accounting system. Many companies use a perpetual inventory system only to track inventory quantities. They then use a periodic inventory system to value inventory. Production costs might be tracked by raw materials and conversion costs. At year-end inventory is valued using the entity's chosen valuation method (LIFO, FIFO, Retail Method, etc.). The cost of goods sold is determined by adding production costs to beginning inventory and subtracting ending inventory.

The accuracy of cost of goods sold (EO2, C2, VA2, and PD2) depends on controls over (1) the accumulation of production costs and (2) the valuation of ending inventory. In a strong system of internal control there is usually an independent review of manufacturing variances. If variances are due to inefficient production, they should be treated as a period cost and charged directly to cost of goods sold. If variances occur because standard costs no longer reflect the actual cost of production, an argument can be made for including an appropriate portion of the variances in inventory. There should also be an independent review of the valuation of inventory at the end of the year.

Finally, internal controls over disclosure objectives (PD3-PD6) require the diligent work of an effective disclosure committee.

[LEARNING CHECK

16-1 a. Describe the nature of the production cycle.
  b. Identify the major transaction class within this cycle.
  c. Name three other cycles that interface with the production cycle.

16-2 a. Identify several transaction class audit objectives for the production cycle.
  b. Identify several account balance audit objectives for the production cycle.

16-3 a. Discuss materiality from the perspective of the production cycle.
  b. Discuss inherent risk from the perspective of the production cycle.
  c. Describe three analytical procedures an auditor might use when auditing the production cycle, and describe how each analytical procedure might identify a potential misstatement in the financial statements.

16-4   a. Explain several control environment factors that impact the production cycle.

        b. Identify several unique elements of an entity's accounting information system that pertain to the production cycle.

16-5   Identify the documents, records, and computer files that provide a basis of authorization and control in the four functions that culminate in transferring production to finished goods.

16-6   What controls are important in determining and recording manufacturing costs?

16-7   What controls are important in protecting inventories and maintaining the correctness of inventory balances?

[KEY TERMS

Completed production report, p. 750	Production cycle, p. 744
Daily production report, p. 750	Production order, p. 750
Finished goods inventory master file, p. 750	Raw materials inventory master file, p. 750
Manufacturing transactions, p. 744	Standard cost master file, p. 750
Material requirements report, p. 750	Time ticket, p. 750
Materials issue slip, p. 750	Work-in-progress inventory master file, p. 750
Move ticket, p. 750	

PRELIMINARY AUDIT STRATEGIES

Audit Decision 4

■ What factors are involved in determining an acceptable level of tests of details risk for inventory assertions?

Figure 16-7 summarizes some key issues related to preliminary audit strategies for the audit of inventory. Inventory audits usually face significant inherent risks for the existence and occurrence assertion and the valuation and allocation assertion. If internal controls are strong, auditors often think about moving the timing of inventory observations to an interim date and they can reduce the extent of inventory observations. If internal controls are weak, inventory observations should be performed at year-end and the extent of inventory observations should be increased.

POSSIBLE SUBSTANTIVE TESTS OF INVENTORY ASSERTIONS

Audit Decision 5

■ How does the auditor determine the elements of an audit program for substantive tests to achieve specific audit objectives for inventory?

Possible substantive tests of inventory balance assertions and the specific account balance audit objectives to which they relate are shown in Figure 16-8. Evidence from some of the tests applicable to merchandise inventory and to manufactured finished goods inventories also relates to objectives for the corresponding cost of goods sold accounts because of the reciprocal relationship of these accounts. Each of the substantive tests is discussed in a following section, together with selected comments about how the tests can be tailored based on the acceptable level of detection risk to be achieved.

Initial Procedures

An essential initial procedure involves obtaining an understanding of the entity's business and industry. This allows the auditor to develop a knowledgeable

Figure 16-7 ■ Preliminary Audit Strategies for Inventory

Assertion	Inherent Risk	Control Risk	Analytical Procedures Risk	Test of Details Risk
Existence and Occurrence	Maximum: There are significant inherent risks associated with the susceptibility of inventory to theft and inventory counts may be overstated as part of fraudulent financial reporting to improve gross margins.	Low: A strong perpetual inventory system with regular test counts of the physical against the perpetual inventory.	High: Analytical procedures are often too blunt to restrict detection risk to a low level for the existence of inventory.	Moderate: If internal controls are strong the auditor may observe the existence of inventory prior to year-end. Extent of testing depends on the level of test of details risk.
Completeness	Moderate to High: Understatements of inventory may result from poor inventory counts or cutoff errors.	Low: A strong perpetual inventory system with regular test counts of the physical against the perpetual inventory.	High: Analytical procedures are often too blunt to restrict detection risk to a low level for the completeness of inventory.	Moderate: If internal controls are strong the auditor may test the completeness of inventory during inventory observations prior to year-end.
Rights and Obligations	High: A company may have consignment inventory on hand that it does not own, or inventory may be pledged as security for a loan.	Moderate or Low: A perpetual inventory system must track consignment inventory, and regular test counts should be made. The perpetual should also be compared with monthly statements from vendors.	Maximum: Analytical procedures are not directed at the rights and obligations assertion.	Low: Direct confirmation of borrowing arrangements will include information about assets pledged as security for loans. The auditor will also read the contracts to understand terms of borrowing.
Valuation or Allocation	Maximum: Significant inherent risks associated with valuation issues, including the appropriate application of valuation methods (LIFO, FIFO, etc.) and lower of cost or market issues.	Moderate or Low: Figure 16-6 explains a number of controls over the value of manufactured inventory. An effective disclosure committee should regularly review lower of cost or market issues.	High: Analytical procedures are often too blunt to provide restrict detection risk to a low level for the valuation assertion.	Low: The auditor must substantively test the valuation at historical cost and lower of cost or market issues. Extent of testing depends on the level of test of details risk.
Presentation or Disclosure	Moderate: Inventory disclosures are straightforward and not extensive.	Moderate or Maximum: Primary control is the involvement of an effective disclosure committee.	Maximum: Analytical procedures are not directed at disclosures.	Very Low: The auditor will often perform tests of details to evaluate the quality and accuracy of financial statement disclosures. The auditor will also read the contracts to understand terms of borrowing.

Figure 16-8 ■ Possible Substantive Tests of Inventory Assertions

Category	Substantive Test	Specific Audit Objectives

Initial Procedures	1. Obtain an understanding of the business and industry and determine:
	  a. The significance of cost of sales and inventory to the business
	  b. Key economic drivers that influence the entity's cost of sales gross margins and the possibility of obsolete inventory.
	  c. The extent to which the client has consignment inventories (in or out)
	  d. The existence of purchase commitments and concentration of activities with suppliers.
	2. Perform initial procedures on inventory balances and records that will be subjected to further testing.
	  a. Trace beginning inventory balances to prior year's working papers.
	  b. Review activity in inventory accounts and investigate entries that appear unusual in amount or source.
	  c. Verify totals of perpetual records and other inventory schedules and their agreement with general ledger balances.
		All
		
		VA3
		EO3, VA3, PD3
		
		VA3

Analytical Procedures	3. Perform analytical procedures.
	  a. Review industry experience and trends.
	  b. Examine analysis of inventory turnover.
	  c. Review relationship of inventory balances to recent purchasing, production, and sales activities.
	  d. Compare inventory balances to anticipated sales volume.
		All

Tests of Details of Transactions	4. On a test basis, vouch entries in inventory to supporting documentation (e.g., vendor's invoices, manufacturing cost records, completed production reports, and sales and sales return records). 5. On a test basis, trace data from purchases, manufacturing, completed production, and sales records to inventory accounts. 6. Test cutoff of purchases and sales returns (receiving), movement of goods through manufacturing departments (routing), and sales (shipping).	EO1, EO2, VA1, V2, PD1, PD2 C1, C2 EO1, EO2, C1, C2

Tests of Details of Balances	7. Observe client's physical inventory count.
	  a. Decide on timing and extent of tests.
	  b. Evaluate adequacy of clients inventory taking plans.
	  c. Observe care taken in client's counts and make test counts.
	  d. Look for indications of slow-moving, damaged, or obsolete inventory.
	  e. Account for all inventory tags and count sheets used in physical count.
	8. Test clerical accuracy of inventory listings.
	  a. Recalculate totals and extensions of quantities times unit prices.
	  b. Trace test counts (from item 7c) to listings.
	  c. Vouch items on listings to inventory tags and count sheets.
	  d. Reconcile physical counts to perpetual records and general ledger balances and review adjusting entries.
	9. Test inventory pricing.
	  a. Examine vendors' paid invoices for purchased inventories.
	  b. Examine propriety of direct labor and overhead rates, standard costs, and disposition of variances pertaining to manufactured inventory.
	10. Confirm inventories at locations outside the entity.
	11. Examine consignment agreements and contracts.
	12. Based on the tests of beginning inventory, production costs, and ending inventory, determine the appropriateness of cost of sales.
		
		EO3, C3
		EO3, C3
		EO3, C3
		VA4
		EO3, C3
		
		VA3
		C3
		EO3
		EO3, C3, VA3, PD3
		
		VA3
		VA3
		
		EO3, C3, RO1
		RO1
		EO2, C2, VA2, PD2

(continues)

Figure 16-8 ■ (Continued)

Category	Substantive Test	Specific Audit Objectives
Tests of Details of Balances: Accounting Estimates	13. Evaluate the net realizable value of inventory:	
	a. Examine sales invoices after year-end and perform lower of cost or market test.	VA4
	b. Compare inventories with entity's current sales catalogue and sales reports.	VA4
	c. Inquire about slow-moving, excess, or obsolete inventories and determine need for write-down.	VA4
	d. Evaluate management's process for estimating the net realizable value of inventory using hindsight.	VA4
	e. Evaluate the net realizable value of inventory given information about: • Industry trends • Inventory turnover trends • Specific slow-moving inventory	VA4
Required Procedure	14. Observation of physical inventory count included as step 7 above.	EO3, C3
Presentation and Disclosure	15. Compare statement presentation with GAAP.	
	a. Confirm agreements for assigning and pledging inventories.	PD3, PD6
	b. Review presentation and disclosure for inventories in drafts of the financial statements and determine conformity with GAAP.	PD3, PD6
	c. Evaluate the completeness of presentation and disclosures for inventories in drafts of financial statements to determine conformity to GAAP by reference to disclosure checklist.	PD4
	d. Read disclosures and independently evaluate their classification and understandability.	PD5

perspective about the entity and set the context for the evaluation of analytical procedures and tests of details. If the client is a manufacturer, it is particularly important to understand the mix of fixed costs and variable costs involved in the manufacturing process. If a manufacturer is particularly capital intensive, it will need a high volume of activity, perhaps operating at 80 to 90 percent of capacity, to achieve breakeven profitability. If the entity is a retailer, it is important to understand the sources of supply of products and the role the client plays in the distribution chain. The auditor also should understand the importance of consignment inventories, whether consignments in or consignments out, to the client's business.

In tracing beginning inventory balances to prior-year working papers, the auditor should make certain that any audit adjustments agreed upon in the prior year did in fact get recorded. In addition, current-period entries in the general ledger inventory accounts should be scanned to identify any postings that are unusual in amount or nature and require special investigation. Initial procedures also involve determining that the detailed perpetual or other inventory schedules tie in with the general ledger balances. Additional work on inventory listings prepared on the basis of the physical inventory is discussed in a later section dealing with tests of details of balances.

Analytical Procedures

The application of analytical procedures to inventories uses the auditor's knowledge of the entity and its environment to develop expectations about the financial statements. This knowledgeable perspective is effective in identifying accounts that may be misstated. Suggested analytical procedures are presented in Figure 16-4 and by the steps shown in Figure 16-8. A review of industry experience and trends may be essential in developing expectations to be used in evaluating analytical data for the client. For example, knowing that a sharp drop in the client's inventory turnover ratio mirrors what is happening in the industry may help the auditor in concluding that the drop is not indicative of errors pertaining to existence or occurrence or completeness of the client data used in calculating the inventory turnover ratio, but may instead be indicative of a valuation problem related to a drop in demand that is likely to be followed by falling market prices. A review of relationships of inventory balances to recent purchasing, production, and sales activities should also aid the auditor in understanding changes in inventory levels. For example, an increase in the reported level of finished goods inventory when purchasing, production, and sales levels have remained steady might be indicative of misstatements related to the existence or valuation of the finished goods inventory. In addition to the calculation of an overall inventory turnover ratio for each inventory account, it may be appropriate to calculate the ratio for disaggregated data, such as by product line.

Because of the reciprocal relationship between inventories and cost of goods sold, these procedures may provide evidence useful in determining the fairness of management's assertions pertaining to both accounts. For example, an unexpectedly high inventory turnover ratio or an unexpectedly low gross margin might be caused by an overstatement of cost of goods sold and corresponding understatement of inventories. The auditor should also understand and evaluate the degree to which manufacturing costs are fixed and variable, and the relationship between costs, volume, and gross profit. Conversely, conformity of these ratios with expectations may provide some limited assurance of the fairness of the historical data used in the calculations unless evidence from other sources is contradictory. Finally, analysis of inventory levels and ratios based on anticipated sales volume in the subsequent period may be useful in conjunction with the market valuation tests discussed in a later section.

Tests of Details of Transactions

These tests involve the procedures of vouching and tracing to obtain evidence about the processing of individual transactions that affect inventory balances. Special consideration is given to determining the propriety of the cutoff of inventory transactions at the end of the accounting period.

Test Entries to Inventory Accounts

Some or all of this type of testing may be done as part of dual-purpose tests during interim work. Examples of vouching recorded entries in inventory accounts include the vouching of

- Debits in merchandise or raw materials inventories to vendors' invoices, receiving reports, and purchase orders.
- Debits in work-in-process or finished goods inventories to manufacturing cost records and production reports.
- Credits to merchandise and finished goods inventories to sales documents and records.

■ Credits to raw materials and work-in-process inventories to manufacturing cost records and production reports.

Recall that vouching entries that increase inventory balances provides evidence about the existence and valuation of the inventory at the time of the transaction. Vouching entries that decrease inventory balances to determine the propriety of the inventory reductions provides further evidence about the valuation assertion for cost of goods sold. Tracing documentation for purchases and the cost of factors added to production to entries in the inventory accounts provides evidence for the completeness and valuation inventory assertions. Tracing documentation of transactions that decrease inventory balances, such as sales, to determine that entries were recorded and at the right amounts provides further evidence for the existence and valuation assertions for inventory. Tracing and vouching also contribute evidence for the rights and obligations (ownership) assertion for inventories.

Test Cutoff of Purchases, Manufacturing, and Sales Transactions

The purpose and nature of sales and purchases cutoff tests are explained in Chapters 14 and 15, respectively, in connection with the audit of accounts receivable and accounts payable balances. Both tests are important in establishing that transactions occurring near the end of the year are recorded in the correct accounting period. In a manufacturing company, it must also be determined that entries are recorded in the proper period for the transfer of costs for goods moved between (1) stores and production departments, (2) one production department and another, or (3) production departments and finished goods.

In each case, the auditor must ascertain through inspection of documents and physical observation that the paperwork cutoff and the physical cutoff for inventory taking are coordinated. For example, if the auditor determines that an entry transferring the cost of the period's last lot of completed production to finished goods has been recorded, he or she should determine that the goods, even if in transit, were included in the physical inventory of finished goods only—that is, that they were neither counted as part of work in process, nor double counted, nor missed altogether. Evidence from these cutoff tests relates to both the existence or occurrence and completeness assertions for inventory balances and cost of goods sold.

Tests of Details of Balances

Figure 16-8 shows a number of tests of balances related to the requirement of observing the client's physical inventory.

Observation of the Client's Physical Inventory Count

The observation of inventories has been a generally accepted auditing procedure for more than 60 years. This procedure is required whenever inventories are material to a company's financial statements and it is practicable and reasonable. The observation of inventories may prove to be inconvenient, time consuming, and difficult for the auditor, but it is seldom impracticable and unreasonable.

In performing this auditing procedure, the client has responsibility for the taking of the inventory. AU 331, *Inventories,* states that from this substantive test, the auditor obtains direct knowledge of the effectiveness of the client's inventory tak-

seeing is believing

During the 1930s, audit evidence for inventories was usually restricted to obtaining a certification from management as to the correctness of the stated amount. In 1938, the discovery of a major fraud in the McKesson & Robbins Company, a major pharmaceutical firm, caused a reappraisal of the auditor's responsibilities for inventories. The company's December 1937 financial statements "certified" by a national public accounting firm reported $87 million of total assets. Of this amount, $19 million was subsequently determined to be fictitious: $10 million in inventory and $9 million in receivables. The auditors were exonerated of blame because they had complied with existing auditing standards. However, promptly thereafter, in Statement on Auditing Procedure No. 1, auditing standards were changed to include physical observation of inventories.

Source: SEC Financial Reporting Release No. 1.

ing and the measure of reliance that may be placed on management's assertions as to the quantities and physical condition of the inventories. The primary audit considerations applicable to this required procedure are explained in the following subsections.

Timing and Extent of the Test

The timing of an inventory observation depends on the client's inventory system and the effectiveness of internal controls. In a periodic inventory system, quantities are determined by a physical count, and all counts are made as of a specific date. The date should be at or near the balance sheet date, and the auditor should ordinarily be present on the specific date.

In a perpetual inventory system with effective internal controls, physical counts may be taken and compared with inventory records at interim dates. When the perpetual records are well kept and comparisons with physical counts are made periodically by the client, the auditor should be present to observe a representative sample of such counts. In such cases, this procedure may occur either during or after the end of the period under audit. In companies where inventories are at multiple locations, the auditor's observations ordinarily should encompass all significant inventory locations.

Inventory-Taking Plans

The taking of a physical inventory by a client is usually done according to a plan or a list of instructions. The client's instructions should include such matters as the:

- Names of employees responsible for supervising the inventory taking
- Date of the counts
- Locations to be counted
- Detailed instructions on how the counts are to be made
- Use and control of prenumbered inventory tags and summary (compilation) sheets

- Provisions for handling the receipt, shipment, and movement of goods during the counts if such activity is unavoidable
- Segregation or identification of goods not owned

The auditor must do advanced planning if an inventory observation is to be done efficiently and effectively. An experienced auditor usually has the responsibility for (1) planning the procedure, (2) determining the manpower needs, and (3) assigning members of the audit team to specific locations. Each observer should be provided with a copy of the client's inventory plans and written instructions of his or her duties.

Performing the Test

In observing inventories, the auditor should:

- Scrutinize the care with which client employees are following the inventory plan.
- See that all merchandise is tagged and no items are double tagged.
- Determine that prenumbered inventory tags and compilation sheets are properly controlled.
- Make some test counts and trace quantities to compilation sheets.
- Be alert for empty containers and hollow squares (empty spaces) that may exist when goods are stacked in solid formations.
- Watch for damaged and obsolete inventory items.
- Appraise the general condition of the inventory.
- Identify the last receiving and shipping documents used and determine that goods received during the count are properly segregated.
- Inquire about the existence of slow-moving inventory items.

The extent of the auditor's test counts depends, in part, on the care exercised by client employees in taking the inventory, the nature and composition of the inventory, and the effectiveness of controls pertaining to both the physical safeguarding of the inventory and the maintenance of perpetual records. Ordinarily, the auditor will stratify the inventory items to include the items of highest dollar value in the count and take a representative sample of other items. Perpetual inventory records are helpful in identifying the high-value items and selecting the sample items.

In making test counts, the auditor should record the count and give a complete and accurate description of the item (identification number, unit of measurement, location, etc.) in the working papers as shown in Figure 16-9. Such data are essential for the auditor's comparison of the test counts with the client's counts, and the subsequent tracing of the counts to inventory summary sheets and perpetual inventory records. After the inventory has been counted, the auditor needs to make a listing of all tags (used or unused) or summary sheets and obtain sufficient information so that no inventory can be added to the count after the auditor has observed inventory. Several significant frauds have occurred, overstating inventory, when the auditor has not adequately controlled the count sheets or tags.

On conclusion of the observation procedure, a designated member of the audit team should prepare an overall summary. The summary should include a description of such matters as (1) departures from the client's inventory-taking plan, (2)

Figure 16-9 ■ Inventory Test Counts Working Paper

Highlift Company

W/P Ref. *F – 2*
Raw Materials Test Counts
December 31, 20X1

Prepared By: *W.C.B.* Date: *12/31/X1*
Reviewed By: *R. E. Z.* Date: *1/25/X2*

Tag No.	Inventory Sheet No.	Inventory Number	Inventory Description	Client Count	Auditor Count	Difference
6531	15	1-42-003	back plate	125	125 (a)	0
8340	18	1-83-012	1/4" copper plate	93	93 (a)	0
1483	24	2-11-004	Single end wire	1325 yds.	1321 yds. (a)	4 yds. (b)
4486	26	2-28-811	Copper tubing	220	220 (a)	0
3334	48	4-26-204	Side plate	424	424 (a)	0
8502	64	7-44-310	1/2" copper wire	276 ft.	276 ft. (a)	0
8844	68	7-72-460	3/8" copper wire	419 ft.	419 ft. (a)	0
6295	92	3-48-260	Front plate	96	69 (a)	27 (b)

(a) Traced to client's inventory summary sheet (F-4) noting corrections for all differences.
(b) Each difference was corrected by the client. The net effect of the corrections was to increase inventory by $840. If similar errors existed in the unsampled portion of the population (F-5), the projected misstatement would amount to $26,460, which is considered to be immaterial. Pass further investigation.

the extent of test counts and any material discrepancies resulting therefrom, and (3) conclusions on the accuracy of the counts and the general condition of the inventory.

Inventories Determined by Statistical Sampling

A company may have inventory controls or use methods of determining inventories, such as statistical sampling, that do not require an annual physical count of every item of inventory. Such methods do not relieve the auditor of the responsibility to observe the taking of inventories. It is still necessary to observe such counts as deemed necessary in the circumstances. In addition, the auditor must obtain evidence on the appropriateness of the method used to determine inventory quantities. When the client uses statistical sampling methods, AU 331.11 indicates that the auditor must ascertain that (1) the sampling plan has statistical validity, (2) it has been properly applied, and (3) the results in terms of precision and reliability are reasonable in the circumstances.

Observation of Beginning Inventories

To express an unqualified opinion on the income statement, the auditor must observe the taking of both the beginning and ending inventories. On a recurring audit engagement, this requirement is met by observing the ending inventory of each year. However, in the initial audit of an established company, the auditor may either be appointed after the beginning inventory has been taken or be asked to report on the financial statements of one or more prior periods. In such circumstances, it is impracticable and unreasonable for the auditor to have observed the inventory taking, and generally accepted auditing standards permit the auditor to verify the inventories by other auditing procedures.

When the client has been audited by another firm of independent auditors in the prior period(s), the other procedures may include a review of the predecessor auditor's report and/or working papers and a review of the client's inventory summaries for the prior period(s). If the client has not been audited previously, the auditor may be able to obtain audit satisfaction by reviewing the summaries of any client counts, testing prior inventory transactions, and applying gross profit tests to the inventories. Such procedures are appropriate only when the auditor is able to verify the validity and propriety of the ending inventory for the period under audit.

When inventories have been observed, the auditor may be able to issue a standard audit report. This is also permissible when the auditor has used alternative substantive tests to verify the beginning inventory. However, when sufficient evidence has not been obtained as to the beginning inventories or the auditor is unable to observe the taking of ending inventories, the auditor has a scope limitation and should issue a qualified opinion or a disclaimer of opinion as discussed in Chapter 2.

Test Clerical Accuracy of Inventory Listings

After the physical inventory has been taken, the client uses the inventory tags or count sheets to prepare or compile a listing or listings of all items counted. The inventory items are then priced to arrive at the total dollar valuation of the inventory on hand. Because this listing serves as the client's basis for any entries required to adjust recorded inventories to agree with those on hand, the auditor must perform certain tests to determine that the listing is clerically accurate and that it accurately represents the results of the physical counts.

Tests of clerical accuracy include recalculating the totals shown on the inventory listings and verifying the accuracy of the extensions of quantities times unit prices on a test basis. To determine that the list accurately represents the results of the count, the auditor traces his or her own test counts to the inventory listings, and vouches items on the listings to the inventory tags and count sheets used in the physical inventory. The physical counts are then compared on a test basis with amounts per perpetual records, when applicable, and any differences are noted, investigated, and traced to adjusting entries when required. This test provides evidence for the existence or occurrence, completeness, and valuation or allocation assertions.

Test Inventory Pricing

This test involves examining supporting documentation for both the cost and market value of inventories. Thus, it relates primarily to the valuation or allocation assertion. It also involves determining that the costing procedures used are consistent with those used in prior years. A review of perpetual inventory records and inquiry of the client should enable the auditor to determine both the basis and costing methods used in pricing inventory quantities. The consistency of the pricing, in turn, can be established by recourse to last year's working papers on a recurring audit and/or to the prior year's financial statements. This step in the verification of pricing includes a review of the pricing of obsolete and damaged goods to ascertain that they are not valued in excess of net realizable value at the statement date. Evidence in support of unit costs varies with the nature of the inventory. For items purchased for resale, use, or consumption (merchandise inventory, raw materials, and supplies), costs should be vouched to representative vendor invoices. If the client is unable to produce vendor invoices for the quantity in inventory, it would indicate a potential existence problem with inventories.

Test Cost of Manufactured Inventories

The nature and extent of the auditor's pricing tests of work in process and finished goods depend on the reliability of the client's cost accounting records and the methods used by the client in accumulating such costs. The auditor should review the methods for propriety as well as for accuracy and consistency of application. For example, when standard costs are used, the auditor should test the calculation of the standards, compare the calculations with engineering specifications, determine that the standards are current, and evaluate whether the standards approximate actual costs by examining the variance accounts. When variance accounts have large balances, the auditor must consider whether fair presentation requires a pro rata allocation to inventories and cost of goods sold, rather than simply charging the variances to cost of goods sold.

When client assertions about the nature of the inventory pertain to highly technical matters, the auditor may require the assistance of an outside expert. This might occur, for example, in an oil company with different grades of gasoline and motor oil, or in a jewelry store with different carat diamonds and different jeweled watches. As explained in Chapter 7, the auditor may use the work of a specialist as an auditing procedure to obtain competent evidential matter, when he or she is satisfied about the qualifications and independence of the expert.

Confirm Inventories at Locations Outside the Entity

When client inventories are stored in public warehouses or with other outside custodians, the auditor should obtain evidence as to the existence of the inventory by direct communication with the custodian. This type of evidence is deemed sufficient except when the amounts involved represent a significant proportion of current or total assets. When this is the case, AU 331.14, *Inventories,* states that the auditor should apply one or more of the following procedures:

- Test the owner's procedures for investigating the warehouseman and evaluating the warehouseman's performance.
- Obtain an independent accountant's report on the warehouseman's control procedures relevant to custody of goods and, if applicable, pledging of receipts, or apply alternative procedures at the warehouse to gain reasonable assurance that information received from the warehouseman is reliable.
- Observe physical counts of the goods, if practicable and reasonable.
- If warehouse receipts have been pledged as collateral, confirm with lenders pertinent details of the pledged receipts (on a test basis, if appropriate).

This test also provides evidence about the rights and obligations assertion. In addition, it will result in evidence as to the completeness assertion if the custodian confirms more goods on hand than stated in the confirmation request. Confirming inventories does not provide any evidence about the value of the inventory because the custodian is not asked to report on the cost, condition, or market value of the goods stored in the warehouse.

Examine Consignment Agreements and Contracts

Goods on hand may be held for customers, at their request, after a sale has occurred. Goods may also be held on consignment. Thus, management is requested to segregate goods not owned during the inventory taking. In addition, the auditor usually requests a written assertion on ownership of inventories in the client representation letter. This letter is illustrated in Chapter 19.

The auditor should also inquire of management as to any goods held on consignment. When consignments exist, the agreement should be examined for terms and conditions. If the client has shipped goods on consignment, the auditor should review the documentation to determine that goods held by the consignee are included in the consignor's inventory at the balance sheet date.

As to be expected, the evidence obtained from this test relates to the rights and obligations assertion. For goods held on consignment, the test also provides evidence concerning the presentation and disclosure assertion.

Tests of Details of Accounting Estimates

The audit of accounting estimates is particularly challenging because of their prospective nature. When auditing inventory, the auditor must determine whether it is appropriate to write down the value of inventory below cost because the inventory is obsolete or slow moving, and whether conditions would cause the client to sell inventory at such a price that it would experience a loss on its sale.

The auditor's responsibility for quality is limited to that of a reasonably informed observer. This means that the auditor is expected to determine whether the inventory appears to be in condition for sale, use, or consumption, and whether there are any obsolete, slow-moving, or damaged goods. The auditor obtains evidence of general condition or obsolescence by:

- Observing the client's inventory taking
- Scanning perpetual inventory records for slow-moving items
- Reviewing quality control production reports

In addition, the auditor will use hindsight to the extent possible and review the sale of inventory after year-end to determine the reasonableness of costs compared to subsequent sales prices. For example, the auditor will usually:

- Compare the cost of inventory items with the entity's current sales catalog and sale reports
- Review inventory turnover after year-end
- Consider whether a change in replacement costs is an indicator of changing market conditions
- Make inquiries of the client about slow-moving and obsolete inventory and the realizable value of inventory through sales

When the evidence suggests a decline in the realizable value of the goods, an appropriate write-down below cost is required by GAAP.

Comparison of Statement Presentation with GAAP

It is customary to identify the major inventory categories in the balance sheet and the cost of goods sold in the income statement. In addition, there should be disclosure of the inventory costing method(s) used, the assignment or pledging of inventories, and the existence of major purchase commitments.

Evidence pertaining to statement presentation and disclosure is usually provided by the substantive tests described above. Further evidence may be obtained, as needed, from a review of the minutes of board of directors' meetings and from inquiries of management. Based on the evidence and a comparison of the client's financial statements with applicable accounting pronouncements, the auditor determines the propriety of the presentation and disclosures.

Inquiry of management is also used to determine the existence of binding contracts for future purchases of goods. When such commitments exist, the auditor should examine the terms of the contracts and evaluate the propriety of the company's accounting and reporting. When material losses exist on purchase commitments, they should be recognized in the statements, together with a disclosure of the attendant circumstances as noted in the discussion of accounts payable in the previous chapter.

Based on the evidence obtained from some combination of the foregoing substantive tests, the auditor should be able to satisfy each of the audit objectives for inventories.

[LEARNING CHECK

16-8 What factors should be considered by an auditor in specifying the acceptable level of detection risk for assertions pertaining to (a) merchandise inventory and (b) manufactured finished goods inventory?

16-9 Indicate several ratios and their formulas that may be used in applying analytical procedures to inventory balances.

16-10 a. Identify five tests of details of balances that may be applied to inventories.

   b. For the test of observing the client's physical inventory count, indicate (1) when this test is required, (2) factors that affect the timing and extent of the test, (3) what should be considered in evaluating the client's inventory-taking plans, and (4) what the auditor should do during the actual taking of the physical inventory.

16-11 a. What documents and other information does the auditor use in performing an inventory pricing test?

   b. How are confirmations used in the audit of inventory balances?

16-12 a. Explain the nature of the assertion being tested when the auditor evaluates the net realizable value of inventory.

   b. Identify the audit procedures that an auditor would perform to evaluate the net realizable value of inventory.

[AUDITING THE PERSONNEL SERVICES CYCLE]

An entity's **personnel services cycle** involves the events and activities that pertain to executive and employee compensation. The types of compensation include

Audit Decision 6

■ **What is the nature of the personnel services cycle, and how are specific audit objectives developed for the personnel services cycle?**

salaries, hourly and incentive (piecework) wages, commissions, bonuses, stock options, and employee benefits (e.g., health insurance and paid vacations). The major class of transactions in this cycle is **payroll transactions.** Accounts affected by these transactions are shown in Figure 16-10. In many companies, payroll is recorded when paid, and payroll taxes are accrued at the same time. If the pay period does not match up with the end of the quarter or fiscal year, accruals should be made for payroll payable.

The personnel services cycle interfaces with two other cycles. The paying of the payroll and the payment of payroll taxes relate to cash disbursements transactions in the expenditure cycle. The audit of the imprest payroll bank account used for payroll disbursements is covered in Chapter 18. The distribution of factory labor costs to work in process pertains to the production cycle. The remainder of this section focuses primarily on hourly compensation to employees and related payroll taxes, and on important measurement and disclosure issues related to stock options and pension plans.

AUDIT OBJECTIVES

Selected specific audit objectives for the personnel services cycle are shown in Figure 16-11. The procedures used by the auditor to meet these objectives are described in the remainder of this chapter.

UNDERSTANDING THE ENTITY AND ITS ENVIRONMENT

Audit Decision 7

■ **What audit planning decisions should be made when developing an audit program for the personnel services cycle?**

Detailed statistics on labor costs by industry are not as readily available as other financial statistics without belonging to a specific trade association. However, some industries, such as the school district, are labor intensive. The audit of personnel services may represent 80 to 90 percent of the total annual budget for a school district. The hotel industry is a service industry that also depends on effective utilization of personnel. Today, the majority of employment in the U.S. economy is in the service sector.

Personnel services may be of varying importance to manufacturers, wholesalers, and retailers. Some industries may differ widely on the labor intensiveness of the manufacturing process. Furthermore, some manufacturers continue to have defined benefit pension plans that have significant inherent risks associated with

Figure 16-10 ■ Key Transactions in the Personnel Services Cycle

Debit	Credit
Compensation expense (including salaries, wages, commissions, bonuses, stock options and stock appreciation rights, and employee benefits)	Imprest payroll bank account (for net payroll)
	Accrued benefits payable
Direct labor costs	Liabilities for amounts withheld from employees
Manufacturing labor (indirect labor costs)	Accrued payroll taxes payable
Payroll tax expense	

Figure 16-11 ■ Selected Specific Audit Objectives for the Personnel Services Cycle

Specific Audit Objectives

Transaction Objectives

Occurrence. Recorded employee compensation, benefits, and payroll tax expenses relate to compensation for services rendered during the year **(EO1).**

Completeness. Recorded employee compensation, benefits, and tax expenses include all such expenses incurred for personnel services during the year **(C1).**

Accuracy. Employee compensation, benefits, and payroll tax expenses are accurately computed and recorded **(VA1).**

Cutoff. Employee compensation, benefits, and payroll tax expenses have been recorded in the correct accounting period **(EO1 and C1).**

Classification. Employee compensation, benefits, and payroll tax expenses are properly identified and classified in the income statement **(PD1).**

Balance Objectives

Existence. Employee compensation, benefits, and payroll tax liabilities represent amounts owed at the balance sheet date **(EO2).**

Completeness. Employee compensation, benefits, and payroll tax liabilities include all such amounts owed at the balance sheet date **(C2).**

Rights and Obligations. Employee compensation, benefits, and payroll tax liabilities are obligations of the reporting entity **(RO1).**

Valuation or Allocation. Employee compensation, benefits, and payroll tax liabilities are accurately computed and recorded **(VA2).**

Disclosure Objectives

Occurrence and Rights and Obligations. Disclosed employee compensation and benefits transactions and balance have occurred and pertain to the entity **(PD3).**

Completeness. All employee compensation and benefits disclosures that should have been included in the financial statements have been included **(PD4).**

Classification and Understandability. All employee compensation and benefits information is appropriately presented and described and information in disclosures is clearly expressed **(PD5).**

Accuracy and Valuation. All employee compensation and benefits information is disclosed accurately and at appropriate amounts **(PD6).**

the measurement of pension costs and pension disclosures. Other compensation plans may include stock options that present their own measurement and disclosure risks for auditors. Before proceeding with the audit of personnel services, it is important for the auditor to understand:

■ The importance of personnel services to the overall entity (e.g., is the entity labor intensive or capital intensive?).

■ The nature of compensation, as hourly compensation requires a different control system than salaried compensation.

■ The importance of various compensation packages such as bonuses, stock options and stock appreciation rights, and pension agreements.

If an entity's compensation is primarily salary based and demonstrates a predictable relationship to the delivery of services, the auditor might emphasize analytical procedures in the development of audit strategy. If compensation expenses are based on hourly pay, and show a high degree of variability throughout the period, the auditor may emphasize a lower assessed level of control risk approach.

ANALYTICAL PROCEDURES

The auditor usually will perform analytical procedures early in the audit of the personnel services cycle because they are cost effective. Examples of analytical procedures that the auditor might use are presented in Figure 16-12. Analytical procedures may be useful in identifying potential fraud such as when gross payroll per employee exceeds the auditor's expectations. This type of procedure is most effective when the auditor is able to use generalized audit software, sort employees by category, and then evaluate the average pay by category of employees. For example, if the auditor was performing this test for a professional baseball team, professional ballplayers should be segregated from front office personnel, which in turn is segregated from employees who vend hot dogs at the ball games. If every class of employees is lumped together, the analytical procedure quickly becomes ineffective.

In some cases, the auditor may be able to develop accurate expectations regarding an organization's payroll. In a university, for example, the auditor may be able to develop accurate estimates of the number of full-time faculty and gross pay for those faculty in a school or college given the number of full-time-equivalent students. As the auditor is able to develop more reliable expectations, he or she may place more assurance on that evidence and assess analytical procedures risk at a lower level than if expectations were rather broad and general. As stated above, the use of generalized audit software may allow for the development of more accurate expectations when auditing the personnel services cycle.

INHERENT RISK

The auditor is rarely concerned about the completeness assertion in the payroll cycle because most employees quickly follow up with their employers if they are not paid. However, payroll fraud (existence or occurrence) is a major concern for the auditor. Fraud may occur at two levels. Employees involved in preparing and paying the payroll may process data for fictitious employees and then divert the paychecks to their own use. When there is frequent turnover of personnel in a company, there is the risk that a terminated employee is continued on the payroll. Alternatively, management may overtly misclassify or "pad" labor cost in government contract work to defraud the agency.

Pay periods may be weekly, bimonthly, or monthly. In each case, the volume of payroll transactions may be high. For factory workers, gross earnings may be based on time and/or productivity. Thus, the computations may be complex, and inherent risk for the valuation or allocation assertion may be high. Significant valuation issues also exist in accounting for stock options and for defined benefit pension plans.

Finally, a company's benefit plans might involve stock options, stock appreciation rights, or pension plans that involve both significant measurement and disclosures issues. Hence, inherent risk may be high for the existence or occurrence, valuation or allocation, and presentation and disclosure assertions.

Figure 16-12 ■ Analytical Procedures Commonly Used to Audit the Personnel Services Cycle

Ratio	Formula	Audit Significance
Average payroll cost per employee classification	Total payroll costs for an employee group divided by the number of employees in the group	Reasonableness test of gross payroll for a group of employees. Many companies have more than one class of employee, and it is important to evaluate the reasonableness of payroll based on employee class.
Revenue per employee	Total revenue ÷ the number of full-time employees	This may be a measure of productivity per employee. This is particularly important in services industries and would be compared with industry statistics.
Total payroll costs as a percentage of revenues	Total payroll expenses ÷ total revenues	Reasonableness test of payroll costs. This is often compared with industry statistics.
Payroll tax expense as a percentage of gross payroll	Total payroll tax expenses ÷ gross payroll	Reasonableness test of payroll taxes. This can often be compared with standard tax rates.
Compare payroll expenses (salaries and wages, commissions, bonuses, employee benefits, etc.) with prior-year expenses or budgets	Current-year payroll expenses ÷ prior-year payroll expenses	Reasonableness test for payroll expenses if the ratio is significantly different from 1.0
Compare current year payroll liability with prior-year payroll liability	Current-year payroll tax liability ÷ prior-year payroll tax liability adjusted for growth in payroll volume	Reasonableness test for payroll liability if the ratio is significantly different from 1.0
Compute ratio of payroll tax expense to total payroll expenses	Payroll tax expense ÷ total payroll expense	Reasonableness test for payroll tax expense based on prior-year ratio of payroll tax expense to total payroll.
Employee benefits expenses as a percentage of gross payroll	Total benefits expenses ÷ gross payroll	Reasonableness test of benefits expenses. This is often compared with industry statistics.

CONSIDERATION OF INTERNAL CONTROLS

Audit Decision 8

■ What should be considered in evaluating control activities for personnel services cycle transactions?

As for other major transaction cycles, all five components of internal controls are relevant to the personnel services cycle. Several control environment factors have direct relevance. Overall responsibility for personnel matters is often assigned to a vice president of industrial or labor relations, or a manager of human or personnel resources. The human resources department is usually responsible for authorizing employment of personnel and for authorizing salaries, wages, and benefits. The board of directors usually sets officers' salaries and other forms of officer compensation. Departments that may be significantly involved in the processing of payroll transactions include timekeeping, payroll, and the treasurer's office. Personnel polices and practices should ensure that individuals involved in payroll functions are knowledgeable about state and federal payroll laws and regulations and applicable provisions of labor contracts. Finally, a sound control environment establishes an appropriate level of accountability for the use of the entity's personnel resources.

In addition to a strong control environment, at this stage we assume that the entity has sound risk assessment procedures and effective monitoring of the system of internal control. The following discussion focuses on the accounting system aspects of the information and communication component, and on effective control activities. The discussion further assumes that an entity has good segregation of duties and that computer general controls are effective, so that the focus of the discussion is on programmed application control procedures.

Common Documents and Records

The following documents and records are important in executing and recording payroll transactions:

- **Personnel authorization.** Memo issued by personnel department indicating the hiring of an employee and each subsequent change in the employee's status for payroll purposes.
- **Clock card.** Form used by each employee to record hours worked daily during a pay period. It is used with time clocks that record the time on the card. This and the following form may be replaced in modern systems with an employee badge that is inserted into a terminal to cause an electronic record of the time to be made.
- **Time ticket.** Form used to record time worked by an employee on specific jobs. Time worked is often machine imprinted.
- **Payroll register.** Report showing each employee's name, gross earnings, payroll deductions, and net pay for a pay period. It provides the basis for paying employees and recording the payroll.
- **Imprest payroll bank account.** Account to which a deposit equal to the total net payroll is made each pay period, and on which checks for salaries and wages for employees are drawn.
- **Payroll check.** Order drawn on a bank to pay an employee. It is accompanied by a detachable memo indicating gross earnings and payroll deductions.
- **Labor cost distribution summary.** Report showing the account classifications for gross factory earnings for each pay period.
- **Payroll tax returns.** Forms prescribed by tax authorities for filing with payments of taxes withheld from employees, and employer's payroll taxes for social security and federal and state unemployment.
- **Employee personnel file.** Holds pertinent employment data for each employee and contains all personnel authorizations issued for the employee, job evaluations, and disciplinary actions, if any.
- **Personnel data master file.** Computer file containing current data on employees needed for calculating payroll such as job classification, wage rate, and deductions.
- **Employee earnings master file.** Computer file containing each employee's gross earnings, payroll deductions, and net pay for the year to date by pay periods.

Functions and Related Controls

The processing of payroll transactions involves the following **payroll functions:**

- Initiating payroll transactions, including:
  - Hiring employees
  - Authorizing payroll changes
- Receipt of services, including preparing attendance and timekeeping data
- Recording and paying payroll transactions, including:
  - Preparing and recording the payroll
  - Paying the payroll and protecting unclaimed wages
  - Filing payroll tax returns

Each function is explained below. Where applicable, reference is made to the flowchart in Figure 16-13, which shows a representative system for processing payroll transactions. In this case, the company is using on-line entry/on-line processing for payroll authorization changes, and batch entry/batch processing for preparing the payroll. Figure 16-14 provides sample control procedures related to the functions discussed below.

In the flowchart, it should be observed that responsibility for executing and recording payroll is spread over several departments. This segregation of duties contributes significantly to reducing the risk of payments to fictitious employees or excessive payments to actual employees due to inflated rates or hours.

Initiating Payroll Transactions

Hiring Employees

The hiring of employees is done in the personnel department. All hirings should be documented on a personnel authorization form. The form should indicate the job classification, starting wage rate, and authorized payroll deductions. In the system shown in Figure 16-13, authorized individuals in the personnel department gain access to the personnel data master file by entering a password on an on-line terminal before entering data on new hires. Periodically, a computer-generated log of all changes to the master file is printed and independently checked by a personnel manager not involved in entering the data into the computer. One copy of the personnel authorization form is placed in the employee's personnel file in the personnel department.

Controls over adding new hires to the personnel data master file reduce the risk of payroll payments to fictitious employees. Thus, they relate to existence or occurrence and rights and obligations assertions for payroll transactions.

Authorizing Payroll Changes

The request for a change in job classification or a wage rate increase may be initiated by the employee's supervisor. However, all changes should be authorized in writing by the personnel department before being entered in the personnel data master file. Other controls over entering the changes in the computer and distributing the change forms are the same as those discussed above for new hires. These controls over payroll changes help to ensure the accuracy of the payroll and relate to the valuation or allocation assertion as well as rights and obligations.

Figure 16-13 ■ System Flowchart—Payroll Transactions

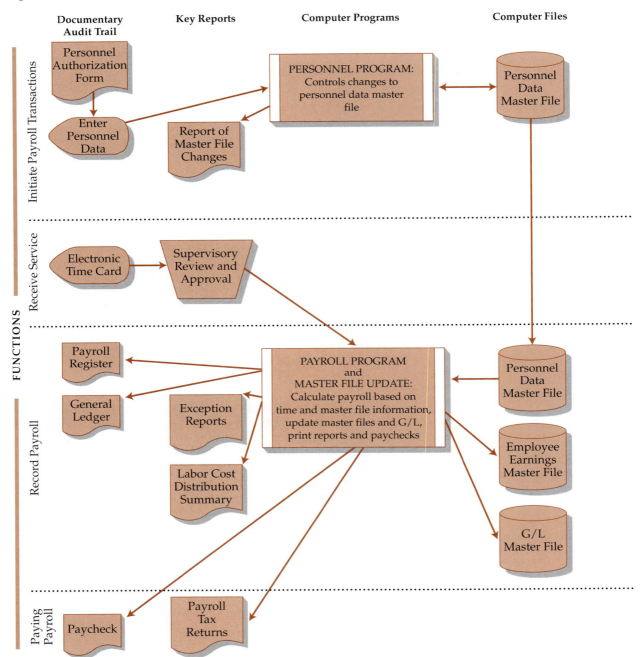

Figure 16-14 ■ Control Risk Considerations—Payroll Transactions

Function	Potential Misstatement	Computer Control[a] (Manual Controls in Italics)	EO1	C1	VA1	PD1
Initiating Payroll Transactions						
Hiring employees	Fictitious employees may be added to the payroll.	*Personnel department authorizes all new hires.*	P	P		
		Only a few key employees in personnel can add a new employee to the master payroll file.	P	P		
		Computer reports all changes to the personnel data master file. *Management in personnel reviews report of all master file changes.*	D	D		
Authorizing payroll changes	Employees may receive unauthorized rate increases.	*Personnel department authorizes all rate changes to the personnel data master file.*			P	
	Terminated employees may remain on the payroll.	*Personnel department removes terminated employees from the personnel data master file.*	P			
		Only a few key employees in personnel can change information on the personnel data master file	D	D		
		Management in personnel department reviews all changes to the personnel data master file.	D	D	D	D
Receipt of Services						
Preparing attendance and time-keeping data	Employees may be paid for hours not worked. / Employees may not be paid for hours worked.	*Use of time clock procedures and supervisory approval of time tickets.*	P	P		
Recording Payroll Transactions						
Preparing and recording the payroll	Payroll data may be lost during submission to IT.	Batch total of hours worked prepared by payroll department and verified by the computer.	D	D	D	D
	Payroll transactions may include incorrectly keyed or invalid data.	Computer limit test on the number of hours worked and the amount of each payroll check.	D	D	D	D
		Data submitted for processing is compared with the master payroll file.	D		D	D
Paying Payroll						
Paying the payroll and protecting unclaimed wages	Payroll check may be distributed to unauthorized recipients.	*Employee identification needed to receive payroll check.*	D	D	D	D
Filing payroll tax returns	Payroll tax returns may not be filed on a timely basis.	*Assignment of responsibility for timely filing of returns.*		P	P	
		Review of timely filing of return by accounting management.		D	D	
Management Control						
	Payroll may be recorded for services not received; they may be posted to the wrong account or in the wrong amount.	An appropriate level of management reviews all purchases charged to their responsibility center on a timely basis reviewing employees, amounts, and accounts charged.	D	D	D	D

[a] All computer controls assume that exceptions are either printed on an exception report for followup or an error message appears during input and the transaction cannot be processed without correction and acceptance.

P = potential control to prevent misstatement or unauthorized use of resources.

D = potential control to detect misstatement or unauthorized use of resources.

The personnel department should also issue a termination notice on completion of an individual's employment. Prompt updating of the personnel data master file is vital in preventing terminated employees from continuing on the payroll. Thus, this control relates to existence or occurrence assertions.

Receiving Services

Preparing Attendance and Timekeeping Data

In many companies, a timekeeping department is responsible for this function. Time clocks are frequently used to record time worked by an employee when a clock card or employee badge is inserted in the clock. To prevent one employee from "punching in" for another employee, security personnel should supervise the clock card procedures.

For factory employees, clock card hours must be supported by time tickets showing the type of work done (direct or indirect labor) and the jobs to which direct labor hours are to be charged. All time worked should be approved in writing by a supervisor. Timekeeping then reconciles the approved time tickets and clock cards and forwards them to payroll for use in preparing the payroll.

By ensuring that accurate data are accumulated on time worked, controls over the timekeeping function relate to the existence or occurrence, completeness, and valuation or allocation assertions for payroll transactions. Supervisory approval of the labor classification relates to the presentation and disclosure assertion. The timekeeping function is not shown in Figure 16-13.

Recording and Paying Payroll

Preparing the Payroll

Figure 16-14 illustrates typical controls in a basic system for preparing the payroll. Information from electronic time cards should be forwarded to the supervisor for review and electronic approval. The file is then electronically forwarded to payroll for processing. In some systems, a batch total can be prepared that will compare the total number of transactions submitted for processing with the number of individual electronic time cards to test the accuracy of the data submitted for processing.

The payroll program sorts payroll transactions by employee number, and the data are subjected to an edit check routine. This includes a check for valid employee number and a limit or reasonableness check on the hours worked. The output of this run consists of valid payroll transactions and an exceptions and control report that is sent to data control. Data control compares the control totals with the batch control log, informs the payroll department of exceptions discovered by the edit routine, and follows up to see that payroll submits corrected data. These controls over the data entry process preceding the calculation of the payroll contribute to the existence or occurrence, completeness, and valuation or allocation assertions for payroll transactions.

In the system shown in Figure 16-13, the program uses data from the valid payroll transactions, and the personnel data and employee earnings master files, to calculate payroll and prepare the payroll register and payroll checks. This program also records the payroll as described in the next section.

Recording the Payroll

As the gross pay, deductions, and net pay are calculated for each employee, the program updates the employee earnings master file and accumulates totals for the payroll journal entry that is generated and entered in the general ledger master file at the conclusion of the run. The following printed outputs of this run are sent to data control:

- An exceptions and control report that is reviewed by data control before distributing the other printed output.
- A copy of the payroll register that is returned along with the clock cards and time tickets to the payroll department for comparison with the original batch transmittal data.
- A second copy of the payroll register and prenumbered payroll checks that are sent to the treasurer's office.
- A general ledger summary that is sent to accounting showing the payroll entry generated by the payroll program.

Proper review of each of these outputs by the appropriate personnel contributes to control over misstatements in all five assertion categories.

Paying the Payroll and Protecting Unclaimed Wages

The preceding section indicates a copy of (1) the payroll register and (2) the payroll checks are sent to the treasurer's office where these functions are commonly performed. Applicable controls include the following:

- Payroll checks should be signed and distributed by authorized treasurer's office personnel not involved in preparing or recording the payroll.
- Access to check signing machines and signature plates should be restricted to authorized individuals.
- Payroll checks should be distributed only on proper identification of employees.
- Unclaimed payroll checks should be stored in a safe or vault in the treasurer's office.

Collectively, these controls pertain to all five categories of assertions.

Another important control over paying the payroll in most large companies is the use of an imprest payroll bank account on which all payroll checks are drawn. Control procedures and substantive tests pertaining to this account are explained in Chapter 18.

Filing Payroll Tax Returns

Payroll tax returns must be filed for amounts withheld from employees for federal income taxes and social security, and for the social security and federal and state unemployment taxes levied on the employer. Returns must be filed on a timely basis to avoid penalties and interest payments, and possibly even criminal charges. Thus, responsibility should be clearly assigned for performing this function according to a schedule that conforms to federal and state filing and payment deadlines.

LEARNING CHECK

16-13 a. Describe the nature of the personnel services cycle.
b. What cycles interface with this cycle?

16-14 a. Explain the materiality and inherent risk associated with the personnel services cycle.
b. What is the auditor's usual audit strategy for this cycle? Why?

16-15 State the audit objectives that pertain to management's assertions about personnel services transactions and balances.

16-16 Identify several analytical procedures that the auditor might use in the personnel services cycle and explain their audit significance.

16-17 Identify important aspects of the control environment, risk assessment, and monitoring components of internal controls as they relate to the personnel services cycle.

16-18 Identify the functions in processing payroll transactions.

16-19 a. Indicate the responsibilities of the personnel department in the processing of payroll transactions.
b. Describe the control procedures in preparing attendance and timekeeping data.

16-20 Explain the tests of control that involve (a) terminated employees and (b) witnessing a payroll distribution.

16-21 Using the information in Figure 16-14, develop a test of controls for each assertion related to the personnel services cycle.

KEY TERMS

Clock card, p. 774
Employee earnings master file, p. 774
Employee personnel file, p. 774
Imprest payroll bank account, p. 774
Labor cost distribution summary, p. 774
Payroll check, p. 774
Payroll functions, p. 775

Payroll register, p. 774
Payroll tax returns, p. 774
Payroll transactions, p. 770
Personnel authorization, p. 774
Personnel data master file, p. 774
Personnel services cycle, p. 769
Time ticket, p. 774

PRELIMINARY AUDIT STRATEGIES

Audit Decision 9
■ What factors are involved in determining an acceptable level of tests of details risk for payroll balance assertions?

Figure 16-15 summarizes some key issues related to preliminary audit strategies for the audit of the personnel services cycle. The most important inherent risk is associated with the overstatement of personnel services costs due to fictitious employees or the overstatement of hours worked. However, this is also a cycle of routine transactions where internal controls should control inherent risks. As a result, substantive tests focus on tests of transactions and test of balances at an interim date. Finally, tests must also be performed regarding benefits, pension plan disclosures, and stock options.

Figure 16-15 ■ Preliminary Audit Strategies for the Personnel Services Cycle

Assertion	Inherent Risk	Control Risk	Analytical Procedures Risk	Test of Details Risk
Existence and Occurrence	High: There are important inherent risks associated with fictitious employees being put on the payroll, overreporting of hours worked, and (in some instances) overreporting payroll costs on cost plus contracts.	Low: A strong system of internal control, including controls over the payroll master file, should minimize the risk of fictitious employees or unauthorized hours in routine payroll transactions.	Moderate: Analytical procedures may provide a reasonableness test for overstatements if there are good controls over information regarding number of employees and hours worked.	High: The auditor might perform moderately extensive test transactions at an interim date regarding the existence of and update tests of controls at final. The auditor will refer to the results of an ERISA audit with respect to pension balances.
Completeness	Moderate: If employees are not paid, they are likely to complain, minimizing the risk of unrecorded payroll. There may be some inherent risk of unrecorded payroll taxes and other benefits.	Low: A strong system of internal control, including controls over the payroll master file, should minimize the risk of completeness problems with routine payroll transactions.	Moderate: Analytical procedures may provide a reasonableness test for understatements if there are good controls over information regarding number of employees and hours worked.	Very High: The auditor may perform some tests of transactions to ensure that all payroll transactions are recorded.
Rights and Obligations	Moderate: It is unusual for entities to record obligations that they do not owe.	Low: A strong system of internal control should ensure that payroll liabilities are the obligations of the entity.	Maximum: Analytical procedures are not directed at the rights and obligations assertion.	High: The auditor will perform test of balances at an interim date to ensure that the obligations are the obligations of the entity.
Valuation or Allocation	Moderate: Payroll calculations are not complex.	Low: A strong system of internal control, including controls over the payroll master file, should minimize the risk of valuation problems with routine payroll transactions.	Moderate to High: Analytical procedures may provide a reasonableness test about the valuation of problems regarding gross payroll.	Low to High: The extensiveness of tests transactions at an interim date depends on controls and the results of analytical procedures. The auditor will refer to the results of an ERISA audit with respect to pension balances and recalculate stock option information.
Presentation and Disclosure	High: There are significant disclosures associated with stock options and employee benefits plans.	Moderate or Maximum: Primary control is the involvement of an effective disclosure committee.	Maximum: Analytical procedures are not directed at disclosures.	Very Low: The auditor will often perform tests of details to evaluate the quality and accuracy of financial statement disclosures.

SUBSTANTIVE TESTS OF THE PERSONNEL SERVICES CYCLE

Audit Decision 10

■ How does the auditor determine the elements of an audit program for substantive tests to achieve specific audit objectives for payroll balances?

Substantive tests of payroll transactions are often performed at an interim date as part of a dual purpose test. Substantive tests of payroll balances are normally performed at or near the balance sheet date. The balances include accrued liabilities for salaries, wages, commission, bonuses, employee benefits, and payroll taxes, and the related expense accounts. The imprest payroll account balance is considered in Chapter 18. Possible substantive tests of the personnel services cycle and the specific account balance audit objectives to which they relate are shown in Figure 16-16. Each of the substantive tests is discussed in a following section, together with selected comments about how the tests can be tailored based on the acceptable level of detection risk to be achieved.

Initial Procedures

An essential initial procedure involves obtaining an understanding of the entity's business and industry, and expected payroll costs. This allows the auditor to develop a knowledgeable perspective about the entity and to set the context for evaluating analytical procedures and tests of details. If the client is a manufacturer, it is particularly important to understand the mix payroll costs versus other manufacturing costs and how this interacts with the production cycle. It is also important to understand incentive compensation agreements and the degree to which these agreements might influence behavior relating to other cycles (e.g., compensating executive only on the level of revenues). Finally, the auditor also needs to understand the nature of pension agreements, stock options, and other employee benefit costs.

In tracing beginning payroll and payroll tax payable balances to prior-year working papers, the auditor should make certain that any audit adjustments agreed upon in the prior year did in fact get recorded. In addition, current-period entries in the general ledger inventory accounts should be scanned to identify any postings that are unusual in amount or nature and require special investigation. Initial procedures also involve determining that the detailed subsidiary ledgers for payroll liabilities tie in with the general ledger balances.

Analytical Procedures

The importance of analytical procedures was discussed earlier in the chapter. The auditor's goal is to develop an expectation of accrued payroll account balances and the relationship between payroll costs and hours worked. Several analytical procedures that can be performed to provide evidence about payroll accruals are shown in Figure 16-12. The auditor should be alert to signals of unrecorded payroll liabilities. Analytical procedures are performed in the final stages of the engagement to ensure that the evidence evaluated in details tests is consistent with the overall picture reported in the financial statements.

Tests of Details of Transactions

These tests involve the procedures of vouching and tracing to obtain evidence about the processing of individual personnel services transactions. Special con-

Figure 16-16 ■ Possible Substantive Tests of Personnel Services Assertions

Category	Substantive Test	Specific Audit Objectives

Initial Procedures	1. Obtain an understanding of the business and industry and determine:
	  a. The significance of payroll costs to the business
	  b. Key economic drivers that influence payroll costs
	  c. The extent to which the client has defined benefit pension plans or uses other incentive compensation plans.
		All

	2. Perform initial procedures on inventory balances and records that will be subjected to further testing.	
	a. Trace beginning accrued payroll balances to prior year's working papers.	VA3
	b. Review activity in payroll accounts and investigate entries that appear unusual in amount or source.	EO3, VA3, PD3
	c. Verify totals of payroll registers and other subsidiary ledgers for agreement with general ledger balances.	VA3

Analytical Procedures	3. Perform analytical procedures:
	  a. Review industry experience and trends.
	  b. Examine analysis of payroll costs.
	  c. Review relationship of payroll costs to recent production and sales activities.
		All

Tests of Details of Transactions	4. On a test basis, vouch payroll transactions to supporting documentation. (e,g., time cards, employee contracts, bonus arrangements, and incentive compensation agreements).	EO1, EO2, VA1, V2, PD1, PD2
	5. On a test basis, vouch payroll tax transactions to supporting documentation (e,g., underlying gross payroll and calculation of payroll taxes).	EO1, EO2, VA1, V2, PD1, PD2
	6. Verify officer compensation to board of director authorization.	EO1, EO2, VA1, V2, PD1, PD2
	7. On a test basis, trace data from time cards and contracts to the payroll register.	C1, C2
	8. Test payroll cutoff at the end of the month (year) based on time periods worked and payroll accrual if month (year) end and the end of the payroll period do not match up.	EO1, EO2, C1, C2
Tests of Details of Balances	9. Recalculate accrued payroll liabilities at year-end to underlying payroll records.	EO2, C2, VA2, PD2
	10. Recalculate accrued payroll tax liabilities and vouch to subsequent cash disbursements.	EO2, C2, VA2, PD2
	11. Determine that accrued payroll payables are the obligations of the entity.	RO1
Tests of Details of Balances: Accounting Estimates	12. Determine method of accounting for stock options, and recalculate stock option expense (or disclosure information).	EO1, EO2, VA1, V2, PD1, PD2
Presentation and Disclosure	13. Compare statement presentation with GAAP.	
	a. Compare pension plan disclosures to results of ERISA audit.	PD3, PD6
	b. Review presentation and disclosure for payroll costs (pensions, stock options, and other compensation arrangements) in drafts of the financial statements and determine conformity with GAAP.	PD3, PD6
	c. Evaluate the completeness of presentation and disclosures for personnel services activities in drafts of financial statements to determine conformity to GAAP by reference to disclosure checklist.	PD4
	d. Read disclosures and independently evaluate their classification and understandability.	PD5

sideration is given to payroll taxes, benefits and pension costs, incentive compensation agreements, and determining the propriety of the cutoff of payroll transactions at the end of the accounting period.

Test Entries to Payroll Accounts

Some or all of this type of testing may be done as part of dual-purpose tests during interim work. Examples of vouching recorded entries in payroll accounts include the vouching of

- Debits in the payroll register, including the appropriateness of classification of payroll costs charged to various manufacturing activities.
- The determination of the costs associated with various incentive compensation agreements.
- The determination of pension costs, including the use of an actuary to determine the costs for defined benefit pension plans.
- The determination of the expense associated with stock options using an options pricing model (which might be recorded as an expense or disclosed in the notes to the financial statements).
- The determination of authorization of officers' compensation by the board of directors.

Recall that vouching entries in the payroll register provides evidence about the existence and occurrence and valuation of payroll at the time of the transaction. Tracing documentation for payroll transactions provides evidence for the completeness and valuation of personnel services assertions.

Officers' compensation is audit sensitive for the following two reasons: (1) separate disclosure of officers' compensation is required in 10-K reports that public companies file with the SEC, and (2) officers may be able to override controls and receive salaries, bonuses, stock options, and other forms of compensation in excess of authorized amounts. For these reasons, board of directors' authorizations for officers' salaries and other forms of compensation should be compared with recorded amounts. This test pertains to objectives related to each category of assertions.

Test Cutoff of Personnel Service Transactions

Depending on how pay periods are determined, there may be a risk of misstatement associated with cutoff problems. If employees are paid every two weeks and payroll is recorded when paid, it is possible that almost two weeks worth of payroll costs have not been recorded at month, quarter, or year-end. The auditor should determine management's procedures for accruing personnel services costs, including the costs of gross payroll, payroll taxes, and other benefits and test the completeness and accuracy of payroll accruals.

Test of Details of Balances and Disclosures

Tests of details of balances focus on the following procedures:

- Recalculating accruals
- Auditing employee benefits and pension plans
- Auditing stock options and stock appreciation rights

Recalculate Accrued Payroll Liabilities

It is necessary for many companies to make a variety of accruals at the balance sheet date for amounts owed to officers and employees for salaries and wages, commissions, bonuses, vacation pay, and so on, and for amounts owed to government agencies for payroll taxes. Although the auditor's primary concern for payroll expenses for the year is with overstatement, for the year-end accruals the primary concern is with understatement. Also of concern is consistency in the methods of calculating the accruals from period to period.

In obtaining evidence concerning the reasonableness of management's accruals, the auditor should review management's calculations or make independent calculations. Accruals for payroll taxes should be compared with amounts shown on payroll tax returns. Additional evidence can be obtained by examining subsequent payments made on the accruals prior to the completion of fieldwork. Evidence obtained from these tests pertains primarily to objectives related to the valuation or allocation assertion.

Auditing Employee Benefits and Pension Plans

Many companies offer significant pension and postretirement benefits to employees. A number of manufacturing companies have defined benefit pension plans that present significant issues with respect to the measurement of pension expenses, as well as pension disclosures. The most significant risks are associated with misstatements in the valuation or allocation assertion (determining pension expenses), and the presentation and disclosure assertions (disclosure in the pension footnote). Defined benefit pension plans are normally subject to requirements of the Employee Retirement Income Security Act (ERISA) of 1974, which usually requires a separate audit of the pension plan. The financial statement auditor can usually refer to the results of the ERISA audit when auditing pension expenses and disclosures. When completing the ERISA audit, the auditor will usually employ an outside expert to audit the important actuarial assumptions that are needed to determine pension expenses and the projected benefit obligation. When auditing pension expenses, the auditor should also evaluate the reasonableness of the key actuarial estimates such as the discount rate that is used to determine the projected benefit obligation and the long-term rate of return assumption used for the expected return on plan assets. The discount rate should be in line with current annuity purchase rates or high-quality fixed income investments. The long-term rate of return assumption should reflect the actual and anticipated returns for the plan's assets.

Auditing Stock Options and Stock Appreciation Rights

A common form of employee compensation for many companies involves the use of stock options. The auditor should determine (1) the types of incentive compensation plans used to compensate employees and officers, (2) how compensation expense is determined, and how compensation expense is allocated to various accounting periods, and (3) the adequacy of disclosure related to incentive compensation plans.

First, the auditor should determine the incentive compensation methods used by the client and read the underlying contracts to identify significant terms associated with incentive compensation plans. Common methods include the use of both incentive stock options and, in some cases, stock appreciation rights. Stock appreciation rights are often used for key employees to provide them with sufficient cash to exercise stock options and hold the stock, rather than selling the stock to obtain sufficient cash to exercise the option.

With respect to accounting for compensation expense, most companies structure their stock option plans to meet the requirements of APB No. 25, so that they may use the intrinsic value approach and report no compensation expense associated with the use of stock options. Stock appreciation rights, however, require the recognition of compensation expense, regardless of whether the right is exercised during the period. The auditor needs to carefully evaluate the appropriateness of the application of GAAP in the context of the terms of contracts associated with stock options and stock appreciation rights.

The most significant issue associated with incentive compensation plans relates to adequate disclosures in the financial statements. FASB No. 123 requires these companies to disclose pro forma net income and earnings per share as if the fair value approach were used. As a result, the auditor must audit the valuation model used to determine the fair value of the stock options. When evaluating fair presentation in the financial statements, the auditor evaluates assumptions that include the risk-free rate, the expected life of the option, the expected volatility of the stock price, and expected dividends.

The auditor should also evaluate the fair presentation of disclosures, including general descriptions of the plan, and the number and weighted-average exercise prices of options that were outstanding at the beginning and end of the year, as well as options granted, exercised, forfeited, or expired during the year.

LEARNING CHECK

16-22 a. What is the likely acceptable level of detection risk for payroll expense account assertions? Why?

b. What effect does this have on the design of substantive tests for payroll assertions?

16-23 a. What procedures should be performed to obtain evidence about the reasonableness of management's accrued payroll liabilities?

b. Why is officers' compensation audit sensitive, and what tests should be performed on such compensation?

c. Explain how the auditor should test the appropriateness of accrued pension costs and pension expenses.

d. Explain how the auditor should test the appropriateness of stock compensation expense.

OTHER SERVICES IN THE PRODUCTION AND PERSONNEL SERVICES CYCLES

Inventory management is a core process that every manufacturing, wholesaling, and retailing company must manage well in order to attain profitability and cash flow goals. When the auditor evaluates issues such as the net realizable value of inventory, he or she should consider the client's business risks and the risk of substitute products or competitors taking market share. This knowledge might lead to a risk assessment assurance service.

Audit Decision 11

■ **How does the auditor use the knowledge obtained during the audit of the production and personnel services cycles to support other assurance services?**

Furthermore, the auditor's analytical procedures will address the effectiveness of the inventory management process. Usually, the auditor will evaluate an entity's inventory turn days. Figure 16-3 points out the wide variation in inventory turn days for three different industries. If a client ranks near the bottom of the industry, the CPA will usually try to address the issue of how the client could improve the inventory management process. CPAs regularly make recommendations for improvements in information systems that allow management to better monitor and control inventory shrinkage and better match inventory quantities with demand. However, the CPA must take care to focus on recommendations for the client and not cross the line of making management decisions or engaging in implementation issues that would impair the auditor's independence.

Personnel management is a core process for many companies. Today, most of the employment in the United States is in the service sector rather than in manufacturing. Many companies in the service sector track revenue per employee. Retailers often track both revenue per square foot and revenue per employee. When performing the audit, many CPAs monitor this statistic and evaluate performance relative to others in the industry. CPAs who understand the industry can often help clients identify opportunities that may exist in growing revenue per employee.

When auditing expenses and profitability, a CPA will often evaluate employee productivity statistics. As employees are more productive, companies will often obtain better profitability in an industry. Having a means to evaluate employee productivity (often the productivity of employee teams or departments) is particularly important in service organizations. CPAs are often skilled at developing the means to hold responsibility centers accountable for their use of resources—in this case the payroll resource. CPAs may assist clients by (1) suggesting appropriate measures of employee productivity or by (2) identifying steps that a client may take to improve employee productivity. For example, a manufacturing company may monitor the number of units produced per employee (excluding defects and rework). A service organization, such as a software company, may evaluate the number of new product innovations that are adopted by the marketplace that come from a product development team. A university may monitor outcomes such as the amount of grants and contracts obtained by a department's faculty member or a department's student–faculty ratios, student retention rates, and graduation rates. CPAs may work with clients to develop an appropriate set of performance measures as part of a performance measurement assurance service.

[FOCUS ON AUDIT DECISIONS]

This chapter focuses on the practical aspects of auditing the production and personnel services cycles. The chapter pays particular attention to audit planning concerns related to the production and personnel services cycles, specific internal controls that are tailored to these cycles, and substantive tests for each cycle. Figure 16-17 summarizes the audit decisions discussed in Chapter 16 and provides page references indicating where these decisions are discussed in more detail.

Figure 16-17 ■ Summary of Audit Decisions Discussed in Chapter 16

Audit Decision	Factors That Influence the Audit Decision	Chapter References
D1. What is the nature of the production cycle, and how are specific audit objectives developed for the production cycle?	The production cycle focuses on the audit of inventory for a manufacturer. It includes the purchases of raw materials, payment for direct and indirect labor, and the process of determining total production costs, the cost of ending inventory and of cost of goods sold. Figure 16-2 uses the framework developed in Chapter 6 to determine the specific audit objectives for the purchases cycle.	pp. 744–745
D2. What audit planning decisions should be made when developing an audit program for the production cycle?	Figure 16-3 illustrates how the auditor would use knowledge of the entity and its environment in the context of five example industries, each with different characteristics and risks. This knowledge is used to (1) develop expectations of the financial statements and (2) assess the risk of material misstatement. Figure 16-4 presents a number of analytical procedures that are commonly used when auditing inventory and the production cycle, along with a discussion of their audit significance. Many assertions in the production cycle involve important inherent risks. Some key risks are identified below and discussed in more detail in the chapters. Does the inventory actually exist (E&O)? Significant financial frauds have stemmed from phantom inventory. Is all inventory counted (C)? Does the client hold consignment inventory or have inventory on consignment out (RO)? There are significant valuation issues associated with accounting for production costs (VA). Additional inherent risk factors are discussed in the chapter.	pp. 745–749
D3. What should be considered in evaluating control activities for the production cycle transactions?	The primary functions in the production cycle include initiating production, producing inventory, and recording inventory. Figure 16-5 provides an overview of the accounting system for the production cycle, and Figure 16-6 identifies a number of example control activities that can control the financial reporting process for this cycle.	pp. 749–756
D4. What factors are involved in determining an acceptable level of tests of details risk for inventory assertions?	Figure 16-7 explains one possible preliminary audit strategy for each assertion in the production cycle for the audit of inventory. This figure provides a summary of how inherent risk, control risk, and detection risk may influence test of details risk for inventory.	p. 757
D5. How does the auditor determine the elements of an audit program for substantive tests to achieve specific audit objectives for inventory?	This section of the chapter uses the framework developed in Chapter 12 to develop substantive tests for each specific audit objective in the production cycle. These are summarized in Figure 16-8 and explained in depth in the chapter discussion. Particular focus is given to tests of the existence of inventory.	pp. 757–769
D6. What is the nature of the personnel services cycle, and how are specific audit objectives developed for the personnel services cycle?	The personnel services cycle includes executive compensation, employee compensation, salaried wages, hourly wages, incentive compensation plans, bonuses, stock options, and other benefits. Figure 16-11 uses the framework developed in Chapter 6 to determine the specific audit objectives for the personnel services cycle.	pp. 769–770

(continues)

Figure 16-17 ■ (Continued)

Audit Decision	Factors That Influence the Audit Decision	Chapter References
D7. What audit planning decisions should be made when developing an audit program for the personnel services cycle?	Various industries vary significantly in their labor intensiveness. The personnel services cycle is particularly important in the service sector that dominates the United States economy. The chapter discussion focuses on how this knowledge is used to (1) develop expectations of the financial statements and (2) assess the risk of material misstatement. Figure 16-12 presents a number of analytical procedures that are commonly used when auditing the personnel services cycle, along with a discussion of the significance of each ratio. There are a number of important inherent risks in the personnel services cycle. Risks include fictitious employees on the payroll, the overstatement of hours worked, cutoff problems if the pay period does not coincide with month or year-end, and valuation issues associated with stock options and accounting for pension plans. In addition, the auditor needs to be alert to padding of labor costs in cost plus contracts.	pp. 770–773
D8. What should be considered in evaluating control activities for personnel services cycle transactions?	Most personnel service transactions are routine transactions where risks can be controlled by an effective system of internal control. The key functions in the payroll cycle include initiating payroll transactions, the receipt of services, and recording and paying payroll transactions. Figure 16-13 provides an overview of the personnel services cycle, and Figure 16-14 explains control activities commonly found in the personnel services cycle. The chapter discussion addresses the common functions, documents, and controls found in many companies.	pp. 773–779
D9. What factors are involved in determining an acceptable level of tests of details risk for payroll balance assertions?	Figure 16-15 explains the details behind a preliminary audit strategy for each assertion in the personnel services cycle. This figure provides a summary of how inherent risk, control risk, and detection risk may influence test of details risk for payroll balances.	pp. 780–781
D10. How does the auditor determine the elements of an audit program for substantive tests to achieve specific audit objectives for payroll balances?	This section of the chapter uses the framework developed in Chapter 12 to develop substantive tests for each specific audit objective in the personnel services cycle. Figure 16-16 provides an example of substantive tests normally performed in the personnel services cycle. These examples are explained in more depth in the chapter.	pp. 782–786
D11. How does the auditor use the knowledge obtained during the audit of the production and personnel services cycles to support other assurance services?	Once the auditor has completed an audit of the production and personnel services cycles, the auditor should have information that supports an audit opinion, recommendations about improvements in internal controls, and knowledge that may be relevant to other client services. This final section of the chapter provides examples of how knowledge obtained while auditing the expenditure cycle can be used to support other assurance services that clients value.	pp. 786–787

objective questions

Objective questions are available for the student at www.wiley.com/college/boynton

comprehensive questions

16-24   **(Analytical procedures)** Circuits Technology, Inc. (CTI) resells, installs and provides computer networking products (client software, gateway hardware and software, and twinax hardware) to other businesses. Exhibit 16-24 provides some summary information from CTI's financial statements.

EXHIBIT 16-24 CTI SELECTED FINANCIAL INFORMATION ($000)

	20x1	20x2	20x3	20x4	20x5
Accounts Receivable, net	$ 837	$ 1,335	$ 1,121	$ 962	$ 822
Inventory	$ 1,025	$ 1,327	$ 1,099	$ 1,003	$ 1,027
Accounts Payable	$ 164	$ 380	$ 225	$ 201	$ 175
Sales	$ 3,780	$ 5,638	$ 4,623	$ 4,022	$ 3,095
Cost of Sales	$ 1,812	$ 2,691	$ 2,399	$ 1,923	$ 1,859
Gross Margin	$ 1,968	$ 2,947	$ 2,224	$ 2,099	$ 2,046

Required

a. Calculate purchases, gross margin, inventory turn days, accounts receivable turn days, and accounts payable turn days for the years ended 20x2, 20x3, 20x4, 20x5.

b. Describe the trends identified by performing analytical procedures in the gross operating cycle, the net operating cycle, and gross margin.

c. If tolerable misstatement is $45,000 for inventory, develop an expectation range for inventory turn days.

d. With respect to inventory, what might these trends indicate about the potential misstatement in inventory?

16-25   **(Analytical procedures—production and personnel services cycles)** The following information was taken from the accounting records for Aurora Manufacturing, Inc. The market for Aurora's products has been very competitive in 20X4, and the company was able to raise prices only 3.7 percent.

	UNAUDITED 20x4	AUDITED 20x3	AUDITED 20x2
Sales	$ 12,005,336	$ 10,291,333	$ 8,892,133
Cost of Raw Materials Used	$ 3,923,336	$ 3,173,333	$ 2,800,000
Direct Labor Cost	$ 1,696,081	$ 1,364,314	$ 1,190,000
Cost of Payroll Taxes and Benefits	$ 580,060	$ 439,309	$ 383,180
Indirect Costs	$ 1,088,885	$ 1,094,930	$ 962,100
	$ 7,288,362	$ 6,071,886	$ 5,335,280
Beginning Inventory	$ 330,587	$ 274,764	$ 156,577
Ending Inventory	$ 470,016	$ 330,587	$ 274,764
Capacity	10,000,000	10,000,000	10,000,000
Units Produced	8,780,800	7,840,000	7,000,000
Units Sold	8,750,000	7,775,000	6,850,000

Beginning Inventory	415,000	350,000	200,000
Ending Inventory	445,800	415,000	350,000
Direct Labor Hours	92,429	76,863	70,000
Number of Manufacturing Employees	46	38	35
Labor Cost Including Benefits	$ 2,276,140	$ 1,803,623	$ 1,573,180
Tons of Raw Material Used	7,473	6,222	5,600
Tons of Ending Raw Materials Inventory	21	18	16

Required

a. Calculate the following ratios for years 2, 3, and 4:
- Cost of goods sold
- Gross profit percentage
- Inventory turn days (ending inventory / cost of sales* 365)
- Number of units per ton of raw materials
- Number of units per direct labor hour
- Cost of raw materials produced per ton
- Cost of direct labor per hour
- Payroll taxes and benefits as a percent of direct labor cost
- Cost per unit of ending inventory

b. Describe the trends in raw materials costs and direct labor costs. Are these results consistent with the trends in gross profit margin and inventory turnover? What are the implications of the resulting ratios for the auditor's audit strategy in year 4? What specific audit objectives are likely to be misstated? How should the auditor respond in terms of potential audit tests?

16-26 **(Evaluation of internal controls—raw materials and supplies inventory)** The Jameson Company produces a variety of chemical products for use by plastics manufacturers. The plant operates on two shifts, five days per week, with maintenance work performed on the third shift and on Saturdays as required.

An audit conducted by the staff of the new corporate internal audit department has recently been completed, and the comments on inventory control were not favorable. Audit comments were particularly directed to the control of raw material ingredients and maintenance materials.

Raw material ingredients are received at the back of the plant, signed for by one of the employees of the batching department, and stored near the location of the initial batching process. Receiving tallies are given to the supervisor during the day, and he forwards the tallies to the inventory control department at the end of the day. The inventory control department calculates ingredient use using weekly reports of actual production and standard formulas. Physical inventories are taken quarterly. Purchase requisitions are prepared by the inventory control department and rush orders are frequent. In spite of the need for rush orders, the production superintendent regularly gets memos from the controller stating that there must be excessive inventory because the ingredient inventory dollar value is too high.

Maintenance parts and supplies are received and stored in a storeroom. There is a storeroom clerk on each of the operating shifts. Storeroom requisitions are to be filled out for everything taken from the storeroom; however, this practice is not always followed. The storeroom is not locked when the clerk is out because of the need to obtain parts quickly. The storeroom is also open during the third shift for the maintenance crews to get parts as needed. Purchase requisitions are prepared by the storeroom clerk, and physical inventory is taken on a cycle count basis. Rush orders are frequent.

Required

a. Identify the weaknesses in Jameson Company's internal control procedures used for (1) ingredients inventory and (2) maintenance material and supplies inventory.

b. Recommend improvements that should be instituted for each of these areas.

ICMA

16-27   **(Substantive tests and related assertions—inventory balances)** In performing substantive tests of inventory balances in the audit of the Henning Company, Karlene Kerr, CPA, recognizes that the following potential misstatements may occur or exist:

1. All inventory items are not counted or tagged.

2. Extension errors are made on the client's inventory summaries.

3. Purchases received near the balance sheet date may be included in the physical count but may not be booked.

4. Obsolete and damaged goods are not noticed in warehouse.

5. Inventory stored in a public warehouse may not exist.

6. Client personnel may incorrectly count the inventory.

7. The lower-of-cost-or-market method may be incorrectly applied.

8. Empty containers or hollow squares may be included in the inventory.

9. Goods held on consignment may be included as inventory.

10. Losses on purchase commitments may not be recognized.

Required

a. Identify the substantive test that should detect each error.

b. For each test, indicate the financial statement assertion(s) to which it pertains.

c. Indicate the type of audit procedures (i.e., inspection of tangible assets, confirmations) used for each substantive test. (Use a tabular format for your answers with one column for each part.)

16-28   **(Audit procedures for cost/standard cost system)** The client's cost system is often the focal point in the CPA's audit of the financial statements of a manufacturing company.

Required

a. For what purpose does the CPA review the cost system?

b. The Summerfield Manufacturing Company employs standard costs in its cost accounting system. List the auditing procedures that you would apply to satisfy yourself that Summerfield's cost standards and related variance amounts are acceptable and have not distorted the financial statements. (Confine your auditing procedures to those applicable to materials.)

AICPA

16-29   **(Computer-assisted substantive tests for inventory)** An auditor is conducting an audit of the financial statements of a wholesale cosmetics distributor with an inventory consisting of thousands of individual items. The distributor keeps its inventory in its own distribution center and two public warehouses. An inventory computer file is maintained on a computer disk and at the end of each day the file is updated. Each record of the inventory file contains the following data:

1. Item number

2. Location of item

3. Description of item

4. Quantity on hand

5. Cost per item

6. Date of last purchase

7. Date of last sale

8. Quantity sold during year

The auditor is planning to observe the distributor's physical count of inventories as of a given date. The auditor will have available a computer tape of the data on the inventory file on the date of the physical count and a general-purpose computer software package.

Required

The auditor is planning to perform inventory substantive tests. Identify the inventory tests and describe how use of the general-purpose software package and the tape of the inventory file data might be helpful to the auditor in performing such tests. (*Hint:* You may wish to refer to Chapter 12 as well as this chapter in answering this question.) Organize your answer as follows:

INVENTORY SUBSTANTIVE TEST	HOW GENERALIZED AUDIT SOFTWARE MIGHT BE HELPFUL FOR SUBSTANTIVE TESTS
1. Observe the physical count, making and recording test counts when applicable.	1. Determine which items are to be test counted by selecting a random sample of a representative number of items from the inventory file as of the date of the physical count.

AICPA

16-30   **(Computer-assisted substantive tests for inventory)** Brown, CPA, is auditing the financial statements of Big Z Wholesaling, Inc., a continuing audit client, for the year ended January 31, 20X2. On January 5, 20X2, Brown observed the tagging and counting of Big Z's physical inventory and made appropriate test counts. These test counts have been recorded on a computer file. As in prior years, Big Z gave Brown two computer files. One file represents the perpetual inventory (FIFO) records for the year ended January 31, 20X2. The other file represents the January 5 physical inventory count. Assume:

- Brown issued an unqualified opinion on the prior year's financial statements.
- All inventory is purchased for resale and located in a single warehouse.
- Brown has appropriate computerized audit software.
- The perpetual inventory file contains the following information in item number sequence:
  - Beginning balances at February 1, 20X1: Item number, item description, total quantity, and prices.
  - For each item purchased during the year: Date received, receiving report number, vendor, item number, item description, quantity, and total dollar amount.
  - For each item sold during the year: Date shipped, invoice number, item number, item description, quantity shipped, and dollar amount of the cost removed from inventory.
  - For each item adjusted for physical inventory count differences: date, item number, item description, quantity, and dollar amount.
  - The physical inventory file contains the following information in item number sequence: tag number, item number, item description, and count quantity.

Required

Describe the substantive auditing procedures Brown may consider performing with computerized audit software using Big Z's two computer files and Brown's computer file of test counts. The substantive auditing procedures described may indicate the reports to be printed out for Brown's followup by subsequent application of manual procedures. Do not describe subsequent manual auditing procedures.

Group the procedures by those using (a) the perpetual inventory file and (b) the physical inventory and test count files. (*Hint:* You may wish to refer to Chapter 12 as well as this chapter in answering this question.)

AICPA

16-31 **(PPS statistical sampling for inventory balance)** In auditing the December 31, 20X1, physical inventory being taken by employees in the Sutter Company, you decide to use PPS sampling for variables to determine that the inventory is not materially misstated. Thus far, the following information has been compiled:

Book value of inventory	$2,960,000
Tolerable misstatement	$200,000
Population size	6,511
Estimated standard deviation	$100
Desired risk of incorrect acceptance	5%
Anticipated misstatement	$50,000

Required

a. Calculate sample size and the sampling interval.

b. Assume that three items in the sample contained errors as follows:

Part Number	Book Value	Audit Value
40965	$15,700	$12,560
41139	$56,000	$50,400
47622	$23,200	$22,040

Calculate the projected error and the allowance for sampling risk.

c. What conclusion is supported by the sample results? Explain.

16-32 **(Internal control questionnaire—payroll)** Butler, CPA, has been engaged to audit the financial statements of Young Computer Outlets, Inc., a new client. Young is a privately owned chain of retail stores that sells a variety of computer software and video products. Young uses an in-house payroll department at its corporate headquarters to compute payroll data, and to prepare and distribute payroll checks to its 300 salaried employees.

Butler is preparing an internal control questionnaire to assist in obtaining an understanding of Young's internal control structure and in assessing control risk.

Required

Prepare a "Payroll" segment of Butler's internal control questionnaire that would assist in obtaining an understanding of Young's internal control structure and in assessing control risk. Do not prepare questions relating to cash payrolls, IT applications, payments based on hourly rates, piecework, commissions, employee benefits (pensions, health care, vacations, etc.), or payroll tax accruals other than withholdings.

Use the format in the following example:

QUESTIONS	YES	NO
1. Are paychecks prenumbered and accounted for?		
2.		
3.		

16-33   **(Control activities in payroll processing)** As part of the audit of Manor Company, you are assigned to review and test the payroll transactions of the Galena plant. Your tests show that all numerical items were accurate. The proper hourly rates were used, and the wages and deductions were calculated correctly. The payroll register was properly footed, totaled, and posted.

Various plant personnel were interviewed to ascertain the payroll procedures being used in the department. You determine that

1. The payroll clerk receives the time cards from the various department supervisors at the end of each pay period, checks the employee's hourly rate against information provided by the personnel department, and records the regular and overtime hours for each employee.

2. The payroll clerk sends the time cards to the plant's data processing department for compilation and processing.

3. The data processing department returns the time cards with the printed checks and payroll register to the payroll clerk on completion of the processing.

4. The payroll clerk verifies the hourly rate and hours worked for each employee by comparing the detail in the payroll register to the time cards.

5. If errors are found, the payroll clerk voids the computer-generated check, prepares another check for the correct amount, and adjusts the payroll register accordingly.

6. The payroll clerk obtains the plant signature plate from the accounting department and signs the payroll checks.

7. An employee of the personnel department picks up the checks and holds them until they are delivered to the department supervisors for distribution to the employees.

Required

a. Identify the shortcomings in the payroll procedures used in the payroll department of the Galena plant and suggest corrective actions.

b. Identify the weaknesses, if any, that you believe are material and the reasons why.

ICMA (adapted)

16-34   **(Potential misstatements/control activities for payroll)** The Kowal Manufacturing Company employs about 50 production workers and has the following payroll procedures.

The factory foreman interviews applicants and on the basis of the interview either hires or rejects the applicants. When the applicant is hired, a W-4 form (Employee's Withholding Exemption Certificate) is prepared and given to the foreman. The foreman writes the hourly rate of pay for the new employee in the corner of the W-4 form and then gives the form to a payroll clerk as notice that the worker has been employed. The foreman verbally advises the payroll department of rate adjustments.

A supply of blank time cards is kept in a box near the entrance to the factory. Each worker takes a time card on Monday morning, fills in his or her name, and notes in pencil on the time card the daily arrival and departure times. At the end of the week, the workers drop the time cards in a box near the door to the factory.

The completed time cards are taken from the box on Monday morning by a payroll clerk. Two payroll clerks divide the cards alphabetically between them, one taking the A to L section of the payroll and the other taking the M to Z section. Each clerk is fully responsible for her section of the payroll. She computes the gross pay, deductions, and net pay, posts the details to the employee's earnings records, and prepares and numbers the payroll checks. Employees are automatically removed from the payroll when they fail to turn in a time card.

The payroll checks are manually signed by the chief accountant and given to the foreman. The foreman distributes the checks to the workers in the factory and arranges for the delivery of the checks to the workers who are absent. The payroll bank account is reconciled by the chief accountant, who also prepares the various quarterly and annual payroll tax reports.

Required

a. Identify the misstatements that may occur in the Kowal Company's procedures.

b. For each misstatement in (a) above, give your recommended improvements.

AICPA (adapted)

16-35   **(Potential misstatements/tests of controls—payroll)** The following questions are included in the internal control questionnaire on control procedures for payroll transactions in the Pena Company:

1. Are pay rates, payroll deductions, and terminations authorized by the personnel department?

2. Are time clocks and clock cards used?

3. Is there supervisory approval of time worked by each employee?

4. Are payroll checks signed and distributed by treasurer office personnel?

5. Is there internal verification of payroll checks with payroll register data?

6. Are unclaimed wages controlled by a treasurer's office employee?

7. Is access restricted to personnel and employee earnings master files?

8. Are hirings authorized by personnel department?

9. Is time clock punching supervised?

10. Is responsibility assigned for the timely filing of payroll tax returns and payment of payroll taxes?

Required

a. Identify a misstatement that may occur if a *No* answer is given to each question.

b. Identify a possible test of controls assuming a *Yes* answer is given to each question. (Present your answers in tabular form using separate columns for each part.)

16-36   **(Additional services—inventory and personnel services cycle)** Most CPAs audit many clients, often in the same or similar industries. When clients hire CPAs, they want to know what the CPA can tell them to help them improve their business.

Required

Assume that you are auditing a company that assembles and retails personal computers. You have completed the audit and are prepared to give the client an unqualified audit opinion.

a. With respect to inventory and the personnel services cycle, list several sources of information that will assist you in benchmarking the company's performance.

b. Using the following table, (1) identify evidence that the auditor would obtain while performing the audit, (2) identify the audit objectives to which the evidence pertains, and (3) develop an example of how the evidence would support value-added services for the client.

PRODUCTION CYCLE

EVIDENCE OBTAINED DURING THE AUDIT	AUDIT OBJECTIVE SATISFIED WITH THE EVIDENCE	EXAMPLE OF HOW EVIDENCE WOULD SUPPORT OTHER SERVICES
1.		
2.		

PERSONNEL SERVICES CYCLE

EVIDENCE OBTAINED DURING THE AUDIT	AUDIT OBJECTIVE SATISFIED WITH THE EVIDENCE	EXAMPLE OF HOW EVIDENCE WOULD SUPPORT OTHER SERVICES
1.		
2.		

cases

16-37   **(Mt. Hood Furniture—PPS sampling problem)** Complete Case 13-35 at the end of Chapter 13, which involves this application of PPS sampling to the inventory of Mt. Hood Furniture.

16-38   **(Risk assessments and substantive tests for the production cycle)** Circuits Technologies, Inc.

Part I: Company History and Background

You are about to begin the audit of Circuits Technology Inc. for the year ended December 31, 2002. Circuits Technology Inc. (CTI), resells, installs, and provides computer networking products (client software, gateway hardware and software, and twinax hardware) to other businesses. Jessica Freeman founded the business in the late 1980s and grew the business to a stable and profitable enterprise in a major metropolitan area. Jessica owns 60 percent of the business, and four other shareholders (a brother, a sister, her father, and a friend) own 10 percent each. The minority shareholders contributed capital to the company when it was getting started, and the owners make up the board of directors. They usually meet only once a year to discuss dividends to be declared. During the rest of the year, the minority owners leave the day-to-day management decisions to Jessica as she also has controlling interest in the company.

The business grew rapidly during the 1990s. In 1999, near the end of the company's growth stage, Jessica was approached about merging the business with a larger company, but she decided that she did not want to merge the company, even if it meant limiting the growth of the business. CTI was her baby. Jessica enjoyed being CEO, she knew the business inside and out, and she did not want to be subordinate to someone else. The business was organized as a Subchapter S Corporation, and it was distributing a nice return to shareholders, so family members and friends were happy with her decisions. Jessica had her fingers in every aspect of the business, and she was boss.

Question 16-24 provides a history of CTI's last five years' financial history. CTI was a solid performing business up until 2001. Then the entire industry slowed down. All the demand that had been generated by the Y2K issues had been met, and the steady business and cash flow did not come as easily. Jessica and her sales staff had to work harder to close deals, and the industry became more competitive.

Rob Kaiser, the CFO, began complaining about Jessica's increasing intrusion into the company's finances in late 2000. During the period of steady performance, he and Jessica met quarterly to discuss the company's performance and finances. They would go over the entity's operating performance, its investing activities, and cash management, and the primary focus of attention was the annual distribution of earnings to shareholders. On occasion Jessica would want to structure a client contract in a particular way, or she would come in and insist on an additional discount for a particular customer, but Jessica had let Rob manage the finances of the business.

Now things had changed, particularly in the competitive environment where numerous vendors were chasing each customer. Jessica regularly discussed the accounting for particular transactions. It was not uncommon for her to come in and tell someone in accounting to change a sales invoice to offer a particular price discount to a customer. Furthermore, there were often heated discussions between Rob and Jessica over the monthly financial statements. Jessica knew the business and sometimes would not accept his explanations for draft financial statements that showed performance falling below Jessica's expectations. She had built the business, was involved in key decisions, and knew what profit margins should result. For example, gross margins should not fall below 52 percent as they did in 2000. In her view this was due to problems in the accounting system.

In some cases, Jessica was correct. Accounting was not a high priority. The first priority had to be sales and customer satisfaction. Jessica swallowed hard when she had to hire Rob, but it was clear that it would be more cost effective to hire someone in-house to manage finances than to subcontract to a CPA firm. However, accounting never had a significant budget. It could invest in technology and software, but it was always several people short of full staffing for the accounting system. Bob and his two salaried employees were cross-trained on most aspects of the accounting system, and everyone worked long hours. As a result, errors happened. The previous audit surfaced problems in the purchasing cycle, and some vendor's invoices had been paid twice. These problems usually surrounded rush purchases for clients where the vendor was asking for significant up-front payments. The audit also noted some cutoff problems in sales and purchases, and proposed an audit adjustment to the allowance for doubtful accounts. In Rob's opinion, this was the result of his department being stretched too thin.

In recent years, Jessica has paid considerable attention to the financial performance in the last two quarters of the year. Her major concern has focused on the company's profitability and ability to pay shareholder distributions. During the year-end close last year, Jessica was stopping by Rob's office daily to ask about the journal entries that were being made that day and their impact on earnings. This just added to the pressure on Rob to "get the job done."

Rob was also concerned about managing the relationship with First State Bank. Over the years the business relationship changed from one where CTI had significant deposits with First State Bank and used occasional seasonal borrowing to one where the line of credit has not been retired in the last 18 months. First State Bank, which had previously been satisfied with reviewed financial statements, now would like to have audited financial statements. This is another cost that Jessica and Rob don't want, but they have no choice. Furthermore, First State Bank established the following debt covenants.

- Dividends are restricted to 90 percent of net income.
- CTI must keep a minimum current ratio of 2.50 : 1.
- CTI must keep a minimum quick ratio of 1.2 : 1.
- CTI's debt to equity ratio cannot exceed 1.00 : 1.

Rob kept tight control on cash. An independent bank reconciliation was performed monthly. Furthermore, Bob closely tracked when vendor payments were due. With the exception of 1999, he had been able to keep the accounts payable turn days somewhere between 30 and 38 days. Rob would have liked to collect receivables faster, but the nature of the company's service, which involves installation of hardware and software to the customer's satisfaction, resulted in collection periods approaching 90 days. The company did not rely on programmed control procedures to monitor individual transactions. CTI did not have the staff to follow up on exception reports that might be generated by the accounting system. The primary controls in place involved Rob's independent review of transactions on a monthly basis. In addition, Jessica kept a close eye on revenues, expenses, and profit margins, and she demanded explanations from Rob when actual results deviated from her expectations.

Required

1. Evaluate the effectiveness of the CTI's control environment.

2. Analytical procedures: Complete Question 16-24.

3. Assess risk at the financial statement level.
   a. Evaluate inherent risk at the financial statement level.
   b. Evaluate the risk of fraud. Specifically consider each aspect of the fraud triangle; (1) incentives and pressures, (2) opportunity, and (3) attitudes and rationalization.

4. What is the potential for the effectiveness of the management performance reviews performed by Rob and Jessica with respect to the following assertions?
   - Existence of inventory
   - Valuation of inventory and cost of sales

5. Prepare a letter with any internal control recommendations that you have for management. Each specific recommendation should describe the current system, explain the risk involved, and make specific recommendations for improvement. You may assume that issues have already been discussed with management regarding the audit adjustments found in prior audits, so focus your attention on other issues that are of concern to you.

Part II: Substantive Tests

CTI prices its inventory at FIFO. You select a random sample of 35 items for price testing and find the following results as of year-end, 2002 (see Exhibit 16-38 on page 800). The total value of inventory is $1,027,000. You should assume that errors exist in the unsampled portion of the population in the same proportion that they exist in the sample.

Required

6. Evaluate the implications of the evidence you noted above.
   - What are the implications of your direct findings for fair presentation in the financial statements? You may assume that it is your best guess that errors found in your sample are representative of errors that would exist in items that you did not sample.
   - Based on your findings, what additional audit procedures should be performed, if any?

7. What issues do you want to discuss with company management and the board of directors? Draft your management letter comments regarding the issues that you want to discuss with the company management, and indicate (in the margin) who you would have the conversations with.

8. As the auditor for CTI, what conversations or correspondence, if any, should you have with First State Bank?

EXHIBIT 16-38

	SKU #	QUANTITY PER CLIENT	PRICE PER CLIENT	QUANTITY × PRICE	QUANTITY PER AUDITOR	PRICE PER AUDITOR	QUANTITY × PRICE
1	10001	6	$ 1,252.00	$ 7,512.00	6	$ 1,252.00	$ 7,512.00
2	10269	4	$ 1,275.00	$ 5,100.00	4	$ 1,275.00	$ 5,100.00
3	10537	7	$ 1,279.00	$ 8,953.00	7	$ 1,279.00	$ 8,953.00
4	10805	8	$ 2,200.00	$ 17,600.00	8	$ 1,200.00	$ 9,600.00
5	11073	3	$ 1,400.00	$ 4,200.00	3	$ 1,400.00	$ 4,200.00
6	11341	8	$ 1,410.00	$ 11,280.00	8	$ 1,410.00	$ 11,280.00
7	11609	4	$ 1,400.00	$ 5,600.00	4	$ 1,400.00	$ 5,600.00
8	11877	9	$ 810.00	$ 7,290.00	9	$ 510.00	$ 4,590.00
9	12145	10	$ 750.00	$ 7,500.00	10	$ 500.00	$ 5,000.00
10	12413	9	$ 750.00	$ 6,750.00	9	$ 750.00	$ 6,750.00
11	12681	8	$ 800.00	$ 6,400.00	8	$ 800.00	$ 6,400.00
12	12949	7	$ 1,800.00	$ 12,600.00	7	$ 800.00	$ 5,600.00
13	13217	4	$ 2,750.00	$ 11,000.00	4	$ 1,750.00	$ 7,000.00
14	13485	5	$ 2,750.00	$ 13,750.00	5	$ 1,750.00	$ 8,750.00
15	13753	6	$ 800.00	$ 4,800.00	6	$ 800.00	$ 4,800.00
16	14021	2	$ 800.00	$ 1,600.00	2	$ 800.00	$ 1,600.00
17	14289	3	$ 900.00	$ 2,700.00	3	$ 900.00	$ 2,700.00
18	14557	1	$ 900.00	$ 900.00	1	$ 900.00	$ 900.00
19	14825	5	$ 1,000.00	$ 5,000.00	5	$ 900.00	$ 4,500.00
20	15093	18	$ 1,000.00	$ 18,000.00	18	$ 1,000.00	$ 18,000.00
21	15361	16	$ 1,250.00	$ 20,000.00	16	$ 1,000.00	$ 16,000.00
22	15629	14	$ 1,250.00	$ 17,500.00	14	$ 1,000.00	$ 14,000.00
23	15897	9	$ 2,000.00	$ 18,000.00	9	$ 1,750.00	$ 15,750.00
24	16165	5	$ 2,000.00	$ 10,000.00	5	$ 1,750.00	$ 8,750.00
25	16433	2	$ 3,000.00	$ 6,000.00	2	$ 3,000.00	$ 6,000.00
26	16701	8	$ 250.00	$ 2,000.00	8	$ 250.00	$ 2,000.00
27	16969	8	$ 275.00	$ 2,200.00	8	$ 275.00	$ 2,200.00
28	17237	8	$ 270.00	$ 2,160.00	8	$ 270.00	$ 2,160.00
29	17505	15	$ 200.00	$ 3,000.00	15	$ 100.00	$ 1,500.00
30	17773	12	$ 400.00	$ 4,800.00	12	$ 250.00	$ 3,000.00
31	18041	12	$ 410.00	$ 4,920.00	12	$ 250.00	$ 3,000.00
32	18309	11	$ 400.00	$ 4,400.00	11	$ 310.00	$ 3,410.00
33	18577	9	$ 410.00	$ 3,690.00	9	$ 310.00	$ 2,790.00
34	18845	6	$ 750.00	$ 4,500.00	6	$ 650.00	$ 3,900.00
35	19113	4	$ 750.00	$ 3,000.00	4	$ 750.00	$ 3,000.00
Total				$ 264,705.00			$ 216,295.00

Additional Findings for Part 6

In addition, you find a journal entry where Rob has capitalized half of December's payroll for six network installers who work on two contracts as part of work in progress. Gross payroll amounts to $15,600 plus 35 percent for the cost of payroll taxes and benefits. The total of payroll included in work in process amounted to $21,060. Further investigation shows that the client was billed for all work performed on those contracts as of December 31, 2002.

professional simulations

The Vane Corporation is a manufacturing concern that has been in business for the past 18 years. During this period, the company has grown from a very small family-owned operation to a medium-sized manufacturing concern with several departments. Despite this growth, a substantial number of the procedures employed by Vane Corporation have been in effect since the business was started.

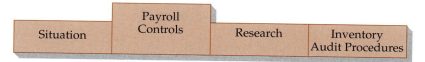

Under the supervision of a new CFO, Roger Bowman, Vane is in the process of planning to upgrade its systems. In this process, they are looking for your input as their auditor. The payroll function that has been in place for a number of years operates in the following manner.

Each worker picks up a weekly time card on Monday morning and writes in his name and identification number. These blank cards are kept near the factory entrance. The workers write on the time card the time of their daily arrival and departure. The workers also complete a job time ticket for each individual job they work on each day. The job time tickets are collected daily and sent to cost accounting, where they are used to prepare a cost distribution analysis. On the following Monday, the factory foremen collect the completed cards for the previous week and send them to data processing.

In data processing, the time cards are used to input hours worked and prepare paychecks weekly. Payroll is processed with access to the master payroll file, which includes worker identification numbers and wage rates. The checks are written by the computer on the regular checking account and imprinted with the treasurer's signature. After the payroll file is updated and the checks are prepared, the checks are sent to the factory foremen, who distribute them to the workers or hold them for the workers to pick up later if they are absent.

The foremen notify data processing of new employees and terminations. Any changes in hourly pay rate or any other changes affecting payroll are usually communicated to data processing by the foremen. Further analysis of the payroll function reveals the following:

1. A worker's gross wages never exceed $2000 per week.

2. Raises never exceed $0.55 per hour for the factory workers.

3. No more than 20 hours of overtime are allowed each week.

4. The factory employs 150 workers in ten departments.

Based on a system walkthrough and inquiries of people who work in the system you have also identified the following errors and inconsistencies that have been encountered in the past few pay periods:

1. A workers's paycheck was not processed properly because he had transposed two numbers in his identification number when he filled out his time card.

2. A worker was issued a check for $2,531.80 when it should have been $253.81.

3. One worker's paycheck was not written, and this error was not detected until the paychecks for that department were distributed by the foreman.

4. One worker received a paycheck for an amount considerably larger than he should have. Further investigation revealed that 84 had been punched instead of 48 for hours worked.

5. In processing nonroutine changes, a computer operator included a pay rate increase for one of his friends in the factory. This was discovered by chance by another employee.

For the following three assertions identify whether you believe Vane has sufficient internal controls or whether it has a significant deficiency in internal controls. For each assertion with a significant deficiency, develop a recommendation to improve the adequacy of control activities. Use the following format.

ASSERTION	ADEQUACY OF CONTROLS	RECOMMEND IMPROVEMENTS FOR SIGNIFICANT DEFICIENCIES
Existence and Occurrence	Controls are sufficient ○ A significant deficiency exits ○	
Completeness	Controls are sufficient ○ A significant deficiency exits ○	
Valuation or Allocation	Controls are sufficient ○ A significant deficiency exits ○	

Situation | Payroll Controls | Research | Inventory Audit Procedures

Vane's new CFO, Roger Bowman, has decided to use statistical sampling to estimate the quantities of inventory on hand at year-end, rather than count the entire inventory. Is it appropriate for Roger to not count the entire inventory? What are the audit implications if Roger proceeds to use statistical sampling to estimate the quantities of inventory on hand? Cut and paste the U.S. auditing standards sections that apply to this issue.

Situation | Payroll Controls | Research | Inventory Audit Procedures

Audit procedure

A. Understand the key economic drivers that influence the entity's cost of sales, gross margins, and the possibility of obsolete inventory.

B. On a test basis, trace data from purchases, manufacturing, completed production, and sales records to inventory accounts.

C. Vouch the items on the final inventory listing to inventory tags, count sheets, and test counts taken during the inventory observation.

D. Trace test counts taken during the inventory observation to the final inventory listing.

E. Examine sales invoices after year-end and determine the net realizable value of inventory.

F.   Confirm inventories at locations outside the entity.

G.   Based on tests of beginning inventory, production costs, and ending inventory, determine the appropriateness of cost of goods sold.

H.   Confirm agreements for assigning and pledging inventories.

I.   Examine vendors paid invoices for purchased inventory prior to year-end.

J.   Evaluate the completeness of presentation of disclosures to determine conformity with GAAP by reference to a disclosure checklist.

Determine the audit procedure that best addresses the following risks.

Risk	(A)	(B)	(C)	(D)	(E)	(F)	(G)	(H)	(I)	(J)
1. Inventory that was counted and on hand at year-end may not be included in the final inventory listing.	○	○	○	○	○	○	○	○	○	○
2. Inventory quantities may be correct, but inventory may be incorrectly valued at FIFO.	○	○	○	○	○	○	○	○	○	○
3. Inventory that is said to be on hand in a public warehouse may not exist.	○	○	○	○	○	○	○	○	○	○
4. Inventory may have to be sold at a loss in order to move inventory.	○	○	○	○	○	○	○	○	○	○
5. All manufacturing costs may not be included in the underlying accounting records supporting costs of sales.	○	○	○	○	○	○	○	○	○	○

AUDITING THE INVESTING AND FINANCING CYCLES

[17]

WORLDCOM AND ENRON: LESSONS FOR THE INVESTING AND FINANCING CYCLES

In June of 2002, WorldCom announced that during the previous two years $3.8 billion in costs had been capitalized rather than expensed. This is only half the story. Eventually we learned that WorldCom overstated earnings by more than $7.2 billion during the period of 1999 through the first quarter of 2002. WorldCom overstated earnings by approximately $3.3 billion for 1999 and 2000 combined, $3.0 billion for the year ended 2001, and $797 million for the first quarter of 2002.

The cost of capacity is a major expense for telephone companies. During the 1998–2002 period, many telephone companies were investing in increased capacity in terms of both fiber-optic lines and the ability to deliver cellular telephone service. Some of the capacity was purchased, and other access to capacity was rented. During this period of time, WorldCom reported better profit margins than anyone in the industry. Unfortunately, the reported profitability was driven by overstating long-term assets by some $7.2 billion.

The heroes in the WorldCom story were the internal auditors, who realized that capital expenditures exceeded the amounts authorized by the board of directors by over $2 billion. Internal auditors also uncovered over $500 million in capitalized costs that were not supported by vendor's invoices, and they showed a tenacity in understanding issues that were not clearly explained by others in the accounting staff. If the internal auditors were heroes, a number of accountants also played the role of villain. The SEC has brought suit against Scott Sullivan, the CFO; David Meyers, the controller; Buford Yates Jr., director of General Accounting; and Betty Vinson and Troy Normand, accountants in general accounting for WorldCom.

The Enron scandal is also about financing and investing activities. A significant component of the Enron story revolved around the use of special-purpose entities that allowed Enron to move both assets and debt off the balance sheet. Some estimates put the amount of off-balance sheet debt at over $20 billion. When Enron needed to borrow because of poor operating cash flows, it had no more borrowing capacity. It could not retire debt as it came due, and shareholders lost billions of dollars in the decline of the value of their shares. The critical aspect of Enron's fraudulent financial reporting was the failure to report how highly leveraged the company really was.

These two major companies that engaged in fraudulent financial reporting did so with issues directly related to the investing and financing cycle. Chapter 17 explains the auditor procedures that should have been performed to uncover these frauds.

Sources: SEC Accounting and Auditing Enforcement Release 1678 and related enforcement releases (1585, 1635, 1642, 1650, 1678, 1977). Bethany McLean and Peter Elkind, *The Smartest Guys in the Room,* (New York: Penguin Group (USA), 2003).

[PREVIEW OF CHAPTER 17]

Chapters 14, 15, and 16 focused on operating activities. This chapter focuses on investing and financing activities (using the FASB definitions of investing and financing activities in FASB 95, Statement of Cash Flows). The following diagram provides an overview of the chapter organization and content.

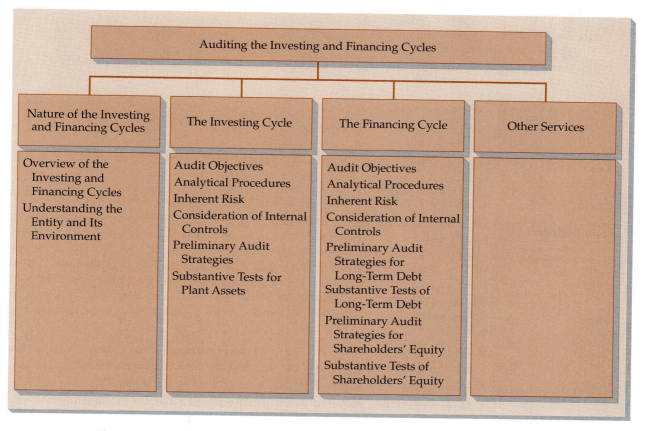

Chapter 17 focuses on the following aspects of the auditor's decision process associated with auditing investing and financing activities.

focus on audit decisions

After studying this chapter you should understand the factors that influence the following audit decisions.

D1. What is the nature of the investing and financing cycles?

D2. How does understanding the entity and its environment influence audit planning decisions in the investing and financing cycles?

D3. How are specific audit objectives developed for the audit of plant assets in the investing cycle?

D4. What audit planning decisions should be made when developing an audit program for the plant assets?

D5. What factors are involved in determining an acceptable level of tests of details risk for plant assets?

D6. How does the auditor determine the elements of an audit program for substantive tests to achieve specific audit objectives for plant assets?

D7. How are specific audit objectives developed for long-term debt and shareholders' equity in the financing cycle?

D8. What audit planning decisions should be made when developing an audit program for the financing cycle?

D9. What is involved in determining a preliminary audit strategy and planning an audit program for substantive tests for long-term debt?

D10. What is involved in determining a preliminary audit strategy and planning an audit program for substantive tests for shareholders' equity?

D11. How does the auditor use the knowledge obtained during the audit of the investing and financing cycles to support other assurance services?

NATURE OF THE INVESTING AND FINANCING CYCLES

OVERVIEW OF THE INVESTING AND FINANCING CYCLES

Audit Decision 1

■ What is the nature of the investing and financing cycles?

On a regular basis management makes decisions about how it uses resources to accomplish its goals. Resources may be deployed on operations and on management of key processes. Resources may also need to be deployed on capital expenditures necessary to support the continuation and growth of operations. Often these capital expenditures are of such magnitude that the entity needs to seek additional financing to acquire necessary assets. The auditor usually wants to obtain answers to the following questions when auditing investing and financing activities:

■ What assets are necessary to support the operations of the entity, and what are management's long-range plans for growing the entity's asset base?

■ What assets were acquired, or disposed of, during the period?

■ How were newly acquired assets financed, and what are management's long-range plans for financing the entity's growth?

These questions directly address an entity's investing and financing activities.

Investing activities are the purchase and sale of land, buildings, equipment, and other assets not generally held for resale. In addition, investing activities include the purchase and sale of financial instruments not intended for trading purposes (discussed in Chapter 18). An entity acquires these assets because they support its operations and core processes. As a rule of thumb, most businesses will acquire new assets if the rate of return generated by those assets exceeds the after-tax marginal cost of debt financing associated with acquiring additional assets. The first step in auditing investing activities involves understanding the assets that are needed to support the entity's operations (e.g., machinery, equipment, facilities, land, or natural resources) and the rate of return that a company expects to achieve from its underlying asset base.

The second step in auditing investing activities involves determining what assets were acquired during the period. Usually the growth in fixed assets should demonstrate a consistent relationship with the growth in revenues, accounting for some start-up period. Long-term assets are fairly stable for most entities. In other words, most of the fixed assets that existed at the end of the year also existed at the beginning of the year. Hence, the auditor often focuses audit strategy on auditing the changes in long-term assets rather than the entire population of long-term assets.

Financing activities include transactions and events whereby cash is obtained from or repaid to creditors (debt financing) or owners (equity financing). Financing activities would include, for example, acquiring debt, capital leases, issuing bonds, or issuing preferred or common stock. Financing activities would also include payments to retire debt, reacquiring stock (treasury stock), and the payment of dividends. If the auditor knows the changes that have occurred in investing activities, the changes in financing activities often are predictable. If, for example, an entity finances equipment with a capital lease, the values of the additional asset and debt are directly related. The population of debt and equity instruments is also usually small. For example, a public company may have approximately 50 different notes payable, and only one to three classes of equity securities, which are small population sizes. As a result, audit strategy often focuses on auditing the population of debt and equity at year-end.

UNDERSTANDING THE ENTITY AND ITS ENVIRONMENT

Audit Decision 2

■ How does understanding the entity and its environment influence audit planning decisions in the investing and financing cycles?

When the auditor develops a business-based approach to investing activities she or he studies the linkage between long-term assets and the financing used to acquire those investments. If a company engages in a major expansion of plant assets, it must also consider how it will finance the acquisition. The auditor must also be alert to the possible use of variable interest entities in highly leveraged deals that put both the property and the financing off balance sheet, and raise questions about whether the variable interest entity should be consolidated. It is essential that the auditor understand how assets support the operations of the entity, what new assets were acquired, and how they were financed. Figure 17-1 provides summary financial information related to financing and investing activities for the industries that have been discussed throughout Part 4 of the text.

There is a sizable variation between industries in the importance of financing and investing activities to the entity's operations. Hence, industry knowledge is important to developing expectations regarding the financial statements. In many of these industries investments in property, plant, and equipment are material, and carefully controlled. Because new investments are often accompanied by additional debt or equity financing, it is a common audit strategy to have the same individual audit both investing and financing activities.

[THE INVESTING CYCLE]

The following discussion focuses on **plant assets** (property, plant, and equipment). The logic that applies to the audit of plant assets is essentially the same as the logic that would apply to long-term assets such as natural resources or goodwill that may result in a merger or acquisition. Investing activities associated with investing in monetary assets are discussed in Chapter 18.

Figure 17-1 ■ Understanding an Entity's Investing and Financing Activities

Example Industry Traits	Developing a Knowledgeable Perspective about the Entity's Financial Statements (Industry Median)	Assessing the Risk of Material Misstatement
Mfg. of Construction Machinery and Equipment • Fixed assets are material. Fixed assets are a lower percentage of total assets only because of the significance of receivables and inventory. • Fixed assets are commonly financed with financing debt.	Net Fixed Assets as a % of Total Assets: 23.1% Operating Debt as a % of Total Assets: 29.7% Financing Debt as a % of Total Assets: 28.1% Equity as a % of Total Assets: 42.2% Sales to Net Fixed Assets: 10.0 Sales to Total Assets: 2.0	• There is little risk of asset obsolescence. • Debt tends to be stable and concentrated with a few sources.
Computer Mfg. • Fixed assets are a nominal portion of business model which is driven by technology. • Equity and reinvested earnings have been a significant source of financing. • There is an equity need for early-growth-stage companies.	Net Fixed Assets as a % of Total Assets: 15.2% Operating Debt as a % of Total Assets: 34.2% Financing Debt as a % of Total Assets: 27.0% Equity as a % of Total Assets: 38.8% Sales to Net Fixed Assets: 25.7 Sales to Total Assets: 2.3	• Chip manufacturers, rather than computer manufacturers, have a higher degree of obsolescence of production technology. • Debt tends to be stable and concentrated with a few sources.
Retail Grocer • Fixed assets are a significant portion of business model. • Sales are driven by sq. ft. of retail space. • Store size influences product mix. • Fixed assets are often financed with long-term debt.	Net Fixed Assets as a % of Total Assets: 40.9% Operating Debt as a % of Total Assets: 32.2% Financing Debt as a % of Total Assets: 38.6% Equity as a % of Total Assets: 29.2% Sales to Net Fixed Assets: 13.3 Sales to Total Assets: 5.0	• Locations are key to sales, and poor locations may create possible store closings and discontinued operations. • Debt tends to be stable and concentrated with a few sources.
Hotel • This is a very fixed assets-intense industry, and profitability often depends on the quality and location of properties. • Long-term assets are normally debt financed.	Net Fixed Assets as a % of Total Assets: 74.4% Operating Debt as a % of Total Assets: 21.8% Financing Debt as a % of Total Assets: 70.3% Equity as a % of Total Assets: 7.9% Sales to Net Fixed Assets: 0.7 Sales to Total Assets: 0.6	• There is higher risk with a high volume of property transactions. • Poor property performance may represent asset impairment situations. • There is a higher risk that both the property and financing will be put in an off-balance sheet variable interest entity.
Local School District • Fixed asset intense, but fixed assets are often kept in place for long periods. Asset life is often longer than financing period for bonds issued. • There is risk if student age population decreases.	Net Fixed Assets as a % of Total Assets: 49.5% Operating Debt as a % of Total Assets: 18.9% Financing Debt as a % of Total Assets: 23.7% Equity as a % of Total Assets: 57.4% Sales to Net Fixed Assets: 1.3 Sales to Total Assets: 0.7	• There are few property transactions in a given year. • Public bonding is usually used for debt, which is backed by tax levies. • Possible asset impairment occurs if student population decreases rapidly.

AUDIT OBJECTIVES

Audit Decision 3

■ How are specific
audit objectives
developed for the
audit of plant assets
in the investing
cycle?

The classes of transactions associated with the audit of plant assets include (1) **acquiring fixed assets** (whether purchased or manufactured), (2) **disposals of fixed assets** (sale or trade-in of fixed assets), (3) **repair and maintenance transactions** (which might include transactions which should be capitalized) discounts, and (4) **depreciation expense** (the matching of the cost of fixed assets with revenues). The specific audit objectives for the audit of fixed assets in the investing cycle are presented in Figure 17-2. Each of the objectives is derived from management's implicit or explicit assertions about fixed assets transactions, balances and disclsoures. These objectives are the primary ones for this cycle in most audits. They are not intended to be all-inclusive for all client situations.

To achieve each of these specific audit objectives, the auditor employs various parts of the audit planning and testing methodologies described in Parts 2 and 3 of this book, as illustrated in the previous three chapters. This includes under-

Figure 17-2 ■ Selected Specific Audit Objectives for the Investing Cycle (Plant Assets)

Specific Audit Objectives

Transaction Objectives

Occurrence. Recorded acquisitions of plant assets **(EO1)**, disposals of plant assets **(EO2)**, and repair and maintenance transactions **(EO3)** represent transactions that occurred during the year.

Completeness. All acquisitions of plant assets **(C1)**, and disposals of plant assets **(C2)** and repair and maintenance transactions **(C3)** that occurred during the period were recorded.

Accuracy. Acquisitions of plant assets **(VA1)**, disposals of plant assets **(VA2)**, and repair and maintenance transactions **(VA3)** are accurately valued using GAAP and correctly journalized, summarized, and posted. Transactions for depreciation expense are properly valued **(VA4)**.

Cutoff. All acquisitions of plant assets **(EO1 and C1)**, and disposals of plant assets **(EO2 and C2)**, and repair and maintenance transactions **(EO3 and C3)**, have been recorded in the correct accounting period.

Classification. All acquisitions of plant assets **(PD1)**, and disposals of plant assets **(PD2)**, and repair and maintenance transactions **(PD3)** have been recorded in the proper accounts.

Balance Objectives

Existence. Recorded plant assets represent productive assets that are in use at the balance sheet date **(EO4)**.

Completeness. Plant assets balances include the effects of all applicable transactions during the period **(C4)**.

Rights and Obligations. The entity owns or has rights to all recorded plant assets at the balance sheet date **(RO1)**.

Valuation and Allocation. Plant assets balances are stated at cost **(VA5)** less accumulated depreciation **(VA6)** and are written down for material impairments **(VA7)**.

Disclosure Objectives

Occurrence and Rights and Obligations. Disclosed plant and equipment events and transactions have occurred and pertain to the entity **(PD4)**.

Completeness. All PP&E disclosures that should have been included in the financial statements have been included **(PD5)**.

Classification and Understandability. All PP&E information is appropriately presented and described and information in disclosures is clearly expressed **(PD6)**.

Accuracy and Valuation. PP&E information is disclosed accurately and at appropriate amounts **(PD7)**.

standing relevant analytical procedures, assessing inherent risk, and assessing control risk when developing audit strategies.

ANALYTICAL PROCEDURES

Audit Decision 4

■ What audit planning decisions should be made when developing an audit program for the plant assets?

Analytical procedures are required as part of audit planning, they are cost effective, and they may assist the auditor in identifying assertions that may be misstated. Figure 17-3 presents some example analytical procedures along with an explanation of the problems that they might identify. Plant assets should be relatively stable, and as a result, analytical procedures may provide assurance about the fair presentation in the financial statements. However, the auditor should show an appropriate level of professional skepticism when evaluating the appropriateness of depreciation expense, as well as policies regarding whether a lease is a capital lease or an operating lease, and whether costs should be capitalized or directly expensed.

INHERENT RISK

Inherent risk for long-lived assets is a complex issue. On one hand, inherent risk for the existence assertion is often low because fixed assets are not vulnerable to theft. On the other hand, if incentives to improve earnings are present there is a higher risk that management may attempt to capitalize expenses. The completeness assertion may represent a significant inherent risk if a company uses a form of off-balance sheet financing that places the property and debt in a variable interest entity. The completeness assertion may also be high risk if it is difficult to determine whether the economic substance of a lease is an operating lease or a

Figure 17-3 ■ Analytical Procedures Commonly Used to Audit Plant Assets

Ratio	Formula	Audit Significance
Fixed asset turnover	Net sales ÷ average fixed assets	An unexpected increase in fixed asset turnover may indicate the failure to record or capitalize depreciable assets.
Total asset turnover	Net sales ÷ average total assets	An unexpected increase in total asset turnover may indicate the failure to record or capitalize depreciable assets.
Return on total assets	(Net income+(interest × (1-tax rate))) ÷ average total assets	An unexpected increase in return on assets may indicate the failure to record or capitalize depreciable assets.
Depreciation expense as a percent of property, plant, and equipment	Depreciation expense ÷ average property plant and equipment	An unexpected increase or decrease in the depreciation expense as a percent of depreciable assets may indicate an error in calculating depreciation.
Repair expenses to net sales	Repair and maintenance expense ÷ net sales	An unexpected increase in repair and maintenance expense may indicate the possibility that assets that should have been capitalized have been expensed.

improving earnings by managing depreciation estimates

In February 1998, Waste Management announced that it would take a pretax charge of $3.54 billion. The size of the charge stunned the investment community, and soon thereafter the SEC began an investigation into Waste Management's accounting practices. The cause of the write-off was to correct for an accumulation of understated accounting estimates over the prior decade. With hindsight it was determined that early in the 1990s Waste Management changed its depreciation policies at the direction of its president, Phil Rooney. In order to improve the company's earnings picture, the company began stretching the depreciation schedules on trucks (which cost about $150,000 each) from an industry standard 8–10 years to 10–12 years. Standard industry practice was to claim no salvage value on garbage hauling equipment, and Waste Management claimed approximately $25,000 per truck. For an individual piece of equipment, these seem like small changes. In aggregate, they were significant. Waste Management was a capital-intensive company with heavy fixed costs. In order to show positive results to Wall Street, Waste Management consciously stretched depreciation schedules, decreased its expenses, and improved earnings. A few years later the problem resulted in an accumulated overvaluation of assets of $3.5 billion.

Depreciation is an important accounting estimate. In this case Waste Management followed accounting practices different from others in the industry, resulting in lower depreciation charges and higher earnings. However, these accounting changes did not improve Waste Management's cash flow. Eventually, the economic substance of Waste Management's business caught up with the company, and significant write-downs were necessary. When auditing plant assets, it is important for the auditor to use his or her knowledge of the business and industry to test the reasonableness of both estimated useful lives and salvage values.

Source: Peter Elkind, "Garbage In, Garbage Out," *Fortune,* May 25, 1998, pp. 130–138.

capital lease. The rights and obligations assertion is significant because assets are usually pledged as collateral for underlying debt. Inherent risk for the valuation assertion is also high or maximum depending on the industry and the degree of difficulty associated with estimating useful lives and salvage values for depreciation methods and the extent to which the value of long-lived assets is impaired. Finally, fixed assets disclosures are relatively straightforward, and misstatements represent only a moderate inherent risk.

CONSIDERATION OF INTERNAL CONTROLS

The same aspects of internal controls that establish a high level of control consciousness such as a strong control environment, effective risk assessment, effective accountability for the use of resources, and monitoring of the control system are important in the context of accounting for plant assets. Specific control activities are discussed in the following paragraph. Although some of these transactions are routine, many are not, and the involvement of an effective disclosure committee is important for many of these assertions.

One of the key transactions associated with plant assets is the initial accounting for the acquisition of plant assets. The features of the accounting system and specific control procedures associated with the expenditure cycle discussed in Chapter 15 apply to the acquisition of furniture or equipment and the purchase of repair and maintenance. Hence, the controls described in Chapter 15 over the existence (EO1, EO3), completeness (C1, C3), accuracy (VA1, VA3), cutoff (EO1, C1, EO3, C3), and classification of purchases and repair and maintenance transactions (PD1, PD3) should control the acquisition of fixed assets. The disclosure committee should regularly review the entity's policies for determining whether a purchase, or new lease, should be capitalized or expensed (PD1, PD3). Transactions that are individually material, such as the acquisition of land or buildings, or major capital expenditures, are usually subject to separate controls including capital budgets and authorization by the board of directors (EO1). As a result, control risk may be low for many assertions. Finally, the disclosure committee should be involved in reviewing depreciation policies for new assets and the reasonableness of assumptions about useful lives and salvage values (VA4, VA6). Once deprecation polices are determined, computer programs are used to calculate depreciation expense, and these programs usually include reasonableness tests such as limit tests of checks to ensure that assets are not overdepreciated (e.g., the book value of assets should be greater than zero) (VA4).

Controls over the disposition of assets should include specific controls for the authorization for the sale, or trade-in, of fixed assets (EO2). Because the sale, or trade-in, of fixed assets is less routine, the disclosures committee should become more involved in reviewing the completeness and accuracy of accounting for these transactions (EO2, C2, VA2, PD2).

Controls over fixed asset balances often include physical controls over fixed assets as well as the maintenance of a fixed asset inventory that is periodically checked against existing assets (EO4, C4). Controls over the valuation of assets at historical cost (VA5) are directly related to the controls over the valuation of recorded transactions (VA1–VA4). The disclosures committee also has responsibility for reviewing specific transactions where property and debt reside in variable interest entities and for determining whether such transactions are properly accounted for (EO4, C4). The disclosures committee should also review any rights or obligations issues (RO1) and issues surrounding asset impairment (VA7) on a regular basis. Finally, the disclosures committee should review all financial statement disclosures before they are presented to the auditor (PD4, PD5, PD6, and PD7).

PRELIMINARY AUDIT STRATEGIES

Audit Decision 5

■ What factors are involved in determining an acceptable level of tests of details risk for plant assets?

Figure 17-4 summarizes some key issues related to preliminary audit strategies for the audit of plant assets. Auditors may follow very different approaches for public and private companies. Public companies with ongoing construction projects or acquisitions may have effective controls over these expenditures. However, most private companies do not have a disclosure committee, and as a result the auditor is likely to follow a primarily substantive approach for most, if not all, assertions.

An important aspect of fixed assets is that the balance is fairly stable over time. For most entities, the entire inventory that was present at the prior year-end is now gone. Yet most of the fixed assets that were present at the prior year-end are still present. As a result, many substantive tests focus on auditing the ending balance by tying beginning balance to the prior year's audit and then auditing the transactions during the year.

Figure 17-4 ■ Preliminary Audit Strategies for Plant Assets

Assertion	Inherent Risk	Control Risk	Analytical Procedures Risk	Test of Details Risk
Existence and Occurrence	Moderate to Maximum: On one hand, the risk of misappropriation of fixed assets is small. On the other hand, there is a significant risk that items that should be expensed are capitalized.	Low to High: Controls over the occurrence of fixed asset acquisition are often effective, as are physical controls over fixed assets. Controls over accounting policy regarding the capitalization of costs depend on disclosure committee effectiveness.	Moderate to High. Analytical procedures are more effective at signaling problems with unintentional misstatements than with fraudulent financial reporting. As a result, analytical procedures may not provide assurance about the existence of fixed assets.	Low to Moderate. Tests of details usually focus on tests of transactions. Vouching fixed asset transactions and inspecting acquired assets can be performed at an interim date and updated in final stages of the audit.
Completeness	Moderate to Maximum: There may be a significant risk associated with the acquisition of properties through the use of variable interest entities. There is also a moderate inherent risk that purchases may not be recorded.	Moderate to Maximum: Controls over accounting for off balance sheet financing depend on the effectiveness of the disclosure committee. Other risks relate to controls over completeness of purchases.	Moderate to High. Analytical procedures are more effective at signaling problems with unintentional misstatements than with fraudulent financial reporting. As a result, analytical procedures may not provide assurance about the completeness of fixed assets.	Low to Moderate. Tests of details usually focus on review of authorization of major capital expenditures by the board of directors, plus inquiry, observation, plant tours, and reading contracts and leases.
Rights and Obligations	Moderate: Fixed assets are often pledged as collateral for loans that are used to finance fixed asset acquisition.	Moderate to Maximum: Controls over disclosure of rights and obligations depend on disclosure committee effectiveness.	Maximum. Analytical procedures are usually not directed at rights and obligations issues.	Low: Confirmations of lenders of assets pledged as collateral are usually obtained as part of auditing financing activities.
Valuation or Allocation	High to Maximum: The major valuation issues are associated with the reasonableness of deprecation estimates along with the issue of impairment tests of fixed assets.	Moderate to Maximum: Controls over accounting estimates such as depreciation and the need for write-downs are associated with the impairment of fixed assets that depend on disclosure committee effectiveness.	Moderate to High. Analytical procedures are more effective as signaling problems with unintentional misstatements than with fraudulent financial reporting. As a result, analytical procedures may not provide assurance about the valuation of fixed assets.	Low: Auditors need to test the reasonableness of useful lives, salvage values, and depreciation expense estimates. Auditors must evaluate whether the value of fixed assets is impaired.
Presentation and Disclosure	Moderate: Disclosures related to fixed assets are not complex.	Moderate to Maximum. Controls over disclosures depend on disclosure committee effectiveness.	Maximum: Analytical procedures are not directed at disclosures.	Low: The auditor will often perform tests of details to evaluate the quality and accuracy of financial statement disclosures.

Audit Decision 6

■ How does the auditor determine the elements of an audit program for substantive tests to achieve specific audit objectives for plant assets?

SUBSTANTIVE TESTS FOR PLANT ASSETS

Possible substantive tests for plant asset balances in a recurring engagement and the specific account balance audit objectives to which the tests relate are shown in Figure 17-5. Each substantive test is explained in the following sections.

Initial Procedures

An important initial procedure involves obtaining an understanding of the business and industry. Industries that are very capital intensive usually have heavy fixed operating costs and require significant volume to break even. As discussed earlier in the chapter, it is important for the auditor to understand how assets support core activities of the entity and the generation of earnings. This understanding of the economic substance behind plant assets transactions provides the context for evaluating the reasonableness of evidence collected during the audit.

Before performing other substantive tests in the audit program, the auditor determines that the beginning general ledger balance for plant asset accounts agrees with the prior period's working papers. Among other things, this comparison will confirm that any adjustments determined to be necessary at the conclusion of the prior audit and reflected in the prior period's published financial statements were also properly booked and carried forward. Next, the auditor should test the mathematical accuracy of client-prepared schedules of additions and disposals and reconcile the totals with changes in the related general ledger balances for plant assets during the period. In addition, the auditor should test the schedules by vouching items on the schedules to entries in the ledger accounts and tracing ledger entries to the schedules to determine that they are an accurate representation of the accounting records from which they were prepared. The schedules may then be used as the basis for several of the other audit procedures. Figure 17-6 illustrates an auditor's lead sheet schedule for plant assets and accumulated depreciation.

Substantive Analytical Procedures

An important part of the investing cycle is determining that the financial information subjected to audit is consistent with the auditor's expectations. The earlier discussions regarding knowledge of the business and industry and analytical procedures addressed procedures that the auditor might perform to assess the reasonableness of balances for plant assets, depreciation expense, repair and maintenance expense, and expenses associated with operating leases (see Figure 17-3). When performing analytical procedures, the auditor should maintain an appropriate level of professional skepticism and investigate abnormal results. If the results of analytical procedures are consistent with the auditor's expectations, audit strategy might be modified to reduce the extent of details tests of transactions and balances discussed below.

Tests of Details of Transactions

These substantive tests cover three types of transactions related to plant assets: (1) additions, (2) disposals, and (3) repairs and maintenance.

Figure 17-5 ■ Possible Substantive Tests of Plant Asset Assertions

Category	Substantive Test	Specific Audit Objectives

Initial Procedures	1. Obtain an understanding of the entity and its environment and determine:
	  a. The significance of plant assets, and changes in plant assets, to the entity.
	  b. Key economic drivers that influence the entity's acquisition of plant assets.
	  c. Industry standards for the extent to which the entity is capital intensive and the impact of plant assets on earnings.
	  d. Understand the degree to which the company has used variable interest entities and operating leases to finance assets.
	2. Perform initial procedures on plant assets balances and records that will be subjected to further testing.
	  a. Trace beginning balance for plant assets and accumulated depreciation to prior year's working papers.
	  b. Review activity in general ledger accounts for plant assets and depreciation expense and investigate entries that appear unusual in amount or source.
	  c. Obtain client-prepared schedules of plant asset additions, retirements, and depreciation expense, and determine that they accurately represent the underlying accounting records from which they were prepared by:
	    i. Footing and crossfooting the schedules and reconciling the totals with increases or decreases in the related general ledger balances during the period.
	    ii. Testing agreement of items on schedules with entries in related general ledger accounts.
		All
		
		EO4, C4
		
		EO1, EO4
		
		VA4
		
		VA1, VA2, VA3

Analytical Procedures	3. Perform analytical procedures:
	  a. Develop an expectation for plant assets using knowledge of the industry and the entity's business activity.
	  b. Calculate ratios:
	    i. Fixed asset turnover
	    ii. Depreciation expense as a percent of sales
	    iii. Repair and maintenance expense as a percent of sales
	    iv. Rate of return on assets
	  c. Analyze ratio results relative to expectations based on prior years, industry data, budgeted amounts, or other data.
		All

Tests of Details of Transactions	4. Vouch plant asset additions to supporting documentation. 5. Vouch plant asset disposals to supporting documentation. 6. Vouch a sample of entries to repairs and maintenance expense. 7. Vouch the recording of new capital lease and operating leases to underlying contracts.	EO1, VA1, PD1, EO4, VA4 EO2, VA2, PD2, EO4, VA4 EO3, VA3, PD3, EO4, VA4 EO1, C1, VA1, PD1

Tests of Details of Balances	8. Inspect plant assets.
	  a. Inspect plant asset additions.
	  b. Tour other plant assets and be alert to evidence of additions and disposals not included on client's schedules and to conditions that bear on the proper valuation and classification of the plant assets.
	9. Examine title documents and contracts.
		
		EO4
		EO4, C1, C2, C4
		
		RO1

Tests of Details of Accounting Estimates	10. Evaluate the fair presentation of depreciation expense by evaluating the appropriateness of useful lives and estimated salvage values. 11. Determine if any significant events have resulted in an impairment of the value of plant assets.	VA6 VA7

Tests of Details of Presentation and Disclosure	12. Compare statement presentation with GAAP.
	  a. Determine that plant assets and related expenses, gains, and losses are properly identified and classified in the financial statements.
	  b. Determine the appropriateness of disclosures related to the cost, book value, depreciation methods, and useful lives of major classes of plant assets, the pledging of plant assets as collateral, and the terms of lease contracts.
	  c. Evaluate the completeness of presentation and disclosures for plant assets in drafts of financial statements to determine conformity to GAAP by reference to disclosure checklist.
	  d. Read disclosures and independently evaluate their classification and understandability.
		
		PD4, PD7
		
		PD4, PD7
		
		PD5
		
		PD6

Figure 17-6 ■ Plant Asset and Accumulated Depreciation Lead Schedule

Highlift Company
Property, Plant, and Equipment and Accumulated Depreciation
Lead Schedule
December 31, 20X1

W/P Ref: G

Prepared by: C.J.Y. Date: 2/4/x2
Reviewed by: R.C.P. Date: 2/12/x2

W/P Ref.	Acct. No.	Account Title	Asset Cost					Accumulated Depreciation				
			Balance 12/31/X0	Additions	Disposals	Adjustments DR/(CR)	Balance 12/31/X1	Balance 12/31/X0	Provisions	Disposals	Adjustments (DR)/CR	Balance 12/31/X1
G-1	301	Land	450,000✓				450,000					
G-1	302	Buildings	2,108,000✓	125,000		㉑(25,000)	2,208,000	379,440✓	84,320		㉑(1,000)	462,760
G-3	303	Mach. and equip.	3,757,250✓	980,000	370,000	㉑ 25,000	4,392,250	1,074,210✓	352,910	172,500	㉑ 1,000	1,255,620
G-4	304	Furn. and fixtures	853,400✓	144,000	110,000		887,400	217,450✓	43,250	21,000		239,700
			7,168,650	1,249,000	480,000	0	7,937,650	1,671,100	480,480	193,500	0	1,958,080
			F	F	F	F	FF	F	F	F	F	FF

✓ Traced to general ledger and 12/31/X0 working papers

F Footed

FF Crossfooted and footed

㉑ To reclassify cost and related accumulated depreciation for purchased addition recorded in Buildings account that should have been recorded in Machinery and Equipment account. See adjusting entry #21 on W/P AE-4

Vouch Plant Asset Additions

All major additions should be supported by documentation in the form of authorizations in the minutes, vouchers, invoices, contracts, and canceled checks. The recorded amounts should be vouched to supporting documentation (EO1). If there are numerous transactions, the vouching may be done on a test basis. In performing this test, the auditor ascertains that appropriate accounting recognition has been given to installation, freight, and similar costs. For construction in progress, the auditor may review the contract and documentation in support of construction costs.

When plant assets are acquired under a capital lease, the cost of the property and the related liability should be recorded at the present value of the future minimum lease payments (VA1). The accuracy of the client's determination of the present value of the lease liability should also be verified by recomputation. Vouching additions provides evidence about the existence or occurrence (EO1), rights and obligations (RO1), and valuation or allocation assertions (VA1).

Vouch Plant Asset Disposals

Evidence of sales, retirements, and trade-ins should be available to the auditor in the form of cash remittance advices, written authorizations, and sales agreements. Such documentation should be carefully examined to determine the accuracy and propriety of the accounting records, including the recognition of gain or loss, if any. The following procedures may also be useful to the auditor in determining whether all retirements have been recorded (C2):

- Analyze the miscellaneous revenue account for proceeds from sales of plant assets.
- Investigate the disposition of facilities associated with discontinued product lines and operations.
- Trace retirement work orders and authorizations for retirements to the accounting records.
- Review insurance policies for termination or reductions of coverage.
- Make inquiry of management as to retirements.

Evidence that all retirements or disposals have been properly recorded relates to the existence or occurrence (C2), rights and obligations (RO1), and valuation or allocation assertions (VA3). Evidence supporting the validity of transactions that reduce plant asset balances relates to the completeness assertion.

Finally, evidence obtained while auditing disposals of plant assets may assist in the audit of depreciation expense. Significant losses on the disposal of assets may indicate that depreciation estimates may be inadequate. Significant gains may indicate that the client is overly aggressive in depreciating assets (VA4, VA6).

Review Entries to Repairs and Maintenance Expense

The auditor's objectives in performing this test are to determine the propriety and consistency of the charges to repairs expense. Propriety involves a consideration of whether the client has made appropriate distinctions between capital and revenue expenditures. Accordingly, the auditor should scan the individual charges to identify those that are sufficiently material to be capitalized. For these items, the auditor should examine supporting documentation, such as the vendor's invoice, company work order, and management authorization to determine the propriety of the charge or the need for an adjusting entry (EO3). The auditor should also consider other expenses that an entity might have capitalized, such as line costs in a telecommunications company or the capitalization of interest costs.

Consistency involves a determination of whether the company's criteria for distinguishing between capital items and expenditures are the same as in the preceding year. This substantive test provides important evidence concerning the completeness assertion (C4) for plant assets because it should reveal expenditures that should be capitalized. Analyzing the entries to repairs expense also results in evidence about the valuation of the plant assets. In addition, the analysis may reveal misclassifications in the accounts that related to the presentation and disclosure assertion (PD1, PD3).

Tests of Details of Balances

Two procedures in this category of substantive tests are: (1) inspect plant assets, and (2) examine title documents and contracts.

Inspect Plant Assets

The inspection of plant assets enables the auditor to obtain direct personal knowledge of their existence (EO4). In a recurring engagement, detailed inspections may be limited to items listed on the schedule of plant asset additions. However, the auditor should take a tour of other plant assets during which he or she should be alert to other evidence relevant to plant assets. For example, the astute auditor will look for indications of additions or retirements not listed on the schedules (C1, C2, C4), which relates to the completeness and existence assertions, respectively, and to evidence regarding the general condition of other plant assets and whether they are currently being used, which relates to the valuation or allocation and presentation and disclosure assertions.

Examine Title Documents and Contracts

The ownership of vehicles may be established by examining certificates of title, registration certificates, and insurance policies. For equipment, furniture, and fixtures, the "paid" invoice may be the best evidence of ownership (RO1). Evidence of ownership in real property is found in deeds, title insurance policies, property tax bills, mortgage payment receipts, and fire insurance policies. Verification of ownership in real property can also be substantiated by a review of public records. When this form of additional evidence is desired, the auditor may seek the help of an attorney. The examination of ownership documents contributes to the existence or occurrence and rights and obligations assertions for plant assets.

Lease agreements convey to a lessee the right to use property, plant, or equipment, usually for a specified period of time. For accounting purposes, leases may be classified as either capital leases or as operating leases. The auditor should read the lease agreement to determine the proper accounting classification of the lease in accordance with Financial Accounting Standards Board pronouncements (PD1, PD4-7). When a capital lease exists, both an asset and a liability should be recognized in the accounts and statements. In addition to the existence or occurrence and rights and obligations assertions, the examination of lease contracts pertains to the presentation and disclosure assertion owing to the disclosures that are required under GAAP. The auditor should also examine contracts governing construction in progress, when applicable, to obtain evidence relevant to evaluating the client's accounting and reporting for the related assets.

Tests of Details of Accounting Estimates

Two important tests of accounting estimates include substantive tests to (1) review provisions for depreciation (VA4, VA6) and (2) evaluate impairments of plant assets (VA7).

Review Provisions for Depreciation

In this test, the auditor seeks evidence on the reasonableness, consistency, and accuracy of depreciation charges. An essential starting point for the auditor in making this test is to ascertain the depreciation methods used by the client during the year under audit. The identity of the methods can be obtained from a review of depreciation schedules prepared by the client and inquiry of the client. The auditor must then determine whether the methods currently in use are consistent with the preceding year. On a recurring audit, this can be established by a review of last year's working papers.

Determination of the reasonableness of depreciation provisions involves consideration of such factors as (1) the client's past history in estimating useful lives and (2) the remaining useful lives of existing assets. The auditor's verification of accuracy is achieved through recalculation. Ordinarily, this is done on a selective basis by recomputing the depreciation on major assets and testing depreciation taken on additions and retirements during the year. Evidence of unusual gains and losses on the retirement of assets may indicate that depreciation estimates may be misstated. This substantive test provides evidence about all the financial statement assertions except the rights and obligations assertion.

Impairment of Plant Assets

Events may occur between acquiring and retiring an asset that affect the valuation assertion and require an immediate writedown of the asset as addressed in FASB 121, Accounting for the Impairment of Long-Lived Assets and for Long-Lived Assets to Be Disposed Of. The auditor should evaluate whether the client has appropriately accounted for the impairment of plant assets when there has been a material change in the way an asset is used, or when there has been a material change in the business environment. The evidence to evaluate impairment is based on an estimate of the undiscounted future cash flows from the asset. Based on the criteria established in FASB 121, an auditor should consider that the value of an asset is impaired when the undiscounted future cash flows from an asset are less than the book value of the asset.

Tests of Details of Presentation and Disclosure

The financial statement presentation requirements for plant assets are moderately extensive (PD4-7). For example, the financial statements should show depreciation expense for the year, the cost and book value for major classes of plant assets, and the depreciation method(s) used. Evidence concerning these matters is acquired through the substantive tests described in the preceding sections.

Property pledged as security for loans should be disclosed. Information on pledging may be obtained from reviewing the minutes and long-term contractual agreements, confirming debt agreements, and making inquiries of management. The appropriateness of the client's disclosures related to assets under lease can be determined by recourse to the authoritative accounting pronouncements and the related lease agreements.

[LEARNING CHECK

17-1   Describe the nature of the investing and financing cycles and identify the major classes of transactions in the cycle.

17-2   Identify three questions that the auditor wants to obtain answers to, and explain why they are important to developing an audit strategy for investing and financing activities.

17-3   Compare and contrast the importance of investing and financing activities for the average company in the hotel industry versus the average company involved in computer assembly.

17-4   a. State the audit objectives for each management assertion that pertains to the audit of plant assets.
   b. How would the audit objectives for plant assets compare with audit objectives for investments in natural resources or intangible assets?

17-5   a. Identify three analytical procedures that an auditor might perform with respect to plant assets and explain how they might assist in identifying potential misstatements.
   b. Discuss the factors that would influence the auditor's consideration of inherent risk for plant assets.
   c. What is the relationship between internal control in the expenditure cycle and plant assets? What specific controls might apply to plant assets that might not apply to routine expenditures?

17-6   a. Contrast the auditor's responsibilities in verifying the beginning plant asset balance between a first time and a repeat audit engagement.
   b. Identify the substantive tests of plant assets that apply to three or more assertions.

17-7   Distinguish among the following substantive tests of plant assets and indicate the assertions to which each test pertains:
   a. Apply analytical procedures.
   b. Inspect plant assets.
   c. Examine title documents and lease contracts.
   d. Vouch plant asset additions.

17-8   What procedures may be helpful in determining whether all retirements of plant assets have been recorded?

17-9   a. What factors should the auditor consider in reviewing depreciation entries and computations?
   b. What factors should the auditor consider in determining whether the value of assets has been impaired?

[KEY TERMS

Acquiring fixed assets, p. 809
Depreciation expense, p. 809
Disposals of fixed assets, p. 809
Financing activities, p. 807

Investing activities, p. 806
Plant assets, p. 807
Repair and maintenance transactions, p. 809

[THE FINANCING CYCLE]

Significant investing transactions are usually accompanied by significant financing transactions. The **financing cycle** includes two major transaction classes as follows:

- **Long-term debt transactions** include borrowings from bonds, mortgages, notes, and loans, and the related principal and interest payments.
- **Stockholders' equity transactions** include the issuance and redemption of preferred and common stock, treasury stock transactions, and dividend payments.

Bond and common stock issues typically represent the primary sources of capital funds. Accordingly, attention is focused primarily on these two sources of financing.

The financing cycle interfaces with the expenditure cycle when cash is disbursed for bond interest, the redemption of bonds, cash dividends, and the purchase of treasury stock. The accounts used in recording financing cycle transactions include:

LONG-TERM DEBT TRANSACTIONS	STOCKHOLDERS' EQUITY TRANSACTIONS
Bonds, Mortgages, Notes, and Loans Payable	Preferred Stock
Bond Premium (Discount)	Common Stock
Interest Payable	Treasury Stock
Interest Expense	Paid-in Capital
Gain (Loss) on Retirement of Bonds	Retained Earnings
	Dividends
	Dividends Payable

AUDIT OBJECTIVES

Audit Decision 7

■ How are specific audit objectives developed for long-term debt and shareholders' equity in the financing cycle?

For each of the five categories of financial statement assertions, Figure 17-7 lists a number of specific account balance audit objectives pertaining to accounts affected by financing transactions outlined above. Considerations and procedures relevant to meeting these objectives are explained in the following sections.

ANALYTICAL PROCEDURES

Audit Decision 8

■ What audit planning decisions should be made when developing an audit program for the financing cycle?

Given that the auditor understands the entity's investing activities and the nature of the business, the entity's financing activities should be predictable. Figure 17-8 presents some example analytical procedures along with an explanation of the problems that they might identify. These analytical procedures provide indicators of the entity's need for financing, its ability to service debt, and the reasonableness of interest costs (including both interest expense and capitalized interest).

INHERENT RISK

The risk of misstatements in executing and recording financing cycle transactions is usually moderate. The major risk is associated with the completeness assertion. These risks involve the usual risks of unrecorded liabilities along with the use of variable interest entities for off-balance sheet financing (both are completeness assertion problems). Another significant inherent risk relates to equity instruments that behave like debt. These should not be classified as shareholders' equity

Figure 17-7 ■ Selected Specific Audit Objectives for the Financing Cycle (Debt and Equity)

Specific Audit Objectives

Transaction Objectives

Occurrence. Recorded debt **(EO1)**, interest cost **(EO2)**, and equity **(EO3)** represent transactions that occurred during the year.

Completeness. All debt **(C1)** and interest costs incurred **(C2)** and equity transactions **(C3)** that occurred during the period were recorded.

Accuracy. Debt **(VA1)**, interest costs **(VA2)**, and equity transactions **(VA3)** transactions are accurately valued using GAAP and correctly journalized, summarized, and posted.

Cutoff. All debt **(EO1 and C1)**, interest cost **(EO2 and C2)**, and equity transactions **(EO3 and C3)** have been recorded in the correct accounting period.

Classification. All debt **(PD1)**, interest cost **(PD2)**, and equity transactions **(PD3)** have been recorded in the proper accounts.

Balance Objectives

Existence. Recorded debt **(EO4)** and equity **(EO5)** exist at the balance sheet date.

Completeness. All debt **(C4)** and equity **(C5)** is recorded at the balance sheet date.

Rights and Obligations. All recorded debt balances are the obligations of the entity **(RO1)**, and equity balances represent owner's claims on the reporting entity's assets **(RO2)**.

Valuation and Allocation. Debt **(VA4)** and equity **(VA5)** balances are properly valued in accordance with GAAP.

Disclosure Objectives

Occurrence and Rights and Obligations. Debt **(PD4)** and equity **(PD8)** disclosures have occurred and pertain to the entity.

Completeness. All debt **(PD5)** and equity **(PD9)** disclosures that should have been included in the financial statements have been included.

Classification and Understandability. All debt **(PD6)** and equity **(PD10)** information is appropriately presented and described and information in disclosures is clearly expressed.

Accuracy and Valuation. Debt **(PD7)** and equity **(PD11)** information is disclosed accurately and at appropriate amounts.

in the financial statements. In many companies, these debt and equity transactions occur infrequently. In addition, board of director authorizations are required for most transactions, and company officers participate in their execution. The routine transactions in this cycle include the payment of principal and interest (which should be covered by controls in the expenditure cycle) and the payment of dividends (which are often handled by outside agents).

CONSIDERATION OF INTERNAL CONTROLS

The applicability of the internal control components to financing cycle transactions and balances is similar in many respects to that described earlier for the investing cycle. In the control environment, for instance, responsibility for the transactions is usually assigned to the treasurer or chief financial officer who must possess the integrity and competence to perform these duties. Major transactions will require authorization by the board of directors, and the board's audit committee may closely monitor activities and controls in this cycle.

The accounting system element of the information and communication component will generally provide for subsidiary ledgers for both bonds payable and capital stock. These may be maintained by entity personnel or outside agents.

Figure 17-8 ■ Analytical Procedures Commonly Used to Audit the Financing Cycle

Ratio or Other Financial Information	Formula	Audit Significance
Free Cash Flow	Cash Flow from Operation less Capital Expenditures	Negative free cash flows indicate the need for expected financing to prevent drawing down on cash or investments.
Interest-Bearing Debt to Total Assets	Interest-Bearing Debt ÷ Total Assets	Provides a reasonableness of the entity's proportion of debt that may be compared with prior years' experience or industry data.
Shareholders' Equity to Total Assets	Shareholders' Equity ÷ Total Assets	Provides a reasonableness of the entity's proportion of equity that may be compared with prior years' experience or industry data.
Comparing Return on Assets with the Incremental Cost of Debt	Is ROA > the incremental cost of debt? $ROA = (Net\ Income + (Interest \times (1\text{-}tax\ rate)))/Average\ Total\ Assets$	If a company is able to generate a higher rate of return on assets than its incremental cost of debt, this is a signal that an entity may use debt financing to expand the assets and earnings of the entity.
Return on Common Equity	(Net Income – Preferred Dividends) ÷ Average Common Shareholders' Equity	Provides a reasonableness test of shareholder's equity given the company's earnings and financing structure.
Current Portion of Debt and Dividends to Cash Flow from Operations	(Current Portion of Debt + Dividends) ÷ Cash Flow from Operations	A test of the entity's ability to service its financing obligations. Ratios less than 1.0 indicate potential liquidity problems.
Times Interest Earned	Income before Interest and Income Taxes ÷ (Interest Expense + Capitalized Interest)	A test of the entity's ability to generate earnings to cover cost of debt service. Ratios less than 1.0 indicate that the entity's earnings are insufficient to cover financing costs.
Interest Expense to Interest-Bearing Debt	(Interest Expense + Capitalized Interest) ÷ Average Interest Bearing Debt	A reasonableness test of recorded interest expense that should approximate the entity's average cost of debt capital.

Applications of each category of control activities can be found in the financing cycle and are commented upon in the next two sections.

Common Documents and Records

Several of the documents described in the investing cycle, such as stock and bond certificates and a bond indenture, are also important in the financing cycle except the perspective is changed from that of the investor to the issuer. As noted above, separate bondholder and stockholder subsidiary ledgers may be maintained. In addition, financing cycle transactions may involve entries in the general journal and cash receipts and disbursements journals for the issuance and retirement of debt and equity securities, the accrual and payment of interest, and the declaration and payment of dividends.

Functions and Related Controls

The following **financing functions** and related control activities are associated with the financing cycle:

- *Authorizing bonds and capital stock.* The board of directors usually authorizes financing transactions based on its strategic plans and investing activities.
- *Issuing bonds and capital stock.* Issues are made in accordance with board of directors authorizations and legal requirements, and proceeds are promptly deposited intact; unissued bond and stock certificates are physically safeguarded.
- *Paying bond interest and cash dividends.* Payments are made to proper payees in accordance with board of directors or management authorizations.
- *Redeeming and reacquiring bonds and capital stock.* Transactions are executed in accordance with board of directors authorizations; treasury stock certificates are physically safeguarded.
- *Recording financing transactions.* Transactions are correctly recorded as to amount, classification, and accounting period based on supporting authorizations and documentation; the duties of executing and recording financing transactions are segregated; periodic independent checks are made of agreement of subsidiary ledgers and control accounts, including confirmation with the **bond trustee** or **transfer agent,** if applicable.

Major financing transactions (authorizing and issuing debt, bonds, or capital stock) usually require involvement of the board of directors (EO1, EO3). Controls over the routine payment of principal and interest are usually subject to the standard internal controls in the expenditure cycle (EO2, VA2, PD2). Dividends require board of directors authorization and are usually handled by an outside transfer agent (EO3, VA3, PD3). Controls over the completeness of transactions usually involve the regular review of the disclosure committee, particularly with respect to accounting for any transactions involving variable interest entities (C1-3, PD1-3). An independent review of the amortization of bond premium or discounts also falls within the responsibilities of a disclosures committee. This review is usually performed when the bond is issued (VA1-2).

Management normally maintains subsidiary records of loan balances. It is common for the Treasury Department to establish independent checks of such balances against monthly statements sent by lenders (EO4, C4, RO1, VA4). Equity transactions are usually rare. In a private company the Treasury Department usually maintains controls over stock certificates. Public companies usually outsource these transactions to a transfer agent. Often a quarterly reconciliation is sufficient (EO5, C5, RO2, VA5). Finally, the disclosure committee should review all financial statement disclosures before they are presented to the auditor (PD4-11).

PRELIMINARY AUDIT STRATEGIES FOR LONG-TERM DEBT

Audit Decision 9

■ What is involved in determining a preliminary audit strategy and planning an audit program for substantive tests for long-term debt?

Figure 17-9 summarizes some key issues related to preliminary audit strategies for the audit of long-term debt. This is an area where the significant inherent risk is a risk of unrecorded liabilities. Auditors will want to ascertain whether financing and investing activities are consistent with each other. Auditors may follow slightly different approaches for public and private companies. Public companies will often have effective controls over borrowing. However, most private companies may

Figure 17-9 ■ Preliminary Audit Strategies for Long-Term Debt

Assertion	Inherent Risk	Control Risk	Analytical Procedures Risk	Test of Details Risk
Existence and Occurrence	Moderate: The existence of recorded debt is not a significant inherent risk.	Low: The Treasury Department should regularly compare existing debt with monthly statements from lenders.	Moderate: Comparing financial data and linking investing activities with financing activities disclose misstatements.	High: The auditor will usually directly confirm borrowing arrangements with lenders.
Completeness	Maximum: There is a significant inherent risk associated with unrecorded liabilities. This is an important risk if a company uses a variable interest entity to finance property acquisitions.	Moderate or High: Primary controls include involvement of the board of directors and effective disclosure committees.	High: Comparison of financial numbers may not necessarily disclose unrecorded liabilities.	Low: Direct confirmation of borrowing arrangements, including entities that have lent funds in the past but currently have zero balances.
Rights and Obligations	High: An important inherent risk represents understanding the collateral that may be pledged as security for a loan.	Moderate or High: Primary control is the involvement of an effective disclosures committee.	Maximum: Analytical procedures are not directed at the rights and obligations assertion.	Low: Direct confirmation of borrowing arrangements will include information about assets pledged as security for loans. The auditor will also read the contracts to understand terms of borrowing.
Valuation or Allocation	Moderate: The valuation of recorded debt is not high. The calculations associated with debt are not complex.	Moderate or Low: Independent review of principal and interest calculations.	Moderate or low: Analytical procedures are often used to test the reasonableness of interest expense.	High: The auditor will usually directly confirm amounts of outstanding borrowing and accrued interest with lenders.
Presentation and Disclosure	High or Maximum: There are numerous debt disclosures that need to be addressed.	Moderate or Maximum: Primary control is the involvement of an effective disclosures committee.	Maximum: Analytical procedures are not directed at disclosures.	Low: The auditor will often perform tests of details to evaluate the quality and accuracy of financial statement disclosures. The auditor will also read the contracts to understand terms of borrowing.

have neither a significant treasury function nor an effective disclosure committee. Even with strong controls, debt instruments are usually small in number, even for large companies. This makes confirmation of debt a cost-effective audit approach.

SUBSTANTIVE TESTS OF LONG-TERM DEBT

Figure 17-10 shows a list of possible substantive tests of long-term debt balances together with the specific audit objectives to which each test relates. As in the case

Figure 17-10 ■ Possible Substantive of Long-Term Debt Assertions

Category	Substantive Test	Specific Audit Objectives

Initial Procedures	1. Obtain an understanding of the business and industry and determine:
	    a. The significance of various sources of financing (debt and equity) to the entity
	    b. Key economic drivers that influence the entity's need for financing and its ability to service the cost of debt and equity.
	    c. Industry standards for the extent to which the industry uses debt and equity financing and the impact of debt on earnings.
	    d. Understand the degree to which the company has used variable interest entities and operating leases to finance assets.
	 2. Perform initial procedures on long-term debt balances and records that will be subject to further testing.
	    a. Trace beginning balance for long-term debt accounts to last year's working papers.
	    b. Review activity in all long-term debt and related income statement accounts and investigate entries that appear unusual in amount or source.
	    c. Obtain client-prepared schedules of long-term debt and determine that they accurately represent the underlying accounting records from which they were prepared by:
	      i. Footing and crossfooting the schedules and reconciling the totals with increases or decreases in related subsidiary and general ledger balances.
	      ii. Testing agreement of items on schedules with entries in related subsidiary and general ledger accounts.
		All
		
		 VA4
		
		 EO1, EO4
		
		 VA4
		
		 VA4
		 VA4

Analytical Procedures	3. Perform analytical procedures:
	    a. Calculate ratios: (see Figure 17-8)
	    b. Analyze ratio results relative to expectations based on prior year, budget, industry, or other data.
		All

Tests of Details of Transactions	4. Vouch a sample of entries in long-term debt and related interest expense accounts.	EO1, VA1, PD1 EO2, VA2, PD2
Tests of Details of Balances	5. Review authorizations and contracts for long-term debt. 6. Confirm debt with lenders and bond trustees. 7. Recalculate interest expense.	EO4, C1, C4, RO1, VA4 EO4, C1, C4, RO1, VA4 EO2, C2, VA2, PD2

Presentation and Disclosure	8. Compare statement presentation with GAAP.
	    a. Determine that long-term debt balances are properly identified and classified in the financial statements.
	    b. Determine the appropriateness of disclosures concerning all terms, covenants, and retirement provisions pertaining to long-term debt.
	    c. Evaluate the completeness of presentation and disclosures for long-term debt in drafts of financial statements to determine conformity to GAAP by reference to disclosure checklist.
	    d. Read disclosures and independently evaluate their classificaiton and understandability.
		
		 PD4, PD7
		
		 PD4, PD7
		
		 PD5
		
		 PD6

of accounts payable in Chapter 15, the auditor is primarily concerned about the understatement (completeness assertion) of long-term debt. The auditor relies primarily on (1) direct communication with outside independent sources, (2) review of documentation, and (3) recomputations in obtaining sufficient competent evidential matter about the assertions pertaining to long-term debt balances. Audit working papers, such as the analysis of long-term notes payable and interest in Figure 17-11, are used to document the auditor's tests. Each of the substantive tests is explained in a following section.

Initial Procedures

As shown in Figure 17-10, the familiar initial procedures are applicable to long-term debt balances. It is important to obtain an understanding of the business and industry, and determine the entity's need for external financing and its ability to service debt. Because financing is so clearly linked to investing activities, the auditor may perform these procedures simultaneously.

The schedules associated with long-term debt may include separate schedules of long-term notes payable to banks, obligations under capital leases, and listings of registered bondholders prepared by bond trustees. As in each of the previous listings of possible substantive tests, these procedures pertain to the mathematical and clerical accuracy component of the valuation or allocation assertion, and are performed preparatory to using the long-term debt schedules as a basis for additional substantive tests.

Analytical Procedures

An important part of auditing long-term debt is determining that the financial information subjected to audit is consistent with the auditor's expectations. The earlier discussions regarding knowledge of the entity and its environment and analytical procedures risk addressed procedures that the auditor might perform to assess the reasonableness of financial statement information regarding long-term debt and interest expense (Figure 17-8). The auditor should also evaluate the disclosures regarding the maturities of debt and debt covenants. As part of the auditor's responsibilities with respect to evaluating whether an entity is a going concern, the auditor will evaluate the entity's ability to generate sufficient cash flow to meet commitments regarding interest expenses (including capitalized interest), debt maturities, and debt covenants. When performing analytical procedures, the auditor should maintain an appropriate level of professional skepticism and investigate abnormal results.

Tests of Details of Transactions

For bonds, the auditor should obtain evidence on both the face value and net proceeds of the obligation at the date of issue. Issuances of debt instruments should be traced to cash receipts as evidenced by brokers' advices. Payments on principal of long-term debt can be verified by an examination of vouchers and canceled checks; payments in full can be validated by an inspection of the canceled notes or bond certificates. When installment payments are involved, their propriety can be traced to repayment schedules. Bonds may also be converted into stock. Evidence of such transactions is available in the form of canceled bond certificates and the issuance of related stock certificates.

Figure 17-11 ■ Notes and Interest Payable Working Paper

WILLIAMS COMPANY
LONG-TERM PAYABLE AND ACCRUED INTEREST
DECEMBER 31, 20X1

W/P REF: N-3
PREPARED BY: CJL DATE: 1/24/X2
REVIEWED BY: RCP DATE: 1/30/X2

ACCTS. 220, 225, 475

DESCRIPTION	NOTES PAYABLE				INTEREST PAYABLE			
	BALANCE 1/1/X1	ADDITIONS	PAYMENTS	BALANCE 12/31/X1	BALANCE 1/1/X1	EXPENSE	PAYMENTS	BALANCE 12/31/X1
10% NOTE PAYABLE TO CULVER NATIONAL BANK, DUE $100,000 PER YEAR TO 7/1/X3 ①	300,000 √		100,000 ø	200,000 Ⓒ y	15,000 y	25,000 Ⓡ	30,000 ø	10,000
9% NOTE PAYABLE TO FIRST TRUST COMPANY, DUE 9/1/X3 ②		250,000 √ ø		250,000 Ⓒ y		7,500 Ⓡ		7,500
	300,000	250,000	100,000	450,000	15,000	32,500	30,000	17,500 y
	F	F	F	FF To N-1	F	F To N-5	F	FF To N-1

① Long-term investments in stock of Afton Co. and Boltry Inc pledged as security-see confirmation received from bank-Q-4
② Land and building pledged as security-see bank confirmation-Q-5
√ Traced to prior years working papers
y Traced to ledger at 12/31/X1
Ⓒ Confirmed by bank-see Q-4 and Q-5
ø Examined copy of note
→ Traced to cash journal and supporting documentation
Ⓡ Recomputed interest expense-no exception
F Footed
FF Footed and crossfooted

When bond interest is paid by an independent agent, the auditor should examine the agent's reports on payments. The vouching of entries to long-term debt accounts provides evidence about the following four assertions: existence or occurrence (EO1-2), completeness (C1-2), rights and obligations (RO1), and valuation or allocation (VA1-2). Again, the completeness assertion is addressed only in the sense that vouching debits to long-term debt provides evidence that entries made to reduce debt balances are not invalid. Vouching recorded entries will not reveal unrecorded long-term debt.

Tests of Details of Balances

There are three substantive tests in this category: (1) review authorizations and contracts for long-term debt, (2) confirm debt with lenders and bond trustees, and (3) recalculate interest expense.

Review Authorizations and Contracts

The authority of a corporation to enter into a contractual agreement to borrow money through the issuance or incurrence of long-term debt rests with the board of directors. Accordingly, evidence of authorizations should be found in the minutes of board meetings. Normally, the auditor reviews only the authorizations that have occurred during the year under audit because evidence of the authorizations for debt outstanding at the beginning of the year should be in the permanent working paper file.

Authorization for the debt issue should include reference to the applicable sections of the bylaws that pertain to such financing. It may also include the opinion of the company's legal counsel on the legality of the debt. The review of contracts should also include the details of covenants and the entity's compliance therewith, and the details of obligations under capital leases. Evidence obtained from this test may pertain to all five assertion categories (see Figure 17-10).

Confirm Debt

The auditor is expected to confirm the existence and nature of long-term debt by direct communication with lenders and bond trustees. Notes payable to banks in which the client has an account are confirmed as part of the confirmation of bank balances as explained in Chapter 18. Other notes are confirmed with the holders by separate letter. Such requests should be made by the client and mailed by the auditor. The existence of mortgages and bonds payable normally can be confirmed directly with the trustee. Each confirmation should include a request for the current status of the debt and current year's transactions. All confirmation responses should be compared with the records, and any differences should be investigated. Confirming long-term debt and key requirements of the contract relates to all assertion categories (see Figure 17-10).

Recalculate Interest Expense

Evidence of interest expense and accrued interest payable is easily obtainable by the auditor. The auditor reperforms the client's interest calculations and traces interest payments to supporting vouchers, canceled checks, and confirmation responses. Accrued interest, in turn, is verified by identifying the last interest payment date and recalculating the amount booked by the client.

When bond interest coupons are involved, the auditor can examine the canceled coupons and reconcile them to the amount paid. When bonds are originally sold at a premium or discount, the auditor should review the client's amortization schedule and verify the recorded amount of amortization by recalculation. This test is directed primarily at the existence or occurrence (EO1,2), valuation or allocation (VA1,2), and completeness assertions (C1,2) for interest expense and interest payable. It also provides evidence about the rights and obligations assertion (RO1) for interest payable.

Tests of Details of Presentation and Disclosure

In evaluating the appropriateness of the client's classification and disclosure of long-term debt, the auditor should be aware of applicable FASB Statements on Financial Accounting Standards (SFASs). The foregoing tests of inspecting and reading debt contracts and confirming the terms of debt provide the client data for use in the comparison. This test relates to the presentation and disclosure assertion (PD4-7).

[LEARNING CHECK

17-10 a. Describe the nature of the financing cycle.
b. Identify other cycles that interface with the financing cycle.

17-11 State the specific audit objectives that apply to the financing cycle.

17-12 a. Discuss the issues associated with materiality and inherent risk as they relate to the financing cycle.
b. Identify four analytical procedures that the auditor might perform and explain how they might assist in evaluating the reasonableness of debt and equity balances and transactions.

17-13 Discuss the applicability of the internal control structure components to financing cycle transactions.

17-14 State and describe the functions that relate to financing cycle transactions.

17-15 What factors pertain to determining the acceptable level of detection risk for long-term debt transactions?

17-16 What substantive tests apply to the existence and valuation assertions for long-term debt balances?

17-17 Describe the nature of each of the following substantive tests and indicate the assertions to which each relates:
a. Vouch entries to long-term debt accounts.
b. Confirm debt.
c. Recalculate interest expense.

[KEY TERMS

Bond trustee, p. 824
Financing cycle, p. 821
Financing functions, p. 824
Long-term debt transactions, p. 821

Stockholders' equity transactions, p. 821
Transfer agent, p. 824

PRELIMINARY AUDIT STRATEGIES FOR SHAREHOLDERS' EQUITY

Figure 17-12 summarizes some key issues related to preliminary audit strategies for the audit of shareholders' equity. The highest inherent risk is associated with the presentation and disclosure assertion. Some companies use equity instruments that behave like debt and should not be classified in shareholders' equity.

Figure 17-12 ■ Preliminary Audit Strategies for Shareholders' Equity

Assertion	Inherent Risk	Control Risk	Analytical Procedures Risk	Test of Details Risk
Existence and Occurrence	Moderate: The existence of recorded equity transactions and balances is not a significant inherent risk.	Low: Routine stock transactions are usually handled by a registrar or transfer agent.	High: Comparison of financial numbers may not necessarily disclose misstatements in equity accounts.	High: The auditor will usually directly confirm equity transactions and balances with the registrar or transfer agent.
Completeness	Moderate: There is only a modest risk associated with unrecorded equity transactions.	Low: Routine stock transactions are usually handled by a registrar or transfer agent. The auditor is normally involved in a new registration statement associated with new issues of stock. These transactions often have significant board of directors oversight.	High: Comparison of financial numbers may not necessarily disclose misstatements in equity accounts.	High: The auditor will usually directly confirm equity transactions and balances with the registrar or transfer agent.
Rights and Obligations	High: An important inherent risk represents understanding the collateral that may be pledged as security for a loan.	Low: Routine stock transactions are usually handled by a registrar or transfer agent.	Maximum: Analytical procedures are not directed at the rights and obligations assertion.	Low: The auditor will usually directly confirm equity transactions and balances with the registrar or transfer agent.
Valuation or Allocation	Moderate: The valuation of recorded equity is not high. The calculations associated with equity are not complex.	Low: Routine stock transactions are usually handled by a registrar or transfer agent.	High: Comparison of financial numbers may not necessarily disclose misstatements in equity accounts.	High: The auditor will usually directly confirm equity transactions and balances with the registrar or transfer agent.
Presentation and Disclosure	High or Maximum: Some companies use equity instruments that are in economic substance debt. These should not be included in shareholders' equity.	Moderate or Maximum: Primary control is the involvement of an effective disclosure committee.	Maximum: Analytical procedures are not directed at disclosures.	Low: The auditor will often perform tests of details to evaluate the quality and accuracy of financial statement classifications and disclosures.

For most assertions related to shareholders' equity, substantive tests of transactions and balances are cost effective and efficient.

SUBSTANTIVE TESTS OF STOCKHOLDERS' EQUITY

Figure 17-13 shows a list of possible substantive tests of stockholder's equity balances together with the specific audit objectives to which each test relates. The auditor relies primarily on (1) direct communication with outside independent sources and (2) review of documentation to obtain sufficient competent evidential matter about the assertions pertaining to shareholders' equity. Audit working papers, such as the analysis of shareholders' equity in Figure 17-15, are used to document the auditor's tests. Each of the substantive tests is explained in a following section.

Initial Procedures

The auditor should obtain an understanding of the business and industry and determine (1) the entity's need for external financing and (2) the desirability of using equity financing to support the growth of the entity. Equity financing might be used either to support investing activities or to support needed investments in working capital (e.g., growth in inventories and receivables needed to grow the entity).

The schedules referred to in Figure 17-13 for this group of procedures might include a trial balance of the stockholders' ledger or listings of stockholders supplied by the registrar and transfer agent. The auditor should test the agreement of the data in the schedules with any underlying accounting records and verify that the schedules or subsidiary ledgers agree with general ledger control accounts. This evidence pertains to the mathematical and clerical accuracy component of the valuation or allocation assertion.

Analytical Procedures

Figure 17-14 presents several ratios commonly used to evaluate the reasonableness of stockholders' equity. The financial relationships expressed in these ratios may be helpful in evaluating the reasonableness of stockholders' equity balances. The evidence obtained from these analytical procedures pertains to the existence or occurrence, completeness, and valuation or allocation assertions.

Tests of Details of Transactions

This category of tests includes vouching entries in the paid-in capital and retained earnings accounts as explained in the following sections.

Vouch Entries to Paid-in Capital Accounts

Each change in a capital stock account should be vouched to supporting documentation. For a new issue of stock, the auditor can examine remittance advices of the cash proceeds from the issue. If the consideration for the shares was other than cash, the auditor should carefully examine the basis for the valuation, such as the market value of the consideration received or given. For the shares issued, market quotations may be useful in determining the propriety of the valuation; when the value of the property received is used, an appraisal may be necessary.

Figure 17-13 ■ Possible Substantive Tests of Stockholders' Equity Assertions

Category	Substantive Test	Specific Audit Objectives

Initial Procedures	1. Obtain an understanding of the business and industry and determine:
	  a. The significance of various sources of financing (debt and equity) to the entity
	  b. Key economic drivers that influence the entity's need for financing and its ability to obtain equity capital and pay dividends.
	  c. Industry standards for the extent to which the industry uses equity financing.
	2. Perform initial procedures on stockholders' equity balances and records that will be subject to further testing.
	  a. Trace beginning balance for stockholders' equity accounts to last year's working papers.
	  b. Review activity in stockholders' equity accounts and investigate entries that appear unusual in amount or source.
	  c. Obtain client-prepared schedules of changes in stockholders' equity balances and determine that they accurately represent the underlying accounting records from which they were prepared by:
	    i. Footing and crossfooting the schedules and reconciling the totals with increases or decreases in related subsidiary and general ledger balances.
	    ii. Testing agreement of items on schedules with entries in related subsidiary and general ledger accounts.
		All
		
		VA5
		
		EO3
		
		VA5
		
		VA5
		
		VA5

Analytical Procedures	3. Perform analytical procedures:
	  a. Calculate ratios
	    • Return on common stockholders' equity
	    • Equity to total liabilities and equity
	    • Dividend payout rate
	    • Earnings per share
	    • Sustainable growth rate
	4. Analyze ratio results relative to expectations based on prior-year, budget, industry, or other data.
		All
		
		All

Tests of Details of Transactions	5. Vouch entries in paid-in capital account. 6. Vouch entries in retained earnings.	EO3, VA3, PD3 EO3, VA3, PD3
Tests of Details of Balances	7. Review articles of incorporation and bylaws. 8. Review authorizations and terms of stock issues. 9. Confirm shares outstanding with registrar and transfer agent. 10. Inspect stock certificate book. 11. Inspect certificates of shares held in treasury.	All EO5, C3, C5, RO2 EO5, C3, C5, VA5 EO5, C3, C5, RO2 EO5, C3, C5, RO2

Presentation and Disclosure	12. Compare statement presentation with GAAP.
	  a. Determine that stockholders' equity balances are properly identified and classified in the financial statements.
	  b. Determine the appropriateness of disclosures concerning all changes in stockholders' equity account balances during the period, par or stated values, dividend and liquidation preferences, dividends in arrears, stock option plans, conversion features, and treasury shares.
	  c. Evaluate the completeness of presentation and disclosures for stockholders' equity in drafts of financial statements to determine conformity to GAAP by reference to disclosure checklist.
	  d. Read disclosures and independently evaluate their understandability.
		PD8, PD11
		PD8, PD11
		
		PD9
		
		PD10
		
		PD10

Figure 17-14 ■ Analytical Procedures Commonly Used to Audit Shareholders' Equity

Ratio or Other Financial Information	Formula	Audit Significance
Return on common stockholders' equity	(Net income – preferred dividends) / average common stockholders' equity	Provides a measure of the rate of return generated on the common shareholders' investment. Auditors should understand the competitiveness factors that allow a company to obtain a unusually high return.
Equity to total liabilities and equity	Stockholders' equity / (stockholders' equity + total liabilities)	Provides a reasonableness of the entities' proportion of equity that may be compared with prior years' experience or industry data.
Dividend payout rate	Cash dividends / net income	Auditors would normally expect low-dividend payout rates for high-growth companies that need reinvested earnings to fund investments in working capital and long-term assets.
Earnings per share	Net income / weighted average common shares outstanding	Earnings per share is useful for comparisons with price per share. This ratio can be compared with industry price earnings ratios for reasonableness.
Sustainable growth rate	Return on common equity * (1- dividend payout rate)	Provides an estimate of rate of sales growth that can be obtained without changing the entity's profitability or financing structure. The auditor should expect changes in the financing structure when sales grow significantly faster than the sustainable growth rate.

An analysis of a capital stock account is illustrated in Figure 17-15. Similar analyses are prepared for treasury stock and other stockholders' equity accounts.

The auditor should exercise care in determining the propriety of the accounting treatment for shares issued as part of stock option, stock warrant, or stock conversion plans or in connection with a stock split. Documentation of the cost of treasury stock should be available to the auditor in the form of authorizations in the minutes, disbursement vouchers, and canceled checks.

Evidence from vouching of entries to capital stock accounts relates most closely to the existence or occurrence, rights and obligations, and valuation or allocation assertions.

Vouch Entries to Retained Earnings

Each entry to retained earnings except the posting of net income (or net loss) should be vouched to supporting documentation. Entries for dividend declarations and retained earnings appropriations are traced to the minutes book. In determining the propriety of the distribution, the auditor should:

■ Establish that preferential or other rights of stockholders and any restrictions on dividend distributions have been recognized.

Figure 17-15 ■ Capital Stock Working Paper

Prepared by: *A.E.R.*   Date: *1/12/x2*

Reviewed by: *R.C.P.*   Date: *1/12/x2*

Willems Company   *P-2*

Capital Stock $100 par

Acc. # 600   12/31/x1

	Authorized	Shares Issued and outstanding	Amount	
Balances, 1/1/x1	10000 ✓	5000 ✓	500000 ✓	
Shares issued at par for cash on 4/1/x1		1000 √	100000 √∅	
Balances, 12/31/x1	10000	6000 C	600000	To P-1

✓ Traced to prior years working papers

√ Traced to approval per minutes of Board of Directors meeting on 3/20/x1

∅ Traced proceeds to cash receipts

C Confirmed by First Trust Company transfer agent for the company - See P-3

Reviewed minutes of all Board of Directors meetings for evidence of capital stock transactions. Only reference was to transaction of 4/1/x1 as per above.

- Establish the number of shares outstanding on the date of record and verify the accuracy of the total dividend declaration by recalculation.
- Ascertain the propriety of the entry to record the declaration.
- Trace dividend payments to canceled checks and other documentation.

The client is also expected to furnish support for any prior-period adjustments. Vouching enables the auditor to ascertain whether (1) a proper distinction has been made between paid-in capital and retained earnings and (2) applicable legal and contractual requirements have been met. In addition to the valuation or allocation assertion, this test also relates to the existence or occurrence and rights and obligations assertions.

Tests of Details of Balances

Substantive tests in this category are explained in the next five sections.

Review Articles of Incorporation and Bylaws

Copies of the articles of incorporation and the bylaws should be in the auditor's permanent working paper file in the audit of a continuing client. The auditor should inquire of management and the client's legal counsel about changes in either or both of the documents. Preferably, the responses from both parties should be in writing.

In the initial audit of a corporation, the auditor will make an extensive review of the articles and bylaws and note key matters in his working papers. This substantive test is designed to determine that capital stock has been legally issued and that the board of directors has been acting within the scope of its authority. Thus, this test provides important evidence about the existence or occurrence and rights and obligations assertions.

Review Authorizations and Terms of Stock Issues

All stock issues, stock reacquisitions, and dividend declarations should be authorized by the board of directors. Accordingly, a review of the minutes should provide evidence of stockholders' equity transactions authorized during the year.

Different classes of stock may contain restriction provisions or convey preferences in dividend declarations and liquidation. The auditor should examine each issue for such terms and make appropriate notations in the working papers. This substantive test relates to the existence or occurrence and rights and obligations assertions.

Confirm Shares Outstanding with Registrar and Transfer Agent

When the client uses a **registrar,** the auditor should confirm total shares authorized, issued, and outstanding at the balance sheet date with the registrar. Confirmation with the **transfer agent,** in turn, provides evidence of shares held by each stockholder. The confirmation responses are then compared with the capital stock accounts and the stockholders' ledger. The confirming of shares outstanding relates to the following three assertions: existence or occurrence, completeness, and rights and obligations.

Inspect Stock Certificate Book

This test is required when the client serves as its own transfer agent. Several steps are involved in the test. First, the auditor should examine the stock certificate book to determine that (1) stubs for shares issued and outstanding have been properly filled out, (2) canceled certificates are attached to original stubs, and (3) all unissued certificates are intact. Second, the auditor should ascertain that the changes during the year have been correctly recorded in the individual stockholders' accounts in the subsidiary ledger. When there are numerous issuances and cancellations, this comparison may be done on a test basis. Third, the auditor should reconcile the total shares issued and outstanding as shown in the stock certificate book with total shares reported in the stockholders' ledger and capital stock accounts. This test relates to the same assertions as confirming shares with the registrar and transfer agent.

Inspect Certificates of Shares Held in Treasury

If capital stock is held in the treasury, the auditor should count the certificates at the same time other securities are counted. Ideally, the count should be made at the balance sheet date. If this is not possible, there must be a reconciliation from the date of the count to the balance sheet date. The number of shares held should also be agreed to the shares shown in the treasury stock account. In inspecting the certificates, the auditor should note in the working papers the number of shares acquired during the year for subsequent tracing to the cash records.

This test pertains to the following three assertions: existence or occurrence, completeness, and rights and obligations.

Tests of Details of Presentation and Disclosure

APB Opinion No. 12 provides that disclosure of changes in the separate accounts comprising stockholders' equity is required to make the financial statements sufficiently informative. Such disclosure may be made in the basic statements and notes thereto or be presented in a separate statement.

Disclosures related to the equity section include details of stock option plans, dividends in arrears, par or stated value, and dividend and liquidation preferences. The auditor obtains evidence about the presentation and disclosure assertion from the foregoing tests and from a review of the corporate minutes for provisions and agreements affecting the stockholders' equity accounts. In reviewing the minutes, the auditor should note whether any shares of stock have been reserved for stock option or similar plans, commitments for future issuance of stock in the purchase of or merger with another company, and restrictions limiting dividend payments or requiring minimum working capital requirements. Relevant evidence may also be obtained from discussions and communications with legal counsel.

When evaluating the appropriateness of the client's classification and disclosure of shareholders' equity, the auditor should be aware of applicable FASB Statements on Financial Accounting Standards (SFASs). For example, SFAS No. 150, *Accounting for Certain Financial Instruments with Characteristics of Both Liabilities and Equity,* indicates that some equity instruments used by companies behave more like debt than equity and, therefore, should not be classified as shareholders' equity. The foregoing tests of shareholders' equity should provide the basis for evaluating disclosures. This test relates to the presentation and disclosure assertion (PD8–11).

[OTHER SERVICES]

Audit Decision 11

■ How does the auditor use the knowledge obtained during the audit of the investing and financing cycles to support other assurance services?

When the auditor has completed the audit of investing activities, the auditor is in a position to evaluate the entity's investments relative to others in the industry. Auditors are uniquely positioned to provide two important services. First, the auditor can evaluate how effective the entity has been in utilizing its assets to generate sales, profits, and cash flows, and accomplish the entity's goals. This is an important performance measurement service. Second, the auditor is then positioned to provide independent advice by evaluating the entity's planned investing activities and determining whether the planned steps best support its goals.

Auditors also have significant knowledge and experience in understanding the sources of financing used by various entities to finance strategic investments. Auditors have knowledge of the advantages and disadvantages of bank financing, mortgage financing, lease financing, financing that may be available from insurance companies or other entities, or various classes of preferred stock. CPAs are in an excellent position to advise clients on how to finance important investments.

Finally, many investments are accomplished through merger or acquisition. Many CPA firms are experts in guiding a company through a merger or acquisition. This service would include identifying possible acquisitions candidates, helping an entity evaluate the potential benefits and risks associated with an acquisition, as well as how to structure the acquisition. Each of the foregoing represents possible services that build on the knowledge obtained during an audit of the investing and financing cycle.

[LEARNING CHECK

17-18 What considerations apply to determining the acceptable level of detection risk for stockholders' equity balances?

17-19 What substantive tests apply to the existence or occurrence and completeness assertions for stockholders' equity balances?

17-20 Identify the ratios that may be used in applying analytical procedures to stockholders' equity balances.

17-21 Identify three different value-added services that a CPA might perform for a client, related to the investing and financing cycles.

[KEY TERMS

Registrar, p. 836   Transfer agent, p. 836

[FOCUS ON AUDIT DECISIONS]

This chapter focuses on the practical aspects of auditing the investing and financing cycles. The chapter pays particular attention to audit planning concerns related to the investing and financing cycles, specific internal controls that are tailored to each cycle, and substantive tests for each cycle. Figure 17-16 summarizes the audit decisions discussed in Chapter 17 and provides page references indicating where these decisions are discussed in more detail.

Figure 17-16 ■ Summary of Audit Decisions Discussed in Chapter 17

Audit Decision	Factors that Influence the Audit Decision	Chapter References
D1: What is the nature of the investing and financing cycles?	This chapter discusses audit procedures for items normally found in the investing and financing sections of the statement of cash flows. Investing activities are the purchase and sale of land, buildings, equipment, and other assets not generally held for resale. In addition, investing activities include the purchase and sale of financial instruments not intended for trading purposes (discussed in Chapter 18). Financing activities include transactions and events whereby cash is obtained from or repaid to creditors (debt financing) or owners (equity financing). The chapter illustrates the audit of investing activities in the context of plant assets. It illustrates the audit of financing activities in the context of long-term debt and shareholders' equity accounts.	pp. 806–807
D2: How does understanding the entity and its environment influence audit planning decisions in the investing and financing cycles?	Investing and financing activities are often linked closely together. When companies acquire long-term assets, they normally use some form of financing activity to fund the acquisition. These accounts are often audited together because the business linkage between these transactions is so closely tied together.	p. 807
D3: How are specific audit objectives developed for the audit of plant assets in the investing cycle?	Figure 17-2 uses the framework discussed in Chapter 6 to develop specific audit objectives for the audit of plant assets.	pp. 809–810
D4: What audit planning decisions should be made when developing an audit program for the plant assets?	Figure 17-3 presents a number of analytical procedures that are commonly used when auditing plant assets, along with a discussion of their audit significance. Almost every assertion in the investing cycle for plant assets involves important inherent risks. Some key risks are identified below and discussed in more detail in the chapters. (E&O) Capitalizing items that should be expensed; (C) the use of variable interest entities to acquire the use of assets and keep assets and debt off the balance sheet; (RO) long-term assets are often pledged as collateral for financing; (VA) accounting estimates of depreciation and asset impairment. Additional inherent risk factors are discussed in the chapter.	pp. 810–812
D5: What factors are involved in determining an acceptable level of tests of details risk for plant assets?	Figure 17-4 outlines one possible preliminary audit strategy for each assertion in the investing cycle for plant assets. Because there is often little turnover of plant assets, audit strategies often focus on tests of transactions for plant assets.	pp. 812–813
D6: How does the auditor determine the elements of an audit program for substantive tests to achieve specific audit objectives for plant assets?	This section uses the framework developed in Chapter 12 to design substantive tests for plant assets. Figure 17-5 focuses on the nature of substantive tests for plant assets. It summarizes the initial procedures, analytical procedures, tests of details of transactions, tests of details of balances, tests of details of accounting estimates, and tests of details of disclosures relevant to the expenditure cycle. The chapter discussion explores these tests in more detail.	pp. 814–820

(continues)

Figure 17-16 ■ (Continued)

Audit Decision	Factors that Influence the Audit Decision	Chapter References
D7: How are specific audit objectives developed for long-term debt and shareholder's equity in the financing cycle?	Figure 17-7 uses the framework discussed in Chapter 6 to develop specific audit objectives for the audit of long-term debt and shareholders' equity.	p. 821
D8: What audit planning decisions should be made when developing an audit program for the financing cycle?	Figures 17-8 and 17-14 present a number of analytical procedures that are commonly used when auditing financing cycle accounts, along with a discussion of their audit significance. The primary inherent risk factor for long-term debt is associated with the completeness assertion associated with unrecorded liabilities and off-balance sheet financing. Some equity instruments behave like debt and should not be classified in shareholders' equity. Other inherent risk factors are included in the chapter discussion.	pp. 821–824
D9: What is involved in determining a preliminary audit strategy and planning an audit program for substantive tests for long-term debt?	Figure 17-9 outlines one possible preliminary audit strategy for each assertion in the financing cycle for long-term debt. This section also uses the framework developed in Chapter 12 to design substantive tests for the financing cycle. Figure 17-10 focuses on the nature of substantive tests for long-term debt. It summarizes the initial procedures, analytical procedures, tests of details of transactions, tests of details of balances, and tests of details of disclosures relevant to the expenditure cycle. The chapter discussion explores these tests in more detail.	pp. 824–830
D10: What is involved in determining a preliminary audit strategy and planning an audit program for substantive tests for shareholders' equity?	Figure 17-12 outlines one possible preliminary audit strategy for each assertion in the financing cycle for shareholders' equity. This section also uses the framework developed in Chapter 12 to design substantive tests for stockholders' equity. Figure 17-13 focuses on the nature of substantive tests for shareholders' equity. It summarizes the initial procedures, analytical procedures, tests of details of transactions, tests of details of balances, and tests of details of disclosures relevant to the expenditure cycle. The chapter discussion explores these tests in more detail.	pp. 831–837
D11: How does the auditor use the knowledge obtained during the audit of the investing and financing cycles to support other assurance services?	Once the auditor has completed an audit of the investing and financing cycle, the auditor should have information that supports an audit opinion as well as recommendations related to improvements in internal controls. In addition, the auditor probably has obtained knowledge that may be relevant to other client services. This final section of the chapter provides examples of how knowledge obtained while auditing the financing and investing cycles can be used to provide other services that client's value.	p. 888

objective questions

Objective questions are available for the student at www.wiley.com/college/boynton

comprehensive questions

17-22   **(Internal controls for plant assets)** Harris, CPA, has accepted an engagement to audit the financial statements of Grant Manufacturing Co., a new client. Grant has an adequate control environment and a reasonable segregation of duties. Harris is about to assess control risk for the assertions related to Grant's property and equipment.

Required

Describe the key internal control structure policies and procedures related to Grant's property, equipment, and related transactions (additions, transfers, major maintenance and repairs, retirements, and dispositions) that Harris may consider in assessing control risk.

AICPA

17-23   **(Audit objectives for plant assets)** Rivers, CPA, is the auditor for a manufacturing company with a balance sheet that includes the caption "Property, Plant & Equipment." The company's management has asked Rivers if audit adjustments or reclassifications are required for the following material items that have been included in or excluded from "Property, Plant & Equipment":

1. A tract of land was acquired during the year. The land is the future site of the client's new headquarters, which will be constructed in the following year. Commissions were paid to the real estate agent used to acquire the land, and expenditures were made to relocate the previous owner's equipment. These commissions and expenditures were expensed and are excluded from "Property, Plant & Equipment."

2. Clearing costs were incurred to make the land ready for construction. These costs were included in "Property, Plant & Equipment."

3. During the land clearing process, timber and gravel were recovered and sold. The proceeds from the sale were recorded as other income and are excluded from "Property, Plant & Equipment."

4. A group of machines was purchased under a royalty agreement that provides royalty payments based on units of production from the machines. The cost of the machines, freight costs, unloading charges, and royalty payments were capitalized and are included in "Property, Plant & Equipment."

Required

a. Identify the audit objectives (assertions) for "Property, Plant & Equipment" and indicate the principal substantive tests pertaining to each.

b. Indicate whether each of the items numbered 1 to 4 above requires one or more audit adjustments or reclassifications, and explain why such adjustments or reclassifications are required or not required. Organize your answers as follows:

ITEM NUMBER	IS AN AUDIT ADJUSTMENT OR RECLASSIFICATION REQUIRED? (YES OR NO)	REASONS WHY AUDIT ADJUSTMENT OR RECLASSIFICATION IS REQUIRED OR NOT REQUIRED

AICPA (adapted)

17-24   **(Substantive tests for plant assets)** Pierce, an independent auditor, was engaged to audit the financial statements of Mayfair Construction Incorporated for the year ended December 31, 20X3. Mayfair's financial statements reflect a substantial amount of mobile construction equipment used in the firm's operations. The equipment is accounted for in a subsidiary ledger. Pierce performed a study and evaluation of the internal control structure and found it satisfactory.

Required

Identify the substantive tests that Pierce should utilize in examining mobile construction equipment and related depreciation in Mayfair's financial statements.

AICPA

17-25   **(Substantive tests, assertions, and types of evidence for financing cycle transactions)** The following transactions and events relate to financing cycle transactions in Weber Inc.

1. Declare cash dividend on common stock.

2. Issue bonds.

3. Pay bond interest.

4. Purchase 500 shares of treasury stock.

5. Pay cash dividend declared in (1) above.

6. Issue additional common stock for cash.

7. Accrue bond interest payable at year-end.

8. Redeem outstanding bonds.

9. Establish appropriation for bond retirement.

10. Announce a two-for-one stock split.

Required

a. Identify the substantive test that should verify each transaction or event.

b. For each test, indicate the financial statement assertion(s) to which it pertains.

c. Indicate the type of evidence obtained from the substantive test (i.e., physical, confirmation, documentary, written representation, mathematical, oral, or analytical). Use a tabular format for your answers, with one column for each part.

17-26   **(Substantive tests and disclosures for long-term debt)** Andrews, CPA, has been engaged to audit the financial statements of Broadwall Corporation for the year ended December 31, 20X1. During the year, Broadwall obtained a long-term loan from a local bank pursuant to a financing agreement that provided that the

1. Loan was to be secured by the company's inventory and accounts receivable.

2. Company was to maintain a debt-to-equity ratio not to exceed two to one.

3. Company was not to pay dividends without permission from the bank.

4. Monthly installment payments were to commence July 1, 20X1.

In addition, during the year the company also borrowed, on a short-term basis, from the president of the company, including substantial amounts just prior to the year-end.

Required

a. For purposes of Andrews' audit of the financial statements of Broadwall Corporation, what substantive tests should Andrews employ in examining the described loans? Do not discuss internal control.

b. What are the financial statement disclosures that Andrews should expect to find with respect to the loans from the president?

AICPA

17-27 **(Substantive tests for stockholders' equity balances)** Jones, CPA, the continuing auditor of Sussex, Inc., is beginning the audit of the common stock and treasury stock accounts. Jones has decided to design substantive tests with control risk at the maximum level.

Sussex has no par, no stated value common stock, and acts as its own registrar and transfer agent. During the past year, Sussex both issued and reacquired shares of its own common stock, some of which the company still owned at year-end. Additional common stock transactions occurred among the shareholders during the year.

Common stock transactions can be traced to individual shareholders' accounts in a subsidiary ledger and to a stock certificate book. The company has not paid any cash or stock dividends. There are no other classes of stock, stock rights, warrants, or option plans.

Required

What substantive tests should Jones apply in examining the common stock and treasury stock accounts?

AICPA

17-28 **(Confirmation of stock outstanding)** You are engaged in doing the audit of a corporation whose records you have not previously audited. The corporation has both an independent transfer agent and a registrar for its capital stock. The transfer agent maintains the record of stockholders, and the registrar checks that there is no overissue of stock. Signatures of both are required to validate certificates.

It has been proposed that confirmations be obtained from both the transfer agent and the registrar as to the stock outstanding at the balance sheet date. If such confirmations agree with the books, no additional work is to be performed as to capital stock.

Required

If you agree that obtaining the confirmations as suggested would be sufficient in this case, give the justification for your position. If you do not agree, state specifically all additional steps you would take and explain your reason for taking them.

AICPA

cases

17-29 The Lewis Company is a biotechnology company that has recently received U.S. Food and Drug Administration (FDA) approval for a new drug that treats Parkinson's disease, and sales are showing early signs of success. On the wave of this success, the Lewis Company acquired a patent for a related drug from Brown and Harley, another biotechnology company, that is designed to treat Alzheimer's disease. Brown and Harley has completed successful animal tests with the patented drug known as AZH. Now that Lewis has acquired the patent, Lewis will have to take the drug through human trials and obtain FDA approval, a process that could take two to four years.

Lewis agreed to pay Brown and Harley $10 million for the patent on February 29, 20X0. Brown and Harley's book value associated with the patent was only $500,000. Lewis acquired the patent from Brown and Harley for $1 million in cash and $9 million in 9%, preferred stock redeemable on February 29, 20X4. Lewis accounted for the transaction by debiting an asset account for the patent in the amount of $10 million, with an intent to amortize the patent over 16 years, the remaining legal life of the patent, crediting cash for $1 million, and crediting shareholders' equity accounts for $9 million.

Required

a. What is the economic substance of the patent acquired by the Lewis Company? In your opinion, has the Lewis Company accurately accounted for the investing side of the transaction?

b. Describe the audit procedures that you would perform in 20X0 to audit the patent. For each procedure, describe how the procedure satisfies the audit of management's financial statement assertions.

c. What is the economic substance of the preferred stock issued by the Lewis Company? In your opinion, has the Lewis Company accurately accounted for the financing side of the transaction?

d. Describe the audit procedures that you would perform in 20X0 to audit the preferred stock. For each procedure, describe how the procedure satisfies the audit of management's financial statement assertions.

professional simulations

Your client, Alpha Net Universal (ANU), was founded in 1992. It went public with an IPO in 1998 and it had a very profitable run for the next ten years. ANU's most recent product as been so successful that ANU is planning on expanding the technology into other business and engineering applications and it is looking for new facilities. Russell Craig (ANU's CFO) is very pleased to be looking for real estate in late 20X3 as the local commercial real estate market is depressed and property values are low. Russell feels that if he had to rent in this market he would pay about $15.00 a square foot per year for space that would fit the company's needs. He is close to completing the negotiation of a lease transaction, and he wants to confirm his understanding regarding the accounting for the transaction. Russell expects that if ANU goes forward with the lease, it will close on December 31, 20X3.

Exhibit 17-30 provides a working paper (lead schedule) for the audit of ANU's property, plant and equipment. Explain the auditing procedures that should be performed associated with the legend identified as a) through h). Use the following format.

Legend	Audit Procedure
a)	
b)	
c)	
d)	
e)	
f)	
g)	
h)	

EXHIBIT 17-30 PLANT ASSET AND ACCUMULATED DEPRECIATION LEAD SCHEDULE

Alpha Net Universal

Property Plant and Equipment and Accumulated Depreciation

Lead Schedule

December 31, 21X3

W/P Ref: **G**

Prepared by: *CJG*   Date: 2/4/X4

Reviewed By: *RCP*   Date: 2/12/X4

Account Title Asset Cost	Balance 112/31/x2	Additions	Disposals	Adjustments Dr (Cr)	Balance 12/31/X3
Land	$ 550,000 c)	$ 50,000 d)		$ (25,000) f)	$ 575,000
Buildings	$ 2,150,000 c)	$ 250,000 d)		$ 25,000 f)	$ 2,425,000
Machinery and Equipment	$ 3,650,000 c)	$ 945,000 d)	$ 365,000 e)		$ 4,230,000
Furniture and Fixtures	$ 825,000 c)	$ 123,000 d)	$ 55,000 e)		$ 893,000
Capital Leases	$ 1,175,000 c)				$ 1,175,000
Total	$ 8,350,000	$ 1,368,000	$ 420,000	$ ———	$ 9,298,000
	a)	a)	a)	a)	b)

Accumulated Depreciation	Balance 112/31/x2	Provisions	Disposals	Adjustments Dr (Cr)	Balance 12/31/X3
Land	$ ——— c)				$ ———
Buildings	$ 380,000 c)	$ 85,000 g)			$ 465,000
Machinery and Equipment	$ 1,075,000 c)	$ 352,800 g)	$ 171,250 h)		$ 1,256,550
Furniture and Fixtures	$ 212,250 c)	$ 123,000 g)	$ 23,000 h)		$ 312,250
Capital Leases	$ 470,000 c)	$ 117,500 g)			$ 587,500
Total	$ 2,137,250	$ 678,300	$ 194,250	$ ———	$ 2,621,300
	a)	a)	a)	a)	b)

Situation	Audit Procedures	FARS Research	Audit Report

A real estate development company, Shailer Construction, has recently completed construction of a 35,000 square foot facility that would fit ANU's needs. The fair market value of the land and buildings is currently $10 million. ANU and Shailer Construction have found permanent funding for the transaction from a major commercial bank, Portland Commercial Bank (PCB). Following is a summary of the key aspects of the transaction.

■ Shailer Enterprises, a special purpose entity, will purchase the completed building from Shailer Construction for $10 million. Shailer Enterprises will be funded with $1 million in equity provided by Shailer Construction, and $9 million in a loan from PCB (based on the investment grade credit rating of the lessee, ANU). PCB will lend the $9 million to Shailer Enterprises at a floating interest rate of the prime rate plus one percent. Shailer will pay interest only on the loan until it comes due in six years on December 31, 20X9; however, PCB will consider renewing the loan for another six-year period based on the economic circumstances at the time.

■ ANU will lease the property from Shailer Enterprises in a noncancelable lease that expires on December 31, 20X9. ANU will be committed to a fixed monthly payment amounting to $10,000 plus a variable lease component amounting to the prime rate plus one percent on the $9 million principal of the loan.

- ANU will agree to pay all the cost of operation of the facility, including leasehold improvements, utilities, insurance, property taxes, and any other operating costs. In addition, ANU is responsible for any risks due to environmental conditions that may be created during the term of the lease, damage, or destruction. ANU has full responsibility to manage, maintain, and operate the property.

- At the end of the lease (December 31, 20X9), ANU will have three options.
  1. ANU can elect to extend the term of the lease, subject to ANU's credit standing, and ANU's ability to extend or restructure the debt and equity transactions with Shailer and lenders.
  2. ANU can purchase the property for $10 million. If the $10 million price is so significantly below market value that is deemed to be a bargain purchase, then ANU agrees to pay an additional amount to Shailer Enterprises, agreed upon by both parties, so that it will not be a bargain purchase.
  3. If ANU does not extend the lease term or purchase the property, it must vacate the property, and make a contingent rent payment that is capped in the amount of $5 million that will be used to retire the principal on the loan. ANU, as an agent of Shailer Enterprises, is responsible for finding a third party to purchase the property and ANU will bear all the costs of the sale. Once the property is sold, the proceeds will be used to (1) retire the remaining principal and interest due on the loan, and (2) pay Shailer Enterprises $1 million. The remainder of the proceeds will go to ANU.

- ANU will also agree to a lease covenant that it will maintain $5 million in long-term investments as security for any potential contingent rent that may be due at the end of the lease. These funds will be invested in government securities and managed and held in safekeeping by PCB.

Russell Craig wants you to confirm his understanding that under SFAS #13 and EITF 90-15 this is an operating lease. He plans to record lease payments as an expense along with other operating costs of the facility. Furthermore, he plans to disclose all the normal disclosures associated with operating lease, and he further will disclose the related restrictions on the $5 million of long-term investments. Cut and paste all appropriate sections of accounting standards that apply to the accounting for the lease that Mr. Craig is considering.

Situation	Audit Procedures	FARS Research	Audit Report

Draft the audit opinion that you would write if ANU accounts for this lease as proposed by Mr. Craig.

[18] AUDITING INVESTMENTS AND CASH BALANCES

WHERE'S THE CASH? AUDITOR'S UNCOVER MASSIVE FRAUD

From August 2003 through November 2003, Parmalat Finanziaria, S.p.A. (Parmalat), an Italian milk products company, offered $100 million of unsecured Senior Guaranteed Notes to U.S. investors. The $100 million note offering failed after Parmalat's auditors raised questions about certain Parmalat accounts.

Massive fraudulent financial reporting was uncovered when Parmalat's auditors sent a bank confirmation to confirm cash on hand at the Bank of America and the bank replied that there was no such account. In the previous financial statements Parmalat purported to hold approximately $4.9 billion of cash and marketable securities at the Bank of America in New York City in the name of Bonlat Financing Corporation, a wholly owned subsidiary incorporated in the Cayman Islands. Bonlat's auditors certified the subsidiary's 2002 financial statements were based upon a false confirmation that Bonlat held these assets at the Bank of America. However, the bank account did not exist, and the bank confirmation upon which Bonlat's auditors relied had been forged.

It subsequently came to light that Parmalat overstated cash and marketable securities by at least 2.4 billion Euros for the year ended 2002 and by at least 2.95 billion Euros for the year ended 2003. This chapter explores audit procedures that are normally used to audit investments and cash balances. Some of these procedures eventually brought this massive fraud to public scrutiny.

Sources: Accounting and Auditing Enforcement Release 1936, December 30, 2003, and Accounting and Auditing Enforcement Release 2065, July 28, 2004.

[PREVIEW OF CHAPTER 18]

This chapter focuses on the audit of two very liquid assets: investments in marketable securities and cash balances. This chapter completes the discussion of investing activities, begun in Chapter 17, with an examination of an entity's investments in securities. This discussion centers on entities other than those in the financial services sector (where investments in the securities of other companies are core operating activities). Finally, the chapter discusses the audit of cash balances, which result from the cumulative effects of the revenue, expenditure, production, personnel, investing, and financing cycles. Attention is also given to two types of fraud involving cash—*kiting,* which involves interbank transfers, and *lapping,* which involves misappropriating cash receipts. The following diagram provides an overview of the chapter organization and content.

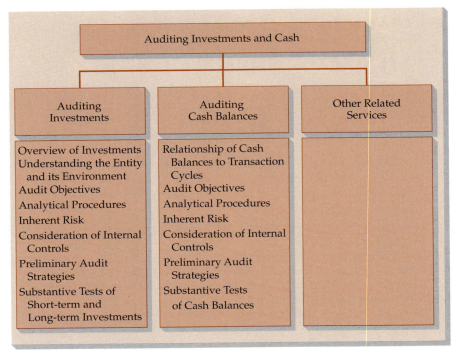

Chapter 18 focuses on the following aspects of the auditor's decision process associated with auditing investment and cash balances.

focus on audit decisions

After studying this chapter you should understand the factors that influence the following audit decisions.

D1. What is the nature of short-term and long-term investments, and how are specific audit objectives developed for short-term and long-term investments?

D2. What audit planning decisions should be made when developing an audit program for the audit of short-term and long-term investments?

D3. What factors are involved in determining an acceptable level of tests of details risk for short-term and long-term investments?

D4. How does the auditor determine the elements of an audit program for substantive tests to achieve specific audit objectives for short-term and long-term investments?

D5. What is the relationship of the transaction cycles to cash balances, and how are specific audit objectives developed for cash balances?

D6. What audit planning decisions should be made when developing an audit program for the audit of cash balances?

D7. What factors are involved in determining an acceptable level of tests of details risk for cash balance assertions?

D8. How does the auditor determine the elements of an audit program for substantive tests to achieve specific audit objectives for substantive tests for cash balances?

D9. What is the fraud known as kiting, and how can the auditor detect it?

D10. What is the fraud known as lapping, and how can the auditor detect it?

D11. What are the roles of confirmations and the use of a bank cutoff statement in the audit of cash balances?

D12. How might the auditor use the knowledge obtained during the audit of investments and cash balances to deliver other services to clients?

[AUDITING INVESTMENTS]

OVERVIEW OF INVESTMENTS

Audit Decision 1

■ What is the nature of short-term and long-term investments, and how are specific audit objectives developed for short-term and long-term investments?

On June 30, 2004, Microsoft reported total cash and short-term investments of $60.52 billion. Microsoft reports that the short-term investments are generally in liquid, investment-grade securities. Although Microsoft had an unusually high proportion of investments for a company that is not in the business of trading securities, many companies make similar investments while they are waiting to invest excess cash in other forms of productive assets. An entity's investment activities represent activities relating to the ownership of securities issued by other entities. These securities include certificates of deposit (CDs), preferred and common stocks, and corporate and government bonds. This chapter focuses on investments in common stock and corporate bonds.

Investing in marketable securities interfaces with two other cycles. Dividends and interest received on investments involve cash receipts transactions discussed in this text as part of the revenue cycle. A purchase of securities with cash involves cash disbursements transactions discussed in this text as part of the expenditure cycle. These transactions may be subjected to the same controls as other cash receipts and disbursements transactions as discussed in Chapters 14 and 15, as well as additional controls applicable only to **investing transactions** as discussed in later sections.

The following accounts are used in recording short-term and long-term investing transactions and the resulting income statement effects of those investments:

BALANCE SHEET ACCOUNTS	INCOME STATEMENT ACCOUNTS
Investments in equity and debt securities classified as trading or available-for-sale securities	Dividend revenue (from equity investments not accounted for by the equity method)
Market adjustment accounts for the above asset accounts (when there is an accumulated difference between cost and fair value of investment in equity and debt securities)	Interest revenue (on investment in debt securities)
Cumulative unrealized holding gains and losses on equity and debt securities classified as available-for-sale securities (equity account)	Realized gains and losses (on equity and debt security transactions)
Investments in equity securities accounting for by the equity method (investor exercises significant influence over investee)	Unrealized holding gains and losses on equity and debt securities classified as trading (changes in fair value during the current period)
Investments in equity securities accounting for at cost (fair value not determinable)	Equity in investee's earning (for investments account for by the equity method)
Investments in debt securities classified as held-to-maturity (carried at amortized cost)	

The variety of accounts listed above indicates that the auditor must be familiar with the many dimensions of valuation, classification, and disclosures pertaining to investments in equity and debt securities.

Figure 18-1 ■ Selected Specific Audit Objectives for Short-term and Long-term Investments

Specific Audit Objectives

Transaction Objectives

Occurrence. Recorded purchases **(EO1)** and sales **(EO2)** of investments, and investment revenues, realized gains and losses, and unrealized gains and losses **(EO3)** resulted from transactions that occurred during the period.

Completeness. The effects of all investment purchases **(C1)**, sales **(C2)**, and income transactions and events **(C3)** that occurred during the period were recorded.

Accuracy. Recorded purchases **(VA1)** and sales **(VA2)** of investments, and investment revenues, realized gains and losses, and unrealized gains and losses **(VA3)** accurately valued using GAAP and correctly journalized, summarized, and posted.

Cutoff. Recorded purchases **(EO1 and C1)** and sales **(EO2 and C2)** of investments, and investment revenues, realized gains and losses, and unrealized gains and losses **(EO3 and C3)** have been recorded in the correct accounting period.

Classification. All purchases **(PD1)** and sales **(PD2)** of investments, and investment revenues, realized gains and losses, and unrealized gains and losses **(PD3)** have been recorded in the proper accounts.

Balance Objectives

Existence. Recorded short-term and long-term investments represent investments that exist at the balance sheet date **(EO4)**.

Completeness. All short-term and long-term investments are included in the balance sheet investment accounts **(C4)**.

Rights and Obligations. The entity owns or has rights to all recorded short-term and long-term investments **(RO1)**.

Valuation and Allocation. Short-term and long-term investments are reported on the balance sheet at fair value, cost, amortized cost, or the amount determined by the equity method, as appropriate for particular investments **(VA4)**.

Disclosure Objectives

Occurrence and Rights and Obligations. Disclosed short-term and long-term investment events and transactions have occurred and pertain to the entity **(PD4)**.

Completeness. All short-term and long-term investment disclosures that should have been included in the financial statements have been included **(PD5)**.

Classification and Understandability. All short-term and long-term investment information is appropriately presented and described, and information in disclosures is clearly expressed **(PD6)**.

Accuracy and Valuation. Short-term and long-term investment information is disclosed accurately and at appropriate amounts **(PD7)**.

AUDIT OBJECTIVES

For each of the five categories of financial statement assertions, Figure 18-1 lists a number of specific audit objectives pertaining to accounts affected by short-term and long-term investment transactions. Considerations and procedures relevant to meeting these objectives are explained in the following sections.

UNDERSTANDING THE ENTITY AND ITS ENVIRONMENT

The significance of investments in short-term and long-term securities depends in large part on an entity's ability to generate free cash flow (cash flow from operations less capital expenditures). Companies with significant free cash flow must

Audit Decision 2

■ What audit planning decisions should be made when developing an audit program for the audit of short-term and long-term investments?

regularly address how to invest excess cash. Some companies may have times in their annual business cycle when they are generating sufficient cash flow that they seek short-term investments to generate some earnings on their excess cash. For example, if a school district receives a property tax remittance in one lump sum, it will want to find a secure investment opportunity to generate income as it progressively draws down on the investment to cover operating costs. Knowledge of an entity's sources of cash flow should assist the auditor in developing expectations regarding short-term and long-term investments.

ANALYTICAL PROCEDURES

Within an industry, the audit of investments will vary significantly from one company to another. For example, various companies in the retail grocery business face the same challenges in inventory management, which allows for effective industry comparisons. However, each retail grocer may have varying amounts of excess cash to invest in the securities of other companies, so it is more difficult to make meaningful comparisons with industry data. As a result, it is more difficult to obtain independent, reliable data to develop an expectation. Auditors may compare current-year and prior-year balances, or they may compare actual results for the amount of investments and investment income with budgets or other documentation of management's plans.

Unexpected differences might indicate misstatements pertaining to the existence or occurrence, completeness, valuation or allocation, and presentation and disclosure assertions. For example, a higher-than-expected rate of return on trading securities might be found to have been caused by erroneously recording the unrealized gain from an increase in the fair value of available-for-sale securities in the income account for trading securities rather than in the equity account for unrealized gains on available-for-sale securities. Similarly, a lower-than-expected rate of return on an equity method investment might result from an error in recording (1) the investor's share of the investee's earnings or (2) amortization of the excess of the investor's cost over the underlying book value of the investment.

INHERENT RISK

Inherent risk for investments is affected by many factors. The volume of investing transactions is generally quite low. However, securities are susceptible to theft, and the accounting for investments can become complex. Examples of the latter include certain equity method investments for which the acquisition costs exceed book values, and the accounting required when certain investments are reclassified from one category to another. In addition, certain inherent risks are more challenging to address with controls, and afford management an opportunity for manipulating the reporting for investments. Specifically, the proper classification of an investment may be contentious, which in turn affects the valuation method, income effects, and disclosure requirements applicable to the investment. For example, the accounting treatment of debt securities classified as *held-to-maturity* versus *available-for-sale* is quite different, as is the treatment of equity securities classified as *available-for-sale* versus *trading*. By misrepresenting the appropriate classification of an investment, management can defer or accelerate the recognition of unrealized gains and losses in income. Moreover, fair values, when required, may be difficult to determine or they may be volatile. Thus, these factors, when applicable, may contribute to high levels of inherent risk for the valuation or allocation and presentation and disclosure assertions.

CONSIDERATION OF INTERNAL CONTROLS

The understanding of several *control environment* factors is relevant to the audit of the investing cycle. For example, the authority and responsibility for investing transactions should be assigned to a company officer such as the treasurer. This individual should be a person who (1) is of unquestioned integrity, (2) possesses the knowledge and skills required of a person charged with executing such transactions, (3) realizes the importance of observing all prescribed control procedures, and (4) can assist other participating members of management in making initial and ongoing assessments of risks associated with individual investments.

The *information and communication system* must capture and retain all the necessary cost, fair value, and other data required for each method of accounting for the various categories of investments in equity and debt securities, both at acquisition and at subsequent reporting dates. Thus, accounting personnel must be familiar with these requirements and be capable of implementing them. Separate subsidiary investment ledgers may be maintained for the various categories of investments.

Each category of control activities applies to investments. Several common documents and records used in investing activities are explained in the next section, followed by descriptions of important investing functions and selected control activities pertaining to each. In a strong system of internal controls, an investment committee sets investing policy and reviews investing transactions. In addition, internal auditors and the board of directors should closely monitor the effectiveness of controls over investing activities.

Common Documents and Records

The documents and records applicable to this cycle are

- **Stock certificate.** An engraved, prenumbered form showing the number of shares of stock owned by a shareholder in a corporation. This document provides evidence for the existence or occurrence assertion.
- **Bond certificate.** An engraved, prenumbered form showing the number of bonds owned by a bondholder.
- **Bond indenture.** A contract stating the terms of bonds issued by a corporation.
- **Broker's advice.** A document issued by a broker specifying the exchange price of investing transactions; it is the primary source document for recording investing transactions. The advice provides evidence for the valuation or allocation assertion.
- **Broker's statement.** A monthly statement issued by a broker specifying securities held in safekeeping by the broker, their cost, and their fair-market value at the end of the month. In addition, the monthly statement usually summarizes any transactions that took place during the month.
- **Books of original entry.** The general journal is often used to record such items as the accrual of bond interest revenue, market adjustments under the fair-value method, and income earned under the equity method of accounting. The cash receipts journal is used to record the proceeds from sales transactions and the

receipt of interest and dividends. The voucher and check registers are used in purchasing and paying for the cost of securities.

■ **Investment subsidiary ledger.** Separate subsidiary ledgers may be used for each different class of investments when the company has a portfolio consisting of many different investments.

Functions and Related Controls

Activities in the investing cycle include the following **investing functions** and related controls:

■ *Authorize investment transactions:*

- ■ *Purchasing securities.* Purchases are made in accordance with management's authorizations.

- ■ *Selling securities.* Sales are made in accordance with management's authorizations.

■ *Receive or deliver securities:*

- ■ *Receiving/safeguarding/delivering securities.* Securities are usually held in safekeeping by a broker, who is responsible for the safekeeping of securities along with the receipt and delivery of securities for the entity. In rare instances securities are stored in safes or vaults, and access should be restricted to authorized personnel; securities should be periodically inspected, and counted and compared with recorded balances.

- ■ *Receiving periodic income.* Dividend and interest checks are promptly deposited intact. When securities are held in safekeeping, dividend and interest income is deposited directly to the entity's account by the broker.

■ *Record transactions:*

- ■ *Recording purchases, sales, and income.* Transactions are recorded based on appropriate supporting documentation; the duties of recording transactions and maintaining custody of the securities are segregated. Comparing recorded transactions to underlying information on a broker's advice normally controls the occurrence, accuracy, and cutoff objectives. An investment committee (that has individuals with knowledge of investing activities and an understanding of accounting for investing activities) is usually responsible for evaluating the classification of securities.

- ■ *Recording market adjustments and reclassifications.* Changes in fair values and in circumstances pertaining to the proper classification of investments are periodically analyzed and recorded. The investment committee should review the classification, valuation, and unrealized gains and losses on trading securities on a monthly or quarterly basis.

- ■ *Reviewing purchases, sales, and income transactions.* This review by an investment committee provides independent checks on the accounting function.

■ *Settle transactions:*

- ■ *Receiving cash.* Control procedures should provide reasonable assurance that documentation establishing accountability is created for cash receipts from the sale of investments and for the transfer of funds from a brokerage account to the primary checking account. See controls over cash receipts discussed in Chapter 14.

■ *Disbursing cash.* Cash disbursements to settle purchases of investments should include comparisons of disbursements with underlying brokerage advices and controls over the transfer of funds to a brokerage account from the primary checking account. See controls over cash disbursements discussed in Chapter 15.

■ *Assessing investment performance and reporting.* Performance reviews are made by management and an independent investment committee to detect poor investment performance and/or erroneous reporting, including comparisons of investment balances and rates of return for various classes of investments with budgeted amounts, and reviews of the propriety of the classification of individual investments.

Careful consideration of the foregoing descriptions of investing functions should suggest a variety of potential misstatements that could occur in investment balances.

LEARNING CHECK

18-1 Describe the nature of investments in the securities of other entities.

18-2 State the audit objectives for each of the management assertions that pertain to the audit of investments.

18-3 a. Shad Sloan contends that investments are seldom material to the financial statements. Is Shad correct? Explain.

  b. Keri Kline states that it is difficult to compare investing activities with industry norms in auditing investments. Is Keri right? Explain.

18-4 Describe the applicability of internal control structure components to the investing cycle.

18-5 a. Identify and describe the functions that pertain to investing cycle transactions.

  b. Using your knowledge of internal control design, explain how each assertion would be controlled for investing activities.

KEY TERMS

Bond certificate, p. 852
Bond indenture, p. 852
Books of original entry, p. 852
Broker's advice, p. 852
Broker's statement, p. 852

Investing functions, p. 853
Investing transactions, p. 849
Investment subsidiary ledger, p. 853
Stock certificate, p. 852

Audit Decision 3

■ **What factors are involved in determining an acceptable level of tests of details risk for short-term and long-term investments?**

PRELIMINARY AUDIT STRATEGIES

Figure 18-2 summarizes some key issues related to preliminary audit strategies for the audit of short-term and long-term investments. This is an audit area where the population of investing transactions is often small. As a result of small population sizes, many auditors will follow a primarily substantive approach. Nevertheless, auditors of public companies need to perform sufficient tests of controls to support an opinion on internal controls. Controls over cash receipts and cash dis-

Figure 18-2 ■ Example Preliminary Audit Strategies for Investments

Assertion	Inherent Risk	Control Risk	Analytical Procedures Risk	Test of Details Risk
Existence and Occurrence	Maximum: Short-term and long-term investments represent liquid resources that may be susceptible to misappropriation.	Low: Strong controls over cash disbursements and cash receipts investment transactions. Additional controls include monthly comparison of subsidiary records with broker's statements.	High: Comparing financial data for year-to-year comparison of balances and investment income.	Low: The auditor will usually directly confirm investments and investment activity with brokers, or compare with broker's statements.
Completeness	Moderate to Maximum: Completeness problems may result if funds intended for investment are misappropriated.	Low: Strong controls over cash disbursements and cash receipts investment transactions. Additional controls include monthly comparison of subsidiary records with broker's statements.	High: Comparing financial data for year-to-year comparison of balances and investment income.	Moderate: The auditor will usually directly confirm investments and investment activity with brokers, or compare with broker's statements.
Rights and Obligations	Moderate to High: Securities may be pledged as collateral for loans.	Moderate: Primary control is the involvement of an effective investment committee that reviews investment transactions.	Maximum: Analytical procedures are not directed at the rights and obligations assertion.	Moderate: The auditor will usually directly confirm investments and investment activity with brokers, or compare with broker's statements.
Valuation or Allocation	High to Maximum: The major valuation issues are associated with the fair value of trading investments and accounting for unrealized gains and losses.	Moderate or High: Controls over routine transactions are related to controls over cash disbursements and cash receipts. Primary control over estimates includes effective involvement of independent investment or disclosures committees.	High: Comparing financial data for year-to-year comparison of balances and investment income.	Low: The auditor will usually directly confirm investments and investment activity with brokers, or compare with broker's statements. Often fair values can readily be tested to independent sources.
Presentation and Disclosure	Moderate to High: Classification issues exist with respect to credit balances. Also, there are important disclosures related to compensating balance agreements and other restrictions on cash.	Moderate or Maximum: Primary control is the involvement of an effective investment or disclosure committee.	Maximum: Analytical procedures are not directed at disclosures.	Low: The auditor will often perform tests of details to evaluate the quality and accuracy of financial statement disclosures.

bursements are usually tested as part of the revenue and expenditure cycles. The following discussion focuses on a preliminary audit strategy developed for a private company.

SUBSTANTIVE TESTS OF SHORT-TERM AND LONG-TERM INVESTMENTS

Audit Decision 4

■ How does the auditor determine the elements of an audit program for substantive tests to achieve specific audit objectives for short-term and long-term investments?

A list of possible substantive tests of investments and the specific audit objectives to which they relate is presented in Figure 18-3. Note that the tests of details of balances category contains the largest number of possible tests, and that a variety of tests can contribute to achieving the low acceptable levels of detection risk that may be needed for the valuation or allocation and presentation and disclosure assertions. Each of the tests is explained in a following section.

Initial Procedures

The series of procedures in this category as shown in Figure 18-3 follows the pattern established for major accounts in the other cycle chapters. That is, first, the auditor obtains an understanding of the entity and its environment. It is important for the auditor to understand the economic drivers that allow an entity to engage in investing activities, such as an entity's policy for investing excess cash, its financing activities, and its ability to generate free cash flow. Second, agreement of beginning investment balances with audited amounts in the prior year's working papers is verified. Next, the activity in investment-related accounts is reviewed to determine the presence of any entries that are unusual in nature or amount that should be investigated. Then, client-prepared schedules of all investments, or additions and disposals in the current period, are checked for mathematical accuracy and agreement with the underlying accounting records. The latter procedure includes determining that schedules and subsidiary investment ledgers agree with related general ledger control account balances. The schedules can then serve as the basis for additional substantive tests.

Analytical Procedures

Analytical procedures for investment balances involve the interrelationship of specific accounts within the current period and comparisons with prior-year data, budgeted amounts, or other expectations. For example, the percentage of short- and long-term investment balances to current and total assets, respectively, and rates of return on various classes of investments can be compared with expectations. When performing analytical procedures in investment income, it is important to understand the entity's investment policy regarding the proportion of investments in government securities, corporate bonds, and equity securities. The auditor should evaluate the reasonableness of investment income for each class of investments separately, based on recent market performance. The effectiveness of analytical procedures discussed earlier in the chapter may reduce the amount of evidence needed from other substantive tests.

Tests of Details of Transactions

Tests of details of transactions may be particularly effective as an audit approach when the entity has a low volume of transactions. These substantive tests consist

Figure 18-3 ■ Possible Substantive Tests of Short-Term and Long-Term Investments

Category	Substantive Test	Specific Audit Objectives

Initial Procedures	1. Obtain an understanding of the entity and its environment and determine:
	  a. The significance of investment balances and transactions to the entity.
	  b. The entity's policies for investing surplus cash balances.
	  c. Key economic drivers that influence the entity's acquisition of investments, including the entity's ability to utilize cash flowing from financing activities to generate free cash flow.
	  d. Industry standards for the extent to which investments are important to the entity and their impact on earnings.
	2. Perform initial procedures on investment balances and records that will be subjected to further testing.
	  a. Trace beginning balance for investment assets and equity accounts to prior year's working papers.
	  b. Review activity in all investment-related balance sheet and income statement accounts and investigate entries that appear unusual in amount or source.
	  c. Obtain client-prepared schedules of investments, and determine that they accurately represent the underlying accounting records from which they were prepared by:
	    i. Footing and crossfooting the schedules and reconciling the totals with related subsidiary and general ledger balances.
	    ii. Testing agreement of items on schedules with entries in related subsidiary and general ledger accounts.
		All
		
		VA4
		
		All
		
		VA4
		
		VA4

Analytical Procedures	3. Perform analytical procedures:
	  a. Calculate ratios:
	    i. Short-term investments to total assets.
	    ii. Long-term investments to total assets.
	    iii. Rates of return by investment classification.
	  b. Analyze ratio results relative to expectations based on prior years, budgeted, or other data.
		All

Tests of Details of Transactions	4. On a test basis, vouch entries in investment and related income and equity accounts.	EO1-3, C1-3, VA1-3, PD1-3

Tests of Details of Balances	5. Inspect and count securities on hand.
	6. Confirm securities held by others.
	7. Recalculate investment revenue earned.
	8. Determine the appropriate classification of held-to-maturity securities, trading securities, and available-for-sale securities by reference to:
	  a. Documentation of management's stated intent.
	  b. Whether management's actions are consistent with management's stated intent.
	  c. Management's ability to hold debt securities to maturity.
	  d. Written representation from management confirming the proper classification of securities.
	9. Obtain evidence corroborating the fair value of investments at balance sheet date, including, but not limited to:
	  a. Quoted market prices obtained from financial publications.
	  b. Fair-value estimates obtained from broker dealers and other third-party sources.
	  c. Evaluation of the appropriateness of valuation models.
		EO4, C4, RO1
		EO4, C4, RO1
		EO4, C4, VA4
		PD4
		
		VA4

Presentation and Disclosure	10. Compare statement presentation with GAAP.
	  a. Determine the investment balances are properly identified and classified in the financial statements.
	  b. Determine the appropriateness of disclosures concerning the valuation bases for investments, realized and unrealized gain or loss components, related party investments, and pledged investments.
	  c. Evaluate the completeness of presentation and disclosures for investments in drafts of financial statements to determine conformity to GAAP by reference to disclosure checklist.
	  d. Read disclosures and independently evaluate their classification and understandability.
		PD4, PD7
		
		PD4, PD7
		
		PD6
		
		PD6

of vouching the individual debits and credits in the various investment accounts. For example, debits to asset accounts for acquisition transactions can be vouched to brokers' advices and canceled checks. Other debits to the investment accounts or related market adjustment accounts can be vouched to documentation verifying increases in fair values to be recognized in the accounts. Credits posted to asset accounts can be vouched to bank or broker's advices evidencing the sale of investments, or to documentation of decreases in fair values to be recognized in the accounts. Similarly, entries to income statement and equity accounts for realized and unrealized gains and losses can be vouched to documentation of sales transactions or changes in fair values based on independently published market values. Entries for major purchases and sales of investments can often be vouched to authorizations in the minutes of the board of directors.

For investments accounted for by the equity method, post-acquisition debits can be vouched to documentation showing the investor's share of the investee's earnings. Credits can be vouched to documentation of dividends received from investees or to worksheets showing the calculation of the periodic amortization of the excess of cost over underlying book value. Audited financial statements of the investee generally constitute sufficient evidence regarding the underlying net assets and the results of operations of the investee. If the financial statements of the investee are not audited, the auditor should apply, or should request that the client arrange with the investee to have the investee's auditor apply, appropriate auditing procedures to such financial statements, considering the materiality of the investment in relation to the financial statements of the client.

Knowledge of the proper accounting for investing activities affecting other investment balances will inform the auditor as to the sources to which the debits and credits can be vouched. Depending on the particular debits or credits being vouched, careful examination of the supporting documentation can provide evidence bearing on any of the five categories of assertions. For example, brokers' advices provide evidence about the existence or occurrence of transactions, the transfer of ownership of securities, and the valuation of the securities at the transaction date. Documentation may also be helpful in determining that the debits and credits have been made to the proper accounts (proper classification).

Tests of Details of Balances

Three substantive tests in this category are explained in the following subsections.

Inspect and Count Securities on Hand

This test ordinarily is performed simultaneously with the auditor's count of cash and other negotiable instruments. In performing the test, (1) the custodian of the securities should be present throughout the count, (2) a receipt should be obtained from the custodian when the securities are returned, and (3) all securities should be controlled by the auditor until the count is completed.

In inspecting securities, the auditor should observe such matters as the certificate number on the document, name of owner (which should be the client, either directly or through endorsement), description of the security, number of shares (or bonds), and name of issuer. These data should be recorded as part of the auditor's analysis of the investment account. Figure 18-4 illustrates an audit working paper for one class of equity securities. For securities purchased in prior years, the data should be compared with those shown on last year's working papers. A lack of

Figure 18-4 ■ Available-for-Sale Securities Working Paper

Williams Company
Available for Sale Securities
December 31, 20X1

Prepared By: A.E.R. Date: 2/3/X2
Reviewed By: R. E. G. Date: 2/10/X2
W/P Ref. H-2

DESCRIPTION	CTF. NO.	DATE ACQUIRED	NO. OF SHARES	COST PER SHARE	BALANCES 1/1/x1	PURCHASES	SALES	BALANCES 12/31/x1	MKT PRICE PER SHARE	MKT VALUE 12/31/x1	DIVIDEND INCOME
General Mfg. Co.	C2779	4/21/x0	900	$ 22.00	$ 19,800 a			$ 19,800 d	$ 24.50 e	$ 22,050 d	$ 675 f
Metropolitan Edison	M82931	9/21/x0	500	$ 33.20	$ 16,600 a		$ 16,600 c	$ — d	d	d	$ 127
Pacific Papers, Inc.	54942	2/14/x1	200	$ 18.50	$ —	$ 3,700 c		$ 3,700 d	$ 17.00 e	$ 3,400 d	$ — f
Warrenton Corp.	7336	7/19/x0	400	$ 27.25	$ 10,900 a			$ 10,900 d	$ 29.25 e	$ 11,700 d	$ 120 f
					$ 47,300 a	$ 3,700	$ 16,600	$ 34,400 b		$ 37,150	$ 922 b
					F	F	F	FF	F	F	F
								to H-1		to H-1	to R-1

Fair Value over (under) cost at 12/31/x1
Balance in Market Adjustment – Available for Sale Securities Account: 12/31/x1 .... $ 2,750

Current Adjustment Required : Increase (Decrease) .... $ 1,250
.... $ 1,500   AE

F) Footed
FF) Footed and Crossfooted
a) Agreed to prior year's working papers
b) Traced to general ledger
c) Vouched to brokers' advices and board of directors' authorization
d) Extension checked
e) Per market quotation in *Wall Street Journal* 1/2/x2
f) Dividend rates check to Standard and Poor's; dividends received to cash receipts journal

AE: Adjusting entry posted to W/P AE – 2
Market Adjustment Available-for-Sales Securities .... $ 1,500
 Unrealized Gain (Loss) in Available for Sale Securities .... $ 1,500

agreement between the certificate numbers may be indicative of unauthorized transactions for those securities. When the count is not made on the balance sheet date, the auditor should prepare a reconciliation from the date of count to the statement date by reviewing any intervening security transactions.

Confirm Securities Held by Others

Material securities held by outsiders for safekeeping should be confirmed. Confirmations should be requested as of the date securities held by the client are counted. The confirmation process for securities is identical with the steps required in confirming receivables. Thus, the auditor must control the mailings and receive the responses directly from the custodian. The data confirmed are the same as the data that should be noted when the auditor is able to inspect the securities. Securities may also be held by creditors as collateral against loans or be placed in escrow by court order. In such cases, the confirmation should be sent to the indicated custodian.

Recalculate Investment Revenue Earned

Income from investments is verified by documentary evidence and recalculation.

- Dividends on all stocks listed on stock exchanges and many others are included in published investment services. The auditor can independently verify the dividend revenue by reference to the declaration date, amount, and payment date shown in the record book. The verification of dividend income is usually incorporated into the schedule of investments, as illustrated in Figure 18-4.
- Interest earned and interest collected on investments in bonds can be verified by examining the interest rates and payment dates indicated on the bond certificate. In addition, the auditor reviews the client's amortization schedule for bond premium and discount and recalculates the amount amortized, if any.
- Verification of the investor's share of investee earnings for equity method investments was discussed as part of vouching entries in the earlier section on tests of details of transactions. Recalculation of investment revenue balances pertains primarily to the valuation or allocation assertion.

Tests of Details of Accounting Estimates

When auditing investments, the auditor must apply significant audit judgment with respect to evaluating (1) the proper classification of investments and (2) the fair value of investments. The professional guidance provided by AU 332, *Auditing Derivative Instruments, Hedging Activities, and Investments in Securities,* is discussed below.

Proper Classification of Investments

The appropriateness of the client's application of FASB No. 115, *Accounting for Certain Investments in Debt and Equity Securities,* depends on the entity's classification of securities as:

- Held-to-maturity securities, which are reported at amortized cost.
- Trading securities, which are reported at fair value, with unrealized gains and losses included in earnings.

- Available-for-sale securities, which are reported at fair value with unrealized gains and losses excluded from earnings and reported in a separate equity account.

The auditor should determine whether management's investment activities corroborate or conflict with management's stated intent. For example, sales of investments classified in the held-to-maturity category should cause the auditor to question the appropriateness of management's classification of other investments in that category. The auditor should also consider management's ability to hold a debt security to maturity given the client's financial position, working capital needs, and ability to generate operating cash flow. Finally, the auditor ordinarily should obtain written representation from management confirming the appropriate classification of securities.

Auditing the Fair Value of Investments

If investments are carried at their fair value, the auditor should obtain evidence corroborating the fair value. Common sources for corroborating the fair value of securities include quoted market prices obtained from financial publications or fair-value estimates obtained from broker-dealers and other third-party sources. In the case of investments valued using a valuation model, the auditor does not function as an appraiser and is not expected to substitute his or her judgment for that of the entity's management. Rather, the auditor generally should assess the reasonableness and appropriateness of the model. The auditor may consider it necessary to involve a specialist in assessing the entity's fair-value estimates or related models.

GAAP requires management to determine whether a decline in fair value below the amortized cost basis of certain investments is other than temporary, which often involves the estimation of the outcomes of future events. The auditor should evaluate whether management has considered relevant information in determining whether an other-than-temporary impairment condition exists. Example factors that may indicate an other-than-temporary impairment condition include the following:

- Fair value is significantly below cost.
- The decline in value is attributable to specific adverse conditions affecting a particular investment.
- A debt security has been downgraded by a rating agency.
- The financial condition of the issuer has deteriorated.
- Dividends have been reduced or eliminated, or scheduled interest payments on debt securities have not been made.

The auditor should obtain evidence about such conditions and whether they tend to corroborate or conflict with management's conclusions.

Tests of Details of Presentation and Disclosure

The foregoing substantive tests should provide much of the evidence needed by the auditor to determine whether investment balances are properly identified and classified in the financial statements. However, regarding classification as to current or noncurrent, or trading versus available-for-sale, the auditor must also make inquiries of management concerning its intentions regarding holding periods and so on. In the case of debt securities classified as held-to-maturity, the auditor must also assess the entity's ability to hold the investment until maturity. Most auditors use checklists as an aid in determining that all required disclosures are made concerning valuation bases for investments, the various components of realized and unrealized gains and losses, related party investments, and securities that have been pledged as collateral.

[LEARNING CHECK

18-6   What factors are relevant in determining the acceptable level of detection risk for investment balances?

18-7   a. What precautions should be taken in counting and inspecting securities?
b. Identify the financial statement assertions affected by this test.

18-8   What data should be shown in the working papers concerning securities that have been examined by the auditor?

18-9   a. Indicate the form and timing of confirming securities held by outside custodians.
b. State the financial statement assertions affected by this test.

[AUDITING CASH BALANCES]

Cash balances include undeposited receipts on hand, cash in bank in general checking and savings accounts, and imprest accounts such as petty cash and payroll bank accounts. This represents cash needed to settle obligations and pay payroll, and most entities will move surplus cash to some form of interest-earning investment. Certain balances, such as certificates of deposits, bond sinking fund cash, certain foreign currency balances, and other accounts that have restrictions on their use, should ordinarily be classified as investments.

RELATIONSHIP OF CASH BALANCES TO TRANSACTION CYCLES

Audit Decision 5
■ What is the relationship of the transaction cycles to cash balances, and how are specific audit objectives developed for cash balances?

Five transaction cycles relate directly to general cash balances, as shown in Figure 18-5. The cycles are revenue, expenditure, financing, investing, and personnel services. The production cycle does not have transactions that relate directly to cash. Note that the financing and investing cycles both increase and decrease cash, whereas the revenue cycle increases, and the expenditure and personnel services cycles decrease, cash. For many entities, the volume of revenue and expenditure cycle transactions is large and can also be large for the personnel services cycle. The volume and size of individual cash transactions in the financing and investing cycles vary greatly from one entity to another and can also vary greatly from year to year for a single entity.

AUDIT OBJECTIVES

Because (1) internal control considerations pertaining to the various transaction classes that affect cash and (2) the related transaction class audit objectives for

Figure 18-5 ■ Relationship of Transaction Cycles to Cash

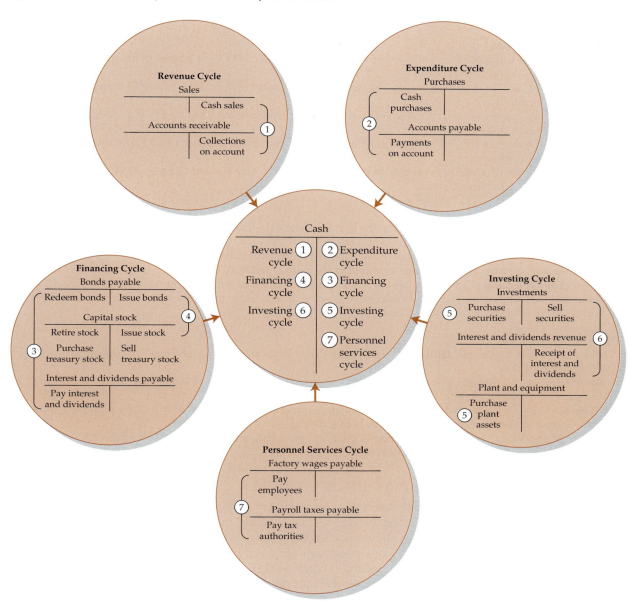

those transactions are addressed in the previous four chapters, this chapter focuses primarily on substantive tests for cash balances. Chapters 14 and 15 have explained internal controls and tests of transactions for cash receipts and cash disbursements. Accordingly, Figure 18-6 only includes account balance audit objectives for cash balances and disclosures. The substantive tests used to meet these objectives are explained later in the chapter.

Figure 18-6 ■ Selected Specific Audit Objectives for Cash

Specific Audit Objectives

Transaction Objectives

Occurrence. See Chapter 14 for audit objectives related to cash receipts and Chapter 15 for audit objectives related to cash disbursements.

Completeness. See Chapter 14 for audit objectives related to cash receipts and Chapter 15 for audit objectives related to cash disbursements.

Accuracy. See Chapter 14 for audit objectives related to cash receipts and Chapter 15 for audit objectives related to cash disbursements.

Cutoff. See Chapter 14 for audit objectives related to cash receipts and Chapter 15 for audit objectives related to cash disbursements.

Classification. See Chapter 14 for audit objectives related to cash receipts and Chapter 15 for audit objectives related to cash disbursements.

Balance Objectives

Existence. Recorded cash balances exist at the balance sheet date **(EO1)**. Year-end transfers of cash between banks are recorded in the proper period **(EO2)**.

Completeness. Recorded cash balances include the effects of all transactions that have occurred **(C1)**. Year-end transfers of cash between banks are recorded in the proper period **(C2)**.

Rights and Obligations. The entity has legal title to all cash balances shown at the balance sheet date **(RO1)**.

Valuation and Allocation. Recorded cash balances are realizable at the amounts stated on the balance sheet and agree with supporting schedules **(VA1)**.

Disclosure Objectives

Occurrence and Rights and Obligations. Disclosed cash events and transactions have occurred and pertain to the entity **(PD1)**.

Completeness. All cash disclosures that should have been included in the financial statements have been included **(PD2)**.

Classification and Understandability. All information about cash balances is appropriately presented and described, and information in disclosures is clearly expressed **(PD3)**.

Accuracy and Valuation. Cash information is disclosed accurately and at appropriate amounts **(PD4)**.

ANALYTICAL PROCEDURES

Audit Decision 6

■ What audit planning decisions should be made when developing an audit program for the audit of cash balances?

Management's operating, investing, and financing decisions and strategies significantly affect cash balances. Consequently, in some audits these balances may not be expected to show a stable or predictable relationship with other current or historical financial or operating data. Well-managed companies regularly develop cash budgets, projecting (1) cash receipts based on anticipated collection of receivables, (2) cash disbursements for operating needs, and (3) investing and financing activities. Effective analytical procedures involve comparing cash balances with forecasts or budgets, or with company policies regarding minimum cash balances and the investment of surplus cash. It is usually more effective to compare cash balances with budgets and company policies because the individual cash needs of various entities are often unique. Auditors normally do not expect to obtain significant assurance from analytical procedures applied to cash balances.

INHERENT RISK

The high volume of transactions alone contributes to a significant level of inherent risk for certain cash balance assertions, particularly existence or occurrence and completeness. In addition, the nature of cash balances makes them suscepti-ble to theft as numerous kinds of fraudulent schemes involving cash have borne out. In contrast to receivables or inventories, however, the risks pertaining to the rights and obligations, valuation or allocation, and presentation and disclosure assertions for cash are minimal due to the absence of complexities involving rights, accounting measurements, estimates, and disclosures.

CONSIDERATION OF INTERNAL CONTROLS

Internal controls related to cash receipts and cash disbursements were discussed in Chapters 14 and 15, respectively. The student should review the discussion in these chapters regarding the internal control elements of the control environment, risk assessment, information and communication, control procedures, and moni-toring, including the discussion of key documents and records and common func-tions and controls. Cash receipts and disbursements often represent routine trans-actions that can be controlled by a sound system of internal controls, which may allow the auditor to assess control risk at a low level. Because of the susceptibility of cash balances to theft, many auditors carefully evaluate internal controls over cash, and ensure that significant deficiencies in internal control are clearly com-municated to management.

[LEARNING CHECK

18-10 Identify several types of cash accounts that should be included as cash bal-ances on the balance sheet and several others that should not.

18-11 Which transaction cycles relate directly to cash and how?

18-12 a. State the account balance audit objectives for cash that are associated with each category of financial statement assertions.
b. Indicate the relative degree of inherent risk associated with each asser-tion category for cash balances.

18-13 Cash balances often constitute a very small percentage of an entity's cur-rent or total assets. Why is significant effort allocated to testing controls and performing audit procedures for cash balances?

18-14 What special considerations relate to applying the concepts of materiality and preliminary audit strategies to the audit of cash balances?

PRELIMINARY AUDIT STRATEGIES

Audit Decision 7

■ What factors are involved in determin-ing an acceptable level of tests of details risk for cash balance assertions?

Figure 18-7 summarizes some key issues related to preliminary audit strategies for the audit of cash balances. In this section and the following subsections, the term *cash balances* refers only to cash on hand and in bank, excluding petty cash and other imprest funds. Controls over cash receipts and cash disbursements are usu-ally tested as part of the revenue and expenditure cycles. The audit strategy is highly dependent on tests of effectiveness of internal controls. If internal controls are strong, the auditor may perform less extensive substantive tests and place a greater degree of reliance on internal documentation.

Some small business owners want the auditor to carefully audit cash to provide them assurance about the validity of cash balances. As a result, the auditor will follow a primarily substantive approach emphasizing tests of details even when

Figure 18-7 ■ Example Preliminary Audit Strategies for Cash

Assertion	Inherent Risk	Control Risk	Analytical Procedures Risk	Test of Details Risk
Existence and Occurrence	Maximum: Cash involves a high volume of transactions, and it is highly susceptible to misappropriation.	Low: Strong controls over cash disbursements and cash receipts. Additional controls include independent monthly bank reconciliations.	High: Comparing financial data for year-to-year and comparison of cash balances with cash budgets and forecasts.	Low: The auditor will usually directly confirm bank balances, and tests of bank reconciliation depend on quality of internal controls.
Completeness	Moderate to Maximum: Completeness problems may result if schemes involving the misappropriation of assets are not recorded.	Low: Strong controls over cash disbursements and cash receipts investment transactions. Additional controls include independent monthly bank reconciliation.	High: Comparing financial data for year-to-year and comparison of cash balances with cash budgets and forecasts.	Low: The auditor will usually directly confirm bank balances, and tests of bank reconciliation depend on quality of internal controls.
Rights and Obligations	Low: Significant rights issues do not exist with respect to cash balances.	N/A	Maximum: Analytical procedures are not directed at the rights and obligations assertion.	Moderate: The auditor will usually directly confirm bank balances and any restrictions on cash.
Valuation or Allocation	Moderate: Significant valuation issues do not exist with respect to cash balances.	Low: Strong controls over cash disbursements and cash receipts. Additional controls include independent monthly bank reconciliations.	High: Comparing financial data for year-to-year and comparison of cash balances with cash budgets and forecasts.	Moderate: The auditor will usually directly confirm bank balances. Tests of bank reconciliation depend on quality of internal controls.
Presentation and Disclosure	Moderate to High: There may be concerns about classification of credit balances.	Moderate or Maximum: Primary control is the involvement of an effective disclosure committee.	Maximum: Analytical procedures are not directed at disclosures.	Low: The auditor will often perform tests of details to evaluate the quality and accuracy of financial statement disclosures.

the audit risk model might indicate that such an approach is not necessary because of the effectiveness of internal controls. Other clients may rely on the CFO, or an internal audit department, to carefully review or audit cash balances and may ask the auditor to design the scope of the audit of cash balances based only on what is necessary to issue an opinion on fair presentation in the financial statements.

SUBSTANTIVE TESTS OF CASH BALANCES

A listing of possible substantive tests to achieve the specific audit objectives for cash balances is presented in Figure 18-8. Not all of the tests are performed in every audit. Each of the tests is explained in a following section, including comments on when certain of the tests might be omitted and how some of them can be tailored based on applicable risk factors.

Figure 18-8 ■ Possible Substantive Tests of Cash Balance Assertions

Category	Substantive Test	Specific Audit Objectives

Initial Procedures	1. Obtain an understanding of the business and industry and determine:
	  a. The significance of cash balances and transactions to the entity.
	  b. The entity's policies for forecasting cash balances and investing surplus cash balances.
		All

	2. Perform initial procedures on cash balances and records that will be subjected to further testing.	VA1
	a. Trace beginning balance for cash on hand and in bank to prior year's working papers.	All
	b. Review activity in general ledger accounts for cash and investigate entries that appear unusual in amount or source.	VA1
	c. Obtain client-prepared schedules of cash on hand and in bank, verify mathematical accuracy, and determine agreement with general ledger.	

Analytical Procedures	3. Perform analytical procedures:
	  a. Compare cash balances with budgeted amounts, prior-year balances, or other expected amounts.
	  b. Calculate cash as a percent of current assets and compare with expectations.
		All

Tests of Details of Transactions	4. Perform cash cutoff tests (note these test may have been performed as part of the audit programs for accounts receivable and accounts payable):
	  a. Observe that all cash received through the close of business on the last day of the fiscal year is included in cash on hand or deposits in transit and that no receipts of the subsequent period are included, or
	  b. Review documentation such as daily cash summaries, duplicate deposit slips, and bank statements covering several days before and after year-end date to determine proper cutoff.
		EO2, C2

	c. Observe the last check issued and mailed on the last business day of the fiscal year and trace to accounting records to determine the accuracy of the cash disbursements cutoff, or	EO2, C2
	d. Compare dates on checks issued for several days before and after the year-end date to the dates the checks were recorded to determine proper cutoff.	EO2, C2, VA1

(continues)

Figure 18-8 ■ (Continued)

Category	Substantive Test	Specific Audit Objectives
Tests of Details of Balances	5. Trace bank transfers for several days before and after the year-end date to determine that each transfer is properly recorded as a disbursement and a receipt in the same accounting period and is properly reflected in bank reconciliations when applicable.	
	6. Prepare proof of cash for any bank accounts the entity has been unable to reconcile or for which there is a high risk that fraudulent transactions have occurred.	
	7. Count undeposited cash on hand and determine that such amounts are included in cash balances.	EO1, C1, RO1, VA1
	8. Confirm bank deposit and loan balances with banks.	EO1, C1, RO1, VA1
	9. Confirm other arrangements with banks such as lines of credit, compensating balance agreements, and loan guarantees or other parties.	EO1, C1, RO1, VA1
	10. Obtain, scan, review, and prepare bank reconciliations as appropriate.	EO1, C1, RO1, VA1
	11. Obtain and use bank cutoff statements to verify bank reconciliation items, detect any unrecorded checks that have cleared the bank, and look for evidence of window dressing.	EO1, C1, RO1, VA1
Presentation and Disclosure	12. Compare statement presentation with GAAP.	
	a. Determine that cash balances are properly identified and classified in the financial statements.	PD1, PD4
	b. Determine that bank overdrafts are reclassified as current liabilities.	PD1, PD4
	c. Make inquiries of management, review correspondence with banks, and review minutes of board of directors meetings to determine matters requiring disclosure such as lines of credit, loan guarantees, compensating balance agreements, or other restrictions on cash balances.	PD1, PD4
	d. Evaluate the completeness of presentation and disclosures for cash in drafts of financial statements to determine conformity to GAAP by reference to disclosure checklist.	PD2
	e. Read disclosures and independently evaluate their classification and understandability.	PD3

Initial Procedures

Audit Decision 8

■ How does the auditor determine the elements of an audit program for substantive tests to achieve specific audit objectives for substantive tests for cash balances?

Before proceeding with details tests of cash balances, the auditor should ensure that he or she has obtained an understanding of the entity and its enviornment and the importance of cash balances to the entity. For example, the auditor might understand the volume of transactions going through various cash accounts, the entity's ability to generate positive cash flow from operations, policies for forecasting or budgeting cash, and policies for investing surplus cash. The starting point for verifying cash balances is tracing the current period's beginning balances to the ending audited balances in the prior year's working papers (when applicable). Next, the current period's activity in the general ledger cash accounts should be reviewed for any significant entries that are unusual in nature or amount that require special investigation. In addition, any schedules prepared by the client showing summaries of undeposited cash receipts at different locations and/or summaries of bank balances are obtained. The mathematical accuracy of any such schedules should be determined and their agreement with related cash balances in the general ledger checked. This test provides evidence about the valuation or allocation assertion.

Analytical Procedures

As previously discussed, the effectiveness of analytical procedures varies significantly from client to client. The effectiveness of analytical procedures discussed earlier in the chapter may reduce the amount of evidence needed from other substantive tests relative to that required when the data do not conform to reasonable expectations developed from cash budgets or forecasts, or company policies regarding the investment of surplus cash.

Tests of Details of Transactions

As discussed previously in Chapters 14 and 15, some substantive tests of details involving the tracing and vouching of cash receipts and cash disbursements transactions are ordinarily performed concurrently with tests of controls as dual-purpose tests. The evidence from such tests should be combined with the evidence from the procedures discussed here in reaching a conclusion as to the fair presentation of cash balances. In the next two subsections, consideration is given to two tests of transactions that are generally performed at or near the balance sheet date.

Perform Cash Cutoff Tests

A proper cutoff of cash receipts and cash disbursements at the end of the year is essential to the proper statement of cash at the balance sheet date. Two **cash cutoff tests** are performed: (1) a cash receipts cutoff test, which is explained in Chapter 14, and (2) a cash disbursements cutoff test, as explained in Chapter 15. The use of a bank cutoff statement, described below, is also helpful in determining whether a proper cash cutoff has been made. Cash cutoff tests are directed primarily at the financial statement assertions of existence or occurrence and completeness.

Trace Bank Transfers

Audit Decision 9

■ What is the fraud known as kiting, and how can the auditor detect it?

Many entities maintain accounts with more than one bank. A company with multiple bank accounts may make authorized transfers of money between bank accounts. For example, money may be transferred from a general bank account to a payroll bank account for payroll checks that are to be distributed on payday. When a bank transfer occurs, several days (called the float period) generally will elapse before the check clears the bank on which it is drawn. Thus, cash on deposit per bank records will be overstated during this period because the check will be included in the balance of the bank in which it is deposited and will not be deducted from the bank on which it is drawn. Bank transfers may also result in a misstatement of the bank balance per books if the disbursement and receipt are not recorded in the same accounting period.

Intentionally recording a bank transfer as a deposit in the receiving bank while failing to show a deduction from the bank account on which the transfer check is drawn is a form of fraud known as **kiting.** Kiting may be used to conceal a cash shortage or overstate cash in bank at the statement date.

An auditor requires evidence on the validity of bank transfers or, conversely, of misstatements therein. This is obtained by preparing a **bank transfer schedule.** Data for the schedule are obtained from an analysis of the cash entries per books and applicable bank and cutoff bank statements. The schedule lists all transfer checks issued at or near the end of the client's fiscal year, and shows the dates that the checks were recorded by the client and the bank, as illustrated in Figure 18-9.

Figure 18-9 ■ Bank Transfer Schedule

Check No.	Bank Accounts		Amount	Disbursement Date		Receipt Date	
	From	To		Per Books	Per Bank	Per Books	Per Bank
4100	General	Payroll	$ 50,000	12/31	1/3	12/31	1/2
4275	General	Branch #1	$10,000	12/31	1/4	1/2	1/2
4280	General	Branch #2	$20,000	1/2	1/2	12/31	12/31
B403	Branch #4	General	$ 5,000	1/2	1/3	1/3	12/31

If we assume all checks are issued on December 31, check 4100 in Figure 18-9 has been handled properly because both book entries were made in December and both bank entries occurred in January. This check would be listed as an outstanding check in reconciling the general bank account at December 31 and as a deposit in transit in reconciling the payroll bank account. Check 4275 illustrates a transfer check in transit at the closing date. Cash per books is understated $10,000 because the check has been deducted from the balance per books by the issuer in December, but has not been added to the Branch #1 account per books by the depositor until January. Thus, an adjusting entry is required at December 31 to increase the branch balance per books.

Checks 4280 and B403 illustrate the likelihood of kiting because these December checks were not recorded as disbursements per books until January, even though they were deposited in the receiving banks in December. Check 4280 results in a $20,000 overstatement of cash in bank because the receipt per books occurred in December, but the corresponding book deduction was not made until January. Check B403 may illustrate an attempt to conceal a cash shortage because the bank deposit occurred in December presumably to permit reconcilement of bank and book balances, and all other entries were made in January.

Kiting is possible when weaknesses in internal controls allow one individual to issue and record checks (i.e., improper segregation of duties), or there is collusion between the individuals who are responsible for the two functions. In addition to tracing bank transfers, kiting may be detected by (1) obtaining and using a bank cutoff statement (as discussed in a later section) because the kited check clearing in January will not appear on the list of outstanding checks for December and (2) performing a cash cutoff test because the last check issued in December will not be recorded in the check register.

Count Cash on Hand

Undeposited cash receipts and change funds are ordinarily considered cash on hand. To properly perform **cash counts,** the auditor should:

■ Control all cash and negotiable instruments held by the client until all funds have been counted.

■ Insist that the custodian of the cash be present throughout the count.

■ Obtain a signed receipt from the custodian on return of the funds to the client.

■ Ascertain that all undeposited checks are payable to the order of the client, either directly or through endorsement.

---

vault teller lacked cents

A long-term bank employee worked as a vault teller in a large commercial bank vault that contained large quantities of bagged coins. In previous audits, he had observed that the auditors selected bags positioned in the front rows of the bins for test counting because moving the front bags and counting the bags in the back of the bins were physically difficult. The vault teller devised a scheme to put pennies in the quarter bags in the back rows. A newly hired staff auditor misunderstood the audit instructions and attempted to physically count all bagged coins. On opening all the quarter bags, much to the dismay of the vault teller, the auditor discovered the irregularity which amounted to a $3,800 vault shortage. The vault teller confessed to the scheme and was prosecuted. New procedures were implemented to include periodic test counts and to open bags to verify correct denominations.

Source: Hilliard T. Steele, ed., "Fraud Findings," *The Internal Auditor* (April 1990), p. 67.

The control of all funds is designed to prevent transfers by the client of counted funds to uncounted funds. The sealing of funds and the use of additional auditors are often required when cash is held in many locations. The safeguards pertaining to the custodian serve to minimize the possibility, in the event of a shortage, of the client claiming that all cash was intact when released to the auditor for counting.

Tests to Detect Lapping

Audit Decision 10

■ What is the fraud known as lapping, and how can the auditor detect it?

Lapping is a form of fraud that results in the deliberate misappropriation of cash receipts. It may involve either a temporary or a permanent abstraction of cash receipts for the personal use of the individual perpetrating the unauthorized act. Lapping is usually associated with collections from customers, but it may also involve other types of cash receipts. Conditions conducive to lapping exist when an individual who handles cash receipts also maintains the accounts receivable ledger. The auditor should assess the likelihood of lapping in obtaining an understanding about the segregation of duties in the receiving and recording of collections from customers.

To illustrate lapping, assume on a given day that cash register tapes totaled $600 and mail receipts opened by the lapper consisted of one payment on account by check for $200 from customer A. The lapper would proceed to take $200 in cash and destroy all evidence pertaining to the mail receipt except for the customer's check. The cash receipts journal entry would agree with the register tape ($600), and the deposit slip would show cash $400 and A's check for $200. These facts can be tabulated as follows:

ACTUAL RECEIPTS		DOCUMENTATION		JOURNAL ENTRY		BANK DEPOSIT SLIP	
Cash	$600	Cash Tape	$600	Cash Sales	$600	Cash	$400
A check	$200		$ —		$ —	A check	$200
	$800		$600		$600		$600

In an effort to conceal the shortage, the defrauder usually attempts to (1) keep bank and book amounts in daily agreement so that a bank reconciliation will not detect the irregularity and (2) correct the customer's account within three to four days of actual collection so that any discovered discrepancy in the customer's account can be explained as a delay in receiving the money or posting. To accomplish the latter, the abstraction is shifted to another customer's account several days later as follows:

ACTUAL RECEIPTS		DOCUMENTATION		JOURNAL ENTRY		BANK DEPOSIT SLIP	
Cash	$500	Cash Tape	$500	Cash Sales	$500	Cash	$400
B check	$300	A check	$200	A check	$200	B check	$300
	$800		$700		$700		$700

The total shortage is now $300—$200 from the first example plus $100 from the second example.

Tests to detect lapping are performed only when control risk for cash receipts transactions is moderate or high. There are three procedures that should detect lapping.

- *Confirm Accounts Receivable.* This test will be more effective if it is performed on a surprise basis at an interim date. Confirming at this time will prevent the individual engaged in lapping from bringing the "lapped" accounts up to date. Confirmation at the balance sheet date may be ineffective because the "lapper" may anticipate this procedure and adjust the "lapped" accounts to their correct balances at this date.
- *Make a Surprise Cash Count.* The cash count will include coin, currency, and customer checks on hand. The auditor should oversee the deposit of these funds. Subsequently, the details of the deposit shown on the duplicate deposit slip should be compared with cash receipts journal entries and postings to the customers' accounts.
- *Compare Details of Cash Receipts Journal Entries with the Details of Corresponding Daily Deposit Slips.* This procedure should uncover discrepancies in the details such as those shown in the two examples above. When there is appropriate segregation of duties in the handling of mail receipts, some auditors prefer to use prelists in this procedure. In such a case, the dates of the actual collections are compared with the dates of the postings of the collections to the accounts receivable ledger.

Tests of Details of Balances

Confirm Bank Deposit and Loan Balances

Audit Decision 11

■ What are the roles of confirmations and the use of a bank cutoff statement in the audit of cash balances?

It is customary for the auditor to obtain a **bank confirmation** for cash on deposit and loan balances as of the balance sheet date. Figure 18-10 illustrates a *Standard Form to Confirm Account Balance Information with Financial Institutions*. This form was jointly developed and approved by the American Bankers Association, the AICPA, and the Bank Administration Institute. Notice that the form requests information about the following three items: (1) deposit balances, (2) loan balances, and (3) other deposit or loan accounts that may have come to the attention of the authorized bank official.

Figure 18-10 ■ Standard Confirmation Form for Bank Balances

STANDARD FORM TO CONFIRM ACCOUNT
BALANCE INFORMATION WITH FINANCIAL INSTITUTIONS

ORIGINAL
To be mailed to accountant

CUSTOMER NAME

We have provided to our accountants the following information as of

the close of business on_____, 20___, regarding our deposit and loan balances. Please confirm the accuracy of the information, noting any exceptions to the information provided. If the balances have been left blank, please complete this form by furnishing the balance in the appropriate space below.* Although we do not request nor expect you to conduct a comprehensive, detailed search of your records, if during the process of completing this confirmation additional information about other deposit and loan accounts we may have with you comes to your attention, please include such information below. Please use the enclosed envelope to return the form directly to our accountants.

Financial Institution's Name and Address   [   ]

[   ]

1. At the close of business on the date listed above, our records indicated the following deposit balance(s):

ACCOUNT NAME	ACCOUNTS NO.	INTEREST RATE	BALANCE*

2. We were directly liable to the financial institution for loans at the close of business on the date listed above as follows:

ACCOUNTS NO./ DESCRIPTION	BALANCE*	DATE DUE	INTEREST RATE	DATE THROUGH WHICH INTEREST IS PAID	DESCRIPTION OF COLLATERAL

_____ (Customer's Authorized Signature)   _____ (Date)

The information presented above by the customer is in agreement with our records. Although we have not conducted a comprehensive, detailed search of our records, no other deposit or loan accounts have come to our attention except as noted below.

_____ (Financial Institution Authorized Signature)   _____ (Date)

_____ (Title)

EXCEPTIONS AND/OR COMMENTS

Please return this form directly to our accountants: [   ]

*Ordinarily, balances are intentionally left blank if they are not available at the time the form is prepared.   [   ]

Approved 1990 by American Bankers Association, American Institute of Certified Public Accountants, and Bank Administration Institute. Additional forms available from: AICPA – Order Department, P.O. Box 1003, NY, NY 10108-1003

The confirmation request is prepared in duplicate and signed by an authorized check signer of the client. Both copies are sent to the bank, and the original is returned to the auditor. To assure the competency of the evidence from this procedure, the auditor should personally mail the request in his or her own return address envelope, and the response should be returned directly to the auditor by the bank. Bank confirmation requests should be sent to all banks in which the client has an account, including those that may have a zero balance at the end of the year.

Confirm Other Arrangements with Banks

Other arrangements with banks include such matters as lines of credit, compensating balances, and contingent liabilities. The arrangements for establishing a line of credit with a bank may require the borrower to maintain a cash balance with the bank. The amount may be an agreed-on-percentage of the amount borrowed, or it may be a specified dollar amount. The required minimum amount is referred to as a **compensating balance.** A contingent liability may exist when the client is the guarantor of a loan made by the bank to a third party.

If, after assessing inherent and control risk, the auditor believes such arrangements may exist, he or she should send a confirmation letter to the bank. The letter should specifically identify the information requested and be signed by the client. The AICPA has developed standard confirmation letters for the three arrangements identified above. Preferably, the letter should be sent to the bank official who is in charge of the client's relationship with the bank. Directing the letter to such an individual will expedite the confirmation process and enhance the quality of the evidence the auditor obtains. The auditor's request for information on line of credit and contingent liabilities does not require the respondent to make a detailed search of the bank's records.

Scan, Review, or Prepare Bank Reconciliations

Scanning, testing, or preparing a bank reconciliation establishes the correct cash in the bank balance at the balance sheet date. When the acceptable level of detection risk is high, the auditor may scan the client-prepared **bank reconciliation** and verify the mathematical accuracy of the reconciliation. If detection risk is moderate, the auditor may review the client's bank reconciliation. The review will normally include

- Comparing the ending bank balance with the balance confirmed on the bank confirmation form
- Verifying the validity of deposits in transit and outstanding checks
- Establishing the mathematical accuracy of the reconciliation
- Vouching reconciling items such as bank charges and credits and errors to supporting documentation
- Investigating old items such as checks outstanding for a long period of time and unusual items

The working paper for an auditor review of a bank reconciliation prepared by the client (PBC) is illustrated in Figure 18-11.

When detection risk is low, the auditor may prepare the bank reconciliation using bank data in the client's possession. When detection risk is very low or the

Figure 18-11 ■ Review of Client-Prepared Bank Reconciliation

Bates Company
W/P Ref. A-1
Bank Reconciliation – City Bank – General Accounts
December 31, 20X1
(PBC)

Prepared By: *C.J.B.* Date: 1/15/X2
Reviewed By: *R. E. Z.* Date: 1/25/X2

Acct # 110
Bank Account No. 12345-642
Balance per Bank .... $ 120,262.47 a
Deposits in Transit

	Per books	Per bank		
	12–30	1–2	$ 8,425.15 b	
	12–31	1–7	$ 17,844.79 b	$ 26,269.94 F
Outstanding Checks:		1047	$ 225.94 b	
		1029	$ 21,600.00 b	
		1435	$ 47.25 b	
		1436	$ 1,428.14 b	
		1437	$ 1,000.00 b	
		1440	$ 832.08 b	
		1441	$ 41.08 b	$ (25,174.49) F

Add NSF Check: R. Zim 12/29 .... $ 200.00 c

Balance per Books .... $ 121,557.92 F, d

To A

F) Footed
a) Agreed to bank statement and bank confirmation
b) Traced to cutoff bank statement
c) Traced to bank statement and debit memo. Cash balance at year-end was overstatated by $200 and receivables were understated by the same amount. Immaterial. Pass further investigation.
d) Traced to general ledger

auditor suspects possible material misstatements, the auditor may obtain the year-end bank statement directly from the bank and prepare the bank reconciliation. To do so, the auditor must request the client to instruct the bank to send the bank statement and accompanying data (paid checks, debit memos, etc.) directly to the auditor. This procedure will prevent the client from making alterations of the data to cover any misstatements.

The evidence provided by a bank reconciliation alone is generally not considered sufficient to verify the balance of cash in bank because of uncertainties concerning the following two most important reconciling items: (1) deposits in transit and (2) outstanding checks. Such evidence is obtainable only by tracing these items to the bank statement in the next accounting period. The procedure of obtaining a bank cutoff statement is designed, in part, for this purpose. When the cutoff statement validates these and other reconciling items, the reliance that an auditor can place on a bank reconciliation is significantly enhanced.

Obtain and Use Bank Cutoff Statements

A **bank cutoff statement** is a bank statement as of a date subsequent to the date of the balance sheet. The date should be at a point in time that will permit most of the year-end outstanding checks to clear the bank. Usually, the date is seven to ten business days following the end of the client's fiscal year.

The client must request the cutoff statement from the bank and instruct that it be sent directly to the auditor. On receipt of the cutoff statement, with enclosed canceled checks and bank memoranda, the auditor should:

■ Trace all prior-year dated checks to the outstanding checks listed on the bank reconciliation

■ Trace deposits in transit on the bank reconciliation to deposits on the cutoff statement

■ Scan the cutoff statement and enclosed data for unusual items

The tracing of checks is designed to verify the list of outstanding checks. In this step, the auditor may also find that a prior-period check not on the list of outstanding checks has cleared the bank and that some of the checks listed as outstanding have not cleared the bank. The former may be indicative of an irregularity known as kiting, which is explained on page 869; the latter may be due to delays in (1) mailing the checks by the client, (2) depositing the checks by the payees, and (3) processing the checks by the bank. The auditor should investigate any unusual circumstances.

When the aggregate effect of uncleared checks is material, it may be indicative of an irregularity known as **window dressing,** which is a deliberate attempt to overstate a company's short-term solvency.[1] In such a case, the auditor should trace the uncleared checks to the check register and supporting documentation and, if necessary, make inquiries of the treasurer.

The tracing of deposits in transit to the cutoff statement is normally a relatively simple matter because the first deposit on the cutoff statement should be the deposit in transit shown on the reconciliation. When this is not the case, the auditor should determine the underlying circumstances for the time lag from the treasurer and corroborate his or her explanations.

In scanning the cutoff statement for unusual items, the auditor should be alert for such items as unrecorded bank debits and credits and bank errors and corrections.

Inasmuch as the auditor obtains the cutoff statement directly from an independent source outside the client's organization, it provides a high degree of competent corroborating information about the validity of the year-end bank reconciliation and the existence or occurrence, completeness, rights and obligations, and valuation or allocation assertions for cash in bank.

Tests of Details of Presentation and Disclosure

Cash should be correctly identified and classified in the balance sheet. For example, cash on deposit is a current asset. However, bond sinking fund cash is a long-term investment. In addition, there should be appropriate disclosure

---

[1] Assume at the balance sheet date, the client's balances show current assets of $800,000 and current liabilities of $400,000. If $100,000 of checks to short-term creditors have been prematurely entered, the correct totals are current assets of $900,000 and current liabilities of $500,000, which results in a 1.8:1 current ratio instead of the reported 2:1.

of arrangements with banks such as lines of credit, compensating balances, and contingent liabilities. A bank overdraft is normally reported as a current liability.

The auditor determines the appropriateness of the statement presentation from a review of the draft of the client's statements and the evidence obtained from the foregoing substantive tests. In addition, the auditor should review the minutes of board of directors meetings and make inquiry of management for evidence of restrictions on the use of cash balances.

LEARNING CHECK

18-15 a. Identify three different tests of details of transactions that can be performed in auditing cash balances.
b. Which of these tests need not be performed when control risk pertaining to cash transactions and balances is low and the entity's bank accounts have been reconciled?

18-16 a. What is meant by the term *kiting?*
b. What procedures can the auditor use to detect kiting?

18-17 What precautions should the auditor take in counting cash on hand?

18-18 a. What is lapping?
b. What circumstance is conducive to lapping?

18-19 a. What precautions are taken by the embezzler to prevent detection of lapping?
b. What tests can the auditor use to detect lapping?

18-20 a. What types of information does the auditor seek to have confirmed on the standard form to confirm account balance information with financial institutions?
b. What assertions are addressed by the confirmation data?

18-21 a. What is a *compensating balance?*
b. What is the auditor's primary source of evidence about this item, and to what assertion does it pertain?

18-22 How may the auditor vary his or her work on bank reconciliations based on the applicable acceptable level of detection risk?

18-23 a. What safeguards should the auditor take in obtaining a bank cutoff statement?
b. For what purposes does the auditor use a bank cutoff statement?

18-24 Identify several considerations the auditor should make regarding management's presentation and disclosure of cash balances.

KEY TERMS

Bank confirmation, p. 872
Bank cutoff statement, p. 875
Bank reconciliation, p. 874
Bank transfer schedule, p. 869
Cash counts, p. 870

Cash cutoff tests, p. 869
Compensating balance, p. 874
Kiting, p. 869
Lapping, p. 871
Window dressing, p. 876

[OTHER RELATED SERVICES]

Audit Decision 12

■ How might the auditor use the knowledge obtained during the audit of investments and cash balances to deliver other services to clients?

Not every company follows the practices of most well-managed companies of forecasting cash balances and developing policies of the investment of surplus cash. CPAs understand the opportunities available to companies to invest surplus cash for short periods of time when it is not needed to pay current obligations, sometimes even on an overnight basis. Furthermore, electronic spreadsheets make it easier for CPAs to develop models to forecast cash balances on a month-by-month basis. Following are some important value-added opportunities that CPAs may provide using the knowledge obtained during the audit of marketable securities and cash balances.

■ Determine key assumptions regarding cash collections and the payment of operating expenses that influence the forecasting of cash balances.

cash balances in freefall

An outside director of a not-for-profit approached a CPA friend with a problem. The chairwoman of the board of directors was concerned about what she had seen in recent monthly financial statements. The not-for-profit was a social service agency that subcontracted with the state and county to deliver three programs that provided services to children, services to women moving from the state's corrections program back to the community, and services to the elderly. She stated that in recent months the entity's cash balances "were in freefall." Several month ago, they had over $500,000 in cash and investments. Now most of it was gone, and the chief accounting officer was talking with her about the need to draw on a line-of-credit with the bank to pay bills, for the first time in over three years. Internal controls were good, and the entity received only minor reportable conditions associated with the annual audit that was just completed.

The CPA volunteered to perform a free consulting engagement to help her friend identify the problem. The CPA identified two major problems that caused the decline in cash balances.

First, the entity agreed to contract changes with the state and county whereby it would be reimbursed for the services it provided at a rate per person served rather than the previous monthly lump-sum amount. The previous lump sum was sufficient to cover the entity's fixed payroll and operating costs, but now that the entity was being reimbursed on a per-person basis, some months the reimbursement from the state or county was insufficient to cover the organization's costs.

Second, the entity had been paid its lump sum by the state or county in time to use the cash to pay its payroll and operating expenses. Now the organization had to incur the costs, provide services, and then bill the state or county for each person served. Rather than receiving cash before paying for its costs, it delivered services, billed for services, and waited four to six weeks for cash to come in. Furthermore, many of the managers who were good at providing social services were slow to prepare their billings to the state or county, delaying cash flow for a longer period.

The auditor focused on internal controls over cash, rather than on the entity's business practices. The internal controls were strong, while the entity's business practices were weak. During the subsequent year the audit was put up for bid, and the CPA who recommended that the social service agency negotiate an advance from the state and county to cover its cash flow needs won the engagement. In the subsequent years the CPA helped train the organization's managers to behave more like a for-profit organization as it now had heavy fixed costs that had to be recovered on a fee for each person served.

- Assist management in the development of models to forecast cash balances, needed borrowing, or potential surplus cash balances available for investment.
- Identify opportunities for changes in business practices, such as changes in credit policy or changes in inventory management, which will improve cash flow.
- Assist management in developing policies for the short-term investment of excess cash.
- Identify opportunities for improving the rate of return on short-term investments of excess cash.

Each of these steps can help an entity improve its cash management practices.

FOCUS ON AUDIT DECISIONS

This chapter focuses on the audit of two very liquid assets: short-term and long-term investments and cash. Figure 18-12 summarizes the audit decisions discussed in Chapter 18 and provides page references indicating where these decisions are discussed in more detail.

Figure 18-12 ■ Summary of Audit Decisions Discussed in Chapter 18

Audit Decision	Factors That Influence the Audit Decision	Chapter References
D1. What is the nature of short-term and long-term investments, and how are specific audit objectives developed for short-term and long-term investments?	Short-term and long-term investments include investing in the debt and equity securities of another entity. This audit area also includes related interest and dividend income. Figure 18-1 uses the framework discussed in Chapter 6 to develop the specific audit objectives that are tailored to short-term and long-term investments. In order to collect sufficient, competent evidence, the auditor must obtain evidence for each audit objective.	pp. 849–850
D2. What audit planning decisions should be made when developing an audit program for the audit of short-term and long-term investments?	A key aspect of understanding an entity's investments in debt and equity securities relates to its ability to generate free cash flows. The ability to generate free cash flow may be seasonal and depends on an entity's competitive advantage in the marketplace.	pp. 850–854
	Each company's ability to generate cash flow is so unique that industry information may not be a good benchmark for comparing a company. It may be more effective to develop expectations using cash budgets or forecasts.	
	The most significant inherent risk revolves around the classification of investments as held-to-maturity, available-for sale, or trading securities. Additional inherent risks relate to the fact that investments may be susceptible to misappropriation, and some investments should be valued at fair value.	
	The chapter discussion identifies specific controls associated with four functions: (1) authorizing investment transactions, (2) receiving or delivering securities, (3) recording transactions, and (4) settling transactions. The suggested controls are similar to those suggested in previous chapters with modifications for documents and records that are tailored to investments in debt and equity securities.	

(continues)

Figure 18-12 ■ (Continued)

Audit Decision	Factors That Influence the Audit Decision	Chapter References
D3. What factors are involved in determining an acceptable level of tests of details risk for short-term and long-term investments?	Figure 18-2 outlines one possible preliminary audit strategy for each assertion for investments. The audit of short-term investments often focuses on tests of balances due to significant turnover in these accounts. However, the audit of long-term investments may have low turnover and focus on tests of transactions.	pp. 854–856
D4. How does the auditor determine the elements of an audit program for substantive tests to achieve specific audit objectives for short-term and long-term investments?	This section uses the framework developed in Chapter 12 to design substantive tests for the investing cycle. Figure 18-3 summarizes substantive tests for investments. It summarizes the initial procedures, analytical procedures, tests of details of transactions, tests of details of balances, tests of details of accounting estimates, and tests of details of disclosures relevant to the investing cycle. The chapter discussion explores these tests in more detail.	pp. 856–862
D5. What is the relationship of the transaction cycles to cash balances, and how are specific audit objectives developed for cash balances?	Figure 18-5 provides a graphic illustration of how the other transaction cycle interacts with cash. The revenue cycle, expenditure cycle, financing cycle, investing cycle, and personnel services cycle all have transactions that flow through cash balances. Controls over these other cycles are important to controls over cash. Figure 18-6 presents specific audit objectives for cash balances.	pp. 862–864
D6. What audit planning decisions should be made when developing an audit program for the audit of cash balances?	Cash balances are more related to an entity's cash management practices than to specific industry issues. However, when a company is profitable and generating free cash flow, it is more likely that excess cash will be invested in short-term and long-term investments.

Well-managed companies regularly develop cash budgets, projecting (1) cash receipts based on anticipated collection of receivables, (2) cash disbursements for operating needs, and (3) investing and financing activities. Effective analytical procedures involve comparing cash balances with forecasts or budgets, or with company policies regarding minimum cash balances and the investment of surplus cash.

The high volume of transactions and the susceptibility to theft contribute to a significant level of inherent risk for existence or occurrence and completeness assertions. However, the risks pertaining to the rights and obligations, valuation or allocation, and presentation and disclosure assertions for cash are minimal due to the absence of complexities involving rights, accounting measurements, estimates, and disclosures.

Cash receipts and disbursements often represent routine transactions that can be controlled by a sound system of internal controls. Because of the susceptibility of cash balances to theft, many auditors carefully evaluate internal controls over cash, and ensure that significant deficiencies in internal control are clearly communicated to management. Internal controls over cash receipts and cash disbursements were previously discussed in Chapters 14 and 15, respectively. | pp. 864–865 |

(continues)

Figure 18-12 ■ (Continued)

Audit Decision	Factors That Influence the Audit Decision	Chapter References
D7. What factors are involved in determining acceptable level of tests of details risk for cash balance assertions?	Figure 18-7 outlines one possible preliminary audit strategy for each assertion for cash balances. Audit strategies focus on the audit of cash balances and are influenced by the entity's system of internal controls.	pp. 865–868
D8. How does the auditor determine the elements of an audit program for substantive tests to achieve specific audit objectives for substantive tests for cash balances?	This section of the chapter uses the framework developed in Chapter 12 to develop substantive tests for each specific audit objective in the expenditure cycle. These are summarized in Figure 18-8 and explained in depth in the chapter discussion.	pp. 868–869
D9. What is the fraud known as kiting, and how can the auditor detect it?	Intentionally recording a bank transfer as a deposit in the receiving bank while failing to show a deduction from the bank account on which the transfer check is drawn is an irregularity known as *kiting*. To test for kiting a auditor needs to perform substantive tests of bank transfers before and after year-end. Figure 18-9 provides examples of bank transfers that involve kiting (examples 3 and 4).	pp. 869–871
D10. What is the fraud known as lapping, and how can the auditor detect it?	*Lapping* is fraud that results in the deliberate misappropriation of cash receipts. Conditions conducive to lapping exist when an individual who handles cash receipts also maintains the accounts receivable ledger, and the individual usually credits one customer's cash receipt to a customer from whom funds were misappropriated. The chapter discussion explains how lapping is often detected.	pp. 871–872
D11. What are the roles of confirmations and the use of a bank cutoff statement in the audit of cash balances?	Bank confirmations are an important tool when testing the existence of cash balances. If internal controls are poor, an auditor may request a bank cutoff statement. A bank cutoff statement is a bank's statement as of a date subsequent to the balance sheet date. It is used to obtain evidence of the validity of items shown on a client's bank reconciliation.	pp. 872–877
D12. How might the auditor use the knowledge obtained during the audit of investments and cash balances to deliver other services to clients?	When auditing investments and cash balances, auditors may recognize opportunities to improve cash management activities. The chapter discussion addresses a number of activities that may help an entity improve its cash management practices.	pp. 878–879

objective questions

Objective questions are available for the student at www.wiley.com/college/boynton

18-25   **(Controls and substantive tests for investment transaction)** You have been assigned to audit the "investments" account of one of your firm's older clients, the D Company. During the prior year, your client received more than $1 million from the sale of all its stock in a subsidiary. The proceeds from this sale were promptly invested in time certificates of deposit (CDs) having various maturities. More than one year has elapsed since the sale of the stock, and your client continues to invest the funds in CDs. Investment decisions are made by the company treasurer, who also is responsible for custody of the CDs.

During the current year, D's treasurer obtained $100,000 from the surrender of a CD at maturity and invested the proceeds in another six-month certificate having an interest rate of 10 percent. This transaction was recorded on the books of the company as being for a CD bearing an interest rate of 8 percent. At the end of the six months, the treasurer redeemed this CD for its $105,000 maturity value. On the books of the company, the transaction was recorded as having been for $104,000, and the treasurer deposited that amount in the company's bank account prior to reinvesting the proceeds in another security.

Required

a. What internal controls could have prevented or permitted detection of the treasurer's action?

b. What substantive tests could you perform to discover this irregularity?

18-26   **(Substantive tests of investment balances)** In verifying investing cycle balances in the Travis Company, C.J. Kupec, CPA, recognizes that the following misstatements may occur or exist:

1. A mathematical error is made in accruing interest earned.
2. A 25 percent common stock investment in an affiliated company is accounted for on the cost basis.
3. Securities held by an outside custodian are in the treasurer's name.
4. Securities on hand at the beginning of the year are diverted to personal use in July and are replaced in December.
5. An authorized purchase is recorded at cost, and the broker's fee is expensed.
6. Ten shares of stock reported to be on hand are missing.
7. Marketable equity securities are reported at cost, which is above market.
8. The schedule of marketable securities does not reconcile to the general ledger accounts.
9. Gain on a sale of securities is reported net of taxes.
10. Securities pledged as collateral on a bank loan are not disclosed.

Required

a. Identify the substantive test that should detect each misstatement.

b. For each test, indicate the financial statement assertion(s) to which it pertains.

c. Indicate the type of evidence obtained from the substantive test (i.e., physical, confirmation, documentary, written representation, mathematical, oral, or analytical). (Use a tabular format for your answers with one column for each part.)

18-27   **(Investments—audit objectives, confirmations, disclosures)** As a result of highly profitable operations over a number of years, Eastern Manufacturing Corporation accumulated a substantial investment portfolio. In the audit of the financial statements for the year ended December 31, 20X0, the following information came to the attention of the corporation's independent auditor (CPA):

1. The manufacturing operations of the corporation resulted in an operating loss for the year.

2. In 20X0, the corporation placed the securities making up the investment portfolio with a financial institution that will serve as custodian of the securities. Formerly, the securities were kept in the corporation's safe deposit box in the local bank.

3. On December 22, 20X0, the corporation sold and then repurchased on the same day a number of securities that had appreciated greatly in value.

Management stated that the purpose of the sale and repurchase was to establish a higher cost and book value for the securities and to avoid the reporting of a loss for the year.

Required

a. List the audit objectives of the CPA's examination of the investment account.

b. Under what conditions would the CPA accept a confirmation of the securities on hand from the custodian in lieu of inspecting and counting the securities?

c. What disclosure, if any, of the sale and repurchase of the securities would the CPA recommend for the financial statements?

AICPA

18-28 **(Evaluation of working paper for investments)** The schedule on page 886 was prepared by the controller of World Manufacturing, Inc., for use by the independent auditors during their audit of World's year-end financial statements. All procedures performed by the audit assistant were noted in the "Legend" section at the bottom. The schedule was properly initialed, dated, and indexed, and then submitted to a senior member of the audit staff for review. Internal control was reviewed and is considered satisfactory.

Required

a. What information that is essential to the audit of marketable securities is missing from this schedule?

b. What are the essential substantive tests that were noted as having been performed by the audit assistant?

AICPA

18-29 **(Audit program for cash balances)** MLG Company's auditor received directly from the banks confirmations and cutoff statements with related checks and deposit tickets for MLG's three general-purpose bank accounts. The auditor determined that control risk for cash balance assertions was low. The proper cutoff of external cash receipts and disbursements was established. No bank accounts were opened or closed during the year.

Required

Prepare the audit program of substantive procedures to verify MLG's bank balances. Ignore any other cash accounts.

AICPA (adapted)

18-30 **(Cash irregularities)** The Patricia Company had poor internal control over its cash transactions. Facts about its cash position at November 30, 20X0, were as follows:

The cashbook showed a balance of $18,901.62, which included undeposited receipts. A credit of $100 on the bank's records did not appear on the books of the company. The balance per bank statement was $15,550. Outstanding checks were: #62 for $116.25, #183 for $150, #284 for $253.25, #8621 for $190.71, #8623 for $206.80, and #8632 for $145.28.

The cashier abstracted all undeposited receipts in excess of $3,794.41 and prepared the reconciliation shown on page 887:

World Manufacturing Inc. Marketable Securities Year Ended December 31, 20X1

Description of Security	CORP. %	YR. DUE	Serial No.	Face Value of Bonds	Gen. Ledger 1/1	Purch. in 20X1	Sold in 20X1	Cost	Gen. Ledger 12/31	12/31 Market	Pay Date(s)	Amt. Rec	Accruals 12/31
BONDS													
A	6	91	21-7	10,000	9,400 a				9,400	9,400	1/15 7/15	300 b, d 300 b, d	275
D	4	83	73-0	30,000	27,500 a				27,500	26,220	12/1	1,200 b, d	100
G	9	98	16-4	5,000	4,000 a				4,000	5,080	8/1	450 b, d	188
Rc	5	85	08-2	70,000	66,000 a		57,000 b, c	66,000					
Sc	10	99	07-4	100,000		100,000 c, e			100,000	101,250	7/1	5,000 b, d	5,000
					106,900 a, f	100,000 f	57,000 f	66,000 f	140,900 f	141,650 f		7,250 f	5,563 f
									f, g	f		f	f
STOCKS													
P 1,000 shs. Common			1,044	7,500 a					7,500	7,600	3/1 6/1 9/1 12/1	750 b, d 750 b, d 750 b, d 750 b, d	250
U 50 shs. Common			8,530	9,700 a					9,700	9,800	2/1 8/1	800 b, d 800 b, d	667
				17,200 a, f					17,200	17,400		4,600	917
									f	f, g		f	f

Legends and comments relative to above:

a = Beginning balances agreed to 19X0 working papers.
b = Traced to cash receipts.
c = Minutes examined (purchase and sales approved by the board of directors).
d = Agreed to 1099 (tax form).
e = Confirmed by tracing to broker's advice.
f = Totals footed.
g = Agreed to general ledger.

Balance per books, November 30, 20X2		$ 18,901.62
Add: Outstanding Checks		
8621	$ 190.71	
8623	$ 206.80	
8632	$ 145.28	$ 442.79
		$ 19,344.41
Less Undeposited receipts		$ (3,794.41)
Balance per bank, November 30, 20X2		$ 15,500.00
Deducted: Unrecorded credit		$ 100.00
True cash, November 30, 20X2		$ 15,450.00

Required

a. Prepare a working paper showing how much the cashier abstracted.

b. How did he attempt to conceal his theft?

c. Using only the information given, name two specific features of internal control that were apparently lacking.

AICPA

18-31 **(Substantive tests for cash balances)** You are the in-charge accountant examining the financial statements of the Gutzler Company for the year ended December 31, 20X0. During late October 20X0, you, with the help of Gutzler's controller, completed an internal control questionnaire and prepared the appropriate memoranda describing Gutzler's accounting procedures. Your comments relative to cash receipts are as follows:

All cash receipts are sent directly to the accounts receivable clerk with no processing by the mail department. The accounts receivable clerk keeps the cash receipts journal, prepares the bank deposit slip in duplicate, posts from the deposit slip to the subsidiary accounts receivable ledger, and mails the deposit to the bank.

The controller receives the validated deposit slips directly (unopened) from the bank. He also receives the monthly bank statement directly (unopened) from the bank and promptly reconciles it.

At the end of each month, the accounts receivable clerk notifies the general ledger clerk by journal voucher of the monthly totals of the cash receipts journal for posting to the general ledger.

Each month, with regard to the general ledger cash account, the general ledger clerk makes an entry to record the total debits to cash from the cash receipts journal. In addition, the general ledger clerk on occasion makes debit entries in the general ledger cash account from sources other than the cash receipts journal (e.g., funds borrowed from the bank).

In the audit of cash receipts you have already performed certain of the standard auditing procedures listed below. The extent to which these procedures were performed is not relevant to the question.

1. Total and cross-total all columns in the cash receipts journal.

2. Trace postings from the cash receipts journal to the general ledger.

3. Examine remittance advices and related correspondence to support entries in the cash receipts journal.

Required

Considering Gutzler's internal control over cash receipts and standard auditing procedures already performed, list all other auditing procedures and reasons therefore which should be performed to obtain sufficient audit evidence regarding cash receipts. Do not discuss the procedures for cash disbursements and cash balances. Also do not discuss the extent to which any of the procedures are to be performed. Assume adequate controls exist to assure that all sales transactions are recorded. Organize your answer sheet as follows:

OTHER AUDIT PROCEDURES	REASONS FOR OTHER AUDIT PROCEDURES

AICPA

18-32   **(Bank transfer schedule; kiting)** The LMN Company maintains three bank accounts: City Bank-Regular, City Bank-Payroll, and Metro Bank-Special. Your analysis of cash disbursements records for the period June 23 to July 6 reveals the following bank transfers:

CHECK NO.	DATE OF CHECK	BANK DRAWN ON	PAYEE	AMOUNT
2476	June 23	Regular	Payroll	$100,000
2890	June 25	Regular	Payroll	200,000
3140	June 28	Regular	Special	100,000
A1006	June 29	Special	Payroll	50,000
A1245	June 30	Special	Regular	25,000
3402	June 30	Regular	Special	125,000

You determine the following facts about each of the first five checks: (1) the date of the cash disbursements journal entry is the same as the date of the check, (2) the payee receives the check two days later, (3) the payee records and deposits the check on the day it is received, and (4) it takes five days for a deposited check to clear banking channels and be paid by the bank on which it is drawn. Check 3402 was not recorded as a disbursement until July 1. This check was picked up by the payee on the date it was issued, and it was included in the payee's after-hours bank deposit on June 30.

Required

a. What are the purposes of the audit of bank transfers?

b. Prepare a bank transfer schedule as of June 30 using the format illustrated in Figure 18-9.

c. Prepare separate adjusting entries for any checks that require adjustment.

d. In the reconciliation for the three bank accounts, indicate the check numbers that should appear as (1) an outstanding check or (2) a deposit in transit.

e. Which check(s) may be indicative of kiting?

18-33   **(Procedures to detect lapping)** During the year, Strang Corporation began to encounter cash flow difficulties, and a cursory review by management revealed receivable collection problems. Strang's management engaged Stanley, CPA, to perform a special investigation. Stanley studied the billing and collection cycle and noted the following:

The accounting department employs one bookkeeper who receives and opens all incoming mail. This bookkeeper is also responsible for depositing receipts, filing remittance advices on a daily basis, recording receipts in the cash receipts journal, and posting receipts in the individual customer accounts and the general ledger accounts. There are no cash sales. The bookkeeper prepares and controls the mailing of monthly statements to customers.

The concentration of functions and the receivable collection problems caused Stanley to suspect that a systematic defalcation of customers' payments through a delayed posting of remittances (lapping of accounts receivable) is present. Stanley was surprised to find that no customers complained about receiving erroneous monthly statements.

Required

Identify the procedures that Stanley should perform to determine whether lapping exists. Do not discuss deficiencies in the internal control structure.

AICPA

cases

18-34   **(Substantive tests of investment balances)** The Jones Company, located in Chicago, has been your client for many years. The company manufactures light machinery and has a calendar year closing. At December 31, 20X1, and 20X2, the following items appeared in the accounts applicable to investment securities. Investments in securities represent approximately 8 percent of total assets. Income from securities represents approximately 3 percent of income before federal income tax.

BALANCE SHEET ACCOUNTS	20X0	20X1
U.S. government certificates of indebtedness,		
3% series D dated May 15, 20X0, due May 15, 20X2		
(at cost)	$300,000	$300,000
Available-for-sale equity securities (at fair value):		
50 shares of AP Company	5,800	5,000
100 shares of UC Corporation	—	8,000
75 shares of IC Corporation	12,000	—
Investment in a 60% owned subsidiary—SUB, Inc.	50,000	50,000
Unrealized gain (loss) on available-for-sale securities		
(equity account)	1,450	(1,075)
Accrued interest receivable	1,125	1,125

INCOME STATEMENT ACCOUNTS		
Interest income	9,000	9,000
Gain (loss) on sale of securities	(–2,000)	3,000
Dividend income	13,000	14,000

The U.S. government securities shown above are held at the Utah Banking Company. The AP Company securities are held in the Jones Company's safe, and the UC Corporation securities are in a safety deposit box at the Chicago Bank Company, which is the company's bank. Access to the company's safe is limited to the treasurer or his assistant. Access to the safety deposit box is limited to any two of the treasurer, the assistant treasurer, or the controller. The securities of SUB, Inc., are also held by the Chicago Bank Company as collateral for a loan that the Jones Company has outstanding. SUB, Inc., has a June 30 closing and is audited by your firm.

Your tests of internal control indicate unusual strengths in the areas of cash receipts and cash disbursements. The treasurer is responsible for the physical control of securities, whereas the controller is responsible for the recording of all transactions affecting securities. An assistant to the assistant controller maintains an investment ledger that shows the name of each investment, the number of shares held or the face value of bonds, the date of purchase and sale, if applicable, the cost, the physical location of the securities, and the income thereon. This person prepares monthly statements of securities on hand showing their description and cost. All purchases and sales of securities are authorized by the company's finance committee. The following audit program has been prepared for the examination of securities at December 31, 20X1.

1. *U.S. Government Securities*
   a. Prepare a schedule of the securities at December 31, 20X1.
   b. Obtain direct confirmation from the Utah Banking Company as to description and amount of securities held.

    c. Trace the confirmation to the schedule and so indicate.
    d. Verify the interest earned for the year and accrued interest receivable at December 31, 20X1.
    e. Trace the appropriate totals to the general ledger accounts.

2. *Available-for-Sale Equity Securities*
    a. Prepare an analysis of the securities account for the year under audit, including the market value of the securities at December 31, 20X1.
    b. Count AP Company securities at the company's office at the close of business on December 31, 20X1. Inspection of the securities should be in the presence of client's representative. Note the time of count, name of client's representative, and name of the auditor on the count sheet. Accompanied by the client's representative, inspect the UC Corporation securities at the Chicago Bank Company. Inspection should be completed at the close of business on December 31, 20X1. The same information should be shown on this count sheet as is indicated to be appropriate for the count sheet mentioned above. The count sheets should show the number of shares, the full name of security, and the type of security (preferred or common shares).
    c. Vouch purchases and sales by reference to brokers' advices. Compare authorizations of the finance committee to the schedule.
    d. Compare dividends received for the year with a published dividend record.
    e. Verify the recorded gain or loss on sale of securities.
    f. Trace the appropriate totals on the schedule to the general ledger accounts.

3. *Investment in 60% Owned Subsidiary-SUB, Inc.*
    a. Request the Chicago Bank Company to confirm that it holds the securities for SUB, Inc., as collateral for a loan. The amount payable to the bank may be confirmed concurrently.
    b. Review the monthly statements of SUB, Inc., since your latest examination and compare them with the audited statements at June 30. Obtain an explanation of all unusual transactions and fluctuations.
    c. Discuss the December 31, 20X1, financial statements with the management of the company. Inquire as to material amounts not recorded.
    d. Establish that the intercompany accounts are in agreement at December 31.
    e. Record the company's equity in the assets and net income of SUB, Inc., at December 31, 20X1.

Required

a. List the substantive tests that you believe are appropriate and identify the assertions to which each test relates.

b. List the substantive tests that you believe are inappropriate and give the reasons for your conclusion.

c. List additional substantive tests, if any, that you believe are appropriate and state why.

professional simulation

| Situation | Research | Audit Planning | Audit Procedures |

The Vane Corporation is a manufacturing concern that has been in business for the past 18 years. During this period, the company has grown from a very small family-owned operation to a medium-sized manufacturing concern with several departments. Despite this growth, a substantial number of the procedures employed by Vane Corporation have been in effect since the business was started.

Generally accepted accounting principles require that management's intent and ability be considered in valuing certain securities; for example, whether —

■ Debt securities are classified as held-to-maturity and reported at their cost depend on management's intent and ability to hold them to their maturity.

■ Equity securities are reported using the equity method depend on management's ability to significantly influence the investee.

■ Equity securities are classified as trading or available-for-sale depend on management's intent and objectives in investing in the securities.

Cut and paste the U.S. auditing standards sections that explain the evidence that an auditor should obtain to evaluate assertions about securities based on management's intent and ability.

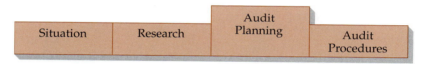

You have been asked to prepare a training session for new audit staff on the audit of cash balances. You have been asked to explain how the audit of cash balances at year-end will differ if the client has good internal controls over cash transactions and bank balances versus a client that has weak internal controls over cash transactions and bank balances. Prepare a memo outlining contrasting the audit of cash balances at year-end for each of these two situations.

To: Audit File

Re: Staff Training for Audit of Cash Balances

From: CPA Candidate

GOOD INTERNAL CONTROLS OVER CASH TRANSACTIONS AND CASH BALANCES	WEAK INTERNAL CONTROLS OVER CASH TRANSACTIONS AND CASH BALANCES

Exhibit 18-35 provides a working paper (lead schedule) for the audit of Vane's bank balance. Explain the auditing procedures that should be performed associated with the legend identified as a) through i). Use the following format.

LEGEND	AUDIT PROCEDURE
a)	
b)	
c)	
d)	
e)	
f)	
g)	
h)	
i)	

EXHIBIT 18-35 AUDIT OF CASH IN BANK

Vane Corporation
Cash in Bank
December 31, 20X3

Prepared by: *CJG*   W/P Ref: B-1
Reviewed By: *RCP*   Date: 2/4/X4
                      Date: 2/12/X4

Balance per bank		$ 18,375.91 a)
Deposits in Transit		
12/30	$ 1,471.10 b)	
12/31	$ 2,840.69 b)	$ 4,311.79 i)
Subtotal		$ 22,687.70 i)
Outstanding checks		
837	$ 6,000.00 c)	
1941	$ 671.80	
1966	$ 320.00	
1984	$ 1,855.42 c)	
1985	$ 3,621.22 c)	
1987	$ 2,576.89 c)	
1991	$ 4,420.88 c)	$ (19,466.21) i)
Subtotal		$ 3,221.49 i)
NSF check returned 12/29		$ 200.00 d)
Bank charges		$ 550.00 e)
Error Check No. 1932		$ 148.10 f)
Customer note collected by the bank ($2,750 plus $275 interest)		$ (3,025.00) g)
Balance per books		$ 550.09 h)
		i)

PART

[5]

COMPLETING THE AUDIT, REPORTING, AND OTHER SERVICES

COMPLETING THE AUDIT AND POSTAUDIT RESPONSIBILITIES

AUDITOR'S RESPONSIBILITIES FOR EVENTS OCCURRING AFTER BALANCE SHEET DATE

On February 6, 2002, PriceWaterhouseCoopers LLP issued an unqualified opinion on the financial statements of Adolph Coors Company for the years ended December 30, 2001, and December 31, 2000. The balance sheet showed total assets of approximately $1.7 billion, current liabilities of approximately $0.5 billion, long-term liabilities of approximately $0.25 billion, and shareholders' equity of approximately $0.95 billion. Net income was approximately $123 million, and cash flow from operations was approximately $193 million.

Management disclosed in a note to the financial statements that on February 2, 2002 (approximately one month after the balance sheet date) it had purchased 100 percent of the shares of Bass Holdings, Ltd., in the United Kingdom for approximately $1.7 billion. Coors added $2.3 billion to its assets base and accepted over $600 million in debt for the net assets of $1.7 billion. Adolph Coors Company financed the $1.7 billion acquisition with approximately $1.5 billion in debt. The reported financial statements as of December 30, 2001, show a favorable debt to equity ratio of approximately 0.79:1. After reading the subsequent events footnote, the company looks very different with an additional $1.5 billion in debt.

This was what auditors call a type 2 subsequent event. The event did not exist as of the balance sheet date and should not affect the December 30, 2001, balance sheet. However, the event occurred prior to the date of the auditor's report, and it is clearly material to the financial statements. As a result, it was rightly disclosed in the notes to the statements.

This event was quite obvious. It would have been announced in the financial press, and it is clearly material to the financial statements. It is appropriate to ask about the auditor's responsibility to search for such events. Does the auditor have to design audit procedures to look for such events? When should such audit procedures be performed? This responsibility and other similar responsibilities are discussed further in this chapter.

[PREVIEW OF CHAPTER 19]

Many aspects of interim and year-end audit testing have been discussed in previous chapters. This chapter is concerned with four important additional areas of activity in a financial statement audit. The following diagram provides an overview of the chapter organization and content.

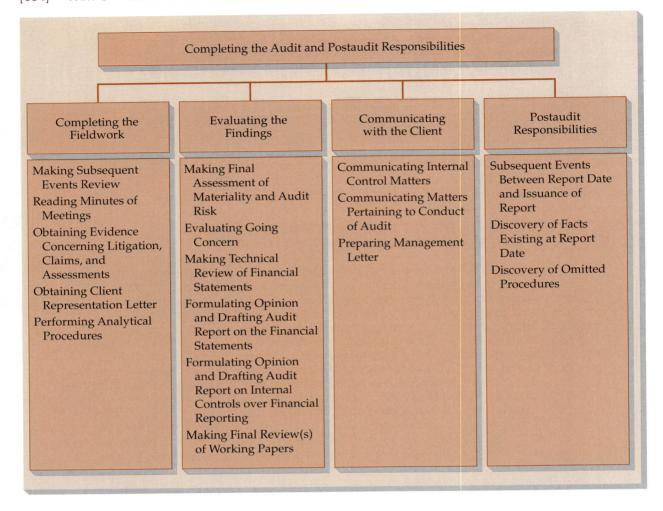

D10. What is the purpose of a final review of working papers?

D11. What internal control weaknesses should be reported to management and to the public?

D12. What other matters should be communicated to the audit committee associated with a financial statement audit?

D13. What is the auditor's responsibility for events that occur between report date and issuing the audit report?

D14. What is the auditor's responsibility for events that existed at balance sheet date but were not discovered until after the report was issued?

D15. What is the auditor's responsibility for the discovery of omitted procedures after report date?

Procedures performed to complete the audit have the following distinctive characteristics: (1) they do not pertain to specific transaction cycles or accounts, (2) they are performed after the balance sheet date, (3) they involve many subjective judgments by the auditor, and (4) they are usually performed by audit managers or other senior members of the audit team who have extensive audit experience with the client.

This is the last opportunity for the auditor to step above the transaction level and take a holistic look at the financial statements and determine that they represent the underlying business dynamics. The adage, "last but not least," applies to completing the audit. Indeed, the decisions made, and conclusions reached, by the auditor in completing the audit often have a direct impact on the opinion to be expressed on the client's financial statements.

In completing the audit, the auditor frequently works under tight time constraints, particularly as clients seek the earliest possible date for the issuance of the audit report. Although time may not be the auditor's ally, the auditor must take the time to make sound professional judgments and to express the opinion appropriate in the circumstances. For purposes of discussion, the auditor's responsibilities in completing the audit are divided into the following three categories: (1) completing the fieldwork, (2) evaluating the findings, and (3) communicating with the client.

COMPLETING THE FIELDWORK

In completing the fieldwork, the auditor performs specific auditing procedures to obtain additional audit evidence. The procedures are:

- Making subsequent events review
- Reading minutes of meetings
- Obtaining evidence concerning litigation, claims, and assessments
- Obtaining client representation letter
- Performing analytical procedures

The procedures do not have to be performed in the foregoing sequence. Each procedure is explained in a following section.

MAKING SUBSEQUENT EVENTS REVIEW

Audit Decision 1

■ What are the auditor's responsibilities with respect to subsequent events?

The auditor's responsibility for assessing the fairness of a client's financial statements is not limited to an examination of events and transactions that occur up to the balance sheet date. AU 560, *Subsequent Events,* states that the auditor also has specified responsibilities for events and transactions that (1) have a material effect on the financial statements and (2) occur after the balance sheet date but prior to the issuance of the financial statements and the auditor's report. These occurrences are referred to as **subsequent events.**

As shown in Figure 19-1, the time frame for a subsequent event extends from the balance sheet date to the issuance of the auditor's report. Figure 19-1 also identifies a **subsequent events period,** which extends from the balance sheet date to the end of fieldwork. During this period, the auditor is required under GAAS to obtain reasonable assurance regarding the discovery of subsequent events. As explained later in the chapter, the auditor has no responsibility to discover subsequent events that occur between the end of fieldwork and the issuance of the audit report.

Types of Events

AU 560.03 and 560.05 indicate that there are two types of subsequent events.

- **Type 1 subsequent events** provide additional evidence with respect to conditions that existed at the date of the balance sheet and affect the estimates inherent in the process of preparing financial statements.
- **Type 2 subsequent events** provide evidence with respect to conditions that did not exist at the date of the balance sheet but arose subsequent to that date.

Type 1 events require adjustment of the financial statements. Type 2 events require disclosure in the statements, or in very material cases, attaching pro-forma (as if) data to the financial statements. The following examples are illustrative of the two types of events:

Figure 19-1 ■ Subsequent Events Time Dimensions

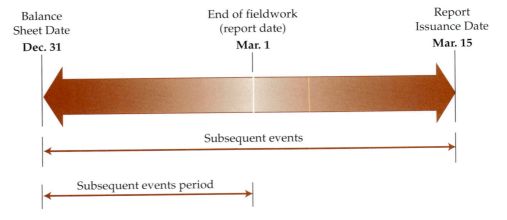

TYPE 1	TYPE 2
Realization of recorded year-end assets, such as receivables and inventories, at a different amount than recorded	Issues of long-term bonds or preferred common stock
	Purchase of a business
Settlement of recorded year-end estimated liabilities, such as litigation and product warranties, at a different amount than recorded	Casualty losses resulting from fire or flood

An example may help in distinguishing between the two types of events. Assume that a major customer becomes bankrupt on February 1, 20X1, and that the client considered the customer's balance to be totally collectable in making its estimate of potentially uncollectable accounts in its December 31, 20X0, statements. If, on review of the subsequent event, the auditor determines that the bankruptcy was attributable to the customer's deteriorating financial position that existed (but was unknown to the client) at the balance sheet date, the client should be requested to adjust the December 31, 20X0, statements for the loss. If, on the other hand, the auditor determines that the customer was financially sound at December 31 and the bankruptcy resulted from a fire or similar catastrophe that occurred after the balance sheet date, only disclosure in the notes to the December 31 statements is needed. Ordinarily, type 1 events require adjustment because they typically represent conditions that have accumulated over an extended period of time.

Auditing Procedures in the Subsequent Period

The auditor should identify and evaluate subsequent events up to the date of the auditor's report, which should be as of the end of fieldwork. This responsibility is discharged in the following two ways: (1) by being alert for subsequent events in performing year-end substantive tests such as cutoff tests and searching for unrecorded liabilities and (2) by performing the following auditing procedures specified in AU 560.12 at or near the completion of fieldwork:

- Read the latest available interim financial statements and compare them with the statements being reported on and make other comparisons appropriate in the circumstances.
- Inquire of management having responsibility for financial and accounting matters as to
  - Any substantial contingent liabilities or commitments existing at the balance sheet date or date of inquiry.
  - Any significant changes in capital stock, long-term debt, or working capital to the date of inquiry.
  - The current status of items previously accounted for on the basis of tentative, preliminary, or inconclusive data.
  - Whether any unusual adjustments have been made since the balance sheet date.
- Read minutes of meetings of directors, stockholders, and other appropriate committees.
- Inquire of client's legal counsel concerning litigation, claims, and assessments.

■ Obtain letter of representation from client about subsequent events that would, in its opinion, require adjustment or disclosure.

■ Make additional inquiries or perform additional procedures considered necessary in the circumstances.

The procedures pertaining to legal counsel and the representation letter are explained later in the chapter.

Effects on Auditor's Report

The failure to record or properly disclose subsequent events in the financial statements will result in a departure from the auditor's standard report. Depending on materiality, the auditor should express either a qualified opinion or an adverse opinion because the financial statements are not presented fairly in conformity with GAAP.

READING MINUTES OF MEETINGS

The minutes of meetings of stockholders, the board of directors, and its subcommittees, such as the finance committee and the audit committee, may contain matters that have audit significance. For example, the board of directors may authorize issue of a new bond, purchase of treasury stock, payment of a cash dividend, or discontinuance of a product line. Each of these circumstances affects management's assertions in the financial statements. The auditor should determine that all minutes of board meetings held during the period under audit and during the period from the balance sheet date to the end of fieldwork have been provided for his or her review. The reading of minutes is ordinarily done as soon as they become available in order to give the auditor the maximum opportunity to assess their significance to the audit. For example, information learned from the minutes might cause the auditor to modify planned substantive tests, or to request the client to include the disclosure of a subsequent event in the financial statements. The auditor's reading of the minutes should be documented in the working papers.

OBTAINING EVIDENCE CONCERNING LITIGATION, CLAIMS, AND ASSESSMENTS

Audit Decision 2

■ What evidence does an auditor need about litigation, claims, and assessments (LCA)?

The FASB in SFAS 5, *Accounting for Contingencies*, defines a contingency as an existing condition, situation, or set of circumstances involving uncertainty as to possible gain (gain contingency) or loss (loss contingency) that will be resolved when one or more future events occur or fail to occur. Gain contingencies, such as a client's claim against others for patent infringement, present only a relatively small problem for the auditor because under GAAP they normally are not recorded until they are realized. Loss contingencies, on the other hand, often represent a significant problem for the auditor. Depending on subjective evaluations of the likelihood of future payment, GAAP requires that loss contingencies either be (1) recorded as contingent liabilities, (2) disclosed in the notes to the financial statements, or (3) ignored. These contingencies include potential liabilities from income tax disputes; product warranties; guarantees of obligations of others; and litigation, claims, and assessments.

The auditor's concerns about contingent liabilities are not limited to completing the audit. During audit testing and particularly in searching for unrecorded liabilities (see Chapter 15), the auditor should be alert for the possibility of contingent liabilities. Moreover, in reading the minutes of board of directors' meetings and in reviewing contracts, the auditor should look for circumstances that may indicate contingencies that should be investigated. GAAS does not specify auditing requirements for all contingencies. However, GAAS does contain requirements for auditing litigation, claims, and assessments. These requirements are usually met at the time of completing the audit because the auditor desires that the evidential matter be obtained as close to the end of fieldwork as is feasible.

Audit Considerations

AU 337.04, *Inquiry of a Client's Lawyer Concerning Litigation, Claims, and Assessments,* states that the auditor should obtain evidence on **litigation, claims, and assessments (LCA):**

1. The existence of a condition, situation, or set of circumstances indicating an uncertainty as to the possible loss to an entity arising from litigation, claims, and assessments.
2. The period in which the underlying cause for legal action occurred.
3. The degree of probability of an unfavorable outcome.
4. The amount or range of potential loss.

Because LCAs usually are within the direct knowledge of management, management is the primary source of information about such matters. Accordingly, the auditor should (a) inquire of and discuss with management its means of identifying LCA, (b) obtain from management a description and evaluation of LCA that existed at the balance sheet date, and (c) obtain assurance from management, preferably in writing, of the existence of any unasserted claims. In addition, the auditor should examine documents in the client's possession concerning LCA. The auditor may also obtain information about LCA through reading minutes of board of directors' meetings, contracts and loan agreements, and bank confirmation responses concerning loan guarantees.

Letter of Audit Inquiry

It should be recognized that an auditor normally does not possess sufficient legal skills to make an informed judgment about all LCAs. Thus, AU 337.08 indicates that a **letter of audit inquiry** to the client's lawyer(s) is the auditor's primary means of obtaining corroboration of the information about LCA furnished by management. It should assist the auditor in obtaining evidence about the four items identified in AU 337.04 (see preceding paragraph). Appendix A to AU 337 provides an illustrative audit inquiry letter to legal counsel. Management should send the letter to each lawyer who has been engaged by the client and has given substantive attention during the year to LCA or significant unasserted claims that may be material. The letter should ask the lawyer to respond directly to the auditor.

Effects of Responses on Auditor's Report

The lawyer's responses may have no effect on the auditor's report. That is, the auditor may issue a standard report with an unqualified opinion. This can occur when the responses indicate that, based on a reasonable investigation of the matters at issue, there is (1) a high probability of a favorable outcome or (2) the matters at issue are immaterial.

In some cases, the lawyer's response may indicate significant uncertainty about the likelihood of an unfavorable outcome of LCA or the amount or range of potential loss. For example, the matter may be only in the initial stage of litigation, and there may be no historical experience of the entity in similar litigation. In this situation, the auditor may conclude that the financial statements are affected by an uncertainty that is not susceptible to reasonable estimation at the balance sheet date. If the uncertainty is adequately disclosed in the financial statements, the auditor's report should contain an unqualified opinion.

A lawyer's refusal to respond to a letter of audit inquiry is a limitation on the scope of the audit. Depending on the materiality of the items, the auditor should express a qualified opinion or disclaim an opinion on the financial statements. The auditor may obtain assistance about LCA from the client's legal department. However, because of possible management bias, such help is not a substitute for corroborating information that an outside lawyer refuses to furnish.

OBTAINING CLIENT REPRESENTATION LETTER

Audit Decision 3

■ What is the purpose of a client representation letter, and what should be included in the letter?

The auditor is required to obtain certain written representations from management in meeting the third standard of fieldwork. This is accomplished through a **client representation letter,** commonly referred to as a **rep letter.** AU 333, *Management Representations,* explains that representations are part of evidential mater, but they are not a substitute for the application of the auditing procedures necessary to afford a reasonable basis for an opinion. Management representations:

- Confirm oral representations given to the auditor
- Document the continuing appropriateness of such representations
- Reduce the possibility of misunderstandings concerning management's representations

A rep letter may complement other auditing procedures. For example, a rep letter may complement a letter of audit inquiry of a lawyer by containing management's statements that LCAs are properly accounted for and that there are no unasserted claims or assessments that require disclosure in the financial statements. In some cases, however, a rep letter may be the primary source of audit evidence. For instance, when a client plans to discontinue a line of business, the auditor may not be able to corroborate this event through other auditing procedures. Accordingly, the auditor should request management to indicate its intent in the rep letter.

If a representation made by management is contradicted by other audit evidence, the auditor should investigate the circumstances and consider the reliability of the representation made. For example, management's representations about the classification of held-to-maturity securities may be contradicted by management's sale of such securities. In addition, based on the circumstances, the auditor should consider whether his or her reliance on management's representations relating to other aspects of the financial statements is appropriate and justified.

Content of Representation Letter

AU 333.06 provides guidance on four major categories of specific representations that should be included in a rep letter. The rep letter should include representations about:

- Management's responsibility for the financial statements
- Completeness of information and evidence furnished to the auditor
- Issues regarding revenue recognition, accounting estimates, and disclosures
- Subsequent events

For example, under management's responsibility for the financial statements, management should acknowledge that they are responsible for adjusting the financial statements for material misstatements detected by the auditor, and that any uncorrected misstatements aggregated by the auditor during the current engagement are immaterial, both individually and in aggregate, to the financial statements taken as a whole. Figure 19-2 presents an illustrative rep letter that includes representations related to each of these four major categories. Rep letters should be prepared on the client's stationery, addressed to the auditor, and dated as of the date of the auditor's report. Normally, the chief executive officer and the chief financial officer sign the rep letter. In many audits, the auditor will draft the representations, but management must acknowledge responsibility for these important representations by discussing the items with the auditor and by signing the letter.

Effects on the Auditor's Report

When the auditor obtains a rep letter and he or she is able to corroborate management's representations, a standard audit report can be issued. However, there is a limitation on the scope of the audit when the auditor is unable to (1) obtain a rep letter or (2) support a management representation that is material to the financial statements by other auditing procedures. A scope limitation will result in a departure from the auditor's standard report with either a qualified opinion or a disclaimer of opinion. Management's refusal to furnish written representations may be sufficient, in the auditor's judgment, to cause the auditor to withdraw from the engagement.

PERFORMING ANALYTICAL PROCEDURES

Audit Decision 4

■ What is the purpose of performing analytical procedures at the final stages of an engagement?

Earlier chapters have explained and illustrated the application of analytical procedures in audit planning and in performing year-end substantive tests. It will be recalled that analytical procedures involve the use of ratios and other comparative techniques. Analytical procedures are also required in completing the audit as an **overall (or final) review** of the financial statements. SAS 56, *Analytical Procedures* (AU 329.22), states that the objective of the overall review is to assist the auditor in assessing conclusions reached in the audit and in evaluating the financial statement presentation taken as a whole.

In making an overall review, the auditor reads the financial statements and accompanying notes and considers the adequacy of the evidence gathered in response to unusual or unexpected balances and relationships (1) anticipated in planning the audit or (2) identified during the audit in substantive testing.

Figure 19-2 ■ Client Representation Letter

Letterhead of Melville Co., Inc.
Route 32
Midtown, New York 11746

February 14, 20x8
Reddy & Abel, Certified Public Accountants

Dear Sirs:

We are providing this letter in connection with your audit of the balance sheets, income statements, and statement of cash flows. Melville Co., Inc. as of December 31, 20x7 and 20x6 and for the years then ended, for the purpose of expressing an opinion as to whether the financial statements present fairly in all material respects, the financial position, results of operation, and cash flows of Melville Co., Inc. in conformity with Generally Accepted Accounting Principles.

Certain representations in this letter are described as being limited to matters that are material. Items are considered material, regardless of size, if they involve an omission or misstatement of accounting information that, in light of surrounding circumstances, makes it probable that the judgment of a reasonable person relying on the information would be changed or influenced by the omission or misstatement.

We confirm to the best of our knowledge and belief, on February 14, 20x8, the following representations made to you during your audit(s).

1. The financial statements referred to above are fairly presented in conformity with Generally Accepted Accounting Standards.
2. We have made available to you all —
   a. Financial records and related data.
   b. Minutes of meetings of stockholders, directors, and committees of directors, or summaries of actions of recent meetings for which minutes have not yet been prepared.
3. There have been no communications from regulatory agencies concerning noncompliance with or deficiencies in financial reporting practices.
4. There are no material transactions that have not been properly recorded in the accounting records underlying the financial statements.
5. There has been no —
   a. Fraud involving management or employees who have significant roles in internal control.
   b. Fraud involving others that could have a material effect on the financial statements.
6. The company has no plans or intentions that may materially affect the carrying value or classification of assets and liabilities.
7. We believe the effects of any uncorrected financial statement misstatements aggregated by the auditor during the current engagement and pertaining to the latest period presented are immaterial, both individually and in the aggregate, to the financial statements taken as a whole.
8. The following have been properly recorded or disclosed in the financial statements.
   a. Related party transactions, including sales purchases, loans, transfers, leasing arrangements, and guarantees, and amounts receivable from or payable to related parties.
   b. Guarantees, whether written or oral, under which the company is contingently liable.
   c. Significant estimates and material concentrations known to management that are required to be disclosed in accordance with the AICPA's Statement of Position 94-6 *Disclosure of Certain Risks and Uncertainties.*
9. There are no —
   a. Violations or possible violations of laws or regulations whose effects should be considered for disclosure in the financial statements or as a basis for recording a loss contingency.
   b. Unasserted claims or assessments that our lawyer has advised us are probable of assertion and must be disclosed in accordance with Financial Accounting Standards Board (FASB) Statement No. 5.
   c. Other liabilities or gain or loss contingencies that are required to be accrued or disclosed by FASB Statement No. 5.
10. The company has satisfactory title to all owned assets, and any liens, encumbrances, or pledges of assets as collateral for loans are adequately disclosed in the notes to the financial statements.
11. The company has complied with all aspects of contractual agreements that would have a material effect on the financial statements in the event of noncompliance.
12. Debt securities that have been classified as held-to-maturity have been so classified due to the company's intent to hold such securities to maturity and the company's ability to do so. All other debt securities appropriately have been classified as available-for-sale or trading.
13. Provision has been made to reduce excess or obsolete inventories to their estimated net realizable value.
14. Capital stock reserved for options, warrants, conversions, or other requirements has been properly disclosed.

To the best of our knowledge and belief, no events have occurred subsequent to the balance sheet date and through the date of this letter that would require adjustments to or disclosure in the aforementioned financial statements.

_____
Mr. Thomas Thorp, President, and CEO

_____
Ms. Marilyn Johnson, CFO

do the financial statements make sense?

An important additional objective of the overall review in one Big Four firm is: Do the financial statements make sense from the point of view of users of the statements? The focus is not on unusual relationships but on whether the impression a user is likely to obtain, based solely on the financial statements, is consistent with the auditor's accumulated knowledge of the entity. In meeting this objective, the firm requires the auditor to consider business ratios and other rules of thumb commonly used in the particular industry because these are the measures that users ordinarily use to evaluate the entity. As in other types of overall reviews, the findings may result in recommendations for changes in presentation and disclosures in the financial statements, additional auditing procedures, or changes in the audit opinion.

Source: KPMG, Peat Marwick, Audit Manual—U.S. (May 1988), pp. II–146–147.

Analytical procedures are then applied to the financial statements to determine whether any additional unusual or unexpected relationships exist. If such relationships exist, additional auditing procedures should be performed in completing the audit.

Analytical procedures in the overall review should be performed by an individual having comprehensive knowledge of the client's business and industry such as a partner or manager on the audit. A variety of analytical procedures may be used. The procedures should be

- Applied to critical audit areas identified during the audit
- Based on the financial statement data after all audit adjustments and reclassifications have been recognized

In making an overall review of the fair presentation in the financial statements, company data may be compared with (1) expected entity results based on the underlying business dynamics, (2) available data on industry performance, and (3) relevant nonfinancial data such as units produced or sold and the number of employees. An overall review would ordinarily compare an entity's reported financial performance with its strategic goals for revenues, customers, and market share, for the efficiency of core processes, and the correspondence of nonfinancial measures with the overall picture reported in the financial statements.

[LEARNING CHECK

19-1 Identify the three categories of activities that pertain to completing the audit.

19-2 List the activities involved in completing fieldwork.

19-3 a. Distinguish between the terms *subsequent events* and *subsequent events period.*

b. Define the two types of subsequent events and indicate the accounting treatment of each type.

c. What is the auditor's responsibility for subsequent events?

19-4 a. What evidence is required in an audit of litigation, claims, and assessments?

b. What is a letter of audit inquiry?

c. What effects may a lawyer's failure to respond to a letter of audit inquiry have on the audit report?

19-5 a. What objectives are met in obtaining a client representation letter?

b. What is the impact of a client's refusal to provide a rep letter?

19-6 a. What are the objectives of making an overall review?

b. Who should make this review?

c. How should analytical procedures be used in this review?

KEY TERMS

Client representation letter, p. 900
Letter of audit inquiry, p. 899
Litigation, claims, and assessments (LCA), p. 899
Overall (or final) review, p. 901

Rep letter, p. 900
Subsequent events, p. 896
Subsequent events period, p. 896
Type 1 subsequent events, p. 896
Type 2 subsequent events, p. 896

EVALUATING THE FINDINGS

The auditor has the following two objectives in evaluating the findings: (1) determining the type of opinion to be expressed and (2) determining whether GAAS has been met in the audit. To meet these objectives, the auditor completes the following steps:

- Making final assessment of materiality and audit risk
- Evaluating whether there is substantial doubt about the entity's ability to continue as a going concern
- Making technical review of financial statements
- Formulating opinion and drafting audit report on financial statements
- Formulating opinion and drafting audit report on internal controls over financial reporting (for public companies)
- Making final review(s) of working papers

These steps are performed in the order in which they are listed.

MAKING FINAL ASSESSMENT OF MATERIALITY AND AUDIT RISK

Audit Decision 5

■ What should be addressed in the process of making a final assessment of materiality and audit risk?

In formulating an opinion on the financial statements, the auditor should assimilate all the evidence gathered during the audit. An essential prerequisite in deciding on the opinion to express is a final assessment of materiality and audit risk. The starting point in this process is to total the misstatements found in examining all accounts that were not corrected by the client. In some cases, the uncorrected misstatements may have been individually immaterial so that no correction was requested by the auditor. In other cases, the client may have been unwilling to make the corrections that were requested. The next step in the process is to determine the effects of the total misstatements on net income and other financial statement totals to which the misstatements pertain, such as current assets or current liabilities.

The auditor's determination of misstatements in an account should include the following components:

- Uncorrected misstatements specifically identified through substantive tests of details of transactions and balances (referred to as **known misstatement**)
- Projected uncorrected misstatements estimated through audit sampling techniques
- Estimated misstatements detected through analytical procedures and quantified by other auditing procedures

The total of these components for an account is called **likely misstatement.** The sum of the likely misstatement in all accounts is called **aggregate likely misstatement.** The auditor's assessment of aggregate likely misstatement may also include the effect on the current period's financial statements of any uncorrected likely misstatements from a prior period. When including them this may lead to the conclusion that there is an unacceptably high risk that the current period's financial statements are materially misstated. A working paper illustrating one approach to analyzing aggregate likely misstatement is shown in Figure 19-3.

The data that have been accumulated are then compared with the auditor's preliminary judgments concerning materiality that were made in planning the audit. As explained in Chapter 8, planning materiality extends to both the individual account balance and the financial statement levels. If any adjustments in planning materiality have been made during the course of the audit, they should, of course, be included in this assessment.

In planning the audit, the auditor specified an acceptable level of audit risk. As aggregate likely misstatement increases, the risk that the financial statements may be materially misstated also increases. When the auditor concludes that audit risk is at an acceptable level, he or she can proceed to formulate the opinion supported by the findings. However, if the auditor believes that audit risk is not acceptable, he or she should either (1) perform additional substantive tests or (2) convince the client to make the corrections necessary to reduce the risk of material misstatement to an acceptable level.

EVALUATING GOING CONCERN

Audit Decision 6

■ What should the auditor consider when evaluating whether an entity is a going concern?

AU 341, *The Auditor's Consideration of an Entity's Ability to Continue as a Going Concern,* establishes a responsibility for the auditor to evaluate whether there is substantial doubt about the client's ability to continue as a going concern for a reasonable period of time, not to exceed one year beyond the date of the financial statements being audited (generally one year from the balance sheet date). Ordinarily, information that would raise **substantial doubt** about the going-concern assumption relates to the entity's inability to continue to meet its obligations as they become due without substantial disposition of assets outside the ordinary course of business, restructuring of debt, externally forced revisions of its operations, or similar actions.

The auditor normally evaluates whether there is substantial doubt about the client's ability to continue as a going concern based on the results of normal audit procedures performed in planning, in gathering evidence to support various audit objectives, and in completing the audit. It may be necessary to obtain

Figure 19-3 ■ Analysis of Aggregate Likely Misstatement Working Paper

Ambient Corporation
Analysis of Aggregate Likely Misstatements
December 31, 20X1

W/P Ref. A-5
Prepared By: A.E.R.   Date: 2/12/X2
Reviewed By: R. E. G.   Date: 2/16/X2

W/P Ref	Acct. No.	Description Acquired	DEBIT Assets Current	Non-Current	(CREDIT) Liabilities Current	Non-Current	Shareholders' Equity	Pretax Earnings	Income Tax Expense
Uncorrected Known Misstatements									
D-1	1590	Accumulated Depreciation		$ 3,500					
	4590	Depreciation Expense					$ (3,500)	$ (3,500)	
	2295	Income Taxes Payable			$ (1,225)		$ 1,225		$ 1,225
		Overstatement of Depreciation Expense							
Uncorrected Projected Misstatements									
C-1	4200	Cost of Goods Sold					$ 8,000	$ 8,000	
	1200	Inventory	$ (8,000)						
	2295	Income Taxes Payable			$ 2,800		$ (2,800)		$ (2,800)
		Overstatement of Ending Inventory Projected from Statistical Sample							
		Aggregate Likely Misstatement	$ (8,000)	$ 3,500	$ 1,575	$ —	$ 2,925	$ 4,500	$ (1,575)
		Final Balance from Trial Balance	$ 400,000	$ 735,000	$ 225,000	$ 375,000	$ 535,000	$ 150,000	$ 75,000
		Aggregate Likely Misstatement %	2.0%	0.5%	0.7%	0.0%	0.5%	3.0%	2.1%

Conclusion: The likely misstatements listed above are deemed to be immaterial, either individually or in their aggregate effects on the individual accounts, the financial statements categories, or the financial statement totals to which they relate.

additional information to support information that mitigates the auditor's doubt.

If the auditor believes there is substantial doubt about the entity's ability to continue as a going concern for a reasonable period of time, he or she should take the following steps. The auditor should (1) obtain information about management's plans that are intended to mitigate the effect of such conditions or events, and (2) assess the likelihood that such plans can be effectively implemented.

If, after evaluating management's plans, the auditor concludes there is substantial doubt about a going concern, he or she should (1) consider the adequacy of disclosure about the entity's possible inability to continue as a going concern for a reasonable period of time, and (2) include an explanatory paragraph (following the opinion paragraph) in the audit report to reflect his or her conclusion. If the auditor concludes that substantial doubt does not exist, he or she should still consider the need for disclosure. Some of the information that might be disclosed includes:

- Pertinent conditions and events giving rise to the assessment of substantial doubt about the entity's ability to continue as a going concern for a reasonable period of time
- The possible effects of such conditions and events
- Management's evaluation of the significance of those conditions and events and any mitigating factors
- Possible discontinuance of operations
- Management's plans (including relevant prospective financial information)
- Information about (a) the recoverability or classification of recorded asset amounts or, (b) the amounts or classification of liabilities

If, after considering identified conditions and management's plans, the auditor concludes that substantial doubt about the entity's ability to continue as a going concern for a reasonable period of time remains, the audit report is normally an unqualified audit opinion with an explanatory paragraph about the uncertainty (following the opinion paragraph) to reflect that conclusion. The auditor's conclusion about the entity's ability to continue as a going concern should be expressed through the use of the phrase "substantial doubt about its [the entity's] ability to continue as a going concern." If the auditor concludes that the entity's disclosures with respect to the entity's ability to continue as a going concern are inadequate, a departure from generally accepted accounting principles exists. This may result in either a qualified (except for) or an adverse opinion.

MAKING TECHNICAL REVIEW OF FINANCIAL STATEMENTS

Audit Decision 7

- What is the purpose of a technical review of the financial statements?

Public accounting firms have detailed financial statement checklists that are completed by the auditor who performs the initial review of the financial statements. The purpose of the **financial statement checklist** is to help the auditor evaluate financial statement disclosure assertions. The manager and partner in charge of the engagement then review the completed checklist and the financial statements. Prior to the release of the audit report on a publicly held client, there should also be a technical review of the statements by a partner who was not a member of the audit team.

The checklists include matters pertaining to the form and content of each of the basic financial statements as well as to required disclosures. Most firms now have separate checklists for SEC and non-SEC clients. The completed checklist and the findings of the reviewers should be included in the working papers.

FORMULATING OPINION AND DRAFTING AUDIT REPORT ON THE FINANCIAL STATEMENTS

Audit Decision 8

■ What are the key steps involved in forming an opinion and drafting a report on the financial statements?

During the course of an audit engagement, a variety of audit tests are performed. These tests often are performed by staff personnel whose participation in the audit may be limited to a few areas or accounts. As the tests for each functional area or statement item are completed, the staff auditor is expected to summarize his or her findings.

It is necessary in completing the audit for the separate findings to be summarized and evaluated for the purpose of expressing an opinion on the financial statements taken as a whole. The ultimate responsibility for these steps rests with the partner in charge of the engagement. In some cases, the audit manager makes the initial determinations that are then carefully reviewed by the partner.

Before reaching a final decision on the opinion, a conference generally is held with the client. At this meeting, the auditor reports the findings orally and attempts to provide a rationale for proposed adjustments and/or additional disclosures. Management, in turn, may attempt to defend its position. In the end, some agreement is generally reached on the changes to be made, and the auditor can proceed to issue an unqualified opinion. When such an agreement is not obtained, the auditor may have to issue another type of opinion. Communication of the auditor's opinion is made through an audit report. The various types of auditors' reports were previously discussed in Chapter 2.

FORMULATING OPINION AND DRAFTING AUDIT REPORT ON INTERNAL CONTROLS OVER FINANCIAL REPORTING

Audit Decision 9

■ What are the key steps involved in forming an opinion and drafting a report on internal controls over financial reporting?

Recall from Chapter 2 that public companies must make an assertion about the adequacy of their system of internal control over financial reporting. The auditor of a public company must then form an opinion (1) about the fairness of management's assertion and (2) about the adequacy of internal controls over financial reporting as of balance sheet date. During the course of an audit engagement, staff personnel whose participation in the audit may be limited to a few areas or accounts, perform a variety of tests of controls. It is necessary in completing the audit for the separate findings to be summarized and evaluated for the purpose of expressing an opinion on the system of internal control over financial reporting. If the auditor believes that a material weakness exists (more than a remote chance that a material misstatement, individually or in aggregate, could occur in interim or annual financial statements), the auditor must express an adverse opinion on the effectiveness of the system of internal control over financial reporting. The ultimate responsibility for these steps rests with the partner in charge of the engagement. In some cases, the audit manager makes the initial determinations, which are then carefully reviewed by the partner.

Auditors often perform tests of controls at an early interim date to determine whether material weaknesses exist and to give management time to correct such weakness prior to year-end. Before reaching a final decision on the opinion, a conference generally is held with the client. At this meeting, the auditor reports the findings orally and attempts to provide a rationale regarding internal control weaknesses. However, if the auditor continues to feel that a material weakness exists at the balance sheet date, the auditor must express an adverse opinion on the effectiveness of internal controls over financial reporting. The auditor's opinion is communicated through an audit report on internal controls over financial reporting. The various types of auditors' reports were previously discussed in Chapter 2.

MAKING FINAL REVIEW(S) OF WORKING PAPERS

Audit Decision 10

■ What is the purpose of a final review of working papers?

In Chapter 6 the first-level review of working papers by a supervisor was explained. This review is made to evaluate the work done, the evidence obtained, and the conclusions reached by the preparer of the working paper. Additional reviews of the working papers are made at the end of fieldwork by members of the audit team. The levels of review that may be made in completing the audit are shown in the following table:

REVIEWER	NATURE OF REVIEW
Manager	Reviews working papers prepared by seniors and reviews some or all of the working papers reviewed by seniors.
Partner in charge of the engagement	Reviews working papers prepared by managers and reviews other working papers on a selective basis.

The partner's review of the working papers is designed to obtain assurance that

■ The work done by subordinates has been accurate and thorough.

■ The judgments exercised by subordinates were reasonable and appropriate in the circumstances.

■ The audit engagement has been completed in accordance with the conditions and terms specified in the engagement letter.

■ All significant accounting, auditing, and reporting questions raised during the audit have been properly resolved.

■ The working papers support the auditor's opinion.

■ GAAS and the firm's quality control policies and procedures have been met.

Detailed checklists covering the above matters are commonly used in performing the review of working papers.

Some firms require an independent **"cold" (or second) review** of the working papers by a partner who did not participate in the audit. Such reviews are mandatory in audits of SEC registrants. The rationale for a second partner review is based on the objectivity of the reviewer who may challenge matters approved by earlier reviewers. Thus, the review provides additional assurance that all GAAS have been met in the engagement.

[LEARNING CHECK

19-7   a. What are the two objectives to be achieved in evaluating the findings?

b. List four steps in meeting these objectives.

19-8 a. What are the purposes of the auditor's final assessment of materiality and audit risk?

b. Distinguish between the terms *known misstatement, likely misstatement,* and *aggregate likely misstatement.*

19-9 a. Describe the auditor's responsibility to evaluate an entity's ability to continue as a going concern for a reasonable period of time.

b. What evidence should an auditor use to evaluate a going concern?

c. If the auditor concludes that there is substantial doubt about an entity's ability to continue as a going concern for a reasonable period of time, what should be disclosed in the financial statements?

d. How does substantial doubt about going concern influence the auditor's opinion on the financial statements?

19-10 What is included in the technical review of the financial statements, what aids are used in the review, and who makes the review?

19-11 a. How and by whom is the opinion on the financial statements formulated, and how is it communicated?

b. How are proposed adjustments and disclosures generally resolved?

19-12 a. How and by whom is the opinion on the internal controls over financial reporting formulated, and how is it communicated?

b. Can an auditor resolve material weaknesses in internal control the same way material misstatements in the financial statements are discussed and resolved?

19-13 a. Identify the primary reviewers of working papers and the nature of their reviews.

b. What are the objectives of the engagement partner's review?

c. Why may a second partner review be desirable?

[KEY TERMS

Aggregate likely misstatement, p. 905
"Cold" (or second) review, p. 909
Financial statement checklist, p. 907

Known misstatement, p. 905
Likely misstatement, p. 905
Substantial doubt, p. 905

[COMMUNICATING WITH THE CLIENT]

The auditor's communications with the client at the conclusion of the audit involves the audit committee (or the board of directors) and management. The communications to the audit committee involve matters pertaining to (1) the client's internal controls and (2) the conduct of the audit. The communication to management and the audit committee is normally in the form of a management letter.

Audit Decision 11

■ What internal control weaknesses should be reported to management and to the public?

COMMUNICATING INTERNAL CONTROL MATTERS

During an audit, the auditor may become aware of matters relating to the internal controls over financial reporting that are less than a material weakness that should be of interest to the client's audit committee or to individuals with equivalent authority and responsibility. Both AU 325, *Communication of Internal Control*

Related Matters Noted in an Audit, and PCAOB Standard No. 2, *An Audit of Internal Control over Financial Reporting Conducted in Conjunction with a Financial Statement Audit,* require the auditor to communicate significant deficiencies in internal controls, which are defined as follows:

A **significant deficiency** is an internal control deficiency that adversely affects the company's ability to initiate, record, process, or report external financial data reliably in accordance with GAAP. A significant deficiency could be a single deficiency, or a combination of deficiencies, that results in more than a remote likelihood that a misstatement of the annual or interim financial statements that is more than inconsequential in amount will not be prevented or detected.

A significant deficiency may pertain to any internal control element. The designation of a significant deficiency is influenced by the likelihood of a misstatement (more than remote) and the magnitude of possible misstatement (more than inconsequential), as explained in Chapter 2.

For private companies, AU 325.04 indicates that the auditor is not required to search for significant deficiencies. He or she may become aware of a significant deficiency by obtaining an understanding of internal controls, performing tests of controls, performing substantive tests, or otherwise during the audit.

The communication preferably should be in writing. The distribution of the report should ordinarily be restricted to the audit committee, management, and others within the organization. However, when such a report is required by governmental authorities, AU 325.11 states that any report issued on significant deficiencies should:

- Indicate that the purpose of the audit is to report on the financial statements and not to provide assurance on the internal controls
- Include the definition of a significant deficiency
- Include the restriction on distributions

AU 325.12 illustrates the sections of a letter on internal control for private companies that includes the following language:

In planning and performing our audit of the financial statements of ABC Corporation for the year ended December 31, 20X1, we considered internal control in order to determine our auditing procedures for the purpose of expressing our opinion on the financial statements and not to provide assurance on internal control. However, we noted certain matters involving the internal control and its operation that we considered to be significant deficiencies under standards established by the American Institute of Certified Public Accountants. A significant deficiency is an internal control deficiency that adversely affects the company's ability to initiate, record, process, or report external financial data reliably in accordance with GAAP. A significant deficiency could be a single deficiency, or a combination of deficiencies, that results in more than a remote likelihood that a misstatement of the annual or interim financial statements that is more than inconsequential in amount will not be prevented or detected.

(Include paragraphs to describe the reportable conditions noted.)

This report is intended solely for the information and use of the audit committee (board of directors, board of trustees, or owners in owner-managed enterprises), management, and others within the organization (or specified regulatory agency or other specified third party).

The communication should be made in a timely manner either during the audit or after its conclusion.

The following additional factors may affect the content of the report:

- Because of the potential for misinterpretation of the highly limited degree of assurance provided by the report, the auditor should not state in the report that no significant deficiencies in internal control over financial reporting were noted.
- By agreement with the client, the report may (1) exclude significant deficiencies already known to the audit committee and (2) include matters that do not qualify as significant deficiencies.

Recall that a significant deficiency may be of such magnitude as to be a material weakness, which is defined as follows:

A **material weakness** is a significant deficiency that, by itself, or in combination with other significant deficiencies, results in more than a remote likelihood that a material misstatement of the annual or interim financial statements will not be prevented or detected.

If even one material weakness exists in a public company, the auditor is required to issue an adverse opinion on internal controls over financial reporting. In a private company, however, the auditor is not required by GAAS to separately identify and communicate material weaknesses in the report to the audit committee. However, when either by client request or by auditor choice material weaknesses are identified and described in the report, two additional paragraphs are required as part of the auditor's letter. The first paragraph should contain a definition of the term *material weakness* and a description of the deficiencies in internal control that are material weaknesses. As indicated in AU 325.16, the second additional paragraph should describe the limitations of the auditor's work as follows:

Our consideration of internal control would not necessarily disclose all matters in internal control that might be a significant deficiency and, would not necessarily disclose all reportable conditions that are also considered to be material weakness as defined above. However, none of the significant deficiencies described above is believed to be a material weakness.

When the preceding paragraph is included in the report and none of the reportable conditions are considered to be material weaknesses, a statement to this effect is added to the paragraph (see sample above).

Following is an example internal control recommendation.

Cash

Issue

As part of a strong system of internal controls, there should be an appropriate segregation of duties. This ensures that no one employee has access to both physical assets and the related accounting records or to all phases of a transaction.

Finding

Cash receipts are processed by an accounting employee who summarizes the receipts, prepares the deposit slip, and posts the cash to accounts receivable. A cash receipts journal is prepared by the accounting manager who also reconciles the bank accounts.

Recommendation

We suggest that the company establish certain internal control policies with regard to segregation of duties within the area of cash receipts. None of the following duties should be performed by the same person:

- Receive and open mail and run tape of cash receipts.
- Prepare deposit slip from cash receipts.
- Post transactions to accounts receivable, reconciling any differences between tape and deposit slip.
- Reconcile bank accounts.

COMMUNICATING MATTERS PERTAINING TO CONDUCT OF AUDIT

Audit Decision 12

■ What other matters should be communicated to the audit committee associated with a financial statement audit?

AU 380, *Communication with Audit Committees,* requires the auditor to communicate certain matters pertaining to the conduct of the audit to those who have responsibility for overseeing the financial reporting process. Normally, this responsibility is assigned to an audit committee of the board of directors or to a group with equivalent authority such as a finance committee. The communication may be oral or written, and it may occur during or shortly after the audit. When the communication is in writing, the report should indicate that it is intended for the audit committee or the board of directors and, if appropriate, management. AU 380.06-.14 state that the communication with the audit committee may include the following matters:

- *Auditor's responsibility under GAAS* including the assurance provided by an audit that the financial statements are free of material misstatements, concepts of materiality used in the audit, and types of audit tests performed.
- *Significant accounting policies* such as management's initial selection and changes in policies, accounting methods used for significant unusual transactions, and effects of policies in areas that lack authoritative guidance or consensus.
- *Auditor's judgments about the quality of the entity's accounting principles.* The discussion would normally include management as an active participant since it has primary responsibility for establishing accounting principles. An open and frank discussion should include such matters as the consistency of application of accounting policies, the clarity and completeness of the entity's financial statements, and items that have a significant impact on the representational faithfulness, verifiability, and neutrality of the accounting information included in the financial statements. Examples include (1) the selection of new policies or changes to accounting policies, (2) estimates, judgments, and uncertainties, (3) unusual transactions, and (4) accounting policies related to significant financial statement items, including the timing

of transactions and the period in which they are recorded, or accounting practices that may be unique to an industry.

■ *Management judgments and accounting estimates* including the basis for judgments and the process for making accounting estimates.

■ *Significant audit adjustments* that individually, or in the aggregate, have an important effect on the entity's financial reporting process.

■ *Disagreements with management* that are significant to the financial statements or the auditor's report, and disagreements that pertain to the application of accounting principles and the basis for management's judgments about accounting estimates.

■ *Consultation with other accountants* on auditing and accounting matters.

■ *Major issues discussed with management prior to retention* including those pertaining to accounting principles and auditing standards.

■ *Difficulties encountered in performing the audit* such as unreasonable delays by management in permitting the commencement of the audit and in providing needed information, unavailability of client personnel, and failure of the client to complete client-prepared schedules in a timely manner.

In addition, as explained previously, the auditor must communicate reportable conditions in a company's internal control structure to the audit committee.

PREPARING MANAGEMENT LETTER

During the course of an audit engagement, auditors observe many facets of the client's business organization and operations. At the conclusion of an audit, many auditors believe it is desirable to write a letter to management, known as a **management letter,** that may include recommendations beyond improvements in the system of internal control. These recommendations usually relate to improving the efficiency and effectiveness of the company's operations. The issuance of such letters has become an integral part of the services rendered by auditors to their clients. A management letter tangibly demonstrates the auditor's continuing interest in the welfare and future of the client. Communicating matters in addition to significant deficiencies in internal control is not required by GAAS.

Matters that are relevant to management letters should be noted in the audit working papers as the audit progresses to ensure that they are not overlooked. Subsequently, the working papers should provide adequate documentation of the management letter comments. Such support will also be useful in any discussions with management about the comments.

Management letters should be carefully prepared, well organized, and written in a constructive tone. Prompt issuance of the letters creates a favorable impression and may encourage both an early and a positive response by management. Management letters may include comments on

■ Internal control matters
■ Recommendations regarding the management of resources and other services noted during the audit
■ Tax-related matters

A summary of the auditor's responsibilities in completing the audit is presented in Figure 19-4.

Figure 19-4 ■ Summary of Auditor's Responsibilities in Completing the Audit

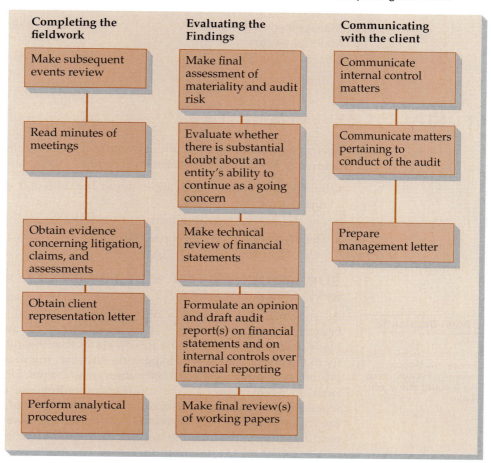

LEARNING CHECK

19-14   What parties are involved in the auditor's communications with the client at the conclusion of the audit?

19-15   a. Distinguish between reportable conditions and material weaknesses.
        b. What are the essential requirements for a report issued on reportable conditions?

19-16   What are the effects on a report on reportable conditions when the auditor separately identifies and describes material weaknesses?

19-17   a. Indicate the form and timing of the auditor's communication with the audit committee on the conduct of the audit.
        b. What matters should be included in the communication?

19-18   a. What purpose is served by a management letter?
        b. List the types of data that may be included in a management letter.

KEY TERMS

Management letter, p. 918
Material weakness, p. 916

Significant deficiency, p. 915

POSTAUDIT RESPONSIBILITIES

This section pertains to the auditor's responsibilities following the completion of fieldwork. **Postaudit responsibilities** include consideration of

- Subsequent events occurring between the date and issuance of the auditor's report
- The discovery of existing facts
- The discovery of omitted procedures

SUBSEQUENT EVENTS BETWEEN REPORT DATE AND ISSUANCE OF REPORT

Audit Decision 13

■ What is the auditor's responsibility for events that occur between report date and issuing the audit report?

As shown in Figure 19-1, a time interval of several weeks typically elapses between the end of fieldwork and the issuance of the audit report. AU 530, *Dating of the Independent Auditor's Report,* states that the auditor has no responsibility to make any inquiries or to perform any auditing procedures during this time period to discover any material subsequent events. However, if knowledge of such an event comes to the auditor's attention, he or she should consider whether there should be disclosure in or adjustment of the financial statements for the event. When adjustment is required and management appropriately modifies the statements, the auditor may issue a standard audit report. When management makes required disclosure, the auditor may also issue a standard report, providing the report is redated to coincide with the date of the subsequent event.

Alternatively, the auditor may use **dual dating** in the audit report. Under this course of action, the original date is retained except for the dating of the subsequent event. The dual date is indicated in the audit report immediately below the signature of the firm. Assuming the original date of the auditor's report was February 28 and the date of the subsequent event is March 7, the dual dating would appear as follows:

February 28, 20x1, except for the information in Note A for which the date is March 7.

Dual dating is the most common practice because redating of the entire report extends the auditor's overall responsibility beyond the completion of fieldwork. Under redating, the auditor should extend the subsequent events review procedures to the later date.

DISCOVERY OF FACTS EXISTING AT REPORT DATE

Audit Decision 14

■ What is the auditor's responsibility for events that existed at balance sheet date but were not discovered until after the report was issued?

The auditor has no responsibility for the postaudit discovery of facts existing (but unknown) at the date of the audit report. However, AU 561, *Subsequent Discovery of Facts Existing at the Date of the Auditor's Report*, indicates that if (1) the auditor becomes aware of such facts and (2) the facts may have affected the report that was issued, the auditor is required to ascertain the reliability of the information. When the investigation confirms the existence of the fact and the auditor believes the information is important to those relying or likely to rely on the financial statements, the auditor should take steps to prevent future reliance on the audit report.

The preferred result is the preparation of revised statements by the client and the issuance of a revised audit report as soon as practicable. If the client refuses to disclose the newly discovered facts, the auditor should notify each member of the board of directors of such refusal. In addition, AU 561.08 states that the auditor should take the following steps to prevent further reliance on the report:

■ Notify the client that the audit report must no longer be associated with the financial statements.

■ Notify the regulatory agencies having jurisdiction over the client that the report should no longer be relied on.

■ Notify (generally via the regulatory agency) each individual known to be relying on the statements that the report should no longer be relied on.

AU 561.09 provides guidelines for the auditor in notifying parties other than the client. When the auditor has been able to make a satisfactory investigation and has determined that the information is reliable, he or she should describe the effects the subsequently acquired information would have had on the financial statements and the auditor's report. When the client has not cooperated and the auditor has been unable to make a satisfactory investigation, without disclosing the specific information, the auditor should (1) indicate the lack of cooperation and (2) state that if the information is true, the audit report should no longer be relied on.

DISCOVERY OF OMITTED PROCEDURES

Audit Decision 15

■ What is the auditor's responsibility for the discovery of omitted procedures after report date?

After the date of the audit report, the auditor may conclude that one or more auditing procedures considered necessary in the circumstances was omitted from the audit. Auditing standards do not require the auditor to conduct any postaudit reviews of his or her work. However, discovery of an omitted procedure may result from a postengagement review performed during a firm's quality control inspection program or during an outside peer review.

On discovery of an omitted procedure, the auditor should assess its importance to his or her ability to currently support the opinion expressed on the financial statements. A review of the working papers and a reevaluation of the overall scope of the audit may enable the auditor to conclude that he or she can still support the previously expressed opinion. Alternatively, AU 390.05, *Consideration of Omitted Procedures after the Report Date*, indicates that if the auditor decides that the opinion cannot be supported and he or she believes persons are currently relying on the report, the auditor should promptly perform the omitted procedures or alternative procedures that would provide a satisfactory basis for the opinion.

When a satisfactory basis for an opinion is obtained and the evidence supports the opinion expressed, the auditor has no further responsibility. However, if the performance of the omitted procedures reveals facts existing at the report date that would have changed the previously expressed opinion, the auditor should follow the notification procedures described in the last paragraph of the preceding section to prevent further reliance on the report. If the auditor is unable to perform the omitted or alternative procedures, he or she should consult an attorney to determine an appropriate course of action.

LEARNING CHECK

19-19 a. Explain the auditor's responsibility for discovery of subsequent events occurring after completion of fieldwork but before issuance of the audit report.

b. When such an event occurs and is appropriately reflected in the financial statements, what are the auditor's alternatives with respect to dating the audit report and the conditions applicable to each alternative?

19-20 a. What responsibility does the auditor have for the postaudit discovery of facts existing at the date of the auditor's report?

b. Identify the steps the auditor should take when the client refuses to make disclosure of the newly discovered facts.

19-21 What information should the auditor include in a notification of parties other than the client about the postaudit discovery of facts when he or she has been (a) able and (b) unable to make a satisfactory investigation of the facts?

19-22 a. What responsibility does the auditor have upon discovery of omitted procedures after the report date?

b. Indicate the possible consequences of the auditor's investigation of omitted procedures.

KEY TERMS

Dual dating, p. 916   Postaudit responsibilities, p. 916

FOCUS ON AUDIT DECISIONS

This chapter focuses on (1) procedures performed in completing fieldwork, (2) evaluating audit findings, (3) communicating with the client, and (4) postaudit responsibilities. Figure 19-5 summarizes the audit decisions discussed in Chapter 19 and provides page references indicating where these decisions are discussed in more detail.

Figure 19-5 ■ Summary of Audit Decisions Discussed in Chapter 19

Audit Decision	Factors that Influence the Audit Decision	Chapter References
Completing Fieldwork		
D1. What are the auditor's responsibilities with respect to subsequent events?	Figure 19-1 graphically depicts the subsequent events period. Type 1 subsequent events provide additional evidence about conditions that existed at balance sheet date and affect the estimates inherent in the financial reporting process. They require adjustment of the financial statements. Type 2 subsequent events provide evidence about conditions that did not exist at balance sheet date but arose subsequent to that date. Type 2 subsequent events require disclosure. Important audit procedures should include: ■ Read the latest interim financial statements after year-end. ■ Inquire of management about (a) any substantial contingent liabilities or commitments, (b) any significant changes in capital stock, long-term debt, or working capital, (c) the current status of items previously accounted for on the basis of tentative data, (d) whether any unusual adjustments have been made since balance sheet date. ■ Read minutes of meetings of directors, stockholders, and other appropriate committees. ■ Inquire of client's legal counsel concerning litigation, claims, and assessments. ■ Obtain letter of representation from client about subsequent events that would, in its opinion, require adjustment or disclosure. ■ Make additional inquiries or perform additional procedures considered necessary in the circumstances.	pp. 896–898
D2. What does an auditor need evidence about with respect to litigation, claims, and assessments (LCA)?	With respect LCA, the auditor should obtain evidence about (1) the existence of a condition, situation, or set of circumstances indicating an uncertainty as to the possible loss to an entity arising from litigation, claims, and assessments; (2) the period in which the underlying cause for legal action occurred; (3) the degree of probability of an unfavorable outcome; and (4) the amount or range of potential loss. Evidence is obtained both from management and the client's lawyer(s).	pp. 898–900
D3. What is the purpose of a client representation letter and what should be included in the letter?	A client rep letter documents a number of important understandings with the client, including (1) management's responsibility for the financial statements, (2) the completeness of information and evidence furnished to the auditor, (3) issues regarding revenue recognition, accounting estimates, and disclosures, and (4) issues about subsequent events. Figure 19-2 provides an example rep letter.	pp. 900–901

(continues)

Figure 19-5 ■ (Continued)

Audit Decision	Factors that Influence the Audit Decision	Chapter References
D4. What is the purpose of performing analytical procedures at the final stages of an engagement?	The auditor performs analytical procedures to evaluate the reasonableness of other decisions reached at the conclusion of the engagement. The auditor performs a test to make sure the financial statements are consistent with his or her knowledge of the business dynamics, and other information obtained during the audit.	pp. 901–903
Evaluating Findings		
D5. What should be addressed in the process of making a final assessment of materiality and audit risk?	At the end of the engagement, the auditor needs to aggregate audit findings to determine if audit evidence indicates the existence of material misstatements. The auditor should consider both known misstatements and projected or likely misstatements. Figure 19-3 provides an example of how auditors might aggregate audit findings. The auditor assesses risk at the assertion level. At the end of the audit, the auditor needs to review the risk assessments and evidence obtained to ensure that audit risk is reduced to a sufficiently low level.	pp. 904–905
D6. What should the auditor consider when evaluating whether an entity is a going concern?	The auditor needs to assess whether there is *substantial doubt* about an entity's ability to continue as a going concern in every audit. The chapter provides examples of the types of situations that represent substantial doubt and explains the process of evaluating going concern.	pp. 905–907
D7. What is the purpose of a technical review of the financial statements?	A technical review is usually performed by a manager or partner to determine compliance with GAAP. Auditors normally use detailed financial statement checklists to guide the evaluations of the completeness and accuracy of financial statement disclosures.	pp. 907–908
D8. What are the key steps involved in forming an opinion and drafting a report on the financial statements?	Ultimately, the engagement partner must evaluate the audit evidence obtained and make a decision about the opinion that should be rendered on the financial statements. If misstatements aggregate to a material amount, the auditor will normally meet with the client, present the audit findings and rationale, and allow the client to adjust the financial statements and receive an unqualified opinion. The various types of opinions were explained in Chapter 2.	p. 908
D9. What are the key steps involved in forming an opinion and drafting a report on internal controls over financial reporting?	When considering an opinion on internal control (for a public company), the auditor must evaluate deficiencies in internal control in terms of the probability that a deficiency will allow a misstatement to occur and the magnitude of the potential misstatement. The auditor will normally test controls and identify any material weaknesses in internal control at an interim date to give the client an opportunity to improve internal controls. If a material weakness exists at balance sheet date, the auditor will have to issue an adverse report on the effectiveness of internal controls over financial reporting. The various types of opinions were explained in Chapter 2.	pp. 908–909

(continues)

Figure 19-5 ■ (Continued)

Audit Decision	Factors that Influence the Audit Decision	Chapter References
D10. What is the purpose of a final review of working papers?	The final review of working papers is performed to obtain assurance that (1) the work done by subordinates has been accurate and thorough, (2) the judgments exercised by subordinates were appropriate in the circumstances, (3) the audit engagement has been completed in accordance with the conditions specified in the engagement letter, (4) all significant accounting, auditing, and reporting questions raised during the audit have been properly resolved, (5) the working papers support the auditor's opinion, and (6) GAAS and the firm's quality control policies and procedures have been met.	p. 909
Communicating with the Client		
D11. What internal control weaknesses should be reported to management and to the public?	In an audit of internal controls for a public company, material weaknesses are communicated in an auditor's report on internal controls, and significant deficiencies must be communicated to the audit committee. In a private company audit, both material weaknesses and significant deficiencies should be reported to the audit committee, or its equivalent.	pp. 910–913
D12. What other matters should be communicated to the audit committee associated with a financial statement audit?	Other required communications with the audit committee, or its equivalent, include (1) the auditor's responsibility under GAAS, (2) significant accounting policies, (3) the auditor 's judgments about the quality of the entity's accounting principles, (4) management judgments and accounting estimates, (5) significant audit adjustments, (6) disagreements with management, (7) consultation with other accounts, and (8) difficulties encountered in performing the audit.	pp. 913–915
Postaudit Responsibilities		
D13. What is the auditor's responsibility for events that occur between report date and issuing the audit report?	The auditor is not required to search for subsequent events that happen after report date. If the auditor finds important type 2 events after report date, they are normally disclosed in the financial statements, and report date for the subsequent event note is different from report date on the financial statements (dual dating).	p. 916
D14. What is the auditor's responsibility for events that existed at balance sheet date but were not discovered until after the report was issued?	The auditor has no responsibility to search for subsequent events after report date. If (1) the auditor becomes aware of such facts and (2) the facts may have affected the report that was issued, the auditor is required to ascertain the reliability of the information. When the investigation confirms the existence of the fact and the auditor believes the information is important to those relying or likely to rely on the financial statements, the auditor should take steps to prevent further reliance on the audit report.	p. 917
D15: What is the auditor's responsibility for the discovery of omitted procedures after report date?	If peer review or other quality control inspection programs determine that important procedures were omitted from an audit, the auditor should promptly perform the omitted procedures. If the evidence obtained supports the opinion expressed, the auditor has no other responsibilities. If the evidence causes the auditor to change his or her opinion, the auditor should take steps to prevent further reliance on the audit report.	pp. 917–918

objective questions

Objective questions are available for the student at www.wiley.com/college/boynton

comprehensive questions

19-23 **(Subsequent events)** Green, CPA, is auditing the financial statements of Taylor Corporation for the year ended December 31, 20X1. Green plans to complete the fieldwork and sign the auditor's report about May 10, 20X2. Green is concerned about events and transactions occurring after December 31, 20X1, that may affect the 20X1 financial statements.

Required

a. What are the general types of subsequent events that require Green's consideration and evaluation?

b. What are the auditing procedures Green should consider performing to gather evidence concerning subsequent events?

19-24 **(Subsequent events/client representation letter/management letter)** Charles Jones is the controller of Precision Tool & Die Corporation, a closely held firm. The principal owners of the company are seeking to retire soon and to sell their share interests. As audited financial statements will be needed during the process, the firm of Higgins & Clark has been hired to audit the financial statements for the fiscal year ended November 30, 20X8.

At a recent meeting with the owners, Jones presented a status report on the audit. Most of the fieldwork has been completed, and the preliminary financial statements will be prepared within the next 10 days. Higgins & Clark has targeted a report issue date of January 15, 20X9. In response to a query regarding work remaining to be done, Jones identified the following three major tasks that must be accomplished:

■ A subsequent events review

■ The client representation letter

■ The management letter

Required

a. 1. Describe the purpose of a subsequent events review.
   2. Describe the two actions that might be taken upon discovery of a material subsequent event and the potential effect of each action on the firm's financial statements.

b. 1. Describe the purpose of the client representation letter.
   2. Identify four items that may appear in a client representation letter.

c. 1. Define the purpose served by the management letter.
   2. Identify three major subjects that may be addressed in the management letter.

ICMA

19-25 **(Subsequent events)** In connection with the audit of Flowmeter, Inc., for the year ended December 31, 20X0, Hirsch, CPA, is aware that certain events and transactions that took place after December 31, 20X0, but before Hirsch issues his report dated February 8, 20X1, may affect the company's financial statements.

The following material events or transactions have come to his attention.

1. On January 3, 20X1, Flowmeter, Inc., received a shipment of raw materials from Canada. The materials had been ordered in October 20X0 and shipped FOB shipping point in November 20X0.

2. On January 15, 20X1, the company settled and paid a personal injury claim of a former employee as the result of an accident that occurred in March 20X0. The company had not previously recorded a liability for the claim.

3. On January 25, 20X1, the company agreed to purchase for cash the outstanding stock of Porter Electrical Company. The acquisition is likely to double the sales volume of Flowmeter, Inc.

4. On February 1, 20X1, a plant owned by Flowmeter, Inc., was damaged by a flood, resulting in an uninsured loss of inventory.

5. On February 5, 20X1, Flowmeter, Inc., issued and sold to the general public $2 million in convertible bonds.

Required

For each of the above events or transactions, indicate the audit procedures that should have brought the item to the attention of the auditor and the form of disclosure in the financial statements including the reasons for such disclosure. Organize your answers in the following format:

ITEM NO.	AUDIT PROCEDURES	REQUIRED DISCLOSURES AND REASONS

AICPA

19-26 **(Litigation, claims, and assessments)** Young, CPA, is considering the procedures to be applied concerning a client's loss contingencies relating to litigation, claims, and assessments.

Required

What substantive audit procedures should Young apply when testing for loss contingencies relating to litigation, claims, and assessments?

AICPA

19-27 **(Litigation, claims, and assessments)** During an audit engagement, an auditor is expected to communicate with lawyers concerning litigation, claims, and assessments. Listed below are five situations regarding LCA. The last clause or sentence of each case states a conclusion.

1. If the client's lawyer is silent on certain aspects of an attorney's letter request, the auditor may infer the response is complete.

2. Letters of audit inquiry ask for the lawyer's evaluation of the probable outcome of matters reported in the response. If the lawyer's response does not contain this evaluation, the auditor should conclude the scope of the audit has been restricted.

3. The Top Dollar Corporation is involved in litigation for which the potential liability is so great that an unfavorable judgment at or near the claimed amount would seriously impair its operations. This is how the company's attorneys answered the legal confirmation request: "Although no assurance can be given as to the outcome of this action, based on the facts known by us to date, in the confidence of the attorney/client relationship and otherwise, and our understanding of the present law, we believe the company has good and meritorious defense to the claims asserted against it and should prevail." On this basis, the independent auditor may issue an unqualified opinion.

4. In situations where the auditor has orally discussed matters involving litigation with the client's legal counsel and obtained his oral opinion on the outcome of disputed matters, it is not necessary to obtain written confirmation of these oral opinions if the auditor has summarized the attorney's opinion in a memo to the working papers.

5. For the past 10 years, XYZ Company has used the services of JJH&I for its primary legal advice and in many significant matters of litigation. Ninety-five percent of JJH&I's legal fees originate from services performed for XYZ Company. At December 31, JJH&I was handling litigation involving great potential liability to the company and has now responded to the auditor's letter of inquiry. If we assume full disclosure, complete reliance can be placed on this response.

Required

For each case, indicate whether you agree or disagree with the conclusion and the reason(s) therefor.

19-28 **(Client representation letter)** During the audit of the annual financial statements of Amis Manufacturing, Inc., the company's president, R. Alderman, and Luddy, the auditor, reviewed matters that were supposed to be included in a written representation letter. On receipt of the following client representation letter, Luddy contacted Alderman to state that it was incomplete:

To E. K. Luddy, CPA

In connection with your audit of the balance sheet of Amis Manufacturing, Inc., as of December 31, 20X5, and the related statements of income, retained earnings, and changes in cash flows for the year then ended, for the purpose of expressing an opinion as to whether the financial statements present fairly the financial position, results of operations, and changes in cash flows of Amis Manufacturing, Inc., in conformity with generally accepted accounting principles, we confirm, to the best of our knowledge and belief, the following representations made to you during your audit. There were no

- Plans or intentions that may materially affect the carrying value or classification of assets and liabilities.
- Communications from regulatory agencies concerning noncompliance with, or deficiencies in, financial reporting practices.
- Agreements to repurchase assets previously sold.
- Violations or possible violations of laws or regulations whose effects should be considered for disclosure in the financial statements or as a basis for recording a loss contingency.
- Unasserted claims or assessments that our lawyer has advised are probable of assertion and must be disclosed in accordance with Statement of Financial Accounting Standards No. 5.
- Capital stock repurchase options or agreements or capital stock reserved for options, warrants, conversions, or other requirements.
- Compensating balance or other arrangements involving restrictions on cash balances.

R. Alderman, President

Amis Manufacturing, Inc.

March 14, 20X6

Required

Identify the other matters that Alderman's representation letter should specifically confirm.

AICPA

19-29 **(Analytical procedures in overall review)** In auditing the financial statements of a manufacturing company that were prepared from data processed by electronic data processing equipment, the CPA has found that his traditional "audit trail" has been obscured. As a result, the CPA may place increased emphasis on overall checks of the data under audit.

These overall checks, which are also applied in auditing visibly posted accounting records, include the computation of ratios, which are compared with prior-year ratios or industry-wide norms. Examples of such overall checks or ratios are the computation of the rate of inventory turnover and the computation of the number of days' sales in receivables.

Required

a. Discuss the advantages to the CPA of the use of ratios as overall checks in an audit.

b. In addition to the computations given above, list the ratios that a CPA may compute during an audit as overall checks on balance sheet accounts and related nominal accounts. For each ratio listed, name the two (or more) accounts used in its computation.

c. When a CPA discovers that there has been a significant change in a ratio when compared with the prior year's ratio, he considers the possible reasons for the change. Give the possible reasons for the following significant changes in ratios:

1. The rate of inventory turnover (ratio of cost of sales and average inventory) has decreased from the prior year's rate.

2. The number of days' sales in receivables (ratio of average daily accounts receivable and sales) has increased over the prior year.

AICPA

19-30   **(Significant deficiency/material weaknesses)** On completing the work on the internal control of the Klima Corporation in the 20X4 audit, an inexperienced staff member was asked to prepare the communication for the audit committee. The audit team concluded that there were several reportable conditions but no material weaknesses. The first and last paragraphs of the staff member's draft were as follows:

> To the Audit Committee:
>
> In completing our audit of the financial statements of the Klima Corporation for the year ended December 31, 20X4, we considered its internal control environment in order to determine our auditing procedures for the purpose of expressing our opinion on the financial statements and not to express an opinion on internal controls. However, we noted certain matters involving the design and effectiveness of the system of internal control that we consider to be reportable conditions under GAAS established by the American Institute of Certified Public Accountants. Reportable conditions involve matters coming to our attention relating to potential weaknesses in the design or operation of internal control that, in our judgment, could adversely affect the organization's ability to prepare financial statements in conformity with GAAP.
>
> …
>
> This report is intended solely for the audit committee and others within the organization.

Required

a. List the deficiencies in the report. For each deficiency, indicate the proper wording. Use the following format for your answers: (*Note:* Do not write a proper report.)

DEFICIENCY	PROPER WORDING

b. Distinguish between a reportable condition and a material weakness.

c. Indicate the effects on the report when the auditor wishes to inform the audit committee that identified reportable conditions are not material weaknesses.

19-31   **(Management letter)** The major result of a financial audit conducted by an independent accountant is the expression of an opinion by the auditor on the fairness of the financial statements. Although the auditor's report containing the opinion is the best known report issued by the independent auditor, other reports are often prepared during the course of a normal audit. One such report is the management letter (informal report).

Required

a. What is the purpose of a management letter?

b. Identify the major types of information that are likely to be covered in a management letter. Support your answer with a detailed example of one of the types identified above.

ICMA

19-32   **(Subsequent events/postaudit discovery of facts)** The fiscal year of the Edie Company ends on December 31. Your audit report, dated February 26, is to be delivered to the client on March 9. Listed below are events that occur or are discovered from the date of the balance sheet to June 30 of the following year. Assume each event has a material effect on the financial statements.

1. Jan 15   Inventory is sold at a price below December 31 net realizable value.

2. Jan 20   A major customer becomes bankrupt from ongoing net losses.

3. Jan 31   The board of directors authorizes the acquisition of a company as a subsidiary.

4. Feb 10   A fire destroys a major company warehouse.

5. Feb 25   A lawsuit is decided against the company for an accident that occurred on October 10. The damages are three times higher than estimated on December 31.

6. Feb 28   The board of directors authorizes a two-for-one stock split.

7. Mar 7   A foreign government expropriates a major foreign subsidiary following the unexpected overthrow of the government.

8. Mar 31   A court rules that a minority group is the rightful legal owner of land on which an operating division is located.

Required

a. Identify each event as a (1) type 1 subsequent event during the subsequent events period, (2) type 2 subsequent event during the subsequent events period, (3) type 1 subsequent event occurring after fieldwork but before issuance of report, (4) type 2 subsequent event occurring after fieldwork but before issuance of report, or (5) postaudit discovery of facts existing at date of report.

b. Explain your audit responsibilities for each category in (a).

c. Indicate how you would obtain knowledge of each of the eight items.

d. What additional responsibilities does an auditor have for the postaudit discovery of facts if the client refuses to make required disclosures?

cases

19-33   **(Mt. Hood Furniture, Inc., completing the audit)** Complete the following requirements based on the following information on Mt. Hood Furniture. Fieldwork was completed on February 28, 20X4.

Required

a. Evaluate the fair presentation of the following two subsequent events.
   1. On January 20, 20X4, Dealer No. 55 filed for bankruptcy protection based on the fact that it was having financial difficulties.
   2. Robert Saws owns the land under the manufacturing and sales facilities of Mt. Hood Furniture. On January 15, 20X4, Saws agreed to sell the land back to Mt. Hood Furniture for $2.0 million. Appraisals of the land ranged from $1.8 million to $2.25 million. Mt. Hood will pay $250,000 down and annual installments of $250,000 plus interest at 8 percent.

b. Based on your findings in other aspects of this case, prepare an analysis of aggregate likely misstatements similar to that shown in Figure 19-3.

c. Draft a representation letter for discussion with the CEO, Conrad Saws, and the CFO, Julia Anderson.

d. Draft a letter communicating internal control related matters to Mt. Hood Furniture, Inc. based on your review of internal controls in prior chapters.

e. Evaluate whether you have substantial doubt about the ability of Mt. Hood Furniture, Inc. to continue as a going concern for a reasonable period of time. Summarize your conclusions in a memo to the working papers. Discussions with Conrad Saws, James Doyle, and Julia Anderson disclose the following information. Your professor will provide you with projected financial statements that Julia Anderson has prepared based on the following assumptions.
   - Sales growth is planned at 10 percent per year for the next few years to improve operating cash flows.
   - The company believed it could maintain a 28 percent gross profit margin and achieve the expected sales growth.
   - Fixed assets acquisition would average about $500,000 per year, and depreciation would increase approximately $50,000 per year.
   - Selling expenses would average approximately 12 percent of sales revenues.
   - General and administrative expenses were relatively fixed but could grow at approximately 6 percent per year.
   - Other operating expenses were relatively fixed but could grow at approximately 4 percent per year.
   - The effective tax rate for combined federal and state income taxes was estimated at 40 percent. The deferred portion of income tax expenses was expected to be approximately 5 percent of total tax expenses.

   Company targets for the operating cycle were as follows.

	20X4	20X5
Account Receivable Turn Days	69	66
Inventory Turn Days	90	90
Accounts Payable Turn Days	55	50

   - Prepaid expenses, accrued payroll, and accrued expenses were expected to grow at approximately 4 percent per year.
   - The company would have to maintain the following ratios with respect to debt covenants.
     - Current ratio: 1.75:1
     - Quick ratio: 0.9:1
     - Debt to net worth: 2.0:1
     - Dividends to net income: 0.25:1

19-34   **(Letter of audit inquiry)** Cole & Cole, CPAs, are auditing the financial statements of Consolidated Industries Co. for the year ended December 31, 20X2. On April 2, 20X3, an inquiry letter to J. J. Young, Consolidated's outside attorney, was drafted to corroborate the information furnished to Cole by management concerning pending and threatened litigation, claims, and assessments, and unasserted claims and assessments. On May 6, 20X3, C. R. Brown, Consolidated's chief financial officer, gave Cole a draft of the inquiry letter below for Cole's review before mailing it to Young.

May 6, 20X3

J. J. Young, Attorney at Law

123 Main Street

Anytown, USA

Dear J. J. Young:

In connection with an audit of our financial statements at December 31, 20X2, and for the year then ended, management of the Company has prepared, and furnished to our auditors, Cole & Cole, CPAs, 456 Broadway, Anytown, USA, a description and evaluation of certain contingencies, including those set forth below involving matters with respect to which you have been engaged and to which you have devoted substantive attention on behalf of the Company in the form of legal consultation or representation. Your response should include matters that existed at December 31, 20X2. Because of the confidentiality of all these matters, your response may be limited.

In November 20X2, an action was brought against the Company by an outside salesman alleging breach of contract for sales commissions and pleading a second cause of action for an accounting with respect to claims for fees and commissions. The causes of action claim damages of $300,000, but the Company believes it has meritorious defenses to the claims. The possible exposure of the Company to a successful judgment on behalf of the plaintiff is slight.

In July 20X0, an action was brought against the Company by Industrial Manufacturing Co. (Industrial) alleging patent infringement and seeking damages of $20,000,000. The action in U.S. District Court resulted in a decision on October 16, 20X2, holding that the Company infringed seven Industrial patents and awarded damages of $14,000,000. The Company vigorously denies these allegations and has filed an appeal with the U.S. Court of Appeals for the Federal Circuit. The appeal process is expected to take approximately two years, but there is some chance that Industrial may ultimately prevail.

Please furnish to our auditors such explanation, if any, that you consider necessary to supplement the foregoing information, including an explanation of those matters as to which of your views may differ from those stated and an identification of the omission of any pending or threatened litigation, claims, and assessments or a statement that the list of such matters is complete. Your response may be quoted or referred to in the financial statements without further correspondence with you.

You also consulted on various other matters considered pending or threatened litigation. However, you may not comment on these matters because publicizing them may alert potential plaintiffs to the strengths of their cases. In addition, various other matters probable of assertion that have some chance of an unfavorable outcome, as of December 31, 20X2, are unasserted claims and assessments.

C. R. Brown

Chief Financial Officer

Required

Describe the omissions, ambiguities, and inappropriate statements and terminology in Brown's letter.

AICPA

professional simulations

Situation			
	Events Subsequent to Balance Sheet Date	Research	Going Concern

Jose Rojas is an audit partner in a large southwestern office of a national accounting firm. He is completing the audit of Southwest Medical Laboratories (SML), a pharmaceutical company that has several manufacturing locations in North America. You are the in-charge accountant on the SML engagement and are faced with the following issues that need to be resolved before you can complete your report on the financial statements.

Situation	Events Subsequent to Balance Sheet Date	Research	Going Concern

Following is a list of events that occurred subsequent to SML's year-end, June 30, 20X1. You have completed fieldwork on August 21, 20X1 and anticipate issuing your audit report on August 30, 20X1. Identify the type of event that each event represents using the following coding:

a. A type I subsequent event
b. A type II subsequent event
c. A subsequent event occurring after the completion of fieldwork but before issuance of report
d. A subsequent discovery of facts existing at the date of the auditor's report
e. A subsequent discovery of omitted audit procedures after the report date

	a.	b.	c.	d.	e.
1. On August 25, 20X1 you read in the morning paper that the Board of Directors of SML has decided to lay off 100 workers at one of its manufacturing locations due to reduced sales of the product manufactured at the facility. On August, 20X1 all the remaining workers went on strike.	○	○	○	○	○
2. The SML engagement is selected for peer review in October of 20X1. The peer reviewer disagrees with your professional judgment not to send a confirmation on a major account payable to the construction company building a new manufacturing facility in Mexico. In response to the comment you contact the construction company and learn that material invoices were not recorded, understating construction-in-progress and accounts payable.	○	○	○	○	○
3. On August 21, 20X1 the company signed an agreement to purchase 100 percent of the assets and research and development of Unicorn Research Inc. for $7 million. SML issued new common stock to the shareholders of Unicorn amounting to $3 million and added new debt from available lines of credit in the amount of $4 million.	○	○	○	○	○

4. On August 15, 20X1 SML paid a $200,000 personal injury claim of an employee as a result of an accident that occurred in May of 20X1. The claim was covered in the letter regarding litigation, claims and assessments from the client's lawyer who indicated that is was probable that the company would settle the claim. SML had not previously recorded a liability for the claim.

○ ○ ○ ○ ○

5. On September 22, 20X1 SML had to make good on a guarantee of a third parties investment in United Medical Labs (UML), and unconsolidated subsidiary. SML's CFO determines that as of the end of the first quarter SML should consolidate UML in its financial statements. Your firm had previously read contracts regarding this investment and had not received any evidence of the guarantee. Inquiries of management about contingent liabilities also did not surface the guarantee. Had you known about the guarantee you believe that UML should be consolidated in SML's financial statements as of June 30, 20X1.

○ ○ ○ ○ ○

6. On June 29, 20X1 SML reached an agreement with to sell certain patents to Houston Research for $1 million. Papers were signed on June 29, 20X1 and final documents were received from the lawyers on July 6, 20X1. The sale was recorded on July 8, 20X1 after documents were received from the lawyers.

○ ○ ○ ○ ○

7. On August 3, 20X1 SML was denied U.S. Food and Drug Administration approval for a cancer drug that it has been working on for the past five years. The application was submitted on the U.S. Food and Drug Administration on January 15, 20X1. The company had built an inventory of $1 million of the cancer drug as of June 30, 20x1.

○ ○ ○ ○ ○

Situation	Events Subsequent to Balance Sheet Date	Research	Going Concern

Following is list events that occurred subsequent to SML's year-end, June 30, 20X1. In the space provided in the table below indicate the appropriate U.S. auditing standards paragraph(s), AU reference, which explains the auditor's responsibility to plan procedures to find each event.

AU Reference

1. On August 25, 20X1 you read in the morning paper that the Board of Directors of SML has decided to lay off 100 workers at one of its manufacturing locations due to reduced sales of the product manufactured at the facility. On August 27, 20X1 all the remaining workers went on strike.
2. The SML engagement is selected for peer review in October of 20X1. The peer reviewer disagrees with your professional judg-

AU Reference

ment not to send a confirmation on a major account payable to the construction company building a new manufacturing facility in Mexico. In response to the comment you contact the construction company and learn that material invoices were not recorded, understating construction-in-progress and accounts payable.

3. On August 21, 20X1 the company signed an agreement to purchase 100 percent of the assets and research and development of Unicorn Research Inc. for $7 million. SML issued new common stock to the shareholders of Unicorn amounting to $3 million and added new debt from available lines of credit in the amount of $4 million.

4. On August 15, 20X1 SML paid a $200,000 personal injury claim of an employee as a result of an accident that occurred in May of 20X1. The claim was covered in the letter regarding litigation, claims, and assessments from the client's lawyer who indicated that is was probable that the company would settle the claim. SML had not previously recorded a liability for the claim.

5. On September 22, 20X1 SML had to make good on a guarantee of a third party's investment in United Medical Labs (UML), and unconsolidated subsidiary. SML's CFO determines that as of the end of the first quarter SML should consolidate UML in its financial statements. Your firm had previously read contracts regarding this investment and had not received any evidence of the guarantee. Inquiries of management about contingent liabilities also did not surface the guarantee. Had you known about the guarantee you believe that UML should be consolidated in SML's financial statements as of June 30, 20X1.

6. On June 29, 20X1 SML reached an agreement to sell certain patents to Houston Research for $1 million. Papers were signed on June 29, 20X1 and final documents were received from the lawyers on July 6, 20X1. The sale was recorded on July 8, 20X1 after documents were received from the lawyers.

7. On August 3, 20X1 SML was denied U.S. Food and Drug Administration approval for a cancer drug that it has been working on for the past five years. The application was submitted on the U.S. Food and Drug Administration on January 15, 20X1. The company had built an inventory of $1 million of the cancer drug as of June 30, 20x1.

| Situation | Events Subsequent to Balance Sheet Date | Research | Going Concern |

Following is a brief summary of SML's financial condition, results of operations, and cash flows for the year ended June 30, 20X1.

Southwest Medical Laboratories

Summary Financial Information

General Ledger Information as of June 30, 20x1

Current Assets	$ 6,000,000	Revenue	$ 7,000,000
Long-term Assets	$ 4,000,000	Net Loss	$<3,500,000>
Total Assets	$ 10,000,000		
		Cash Flow from Operations	$<2,500,000>
Current Liabilties	$ 5,500,000		
Long-term Liabiltiies	$ 3,500,000		
Total Liabilities	$ 9,000,000	Available Lines of Credit	$ 4,500,000
Contributed Capital	$ 9,000,000		
Retained Earnings	$ (8,000,000)		
Total Equity	$ 1,000,000		
Total Liabilities and Equity			

SML expected that the approval of its new cancer drug would increase operating cash flow by $3.5 million dollars a year. In addition, the acquisition of Unicorn research should increase operating cash flow by approximately $700,000 a year. They also received $1 million from the sale of patent on July 8, 20X1.

Prepare a memo to the audit file evaluating SML's ability to continue as a going concern as of report date.

To: Audit File

Re: SML Going Concern Evaluation

From: CPA Candidate

ATTEST AND ASSURANCE SERVICES, AND RELATED REPORTS

A BUSY DAY WITH LOTS OF QUESTIONS

Keith Lewis was an assurance partner in a large local CPA firm in his community. On the way home, the reflected on what he thought had been one of the most unique days in his career.

It began with a question from an audit client that had significant debt covenants with the local bank. The client wanted to impress the bank and had come in to ask if Keith could audit the company's compliance with debt covenants as well as the financial statements. Keith responded that he thought he could only give negative assurance on the compliance with debt covenants, in addition to positive assurance on the financial statements, but he would get back to the client the following day.

A second client called an hour later with another unusual request. This client was about to sign a rental agreement. The rent was based on gross sales, and called for an annual audit of sales from that particular location. Keith's firm audited the financial statements that included sales from 12 stores. Could it perform an audit of only sales for only the one store? Keith responded that it would have to be a separate engagement, but that his firm could perform the audit.

Over lunch with a prospective client. Keith learned that the entity kept its records on a cash basis of accounting. The bank wanted an audit, and was willing to accept cash basis financial statements. The client was concerned that cash basis statements were not GAAP and did not want to set up another set of books. Could Keith's firm audit the cash basis financial statements without giving a qualified or an adverse opinion? Keith responded that cash basis statements were another comprehensive basis of accounting and that he could issue an unqualified opinion on cash basis financial statements. Keith said that his firm had just completed a similar engagement for a company that used the federal income tax basis of accounting.

After lunch, Keith had a meeting with another audit client. The client was considering a business expansion and wanted Keith's firm to advise the client on the business risks involved. He felt that Keith's firm had asked questions about business risk when performing the audit, and wondered what other services the firm could perform. Keith briefly explained a service called CPA Risk Advisory and said that he would put together a proposal for the client.

In addition to reviewing regular audit working papers, Keith had had four requests for assurance services that were not for traditional audits. Keith reflected back on the fact that the profession had changed and grown substantially from his first days in the profession. What requests would he receive tomorrow?

Over the years, CPAs have earned a reputation for independence, integrity, and objectivity. This reputation has created opportunities for a wide array of assurance services.

Chapter 20 describes many of these nontraditional attest and assurance services offered by CPAs.

[PREVIEW OF CHAPTER 20]

Chapters 1 through 20 focus on the process of auditing financial statements that are prepared in accordance with GAAP. The financial statement audit is the cornerstone of a variety of services offered by CPAs, as well as the reason for the regulatory franchise associated with granting CPA licenses. Based largely on the skills, experience, and reputation that CPAs have acquired as auditors, businesses, regulatory agencies, and others have increasingly turned to the public accounting profession for a widening range of other types of attest and nonattest services. These are explained in more detail in this chapter. The following diagram provides an overview of the chapter organization and content.

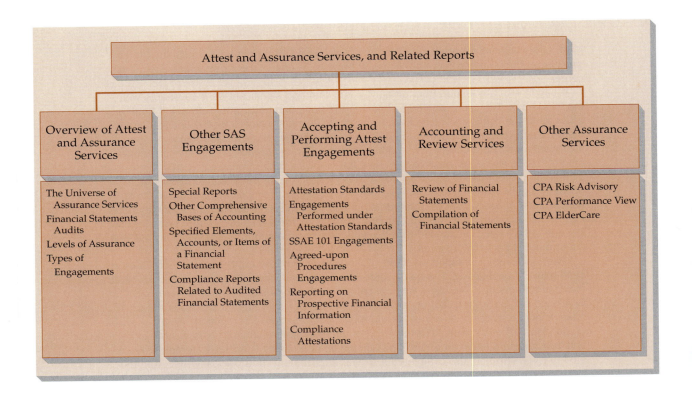

Attest and Assurance Services, and Related Reports				
Overview of Attest and Assurance Services	**Other SAS Engagements**	**Accepting and Performing Attest Engagements**	**Accounting and Review Services**	**Other Assurance Services**
The Universe of Assurance Services Financial Statements Audits Levels of Assurance Types of Engagements	Special Reports Other Comprehensive Bases of Accounting Specified Elements, Accounts, or Items of a Financial Statement Compliance Reports Related to Audited Financial Statements	Attestation Standards Engagements Performed under Attestation Standards SSAE 101 Engagements Agreed-upon Procedures Engagements Reporting on Prospective Financial Information Compliance Attestations	Review of Financial Statements Compilation of Financial Statements	CPA Risk Advisory CPA Performance View CPA ElderCare

focus on audit decisions

After studying this chapter you should understand the factors that address the following audit decisions:

D1. What opinions can be used in an audit of the basic financial statements?

D2. What are the primary options in terms of level of service that might be available for an attest engagement?

D3. What are the professional standards that cover most audit and attest engagements?

D4. Under what circumstances can an auditor audit and report on financial statements prepared in accordance with an other comprehensive basis of accounting?

D5. Under what circumstances can an auditor audit and report on an individual element, account, or item of the financial statements?

D6. Under what circumstances can an auditor audit and report on compliance with contractual agreements?

D7. What are the attestation standards, and how do they compare with GAAS?

D8. What are the basic principles for a WebTrust engagement?

D9. What are the basic principles and criteria for a SysTrust engagement?

D10. What conditions must be met in order to accept an agreed-upon procedures engagement?

D11. What is the difference between a financial forecast and a projection, and what levels of assurance can be provided on prospective financial statements?

D12. What assurance can be provided in a compliance attestation performed in accordance with SSAEs?

D13. What procedures should be performed to support a review and a compilation of the financial statements?

D14. What language should be used for a review and a compilation report?

D15. What are the types of services that might be performed as part of a CPA Risk Advisory engagement?

D16. What are the types of services that might be performed as part of a CPA Performance View engagement?

D17. What are the types of services that might be performed as part of a CPA ElderCare engagement?

OVERVIEW OF ATTEST AND ASSURANCE SERVICES

UNIVERSE OF ASSURANCE SERVICES

Recall from Chapter 1 that CPAs perform a wide range of assurance services. **Assurance services** are independent professional services that improve the quality of information, or its context, for decision makers. The universe of assurance services is depicted in Figure 20-1, and it includes audits, attest services, compilation and review services, and other assurance services.

The audit is the most valued and respected service offered by CPAs. The financial statement audit is the primary subject matter of this book. Other attest services have been offered and accepted in the marketplace. An audit of internal controls over financial reporting began as an attest service. Today, CPAs perform other attest services such as attesting to a financial projection or forecast, or performing an agreed-upon procedures engagement. This chapter explores the full universe of assurance services. It explains the various assurance services, the level of assurance that each service provides, and the types of report that may be issued by CPAs.

FINANCIAL STATEMENT AUDITS

Audit Decision 1

■ What opinions can be used in an audit of the basic financial statements?

The financial statement audit has been the cornerstone of the accounting profession. In most states the CPA license gives CPAs a monopoly to audit financial statements. By performing financial statement audits, CPAs have developed a reputation for independence, integrity, and objectivity. Chapter 2 discussed auditor responsibilities and auditor reports. Appendix 2A provides a number of examples of audit reports, along with a narrative that explains the meaning of each report and the auditor's criteria for using a report. Figure 20-2 summarizes some of the key examples contained in Chapter 2.

Figure 20-1 ■ Universe of Assurance Services

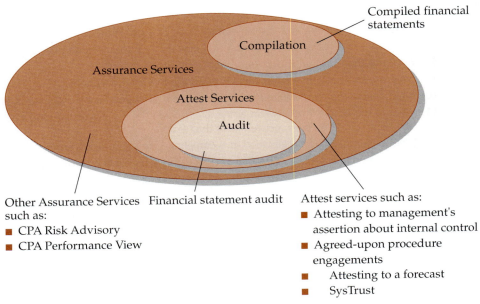

Compiled financial statements

Compilation

Assurance Services

Attest Services

Audit

Other Assurance Services such as:
■ CPA Risk Advisory
■ CPA Performance View

Financial statement audit

Attest services such as:
■ Attesting to management's assertion about internal control
■ Agreed-upon procedure engagements
■ Attesting to a forecast
■ SysTrust

Figure 20-2 ■ A Summary of Examples of Common Audit Reports

Report	Example
Standard report on audited financial statements	Figure 2-3, page 65
Departures from the standard report on audited financial statements	Figure 2-4, page 71
Unqualified opinion on the financial statements with explanatory language regarding going concern	Appendix 2A, page 85
Unqualified opinion on the financial statements with explanatory language regarding a change in accounting principles accounted for in conformity with GAAP	Appendix 2A, page 86
Unqualified opinion on the financial statements with opinion based in part on report of another auditor where there is no scope limitation or nonconformity with GAAP	Appendix 2A, page 87
Unqualified opinion on the financial statements with emphasis of a matter by the auditor	Appendix 2A, page 88
Qualified opinion for departure from GAAP	Appendix 2A, page 89
Qualified opinion for scope limitation	Appendix 2A, page 90
Adverse opinion for departure from GAAP	Appendix 2A, page 91
Disclaimer of opinion for scope limitation	Appendix 2A, page 92
Unqualified opinion—other comprehensive basis of accounting	Appendix 2A, page 93
Standard audit report on internal controls over financial reporting	Figures 2-5, page 73

LEVELS OF ASSURANCE

Audit Decision 2

■ What are the primary options in terms of level of service that might be available for an attest engagement?

The CPA profession has developed a number of services that build upon the financial statement audit. Some of these services provide audit level assurance on other assertions. Some of these services provide less than audit-level assurance on financial statements. Figure 20-3 depicts an Assurance/Service Matrix that shows how the CPAs reputation for independence, integrity, and objectivity has resulted in expanding the levels of assurance and the types of engagements offered by CPAs. The core service discussed in this book, the audit of GAAP financial statements, is depicted in the upper-left corner of the Assurance/Service Matrix. The following discussion provides an overview of the four basic levels of assurance offered by CPAs and the types of engagements on which these levels of assurance might be rendered.

The four basic levels of assurance can be described as follows:

■ **Audit or examination-level assurance,** where the intent of the engagement is a positive expression of an opinion by the CPA regarding an assertion by management governed by professional standards.

■ **Review-level assurance,** where the intent of the engagement is for the CPA to express **negative assurance** that nothing came to his or her attention that led the CPA to believe that the assertion by management governed by professional standards would be misleading.

■ **Agreed-upon procedures,** where the intent of the engagement is for the CPA to provide a summary of findings based on agreed-upon procedures applied to an assertion by management governed by professional standards. The level of assurance may vary depending on the procedures applied to the assertion.

■ **No assurance,** where the intent of the engagement is to assist management in the preparation of information included in an assertion governed by professional standards. Chapter 1 refers to these services as **accounting and compilation**

Figure 20-3 ■ Assurance/Service Matrix

Assurance	SAS Engagements				SSAE Engagements							SSARS Engagements	
	GAAP F/S	OCBOA F/S	F/S Elements	Compliance Reports	General Attest	Agreed-Upon Procedures	Prospective F/S	Proforma	Internal Control	Compliance	MD & A	GAAP F/S	OCBOA F/S
Audit/Examination (100%)	✓	✓	✓		✓		✓	✓	✓	✓	✓		
Review			✓		✓		✓			✓		✓	✓
Agreed-upon Procedures					✓	✓	✓			✓			
Unaudited/Compilation (0%)	✓				✓							✓	✓

services. The CPA will explicitly state that no assurance is provided in his or her report associated with management's assertion.

Each of these levels of assurance will be discussed in detail throughout this chapter.

TYPES OF ENGAGEMENTS

Audit Decision 3

■ What are the professional standards that cover most audit and attest engagements?

All the types of engagements discussed in this chapter are covered by professional standards developed by the AICPA and are summarized in Figure 20-3. These professional standards promote uniformity in quality of practice and enhance users' understanding of the differences in the types of services rendered and the levels of assurance associated with them. CPAs who perform many of these types of services must also subject their practices to regular peer review. The basic professional standards issued by the Auditing Standards Board that relate to these services are as follows:

■ **Statements on Auditing Standards (SAS).** The SASs are interpretations of generally accepted auditing standards and generally relate to management's assertions about elements contained in the financial statements. The types of engagements discussed in this chapter include reporting on financial statements prepared on a comprehensive basis of accounting other than GAAP, reporting on specified elements, accounts, or items of a financial statement, and compliance reports related to audited financial statements.

■ **Statements on Standards for Attestation Engagements (SSAE).** The SSAEs establish a broad framework for a variety of attest services increasingly demanded of the accounting profession. The standards and related interpretive commentary are designed to provide professional guidelines that will enhance both consistency and quality in the performance of such services. This chapter provides an overview of attestation standards and discusses reporting on many of the services covered by attestation standards.

■ **Statements on Standards for Accounting and Review Services (SSARS).** The SSARSs define the services associated with the review or the compilation of financial statements of a nonpublic entity and provide guidance to accountants concerning the standards and procedures applicable to these two engagements. These services are available only to nonpublic entities; this chapter will discuss both the review and the compilation service.

The remainder of the chapter discusses special reports covered by SASs, attest engagements covered by the SSAEs, and financial statements engagements for nonpublic companies covered by the SSARSs. It concludes with a brief section on other assurance services.

OTHER SAS ENGAGEMENTS

SPECIAL REPORTS

Special reports are reports resulting from the audit of, or application of agreed-upon procedures to, historical financial data other than financial statements prepared in conformity with GAAP. AU 623, *Special Reports,* indicates that the term *special reports* applies to auditors' reports on

■ Financial statements that are prepared in conformity with a comprehensive basis of accounting other than generally accepted accounting principles

- Specified elements, accounts, or items of a financial statement
- Compliance with aspects of contractual agreements or regulatory requirements related to audited financial statements
- Financial presentations to comply with contractual agreements or regulatory provisions
- Financial information presented in prescribed forms or schedules that require a prescribed form of auditors' report

Special reports based on an audit are similar to the auditor's standard report in that they usually contain an introductory paragraph, a scope paragraph, and an opinion paragraph. However, as explained and illustrated below, special reports have wording that differs from the language in the auditor's standard report. In addition, the "standard" special report may have four or even five paragraphs depending on the circumstances. The explanation of special reports in this chapter is limited to the first three items in the foregoing list.

OTHER COMPREHENSIVE BASES OF ACCOUNTING

Audit Decision 4

- Under what circumstances can an auditor audit and report on financial statements prepared in accordance with an other comprehensive basis of accounting?

Four comprehensive bases of accounting other than GAAP are recognized in AU 623.04:

- A basis used to comply with the requirements or financial reporting provisions of a governmental regulatory agency
- A basis used to file the entity's income tax return
- The cash receipts and disbursements basis of accounting and modifications of the cash basis having substantial support
- A basis that uses a definite set of criteria that has substantial support such as the price-level basis of accounting

The use of an **other comprehensive basis of accounting (OCBOA)** is common. Many companies subject to regulatory bodies keep their accounts solely on the basis prescribed by the agency. For example, railroads conform with the requirements of the Interstate Commerce Commission (ICC), public utilities use the basis set forth by the Federal Energy Regulatory Commission, and insurance companies follow state insurance commission accounting requirements. In addition, many small companies and individual practitioners, such as doctors, lawyers, and CPAs, use the income tax, cash, or modified cash basis of accounting. When an entity uses a basis other than GAAP, the notes to the financial statements should indicate the basis of accounting.

All of the 10 GAAS are applicable whenever the auditor audits and reports on any financial statement, regardless of the basis of accounting used in preparing the statement. The major difference in this case is that the statements are not intended to present fairly financial position, and so forth, in conformity with GAAP. However, the first standard of reporting is satisfied by indicating whether the statements are presented fairly in conformity with the basis of accounting used.

The auditor's special report on financial statements prepared on an OCBOA should contain four paragraphs:

- An *introductory paragraph* that is the same as in the auditor's standard report except that more distinctive titles should be used for the financial statements, such as statement of assets and liabilities arising from cash transactions.

- A *scope paragraph* that is the same as in the auditor's standard report.
- An *explanatory paragraph* following the scope paragraph that states the basis of presentation and refers to the note to the financial statements that describes the comprehensive basis of accounting other than GAAP.
- An *opinion paragraph* that expresses the auditor's opinion (or disclaims an opinion) on whether the financial statements are presented fairly, in all material respects, in conformity with the basis of accounting described.

As in the case of financial statements prepared in conformity with GAAP, the auditor's special report on statements prepared on an OCBOA may contain additional explanatory language when (1) the auditor cannot express an unqualified opinion or (2) circumstances require explanatory language with an unqualified opinion. An example of a special report on financial statements prepared on a cash basis of accounting is illustrated in Figure 20-4. Notice that distinctive language is used in describing the financial statements in the introductory paragraph and in the wording of the opinion paragraph.

Audit Decision 5

■ Under what circumstances can an auditor audit and report on an individual element, account, or item of the financial statements?

SPECIFIED ELEMENTS, ACCOUNTS, OR ITEMS OF A FINANCIAL STATEMENT

An auditor is not limited to auditing entire financial statements. A CPA can audit an element of the financial statements, an account, or an item in the financial statements. These engagements may include audits of rentals, royalties, profit participation plans, or the provision for income taxes. A special report may be issued on

Figure 20-4 ■ Special Report—Cash Basis of Accounting

Independent Auditor's Report

We have audited the accompanying statements of assets and liabilities arising from cash transactions of XYZ Company as of December 31, 20X2 and 20X1, and the related statements of revenue collected and expenses paid for the years then ended. These financial statements are the responsibility of the company's management. Our responsibility is to express an opinion on these financial statements based on our audits.

We conducted our audits in accordance with auditing standards generally accepted in the United States of America. Those standards require that we plan and perform the audit to obtain reasonable assurance about whether the financial statements are free of material misstatement. An audit includes examining, on a test basis, evidence supporting the amounts and disclosures in the financial statements. An audit also includes assessing the accounting principles used and significant estimates made by management, as well as evaluating the overall financial statement presentation. We believe our audits provide a reasonable basis for our opinion.

As described in note X, these financial statements were prepared on the basis of cash receipts and disbursements, which is a comprehensive basis of accounting other than generally accepted accounting principles.

In our opinion, the financial statements referred to above present fairly, in all material respects, the assets and liabilities arising from cash transactions of XYZ Company as of December 31, 20X2 and 20X1, and its revenue collected and expenses paid during the years then ended, on the basis of accounting described in note X.

Source: AU 623.08.

these data as a result of an audit to obtain reasonable assurance about their fair presentation.

An audit culminates in the expression of an opinion on the fairness of the presentation of the specified elements, accounts, or items. The specified data may be presented in conformity with GAAP or an OCBOA, or on the basis of an agreement such as a lease contract. All 10 GAAS are applicable when the specified data are presented in conformity with GAAP or an OCBOA. Otherwise, the first reporting standard is inapplicable. An engagement to express an opinion on specified elements, accounts, or items may be made in conjunction with the audit of the financial statements or in a separate engagement.

Distinctive wording is required in the introductory, scope, and opinion paragraphs of the special report because the auditor is not reporting on the financial statements taken as a whole. A special report on a royalty contract is illustrated in Figure 20-5. In describing the basis of presentation (paragraph 3), if considered necessary, the auditor may include any significant interpretations of the contract made by the company's management. In expressing an opinion, AU 623.13 indicates that the auditor should recognize that the concept of materiality must be related to each individual element, account, or item being reported on rather than

Figure 20-5 ■ Special Report on Royalties: Separate Audit Engagement; Audited Data Presented per Agreement

Independent Auditor's Report

We have audited the accompanying schedule of royalties applicable to engine production of the Q division of XYZ Corporation for the year ended December 31, 20X2, under the terms of a license agreement dated May 14, 20XX, between ABC Company and XYZ Corporation. This schedule is the responsibility of XYZ Corporation's management. Our responsibility is to express an opinion on this schedule based on our audit.

We conducted our audit in accordance with auditing standards generally accepted in the United States of America. Those standards require that we plan and perform the audit to obtain reasonable assurance about whether the schedule of royalties is free of material misstatement. An audit includes examining, on a test basis, evidence supporting the amounts and disclosures in the schedule. An audit also includes assessing the accounting principles used and significant estimates made by management, as well as evaluating the overall schedule presentation. We believe our audit provides a reasonable basis for our opinion.

We have been informed that, under XYZ Corporation's interpretation of the agreement referred to in the first paragraph, royalties were based on the number of engines produced after giving effect to a reduction for production retirements that were scrapped, but without a reduction for field returns that were scrapped, even though the field returns were replaced with new engines without charge to the customer.

In our opinion, the schedule of royalties referred to above presents fairly, in all material respects, the number of engines produced by the Q division of XYZ Corporation during the year ended December 31, 20X2, and the amount of royalties applicable thereto, under the license agreement referred to above.

This report is intended solely for the information and use of the boards of directors and management of XYZ Corporation and ABC Company and should not be used by anyone other than these parties.

Source: AU 623.18.

to the financial statements taken as a whole. Furthermore, the auditor should not express an opinion on the specified data when he or she has expressed an adverse opinion or disclaimed an opinion on the financial statements unless the specified data constitute only an insignificant portion of the financial statements. Finally, the use of the report is limited to parties who understand the royalty agreement.

COMPLIANCE REPORTS RELATED TO AUDITED FINANCIAL STATEMENTS

Audit Decision 6

■ Under what circumstances can an auditor audit and report on compliance with contractual agreements?

Companies may be required by contractual agreements or regulatory agencies to furnish compliance reports by independent auditors. For example, bond indentures often impose a variety of obligations on borrowers such as payments to sinking funds, maintenance of a minimum current ratio, and restrictions on dividend payments. In addition to requiring audited financial statements, lenders or their trustees often request assurance from the independent auditor that the borrower has complied with the accounting and auditing covenants of the agreement. The auditor satisfies this request by giving *negative assurance* on compliance by stating that "nothing came to our attention which would indicate that the company is not in compliance." AU 623.19 states that this assurance should not be given unless the auditor has audited the financial statements to which the agreements or regulatory requirements relate.

Furthermore, such assurance should not extend to covenants that relate to matters that have not been subjected to the audit procedures performed in the financial statement audit, and should not be given when the audit resulted in an adverse opinion or a disclaimer of opinion.

The auditor's assurance on compliance may be given in a separate report or in one or more explanatory paragraphs following the opinion paragraph of the report on the audited financial statements. The report language should restrict the distribution of the information on negative assurance to parties within the entity (such as the board of directors), parties to the loan agreement, or the regulatory agency. A separate report on debt compliance is illustrated in Figure 20-6.

Figure 20-6 ■ Special Report on Debt Compliance Given as a Separate Report

Independent Auditor's Report

We have audited, in accordance with auditing standards generally accepted in the United States of America, the balance sheet of XYZ Company as of December 31, 20X2, and the related statements of income, retained earnings, and cash flows for the year then ended, and have issued our report thereon dated February 16, 20X3.

In connection with our audit, nothing came to our attention that caused us to believe that the company failed to comply with the terms, covenants, provisions, or conditions of sections XX to XX, inclusive of the indenture dated July 20, 20X0, with ABC Bank insofar as they relate to accounting matters. However, our audit was not directed primarily toward obtaining knowledge of such noncompliance.

This report is intended solely for the information and use of the boards of directors and management of XYZ Company and ABC Bank and is not intended to be and should not be used by anyone other than these specified parties.

Source: AU 623.21.

LEARNING CHECK

20-1   a. Describe four basic levels of assurance that can be rendered by CPAs in a variety of engagements.

       b. Identify three groups of professional standards that are issued by the Auditing Standards Board. Briefly describe the types of professional services that are covered by each group of standards.

20-2   a. What types of reports are encompassed by the term *special reports* as described in AU 623?

       b. State the common characteristics of the types of data covered by special reports.

20-3   a. When is a basis of accounting considered to be an other comprehensive basis of accounting (OCBOA)?

       b. Explain the effects on the auditor's standard report when reporting on financial statements prepared on an OCBOA.

20-4   a. Describe the types of circumstances when the auditor would be asked to report on specified elements, accounts, or items of a financial statement.

       b. Describe the auditor's report for an engagement where he or she audits specified elements, accounts, or items of a financial statement.

20-5   a. Under what circumstances may an auditor provide negative assurance in a compliance report related to audited financial statements?

       b. What are the reporting options for conveying negative assurance in these circumstances?

KEY TERMS

Accounting and compilation services, p. 937
Agreed-upon procedures, p. 937
Assurance services, p. 935
Audit or examination-level assurance, p. 937
Negative assurance, p. 937
No assurance, p. 937
Other comprehensive basis of accounting (OCBOA), p. 939

Special reports, p. 938
Review-level assurance, p. 937
Statements on Auditing Standards (SAS), p. 938
Statements on Standards for Accounting and Review Services (SSARS), p. 938
Statements on Standards for Attestation Engagements (SSAE), p. 938

ACCEPTING AND PERFORMING ATTEST ENGAGEMENTS

Audit Decision 7

■ What are the attestation standards, and how to they compare with GAAS?

In 1986, the AICPA issued the first in a new series of authoritative statements entitled **Statements on Standards for Attestation Engagements (SSAE),** which are intended to provide guidance and establish a broad framework for performing and reporting on attest services. **Attest services** are engagements in which a certified public accountant in the practice of public accounting (often referred to as the practitioner) is engaged to issue or does issue an examination, a review, or an agreed-upon procedures report on subject matter, or an assertion about the subject matter (the assertion), that is the responsibility of another party.

A CPA should accept only those **attest engagements** that can be completed in accordance with the attestation standards described in the next section. In performing an attest engagement, a CPA (1) gathers evidence to support the assertion, (2) objectively assesses the measurements and communications of the individual making the assertion, and (3) reports the findings. Thus, because they are concerned primarily with the basis and support for written assertions, attest services are analytical, critical, and investigative in nature.

A variety of services do not involve attesting to the reliability of a written assertion that is the responsibility of another party. Examples of CPA services that would not be considered attest engagements include

■ Management consulting engagements in which the practitioner is engaged to provide advice or recommendations to a client.

■ Engagements in which the practitioner is engaged to advocate a client's position—for example, tax matters being reviewed by the Internal Revenue Service.

■ Tax engagements in which a practitioner is engaged to prepare tax returns or provide tax advice.

■ Engagements in which the practitioner compiles financial statements, because he or she is not required to examine or review any evidence supporting the information furnished by the client and does not express any conclusion on its reliability.

■ Engagements in which the practitioner's role is solely to assist the client—for example, acting as the company accountant in preparing information other than financial statements.

■ Engagements in which a practitioner is engaged to testify as an expert witness in accounting, auditing, taxation, or other matters.

■ Assurance services such as CPA Risk Advisory or CPA Performance View (see pp. 965–968).

ATTESTATION STANDARDS

In an attest engagement, the CPA must meet the 11 general **attestation standards** presented in SSAE 1. These standards are shown in Figure 20-7 where they are compared with the 10 generally accepted auditing standards (GAAS) with which we are already familiar.

As the figure shows, the attestation standards, like GAAS, are classified into three categories: general, fieldwork, and reporting. Comparison of the standards in each category reveals that the attestation standards are a natural extension of GAAS to accommodate the broader array of attest services. However, several significant conceptual differences between the two sets of standards may be observed. Specifically, the attestation standards:

■ Extend the attest function beyond historical financial statements. Thus, the standards omit references to financial statements and to GAAP.

■ Allow the CPA to give assurances on the assertions below the level of the "positive expression of opinion" associated with the traditional financial statement audit.

■ Provide for attest services tailored to the needs of specific users based on "agreed-upon procedures" and "limited-use" reports.

Figure 20-7 ■ Attestation Standards Compared with GAAS

Attestation Standards	General Accepted Auditing Standards
General Standards	
1. The engagement shall be performed by a practitioner or practitioners having adequate technical training and proficiency in the attest function.	1. The audit is to be performed by a person or persons having adequate technical training and proficiency as an auditor.
2. The engagement shall be performed by a practitioner or practitioners having adequate knowledge in the subject matter of the assertion.	
3. The practitioner shall perform the engagement only if he or she has reason to believe that the subject matter is capable of evaluation against criteria that are suitable and available to users.	
4. In all matters relating to the engagement, an independence in mental attitude shall be maintained by the practitioner or practitioners.	2. In all matters relating to the assignment, an independence in mental attitude is to be maintained by the auditor or auditors.
5. Due professional care shall be exercised in the performance of the engagement.	3. Due professional care is to be exercised in the planning and performance of the examination and the preparation of the report
Standards of Fieldwork	
1. The work shall be adequately planned and assistants, if any, shall be properly supervised.	1. The work is to be adequately planned and assistants, if any, are to be properly supervised.
	2. A sufficient understanding of the entity and its environment, including its internal control, should be obtained to assess the risk of material misstatement of the financial statements whether due to error or fraud, and to design the nature, timing and extent of further audit procedures.
2. Sufficient evidence shall be obtained to provide a reasonable basis for the conclusion that is expressed in the report.	3. Sufficient competent audit evidence should be obtained through audit procedures performed to afford a reasonable basis for an opinion regarding the financial statements under audit.
Standards of Reporting	
1. The report shall identify the assertion being reported on and state the character of the engagement.	1. The report shall state whether the financial statements are presented in accordance with generally accepted accounting principles.
2. The report shall state the practitioner's conclusion about the reliability of the assertion based on the established or stated criteria against which it was measured.	2. The report shall state whether such principles have been consistently observed in the current period in relation to the preceding period.
3. The report shall state all of the practitioner's significant reservations about the engagement and the assertion.	3. Informative disclosures in the financial statements are to be regarded as reasonably adequate unless otherwise stated in the report.
4. The report shall state that the use of the report is restricted to specified parties under the following circumstances: • When the criteria used to evaluate the subject matter are determined by the practitioner to be appropriate only for a limited number of parties who either participated in their establishment or can be presumed to have an adequate understanding of the criteria • When the criteria used to evaluate the subject matter are available only to specified parties • When reporting on subject matter and a written assertion has not been provided by the responsible party • When the report is on an attest engagement to apply agreed-upon procedures to the subject matter.	4. The report shall either contain an expression of opinion regarding the financial statements, taken as a whole, or an assertion to the effect that an opinion cannot be expressed. When an overall opinion cannot be expressed, the reasons therefor should be stated. In all cases where an auditor's name is associated with financial statements, the report should contain a clear-cut indication of the character of the auditor's examination, if any, and the degree of responsibility he is taking.

Source: Introduction to Attestation Standards.

The two new general standards (numbers 2 and 3) establish the boundaries for attest services. This type of service is limited to engagements in which (1) the CPA has adequate knowledge of the subject matter of the assertion and (2) the assertion is capable of evaluation against criteria that are suitable to users. Though not explicitly stated in the general standards, the definition of an attest engagement given in SSAE 1 requires that the assertion be in writing.

The second standard of fieldwork under GAAS requires the auditor to obtain an understanding of internal control, however, obtaining an understanding of internal control is not applicable in all attest engagements.

The separate GAAS reporting standards pertaining to consistency and informative disclosures are encompassed, when applicable, in the second attestation standard of reporting which requires a conclusion as to whether the assertions are presented in conformity with established criteria. The fourth attestation standard of reporting explicitly acknowledges the "limited-use" attribute of many attestation reports that impose restrictions on their distribution.

ENGAGEMENTS PERFORMED UNDER ATTESTATION STANDARDS

Figure 20-8 provides a summary of engagements that a CPA can perform under Statements on Standards for Attestation Engagements (SSAEs). This figure provides an overview of the attest services and describes the levels of assurance associated with each attest service. The following discussion focuses on four of these engagements:

- SSAE 101 engagements
- Agreed-upon procedures engagements
- Prospective financial information (forecast and projections)
- Compliance attestations

The standards for reporting on internal controls for public companies are governed by PCAOB Standard No. 2, *An Audit of Internal Control over Financial Reporting Conducted in Conjunction with an Audit of Financial Statements.*

SSAE 101 ENGAGEMENTS

Early in 2000, the AICPA Assurance Services Executive Committee endorsed principles and criteria for two types of engagements, CPA **WebTrust** and CPA **SysTrust.** Both of these assurance services are designed to meet the needs expressed by decision makers for assurance about the reliability of information systems, particularly those associated with electronic commerce. Each of these services results in a report issued under SSAE 101.

CPA WebTrust

Audit Decision 8

■ What are the basic principles for a WebTrust engagement?

Electronic commerce (e-commerce) grew dramatically in the last two decades. The growth of the World Wide Web has been accompanied by many businesses using the Web to conduct business, to both market and sell their products to customers. However, many consumers perceive that the risks of doing business electronically outweigh the advantages of e-commerce.

Figure 20-8 ■ Summary of Engagements Covered by Statements on Standards for Attestation Engagements

SSAE Section	Nature of Attest Engagement	Type of Assurance
101	Attest Engagements—This section sets forth attestation standards and provides guidance to a practitioner regarding general attest engagements. The standard establishes a framework for general attest engagements developed around the attestation standards explained in Figure 20-7. Two assurance services performed under SSAE 101 include WebTrust and SysTrust.	Examination Review Agreed-upon Procedures
201	Agreed-upon Procedure Engagements—This section sets forth attestation standards and provides guidance to a practitioner concerning performance and reporting in all agreed-upon procedures engagements, except those covered by other specific professional standards.	Agreed-upon Procedures
301	Financial Forecasts and Projections A **financial forecast** is a prospective financial statement that presents, to the best of the responsible party's knowledge and belief, an entity's expected financial position, results of operations, and cash flows. A **financial projection** is a prospective financial statement that presents, to the best of the responsible party's knowledge and belief, given one or more hypothetical assumptions, an entity's expected financial position, results of operations, and cash flows.	Examination Agreed-upon Procedures Compilation
401	Reporting on Pro Forma Information The objective of **pro forma financial information** is to show what the significant effects on historical financial information might have been had a consummated or proposed transaction (or event) occurred at an earlier date. Pro forma financial information is commonly used to show the effects of transactions such as a business combination, the disposition of a significant portion of the business, or a change in the form of business organization or status as an autonomous entity.	Examination Review
501	Reporting on an Entity's Internal Controls—This section provides guidance regarding: • Conditions that must be met for a practitioner to accept an engagement to examine the effectiveness of an entity's internal control; the prohibition of acceptance of an engagement to review such subject matter. • Engagements to examine the design and operating effectiveness of an entity's internal control. • Engagements to examine the design and operating effectiveness of a segment of an entity's internal control. • Engagements to examine only the suitability of design of an entity's internal control (no assertion is made about the operating effectiveness of the internal control). • Engagements to examine the design and operating effectiveness of an entity's internal control based on criteria established by a regulatory agency.	Examination
601	Compliance Attestations—This section provides guidance for engagements related to management's written assertion about either • An entity's compliance with requirements of specified laws, regulations, rules, contracts, or grants, or • The effectiveness of an entity's internal control over compliance with specified requirements.	Examination Agreed-upon Procedures
701	Management's Discussion and Analysis—This section sets forth attestation standards and provides guidance to a practitioner concerning the performance of an attest engagement with respect to management's discussion and analysis (MD&A) prepared pursuant to the rules and regulations adopted by the Securities and Exchange Commission (SEC), which are presented in annual reports to shareholders and in other documents.	Examination Review

These risks include concerns about

- An entity's **business and information privacy practices**—that is, whether the entity discloses its business and information privacy practices for e-commerce transactions and executes transactions in accordance with its disclosed practices.
- **Transaction integrity**—that is, whether the entity maintains effective controls to provide reasonable assurance that customers' transactions using e-commerce are completed and billed as agreed.
- **Information protection**—that is, whether the entity maintains effective controls to provide reasonable assurance that the private customer information obtained as a result of e-commerce is protected from uses not related to the entity's business.

WebTrust was developed jointly by the AICPA and the Canadian Institute for Chartered Accountants (CICA) to provide assurance to e-commerce consumers about these risks.

The principles followed in a WebTrust engagement are summarized in Figure 20-9 along with example criteria. Three WebTrust principles were developed around the risks of (1) business and information privacy practices, (2) transaction integrity, and (3) information protection. In the United States a WebTrust engagement is performed as an attest engagement under SSAE 101. The WebTrust client makes an assertion about whether it met the WebTrust principles and criteria, and about its business practices, its internal controls related to executing the transaction as agreed with a customer using e-commerce, and its internal controls related to the privacy of customer information. Organizations that use the WebTrust service and seal include the American Red Cross, Baltimore Technologies, Bell Canada, and Verisign.

CPA SysTrust

Audit Decision 9

- What are the basic principles and criteria for a SysTrust engagement?

A current trend in business practices involves outsourcing services that are important to an organization but are not part of the organization's core competencies. Organizations are also entering into strategic alliances to more efficiently and effectively accomplish organizational goals. For example, many of the state CPA societies have entered into a shared-services network to develop a common database and join together many of their common backroom functions. Through this alliance, state CPA societies will be able to put together the resources to accomplish what no one could accomplish individually. As organizations enter into these alliances, partnerships, joint venture agreements, and outsourcing arrangements, they have concerns about the reliability of the data and information that they share in common. Will member data be adequately safeguarded? Does the underlying system produce reliable information to support decision making? SysTrust was developed jointly by the AICPA and the CICA to provide this level of assurance about system reliability.

Figure 20-10 summarizes the SysTrust principles and criteria. The goal is to provide the user of a SysTrust report with assurance about the overall reliability of the system used for decision making, as defined by these four characteristics. The CPA can attest to all four SysTrust principles or any one SysTrust principle.

For each principle the criteria are organized into three categories. The first is *communications*, which addresses whether the entity has defined performance

Figure 20-9 ■ WebTrust Principles

Business and Information Privacy Practices	The entity discloses its business and information privacy practices for e-commerce transactions and executes transactions in accordance with its disclosed practices. *Example Criteria*
	• The entity discloses descriptive information about the nature of the goods that will be shipped or the services that will be provided, including, but not limited to, the following:
	  • Condition of goods (meaning, whether they are new, used, or reconditioned).
	  • Description of services (or service contract).
	• The entity discloses the terms and conditions by which it conducts its e-commerce transactions including but not limited to the following:
	  • Time frame for completion of transactions (transaction means fulfillment of orders where goods are being sold and delivery of service where a service is being provided).
	• The entity discloses on its web site (and/or in information provided with the product) where customers can obtain warranty, repair service, and support related to the goods and services purchased on its web site.
	• The entity discloses on its web site its information privacy practices. These practices include but are not limited to the following disclosures.

Transaction Integrity	The entity maintains effective controls to provide reasonable assurance that customers' transactions using e-commerce are completed and billed as agreed. *Example Criteria*
	• The entity maintains controls to provide reasonable assurance that:
	  • Each request or transaction is checked for accuracy and completeness.
	  • Positive acknowledgment is received from the customer before the transaction is processed
	• The entity maintains controls to provide reasonable assurance that:
	  • Sales prices and all other costs/fees are displayed for the customer before processing the transaction.
	  • Transactions are billed and electronically settled as agreed.

Information Protection	The entity maintains effective controls to provide reasonable assurance that private customer information obtained as a result of e-commerce is protected from uses not related to the entity's business. *Example Criteria* • The entity maintains controls to protect transmissions of private customer information over the Internet from unintended recipients. • The entity maintains controls to protect private customer information obtained as a result of e-commerce and retained in its system from outsiders.

objectives, policies, and standards for each principle. The second is *procedures*, which addresses whether the entity uses procedures, people, software, data, and infrastructure to achieve each principle. The final area is *monitoring*, which addresses whether an entity monitors the system and takes actions to achieve compliance with the principles.

In the United States, a SysTrust engagement is performed as an attest engagement under either AT 101, *Attest Engagements*, or AT 201, *Agreed-Upon Procedures Engagements.* The SysTrust client makes an assertion about whether it met the SysTrust principles and criteria. In other words, management makes an assertion

Figure 20-10 ■ SysTrust Principles and Criteria

SysTrust Principles	Broad SysTrust Criteria
Availability: The system is available for operation and use at times set forth in the service-level statements or agreements.	1. The entity has defined and communicated performance objectives, policies, and standards for system availability. 2. The entity utilizes procedures, people, software, data, and infrastructure to achieve system availability objectives in accordance with established policies and standards. 3. The entity monitors the system and takes action to achieve compliance with system availability objectives, policies, and standards.
Security: The system is protected against unauthorized physical and logical access.	1. The entity has defined and communicated performance objectives, policies, and standards for system security. 2. The entity utilizes procedures, people, software, data, and infrastructure to achieve system security objectives in accordance with established policies and standards. 3. The entity monitors the system and takes action to achieve compliance with system security objectives, policies, and standards.
Integrity: Systems processing is complete, accurate, timely, and authorized.	1. The entity has defined and communicated performance objectives, policies, and standards for system processing integrity. 2. The entity utilizes procedures, people, software, data, and infrastructure to achieve system processing integrity objectives in accordance with established policies and standards. 3. The entity monitors the system and takes action to achieve compliance with system processing integrity objectives, policies, and standards.
Maintainability: The system can be updated when required in a manner that continues to provide for system availability, security, and integrity.	1. The entity has defined and communicated performance objectives, policies, and standards for system maintainability. 2. The entity utilizes procedures, people, software, data, and infrastructure to achieve system maintainability objectives in accordance with established policies and standards. 3. The entity monitors the system and takes action to achieve compliance with system maintainability objectives, policies, and standards.

Source: AICPA/CICA SysTrust™ Principles and Criteria for Systems Reliability, Version 2.0, AICPA/CICA, 2001.

about the reliability of the system in terms of availability, security, integrity, and maintainability. According to the *AICPA/CICA SysTrust Principles and Criteria for Systems Reliability, Version 2.0,* the CPA may report on either of the following:

■ Management's assertion that it maintained effective controls over the reliability of the system during the period covered by the report.

■ The subject matter—that is, the effectiveness of controls over the system's reliability during the period covered by the report. If one or more criteria have not been achieved, the practitioner can issue a qualified or adverse report.

However, when issuing a qualified or adverse report, the practitioner should report directly on the subject matter rather than on the assertion. Since the concept of system reliability is dynamic rather than static, SysTrust reports will always cover a historical period of time as opposed to a point in time. Although the determination of an appropriate period should be at the discretion of the CPA and the reporting entity, the AICPA/CICA report on principles and criteria suggests that reporting periods of less than three months generally would not be deemed meaningful.

AGREED-UPON PROCEDURES ENGAGEMENTS

<table>
<tr><td>**Audit Decision 10**</td></tr>
<tr><td>■ What conditions must be met in order to accept an agreed-upon procedures engagement?</td></tr>
</table>

The application of **agreed-upon procedures** does not constitute an audit. This type of service might occur, for example, in a proposed acquisition when the prospective purchaser asks the accountant only to reconcile bank balances and confirm the accounts receivable. AT 201, *Agreed-upon Procedure Engagements,* states that an independent accountant may accept an engagement to apply agreed-upon procedures to specified elements, accounts, or items in a financial statement under the conditions identified in Figure 20-11.

In order to ensure that all the specified parties understand the agreed-upon procedures and take responsibility for the sufficiency of those procedures, the accountant will ordinarily communicate directly with and obtain affirmative acknowledgment from each of the specified parties. The accountant's responsibility in an agreed-upon procedures engagement is to carry out the procedures and report the findings in accordance with the applicable general, fieldwork, and reporting standards.

An accountant should present the results of applying agreed-upon procedures to specific subject matter in the form of a **report of procedures and findings.** The CPA should not give negative assurance in the report of findings and should avoid vague or ambiguous language in reporting findings. Figure 20-12 provides some examples of appropriate and inappropriate descriptions of findings.

Figure 20-11 ■ Conditions for Accepting an Agreed-Upon Procedures Engagement

a. The practitioner is independent.
b. One of the following conditions is met.
  (1) The party wishing to engage the practitioner is responsible for the subject matter, or has a reasonable basis for providing a written assertion about the subject matter when the nature of the subject matter is such that a responsible party does not otherwise exist.
  (2) The party wishing to engage the practitioner is not responsible for the subject matter but is able to provide the practitioner, or have a third party who is responsible for the subject matter provide the practitioner with evidence of the third party's responsibility for the subject matter.
c. The practitioner and the specified parties agree upon the procedures performed or to be performed by the practitioner.
d. The specified parties take responsibility for the sufficiency of the agreed-upon procedures for their purposes.
e. The specific subject matter to which the procedures are to be applied is subject to reasonably consistent measurement.
f. Criteria to be used in the determination of findings are agreed upon between the practitioner and the specified parties.
g. The procedures to be applied to the specific subject matter are expected to result in reasonably consistent findings using the criteria.
h. Evidential matter related to the specific subject matter to which the procedures are applied is expected to exist to provide a reasonable basis for expressing the findings in the practitioner's report.
i. Where applicable, the practitioner and the specified parties agree on any materiality limits for reporting purposes.
j. Use of the report is restricted to the specified parties.
k. For agreed-upon procedures engagements on prospective financial information, the prospective financial statements include a summary of significant assumptions.

Figure 20-12 ■ Descriptions of Findings and Conclusions

Agreed-upon Procedures	Appropriate Description of Findings	Inappropriate Description of Findings
Inspect the shipment dates for a sample (agreed-upon) of specified shipping documents, and determine whether any such dates were subsequent to December 31, 20XX.	No shipment dates shown in the sample of shipping documents were subsequent to December 31, 20XX.	Nothing came to my attention as a result of applying that procedure.
Calculate the number of blocks of streets paved during the year ended September 30, 20XX, shown on contractors' certificates of project completion; compare the resultant number to the number in an identified chart of performance statistics.	The number of blocks of streets paved in the chart of performance statistics was Y blocks more than the number calculated from the contractors' certificates of project completion.	The number of blocks of streets paved approximated the number of blocks included in the chart of performance statistics.
Inspect the quality standards classification codes in identified performance test documents for products produced during a specified period; compare such codes to those shown in an identified computer printout.	All classification codes inspected in the identified documents were the same as those shown in the computer printout except for the following: [List all exceptions.]	All classification codes appeared to comply with such performance documents.

Source: AT 201.26.

AT 201.31 states that the accountant's report should contain the following elements:

- A title that includes the word *independent*
- Identification of the specified parties
- Identification of the subject matter (or the written assertion related thereto) and the character of the engagement
- Identification of the responsible party
- A statement that the subject matter is the responsibility of the responsible party
- A statement that the procedures performed were those agreed to by the specified parties identified in the report
- A statement that the agreed-upon procedures engagement was conducted in accordance with attestation standards established by the AICPA
- A statement that the sufficiency of the procedures is solely the responsibility of the specified parties and a disclaimer of responsibility for the sufficiency of those procedures
- A list of the procedures performed (or reference thereto) and related findings.
- Where applicable, a description of any agreed-upon materiality limits
- A statement that the practitioner was not engaged to and did not conduct an examination of the subject matter, the objective of which would be the expression of an opinion, a disclaimer of opinion on the subject matter, and a statement that if the practitioner had performed additional procedures, other matters might have come to his or her attention that would have been reported

- A statement of restrictions on the use of the report because it is intended to be used solely by the specified parties
- Where applicable, reservations or restrictions concerning procedures or findings
- Where applicable, a description of the nature of the assistance provided by a specialist
- The manual or printed signature of the practitioner's firm
- The date of the report

REPORTING ON PROSPECTIVE FINANCIAL INFORMATION

Prospective financial information is generally provided in public offerings of bonds and other securities. In addition, banks and other lending institutions often insist on projections of future earnings in extending credit to individuals and companies, and governmental agencies sometimes require forecasts in applications for grants and government contracts. To enhance the reliability of the prospective financial information, CPAs may be asked to become associated with such data.

Types of Prospective Financial Information

Audit Decision 11

■ What is the difference between a financial forecast and a projection, and what levels of assurance can be provided on prospective financial statements?

AT 301.08 recognizes two types of **prospective financial information** as follows:

- *Financial forecast*—Prospective financial statements that present, to the best of the responsible party's knowledge and belief, an entity's expected financial position, results of operations, and cash flows. A financial forecast is based on the responsible party's assumptions reflecting the conditions it expects to exist and the course of action it expects to take. A financial forecast may be expressed in specific monetary amounts as a single-point estimate of forecasted results or as a range, where the responsible party selects key assumptions to form a range within which it reasonably expects, to the best of its knowledge and belief, the item or items subject to the assumptions to actually fall. When a forecast contains a range, the range is not selected in a biased or misleading manner, for example, a range in which one end is significantly less expected than the other.
- *Financial projection*—Prospective financial statements that present, to the best of the responsible party's knowledge and belief, given one or more hypothetical assumptions, an entity's expected financial position, results of operations, and cash flows. A financial projection is sometimes prepared to present one or more hypothetical courses of action for evaluation, as in response to a question such as, "What would happen if…?" A financial projection is based on the responsible party's assumptions reflecting conditions it expects would exist and the course of action it expects would be taken, given one or more hypothetical assumptions. A projection, like a forecast, may contain a range.

A financial forecast and a financial projection differ in terms of assumptions and the expected course of action. A forecast is based on conditions expected to exist and the course of action expected to be taken. In contrast, a projection involves one or more hypothetical courses of action. Both a forecast and a projection may be stated either as a single-point estimate or as a range. The two types of prospective financial information also differ as to use; a forecast is appropriate for general use, whereas a projection is for limited use by the entity alone or by the entity and third parties with whom the entity is negotiating directly.

A CPA may accept an engagement to perform one of three types of services pertaining to prospective financial statements when third-party use is anticipated: (1) compilation (preparation), (2) examination, and (3) application of agreed-upon procedures. The compilation does not result in the expression of any assurance (positive or negative) on the prospective statements. The other types of service constitute attestation engagements in which the CPA must satisfy the 11 attestation standards.

Examination of Prospective Financial Statements

AT 301.29 indicates that an **examination** of prospective financial statements involves (1) evaluating the preparation of the prospective financial statements, (2) evaluating the support underlying the assumptions, (3) evaluating the presentation of the prospective financial statements for conformity with AICPA presentation guidelines, and (4) issuing an examination report.

Standard Report on Prospective Financial Statements

AT 301.33 provides that the CPA's standard report on an examination of prospective financial statements should include:

- A title that includes the word *independent*
- Identification of the prospective financial statements presented
- Identification of the responsible party and a statement that the prospective financial statements are the responsibility of the responsible party
- A statement that the practitioner's responsibility is to express an opinion on the prospective financial statements based on his or her examination
- A statement that the examination of the prospective financial statements was conducted in accordance with attestation standards established by the American Institute of Certified Public Accountants and, accordingly, included such procedures as the practitioner considered necessary in the circumstances
- A statement that the practitioner believes that the examination provides a reasonable basis for his or her opinion
- The practitioner's opinion that the prospective financial statements are presented in conformity with AICPA presentation guidelines and that the underlying assumptions provide a reasonable basis for the forecast or a reasonable basis for the projection given the hypothetical assumptions
- A caveat that the prospective results may not be achieved
- A statement that the practitioner assumes no responsibility to update the report for events and circumstances occurring after the date of the report
- The manual or printed signature of the practitioner's firm
- The date of the examination report

The suggested wording of a standard report on the examination of a financial forecast is illustrated in Figure 20-13.

Departures from Standard Report

As in the case of reports on historical financial statements, other types of opinions may be expressed on prospective financial statements. The circumstances and their effects on the CPA's opinion are as follows:

Figure 20-13 ■ Standard Report on Examination of Financial Forecast

Independent Accountant's Report
We have examined the accompanying forecasted balance sheet, statements of income, retained earnings, and cash flows of XYZ Company as of December 31, 20XX, and for the year then ending. XYZ Company's management is responsible for the forecast. Our responsibility is to express an opinion on the forecast based on our examination.   Our examination was conducted in accordance with attestation standards established by the American Institute of Certified Public Accountants and, accordingly, included such procedures as we considered necessary to evaluate both the assumptions used by management and the preparation and presentation of the forecast. We believe that our examination provides a reasonable basis for our opinion.   In our opinion, the accompanying forecast is presented in conformity with guidelines for presentation of a forecast established by the American Institute of Certified Public Accountants, and the underlying assumptions provide a reasonable basis for management's forecast. However, there will usually be differences between the forecasted and actual results, because events and circumstances frequently do not occur as expected, and those differences may be material. We have no responsibility to update this report for events and circumstances occurring after the date of this report.   *Source:* AT 301.34.

- If, in the practitioner's opinion, the prospective financial statements depart from AICPA presentation guidelines, he or she should express a qualified opinion or an adverse opinion. However, if the presentation departs from the presentation guidelines because it fails to disclose assumptions that appear to be significant, the practitioner should express an adverse opinion.
- If the practitioner believes that one or more significant assumptions do not provide a reasonable basis for the forecast, or a reasonable basis for the projection given the hypothetical assumptions, he or she should express an adverse opinion.
- If the practitioner's examination is affected by conditions that preclude application of one or more procedures he or she considers necessary in the circumstances, he or she should disclaim an opinion and describe the scope limitation in his or her report.

In each case, the report should contain an explanatory paragraph that describes the circumstances.

COMPLIANCE ATTESTATIONS

Audit Decision 12

■ What assurance can be provided in a compliance attestation performed in accordance with SSAEs?

Another area in which CPAs are increasingly being asked by regulatory bodies and others to perform additional services is in regard to an entity's **compliance with specified requirements** such as laws, regulations, contracts, rules, or grants. These requirements may be financial or nonfinancial in nature. For example, the Federal Depository Insurance Corporation Improvement Act of 1991 (FDICIA) requires certain insured depository institutions to engage independent accountants to perform agreed-upon procedures to test an institution's compliance with certain FDIC-designated "safety and soundness" laws and regulations. A nonfinancial example is the Environmental Protection Agency's (EPA) requirement that certain entities engage independent accountants to perform agreed-upon procedures regarding compliance with an EPA regulation that gasoline contain at least 2 percent oxygen.

Examination Engagements

The objective of the practitioner's examination procedures applied to an entity's compliance with specified requirements is to express an opinion on an entity's compliance, based on the specified criteria. To express such an opinion, the practitioner accumulates sufficient evidence about the entity's compliance with specified requirements, thereby restricting attestation risk to an appropriately low level. The CPA should consider attestation risk the same way he or she would consider audit risk. The attestation standards provide guidance on assessing inherent risk (including the risk of fraud), control risk, and detection risk. Furthermore, in an examination of an entity's compliance with specified requirements, the practitioner's consideration of materiality is affected by (a) the nature of the compliance requirements, which may or may not be quantifiable in monetary terms, (b) the nature and frequency of noncompliance identified with appropriate consideration of sampling risk, and (c) qualitative considerations, including the needs and expectations of the report's users. Most of the same logic that is used in an audit, including the consideration of subsequent events, applies to an examination of compliance with specified requirements.

Figure 20-14 provides an example of an examination report associated with an entity's compliance with specified requirements.

Agreed-upon Procedures Engagements

The AICPA issued *Compliance Attestation* (AT 601) to provide guidance to CPAs engaged to perform agreed-upon procedures on management's written assertions about (1) an entity's compliance with specified requirements, (2) the effectiveness of an entity's internal control over compliance (i.e., the process by which management obtains reasonable assurance of compliance with specified requirements), or

Figure 20-14 ■ Examination Report for Compliance with Specified Requirements

Independent Accountant's Report
We have examined [name of entity]'s compliance with [list specified compliance requirements] during the [period] ended [date]. Management is responsible for [name of entity]'s compliance with those requirements. Our responsibility is to express an opinion on [name of entity]'s compliance based on our examination.

Our examination was conducted in accordance with attestation standards established by the American Institute of Certified Public Accountants and, accordingly, included examining, on a test basis, evidence about [name of entity]'s compliance with those requirements and performing such other procedures as we considered necessary in the circumstances. We believe that our examination provides a reasonable basis for our opinion. Our examination does not provide a legal determination on [name of entity]'s compliance with specified requirements.

In our opinion, [name of entity] complied, in all material respects, with the aforementioned requirements for the year ended December 31, 20XX.

Source: AT 601.56. |

(3) both. The practitioner's procedures generally may be as limited or as extensive as the specified users desire, as long as the specified users:

- Agree upon the procedures performed or to be performed, and
- Take responsibility for the sufficiency of the agreed-upon procedures for their purposes.

To reduce the risk of misunderstandings between users and independent accountants, ordinarily the practitioner should communicate directly with and obtain affirmative acknowledgment from each of the specified users.

[LEARNING CHECK

20-6   a. Define an attest engagement.
   b. State the three major activities involved in performing an attest engagement.

20-7   a. How are attestation standards classified?
   b. Indicate the principal differences between the attestation standards and GAAS.

20-8   a. Identify six types of attest engagements that have been recognized in professional standards.
   b. Indicate the levels of assurance associated with each type.

20-9   a. Briefly describe the service known as CPA WebTrust.
   b. Describe three risks associated with electronic commerce that are addressed in a WebTrust engagement. How do these risks relate to the principles associated with a WebTrust engagement?
   c. What professional standards apply to a WebTrust engagement?
   d. Briefly describe the key components of the attest report associated with a WebTrust engagement.

20-10   a. Briefly describe the service known as CPA SysTrust.
   b. Identify four broad principles associated with a SysTrust engagement.
   c. Describe the three categories of criteria associated with each principle in a SysTrust engagement.
   d. What professional standards apply to a SysTrust engagement?
   e. Briefly describe the key components of the attest report associated with a SysTrust engagement.

20-11   a. What conditions should be met in order to accept an agreed-upon procedures engagement?
   b. What should be included in a practitioner's report on agreed-upon procedures?

20-12   a. Identify and distinguish between two types of prospective financial information.
   b. What matter should be covered in an accountant's examination report on prospective financial statements?
   c. Describe the conditions that result in a departure from the standard report for an examination of a financial forecast. What reports should be issued in each case?

20-13   a. What conditions must be met for an independent accountant to perform an agreed-upon procedures compliance attestation?

b. Who determines the procedures in an agreed-upon procedures compliance attestation?

c. Compare and contrast a financial statement audit and an examination of a compliance attestation.

[KEY TERMS

Agreed-upon procedures, p. 951
Attest engagements, p. 944
Attest services, p. 943
Attestation standards, p. 944
Availability, p. 950
Business and information privacy practices, p. 948
Compliance with specified requirements, p. 955
Examination, p. 954
Financial forecast, p. 947
Financial projection, p. 947
Information protection, p. 948
Integrity, p. 950

Maintainability, p. 950
Pro forma financial information, p. 947
Prospective financial information, p. 953
Report of procedures and findings, p. 951
Security, p. 950
Statements on Standards for Attestation Engagements (SSAE), p. 943
SysTrust, p. 946
Transaction integrity, p. 948
WebTrust, p. 946

[ACCOUNTING AND REVIEW SERVICES]

The Statements and Standards for Accounting and Review Services (SSARSs) were first developed in 1979 at a time when CPAs could provide only two levels of assurance on financial statements. CPAs could either audit financial statements, providing reasonable assurance that the financial statements were free of material misstatement, or provide no assurance about whether the financial statements were free of material misstatements in the form of unaudited financial statements. The SSARS review service was originally developed as a lower-cost and lower-assurance alternative to an audit of the financial statements of nonpublic companies. SSARSs were developed to meet the needs of small business and the users of financial statements on nonpublic companies.

The codification of Statements on Standards for Accounting and Review Services is referred to by AR section numbers associated with accounting and review services. AR 100.04 defines **nonpublic companies** as any entity other than (a) one whose securities trade in a public market either on a stock exchange (domestic or foreign) or in the over-the-counter market, including securities quoted only locally or regionally, (b) one that makes a filing with a regulatory agency in preparation for the sale of any class of its securities in a public market, or (c) a subsidiary, corporate joint venture, or other entity controlled by an entity covered by (a) or (b). SSARSs also provide guidance on reporting on personal financial statements and include an exemption for the preparation of personal financial statements that are included in written personal financial plans prepared by an accountant.

The following discussion focuses on two common types of engagements for nonpublic companies: a review and a compilation of financial statements. Students should also note that because these services are performed for nonpublic companies, often these engagements involve the review or compilation of OCBOA financial statements. Figure 20-15 summarizes the assurance provided by review and compilation services and the procedures that support that level of assurance. In any engagement performed under SSARS, the accountant should establish an understanding with the entity, preferably in writing, regarding the services to be performed. The understanding should include a description of the nature and limitations of the services to be performed and a description of the report the accountant expects to render. These services are substantially less than an audit. As a result, the understanding should also provide

- That the engagement cannot be relied upon to disclose errors, fraud, or illegal acts.
- That the accountant will inform the appropriate level of management of any material errors that come to his or her attention and any fraud or illegal acts that come to his or her attention, unless they are clearly inconsequential.

REVIEW OF FINANCIAL STATEMENTS

Audit Decision 13

■ What procedures should be performed to support a review and a compilation of the financial statements?

The purpose of a **review engagement** of the financial statements of a nonpublic entity is to perform inquiry and analytical procedures that provide the accountant with a reasonable basis for expressing limited assurance that there are no material modifications that should be made to the statements in order for them to be in conformity with GAAP (or OCBOA, if applicable). Figure 20-15 outlines the procedures that an accountant performs in supporting the expression of limited assurance on the financial statements.

The accountant's procedures are based primarily on inquiry and analytical procedures. The accountant should possess knowledge of the accounting principles and practices used by the industry and knowledge of the business, its organization and operating characteristics, and the nature of its assets, liabilities, revenues, and expenses that support effective use of inquiry and analytical procedures. Knowledge of the business often includes understanding the entity's products and services and important operating characteristics of the organization.

Analytical procedures are similar to those performed at the planning stages of an audit. The auditor should develop expectations considering the overall economy, the client's industry, and the client's business, before comparing actual results with expectations. Effective analytical procedures then lead to pointed inquiry about significant differences.

The accountant usually focuses on understanding the entity's strategy by making inquiries about actions taken at its board of directors meeting. Furthermore, the accountant makes inquiries of persons who have responsibility for financial and accounting matters about the entity's accounting principles and system of accounting for transactions and for developing information for the financial statements, and about such issues as changes in the entity's business activities or accounting practices or about subsequent events. Other inquiries should include:

- Unusual or complex situations that may have an effect on the financial statements.

Figure 20-15 ■ Summary of Accounting and Review Services

Review	Compilation
Assurance Express limited assurance that there are no material modifications that should be made to the statements in order for them to be in conformity with GAAP (or OCBOA, if applicable).	**Assurance** Presenting in the form of financial statements information that is the representation of management without undertaking to express any assurance on the statements.

Procedures
• The accountant should possess a level of knowledge of the accounting principles and practices of the industry in which the entity operates and an understanding of the entity's business that will provide him, through the performance of inquiry and analytical procedures, with a reasonable basis for expressing limited assurance that there are no material modifications that should be made to the financial statements in order for the statements to be in conformity with generally accepted accounting principles.
• The accountant's understanding of the entity's business should include a general understanding of the entity's organization, its operating characteristics, and the nature of its assets, liabilities, revenues, and expenses. This would ordinarily involve a general knowledge of the entity's production, distribution, and compensation methods, types of products and services, operating locations, and material transactions with related parties.
• The accountant's inquiry and analytical procedures should ordinarily consist of the following:
  ○ Inquiries concerning the entity's accounting principles and practices and the methods followed in applying them.
  ○ Inquiries concerning the entity's procedures for recording, classifying, and summarizing transactions, and accumulating information for disclosure in the financial statements, including the status of uncorrected misstatements identified in previous engagements.
  ○ Analytical procedures designed to identify relationships and individual items that appear to be unusual. The auditor should consider the general economy, the client's entire industry, and the client's company when evaluating results.
  ○ Inquiries concerning actions taken at meetings of stockholders, board of directors, committees of the board of directors, or comparable meetings that may affect the financial statements.
  ○ Inquiries about management's knowledge about any actual or suspected fraud that could have a material effect on the financial statements.
  ○ Inquiries about unusual or complex situations that may have an effect on the financial statements.
  ○ Inquiries about significant transactions occurring or recognized near the end of the reporting period, and inquiries about subsequent events.
  ○ Reading the financial statements to consider, on the basis of information coming to the accountant's attention, whether the financial statements appear to conform with generally accepted accounting principles.
  ○ Inquiries of persons having responsibility for financial and accounting matters concerning (1) whether the financial statements have been prepared in conformity with generally accepted accounting principles consistently applied, (2) changes in the entity's business activities or accounting principles and practices, (3) matters as to which questions have arisen in the course of applying the foregoing procedures, and (4) events subsequent to the date of the financial statements that would have a material effect on the financial statements.
• The accountant is required to obtain a representation letter from members of management whom the accountant believes are responsible for and knowledgeable, directly or through others in the organization, about the matters covered in the representation letter.
	Procedures
	• The accountant should possess a level of knowledge of the accounting principles and practices of the industry in which the entity operates that will enable him to compile financial statements that are appropriate in form for an entity operating in that industry.
	• The accountant should possess a general understanding of the nature of the entity's business transactions, the form of its accounting records, the stated qualifications of its accounting personnel, the accounting basis on which the financial statements are to be presented, and the form and content of the financial statements.
	• The accountant should read the compiled financial statements and consider whether such financial statements appear to be appropriate in form and free from obvious material errors.

- Significant transactions occurring or recognized near the end of the reporting period.
- The status of uncorrected misstatements identified during the previous engagement.
- Questions that have arisen in the course of applying the review procedures.
- Management's knowledge of any actual or suspected fraud that affects the entity and involves management or others where the fraud could have a material effect on the financial statements.
- Significant journal entries and other adjustments.
- Communications from regulatory agencies.

AR 100.30 states that a review does not contemplate obtaining an understanding of internal control or assessing control risk, tests of accounting records and of responses to inquiries by obtaining corroborating evidential matter, and certain other procedures ordinarily performed during an audit. Thus, a review does not provide assurance that the accountant will become aware of all significant matters that would be disclosed in an audit. However, if the accountant becomes aware that information coming to his or her attention is incorrect, incomplete, or otherwise unsatisfactory, he or she should perform the additional procedures he or she deems necessary to achieve limited assurance that there are no material modifications that should be made to the financial statements in order for the statements to be in conformity with GAAP or OCBOA.

A sample standard review report recommended in AR 100.40 is shown in Figure 20-16.

<table>
<tr><td>

Audit Decision 14

- What language should be used for a review and a compilation report?

</td></tr>
</table>

COMPILATION OF FINANCIAL STATEMENTS

The purpose of a **compilation engagement** is to present in the form of financial statements information that is the representation of management without undertaking to express any assurance on the statements. Many small businesses rely on

Figure 20-16 ■ Accountant's Report on SSARS Review of Financial Statements

Independent Accountant's Report

I (we) have reviewed the accompanying balance sheet of XYZ company as of December 31, 20XX, and the related statements of income, retained earnings, and cash flows for the year then ended, in accordance with Statements on Standards for Accounting and Review Services issued by the American Institute of Certified Public Accountants. All information included in these financial statements is the representation of management (owners) of XYZ company.

A review consists principally of inquiries of company personnel and analytical procedures applied to financial data. It is substantially less in scope than an audit in accordance with generally accepted auditing standards, the objective of which is the expression of an opinion regarding the financial statements taken as a whole. Accordingly, I (we) do not express such an opinion.

Based on my (our) review, I am (we are) not aware of any material modifications that should be made to the accompanying financial statements in order for them to be in conformity with generally accepted accounting principles.

Source: AR 100.40.

assistance from their CPAs to prepare financial information for their use in either managing the company or in submitting information about the company to a bank in support of a request for financing. CPAs perform the same types of services for small businesses that a CFO or controller might perform in preparing information for management of a large company.

The compilation engagement is directed at assisting management in the preparation of financial information—not at providing assurance about whether the information is free of material misstatement. As a result, it is important for the auditor to reach an understanding with the client about the purpose of the engagement and the fact that a compilation cannot be relied upon to find errors or fraud.

The accountant's procedures associated with a compilation engagement are directed at preparing information, not providing assurance about the information. As a result, the procedures depicted in Figure 20-15 focus on the accountant's knowledge of the accounting principles and practices of the industry, and an understanding of the nature of the entity's business transactions, the form of its accounting records, the stated qualifications of its accounting personnel, the accounting basis on which the financial statements are to be presented, and the form and content of the financial statements. With this knowledge the accountant should assess whether the entity needs other accounting services either in connection with the compilation or as a separate service. For example, the client may need assistance from the CPA in providing various bookkeeping or data processing services, in preparing a working trial balance, or in adjusting the general ledger.

When performing a compilation, AR 100.09 states that the accountant is not required to make inquiries or perform other procedures to verify, corroborate, or review information supplied by the entity. However, the accountant may have made inquiries or performed other procedures.

The results of such inquiries or procedures, knowledge gained from prior engagements, or the financial statements on their face may cause the accountant to become aware that information supplied by the entity is incorrect, incomplete, or otherwise unsatisfactory for the purpose of compiling financial statements. In these circumstances, the accountant should obtain additional or revised information. If the entity refuses to provide additional or revised information, the accountant should consider whether modification of his or her standard report is adequate to disclose the departure, or whether he or she should withdraw from the compilation engagement.

A sample standard compilation report recommended in AR 100.14 is shown in Figure 20-17. In some cases, management may want the accountant to compile finan-

Figure 20-17 ■ Accountant's Report on Compilation of Financial Statements

I (we) have compiled the accompanying balance sheet of XYZ Company as of December 31, 20XX, and the related statements of income, retained earnings, and cash flows for the year then ended, in accordance with Statements on Standards for Accounting and Review Services issued by the American Institute of Certified Public Accountants.

A compilation is limited to presenting in the form of financial statements information that is the representation of management (owners). I (we) have not audited or reviewed the accompanying financial statements and, accordingly, do not express an opinion or any other form of assurance on them.

Source: AR 100.14.

cial statements so that management can monitor the business, and management may decide that it does not need full disclosure financial statements for this purpose. As a result, management may ask the accountant to prepare financial statements that omit substantially all disclosures, or the statement of cash flows. When the accountant concludes that the omissions were not intended to mislead users, the only change from the standard report is the addition of the following paragraph.

Management has elected to omit substantially all of the disclosures (and the statement of cash flows) required by generally accepted accounting principles. If the omitted disclosures were included in the financial statements, they might influence the user's conclusions about the company's financial position, results of operation, and cash flows. Accordingly, these financial statements are not designed for those who are not informed about such matters.

The above language regarding management's election to omit substantially all disclosures was developed because of the accounting profession's concern that financial statements prepared for management might also be given to bankers or other individuals outside the company. An important service for small business may involve tapping the entity's financial records electronically, preparing financial statements for management, and returning financial statements to the company electronically. When an accountant submits compiled financial statements to his or her client that are not expected to be used by a third party, The CPA may:

- Issue a standard compilation report, and
- Document an understanding with the entity through the use of an engagement letter, preferably signed by management, regarding the services to be performed and the limitations on the use of those financial statements.

LEARNING CHECK

20-14 a. What is the objective of a review engagement of the financial statements of a nonpublic entity?

b. What is involved when a CPA reviews the financial statements of a nonpublic entity?

c. Describe the accountant's report for a review of the financial statements of a nonpublic entity.

20-15 a. What is the objective of a compilation engagement regarding the financial statements of a nonpublic entity?

b. What is involved when a CPA compiles the financial statements of a nonpublic entity?

c. Describe the accountant's report for a compilation of the financial statements of a nonpublic entity that omit substantially all disclosures.

KEY TERMS

Compilation engagement, p. 961
Nonpublic companies, p. 958
Review engagement, p. 959

Statements and Standards for
Accounting and Review Services
(SSARS), p. 958

[OTHER ASSURANCE SERVICES]

Three other assurance service opportunities are discussed in the remainder of this chapter. All of the previous services represent audit or attest services covered by Statements on Auditing Standards, Statements on Standards for Attestation Engagements, or Statements on Standards for Accounting and Review Services. These remaining assurance services lie on a continuum between the attest type engagements discussed above and consulting services. The level of assurance is flexible and depends on the need of the decision maker. Figure 20-18 compares assurance services with attestation services and consulting services.

Attestation services (e.g., audits, reviews, or other attestation engagements) involve providing a written conclusion attesting to the reliability of written information that is used by third parties. There are generally three parties in the engagement: the party preparing the information and determining the informa-

Figure 20-18 ■ Comparison of Attestation, Assurance, and Consulting Services

	Attestation	Assurance	Consulting
Result	Written conclusion about the reliability of the written assertions of another party	Better information for decision makers. Recommendations might be a by-product.	Recommendations based on the objectives of the engagement
Objective	Reliable information	Better decision making	Better outcomes
Parties to the engagement	Not specified, but generally three (the third party is usually external); CPA generally paid by the preparer	Generally three (although the preparer and user might be employed by the same entity); CPA paid by the preparer or user	Generally two; CPA paid by the user
Independence	Required by standards	Included in definition	Not required
Substance of CPA output	Conformity with established or stated criteria	Assurance about reliability or relevance of information. Criteria might be established, stated, or unstated	Recommendations; not measured against formal criteria
Form of CPA output	Written	Some form of communication	Written or oral
Critical information developed by	Asserter	Either CPA or asserter	CPA
Information content determined by	Preparer (client)	Preparer, CPA, or user	CPA
Level of assurance	Examination, review, or agreed-upon procedures	Flexible; for example, it might be compilation level, explicit assurance about usefulness of the information for intended purpose, or implicit from the CPA's involvement	No explicit assurance

tion content, the party using the information, and the CPA. Independence is required by standards such as GAAS or attestation standards, and the CPA prepares a written report expressing his or her conclusions.

At the other end of the spectrum, a consulting engagement is generally a two-party engagement between the CPA and his or her client. The objective of the consulting engagement is to improve organizational outcomes. Each engagement is custom made, and the CPA determines the information content of his or her report in a consulting engagement. Independence is not required, no explicit assurance is provided, and reports may be written or oral. The recommendations in a consulting engagement are not measured against established criteria such as GAAP, OCBOA, or the COSO standards on internal controls.

Assurance services lie along the spectrum between attestation engagements and consulting engagements. As stated earlier, the goal of assurance services is better decision making. When working to improve information for decision makers, the CPA will likely focus on improving the relevance of information, not just its reliability. The criteria used for the engagement will usually be tailored to the decision maker rather than using a one-size-fits-all criterion such as GAAP or OCBOA. Assurance engagements are more flexible than attest engagements; information may be developed by either the CPA or by an entity making an assertion; and the content of information may be determined by either the CPA, the preparer, or the user. The CPA provides an independent conclusion about information. A written report, however, is not required.

Two assurance opportunities discussed in the remainder of the chapter, CPA Risk Advisory and CPA Performance View, represent natural extensions of the financial statement audit. They are also grounded in research supporting the demand for these services, particularly by senior management and the board of directors. The final assurance service discussed in the chapter, CPA ElderCare, might be an extension of tax and financial planning services offered by CPAs.

CPA RISK ADVISORY

Audit Decision 15

■ What are the types of services that might be performed as part of a CPA Risk Advisory engagement?

Recall from Chapter 7 that the auditor should understand an entity's objectives, strategies, and related business risks. **Business risks** result from significant conditions, events, circumstances, or actions that could adversely affect the entity's ability to achieve its objectives and execute its strategies. **CPA Risk Advisory** is an assurance engagement on business risk assessment that might include any of the following types of services:

■ Identification and assessment of primary potential risks faced by a business or entity
■ Independent assessment of risks identified by an entity
■ Evaluation of an entity's systems for identifying and limiting risks

Hence, the nature of the CPA service depends on the risk assessment practices that exist within the entity. The foundation for any of these services is the knowledge about an entity's objectives, strategies, and related business risks obtained while performing the audit, and the decision maker's needs.

Organizations that manage risk well are more likely to achieve or exceed their objectives because they have the capacity and ability to, (1) identify and exploit opportunities, (2) identify and manage risks that could affect achieving their objectives, (3) make good decisions quickly, and (4) respond and adapt to unexpected events. Successful organizations take calculated risks to achieve objectives. They weigh opportunities against threats and act decisively. The traditional, negative definitions of risk—harm, loss, danger, and hazard—are only part of the story. The other and equally important part is opportunity.

Although each organization has its own unique approach to risk management, a number of consistent steps have emerged and represent current best practice.

- Establish the context.
- Identify risks.
- Analyze and assess risks.
- Design strategies for managing risk.
- Implement and integrate risk management.
- Measure, monitor, and report.

These steps can be applied to an entire enterprise, to part of the organization, or to a specific project. Although an enterprisewide program is the most effective, there is considerable value in beginning in a local or limited way.

The decision makers involved in a CPA Risk Advisory service are likely to be management and the board of directors, charged with oversight of the entity's operation and who need to consider the risks faced by the entity. Understanding an entity's business risk is a particularly important part of the strategic planning process for an entity. When the audit client is a small business, the owner–manager often seeks auditors with industry experience so that he or she might tap the CPA's knowledge of how to improve the business. In other words, the owner–manager is seeking the CPA's opinion on how to better manage the entity's business risks. Often, the board of directors, which has less day-to-day experience working with an entity, would like assurance about the entity's business risks because this service might provide leading indicators of an entity's eventual financial performance.

The auditor likely obtains knowledge of each of these risks while performing the financial statement audit. For example, the auditor might obtain knowledge about strategic environment risks associated with changes in customers' tastes and preferences or changes in the competitive environment when auditing the revenue and production cycles. The auditor often obtains knowledge of the risk of adverse changes in the market for the client's products in order to evaluate the net realizable value of the client's inventory. The auditor might obtain knowledge about operating environment risks related to inefficient business practices when auditing the production cycle. The auditor might obtain knowledge about information risks associated with poor-quality financial information when gaining an understanding of the entity's system of internal control. Finally, the auditor also considers these types of risks when evaluating whether an entity is likely to continue as a going concern. Understanding the client's business risks is important to making audit judgments regarding accounting estimates and evaluating the reasonableness of the entity's profitability. Hence, risk assessment services are a natural extension of the financial statement audit.

When performing such services, the independent auditor should be careful to maintain an advisory role. The independent CPA should not make management decisions or take other actions that would impair independence.

CPA PERFORMANCE VIEW

Audit Decision 16

■ What are the types of services that might be performed as part of a CPA Performance View engagement?

CPA Performance View is the AICPA's branded version of performance measurement. The AICPA has recognized performance measurement as a growing area that is well suited to the skill sets of CPAs, and builds on knowledge obtained during an audit. The purpose of a CPA Performance View engagement is to provide assurance regarding an organization's use of both financial and nonfinancial measures to evaluate the effectiveness and efficiency of its activities. These performance measures can be used for assessing performance at any level within an organization, or for assessing the performance of the entity as a whole. Performance measures can also be used to evaluate how the organization is performing in relation to others in the same industry.

The report of the AICPA Special Committee on Assurance Services discusses a spectrum of services that CPAs can provide. Each service could be performed as a separate engagement, or several could be combined into one engagement. The potential services are as follows:

For Organizations that Have Performance Measurement Systems

■ Assessing the reliability of information being reported from the organization's performance measurement system.

■ Assessing the relevance of the performance measures (that is, how well they inform management about achievement of the performance objectives they have set).

For Organizations that Do Not Have Performance Measurement Systems

■ Identifying relevant performance measures.

For All Organizations

■ Providing advice on how the organization can improve its performance measurement system and its actual results.

Potential users of CPA Performance View might include senior management and the board of directors. Senior management might use these services to: (1) assess whether their systems are properly measuring activities that are relevant to and consistent with their strategic objectives, (2) evaluate their employees, (3) measure actual performance against their objectives, or (4) identify those activities, processes, or functions that provide the best opportunities for improvement in performance. The board of directors might use this service to assist them with their oversight responsibilities.

Many organizations track their success based solely on past financial performance. Although an organization's history is an excellent way to see where it has been, it does not say much about where it is going. If a company earned $250,000 or $2 billion last year, what in the financial statements leads you to believe it will accomplish the same or better next year? Traditional performance tracking methods focus on sales, net income, gross margin, return on assets, asset turnover, and so on, but do not provide the needed information to anticipate the future. It is great news that gross margins are remaining high or increasing, but if customers are unhappy with service and are switching to competitors, what good is the information about margins? Although financial

Figure 20-19 ■ The Balanced Scorecard Approach to Performance Measurement

Customer Perspective
Example Goals
- Product quality

- Customer Satisfaction

- New Customer Acquisition

Example Meausres
- Measure of warranty claims
- Summary of product evaluation by independent rating agencies
- Measure of on-time delivery
- Customer satisfaction surveys
- Report of new customers ranked by volume of activity or gross profit margins

Internal Perspective
Example Goals
- Manufacturing efficiency
- Manufacturing effectiveness
- Service effectiveness

Example Measures
- Product cycle time
- Defects per million
- Transaction requests not fulfilled

Innovation Perspective
Example Goals
- Product innovation

Example Measures
- Percent of revenues from new products
- Number of suggestions made and implemented

Financial Perspective
Example Goals
- Revenue goals
- Overall financial goals

Example Measures
- Revenues by product mix
- Return on investment
- Cash flow generation

measures provide an accurate and detailed history, they do not provide guidance for the future.

CPA Performance View is a system that merges the standard financial measures with leading indicators, such as customer satisfaction, employee training and satisfaction, product quality, sales calls, and proposals delivered. By joining the two, an entity will have the ability to identify critical decision points that can lead to organizational change and better performance.

The balanced scorecard system suggested by Kaplan and Norton[1] has received considerable attention as an alternative system of performance measures. Under the balanced scorecard approach, an entity develops goals in each of four areas: (1) the customer perspective, (2) the internal perspective, (3) the innovation perspective, and (4) the financial perspective. It then develops performance measures relevant to its goals. Figure 20-19 provides some examples of how an organization might set goals and develop internal measures that are associated with those goals.

---

[1] Robert S. Kaplan and David P. Norton, *The Balanced Scorecard—Translating Strategy into Action* (Boston, MA: Harvard Business School Press, 1996).

CPA ELDERCARE

Audit Decision 17

■ What are the types of services that might be performed as part of a CPA ElderCare engagement?

The purpose of a **CPA ElderCare** engagement is to assure family members that elderly relatives no longer able to be totally independent are receiving the type of care they need. CPA ElderCare (ElderCare) might result in three different types of engagements.

1. *Attestation engagements,* such as a compliance attestation where the CPA performs tests of a health care facility's assertion that it complied with stated regulations or policies in accordance with AT 601, *Compliance Attestations.* Alternatively, the CPA might perform an agreed-upon procedure attestation where the CPA issues a report of procedures and findings associated with the measurable care-giving performance (AT 201, *Agreed-Upon Procedure Engagements*). An attest service might also include a review of the financial performance of a trust in accordance with AR 100, *Compilation and Review of Financial Statements.*
2. *Direct services,* such as paying bills for elderly individuals or ensuring that expected revenues are received in the process of managing an elderly individual's checking account. Performing direct services for an elderly client may impair independence associated with other services for that client.
3. *Consulting Services,* such as assisting the elderly or their families in determining the range of housing and care alternatives. Consulting services might also include performing such services as helping a family member monitor care or financial services such as estate planning or establishing a trusteeship. Figure 20-20 provides a listing of possible services that could be provided under the umbrella of an ElderCare engagement. The customer, or decision maker, of ElderCare services may be either an elderly individual who needs some form of assistance or care, or the family of an elderly individual who would like periodic reports on the care of an elderly relative.

The AICPA Special Committee on Assurance Services stated that one of the megatrends that will continue to affect the United States is the aging of the population. The Report of the AICPA Special Committee on Assurance Services reads as follows:

> The U.S. Bureau of the Census estimates that by the year 2000 16.6 million people in the United States will be 75 years of age or older; approximately 4.3 million people in the United States will be aged 85 and over. Many of these people will be widows who did not handle finances while their spouses were living. It is also estimated that persons age 65 and over controlled between $11 trillion and $13 trillion of wealth. Increasingly, people are living to ages where assistance is needed in remaining in their own homes or for institutional care. In the past, they normally relied on members of their families, many of whom lived close by, for this assistance. But now, younger adults often find it necessary for both spouses to work outside the home to provide an acceptable standard of living. As a result, the younger generation does not have the time available to care for aging parents. And as our society has become mobile in following job opportunities, many family members now live far away from their elders as the latter begin to require care and assistance.

The knowledge and experience that an auditor brings in performing a variety of audit and attestation engagements lend instant credibility to these new services. Auditors are skilled in evaluating financial and nonfinancial assertions and have experience in using experts, when necessary, to ensure that appropriate evidence is

Figure 20-20 ■ CPA ElderCare Services

Assurance Services
Financial
- Review and report on financial transactions
- Test for asserter's adherence to established criteria
- Review investments and trust activity
- Audit third-party calculations, such as pension, insurance, and annuity payouts
- Review reports from fiduciaries

Nonfinancial
- Measure and report on care provider performance against established goals
- Evaluate and report on the performance of other outside parties, such as contractors

Direct Services
Financial
- Receive, deposit, and account for client receipts
- Ensure expected revenues are received
- Make appropriate disbursements
- Submit claims to insurance companies
- Confirm accuracy of provider bills and appropriate reimbursements
- Protect the elderly by controlling the checkbook and other assets
- Provide income tax planning and return preparation
- Provide gift tax return preparation
- Prepare employment tax returns for caregivers and other household help

Nonfinancial
- Arrange for transportation, housekeeping, and other services
- Manage real estate and other property
- Visit and report on elderly on behalf of children in distant locations

Consulting Service
Financial
ElderCare Planning for
- Housing and support service needs

- Declining competency
- Death or disability of one or both spouses
- Alternative costs of retirement communities and other housing
- Housing and care alternatives
- Services available in the community
- Estate planning

Fiduciary planning for
- Financial power of attorney
- Health care power of attorney
- Guardianship
- Trusteeship
- Living wills
- Advanced medical directives

Evaluation of health care financing options for
- Medicare and Medicaid
- LTC insurance
- Medigap insurance
- HMOs
- Annuities
- Viatical insurance settlements
- Reverse mortgages
- Sales/leaseback of home
- Flexible spending accounts

Nonfinancial
Family facilitation
- Mediate/arbitrate family disputes
- Provide objectivity for highly emotional issues
- Act as a "go-between" between parent and child

Coordination of support and health care services
- Lead a team of health care, legal, and other professionals

Other consulting services
- Help family monitor care
- Establish standards of care expected
- Communicate expectations to care providers
- Establish performance measurement systems

Source: Karen Duggan, George Lewis, and Ann Elizabeth Sammon, "Opportunity Knocks: CPA ElderCare Services," *Journal of Accountancy,* December 1999, pp. 43–51.

obtained to support the auditor's expression of assurance. In some cases, the CPA may coordinate a team that includes other professionals such as geriatric care managers or social workers. When performing attestation services, the auditor needs to ensure that he or she has followed relevant professional standards and is independent.

The CPA who performs direct services for the client will often not be independent by the nature of the engagement. Nevertheless, this may be the best way to serve the decision-making needs of the elderly, or their family, who need the direct services of a trusted individual. CPAs who perform tax and personal financial planning services might be ideally positioned to assist clients who need these direct services.

[LEARNING CHECK

20-16 a. Describe the purpose of a risk assessment engagement. Who are the most likely customers of a risk assessment engagement?

b. Identify three major types of services associated with a risk assessment engagement.

c. Identify a useful way to categorize business risks.

d. Describe activities performed in the financial statement audit that prepare auditors for performing a business risk engagement.

20-17 a. Describe the purpose of a performance measurement engagement. Who are the most likely customers of a performance measurement engagement?

b. Identify several services that a CPA might offer in a performance measurement engagement.

c. What are the elements of the balanced scorecard? Give an example of each.

d. Describe activities performed in the financial statement audit that prepare auditors for performance measurement engagement.

20-18 a. Describe the purpose of a CPA ElderCare engagement. Who are the most likely customers of a CPA ElderCare engagement?

b. Describe three types of services that might be performed as part of a CPA ElderCare engagement. Provide an example of each.

c. Describe an important trend that motivates the need for CPA ElderCare engagements.

[KEY TERMS

Business risks, p. 965
CPA ElderCare, p. 969

CPA Performance View, p. 967
CPA Risk Advisory, p. 965

[FOCUS ON AUDIT DECISIONS]

This chapter focuses on a variety of services that represent an extension of the basic audit service. Figure 20-21 summarizes the audit decisions discussed in Chapter 20 and provides page references indicating where these decisions are discussed in more detail.

Figure 20-21 ■ Summary of Audit Decisions Discussed in Chapter 20

Audit Decision	Factors that Influence the Audit Decision	Chapter References
D1. What opinions can be used in an audit of the basic financial statements?	This is primarily covered in Chapter 2. See Figures 20-2 and 2-4.	pp. 935–936
D2. What are the primary options in terms of level of service that might be available for an attest engagement?	• Audit or examination level of assurance (reasonable assurance) • Review-level assurance (negative assurance) • Agreed-upon procedures assurance • No assurance	pp. 937–938
D3. What are the professional standards that cover most audit and attest engagements?	• Statements on Auditing Standards • Statements on Standards for Attestation Engagements • Statements on Standards for Accounting and Review Services	p. 938
D4. Under what circumstances can an auditor audit and report on financial statements prepared in accordance with an other comprehensive basis of accounting?	GAAS recognizes four comprehensive bases of accounting other than GAAP: • A basis used to comply with the requirements of a regulatory agency • A basis used to file the entity's income tax return • The cash receipts and disbursements basis of accounting • A basis that uses a definite set of criteria with substantial support such as the price-level basis of accounting	pp. 939–940
D5. Under what circumstances can an auditor audit and report on an individual element, account, or item of the financial statements?	An auditor is not limited to auditing the entire financial statements. An engagement to express an opinion on specified elements, accounts, or items may be made in conjunction with the audit of the financial statements or as a separate engagement. However, the report should include language that limits the use of the report to those who specifically need and understand the purpose of the engagement.	pp. 940–942
D6. Under what circumstances can an auditor audit and report on compliance with contractual agreements?	When an auditor audits the financial statements as a whole, the auditor may also provide review-level assurance that nothing came to the auditor's attention that led the firm to believe that the company was not in compliance with a contractual agreement.	p. 942
D7. What are the attestation standards, and how do they compare with GAAS?	Figure 20-7 identifies the five general standards, two fieldwork standards, and four reporting standards and compares them with GAAS.	pp. 943–947
D8. What are the basic criteria for a WebTrust engagement?	A WebTrust engagement addresses the risk associated with (1) business and information privacy practices, (2) transaction integrity, and (3) information protection.	pp. 946–948
D9. What are the basic principles and criteria for a SysTrust engagement?	A SysTrust engagement addresses four basic principles: (1) system availability, (2) system security, (3) system integrity, and (4) system maintainability. Each principle is organized into three criteria: communications, procedures, and monitoring.	pp. 948–951
D10. What conditions must be met in order to accept an agreed-upon procedures engagement?	The assurance provided by an agreed-upon procedures engagement depends on the procedures performed. As a result, Figure 20-11 outlines 11 conditions that are important to the acceptance of an agreed-upon procedures engagement.	pp. 951–953

(continues)

Figure 20-21 ■ (Continued)

Audit Decision	Factors that Influence the Audit Decision	Chapter References
D11: What is the difference between a financial forecast and a projection, and what levels of assurance can be provided on prospective financial statements?	A financial forecast represents an entity's best estimate of financial position, results of operations, and cash flows. A financial projection represents the financial position, results of operations, and cash flows that result from given hypothetical assumptions. A projection is a "what if" scenario. An auditor may provide examination, agreed-upon procedures, or compilation-level assurance (no assurance) on a forecast or projection.	pp. 953–955
D12. What assurance can be provided in a compliance attestation performed in accordance with SSAEs?	An auditor can audit compliance with laws, regulations, grants, or contracts under the Statements on Standards for Attestation Engagements. An auditor can provide either examination-level assurance or agreed-upon procedures assurance.	pp. 955–957
D13. What procedures should be performed to support a review and a compilation of the financial statements?	Figure 20-15 outlines the procedures required in both a compilation and a review engagement under Statements on Standards for Accounting and Review Services.	pp. 958–961
D14. What language should be used for a review and a compilation report?	Figure 20-16 provides an example review report, and Figure 20-17 provides an example compilation report.	pp. 961–963
D15. What are the types of services that might be performed as part of a CPA Risk Advisory engagement?	CPA Risk Advisory is an assurance engagement on business risk assessment that might include any of the following types of services: • Identification and assessment of primary potential risks faced by a business or entity • Independent assessment of risks identified by an entity • Evaluation of an entity's systems for identifying and limiting risks	pp. 963–966
D16. What are the types of services that might be performed as part of a CPA Performance View engagement?	The potential services in a CPA Performance View Engagement include: *For Organizations that Have Performance Measurement Systems* • Assessing the reliability of information being reported from the organization's performance measurement system. • Assessing the relevance of the performance measures (that is, how well they inform management about achievement of the performance objectives they have set). *For Organizations that Do Not Have Performance Measurement Systems* • Identifying relevant performance measures. *For All Organizations* • Providing advice on how the organization can improve its performance measurement system and its actual results.	pp. 967–968
D17. What are the types of services that might be performed as part of a CPA ElderCare engagement?	The purpose of a CPA ElderCare engagement is to assure family members that elderly relatives no longer able to be totally independent are receiving the type of care and services they need. Figure 20-20 provides examples of a wide range of ElderCare services.	pp. 969–971

objective questions

Objective questions are available for the student at www.wiley.com/college/boynton

comprehensive questions

20-19 **(Special reports)** Jiffy Clerical Services is a corporation that furnishes temporary office help to its customers. Billings are rendered monthly based on predetermined hourly rates. You have examined the company's financial statements for several years. Following is an abbreviated statement of assets and liabilities on the modified cash basis as of December 31, 20X0:

Assets	
Cash	$ 20,000
Advances to employees	$ 1,000
Equipment and autos, less accumulated deprecation	$ 25,000
Total assets	$ 46,000
Liabilities	
Employees' payroll taxes withheld	$ 8,000
Bank loan payable	$ 10,000
Estimated income taxes on cash basis profits	$ 10,000
Total liabilities	$ 28,000
Net Assets	$ 18,000
Represented by	
Common stock	$ 3,000
Cash profits retained in the business	$ 15,000
	$ 18,000

Unrecorded receivables were $55,000 and payables were $30,000.

Required

a. Prepare the report you would issue covering the statement of assets and liabilities as of December 31, 20X0, as summarized above, and the related statements of cash revenue and expenses for the year ended that date.

b. Briefly discuss and justify your modifications of the conventional report on accrual basis statements.

20-20 **(Special reports)** Young and Young, CPAs, completed an audit of the financial statements of XYZ Company, Inc., for the year ended June 30, 20X3, and issued a standard unqualified auditor's report dated August 15, 20X3. At the time of the engagement, the board of directors of XYZ requested a special report attesting to the adequacy of the provision for federal and state income taxes and the related accruals and deferred income taxes as presented in the June 30, 20X3, financial statements.

Young and Young submitted the appropriate special report on August 22, 20X3.

Required

Prepare the special report that Young and Young should have submitted to XYZ Company, Inc.

AICPA

20-21 **(Compliance report based on audit)** In addition to examining the financial statements of the ABC Company at December 31, 20X0, the auditor agrees to review the loan agreement dated July 1, 20X0, with the Main Street Bank to determine whether the borrower is complying with the terms, provisions, and requirements of sections 14 to 30 inclusive. The auditor finds that the ABC Company is in full compliance with the loan agreement.

Required

a. Prepare a report on compliance with contractual provisions, assuming it is to be a separate report.

b. Indicate how the report on compliance would differ if it were included as part of the auditor's report on the financial statements.

20-22 **(WebTrust)** One of your clients, Green Golf, Inc., is a retailer of golf equipment. Over the last five years 50 percent of the company's business, and most of the company's growth, have come from a shift from retail store sales to catalogue sales. The company has established a web site for business-to-customer transactions, yet the customer response has reached only about 30 percent of projected sales. You are aware of your client's frustrations in carving out an electronic commerce market presence, and you and your audit manager have arranged a lunch with the client to discuss WebTrust.

Required

a. Describe how a WebTrust engagement might benefit your client in his efforts to expand his use of electronic commerce in the business-to-consumer environment.

b. What assurance must your client be prepared to offer the consumer as part of a WebTrust engagement?

c. If your client is making a statement to the public about his electronic commerce practices, why does he need a report from his CPAs about those practices?

d. Describe the inherent limitations involved in a WebTrust engagement.

20-23 **(SysTrust)** During a recent staff training session the audit partners, managers, seniors, and staff were discussing the new assurance service opportunity associated with SysTrust. Your client base includes specializations in small manufacturing companies that do outsourcing work for the auto industry, retailers, and financial institutions with trust departments. Answer the following questions that are raised during the discussion.

Required

a. What clients are most likely to be interested in a SysTrust engagement? Describe how decision makers would benefit from a SysTrust engagement.

b. What specific assurances are provided by a company that hires a CPA to attest to its assertions about SysTrust principles and criteria?

c. Assume that your CPA firm sells time on your accounting system to your small-business clients where they can log onto your system and maintain their own general ledger. Can you offer your clients a SysTrust report on the reliability of your general ledger system that you make available for their use?

20-24 **(Agreed-upon procedures)** Health Equipment Company (HEC) has acquired the rights to manufacture and sell certain health diagnostic equipment in the 13 Eastern states from Human Diagnostic, Inc., in exchange for paying a 15 to 25 percent royalty on the machinery sold, depending on the type of equipment sold. The contract allows Human Diagnostics, Inc. (HDI) to come in and audit royalties paid at any time. In the third year of the contact HDI was concerned that they had not received adequate royalties, so they hired Fred Fastfoot, CPA, to audit royalties paid. At Fred Fastfoot's suggestion, HDI signed an engagement letter to have Fred perform an agreed-upon procedures engagement, and the engagement letter outlined the procedures to be performed. Upon obtaining a signed engagement letter from HDI, Fred wrote HEC asking for information to allow him to perform an agreed-upon procedures engagement.

After three weeks Fred had received no information from HEC. Fred send a second request and threatened to turn the matter over to HDI's attorney if the information was not received. A week later partial information arrived. HEC also stated that it felt that some of the information requested was outside the scope of the contract. Fred was able to perform some of the agreed-upon procedures but not others. Advocating for HDI's position, Fred send a third request to HEC only to receive a reply from HEC that it did not feel that the information was relevant to the scope of the contract. After discussions with HDI, Fred turned over all the information that he received from HEC to HDI. At the same time, HDI asked Fred to discontinue the engagement and HDI proceeded to bring litigation against HEC.

Required

Identify the inappropriate actions of Fred Fastfoot, CPA, and indicate what Fred should have done to avoid each inappropriate action. Organize your answer sheet as follows:

INAPPROPRIATE ACTION	WHAT FRED SHOULD HAVE DONE TO AVOID INAPPROPRIATE ACTION

20-25 **(Reporting on prospective financial statements)** Clients sometimes call on an accountant to report on or assemble prospective financial statements for use by third parties.

Required

a. 1. Identify the types of engagements that an accountant may perform under these circumstances.
   2. Explain the difference between "general use" and "limited use" of prospective financial statements.
   3. Explain what types of prospective financial statements are appropriate for "general use" and what types are appropriate for "limited use."

b. Describe the contents of the accountant's standard report on a compilation of a financial projection.

AICPA

20-26 **(Situations involving unaudited, compiled, or reviewed financial statements)** The limitations of the CPA's professional responsibilities when he or she is associated with unaudited financial statements are often misunderstood. These misunderstandings can be substantially reduced by carefully following professional pronouncements in the course of the work and taking other appropriate measures.

Required

The following list describes seven situations the CPA may encounter or contentions he or she may have to deal with in the association with and preparation of unaudited financial statements. Briefly discuss the extent of the CPA's responsibilities and, if appropriate, the actions that should be taken to minimize any misunderstandings. Number your answers to correspond with the numbering in the following list.

1. The CPA was engaged by telephone to perform write-up work including the preparation of financial statements. The client believes that the CPA has been engaged to audit the financial statements and examine the records accordingly.

2. A group of businessmen who own a farm that is managed by an independent agent engage a CPA to prepare quarterly unaudited financial statements for them. The CPA prepares the financial statements from information given by the independent agent. Subsequently, the businessmen find the statements were inaccurate because their independent agent was embezzling funds. The businessmen refuse to pay the CPA's fee and blame the CPA for allowing the situation to go undetected, contending that the CPA should not have relied on representations from the independent agent.

3. In comparing the trial balance with the general ledger, the CPA finds an account labeled "audit fees" in which the client has accumulated the CPA's quarterly billings for accounting services, including the preparation of quarterly unaudited financial statements.

4. Unaudited financial statements were accompanied by the following letter of transmittal from the CPA: We are enclosing your company's balance sheet as of June 30, 20X0, and the related statements of income and retained earnings and cash flows for the six months then ended that we have reviewed.

5. To determine appropriate account classification, the CPA reviewed a number of the client's invoices. The CPA noted in the working papers that some invoices were missing but did nothing further because the CPA felt they did not affect the unaudited financial statements he or she was preparing. When the client subsequently discovered that invoices were missing, the client contended that the CPA should not have ignored the missing invoices when preparing the financial statements and had a responsibility to at least inform the client that they were missing.

6. The CPA has prepared a draft of unaudited financial statements from the client's records. While reviewing this draft with the client, the CPA learns that the land and building were recorded at appraisal value.

7. The CPA is engaged to review, but not audit, the financial statements prepared by the client's controller. During this review, the CPA learns of several items that by Generally Accepted Accounting Principles would require adjustment of the statements and footnote disclosures. The controller agrees to make the recommended adjustments to the statements but says that he or she is not going to add the footnotes because the statements are unaudited.

AICPA

20-27   **(Compilation and review engagements)** Ann Martin, CPA, has been asked by Harry Adams, owner of Adams Cleaners, to prepare the company's annual financial statements from the company's records. Adams, who is unfamiliar with the services of a CPA, also requests Ms. Martin to add as much prestige to the statements as possible in the form of an opinion or some type of assurance.

Required

a. Explain the nature and limitations of an engagement to compile financial statements.

b. Write the accountant's report on a compilation of financial statements.

c. Explain the type of assurance that may be given if Martin is engaged to review Adams's financial statements.

d. Explain why an opinion cannot be expressed.

20-28   **(Evaluate compilation report)** The following report was drafted on October 25, 20X0, by Major, CPA, at the completion of the engagement to compile the financial statements of Ajax Company for the year ended September 30, 20X0. Ajax is a nonpublic entity in which Major's child has a material direct financial interest. Ajax decided to omit substantially all of the disclosures required by generally accepted accounting principles because the financial statements will be for management's use only. The statement of cash flows was also omitted because management does not believe it to be a useful financial statement.

> To the Board of Directors of Ajax Company:
>
> I have compiled the accompanying financial statements of Ajax Company as of September 30, 20X0, and for the year then ended. I planned and performed the compilation to obtain limited assurance about whether the financial statements are free of material misstatements.
>
> A compilation is limited to presenting information in the form of financial statements. It is substantially less in scope than an audit in accordance with generally accepted auditing standards, the objective of which is the expression of an opinion regarding the financial statements taken as a whole. I have not audited the accompanying financial statements and, accordingly, do not express any opinion on them.
>
> Management has elected to omit substantially all of the disclosures required by generally accepted accounting principles. If the omitted disclosures were included in the financial statements, they might influence the user's conclusions about the Company's financial position, results of operations, and changes in financial position.
>
> I am not independent with respect to Ajax Company. This lack of independence is due to my child's ownership of a material direct financial interest in Ajax Company.
>
> This report is intended solely for the information and use of the Board of Directors and management of Ajax Company and should not be used for any other purpose.
>
> Major, CPA

Required

Identify the deficiencies contained in Major's report on the compiled financial statements. Group the deficiencies by paragraph where applicable. Do not redraft the report.

20-29   **(Business risk assessment)** You have just acquired a new small-business client that dominates the retail marketplace for high-end stereo and television equipment in three small, but growing, communities. The business also works closely with several local builders and sells a service where it installs audio equipment in new homes. The long-time owner of the company has just retired, and his daughter has recently taken the reins as owner–manager. She is considering how to expand the business. In particular, she is looking into business opportunities to open stores in larger markets, as growth is limited by community size in the current locations.

Required

a. Describe the nature of a risk assessment service that you could offer the new owner–manager as she develops a plan to expand the business.

b. Explain the competitive advantages you bring to a risk assessment engagement as a CPA and the company's auditor.

c. It is often useful to categorize business risk into three categories: (1) strategic environment risks, (2) operating environment risks, and (3) information risks. For each category identify two specific risks that the new owner–manager should consider in the context of opening a new store in a larger market. Also identify a service you can perform to assist the owner–manager with these risks without violating AICPA independence rules for this nonpublic company. Use the following format.

RISK IDENTIFICATION	SERVICE TO ASSIST CLIENT
Strategic environment risk	Describe service to assist client
•	•
•	•
Operating environment risk	Describe service to assist client
•	•
•	•
Information risk	Describe service to assist client
•	•
•	•

case

20-30 **(Evaluate compilation engagement performance)** Brown, CPA, received a telephone call from Calhoun, the sole owner and manager of a small corporation. Calhoun asked Brown to prepare the financial statements for the corporation and told Brown that the statements were needed in two weeks for external financing purposes. Calhoun was vague when Brown inquired about the intended use of the statements. Brown was convinced that Calhoun thought Brown's work would constitute an audit. To avoid confusion, Brown decided not to explain to Calhoun that the engagement would only be to prepare the financial statements. Brown, with the understanding that a substantial fee would be paid if the work were completed in two weeks, accepted the engagement and started the work at once.

During the course of the work, Brown discovered an accrued expense account labeled "professional fees" and learned that the balance in the account represented an accrual for the cost of Brown's services. Brown suggested to Calhoun's bookkeeper that the account name be changed to "fees for limited audit engagement." Brown also reviewed several invoices to determine whether accounts were being properly classified. Some of the invoices were missing. Brown listed the missing invoice numbers in the working papers with a note indicating that there should be a followup on the next engagement. Brown also discovered that the available records included the fixed asset values at estimated current replacement costs. Based on the records available, Brown prepared a balance sheet, income statement, and statements of stockholders' equity. In addition, Brown drafted the footnotes but decided that any mention of the replacement costs would only mislead the readers. Brown suggested to Calhoun that readers of the financial statements would be better informed if they received a separate letter from Calhoun explaining the meaning and effect of the estimated replacement costs of the fixed assets. Brown mailed the financial statements and footnotes to Calhoun with the following note included on each page:

The accompanying financial statements are submitted to you without complete audit verification.

Required

Identify the inappropriate actions of Brown and indicate what Brown should have done to avoid each inappropriate action. Organize your answer sheet as follows:

INAPPROPRIATE ACTION	WHAT BROWN SHOULD HAVE DONE TO AVOID INAPPROPRIATE ACTION

AICPA

professional simulation

Jennifer Robben is a partner in the CPA firm of Robben, Harrison and Co. During the course of a year she receives a number of requests from clients for various services. The following questions address the firm's ability to provide these services in accordance with professional standards.

Following is list of various engagements that a client might ask a CPA to perform. Identify the professional standards that provide guidance on performing the engagement.

a. Statements on Auditing Standards

b. Statements on Standards for Attestation Engagements

c. Statements on Standards for Accounting and Review Services

d. The engagement is not appropriate under current professional standards

	a.	b.	c.	d.
1. A private company client would like to have your accounting firm provide reasonable assurance that a financial forecast of the next year's financial position, results of operations, and cash flows will be achieved.	○	○	○	○
2. A private company needs to provide a bank with financial statements. It does not want to pay for an audit, and the bank is willing to accept less than audited financial statements. Can your firm provide negative assurance that your firm is not aware of any material modifications that need to be made to the financial statements in order for them to be in accordance with GAAP?	○	○	○	○
3. A public company would like you to perform agreed-upon procedures regarding a royalty payable where the client owes royalties based on the number of parts produced under a licensing agreement.	○	○	○	○

4. A private company would like to have you audit financial statements prepared on a federal income tax basis of accounting. ○ ○ ○ ○

5. A public company would like to have you provide a report to lenders providing them with some level of assurance that the company complied with terms, covenants, and provisions of a debt agreement. ○ ○ ○ ○

6. A local casino would like to provide a report to the public that provides reasonable assurance that that payout rate on its slot machines was greater than or equal to 97 percent. ○ ○ ○ ○

7. A private company client would like to you compile a financial projection, with no assurance, that would project financial position, results of operations and cash flows based on assumptions agreed upon by the client and the bank. ○ ○ ○ ○

8. A public company in the petroleum industry would like to have your firm conduct an agreed-upon procedures engagement to the Environmental Protection Agency (EPA) that it complied with the EPA regulation that its gasoline product contained at least 2 percent oxygen. ○ ○ ○ ○

Situation	Various Assurance Engagements	Research

Following is list of engagements that were requested of Jennifer Robben during the last year. In the space provided in the table below indicate the appropriate professional standard paragraph(s) that provide example reports relevant to each engagement.

Professional Standard Reference

1. A private company client would like to have your accounting firm provide reasonable assurance that a financial forecast of the next year's financial position, results of operations, and cash flows will be achieved. _____

2. A private company needs to provide a bank with financial statements. It does not want to pay for an audit, and the bank is willing to accept less than audited financial statements. Can your firm provide negative assurance that your firm is not aware of any material modifications that need to be made to the financial statements in order for them to be in accordance with GAAP? _____

3. A public company would like you to perform agreed-upon procedures regarding a royalty payable where the client owes royalties based on the number of parts produced under a licensing agreement. _____

4. A private company would like to have you audit financial statements prepared on a federal income tax basis of accounting. _____

5. A public company would like to have you provide a report to lenders providing them with some level of assurance that the company complied with terms, covenants, and provisions of a debt agreement. _____

6. A local casino would like to provide a report to the public that provides reasonable assurance that that payout rate on its slot machines was greater than or equal to 97 percent. _____

7. A private company client would like to you compile a financial projection, with no assurance, that would project financial position, results of operations and cash flows based on assumptions agreed upon by the client and the bank. _____

8. A public company in the petroleum industry would like to have your firm conduct an agreed-upon procedures engagement to the Environmental Protection Agency (EPA) that it complied with the EPA regulation that its gasoline product contained at least 2 percent oxygen. _____

[21] INTERNAL, OPERATIONAL, AND GOVERNMENTAL AUDITING

UNDERSTANDING THE RISK OF FRAUD IN GOVERNMENTAL AUDITS

Many auditors need to be conversant with both GAAS and generally accepted government auditing standards (GAGAS). GAGAS applies to audits and attestation engagements of government entities, programs, activities, and functions, and to government assistance administered by contractors, nonprofit entities, and other nongovernmental entities. As a result, GAGAS applies to many state and local governments and not-for-profit entities that receive federal awards.

The auditor that audits a small city, or a not-for-profit entity, and that receives a federal award must plan and perform an audit in accordance with GAGAS. GAGAS, like GAAS, requires auditors to consider the risk of fraud. Abraham Akresh, CPA (assistant director in the Financial Management and Assurance Team of the U.S. General Accounting Office), has suggested three important risks that an auditor should consider when assessing the risk of fraud.

1. Risk of management misrepresentation of financial statements
2. Risk of material misappropriation of assets—by employees
3. Risk of material misappropriation of assets—by people outside the organization

Akresh makes the following suggestions regarding the risk of fraud in governmental audits.

- The risk of management misrepresentation of financial statements is usually low, especially in the federal government, since there are no stockholders and financial statements are rarely used for investment decisions. There might be some risk in state and local governments, but it is usually less than for SEC registrants as there are no stock options or bonuses based on financial statements.

- The risk of material misappropriation of assets by employees may range from low to high because of materiality considerations. In a larger city it takes lots of theft to be material. It may not take a lot of theft to be material to a small city or not-for-profit entity. In addition, auditors should consider the qualitative aspects. Nevertheless, entities need strong controls to prevent or detect these misappropriations. Because small entities, such as not-for-profit organizations and some local governments, often lack appropriate controls, fraud risk often increases. For example, auditors should be alert for abuse of travel or purchase cards by employees. Many governments give employees credit cards to be used for the entity's purposes. This increased opportunity for fraud exists because many employees are given credit cards to "reduce red tape" in procurement. However, they may be used for personal purposes by employees who rationalize that their pay is low.

■ The risk of material misappropriation of assets by people outside the organization is often a major consideration when the entity makes grants or pays benefits. Entities need strong controls in this area, including specific controls over the existence and occurrence assertion. For example, auditors should be alert to conflicts of interest among procurement officials and to the awarding of contracts based on fraudulent data. Auditors should also be alert to benefit payments made to deceased retirees.

These types of risks should regularly be considered as part of the auditor's brainstorming session. Auditors might also brainstorm on how to use generalized audit software to scan an entire population of expenditure to identify items likely to represent fraud.

Source: Abraham Akresh, *AICPA Pre-Certification Education Executive Committee Fraud Education Task Force,* American Institute of Certified Public Accountants, Inc., New York, New York, 2004.

[PREVIEW OF CHAPTER 21]

Thus far in this textbook, the focus has been primarily on financial statement audits for nongovernmental entities made by independent auditors. In this chapter, attention is directed to other types of auditing. For each type of auditing, consideration is given to its objectives, scope, and applicable standards. The following diagram provides an overview of the chapter organization and content.

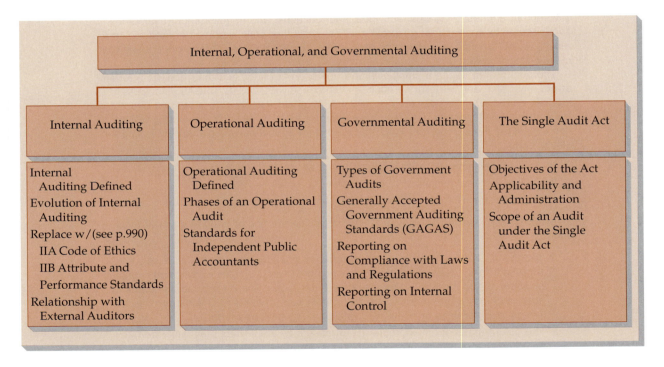

Internal, Operational, and Governmental Auditing			
Internal Auditing	**Operational Auditing**	**Governmental Auditing**	**The Single Audit Act**
Internal Auditing Defined Evolution of Internal Auditing Replace w/(see p.990) IIA Code of Ethics IIB Attribute and Performance Standards Relationship with External Auditors	Operational Auditing Defined Phases of an Operational Audit Standards for Independent Public Accountants	Types of Government Audits Generally Accepted Government Auditing Standards (GAGAS) Reporting on Compliance with Laws and Regulations Reporting on Internal Control	Objectives of the Act Applicability and Administration Scope of an Audit under the Single Audit Act

focus on auditor knowledge

After studying this chapter you should understand the following aspects of an auditor's knowledge base:

K1. Know the definition of internal auditing and the IIA professional practices framework.

K2. Know the IIA code of ethics, attribute standards, and performance standards.

K3. Know the definition of operational auditing and describe the phases of an operational audit.

K4. Know the standards that independent public accountants should follow in performing operational audits.

K5. Know the three types of governmental audits.

K6. Know the general standards, additional fieldwork standards, and additional reporting standards associated with generally accepted governmental auditing standards (GAGAS) for financial audits and performance audits.

K7. Know the objectives and applicability of the Single Audit Act.

K8. Know the components of a single audit and the procedures and reports associated with each.

INTERNAL AUDITING

Chapter 1 introduced internal auditing, and Chapter 10 explained how internal auditing is an important part of the monitoring component of an entity's system of internal control. As explained in the following sections, internal auditing also provides other valuable services to an entity.

INTERNAL AUDITING DEFINED

The Institute of Internal Auditors (IIA) defines internal auditing as:

Internal auditing is an independent, objective assurance and consulting activity designed to add value and improve an organization's operations. It helps an organization accomplish its objectives by bringing a systematic, disciplined approach to evaluate and improve the effectiveness of risk management, control, and governance processes.

Auditor Knowledge 1

■ Know the definition of internal auditing and the IIA professional practices framework.

The essential parts of this definition are as follows:

- *Internal* indicates that auditing activities are carried on within organizations. Today employees of the organization may conduct internal audit activities, or they may be outsourced to other professionals outside the organization who serve the entity.
- *Independent and objective* makes it clear that the auditor's judgment has value when it is free of bias.
- *Systematic, disciplined approach* implies that the internal auditor follows professional standards that guide internal audit work.
- *Helps an organization accomplish its objectives* indicates that internal auditing exists to aid or benefit the entire organization and is guided by the organization's goals and objectives. Some specific ways in which internal auditors add value include a focus on the improvement of *the organization's operations and the effectiveness of risk management, control, and governance processes.*

Internal auditing is part of the monitoring function of internal control that examines and evaluates the adequacy and effectiveness of other controls.

EVOLUTION OF INTERNAL AUDITING

Internal auditing has evolved into a highly professional activity that extends to the appraisal of the efficiency and effectiveness of all phases of a company's operations, both financial and nonfinancial. Internal auditors were primarily responsible for finding the financial fraud at WorldCom. Today many companies have an internal auditing department, the director/manager of the internal audit function may have senior management status, and internal audit has a reporting responsibility directly to the board of directors or its audit committee.

Passage of the Foreign Corrupt Practices Act in 1977 added emphasis to internal auditing. This Act requires companies to maintain effective internal control systems. Companies subject to this Act quickly realized that an expanded internal auditing function provided the best assurance of compliance. Accordingly, budgets for internal auditing were dramatically enlarged, and the size and quality of internal auditing departments were significantly increased.

The growth and importance of internal auditing to a company has been accompanied by increased professional recognition for the internal auditor. The Institute of Internal Auditors (IIA) was formed in 1941, and its current membership is approximately 70,000 internal auditors in 120 countries. In 1972, the IIA administered its first Certificate of Internal Auditors' Examination. The examination takes two days and consists of four parts:

- The internal auditor's role in governance, risk, and control
- Conducting an internal audit engagement
- Business analysis and information technology
- Business management skills

To become a certified internal auditor (CIA), an individual must pass the examination and have a minimum of two years of experience as an internal auditor or the equivalent. The criteria for internal auditing experience include auditing experience in public accounting. To retain the CIA certificate, the individual must comply with the IIA's practice standards and code of ethics and meet continuing professional education requirements. Certified internal auditors are not licensed by any governmental agency.

In 1999, the Institute of Internal Auditors' board of directors took several steps to prepare the IIA for the twenty-first century. In June of 1999 it approved a new definition of internal auditing (presented above), a new professional practices framework, and a new Code of Ethics. Figure 21-1 summarizes the new professional practices framework.

IIA CODE OF ETHICS

Like the AICPA Code of Professional Ethics, the IIA Code of Ethics is divided into both ethical principles and ethical rules. Although internal auditors cannot be independent in the same way as external auditors, the IIA places significant emphasis on integrity and objectivity in both the principles and rules. The other two main features address confidentiality of information and internal auditor competency. Figure 21-2 presents the IIA Code of Ethics.

IIA ATTRIBUTE AND PERFORMANCE STANDARDS

The new framework presented three new sets of standards:

Figure 21-1 ■ IIA Professional Practices Framework

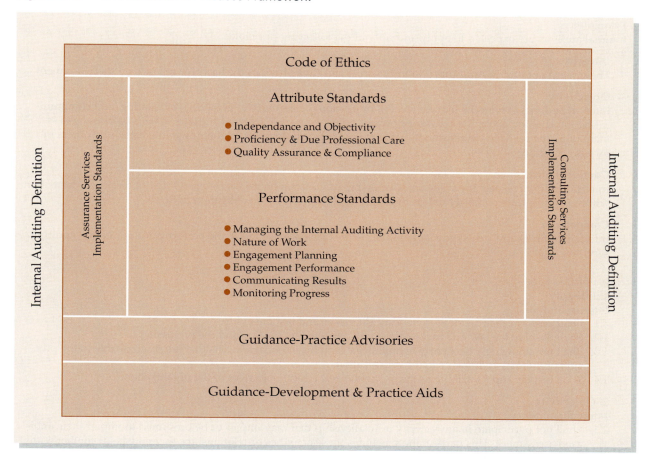

■ **Attribute Standards** that address the characteristics of organizations and individuals performing internal audit services.

■ **Performance Standards** that describe the nature of internal audit services and
provide quality criteria against which the performance of these services can be
measured.

■ **Implementation Standards** that apply the attribute and performance standards
to specific types of services (e.g., a compliance audit, a fraud investigation, a
control self-assessment project).

Figure 21-3 summarizes the current attribute and performance standards. The full
set of attribute, performance, and implementation standards can be found at
www.theiia.org.

The attribute standards are similar to the general standards of generally
accepted auditing standards. In addition to proficiency, independence, and due
professional care, the standards address issues of importance to internal auditors.
Standard 1100 creates a framework for the charter and authority for internal auditors. Standard 1300 explicitly writes the concepts of quality control into the attrib-

Figure 21-2 ■ IIA Code of Ethics

Principles

Internal auditors are expected to apply and uphold the following principles:

Integrity

The integrity of internal auditors establishes trust and thus provides the basis for reliance on their judgment.

Objectivity

Internal auditors exhibit the highest level of professional objectivity in gathering, evaluating, and communicating information about the activity or process being examined. Internal auditors make a balanced assessment of all the relevant circumstances and are not unduly influenced by their own interests or by others in forming judgments.

Confidentiality

Internal auditors respect the value and ownership of information they receive and do not disclose information without appropriate authority unless there is a legal or professional obligation to do so.

Competency

Internal auditors apply the knowledge, skills, and experience needed in the performance of internal auditing services.

Rules of Conduct

1. Integrity

Internal auditors:

1.1. Shall perform their work with honesty, diligence, and responsibility.
1.2. Shall observe the law and make disclosures expected by the law and the profession.
1.3. Shall not knowingly be a party to any illegal activity, or engage in acts that are discreditable to the profession of internal auditing or to the organization.
1.4. Shall respect and contribute to the legitimate and ethical objectives of the organization.

2. Objectivity

Internal auditors:

2.1. Shall not participate in any activity or relationship that may impair or be presumed to impair their unbiased assessment. This participation includes those activities or relationships that may be in conflict with the interests of the organization.
2.2. Shall not accept anything that may impair or be presumed to impair their professional judgment.
2.3. Shall disclose all material facts known to them that, if not disclosed, may distort the reporting of activities under review.

3. Confidentiality

Internal auditors:

3.1. Shall be prudent in the use and protection of information acquired in the course of their duties.
3.2. Shall not use information for any personal gain or in any manner that would be contrary to the law or detrimental to the legitimate and ethical objectives of the organization.

4. Competency

Internal auditors:

4.1. Shall engage only in those services for which they have the necessary knowledge, skills, and experience.
4.2. Shall perform internal auditing services in accordance with the *Standards for the Professional Practice of Internal Auditing.*
4.3. Shall continually improve their proficiency and the effectiveness and quality of their services.

Adopted by The IIA Board of Directors, June 17, 2000.

Figure 21-3 ■ IIA Attribute and Performance Standards

Attribute Standards

1000   **Purpose, Authority, and Responsibility:** The purpose, authority, and responsibility of the internal audit activity should be formally defined in a charter, consistent with the Standards, and approved by the board.

1100   **Independence and Objectivity:** The internal audit activity should be independent, and internal auditors should be objective in performing their work.

1200   **Proficiency and Due Professional Care:** Engagements should be performed with proficiency and due professional care.

1300   **Quality Assurance and Improvement Program:** The chief audit executive should develop and maintain a quality assurance and improvement program that covers all aspects of the internal audit activity and continuously monitors its effectiveness. This program includes periodic internal and external quality assessments and ongoing internal monitoring. Each part of the program should be designed to help the internal auditing activity add value and improve the organization's operations and to provide assurance that the internal audit activity is in conformity with the Standards and the Code of Ethics.

Performance Standards

2000   **Managing the Internal Audit Activity:** The chief audit executive should effectively manage the internal audit activity to ensure it adds value to the organization.

2100   **Nature of Work:** The internal audit activity should evaluate and contribute to the improvement of risk management, control, and governance processes using a systematic and disciplined approach.

2200   **Engagement Planning:** Internal auditors should develop and record a plan for each engagement, including the scope, objectives, timing, and resource allocations.

2300   **Performing the Engagement:** Internal auditors should identify, analyze, evaluate, and record sufficient information to achieve the engagement's objectives.

2400   **Communicating Results:** Internal auditors should communicate the engagement results.

2500   **Monitoring Progress:** The chief audit executive should establish and maintain a system to monitor the disposition of results communicated to management.

2600   **Management's Acceptance of Risks:** When the chief audit executive believes that senior management has accepted a level of residual risk that may be unacceptable to the organization, the chief audit executive should discuss the matter with senior management. If the decision regarding residual risk is not resolved, the chief audit executive and senior management should report the matter to the board for resolution.

---

ute standards. Quality control is addressed by a separate set of quality control standards for external CPAs.

A number of the performance standards are similar to the fieldwork standards and reporting standards of GAAS. However, a few standards are unique to internal audit engagements. Standard 2000 sets the tone for all the following standards by stating that internal audit should add to the value of the organization. Standard 2500 addresses the importance of monitoring the issues that the internal auditor reports to management. Finally, standards 2600 addresses the issue of residual business risk. When the chief audit executive believes that the organization has taken on an unacceptable level of business risk, the auditor has a responsibility to take this conclusion first to senior management and then to the board of directors if it is not satisfactorily resolved at the senior management level.

RELATIONSHIP WITH EXTERNAL AUDITORS

Usually, a close relationship exists between internal auditors and an entity's outside independent auditors. As indicated in an earlier chapter, the work of internal auditors may be a supplement to, but not a substitute for, the work of independent auditors in a financial statement audit. As noted above, one responsibility of the director of internal auditing is to coordinate the work of internal auditors with the work of the external auditor. It is not uncommon in practice for the external auditor to review the internal auditing department's planned work program for the year to minimize duplication of effort.

Although they often have a close working relationship, the following important differences exist between the two types of auditors:

	INTERNAL AUDITORS	EXTERNAL AUDITORS
Employer	Companies and governmental units	CPA firms
National organization	Institute of Internal Auditors (IIA)	American Institute of Certified Public Accountants (AICPA)
Certifying designation	Certified Internal Auditor (CIA)	Certified Public Accountant (CPA)
License to practice	No	Yes
Primary responsibility	To board of directors	To third parties
Scope of audits	All activities of an organization	Primarily financial statements

[LEARNING CHECK

21-1 a. Is internal auditing a management or an accounting function? Explain.
      b. Jill Jensen is confused as to the scope and primary beneficiary of internal auditing. Clarify these points for Jill.

21-2 a. State the requirements for becoming a certified internal auditor.
      b. What must a CIA do to retain the certificate?

21-3 a. What is the objective of internal auditing?
      b. The scope of internal auditing is limited to financial statement audits. Do you agree? Explain.

21-4 a. Identify the two sets of standards in the new IIA Professional Practices Framework and describe the purpose of each.
      b. Identify the basic categories of the attribute and performance standards. Briefly describe the purpose of each set of standards.

21-5 How does the independence of an internal auditor differ from that of an external auditor?

[KEY TERMS

Attribute standards, p. 987
Implementation standards, p. 987

Internal auditing, p. 985
Performance standards, p. 987

OPERATIONAL AUDITING

Auditor Knowledge 3

■ **Know the definition of operational auditing and describe the phases of an operational audit.**

Operational auditing has been used in the past to identify a variety of activities that include evaluating management's performance, management's planning and quality control systems, and specific operating activities and departments. As suggested by its name, this type of auditing pertains to an entity's nonfinancial operations. Operational audits of nongovernmental units are generally made by internal auditors. However, in some cases, external auditors may be engaged to perform the audit.

OPERATIONAL AUDITING DEFINED

A IIA publication defines operational auditing as follows:

> **Operational auditing** is the systematic process of evaluating an organization's effectiveness, efficiency, and economy of operations under management's control and reporting to appropriate persons the results of the evaluation along with recommendations for improvements.[1]

The essential parts of this definition are as follows:

■ *Systematic process.* As in the case of a financial statement audit, an operational audit involves a logical, structured, and organized series of steps or procedures. This aspect includes proper planning, as well as obtaining and objectively evaluating evidence pertaining to the activity being audited.

■ *Evaluating an organization's operations.* The evaluation of operations should be based on some established or agreed-upon criteria. In operational auditing, the criteria are often expressed in terms of performance standards established by management. However, in some cases, the standards may be set by a governmental agency or by industry. These criteria frequently are less clearly defined than the criteria used in financial statement audits. Operational auditing measures the degree of correspondence between actual performance and the criteria.

■ *Effectiveness, efficiency, and economy of operations.* The primary purpose of operational auditing is to help management of the audited organization to improve the effectiveness, efficiency, and economy of operations. Thus, operational auditing focuses on the future. This is in direct contrast to a financial statement audit, which has a historical focus.

■ *Reporting to appropriate persons.* The appropriate recipient of an operational audit report is management or the individual or agency that requested the audit. Except when the audit is requested by a third party, the distribution of the report remains within the entity. In most cases, the board of directors or its audit committee receives copies of operational audit reports.

■ *Recommendations for improvement.* Unlike financial statement audits, an operational audit does not end with a report on the findings. It extends to making

---

[1] Darwin J. Casler and James R. Crockett, *Operational Auditing: An Introduction* (Altamonte Springs, FL: Institute of Internal Auditors, 1982), p. 14.

recommendations for improvement. Developing recommendations is, in fact, one of the most challenging aspects of this type of auditing.

PHASES OF AN OPERATIONAL AUDIT

There are more phases in an operational audit than in a financial statement audit. The similarities and differences in the phases between these two types of audits are shown in Figure 21-4. Each of the phases of an operational audit is explained in the following sections.

Select Auditee

Like many other activities within an entity, operational auditing is usually subject to budgetary or economic constraints. It is important, therefore, that the resources for operational auditing be put to the best use. Selecting the auditee begins with a preliminary study (or survey) of potential auditees within an entity to identify the activities that have the highest audit potential in terms of improving the effectiveness, efficiency, and economy of operations. In essence, the preliminary study is a screening process that results in a ranking of potential auditees.

The starting point of the preliminary study is to obtain a comprehensive understanding of the entity's organizational structure and operating characteristics. In addition, the auditor should be knowledgeable of the industry in which the entity operates and the nature and extent of applicable government regulations. Attention is next focused on the activity, unit, or function that could be audited. An understanding of the potential auditees is obtained by:

■ Reviewing background file data on each auditee
■ Touring the auditee's facilities to ascertain how it accomplishes its objectives
■ Studying relevant documentation about the auditee's operations such as policies and procedures manuals, flowcharts, performance and quality control standards, and job descriptions
■ Interviewing the manager of the activity about specific problem areas (often called the entry interview)

Figure 21-4 ■ Financial Statement vs. Operational Audits

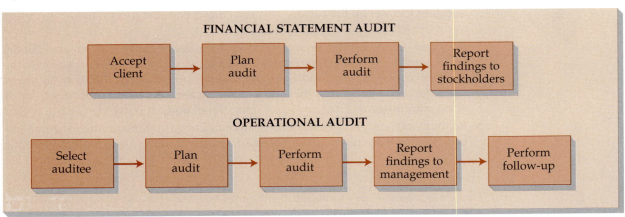

- Applying analytical procedures to identify trends and unusual relationships
- Conducting mini audit probes (or tests) to confirm or clarify the auditor's understanding of potential problems

The auditor's understanding of each auditee should be documented through completed questionnaires, flowcharts, and narrative memoranda. Based on this understanding, the auditor prepares a preliminary study report or memorandum, which summarizes the findings and includes a recommendation as to the auditee(s) that should be audited. The report is for the exclusive use of the internal auditing department. It is not a report for management.

Plan Audit

Careful audit planning is essential to both the effectiveness and efficiency of an operational audit. Planning is especially critical in this type of an audit because of the diversity of operational audits. The cornerstone of audit planning is the development of an audit program. The program must be tailor-made to the circumstances found in the auditee in the preliminary study phase of the audit. As in the case of a financial statement audit, the audit program contains a set of procedures designed to obtain evidence pertaining to one or more objectives. The evidence examined is usually based on samples of data. Thus, consideration should be given in audit planning to the use of statistical sampling techniques. In addition, the auditor should recognize when computer-assisted techniques will be cost efficient.

Audit planning also includes selecting the audit team and scheduling the work. The audit team must include auditors who have the technical expertise needed to meet the audit objective(s). The work should be scheduled in consultation with the auditee to obtain the maximum cooperation from the auditee's personnel during the audit.

Perform Audit

During the audit, the auditor makes an extensive search for facts pertaining to the problems identified in the auditee during the preliminary study. Making the audit is the most time-consuming phase of an operational audit. This phase is often referred to as *making the in-depth audit.*

In an operational audit, the auditor relies primarily on inquiry and observation. A common approach is to develop a questionnaire for the auditee and to use it as a basis for interviewing the auditee's personnel. From the inquiries, the auditor expects to obtain opinions, comments, and suggested solutions to the problems. Effective interviewing is indispensable in an operational audit. Through observation of the auditee's personnel, the auditor may be able to detect inefficiencies and other conditions that are contributing to the problem(s).

The auditor must also use analysis in an operational audit. For this purpose, analysis involves the study and measurement of actual performance in relation to some criteria. The criteria may be internally developed by the entity such as stated productivity goals and budgets. Alternatively, the criteria may be externally generated in the form of industry standards or be derived by the auditor from previous audits of similar activities. Analysis provides a basis for determining the degree to which the auditee is meeting specified objectives.

The work done, the findings, and the recommendations should be documented in working papers. As in a financial statement audit, the working papers represent the primary support for the auditor's report. The in-charge auditor normally has the responsibility for reviewing the working papers both during and at the completion of the examination. Reviews during the audit are helpful in monitoring progress, whereas the review at the end of the audit ensures the overall quality of the work.

Report Findings

Operational auditing is similar to other types of auditing in that the final product of the audit is an audit report. There are, however, many unique circumstances pertaining to reporting in an operational audit. For example, in contrast to the standard language contained in the auditor's report in a financial statement audit, the language of the report in an operational audit varies for each auditee. The report should contain:

- A statement of the objectives and scope of the audit
- A general description of the work done in the audit
- A summary of the findings
- Recommendations for improvement
- Comments of the auditee

The report is generally drafted by the in-charge auditor. The draft is then discussed with the manager of the audited unit. This discussion serves several important purposes: (1) it gives the auditor an opportunity to test the accuracy of the findings and the appropriateness of the recommendations, and (2) it enables the auditor to obtain the auditee's comments for inclusion in the report. The initial draft is then revised as necessary, and the final draft is prepared.

In some cases, the recommendations may just suggest the need for further study of the problems. The inclusion of the auditee's comments is optional. Ordinarily, they are included only when the auditee disagrees with the findings and recommendations.

The auditor's findings basically result in constructive criticism. In writing the report, the auditor should be sensitive to the recipient's reactions. When the language is less threatening, the response of the recipient to the report is likely to be more positive. Ordinarily, copies of operational auditing reports are sent to senior management and to the audit committee. If the report is long and detailed, the report may begin with an executive summary of the findings and recommendations.

Perform Follow-up

The final or follow-up phase of an operational audit is for the auditor to follow up on the auditee's response to the audit report. Ideally, the policies of the entity should require the manager of the audited unit to respond to the report in writing within a specified time period. However, the follow-up should extend to determining the adequacy of the measures taken by the auditee in implementing the recommendations. Practice Standard 440 of the IIA states that internal auditors should follow-up to ascertain that appropriate action has been taken on the report findings. The failure of the auditor to receive an appropriate response should be communicated to senior management.

STANDARDS FOR INDEPENDENT PUBLIC ACCOUNTANTS

Based on their expertise and experience, independent public accountants are qualified to perform operational audits. In 1982, the AICPA appointed the Special Committee on Operational and Management Auditing to study the involvement of independent accountants in operational auditing. The Committee concluded in its report entitled *Operational Audit Engagements* that an operational audit engagement is a distinct form of management consulting services (MCS). It also made the following observations (p. 1):

■ Independent accountants will increasingly be asked to provide this service for both private sector and governmental clients.

■ This type of service provides independent evaluation and advice to boards of directors, senior management, and elected officials who are being held to high standards of responsibility and stewardship.

■ The experience gained in public accounting in the diagnostic and fact-finding aspects of financial auditing and management consulting services provides an excellent background for performing operational audits.

Management consulting services have become an important part of the services performed today by many CPA firms.

In performing operational audits, independent CPAs should follow the practice standards for MCS engagements established by the Management Consulting Services Executive Committee of the AICPA. The independent accountant must also comply with Rule 201, General Standards, of the AICPA's *Code of Professional Conduct*, which is explained in Chapter 3. Care must be taken not to make management decisions when performing an operational audit or independence might be impaired. When the audit is conducted for governmental entities, the independent auditor must also follow applicable government *performance audit standards* described later in the chapter.

[LEARNING CHECK

21-6 a. Like internal auditing, operational auditing involves independent appraisal. Do you agree? Explain.

b. The scope of operational auditing is similar to the scope of internal auditing. Is this true? Explain.

21-7 a. Identify the phases of an operational audit.

b. How do these phases differ from a financial statement audit?

21-8 Explain the auditor's responsibilities in (a) selecting the auditee and (b) reporting the findings.

21-9 Identify the applicable standards when a CPA performs an operational audit.

[KEY TERM

Operational auditing, p. 991

GOVERNMENTAL AUDITING

Governmental auditing includes all audits made by government audit agencies and all audits of governmental organizations. Government audit agencies include the U.S. General Accounting Office, the Defense Contract Audit Agency, and state audit agencies. Audits of governmental organizations include audits of state and local government units made by federal government auditors and independent public accountants. In some cases, these audits may include specific programs, activities, functions, and funds. Audits of governmental organizations are premised largely on the concept that the officials and employees who manage public funds are accountable to the public. Our interest here is in the audits of governmental organizations.

TYPES OF GOVERNMENT AUDITS

Three types of government audits are identified in Government Auditing Standards:

■ **Financial audits** are primarily concerned with providing reasonable assurance about whether financial statements are presented fairly in all material respects in conformity with generally accepted accounting principles (GAAP), or with a comprehensive basis of accounting other than GAAP. Other objectives of financial audits, which provide for different levels of assurance and entail various scopes of work, may include

- providing special reports for specified elements, accounts, or items of a financial statement
- reviewing interim financial information
- issuing letters for underwriters and certain other requesting parties
- reporting on the processing of transactions by service organizations
- auditing compliance with regulations relating to federal award expenditures and other governmental financial assistance in conjunction with or as a by-product of a financial statement audit

Financial audits are performed under the American Institute of Certified Public Accountants' (AICPA) generally accepted auditing standards for fieldwork and reporting, as well as the related AICPA Statements on Auditing Standards (SAS). GAGAS prescribe general standards and additional fieldwork and reporting standards beyond those provided by the AICPA when performing financial audits.

■ **Attestation engagements** concern examining, reviewing, or performing agreed-upon procedures on a subject matter or an assertion about a subject matter and reporting on the results. The subject matter of an attestation engagement may take many forms, including historical or prospective performance or condition, physical characteristics, historical events, analyses, systems and processes, or behavior. Attestation engagements can cover a broad range of financial or nonfinancial subjects and can be part of a financial audit or performance audit. Possible subjects of attestation engagements could include reporting on

- an entity's internal control over financial reporting
- an entity's compliance with requirements of specified laws, regulations, rules, contracts, or grants

- the effectiveness of an entity's internal control over compliance with specified requirements, such as those governing the bidding for, accounting for, and reporting on grants and contracts
- management's discussion and analysis (MD&A) presentation
- prospective financial statements or pro forma financial information
- the reliability of performance measures
- final contract cost
- allowability and reasonableness of proposed contract amounts and specific procedures performed (agreed-upon procedures)

■ **Performance audits** entail an objective and systematic examination of evidence to provide an independent assessment of the performance and management of a program against objective criteria as well as assessments that provide a prospective focus or that synthesize information on best practices or cross-cutting issues. Performance audits provide information to improve program operations and facilitate decision making by parties with responsibility to oversee or initiate corrective action, and improve public accountability. Performance audits encompass a wide variety of objectives, including objectives related to assessing program effectiveness and results; economy and efficiency; internal control; compliance with legal or other requirements; and objectives related to providing prospective analyses, guidance, or summary information. Performance audits may entail a broad or narrow scope of work and apply a variety of methodologies; involve various levels of analysis, research, or evaluation; generally provide findings, conclusions, and recommendations; and result in the issuance of a report.

Auditors performing such engagements, whether employed by government auditing agencies or by CPA firms, must be careful to observe all applicable AICPA and government auditing standards as discussed in the remaining sections of this chapter.

GENERALLY ACCEPTED GOVERNMENT AUDITING STANDARDS (GAGAS)

The U.S. General Accounting Office (GAO) establishes audit standards for audits of government organizations, programs, activities, functions, and government funds received by nongovernment organizations. The standards pertain to the auditor's professional qualifications, the quality of audit effort, and the characteristics of professional and meaningful audit reports. The GAO audit standards must be followed by auditors and audit organizations when required by law, regulation, agreement or contract, or policy. Audit organizations consist of government audit agencies and nongovernment entities such as public accounting firms and consulting firms.

The GAO audit standards are recognized as **generally accepted government auditing standards (GAGAS).** The GAO standards are commonly referred to as the **Yellow Book standards** because of the color of the pamphlet in which they are published. GAGAS include the AICPA generally accepted auditing standards for fieldwork and reporting. As they are issued, any relevant new AICPA auditing and attestation standards will be adopted and incorporated into GAGAS unless the GAO excludes them by formal announcement. Independent auditors who are members of the AICPA must follow GAGAS in government audits or be in violation of the AICPA *Code of Professional Conduct.*

GAGAS are classified into the following six categories: (1) general standards; (2) fieldwork standards for financial audits; (3) reporting standards for financial audits; (4) general, fieldwork, and reporting standards for attestation engagements; (5) fieldwork standards for performance audits, and (6) reporting standards for performance audits. The standards in the first three categories are identified and discussed in the following sections. The performance audit standards in the last two categories are presented in Figure 21-5 for information purposes only and are not discussed further here. Standards for attestation engagements are also beyond the scope of this discussion. Further information about these standards can be found at http://www.gao.gov/govaud/yb/2003/html/TOC.html.

General Standards

The general category of GAGAS pertains primarily to the qualifications of the auditor and audit organizations. These standards apply to both types of government audits. There are four standards in this category:

Figure 21-5 ■ Fieldwork and Reporting Standards for Performance Audits

Fieldwork Standards	Reporting Standards
1. Planning Work is to be adequately planned. **2. Supervision** Staff are to be properly supervised. **3. Evidence** Sufficient, competent, and relevant evidence is to be obtained to provide a reasonable basis for the auditors' findings and conclusions. **4. Audit Documentation** Auditors should prepare and maintain audit documentation. Audit documentation related to planning, conducting, and reporting on the audit should contain sufficient information to enable an experienced auditor, who has had no previous connection with the audit, to ascertain from the audit documentation the evidence that supports the auditors' significant judgments and conclusions. Audit documentation should contain support for findings, conclusions, and recommendations before auditors issue their report.	**1. Form** Auditors should prepare audit reports communicating the results of each audit. **2. Report Contents** The audit report should include the objectives, scope, and methodology; the audit results, including findings, conclusions, and recommendations, as appropriate; a reference to compliance with generally accepted government auditing standards; the views of responsible officials; and, if applicable, the nature of any privileged and confidential information omitted. **3. Report Quality Elements** The report should be complete, accurate, objective, convincing, and as clear and concise as the subject permits. **4. Report Issuance and Distribution** Government auditors should submit audit reports to the appropriate officials of the audited entity and to the appropriate officials of the organizations requiring or arranging for the audits, including external funding organizations, such as legislative bodies, unless legal restrictions prevent it. Auditors should also send copies of the reports to other officials who have legal oversight authority or who may be responsible for acting on audit findings and recommendations, and also to others authorized to receive such reports. Unless the report is restricted by law or regulation, or contains privileged or confidential information, auditors should clarify that copies are made available for public inspection. Nongovernment auditors should clarify report distribution responsibilities with the party contracting for the audit and follow the agreements reached.

Source: Government Auditing Standards, Chapters 7 and 8.

- *Independence.* In all matters relating to the audit work, the audit organization and the individual auditors, whether government or public, should be free from personal and external impairments to independence, should be organizationally independent, and should maintain an independent attitude and appearance.

- *Professional judgment* should be used in planning and performing audits and attestation engagements and in reporting the results.

- *Competence.* The staff assigned to perform the audit or attestation engagement should collectively possess adequate professional competence for the tasks required.

- *Quality control and assurance.* Each audit organization performing audits and/or attestation engagements in accordance with GAGAS should have an appropriate internal quality control system in place and should undergo an external peer review.

The general standards address the fundamental requirements for ensuring the credibility of audit results. Credibility is essential to all audit organizations. These general standards encompass the independence of the audit organization and its individual auditors; the exercise of professional judgment in the performance of work and the preparation of related reports; the competence of audit staff, including the need for their continuing professional education; and the existence of quality control systems and external peer reviews.

These general standards provide the underlying framework that is critical in effectively applying the fieldwork and reporting standards when performing the detailed work associated with audits or attestation engagements. Therefore, these general standards are required to be followed by all auditors and audit organizations, both government and nongovernment, performing work under generally accepted government auditing standards (GAGAS).

Fieldwork Standards for Financial Audits

The GAGAS fieldwork standards incorporate the three AICPA fieldwork standards without modification. Also incorporated, by reference, are all of the related SASs issued by the AICPA that may be viewed as interpretations of the fieldwork standards. Complementing these standards, GAGAS include five additional fieldwork standards as follows:

- *Auditor communication.* Auditors should communicate information regarding the nature, timing, and extent of planned testing and reporting and the level of assurance provided to officials of the audited entity and to the individuals contracting for or requesting the audit.

- *Considering the results of previous audit and attestation engagements.* Auditors should consider the results of previous audits and attestation engagements and follow up on known significant findings and recommendations that directly relate to the objectives of the audit being undertaken.

- *Detecting material misstatements resulting from violations of contract provisions or grant agreements, or from abuse.*
  - Auditors should design the audit to provide reasonable assurance of detecting material misstatements resulting from violations of provisions of contracts or grant agreements that have a direct and material effect on the deter-

mination of financial statement amounts or other financial data significant to the audit objectives. If specific information comes to the auditors' attention that provides evidence concerning the existence of possible violations of provisions of contracts or grant agreements that could have a material indirect effect on the determination of financial statement amounts, auditors should apply audit procedures specifically directed to ascertain whether violations of provisions of contracts or grant agreements have occurred or are likely to have occurred.

■ Auditors should be alert to situations or transactions that could be indicative of abuse, and if indications of abuse exist that could significantly affect the financial statement amounts or other financial data, auditors should apply audit procedures specifically directed to ascertain whether abuse has occurred and the effect on the financial statement amounts or other financial data.

■ *Developing elements of a finding.* Audit findings, such as deficiencies in internal control, fraud, illegal acts, violations of provisions of contracts or grant agreements, have often been regarded as containing the elements of criteria, condition, and effect, plus underlying cause when problems are found.

■ *Audit documentation.* Documentation related to planning, conducting, and reporting on the audit should contain sufficient information to enable an experienced auditor who has had no previous connection with the audit to ascertain from the audit documentation the evidence that supports the auditors' significant judgments and conclusions. Audit documentation should contain support for findings, conclusions, and recommendations before auditors issue their report.

The first additional GAGAS standard broadens who the auditor must communicate with when establishing an understanding regarding the audit. GAGAS requires that the individuals contracting for, or requesting, the audit services be involved in establishing an understanding. Specific information should be communicated regarding the nature and extent of testing and reporting on compliance with laws and regulations and internal control over financial reporting to reduce the risk that the needs or expectations of parties involved may be misinterpreted.

The second additional standard recognizes the GAO's conclusion that much of the benefit from audit work is not in the findings reported or recommendations made, but in their effective resolution, which is a responsibility of the auditee's management. This additional standard establishes part of a process to track the status of previous findings and resolutions and is intended to help auditors ensure that the benefits of their work are realized.

The third additional standard recognizes that governmental organizations are often subject to more specific rules and regulations than entities in the private sector and that noncompliance can have material effects on the financial statements. This standard is patterned after GAAS requirements regarding auditors' responsibilities for detecting irregularities and illegal acts, and under GAGAS, auditors have the same responsibility for detecting material misstatements arising from other types of noncompliance as they do from illegal acts.

The fourth additional standard recognizes that the elements needed for a finding depend entirely on the objectives of the audit. Thus, a finding or set of findings is complete to the extent that the audit objectives are satisfied. When problems are identified, auditors should plan audit procedures to develop the elements of the finding into the auditors' report.

The final additional standard regarding audit documentation codifies a requirement that audit working papers should contain support for findings, conclusions, and recommendations before auditors issue their report.

GAGAS do not prescribe additional internal control standards for financial statement audits. However, the *Yellow Book* does include guidance on applying the second standard of fieldwork of GAAS when considering the control environment, safeguarding controls, controls over compliance with laws and regulations, and control risk assessments in government audits. The Yellow Book also provides additional guidance on setting materiality. Specifically, it states that in an audit of a government entity or an entity that receives government assistance, it may be appropriate to set materiality levels lower than in audits of other entities because of the public accountability of the auditee, the various legal and regulatory requirements, and the visibility and sensitivity of government programs, activities, and functions.

All AICPA standards (SASs and SSAEs) that apply to financial related audits are also incorporated by reference into GAGAS.

Reporting Standards for Financial Audits

Complementing the AICPA's four generally accepted reporting standards and related SASs, all of which are incorporated into GAGAS by reference, the *Yellow Book* includes the following six additional reporting standards:

- *Reporting auditors' compliance with GAGAS.* Audit reports should state that the audit was made in accordance with generally accepted government auditing standards.

- *Reporting on internal control and on compliance with laws, regulations, and provisions of contracts or grant agreements.* When providing an opinion or a disclaimer on financial statements, auditors should include in their report on the financial statements either a (1) description of the scope of the auditors' testing of internal control over financial reporting and compliance with laws, regulations, and provisions of contracts or grant agreements and the results of those tests or an opinion, if sufficient work was performed, or (2) reference to the separate report(s) containing that information. If auditors report separately, the opinion or disclaimer should contain a reference to the separate report containing this information and state that the separate report is an integral part of the audit and should be considered in assessing the results of the audit.

- *Reporting deficiencies in internal control, fraud, illegal acts, violations of provisions of contracts or grant agreements, and abuse.* For financial audits, including audits of financial statements in which the auditor provides an opinion or disclaimer, auditors should report, as applicable to the objectives of the audit, (1) deficiencies in internal control considered to be reportable conditions as defined in AICPA standards, (2) all instances of fraud and illegal acts unless clearly inconsequential, and (3) significant violations of provisions of contracts or grant agreements and abuse. In some circumstances, auditors should report fraud, illegal acts, violations of provisions of contracts or grant agreements, and abuse directly to parties external to the audited entity.

- *Reporting views of responsible officials.* If the auditors' report discloses deficiencies in internal control, fraud, illegal acts, violations of provisions of contracts or grant agreements, or abuse, auditors should obtain and report the views of responsible officials concerning the findings, conclusions, and recommendations, as well as planned corrective actions.

■ *Reporting privileged and confidential information.* If certain pertinent information is prohibited from general disclosure, the audit report should state the nature of the information omitted and the requirement that makes the omission necessary.

■ *Report issuance and distribution.* Government auditors should submit audit reports to the appropriate officials of the audited entity and to appropriate officials of the organizations requiring or arranging for the audits, including external funding organizations such as legislative bodies, unless legal restrictions prevent it. Auditors should also send copies of the reports to other officials who have legal oversight authority or who may be responsible for acting on audit findings and recommendations and to others authorized to receive such reports. Unless the report is restricted by law or regulation, or contains privileged and confidential information, auditors should clarify that copies are made available for public inspection. Nongovernment auditors should clarify report distribution responsibilities with the party contracting for the audit and follow the agreements reached.

The first additional reporting standard requires that the audit report on financial statements explicitly state that the audit was conducted in accordance with GAGAS whenever the report is submitted to comply with a legal, regulatory, or contractual requirement for a GAGAS audit. This standard does not prohibit issuing a report that does not refer to GAGAS when the auditee needs an audit report for purposes other than complying with requirements calling for a GAGAS audit.

The second additional standard does not require the auditor to report on internal controls over financial reporting similar to the report for public companies. It does, however, require the auditor to report the scope of tests of controls over both financial reporting and compliance with laws and regulations.

The third additional reporting standard expands the scope of the report beyond fair presentation in the financial statements. The auditor must also report known internal control deficiencies, fraud, illegal acts, or violation or abuse of contract provisions.

The fourth additional reporting standard provides an opportunity for management to respond to the auditor's findings. It recognizes that one of the most effective ways to ensure that a report is fair, complete, and objective is to obtain advance review and comments by responsible officials of the audited entity and others, as may be appropriate. Including the views of responsible officials results in a report that presents not only the deficiencies in internal control, fraud, illegal acts, violations of provisions of contracts or grant agreements, or abuse the auditors identified but also what the responsible officials of the audited entity think about the deficiencies in internal control, fraud, illegal acts, violations of provisions of contracts or grant agreements, or abuse, and what corrective actions officials of the audited entity plan to take. Auditors should include in their report a copy of the officials' written comments or a summary of the comments received.

The fifth additional standard recognizes that certain information may be prohibited from general disclosure by federal, state, or local laws or regulations. The report distribution requirements detailed in the final additional standard make it important for the engaging organization and the auditor to have a clear understanding as to which officials or organizations will receive the report and who will make the distribution.

In reporting on financial related audits, auditors should follow all applicable portions of the GAAS and GAGAS reporting standards for financial audits as well as applicable portions of the AICPA's SASs, and SSAEs such as those discussed in Chapter 20. For financial related audits not covered by the above, the GAGAS reporting standards for performance audits (see Figure 21-5) should be followed.

REPORTING ON COMPLIANCE WITH LAWS AND REGULATIONS

The second additional reporting standard requires that either the auditors' reports on financial statements or a separate report referred to therein include the same information on irregularities and illegal acts that is reported to audit committees under AICPA standards. Other instances of noncompliance that are material to the financial statements such as violations of contract provisions or grant agreements must also be reported. Examples of the latter include failure of grantees to contribute their own resources pursuant to matching requirements, violations of restrictions on the purposes for which funds can be expended, and improper allocations of indirect costs. When noncompliance is found, the manner of reporting should provide the reader with a basis for judging the prevalence and consequences of such conditions by referring to such variables as the number of cases examined, frequency of noncompliance, dollar value, and so on.

This standard also requires auditors to report irregularities or illegal acts directly to external parties in two circumstances when the auditee fails to do so as soon as practicable after the auditor has communicated the matter to the auditee's governing body: (1) when the auditee is required by law or regulation to report such events to external parties and (2) when an auditee that receives assistance from a government agency fails to report to the agency an irregularity or illegal act involving that assistance. When laws, regulations, or policies require auditors to report indications of certain types of irregularities or illegal acts to law enforcement or investigatory authorities, they should consult with those authorities and/or legal counsel to determine whether broader reporting would compromise investigative or legal proceedings already underway. In such cases, auditors may limit their reporting to information that is already part of the public record.

Extensive guidance on **compliance auditing, compliance attestation,** and reporting thereon is provided in AU 801, *Compliance Auditing Considerations in Audits of Governmental Entities and Recipients of Governmental Financial Assistance,* and AT 601, *Compliance Attestations.* A sample compliance report is presented in Figure 21-6. Based on AT 600.54, the CPA's report on an examination of a compliance attestation, which is ordinarily addressed to the entity, should include the following:

- A title that includes the word *independent.*
- Identification of the specified compliance requirements, including the period covered, and of the responsible party.
- A statement that compliance with the specified requirements is the responsibility of the entity's management.
- A statement that the practitioner's responsibility is to express an opinion on the entity's compliance with those requirements or on management's assertion on such compliance based on his or her examination.

- A statement that the examination was conducted in accordance with attestation standards established by the American Institute of Certified Public Accountants and, accordingly, included examining, on a test basis, evidence about the entity's compliance with those requirements and performing such other procedures as the practitioner considered necessary in the circumstances.
- A statement that the practitioner believes the examination provides a reasonable basis for his or her opinion.
- A statement that the examination does not provide a legal determination on the entity's compliance.
- The practitioner's opinion on whether the entity complied, in all material respects, with specified requirements based on the specified criteria.
- A statement restricting the use of the report to the specified parties under the following circumstances:
  - When the criteria used to evaluate compliance are determined by the practitioner to be appropriate only for a limited number of parties who either par-

Figure 21-6 ■ Example Report on Compliance

Independent Accountant's Report

[Introductory paragraph]

We have examined [name of entity]'s compliance with [list specified compliance requirements] during the [period] ended [date]. Management is responsible for [name of entity]'s compliance with those requirements. Our responsibility is to express an opinion on [name of entity]'s compliance based on our examination.

[Scope paragraph]

Our examination was conducted in accordance with attestation standards established by the American Institute of Certified Public Accountants and, accordingly, included examining on a test basis, evidence about [name of entity]'s compliance with those requirements and performing such other procedures as we considered necessary in the circumstances. We believe that our examination provides a reasonable basis for our opinion. Our examination does not provide a legal determination on [name of entity]'s compliance with specified requirements.

[Opinion paragraph]

In our opinion, [name of entity] complied, in all material respects, with the aforementioned requirements for the year ended December 31, 20XX.

[Restricted use paragraph]

This report is intended solely for the information and use of [list specific parties] and is not intended to be used by anyone other than these specified parties.

_____

[Signature]

_____

[Date]

Source: AT 600.56.

ticipated in their establishment or can be presumed to have an adequate understanding of the criteria.

- ■ When the criteria used to evaluate compliance are available only to the specified parties
- ■ The manual or printed signature of the practitioner's firm.
- ■ The date of the examination report.

REPORTING ON INTERNAL CONTROL

As indicated in the second additional reporting standard, GAGAS requires auditors to report deficiencies in internal control that they consider to be significant deficiencies (as discussed in Chapters 11 and 19 of this text). Examples of significant deficiencies may include:

- ■ Absence of appropriate segregation of duties consistent with appropriate control objectives.
- ■ Evidence of failure to safeguard assets from loss, damage, or misappropriation.
- ■ Absence of a sufficient level of control consciousness within the organization.
- ■ Failure to follow up and correct previously identified deficiencies in internal control.

Furthermore, GAGAS requires that significant deficiencies that constitute material weaknesses be so identified, a requirement that is optional under GAAS. When there are deficiencies that do not qualify as reportable conditions, they should be communicated to the auditee, preferably in writing such as in a management letter. When this occurs, reference should be made to the communication in the auditor's report on controls.

The report on controls does not express any form of assurance on the effectiveness of the internal control. Additional guidance on reporting on the internal control of a governmental entity, including the suggested content and format of separate reports suitable for a variety of circumstances, can be found in AT 501.

[LEARNING CHECK

21-10 a. Explain the scope of governmental auditing.
   b. Identify the types of government audits.
21-11 a. What agency establishes audit standards for government audits?
   b. What is the relationship between GAGAS and GAAS?
21-12 a. Identify the categories of GAGAS.
   b. State the general standards that apply to all government audits.
21-13 a. Identify the supplemental fieldwork standards that apply in a financial statement audit.
   b. What reports are required by the supplemental reporting standards in a financial statement audit?
21-14 a. Indicate the nature of each paragraph of the auditor's unqualified report on compliance with applicable laws and regulations.
   b. Identify the requirements for reporting on internal control under GAGAS that differ or are in addition to GAAS.

[KEY TERMS

Attestation engagements, p. 996
Compliance attestation, p. 1003
Compliance auditing, p. 1003
Financial audits, p. 996
Generally accepted government
   auditing standards (GAGAS),
   p. 997

Governmental auditing, p. 996
Performance audits, p. 997
Yellow Book standards, p. 997

[THE SINGLE AUDIT ACT]

Auditor Knowledge 7

■ Know the objec-
tives and applicability
of the Single Audit
Act.

The **Single Audit Act,** passed by Congress in 1984 and amended in 1996, established the concept of a single organizationwide government audit (the **single
audit**) encompassing both financial and compliance audits. The Act reduces the
need for federal agencies to conduct, and for recipients of federal financial assistance to undergo, multiple separate financial and compliance audits.

OBJECTIVES OF THE ACT

Section 1(a) of the Act states that the Act's objectives are to:

■ Improve the financial management of state and local governments and nonprofit organizations with respect to federal financial assistance programs.
■ Establish uniform requirements for audits of federal financial assistance provided to state and local governments.
■ Promote the efficient and effective use of audit resources.
■ Ensure that federal departments and agencies, to the maximum extent practicable, rely on and use audit work done pursuant to the requirements of the Single Audit Act.

    As implemented, the Act also has become an instrument for ensuring that the
recipients of federal financial assistance comply with several significant national
policies pertaining to such matters as wages, work conditions, and civil rights as
explained further in a subsequent section.

APPLICABILITY AND ADMINISTRATION

Under the Act, state and local governments and nonprofit organizations that
receive $500,000 or more in federal financial assistance in any fiscal year, either
directly from a federal agency or indirectly through another state or local government entity, are required to have a single annual audit pursuant to the Act. The
Federal Office of Management and Budget (OMB) is authorized to adjust the
threshold amount every two years. The Act adds to the requirements contained in
the *Yellow Book* standards, with special emphasis on defined major federal financial assistance programs.

    Federal financial assistance is broadly defined in the Act as assistance pro-
vided by a federal government agency in the form of grants, contracts, loans, loan

guarantees, property, cooperative agreements, interest subsidies, insurance, or direct appropriations, but not direct federal cash assistance to individuals. The auditor shall use a risk-based approach to determine which federal programs are **major programs.** The risk-based approach shall include consideration of: (1) current and prior audit experience, (2) oversight by federal agencies and pass-through entities, and (3) the inherent risk of the federal program. *OMB Circular A-133, Audits of States, Local Governments, and Non-Profit Organizations,* provides additional specific guidance on implementing these three criteria. Programs not qualifying as major programs are designated **nonmajor programs.**

The director of the Office of Management and Budget (OMB) has prescribed policies, procedures, and guidelines to implement the Act in *OMB Circular A-128—Audits of State and Local Governments.*[2] The director also designates cognizant agencies to monitor compliance with the Act. A **cognizant agency** is a federal agency that has the responsibility for implementing the requirements for single audits for a particular state or local government. The cognizant agency represents the collective interests of all federal government agencies in the results of the audit. The responsibilities of the agency include providing technical advice and liaison to state and local governments and independent auditors. Thus, the governmental unit can work directly with one agency rather than with several.

SCOPE OF AN AUDIT UNDER THE SINGLE AUDIT ACT

<table>
<tr><td>

Auditor Knowledge 8

■ Know the components of a single audit and the procedures and reports associated with each.

</td></tr>
</table>

The scope of an audit conducted as specified in the Act and *OMB Circular A-133, Audits of States, Local Governments, and Non-Profit Organizations,* has two components and five procedures, as outlined in Figure 21-7.

General

In general, the audit shall be conducted in accordance with GAGAS. The auditor shall cover the entire operations of the auditee; or at the option of the auditee, the audit shall include a series of audits that cover departments, agencies, and other organizational units that expended or administered federal awards during the year. Each separate audit shall encompass the financial statements and schedule of expenditure of federal awards for each department, agency, or other governmental unit.

Financial Statements

The auditor shall determine whether the financial statements of the auditee are presented fairly in all material respects in conformity with generally accepted accounting principles. The auditor shall also determine whether a schedule of expenditures of federal awards is presented fairly in all material respects in relation to the auditee's financial statements taken as a whole.

---

[2] A companion document, *OMB Circular A-133—Audits of Institutions of Higher Education and Other Nonprofit Institutions,* prescribes audit requirements for institutions of higher education and other nonprofit institutions that receive federal awards of $500,000 or more per year. (The definition of federal award is slightly broader than the definition of federal financial assistance.) To assist auditors in complying with *OMB Circular A-133,* the AICPA has issued Statement of Position 92-9, *Audits of Not-for-Profit Organizations Receiving Federal Awards.* These materials are beyond the scope of this chapter.

Figure 21-7 ■ Summary of Auditors Responsibilities under the Single Audit Act

Component	Procedures Performed	Report Issued
Financial statement audit	1. Audit of the financial statements in accordance with GAAS and the general standards of GAGAS.	1a. Opinion on the financial statements. 1b. Report on supplementary schedule of federal financial assistance.
	2. Audit of the financial statements in accordance with the additional GAGAS standards of fieldwork and reporting.	2a. Report on internal control based on the audit. 2b. Report on compliance with laws and regulations that may have a material effect on the financial statements.
Audit of federal financial assistance	3. Procedures to obtain understanding of the internal control over federal financial assistance test of controls, and to support an assessment of control risk at a low level.	3a. Report on internal controls over federal financial assistance.
	4. Tests of compliance with general requirements applicable to all federal financial assistance programs and specific requirements applicable to major federal financial assistance programs.	4a. Report on compliance with general requirements applicable to federal financial assistance programs. 4b. Opinion on compliance with specific requirements applicable to each major federal financial assistance program. 4c. Schedule of findings and questioned costs.
	5. Performance of procedures to assess the reasonableness of summary schedule of prior findings and current follow-up.	5a. Report, as a current-year finding, when the auditor concludes that the summary of prior findings materially misstates their status.

Source: AU 801.102 (Adapted).

Internal Controls

In addition to the requirements of GAGAS, the auditor shall perform procedures to obtain an understanding of internal control over federal programs sufficient to plan the audit to support a low assessed level of control risk for major programs. In general, the auditor shall also plan to test the system of internal control over major programs to support a low assessed level of control risk for the assertions relevant to the compliance requirements for each major program.

Compliance

In addition to the requirements of GAGAS, the auditor shall determine whether the auditee has complied with laws, regulations, and the provisions of contracts or grant agreements that may have a direct and material effect on each of its major programs. The OMB produces a Compliance Supplement that describes the principal compliance requirements applicable to most federal programs. The compliance testing shall include tests of transactions and such other auditing procedures necessary to provide the auditor sufficient evidence to support an opinion on compliance. The auditor should set the scope of the audit to address specific requirements such as the following:

- Types of services allowed or not allowed, which specifies the types of goods or services that entities may purchase with federal assistance.
- Eligibility, which specifies the characteristics of individuals or groups to which entities may give financial assistance.
- Matching, which specifies amounts entities should contribute from their own resources toward projects for which financial assistance is provided.
- Reporting, which specifies other reports entities must file.
- Special tests and provisions, which might include such requirements as holding hearings regarding the proposed use of funds and deadlines for expending funds.
- The materiality of any findings of noncompliance is evaluated in the context of the program to which the findings relate rather than the overall financial statements.

Audit Follow-up

The auditor shall follow-up on prior audit findings and perform procedures to assess the reasonableness of a summary schedule of prior audit findings prepared by the auditee. The auditor should report as a current-year audit finding, when the auditor concludes that the summary schedule of prior audit findings materially misrepresents the status of any prior audit finding. The auditor shall also perform audit follow-up procedures regardless of whether a prior audit finding relates to a major program in the current year.

Reporting Requirements

The auditor's report(s) may be in the form of either combined or separate reports. In addition to guidance provided in *OMB Circular A-133*, the auditor should consider the following:

- AU 801, *Compliance Auditing Considerations in Audits of Governmental Entities and Recipients of Governmental Financial Assistance*
- AT 101, *Attest Engagements*
- AT 601, *Compliance Attestation*

The content of the auditor's reports is discussed below.

Opinion on Financial Statements

First, the auditor shall issue an opinion (or disclaimer of opinion) as to whether the financial statements are presented fairly in all material respects in conformity with generally accepted accounting principles. As part of this requirement, the auditor shall issue an opinion (or disclaimer of opinion) as to whether the Schedule of Expenditures of Federal Awards is presented fairly in all material respects in relation to the financial statements taken as a whole.

Figure 21-8 ■ Summary of Auditor Knowledge Discussed in Chapter 21

Auditor Knowledge	Summary	Chapter References
K1. Know the definition of internal auditing and the IIA professional practices framework.	The IIA defines internal auditing as an independent, objective assurance and consulting activity designed to add value and improve an organization's operations. It helps an organization accomplish its objectives by bringing a systematic, disciplined approach to evaluate and improve the effectiveness of risk management, control, and governance processes. Figure 21-1 provides a graphic depiction of the IIA professional practices framework.	pp. 985–986
K2. Know the IIA code of ethics, attribute standards, and performance standards.	Figure 21-2 summarizes the IIA code of professional ethics. Figure 21-3 summarizes the IIA attribute and performance standards. These are explained in more detail in the chapter discussion.	pp. 986–990
K3. Know the definition of operational auditing and describe the phases of an operational audit.	The IIA has defined operational auditing as the systematic process of evaluating an organization's effectiveness, efficiency, and economy of operations under management's control and reporting to appropriate persons the results of the evaluation along with recommendations for improvements. The chapter discussion explains five phases of an operational audit: (1) select the auditee, (2) plan the audit, (3) perform the audit, (4) report findings to management and (5) perform follow-up.	pp. 991–994
K4. Know the standards that independent public accountants should follow in performing operational audits.	The independent CPA should follow Management Consulting Services standards when performing an operational audit.	p. 995
K5. Know the three types of governmental audits.	The three types of governmental audits are (1) financial audits, (2) attestation engagements, and (3) performance audits. These are explained in more detail in the chapter discussion.	pp. 996–997
K6. Know the general standards, additional fieldwork standards, and additional reporting standards associated with generally accepted governmental auditing standards (GAGAS) for financial audits and performance audits.	The four general standards address (1) independence, (2) professional judgments, (3) competence, and (4) quality control and assurance. The additional fieldwork standards for financial audits are (1) auditor communication, (2) considering the results of previous engagements, (3) detecting material misstatements resulting from violations of contract provisions or grant agreements or from abuse, (4) developing elements of a finding, and (5) audit documentation. The additional reporting standards for financial audits are (1) reporting auditors' compliance with GAGAS, (2) reporting on internal control and on compliance with laws, regulations, and provisions of contracts or grant agreements, and (3) reporting deficiencies in internal control, fraud, illegal acts, violations of provision of contracts or grand agreements, and abuse. The additional requirements for financial audits are discussed in more detail in the chapter. The additional fieldwork and reporting standards for performance audits are summarized in Figure 21-5.	pp. 997–1005

(continues)

Figure 21-8 ■ (Continued)

Auditor Knowledge	Summary	Chapter References
K7. Know the objectives and applicability of the Single Audit Act.	The objectives and applicability of the Single Audit Act are to (1) improve the financial management of state and local governments and nonprofit organizations with respect to federal financial assistance programs, (2) establish uniform requirements for audits of federal financial assistance provided to state and local governments, (3) promote the efficient and effective use of audit resources, and (4) ensure that federal departments and agencies, to the maximum extent practicable, rely on and use audit work done pursuant to the requirements of the Single Audit Act. The Single Audit Act applies to state and local governments and not-for-profit entities that receive over $500,000 in federal financial assistance in a fiscal year.	pp. 1006–1007
K8. Know the components of a single audit and the procedures and reports associated with each.	The Single Audit Act has five major components: (1) general, (2) financial statements, (3) internal controls, (4) compliance, and (5) audit follow-up. Figure 21-7 provides a summary of the auditor's responsibility under the Single Audit Act.	pp. 1007–1011

objective questions

Objective questions are available for the student at www.wiley.com/college/boynton

comprehensive questions

21-21 **(Internal auditing practice standards)** Standards for the Professional Practice of Internal Auditing have been established by the Institute of Internal Auditors. Listed below are specific policies adopted by the Marco Corporation for its internal auditors:

1. Internal auditors must comply with the Institute of Internal Auditor Code of Ethics.

2. Internal auditors should periodically inspect the safeguards over inventories and cash.

3. Internal auditors should have valid evidence for audit findings.

4. Inexperienced internal auditors must be supervised by certified internal auditors.

5. Internal auditors should attend professional seminars on EDP.

6. Internal auditors should be unbiased in performing audits.

7. Internal auditors should make a study of the efficiency of personnel in the receiving department.

8. Internal auditors should make postaudit reviews of actions taken by a department following an audit.

9. Internal auditors should periodically review the company's compliance with federal governmental regulations.

10. Internal auditors' reports of audit findings should be communicated to appropriate levels of management.

11. The director of internal auditing should plan the activities for the year.

12. Internal auditors should exercise due care in doing each audit.

13. A quality assurance program should be established and maintained.

14. All new internal auditors must be college graduates.

15. There should be a statement of purpose, authority, and responsibility for the internal audit department.

Required

a. Identify and state the specific IIA practice standard that pertains to each policy.

b. For each specific standard identified in (a) above, identify the related category of general standard (independence, professional proficiency, scope of work, performance of audit work, and management of the internal auditing department). Use the following format for your answers:

Policy No.	Specific Standard (a)	General Standard (b)

21-22   **(Internal auditing standards)** The Standards for the Professional Practice of Internal Auditing contain general standards for independence and performance of audit work.

Required

a. State the general and specific standards that pertain to independence.

b. How, if at all, does the standard of independence for internal auditors differ from the standard of independence for independent auditors?

c. State the general and specific standards that relate to the performance of audit work.

d. Identify four guidelines that apply to the specific standard pertaining to planning.

e. Identify four guidelines that apply to the specific standard of communicating results.

21-23   **(Internal auditing scope-of-work standards)** You are a senior internal auditor for a savings and loan association. You are discussing the preliminary findings of your audit with the branch manager. Some of the findings you feel need to be investigated further are:

1. The branch seems to have too many tellers.

2. No security officer has been appointed, and camera surveillance seems to be insufficient.

3. Although the association does not have a specific dress code, the attire of the branch personnel appears to be too casual, even after considering a recent directive to conserve energy during the summer months.

4. Some of the branch loan officers appear to lack adequate qualifications.

5. Some customers are not charged penalties for late payments on loans.

6. Granting new home mortgages seems to be encouraged in spite of an association policy to discourage expanded activity in this area.

Required

On your answer sheet, list the title of each of the specific scope-of-work standards as set forth in the Standards for the Professional Practice of Internal Auditing and to the right of each specific standard, list the number(s) of the finding above that apply.

IIA

21-24 **(Operational auditing)** Enclosure Products, a large, nationwide organization, manufactures and markets several lines of equipment used in packaging. Product reliability and customer service are considered critical to the company's success. The Customer Service Department is charged with the following responsibilities:

- Providing prospective customers with product information.
- Monitoring the adequacy of spare parts availability.
- Providing information to customers about equipment operation and maintenance.
- Preparing and providing customer training courses.
- Providing backup service and support in the event of critical breakdowns.
- Handling warranty claims.
- Maintaining general liaison with customers.

The company recently computerized its Customer Service Department to improve operational efficiency and customer satisfaction. This change represented a sizable investment by Enclosure Products. The new system includes management information to monitor performance in the areas listed above. The Audit Committee of Enclosure Products' board of directors has requested that the Internal Audit Department perform an operational audit of the Customer Service Department. The Audit Committee has asked that the audit objectives include evaluation of the following:

- Security of assets, including computer information.
- Compliance with applicable laws and company policies.
- Reliability of financial records.
- Effectiveness of performing assigned responsibilities.
- Determination of the value of the spare parts inventory.

Required

a. Explain why each of the five audit objectives suggested by the Audit Committee is, or is not, appropriate for an operational audit of Enclosure Products' Customer Service Department.

b. Outline the basic procedures for performing an operational audit.

ICMA (adapted)

21-25 **(Operational auditing)** Janet Joebert is an internal auditor for the Beamer Company. Janet is assigned to conduct an operational audit on the company's receiving department. This is to be Janet's first operational audit. In preparing for the audit, she asks the following questions:

1. What are the similarities and differences between the phases of an operational audit and the phases of a financial statement audit?
2. What is involved in making a preliminary study?
3. What are the key factors in making the examination?
4. What are the essential elements of the report on audit findings?
5. What is the nature and extent of performing a follow-up on the audit?

Required

a. Answer Janet's questions.

b. If Janet were a CPA in public practice, what standards would she have to follow in conducting the operational audit?

21-26   **(Government auditing standards)** Generally accepted government auditing standards (GAGAS) for a financial statement audit are classified into three categories: general, field-work, and reporting. The following statements relate to the specific GAGAS:

1. Due professional care should be used in conducting the audit and in preparing related reports.

2. Working papers should contain sufficient information to ascertain that the evidence supports the auditor's significant conclusions and judgments.

3. The auditor's report on financial statements should either describe the scope of the auditor's testing of compliance with internal controls and present the results of those tests or refer to separate reports containing that information.

4. Planning should include following up on known and material findings and recommendations from previous audits.

5. Auditors should communicate certain information to the audit committee or individuals with whom they have contracted for the audit.

6. The staff assigned to conduct the audit should collectively possess adequate professional proficiency for the tasks required.

7. The auditors should prepare a written report on their tests of compliance with applicable laws and regulations.

8. The auditor should also be aware of the possibility of illegal acts that could have an indirect and material effect on the financial statements.

9. Audit organizations conducting government audits should have an appropriate internal quality control system in place.

10. A record of the auditors' work should be retained in the form of working papers.

11. A statement should be included in the auditors' report that the audit was made in accordance with generally accepted government auditing standards.

12. In all matters relating to the audit work, the audit organization and the individual auditors should be free from personal and external impairments to independence.

13. The auditor should design audit steps and procedures to provide reasonable assurance of detecting errors, irregularities, and illegal acts.

14. Written audit reports are to be submitted by the audit organization to the appropriate officials of the organization audited.

15. If certain information is prohibited from general disclosure, the report should state the nature of the information omitted.

Required

a. Indicate the category and specific standard to which each of the statements pertains.

b. Explain the relationship of GAAS to the above standards.

c. Identify the reports that should be issued in a financial audit.

21-27   **(Single Audit Act)** Laura Level, CPA, is assigned to the single audit of the city of Plainville. This is Laura's first single audit. As the manager on the audit, you decide to test Laura on her understanding of the Single Audit Act and the auditing requirements of that Act. Your questions to Laura are:

1. What criteria determine whether the city of Plainville must have a single audit?

2. What are the objectives of the Single Audit Act?

3. What is the role of the director of the Office of Management and Budget in the audit?

4. What is a cognizant agency? What are the responsibilities of this agency in the audit?

5. What are the audit objectives of the Act?

6. What audit reports are required on the city's federal financial assistance programs?

7. How may the required reports be issued?

Required

Supply the answers that Laura should give.

21-28 **(Single Audit Act)** Jones and Baker, a CPA firm, has a number of governmental audit clients. Some of the clients have federal government financial assistance programs.

Required

a. What responsibility does the auditor have for reporting on compliance under the Single Audit Act?

b. What responsibility does the auditor have for testing compliance in (1) major and (2) nonmajor federal financial assistance programs?

cases

21-29 **(Objectivity in internal auditing)** Lajod Company has an Internal Audit Department consisting of a manager and three staff auditors. The manager of Internal Audits, in turn, reports to the corporate controller. Copies of audit reports are routinely sent to the board of directors as well as the corporate controller and the individual responsible for the area or activity being audited.

The manager of Internal Audits is aware that the external auditors have relied on the internal audit function to a substantial degree in the past. However, in recent months, the external auditors have suggested there may be a problem related to the objectivity of the internal audit function. This objectivity problem may result in more extensive testing and analysis by the external auditors.

The external auditors are concerned about the amount of nonaudit work performed by the Internal Audit Department. The percentage of nonaudit work performed by the internal auditors in recent years has increased to about 25 percent of their total hours worked. A sample of five recent nonaudit activities is as follows:

1. One of the internal auditors assisted in the preparation of policy statements on internal control. These statements included such items as policies regarding sensitive payments and standards of internal control for systems.

2. The bank statements of the corporation are reconciled each month as a regular assignment for one of the internal auditors. The corporate controller believes this strengthens the internal control function because the internal auditor is not involved in the receipt and disbursement of cash.

3. The internal auditors are asked to review the budget data in every area each year for relevance and reasonableness before the budget is approved. In addition, an internal auditor examines the variances each month, along with the associated explanations. These variance analyses are prepared by the corporate controller's staff after consultation with the individuals involved.

4. One of the internal auditors has recently been involved in the design, installation, and initial operation of a new computer system. The auditor was concerned primarily with the design and implementation of internal accounting controls and the computer appli-

cation controls for the new system. The auditor also conducted the testing of the controls during the test runs.

5. The internal auditors are frequently asked to make accounting entries for complex transactions before the transactions are recorded. The employees in the accounting department are not adequately trained to handle such transactions. In addition, this serves as a means of maintaining internal control over complex transactions.

The manager of Internal Audits has always made an effort to remain independent of the corporate controller's office and believes the internal auditors are objective and independent in their audit and nonaudit activities.

Required

a. Define objectivity as it relates to the internal audit function.

b. For each of the five situations outlined above, explain whether the objectivity of Lajod Company's Internal Audit Department has been materially impaired. Consider each situation independently.

c. The manager of Audits reports to the corporate controller.
   1. Does this reporting relationship result in a problem of objectivity? Explain your answer.
   2. Would your answer to any of the five situations in requirement (b) above have changed if the manager of Internal Audits reported to the board of directors? Explain your answer.

ICMA (adapted)

professional simulation

Jennifer Robben is a partner in the CPA firm of Robben, Harrison and Co. The firm has been asked to propose on a compliance engagement for R.E. Fine and Company, and local refinery of petroleum products. The proposed engagement includes performing both an audit of R.E. Fine's financial statements and an examination of its compliance with state laws regarding the handling of hazardous waste.

You have been asked to research the requirements associated with examination procedures applied to R.E. Fine's compliance with state laws regarding the handling of hazardous waste materials. Jennifer recognizes that to express an opinion on an entity's compliance with specified criteria the firm needs to plan an engagement to accumulate sufficient evidence about the entity's compliance with specified requirements. Cut and paste the appropriate sections of professional standards that explain what should be covered in planning such an attestation engagement.

Upon completing the examination of R.E. Fine's compliance with state laws regarding the handling of hazardous waste materials you have reached a conclusion that R.E. Fine complied, in all material respects, with the aforementioned requirements for the year ended December 31, 20X8. Draft the independent accountant's report that communicates this conclusion in accordance with appropriate professional standards.

INDEX

STATEMENTS ON AUDITING STANDARDS